# Advance Praise for *The Handbook of Organizational Consulting Psychology*

"Rodney Lowman has done it again! He has edited a book that is unique, comprehensive, and aimed squarely at the science and practice of psychology in organizations. This book shows a remarkable breadth of coverage: science and practice, topics both traditional and cutting edge, issues within and across levels, all by contributors with extensive and diverse experience in organizational consulting. There's something here for anyone interested in a psychological approach to consulting in organizations."
— *Rosemary Hays-Thomas, professor of psychology, The University of West Florida*

"*The Handbook of Organizational Consulting Psychology* addresses a longtime need for a new, comprehensive, major work in consulting psychology. It is broad in scope and clearly integrates topics in consulting psychology that are at the core of the field and that reflect recent innovations in the application of consulting principles and techniques. The scope and depth of this book are not only timely but also unique. I would expect this book to become an essential reference for all consulting psychologists."
— *Clyde A. Crego, director, Counseling & Psychological Services, California State University Long Beach and University of Southern California; former president, APA Division of Consulting Psychology and APA fellow*

"My one-word reaction: WOW! Aptly entitled a handbook, it could nevertheless well serve as a basic text in the field. It may have its greatest benefit to those who are transiting from more specialized work into organizational consulting, since it lays out a broad range of issues that one may encounter and ought to be prepared to deal with along with some practical advice on how to handle them."
— *Kenneth H. Bradt, consulting psychologist and past president, Society of Consulting Psychology, APA*

"This handbook is a rock for consulting psychologists to stand on. For psychologists who want to be confident in their knowledge of consulting and ethical in what they recommend, this book must be studied and always kept close at hand. The editors have selected highly competent authors who have a depth of specialized knowledge of consulting and state it clearly and boldly."
— *Donald Clifton, past president and chairman of the board, The Gallup Corporation*

" 'One-stop shopping' has become an American obsession, and for this book the term is richly deserved. This is indeed the 'Wal-Mart' of organizational

consulting psychology—and that is meant as a hearty compliment! For the first time in more than 30 years of looking at the literature for what can help me to be a better organizational consultant, I find in one place a foundation for both intellectual knowledge and practice skill-building. There's comfort in the 'elder wisdom' of such key figures in the field as Harry Levinson— writing both on assessment and on its linkage to intervention. And there's good attention to current trends such as executive coaching and use of the concept of emotional intelligence. There simply is no better place to start for both the new consultant and the experienced practitioner."
— *Thomas E. Backer, president, Human Interaction Research Institute; past-president, APA Division of Consulting Psychology; founding editor, Consultation*

"Rodney Lowman has written a seminal book for both new and experienced organizational and consulting psychologists. *The Handbook* clearly defines the parameters for the new specialty of consulting psychology. The cutting-edge issues of consulting and assessment of individuals, groups, and organizations in business are addressed by the leaders in the field. Of particular interest is the chapter linking research to actual interventions. Both experienced and beginning consultants will greatly appreciate the chapter on interventions that work and those that don't work and measuring the impact of consulting. *The Handbook* addresses the key issues in consulting psychology and is a must-read for anyone practicing in the field today."
— *Lilli Friedland, president, Executive Advisors*

"*The Handbook of Consulting Psychology* is a much-needed addition to the psychological literature and a necessary adjunct to the professionalization of the field. It reflects the diversity of style and niche found in the Society of Consulting Psychology itself. It's comprehensive and represents the best current thinking about a wide range of topics that the field has to offer."
— *John E. Deleray, consulting psychologist*

"A bold and seminal work in the rapidly emerging field of consulting psychology, this handbook stands as a beacon of light for psychologists who wish to apply their discipline to helping organizations and the individuals that comprise them to be more effective. Guided by the needs of the customer, Dr. Lowman has effectively cut across and brought together heretofore largely independent domains of research and practice in psychology, specifying the relevant theoretical underpinnings and the knowledge and skill competencies that practitioners must have to be effective. Hopefully this handbook will spawn more cross-area research in psychology, helping to unleash the power of a more unified discipline for organizations."
— *Vicki V. Vandaveer, consulting psychologist and chief executive officer, The Vandaveer Group.*

*The California School of Organizational Studies*
## Handbook of Organizational Consulting Psychology

# The California School of Organizational Studies
# Handbook of Organizational Consulting Psychology

*A Comprehensive Guide to Theory, Skills, and Techniques*

Rodney L. Lowman, Editor

JOSSEY-BASS
A Wiley Imprint
www.josseybass.com

Published by Jossey-Bass
A Wiley Imprint
989 Market Street, San Francisco, CA 94103-1741 www.josseybass.com

Jossey-Bass books and products are available through most bookstores. To contact Jossey-Bass directly call our Customer Care Department within the U.S. at 800-956-7739, outside the U.S. at 317-572-3993 or fax 317-572-4002.

Jossey-Bass also publishes its books in a variety of electronic formats. Some content that appears in print may not be available in electronic books.

**Citation: Lowman, R. L. (Ed.) (2002). *Handbook of organizational consulting psychology*. San Francisco: Jossey-Bass.**

**Library of Congress Cataloging-in-Publication Data:**

The California School of Organizational Studies handbook of organizational consulting psychology : a comprehensive guide to theory, skills, and techniques / Rodney L. Lowman, editor.
    p. cm.
    Includes bibliographical references and index.
    ISBN 978-0-7879-5899-2
      1. Psychology, Industrial. 2. Organizational behavior 3. Organizational change.
    I. Title: Handbook of organizational consulting psychology. II. Lowman, Rodney L.

    HF5548.8 .C18 2002
    158.7—dc21                             2002066098

*For Linda and Marissa with*
*Thanks & Appreciation*

# CONTENTS

# INTRODUCTION

I am excited about this book, and not just for the fact that it is finally completed. The book reflects the depth and breadth of the contemporary state of organizational consulting psychology, an exciting field now coming into its own. In a sense, these chapters, when taken collectively, constitute a coming-of-age story.

As the parent of a child now in college, I can, when I stop to think about it, see the remarkable changes in what just a few years ago was a small bundle of needs concerned with birthday parties, school projects, and holiday presents. Yet, when I dig deeper into memory, the themes of her maturity were always there: creativity, concern with the arts—especially writing and music—interest in teaching, a great sense of humor, and intensity (always there was that).

This book, if you will take the time to read it, first quickly and then slowly and deliberatively, also will stimulate some moments of reflection. As these thirty-one chapters remarkably demonstrate, organizational consulting psychology has also come of age. Consulting psychology as a field now has its own graduate programs, theories, training standards, and literature. It is both a science and a practice, both art and tough-minded outcome. It is a profession that, as typically happens in the development of other new disciplines, has outgrown its parental homes and needs one of its own.

There are those, myself not among them, who would argue that consulting psychology is just a small part of some other field. True, the field borrows heavily from other specialties in psychology and beyond. But with this book it declares independence, the right to stand on its own, to flourish and prosper, or shrivel and wither on its own terms.

It is not hyperbole to stake the claim that thousands of organizations are better today because of the contributions that consulting psychologists have made for them. Consulting psychologists work by assessing and coaching individuals, by creating or improving team functioning, and by improving the quality of the system as a whole. Whether working on the individual, the group, or the organizational level, consulting psychologists are especially well equipped to make better the people side of organizations.

What makes this approach psychology and not, say, business administration or organizational development? Three features seem to be defining: (a) the insistence on measurement, (b) the insistence on assessment, and (c) concern with ethics and values.

I could but will not comment at length on the contributions of these chapters and hopefully of the book as a whole. Because I lived with them for quite a while, I can no longer be impartial about their merits. Still I consider the scope of their achivements I am a little awestruck. The range of contributions is wide—from the wisdom expressed in the simple elegance of a world-eminent consulting psychologist writing at the pinnacle of his career, to the tough-minded statistical rigor of a first author just beginning his.

There is a lot that is not said explicitly in these chapters and I suppose I should make just a bit of that explicit. These chapters clearly say that there is a consulting psychology of organizations, that it is not the same as the psychology of individuals and assuredly not the same as the psychology of disordered individuals. Organizational consulting psychology is based on science, but is mostly about translating science into practice. It respects but builds upon its past. And it combines the discipline of theory building with the reality of practice.

There will be many more books and articles in the years to come, but I hope when it is time to look back on the field's history, this book will have proven to have been a milestone along the way in creating a vibrant and compelling new field of organizational consulting psychology.

Rodney L. Lowman
*Los Angeles, California*
*July 2002*

# PART ONE

# FOUNDATIONS OF ORGANIZATIONAL CONSULTING PSYCHOLOGY

# CHAPTER ONE

# Individual-Level Variables
# in Organizational Consultation

Andrew D. Carson
*Riverside Publishing*

Rodney L. Lowman
*California School of Organization Studies,*
*Alliant International University*

Organizational consulting psychologists work at multiple levels: directly with individuals, as with executive coaching, with dysfunctional or functional groups, or with the organizational system as a whole. Fundamentally, however, organizations are composed of individuals. Consulting psychologists—whatever their level of expertise at the group and organizational levels—are wise to understand people at the individual level if they wish to be effective in their various roles.

## THE CONCEPT OF INDIVIDUAL-LEVEL VARIABLES

This chapter therefore identifies individual-level variables that we feel organizational consulting psychologists should understand. These dimensions are relevant, for example, in conducting assessments or individual coaching. For example, individuals tend to congregate and interact in their work lives with other people who in important psychological respects are similar to themselves (see Holland, 1997; Lowman, 1991, 1993a, 1993b). To some extent, the nature of an organization or occupation is determined by the predominant types of individuals within it, because the types of people (for example, whether intellectual or mechanical, or exuberant and open versus rigid and conservative) will help create the tone and values of the organization. Perhaps of single greatest importance are the individual characteristics of those in leadership roles in the organization (Boudreau, Boswell, & Judge, 2001; Roberts & Hogan, 2001). In addition, individual-level variables retain importance as background or contextual information when working at the group or organizational level, as different change approaches will work either better or worse with different types of individuals or groups of individuals.

Specific aspects of consulting that focus primarily at the individual level, and for which an understanding of individual-level variables are particularly important, include:

- Individual assessment for purposes of selection
- Individual evaluation of fitness for duty
- Interventions to change problematic individual behavior
- Interventions designed to improve or optimize individual-level functioning
- Assessment for purposes of career assessment and counseling

Other chapters in this book (for example, Kilburg, 2002) address specific aspects of the applications of consulting psychology at the individual level. In this introductory chapter, we map the basic variables, or ingredients, demonstrated to have work and organizational relevance in the practice of consulting psychology. Not every individual-level variable will be equally important in each application, but a broad understanding of individual differences—how individuals differ on individual-level variables—will generally make for more effective applications.

This chapter therefore serves as a general introduction on the stable characteristics of people that affect both work adjustment and how individuals seek to fit into groups and organizations. We will discuss these variables in two sets: traits rooted in the structure of personality, and presumably with a relatively larger influence from biological or even genetic factors, and those that appear to have a relatively larger cultural component and are aspects of character. In practice, it is difficult to draw a firm dividing line between these sets of variables. Even so, it is useful for the consulting psychologist to conceptualize a distinction between these two groups of variables, because traits are more difficult to modify, while character may—with effective interventions or policies—change or be changed, at least in its behavioral expressions.

# INDIVIDUAL TRAITS

Over a century of research on differential psychology (see Hough, 2001; Lowman, 1991) has focused on four domains of traits that are relevant for vocational and organizational selection: interests, abilities, personality, and features of psychopathology not already part of these domains. Ability traits have been shown to determine whether one *can* do something (see Carroll, 1993), personality traits the manner of *how* one does something, and interest traits the degree to which one is drawn or naturally motivated to do something. Abilities refer to performance, dimensions of personality to style, and interests to motivation. We shall address the first three areas; those interested in the nature of psychopathology and how it affects work adjustment can refer to Lowman (1989, 1993a).

Much of what we know about the dimensions of individual difference traits derives from factor analytic methods. Our reliance on factor analysis and related methods to identify traits is to some degree ironic and has some limitations. The irony is that the methods to identify psychological variables presumed to be important for specific individuals depend on identifying what is in common *across* individuals. This is not paradoxical, however, since individual uniqueness derives from the idiosyncratic combinations of sets of variables at the individual level that collectively define who a person is. Such variables may also be relevant to organizational behavior and vocational adjustment, but it is difficult for an organizational consulting psychologist to identify them except through careful assessment or finely tuned clinical sensitivities. Other limitations of the methods arise from their inability to identify their relations to, say, biological or social causes. The methods are correlational and simply identify variables that hang together. Also, overly zealous advocates of the methods assume that broad factors identified through the methods are necessarily the most important and represent all the important variables in a domain. Neither is necessarily the case. It may be that particular facets of a broad factor are, in some applied contexts, more important to know and work with than the broad factor itself. Additionally, some important variables may be relatively rare but still important, and factor analytic methods will generally miss these.

## Character and Memes

Characteristics of individuals also exist that are more likely to mature given particular cross-domain or iterative combinations of primary characteristics. Such characteristics also develop only through interaction with, and through acquiring ideas provided by, the groups, organizations, and the wider culture in which the individual matures. Examples include identity, leadership, creativity, entrepreneurial character, and values (and particularly complex combinations of values, such as religious or philosophical beliefs).

Many of these variables may function as memes (see Blackmore, 1999; Brodie, 1996), that is, as "elements of a culture that may be considered to be passed on by non-genetic means, especially imitation" (*Oxford English Dictionary,* cited in Blackmore, p. viii). A term originally coined by Dawkins (1976), memes serve, within individuals, as the means of storage, replication, and transfer of complexes of ideas active at the cultural level. They act as a bridge between the individual, group, and organization. Of course, one might argue that memes constitute an interaction of two ability factors—crystallized intelligence and memory—but advocates of meme theory might argue that memes merely exploit such ability and other resources as a means of replicating themselves across individuals. For example, memes that direct individuals to act in creative ways might be more likely to copy into individuals with particular personality traits (high on openness, and high on the facets of aesthetics, ideas, and fantasy) and interests (artistic). Once incorporated by the individual, a creativity-related meme might serve to maximize behaviors that make use of particular abilities (for example, cultural literacy, ideational fluency, associational fluency, expressional fluency, originality/creativity), which would in turn increase the likelihood of the meme's transmission to others.

With those cautions in mind, we will briefly outline the characteristics of traits identified through research. Readers interested in a systematic treatment beyond this discussion can consult Lowman (1991).

# INTERESTS

Interests refer to individual differences that govern the degree to which one feels that one must do something. Interests therefore relate to the element of motivation (or perhaps compulsion) regarding approach-avoidance behavior. Strong (1955), one of the pioneers of the measurement of interests, stated that they direct us toward "activities for which we have liking or disliking and which we go toward or away from, or concerning which we at least continue or discontinue the status quo; furthermore, they may or may not be preferred to other interests and they may continue varying over time. Or an interest may be defined as a liking/disliking state of mind accompanying the doing of an activity, or the thought of performing the activity" (pp. 138). Interests do not require conscious thought; Strong (1943) said, "they remind me of tropisms. We go toward liked activities, go away from disliked activities" (p. 7).

## Types of Interest Patterns

Holland (1997) extended earlier findings of basic factors of interests into a very popular theory of six main personal orientations, or interest structures. Some authors have challenged the criticality of the six factors, and suggest instead that the number of factors is essentially arbitrary, or that there might exist more important underlying, second-order, or meta-factors (see Lowman & Carson, in press). However, the six factors persist both in the research literature and in most popular treatments. Our present concern is therefore with the six personal orientations (Holland, 1959) that focus on interests, and not with his subsequently proposed vocational personality types (Holland, 1997), which are superordinate constructs that subsume interests as well as abilities, temperaments, values, and other variables. However, we shall refer to the six orientations by the same terms used for vocational personality types: Realistic, Investigative, Artistic, Social, Enterprising, and Conventional. A brief discussion of these variables follows.

Realistic interests lead people to engage in mechanical activities, which extend to technical, hands-on, and outdoor activities that somehow involve mechanical operations, broadly considered. The essential question driving this interest pattern is: how can one manipulate the physical world to make things happen? Realistic interests are satisfied through opportunities to build, to manipulate objects, and to improve or work within the physical world.

Investigative interests lead people to be motivated by and to engage in scientific activities, which include research, mathematics, and related development of novel products. The essential question driving Investigative interests is: why are things (or people) the way they are and how does one know that the answer is correct? Investigative interests are satisfied by opportunities to understand and call for analytical abilities.

Artistic interests lead people to engage in creative activities across a wide range of specific content areas. They include the creation of works of art (visual, musical, literary, or dramatic) and related applications. The essential question driving Artistic interests is: how can one create something beautiful that has never before existed and bring it to the attention of others? Artistic interests are satisfied by opportunities to create.

Social interests motivate people to be involved in people-oriented activities, such as those that may involve teaching, ministering, and especially helping others who are in difficulty. Essentially, Social interests promote behavior that holds the promise of providing the satisfaction that comes with assisting others. The essential question driving Social interests is: how can one help reduce human suffering, regardless of its cause? Social interests are satisfied by opportunities to help, to be involved with people, and to engage others constructively.

Enterprising interests influence people to enjoy and seek out leadership or persuasive roles, and to engage in activities that involve taking charge of groups, setting ambitious goals and persuading others to achieve them. Activities that involve adventure, striving, and clear and measurable outcomes are particularly interesting. The essential question driving Enterprising interests is: how can one realize important ambitions through bringing into alignment the energies of others? Enterprising interests are satisfied by opportunities to influence, persuade, and manage.

Conventional interests, the final of the six patterns, direct people toward activities that involve precise, meticulous, and methodical activities. Such work often involves mathematical or computational tasks, the goal being to create a program or system that, used many times, promotes productive efficiency. The essential question driving Conventional interests is: what are the abstracted requirements of a situation that, properly understood and acted upon, most efficiently reach goals? Conventional interests are satisfied by opportunities to save (as in resources, money, or time).

Holland's interest model is far more sophisticated than the identification of six factors of interests. His carefully researched model looks at a variety of constructs such as interest factor groupings, employment census, and techniques for judging the degree of fit between a person's interest patterns and the work or avocational environment. See Holland (1997) for his complete statement of the theory. Interests have demonstrated marked permanence across a person's life and marked constancy across a variety of cultures. This is probably an artifact of the fact that they have a sizable genetic component (see Gottfredson, 1999; Moloney, Bouchard, & Segal, 1991).

# ABILITIES

Abilities are individual difference characteristics that affect how well one can do something; they predict quality and level of maximal performance (see, for example, Dennis & Tapsfield, 1996). More specifically, abilities sequence and organize thoughts and other abilities to produce behaviors that lead to the effective completion of desired tasks.

Because abilities may speak to what is possible and what potentially obstructs progress toward goal achievement, individuals who wish to believe that only personal will and motivation (or perhaps the quality of educational opportunities) restrain advancement understandably can find the concept of abilities limiting. Out of this concern, among other sources, has emerged a promising literature on skill acquisition that seeks to deconstruct complex achievements into a series of more delimited competencies that can be analyzed and presumably taught. Ericsson (1996), among others (for example, Howe, 1999), has demonstrated this approach to be an alternative at least to the notion of abilities as fixed and delimiting.

Nonetheless, the field of psychology is not yet ready to abandon the construct of abilities. Indeed, psychologists for many decades have sought to discover a reasonably small number of core abilities that appear to support learning and performance across a wide variety of activities. This has led to a debate as to whether abilities arise due to either underlying aptitudes or achievements (with achievements driven by practice, and practice in turn driven largely by interests; Snow, 1998). If abilities arise from aptitudes, then there exists a set of underlying (and presumably cognitive) abilities that affect the ease and rate of learning new material, and perhaps set caps on total learning ability. If abilities arise from achievements, then they are limited directly by practice, and ultimately by interests (motivation). Regardless of their ultimate origin, research has identified several basic abilities that are of interest to the consulting psychologist. Carroll (1993) reviewed the literature on cognitive or intellectual abilities, and, following a reanalysis of a large number of datasets, proposed a structure of such abilities that has proven broadly influential, particularly among those responsible for developing intelligence and ability tests. Although this model largely derived from academic research and has yet to be applied widely to industrial or consulting applications, the model is useful and suggestive. Carroll proposed a three-stratum, hierarchical model of the structure of abilities, with narrow abilities, that is, those that affect a small number of real-life performances at stratum I, broader abilities at stratum II, and general cognitive ability, or *g*, perhaps the most influential of all abilities, at stratum III. The following discussion draws heavily from an adaptation of Carroll's theory by McGrew and Flanagan (1998), who sought to integrate Carroll's theory with those of Cattell (1941, 1957) and Horn (1994). In addition to the broad ability factors discussed here, Table 1.1 lists many of the facets of these abilities as proposed by Carroll, and McGrew and Flanagan, along with related social abilities for which there exists empirical support (social reasoning, business knowledge, psychological knowledge, autobiographical knowledge, biographical knowledge, name-face matching, interpersonal process recall, and reading affect in voice, body language, and facial expressions). These social abilities may be of particular importance in organizational consulting. Rather than create a separate category such as emotional intelligence for such variables, we integrate them directly into the model derived from Carroll's work.

## Intelligence and *g*

General intelligence (popularly called IQ) remains one of, if not the, most important individual difference variables in psychology. It is "a very general mental capability that, among other things, involves the ability to reason, plan, solve problems, think abstractly, comprehend complex ideas, learn quickly, and learn from experience" (Gottfredson, 1994/1997). More than any other single measurable human trait, it predicts important outcomes in the areas of education, work, and general life experience. Intelligence is so important because of the critical importance to a variety of occupational performances of reasoning and decision-making. It becomes even more critical as the settings in which work behavior occurs become more complex, as they are in almost every area of modern life. However, intelligence is not a guarantee of success on the stage of life, and other personal characteristics—such as nonability factors discussed in this chapter—can affect success.

Table 1.1 Individual-Level Ability Traits Important in Consulting.

| Factor | Facet[a] | Facet definition |
|---|---|---|
| g (general cognitive ability) | | |
| Fluid (reasoning) | Induction | Discover underlying rule across instances |
| | Deduction | Given rules and logical steps, solve problem |
| | Quantitative | Use mathematical concepts to reason inductively and deductively |
| Crystallized intelligence | Language development | General development of native language |
| | Foreign language proficiency | General development of foreign language |
| | Foreign language aptitude | Ease of learning foreign language |
| | Lexical knowledge | Vocabulary knowledge via word meanings |
| | Listening | Listen to and understand speech |
| | Communication (real-life) | Speak in real-life situations |
| | Grammatical sensitivity | Understand grammar of native language |
| | General (verbal) information | Range of general knowledge |
| | Cultural literacy | For example, art, music, literature, history |
| | General (science) information | For example, geology, physics, biology, electronics |
| | Business knowledge[b] | For example, marketing, finance, personnel |
| | Psychological knowledge[b] | For example, personality, social, cognitive |
| | Autobiographical knowledge[b] | Of one's own life history |
| | Biographical knowledge[b] | Of eminent individuals, including quotations |
| Memory, short- and long-term | Memory span (short-term) | Immediate recall after a single presentation |
| | Meaningful memory | Ability to remember paired items through meaningful relations |
| | Free-recall memory | Recall unrelated items when presented in long list |
| | Ideational fluency | Produce lots of ideas related to condition or object |
| | Associational fluency | Produce many words or phrases meaningfully related to given concept |
| | Expressional fluency | Rapidly generate and organize words meaningfully into complex ideas |

| | |
|---|---|
| Naming fluency | Rapidly produce names for concepts |
| Sensitivity to problems | Rapidly generate solutions to practical problems |
| Originality/creativity | Rapidly produce clever or original responses to tasks |
| Name-face matching[b] | Recall names associated with faces, and vice versa |
| Interpersonal process recall[b] | Recall flow of interchanges with others, including one's thoughts and affective states |
| **Quantitative knowledge** | |
| Mathematical knowledge | General knowledge about mathematics |
| Mathematical achievement | Measured math achievement |
| **Visual** | |
| Visualization | Mentally manipulate objects to see how they would appear under other conditions |
| Spatial relations (nonsocial) | Maintain orientation with respect to objects in space or manipulate visual patterns |
| Reading facial affect[b] | Perceive affect in facial expressions |
| Reading body language[b] | Perceive affect or meaning in body poses and movement |
| **Auditory** | |
| Reading voice affect[b] | Perceive affect in voices |
| **Reading/writing** | |
| Print comprehension | General literacy, measured by reading vocabulary and reading comprehension tests |
| Writing ability | Write clearly, with good organization |
| English usage knowledge | For example, punctuation, spelling, usage |
| **Processing speed** | |
| Perceptual speed | Rapidly search and compare visual symbols presented contiguously |
| **Reaction time** | |
| Semantic processing speed | Reaction time for decisions requiring encoding and thinking about information |

[a]Does not include all facets of factors identified through research (see McGrew and Flanagan, 1998); only those especially relevant to organizational consulting are listed.

[b]Facets related to social abilities were not part of Carroll's theory (1993); their inclusion here is therefore provisional.

Intelligence is important but is not the only ability that matters in organizational consulting contexts. One problem is how to distinguish intelligence from other abilities, and whether such other abilities in some sense also constitute intelligences. Researchers usually operationalize intelligence as consisting of psychometric *g* (also called general cognitive ability; see Spearman & Jones, 1950), following Spearman's distinction between *g* and specific abilities. Some researchers then define non-*g*, specific abilities, as the variance associated with ability tests once the *g* variance has been removed (Carson, 1998). Other researchers, such as Carroll (1993), Cattell (1957; see McGrew & Flanagan, 1998), and Horn (1994), instead consider specific abilities as facets that are admixtures of *g* and non-*g* specific abilities. Our present discussion follows the latter approach.

## Fluid Intelligence (Reasoning)

This ability helps people reason through problems requiring concentrated attention and careful reasoning of a logical nature. The ability benefits individuals performing novel tasks that cannot be performed automatically; essentially, the individual must create a mental representation of the set of variables or concepts important for completion of the task, and then initiate a set of steps required to successfully perform the task, presumably relying on this mental model in doing so. This ability includes both major approaches to reasoning (inductive and deductive), drawing inferences and considering implications (and making extrapolations), thinking about concepts, and recognizing relationships between elements of problems (and then solving the problems). This ability is broadly important in many work settings, particularly when the worker cannot rely on tried-and-true routines and established skills to get the job done. Organizational consulting psychologists must be high in this ability to succeed, because they constantly confront novel problems that often depend on understanding the relations of many factors for their solution.

## Crystallized Intelligence (Knowledge)

This ability refers to an individual's deep, broad knowledge of a culture and its effective application. In addition to helping people win on televised trivia game shows, this ability provides the raw information materials that support the successful application of more complex behaviors. For example, knowledge enhances leadership and creativity, as discussed later in this chapter.

We suggest that four facets of crystallized intelligence might be especially important in helping individuals contribute and adjust to organizations: business knowledge, psychological knowledge, autobiographical knowledge, and biographical knowledge. That business knowledge is important in business success almost goes without saying. Psychological knowledge, too, aids individuals in both collaborating and competing to attain goals. Autobiographical knowledge helps individuals recall both past actions that worked and those that did not. Finally, biographical knowledge helps individuals do the same through the study of others' lives; one sees this form of knowledge even in the memorization of famous quotations by famous innovators and leaders, a penchant of many business executives. Biographical knowledge is especially important in the creation of paragons, in which one closely studies the biographies of individuals whose characteristics one seeks to emulate through one's own vocational behavior. The consultant may be wise to gain an understanding of the set of paragons that individuals have created, for they serve as important resources guiding individual behavior.

## Memory, Short- and Long-Term

Although Carroll (1993) separates memory processes into short- and long-term broad factors, we combine them for the present discussion, because his short-term factor includes only two facets, memory span and learning abilities, of which only the first is well understood, with the second facet also being associated with the long-term memory factor. Short-term memory is a limited-capacity system; individuals can hold only about seven (plus or minus two) units of information at a time. The ability involves retaining information in immediate awareness for use within a few seconds; an example of its use is remembering phone numbers. People use this ability hundreds of times a day without (generally) realizing it, and any relative deficits can prove irksome, and may require close attention to information and the development of compensatory strategies, such as immediately writing new information down.

Long-term memory, also called long-term storage and retrieval, represents a set of abilities that collectively are like having a good librarian in your mind; the librarian effectively indexes (encodes) information when initially received, stores it in the proper place (long-term memory), and then can help you easily find it when needed (retrieval). Extending the metaphor, the ability does not depend on the size of the library (crystallized or quantitative intelligence), but rather the quality of the librarian. Closely related to this ability might be ideational or associational fluency, likely to be important to creativity.

In addition to the facets of memory discussed by Carroll (1993) and McGrew and Flanagan (1998; see Table 1.1), we suggest two facets of memory that might be important for individuals in organizations but which are not yet well studied in that context: name-face matching, and interpersonal process recall. Some individuals are relatively better at learning associations between names and faces, which provides an advantage in many types of tasks and settings. Interpersonal process recall refers to the ability to encode and recall the process of interactions between individuals, including one's own thoughts and affective states. This is an ability that many counselors and psychologists excel at, but that will also aid managers working through others.

## Quantitative Knowledge

This ability helps one solve math problems correctly. It involves the individual's store of acquired quantitative declarative knowledge (the rules) and procedural knowledge (how to apply the rules in practice). Many jobs require substantial quantitative knowledge.

## Visual (Spatial) Processing

This ability subsumes the variety of narrow abilities that relate to thinking about visual images, including the facets of the generation, storage, retrieval, and transformation of images. Individuals high in this ability might be more likely to think in terms of images rather than, say, words, and can manipulate shapes visually as might be needed by architects, engineers, and electricians. Such individuals might be more likely to draw pictures (or doodle) to represent their thoughts than to put them into words, serving also as an aid to spur further visual thinking. Without some visual imagery to focus and hold their thoughts, individuals high in this ability may be prone to losing their attentional focus.

We suggest two facets of this ability that relate to social skills: reading facial affect and reading body language (see also Robins, 2002). Both can facilitate responsiveness in social interaction and the reception of emotional cues beyond those conveyed by communication through speech.

## Auditory Processing

This ability depends on sound and our sense of hearing. Its exercise involves the production, storage, retrieval, and transformation of sounds. Individuals high in this ability will generally find it easy to acquire and remember information obtained through hearing. We suggest one additional facet of this ability, perceive affect in voices, that enhances the quality of communication through speech.

## Reading/Writing

This ability is not well-defined or researched in the context of broad arrays of abilities, but appears to subsume a number of very narrow component abilities (for example, reading, decoding, and spelling) that, at more complex levels, support such activities as comprehending written passages and writing stories. As with quantitative knowledge, this ability includes both declarative and procedural aspects. Lack of ability in this area can impose steep limitations on advancement through many careers, and some research suggests that an alarmingly high proportion of the American public possesses levels of literacy that are marginal.

## Processing Speed

This is the first of two broad speed abilities, and refers to mental quickness and performing cognitive tasks automatically and efficiently in ways that make minimal demands on mental capacity, especially important when an individual must focus attention and concentration. Processing speed does not refer to simple reactions, but rather to sustaining an efficient and rapid mental process over some duration.

## Decision/Reaction Time or Speed

This second broad speed ability relates to an individual's quickness in making decisions or reacting quickly. It facilitates the speediness of immediate reactions.

Clearly, it will rarely be possible or even desirable to measure all abilities in a particular organizational consulting application. Still, this review of job-relevant abilities implies that it would be very naïve to assume that a single ability trait, even one as broad as intelligence, would be universally applicable. As importantly, occupations, and therefore organizations, are not created tabula rasa. When theories are proposed of such sweeping concepts as organizational learning, it should not be forgotten that organizations, among other things, are the sum (or is it multiplier?) of their individual ability patterns. Some organizations select for and retain only the highest end of the ability spectrum; for others, abilities are less important and the array of talent is more limiting. Such individual difference variables are rarely considered when measuring organizational-level variables that might de facto be influenced by the ability constellation of employees.

# PERSONALITY TRAITS

Personality traits refer to the way people view the world and the manner and style in which they do things, and therefore predict the style as well as the content of behavior. Although some early theorists and researchers (for example, Allport, 1937) discussed the importance of this domain for education, work, and everyday life, most of the discussion of personality was, until the last few decades, primarily focused on psychopathology. Hogan and Roberts (2001) credit the rising importance of personality psychology within organizational psychology to several causes. First, the use of cognitive ability testing may result in adverse impact for some protected classes of job seekers under U.S. law (due mainly to group differences in g; see Herrnstein & Murray, 1994), while well-constructed measures of personality generally do not. Second, the rise of factor-analytically based taxonomies of personality—and especially the five-factor model (probably starting with Tupes & Christal, 1961)—provided a way to organize thousands of different personality measures within a handful of broad groups of traits, which helped to rationalize an otherwise unwieldy literature. Third, various content- and meta-analytic reviews of the literature on personnel and selection demonstrated the important roles that personality traits could play in the prediction of job performance and adjustment. Thus, personality traits, like abilities, predict important work and organizational outcomes, and, like abilities, one may classify them into one of a few broad categories.

## Personality Variables with Consulting Relevance

A major question in discussing the personality variables relevant for organizational consulting psychology is whether one need only focus on the big five personality traits, or whether focus should also extend to the facets, or components, of the big five, and perhaps to other traits as well. Paunonen and Nicol (2001) argue that in many practical applications, one can obtain greater benefits from using the facets instead of focusing only on the broad, overarching factors. However, there is no universally agreed on list of these facets, to parallel the consensus on the big five factors; different authors have proposed different sets (or at least names) of these facets and narrow personality traits. For example, Lowman (1991) describes the organizational importance of such additional personality traits, including achievement orientation, need for power, and masculinity-femininity (or its underlying and more socially acceptable derivatives). Our present discussion of the big five traits and their facets draws from that used in the Revised NEO Personality Inventory (NEO-PI-R; Costa & McCrae, 1992). Although both the measure and its ability to measure facets are not without criticism (see Block, 1995), Piedmont (2001) favorably reviews the empirical support for both the general domain and facet scales, also citing Costa and McCrae's discussion (1995) of the conceptual relations of the domains and their facets. Tinsley (1993) speculated that the personality factor and facet scores of the NEO-PI might overlap with some of the personality and adjustment constructs thought to be important to work adjustment. However, we are mindful that just because the authors of the NEO-PI-R report the existence of a particular facet does not necessarily mean that the facet is viewed as critical for organizational behavior, or that there exists any degree of consensus around its practical usefulness. Therefore, we will note which of these facets have received the most empirical support in organizational research.

**Conscientiousness.** This might be the most important of the big five traits in terms of impact on work performance and adjustment to organizations (Barrick, Mount, & Judge 2001). Costa and McCrae (1992) report that important facets include competence, order, dutifulness, achievement striving, self-discipline, and deliberation, all characteristics that managers generally value in their employees (Fallon, Avis, Kudisch, Gornet, & Frost, 2000; Organ, 1988). Dutifulness is an important construct in the study of organizational issues related to military personnel (for example, Helme, Willemin, & Day, 1971).

**Extraversion/Introversion.** Many authors also describe this trait as being important to organizational adjustment, and for the prediction of job tenure and for influencing how one tries to accomplish work (see, for example, Caldwell & Burger, 1997). Costa and McCrae (1992) report that facets include warmth, gregariousness, assertiveness, activity, excitement seeking, and positive emotions. Many organizational theorists and researchers refer to the constructs warmth (Bass, Valenzi, Farrow, & Solomon, 1975), gregariousness (Hughes, 1956), assertiveness (McNamara & Delamater, 1985), activity (Magee & Hojat, 1998), excitement-seeking (Schroeder, Broach, & Young, 1993), and positive emotions (see Fredrickson, 2000; Staw, Sutton, & Pelled, 1994). Extraversion/introversion describes personality variables of temperament that reflect not so much social gregariousness as need for time to oneself and seeking stimulation internally versus externally (see Zuckerman, 1997).

**Agreeableness.** Although the evidence for its prediction of work-related outcomes is limited (see Barrick et al., 2001) except for jobs involving interpersonal interactions, the personality trait of agreeableness is included in most big five models of personality. Individuals high in this trait are easy to get along with and trust, while individuals low in the trait leave others on edge and wary of direct contact. Researchers and scientists typically are low on the trait, and may express the trait through skepticism and lack of faith that something is so just because someone says so. There are many other ways to express disagreeableness, just as there are many types of vinegar. Organizational consulting psychologists may encounter this trait (on the low, disagreeable end) through individuals who, for a variety of reasons, seem to have a hard time fitting in. However, individuals at the high end of the trait may, depending on the demands of their role and position, also face difficulties. For example, executives of charitable foundations that give grants find themselves being asked repeatedly for money and faith; if the executive is too agreeable, and cannot learn to say no without regret, he or she will experience enormous stress and ultimately fail. According to Costa and McCrae (1992), facets of the trait include trust, straightforwardness, altruism, compliance, modesty, and tender-mindedness. Most of these constructs have been of interest to organizational researchers, including trust (Coleman & Riley, 1970), straightforwardness (Colyer, 1951), altruism (MacKenzie, Podsakoff, & Fetter, 1991; Magee & Hojat, 1998), compliance (Wicks, 1998), and modesty (Wosinska, Dabul, Whetstone-Dion, & Cialdini, 1996).

**Openness to Experience.** This trait also has had mixed results in predicting occupational outcomes (see Barrick et al., 2001), and appears to be a complex trait (for example, Ferguson & Patterson, 1998). Presumably, the trait's importance will vary in importance depending on the nature of the organization's or work unit's mission. It may also predict more to career choice than to occupational performance issues (Tokar, Vaux, & Swanson, 1995). Individuals low on the trait would be expected to be more likely to focus on the practical side and to eschew imagination; this can be very useful when the purpose of the organization is to focus on unexciting details and just get the job done. On the other hand, in organizations that require flexibility of response and must foster independent and creative problem solving, individuals high on the trait can prove very important. An interesting aspect of this trait is that it seems to be positively correlated to measures of intelligence (g) (Carson, Stalikas, & Bizot, 1997; Kline, 2001). Costa and McCrae (1992) describe the facets of this trait as fantasy, aesthetics, feelings, actions, ideas, and values. Although organizational researchers and theorists have explored issues related to many of these facets at an abstract or organizational level, or perhaps in terms of characteristics of the leaders of organizations (especially in relation to factors that support charismatic or transformative leadership), the facets (as traits) seem not to have been heavily researched among the general membership of organizations.

**Neuroticism.** Neuroticism, along with extraversion/introversion, was one of the earliest of the broad personality traits identified by researchers (Roberts & Hogan, 2001). People on the high end of the trait tend to be anxious, become depressed, have poor self-concept, and experience negative emotions. Work can be adversely affected by neuroticism (Lowman, 1989) except, to some extent, in certain creative occupations in which neuroticism may be both expected and, within limits, even enhance performance (Lowman, 1993a). Facets reported by Costa and McCrae (1992) include anxiety, angry hostility, depression, self-consciousness, impulsiveness, and vulnerability. Anxiety (Davids & Mahoney, 1957) and self-consciousness (Buss, 1980) have served as a focus in organizational research. Although angry hostility per se has not received attention from organizational researchers, workplace violence and its causes certainly have (see Neuman & Baron, 1998), along with personality correlates of other hostile workplace behavior (Calabrese, 2000). Depression has been researched extensively in organizational contexts (see Lowman, 1993a), although apparently not as a dispositional style. Finally, impulsiveness seems to have received little attention from organizational consultants except as a feature of various disorders, such as narcissism (for example, Levinson, Sabbath, & Connor, 1992). Judge and Bono (2001) argue that neuroticism should be conceptualized even more broadly, also incorporating emotional stability and negative emotionality, along with other tendencies related to core self-evaluation, such as self-esteem, generalized self-efficacy, and locus of control.

**Other Personality Issues.** An unresolved question in the study of personality traits is the degree to which they rest on underlying temperaments, presumed to be present from birth. Strelau (1998) provides an excellent review of this literature, essentially concluding that although there may be some evidence that each of the big five broad personality traits may rest to some degree on underlying temperamental variables, the strongest evidence points to just two areas of personality: extraversion and neuroticism. Because these traits have relatively strong linkages to underlying, physiologically determined temperaments, they might be especially resistant to modification in adulthood. Of course, any worker might act the part for a while (what Helmreich & Wilhelm, 1987, called the "honeymoon effect"), but perhaps especially in these traits, individuals will revert to temperamental type over time. Readers interested in learning more about the role of personality in organizations are directed to Lowman (1991) and Roberts and Hogan (2001).

As with occupational interests, complex patterns are as important as measuring individual variables (George & Zhou, 2001; Roberts and Hogan 2001). Configurations of personality traits and their patterns in relationships to particular organizational variables might help moderate the impact of single dimensions of personality. Similarly, most personality traits are not linear (for example, good to bad) in their influence on work outcomes: too much aggressiveness might, depending on the job, organization, or culture, be as problematic as too little.

## INTERDOMAIN RELATIONSHIPS

If patterns of variables are important within a single domain (such as personality or interests), they are even more important—but far less studied—across domains. Pioneering work in examining, at the individual-level analysis, interdomain relationships has been offered by certain researchers (for example, Ackerman & Heggestad, 1997; Ackerman, Kyllonen, & Roberts, 1999; Carson, 1998; Lowman, 1991, 1993b). Much more research is needed before conclusions can reliably be drawn about the effects of interests, personality, and ability as they interact with each other. However, as new studies emerge, in time it will be possible to understand the nuances of interdomain relationships that, it would be expected, sometimes compensate for areas of relative weakness (for example, extraversion for limited intelligence), or that sometimes may add constraints (for example, disagreeableness combined with high intelligence in an interpersonally relevant occupation).

## CONCLUSION

This chapter has served as a Cook's tour of individual-level variables relevant for the work of organizational consulting psychologists, with only brief stops in the various domains of ability, personality, interest, and character. Such a brief survey cannot, of course, go into much depth for any given variable, and we have left out some important ones. For example, we have not addressed life history per se (except for autobiographical knowledge as a facet of crystallized intelligence), and the way that biographical data (biodata) might affect adjustment to work (see Stokes, Mumford, & Owens, 1994). However, we assume that life history achieves this effect mainly through its shaping of the various traits and aspects of character described in this chapter.

We also have not discussed how these individual qualities might appear when viewed through the stories that individuals tell about their work experience, reflecting the importance that many organizational consulting psychologists place on practical methods that are essentially forms of story-elicitation and interpretation. However, such qualitative approaches are methods for assessing the individual-level variables, and are not themselves the variables of interest; in particular, their use is unlikely to uncover any broadly applicable traits beyond those outlined in this chapter. Of course, we could be wrong, and as we have stated, there are likely to exist some traits that are unique or rare that lie outside of the present list.

Finally, although traits might themselves be important for understanding the behavior and experience of individuals in various settings, such as work and school, they do not tell the whole story. As Anne Anastasi (1937), a pioneer in differential psychology, put it, "the individual may be regarded partly as a resultant of his multiple group memberships" (p. 601), as other chapters in this volume will attest. It is therefore through efforts to better understand both the groups of which the individual is a member, as well as the organizations that subsume these groups, that the organizational consulting psychologist can ultimately enhance his or her effectiveness in working with individuals.

# References

Ackerman, P. L., & Heggestad, E. D. (1997). Intelligence, personality, and interests: Evidence for overlapping traits. *Psychological Bulletin, 121,* 219–245.

Ackerman, P. L., Kyllonen, P. C., & Roberts, R. D. (Eds.). (1999). *Learning and individual differences: Process, trait, and content determinants.* Washington, DC: American Psychological Association.

Allport, G. W. (1937). *Personality: A psychological interpretation.* New York: Henry Holt.

Anastasi, A. (1937). *Differential psychology: Individual and group differences in behavior.* Old Tappan, NJ: Macmillan.

Barrick, M. R., Mount, M. K., & Judge, T. A. (2001). Personality and performance at the beginning of the new millennium: What do we know and where do we go next. *International Journal of Selection and Assessment, 9,* 9–30.

Bass, B. M., Valenzi, E. R., Farrow, D. L., & Solomon, R. J. (1975). Management styles associated with organizational, task, personal, and interpersonal contingencies. *Journal of Applied Psychology, 60*(6), 720–729.

Blackmore, S. (1999). *The meme machine.* Oxford, England: Oxford University Press.

Block, J. (1995). A contrarian view of the five-factor approach to personality description. *Psychological Bulletin, 117,* 187–215.

Boudreau, J. W., Boswell, W. R., & Judge, T. A. (2001). Effects of personality on executive career success in the United States and Europe. *Journal of Vocational Behavior, 58,* 53–81.

Brodie, R. (1996). *Virus of the mind: The new science of the meme.* Seattle, WA: Integral Press.

Buss, A. H. (1980). *Self-consciousness and social anxiety.* New York: Freeman.

Calabrese, K. R. (2000). Interpersonal conflict and sarcasm in the workplace. *Genetic, Social, and General Psychology Monographs, 126*(4), 459–494.

Caldwell, D. F., & Burger, J. M. (1997). Personality and social influence strategies in the workplace. *Personality and Social Psychology Bulletin, 23,* 1003–1012.

Carroll, J. B. (1993). *Human cognitive abilities: A survey of factor-analytic studies.* Cambridge, England: Cambridge University Press.

Carson, A. D. (1998). The integration of interests, aptitudes, and personality traits: A test of Lowman's matrix. *Journal of Career Assessment, 6,* 83–105.

Carson, A. D., Stalikas, A., & Bizot, E. B. (1997). Correlations between the Myers-Briggs Type Indicator (MBTI) and measures of aptitudes. *Journal of Career Assessment, 5*(1), 81–104.

Cattell, R. B. (1941). Some theoretical issues in adult intelligence testing. *Psychological Bulletin, 38,* 592.

Cattell, R. B. (1957). *Personality and motivation structure and measurement.* New York: World Book.

Coleman, R. J., & Riley, M. J. (1970). The chief executive: His personality characteristics and the firm's growth rate. *Personnel Journal, 49*(12), 994–1001.

Colyer, D. M. (1951). The good foreman—as his men see him. *Personnel, 28,* 140–147.

Costa, P. T., Jr., & McCrae, R. R. (1992). *Revised NEO Personality Inventory (NEO-PI-R) and NEO Five-Factor Inventory (NEO-FFI) professional manual.* Odessa, FL: Psychological Assessment Resources.

Costa, P. T., Jr., & McCrae, R. R. (1995). Domains and facets: Hierarchical personality assessment using the Revised NEO Personality Inventory. *Journal of Personality Assessment, 64,* 21–50.

Davids, A., & Mahoney, J. T. (1957). Personality dynamics and accident proneness in an industrial setting. *Journal of Applied Psychology, 41,* 303–306.

Dawkins, R. (1976). *The selfish gene.* Oxford University Press.

Dennis, I., & Tapsfield, P. (1996). *Human abilities. Their nature and measurement.* Hillsdale, NJ: Erlbaum.

Ericsson, K. A. (1996). *The road to excellence. The acquisition of expert performance in the arts and sciences, sports, and games.* Hillsdale, NJ: Erlbaum.

Fallon, J. D., Avis, J. M., Kudisch, J. D., Gornet, T. P., & Frost, A. (2000). Conscientiousness as a predictor of productive and counterproductive behaviors. *Journal of Business and Psychology, 15,* 339–349.

Ferguson, E., & Patterson, F. (1998). The five factor model of personality: Openness a distinct but related construct. *Personality and Individual Differences, 24,* 789–796.

Fredrickson, B. L. (2000). Why positive emotions matter in organizations: Lessons from the broaden-and-build model. *The Psychologist-Manager Journal, 4*(2), 131–142.

George, J. M., & Zhou, J. (2001). When openness to experience and conscientiousness are related to creative behavior: An interactional approach. *Journal of Applied Psychology, 86,* 513–524.

Gottfredson, L. S. (1997). Mainstream science on intelligence: An editorial with 52 signatories, history, and bibliography. *Intelligence, 24,* 13–23 (original work published 1994).

Gottfredson, L. S. (1999). The nature and nurture of vocational interests. In M. L. Savickas & A. R. Spokane (Eds.), *Vocational interests: Meaning, measurement, and counseling use* (pp. 57–85). Palo Alto, CA: Davies-Black.

Helme, W. H., Willemin, L. P., & Day, R. W. (1971). *Psychological factors measured in the Differential Officer Battery* (U.S. Army Behavior & Systems Research Lab Technical Research Report No. 1173).

Helmreich, R. L., & Wilhelm, J. A. (1987). *Human performance in aerospace environments: The search for psychological determinants.* Unpublished manuscript, University of Texas, Austin.

Herrnstein, R. J., & Murray, C. (1994). *The bell curve: Intelligence and class structure in American life.* New York: Free Press.

Hogan, J. L., & Roberts, B. W. (2001). Introduction: Personality and industrial and organizational psychology. In B. W. Roberts & R. Hogan (Eds.), *Personality psychology in the workplace* (pp. 3–16). Washington, DC: American Psychological Association.

Holland, J. L. (1959). A theory of vocational choice. *Journal of Counseling Psychology, 6,* 35–45.

Holland, J. L. (1997). *Making vocational choices: A theory of vocational personalities and work environments* (3rd ed.). Odessa, FL: Psychological Assessment Resources.

Horn, J. L. (1994). Theory of fluid and crystallized intelligence. In R. J. Sternberg (Ed.), *Encyclopedia of human intelligence* (pp. 443–451). Old Tappan, NJ: Macmillan.

Hough, L. M. (2001). I/Owes its advances to personality. In B. W. Roberts & R. Hogan (Eds.), *Personality psychology in the workplace* (pp. 19–44). Washington, DC: American Psychological Association.

Howe, M.J.A. (1999). *Genius explained.* Cambridge, England: Cambridge University Press.

Hughes, J. L. (1956). Expressed personality needs as predictors of sales success. *Personnel Psychology, 9,* 347–357.

Judge, T. A., & Bono, J. E. (2001). A rose by any other name: Are self-esteem, generalized self-efficacy, neuroticism, and locus of control indicators of a common construct? In B. W. Roberts & R. Hogan (Eds.), *Personality psychology in the workplace* (pp. 93–118). Washington, DC: American Psychological Association.

Kilburg, R. R. (2002). Individual interventions in consulting psychology. In R. L. Lowman (Ed.), *Handbook of organizational consulting psychology* (pp. 109–138). San Francisco: Jossey-Bass.

Kline, P. (2001). Ability and temperament. In J. M. Collis & S. Messick (Eds.), *Intelligence and personality: Bridging the gap in theory and measurement* (pp. 113–118). Hillsdale, NJ: Erlbaum.

Levinson, H., Sabbath, J., & Connor, J. (1992). Bearding the lion that roared: A case study of organizational consultation. *Consulting Psychology Journal: Practice and Research, 44,* 2–16.

Lowman, R. L. (1989). *Pre-employment screening for psychopathology: A guide to professional practice.* Sarasota, FL: Professional Resource Exchange.

Lowman, R. L. (1991). *The clinical practice of career assessment: Interests, abilities, and personality.* Washington, DC: American Psychological Association.

Lowman, R. L. (1993a). *Counseling and psychotherapy of work dysfunctions.* Washington, DC: American Psychological Association.

Lowman, R. L. (1993b). The inter-domain model of career assessment and counseling. *Journal of Counseling and Development, 71,* 549–554.

Lowman, R. L., & Carson, A. D. (in press). Assessment of interests. In J. Graham & J. Naglieri (Eds.), *Handbook of comprehensive psychological assessment.* New York: Wiley.

MacKenzie, S. B., Podsakoff, P. M., & Fetter, R. (1991). Organizational citizenship behavior and objective productivity as determinants of managerial evaluations of salespersons' performance. *Organizational Behavior & Human Decision Processes, 50*(1), 123–150.

Magee, M., & Hojat, M. (1998). Personality profiles of male and female positive role models in medicine. *Psychological Reports, 82*(2), 547–559.

McGrew, K. S., & Flanagan, D. P. (1998). The intelligence test desk reference (ITDR): Gf-Gc cross battery assessment. Boston: Allyn & Bacon.

McNamara, J. R., & Delamater, R. J. (1985). Note on the social impact of assertiveness in occupational contexts. *Psychological Reports, 56*(3), 819–822.

Moloney, D. P., Bouchard, T. J., Jr., & Segal, N. L. (1991). A genetic and environmental analysis of the vocational interests of monozygotic and dizygotic twins reared apart. *Journal of Vocational Behavior, 39,* 76–109.

Neuman, J. H., & Baron, R. A. (1998). Workplace violence and workplace aggression: Evidence concerning specific forms, potential causes, and preferred targets. *Journal of Management, 24*(3), 391–419.

Organ, D. W. (1988). *Organizational citizenship behavior: The good soldier syndrome.* Lexington, MA: Heath.

Paunonen, S. V., & Nicol, A. A. M. (2001). The personality hierarchy and the prediction of work behaviors. In B. W. Roberts & R. Hogan (Eds.), *Personality psychology in the workplace* (pp. 161–191). Washington, DC: American Psychological Association.

Piedmont, R. L. (2001, May 3). *Test review: The NEO-PI-R.* Retrieved December 14, 2001, from http://aac.ncat.edu/newsnotes/y97fall.html

Roberts, B. W., & Hogan, R. (Eds.). (2001). *Personality psychology in the workplace.* Washington, DC: American Psychological Association.

Robins, S. (2002). A consultant's guide to understanding and promoting emotional intelligence in the workplace. In R. L. Lowman (Ed.), *Handbook of organizational consulting psychology* (pp. 159–184). San Francisco: Jossey-Bass.

Schroeder, D. J., Broach, D., & Young, W. C. (1993). *Contribution of personality to the prediction of success in initial air traffic control specialist training* (Report FAA-AM-93-4 29). Washington, DC: Federal Aviation Administration, Office of Aviation Medicine.

Snow, R. E. (1998). Abilities as aptitudes and achievements in learning situations. In J. J. McArdle & R. W. Woodcock (Eds.), *Human cognitive abilities in theory and practice* (pp. 93–112). Hillsdale, NJ: Erlbaum.

Spearman, C., & Jones, L.L.W. (1950). *Human ability.* Old Tappan, NJ: Macmillan.

Staw, B. M., Sutton, R. I., & Pelled, L. H. (1994). Employee positive emotion and favorable outcomes at the workplace. *Organization Science, 5*(1), 51–71.

Stokes, G. S., Mumford, M. D., & Owens, W. A. (Eds.). (1994). *Biodata handbook: Theory, research, and use of biographical information in selection and performance prediction.* Palo Alto, CA: CPP Books.

Strelau, J. (1998). *Temperament.* New York: Plenum.

Strong, E. K. (1943). *Vocational interests of men and women.* Palo Alto, CA: Stanford University Press.

Strong, E. K. (1955). *Vocational interests 18 years after college.* Minneapolis, MN: University of Minnesota Press.

Tinsley, D. J. (1993). Extensions, elaborations, and construct validation of the theory of work adjustment. *Journal of Vocational Behavior, 43*(1), 67–74.

Tokar, D. M., Vaux, A., & Swanson, J. L. (1995). Dimensions relating Holland's vocational personality typology and the five-factor model. *Journal of Career Assessment, 3,* 57–74.

Tupes, E. C., & Christal, R. E. (1961). Recurrent personality factors based on trait ratings. *Journal of Personality, 60*, 225–251.

Wicks, D. (1998). The dynamics of compliance: Influences on individual responses to institutional expectations (Doctoral dissertation York University, 1998). *Dissertation Abstracts International, 58*(10-A), 3997.

Wosinska, W., Dabul, A. J., Whetstone-Dion, R., & Cialdini, R. B. (1996). Self-presentational responses to success in the organization: The costs and benefits of modesty. *Basic and Applied Social Psychology, 18*(2), 229–242

Zuckerman, M. (1997). The psychobiological basis of personality. In H. Nyborg (Ed.), *The scientific study of human nature: Tribute to Hans J. Eysenck at eighty* (pp. 3–16). New York: Pergamon Press.

# CHAPTER TWO

# Organizational Consulting to Groups and Teams

Arthur M. Freedman
*School of Public Affairs*
*American University*

E. Skipton Leonard
*Personnel Decisions International*

Despite the popularity of organizational teams today, they have not always been so valued (Leonard & Freedman, 2000). In fact, prior to the twentieth century, most scholars in the late nineteenth century viewed collective behavior, shared governance, and decision-making with a good deal of suspicion. Le Bon ([1895] 1960) described the collective behavior of the common man during the French Revolution and the Third Republic as primitive and childlike. In the early industrial revolution when labor was cheap and efficiency less important, production was increased by massing individual workers around individual machines rather than organizing them into teams. Early industrialists might have concluded that there was no advantage to encouraging workers to communicate and interact, thereby risking the development of rebellion and collective resistance to the will of the leadership. It might have been considered wiser to keep workers ignorant and highly dependent on the organizational leadership.

After World War II, Kurt Lewin (1947) and his students launched the field of group dynamics within social psychology. Most of the research that is the foundation for current group and team development methodology was completed in the twenty years following Lewin's untimely death in 1947. The advent of technology that allowed people anywhere in the world to work and share information concurrently has greatly increased the popularity of teams in organizations. Many organizations today are organized around teams as the fundamental structural unit (Mohrman, Cohen, & Mohrman, 1995). By the late 1980s and early

1990s the virtues of high-performance and cross-functional teams were being touted by organizations and organizational theorists alike (for example, Katzenbach & Smith, 1993; Reich, 1987; Vaill, 1989). In the last half-decade of the last century, the popularity of virtual teams using the most advanced communications technology to work collaboratively has created the need to reexamine the basic tenets of group and team theory and practice. This chapter provides the consulting psychologist with fundamental knowledge necessary to consult traditional intact (collocated) teams, as well as the currently popular virtual teams that link members from distant parts of the organization and the world. We will also provide a discussion of future trends for group and team theory and practice.

## UNDERSTANDING GROUPS AND TEAMS

It is practical to conceive of teams and groups as being the extremes of a developmental continuum. In this view, a group is merely an aggregate or collection of individuals, whereas a team is composed of members who are committed to realizing a common mission (task) and have developed a consensual perception of the goals that they must achieve by performing various tasks (McFarland, Leonard, & Morris, 1984). Teams are characterized by interdependency and accountability (Lipnack & Stamps, 1997; Katzenbach & Smith, 1993; Rawlings, 2000), and usually require the continuous integration of the expertise distributed among them (Donnellon, 1996).

Teamwork is the term used to describe the coordination of efforts and integration of expertise among team members who perform the tasks that culminate in achieving the goals that fulfill the team's mission. The degree of required coordination and integration of effort varies widely from team to team. Using a sports team analogy, golf and ski teams require little coordination and integration, while baseball and football teams require moderate to high levels of coordination and integration, respectively (McFarland, Leonard, & Morris, 1984; Keidel, 1984). In business organizations, project teams require greater coordination and integration of effort than do management teams. A high degree of collaboration is expected between members of management teams, but a complete integration of activities and efforts is generally not. The complete removal of functional boundaries between management team members is difficult and probably not desirable. Table 2.1 displays a variety of common team types along a continuum of low, medium, and high requirements for interdependence, collaboration, and communication.

Teams that require more interdependence, collaboration, and communication have more of a feeling of "teamness" (that is, having a group identity, sense of camaraderie, and cohesiveness) than teams lower on those dimensions. These

Table 2.1. Level of Communication Required in Relation to Team Type and Task Requirements.

| *Need for Communication/Collaboration* | | |
| --- | --- | --- |
| Low | Medium | High |
| **Team Type** | | |
| • Committees<br>• Special interest groups<br>• Work groups<br>• Task force<br>• Improvement teams<br>• Department groups | • Cross-functional teams<br>• Leadership teams<br>• Process teams | • Self-directed work teams<br>• Project teams<br>• High-performance team |
| **Team Task Requirements** | | |
| • Individual decision-making<br>• Recommendations<br>• Information sharing | • Team and coordinated individual decisions<br>• Strategic planning<br>• High coordination | • Consensus joint decisions<br>• Accountable team outcome<br>• High level of working together<br>• High level of alignment |

*Source:* Personnel Decisions International, 2001. Used by permission.

are also the kinds of teams that recent authors (for example, Katzenbach & Smith, 1993) have referred to as high-performance teams. It should be kept in mind, however, that there are lots of effective and useful teams in organizations that require more limited or moderate degrees of interdependence, collaboration, and communication. For instance, many task forces meet primarily to do general planning and to distribute the necessary work to individual team members, who then work more or less independently. A high degree of communication and collaboration may not be necessary for these teams.

## Teams From a Systems Perspective

Several decades ago it was common to consider teams as isolated, functional organizational entities without considering the organizational system in which they were embedded. In contemporary project-oriented organizations, viewing teams as isolated units makes no sense at all. Consider the cross-functional team composed of members from many other functional teams. The ripple effect of any decisions made within the cross-functional team across the rest of the organization is enormous by design.

From a systems perspective (Katz & Kahn, 1978; Fuqua & Newman, 2002; Von Bertalanffy, 1968), teams are subsystems within a larger organizational system. Figure 2.1 presents a systems view of an organization with a team-based structure. In this simplified schema, functional team members support the work of project teams. Organizations negotiate in the labor and supplier markets to obtain necessary inputs. These supply inputs are then transformed in the throughput process (work) to produce products that have value in the organization's internal or external customer markets. Subsystems within the organization rely upon interactive feedback loops with the customers, financial, supply, and labor markets to make decisions about level of production, product mix, product timing, financing, purchasing, and hiring.

Mohrman et al. (1995) describe three typical ways that team-based organizations can structure their throughput process. These include the project team structure, in which each member of a team represents a different function and more than one reporting line. In the functional team structure, a project team structure is laid over the formal organizational structure and members continue to report directly to their functional managers. Finally, in the matrix team structure, team members report directly to both project and functional managers.

## Task Accomplishment and System Maintenance

Both task accomplishment and system maintenance are vital to any organizational system, no matter the organizational level. The strategic goals of the organization, no matter how well conceived and initiated, cannot be achieved effectively if the integrity and well-being of all system components degrade as a result of neglect, apathy, or oversight. Analysis of team and organizational success consistently reveals the importance of process and roles to maintain and improve the system's infrastructure, both human and physical. For instance,

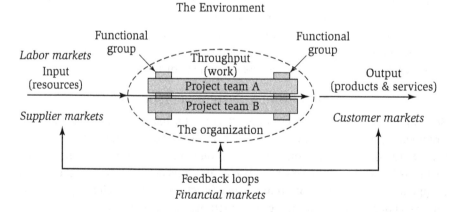

**Figure 2.1 Systems View of a Matrixed Organization.**

early group and team research (for example, Bales, 1950; Beck, 1981) revealed that task and socio-emotional leadership roles are inevitably differentiated as groups and teams struggle to achieve their goals. Without constant investment in physical and human system maintenance, organizations invariably succumb to Newton's second law of thermodynamics (the law of negative entropy)—all systems move toward disorganization, decay, and death without a constant infusion of energy for system maintenance.

## Linking and Coordinating Team Efforts

A common dysfunctional phenomenon in traditional functionally structured organizations is commonly termed "siloing." Without effective linking and coordinating processes, communications tend to travel vertically up and down through the functions with limited cross talk between functions, project teams, and business units, often regardless of their interdependency. Throughout the 1990s, management looked for ways to make the boundaries between functional "silos" more permeable. One common structural solution tried by organizations to neutralize this problem was the creation of cross-functional project management teams, steering committees, and task forces. In theory, these teams typically have planning and coordinating functions, and each team member represents the interests and perspectives of their function or project (Freedman, 2000). The advent of e-mail, intranets, groupware, and tele/videoconferencing has opened up huge possibilities for faster communication over infinite distances to a multitude of involved parties, but has also created a host of new problems for teams.

## Team Communications

When teams members are physically located near each other (collocated), direct face-to-face communications are relatively easy. When team members have visual contact with each other in personal discussions and team meetings, they are able to pick up nonverbal as well as verbal information. Communications theorists (for example, Watzlawick, Beavin, & Jackson, 1967) have long noted that messages have both a *content* aspect (the data of the communication) and a *relationship* aspect (how this communication is to be taken). For instance, "John, take this letter to the mail room," not only instructs John to deliver a letter, but also defines the relationship as a superior giving orders to a subordinate. The quality of the relationship aspect of a communication is frequently delivered by nonverbal behavior or contextual indicators, while the content aspect is usually delivered either verbally or in written form.

Understanding the relationship message usually takes precedence over understanding the content. Most people attach a higher level of importance to the relationship message because it tells them how to understand and what to do with the content. Since relationship messages are frequently delivered through nonverbal and contextual cues, careful attention is directed to these aspects. When there is a contradiction between relationship and content messages, the relationship message is perceived to be more valid. Relationship messages, mostly based on nonverbal behavior (facial expression, body movement, gestures, voice tone, inflection, pitch, volume, context, and others), are perceived as more honest because they are assumed to be under less conscious control than the actual words spoken or written (Watzlawick et al., 1967). The lack of visual and auditory contact, ignorance of cultural behavior styles, and linguistic nuance create significant obstacles to the accurate comprehension of the relationship aspect of messages in virtual teams and cross-functional teams that are trying to communicate over great distances, between different and alien cultures, or using non-native-tongue languages.

## Team Boundaries

In systems theory, boundaries can refer to physical (for example, discontinuities or barriers in space), temporal (beginnings or endings), behavioral (norms and roles), or process (input-throughput-output) features. Teams have a number of boundaries that have practical significance. First, teams have membership boundaries. Membership boundaries are more psychological than physical. As most of us have experienced sometime in our lives, there are times when we are technically counted as a member of a team when we don't feel like or are not perceived as a member of that particular team. Other important team boundaries include space (increasingly less relevant with teams connected only by digital or electronic means, so-called distributed teams), time (full- or part-time membership), primary task (what the team should and shouldn't be doing), and norms and roles (expected and permissible behavior). Effective team leadership cannot occur without managing the particular issues that are relevant to each of these team boundaries.

Norms prescribe the rules (written or unwritten) for behavior and proper ways of acting that have been accepted as legitimate and acceptable for all members of a team. In systems terms, norms (as well as roles) are filters that allow certain kinds of behavior and not others as appropriate and acceptable (Berrien, 1968). Norms are typically based upon commonly held assumptions about the need for the rule or convention (Hall, 1976; Schein, 1992). Within each culture, it can be expected that members understand and accept these assumptions. When cultural boundaries are crossed, however, this expectation is not warranted. Individual members of teams that have cross-organizational, geographical, and cultural boundaries will likely ascribe to different sets of norms that prescribe acceptable role behavior (Hofstede, 1991; Schein, 1992; Trompenaars, 1994). Furthermore, the various organizational subsystems and functional groups that generally have distinctive cultures can create problems in transacting business across internal organizational boundaries.

The assumptions that undergird these norms are seldom surfaced, leading to confusing behavior and considerable misunderstanding (Argyris & Schön, 1992). The lack of agreement regarding norms and assumptions is a formidable obstacle to high performance for teams whose members are distributed across functions, organizations, time zones, and regional or national cultures.

## The Impact of Reward Systems on Teams

Organizations use rewards to create incentives to motivate employees to work hard to achieve goals identified by the organization. Traditionally, most incentives have been linked to individual performance. While this approach does, to some extent, encourage individual achievement, it also sets up the potential for competition with fellow employees because salary and benefit decisions are usually zero-sum situations. Because salary increases come from a fixed pool, giving one person a larger raise necessarily reduces the amount available for others. This is also true for the other forms of rewards for individual performance (for example, recognition, choice assignments, promotions, and the like) (Lawler, 2000).

In most cases, intra-team competition for scarce individual rewards inhibits collaboration, cooperation, and communication, and reduces trust, making teamwork much more difficult. In the past, many organizations that moved from traditional to team-based structures overlooked the need to develop significant rewards for team as well as individual accomplishment (Hackman, 1990). This is especially true for high-performance teams for which the perception of a joint destiny (that is, "we all win or lose together") provides a powerful incentive for collaboration, cooperation, and fearless communication (Lipnack & Stamps, 1997).

## Group and Team Dynamics

One of the paradoxes of teams is that diversity and individuality are prized in assembling teams and then all team members are expected to pull together as if there were no significant differences in team members' interests, loyalties, goals, values, outlooks, or personality makeups (Donnellon, 1996). Each team member must come to terms with the inescapable tension created by the dilemma of simultaneously feeling the desire to behave as a unique individual while at the same time recognizing the need to suppress their individuality (and to make personal sacrifices) in order to coalesce into a cohesive high-performance team (Lipnack & Stamps, 1997; Donnellon, 1996). This dilemma is magnified in cross-functional and management teams in which members are expected to represent separate, distinct, and diverse stakeholder groups while at the same time working together as a unified team with a common mission and joint destiny.

Koestler (1967) uses the term "holon" to express this transcendent notion of being simultaneously a whole in and of itself and a part within larger systems. Resolution of this dilemma allows teams to develop the fluidity and interchangeability of roles that are characteristic of high-performance teams. Teams

mature and develop when members are able to transcend thinking of themselves as either leaders or followers and realize that they must be *both* in order
for the team to reach high performance levels.

**Collective Unconscious and Hidden Agendas.** Bion (1961) noted that the
actual behavior of teams was frequently at odds with the stated purpose of
the group. Bion noted that the group was acting as if the reason for the group's
existence was other than the publicly stated purpose. These mysterious
and often baffling behaviors were termed group dynamics, and represented shared unconscious–motivated behaviors (that is, the group-as-a-whole's
collective unconscious) or conscious but devious behaviors (hidden agendas),
depending upon which psychological persuasion (psychoanalytic versus
behavioral) one ascribed to.

Regardless of which school of psychology theory is used to explain the behavior, the phenomenon noted by Bion and others was clearly observable. At various points, groups seem to operate under some basic assumptions about
the group. While Bion did not posit any particular order to their emergence, the
group seems to act as if the following assumptions are true: *dependency*—
the group acts as if it is helpless and totally dependent upon the task leader to
provide answers and direction; *fight/flight*—the group acts as if the reason that
the group is meeting is either to fight or flee someone or something; *pairing*—the
group acts as if strong bonding between two group members will unify the group
and resolve intra-group conflict and ambivalence toward leadership and authority. The group hopes that effective leadership (a metaphoric messiah) will result
from this union.

## Group and Team Leadership Roles

In common usage, leadership is generally considered along one dimension, task
leadership. After all, if a team is defined as a group of individuals with a common mission, it might seem that leadership is simply influencing others to follow them in the pursuit of particular goals. This common-sense explanation
would hold if it were not for the me-versus-we dilemma just discussed. It is
typical, for example, for some or all team members to resist external efforts to
define the goals and set direction for the team. There are cultural differences in
the degree to which this dynamic occurs, but it can be observed to some degree
in teams in virtually all cultures. Such resistance can lead to emotional conflict
and threaten the integrity and further development of the team. In order for the
team to make progress in defining and achieving its goals, other forms of
leadership inevitably emerge and contribute to a rich and dynamic team interaction. The following typical team leadership roles generally emerge as teams
develop (adapted from Beck, 1981).

**Task Leader.** The task leader knows most about the task and the expectations of the environment. The task leader also helps the group to develop reasonable goals, action plans, accountabilities, rules, communication methods, decision-making styles, and others. She/he also influences evaluation of individual and team performance.

**Emotional Leader.** The emotional leader has the greatest personal investment in the group's task and is usually the best-liked member. He/she is concerned with the smooth running of the team, with active and positive participation, relationships, and interactions. The emotional leader models collaboration and cooperation, supports others, and receives support in return. The emotional leader is most likely to call attention to relational differences in the team's process, and try to resolve or smooth over these difficulties.

**Limits/Assumption-Testing Leader.** The limits/assumption-testing leader facilitates the clarification of assumptions and the testing of limits and boundaries. This person is particularly sensitive to the level of cohesiveness in the team, and to situations in which individual differences are being submerged. These individuals are highly invested in the task. Being willing to take risks, this individual is seen as off-track early in the team's work and frequently becomes the object of negative feelings. As the team matures, however, this leadership is increasingly valued.

**Commitment Leader.** The commitment leader is ambivalent about the task or about participation in the team, and therefore facilitates the team to test the extent of appropriate commitment of team members to each other and to the task. This individual is also sensitive to the team's inconsistencies and inability to set realistic limits and expectations for itself.

In order for the team to achieve its mission (task accomplishment) while holding together in spite of the diversity of personal goals, values, outlooks, and personalities (system maintenance), these roles must emerge. Task leadership pushes for cohesion and alignment of activity. Limits/assumption-testing leadership ensures that individual and stakeholder concerns are not submerged in the quest for alignment and unity of purpose. Commitment leadership challenges the team to develop goals that are relevant and achievable.

Finally, emotional leadership tries to balance competing interests, and encourages harmonious relationships in order to keep internal conflict from causing team disintegration. Team members have skills, attitudes, and personalities that make them more or less suitable for each of these leadership roles (Beck, 1981). Early in a team's life, there is often competition for primacy in enacting these roles (especially the task leadership role) and individuals get locked into one leadership role. As the team matures and moves toward higher performance, team leadership is more fluid and team members may express several leadership roles (Beck, 1981).

## Decision-Making in Groups and Teams

All teams must address the manner in which they make decisions. In traditional hierarchical organizations, decision-making has been the prerogative and responsibility of leadership. Historically, teams formed to perform tasks and missions that were well understood and routinized, or in which speed and coordination were of primary importance, relied primarily upon the formal task leader for decision-making. For these reasons, the task leaders in military, production, surgical, and football teams have retained strong decision-making prerogatives. With the increased use of teams to deal with complex issues in which the quality and acceptance of decisions were more important than speed and integrity of the chain of command, varying forms of group decision-making have increasingly been used. Research on individual versus group decision-making consistently demonstrates that group decisions are generally of higher quality when appropriate procedures are used in situations in which no one person has all the required knowledge and skill (see, for example, Barnlund, 1959; Lane et al., 1982). Although there is little systematic research to support the belief that participation in decision-making increases acceptance of the decision, this is a fundamental tenet of democratic decision-making.

The increase in decision quality and acceptance, however, must be balanced against the additional time required. In many cases the demand for quality and acceptance is not sufficient to warrant a group decision-making procedure (Husband, 1940; Marquart, 1955; Taylor & Faust, 1952). Maier (1970) presents a model that teams can use to decide what level of team involvement in decisions is most appropriate. Decisions that require high levels of acceptance and quality are best made using a rigorous consensus process—everyone must agree with the resulting solution. For solutions that require high levels of acceptance but have lower quality requirements, considerable time can be saved by using a simple majority decision-making rule. Solutions that require high quality but don't have high acceptance requirements are best tackled by a small group of content experts. Finally, decisions with low requirements for both quality and acceptance can be quickly and efficiently made autocratically (the proverbial executive decision) without sacrificing solution effectiveness.

## Team Development

Bennis and Shepard (1956) provided one of the earliest models of group development. In this model, groups move from early phases of dependency and conflict (Bion's basic assumptions of dependency and fight/flight) before resolving authority issues in relation to any perceived leader, making interdependency, intimacy, and creativity possible. After a number of researchers provided variations on the same themes (Mills, 1964; Mann, 1966; Slater, 1966), Tuckman (Tuckman & Jensen, 1977) provided a simplified model, which included the familiar forming, storming, norming, and performing phases of group development.

One criticism of the basic Tuckman model (Tuckman & Jensen, 1977) is that it does not take into account some of the basic differences between the self-analytic groups that early theories were based on, and typical work teams. Some key differences are: the teams are typically launched within already existing organizations, and are staffed by people who are not strangers and need to interact with each other outside of the team and beyond the team's life; teams need to review their work, redefine their mission, deal with the coming and going of members over the life of the team, and periodically renew their commitment to the mission as it evolves. A model, which integrates the research on teams and groups, is presented in Table 2.2.

## Representational and Virtual Teams

The previous section discussed issues related to traditional intact teams, which are collocated and have stable memberships. While some early organizational development (OD) researchers and practitioners (Galbraith, 1973) had advocated the use of representational teams, the problems of integrating and coordinating the efforts of teams that spanned distance and organizational boundaries precluded their widespread use through the late 1980s. Allen (1977), for instance, noted that the probability of team members communicating or collaborating decreases logarithmically with gaps of as little as five to ten meters between offices.

The advent of easier distant communication via tele/videoconferencing, faxes, wireless radios, cell phones and pagers, streaming audio and video, videophones, and the internet/intranets (that is, e-mail, listservs, and interactive websites such as chatrooms) made representational and virtual teams much more feasible. Connell (2002), in a later chapter, provides a detailed discussion of the relevant issues that consulting psychologists need to consider in consulting to virtual teams. The present chapter, therefore, will limit discussion of representational and virtual teams to the systems team development issues that are not treated by Connell (2002).

### Systems Issues in Representational and Virtual Teams

Several issues arise that are specific to consultation work with representational or virtual teams. These include the following.

**Multiple Membership Issues.** Each member of a representational team (for example, cross-functional, leadership teams) has membership in at least one other team. In matrixed organizations, for instance, members of functional units

Table 2.2. An Integrated Model of Team Development.

| Activities/goals | Team challenges |
|---|---|
| **Launching/Forming** | |
| • Given charter from team sponsor<br>• Establishing team membership or criteria for membership<br>• Time boundaries and initial meeting times provided<br>• Clarification of purpose<br>• Building commitment | • Building interest, recruiting members<br>• Coordinating schedules and priorities<br>• Understanding charter |
| **Storming** | |
| • Common goals are clarified, forging a team identity<br>• Team learns how to deal with negative feelings generated by competitive work style and personality differences<br>• Team roles begin to emerge | • Managing conflict<br>• Building consensus<br>• Developing dialogue<br>• Valuing differences |
| **Norming** | |
| • Agreement on procedures for identifying tasks and resources and assigning subtasks<br>• Experimentation with different ways of working together leading to role differentiation | • Avoiding role lock or stereotyping<br>• Finding the right balance between structure and procedure, and spontaneity and experimentation |
| **Performing** | |
| • More efforts to give positive feedback, support, humor, and spontaneity<br>• Spontaneous innovation and creative thinking | • Avoiding overconfidence—team feels superior and able to accomplish anything<br>• Balancing creativity with practical limitations |
| **Reviewing/Renewing/Adjourning** | |
| • Facing realistic limitations of time, resources, and talents of the team members<br>• Facing up to renewing its mission/charter or ending its existence<br>• Group decides for itself what it can tolerate and accomplish, regardless of outside expectations | • Facing realities and candidly reviewing progress<br>• Performing without clear structure, norms, or roles<br>• Becoming self-managing<br>• Keeping from getting discouraged |

*Source:* Adapted from Tuckman and Jensen, 1977; Beck 1981.

may also be members of several project teams. Leadership teams, special examples of representational teams, are comprised of the heads of the important business and functional units in the organization. In both cases, each member serves a linking function between teams that might have interdependent matrix or hierarchical relationships with each other.

Because most members of representational and leadership teams have dual team membership (for example, the cross-business unit and cross-functional/leadership team and the function/unit they represent), they frequently experience split loyalties. For instance, a decision that might be good for the larger organization might have a negative impact on their business unit or function. Furthermore, the amount of joint destiny is diluted by the fact that individual compensation is frequently more related to the performance of the business or functional unit they lead than to the overall performance of the larger organization (Lawler, 2000). Katzenbach (1998), in fact, believes that it is unreasonable to expect a high degree of collaboration and cooperation within leadership teams because of divided loyalties, conflicting executive priorities, changing marketplace demands, confounded accountabilities, and differences in stakeholder expectations.

**Boundary Issues.** Traditional collocated intact work teams have simplified boundary issues by having stable membership, common work and meeting space, the same time zone, and usually the same culture (although this has changed dramatically in the last fifteen years even in intact teams). Stable membership allows the team to go through team development stages together (for example, launching, forming, norming, storming, performing, and adjourning/renewing) and to be in similar biorhythms (it's everyone's morning, afternoon, and others). Meeting face-to-face allows for more efficient communication because members can see nonverbal as well as hear verbal behavior. Stable membership over time also provides transactional experiences that allow members, formally or informally, to test assumptions and negotiate team-based rather than culturally based assumptions.

Representational and virtual teams frequently cross or violate these boundaries, enormously complicating the goal of reaching high performance. Without stable membership, team member priorities are constantly changing, making it difficult to negotiate goals, leadership roles, and group norms. It also becomes difficult to surface and test the kinds of cultural assumptions that various team members, often identified only by voice or e-mail text, are making. The difficulty in identifying and testing cultural assumptions greatly amplifies the kind of dysfunctional basic assumption behaviors noted by Bion (1961), and can easily immobilize the team and significantly inhibit the development of collaboration, trust, interdependency, and, ultimately, creativity and productivity.

**Communication Issues.** The advent of new and radical communications media such as the Internet has allowed representational and virtual teams to span or at least manage many of the boundaries just discussed. These technologies, however, can be as much of a burden as a boon. Though e-mail can be a very efficient method for communicating the content aspect of a message almost instantaneously across the globe, it is a notoriously bad medium for communicating the relationship aspect. To fill the relationship aspect void, socially savvy e-mail authors use analogic "emoticons" to convey their feelings and sentiments (Sanderson, Freeman, Niederst, & Dougherty, 1993)—for example, happiness is expressed as a smiley face lying on its side [(:-)].

**Virtual versus Collocation Issues.** Considerable research indicates that periodic face-to-face contact is necessary for virtual teams to develop into high-performance teams (Armstrong & Cole, 1995; McGrath & Hollinghead, 1994). Face-to-face time spent in complex social interactions is a requisite for team members to discern and test subtle cultural assumptions and personal agendas. These interactions enable team members to calibrate later cyber-messages from team members because they probably can recall nonverbal behavior associated with that person. Face-to-face time also greatly facilitates the negotiation of norms and roles, as well as the development of interpersonal trust based on an assessment of character and competency. A savvy virtual team leader will be sure to schedule lots of white space during face-to-face meetings to allow time for more personal and informal discussions.

**Technology/Behavior Science Integration Issues.** The potential for virtual teamwork is intimately related to the development and global spread of information technology. In many cases, however, the software engineers developing the technology for virtual teams are doing so with limited input and involvement from behavioral scientists and practitioners. The full potential of computer- and Internet-mediated technology for virtual teams will only be realized when software developers, programmers, and IT systems engineers team up with consulting psychologists and end-user populations to design new generations of groupware that can effectively guide distributed, cross-functional virtual team members through the entire life/goal attainment cycle in a cyberspace environment (Galegher, Kraut, & Egido, 1990). For example, as a result of this kind of collaboration, a complex set of nested processes can be designed that would enable teams to drill down to increasingly specific processes for dealing with virtually any challenging organizational issue—from specifying desired states to evaluating the results of a completely executed implementation plan.

## Team Development in Representational and Virtual Teams

There is general agreement that the team development process described by Tuckman (Tuckman & Jensen, 1977) is also applicable to representational and virtual teams (Lipnack & Stamps, 1997; Duarte & Snyder, 1999). There is also a consensus that the time required for representational and virtual teams to coalesce and become a cohesive, creative, and highly productive team is considerably greater than in more traditional, intact teams (Armstrong & Cole, 1995; Lipnack & Stamps, 1997).

Beck (1981) has estimated that collocated intact teams, which have far fewer boundaries to manage and negotiate, take an average of thirteen hours of face-to-face interaction to reach the performing stage of development. It is not surprising, therefore, that De Meyer (1991) and Galegher et al. (1990) were pessimistic that virtual teams could fully form without some degree of face-to-face contact. McGrath (1990), studying computer-mediated conferences, described the team process as chaotic without some face-to-face interaction, especially in the early phases of group formation and problem definition.

Though face-to-face interaction is clearly desirable, the cost of bringing representational and virtual teams together, especially from around the globe, is high. The timing and frequency of face-to-face team meetings are strategic decisions. Lipnack & Stamps (1997) noted the similarity of the Tuckman group development model (Tuckman & Jensen, 1977) and the typical project management cycle—launch, perform, test, and deliver (Lipnick & Stamps, 1993). By overlaying the Tuckman model with the project management cycle, these authors noted that periods of heightened tension, conflict, and team fragmentation occurred predictably during the launching/storming and reviewing/renewing/testing phases of the team's development.

Representational and virtual teams require significant face-to-face time to get beyond basic information sharing to develop into highly performing teams. Teams will receive the greatest payoff from investment in time and money if team members are brought together for a significant period of time (two to three days) during the launching/storming and reviewing/renewing/testing phases of the team's life. By meeting together for several days when the team is initially launched, the team can get the interaction time that Beck (1981) indicates is necessary to successfully traverse the forming, storming, and norming phases. This groundwork is necessary to achieve the cohesiveness, focus, and collaboration required for the high creativity and productivity expected during the mature performing phase of the team's life cycle. Meeting again for several days just prior to delivery of the team's work products will allow team members to reengage with each other, realign themselves regarding mission and deliverables, and celebrate their accomplishments in preparation for adjournment or renewal/redirection.

## Team Success Conditions

In addition to looking at team development over time, it is frequently useful to take a snapshot of a team's functioning at any given time. For this purpose, it is useful to identify the fundamental conditions necessary for team success.

Rawlings (2000) presents a six-factor model for team success (see Figure 2.2) based upon an extensive review of the team literature. Each of these six factors contributes to success at three organizational levels: (1) individual focus—each team member has the capability and commitment necessary to contribute to effective teamwork and performance; (2) team focus—the team has the capabilities and discipline necessary for developing positive teamwork and achieving high performance; and (3) organization focus—the organization and its leaders provide an environment that supports effective teamwork and high performance.

The importance of both task accomplishment and social system maintenance to the success and well-being of any group, team, or social system is a

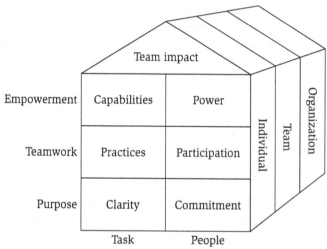

**Clarity**—Clear understanding of its collective purpose and expectations

**Commitment**—Belief in the importance of the work and dedication to high performance

**Practices**—Use of effective processes, tools, and procedures to manage the work

**Participation**—Development of collaborative relationships to ensure full involvement and contribution

**Capabilities**—The right structure, essential competencies, and required resources to succeed

**Power**—The collective will and confidence needed to succeed despite obstacles

**Figure 2.2 Six-Factor Success Model for Team Success.**

*Source:* Copyright 1999 by Personnel Decisions International. Used by permission.

fundamental tenet of systems theory (Berrien, 1968). It should not be surprising, therefore, that both task and relationship factors are included in the team success conditions. This model expresses team success in terms of the interplay between the three required interdependent tasks of the team and the relationship between members. In order to be successful, the team must build: shared purpose and vision (clarity and commitment); teamwork that is characterized by efficient, collaborative work processes and a high degree of trust and participation (practices and participation); and empowerment that is characterized by the team having the structure, capabilities, and resources for collaboration, and the collective will and confidence in one another that the team will succeed (capabilities and power).

# INTERVENTIONS WITH TEAMS

Several types of interventions are possible with groups, and in this section several approaches will be presented.

## Team Building

It is generally assumed that team building is a solution for enhancing the performance of suboptimizing or dysfunctional teams of any kind or type. In this context, the purpose of team building is either corrective in nature or intended to enable suboptimizing teams to realize their potential (Dyer, 1995). For existing teams, the term *team development* seems most appropriate. Alternatively, the members of a new, start-up group—who are, at first, merely an aggregate of individuals—can be convened and trained in participative problem-solving and decision-making methods and processes to prepare them to begin their work. These interventions are properly called *team building* and are intended to enable new teams to climb the learning curve, or ramp up, so they can quickly begin to perform as expected.

Since the 1950s, the teams in question were primarily collocated intact work groups that were accountable for producing routine results by performing some well-known and frequently practiced set of tasks, activities, or functions to achieve a specific set of goals. Some were management teams whose members were responsible for the performance of various interdependent subsystems and intact work teams.

Now and in the future, we are likely to be challenged by the need to adapt our existing concepts, strategies, methods, and skills to deal with multidisciplinary, multifunctional, interdepartmental teams that meet and work sporadically as project teams in unstable face-to-face or virtual realities to achieve uncertain, ambiguous results using homemade strategies and methods.

Most team building or team development interventions use experiential learning methods—case studies, simulations, and exercises—that are intended to assure that team members, as a result of being actively involved in learning from their own shared experiences, will develop an emotional investment in what they have learned, apply it in their real-life work settings, and help each other to do so properly. This is a reasonable but simplistic premise; it ignores cultural barriers to applying classroom learning to the workplace.

Because they should be treated quite differently, it is useful to differentiate family teams from cousin and stranger groups (Shepard, 1964). *Family teams* are composed of members who work together on a regular basis; the members might be collocated. *Cousin groups* are composed of people who work for the same organization and might do the same kinds of work, but do not work together. *Stranger groups* are made up of individuals from different organizations and usually do dissimilar work at different organizational levels.

Team building interventions for cousin and stranger groups were (and still are) usually conducted in off-site retreat settings. Interventions consist of training programs that provide participants with generalized or universal knowledge, concepts, methods, and skills that supposedly lead to enhanced self-awareness of what they do (or don't do) that either contributes to or detracts from high performance in any of their respective back-home teams. The arguable premise is that self-awareness and knowledge is sufficient, by itself, to induce participants to change their work behaviors and achieve higher levels of team effectiveness.

Historically, most team building interventions for new family teams were front-end-loaded. That is, they were trained before they actually began to work together on their actual, real-life work responsibilities. The training usually consisted of a series of simulations, case studies, role plays, and lectures. The learning derived from these experiences was generally universal and prescriptive, or normative. That is, the message was, "This is how you *should* operate in all situations and conditions in order to become a high-performing team (HPT)."

Typically, these prescriptions were formulated without the benefit of a comprehensive organizational diagnosis. Thus, little if any attention was paid to the fit between the team's culture or work processes and the universal prescriptions. Further, the training topics covered everything that the consultant-trainer (CT) or the program's sponsors believed the team members might encounter in their daily work life—for example, communications, goal setting, action planning, group decision-making procedures, leadership functions, conflict management, and feedback. Participants often left such sessions feeling entertained, informed, enthusiastic, and unprepared to recognize and deal with organizational obstacles for using their new skill sets in real life.

Team building was also developed for existing family teams that senior managers believed were underperforming or dysfunctional. The convenient assumption was that this deficit was due to the team members' lack of knowledge or skills. This was often based on informal, unsystematic assessments conducted by managers at a distance without the participation of team members. The interventions were multifaceted, corrective training experiences that were held at retreats (or advances) for three to five days, or spaced half- or full-day sessions on the client system's site ("so we don't completely neglect our routine responsibilities").

Several confounding phenomena became evident when team building interventions were based on the assumption that front-end-loaded or retreat-based training in team building would be as effective as technical skills training. First, not all of the specific concepts, methods, and skills that are taught in team building workshops are needed every day by the team. In fact, most of the palette of HP teamwork skill sets are relevant only on occasion; thus, by the time they are needed, participants often forget when and how to apply them effectively, so they are prematurely rejected (Freedman, 1963). A second confounding variable is that the organization's culture might mitigate against the use of unconventional, state-of-the-art theory, methods, philosophies, and values of building and maintaining HPTs in the real-life workplace (Mager & Pipe, 1997).

A third factor is that such training might enhance team members' insight and awareness of certain team issues, but does not necessarily enable team members to either develop proficiency, or identify when, where, and how to apply these skill set elements. A fourth confounding phenomenon is that training exercises, cases, and simulations are artificial and often abstract or unrelated to the team's actual difficulties in dealing with its goals, work methods, work processes, or results. To maximize the transfer of such training from the classroom to the workplace, CTs had to help team members connect their learning to their team's real-life world. They had to facilitate a theory building process after each training experience to distill and explicate the significant derived concepts, methods, and skills. They then had to assist team members to determine when, under what circumstances and in which situations, the learning experience's results might be properly applied. Thus, transfer of learning from classrooms to workplaces was a difficult and cumbersome three-step process.

## Data-Based Interventions with Teams

An alternative approach insists on an independent assessment of the alignment between the teams' goals, work activities, teamwork processes, and actual results achieved—including what linkage and contextual factors might either enhance or obstruct desired team performance (for example, Dyer, 1995; Reddy, 1994; Schein, 1999). This is consistent with Lewin's dictum that no action should be undertaken without conducting relevant research and no research should be undertaken without taking action (Marrow, 1969). That is, one of the first interventions in any team or intergroup intervention—subsequent to negotiating an initial, mutually acceptable consulting agreement—should be the valid, timely collection and analysis of empirical data. Ideally, data relevant to the team's behavior should also be collected at intervals during the team development process and at the end to evaluate the progress on the team's development goals.

Relevant data can be provided to teams by using standardized or empirical survey instruments, individual or group interviews, observation by process experts, or by technical expert inspection of team work products (Nadler, 1977). Survey research is the most researched data-based approach (for example, Likert, 1961; Fowler, 1993), and, therefore, needs little detailed discussion here.

**360-Degree Feedback for the Team.** This multirater, multilevel survey process provides data from a team's leader and members, sponsors, customers, suppliers, subordinates, senior managers, governmental regulators, and other relevant, significant stakeholders. The type of data collected generally measure fundamental dimensions of team functioning; for example, the team's understanding of the task, the team's commitment to the task, the level and quality of member involvement, the team's use of effective processes, tools, and procedures, the team's structure, competencies, and availability of needed resources, and the team's confidence and determination to succeed (for example, Personnel Decisions International, 2001).

**Self-Assessment.** Another approach is to conduct facilitated discussions with team leaders and members to identify relevant dimensions of their team's functioning (for example, Dyer, 1995; Reddy, 1994; Schein, 1999). Each resulting dimension can be converted into open-ended questionnaires using familiar behavioral indicators. For example:

- To what extent were your ideas and opinions solicited and valued by the other members of your team today?
- What was the quality of the decision(s) that your group made today?
- How committed do you feel to the final decision(s) that your team made today?

When numerical values (anchored by behavioral descriptors) are used, team members can share their perceptions and regularly post their average ratings in their meeting rooms. Posted data provide continuous, highly visible, meaningful performance indicators for team members to discuss and decide what, if anything, they are willing and able to do to improve their self-ratings.

## Organizational Obstacles

Teams do not operate in a vacuum. They are parts of networks of interdependent subsystems, established by their positions within a complex business process or value-chain. Teams require mutual support and cooperation from their interdependent stakeholders.

In either collocated or distributed multifunctional teams, the represented subsystems (for example, departments, product groups, and regions) and their agent-representatives must also actively cooperate and communicate with each other. In the absence of transparency, many teams become suspicious, uncertain, and tentative. They withdraw within their own hardened boundaries and act as if they are under siege. Team members may try to cope by avoiding risks, performing only familiar tasks and activities. Thus, paraphrasing Einstein's definition of insanity, when perceiving external threats, they do what they have always done, hoping this will be sufficient to produce an adaptive response to the challenge of unprecedented circumstances.

Members of represented, cross-functional teams often complain that their back-home managers fail to specify their department's goals and priorities. Or, they haven't been given the resources they need to achieve their objectives. Or, they cannot cope with increasing daily pressure to perform when they also have to do the interdepartmental coordination work that their burnt-out, ineffective, or prematurely retired managers are supposed to do.

Thus, team leaders and members must also achieve proficiency in applying the concepts, methods, and process skills necessary to take the initiative in dealing with the *organizational obstacles* to enabled empowerment. This requires the team to scan both its internal and external environments to identify and track changing environmental variables (for example, shifting political, security, economical, social, governmental, and meteorological conditions) and their stakeholders' responses to these conditions. In periods of unprecedented, discontinuous change, subsystems and stakeholders often try to protect themselves or advance their own interests—often at the expense of the larger organization, and, by default, at the expense of the team.

# THE FUTURE OF TEAMS, TEAMWORK, AND TEAM DEVELOPMENT

The evolution of team development theory and method has been relatively slow since the 1950s. However, two trends appear likely to have a huge impact on the research and practice of group and team development: fast cycle implementation and action learning.

## Fast Cycle Implementation

A comprehensive understanding of group dynamics and the process of converting groups of individuals into HPTs cannot be fully appreciated without a deep appreciation for the contexts within which groups and teams exist (Gillette & McCollum, 1995; Hackman, 1990). Friedlander (1998) described major contextual shifts that have occurred over the past forty years in both the expectations of the consumers of consulting psychology and OD services, and the evolution in the nature of these services. These shifts might have been precipitated by the frequency and intensity of discontinuous, turbulent changes in the external environment.

A parallel shift seems to have occurred regarding the consumers' values. That is, client systems' agents increasingly expect consultants to understand their industry, finance-based strategic business decisions, and the need to accelerate the change process so as to minimize the amount of time it takes to do anything. Anderson's anthology (2000) describes a number of responses to the increasing demand for faster cycle time for diagnosis, design, and delivery of interventions—at the organizational, team (and intergroup), and individual levels. Speed is considered to be a distinctive competitive advantage in most post-industrial organizations. Simultaneously, all parties seem to increasingly understand the need to address the complex interdependencies across vertical organizational levels and lateral subsystem boundaries. The challenge is how to shorten consulting cycle time while optimizing the utility of the individual, team, intersubsystem, and organizational boundary management processes. The new mantra is, "Faster, better, cheaper."

## Action Learning Teams

A second emerging trend is action learning approaches. Until recently, action learning (AL) has not received the recognition and utilization it deserves, although it was developed in 1945. According to Marquardt (1997), AL is an approach to leadership, team, and organizational change and development that utilizes action research (Lewin, 1947) by cross-functional teams composed of high-potential middle managers. AL capitalizes on the needs to deal with real-life organizational issues and be anchored in real-time, and is responsive to cycle time pressure. By paying attention to and learning from their unfolding experience, individual members of AL teams: (a) develop their leadership capabilities; (b) identify and solve real, meaningful organizational problems; (c) enable their organizations to learn how individuals, teams, and total systems can quickly grow and develop; (d) learn the requisite skills to build high performing teams in the future; and (e) gain high levels of self-awareness and self-esteem while (f) earning recognition, appreciation, and respect.

An AL initiative can evolve from either of two organizational needs. The first is the need to develop fully qualified succession candidates. The second is the need to develop employees who can deal creatively and adaptively with unprecedented issues in which there are only ambiguous goals and uncertain methods for creating solutions.

**A Description of AL.** AL works as follows: (a) high-potential individuals from all relevant parts and levels of the organization are selected to join a cadre of participants in an AL initiative; (b) the cadre receives an orientation and introduction to AL theory, strategy, and methods; (c) organizational leaders, serving as sponsors, identify critical, current, unprecedented, organization-wide issues that are to be addressed by AL teams; (d) critical issues are listed and communicated to the cadre along with deadlines for expected results; (e) the cadre is divided into four- to six-person AL teams, each of which is matched to one specific issue for which the team takes responsibility; (f) each AL team meets with its own AL coach (a process-oriented CT) to begin to scope out the issue, and to develop a strategy for studying, analyzing, developing recommendations, presenting recommendations to senior management, and implementing approved recommendations—all within the allocated time parameters; (g) each AL team works in both collocated and distributed modes, in that individual team members take on responsibilities for various tasks, and convene, sometimes in pairs or triads or as a total AL team, and often meet in cyberspace; (h) the AL coach meets with the AL team when they convene for face-to-face progress reviews, analysis, and emergent planning of next steps, when the coach focuses on *how* the team is working and may intervene—primarily by asking process-oriented questions—with the purpose of enabling team members to fully understand and deal with team process issues.

Action learning (Marquardt, 1999; Rothwell, 1999) is similar to Kurt Lewin's action research method (1947) and to the development of the NTL Institute's experiential T-Group (Bradford, Gibb, & Benne, 1964), andragogical learning (Knowles, 1988), double-loop learning (Argyris & Schön, 1992), and participative OD methodology (for example, Cummings & Worley, 2001). The simple elegance of the AL approach is integrating these elements in an innovative manner that yields powerful results. It is also apparent that AL contributes to the reduction in cycle time required to identify and manage unprecedented organizational problems that have no clear-cut ready-made solutions.

While AL has a long history, we believe it is quite likely that the creation and facilitation of AL teams will become increasingly important and recognized as the information age evolves, as an increasing amount of teamwork takes place in cyberspace, and as reduced cycle time becomes more of a competitive necessity than merely a competitive advantage.

# SUMMARY

The second half of the twentieth century saw the emergence of the team as a dominant unit of organizational structure. In fact, in the last decade of the last century, teams and team-based organizations have taken on almost messianic reputations, and are being seen as the salvation for organizations in the information, post-industrial era. This chapter provides consulting psychologists with the current state of knowledge regarding teams. The shift from traditional, intact work teams to representational and virtual teams is discussed. We also discuss the relevant issues for team building interventions. Finally, we provide a look at the future of teams as we start the twenty-first century. In this discussion, new trends in team structures and dynamics made possible by the phenomenal advances in technology are presented. As a caution, the authors warn that introducing technology, no matter how great the potential, without consideration and involvement of the people and human systems that will use and be affected by the technology will lead to disappointing results. The barriers to high performance for representational, distributed, and virtual teams are, in many cases, higher than for more traditional, intact work teams.

## References

Allen, T. (1977). *Managing the flow of technology: Technology transfer and the dissemination of technological information within the R&D organization.* Cambridge, MA: MIT Press.

Anderson, M. (2000). *Fast cycle organization development.* Cincinnati, OH: South-Western.

Argyris, C., & Schön, D. A. (1992). *Theory and practice: Increasing professional effectiveness.* San Francisco: Jossey-Bass.

Armstrong, D. J., & Cole, P. (1995). Managing distances and differences in geographically distributed work groups. In S. Jackson & M. Ruderman (Eds.), *Diversity in work teams* (pp 187–215). Washington, DC: American Psychological Association.

Bales, F. (1950). *Interaction process: A method for the study of small groups.* Reading, MA: Addison-Wesley.

Barnlund, D. A. (1959). A comparative study of individual, majority, and group judgment. *Journal of Abnormal and Social Psychology, 58,* 55–60.

Beck, A. P. (1981). The study of group phase development and emergent leadership. *Group, 5,* 48–54.

Bennis, W. G., & Shepard, H. A. (1956). A theory of group development. *Human Relations, 9,* 415–437.

Berrien, K. F. (1968). *General and social systems.* New Brunswick, NJ: Rutgers University Press.

Bion, W. R. (1961). *Experiences in groups.* New York: Basic Books.

Bradford, L. P., Gibb, J. R., & Benne, K. D. (Eds.). (1964). *T-Group theory and laboratory method: Innovation and re-education.* New York: Wiley.

Connell, J. B. (2002). Organizational consulting to virtual teams. In R. L. Lowman (Ed.), *Handbook of organizational consulting psychology* (pp. 285-311). San Francisco: Jossey-Bass.

Cummings, T. G., & Worley, C. G. (2001). *Organization development and change* (7th ed.). Cincinnati, OH: South-Western.

De Meyer, A. (1991). Tech talk: How managers are stimulating global R&D communication. *Sloan Management Review, 32,* 49–58.

Donnellon, A. (1996). *Team talk: The power of language in team dynamics.* Boston: Harvard Business School Press.

Duarte, D. E., & Snyder, N. T. (1999). *Mastering virtual teams: Strategies, tools, and techniques that succeed.* San Francisco: Jossey-Bass.

Dyer, W. G. (1995). *Team building: Current issues and new alternatives* (3rd ed.). Reading, MA: Addison-Wesley.

Fowler, F. J., Jr. (1993). *Survey research methods* (2nd ed.) Thousand Oaks, CA: Sage.

Freedman, A. M. (1963). *Changes in perceptions of on-the-job problems following human relations laboratory training.* Unpublished master's thesis, Boston University, College of Business Administration.

Freedman, A. M. (2000). Multigroup representation: Representative teams and teams of representatives. *Consulting Psychology Journal, 52,* 63–81.

Friedlander, F. (1998). The evolution of organization development: 1960s to 1990s. *Vision/Action, 17*(1), 10–12.

Fuqua, D. R., & Newman, J. L. (2002). The role of systems theory in consulting psychology. In R. L. Lowman (Ed.), *Handbook of organizational consulting psychology* (pp. 76–105). San Francisco: Jossey-Bass.

Galbraith, J. R. (1973). *Designing complex organizations.* Reading, MA: Addison-Wesley.

Galegher, J., Kraut, R. E., & Egido, C. (Eds.). (1990). *Intellectual teamwork: Social and technological foundations of cooperative work.* Hillsdale, NJ: Erlbaum.

Gillette, J., & McCollum, M. (1995). *Groups in context: A new perspective on group dynamics.* Lanham, MD: University Press of America.

Hackman, J. R. (Ed.). (1990). *Groups that work (and those that don't): Creating conditions for effective teamwork.* San Francisco: Jossey-Bass.

Hall, E. T. (1976). *Beyond culture.* New York: Anchor Books.

Hofstede, G. (1991). *Cultures and organizations: Software of the mind.* New York: McGraw-Hill.

Husband, R. (1940). Cooperative versus solitary problem solution. *Journal of Social Psychology, 11,* 405–409.

Katz, D., & Kahn, R. L. (1978). *The social psychology of organizations* (2nd ed.). New York: Wiley.

Katzenbach, J. R. (1998). *Teams at the top: Unleashing the potential of both teams and individual leaders.* Boston: McKinsey.

Katzenbach, J. R., & Smith, D. K. (1993). *The wisdom of teams: Creating the high performance organization.* New York: HarperCollins.

Keidel, R. W. (1984). Baseball, football, basketball: Models for business. *Organizational Dynamics, 12,* 5–18.

Knowles, M. (1988). *The adult learner: A neglected species* (3rd ed.). Houston: Gulf.

Koestler, A. (1967). *The ghost in the machine.* London: Hutchinson & Co.

Kraut, R. E., Egido, C., & Galegher, J. (1990). Patterns of contact and communication in scientific collaborations. In J. Galegher, R. E. Kraut, & C. Egido (Eds.), *Intellectual teamwork: Social and technological foundations of cooperative work* (pp. 149–171). Hillsdale, NJ: Erlbaum.

Lane, I., Mathews, P., Chancy, C., Effmeyer, R., Reher, R., & Teddlie, C. (1982). Making the goals of acceptance and quality explicit: Effects on group decision. *Small Group Behavior, 13,* 542–554.

Lawler, E. E., III (2000). *Rewarding excellence: Pay strategies for the new economy*. San Francisco: Jossey-Bass.

Le Bon, G. (1960). *The crowd*. New York: Norton. (Originally published 1895.)

Leonard, H. S., & Freedman, A. M. (2000). From scientific management through fun and games to high performing teams: An historical perspective on consulting to team-based organizations. *Consulting Psychology Journal: Practice and Theory. 52*, 3–19.

Lewin, K. (1947). Group decision and social change. In E. Maccoby, T. Newcomb, & E. Hartley, (Eds.), *Readings in social psychology* (pp. 197–211). Austin, TX: Holt, Rinehart and Winston.

Likert, R. (1961). *New patterns of management*. New York: McGraw-Hill.

Lipnack, J., & Stamps, J. (1993). *The teamnet factor: Bringing the power of boundary crossing into the heart of your organization*. New York: Wiley.

Lipnack, J., & Stamps, J. (1997). *Virtual teams: Reaching across space, time, and organizational technology*. New York: Wiley.

Mager, R. F., & Pipe, P. (1997). *Analyzing performance problems or you really oughta wanna: How to figure out why people aren't doing what they should be, and what to do about it* (3rd ed.). Atlanta, GA: Center For Effective Performance.

Maier, N. (1970). *Problem solving and creativity in individuals and groups*. Pacific Grove, CA: Brooks/Cole.

Mann, R. (1966). The development of the member-trainer relationship in self-analytic groups. *Human Relations, 19*, 85–115.

Marquardt, M. J. (1999). *Action learning in action: Transforming problems and people for world-class organizational learning*. Palo Alto, CA: Davies-Black.

Marquart, D. (1955). Group problem solving. *Journal of Social Psychology, 41*, 103–113.

Marrow, A. J. (1969). *The practical theorist: The life and work of Kurt Lewin*. New York: Basic Books.

McFarland, G. K., Leonard, H. S., & Morris, M. M. (1984). *Nursing leadership and management: Contemporary strategies*. New York: Wiley.

McGrath, J. (1990). Time matters in groups. In J. Galegher, R. E. Kraut, & C. Egido, (Eds.), *Intellectual teamwork: Social and technological foundations of cooperative work* (pp. 23–62). Hillsdale, NJ: Erlbaum.

McGrath, J., & Hollinghead, A. (1994). *Groups interacting with technology*. Thousand Oaks, CA: Sage.

Mills, R. (1964). *Group transformation: An analysis of a learning group*. Englewood Cliffs, NJ: Prentice Hall.

Mohrman, S. A., Cohen, S. G., & Mohrman, A. M., Jr. (1995). *Designing team-based organizations: New forms for knowledge work*. San Francisco: Jossey-Bass.

Nadler, D. A. (1977). *Feedback and organization development: Using data-based methods*. Reading, MA: Addison-Wesley.

Personnel Decisions International (2001). *PROFILOR for Teams*. Minneapolis, MN: Author.

Rawlings, D. (2000). Collaborative leadership teams: Oxymoron or new paradigm? *Consulting Psychology Journal: Practice and Theory, 52*, 36–48.

Reddy, W. B. (1994). *Intervention skills: Process consultation for small groups and teams*. San Diego, CA: Pfeiffer.

Reich, R. B. (1987). Entrepreneurship reconsidered: The team as hero. *Harvard Business Review, 3*, 77–83.

Rothwell, W. J. (1999). *The action learning guidebook: A real-time strategy for problem-solving, training design, and employee development*. San Francisco: Jossey-Bass.

Sanderson, D., Freeman, E., Niederst, J., & Dougherty, D. (1993). *Smileys.* Sebastopol, CA: O'Reilly & Assoc.

Schein, E. H. (1992). *Organizational culture and leadership:* A dynamic view (2nd ed.). San Francisco: Jossey-Bass.

Schein, E. H. (1999). *Process consultation revisited: Building the helping relationship.* Reading, MA: Addison-Wesley.

Shepard, H. A. (1964). Exploration on observant participation. In A. P. Bradford, J. R. Gibb, & K. D. Benne (Eds.). *T-group theory and laboratory method: Innovation and re-education* (pp. 370–395). New York: Wiley.

Slater, P. (1966). *Microcosm.* New York: Wiley.

Taylor, D., & Faust, W. (1952). Twenty questions: Efficiency of problem solving as a function of the size of the group. *Journal of Experimental Psychology, 44,* 360–363.

Trompenaars, F. (1994). *Riding the waves of culture: Understanding diversity in global business.* Burr Ridge, IL: Irwin.

Tuckman, B. W., & Jensen, M.A.C. (1977). Stages of small group development revisited. *Group and Organizational Studies, 2,* 419–427.

Vaill, P. (1989). *Managing as a performing art: New ideas for a world of chaotic change.* San Francisco: Jossey-Bass.

Von Bertalanffy, L. (1968). *General systems theory: Foundations, development, applications.* New York: Braziller.

Watzlawick, P., Beavin, J., & Jackson, D. (1967). *Pragmatics of human communications: A study of interaction patterns, pathologies, and paradoxes.* New York: Norton.

# CHAPTER THREE

# The Organizational Level of Analysis:

## Consulting to the Implementation of New Organizational Designs

Susan Albers Mohrman

*Center for Effective Organizations, Marshall School of Business*
*University of Southern California*

During a two-year period, a European electronics firm, Global Solutions, acquired four foreign subsidiaries to bolster its strategy of becoming a global leader selling systems to large global customers. Working with organizational design consultants, it established globally integrated product lines, identified centers of excellence for research and development in four countries, created virtual teams to take advantage of global dispersion to develop twenty-four-hour development processes, and initiated a global supply chain management capability. It introduced state-of-the-art information systems to support globally dispersed work, clarified the missions and accountabilities of global and local teams and business units, and carried out extensive training in cultural diversity and how to operate in and lead dispersed, often cross-functional, teams. Incentive systems were aligned with the performance of global product lines as well as geographic targets. Communication programs were established to convey the new strategy and organizational vision to employees.

One year after defining the strategy and the macro features of the corporation, Global Solutions is struggling to reap the benefits of this elegant design. Far from the vision of global collaboration is the benign neglect shown between co-workers in different locations, independent functioning of contributors who share common goals, and redundant task performance in multiple locations resulting in competing solutions to the same problem. Employees are reluctant to communicate with one another. They have formed strong impressions about each location's failings and limitations, based in large part on the inevitable breakdowns that occur when interdependent work is not well coordinated, and on latent and overt conflicts permeating the planning processes required to stitch the system together.

The general manager of Global Solutions has become increasingly negative about the members of his management team and their willingness and ability to lead their units during this period of change. Even the leaders who helped craft the newly merged organization seem unwilling to change their behavior to effectively coordinate across locations and to provide integrated value to global customers who are looking for global technology solutions. Shadow staffs are being built in different locations to do the work that is in the charters and role descriptions of geographically dispersed individuals and units that can't be relied on to do their share. Trying to deal with what seems to him to be blatant resistance to change, the general manager provides carrots and sticks— incentives and threats—to try to shape behavior in the organization. He begins to replace leaders who don't seem willing to get with the program, and engages another set of consultants to assess the new organization and recommend changes. Yet global integration in general is still slow to emerge, and in fact, work is increasingly being repackaged to be carried out by self-contained and collocated groups. The acquired units are increasingly feeling marginalized as the acquiring company is beginning to use them for limited purposes and is not integrating them into global strategic and operational decision-making processes.

# ORGANIZATIONAL REDESIGN

The case example provides a very realistic introduction to the organizational level of analysis, a major focus of this chapter and one with which the organizational consulting psychologist needs to be familiar. Global Solutions' story captures both the complexity and the difficulty entailed in large-scale organizational redesign—the purposeful change in an organization's form in order to develop new capabilities in a changing market environment. Faced with global customers who require common technical solutions, and with fast-paced competitors drawing on talent from around the world, Global Solutions developed a business strategy to provide compatible products and integrated systems to global customers through the establishment of geographically dispersed product lines and customer-facing teams. Through acquisitions, Global Solutions extended its talent and organizational competency pool globally, and engaged in an extensive redesign process in order to integrate its global assets and provide an organizational architecture (Keidel, 1995; Nadler, Gerstein, & Shaw, 1992) to support a new way of functioning. Yet, despite these changes to the formal design—including aligning rewards and incentives with the desired way of functioning—behavior didn't change accordingly.

Global Solutions is not alone. Organizations today are facing a steady stream of competitive challenges that require strategic change. Simultaneous change occurs in three domains:

1. The business model of the company: the value it delivers to its customers in exchange for the revenue and other resources required for the organization to prosper

2. The technology: tools and methodologies that the organization applies to deliver value to the customer and to manage its own operations

3. The social organization: the design of the organization's structures, processes, and subsystems to support effective performance and enhanced capabilities

Organizational change consultants must understand and contribute both to the crafting of substantive changes in these three domains, and to the ongoing and formidable change implementation challenges facing organizations.

## Organizational Redesign and Organizational Learning

We studied Global Solutions and nine other companies for a three-year period as they embarked on and worked through fundamental change and redesign (Tenkasi, Mohrman, & Mohrman, 1998). We found that such large-scale change poses not only a substantial organizational redesign challenge, but also demands extensive learning by the organization and its members. Whether and how quickly the changes are successfully implemented relates to the effectiveness of the internal learning processes in the organization. Consultants to organization-level change must understand strategic redesign, and provide guidance to line management as it crafts and implements new design features. They must also help the organization establish learning processes to facilitate the transition. Successful change consultation requires a model of change management that goes beyond the pervasive resistance-based conceptualizations that portray the challenge as overcoming resistance to change.

This chapter describes the learning processes that facilitate the implementation of new designs, as well as the leadership roles that create the context for effective learning during transition. It provides a framework for internal and external change agents who are tasked with helping an organization plan and execute the initiatives and interventions to accelerate the transition process.

# THE ORGANIZATION LEVEL OF ANALYSIS: REDESIGN AND LEARNING

In today's dynamic global business environment, the only sustainable competitive advantage is the organization's capacity to learn (Senge, 1990). In order to grow in increasingly competitive markets, organizations must be able to respond to unanticipated market forces and generate new approaches that deliver increased value to customers. They have to be able to reconfigure themselves as needed, shift and broaden their focuses, and work through temporary teams and alliances. They have to be able to shift their organization's design, or architecture. "Those companies that are creative in designing new organizational architectures will be those that gain significant competitive advantage in this new era of change" (Nadler, 1992, p. 8). Organizational transformation has become a prevalent theme, and leading organizations through transformations a critical leadership capability (Bennis & Nanus, 1985; Tichy & Devanna, 1986). Such transformation entails change in many aspects of the organization, including its culture, or meaning system, and at all levels of the organization.

## Multiple Subsystem Change

Organizational transformations occur through simultaneous change in many aspects of the organization, including its structures, processes, and valued outcomes (Ledford, Mohrman, Mohrman, & Lawler, 1989). Just as a building's architecture creates a framework that affects behavior through the shaping of space, and the creation of some opportunities and the constraint of others (Rasmussen, 1991), an organization's design facilitates and encourages some kinds of behaviors and performances while impeding others. Thus redesign is central to most transformations aimed at achieving fundamental change in an organization's capabilities and performance. Such redesign aims at "bringing about a coherence between the goals or purposes for which the organization exists, the patterns of division of labor, inter-unit coordination, and the people who will do the work" (Galbraith, 1977, p. 5).

Figure 3.1 depicts the various aspects of the organization that can be purposefully designed to support the organization's strategy and be mutually consistent (Galbraith, 1995). As the environment changes and the organization needs to perform in a different manner, each of these design elements might need to be redesigned to provide the context for the new behaviors that are necessary to enact the changing strategy:

1. Work processes: The processes that deliver value to the customer can be changed and clarified, and the technologies and tools required to carry out these processes can be developed.

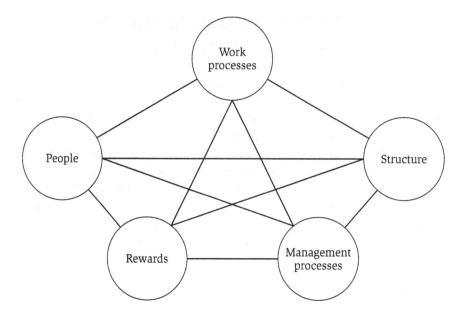

**Figure 3.1 Star Model.**

*Source:* Adapted from Galbraith (1995, p. 12).

2. Structure: Structural units and lateral linkage mechanisms can be changed so that units house complete work processes and there is ongoing coordination and integration across the various units in the organization.

3. Management processes: The direction-setting, communication, decision-making, and performance management processes of the organization can focus attention on key strategic requirements and behaviors, and can clarify, facilitate, and monitor the contribution of all parts of the organization.

4. Rewards: The systems that deliver valued extrinsic outcomes to employees can be crafted to reinforce desired contributions and competencies.

5. People processes: Competency systems, selection and career systems, and development systems can be designed to ensure that the organization has the talent it needs to carry out its strategy.

These design elements all need to be aligned to support a new way of operating. Consultants can help organizational management teams and design teams craft them to fit strategic requirements and work process requirements. In transitions to team structures, for example, the infrastructure and languages for connectivity, the formal leadership for the teams that make up the business unit, and team membership can be prescribed. But changes in behavior, beliefs, and understandings cannot be formally prescribed. They occur through the interactions and experiences of employees in the changing organization. Such deep change cannot be commanded from above. Macro-design interventions define a new playing field, but each subunit and the individuals in the organization need to learn to be effective in the fundamentally altered context.

## Learning at All Levels

Organizational transformation and organizational learning are closely related phenomena. Organizational learning is a collective phenomenon through which organizational members put in place new approaches that enable the organization to perform more effectively and improve performance over time (Tenkasi, Mohrman, & Mohrman, 1998). Achieving effective performance during a time of strategic redirection and organization redesign requires extensive organizational learning. Changing the formal configuration of elements in the organizational system might be essential to organizational transformation but insufficient to yield the desired behavioral changes required to enact new strategies and capabilities. Organizational learning also results from the accumulation of many small, incremental changes that spring up as units within the organizational design and redesign themselves (Weick & Westley, 1996; Levitt & March, 1988). These micro-level changes emerge through the planned and unplanned interactions of individuals in units throughout the organization as they carry out their work within and across reconfigured units, teams, and workgroups.

During transformation, redesign and learning must occur at all levels of the organization (see Figure 3.2). Some aspects of the redesigned organization can be developed through a corporate-level design process and prescribed, but much is emergent. For example, as Global Solutions restructured to develop global product lines and global system capabilities, it acquired new units, redefined and reconfigured its business units, developed globally integrated work, business processes, and information systems, developed metrics focusing on the growth of global accounts and worldwide sales, and put in place career development and reward systems to develop global competencies and reward global functioning. These macro-initiatives were intended to provide the context and infrastructure to support and stimulate new ways of functioning. If that macro-restructuring was to achieve its intended performance, every unit, team, and individual had to develop new approaches to perform differently and relate to and integrate differently with other parts of the organization. Product design teams located in Europe had to develop norms and skills that enabled technical integration with teams in the Americas and Asia that spoke different languages yet had to perform interdependent work.

The locus of organizational learning is the group. The accomplishment of coherence around a targeted set of outcomes and performances requires

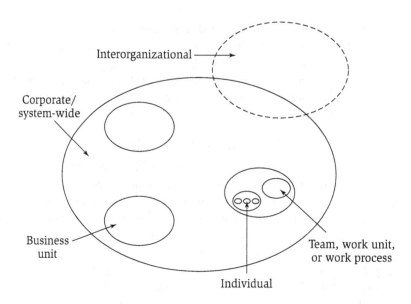

**Figure 3.2 Design at All Systems Levels.**

simultaneous realignment of activities by many people. Successful organizational learning results in altered collective capabilities. We found that units within the same organization vary tremendously in the speed and success of transition, despite the fact that they are exposed to the same company-wide change context and are learning new roles and new ways of doing business within the same overall transition. Some units apparently establish more effective learning processes that enable more rapid adoption of new approaches required for success in the changing macro-organization. The various product and system development teams of Global Solutions, for example, differed greatly in how quickly they developed team approaches to staying aligned with the other teams that were working on related projects. Some teams continued to operate as if their work could be partitioned off from the rest of the global product line. They operated as if they were still in self-contained units with a clear set of requirements that could be achieved with internal focus. Other teams more quickly figured out how their work fit with the work of other teams to create a coherent and compatible set of offerings for global customers. They developed roles and responsibilities for linking to the broader organization and internal processes for adapting to a dynamic family of products.

## Learning and Meaning

The learning required to enable effective performance within a new design often entails change in elements of deep culture (language, behavioral routines, and values). These elements are often embedded and automatic, and are shared and taken for granted by organizational members. They underlie the interpretation, action, and behavior of the organization, and are not easily altered through direct interventions (Ciborra & Schneider, 1992; Sandelands & Stablein, 1987; Drazin & Sandelands, 1992). In Global Solutions, organizational units and individuals who have derived meaning and satisfaction from meeting the particular requirements of a local market might cognitively understand that global reach requires the development of common technical elements that enable compatibility across geographies. However, they might not have a broad enough perspective to understand what elements need to be compatible and why this makes a difference to global customers. They might not know what they have to attend to during the development process. They might not have mental models of what it means to do globally integrated development, and what processes and behaviors will be required to do it successfully. Furthermore, altering one's behavior to foster commonality rather than local optimization and responsiveness throws into question assumptions and values that are deeply held. The very notions of customer responsiveness and technical excellence are redefined; and this requires new understandings of how employees contribute and add value. Decision criteria are changed, and the sense of autonomy and ownership by a particular unit and its members is threatened.

Although the leadership of an organization can articulate a new strategy and design, new guiding principles, and new purposes, managers at the top cannot learn for the rest of the organization. Similarly, consultants can coach the organizational members, and facilitate process and educational interventions, but they cannot learn for the organization. Success in leading an organization through a transition is inextricably dependent on the quality of the ongoing learning processes throughout the organization. Providing a context for learning and sponsoring interventions that stimulate learning is an important leadership function. Helping leaders throughout the organization establish an effective learning environment is a critical change consultation challenge.

Individuals enmeshed in a changing organization face great personal challenges as they adapt to the changes and learn the new capabilities and interaction patterns required for personal success in the changing context. Yet new organizational capabilities need to become embedded not only in individual behavior, but also in collective behavior. Old routines are replaced by new routines, and this is the essence of organizational learning (Levitt & March, 1988). New capabilities are to a large extent relational. Even individual learning occurs in the company of others with whom the individual is interdependent. Individuals and their teammates collectively need to perform new and different functions and accomplish new performances; they need to relate differently to other parts of the organization. Individuals need to operate in a manner that is heedful of and that contributes to a new pattern of activities in their unit and across the larger organization. They perform and learn in that larger context. In Global

Solutions, for example, individual team members need to carry out their development activities with awareness of their expanded interdependencies with work that is being done in different locations, and with focus on the needs of a broader set of actual and potential customers. Control of the technical configuration and functionalities of the products and systems must now be carried out by formal mechanisms rather than through face-to-face interactions among collocated members of self-contained teams. Individuals have to learn how to influence the larger system, participate in virtual meetings, keep up with changes in the larger system, and collaboratively adjust their work in anticipation of system-level effects. They have to develop understanding of a much more complex system in order to participate in it effectively with others.

Perhaps most importantly, individuals must learn how to participate in a learning system and to deal with the uncertainties and ambiguities of being in a dynamic system. Transitions and their associated learning activities are not neat and orderly in the sense of being masterminded from the center and then rolled out. They begin with the identification of the key elements of the new design (for example, global product lines, integration of geographically dispersed development activities, systems customization processes, virtual teams). A series of initiatives and interventions direct attention and activities toward implementation. The new organization literally unfolds through time. At the beginning of a strategic transformation, organizational leaders and members cannot fully predict what is required to support the desired performance capabilities. "Events are set in motion, but the orderliness they will create remains to be discovered" (Weick, 1993, p. 350). Social designs are abstractions that have to be created through action (Perlmutter & Trist, 1986).

## Summary

In summary, the learning interventions that foster accelerated transition must go beyond those that focus on individual learning. Individual education and training might provide basic understanding and skills, but the cognitive, behavioral, and structural learning that is required to enable an organizational unit to operate effectively in a changing organization cannot be reduced to individual learning. Much of the individual learning about how to operate successfully in the changing context occurs in the course of collective learning processes. As the group clarifies how it must function in the changing organization in order to achieve new levels and kinds of performance, it shapes the new context, and its members learn through this collective self-design process how they must contribute in the future. Change consultants need to help the organization craft approaches that result in collective learning and that enhance collective learning capabilities. The next section focuses on the collective learning processes that we found enhance organizational transition.

# LEARNING PROCESSES DURING TRANSITION

In each of the companies that we studied, we compared units that were successfully implementing changes in a relatively accelerated manner with units that were having a more difficult time and apparently lagging behind. Our goal was to explore whether there were systematic differences in the internal learning processes of the accelerated and lagging units. Based on the coding of extensive structured interviews with a cross-section of members of each unit at two points in time, we identified five learning dynamics that were more prevalent in the accelerated units (see Figure 3.3). These dynamics are not discrete processes—rather, they proceed in rich interplay with one another. Each will be described below.

## Developing Shared Meaning

At the beginning of a strategic transition, there is a great deal of uncertainty—about the capability of the organization to achieve success in the changing environment, the nature and desirability of the changes in strategy and organization design that are being undertaken, and on the part of individuals about their own abilities to adapt and be successful as the organization demands new kinds of performance. The orderly and predictable functioning of the past was based on shared meanings that guided decision-making and coordinated activity (Thompson & Tuden, 1959). Now, common beliefs about what will lead to organizational effectiveness and what is expected of employees have been disrupted, and new shared understandings have to be rebuilt. A key task for consultants

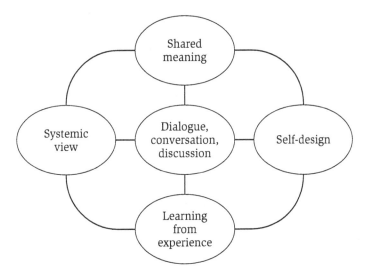

**Figure 3.3 Learning Dynamics During Transition.**

is to guide the system through activities that stimulate and facilitate the development of new shared meaning.

Even the purpose of the organization may have changed. In the case of Global Solutions, for example, the mission had changed from providing products and solutions tailored to the needs of local customers to building platforms and solutions that could serve as the basis for global integration of the customer's activities. Another company in the study was changing from a purpose of developing and providing the best technological products to a sophisticated technological user to a new purpose of developing and providing turnkey systems that could be effectively used by the lay person. This represented a fundamental change in meaning for the engineers and scientists of the company, who had historically focused on whiz-bang technology and assumed that the user would figure out how to apply it.

The meanings of the old system were embedded in the culture of the organization—in its language, its action routines, and its material, structural, and process artifacts (Weick & Westley, 1996). Learning to implement a new design requires building new shared meanings through the development of altered language, new work routines, and new structures and processes. For Global Solutions, for example, a new language, and new communication and coordination routines had to emerge that embody the meaning of global collaboration. New information systems, work and leadership structures, and process tools are organizational artifacts that carry intended meaning, but also are infused with meaning through the collective development of language and routines by organizational members.

During times of great change, when agreement about purposes and cause and effect breaks down, the organization has to operate in a way that allows new shared agreements and meanings to emerge (Weick, 1993). The accelerated change units in our study engaged in processes that enabled members collectively to clarify their understanding of the strategic change and attach meaning to the transition, and in so doing, to establish new work routines and approaches. In one of the software development units of Global Solutions, for example, members came to grips with the meaning of global collaboration by spending time thinking through the ways in which their work affected the ability of a global customer to achieve coordinated operating capability. One of their members had been part of a cross-functional and cross-country team that visited and held focus groups with a number of global customers, and this individual shared his experiences with others in the team. The team identified the reasons why, and purposes for which, their unit would now have to operate with much closer coordination with other units that contributed to the customer solution. Although the term *global collaboration* was being used by management to describe the essence of the redesign, for some of the other units in the company this term was simply an abstract concept that referred to planning activities at a higher organizational level. This software development unit spent time attaching its own meaning to this concept, and in so doing developed a shared understanding and language about the nature and purpose of global collaboration.

## Self-Design

The activities by which the members of a unit determine how they will organize themselves to perform effectively in the changing environment and organizational context are key learning processes. Because the micro-design of many diverse units cannot be centrally determined, implementation cannot be fully accomplished unless each unit goes through a self-design process. Through self-design, the unit translates the overarching intent of the redesign into unit-relevant structures, roles, and practices, and responds to the unanticipated and emergent issues and requirements that become evident as the unit tries to operate in new ways. Self-design is also a key meaning-creating activity; as the members of a unit determine how they will operate, they develop shared ownership and shared meanings that underpin their ability to perform collectively.

Self-design can occur in part through planned consultant-led interventions such as formal team-building activities or large group design activities. However, ongoing response of the group to emergent occurrences and needs lies at the heart of self-design and constitutes the essence of the unit's learning capabilities. In one newly established technical support unit in an aerospace and defense firm in our study, team members convened daily for a brief check-in to discuss transitional issues that had been encountered the previous day. They charted agreements about how they would deal with various kinds of recurring decisions and process requirements. For example, they agreed to processes for defining work and allocating resources (the main resource being their own time) to make sure that team members did not make idiosyncratic agreements with internal and external stakeholders that committed each others' time and depleted capabilities to carry out the new mission. In order to do this, the members of the unit had to come to a shared meaning of what was the core work of the group, and what valued contributions it needed to make so that the system development work that they supported could proceed effectively. They could then design internal processes and delineate roles and relationships to make sure that they could carry out that work effectively.

## Systemic Functioning

The fast-learning units took a more systemic perspective of their work. Consultants can help stimulate this by planning interventions that bring the whole system in the room, such as large group design and implementation sessions, and that focus each part of the organization on how it contributes to the larger whole.

In a stable environment, the different parts of the organizational system have become differentiated, and they have learned to focus on particular performance outcomes and to relate to other parts of the organization through well-worn paths, or routines. When uncertainty is increased, such as during strategic realignments and organizational redesigns, the elements or subunits of the organization might change, as do their relationships to one another and the manner in which any one element needs to perform to support overall system performance. As each unit designs itself, it needs to develop an understanding of where it fits and what it needs to contribute to the effectiveness of the larger system. Learning occurs as the organization considers and strives for a broad array of outcomes that are required for the organization to be effective. Taking a systemic view leads a group to pay attention to more aspects of the system and opens up more avenues for improving performance. It enables appreciation of the whole, rather than of a narrow piece, and creates a framework for seeing interrelationships and patterns that form the basis for learning (Senge, 1990).

One unit in our study was able to contribute to cost and revenue improvements by taking into account concerns not only for the technical capability of the system it was developing, but also for the ease of customer migration to new generations of technology. Previously this unit focused primarily on achieving advanced technology with a quick time to market. Sessions with advanced technology representatives from the business unit and its customers enabled an identification of the various challenges of technology migration from the perspectives of multiple stakeholders. This consultant-facilitated intervention expanded the focus of attention, and the unit was then able to find ways to protect its quick development capabilities while simultaneously delivering broader value to customers. At the same time, technology development took on an expanded meaning, and the unit developed formal linkages to other parts of the organization that were envisioning the next generation of technology and products.

One company in our study stimulated the adoption of a systemic perspective by developing a company-level business model that depicted the outcomes of importance to various stakeholders and to company success. It depicted the key work processes of the organization that deliver value to stakeholders, and the key leverage points for improving performance and competitiveness. Consultants designed and facilitated a series of sessions in which the members of each unit in the organization developed a local version of the business model. This process included the identification of the unit's role in this larger system, as well as important unit-level outcomes, transformation processes, and key leverage points for improving its performance. These business models served as the basis for formulating and reviewing the goals and objectives of the unit, and provided a shared understanding of the system that enabled the unit to identify and focus on improving value-adding activities while de-emphasizing or eliminating non-value-adding work. The business model also provided a framework for identifying needed linkages with other parts of the organization or the larger environment.

## Learning from Experience

The fast-learning units engaged in more ways to learn from experience—both from their own experience and from the experience of other units that were introducing successful change, or from other companies that had made similar transitions. Design transition is by necessity an iterative process. Strategic change leads to the introduction of new design features, and through experience, the organization learns and introduces additional changes and enhancements. The more quickly a unit learns from experience, the faster it can make corrections and introduce new changes in response to ongoing change in the broader organization and market environment. If organization-wide learning dynamics are in place, there are feedback loops so that what is being learned in each unit is input to the larger system level and informs midcourse corrections or ongoing change. Dissemination mechanisms can be built to enable units to learn from each other.

Learning from experience happens naturally. It can be accelerated, however, if the unit consciously adopts learning approaches. Change consultants can help the organization develop and implement ways to learn from experience. They can suggest ways that business units going through change can institutionalize learning routines. Some units experimented with and assessed new approaches before incorporating them into work routines. In one financial services organization, a regional team set aside time in meetings to discuss lessons being learned as members tried new approaches to introducing new products and services to commercial customers. Some units sent members to visit other parts of the organization that were known to be achieving superior outcomes to see how they were accomplishing these results. Organization-wide interventions such as establishing learning fairs or establishing awards for successful replicating of innovative approaches can stimulate the sharing of ideas and openness to new ideas.

## Dialogue

Dialogue is the process that underpins all four of the learning dynamics described above. It is the fundamental process of large-scale change (Barrett, Thomas, & Hocevar, 1995). Dialogue is conversation bringing together multiple perspectives, and enabling the unit to transcend deeply held individual and collective views and create new meaning that goes beyond any individual's previous understanding. Senge (1990) has stressed the importance of dialogue for generative learning, particularly at the collective level. Dialogue underpins the ability to take a broad, systemic perspective through the surfacing of a broader set of knowledge than any one individual would naturally address. It enables the development of new, shared meaning through mutual influence and emergent interpretations. Learning from experience occurs as individuals share their interpretations of events and come to a collective understanding that enables the group to chart a new course of action. Without dialogue, the unit cannot establish shared meaning and agree on new routines (Tenkasi, Mohrman, & Mohrman, 1998).

Global Solutions found that its transition was going very slowly, in part because it envisioned a new way of operating, and instituted a design that required new linkages and processes that cut across many groups in different cultures and with different heritage company routines. Communication was made more difficult by the multiple languages spoken in different locations. One product line, however, stood out from the others in its ability to establish collaboration across geographically dispersed groups. This product line invested in a great deal of early face-to-face meeting time among dispersed members so that they could talk to each other and develop a common understanding of how they would operate as a global product line. The vast majority of time during those meetings was spent in dialogue—talking about purpose, sharing understandings of how the virtual group would handle different kinds of issues, sharing concerns about barriers that might be faced, and learning about each other. These meetings provided a foundation of familiarity that enabled ongoing dialogue, often electronic, as issues emerged and lessons were learned.

## Intervening to Promote Learning During Transition

Many of the learning dynamics that characterized the units with accelerated implementation emerged naturally from within the unit. In one case, a key technical leader prodded the group to come to a common understanding because she feared that otherwise performance would be compromised because the members would be working at cross purposes. In another group, the leader was oriented to learning new approaches and aspired to a global management position. This leader sensed the opportunity for the group to gain visibility in the organization if it could learn quickly how to overcome the barriers and find ways to achieve effective cross-cultural collaboration. He convinced the members that they had a real opportunity to be leaders in the company. In yet another group, one of the members was close friends with someone in another company that had gone through a similar restructuring. She arranged for members of the unit to visit and learn about what they had gone through and what design features they had put in place. The information picked up in that visit provided an initial focus for the ongoing learning processes in the group.

Learning processes do not have to emerge by chance. In several of the companies in our study, change management interventions steered the organization toward collective learning. Change consultants should see their job as helping the organization become a robust learning system, rather than helping the organization overcome resistance to change or implement a particular set of changes. This can be helped by educating leaders about the kinds of learning behavior they need to model and encourage in their groups, and helping leaders to be comfortable managing meaning and engaging in dialogue with their units. Learning can also be stimulated if templates are provided to help shared meaning to develop. Such an approach was utilized by the company mentioned above that developed a business model that became a framework for much of the work in the organization, and put in place performance review processes that required each unit to work through its own systemic business model. Learning can also be encouraged if the macro-design that guides the change is at the level of principles and broad design specifications rather than specified at a very detailed level. Units can be provided with guidance, principles, and processes for carrying out additional design activities locally. Such an approach to minimally specify the design has long been advocated in the socio-technical systems literature; it stresses the need for units to be designed by the people who have to live with the results (for example, Pasmore, 1988). In order to stimulate learning from experience, one company in our study required and provided a template for yearly self-reviews of transition progress by each unit, requiring the unit to invite members of other units to participate in the review and provide third-party observations and suggestions.

In today's dynamic environment, such learning interventions should not be viewed merely as implementation activities for a defined transformation. Rather, they are best seen as building in ongoing learning routines and capabilities to underpin the ability of the organization to change through time. Clearly, change consultants need to work closely with organizational leaders who are ultimately responsible for developing the organization's learning capabilities during transition and beyond. The next section examines the role of leaders during transition.

## LEADER RESPONSIBILITIES DURING TRANSITION

Crafting the strategy and leading change from the top of the organization is necessary but not sufficient during strategic transitions. Yet, it should be clear from the above discussion that successful transition depends on change leadership throughout the organization, and on learning processes within each and every unit. Redesign, strategy formulation, and meaning creation occur at all levels of the system. Consultants cannot be present in all units at all times. Therefore, coaching and teaching the formal leadership of the organization to play strong change leadership roles is a critical consultant function. We found a number of leadership responsibilities that contributed to the acceleration of change and learning. These are important not only for top management, but also for management of the various subunits of the organization. These appear in Figure 3.4, and are briefly described below.

## Focusing the Organization

In the companies and units with the most accelerated transitions, leaders used every opportunity and tool to keep organizational members focused on the desired transition. Some leaders helped their organization develop a vision, continually referred to that vision, and related various actions and plans to it. They found many ways to communicate new expectations, such as in speeches, in video and e-mail communications, and by visiting various teams and work units to talk about the vision and answer questions. They set goals and objectives that related to the vision and held formal reviews of progress. They continually asked questions about how the unit and its members were doing with the changes and what the leader could do to help. Leaders of effective change made it clear that people in the organization, and especially the supervisors and managers, would be held accountable for helping bring about the new capabilities, and they followed up with action through performance appraisals and promotions. Through these focusing activities, leaders not only stimulated the rest of the organizational members to focus on the change, but they showed them how by incorporating the desired change into their own behavior and the way they

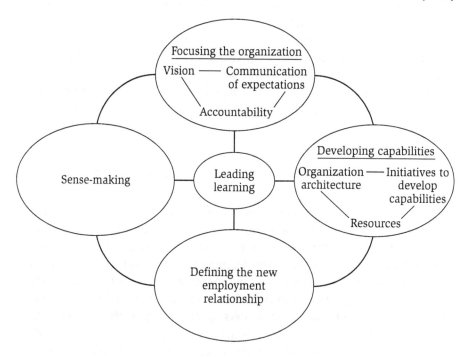

**Figure 3.4 Leader Responsibilities During Transition.**

carried out their formal roles. They demonstrated how the words of the change process get translated into action and artifacts.

## Developing Capabilities

Successful change leaders did not simply command strategic change; they worked to put in place organizational designs, or architectures, to facilitate the changes. This was not limited to a changed structure; rather, successful change leaders understood that new capabilities demanded new work processes, new management processes, and new human resource approaches. They sponsored the initiatives to put these in place, built objectives around the effectiveness of these initiatives, and personally took an interest in making sure these new processes and systems were successful. They also ensured that the organization had access to developmental resources such as training opportunities, team and organization developmental support, and learning interventions. Articulating a new business model, providing the framework and support for each unit to incorporate it, and sponsoring changes in the planning processes of the organization that embody the new understanding of the organization are examples of leadership measures that set up a ripple of learning throughout the organization.

## Sense-Making

Leaders have to help organizational members make sense out of a turbulent and dynamic context. Strategic change is multifaceted, involving simultaneous change to many aspects of the organizational system including market and financial approaches, technology advances, and organizational innovations. There are generally many concurrent initiatives that each work to build a new capability or transform different aspects of the system so they are mutually supportive of new approaches. These initiatives may be experienced by organizational members as unrelated and in some cases contradictory activities. Employees may try to create meaning around each in isolation. For example, Global Solutions was simultaneously putting in place common processes to enable integration across locations, and establishing metrics for each of the development teams in order to clarify accountabilities and track a complex set of related activities. Organizational members focusing on the process development initiatives might interpret the essence of the change to be about uniformity and central control. Those focusing on the team-level metrics might believe the meaning of the change was to encourage each unit to optimize its own performance and not worry about the larger system. As teams were asked to develop a plan for how they could best contribute to an integrated system, a new meaning emerged relating to optimizing the contribution of a unit to the larger system. A key job of the leader is to help the members make sense of what may seem to be a stream of seemingly contradictory and certainly diverse changes and initiatives that are intended in total to gradually change the character of the system.

## Defining the New Employment Relationship

Fundamental change in organizational design results in a change of the employment relationship—the expectations the organization has of its employees and what the employees can expect from the company. In today's world of increasing competitive pressures, change, and complexity, most strategic change requires employees to deal with more complexity and uncertainty. People move beyond their comfortable world of internalized routines and expertise, and return to a learning mode. People are no longer being asked to assume a role in an organization with clear expectations and success criteria; rather, they are being asked to help shape an organization, and are being provided with general and sometimes ambiguous expectations and emerging criteria. In Global Solutions, for example, employees were being asked to deal with a far more complex set of activities and outcomes, to be flexible about work hours in order to work interdependently with people in many different time zones, to exert time and energy overcoming barriers to coordination and communication across cultures, and to be willing to travel and possibly carry out work assignments abroad.

Given these fundamental changes in the demands on employees, organizational leaders need to be very intentional about defining these new expectations and also clarifying what the employee can expect from the company. They need to rethink the inducements side of the employment contract—reward structures, career development opportunities, and other benefits that employees might experience as they contribute to the successful transformation of the company.

## Leading Learning

Leadership behavior sends very powerful messages to employees about how to act and what is valued and expected in the changing organization. Leaders must themselves learn how to carry out their role in a different way, and how to be part of an organization that is operating differently. Managers and team leaders at Global Solutions, for example, were learning the same new business model and global collaboration approaches, and were participating in the same learning activities as the rest of their unit members. The four leader responsibilities described above are ways in which the leader can contribute to and participate in the overall learning processes in the organization. Leaders both model and participate in the learning that must go on in the organization, and build the context for learning throughout the organization.

## Coaching the Leader

A key role of the change consultant is to coach the change leaders of the organization. The change consultant can help set up discrete initiatives such as visioning sessions, team development and large group design sessions, the crafting of a business model, or survey-based assessment and feedback activities. But learning during transition cannot be partitioned into a series of consultant-initiated interventions. Learning has to permeate the system. This can only happen if the leader understands how learning happens and the dynamics that need to be encouraged, and adopts the leadership activities that can catalyze the learning system.

Leaders learn in the same way as all members of the organization: through dialogue, meaning creation, experience, self-design, and through developing a more complete and systemic understanding of the system that they are leading and the context in which it needs to operate. The relationship between the learning capacity of the organization and the ability of leaders to implement strategies that enable the organization to stay on the front edge of change is intuitively obvious. Yet it is not easy to get leaders to focus on the dynamics of change and learning and to be intentional about developing a learning context. Business schools and management development programs do not typically teach these leadership skills.

Effective change consultants need to help the leaders of the organization develop mental models of the learning dynamics in their organization, and provide coaching and feedback to leaders about how their behavior affects the capacity of the organization to learn. Consultants should provide practical approaches to help the leader embed learning in the work and the business processes of the organization, as well as develop leadership practices that model and encourage learning. Leaders can be catalysts for learning, or they can stifle learning and unwittingly reinforce the status quo. They can establish dynamics in which organizational members are helping to define and reach the future state, or they can create a context in which employees do what they are told.

# CONCLUSION

Based on longitudinal research in ten companies going through extensive changes in their business models and organizational designs, this chapter has described the learning processes that can enable accelerated organizational transformation. Understanding these learning dynamics has clear implications for change consultants. In order to help organizations go through successful transformations, consultants must begin to see learning as the essence of change, and their role as helping the company, its various units, and the individuals who constitute it to incorporate learning practices into their routines.

Models of change management have traditionally focused on overcoming resistance to change, and stage models of unfreezing the status quo, transitioning, and institutionalizing a new state (for example, Beckhard & Harris, 1977; Tichy, 1983). In today's dynamic world, organizational transitions entail the formation of new, dynamic forms of organization that require ongoing learning and transformation. It is no longer adequate for consultants to see their role as helping an organization go through a major change. Rather, they need to see the challenge of change as building the learning capabilities of the organization during the course of an iterative and ongoing series of change initiatives and redesign activities. This requires the building of learning dynamics throughout the organization, and helping leaders throughout the organization understand and enact their roles in a learning system. Change unfolds through learning. Any particular change creates a temporary state, one that will once again be altered as the organization learns to be more effective in an environment that is also changing.

Consultant-led organizational design processes and interventions help shape the context for the changes that are required to perform effectively in a changed environment. However, it is through the ongoing learning activities throughout the organization that new meanings are developed to underpin the new practices and interactions that have to be shaped and reshaped through ongoing self-design throughout the organization. Viewing organizational transformation in this manner can increase consultants' effectiveness in working with leaders, design teams, and the myriad of business units, teams, and individuals that must cope with unrelenting change at the same time they must be agents of change and help create the future.

# References

Barrett, F. J., Thomas, G. F., & Hocevar, S. P. (1995). The central role of discourse in large-scale change: A social construction perspective. *Journal of Applied Behavioral Science, 31,* 352–372.

Beckhard, R., & Harris, R. (1977). *Organizational transitions: Managing complex change.* Reading, MA: Addison-Wesley.

Bennis, W. G., & Nanus, B. (1985). *Leaders: Strategies for taking charge.* New York: HarperCollins.

Ciborra, C. U., & Schneider, L. S. (1992). Transforming the routines and contexts of management, work and technology. In P. S. Adler (Ed.), *Technology and the future of work* (pp. 269–291). New York: Oxford University Press.

Drazin, R., & Sandelands, D. (1992). Autogenesis: A perspective on the process of organizing. *Organization Science, 3,* 230–249.

Galbraith, J. R. (1977). *Organization design.* Reading, MA: Addison-Wesley.

Galbraith, J. R. (1995). *Designing organizations: An executive briefing on strategy, structure, and process.* San Francisco: Jossey-Bass.

Keidel, R. W. (1995). *Seeing organizational patterns: A new theory and language of organizational design.* San Francisco: Berrett-Koehler.

Ledford, G. E., Jr., Mohrman, S. A., Mohrman, A. M., Jr., & Lawler, E. E., III. (1989). The phenomenon of large scale change. In A. M. Mohrman, Jr., S. A. Mohrman, G. E. Ledford, Jr., T. G. Cummings, & E. E. Lawler, III, *Large scale organizational change* (pp. 1–32). San Francisco: Jossey-Bass.

Levitt, B., & March, J. G. (1988). Organizational learning. *Annual Review of Sociology, 14,* 319–340.

Nadler, D. A. (1992). Introduction: Organizational architecture: A metaphor for change. In D. A. Nadler, M. S. Gerstein, & R. B. Shaw, *Organizational architecture: Designs for changing organizations* (pp. 1–8). San Francisco: Jossey-Bass.

Nadler, D. A., Gerstein, M. S., & Shaw, R. B. (1992). *Organizational architecture: Designs for changing organizations.* San Francisco: Jossey-Bass.

Pasmore, W. A. (1988). *Designing effective organizations: The socio-technical systems perspective.* New York: Wiley.

Perlmutter, H. V., & Trist, E. (1986). Paradigms for societal transition. *Human Relations, 39*(1), 1–27.

Rasmussen, S. E. (1991). *Experiencing architecture.* Cambridge, MA: MIT Press.

Sandelands, L., & Stablein, R. E. (1987). The concept of organizational mind. In S. Bacharach & N. DiTomaso (Eds.), *Research in the sociology of organizations* (Vol. 5, pp. 135–161). Greenwich, CT: JAI Press.

Senge, P. M. (1990). *The fifth discipline: The art and practice of the learning organization.* New York: Doubleday.

Tenkasi, R. V., Mohrman, S. A., & Mohrman, A. M., Jr. (1998). Accelerating organizational learning during transition. In S. A. Mohrman, J. R. Galbraith, & E. E. Lawler, III, *Tomorrow's organization: Crafting winning capabilities in a dynamic world* (pp. 330–361). San Francisco: Jossey-Bass.

Thompson, J. D., & Tuden, A. (1959). Strategies, structures and processes of organizational decision making. In J. D. Thompson (Ed.), *Comparative studies in organizations* (pp. 195–216). Pittsburgh, PA: University of Pittsburgh Press.

Tichy, N. (1983). *Managing strategic change: Technical, political and cultural dynamics.* New York: Wiley.

Tichy, N. M., & Devanna, M. (1986). *The transformational leader.* New York: Wiley.

Weick, K. E. (1993). Organizational redesign as improvisation. In G. P. Huber & W. H. Glick (Eds.), *Organizational change and redesign: Ideas and insights for improving performance* (pp. 346–382). New York: Oxford University Press.

Weick, K. E., & Westley, F. (1996). Organizational learning: Affirming an oxymoron. In S. R. Clegg, C. Hardy, & W. R. Nord (Eds.), *Handbook of organization studies* (pp. 440–458). Thousand Oaks, CA: Sage.

# CHAPTER FOUR

# The Role of Systems Theory
# in Consulting Psychology

Dale R. Fuqua
*College of Education*
*Oklahoma State University*

Jody L. Newman
*Department of Educational Psychology*
*University of Oklahoma*

Several factors have influenced the current conceptual development and implementation of organizational interventions. Human organizations are becoming increasingly complex. Technological advances have greatly enlarged the environmental influences affecting organizations. Globalization in business and education continues to remove traditional environmental, economic, and social boundaries. The enhanced economy and efficiency afforded by consolidation have encouraged growth in the size of schools, businesses, governmental agencies, and universities. The exponential increase in knowledge, in combination with the increased accessibility to it, has accelerated the rate of change in many settings. In this environment, there has been a continuing trend to employ systems theory and systems thinking as a broad conceptual platform for organizational interventions. It has been widely recognized that systems theory has been the primary conceptual foundation for modern approaches to organizational development (Beckhard, 1969; Brown, Pryzwansky, & Schulte, 1987; French & Bell, 1990; Goodman & Associates, 1982; Fuqua & Kurpius, 1993; Kilburg, 1995; Lawrence & Lorsch, 1969; Lippitt, 1969; Williams, 1978).

## BASIC CONCEPTS IN SYSTEMS THEORY

The term *system* is primarily defined in the *American Heritage Talking Dictionary* (1999) as "a group of interacting, interrelated, or interdependent elements forming a complex whole," which is a meaningful introduction to the topic.

Many volumes have been written about systems theory as it applies to human organizations, and, as is often the case with popular, complex topics, opinions vary regarding what the term refers to in a complete sense. If one were limited to two volumes devoted to the topic, Michael Beer's (1980) and Peter Senge's (1990) treatments of the subject would be good choices. Beer's book does an excellent job of spelling out some fundamental elements of systems theory, and also relates it very effectively to organizational change. Senge referred to systems thinking as the fifth discipline and related it to four other important disciplines: shared vision, mental models, team learning, and personal mastery.

It would be an overwhelming task to review all of the literature related to systems theory. Many of the concepts of systems theory applied to human organizations have been influenced by or borrowed from general systems theory, which is closely related to the early work of Von Bertalanffy (1968) and has a distinct cross-disciplinary focus. Much has been written elsewhere about general systems theory and its value and weaknesses. This chapter is specifically limited to systems theory applied to consulting to human organizations.

## Paradigms of Behavior

There is a remarkable trend across the past 100 years of behavioral science to move from simple, exclusive paradigms toward much more complex, inclusive paradigms for understanding human behavior. Consider the psychoanalytic school of thought in the early 1900s:

Intrapsychic forces $\rightarrow \rightarrow \rightarrow$ Behavior

In this model, observable human behavior was conceptualized as the effect of some unconscious, intrapsychic energy. The therapeutic effort focused on developing a bridge from the unconscious energy to the conscious self-control mechanisms, so the forces could be directed to more desirable behavioral effects. Next, consider the early behavioral models:

Environmental influences $\rightarrow \rightarrow \rightarrow$ Behavior

In the behavioral model, observable behavior was thought to be the result of environmental stimuli and reinforcement contingencies. The therapeutic goal was to change behavior by manipulating the environment. Much later, mediational models were developed and promoted primarily by the early social learning theorists. This model has been symbolized as:

$$S \rightarrow O \rightarrow R$$

In this model, $S$ represents a stimulus condition, $O$ represents the organismic mediation of the stimulus condition, and $R$ symbolizes an observable behavioral response. The arrows reflect that behavior is still viewed as a result of the environment and some internal predisposition.

Kurt Lewin (1951), with his influence on field theory, has had a most notable impact on systems theory. One of his contributions was the following formula:

$$B = f(P, E)$$

That is to say that behavior is a function of the interaction of a person and the environment. Symbolized in a slightly different way, this might appear as:

$$(P \leftrightarrow E) \rightarrow \rightarrow \rightarrow B$$

It is important to pay close attention to the directionality here. The arrow relating the person (internal psychological variables) to the environment is bidirectional. People live and exist in a field (environment or system), and both exert reciprocal effects on one another. Not only are people influenced by the environment, but they are also active shapers of it. Still, though, behavior is viewed as an effect of this bidirectional interaction.

Bandura (1997), from a social cognitive perspective, presents what he refers to as "three major classes of determinants in triadic reciprocal determinism" (p. 6). The three major classes are internal personal factors (P), which include cognitive and affective factors, behavioral factors (B), and factors from the external environment (E). These three sets of factors are presented in the following diagram:

Notice that behavior here is not constructed as an effect, but as a fully functioning class of determinants in reciprocal interaction with the environment and internal personal variables. The most significant aspects of social environments are often the patterns of behavior exhibited by participants. From a systems point of view, the structure of the system can only be seen at times in the behavior of those residing in the system. Trying to apply reductionistic strategies to extricate behavior as an effect from the environment is often not realistic. Similarly, the structure of the environment is often embedded in the cognition and affect of the individual participants. That is where norms, expectations, and standards reside. This principle is essential to understanding the development of systems theory over the past century. We will address the specific features of systems structure subsequently.

Bandura has been one of the most influential thinkers in behavioral science in our time. In presenting his ideas about reciprocal causation, he develops a position of such great importance in the context of systems theory, that we will reproduce it here:

> Human adaptation and change are rooted in social systems. Therefore, personal agency operates within a broad network of sociostructural influences. In agentic transactions, people are both producers and products of social systems. Social structures—which are devised to organize, guide, and regulate human affairs in given domains by authorized rules and sanctions—do not arise by immaculate conception; they are created by human activity. Social structures, in turn, impose constraints and provide resources for personal development and everyday functioning. But neither structural constraints nor enabling resources foreordain what individuals become and do in given situations. For the most part, social structures represent authorized social practices carried out by human beings occupying designated roles [Bandura, 1997, p. 6].

We believe that systems theory has failed at times to meet its potential for producing human good. Too often, systems theory has become an excuse for personal failures, leading some to believe that people are simply products of their environment. The opposite conclusion, in fact, applies. The greatest potential of systems theory is to empower individuals to singularly and collectively take responsibility for the systems in which they work and live, to the end of building and rebuilding human systems to become increasingly responsive to human needs.

Another interesting aspect of systems theory is that it has remained largely theoretical. Specific constructs, measures, and interventions have not operationalized systems theory in a clear, complete, and distinct way. Instead, systems theory is a way of thinking, understanding, and organizing information related to human organizations. Very few successful organizational interventions or strategies could be identified that do not incorporate or rely on ideas from systems perspectives. Systems theory provides a conceptual framework for selecting among, applying, and evaluating the full range of potential organizational interventions. It is not an intervention itself, but is a broad conceptual platform—arguably an essential one—for intervening in organizational settings.

The utility of systems theory is not limited to organization-level interventions. Given the value of systems theory in understanding social systems in general, it is also a useful conceptual framework for individual and small group consultation interventions. Individual problems almost always exist in some social system or context. Small group dynamics are influenced by the larger social system in which the group operates. Individual and small group change efforts will affect and be affected by the social system in which they occur. Effective, sustainable change and development at any level will be more likely when systemic factors are actively considered and integrated into the change effort.

The remainder of this chapter is organized around four major objectives. First, the basic components of a system will be presented and discussed. Second, several key dynamics of systems theory will be reviewed and outlined. Third, some issues related to individual and small group work from a systems perspective will be presented. Fourth, several general aspects of systems thinking in the organizational context will be discussed.

# A CONCEPTUAL MODEL OF AN ORGANIZATIONAL SYSTEM

A completely satisfying visual model of a human/organizational system has been elusive due to the complexity of concepts and relations involved. However, it is possible to represent in diagrammatic form some of the major features of an organization as a system. Figure 4.1 was constructed for this purpose. One of the most fundamental precepts of systems theory is that a system can be conceived of as being comprised of multiple subsystems. The four major subsystems in the figure are labeled in the four blocked arrows, and include the psychosocial, operational, purposive, and methodological subsystems.

It is important to point out that there is no single set of subsystems that might be employed to conceptualize the complex nature of organizations. Instead, there are several ways to label and organize the different aspects of organizations. Historically, several authors have had a significant impact on the particular subsystem structures used in practice. Katz and Kahn (1978) discussed five generic types of subsystems: production, maintenance, managerial, adaptive, and supportive. Kast and Rosenzweig (1974) presented a diagrammatic representation of an organizational system composed of five general areas including goals and values, psychosocial, structural, technical, and managerial subsystems. Beer (1980) presented a social systems model of organizations including people, structures, behavior and process, human outputs, dominant coalitions, and culture. Figure 4.1 also draws heavily from a representation by Kurpius (1985), also discussed by Fuqua and Kurpius (1993).

Even more specifically, it is possible to adapt an organizational model such as the one in Figure 4.1 to any given organization. The focus here, however, is on describing a more general model that might help the consultant organize complex data collection, assessment efforts, and change strategies within a single organization. Adapting the model to fit specific organizational parameters is more of a creative task than a structured one. We begin our discussion of the model by describing the basic subsystems depicted in the figure.

## Purposive Subsystems

At some level, organizations exist to serve some common purpose. In larger organizations this can become a burdensome matter, but in all organizations

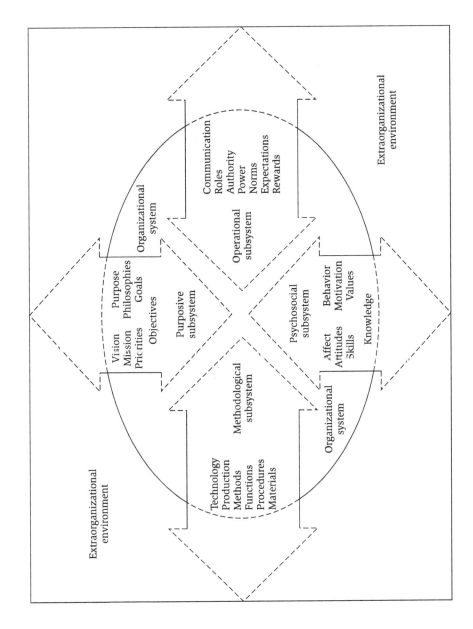

**Figure 4.1 Elements of a Social System.**

the raison d'être is a central organizing framework. Like most organizational structures, there are both formal and informal purposes operating simultaneously. Formal purposes can usually be found in formal written mission statements or related documents. Informal purposes usually are not written down and might not be shared unanimously throughout the organization. For example, a sales unit might agree that the production of high-quality electronic components is the formal purpose of the organization. On the other hand, if measures are taken to improve the quality of the product by slowing production and reducing the number of units available for sale, the formal commitment of sales staff to product quality might quickly decline due to commission-generating goals and objectives at both the individual and unit level. Similarly, an athletic department at a university will routinely ascribe publicly to the highest educational goals for student athletes, but might, at the same time, make unreasonable time demands of student athletes in order to build winning programs. These conflicts in the formal and informal structure can become devastating if not addressed in an intentional way.

The consultant will often begin an informal assessment by asking questions about the purposive subsystem. In the context of organizational life, the purposive subsystem is all of the things, concrete and abstract, formal and informal, collective and individual, that provide meaning and direction for organizational functioning. Consultees will typically respond to questions about organizational purpose, goals, and objectives by producing written documents that largely reflect formal purposes or missions in one form or another. This is a natural and safe way to begin the discussion about these issues. In relatively dysfunctional organizations, disagreement about goals and objectives might very well be difficult to discuss in public group settings. The consultant in some settings is much more likely to learn about conflicting goals, objectives, values, or other internal conflicts about purposes during individual interviews. Conflicts based on the functional direction of an organization can be difficult to discuss in open sessions, especially if other problems are being experienced. Of course, there is great potential for organizational development and increased effectiveness when dimensions like organizational direction and meaning are well integrated and broadly endorsed. In general, broad ownership of, and identity with, the direction of the organization is desirable. Conflict, even at the philosophical level, can and should be conceptualized as a developmental opportunity.

A final issue related to the purposive subsystem is its complexity. It is often driven by contextual factors. For example, the nature of competition can have a substantial bearing on how an organization constructs its direction and mission. The size of an organization is another major factor that will have a direct bearing on the complexity of the purposive subsystem, with larger organizations accommodating a broader range of objectives necessary to be inclusive. The process of establishing goals and objectives in the context of divergent philosophical perspectives in a large social system requires effective planning to ensure a healthy level of inclusion.

## Operational Subsystems

Even in relatively small organizations, the operations of members are framed within certain boundaries for acceptable conduct. Some of these guidelines are drawn from broader socialization processes, but some are specific to the organization. Some of the most important diagnostic areas in organizations are part of the larger subsystem labeled in Figure 4.1 as the operational subsystem. The components listed within this subsystem are key aspects of the broader culture of the organization, and several others could have been added. Careful examination and understanding of these key elements of the social framework of the organization are essential tools for the organizational consultant.

For example, consider the communication dimension. Who is communicating with whom? Are there lines of communication that have been closed or circumvented? What are the patterns of communication? What is the ratio of top-down communications to bottom-up communications? Is there a healthy level of vertical communication? How do communication patterns relate to functions? How does formal communication relate to informal communication? It is useful in a large-scale organizational analysis to actually count types of communication from one area to another, as well as sorting them by form of communication. If the flow of information does not make sense to the consultant as an external observer, it is important to find out why.

The distinction between formal and informal structure is again quite relevant to the operational subsystem. Consider the reward structure in an organization. The usual response to a question about the reward system in an organization includes a presentation from the policy and procedures manual about how members are evaluated for promotion, salary increases, and so forth. This describes the formal reward system in an organization, which is important. In most organizations, though, there are also very important informal rewards that are known to members, but that might not be discussed much in public meetings. In one-on-one interviews, a consultant may learn that there are certain informal rewards that have powerful effects. In one setting, these might include dinner invitations with the CEO or some other high-ranking person. Task assignments to staff can be based on an informal reward system. For example, fewer road assignments might be given to staff members perceived to be closer to a manager on a personal basis. In most settings the subjective nature of such informal rewards can be very impactful in both positive and negative ways. As a consultant, it is critical to evaluate both formal and informal dimensions of the organizational framework.

The distribution of power in organizations is of great importance. In the bureaucratic model of organizations, both power and authority are concentrated at the highest levels of the organization. Based on many different factors, modern theories of organizational behavior favor the distribution of power and authority downward. Beer and Spector (1993) pointed out that "new external demands are overwhelming the capacity of command-and-control organizations to respond" (p. 642). A number of other authors, from different perspectives, have pointed to the limitations of traditional, hierarchical organizational structures in the modern age (Cleveland, 1985; Morgan, 1986; Peters, 1992; Peters & Waterman, 1982; Rogers & Ballard, 1995). Hicks and Peterson (1997) characterized the changing nature of organizations clearly by stating, "The standardization of people and their roles loses its value when the competitive environment is shifting underfoot. Instead of building more structures, organizations are trading functional silos for fluid, responsive processes that are less constrained by formal organizational boundaries" (p. 175). Hicks and Peterson went on to say, "As organizations become flatter, the glue is increasingly composed of common vision and values, organizational purpose, integrated strategies, and core competencies" (p. 175).

A generally important principle is that the people with responsibility for a task and the knowledge necessary for accomplishing it should retain substantial power and authority related to task accomplishment. It is relatively easy to help an organization analyze the codistribution of power and authority, but it is often extremely difficult to reconcile the perceived human needs for control with an ideal distribution of power and authority.

The concept of *equifinality* (that is, the notion that there are multiple possible paths to a given outcome) can be applied here to illustrate the power of systems thinking. Leadership is a major component in the operational subsystem of organizations. Particularly under difficult circumstances, there is serious temptation to blame those in leadership positions, which, unfortunately, is a process in which the leaders themselves sometimes engage. That is not to say that poor leadership does not exist, but that blaming the leadership is sometimes merely scapegoating, or even more often may be only partially fair to the leader. Suppose a leader is having a difficult time implementing some strategic plans. Staff individually might express some doubts about the leader's ability to effectively resolve the process. From the consultant's point of view, the problem might be framed from the perspective of leadership concerns. An alternative (assuming the leader is competent) might be to reframe the problem as one of ineffective communication across the organization. Which of these will likely create more resistance? Which is more likely to encourage an opening of communication? Which is more likely to lead to a successful outcome for all of the parties? Sometimes the same change goals can be realized by entering different subsystems with far fewer negative side effects. This kind of framing is made possible by understanding that leadership and communication are often embedded components of the same system.

## Methodological Subsystems

Important organizational dimensions are involved, even imbedded, in the methods an organization uses to achieve its purposes, goals, and objectives. It is easy to imagine how other important organizational structures like norms, roles, and expectations must interact with the technology and methods of production. For example, in a large printing operation that is dependent on big, expensive computer-operated printing presses, consider the role of the press operators. Most of the other service units are organized around the operation of the presses. From purchasing to shipping functions, success is dependent on the successful operation of the presses. Failure and downtime of the presses can severely impact all others' ability to successfully process and meet contracts. It is not surprising that the role of the press operator is an elevated one in such circumstances. The reward system reflects this elevated role, and so will some social norms surrounding the role. Consultants must recognize the interdependence of structural elements across subsystems in order to effectively identify organizational patterns in a complete and functional way.

The technology, methods, and materials involved in operating an organization vary widely based on the nature of the organization and its mission. Significant alignment of the purposive, operational, and methodological subsystems is an important feature of a well-integrated organization. This is a result of the principle of interdependence, which will be addressed subsequently in more depth. However, the principle of interdependence basically leads to the conclusion that isolated variables that exist in complex sets of interactions cannot be understood fully except in relationship to the whole system of interactions (Beer, 1980; Williams, 1978). Conflicts across these subsystems can be devastating. Significant shifts in the methodological subsystem can be a challenging event in the life of an organization. For example, the implementation of a computerized accountability system in a social service agency might raise basic philosophical questions for professional staff. Likewise, the potential effects of implementing an automated shipping system that will result in the loss of 150 jobs in the plant will be immense. These types of changes in the structural subsystems of the organization require major reconsiderations of other structural dimensions.

## Psychosocial Subsystems

The psychosocial dimension includes the people operating in the organization and their key characteristics. Knowledge bases and skill levels are essential dimensions of individuals' roles in the organization. Attitudes and motivational qualities have a major bearing on the culture of an organization in a reciprocal relationship. Characteristics of individuals within an organization are shaped by the structural aspects of the organization. The formal and informal structures of an organization are also influenced heavily by organizational members' characteristics. This pattern of reciprocal influence between behavior and organizational structure is a key feature of systems theory and will be discussed thoroughly later in the chapter.

Many aspects of the structure of an organization are abstract, while people and their behavior are easily seen and experienced by others in the organization. As a result, there is a fairly strong tendency to interpret organizational problems more in terms of the behavior of individuals and groups in an organization. This sometimes occurs without regard for the structural aspects of the organization that might be contributing as well. From a systems perspective, it is imperative to understand that there is a complex range of inextricable interactions of individual behavior and organizational structure. The important relationship of behavior and organizational structure will be discussed later in some additional detail.

## General Aspects of an Organizational System

In addition to the four major subsystems, Figure 4.1 was designed to highlight other general characteristics of a system. First, the intersection of the four blocked arrows representing the major subsystems characterizes a constant interaction of each subsystem with the other subsystems within the organizational context. The dashed lines that comprise the arrows at their intersection symbolize their permeability. That is, dimensions of each of the subsystems share common aspects and interactions. Just as an example, the kind of leadership roles that are structured into the organization (operational subsystem) will have a direct bearing on the kinds of philosophical perspectives (purposive subsystem) influencing the organization of functions (methodological subsystem), which inevitably affects the motivation of members (psychosocial subsystem). The number of such complex interactions can become overwhelming at the theoretical level. At the practical level, effective consultants, guided by systems thinking, or at least aware of its implications, learn to become skillful at identifying the most relevant interactional patterns in complex fields of interactions.

Notice in Figure 4.1 that the subsystem arrows point outward toward the external organizational environment. These outward points are also comprised of broken lines, reflecting a permeability of boundaries between organizational subsystems and the environment. Historically, there was some discussion about the open system versus closed system nature of organizations (Kast & Rosenzweig, 1974; Katz & Kahn, 1978). Today it is recognized that all human systems are open systems, and that the internal nature of systems is affected in many ways by the near and remote environments in which the systems exist (Beer, 1980). Effective organizations also take their abilities to influence the environment very seriously.

Consider the nature of a manufacturing plant located in a particular community. Generally, the pool of available job applicants will be related to the employment opportunities and the educational system in the community. Social norms will migrate from the community to the work site. Transportation facilities will have a significant bearing, at least potentially, on delivery methods. Prevailing social attitudes will find their way to the work place. Thus, organizations exist within community contexts that extensively affect the organization as a system. Beyond the community, there are national and international environments that can have substantial influences on a local organization. These effects are perhaps easiest to see in terms of competition and market demand. For example, the development of a less expensive production process halfway around the world may create demands for structural changes in a local facility. Even moderate to small organizations benefit from awareness of external environments, especially when this awareness includes monitoring the environment for potentially significant influences. Sometimes the ability to anticipate external influences is a great competitive edge.

The conceptual model in Figure 4.1 is far from complete. However, it does represent several major features of systems theory. It can also be a useful format for organizing a systems analysis. More than occasionally, the use of a systems model such as Figure 4.1 can provide the consultee-organization with a format for self-analysis, data collection, planning, and developmental activities. For example, in many organizations, promotions to leadership roles are given based on performance in professional specializations. Engineers who have great technical knowledge sometimes are promoted into leadership positions where understanding of human factors may be more important than technical knowledge. Good conceptual tools can be of great help in such a situation. Cognitive modeling from a systems theory perspective is one way to empower others who are trying to improve their organizations.

One of the interesting aspects of the diagram in Figure 4.1 is that it can be applied to large or small organizations. It can be applied to whole organizations or to subunits within a larger organization. Systems theory also includes some dynamic principles that generalize well across organizations of different sizes and types. In the next section, attention turns to the nature of some of the fundamental dynamics of systems theory applied specifically to human systems or organizations.

## Systems Dynamics

There are several general principles of activity, energy, influence, and process in human systems that are necessary to systems thinking. In addition to developing some idea of what the generic structures, components, and subsystems are, these principles of systems dynamics are essential to understanding how systems operate and how to intervene in them. There is a synergistic effect when relationships of the parts of a human system interact in complex patterns. In the previous section the assumption that human systems are made up of component structures was made explicit. Now attention turns to how the components interact with one another, and how processes interact with one another and with the structural components of the system.

# INTERACTIONS OF COMPONENTS AND PROCESSES

## Interdependence

If one was restricted to a single word or concept to describe systems theory, *interdependence* would be a good choice. Beer (1980) referred to systems theory as "the ideas that help explain the dynamic interrelationships of several parts of a larger whole as it interacts with its environment" (p. 17). Williams (1978) noted the important implications of interdependence by saying, "The systems approach to studying organizations focuses attention on the fact that, because these variables are always influencing one another, we can understand any given part only by understanding how it influences and is influenced by all the other continually changing parts" (p. 42). The concept of interdependence in systems theory is a broad, inclusive concept that refers to the extensive interconnectedness of all parts of the system to one another.

The consultant working in an organization must be keenly aware of the interdependence of the parts of the system. Simple understanding of events independent of the systemic implications can lead to serious errors in judgment. Quick solutions to problems based on a localized problem definition will often underestimate the systemic nature of many problems due to the general interdependence of the system's parts and processes. It is not always possible or appropriate to move from localized to systemic interventions, but that is a complex matter we address to some extent later in the chapter under the heading of Individual Consultation from a Systems Perspective. Careful analysis of the broader organizational context is always preferred if it is feasible to do so. Maybe a real example will illustrate this point. The first author worked in an incidental role with a unit in a larger organization in which a receptionist-clerk was constantly being criticized for interpersonal problems. She was replaced within a few months by another individual. Soon this second person also developed a reputation as someone with whom it was difficult to work. After the second person was replaced by a third person, who also just happened to be difficult to work with, certain questions arose regarding this particular position. As one might imagine, the position was one with a low salary, poor benefits, and a significant work load with routine paper-processing tasks. Furthermore, the person in this position was responsible for responding to complaints made in person regarding a set of unpopular policies and procedures. Others in the office were rather defensive about the policies and procedures, and no one in the office was willing to share responsibility for receiving complaints. Serial replacements of the personality problem simply sustained system structure that had become dysfunctional regarding some policies and procedures that required more fundamental changes. Obviously, it is the consultee system that must ultimately define the problem as systemic or individual in nature. The task of the consultant is to help the consultee understand their own structure and people accurately enough to know the difference between personality and systems problems. Systems thinking often reveals that problems are just symptoms of systemic interdependence, but that is not always true. Treating symptoms can be expensive in human and economic terms and can serve to limit organizational development. Again, careful, thorough analysis of systemic factors can be very powerful when it is reasonable to do so. Naturally, helping the organization to learn to use this approach is an important goal in the consultation process.

## Closed versus Open Systems

In the physical sciences, there has been some interest in the concept of closed systems, which refers to a system that has impermeable boundaries (Kast & Rosenzweig, 1974). Such closed systems experience entropy, or movement toward a chaotic or random state. Social systems are inherently open systems. Referring back to Figure 4.1, permeability of the social system is symbolized by broken rather than solid lines. Extraorganizational factors are constantly interacting reciprocally with the social system. Furthermore, the concept of social system is actually a multileveled one in which levels of systems can be imbedded. An individual who manages a personnel office for a local company is a family member, an employee of the company, a member of a local church organization, a citizen of the community, and so forth. All of these systems will have some impact on the individual, who will also influence in some ways the various systems. The most important feature of the open systems concept for consultants is to ensure that environmental influences, both near (for example, community) and remote influences (for example, federal legislation, international competition), are addressed in planning activities. The system must be defined relative to functional control, which is sometimes risky and always important. If a consultant is invited to work with a plant to resolve some problem with the shipping and delivery unit, is the client system the shipping department, the plant, or the corporation? Though there are important ethical questions about who comprises the client system, there are also very important functional questions. Where are the resources required to best address the problem? What are the process effects of defining the client system locally (for example, ownership, resistance to change, conflict points)? Realistically, the motivational basis of the consultee group, the nature of the problem, resource or time constraints, and related factors might not allow the consultant access to a full system intervention. Consultants might not always have access to larger systems components in the change effort, but effective consultants must be aware of them and ensure that consultees are as well. Being fully informed about the systems issues is essential in order to provide the consultee system a real choice about response options.

## Residual Effects

The concept of residual effects results directly from the interdependence that exists within a system. Any change in an interdependent system has the potential to create unintended effects in addition to the desired, targeted change. Most practicing consultants could provide personal examples of unintended residual effects of a planned intervention or change strategy because such effects are commonplace. For example, a needs assessment questionnaire designed to help collect information about preferences for various solutions to parking problems can quickly create reverberations throughout an organization about leadership styles, reward systems, and so forth. Discussions about potential reorganization can trigger feelings of powerlessness that can have much broader ramifications for organizational structure and process. Experienced consultants anticipate and plan for residual effects with any organizational intervention. Early in the planning process, provisions for monitoring implementation should include elements designed to monitor the system for residual effects of the intervention. It is important to note that the inevitability of residual effects in human systems is one of several strong reasons for being inclusive in the planning and implementation of interventions.

## Equifinality

Equifinality is a concept with roots in general systems theory. In the context of human systems and their complex, highly interactive nature, many different paths can lead to the same result (Kast & Rosenzweig, 1974), or in problem language, many alternative solutions might exist to a given problem (Brown, Pryzwansky, & Schulte, 1987). Given that consultants often do not have adequate data to determine unequivocally which solution is likely to work best (Blanton, 2000), the availability and consideration of multiple paths to problem solutions must lead to careful deliberation based on the experience of the consultant and consultee group. Due to the complex interdependence of component parts within a human system, the current condition of the system might result from different starting points and different developmental paths. This is not only of great theoretical importance, but also of great potential practical importance. "Not only does the concept of equifinality allow for considering among several alternative intervention targets, but it also allows for constructing powerful multidimensional strategies that can be applied simultaneously at different points in an organizational system" (Fuqua & Kurpius, 1993, p. 609). As an example, suppose a consultant is working with an organization concerned with low staff morale. An effective job enrichment program (Robbins, 1998) aimed at utilizing the skills and knowledge of line staff (psychosocial subsystem) might be paired with a vertical teaming approach to reexamining priorities (purposive subsystem), role reorganization (operational subsystem), and a review of functions and procedures related to roles (methodological subsystem). In this example, the multidimensional nature refers simultaneously to the interventions and the organizational subsystems involved.

## Equilibrium

Historically, emphasis has been placed on the tendency for social systems to seek a state of balance or equilibrium. Perhaps the greatest proponent of the idea of equilibrium or a steady state was Lewin (1951). Social organizations in Lewin's time were obviously much more stable in many ways than organizations of today. Today, competitive organizations are more adaptive and transient than ever before. Still, the application of Lewin's conceptual model of change continues to be a useful way to conceptualize planned organizational change. Figure 4.2 is a representation of Lewin's idea of force field analysis. It is included not only to illustrate the concept of equilibrium, but also because it can be a very helpful planning schema in practice. The first major block in the figure represents some current state of the social system in equilibrium; that is, the problem condition. The second major black represents a futuristic goal condition of the system—the way people would like for the system to be. Both driving and restraining forces in the system are required to hold the system in its current state of equilibrium. Change is conceptualized as the movement from the current state of affairs to the goal state. Initially, this requires the introduction of a state of disequilibrium, which can be introduced by some combination of adding driving forces or removing restraining forces. After the desired state is achieved, the system settles into a new state of equilibrium.

Though force field analysis can be a very useful planning tool, it is also a reminder of a very important dynamic in social systems. There is a strong

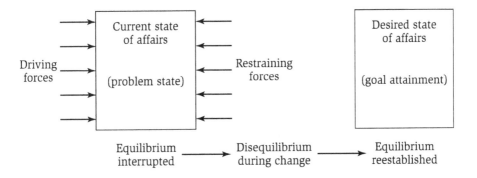

Figure 4.2 **Lewin's Force Field Analysis.**

tendency for systems to become settled into a state of balance or equilibrium. This is to some large extent due to the basic psychological need people have for continuity and control in their environment. Systemic change can be a very stressful process that can interfere with individuals' basic security needs. Recent years have seen an increase in the rate of change demands in many human systems. Tolerance for change and adaptability potential are important characteristics for many organizations. However, the concept of equilibrium is a critical reminder that there are important psychosocial implications of prolonged periods of change and disequilibrium. Effective organizational systems must provide for the basic stability needs of individuals.

## Conflict

Conflict is a basic aspect of all social systems. Conflict can be imbedded between or among structural components. It can also be imbedded between or among subunits of the system. Interpersonal manifestations of conflict are common and predictable. Much has been written about conflict resolution as an organizational intervention strategy. Conflict is mentioned here as a fundamental system dynamic because it must be expected and utilized constantly in systems thinking and systems analysis. Conflict has powerful diagnostic implications. Conflict management and utilization in organizational development must become routine in high-performing organizations. Conflict should be expected as a routine aspect of organizational dynamics. Experienced consultants become quick to recognize conflict and skillful in interpreting it in its interconnectedness with other aspects of the system.

## Differentiation

This concept refers to the general tendency for growth of social systems to include increasing levels of functional specificity. As organizations become larger, they almost inevitably become structurally more complex. Even casual observation of organizations of different sizes would lead one to believe in this concept of differentiation. Implied by this concept is the idea that there is an ideal level of differentiation given a system's size, mission, structure, resources, and circumstances. To some large extent this ought to be a result of rational processes. For example, in a small business with three employees, a director of personnel would not make much sense, for obvious reasons. The level of functional differentiation is a key feature of organizations that is central to understanding the organization systemically.

## Individual Consultation from a Systems Perspective

It may seem ironic to include a section on individual consultation in a chapter on systems theory. In reality, however, there are inevitably going to be times when the consultant encounters circumstances that make an individual focus either necessary or preferred. Fuqua and Newman (1985) delineated several situations in which individual consultation might be most likely to occur:

- When the underlying problems are of an individual nature
- When systems interventions are untimely or unlikely
- When perceptions of problems are limited to individuals
- When a system is highly resistant to change
- When individual behavior change is grossly more efficient given the present condition of the system

As reflected in this list, there are times when intervention at the individual level might be both appropriate and preferred, based on specific parameters of the problem being addressed. At other times, individual intervention might represent a compromise or settling for a less-preferred alternative to a more systems-oriented strategy. Whatever the specific circumstances, it is critical to realize that individual consultation interventions must be based upon sound systems thinking. From a systems perspective, problems, by definition, do not exist in a vacuum. As already noted, subsystems within the organization as a whole are intricately interrelated and interdependent. Situations in which issues or problems are truly isolated to a single individual are probably rare. Tobias (1990) suggested that the idea in consultation is "not only to get to the 'root' of the issue, but to assume that issues have many 'roots' and many 'branches'. . ." (p. 11). In the same vein, Tobias pointed out that in addition to addressing the consultee's immediate presenting problem(s), factors within the organization that both maintain and predispose the organization toward such problems must be identified. Dougherty (1995) argued strongly for maintaining a systems perspective, regardless of the unit or target of change (that is, individual, group, organization, or larger social system). According to Dougherty, even in the case of individual consultation, "the ultimate target in all cases of organizational consultation is the organization . . ." (p. 211). A similar view was advocated by Beckhard (1979), who advocated that all change must be system oriented; that is, it must relate to the broader organization, or at least to significant subsystems within the organization. Thus, even when consultation is directed to the individual level, either by necessity or design, a more meaningful conceptualization of both the problem and the intervention can be achieved by applying a systems perspective.

Fuqua and Newman (1985) proposed a 2 × 2 conceptual model (see Figure 4.3) to represent four possible contexts from which consultation might emerge. The four quadrants in the figure represent the simultaneous perspectives of the individual and the organization regarding the nature of the problem or the appropriate focus of consultation. The four quadrants have been labeled

Organizational
position

|  | Individual problem | Organizational problem |
|---|---|---|
| Individual problem | 1) Individual consultation | 2) Progression |
| Organizational problem | 3) Adaptation | 4) Organizational consultation |

Individual position

**Figure 4.3 Four Approaches to Individual Consultation from a Systems Perspective.**

as individual consultation, progression, adaptation, and organizational consultation. The first quadrant, individual consultation, represents the case in which there is mutual agreement between the individual who will be the focus of the intervention and the organization that the problem is of an individual nature. The focus of the intervention in such a case would be the individual, with the goal of enhancing that person's effectiveness in his or her organizational role. Consider the situation in which a highly qualified engineer is promoted to a managerial position based on technical knowledge and expertise. After a brief period in the new position, it becomes apparent to both the engineer and his or her superiors that a problem exists in the manager's ability to supervise and work effectively with others. There is agreement among all parties that the problem is of an individual nature and that intervention should be focused upon remediating the individual's skill deficit. An intervention such as executive coaching might be pursued.

The second quadrant, described as progression, represents the case in which the individual views the problem as his or her own responsibility, but the organization views it as a system problem. One of the views advanced in this chapter is that, in a majority of cases, a systems focus is superior to the much more limited individual focus, and thus, the term *progression* was selected to reflect progress from a lesser to a more desirable perspective. A progressive context might exist in the following case. Suppose an administrator of a particular unit within a larger organization is instructed by superiors to implement a newly developed employee evaluation system. Suppose further that this unit was not represented among the developers of this new evaluation system, resulting in two critical problems. First, the unique nature of the work done by unit members has not been incorporated into performance criteria in the new system, and second, performance data for employees of the unit that is available does not relate in a meaningful way to the criteria specified in the new evaluation system. Not surprisingly, the administrator's efforts to implement the new evaluation system fail, an outcome for which the administrator readily assumes personal responsibility. Suppose further that the administrator's superiors recognize the broader organization's role in the failure and define the problem at the system level. An intervention broadly involving relevant subsystems within the organization to revisit the evaluation system might be appropriate.

Fuqua and Newman's third quadrant is called adaptation, and refers to the case in which the individual views the problem as systemic, though the organization views the problem as individual in nature. Assuming the organization's perspective remains constant, an adaptive response is required by the individual; that is, he or she might have to accept the inherent limitations of, and proceed with, an intervention that is narrowly focused at the individual level. To illustrate a case of an adaptive response, suppose that a regional sales manager reports a decline in sales for a given quarter, which he or she has reason to believe is related to a decline in the quality of the product being produced and sold. Thus, the sales manager views the problem as a system problem and believes a system-level response would be most appropriate. Upper-level executives, however, might view the problem as resulting from failures of the regional sales manager, thus defining the problem at the individual level. Obviously, the sales manager can attempt to influence this perception in favor of a more system-oriented definition of the problem. However, should such efforts fail, the only alternative available might be to adapt to the organization's definition of the problem. This is obviously not the preferred outcome, and efforts to intervene might be hampered by such a narrow definition of the problem.

Finally, the fourth quadrant in Fuqua and Newman's model represents organizational consultation, the situation in which both the organization and the individual view the problem from a systems perspective. This situation is perhaps the most familiar scenario and the one most widely discussed throughout this book. When there is agreement among parties within the organization that the locus of the problem should be defined systemically, the greatest potential exists for a full mobilization of system resources to achieve the desired outcome. A systems-based consultation will be most appropriate.

The second and fourth quadrants both reflect contexts in which organizational consultation is the most appropriate and preferred approach. As already noted, we believe that, as a general rule, intervention at the system level is preferable to intervention at the individual level. Thus, there are several potential advantages to be gained when progression from individual to organizational consultation occurs. For example, Fuqua and Newman (1985) pointed out that in individual consultation, problem ownership is often limited to the individual, which in many cases might not be appropriate; the range of potential interventions individuals can generate is typically inferior to the range generated by the broader system; and individual consultation, by its very nature, often fails to include those individuals or groups that are most likely to be affected by any change. In addition, the nature and degree of resources that can be mobilized to facilitate intervention are typically greater at the system level than at the individual level. Finally, shared ownership for the definition and resolution of problems can strengthen shared identification with the organizational system.

When individual intervention is unsuccessful, or when system-level intervention is more appropriate and feasible, there are a number of strategies that might be used to mobilize the system to become active in problem definition. Table 4.1 presents four general stages leading to a redefinition of the problem as a systems issue. The stages in Table 4.1 are designed to focus the initial individual consultation on soliciting a wider range of participation in problem definition and resolution.

This perspective emphasizes the use of information and its dissemination to stimulate a system or subsystem to action. Clear and open communication is a critical factor in achieving this objective. The consultant's role during this process is to facilitate the collection and communication of accurate information pertinent to effective problem definition, and to support the individual consultee in the transition from individual to system intervention. Clearly this perspective is based on the assumption that precise, technical information, when thoroughly and effectively organized and communicated, will motivate a system to act. If this assumption proves to be invalid, change is not likely to occur, and underlying motivational problems must be suspected.

Even when adequate motivation exists, conflict and resistance can prove to be major barriers to redefining a problem with broader ownership. The availability of adequate information, widely disseminated, is likely to reduce these human process barriers. Communication and human process strategies, typical to any organizational intervention, might be required to address conflict and reduce resistance to change.

Following the transition from individual to system ownership of a problem, the consultant needs to assess the appropriateness of his or her continuing as a consultant to the system or organization. The original relationship established with the individual consultee might interfere, realistically or perceptually, with the consultant's objectivity from the consultee system's perspective. Whether or not the consultant continues following this transition, some renegotiation of his or her role with both the individual consultee and the consultee system will be required.

Table 4.1 Moving to System Intervention.

| Stages | Objectives | Considerations for implementation | Potential problems |
|---|---|---|---|
| 1) Information gathering | To identify and collect information required to encourage organizational participation in the change effort. | What information is required? How to gain accessibility to information? Who should be involved? How should information be collected? | Too much or too little information. Intentionally restricted accessibility. Personal bias in collection. |
| 2) Information dissemination | To mobilize members of the organization, reduce resistance to change, solicit further participation and input. | Who should be included? How is information to be communicated? What information is to be shared? | Ineffective organization of information. Restricted participation. Closed communication. |
| 3) Appraisal of response | To determine the extent to which information and dissemination is effective in stimulating an organizational response. | How to solicit a response? Is more information required? What is the extent of resistance? | Conflicts of interest. Distortion of communication. Resistance to ownership. Blaming. |
| 4) Define problem locus | To define generally who will be affected by change and who should and will be involved in the planning process. | What range of participation is appropriate? How to proceed with problem definition? | Insufficient information. Interpersonal conflict. Restricted participation. |
| 5) Problem definition | Marks the transition from individual to organizational intervention. | Begin organizational consultation. | Appropriate ownership. Divergent goals and objectives. |

# SYSTEMS THINKING AS INTERVENTION
# IN ORGANIZATIONAL CONTEXTS

"Systems thinking is a discipline for seeing wholes. It is a framework for seeing interrelationships rather than things, for seeing patterns of change rather than static 'snapshots'" (Senge, 1990, p. 69). Systems theory is not a circumscribed set of easily acquired intervention strategies. Instead, it is a way of thinking. It is a broad conceptual system for understanding human organizations. It requires an evolution from positivistic linear thinking toward more complex models. Consider some of the basic assumptions of systems theory already reviewed or suggested, and imagine their implications for consultation practices:

- Organizations are usefully understood as dynamic, whole systems.
- Organizations, including relatively small ones, are comprised of subsystems that interact in complex, multidirectional, and reciprocal interrelationships.
- Human behavior, which is constantly being dramatically influenced by organizational structure, must selectively serve to regulate the structural aspects of an organization. At times it can represent the most influential element of structure.
- Organizations can be greatly influenced by extraorganizational environmental influences that might have complex interrelationships with the internal structure of the organization.
- Changes in any one aspect of the organization might reverberate throughout the system in unintended and unexpected ways.
- People are often unaware of many structural elements of a system, and, in some instances, discussion of informal structure is punishable.
- People can learn very quickly to disassociate from the structure they transmit. Norms for behavior, for example, are primarily maintained within the individuals who might conform to them and even transmit them to others by modeling. The same individuals will attribute the norms to the system.
- Leaders are held responsible for structure, especially when they are unaware of it and it is diffused throughout the system.

If one simply stops with the identification of abstractions such as these, much is lost. These abstractions do reflect the complex nature of systems and the need for understanding. However, their extraordinarily valuable contributions to practice require thoughtful operationalization. This process of operationalization is central to effective consulting. Consulting psychology should ultimately be a vehicle for building and managing social systems that optimize the quality of human life, which includes productivity. Attention, then, is turned to the application of systems theory for this purpose.

Systems theory easily leads to several principles of intervention that can be applied at any level in the social system. They are presented individually as follows.

## Wholistic Understanding

The interconnectedness of people and subsystems is not always easily seen from the inside of organizations. Individuals frequently operate without any observable contact with other units or systems in an organization. The result is that individual interests tend to drive analytical processes. Consultants must be able to empower people to use wholistic views of the organization. This is not only for those in leadership positions. In fact, it is typically more natural for leaders to think systemically than it is for unit-level staff, who might be structurally isolated and passively encouraged to stay that way. Perhaps, the prototypic systems intervention is to help organizational members see the complex patterns of interrelationships that comprise their system.

## Structural versus Behavioral Change

Perhaps the greatest value of systems thinking is its immediate access to structural change as an alternative, supplemental, or complementary approach to managing human environments. It is a natural tendency for people to think about problems in terms of fault and blame reasoning. Social institutions, like families, schools, and churches, all teach socialization objectives primarily at the level of individual responsibilities. Most of the history of the practice of counseling and psychology is tied to individual change, which continues to be true today. As a society, Americans have developed a tendency to think of aberrant behavior as a product of an individual's personal failure. Particularly in dysfunctional systems, discussions of recognized problems are likely to begin with questions of fault, or similarly with attributions of blame. And, it is true that individual choices, failures, and other behaviors can be responsible for the development of system problems. However, from the systems theory point of view, focusing only on individual behavior is an inefficient, misleading and often futile means of problem solving. Referring back to Figure 4.1, the psychosocial subsystem represents the human or behavioral aspects of an organization. The other three subsystems (purposive, operational, and methodological) collectively represent the structure of an organization. Primitive ideas of human organizations emphasize the use of power and authority as centralized commodities that are used to control individual behavior and force compliance. It is true that both structural and behavioral approaches are appropriate in some situations. In practice, both kinds of strategies are often used simultaneously. Furthermore, the principle of interdependence would imply that it is not possible, strictly speaking, to change just behavior or just structure. More progressive and enlightened approaches emphasize the importance of shared decision-making and problem-solving responsibility, and the inclusion of those affected by change efforts in planning the change. From this perspective, the key is to help members of the system take responsibility, not just for their own behavior and circumstances, but also for the structure of the organization and its implications for those who are part of it. The idea is that the structure of the organization should be molded to the psychological and social needs of its members, rather than trying to force unnecessary compliance of individuals to structural demands. Ideally, the result will be to optimize the quality of work life for members in a way that also maximizes realization of the goals and objectives of the organization. "Addressing the system's goals, framework, and methods of operation is a better predictor of *lasting change* than is the practice of changing people" (Kurpius, 1985, p. 369). This is not to say that structural intervention is always preferable, but rather, systems theory provides a basis for considering structural *and* behavioral approaches to helping organizations.

## Inclusion

Given the basic interdependence of people in systems, one is always included or excluded from a change effort. Operating from a systems perspective, the principle of interdependence implies that great influence can be gained by increasing participation in the change process. Not only does inclusion broaden the realm of ownership, it can greatly increase understanding of the problem, the potential solutions, and the likely impact of the various interventions across the system. This can be powerful. Exclusion can also be powerful. It can motivate people to resist change passively or actively. It can increase the sense of isolation and alienation individuals experience. Exclusion can make people suspicious about motives. Valuable human resources and perspectives are lost as a result of excluding people either intentionally or by default. There are times when the scope of a change effort will necessarily be limited by purpose or circumstances. Organizational matters that require rapid responses can limit the scope of involvement of members. Also, members of an organization will often voluntarily exclude themselves from a change effort for legitimate pragmatic reasons, for example, competing priorities. Though inclusion of those to be affected by change in the planning process is a general principle, it needs to be thoughtfully planned in context. In order to promote inclusion, the consultant often has to help people overcome their natural inclinations. Especially in dysfunctional organizations, people might be inclined toward exclusion as a safety or control strategy. Similarly, inclusion of those perceived to be supportive of a preferred agenda might be tempting. Unfortunately, these strategies can only serve to maintain the existing dysfunctional patterns of behavior. Of course, the patterns are often not visible to those who cannot think wholistically.

## Taking Responsibility

We have already indicated that people are often unaware of the structure of the organization in which they exist, and are often isolated in ways that discourage them from understanding their interrelationships with other units. In very dysfunctional systems, people can experience and describe structural issues as something external to them and by which they are being victimized. Usually the most difficult structural issues are actually in the people, but that is not the common perception. For example, a middle-level manager was describing some very difficult conflicts operating in his organization. He had a great deal of energy for discussing the conflict and a great historical explanation for how the conflict had developed. He was asked if he would like forgiveness to be a part of the culture in his work setting. Then he became very quiet. He naturally agreed. In actuality, he was being asked to personally take responsibility for the conflict by addressing a potential structural change. Prior to the focus on forgiveness as a cultural norm, all his energy was being perpetually directed at justifying the existing system, which was very painful and dysfunctional for many people. He could not see the role of his behavior in relation to maintaining the anger and conflict. Of course, this kind of systemic change would require broader participation. The principle of taking responsibility refers to helping organizational members recognize the structural aspects of their systems and supporting them in taking responsibility for the structure that exists. Structural choices require a major shift in relationships of individuals to the organizations that are fundamental to building more caring and functional systems. Naturally, taking responsibility works at the individual, small group, and organizational level.

## Information Accessibility

Power is not evenly distributed in organizations, and so access to information is rarely evenly distributed. It is not at all rare to observe the control of information used as a management strategy. Who should have access to what kinds of information? Who should decide what information is accessible and what information is protected? Most organizations have some strategic information that must be protected. However, the dynamic interdependency that characterizes social systems would suggest that appropriate access to information is essential. The amount of data and information now easily accessible by electronic and other means in even small- to moderate-sized organizations can easily become overwhelming. The management of information systems is a key to building effective organizations. Consultants to organizations should be aware of the central role of information exchange in the work and culture of the organization. Negative corporate phenomena like rumors and secrets can be very destructive, and they often represent counterdependent strategies for coping with a real or perceived lack of access to information. The deliberate construction of planned access to relevant information that is functional for both task accomplishment and the psychological well-being of members is central to systems-based interventions in organizations of any size.

## Problem Attribution

Senge (1990) clearly made two very important points about systems. The first was that "cause and effect are not clearly related in time and space" (p. 63), and the second was that "there is no blame—you and the cause of your problem are part of a single system. The cure lies in your relationship with the enemy" (p. 67). It is a common experience that early in the consultation relationship, consultees have tremendous energy for processing their attributions about the problem for which they are seeking help. Inexperienced consultants often try to actively suppress that bitching, blaming, and complaining phenomenon that is so familiar. Actually, that tends not to work very well for two reasons. First, if one is able to initially suppress it, it continues to seep out at inopportune times. It is as though there is an emotional need for these expressions, and sometimes these are very real needs. Second, the nature of the bitching, blaming, and complaining is very informative for the consultant *and the consultee* regarding the mechanisms that sustain (not cause) the problem. Simple, linear thinking does not work very well in complex systems conceptualized wholistically and assumed to be grossly interdependent. From a systems perspective, blaming others for mutually experienced problems makes little sense. Both the problems and potential solutions derive from the mutual interdependence.

## Collective Efficacy

Bandura (1997) defined perceived collective efficacy as "a group's shared belief in its conjoint capabilities to organize and execute the courses of action required to produce given levels of attainment" (p. 477). He conceived of collective efficacy as a quality that involves the individuals' self-efficacies, but also something that adds up to more than the sum of the self-efficacies of the individuals in the group. In this sense, the construct easily fits into systems thinking. The expectations individuals have regarding goal attainment are heavily influenced by many characteristics of the social groups with which they identify. The structure of large bureaucracies seems impenetrable from individualistic perspectives. Organizational crises, whether internally or externally derived, come in forms that can seem to represent insurmountable challenges when viewed privately. Powerlessness as a psychological experience must infiltrate at the group level to achieve its maximal effect from a systems perspective. This principle explains why in a totalitarian system, authority can ill afford specific acts of freely directed, visible individual attainment. Conversely, organizational consultants often try to help groups within an organization first achieve some limited level of attainment of systemic change. Overcoming limited expectations of influence and responsibility for the social structures we operate within (and that operate in us) can be an important step in building collective efficacy into the social structure of a system. This is a critical goal of organizational consultation at the small-group and organizational levels. Particularly in a period of increasing change demands, both quantitatively and qualitatively, this characteristic of collective efficacy becomes increasingly salient. Building collective successes is key to developing collective efficacy. Furthermore, the consultation process must provide groups ample opportunity to internalize such successes. Persisting in one's powerlessness, however comfortable that may become, is difficult to reconcile with planned change efforts that are successful due to group efforts that are carefully processed and internalized.

# CONCLUSIONS

Systems theory, as it relates to consulting psychology, is a very powerful set of ideas that establishes the framework for conceptualizing human systems from a wholistic perspective. This conceptual framework has led away from simple, linear, deterministic models for explaining how people live and work together. The application of seemingly isolated interventions designed with a singular focus is unrealistic. Systems theory equips the consulting psychologist with an expanded appreciation of the dynamics of interdependence and interconnectedness of component parts of a system that, in interaction, create an entity that is more complex and dynamic than individual components alone. This appreciation is just as influential in intervening with individuals and small groups who exist in systems as it is in intervening with whole systems or communities. It emphasizes the importance of carefully performing preliminary systems analyses that reveal the complex patterns of the system. Without an awareness of the general complexity of systems, individuals are strongly inclined to experience seemingly isolated events as causes or outcomes, when, in fact, these events are part of a much larger systemic pattern. Systems theory leads one to anticipate and plan for residual effects of interventions as well as intended effects. Systems theory implies an inclusive, shared responsibility approach to planning and implementing change efforts.

## References

*American Heritage Talking Dictionary* (3rd ed.) (1999). [CD-ROM]. Boston: Houghton Mifflin.

Bandura, A. (1997). *Self-efficacy: The exercise of control.* New York: Freeman.

Beckhard, R. (1969). *Organization development: Strategies and models*. Reading, MA: Addison-Wesley.

Beckhard, R. (1979). Organization changing through consulting and training. In D. P. Sinha (Ed.), *Consultants and consultant styles* (pp. 17–44). New Delhi, India: Vision Books.

Beer, M. (1980). *Organizational change and development: A systems view*. Santa Monica, CA: Goodyear Publishing.

Beer, M., & Spector, B. (1993). Organizational diagnosis: Its role in organizational learning. *Journal of Counseling and Development, 71*, 642–650.

Blanton, J. S. (2000). Why consultants don't apply psychological research. *Consulting Psychology Journal, 52*, 235–247.

Brown, D., Pryzwansky, W. B., & Schulte, A. C. (1987). *Psychological consultation: Introduction to theory and practice*. Needham Heights, MA: Allyn & Bacon.

Cleveland, H. (1985). The twilight of hierarchy: Speculations on the global information society. *Public Administration Review, 20*, 185–195.

Dougherty, A. M. (1995). *Consultation: Practice and perspectives in school and community settings*. Pacific Grove, CA: Brooks/Cole.

French, W. L., & Bell, C. H. (1990). *Organization development: Behavioral science interventions for organizational improvements*. Englewood Cliffs, NJ: Prentice Hall.

Fuqua, D. R., & Kurpius, D. J. (1993). Conceptual models in organizational consultation. *Journal of Counseling and Development, 71*, 607–618.

Fuqua, D. R., & Newman, J. L. (1985). Individual consultation. *The Counseling Psychologist, 13*, 390–395.

Goodman, P. S., & Associates. (1982). *Changes in organizations: New perspectives on theory, research, and practice*. San Francisco. CA: Jossey-Bass.

Hicks, M. D., & Peterson, D. B. (1997). Just enough to be dangerous: The rest of what you need to know about development. *Consulting Psychology Journal, 49*, 171–193.

Kast, F. E., & Rosenzweig, J. R. (1974). *Organization and management: A systems approach*. New York: McGraw-Hill.

Katz, D., & Kahn, R. L. (1978). *The social psychology of organizations* (2nd ed.). New York: Wiley.

Kilburg, R. R. (1995). Integrating psychodynamic and systems theories in organization development practice. *Consulting Psychology Journal, 47*, 28–55.

Kurpius, D. J. (1985). Consultation interventions: Successes, failures, and proposals. *The Counseling Psychologist, 13*, 368–389.

Lawrence, P. R., & Lorsch, J. W. (1969). *Developing organizations: Diagnosis and action*. Reading, MA: Addison-Wesley.

Lewin, K. (1951). *Field theory in social science: Selected theoretical papers* (D. Cartwright, Ed.). New York: HarperCollins.

Lippitt, G. L. (1969). *Organizational renewal: Achieving viability in a changing world*. Englewood Cliffs, NJ: Prentice Hall.

Morgan, G. (1986). *Images of organization*. Thousand Oaks, CA: Sage.

Peters, T. (1992). *Liberation management: Necessary disorganization for the nanosecond nineties*. New York: Knopf.

Peters, T., & Waterman, R., Jr. (1982). *In search of excellence: Lessons from America's best run corporations*. New York: HarperCollins.

Robbins, S. P. (1998). *Organizational behavior*. Englewood Cliffs, NJ: Prentice Hall.

Rogers, J. L., & Ballard, S. (1995). Aspirational management: Building effective organizations through shared values. *NASPA Journal, 32*, 162–178.

Senge, P. M. (1990). *The fifth discipline: The art and practice of the learning organization*. New York: Doubleday.

Tobias, L. L. (1990). *Psychological consulting to management: A clinician's perspective*. New York: Brunner/Mazel.

Von Bertalanffy, L. (1968). *General systems theory: Foundations, development, applications*. New York: Braziller.

Williams, J. C. (1978). *Human behavior in organizations*. Cincinnati, OH: South-Western.

PART TWO

# INDIVIDUAL LEVEL
# APPLICATIONS

# CHAPTER FIVE

# Individual Interventions in Consulting Psychology

Richard R. Kilburg
*Office of Human Services*
*The Johns Hopkins University*

Bryan Addams (name and identity are assumed) was the president of a medium-sized subsidiary of a large service corporation. He had been recruited to the position approximately seven years before from a competitor with whom he had held a similar position on an interim basis. A loser in the competition for the job in his prior organization, he had landed safely in his current position with a mandate to turn the business around. The parent organization was desperate to see improvement, since the subsidiary was ranked near the bottom of its industry segment in almost every category that could be measured. The CEO of the parent company told Bryan that the rest of the organization depended on how well this unit functioned and that he should do everything he could to change the performance of the business.

Bryan was happy to accept the challenge and moved his family to the home city of the subsidiary. I had coached him in his previous assignment and through the search process, and Bryan asked me to continue to work with him in this new and challenging role. After seven years of very hard and successful work, Bryan had successfully completed the turnaround. The services of the business ranked in the top tier of that segment of the industry, a new cast of energetic and talented leaders had been hired and trained, and the critical dependencies of the parent company were being managed with professionalism and competence. Bryan not only survived a transition in parent company CEOs, he also succeeded in becoming one of the key leaders in the entire organization under his new boss.

During one of our monthly coaching sessions, Bryan told me that he was actively considering stepping down from his position. He had recruited and trained a brilliant young man, Harry Sanchez (name and identity are assumed), who had risen very fast in the organization, and Bryan wanted me to start coaching him as a possible successor. At the age of sixty-two, Bryan told me he wanted to do some different and more family-oriented things with his life, and he seemed ready and willing to step aside and let Harry take over. He wanted to preserve his legacy in the business, but he also felt strongly that Harry was capable of moving the organization to even higher levels of performance.

I arranged to meet Harry and found him to be everything that Bryan had described and more. Bright, ambitious, interpersonally and organizationally savvy, he was ready and willing to take on the assignment as the subsidiary's president. He also shared with me that he saw this as a stepping stone to an eventual job as a CEO in either this or another company. We discussed his part of the transition strategy, and he reformulated it to contain four identifiable parts as a result of our dialogue. First, he would continue to perform his current company duties with careful attention to his contribution to the parent organization. Second, he would look for additional avenues to work in the parent company and in assignments that would draw the CEO's attention. Third, he would work with Bryan to take on additional leadership duties in the subsidiary. Finally, he had been approached by headhunters to apply for the presidencies of at least two other companies in the same industry. He decided that he would pursue these opportunities, and would do so in the open so that both Bryan and the CEO would know that he was being recruited.

Bryan and I continued our work together and paid careful attention to how he coached Harry and his negotiations with the CEO around his own transition. Bryan also started to examine several additional job possibilities that were clearly in line with his desires both to do some meaningful work and to be more available to his family. I continued to coach both of these men through this transition space in their lives and careers. At several points, we had joint conference calls to compare notes, discuss strategy, and troubleshoot problems that had arisen. I have rarely seen two executives work as closely and as successfully together.

Approximately four months into this process, Harry was offered a presidency in a similar organization located in a different section of the country. During a coaching session immediately following that offer, he and I discussed how he could and should approach both organizations. We also discussed the pros and cons of both positions and parent organizations. By the end of our discussion, Harry seemed pretty clear that he strongly preferred to stay in his current company, but would do so only if he were able to succeed Bryan. After considering several alternative ways of managing the process, he decided to approach his current CEO and tell him the truth. Namely, he wanted to move up and felt that he was ready to do so in his own company. If the CEO wanted to initiate a national search for a successor, Harry would understand the need to do so, but he would accept the position he had been offered in the other company. Harry was to orchestrate this discussion with Bryan, who would also talk to the CEO.

Bryan had his own discussions with the CEO, strongly encouraging him to do whatever it took to keep Harry in the company. As it turned out, the CEO agreed completely with Bryan's advice, and he moved very quickly to open formal negotiations with Harry that paralleled those that had been underway for several weeks with the other company. Harry knew that the other company had some additional steps it needed to take before it would finalize an offer, and felt that he could negotiate with his own CEO in good conscience before a final offer was made by the other organization. Recognizing the importance of time, and being a person of considerable integrity and energy, Harry's own CEO successfully concluded negotiations with both Harry and Bryan before the other company put a final offer on the table. Both men ended up with exactly what they wanted personally and professionally. Harry looked forward to the next logical step in what was looking as if it would eventually be a rapid rise to a CEO position in a major company. Bryan was able to capstone his career by solidifying the leadership and organizational gains that seven years of hard work on his part and on the parts of his entire organization had yielded. His boss had broadly welcomed him to stay in his current company in one of several creative and important positions. Bryan was also considering offers in a number of other companies that might result in a better lifestyle for himself and his family. The individual and collaborative coaching processes were successful in assisting both men move their individual agendas forward with clarity and honor. They were also able to be truly and mutually supportive to each other at each step along the way.

The week that the formal announcement was made of Harry's appointment as the president of the subsidiary, I managed to talk briefly with both men. I wanted to make sure they were doing well with the initial shock that sometimes comes with such changes.

"How does it feel?" I asked Harry.

"Actually, it feels pretty good. I told the other company I wasn't coming today and their president was very disappointed. But they still hadn't moved to resolve the issues that had been outstanding."

"So, you think you made the wisest choice?"

"Definitely."

"So, what's next on your agenda?"

"I need to coordinate with Bryan. I formally take over in three months, and I need to finish up several things I've been working on and simultaneously get up to speed on what's on his plate. I'm particularly worried about some recruitment issues and next year's budget."

"Politics, money, and people," I replied.

"What do you mean?" he asked.

"Do your politics right and you can get the money that you need to do the business, especially to hire the right people. Those are the three biggest jobs that you have as a leader."

We spent several minutes talking about the details of the deal he had worked out with the CEO for working capital, and his vision for the next three to five years for the company. He had done a good job in his negotiations, and I thought he had positioned himself well to move the organization forward.

"How did people respond to the announcement?" I then asked him.

"It's funny that you should ask about that. I think everyone responded very well. I've had a lot of people come up and offer me their congratulations, including a number of my peers in the organization. But I'll tell you something, it feels very weird."

"What do you mean?" I asked.

"Every day since the announcement I've felt people's eyes on my back. They are looking at me differently. It feels very strange because I'm the same person as before but they are all acting differently. They seem distant, maybe a little fearful. I can't put my finger on it."

"You are the same person, but you now occupy a very different role. You are now the person in the organization upon whom they all depend."

"Jesus, just that quickly, Bryan is out and I'm in," he said in frustration.

"Harry, we tend to idealize humans and think of ourselves as very special, very different from the other creatures on the planet. Humans are primates, troupe animals. For millions of years, we and all of our ancestors have lived in groups and all of those groups have had leaders. Primatologists have demonstrated that many of the behaviors we see and expect in leaders in modern organizations are the same as those performed in troupes of chimpanzees and gorillas. The leaders in those primate groups set direction, dispense favors, establish status hierarchies, defend the troupe from predators and enemies, lead hunts, and manage conflict."

"So, you're saying I've just become the alpha ape."

"You've just become the leader of your organization and it is comprised of hundreds of primates. They are all now looking to and at you because you hold the position, just as Bryan has for the last seven years. They have begun to adjust to the fact that you will direct them, decide on who is rewarded and punished, defend them, and manage their conflicts with each other. I'm glad to hear that you now feel their eyes on you."

"Why, for God's sake?"

"Because it means you empathize with them and can read nonverbal behavior clearly. These are two skills you will really need as a leader."

"What else will I need?" he asked.

"A lot," I answered.

We went on to discuss how he would spend the next three months and on what he would focus. I suggested that he pick up a copy of Ron Heifetz's book, *Leadership Without Easy Answers* (1994), which deals very well with the issue of leading in primate troupes. We arranged our next conference call and signed off.

Later that week, I talked to Bryan. We started the conversation with his reviewing how his own negotiations with the CEO had gone, the job opportunities that he saw, and what he wanted and needed to do with his family. He seemed excited about the changes on the horizon and wanted to discuss the various options that he was considering. As our conversation moved forward and we explored the situations and scenarios that he had in front of him, I noted that he had not mentioned the announcement. As we neared the end of the conversation, I raised the issue.

"Bryan, I understand from Harry that the formal announcement about the change was made in a letter and in a meeting last week," I said.

"That's right. People took it well."

"What was the impact on you?"

There was a moment of silence on the line as he collected his thoughts. I waited, knowing well that he was quite capable of assessing whether anything else was going on inside of him. Over the years of our work together, I had grown very confident about his capacity for self-awareness and insight.

"It's funny you should ask that question. I've worked so hard to get to this point and looked forward to it. But, I confess that when the announcement was made in the meeting, it felt weird. I was chilled by it, and I've noticed that some people started to act differently almost immediately."

"What have you noticed?"

"Little things mostly; how people look at me in the hall or cafeteria; some folks have stopped approaching me; I've even been told that the rumor mill says that the company is in trouble and I was asked to step down."

"What has been the effect on you?"

"Not much. I really want to make this move in my life, but it all feels a little strange, distant somehow."

"Any other feelings about what you've noticed?" I asked.

"The only other thing I'd say is that I've sometimes found myself a little more irritated than usual. I have a harder time staying with small things that might be important for the long haul but feel insignificant in the moment."

"Are you interested in a response?"

"You know that I always am."

"Well, one thing to keep in mind is my colleague, Harry Levinson's aphorism. 'All change involves loss, and all loss must be grieved.' Even though these changes are ones you have sought and worked for, they still involve you losing things—status, position."

"Money, power. Yes, you are right to remind me. I've kept those things in the background, but I am making sacrifices to be with my family more, and they will need to make sacrifices as well."

"Have you talked with them about that?"

"Oh yes. They do understand, and I think we will be quite okay, if not as well off financially."

"There's one other thing that might be going on as well," I suggested.

"Okay, let me have it."

"Well, you are concentrating on what you are going to do for work in these next few years."

"Yes, that's true."

"Well, the bigger issue might be what are you going to do for the rest of your life. You are moving into late-life transition. The life tables suggest that you have another fifteen to twenty years of time left to you. Have you and your wife talked about how you are going to spend that time?"

A second, longer pause ensued. This is most often a signal that I've touched a client in an important area and that real work has been engaged. I waited again for his reply.

"No. No we haven't. We've talked a lot about where we'll live, what we'll do, and what the children, she, and I need. But we really haven't talked about the rest of our lives or the limitations of time."

"Do you think it would be wise to do that?"

"Yes. And in fact, I've been thinking about taking some time away to just do some reflecting on what I want to do."

"I'd strongly encourage you to do that. I'd also suggest that as you think things through, try to get over to the other side of those fifteen or twenty years and ask yourself the question: when I look back on my life, what do I want to be most proud of, feel best about, feel I've accomplished? If you can figure that out and if there are things that you still want to do, you can use those thoughts to help you and your wife think through how you want to spend some of the time that the two of you have left."

Bryan and I wound up that conversation with a small discussion of how he could raise these issues with his wife. He was very grateful for the talk, and specifically said as he hung up that it had been very useful for him to start thinking about those issues.

# INTRODUCTION

I start this chapter on individual interventions in consulting psychology with this particular case example from my coaching practice because it illustrates so many of the important issues involved with this type of work. Consultation practice nearly always involves working with individuals. I believe that the knowledge and skills required to work with people one-on-one forms the foundation for all consulting work, and that without excellent skills in this area, practitioners will struggle in many aspects of their careers. This is not to say that I believe all consulting psychologists can and will emphasize intensive work with individuals. Indeed, many, if not most, practitioners do not and probably should not undertake the kinds of interventions described in the case example. However, since virtually all consulting engagements involve working with individuals to some degree, if only to form the initial working and contracting alliance with the executive or other person who is negotiating the agreement for services, and in all probability to collect data on what is happening in the organization, it behooves everyone to develop these skills and abilities. The ideas and material that follow in this chapter are provided from a practitioner point of view. Although individual interventions are a core component of the practice of consulting psychology, the research that supports the interventions in this area outside of the traditional domains of work-related assessments and career counseling (Prince and Heiser, 2000) is woefully lacking at present (Kilburg, 2000). As a result, scientific support for the various approaches and issues described leaves much to be desired.

Implied in this case example are a series of issues that this chapter will attempt to discuss in somewhat more detail. First, the challenges Bryan and Harry were experiencing in their lives can be thought of as normal developmental stages in the course of their managerial careers. Bryan, having achieved his capstone position, who had crossed into his sixties, and then made a decision to focus more on his family, illustrated some of the problems and issues faced by individuals when they move into the late-adult-life transition described by Levinson (1978). Similarly, Harry, in his late thirties, on an extremely fast and vertical career ascent, and still not quite at midlife, faced many of the challenges of taking on his first senior executive assignment. Each of these men handled the transition stresses very well, managed their personal relationships with great tact and sensitivity, and thought very carefully about what they needed as individuals, even as they concentrated on meeting the current and future leadership needs of the organization. Working with individuals such as them requires a fundamental understanding of life-span developmental psychology. Without such knowledge, a consultant will have only a partial understanding of what his or her client might be facing at any particular time.

Second, the example demonstrates the importance of multilevel diagnostic acumen. A consultant must be able to watch and listen to the structures, processes, and contents of individual, group, organizational, and community systems, and deconstruct them as they are experienced. Interventions designed and implemented without such sophistication have a much lower probability of succeeding in the long run. The discussions with Harry and Bryan ranged widely over a number of topics during the months of their transition and it was important to constantly think about and review with them the implications of the issues they faced for these various elements of the systems in which they lived.

Third, this situation shows a consultant making several types of interventions in this organizational system with these executives. I coached these two executives as individuals on their particular tasks, responsibilities, and reactions in this situation. I also coached the two of them together as a leadership team managing this transition. Such multimodal interventions are often the rule in consulting engagements, and consultants must have the preparation, experience, and competence to deliver them.

Fourth, both Harry and Bryan faced enormous stresses and emotional demands as they conceptualized and executed this very complex set of strategies. Each of them needed to manage a great deal of anxiety and frustration. And both of them had to come to grips with their inner wishes and dynamics that involved power, control, dependency, autonomy, and competition among other issues. They were savvy, demanding, and mature people who needed and required emotional and professional maturity in their consultant. Clients have real problems and needs, and consultants must be prepared to meet them and simultaneously manage their own needs and problems with courage and prudence.

Fifth, at various times during this engagement, a consultation that in Bryan's case has lasted for over a decade, I had to make significant decisions about when and how to intervene. I am not talking about the normal decisions one makes with a client about what to say during a coaching session. What I am saying is that the decision to begin to coach Harry simultaneously with Bryan and then to coach the two of them together was not taken lightly. I considered referring Harry to another coach and decided against it after I talked at length with both men. Consulting engagements routinely require this type of decision-making, and the outcomes of the assignments depend largely on how successful the practitioner is in making good choices regarding the interventions that are selected.

Sixth, in this assignment, I had to renegotiate the agreement that I had been using with Bryan for some years. We had to discuss confidentiality, methods, goals, and financing. We did this successfully, and I then had to have the same discussion with Harry as we started to work together. The contracting phase of consulting is critical in every assignment, and at times, must be reworked as reality forces new considerations on the people involved.

Seventh, in every consulting assignment in a complex system, practitioners constantly must be mindful of who the client is. In the case example above, it is clear that both Harry and Bryan are specified as clients. However, neither of them was paying for the services out of their pockets. In fact, their company wrote the check. In addition, because the company was a subsidiary of a larger enterprise, the issue of whether and what kinds of allegiances and responsibilities I, as a consultant, might have to these other systems was something I had to keep in mind as the engagement moved forward. These issues get quite complex in various types of individual consulting assignments.

Eighth, the situation in this organization with regard to leadership succession created conflict at many levels. Harry experienced struggles in choosing between the jobs he had been offered, negotiating the details of his appointment, adjustments at home with his family, and changes in the work that he was doing and his relationships with everyone in the company. Similarly, Bryan experienced conflict between his desire to do something different and more aligned with his investments in his family, his ambivalence over leaving a job to which he had become very attached, and over the type of work he would negotiate for himself in the future. Inner conflicts of loyalty, control, competition, and trust were also in evidence. Consulting work nearly always involves addressing conflict inside individual clients, between them and others, and with the systems in which they are employed. Practitioners must have extremely sharp diagnostic and intervention skills in this area, and corresponding degrees of emotional maturity and self-awareness to be able to manage the stresses and strains that normally arise when the complex conflict situations are encountered.

Ninth, any thoughtful review of the previous major points reveals the extreme level of complexity the world of consulting to and with individuals and in organizations routinely produces. Regardless of whether a practitioner works as part of a larger organization or in solo practice, there are often times when these kinds of issues can threaten an individual's knowledge base, skill level, or emotional stability. At such moments, it can be very useful to have a colleague available to help sort through the various issues and difficulties that are being encountered in an effort to insure the consultant's own professional and emotional well-being, as well as to clarify the strategies and methods that should be employed in the engagement to insure success. Such shadow arrangements are quite frequent in the field, yet they are not often discussed in the literature or in training programs. In large organizations in which consultants often practice in teams, such arrangements can and often are formally structured, but they are also informally available. Individuals in solo practice must often make specific arrangements for this type of support in order to insure that they stay on course in their assignments and careers.

Finally, when working with individuals in consulting engagements, practitioners might reach a point at which it is necessary to refer their clients to other professionals for different kinds of services. It is often surprising to me how often executives might need other types of services, and if left to their own devices, they simply would not obtain them. The lives of leaders are very stressful physically, socially, and emotionally for them and their families. Consultants must be prepared and able to intervene when problems of this type are encountered by their clients by confronting the issues as they arise and making appropriate referrals for medical or psychological assistance (Hemfelt, Minirth, & Meier, 1991; O'Neill, 1993).

The remainder of this chapter will review the general types of interventions and skill areas consultants need to master in order to work effectively with individual clients, provide further insight and guidance on the core issues in this type of work, and make recommendations for development for those individuals who are drawn to do this type of work.

# INDIVIDUAL INTERVENTIONS IN CONSULTING PSYCHOLOGY

During the past several years, the Education and Training Committee of Division 13, the Consulting Psychology Division of the American Psychological Association, established a set of guidelines for education and training at the doctoral and post-doctoral level in consulting psychology (American Psychological Association 2000). These guidelines are organized around several core assumptions. First, that the practice of consulting psychology is guided by science in designing, executing, and evaluating the effectiveness of interventions. The guidelines further assume that a practitioner has broad skills and competencies in working with individuals, groups, and organizations as a consultant. Finally, they assume that the competencies with each level of intervention can and do work together as an integrated system that practitioners use in practicing ethically with clients.

There is no need to repeat the guidelines in detail in this chapter. However, they do identify a core set of competencies for consulting work with individuals in organizations that are very important to note. First, in keeping with the emphasis on a consulting practice based on science, the guidelines stress the importance of *assessment* in this work. In the case of individual-level interventions, assessment can focus on a wide variety of areas including: career and vocational interest and direction; job analysis for the purposes of enrichment, redesign, creation, or abolishment; job selection; and job performance and the various components of behavior that contribute to it. Second, interventions are conducted with individuals for *job- and career-related troubles* that they may be encountering. Such problems range from individuals finding themselves in the wrong positions for their interests and talents, to conflicts with bosses, subordinates, and peers, to insufficient self-awareness, knowledge, and skill to do a job or perform a role. Interventions can be designed to assist both the individuals and the systems in which they find themselves cope with and resolve such difficulties. Finally, *coaching services* can be provided to individuals in organizations to assist with a huge variety of challenges (Kilburg, 1996, 2000). Coaching interventions have slowly and surely evolved over time to provide consultants with a set of concepts and tools to help people perform more effectively in their roles at work and in their lives in general (Hudson, 1999). Consultants working with individuals in organizational settings might not be fully competent to perform all of these types of services. However, they should be prepared to recognize when such interventions are necessary and to reach out to other competent colleagues to provide what is needed. Extraordinary amounts of very useful material are readily available to help practitioners develop the knowledge and skills identified in these three areas. Kilburg (2000), Lowman (1993), and Prince and Heiser (2000) are excellent resources to either begin or continue to explore the development of these individual competencies.

# Human Development and Diagnostic Acumen

It is safe to say that effective consulting depends on two major areas of knowledge and skill. First, a practitioner must be able to determine what is happening in, around, and to a human system. Second, the consulting psychologist must be able to design and execute interventions that have a creative, constructive, and demonstrable impact on that human system. After practicing as a consultant, clinician, and manager for three decades, I have come to believe that a thorough knowledge of life-span human development is absolutely critical for anyone wishing to become an interventionist with people and their organizations. Psychology has come a very long way during the past century in identifying the various stages, issues, and problems that can occur in the development of individuals, groups, and organizations (Freud, 1933; Erikson, 1963; Baltes, Standinger, & Lindenberger, 1999; Cartwright and Zander, 1968; Levinson, 1981; Lawler, Nadler, & Cammann, 1980; Levinson, 2002). It is incumbent on practitioners to be thoroughly educated about such issues and their interactions, simply because whenever a consultant is introduced to a new client or client system, assumptions about the developmental levels of the people worked with can never be made.

For example, when a consultant is asked in to coach a high-level executive who may be in danger of career or job derailment in that organization, an assignment that is fairly frequent in the lives of many practitioners, before taking any action, he or she will both want and need to get an accurate picture of how this person functions on the job and in his or her life. This may involve doing paper-and-pencil assessments, conducting interviews with subordinates, peers, superiors, and even family members (Keil, Rimmer, Williams, & Doyle, 1996; Peterson, 1996). It also requires getting a true sense of what is happening in the organization as a whole, and whether the strategies, structures, and processes that are being employed are effective in furthering the goals of the enterprise. All of this then can be used to determine the general level of human development of the individual client, the people and groups with whom he/she engages regularly, and the organization as a whole. When such a determination is made, then a consultant can decide what is the best course of action. In the absence of such a complex dataset, interventions can sometimes be blind, off target, or in the worst case, extremely destructive for the individual and the organization. Keil et al. (1996) provide a good example of how they put such a process to work for their clients.

Assessments of individual, group, and organizational developmental levels provide the foundation for effective design and execution of interventions. The array of contributing factors to the derailment or failure of an individual leader to progress can be enormous (Hogan, Curphy, & Hogan, 1994). The individual can suffer from an undiagnosed physical or mental illness that can impair performance. Similarly, a person can have insufficient knowledge and skills to perform the job to which he or she is assigned. At times, lack of cognitive capacity or education can be the problem that must be addressed. However, very able individuals with sufficient developmental capacity have had their jobs and careers destroyed by dysfunctional group processes, an underdeveloped group of nonsupportive executives, a highly charged and politicized board of directors, or economic or market forces that are beyond the control of an individual or a given company. Interventions in such situations require excellent diagnostic acumen on the part of consultants to prevent such events occurring in the first place or to *re-rail* executives who have failed in assignments or in specific organizations. It is always vital for professionals to retain their objectivity and their curiosity as they move into a consulting engagement. Being able to see, sense, and explore the complex interiors and exteriors of human systems is a key component in being able to intervene successfully with individuals. Knowing just what to do with them or on their behalf requires the ability to determine the possible actions that could be taken, and then to choose and use the right one in the right way. Multilevel diagnostic acumen within a human development conceptual framework is indispensable in consulting practice.

## Multimodal Interventions

Clearly, organizations are quite complex systems. The larger the organization, the more complexity it usually develops (Stacey, 1992, 1996). Consulting assignments with individuals inside of organizations take on unusual characteristics because of the causal connectivity between people, processes, structures, and the actual contents of the work being performed. Making sure that an accurate, developmental assessment is made just begins the work of changing a human system. Once a practitioner knows what needs to be done, the plan must be put into action. When individuals are involved, such plans often require an array of activities to create the desired impact on the person and the organizational situation.

The example that started this chapter illustrated this issue quite nicely. Bryan, a long-term individual coaching client, reached a point in his life and career that led him to first consider and then execute significant changes in his organization and role. That consideration and those changes forced me as the consultant to reconsider my role and activity plan. When he and I initially spoke about meeting with Harry and the possibility of coaching him, I expressed some skepticism about whether I could do that and work with him at the same time. Bryan encouraged me to take just one meeting to help him determine whether his judgment that Harry could do the job was correct. Harry was eager to have the meeting when I talked to him, and I agreed to do that. After an extensive three-hour luncheon during which we covered his views of his career, current leadership strengths, and what he saw were the challenges in the organization, I ended up concurring with Bryan's judgement. Harry and I created an excellent professional connection during that initial meeting. I found him to be very bright, engaged, ambitious, and willing to ask himself hard questions. He responded very well to the observations and issues that I raised during the meeting, saying at the end how stimulated he was by our discussion. As a result, he requested my assistance with his side of the adjustments and changes to come. After discussing some of the complexities of such an arrangement with him, including the issues of confidentiality and conflicts of interest, and receiving a mature and reasoned response to the questions that I raised, I told him that I would be willing to consider it, if Bryan agreed. Bryan did so, enthusiastically. I started to talk with Harry via a monthly telephone conference. As part of the agreement, both men understood that I would push them to get any conflict on the table for the three of us to discuss that arose for them concerning each other or the situation. They agreed to meet often together and keep each other informed of their individual actions and reactions to the situation. They also agreed to a series of joint coaching sessions with me along with individual meetings. The focus of these joint meetings was to be on the transition process, what each of them would do in the company during that time, and the issues that would arise for them as they proceeded with their plans. Because of their long and successful working relationship and their personal and professional maturity, I believed that modifying the consulting agreement in this way could be done without jeopardizing my long-standing work with Bryan.

In this fashion, an individual intervention turned into a second individual intervention and a coaching assignment with an emergent leadership dyad. As the example depicts, this combined intervention significantly aided these two executives in keeping their relationship working effectively and in a mutually supportive fashion through months of complex political, interpersonal, and organizational maneuvers. Both were able to discuss their individual concerns with me and then meet together to identify and solve their mutual problems. Because they really did agree on the goals they had chosen to pursue and on the strategies and roles they would implement to pursue them, misunderstanding and conflict were kept to a minimum. Together, they influenced the senior leaders of the parent company in many major ways, and ended up with agreements that changed their individual roles and insured the succession process they had created. They actually were also able to secure additional resources for their company. This had the long-term effect of improving the adaptive capacity and success of both the subsidiary and the parent company. This illustrates the kind of flexibility that consultants must often display when working inside complex organizations.

As described above, individuals working in complex human systems are embedded in human development ecology. The groups to which the individual belongs strongly influence his or her performance and growth, and vice versa. The individual's relationships with other significant people in the enterprise provide the environmental context in which all interactions and work take place. The long-standing lessons of ecological psychology (Barker, 1968) should inform the intervention decisions that consultants make during their assignments. At times, improving the working capacity and developmental potential of an individual client requires trying to reach many other elements in an organization. The policies, procedures, training opportunities, mentoring capacity, group dynamics, technology interfaces, market demands, and human problems of the people who surround and influence an individual must be taken into account, and when necessary, included in the change strategies designed and implemented by a consultant.

## Human Emotion and Conflict Dynamics in Organizational Settings

Over the years, a number of scholars and consultants have written extensively about the presence and action of psychodynamic issues and processes operating inside organizations (Czander, 1993; Kets deVries, 1984; Levinson, 1981; Schwartz, 1990; Kernberg, 1978, 1979, 1998; Stacey, 1992, 1996; Kilburg, 2000). The literature on this topic is extensive and growing, and any practitioner who works in these settings would be well advised to become familiar with the material and how the dynamic processes manifest themselves inside of, and between, individuals and groups. Working with and within these dynamics presents an ever-present set of challenges and threats to a consulting engagement because they most often manifest themselves in unconscious ways.

Kilburg (2000) extensively discussed these issues and how coaches and consultants can work constructively with psychodynamic challenges when they arise. The key is to understand just how they manifest themselves and what forms they can take in work settings. Figure 5.1 presents a model that can be used both to conceptualize what might be happening in a consulting engagement, and to determine where to intervene. It illustrates that the external and internal worlds of an individual produce the developmental challenges described above. These challenges and demands are processed within the individual by the various psychological structures that arise as a function of normal and traumatic development. The figure depicts these as the rational self, the instinctive self, the conscience, and the ideal self. They are mediated by the complex of current relationships and the past matrix of important internalized others that each person carries around, most often in the form of memories and learned predispositions to perceive events and behavior and respond to them in terms of what happened between themselves and people who are historically important in their lives (Bach, 1994). In consulting with individuals in organizationl contexts, these relationships extend to subordinates, peers, and superiors, and to current and historical people in the person's life outside the enterprise such as spouses, significant others, children, parents,

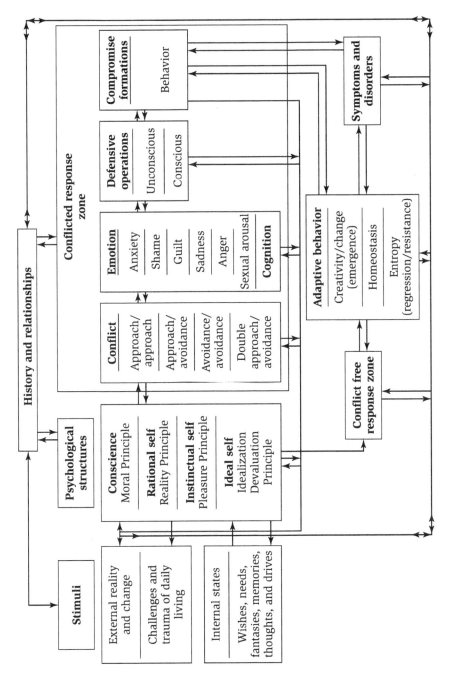

**Figure 5.1 Structure and Process of Psychodynamic Conflict and Adaptation.**

historical mentors, and other people who might have had a major influence on a client.

The most important thing to understand about psychodynamic issues is the idea that humans experience psychological conflict in nearly every area and at every time of their lives. Wurmser (2000) identified six major issues that produce significant conflict in and for humans. First, people struggle with emotions and how to manage them. Key to understanding this area is the fact that people are biologically enhanced to feel and to do so strongly. Sadness, shame, anger, fear, powerlessness, and sexual emotions all operate with astounding influence in every person, and they manifest constantly in individuals who seek the assistance of consultants (Tomkins, 1962–1963). Second, individuals become or are conflicted when their wishes for self-expression and curiosity clash with their fears of others intruding on them, trying to control them, or being empathetically misaligned with them by not understanding who they are or what they need. Such fears can lead to the blocking of the ability to express oneself, an unwillingness to work with others, or difficulties in developing strong and effective relationships. Third, these first two areas can lead to sustained difficulties with maintaining a whole and separate sense of self. For many clients, independence, the ability to work with groups of people, and the capacity to delegate tasks to others with trust and good judgment can be severely compromised by conflicts over the normal boundaries between themselves and the other people in the organization. Fourth, individuals become conflicted over the need to be in control in their own lives and their related fears of being controlled by others. Since nearly every organization is structured around hierarchical layers of increasing power and control (Bedeian & Zammuto, 1991), this issue is constantly present in every consulting engagement with individuals, groups, and organizations. Fifth, many situations in organizations give birth to competitive strivings and triangular relationships. Who will be selected for a promotion, how performance is to be evaluated, who will support a person in their drives to innovate and excel—all become challenges on a daily basis in many enterprises. Understanding such competitive dynamics and how they operate in individuals, groups, and larger systems is vital for practitioners working in consulting assignments. Sixth and finally, people often experience what Wurmser (2000) described as conflicts of loyalty. They are frequently committed to ideals and values that they hold most intensely, and to relationships of incredible complexity. Some of these investments are beneath the surface and remain hidden to an individual. Others are clearly manifested in how they live, think, and feel on a daily basis. When individuals are asked or pressured to take sides where their loyalties divide, the most serious types of conflict can emerge in their personal or organizational lives. Such conflicts can manifest themselves in open fights about the future direction of a business, the right actions to take regarding compensation for leaders, how to treat employees in a merger or acquisition situation, or what to tell a boss when one disagrees with the direction he or she is taking. Here again, consultants are often called in to help individuals think through and cope with such struggles.

Conflict usually produces both thoughts and feelings for anyone who experiences it (Gray, 1994). As described above, the emotions chiefly experienced by people as negative, such as shame, sadness, anxiety, anger, guilt, powerlessness, and hopelessness, are often present in conflict. Even the anticipation of being in a conflict can elicit very strong emotional states. Similarly, thought processes are activated in conflict situations in an effort to understand what is happening and organize responses to any threat. Kegan (1982, 1994), Stacey (1992, 1996), Jaques and Clement (1991), and others have provided excellent descriptions of human thinking as it occurs in organizational settings, and the influence that conflict and threat can have on this most important function. Consultants must realize as they work in and with conflict that their clients' thoughts and feelings might be compromised and contaminated often at an unconscious level, and at times on a conscious level (Kilburg, 2000). Similarly, they must understand that these situations can and often do arouse their own thoughts and feelings, and that these personal responses can significantly and sometimes adversely influence their efforts to assist clients with what they are experiencing.

Figure 5.1 illustrates that defensive operations come into play when humans cope with conflict. Kilburg (2000) reviewed the major defenses and how consultants can work with them when they are experienced in clients. Defenses range from the most primitive, in which threatening people, events, feelings, and thoughts are denied (they literally cease to exist for the person), split (they become part of a bad world that must be responded to often in harsh, extreme, and ineffective ways), or projected (they are experienced as emanating from other people who are seen as hostile and threatening). When these types of defenses are in operation, it is most difficult to achieve good results in a consulting assignment. As Kilburg suggested, consultants must work diligently to insure that they themselves and their clients engage higher-order defenses such as problem solving, humor, and altruism in order to direct their efforts to cope with various situations in positive directions.

When all of these forces and processes work together and often unconsciously in individuals, groups, and organizations, usually a compromise is created to enable the person, group, or organization to manage the conflict and the conditions that produced it. Compromise solutions are easy to recognize when conflicts are overt. People most often try to negotiate a mutually satisfying answer to a problem that they have in common. However, when the conflicts are unconscious and covert, the compromises can be harder to detect and manage. A manager who consistently micromanages the activities of subordinates might well be manifesting such compromise behavior. The model in

Figure 5.1 can provide consultants guidance about what might be happening in these types of situations.

Finally, the model demonstrates that these compromises can lead to creative, homeostatic, or regressive solutions to conflict. Most often, consultants are trying to help clients reach for creative solutions to conflict and challenge. However, in instances in which their clients might be experiencing a more primitive and less functional response to a situation, consultants might merely try to restore a degree of equilibrium to make sure no further injury takes place. In the event that regressive patterns of responses become entrenched, individuals, groups, and organizations can indeed become symptomatic and demonstrate various kinds of dysfunction that consultants may need to confront. These represent the most difficult times and challenges for consultants in working with clients and their organizations. The model also illustrates that humans also experience what has been called a conflict-free zone of functioning. In this zone, people, groups, and organizations often perform at their best because their knowledge, skills, and abilities can be truly focused on the tasks and challenges that they face, and not be spread out in efforts to cope with the sometimes extraordinary complexity that conflict produces. If consultants are not prepared to work in and with this type of dynamic behavior, they will over time be less effective in their efforts to help individual clients and the organizations in which they work. However, they can make significant contributions in many other types of interventions.

Addressing these types of conflict can be some of the most difficult challenges consulting psychologists face. Understanding when and how to engage conflict takes experience and expertise. The major decision rule that I use to guide me is that as long as the client and his or her organization seem to be making progress on what they are trying to accomplish, it is usually unnecessary to examine explicitly whether anything might be going on beneath the surface. In such situations, I usually monitor for signs of latent conflict, but do nothing explicit with anything I note. In the event that I note resistance to change, problems with execution or follow-through, or the appearance of previously unseen emotional responses, I might choose to raise questions about the possibility that conflict might be present. If one or more straightforward discussions about the conflicts do not move the situation forward, I often begin to think that a referral for psychotherapy or some other form of supportive services might be in order. I try to remain quite clear with clients that coaching is not intended to resolve traumas and problems that might be associated with other areas of their lives. When such issues arise, it is usually time to refer them for help they can receive from other professionals.

## Intervention Decisions

Every engagement with an individual client presents a consultant with major challenges about what type of intervention to use, at what time, and in what way, on any issue or problem that is being addressed in the assignment. The largest initial decisions focus on how to conduct an initial contact, explore the client's situation, and negotiate an agreement with a client. Negotiations for the services to be provided in themselves present an interesting set of choices, such as: what to charge; how much time will be involved; and the services to be rendered. Once the engagement is underway, a host of other micro-decisions must be made through the course of an intervention.

Even the smallest issues can have relevance when working in these settings. The time a meeting takes place, the location of where the consultant and client will convene together, who begins a session, and what, if any diagnostic instruments will be used and how—these are all examples of challenges. One can quickly see the subtlety and importance of the capacity of the professional to make mature and reasoned decisions. The type and extent of information available to the consultant is directly influenced by the consistency and quality of these decisions. This in turn profoundly affects the overall quality and effectiveness of consulting work.

As the case example at the beginning of this chapter illustrated, inside each session with a client, consultants face an extraordinary challenge regarding the decisions they make. In my experience, executive and managerial clients are often quite good at decision-making, and bring excellent skills and true experience that might well exceed that of the consultant in many areas. In the best of circumstances, the consultant and client together form a team that is united in its purpose to improve the performance and solve the problems that they identify. Even in this situation, a practitioner must continuously monitor him or herself as well as the client to determine when to listen, ask questions, provide information or advice, challenge, conduct a role play, reframe a situation, empathize, confront, interpret, support, or simply explore what is going on. An abundance of methods and techniques are available to assist in any intervention a consultant might wish to undertake (French & Bell, 1975; Hargrove, 1995).

The example also illustrated that there are times when a consultant must decide to significantly alter an agreement and to take an intervention in a different direction. Moving from an individual intervention to one involving a group or a whole system, or vice versa, creates significant conceptual, operational, and, at times, emotional challenges. The success or failure of a project, the reputation of the consultant, and the economic well-being of the practitioner's family can and do depend on how and how well such decisions are made. At such times, professionals may want to solicit advice from knowledgeable colleagues to assist them in thinking through the consequences of the various choices that they confront.

## Negotiating Agreements

The transition initiated by Bryan in the case example produced a series of major changes in the consulting agreement that I had with him and his company for over a decade. I have found the process of negotiating agreements most often quite easy, but occasionally maddeningly frustrating and complex. The most important issues in completing a successful contracting process are understanding your own needs, strengths, and weaknesses, understanding the needs and capacities of the client, developing a trusting relationship, knowing and using the appropriate negotiation strategies and skills, and most importantly, knowing who the client will be.

I believe that consultants who do not truly know themselves, what they are capable of delivering professionally, where and how they tend to get into interpersonal, psychological, and business trouble, the types of work they most enjoy, what they do poorly, how they feel about money, their time, their personal and professional goals, and the philosophy and strategies by which they conduct their business, are very likely to have trouble in developing functional agreements with their potential or existing clients. A successful agreement begins with the parties recognizing that they both have needs and they both bring value to the bargaining table. The degree to which they understand themselves often determines how well they articulate their positions to each other and then proceed to work through the process. If a consultant does not really know what he or she wants or needs financially from a piece of work, how that work can be conducted successfully, and what business strategy is being followed, the agreement with a client, if reached at all, might well be based on inappropriate or inaccurate assumptions. I have seen this occur most often when consultants, greedy or needy for a contract, over-promise on their capacity to deliver a service and then end up doing a poor job, injuring their reputations, and at times, being fired by their clients. I have also seen able consultants who push organizations for the absolute top dollar on their hourly, daily, or package rates without careful thought as to the long-term consequences for additional work with that enterprise. They sometimes get the agreement and then do not get invited back. So, before entering into a negotiation process, practitioners need to do some homework for and on themselves.

If consultants know and are comfortable with themselves, they can proceed with the process of getting to their client(s) and the needs that he, she, or they might have. Getting the appropriate information can take a good bit of time and effort. It represents an investment in the client organization, in the consultation, and in the professional's business. It is most often time that is largely uncompensated in any direct sense, unless the practitioner builds into his or her fees and charges for a component that captures these investments. Regardless of the amount of time it takes during this process, it is crucial to spend what is necessary to develop a decent understanding of the client's business, the culture, current leadership, the organization's capacities, experience with consultants, and real needs for assistance. This exploration can occur in a reasonably rapid period of time, or in larger assignments, might take multiple quasi-diagnostic meetings (Levinson, 2002).

Once the information is collected, consultants who know themselves and what they are capable of doing well are positioned to discuss their assessment impressions and make suggestions about what services might be appropriate. Practitioners must be prepared to turn down assignments that are inappropriate for them, appear to violate their ethics, or cannot meet their needs. This can often be very difficult when a professional is under some financial pressure. If a consultant is truly unsure of what to do with a client, it is most appropriate to negotiate an initial agreement structured around a more detailed organizational assessment (Levinson, 2002). Such contracts allow a practitioner the luxury of simultaneously gathering much more data to conduct a more elaborate negotiation and to build a greater degree of rapport with the members of the organization. As described above, in the end, the quality of the agreement, indeed of the work itself, depends on the diagnostic acumen of the consultant.

Consulting work is built almost entirely on human relationships. Usually, a purchasing executive or his or her agent might advertise a request for proposals, make a set of formal or informal calls to various individuals or firms to determine capacities and interest, or pursue an individual practitioner based on previous experiences or recommendations from others. Such advertisements need not be formal postings in newspapers or other such outlets. They often come in the form of calls from a representative of the company, in which he or she suggests that you have been identified by the company as someone who might be helpful with a project or problem that the organization is having. From the moment of that initial call to the completion of a body of professional work, practitioners are building, managing, and sometimes repairing relationships with the individuals and groups with whom they will be working. Consultants must be capable of engaging accurate empathy, reasonable amounts of positive regard, good communication, conflict management, problem solving, and diversity management skills from the inception of the relationship (Kilburg, 2000). It really helps to truly like people and enjoy the opportunity to get to know and to work closely with them. Without these abilities and skills, a negotiation process often runs into problems. Many contracts are lost because of the practitioner's inability to form a good relationship with a potential client. It is vital that consultants have enough self-awareness so that they can monitor how they are feeling and reacting to the client, and be prepared to engage the relationship issues with assertiveness, sensitivity, and tact both during the negotiation phase and once service delivery is underway.

The actual negotiation strategies and skills focus on how to establish goals, to specify the work that will be done, the accountability structure that will guide the process, the expectations for and of the client(s), confidentiality management, time expectations, fee and billing arrangements, and depending on the size of the contract, sometimes a host of other details, including who else might be involved. Large companies are now, at times, explicitly or implicitly establishing legal liabilities for consultant's recommendations, and these implications must be considered by practitioners. The easiest processes usually involve person-to-person discussions with the contracting or purchasing manager who arranges payment from a budget under his or her control. It is comparatively simple to clarify needs, expectations, and arrangements under these circumstances, and to have a degree of confidence in the quality of the working relationship in case anything should come up that needs clarification (Block, 1981).

The most difficult negotiations are multiparty in form. In large organizations, purchasing policies, conflict of interest procedures, legal offices, and financial people can often have roles to play in developing an agreement. It takes time, patience, savvy, and determination to work through these kinds of complex organizations. It can sometimes take contacts between half a dozen or more people to arrange for a coaching agreement with an individual client in large organizations. An even more difficult situation arises when the executive with financial control in a project insists on conducting a negotiation through intermediaries in the organization. Again, in some very large organizations, there might well be multiple layers of bureaucracy engaged in the process, and practitioners must be alert and savvy about how to conduct themselves in these situations. Bringing home signed agreements is the lifeblood of a consulting practice. Without the ability to initiate and close business deals, practitioners will not be consultants for long.

Developing a trusting relationship with another person, in this case a potential client, is simultaneously maddeningly complex and quite simple (Block, 1981). I believe that the foundation for trust in human affairs consists of being able to identify and communicate what you will do, and then actually doing it. If these fundamentals are observed in a negotiation process, then you as a consultant will have the opportunity to hear the client's story, perhaps gather some additional information, and successfully complete the contracting phase of the process. During this process, you will also have the opportunity to demonstrate your warmth, positive regard, empathy, and most importantly, your professional skills. When all of these elements are present, clients feel understood, supported, challenged, and that they will be treated with dignity and respect during the engagement. They will know that what a practitioner says will happen. They will then tend to be willing to work together with the consultant in executing the project and managing the problems that inevitably arise, many of which can be frightening, difficult, and even dangerous to the contracting executive. Without the necessary level of trust, agreements can quickly dissolve into a series of protracted communications problems and conflicts. When these kinds of situations arise, any consultant would be wise to ask him or herself whether there is sufficient trust in the relationship. If the answer is no, then ameliorative steps should be undertaken before any additional consulting work is attempted.

## Who Is the Client?

This latter issue necessarily raises one of the most significant ongoing issues in consulting work; namely, who is the client? When doing an individual assessment and coaching intervention with a person who is paying for the services out of his or her own pocket, this question and all of its associated issues can be answered very simply: it is the person who pays the consultant. However, once a consultant enters an organization, the multiple boundary issues and interpersonal, financial, and political complexities begin to escalate quickly. Many consultants are very savvy in managing this issue, particularly as it pertains to the management of confidentiality. They negotiate clear expectations of reporting requirements for the contents of work with individuals in their sessions. This is absolutely necessary when working in complex organizations. However, it often is insufficient.

When practitioners are working with individuals employed by an organization, there are always multiple clients. The specific individual client in the enterprise rarely pays for the services rendered by the professional out of his or her personal funds. This automatically establishes a level of accountability between the consultant and the organization itself. This rarely becomes an overt issue when working with individuals, but it can, in certain circumstances, become critical. For example, an individual can disclose to a consultant that there might be illegal, unethical, or improper conduct happening within the organization that might have significant consequences for the enterprise beyond the impact on the individual client. If consultants have not thought about this contingency, they might be in a severely compromised position when they are forced to decide to keep something quiet for which they themselves could be held legally liable, or to disclose it to someone besides the individual client and risk violating a negotiated understanding. Clients and their superiors can become quite agitated during such episodes, and readily blame the consultant or others for problems that come to the surface in this way. I have generally found it wise to negotiate these expectations and understandings in advance so that individual clients and those others that might be involved in an engagement have some degree of clarity about what to expect if these unusual but critical circumstances arise.

This issue becomes even more complex for consultants who work internally as employees of an organization. In these cases, the supervisory structures and processes can require a practitioner to disclose the progress of a project with an individual to someone to whom he or she reports. Organizational accountabilities can stretch up two or more chains of command and reach into the very highest levels of the organization. At times, professionals can end up working with the superiors of their immediate superiors, and discover information and problems with direct relevance to their own careers. In these circumstances, it is always useful to have clearly articulated policies governing the operation of the consultation service, explicit agreements for the services to be rendered, and strong working relationships with senior management and the general counsel's office. Practitioners must be willing and able to proceed in a sophisticated, sober, and politically sensitive fashion in these situations in order to survive.

## SUPERVISION AND SHADOW CONSULTATIONS

Schroder (1974) and Kilburg (in press) have provided consultants with significant insight into the need for practitioners to create supervisory and shadow consultation arrangements for themselves. The individual consulting assignments described and discussed in this chapter remind us that every individual we work with as consultants is embedded in complex social systems that create multiple demands and, at times, overwhelming stress for them. As we have also seen, these consultations can produce incredible demands on the practitioner as well. Every consultant has limitations of knowledge, skill, emotional resilience, and experience. Each has his or her own psychodynamic history that creates the seedbed for ongoing challenges in life and in professional practice. Finally, we all have different appetites and capacities to endure the stresses and strains of this kind of work. It is perfectly normal and natural for any practitioner to encounter a technical problem in an assignment, and to want and need to turn to someone for assistance and support. It is equally normal for a professional to find him or herself in some kind of intense emotional or interpersonal struggle as a result of the work he or she is doing. I believe that practitioners are wise to anticipate these kinds of stresses and strains, and to make arrangements for professional support and assistance in advance of any specific occurrence.

There are several ways of accomplishing this (Kilburg, in press). First, in consulting firms and internal consulting units, there usually are senior practitioners who can serve as sounding boards and supporters for their subordinates and peers. It is quite customary for these relationships and processes to unfold in natural, nonexplicit ways in the normal conduct of business in these types of settings. In many consulting firms, the supervision and management structures are quite explicit and provide the necessary support. Second, consultants can contract explicitly for supervision or shadowing support with colleagues they respect. Kilburg elaborates these types of arrangements and many of the issues involved. External supervisors and shadow consultants can stimulate the practitioner's continued professional development, help to troubleshoot complex problems and situations, provide emotional support in difficult times and situations, and connect the individual to additional resources that might be helpful in an assignment or for a career. Finally, a significant number of practitioners, particularly those in private practice, choose to establish peer supervision groups to accomplish these objectives. Such groups can provide sustained support for substantial periods of time.

At times, consulting can be a lonely, stressful, and disturbing occupation. As described above, practitioners are almost always in complex, conflict-ridden situations with people in trouble or who are struggling with very demanding problems. As members of the helping professions, they are often ill prepared and have poor resources to handle their own problems. Practitioners can become impaired as a result of their work (Kilburg, Nathan, & Thoreson, 1986). Travel requirements, sleep deprivation, lack of exercise and normal diets, the demands of clients and employing organizations, and the expectations of families can take their toll on individuals over time. Consultants are wise to anticipate these stresses and strains, and to make appropriate arrangements to care for themselves so as to prevent major physical, psychological, and other personal problems.

## REFERRING CLIENTS FOR OTHER SERVICES

One of the realities of life consists of the fact that every human being has limits. Time, energy, knowledge, skill, ability, experience, motivation, and personal and professional networks can vary for all of us. Clients also have their limits, and one of the ways in which they manage their limits is to hire consultants to help them stretch beyond the barriers that they encounter. Depending on the strength, sophistication, and expertise of the practitioner hired, clients will get some or all of their needs met. In situations in which the negotiations and execution of the consulting project have gone well, the issue of making additional referrals might never come up. However, there will be instances that come up periodically that will require a consultant to consider helping a client connect with someone else who can better assist with a problem (Kilburg, 2000).

Making such a referral requires the consultant to rely on the complex diagnostic skills already discussed above. If the assessment indicates that something else is needed, then problem solving, communication, and conflict management skills will be called into play. Simply because a consultant tells a client that something else might be needed never guarantees that action will be taken. The client must agree with the assessment and the recommendation for action, and be willing and able to take the necessary steps to solve the problem identified. Clients may resist the recommendation, disagree with what the consultant suggests, or be unwilling or unable to comply because of a host of reality-based reasons. Often they complain about the lack of time or money to undertake additional activities, or they express resentment or anxiety about the recommendations. Consultants need to be patient and steadfast in these circumstances in order to work through the resistance and insure that the client solves the problems that are identified.

Making an additional referral calls for maturity on the part of the consultant as well. Realizing one's limits, being able to publicly acknowledge them, and dealing with the powerful emotions that can be generated in oneself and in clients by the process, are essential in being able to manage these particular challenges in consulting engagements. The situations calling for such referrals can vary widely. When involved in assignments with individual clients, one always confronts the nature of the specific work of that person. There might be many situations that involve the technical aspects of the work with which a client might need assistance. A consulting psychologist might be coaching a senior financial executive on leadership style, the dynamics of a management team, or interpersonal skills, only to discover that the individual is really struggling with particular aspects of bank financing or stock transactions that are beyond the consultant's expertise. Making a referral or suggesting that the individual seek additional assistance in these situations can be extraordinarily helpful for clients who sometimes have difficulty reaching out for help.

One of the most difficult situations in which referrals are required occurs when health, mental health, or chemical dependency problems are uncovered in the course of working with an individual client. Here again, the skills and personal integrity of the practitioner are really put to the test. Identifying that a problem exists, determining what steps ought to be taken, including when and how to involve a supervising executive or other members of an organization's leadership team, and executing the process one decides on are complicated and difficult actions to undertake. Consultants must have knowledge and skill in being able to work through these kinds of issues if they are going to work in individual engagements. This is not to say that they need to be therapists or chemical dependency counselors. Rather, they must know what is involved, be able to help the individual and the organization conceive and implement the correct action that should be undertaken, and help make the right connections for the additional services. Consultants must also be able to manage themselves during such activities by maintaining appropriate boundaries, being mindful of the need for extreme sensitivity for confidentiality, and managing their own anxiety, shame, anger, sadness, and guilt when difficult choices must be made. Often when a practitioner identifies such a problem and helps the individual get the assistance needed, there is extreme gratitude and relief expressed on everyone's part that the problem can finally be surfaced and managed. However, at times, individual clients who are not ready, willing, or able to undertake the necessary steps to address a situation can lose their position, causing significant trauma for everyone involved. Again, the maturity of the consultant is sorely tested in such situations. The advice provided above about seeking external support is particularly relevant for practitioners who find themselves in these types of situations.

# PROFESSIONAL PREPARATION FOR INDIVIDUAL CONSULTING ASSIGNMENTS

In closing this chapter, I want to discuss briefly the types of preparation I think are necessary to practice as a consulting psychologist in these types of engagements. In a sense, the entire chapter has been about the kinds of knowledge, skill, ability, and experiences that consultants must have to be successful in this work. I have come to believe that the average psychologist practitioner, and indeed, the average consultant, is unlikely to obtain all of the training and expertise needed in virtually any graduate education program now offered. The array of what must be known to truly help clients in these types of situations is simply too vast to be incorporated in one program of study. The professional seeking to practice in this area must be committed to a process of life-long learning to acquire the necessary skills, and to developing a network of colleagues who are available to expand his or her knowledge and skill base almost at a moment's notice. What is required is a combination of the preparation received in the typical clinical, counseling, or school psychology program, combined with some of the emphasis obtained in industrial and organizational psychology education, and elements of training in business schools. Practitioners must know how individuals, groups, organizations, and family systems operate. They must have essential skills in the financial management of business enterprises, and knowledge of business, legal, and financial strategies and frameworks. They must know about culture, global political problems and processes, and most importantly how human beings develop as leaders. It takes considerable time to develop such expertise.

In making the above observations, and by implication, recommendations for preparation to consult with individuals in organizational settings, I am not trying to say that practitioners cannot and should not undertake such assignments until they know everything they need to know to practice at an expert level. Indeed, everyone must make a start in the field, and usually does so during their training years. What I am trying to say is that particularly in these types of engagements, the work of a consulting psychologist will be extraordinarily visible. Leaders in organizations are usually very knowledgeable and skillful. They recognize quickly who can help them and why (Jaques & Clement, 1991). They also recognize the opposite, and if they cannot do that, they don't rise to positions of greater influence. Practitioners must in all cases be honest with themselves about what they know, what they must learn, and how they can supplement their own gaps in preparation, interest, or skill with the expertise of colleagues. If they can do that, they are less likely to make major mistakes and fail in their assignments.

# SUMMARY AND CONCLUSIONS

Consulting with individuals in organizations is exciting, exacting, and difficult work. It is also extremely interesting and can be very rewarding. I hope this chapter has succeeded in illuminating some of the complexities and issues involved. I would encourage anyone who wants to begin or move into this area of practice to seek additional education and training, and to develop a mentoring relationship with a recognized practitioner in the field. Practitioners prepared in clinical, counseling, or school psychology might need to learn a great deal about organizations and management before becoming truly competent to engage in this work. Similarly, those trained in industrial and organizational psychology will need to learn about individual assessment and counseling methods. Acquiring these skills can seem like a daunting task, but with time and careful application of energy, it is possible to do. Everyone who is currently practicing in the field has had to go through the same process. Fortunately, the Society of Consulting Psychology of the American Psychological Association has been steadily developing a variety of resources to help people make progress in a systematic fashion. I strongly encourage individuals with interests in the field to inquire into membership in the Society.

## References

American Psychological Association, Society of Consulting Psychology, Education and Training Committee. (2000). *Guidelines for education and training at the doctoral and post-doctoral level in consulting psychology: Organizational consulting psychology.* Washington, DC: [Author.]

Bach, S. (1994). *The language of perversion and the language of love.* Northvale, NJ: Aronson.

Baltes, B. B., Staudinger, U. M., & Lindenberger, U. (1999). Lifespan psychology: Theory and application to intellectual functioning, *Annual Review of Psychology, 50,* 471–507.

Barker, R. G. (1968). *Ecological psychology: Concepts and methods for studying the environment of human behavior.* Stanford, CA: Stanford University Press.

Bedeian, A. G., & Zammuto, R. F. (1991). *Organizations: Theory and design.* Orlando, FL: Dryden Press.

Block, P. (1981). *Flawless consulting: A guide to getting your expertise used.* San Diego, CA: Pfeiffer.

Cartwright, D., & Zander, A. (1968). *Group dynamics research and theory.* New York: Harper-Collins.

Czander, W. M. (1993). *The psychodynamics of work and organizations: Theory and application.* New York: Guilford Press.

Erikson, E. H. (1963). *Childhood and society* (2nd ed.). New York: Norton.

French, W. L., & Bell, C. H. (1973). *Organization development: Behavioral science interventions for organization improvement.* Englewood Cliffs, NJ: Prentice Hall.

Freud, S. (1933). New introductory lectures on psychoanalysis. *The Standard Edition.* (Vol. 22). London: Hogarth Press.

Gray, P. (1994). *The ego and analysis of defense.* Northvale, NJ: Aronson.

Hargrove, R. (1995). *Masterful coaching: Extraordinary results by impacting people and the way they think and work together.* San Diego, CA: Pfeiffer.

Heifetz, R. A. (1994). *Leadership without easy answers.* Cambridge, MA: Harvard University Press.

Hemfelt, R., Minirth, F., & Meier, P. (1991). *We are driven: The compulsive behaviors America applauds.* Nashville, TN: Nelson.

Hogan, R., Curphy, G. J., & Hogan, J. L. (1994). What we know about leadership: Effectiveness and personality. *The American Psychologist, 49*(6), 493–504.

Hudson, F. M. (1999). *The handbook of coaching: A comprehensive resource guide for managers, executives, consultants, and human resource professionals.* San Francisco: Jossey-Bass.

Jaques, E., & Clement, S. D. (1991). *Executive leadership: A practical guide to managing complexity.* Arlington, VA: Cason Hall.

Kegan, R. (1982). *The evolving self: Problem and process in human development.* Cambridge, MA: Harvard University Press.

Kegan, R. (1994). *In over our heads: The mental demands of modern life.* Cambridge, MA: Harvard University Press.

Kernberg, O. F. (1978). Leadership and organizational functioning: Organizational regression. *International Journal of Group Psychotherapy, 28,* 3–25.

Kernberg, O. F. (1979). Regression in organizational leadership. *Psychiatry, 42,* 24–39.

Kernberg, O. F. (1998). *Ideology, conflict, and leadership in groups and organizations.* New Haven, CT: Yale University Press.

Kets de Vries, M.F.R. (Ed.). (1984). *The irrational executive: Psychoanalytic explorations in management.* Madison, CT: International Universities Press.

Kiel, F., Rimmer, E., Williams, K., & Doyle, M. (1996). Coaching at the top. *Consulting Psychology Journal: Practice and Research. 48*(2), 67–77.

Kilburg, R. R. (Ed.). (1996). Executive coaching [Special issue]. *Consulting Psychology Journal: Practice and Research. 48*(2).

Kilburg, R. R. (2000). *Executive coaching: Developing managerial wisdom in a world of chaos.* Washington, DC: American Psychological Association.

Kilburg, R. R. (in press). Shadow consultation: A reflective approach for preventing practice disasters. *Consulting Psychology Journal: Practice and Research.*

Kilburg, R. R., Nathan, P. E., & Thoreson, R. W. (1986). *Professionals in distress: Issues, syndromes, and solutions in psychology.* Washington, DC: American Psychological Association.

Lawler, E. E., III, Nadler, D. A., & Cammann, C. (1980). *Organizational assessment: Perspectives on the measurement of organizational behavior and the quality of work life.* New York: Wiley.

Levinson, D. J. (1978). *Seasons of a man's life.* New York: Ballantine.

Levinson, H. (1981). *Executive.* Cambridge, MA: Harvard University Press.

Levinson, H. (2002). *Organizational assessment: A step-by-step guide to effective consulting.* Washington, DC: American Psychological Association.

Lowman, R. L. (1993). *Counseling and psychotherapy of work dysfunctions.* Washington, DC: American Psychological Association.

O'Neil, J. R. (1993). *The paradox of success: When winning at work means losing at life.* New York: Putnam.

Peterson, D. B. (1996). Executive coaching at work: The art of one-on-one change. *Consulting Psychology Journal: Practice and Research, 48,* 78–86.

Prince, P. P., & Heiser, L. J. (2000). *Essentials of career interest assessment.* New York: Wiley.

Schroder, M. (1974). The shadow consultant. *The Journal of Applied Behavioral Science, 10,* 579–594.

Schwartz, H. S. (1990). *Narcissistic process and corporate decay: The theory of the organization ideal.* New York: New York University Press.

Stacey, R. D. (1992). *Managing the unknowable: Strategic boundaries between order and chaos in organizations.* San Francisco: Jossey-Bass.

Stacey, R. D. (1996). *Complexity and creativity in organizations.* San Francisco: Berrett-Koehler.

Tomkins, S. S. (1962–1963). *Affect, imagery, and consciousness* (Vols. I-II). New York: Springer.

Wurmser, L. (2000). *The power of the inner judge: Psychodynamic treatment of the severe neuroses.* Northvale, NJ: Aronson.

# CHAPTER SIX

# The Effectiveness of Executive Coaching:

## *What We Know and What We Still Need to Know*

Sheila Kampa
*RHR International*

Randall P. White
*Executive Development Group*

This chapter is borne out of the collaboration of two social scientists who came together as a result of the first's dissertation on executive coaching and leadership. They realized a shared interest in establishing the utility of executive coaching. This mutual interest sparked a dialogue about coaching—what it is, how it is used, how helpful it might be in the lives and careers of executives—that led to this collaborative effort.

In this chapter we attempt to do three things. First, we draw upon previous literature, particularly Kampa-Kokesch and Anderson's review (2001) of the executive coaching literature, to address what coaching is and how it is practiced. In this section of the chapter, we suggest a new, integrative definition of coaching. Second, we seek to answer the question of whether executive coaching has any value—does it work? We do this by examining the results of several empirical studies, drawing out the practical implications. Finally, we outline the questions we believe have been answered by the work in the field to date and suggest directions for the next push in the evaluation of the efficacy of coaching.

Kampa-Kokesch and Anderson (2001) discussed the history of executive coaching, provided a summary of the most common themes in the literature, reviewed the empirical research to date, and in a subsequent paper (in press) compared executive coaching to a general consultation and coaching model. Their review helps inform the first two sections of this chapter. In the first section, the history and themes extracted from the literature by Kampa-Kokesch and Anderson will briefly be summarized and further discussed. The six themes are: (a) definition, (b) purpose, (c) methodologies and techniques, (d) distinctions from therapy and counseling, (e) credentials of coaches, and (f) recipients of executive coaching.

# WHAT IS EXECUTIVE COACHING?

In Kampa-Kokesch and Anderson's review (2001), the most salient points regarding the history of executive coaching seem to be that it is difficult to track because it has only recently received attention in the professional literature, and consultants, particularly those from certain consulting firms, appear to have been conducting some version of developmental (executive) coaching since the 1940s. Kampa-Kokesch and Anderson (in press) demonstrate that executive coaching parallels recognized intervention models, for example Caplan's consultation model (1970) and Kinlaw's general coaching model (1997). With this background, it is difficult to consider executive coaching a fad or passing fancy. We argue that phenomena that exist for over sixty years are not fads. What might be fad-like is the amount of attention executive coaching has recently received both in academic and public literatures. In our opinion, the level of attention might dwindle, but the phenomenon of coaching is likely to remain, particularly since the concept of the coach has been around since the 1500s (see Witherspoon & White, 1996a). Therefore, it is important to decide what exactly executive coaching is and what makes it effective.

## A Definition of Coaching

A critical issue around the definition of executive coaching is that no single consensually validated definition of coaching yet exists. It is difficult to discuss, and even more difficult to study, a phenomenon that is not clearly defined.

Kampa-Kokesch and Anderson (2001, in press) suggested that an integration of Kilburg's definition (2000) with components of Caplan's definition (1970) of consultee-centered administrative consultation (CCAC) and Kinlaw's definition (1997) of general coaching might provide a comprehensive understanding of current executive coaching practices. Kilburg's definition stated that coaching is ". . . a helping relationship formed between a client who has managerial authority and responsibility in an organization and a consultant who uses a wide variety of behavioral techniques and methods to help the client achieve a mutually identified set of goals to improve his or her professional performance and personal satisfaction and, consequently, to improve the effectiveness of the client's organization within a formally defined coaching agreement" (p. 67). Caplan's definition of CACC identifies coaching as consisting of a relationship between a consultant and consultee with the goal of improving the professional functioning of the consultee. Caplan stressed the relationship as the most critical component of the process. Kinlaw (p. 30) defined coaching as ". . . a disciplined personal interaction with one or more persons which produces winning results for individuals, teams, and organizations by focusing and refocusing them on performance goals and facilitating their achievement of these goals." Kinlaw also stressed the importance of the relationship. Because no integrated definition of coaching yet exists, we will attempt to provide one here.

We define executive coaching as a formal, ongoing relationship between an individual or team having managerial authority and responsibility in an organization, and a consultant who possesses knowledge of behavior change and organizational functioning. This relationship has the goal of creating measurable behavior change in the individual or collection of individuals (the team) that results in increased individual and organizational performance, and where the relationship between individual or team and consultant facilitates this change by or through giving direct behaviorally based feedback, creating opportunities for change, and demanding accountability.

## Purpose

Witherspoon and White (1996a, 1996b) stated that high-performance individuals—athletes, performers, and public speakers—have all used coaching as a means of improving their performance. Kampa-Kokesch and Anderson (2001) reviewed additional reasons for using coaching proposed in the literature. These include the rapidly changing global marketplace necessitating continued development (Sperry, 1993), businesses' realization that poor leadership can lead to financial ruin (Kilburg, 1996), and the fact that executives typically receive very little behavioral, as opposed to outcome-based, feedback (Lukaszewski, 1988). Lukaszewski identified the inability to gain access to people who ask questions, provide advice, and give counsel as the greatest difficulty facing senior executives. He noted that most people close to executives are afraid, or do not know how, to confront them regarding their behavior.

We view a major purpose of the executive coach's role as being to provide feedback to the executive about the executive's behavior and its impact on others, both those within and outside the organization (Witherspoon & White, 1996b; O'Neill, 2000). Through this type of feedback, executives can gain increased self-awareness, self-esteem, and better communication with peers and subordinates (Kilburg, 1996), which in turn can lead to increased morale, productivity, and profits for the organization (Smith, 1993). Whether this process does in fact result in these outcomes, however, remains largely unknown—an issue to which we will return. The overall purpose of executive coaching, however, by definition is to increase performance.

## Techniques and Methodologies for Coaching

Kampa-Kokesch and Anderson (2001) reviewed the many existing models of executive coaching. Currently espoused models include: Witherspoon and White's model (1996a) based on four different coaching roles, Kilburg's seventeen-dimensional model (1996) based on systems and psychodynamic theory, Laske's developmental model (1999a), and Waclawski and Church's (1999) model based on feedback utilization. There is considerable overlap in the models used to describe the coaching process, including the stages of executive coaching, which most models agree include relationship building, assessment, intervention, follow-up, and evaluation. These stages are consistent with most consultation interventions (Brown, Pryzwansky, & Schulte, 1998). Kampa-Kokesch and Anderson (2001) also found agreement regarding the desirable assessment techniques and instrumentation, including 360-degree feedback questionnaires, qualitative interviews, and psychological instruments such as personality- and leadership-style inventories (Brotman, Liberi, & Wasylyshyn, 1998; Diedrich, 1996; Harris, 1999; Kiel, Rimmer, Williams, & Doyle, 1996; Kilburg, 1996; Peterson, 1996; Richard, 1999; Saporito, 1996; Tobias, 1996; Witherspoon & White, 1996a). The purpose of such approaches and instruments is to gather data to present to the client. There is further agreement that presenting data, or giving feedback, is a critical component of executive coaching (Diedrich, 1996; Waclawski & Church, 1999; Witherspoon & White, 1996a). Kiel et al. (1996) stated that because executives tend to trust data, they also come to trust coaching more when data are provided. Waclawski and Church (1999) regarded feedback as being so critical, they used it as the crux of their model.

The differences in these models are akin to the differences in theoretical approaches to therapy. For example, there are behavioral, psychodynamic, relational, developmental, existential, and integrationist approaches to therapy (for example, Peltier, 2001). One could argue that the differences between theoretical approaches are in the method of attempting to reach the desired end result. Behaviorists believe that the best approach focuses on behavior; relationists believe that the best approach focuses on the therapeutic alliance. What each approach has in common is that they seek to affect changed behavior or understanding. Executive coaching seeks similar outcomes. How then do coaching and therapy differ from one another?

## Distinguishing Executive Coaching from Counseling and Psychotherapy

Kampa-Kokesch and Anderson (2001) concluded from their review that many of the cited differences between coaching and psychotherapy appear to be logistical in nature—timing, location, frequency of contact—at least when executive coaching is conducted by professionals with psychotherapy training or experience. Kilburg (2000) suggested that the main difference between the two is the depth to which issues are pursued and processed; however, he also stated that the line is not clearly drawn. But what about the frequent situation in which executive coaching is conducted by professionals without psychotherapeutic training or experience? Does this exacerbate any real or perceived differences? We argue not. The intended outcomes of both psychotherapy and executive coaching are behavioral change (though psychotherapy can have additional outcomes that go beyond this; for example, personality reconstruction or enhanced understanding). The fact that the behavioral change sought in executive coaching focuses on change as it relates to effective performance within the organizational or work context (not usually in the broader whole-life context that psychotherapy seeks to address) is probably not especially important, because changes in one sphere of a person's life will most probably have an impact in other spheres. In either case, since executive coaching has the goal of behavior change, social scientists trained in behavioral change and organizational analysis might be most qualified to provide executive coaching services, a point discussed further in the next section.

## Distinguishing Executive Coaching from Consultation

Executive coaching parallels one form of consultation (Caplan, 1970) and consistently follows the natural consultation process (see Brown et al., 1998). As such, we do not see the need to make a distinction. We consider executive coaching one tool in a constellation of consulting tools; executive coaching is just one form of consultation.

## Qualifications to Perform Coaching Services

Kampa-Kokesch and Anderson (2001) highlighted two separate but related ideas from the practice literature on executive coaching. One is the belief that psychologists or social scientists already possess a large number of the skills needed to provide executive coaching, and might therefore be considered the most qualified service providers (see Brotman et al., 1998; Kilburg, 1996; Sperry, 1993, 1996). However, many argue that even though a psychological background provides many of the necessary skills for offering executive coaching services, those skills alone are not sufficient. Some (see Harris, 1999; Kiel et al., 1996; Levinson, 1996; Saporito, 1996; Sperry, 1996; Tobias, 1996) suggest that having an awareness of business, management, executive development, and political issues is also necessary to be effective. Organizations might increasingly consider such a background as they select from the pool of potential coaches. We further suggest that possessing knowledge of the leadership literature is also important in coaching, because most executives are in leadership positions.

These conclusions are tentative at this time. None of these skills or backgrounds have been subjected to empirical tests to determine if they make an actual difference in the effectiveness of coaches. Like much of what has been written about executive coaching, the qualifications of coaches at this time constitute only conceptual or theoretical differences or recommendations. Even now, there is value in considering relative qualifications of persons coaching with different educational or other backgrounds. Until there is an empirical literature base to conclude otherwise, it is reasonable to assume that knowledge of behavioral change, business, and leadership, and the ability to create a trusting and supportive relationship for change to occur, are important factors to use in selecting coaches.

## Recipients of Services

Typical recipients of executive coaching are either people who are solid performers but whose current behaviors are interfering with that performance and putting the company at risk, or people who are targeted for advancement or succession within the organization (Hall, Otazo, & Hollenbeck, 1999; Kampa-Kokesch, 2001; Kampa-Kokesch & Anderson, 2001; Laske, 1999b). Since executive coaching can be an expensive form of executive development, due to the individualized time and attention each executive receives, it follows that those individuals whose technical expertise is valued by the company or those individuals targeted in succession planning exercises are the most likely candidates to receive these services. The ratio of one type of client to the other—faltering executive versus executive targeted for succession—is not clearly established, although some evidence suggests that 30 to 50 percent of executives at senior levels will derail (see Sorcher, 1985; White & DeVries, 1990). Overall, whether the coaching is intended to change behavior for *increased* performance or *improved* performance is a distinction most likely not worth making.

# THE EFFICACY OF COACHING

At this particular stage in the development of the literature on executive coaching as an intervention, there are very few empirical studies evaluating its utility. At the time of this writing, only five studies (Gegner, 1997; Hall et al., 1999; Kampa-Kokesch, 2001; Laske, 1999b; McGovern et al., 2001) investigating the efficacy of executive coaching as defined in this chapter were found using ERIC, PsychLit, and Wilson Business Abstracts, as well as a snowball sampling of references from reviewed studies. Kilburg (1996) provided a brief review of studies that focus on managers as coaches (for example, Coggins, 1991; Dougherty, 1993) and structured coaching programs (for example, Peterson, 1993; Thompson, 1987). He noted that the research conducted in these contexts suggests performance increases in individuals who occupy administrative positions. However, this research did not investigate executive coaching as practiced by consultants in the field. We will therefore review existing research conducted on executive coaching (as defined in this chapter) by consultants in the field who practice it.

Of the five studies included in this chapter, two are dissertations (Kampa-Kokesch, 2001; Laske, 1999b), one a master's thesis (Gegner, 1997), and one sponsored by a consulting firm (McGovern et al., 2001). Some of the studies are less rigorous than others, and, therefore, have greater limitations. The fact that these were field studies, in and of itself, is not a limitation. Gelso and Fretz (1992) identified the field experiment as potentially the most powerful research design because of its rigor and relevance, especially when investigating global factors such as entire treatment packages. Each of these studies (summarized in Table 6.1) provides information about the efficacy of executive coaching.

The five studies provide both quantitative and qualitative data addressing the efficacy of executive coaching. In reviewing the outcomes of these studies, a number of themes appear regarding the efficacy of coaching. There is modest evidence that coaching impacts the following areas: job performance and productivity, learning, self-awareness and development, and leadership effectiveness. There is also consistent evidence that executives find coaching or the coaching experience beneficial (Hall et al., 1999; Gegner, 1997; Kampa-Kokesch, 2001), and that they believe they have received a high return on their investments in coaching (McGovern et al., 2001). Three of the studies have been reviewed in detail by Kampa-Kokesch and Anderson (2001); the remaining two are discussed in more detail in this chapter. Studies are presented as they relate to the categories of job performance and productivity, self-awareness and development, and leadership effectiveness. We recognize that these categories are not mutually distinctive outcomes of coaching, but they are discussed separately for ease of presentation.

## Effect of Coaching on Job Performance and Productivity

There is some qualitative evidence that executive coaching as practiced by consultants in the field increases job performance and productivity. In McGovern et al. (2001), 53 percent of executives reported an increase in productivity during and after coaching, and in Gegner (1997), eight of the twenty-five executives (32 percent) interviewed estimated performance improvement, which they estimated to have improved from 10 to 100 percent (why the remaining thirteen did not provide an estimate was unclear from the study). Clearly, there are limitations to the sample sizes, the failure to gather the same data from all participants, and the subjective nature of the criterion measure used.

Many of the executives surveyed in Kampa-Kokesch (2001) also reported changes in performance and productivity. For example, clients stated that the

**Table 6.1. Summary Table of Empirical Studies.**

| Name of Study | Hall et al. (1999) | Gegner (1997) | Laske (1999b) | Kampa-Kokesch (2001) | McGovern et al. (2001) |
|---|---|---|---|---|---|
| Population | Executives | Executives | Executives | Coaches, executives, direct reports/peers/ supervisors | Executives |
| Sample size | 75 | 48 (quantitative) 27 (qualitative) | 6 | 41 Coaches 50 Clients 62 Direct reports/ peers/supervisors | 100 |
| Control/ comparison group | No | No | No | Yes | No |
| Outcome criteria | Qualitative responses | Increased responsibility and awareness (quantitative); qualitative responses | Change stories | Leadership scores; qualitative responses | Return on investment |
| Quantitative | No | Yes | No | Yes | No |
| Qualitative | Yes | Yes | Yes | Yes | Yes |

most helpful thing about coaching was that it helped them to be more productive, to improve effectiveness, and to accomplish tasks with more ease. The nature of the executive's role—being both task- and relationship-oriented—points to the fact that any type of coaching intervention is designed to affect performance and productivity either directly on the task or by improving relationships. Again, the criterion is limited but not totally without value (see, for example, Miles & Huberman, 1994).

## Individual Learning Factor

Another outcome criterion underlying the efficacy of executive coaching concerns the individual learning that occurs as part of the process. Many in the practice-based literature have identified this as one of the main reasons for the perceived success of coaching (Harris, 1999; O'Brien, 1997; Witherspoon & White, 1996a). Many of the twenty-five executives interviewed by Gegner (1997) reported learning new skills as a result of coaching. Executives in Kampa-Kokesch (2001) and Laske (1999b) also reported learning additional things about themselves and others, which led to the perception of increased self-awareness. We would argue that increased self-awareness can lead to greater intentionality in one's behavior.

## Self-Awareness and Developmental Goals

A third efficacy factor to be considered is the establishment of developmental goals, which there is evidence to suggest are often lacking at the more senior leadership levels in large organizations. Many of the fifty executives surveyed by Kampa-Kokesch (2001) identified developmental goals for, and developmental outcomes established as a result of, coaching. Six of the twenty-five executives (24 percent) interviewed by Gegner (1997) also made statements about the growth they felt they had attained, such as being more open to change and possessing more self-confidence. Anecdotal evidence, particularly with small samples, is suggestive, but not the basis on which to draw substantive conclusions.

A more detailed look at the developmental effects of coaching comes from Laske (1996b), who qualitatively examined the developmental effects of executive coaching on an executive's professional agenda (one of four roles outlined by Witherspoon & White, 1996a). His specific focus was to differentiate behavioral and developmental learning. He did this by interviewing six executives who were identified by their coaches as experiencing developmental change as a result of coaching, suggesting that coaches believe, at least in these six instances, that coaching can affect developmental change. The six executives were interviewed twice, with the first interview focusing on what had significantly changed in the way they performed their organizational functions and what aspects of their professional self-image had most notably been transformed as a result of coaching. The second interview focused on how executives constructed their reality (personal and organizational) based on Kegan's subject-object relations (1994). Laske (1996b) concluded that changes reported by executives did in fact seem to be developmental in nature and not just behavioral or adaptive. He also stated that developmental changes seemed in his sample to be dependent upon the executive's stage and cognitive profile as well as the coach's stage and cognitive profile. This finding, if supported by other, larger and longitudinal studies, might imply that coaching facilitates movement to higher developmental levels only to the extent that the executive is ready for this movement, and to the extent that the coach's own developmental stage and cognitive profile could facilitate this movement.

Laske's study, as the author acknowledged, is limited, including its cross-sectional rather than longitudinal nature. The sample size was small and there was no independent corroboration of the interview findings. Although small sample sizes are not uncommon in exploratory research (see, for example, Strauss & Corbin, 1998) they are more appropriately used to generate hypotheses than reliably to establish group differences.

## Leadership Effectiveness and Coaching

A fourth efficacy factor addresses the degree of impact coaching has on leadership effectiveness. Both quantitative and qualitative data are provided in this study. Kampa-Kokesch (2001) examined the leadership behavior of fifty recipients of executive coaching by having the recipients and their direct reports, peers, or supervisors rate the leadership effectiveness of the recipients being coached. Although this study was conducted by the senior author of this chapter, it is arguably the most empirically rigorous quantitative study investigating the efficacy of coaching, particularly as related to executive leadership, of the small number of empirical studies on coaching thus far reported.

In Kampa-Kokesch (2001), thirteen executive coaching recipients were pre- or early coaching clients (having received zero to three months of coaching, with an average of two months), and twenty-seven were post- or later coaching clients (having received more than three months of coaching, with an average of 23 months). The fifty clients came from a total of twenty-seven different coaches, twenty-five of whom lived and practiced inside the United States. Ten clients reported being self-referred for coaching, and thirty-nine reported being referred through other means. The referral source was not indicative of whether coaching was for remedial or developmental purposes. Reasons for seeking coaching included: relationship difficulties, rapidly changing work environments, personal difficulties interfering with work, executive coaching having been reported as being a positive experience for others in the organization, and strengthening the ability to move forward and make leadership decisions. The instrument used to measure leadership effectiveness was the Multifactor Leadership Questionnaire ×5 (short form), or MLQ5X, which measures transformational and transactional leadership, as well as three outcome variables: effectiveness, extra effort (put forth by others as a result of the leader's leadership style), and satisfaction (Bass & Avolio, 1995).

Few differences were found in this study between the entire pre- and post-groups across all dimensions of the leadership instrument. In fact, only one difference was found (which could therefore have occurred due to chance alone). This occurred on one of the transactional leadership scales, the scale measuring the tendency to avoid performance deviations, errors, and mistakes. The pre- or early coaching group scored higher on this variable than the post- or later coaching group, meaning the pre- or early coaching group tended to avoid performance deviations, errors, and mistakes more frequently than the post or later coaching group. Importantly, the difference on the Management-by-Exception (MEP) variable was statistically significant ($p \leq .05$) and practically meaningful (differences of .50 or more meet that criterion, according to the authors of the MLQ5X; Bass & Avolio, 1995). Additional analyses revealed more between-group differences at higher organizational levels, consistent with other literature using the MLQ (for example, Lowe, Kroek, & Sirvasbramaniam, 1996). These differences, statistically significant and practically meaningful, occurred on three transformational leadership scales: Idealized Influence-Behavior (IIB), measuring charismatic leadership that is behaviorally based and observed by followers; Idealized Influence-Attributed (IIA), measuring charismatic leadership that is attributed to the leader by his/her followers; and Inspirational Motivation (IM), measuring the leader's ability to inspire followers by arousing team spirit and getting them focused on envisioning future organizational goals. These were positive outcomes from the coaching, because a leader's tendency to be viewed as charismatic at higher organizational levels can be important. Furthermore, the ability to positively influence direct reports, arouse team spirit, and get people focused on envisioning future organizational goals all have positive impacts on the effectiveness of an organization. These findings must be put in the context, however, of quite high scores on the transformational leadership variables found among participants in this study (see, for example, Lowe et al., 1996; Yammarino & Bass, 1990).

Limitations of Kampa-Kokesch's study (2001) include the exceptionally low response rate among coaches (2 percent) and the fact that only one instrument was used in this study. Another limitation related to the design of the study was that coaches were asked to identify clients who were just beginning coaching or were within the first three months of coaching. As a result, pre- or early coaching clients had an average of two months of executive coaching, which is arguably enough to effect a change. Also, this study was a field experiment and true randomization did not occur; however, approximation of randomization was present by testing the groups for differences on multiple demographic variables.

## Subjective Reactions to Coaching

A fifth efficacy factor concerns subjective reactions to coaching. Evidence suggests generally positive reactions to coaching (see Hall et al., 1999; Kampa-Kokesch, 2001; Laske, 1999b; McGovern et al., 2001). The seventy-five executives in six different *Fortune* 100 companies interviewed in the Hall et al. study regarding the effectiveness of executive coaching rated coaching as very satisfying (a four on a five-point Likert scale). They reported that the reasons they found coaching beneficial were that they received challenging feedback and helpful examples for behavioral change. They said that the most effective coaching was results-oriented. There was little information reported about the nature of the sample, methodologies used, or analysis conducted. Thus, the results of this study should be regarded as tentative; though, as exploratory work, they suggest that clients find coaching effective for creating behavior change. Executives and stakeholders in the McGovern et al. study were overwhelmingly satisfied with the coaching process. Executives identified the coaching relationships (between consultant and coachee) and the coaching process as factors that contributed to the effectiveness of the coaching. The limitations of McGovern et al. include the fact that a consulting firm—one that offers the service—sponsored the study.

Executives in the Kampa-Kokesch study provided even more detail regarding the benefits of coaching. Their responses clustered around six important themes: self-awareness and development, performance and outcomes, different perspective, objective person, feedback and support, and relationships. The first two areas have been discussed previously, so only the last four will be outlined as they contribute to overall satisfaction with coaching.

With respect to developing different perspectives, some clients reported that the most helpful thing about coaching involved "getting me to look at problems and everyday life in a different way" and learning "how to look at problems and opportunities from all sides and all points of view." With respect to the objective person of the coach, clients said that one of the most helpful things about coaching was "hav[ing] someone to discuss business matters with, someone who can stay objective—an appropriate person . . . to reflect ideas off of, having the ability to discuss what I feel, want to do, or current issues without management judging or using those things against me" and the "one-on-one ability to discuss strengths and weaknesses with a third party outside of office politics." With respect to feedback and support, some clients stated that it was most helpful to receive both positive and negative feedback, to get performance feedback, and to gain support, encouragement, and affirmations. Finally, with respect to relationships, some clients identified a raised awareness regarding the importance of relationships, as evidenced in such statements as "my ability to focus and be able to grow my relationships with other co-workers" and "gaining more insight regarding my colleagues and what makes them tick" as the most helpful outcome from their executive coaching experience.

The Manchester Consulting Group (McGovern et al., 2001) conducted a study designed to examine the effects executive coaching had on an organization's profit and loss. This study used Phillips' (1997) recommended methodology for analyzing program impact by examining expected learning, behavioral change, business results, and return on investment (ROI). Participants were 100 northeastern and mid-Atlantic executives who completed coaching between 1996 and 2000. Their coaching experiences consisted of involvement in customized coaching programs that were either change- or growth-oriented (remedial or developmental in our terms), or a combination of the two. The coaching programs ranged from six to twelve months in duration, and were delivered by coaches who had either Ph.D. or MBA degrees and at least twenty years of organizational development or management experience and training in executive coaching. The sample was balanced to include both genders, an age range from thirty to fifty-nine, and a mixture of races and executive income levels.

Each executive was interviewed over the telephone by one of two independent contractors, who employed a standardized interview protocol (McGovern et al., 2001). During the interviews, executives provided a rating of their overall coaching satisfaction, described their coaching goals, and indicated whether their goals had been met. Respondents were also asked to describe any new behaviors they developed and how often they engaged in these behaviors, and to identify aspects of the coaching they found to be effective or ineffective. Executives also estimated financial gains to the business, and any tangible and intangible benefits of the coaching. Whenever possible, the executive's boss or a sponsor from human resources was also interviewed.

Regarding the overall satisfaction of the coaching process (McGovern et al., 2001), 86 percent of executives and 74 percent of stakeholders reported being "very satisfied" or "extremely satisfied." Learning was categorized into competencies that executives expected to gain as a result of coaching: enhanced leadership skills (14 percent), enhanced management skills (18 percent), increased business agility and credibility (15 percent), better interpersonal skills (35 percent), and fostering personal growth (12 percent).

Behavioral change in this study was measured by asking executives what they were doing differently as a result of coaching. They reported taking specific actions (like proofreading memos before sending them out) to more general activities (like being more strategic when engaged in planning). Executives and stakeholders overwhelmingly reported that the goals established during coaching were met, providing ratings that indicated goals were met "effectively" to "extremely effectively." As might be expected, stakeholder ratings were more conservative than executive ratings. This is a typical pattern (see, for example, Lowe et al., 1996) leading Hogan, Curphy, and Hogan (1994) to conclude that the combination of superior, peer, and direct report ratings are the most accurate ratings of behavior change among subjective estimates of performance.

Regarding the factors that were perceived to have contributed to goal achievement, 84 percent of executives identified the coaching relationship as critical to the success of coaching (McGovern et al., 2001). Other factors that played a part in goal achievement dealt with the tactical process of coaching: having flexible meeting times, engaging in role plays, having the coach sit in on staff meetings, and so on. Factors that detracted from achieving goals included lack of executive availability for coaching, and organizational pressures resulting in the organization not being supportive of the coaching.

Organizational outcomes reported by respondents in this study were positive but not overwhelming. Regarding tangible benefits, 51 percent reported increased productivity; 48 percent reported increased work quality; 48 percent, increased organizational strength; 39 percent, improved customer service; 34 percent, reduced complaints; 32 percent, cost reductions; 22 percent, increased bottom-line profitability; 14 percent, increased top-line revenue; 12 percent, decreased turnover; and 7 percent reported other business effects. The reported intangible benefits were much stronger, with 77 percent of the executives reporting improved relationships with direct reports; 71 percent, improved relationships with stakeholders; 67 percent, improved teamwork; 63 percent, improved relationships with peers; 61 percent, improved job satisfaction, 52 percent, reduced conflict; and 44 percent reported increased organizational commitment. In our experience, these last issues centered around relationships tend to be more critical at senior leadership levels, and by and large have been found as the critical elements of derailment at senior levels (McCall & Lombardo, 1983; McCall, Lombardo, & Morrison, 1988; Morrison, White, & VanVelsor, 1992). Overall, these results suggest that coaching, a relationship-intensive experience, affects other relationships more than it directly affects bottom-line outcomes. Such findings could also help to explain the positive reactions typically experienced by consulting clients.

Concerning subjective estimates of return on investment (see McGovern et al. for the formula used), forty-three of the 100 executives provided a dollar estimate. The remaining executives applied the Total Value Scale of +5 to −5. After adjustments, the ROI estimated by the forty-three executives averaged $100,000, or 5.7 times the investment in coaching. This far exceeded the 25 percent ROI recommended by Phillips (1997) as the minimum return necessary for a program to be considered valuable. Using the Total Value Scale, 74 percent of the executives rated the total value of coaching at +3 or higher, with 54 percent rating it at +4 or higher. Overall, 93 percent of the executives stated that they would recommend coaching to others.

Obvious limitations of the Manchester study (McGovern et al., 2001) include the fact that there was no control group, there were no objective outcome criteria employed, the study measured outcomes at a single point in time, and its results may be perceived as self-serving due to its sponsorship by a consulting firm performing the coaching. Self-ratings of return on investment are also limiting.

## Overall Themes of the Studies

The body of empirical research on executive coaching outcomes so far available is sparse, and existing studies reported here all had limitations, some severe. We believe that the studies reviewed do provide evidence that executive coaching may positively impact individual productivity at the most senior levels, and that this increased productivity is potentially leverageable for the increased productivity of an entire organization. The studies reviewed in this chapter also suggest that coaching results in increased learning, increased self-awareness and development, and more effective leadership, all of which can ultimately affect performance and productivity, and might result in a large return on investment for the business.

These studies have also provided some preliminary evidence about the conditions necessary for successful outcomes in executive coaching. Gegner (1997) reported that the variables of self-efficacy (increased client confidence) and the coach's communication style (actively listening to clients) were the most effective variables of the coaching process. Executives in Gegner (1997), Kampa-Kokesch (2001), and McGovern et al. (2001) identified the coaching relationship as being important to coaching success. Laske (1999b) identified both the client's and the coach's developmental level as being key in creating developmental change in the client, suggesting that they need to be aligned. McGovern et al. (2001) suggested that the ROI can be maximized when coaching is provided by high-caliber coaches. They also suggested six additional conditions to maximize this return, including the need for support from the executive's manager and human resource person, the need for a strong alignment between the executive and stakeholders regarding the significance, implications, and goals of coaching, the need for frequent contact being maintained between stakeholders, and the need for organizational support of the coaching.

# WHERE TO FROM HERE?

We believe that executive coaching, at least at senior levels within organizations, is here to stay. While faddish in the amount of attention it currently draws, the intervention has a long history and parallels general consultation. A variety of factors on both the supplier side—increased interest by therapists unhappy with current developments in psychotherapy—and the consumer side—the tailored nature of the intervention in a fast-paced world—have produced the conditions for continued growth in the use of coaching for executive development. As more practitioners are drawn to learning about executive coaching and more clients use it, the field will be forced to come to terms with what is known and unknown about the effectiveness of this tool. As a step in this direction, we have reported conceptual understandings of coaching. Though no single definition exists, the definitions provided make clearer what we are talking about when referring to executive coaching. Although myriad approaches to coaching exist, there is considerable overlap in the models used. In short, we believe that consulting psychology as a field has some basis for understanding the process of coaching.

Empirically, we know that there is at least preliminary, if limited, evidence supporting the efficacy of coaching. We know there is data suggesting that coaching might impact at least the perception of productivity and performance, self-awareness and development, and leadership effectiveness. We also know that executives consistently find coaching helpful, and in at least one study, report it to have a high ROI. Across the various studies discussed in this chapter, executives identify self-awareness and development, performance and outcomes, different perspective, objective person, feedback and support, and relationships as direct benefits of the coaching they have received.

Much more empirical research is needed, however, before executive coaching can lay claim to an empirical basis for claimed outcomes. Such research can build on the foundation of the studies done so far, but will benefit from: use of control and comparison groups; random assignment of people to conditions; use of multiple criterion measures; careful delineation of the exact nature of the intervention used; increased sample sizes; and consideration of rival hypotheses associated with apparent change. Additional qualitative research, particularly with this population, will also enrich our understanding of coaching outcomes, particularly due to the complexity around executive and organizational effectiveness. In the meantime, claims to the effectiveness of coaching outcomes should be considered in the context of what is, and is not, known at this time.

In terms of the practice of coaching, it is important that qualified, competent people provide coaching. Who these people should be is debatable, but we argue that those who have experience in the business sector, have social science savvy (that is, psychologists from several branches of psychology), and who have leadership knowledge and experience, would probably make first-rate coaches. Anecdotally, at least, it would seem that the best coaches understand human nature and behavior along with adult development (Laske, 1999b). An additional anecdotal factor is that successful coaches are widely read.

It seems to be important that the practice of coaching includes a trusting relationship, an understanding of the person with whom the coach is working, so that difficult and accurate feedback on work-related leadership issues can be provided and a safe environment for behavior change be created. We believe coaching should emphasize work-related issues, including leadership. The point of executive coaching is to help an individual become more effective in his or her current position or to prepare for a subsequent higher profile position. Therefore, the coach needs to have an appreciation for the job the person holds, as well as how this job fits into the overall organizational structure and objectives. We believe, though we acknowledge there is little evidence one way or the other yet to support the contention, that this takes a social scientist who, in thought, word, and deed, can create an atmosphere of trust and respect with the client, and has the knowledge and experience to facilitate behavioral change that positively impacts the business.

In the practical approach to coaching, the principles outlined by McGovern et al. (2001) are useful. In addition, measurable goals must be set, and there must always be open communication between client and coach about any aspect of the coaching process or outcome as well as between coach, client, and client manager. The beauty or art of coaching happens in the interchange, the relationship. If the relationship is effective, if there is chemistry, much insight and self-awareness develops as a result of the dialogue between coach and client. The coaching process also provides honest feedback, which executives often find difficult to obtain, and opportunities in the coaching relationship to try new behaviors. Due to the individualized nature of coaching and the learning that occurs specific to the person, it can prove to be one of the most powerful tools for executive development.

In our experience, if people need lower-level learning—for example, technical knowledge or skills development—they can obtain that from many other sources: books, workshops, mentors, and so on. This is not to say that they could not get it from coaching, but due to the expense—in both time and money—of coaching, it might not be the best method.

For large-scale developmental changes—leadership changes—people can get these from sources other than coaching, too. McCall et al.'s (1988) work emphasizes the important role one's boss plays an executive development. We also know that people can change their behavior, but, depending on the nature of the change, this process is fraught with difficulty, not the least of which is the practice of and subject sustainability of the change. People often act differently after a well-run off-site course that focuses on behavioral change, but they return to their old patterns of behavior shortly thereafter. Coaching provides the potential for follow-through and support that seems to be needed to make lasting behavioral change. It holds people accountable for a longer duration of time so that behavioral change can solidify. A lengthened version of the unfreeze-change-refreeze paradigm (Lewin, 1951) and a chance to practice, to make mistakes, and to get it right, is far more manageable over a sustained period than a single event such as an off-site course.

Empirically, it is still important to ask whether coaching is efficacious, but the question has a different place now because we have some preliminary data suggesting that it is. It is also worth mentioning that we did not find any evidence suggesting it is not. Our limitation in making statements about the usefulness of coaching concerns the fact that there are so few studies yet completed. Obviously, we need more studies to extend the preliminary ones in more situations with more people. In replicating studies, the use of current psychometrics might not be the best method for measuring changes, because it is questionable whether they are sensitive enough to detect differences at the highest levels of leadership. We should also focus more on which factors in the coaching experience make it efficacious and which factors in the relationship between coach and coachee make a difference.

Finally, we need to focus on the outcomes and tie apparent or subjectively perceived outcomes directly to performance and productivity. This is what coaching businesses, boards, and senior executives really want to see. Coaching can give people additional insight, help them move to higher levels of development, and change leadership style, but how do these things affect the organization's profit and loss, however that is measured? We might feel strongly that they do, but we must continue to make the direct link for decision-makers and ourselves so that when asked whether coaching is a viable intervention, we can provide answers to when, where, and how this tool will work, as well as establishing the parameters for a science and study of coaching.

# References

Bass, B. M., & Avolio, B. J. (1995). *Multifactor leadership questionnaire for research permission set manual.* Redwood City, CA: Mind Garden.

Brotman, L. E., Liberi, W. P., & Wasylyshyn, K. M. (1998). Executive coaching: The need for standards of competence. *Counseling Psychology Journal: Practice and Research, 50,* 40–46.

Brown, D., Pryzwansky, W. B., & Schulte, A. C. (1998). *Psychological consultation: Introduction to theory and practice* (4th ed.). Needham Heights, MA: Allyn & Bacon.

Caplan, G. (1970). *Theory and practice of mental health consultation.* New York: Basic Books.

Coggins, M. F. (1991). Facilitating change through peer coaching (Doctoral dissertation, University of Georgia, 1991). *Dissertation Abstracts International, 52*(4), 1209A.

Diedrich, R. C. (1996). An iterative approach to executive coaching. *Counseling Psychology Journal: Practice and Research, 48,* 61–66.

Dougherty, D. C. (1993). Peer coaching: Creating a collaborative environment for change (Doctoral dissertation, University of Oregon, 1993). *Dissertation Abstracts International, 54*(1), 71A.

Gegner, C. (1997). *Coaching: Theory and practice.* Unpublished master's thesis, University of San Francisco, San Francisco, CA.

Gelso, C. J., & Fretz, B. R. (1992). *Counseling psychology.* Orlando, FL: Harcourt Brace.

Hall, D. T., Otazo, K. L., & Hollenbeck, G. P. (1999). Behind closed doors: What really happens in executive coaching. *Organizational Dynamics, 27,* 39–53.

Harris, M. (1999). Look, it's an I-O psychologist . . . no, it's a trainer . . . no, it's an executive coach. *The Industrial-Organizational Psychologist, 36,* 1–5.

Hogan, R., Curphy, G. J., & Hogan, J. L. (1994). What we know about leadership: Effectiveness and personality. *American Psychologist, 49*(6), 493–504.

Kampa-Kokesch, S. (2001). *Executive coaching as an individually tailored consultation intervention: Does it increase leadership?* Unpublished doctoral dissertation, Western Michigan University, Kalamazoo, MI.

Kampa-Kokesch, S., & Anderson, M. (2001). Executive coaching: A comprehensive review of the literature and comparison to a general consultation and general coaching model. *Consulting Psychology Journal: Practice and Research, 53*(4), 205–228.

Kampa-Kokesch, S., & Anderson, M. (in press). Executive coaching: A comparison to a general consultation and general coaching model. *Consulting Psychology Journal: Practice and Research.*

Kegan, R. (1994). *In over our heads: The mental demands of modern life.* Cambridge, MA: Harvard University Press.

Kiel, F., Rimmer, E., Williams, K., & Doyle, M. (1996). Coaching at the top. *Consulting Psychology Journal: Practice and Research, 48*(2), 67–77.

Kilburg, R. R. (1996). Toward a conceptual understanding and definition of executive coaching. *Consulting Psychology Journal: Practice and Research, 48*(2), 134–144.

Kilburg, R. R. (2000). *Executive coaching: Developing managerial wisdom in a world of chaos.* Washington, DC: American Psychological Association.

Kinlaw, D. C. (1997). *Coaching: Winning strategies for individuals and teams.* Brookfield, VT: Gower.

Laske, O. E. (1999a). An integrated model of development coaching. *Consulting Psychology Journal: Practice and Research, 51,* 139–159.

Laske, O. E. (1999b). *Transformative effects of coaching on executive's professional agenda.* Ann Arbor: University of Michigan Press.

Levinson, H. (1996). Executive coaching. *Consulting Psychology Journal: Practice and Research, 48,* 115–123.

Lewin, K. (1951). *Field theory in social science: Selected theoretical papers.* (D. Cartwright, Ed.). New York: HarperCollins.

Lowe, K., Kroek, K. G., & Sirvasbramaniam, N. (1996). Effectiveness correlates of transformational and transactional leadership: A meta-analytic review. *Leadership Quarterly, 7,* 385–425.

Lukaszewski, J. E. (1988). Behind the throne: How to coach and counsel executives. *Training and Development Journal, 42*(10), 32–35.

McCall, M. W., Jr., & Lombardo, M. M. (1983). *Off the track: Why and how successful executives get derailed.* (Technical Report No. 21). Greensboro, NC: Center for Creative Leadership.

McCall, M. W., Jr., Lombardo, M. M., & Morrison, A. M. (1988). *The lessons of experience: How successful executives develop on the job.* San Francisco: New Lexington Press.

McGovern, J., Lindemann, M., Vergara, M., Murphy, S., Barker, L., & Warrenfeltz, R. (2001). Maximizing the impact of executive coaching: Behavioral change, organizational outcomes, and return on investment. *The Manchester Review, 6*(1), 3–11.

Miles, M. B., & Huberman, A. M. (1994). *Qualitative data analysis: An expanded sourcebook* (2nd ed.). Thousand Oaks, CA: Sage.

Morrison, A. M., White, R. P., & VanVelsor, E. (1992). *Breaking the glass ceiling: Can women reach the top of America's largest corporations?* (Rev. Ed.). Reading, MA: Addison-Wesley.

O'Brien, M. (1997). Executive coaching. *Supervision, 58,* 6–8.

O'Neill, M. B. (2000). *Executive coaching with backbone and heart: A systems approach to engaging leaders with their challenges.* San Francisco: Jossey-Bass.

Peltier, B. (2001). *The psychology of executive coaching: Theory and application.* Philadelphia: Brunner-Routledge.

Peterson, D. B. (1993). Skill learning and behavior change in an individually tailored management coaching and training program (Doctoral dissertation, University of Minnesota, 1993). *Dissertation Abstracts International, 54*(3), 1707–1708B.

Peterson, D. B. (1996). Executive coaching at work: The art of one-on-one change. *Consulting Psychology Journal: Practice and Research, 48,* 78–86.

Phillips, J. J. (1997). *Return on investment in training and performance improvement programs.* Houston, TX: Gulf.

Richard, J. T. (1999). Multimodal therapy: A useful model for the executive coach. *Consulting Psychology Journal: Practice and Research, 51,* 24–30.

Saporito, T. J. (1996). Business-linked executive development: Coaching senior executives. *Consulting Psychology Journal: Practice and Research, 48,* 96–103.

Smith, L. (1993). The executive's new coach. *Fortune, 128*(16), 126–128.

Sorcher, M. (1985). *Predicting executive success: What it takes to make it into senior management.* New York: Wiley.

Sperry, L. (1993). Working with executives: Consulting, counseling, and coaching. *Individual Psychology, 49,* 257–266.

Sperry, L. (1996). *Corporate therapy and consultation.* New York: Brunner/Mazel.

Strauss, A. L., & Corbin, J. M. (1998). *Basics of qualitative research: Techniques for developing grounded theory* (2nd ed.). Thousand Oaks, CA: Sage.

Thompson, A. D. (1987). A formative evaluation of an individualized coaching program for business managers and professionals (Doctoral dissertation, University of Minnesota, 1987). *Dissertation Abstracts International, 47*(12), 4339A.

Tobias, L. L. (1996). Coaching executives. *Consulting Psychology Journal: Practice and Research, 48,* 87–95.

Waclawski, J., & Church, A. H. (1999, August). *The 4-3-2-1 coaching model.* Paper presented at the meeting of the Academy of Management Conference, Chicago.

White, R. P., & DeVries, D. L. (1990, Winter). Making the wrong choice: Failure in the selection of senior-level managers. *Issues & Observations,* 1–6.

Witherspoon, R., & White, R. P. (1996a). Executive coaching: A continuum of roles. *Consulting Psychology Journal: Practice and Research, 48,* 124–133.

Witherspoon, R., & White, R. P. (1996b). Executive coaching: What's in it for you? *Training and Development Journal, 50,* 14–15.

Witherspoon, R., & White, R. P. (1997). *Four essential ways that coaching can help executives.* Greensboro, NC: Center for Creative Leadership.

Yammarino, F. J., & Bass, B. M. (1990). Transformational leadership and multiple levels of analysis. *Human Relations, 43,* 975–995.

# CHAPTER SEVEN

# A Consultant's Guide to Understanding and Promoting Emotional Intelligence in the Workplace

Shani Robins

*California School of Organizational Studies*
*Alliant International University*

The primary goal of this chapter is to provide organizational consulting psychologists with the theoretical, empirical, and application tools necessary for understanding emotional intelligence (EI) and applying it to the workplace. This chapter will first provide a working definition of EI, as well as a brief historical review of concepts closely related to EI that have emerged in the last century. The ubiquity of emotions in organizations will then be identified, making explicit the corresponding benefits of increasing EI. I will then discuss the strengths and weaknesses, on both scientific and practical grounds, of the major models and measures of EI, with special consideration of the implications to organizational consulting. Finally, I will describe an illustrative EI consulting intervention in detail. I conclude by suggesting that the consultant's own EI is a key factor in the consultation process itself.

## DEFINING EMOTIONAL INTELLIGENCE AND ITS UTILITY

EI constitutes a set of learnable skills that have cognitive, behavioral, physiological, and social components. These skills can help reduce conflict and facilitate both performance and satisfaction in the workplace (Cherniss & Goleman, 2001; Goleman, 1998). Included among EI skills are the abilities to use verbal and nonverbal cues, context, and knowledge of psychological dimensions to identify and regulate the emotions of oneself and others, to activate emotions at the right time and place and to the right degree, and to apply these processes adaptively in social interactions (Bar-On & Parker, 2000). By increasing EI, an individual will have increased knowledge about such, and greater facility for recognizing and regulating them when they occur in oneself and others.

Training in EI-related skills is quite extensive in U.S. organizations. As an example, General Electric alone reportedly spends over $1 billion a year on social and emotional competencies in leadership programs (Cherniss & Adler, 2000). Preliminary data suggest the value of EI training, but empirically sound outcome studies are needed before definitive conclusions can be drawn. Using broad and preliminary findings, Cherniss and Goleman (2001) provided a cost-benefit analysis on the economic utility of selecting, training, and developing EI-based competencies in organizational settings, and estimate that training in emotional competencies can result in as much as eight times the return on investment (ROI) compared with non-EI-based training. Cherniss estimated that American businesses each year lose between $5.6 and 16.8 billion by not having appropriate EI training (Cherniss, Goleman, Emmerling, Cowan, & Adler, 1998). Such variability in financial benefit estimations suggested by the wide dollar range might derive from the conceptual variability among the EI models and the absence of sufficient outcome studies conducted in organizational settings. Nevertheless, even the low end of estimated benefits of EI training helps explain the extraordinary growth of interest in EI during the last decade, particularly in organizational settings.

Salovey and Mayer (1989) coined the phrase *emotional intelligence* in their original studies on EI. In 1995, the American Dialect Society (1999) selected EI (and its derivative term EQ, or *Emotional Quotient*) as being among the most useful new words or phrases of the year. It was also during this period that Goleman published his popular works (1995, 1998), which catapulted the interest in this topic outside of academic, organizational, and lay circles. To more fully understand EI and its effects, it is useful to consider briefly the nature and functions of emotions.

## The Nature of Emotions

Although there are numerous and diverse definitions of emotions (Ekman & Davidson, 1994; Lewis & Haviland-Jones, 2000), there is also some convergence among definitions. Many conceptualizations of emotion consider the concept to reflect a subjective state that has cognitive, behavioral, and physiological components, interdependent processes between those components, and likely activators and outcomes. Each emotion has a different but overlapping pattern of those components and processes, as well as contextual and temporal patterns that are differentially associated with varied emotions (Lazarus, 1991).

**Emotions as Adaptations.** Whereas the Greeks viewed emotions as irrational animal passions that needed to be constrained, modern theories of emotions posit that emotions are adaptations that have important evolutionary functions that are critical to our survival (Buss, 1999; Darwin, 1965; Lazarus, 1991; Tooby & Cosmides, 1990). The emotion of anger, for instance, serves the adaptive functions of focusing our attention on interpersonal antagonisms, social conflict, cheating, and injustice, thus providing information to oneself for identifying priorities and expectations and modulating action (Schwartz & Clore, 1988). It additionally serves as a method of communicating threat to others (Ekman & Davidson, 1994). Fear, anxiety, and stress, on the other hand, focus our attention towards risks and the necessity of precaution, motivate the decision to flee, and enable flight (Buss, 1999). Evidence that emotions are evolutionary adaptations includes the observations that they appear in the earliest stages of infancy (Lewis, Alessandri, & Sullivan, 1990) and seem to be universal across cultures (Ekman, 1973; Ekman & Davidson, 1994).

Organizational consultants are often called on to develop programs, workshops, and mediation strategies (Gleason, 1997; Moore, 1996) to help attenuate the effects of the so-called negative emotions, particularly anger (Potter-Efron, 1998), an emotion that can result in workplace hostility, violence, and conflict (Averill, 1982; Deutsch & Coleman, 2000; Goleman, 1998; Resnick & Kausch, 1995). Efforts by consultants to reduce the frequency and intensity of an executive's anger or an employee's aggression (Resnick & Kausch, 1995) need to be accompanied by recognition and respect that anger has evolved as an adaptive information processing mechanism that might very well be serving important interpersonal functions within the present system (Robins & Novaco, 1999). As such, any reduction of its frequency and intensity might require either a compensatory reduction of the need for its functions, or finding alternative methods of adapting or satisfying those functions. EI presents a set of skills with the potential to accomplish both. For example, assertiveness in communication can enable grievances to be addressed directly, without the need to escalate to anger. Moreover, the need for anger might be reduced by changing one's cognitive appraisal to less conflict-oriented perceptions (Robins, 1998). Such cognitive-based regulation of emotions is one of the primary components of all EI models (Bar-On & Parker, 2000) and is briefly reviewed below.

**Emotion-Cognition Interactions.** Emotion regulation (Gross, 1998) dates back to the Greeks (Epictetus, 1985), who compared emotions to a storm and considered reasoning to be the tool for calming its waters. In the fifteenth century, monks described the need for even-temperedness, and called for a careful balance of casualness and dignity through self-insight (Ashkanasy, Hartel, & Zerbe, 2000). Gracian in 1647 (as cited in Ashkanasy et al., 2000) noted that the skilled expression and inhibition of emotion at appropriate times enables one to achieve social success in the royal courts, hence the term ingratiate oneself. Contemporary interest in emotions and their regulation through interactions with cognition predates the last century of psychology and is found in the writings of its architects, William James (1884), Freud (1959), and Darwin (1965). Rigorous research on emotions and their treatment occurred in the second half of the twentieth century in both experimental and clinical settings. Overviews of this work can be found in Beck, 1995, Ekman and Davidson, 1994, Ellis, 1993, Lazarus, 1991, LeDoux, 1996, Lewis and Haviland-Jones, 2000, Mayne and Bonanno, 2001, and Meichenbaum, 1990. This research established that how we perceive and interpret a situation will dramatically influence the emotions with which we respond to that situation, as well as the intensity of those emotions.

Our worldview, beliefs, attitudes, and values are the cognitive categories we use to parse and interpret our environment and people's actions. Interpreted as a threat, an action or situation is likely to elicit fear, or to be interpreted as an insult, and will likely result in anger. If interpreted as a compliment, the same behavior might elicit pride or joy. Interpreted as a source of hopelessness, it will likely contribute to depression (see, for example, Beck, 1995; Dalgleish & Power, 1999; Frijda, 1993; Ortony, Clore, & Collins, 1988; Scherer, Schorr, & Johnstone, 2001; Seligman, 1998; Triandis, 1997; Weiner, 1985). In organizations, being terminated might be interpreted as a conflict that activates a strong anger and fear response, because of perceived unfairness and a perceived lack of future options, respectively. Alternatively, someone else, or the same person a year later, might perceive that same occupational position as an obstacle that might have been blocking the expression of the person's development, and consequently might interpret the ostensibly negative event as an opportunity to pursue interests. Neurologically, emotion and cognitive systems that underlie these interactions are highly integrated (Damasio, 1994), providing further evidence as to the powerful influence of cognition on emotion. Indeed, our brain demonstrates considerable plasticity in rerouting its emotional connections and processes based on cognitive learning and behavioral experience (LeDoux, 1996).

Rather than perceive cognition, thinking, reasoning, or intelligence as being in conflict with emotion, leading researchers agree that it is more empirically realistic and useful to conceptualize emotions and cognitions as close, interactive partners. The term EI further highlights this fact, and is thus in and of itself a contribution to both fields. High EI includes developing recognition about which beliefs and attitudes, in which contexts, lead to which frequency and intensity of particular emotions. Moreover, it includes the skills for using that knowledge in regulating emotions. Learning when to interpret events as nonconflictual, and when behaviorally to shift from combative to cooperative communication styles, for example, enables the more adaptive application of EI.

# EMOTIONS IN ORGANIZATIONS AND THE NEED FOR EI

The industrial revolution and the advent of many people working together in close spaces within large corporations presented an emergent need to coordinate individual behavior and control idleness and antagonistic utterances (Taylor, 1947). Whereas in our ancestral past, a fight or flight response likely saved our lives whenever it was activated (Cannon, 1932; Lazarus, 1991), in the industrial age, those same mechanisms have been directed to numerous innocuous events such as copier and computer breakdowns, not getting promotions or pay raises, and long commutes to work, to name a few illustrative frustrations (Goleman, 1995).

Investigations regarding the roles, prevalence, and social and financial implications of emotions in the workplace have been conducted for over a century, but have expanded dramatically in the last decade (Ashforth & Humphrey, 1995; Ashkanasy et al., 2000; Fineman, 2000; Grandey, 2000). A growing body of research culminated in 1998 with the meeting of the First Annual Conference on Emotions and Organizational Life in San Diego, California, and more recently when a special issue of the *Journal of Organizational Behavior* (Fisher & Ashkanasy, 2000) was dedicated to emotions in organizations. Results indicate that the situations most relevant to positive emotions in the workplace are goal achievement, involvement in planning, receiving recognition, coping with a challenge, and acts of colleagues. Negative emotions seem to involve acts of management such as giving mixed messages, acts of colleagues such as lack of support or incompetence, acts of customers, and task problems, such as equipment breaking down or work overload (Ashkanasy et al., 2000).

Among the negative emotions found in the workplace, anger and the consequent aggression present a ubiquitous example (Fitness, 2000). Novaco (1986) and the Centers for Disease Control (1992) described workplace violence as a national epidemic. It is estimated that approximately 18 percent of Americans have witnessed assaults at work, and another 18 percent worry about becoming victims themselves (Toufexis, 1994). The National Crime Victimization Survey (U.S. Department of Justice, Bureau of Justice Statistics, 1998) indicated that annually in the workplace, more than two million Americans were the victims of physical attacks, six million were threatened, and sixteen million were harassed. The incidence of violent behavior among those who were laid off was nearly six times higher than that of their employed peers, even when the research controlled for psychiatric disorders and alcohol abuse. These are worrisome findings given recent trends of budgetary cuts and economic downsizing. It also helps explain why consultants are so often called on to help deal with anger, conflict, and violence in the workplace (Brown, Pryzwansky, & Schulte, 2001; Deutsch & Coleman, 2000). Particular forms of clinical dysfunctions such as narcissism or antisocial and borderline personality disorders have also been argued to be among the individual differences highly associated with workplace distress (Cavaiola & Lavender, 2000).

Despite the evolutionary adaptive nature of emotions to communicate information and motivate action, they can be dysfunctional if they reach pathological frequency and intensity. The cognitive processes that selectively activate emotions seem to have substantial influence over such hijackings. Activating emotions at the right place, at the right time, and to the right extent to facilitate interpersonal and social adaptation thus seems to be a skill, and one that is distinct from the traditional intellectual skills defined as intelligence.

# EI AND OTHER TYPES OF INTELLIGENCE

The study of intelligence developed throughout the twentieth century and was driven largely by testing motivations rather than theoretical questions (Sternberg, 2000). This psychometric approach promulgated tasks that tested the scope of one's vocabulary, reading comprehension, general information, and the ability to complete number series from memory and solve mathematical problems. The accumulated performance on verbal, visual, motor, and memory tasks, and the ability to respond quickly, were considered a general measure of intellectual capacity and one's ability to function and adapt. The extent to which these skills reflected everyday life performance began to be investigated with emerging subfields such as Practical Intelligence (PI; Sternberg & Wagner, 1986). Focus began to shift to definitions of intelligence that had greater ecological validity, such as the extent to which one adapts to social and interpersonal settings in everyday life, copes with conflict, and learns from experience. As the criticisms grew concerning the limits of the classic notions of intelligence, so did the favor grow regarding the notion of multiple intelligences (Cantor & Kihlstrom, 1987; Gardner, 1983, 1993; Sternberg, 1999a, 1999b) and other more inclusive constructs of functioning and adaptation, including wisdom (Baltes & Staudinger, 1996; Robins, 1998, 2000; Sternberg, 1990).

## Multiple Intelligences

The notion of myriad forms of intelligences across diverse domains has been suggested for close to a century (Hunt, 1928; Gardner, 1983, 1993; Sternberg, 1999a, 1999b, 2000; Sternberg & Wagner, 1986; Thorndike, 1936), with Gardner (1983) actually coining the term *"multiple intelligences."* This list of multiple types of intelligences is by no means exhaustive, but does give a flavor of the intellectual history that subtends the emergence of EI.

## Social Intelligence and Social Competence

Early pioneers in the field of the traditional, academic, g-ability intelligence had already envisioned the need to address social ability as part of intelligence, and conceptualized it as understanding others and acting or behaving wisely in relation to and in dealing with them (Thorndike, 1936; Hunt, 1928; Wechsler, 1940). For example, Hunt found that the scores of ninety-eight sales employees on the George Washington Social Intelligence (SI) Test correlated significantly ($r = .61$) with ratings of the ability to get along with people. Others defined SI as the ability to recognize and judge the feelings and motivations of others with empathy (Marlow, 1986), and to be able to do so from nonverbal cues (Sternberg & Smith, 1985). In addition to making sense of and acting on their social environment in purposive ways, SI also meant the ability to adapt to that environment and achieve desired outcomes in important domains (Cantor & Kihlstrom, 1987). Goals and plans are considered in some models to be more important than the behavior itself (Cantor & Kihlstrom, 1987), whereas in models of Social Competence (SC), it is the adaptive outcome that is more central; "SC is the possession and use of the ability to integrate thinking, feeling, and behavior to achieve social tasks and outcomes valued in the host context and culture" (Bar-On & Parker, 2000, p. 32). Although the need for SC seems universal (Buss, 1999), some of the specifics of what constitutes SC seem to be culturally and socially specific (Markus & Kitayama, 1991; Triandis, 1997). For example, extending a greeting to a potential customer or employee as a way of communicating intent to cooperate rather than threaten is quite universal. Whether one uses a handshake or a bow to do so, however, is culture-specific.

## Practical Intelligence

A model of Practical Intelligence (PI) was developed by Sternberg and Wagner (1986) in order to capture a person's analytic, creative, and practical abilities in everyday life. It is conceptually distinct from academic intelligence, which is typically applied to problems that are well defined, are formulated by others, are complete in the information they provide, typically have one correct answer, one or few methods in getting to that answer, are different from ordinary experience, and are likely to elicit little intrinsic interest. The everyday-type problems attributed to PI, on the other hand, are usually intrinsically interesting but poorly defined. They need to be reformulated, lack the necessary information to be solved, and have multiple solutions, as well as multiple methods for arriving at those solutions. PI is sometimes compared to SI (Cantor & Kihlstrom, 1987), but Sternberg points out that although PI deals with everyday problems, and though many are social, they need not be necessarily so. PI includes a person's capacity to recognize and capitalize on their strengths while at the same time compensate for their weaknesses. It includes the ability to accomplish personally valued goals, and to find a more optimal fit between the individual and the demands of the individual's environment by adapting to the environment, shaping it, or selecting a new environment.

### Personal Intelligence

Gardner (1983, 1993) conceptualizes personal intelligence as consisting of intrapersonal intelligence and interpersonal intelligence. The former involves self-awareness and self-regulation, whereas the latter involves social awareness and relationship management. Intrapersonal intelligence in this model involves having access to one's internal emotional states and being able to distinguish subtle differences between states. Interpersonal intelligence involves not one's own feelings, but rather the capacity to read the moods, intentions, and desires of others, sometimes called empathy, and potentially to act on this knowledge. Personal intelligence is correlated with both EI and psychological mindedness (McCallum & Piper, 1997).

## MODELS AND MEASURES OF EI

EI has its direct roots in the literature on social, practical, personal, and multiple intelligence spanning much of the twentieth century. EI emerged more explicitly as a field with the emergence of the concept of Emotional Quotient (EQ) (Bar-On, 1997; Cooper & Sawaf, 1996). The phrase *emotional intelligence* was first used in 1989 (Salovey & Mayer, 1989) and skyrocketed to the public's attention and to organizational domains with the publication of the books titled *Emotional Intelligence* (Goleman, 1995) and *Working with Emotional Intelligence* (Goleman, 1998), respectively. The field has developed considerably since those books' publication, as suggested by the recently published, more scholarly *The Handbook of Emotional Intelligence* (Bar-On & Parker, 2000), and has also been comprehensively applied to the workplace (Cherniss & Goleman, 2001; Weisinger, 1998). An overview comparing and contrasting several prominent models and measures of EI is presented in the following sections, along with their strengths and weaknesses.

The models and measures of EI can be divided into self-report measures and those based on performance. Examples of measures in the former category include those by Bar-On (1997), Mayer, Salovey, and Caruso (2000), Boyatzis, Goleman, and Rhee (2000), and Simmons (1997). Performance-based assessment methodologies require test-takers to identify particular emotions from photographs of facial expressions, videotaped monologues, and written samples (Mayer, DiPaolo, & Salovey, 1990).

## Goleman's Emotional Competence Inventory

Goleman presents a broad model and measure of EI that includes both self- and others' reports (Goleman, 1995, 1998; Boyatzis et al., 2000). Goleman maintains that people's intelligence in solving academic problems says very little about their ability to succeed in solving practical problems in the real world. Fox and Spector (1999) provide interview outcome evidence that job acquisition depends largely on EI rather than IQ. They demonstrate that IQ and EI are distinct and that the latter provides unique contributions to workplace success. These distinctions are supported through extensive research programs (Sternberg, 2000; Sternberg & Wagner, 1986), which have demonstrated that people adept at one may not be so adept in the other (Sternberg, 2000; Rogoff & Lave, 1984), and that there exist individual differences in performance beyond IQ (Murphy, 1996).

Consistent with the intelligence literature (Gardner, 1983; Sternberg, 2000) is Goleman's assertion that only 20 percent of the variance of people's professional, interpersonal, and social success is accounted for by cognitive intelligence tests. Within that literature, it is argued that the remaining 80 percent is explained by personality traits, motivations, and multiple interpersonal and social abilities, of which EI is only one (Bar-On & Parker, 2000; Sternberg, 2000). In contrast, Goleman concludes that most of that 80 percent remaining is explained entirely by EI. Specifically, the more globally encompassing components of Goleman's model of EI (1995) include the ability to monitor oneself and persist in the face of frustrations, to be able to control impulses and delay gratification, and to be able to regulate one's moods and keep distress from swamping the ability to think. According to Goleman (1998), EI additionally emphasizes the capacity for recognizing our own feelings and those of others, for motivating ourselves, and for managing emotions well in ourselves and our relationships.

Based on these competency categories, as well as those obtained from hundreds of validated performance studies of managers, executives, and leaders in North America (Spencer & Spencer, 1993), Boyatzis et al. (2000) developed a comprehensive list of noncognitive competencies, which they factor and cluster analyzed. These results led to their empirically based list of five clusters (Boyatzis et al., 2000). This list includes a Self-Awareness cluster that is comprised of Emotional Awareness, Accurate Self-Assessment, and Self-Confidence; a Self-Management cluster that includes: Self-Control, Trustworthiness, Conscientiousness, and Adaptability; Achievement Orientation (initiative); a Social Awareness Cluster that includes Empathy, Organizational Awareness, and Service Orientation; and a Social Skills cluster that includes Leadership, Communication, Influence, Change Catalyst, Conflict Management, Building Bonds, Teamwork Collaboration, and Developing Others.

These categories comprise the latest version of the Emotional Competence Inventory (ECI) (Boyatzis & Burckle, 1999). This inventory claims to account for a great deal of the noncognitive intelligence variance in organizational performance. Though research as to the validity of this conceptualization of EI is limited, a recent study by Boyatzis (1999) suggests that experienced organizational consultants that were ranked as superior along these EI competencies contributed significantly more profit to the firm from their accounts, as compared to those whose performance ranked as average along these competencies. Moreover, McClelland (1999) demonstrated that the bonuses paid to top executives, associated with their division's financial performance, were highly predictive as to whether they were in the superior rather than the average range of EI competencies as measured by this inventory. Whether the ECI is a useful measure in practical applications, however, might depend on whether the organizational context in which it is used is broad, complex, and varied. In such contexts, numerous and varied competencies are likely to be needed, and tests such as the ECI are more likely to be effective. A major disadvantage of using an all-encompassing net such as the ECI is that it is unclear as to what is being measured, and thus the test might be likely to be less predictive when narrower questions regarding emotional regulation are evaluated.

Sternberg (1999b, 2000), as well as Davies, Stankov, and Roberts (1998), argue that Goleman's conceptualization of EI is indeed too all-encompassing. They note that it is highly correlated with many areas of personality (for example, extroversion) and motivation (for example, achievement drive). Sternberg notes that, in addition to EI, Goleman's model also includes many aspects of social intelligence and PI such as interpersonal skills, flexibility, managing self, and managing others. For the construct of EI, Sternberg favors the considerably more restrictive model of Salovey and Mayer (1989) over that of Goleman. The implication of this distinction to consultation is that in organizational settings that are more clearly emotionally charged, wherein the ability to identify others' emotions and regulate one's own emotions are the paramount competencies needed, the broad brush of the ECI is likely to fall short (Sternberg, 1999b). Rather, a more restrictive model and measure of EI is warranted, which focuses primarily on the identification and regulation of emotion. Mayer and Salovey present the best known of such models.

## Mayer and Salovey: Multifactor EI Scale (MEIS)

Salovey and Mayer (1989) coined the term *emotional intelligence* over a decade ago and defined it narrowly as "the ability to perceive and understand emotional information, or more specifically to monitor one's own and others' feelings and emotions, to discriminate among them, and to use this information to guide one's thinking and actions" (Salovey & Mayer, 1989, p. 189). More recently, Mayer and Salovey (1993), and Mayer, Salovey, and Caruso (2000), identified five components of EI: the accurate perception and adaptive expression of emotion; emotional facilitation of thinking; understanding and analyzing emotions;

employing emotional knowledge; and the reflective regulation of emotions to promote emotional and intellectual growth. Their Multifactor EI Scale (MEIS) (Mayer, Salovey, & Caruso, 2000) was intended to reliably measure these five factors. Its five scales have internal consistency alphas ranging from .81 to .96, with a full-scale alpha of .96.

The MEIS (Mayer & Salovey, 1993) is based on a narrower model than the ECI (Boyatzis et al., 2000). This has the advantage of high construct and content validity in organizational contexts in which the identification and regulation of emotions are of paramount importance and need to dominate the consultant's conceptualization of EI. However, if contexts call for including other constructs (for example, extroversion or personal motivation) as part of the EI measure, Boyatzis et al.'s (2000) model has the advantage of being much broader in scope.

Second, the methods by which the two tests gather information are qualitatively different. The ECI is based on how the person being evaluated is perceived by others, in contrast to the MEIS, which is based on a behavioral measure (the person's ability or performance on an EI-related task such as identifying the emotion of a person in a story or photograph). Because it is performance-based, the MEIS is independent of the person's reputation, making it less susceptible to rater bias.

To elaborate, the methodology of the MEIS involves the person being tested viewing a picture of a face or reading a scenario using interactive multimedia on a computer screen. The person is then asked, "What emotion is the person in the story feeling?." This approach is thought to represent a person's actual EI capacity rather than someone else's opinion of that capacity (Mayer & Salovey, 1993). A correct answer is judged by normative consistencies within our culture, as well as evolutionary cross-cultural universals regarding the categorization and labeling of emotions (Ekman, 1973). This qualitative difference in how the data is acquired suggests that the MEIS is likely to have higher external or ecological validity than the ECI. Additional research is needed, however, to evaluate fully this possible difference.

One way of compensating for the limitations of the self-report approach is to incorporate into an assessment tool a set of validity scales. Such a mechanism was implemented in another prominent EI instrument developed by Bar-On (1997).

## Reuven Bar-On: Emotional Quotient Inventory (EQ-i)

The third prominent model and measure reviewed here are those developed by Bar-On (1997). Bar-On was the first to use the abbreviation EQ (Emotional Quotient), and defined it as "an array of non-cognitive capabilities, competencies and skills that influence one's ability to succeed in coping with environmental demands and pressures" (Bar-On, 1997, p. 14). This conceptualization led to his developing a self-report measure, the Emotional Quotient Inventory (EQ-i).

The advantage of the EQ-i is that it is quite comprehensive, which can also be a disadvantage. As with the ECI, the EQ-i also attempts to measure both personality and intellectual dimensions, as well as emotional dimensions. The scale has 133 items organized in five categories, each of which has several subcategories. The category of *intrapersonal abilities* largely overlaps with the other models' dimensions of emotional perception and expression, and includes the subcategories of Emotional Self-Awareness, Assertiveness, Self-Regard, and Self-Actualization. The second category of *interpersonal abilities* includes Interpersonal Relationships, Social Responsibility, and Empathy. This construct overlaps with Goleman's ECI category of social awareness, but not with Mayer and Salovey's MEIS (1993), which does emphasize social interactions. The category of Adaptability includes problem solving, reality testing, and flexibility. The category of stress management includes stress tolerance and impulse control. And the category of general mood includes happiness and optimism. The latter three categories are largely unique to the EQ model. The EQ-i's four scales have internal consistency alphas ranging from .69 to .89, with a full-scale alpha of .76 (Bar-On, 1997).

Mayer, Salovey, and Caruso (2000) criticized the EQ-i's inclusiveness, noting that the full scale correlates highly with measures of personality (for example, optimism) and mental ability (for example, problem solving), which is why they refer to it as a mixed model. Its inclusiveness, however, might also account for its ability to predict occupational performance, job satisfaction, and the ability to cope with work-related stress (Bar-On, 1997). The contrast between Bar-On's general model of EI and Mayer and Salovey's narrower model might explain the modest correlation between them ($r = .36$; Mayer, Salovey, & Caruso, 2000). A more detailed account comparing their subscales can be found in Bar-On (1997), and Ciarrochi, Chan, and Caputi (2000). The fact that the EQ-i utilizes a self-report measure whereas the MEIS utilizes an ability measure might additionally help explain the low correlation between them. The EQ-i does incorporate several validity scales, including those that assess the respondent's tendency to have exaggerated positive or negative responses. The score is adjusted based on those validity scores.

## Implications for Organizational Consultants

The relatively weak relationship between these scales, which are supposed to be measuring something similar, suggests that they might be measuring somewhat different constructs, or at least different aspects of the same construct. This conclusion has significant implications to both investigators and organizational consultants. Academic researchers studying EI must conceptually and empirically reconcile weak correlations between existing instruments that are all ostensibly measuring EI (Ciarrochi et al., 2000). Either the models or measures need revising, or more apt names for what they are really measuring are needed.

Organizational consultants must therefore be careful not to assume that there is a single, universally accepted measure of EI. It is likely that the three measures of EI reviewed here are measuring divergent skills, and that the format that the measures utilize in data acquisition might impact the validity of that data. In particular, self-report measures of EI (for example, ECI) are more likely to have poor criterion validity and low relation to performance-based measures of EI (for example, MEIS) (Janovics & Christiansen, 2001).

As a practical matter, in organizational settings in which report bias is more likely, performance-based measures of EI are particularly warranted (Smither, 1998). For example, in the area of personnel selection (Cook, 1998), the ECI is likely to be more biased than the MEIS, given the risk of self-assessment distortion among job applicants (Jeanneret & Silzer, 1998). In organizational contexts in which more inclusive measures are useful, the ECI's self-report bias must be weighed against its comprehensive scope, which in this context is advantageous. The EQ-i provides an option for measuring a more comprehensive conceptualization of EI with self-report methods, while at the same time using built-in validity scales to compensate for report bias.

## Other Models of EI

Davis (1996) and Marlow (1986) conceive of EI as social perspective-taking and empathy—the ability to free oneself from one's own view, and to recognize and understand the thoughts, feelings, and motives of the self and others. Indeed, EI, as measured by the MEIS, correlates with self-reported empathy ($r = .43$) (Mayer, Salovey, & Caruso, 2000). Additionally, Bar-On's (1997) conceptualization of EQ explicitly includes empathy among its list of interpersonal abilities, and is shown to be inversely correlated with antisocial characteristics ($r = -.52$) and aggression ($r = -.45$) (Bar-On, 1997). This suggests that the more empathy an individual has, the higher his EI and the less likely he is to act inappropriately or aggressively in social situations. In terms of consulting, these measures of empathy are especially encouraged for implementation in organizational situations wherein frustration, anger, and aggression have historically been found to be frequent or intense. Which measure is most valid in which context has yet to be evaluated.

Cooper (1996) proposed another globally inclusive model of EI that he calls the EQ-Map. He defined EQ as "the ability to sense, understand and effectively apply the power and acumen of emotions as a source of human energy, information, trust, creativity, and influence" (p. 1). He conceptualized EQ using five major dimensions with several subscales in each. Like most EI models, the model includes an Emotional Awareness dimension with the subscales of

Self-Awareness, Emotional Expression, and Emotional Awareness of Others. However, like Goleman's ECI and Bar-On's EQ-i, Cooper's model is highly inclusive. Among its additional dimensions are Competencies that include Intentionality, Creativity, Resilience, Interpersonal Connections, and Constructive Discontent. The EQ-Map also includes a Values and Attitudes Dimension that is composed of Outlook, Compassion, Intuition, Trust, Personal Power, and Integrated Self subscales. Unlike other EI models, it also aims to capture information on the Current Environment of an individual who is attempting to adapt to that environment, operationalized by Cooper in terms of the Life Pressures and Life Satisfaction subscales. This makes it more consistent with systems theory models of emotions (Robins & Novaco, 1999). Also unique to the EQ-Map was Cooper's inclusion of a dimension of Outcomes, which lists General Health, Quality of Life, Relationship Quotient, and Optimal Performance subscales. Given its highly inclusive and comprehensive structure, the EQ-Map is a good measure if more than emotional dimensions are the focus of study. In particular, if a consultant's aim is to also evaluate interpersonal and environmental dimensions, the EQ-Map is likely to be a better choice of comprehensive inventories as compared to the ECI and EQ-i.

Davies et al. (1998) provided an even more limited conceptualization of EI than Mayer and Salovey. They conducted an empirical evaluation of the construct and discriminant validity of EI models using a wide variety of instruments of cognitive aptitudes, verbal abilities, social functioning, and personality variables. They concluded that once personality variables, traditional intelligence, and general cognitive abilities factors are accounted for, there is very little variance left for EI but the "the ability to perceive emotional information in visual and auditory stimuli," which is how they define and measure EI (Davies et. al., 1998, p. 1001). They consequently suggested that the current models of EI might be describing something other than a single, distinct construct. More details on these and other models can be found in Bar-On and Parker (2000), and Cherniss and Goleman (2001).

# CRITICISMS AND LIMITATIONS OF EI

Despite the exuberance regarding EI in both academic and organizational settings, there have also been those who have criticized the construct, due in some part to that very exuberance (Fisher, 1998; Shiller, 2000). Among those critics, Barrett, Miguel, Tan, and Hurud (2001) are perhaps the most ardent skeptics of both the construct of EI as well as its testing, which they perceive to be simply a subset of personality testing. Barrett et al. (2001) presented a comprehensive meta-analysis that they argued provided converging evidence that EI lacks both validity and reliability. They noted that Goleman's assertion that EI is more important than cognitive abilities was based on data that they contend supported exactly the opposite findings. Moreover, they argued that the construct validity and operational measurement of EI constructs is inadequate (Barrett, 1992). In particular, they contended that a scale from one EI test that predicts job performance in one organization cannot be generalized to another test having a scale with the same name (Barrett et al., 2001). In this paper, the authors present a comprehensive set of examples in which EI advocates seemed guilty of selectively reporting and excluding data, making claims without empirical evidence to support those claims, and conveniently relabeling phenomena to support their assertions (Barrett et al., 2001). In reporting these negative EI results from their prodigious meta-analysis, however, they contrasted them with the positive results in which EI dimensions were shown to be highly relevant to predicting successes in the workplace. Thus, although they identified genuine weaknesses that future EI researchers need to address, the field of EI itself also presented a considerable set of positive results (Cherniss & Goleman, 2001) that need to be categorized, quantified, and standardized to better understand the conditions under which those results occur and find a common language to communicate about them in the scientific and consulting literatures.

# EI IN THE WORKPLACE

Despite the diversity among EI models and the heated debates regarding their validity and reliability, there is a growing body of evidence that suggests that whatever EI is, it seems to be relevant to the workplace, can be promoted through training, and potentially has significant implications to the bottom line (Cherniss & Goleman, 2001). A comprehensive review of the effects of EI in the workplace can be found in Goleman (1998), who asserts, for example, that in leadership nearly 90 percent of the competencies necessary for success are social and emotional in nature, including self-confidence, flexibility, empathy, and the ability to get along with others (Lusch & Serpkeuci, 1990; McClelland, 1999; Rosier, 1996; Spencer & Spencer, 1993).

In their comprehensive volume regarding EI in the workplace, Cherniss and Goleman (2001) reported several key findings. Among sales representatives for a large American appliance manufacturer, those who were most *conscientious* (defined by EI-related dimensions such as self-disciplined, careful, and scrupulous) had the largest volume of sales (Cherniss & Goleman, 2001). Concerning hiring, training, and managing performance, it appears that star performers do not have to be at the ceiling on every EI measure in order to demonstrate superior performance, but rather only to pass a threshold on several of the measures across Goleman's four clusters (Cherniss & Goleman, 2001). In terms of hiring at the highest level of the organization, data from over 500 top executive hires across three continents demonstrated that the usual process of just using technical skill and measures of cognitive ability are lacking. Emotional competencies are reported to be better predictors of success (Cherniss & Goleman, 2001), and consequently are recommended to be counted more heavily than one's intellectual ability score as a method for improving senior-level hiring practices. Consultants advising applicants should note that EI predicts both the interviewer's affective response and their likelihood of hire (Fox & Spector, 1999).

Very recent work is beginning to shed light on team-based EI measures [Workgroup EI Profile, Version 3 (WEIP-3)] (Jordan, Ashkanasy, Hartel, & Hooper, in press). These early findings suggest that high EI teams outperform low EI teams, but only in the initial stage of their tasks. Over time, their performance seems to equalize. These results suggest that EI in the workplace provides a similar expertise and cohesiveness that emerges over time experientially. That savings of time for reaching proficient collaboration among group members may significantly enhance the bottom line.

## Selecting for EI

Some studies (see, for example, Harris Education Research Council, 1991) have suggested that more than half of employees lack the motivation to keep learning and improving in their jobs. It is also suggested that 40 percent are not able to work cooperatively with fellow employees, and only 19 percent of those applying for entry-level jobs have sufficient self-discipline in their work habits (Harris Education Research Council, 1991). This implies the need for careful selection of new hires.

An EI competency-based selection program was implemented by L'Oreal for hiring sales people (Spencer & Spencer, 1993). In an interview, applicants were asked to generate several positive and negative situations that they were then asked to resolve. Their responses were analyzed for EI competencies and applicants scoring highest on those were hired. The competency-based-selected employees were estimated to have generated a total of $2,558,360 more revenue annually than their counterparts who were selected by the traditional criterion of cognitive skills and technical knowledge. Such results support the use of EI instruments as screening tools for selecting employees. As is pointed out in other sections, given the weaknesses of any one tool, using multiple tools is likely to provide greater validity.

## Consulting to Increase EI in the Workplace

American industry currently spends over $50 billion each year on training, and four out of five leading-edge companies report that EI is one of the areas they are trying to promote in that training (American Society for Training and Development, 1997; Cherniss & Adler, 2000). Burke and Day (1986) conducted a meta-analysis of the effectiveness of management training programs, many of which are the precursors of today's EI training. They found that human relations training programs were, on average, highly effective as evaluated by both objective measures such as performance and absenteeism, or subjective measures such as self-awareness and behavior ratings by coworkers and supervisors. Such training can result in more than a standard deviation of improvement in performance (Bar-On & Parker, 2000; Latham & Frayne, 1989), an increase that "is worth between 19 percent and 48 percent of economic value added in nonsales jobs and results in a 48 to 120 percent increase in productivity in sales jobs" (Cherniss & Goleman, 2001, p. 48).

Goldstein and Sorcher (1974) pioneered a set of techniques that can be seen as being directly related to modern EI concepts. Their approach used modeling, role playing practice, feedback, and reinforcement, for training supervisors to be more effective in handling the interpersonal aspects of their jobs. Their methods included the use of training videos to simulate the appropriate behaviors for addressing problematic workplace situations. Once key aspects of those behaviors were discussed, the trainee would emulate those behaviors and be reinforced towards mastery-level performance. This type of modeling training has been reported to be highly effective (Russ-Eft & Zenger, 1997).

A more recent trend involves that of executive coaching (Kilburg, 2002; Goldsmith, Lyons, & Freas, 2000), wherein a wide range of managers' and executives' EI competencies are evaluated, and individualized programs for improvement of those competencies are developed and implemented. Outcome studies of such programs indicate that the targeted competencies are significantly improved relative to nontargeted competencies in the same person (Cherniss & Adler, 2000; Peterson, 1996), but far more empirical research is needed (Kampa-Kokesch & White, 2002).

Given results of this kind, MBA programs such as that found in Case Western Reserve University's Weatherhead School of Management have begun to explicitly provide training for social and emotional competencies as part of their curriculum. As a result, compared to their counterparts who proceed through the more traditional program, there is evidence that students who are provided with EI training longitudinally demonstrate positive changes in initiative, flexibility, achievement drive, empathy, self-confidence, persuasiveness, networking, self-control, and group management (Boyatzis, 1996).

Based on the existing research, the Consortium for Research on EI in Organizations has recently empirically identified the factors that most effectively lead to social and emotional learning in work settings (Cherniss et al., 1998), and which constitute the modern EI training protocol. First, given the neural and behavioral entrenchment of emotional pathways, repeated practice is needed to facilitate change with the expectation that it will take time and there will be setbacks. Techniques for maintaining a client's motivation must be implemented regularly.

In the first phase of change using such approaches, a consultant evaluates the competencies that the organization demands and in which the client is apparently lacking (Spencer, McClelland, & Kelner, 1997), and must both enable the client to see the benefits of mastering those competencies as well as socialize him to the process of acquiring them through cognitive, behavioral, and physiological changes. For example, supervisors are more likely to work towards gaining empathy if they feel confident that increasing their empathic responses will produce more committed, motivated, and productive employees (Davis, 1996; Marlow, 1986). One must also evaluate whether the client is committed and realistic as to the requirements for change. If not, more time should be spent on increasing the client's motivation to change. Once the motivation is high, specific, meaningful, and realistic goals are likely to maintain that motivation (Lock & Latham, 1990). These goals should be developed in collaboration with the client so that the consultant is not pursuing goals that are contrary to the client's objectives. Importantly, the organization should provide a supportive environment for developing, practicing, and encouraging the EI competencies. This includes having in place supervisors who will both model and reinforce those competencies (Manz & Sims, 1986).

In the second phase, the client attempts several changes. He seeks to improve his ability to identify his own emotions, and to distinguish them from the emotions of others and improve his ability to use multiple and increasingly subtle cues to identify others' emotions. In this phase, the client additionally attempts to increase his empathy in regarding others' emotions, improve his ability to identify contingencies between cognitive appraisals and emotions, and improve his ability to regulate his emotions. The client also learns to integrate thoughts, emotions, and physiological arousal and behavior to achieve social tasks, increase tolerance for ambiguity and complexity of emotional experiences, identify environmental cues that influence emotions, and develop reward contingencies for practicing higher EI.

Much of this work is quite interpersonal, and a good relationship must therefore be established between the consultant and the client. Because emotional states have behavioral and physiological components and are thus highly experiential (Ekman & Davidson, 1994), a good deal of the EI training needs to be experiential (Robins & Hayes, 1993). This requires repeated practice and role playing, with feedback and homework between sessions to continue practicing the new emotional responses and behavioral techniques. A final step of this phase is to inform clients that setbacks are inevitable and should not be taken as a sign of failure. This can help prevent relapse, which adds considerable value to the training and has been found by management to help increase transfer of skills to the job (Tziner, Haccoun, & Kadish, 1991).

Although clients are, in this model by this phase, able to implement EI competencies, that implementation is not necessarily fluent or automatic. In the third and last phase, therefore, clients need to be encouraged to form social support groups with similar-minded people who also want to practice their EI skills and will provide mutual reinforcement (Powell, 1994). As a last step of an EI intervention, the consultant should evaluate the outcome of that intervention. This includes not just using measures such as the ECI or EQ-i to assess EI competencies gained, but also evaluating the intervention's effectiveness with other measures of performance and productivity (Jeanneret & Silzer, 1998; Smither, 1998). Unfortunately, outcome measures are rarely taken, and when they are, they are usually in the form of participants' opinions of the intervention (American Society for Training and Development, 1997).

As a point of caution, some EI intervention effects might be misleading. For example, American Express implemented an emotional competence program for its financial advisors (Hays, 1999). Although those in the program were reported to have experienced an 18.1 percent increase in business performance, it was only 1.9 percent higher than the 16.2 percent increase for control group members who did not participate in the training. Other EI effects, when promoted in isolation, can actually be detrimental to performance. Emotional regulation of anger, for example, can result in reduced overall levels of functioning. In organizational systems in which anger serves a particular and necessary function (Robins & Novaco, 1999), the unilateral reduction of anger can cause the valuable part of the function no longer to be addressed. An executive's anger, for example, might have come to be the instigating factor for increasing employees' motivation (Steers & Porter, 1991), and eliminating that anger might eliminate the motivation. It is therefore recommended that a systems analysis be conducted prior to undertaking EI interventions, predicting in advance possible adverse perturbations that might result in that system, and addressing system-wide changes in congruence with the EI intervention.

## The Consultant's Own EI

Consulting for EI often necessitates consulting with EI. The consultant must communicate information, not just with technical skill, but with positive role modeling of EI, as well. For example, considerable empathy is often needed in assisting a client with the task of changing his perception of self and others. The general process of consulting involves going into a new domain that is often conflict-ridden, trying to understand the dynamics of that domain, and attempting to facilitate positive outcomes (Hale, 1998). Inevitably, the consultant will run into internal politics, power struggles, animosity, group affiliation pulls and pushes, and the complex emotional currents of the organization (Brown et al., 2001). Although consulting is often interesting, curious, and satisfying, the nature of the job can also promote frustration, anger, and anxiety (Deutsch & Coleman, 2000). If that were not the case, the organization probably wouldn't need a consultant. In order to meet these consulting challenges, one must have the competency of identifying those emotions when they occur in others and oneself, and be able to regulate them (Deutsch & Coleman, 2000). Moreover, emotional responses from employees and executives, if perceived with EI, can provide information that speaks volumes (Brown et al., 2001; Schwarz & Clore, 1988).

The consultation processes themselves thus seem to demand at least a moderate amount of EI. A consultant, particularly if hired to train clients for EI, needs that much more of it as she is also serving as an example for the clients' observational learning. The clients are acquiring EI through factual information acquisition, as well as through observing the emotional responses of the consultant (Russ-Eft & Zenger, 1997). This implies that consultants in the EI realm have a responsibility to continue to develop their own EI competencies, and that organizations should use a consultant's level of EI as part of their process for selection.

## SUMMARY AND CONCLUSIONS

Emotions and EI have been established as being highly relevant aspects of the workplace. The weak relationship between EI scales suggests that they might be measuring somewhat different constructs, or at least different aspects of the same construct. This conclusion has implications to both investigators and organizational consultants. Academic researchers studying EI must reconcile the weak correlations among existing measures that are all ostensibly measuring EI. They need to either converge on a few theoretical models and operationalized measures of EI that improve on those correlations, or rename the existing instruments to more accurately reflect the diverse constructs they are measuring. Concurrently, consultants must recognize that present models and measures of EI are likely to be identifying divergent skills, and thus must decide when and where to apply each scale. Empirical studies of the discriminant and convergent validity of scales based on the existing EI models have barely begun, but already reveal that the comprehensive models of EI seem to include both emotional measures as well as reinvention of older concepts such as personality, whereas the narrower models might indeed be measuring a genuinely novel construct.

As a practical matter, whether or not the more inclusive models and scales are measuring constructs other than EI might be an issue of greater concern to the researcher than to the organizational executive. EI, personality traits, and thinking abilities are all useful for the workplace and need to be measured, regardless of how they are parsed out linguistically. Although the narrower scales are more likely measuring just EI, it is likely rare that an executive would want a potential employee to have only high EI, but not positive personality traits or high intelligence. The exception might be a case wherein emotional regulation skills are a specific priority and the employer does not want to dilute the effects of measuring it with other constructs. Otherwise, the worries about the construct and content validity of the various measures of EI should be left to the academics, whereas the practical usefulness of using multiple measures can be enjoyed by consultants and their clients.

# References

American Dialect Society. (1999). *American Dialect Society: Words of the year.* Retrieved November 2001, from http://www.americandialect.org/woty

American Society for Training and Development. (1997). *Benchmarking forum member-to-member survey results.* Alexandria, VA: Author.

Ashforth, B. E., & Humphrey, R. H. (1995). Emotion in the workplace: A reappraisal. *Human Relations, 48,* 97–125.

Ashkanasy, N. M., Hartel, C.E.J., & Zerbe, W. J. (Eds.). (2000). *Emotions in the workplace: Research, theory, and practice.* Westport, CT: Quorum/Greenwood.

Averill, J. R. (1982). *Anger and aggression: An essay on emotion.* New York: Springer-Verlag.

Baltes, B. B., & Staudinger, U. M. (1996). *Interactive minds: Life-span perspectives on the social foundation of cognition.* Cambridge, MA: Cambridge University Press.

Bar-On, R. (1997). *Bar-On Emotional Quotient Inventory (EQ-i): Technical Manual.* Toronto, Ontario, Canada: Multi-Health Systems.

Bar-On, R., & Parker, J.D.A. (Eds.). (2000). *The handbook of emotional intelligence.* San Francisco: Jossey-Bass.

Barrett, G. V. (1992). Clarifying construct validity: Definitions, processes, and models. *Human Performance, 5,* 13–58.

Barrett, G. V., Miguel, R. F., Tan, J. A., & Hurud, J. M. (2001, April). *Emotional intelligence: The Madison Avenue approach to science and professional practice.* Paper presented at the 16th annual conference of the Society of Industrial and Organizational Psychology, San Diego, CA.

Beck, J. (1995). *Cognitive therapy: Basics and beyond.* New York: Guilford Press.

Boyatzis, R. E. (1996). Competencies can be developed, but not in the way we thought. *Capability, 2,* 25–41.

Boyatzis, R. E. (1999). *The financial impact of competencies in leadership and management of consulting firms.* Cleveland, OH: Case Western Reserve University, Department of Organizational Behavior.

Boyatzis, R. E., & Burckle, M. (1999). *Psychometric properties of the ECI: Technical note.* Boston: Hay/McBer Group.

Boyatzis, R. E., Goleman, D., & Rhee. K. S. (2000). Clustering competence in emotional intelligence: Insights from the Emotional Competency Inventory (ECI). In R. Bar-On & J.D.A. Parker (Eds.), *The handbook of emotional intelligence.* San Francisco: Jossey-Bass.

Brown, D., Pryzwansky, W. B., & Schulte, A. C. (2001). Organizational consultation. In *Psychological consultation: Introduction to theory and practice* (5th ed, pp. 85–107). Needham Heights, MA: Allyn & Bacon.

Burke, M., J. & Day, R. R. (1986). A cumulative study of the effectiveness of managerial training. *Journal of Applied Psychology, 71,* 232–245.

Buss, D. (1999). *Evolutionary psychology: The new science of the mind.* Needham Heights, MA: Allyn & Bacon.

Cannon, W. (1932). *The wisdom of the body.* New York: Norton.

Cantor, N., & Kihlstrom, J. (1987). *Personality and social intelligence.* Hillsdale, NJ: Erlbaum.

Cavaiola, A. A., & Lavender, N. J. (2000). *Toxic coworkers: How to deal with dysfunctional people on the job.* Oakland, CA: New Harbinger.

Centers for Disease Control. (1992). *Homicide in the U.S. workplace: A strategy for prevention and research* (NIOSH Publication No. 92–103). Washington, DC: U.S. Government Printing Office.

Cherniss, C., & Adler, M. (2000*). Promoting emotional intelligence in organizations.* Alexandria, VA: American Society for Training and Development.

Cherniss, C., & Goleman, D. (Eds.). (2001). *The emotionally intelligent workplace: How to select for, measure, and improve emotional intelligence in individuals, groups, and organizations.* San Francisco, CA: Jossey-Bass.

Cherniss, C., Goleman, D., Emmerling, R., Cowan, K., & Adler, M. (1998). *Bringing emotional intelligence to the workplace.* New Brunswick, NJ: Rutgers University, Consortium for Research on Emotional Intelligence in Organizations.

Ciarrochi, J. V., Chan, A.Y.C., & Caputi, P. (2000). A critical evaluation of the emotional intelligence construct. *Personality and Individual Differences, 28,* 539–561.

Cook, M. (1998). *Personnel selection* (3rd ed.). New York: Wiley.

Cooper, R. K. (1996). *EQ map interpretation guide.* San Francisco: AIT and Essi Systems.

Cooper, R. K., & Sawaf, A. (1996). *Executive EQ: Emotional intelligence in leadership and organizations.* New York: Grosset & Dunlap.

Dalgleish, T., & Power, M. J. (Eds.). (1999). *The handbook of cognition and emotion.* New York: Wiley.

Damasio, A. R. (1994). *Descartes' error: Emotion, reason, and the human brain.* New York: Avon.

Darwin, C. (1965). *The expression of the emotions in man and animals.* Chicago: University of Chicago Press. (Original work published 1872)

Davies, M., Stankov, L., & Roberts, R. D. (1998). Emotional intelligence: In search of an elusive construct. *Journal of Personality and Social Psychology, 75,* 989–1015.

Davis, M. H. (1996). *Empathy: A social psychological approach.* Boulder, CO: Westview Press.

Deutsch, M., & Coleman, P. T. (Eds.). (2000). *The handbook of conflict resolution: Theory and practice.* San Francisco CA: Jossey-Bass.

Ekman, P. (1973). Cross-cultural studies of facial expression. In P. Ekman (Ed.), *Darwin and facial expression: A century of research in review* (pp. 169–222). Orlando, FL: Academic Press.

Ekman, P., & Davidson, R. J. (Eds.). (1994). *The nature of emotion: Fundamental questions.* New York: Oxford University Press.

Ellis, A. (1993). Reflections on rational-emotive therapy. *Journal of Consulting and Clinical Psychology, 61,* 199–201.

Epictetus (1985). *Handbook of Epictetus* (N. White, Trans.). Indianapolis, IN: Hackett.

Fineman, S. (Ed.). (2000). *Emotions in organizations* (Vol. 2). Thousand Oaks, CA: Sage.

Fisher, A. (1998). Success secret: A high emotional IQ. *Fortune, 138*(8), 293–298.

Fisher, C. D., & Ashkanasy, N. M. (Eds.) (2000). Emotions in organizations [Special issue]. *Journal of Organizational Behavior, 21*(2).

Fitness, J. (2000). Anger in the workplace: An emotion script approach to anger episodes between workers and their superiors, co-workers, and subordinates. *Journal of Organizational Behavior, 21,* 147–162.

Fox, S., & Spector, P. E. (1999). Relations of emotional intelligence, practical intelligence, general intelligence, and trait affectivity with interview outcomes: It's not all just "G." *Journal of Organizational Behavior, 20,* 1–18.

Freud, S. (1959). The defence neuro-psychoses. In E. Jones (Ed.), *Sigmund Freud: Collected papers* (Vol. 1). New York: Basic Books. (Original work published 1844)

Frijda, N. H. (1993). The place of appraisal in emotion. *Cognition and Emotion, 7,* 357–388.

Gardner, H. (1983). *Frames of mind: The theory of multiple intelligences.* New York: Basic Books.

Gardner, H. (1993). *Multiple intelligence.* New York: Basic Books.

Gleason, S. E. (1997). *Workplace dispute resolution: Directions for the twenty-first century.* East Lansing: Michigan State University Press.

Goldsmith, M., Lyons, L., & Freas, A. (2000). *Coaching for leadership: How the world's greatest coaches help leaders learn.* San Francisco, CA: Jossey-Bass.

Goldstein, A. P., & Sorcher, M. (1974). *Changing supervisory behavior.* New York: Pergamon Press.

Goleman, D. (1995). *Emotional intelligence.* New York: Bantam Books.

Goleman, D. (1998). *Working with emotional intelligence.* New York: Bantam Books.

Grandey, A. (2000). Emotion regulation in the workplace: A new way to conceptualize emotional labor. *Journal of Occupational Health Psychology, 1,* 61–75.

Gross, J. (1998). The emerging field of emotion regulation: An integrative review. *Review of General Psychology, 2,* 271–299.

Hale, J. (1998). *The performance consultant's fieldbook: Tools and techniques for improving organizations and people.* Jossey-Bass: San Francisco.

Harris Education Research Council. (1991). *An assessment of American education.* New York: Author.

Hays, S. (1999, July). American Express taps into the power of emotional intelligence. *Workforce, 78*(7), 72–74.

Hunt, T. (1928). The measurement of social intelligence. *Journal of Applied Psychology, 12,* 317–334.

James, W. (1884). What is an emotion? *Mind, 9,* 188–205.

Janovics, J., & Christiansen, N. D. (2001, April). *Emotional intelligence in the workplace.* Paper presented at the sixteenth annual conference of the Society of Industrial and Organizational Psychology, San Diego, CA.

Jeanneret, R., & Silzer, R. (Eds.). (1998). *Individual psychological assessment: Predicting behavior in organizational settings.* San Francisco: Jossey-Bass.

Jordan, P. J., Ashkanasy, N. M., Hartel, C. E., & Hooper, G. S. (in press). Workgroup emotional intelligence: Scale development and relationship to team process effectiveness and goal focus. *Human Resource Management Review.*

Kampa, S., & White, R. P. (2002). The effectiveness of executive coaching: What we know and what we still need to know. In R. L. Lowman (Ed.), *Handbook of organizational consulting psychology* (pp. 139–158). San Francisco: Jossey-Bass.

Kilburg, R. R. (2002). Individual interventions in consulting psychology. In R. L. Lowman (Ed.), *Handbook of organizational consulting psychology* (pp. 109–138). San Francisco: Jossey-Bass.

Latham, G. P., & Frayne, C. A. (1989). Self-management training for increasing job attendance: A follow-up and a replication. *Journal of Applied Psychology, 74,* 411–416.

Lazarus, R. S. (1991). *Emotion & adaptation.* New York: Oxford University Press.

LeDoux, J. (1996). *The emotional brain: The mysterious underpinnings of emotional life.* New York: Touchstone.

Lewis, M., Alessandri, S. M., & Sullivan, M. W. (1990). Violation of expectancy, loss of control, and anger expressions in young infants. *Developmental Psychology, 26,* 745–751.

Lewis, M., & Haviland-Jones, J. M. (2000). *Handbook of emotions* (2nd ed.). New York: Guilford Press.

Lock, E. A., & Latham, G. P. (1990). *A theory of goal setting and task performance.* Englewood Cliffs, NJ: Prentice Hall.

Lusch, R. F., & Serpkeuci, R. (1990). Personal differences, job tension, job outcomes, and store performance: A study of retail managers. *Journal of Marketing, 54,* 85–101.

Manz, C. C., & Sims, H. P. (1986). Beyond imitation: Complex behavioral and affective linkages resulting from exposure to leadership training models. *Journal of Applied Psychology, 71,* 571–578.

Markus, H. R., & Kitayama, S. (1991). Culture and the self: Implications for cognition, emotion, and motivation. *Psychological Review, 98,* 224–253.

Marlow, H. A. (1986). Social intelligence: Evidence for multidimensionality and construct independence. *Journal of Educational Psychology, 78,* 52–58.

Mayer, J. D., DiPaolo, M. T., & Salovey, P. (1990). Perceiving affective content in ambiguous visual stimuli: A component of emotional intelligence. *Journal of Personality Assessment, 54,* 772–781.

Mayer, J. D., & Salovey, P. (1993). The intelligence of emotional intelligence. *Intelligence, 17,* 433–442.

Mayer, J. D., Salovey, P., & Caruso, E. (2000). Emotional intelligence. In R. J. Sternberg (Ed.), *Handbook of intelligence* (2nd ed., pp. 396–421). Cambridge, England: Cambridge University Press.

Mayne, T. J., & Bonanno, G. A. (2001). *Emotions: Current issues and future directions.* New York: Guilford Press.

McCallum, M., & Piper, W. E. (Eds.). (1997). *Psychological mindedness: A contemporary understanding.* Hillsdale, NJ: Erlbaum.

McClelland, D. C. (1999). Identifying competencies with behavioral-event interviews. *Psychological Science, 9,* 331–339.

Meichenbaum, D. (1990). Evolution of cognitive behavior therapy: Origins, tenets and clinical examples. In J. Zeig (Ed.), *The evolution of psychotherapy: II* (pp. 96–115). New York: Brunner/Mazel.

Moore, C. W. (1996). *The mediation process: Practical strategies for resolving conflict* (2nd ed.). San Francisco: Jossey-Bass.

Murphy, K. R. (1996). *Individual differences and behavior in organizations.* San Francisco: Jossey-Bass.

Novaco, R. W. (1986). Anger as a clinical and social problem. In R. J. Blanchard & D. C. Blanchard (Eds.), *Advances in the study of aggression* (Vol. 2, pp. 1–67). Orlando, FL: Academic Press.

Ortony, A., Clore, G. L., & Collins, A. (1988). *The cognitive structure of emotions.* Cambridge, England: Cambridge University Press.

Peterson, D. B. (1996). Executive coaching at work: The art of one-on-one change. *Consulting Psychology Journal: Practice and Research, 48,* 78–86.

Potter-Efron, R. T. (1998). *Working anger: Preventing and resolving conflict on the job.* Oakland, CA: New Harbinger.

Powell, T. J. (1994). *Understanding self-help: Frameworks and findings.* Thousand Oaks, CA: Sage.

Resnick, P. J., & Kausch, O. (1995). Violence in the workplace and the role of the consultant. *Consulting Psychology Journal: Practice and Research, 47,* 213–222.

Robins, C. J., & Hayes, A. M. (1993). An appraisal of cognitive therapy. *Journal of Consulting and Clinical Psychology, 61,* 205–214.

Robins, S. (1998, June). *Wisdom, adaptation, & automaticity as mediating links in the causal chain of cognitive appraisal and emotion.* Paper presented at the tenth annual convention of the American Psychological Society, Washington, DC.

Robins, S. (2000). *Wisdom therapy: The application of an interdisciplinary concept to organizational and clinical interventions.* Paper presented at the Colloquium Series at the California School of Professional Psychology, San Diego, CA.

Robins, S., & Novaco, R. (1999). A systems conceptualization and treatment of anger. *Journal of Clinical Psychology, 55,* 325–337.

Rogoff, B., & Lave, J. (Eds.). (1984). *Everyday cognition: Its development in social context.* Cambridge, MA: Harvard University Press.

Rosier, R. H. (Ed.). (1996). *The competency model handbook* (Vol. 3). Boston: Linkage.

Russ-Eft, D. F., & Zenger, J. H. (1997). Behavior modeling training in North America: A research summary. In L. J. Bassi & D. F. Russ-Eft (Eds.), *What works* (pp. 89–109). Alexandria, VA: American Society for Training and Development.

Salovey, P., & Mayer, J. D. (1989). Emotional intelligence. *Imagination, Cognition, and Personality, 9,* 185–211.

Scherer, K. R., Schorr, A., & Johnstone, T. (2001). *Appraisal processes in emotion: Theory, methods, research.* Oxford, England: Oxford University Press.

Schwartz, N., & Clore, G. L. (1988). How do I feel about it? The informative function of mood. In K. Fiedler & A. Forgas (Eds.), *Affect, cognition, and social behavior* (pp. 44–62). Toronto, Ontario, Canada: Hogrefe.

Seligman, M.E.P. (1998). *Learned Optimism: How to change your mind and your life* (2nd ed.). New York: Pocket Books.

Shiller, R. J. (2000). *Irrational exuberance.* Princeton, NJ: Princeton University Press.

Simmons, S. M. (Ed.). (1997). *Measuring emotional intelligence.* Arlington, VA: Summit Publishing Group.

Smither, J. W. (Ed.). (1998). *Performance appraisal: State of the art in practice.* San Francisco: Jossey-Bass.

Spencer, L. M., Jr., McClelland, D. C., & Kelner, S. (1997). *Competency assessment methods: History and state of the art.* Boston: Hay/McBer Group.

Spencer, L. M., Jr., & Spencer, S. (1993). *Competence at work. Models for superior performance* New York: Wiley.

Steers, R. M., & Porter, L. W. (Eds.). (1991). *Motivation and work behavior* (5th ed.). New York: McGraw-Hill.

Sternberg, R. J. (1999a). *Handbook of creativity.* Cambridge, England: Cambridge University Press.

Sternberg, R. J. (1999b). *The nature of cognition.* Cambridge, MA: MIT Press.

Sternberg, R. J. (2000). *Handbook of intelligence.* Cambridge, England: Cambridge University Press.

Sternberg, R. J., & Smith, C. (1985). Social intelligence and decoding skills in nonverbal communication. *Social Cognition, 3,* 168–192.

Sternberg, R. J., & Wagner, R. K. (1986). *Practical intelligence.* Cambridge, England: Cambridge University Press.

Taylor, F. W. (1947). *Scientific management.* New York: HarperCollins. (Original work published 1911)

Thorndike, E. L. (1936). Factor analysis of social and abstract intelligence. *Journal of Educational Psychology, 27,* 231–233.

Tooby, J., & Cosmides, L. (1990). The past explains the present: Emotional adaptations and the structure of ancestral environments. *Ethology and Sociobiology, 11,* 375–424.

Toufexis, A. (1994, April 24). Workers who fight firing with fire. *Time, 143,* 36.

Triandis, H. C. (1997). Cross-cultural perspectives on personality. In R. Hogan, J. Johnson, & S. Briggs (Eds.), *Handbook of personality psychology* (pp. 439–464). Orlando, FL: Academic Press.

Tziner, A., Haccoun, R. R., & Kadish, A. (1991). Personal and situational characteristics influencing the effectiveness of transfer of training improvement strategies. *Journal of Occupational Psychology, 64,* 167–177.

U.S. Department of Justice, Bureau of Justice Statistics. (1998, July). *Workplace violence, 1992–1996* (National Crime Victimization Survey NCJ-168634). Washington, DC: Author.

Wechsler, D. (1940). Nonintellective factors in general intelligence. *Psychological Bulletin, 37,* 444–445.

Weiner, B. (1985). An attributional theory of achievement motivation and emotion. *Psychological Review, 92,* 548–573.

Weisinger, H. (1998). *Emotional intelligence at work.* San Francisco: Jossey-Bass.

# CHAPTER EIGHT

# Assessing Candidates
# for Leadership Positions

Andrew N. Garman

*Department of Health Systems Management, Rush University &*
*Department of Organizational & Industrial Psychology*
*The Chicago School for Professional Psychology*

Organizations of all types depend on the performance of employees in key leadership positions to ensure their survival and growth. Key executives typically have decision-making power with a financial impact far larger than their cost to the organization, making decisions about who occupies these positions all the more critical. Boards and hiring managers are willing to pay considerable fees to find and employ the most appropriate people for these critical positions, and will often invest heavily in their development. Unfortunately, surveys regarding management performance often conclude that as many as half or more of managers are seriously underperforming in one or more highly critical areas (DeVries, 1992; Hogan, Raskin, & Fazzini, 1990; Kouzes & Posner, 1993). Why the pervasive shortcomings? One review of the pertinent literature points to the limitations of upper-level executives' facility with personnel selection (Sessa & Campbell, 1997). A more recent survey of 350 companies concluded that less than 44 percent had formal processes in place for nominating or developing high-potential employees (Bennis, 2000). Taken together, these findings suggest that there is room for improvement in the selection and development decisions made within many organizations.

The field of psychology has provided many contributions to the science of assessing candidates for critical organizational positions, and psychologists from a variety of subdisciplines have built practices around providing this type of assessment support. However, developing a safe and effective leadership assessment practice requires more education and experience than most graduate programs in psychology provide, regardless of the specific subdiscipline (Ryan & Sackett, 1992).

The purposes of this chapter are fourfold: (1) to examine the supplementary training needs graduates of individually oriented (for example, clinical and counseling) psychology doctoral programs will likely face in preparing to conduct leadership assessment work; (2) to provide a brief overview of leadership positions within organizations; (3) to provide an overview of the general process typically involved in leadership assessment; and (4) to summarize relevant research on a variety of assessment methods frequently used for this purpose.

# PREPARING TO CONDUCT ASSESSMENTS

In reviewing research on the state of the practice in individual assessment, Ryan and Sackett (1998) concluded that few graduate psychology programs prepare students adequately to conduct individual assessments in organizational settings, and additionally that "many (practicing) assessors are not up to standard" (p. 82). Effective and defensible assessment practices require mastery of several areas that are not a part of the typical doctoral program in clinical or counseling psychology. Of particular importance are three areas elaborated upon here: a solid knowledge of the legal and ethical issues in personnel selection; an understanding of organizational contexts; and a familiarity with the types of methods used for leadership assessment, along with their relative strengths and limitations.

## Legal and Ethical Issues

Assessments from which employment decisions will be made are subject to a host of laws that are not typically covered in clinical and counseling programs. Organizations can and do face stiff civil penalties when their assessment practices are challenged and do not pass certain legal tests (Sharf & Jones, 2000). Psychologists must exercise caution to ensure that their practices are defensible against legal challenges. In the United States, *Uniform Guidelines on Employee Selection Procedures* provides a reference framework for judging the extent to which an assessment practice conforms to federal laws (Equal Employment Opportunity Commission, 1978). The *Guidelines* are particularly relevant to assessment practices at lower managerial levels, where adverse impact (that is, selection procedures that result in protected groups being selected at substantially different rates) can more readily turn into legal challenges. However, because the *Guidelines* are intended to apply to hiring and promotion decisions at *all* levels, psychologists conducting leadership assessments at any organizational level should still be familiar with them as well as the case law affecting assessment at various levels (Jeanneret, 1998). The *Guidelines* also safeguard against many ineffective assessment practices, because they stipulate the necessity of demonstrating that assessments validly relate to the requirements of a given position.

In addition to these guidelines, several professional organizations relevant to psychologists provide testing guidelines that all test users should familiarize themselves with (American Psychological Association, Committee on Psychological Tests and Assessment 1996; American Educational Research Association, American Psychological Association, & National Council on Measurement in Education, 1999; Society for Industrial and Organizational Psychology, 1987). A broader consideration of ethical issues that can arise in individual assessment can be found in the writings of Jeanneret (1998), Lowman (1998), and Sharf and Jones (2000). An examination of the strengths and limitations of doctoral preparation from a variety of psychology disciplines is available in Garman, Zlatoper, and Whiston (1998), and Ryan (1992).

## Organizational Contexts

Psychologists interested in conducting assessments for organizations need to gain familiarity with how organizations work, both from a structural as well as an interpersonal perspective. In terms of structure, a basic familiarity with the principles of organizational design and corporate strategy will be necessary in order to understand the language of the business environment and those who are seeking positions within a given organization. Additionally, psychologists need to develop an understanding of the role and structure of human resource departments. For a cost-effective introduction, numerous graduate textbooks are available on each of these subjects; graduate courses with these titles are an even better option.

In addition to structure, psychologists also need to be familiar with the interpersonal processes that allow these organizations to run. Minimally, a familiarity with organizational behavior (through readings or additional coursework) is needed. Additional familiarity with leadership principles will be very helpful as well.

## Assessment Methods and Tools

Methods used for leadership assessment differ in important ways from clinical assessments. Beyond differences in the legal climate, which has already been discussed, the nature of the referral question is also qualitatively different. For a clinical assessment, a referral question will typically stem from the individual (for example, "Is this person safe to be discharged from the hospital?"). In contrast, for leadership assessment applications, the referral question typically stems from a position to be filled (for example, "Who is most likely to perform well in this position?") From this question, an assessment approach is constructed, then applied uniformly across all candidates for the position. This requires a different approach to the assessment problem, as well as different methods for completing the assessment itself.

In terms of methods, there are few assessment tools originally developed for clinical applications that are legally defensible for use in these organizational contexts. For this reason, most psychologists will need to gain familiarity with a variety of other assessment tools designed specifically for personnel selection decisions. Table 8.1 provides names and websites of a number of major publishers of personnel selection tests, selected due to their frequency of mentioned use in survey research or by assessment colleagues, as well as a number of important professional organizations whose members are involved with leadership assessment work. A useful description of experiences with a number of psychological assessment tools is also provided in Fogli and Whitney (1998).

# OVERVIEW OF LEADERSHIP POSITIONS

What does the prototypical effective leader look like? The most appropriate answer is: it depends (see, for example, Cascio, 1998; Levinson, 1980; Sessa & Taylor, 2000). One cannot define a universal effective leader who will excel in all environments any more than one can design a set of performance metrics that are universally desirable across all positions. However, if our goal is phenomenological understanding rather than assessment per se, then leadership positions can be usefully grouped into several meaningful categories. Taxonomies for leadership positions (see, for example, Freedman, 1998; Mahoney, Jerdee, & Carroll, 1965) typically contain a derivation of, or expansion upon, the following three classifications: entry-level leadership (leaders with one or occasionally two levels of direct reports associated with them); managerial or middle management leadership (leaders whose direct reports also have supervisory responsibility); and upper-level leadership (leaders directly responsible for entire organizations, or for larger departments and operations within very large organizations).

## Entry-Level Leadership Positions

Just as entry-level can be used to describe the first position a person is likely to hold within an organization, entry-level leadership positions are those that a person might assume as the first position in a management career. The supervisor of a group of professionals or service staff is the most common example of this entry-level position; junior managers and managers-in-training comprise a large group of entry-level leaders as well.

**Table 8.1. Resources.**

Major Sources of Assessment Tools for Leadership Positions

| Publisher | Web address | Products |
|---|---|---|
| Bigby, Havis, & Associates, Inc. | www.bigby.com | ASSESS |
| Consulting Psychologists Press, Inc. | www.cpp-db.com | FIRO-B; California Psychological Inventory |
| Hogan Assessment Systems, Inc. | www.hoganassessments.com | Hogan Personality Inventory; Hogan Development Survey (HDS); Motives, Values, Preferences Inventory (MVPI) |
| NCS Assessments, Inc. | www.assessments.ncs.com | 16PF; Guilford-Zimmerman Temperament Survey (GZTS) |
| SHL Group, Inc. | www.shlusa.com | Occupational Personality Questionnaire (OPQ) |

Professional Resources

| Organization | Web address |
|---|---|
| Employment Management Association/Society for Human Resource Management (EMA/SHRM) | www.shrm.org/ema/index.html |
| International Personnel Management Association—Assessment Council (IPMAAC) | www.ipmaac.org |
| Society of Consulting Psychology (SCP) | www.apa.org/divisions/div13/ |
| Society for Industrial and Organizational Psychology (SIOP) | www.siop.org |

**Supervisors.** Persons taking these positions are typically promoted from line-level positions, with the goal of having their experience in the line available to other, less-tenured staff. Although any one supervisor might not make a critical difference to the organization as a whole, the class of position as a whole is often quite pivotal in deciding the effectiveness of the organization. Beyond simply transferring their knowledge to newer coworkers, effective supervisors help to determine whether new employees flourish in the organization, or even whether they will stay with the organization at all.

Individuals assuming supervisory-type leadership positions for the first time are frequently promoted from the rank-and-file of whatever specialty area they had operated in. Such promotions might be influenced more strongly by the candidate's technical skill in their original position than their apparent ability to supervise others. The net effect is, as Hogan, Curphy, and Hogan (1994) describe it, ". . . the organization loses . . . a good scholar or sailor and acquires a supervisor whose talent for management is unknown" (p. 495).

From the perspective of the newly promoted supervisor, this new position can involve an intense struggle to develop new leadership skills, and the transition is frequently described as more of a challenge than they bargained for (see, for example, Freedman, 1998; Garman & Corrigan, 1998). The skill set needed to supervise others is often markedly different from the one that the individual developed to become proficient at the line level; in some instances, the two are practically diametrically opposed. Though a rocky transition does not describe all such promotions, difficulties are especially likely if the employee held a role primarily as an individual contributor, and was used to relying only on his or her own efforts for effective performance. Among the common transitional challenges supervisors face are: renegotiating relationships with coworkers; developing a perspective that balances individual employee needs against organizational realities; and dealing with the hostility of those who may have been passed over for the promotion (Bass, 1990).

Organizations can greatly enhance the success of these transitions by providing formal training in supervisory and managerial skills (Burke & Day, 1986; Niemiec, Sikorski, Clark, & Walberg, 1992; Reither & Pappas, 1998). In addition to skill development provision, these programs can help to acculturate new managers to their new roles in the organization, and provide them with much-needed new sources of social support at a time when their existing supportive relationships with coworkers will need to change.

**Managers-In-Training.** The manager-in-training position is used by many organizations to attract and rapidly develop relatively inexperienced job candidates who are expected to eventually assume management positions (that is, positions above the supervisory level) within the organization. Recent graduates of college and other educational programs are frequently the recruiting targets for these positions. Depending on the organization and the nature of the position, programs for early career high-potentials can involve substantial formal and informal training (Bennis, 2000). As such, individuals enrolled in these programs often represent a substantial investment on the part of the organization, highlighting the need for effective selection procedures.

The pathway to a manager-in-training position depends on the nature of the position and of the organization itself. In some organizations, the manager-in-training position might represent little more than a brief threshold or probationary period for new supervisors. However, in many larger organizations these positions are designed as fast-track placements into which high-potential new hires are slotted. These tracks often promise rapid development and deployment into higher-level positions, creating a talent pool for emerging management needs as well as a recruiting tool for graduates with strong academic records.

The challenges faced by fast-track managers are qualitatively different from those of supervisors. Because many of these individuals are hired from outside of the organization, they do not face the same interpersonal hurdles the supervisors do (that is, there are no preexisting roles and relationships that need to be renegotiated). Their challenges instead might come from their relative inexperience, and the complexity of the positions for which they are training. On both counts, careful assessment of candidate skills and abilities can help ensure that they will successfully complete the training regimen and go on to be successful in these positions.

## Leadership at the Middle-Management Level

For our purposes, middle management refers to positions in which the direct reports have supervisory responsibility, and in which the position reports up to a level somewhere below the top of the organization. Depending on the size of the organization, there might be many layers of middle management, only a single layer, or no layer at all. The nature of middle management will differ to some degree depending on the type of organization, its size, and culture, among other factors, however there are qualities of the middle-manager position that appear to have some universality.

Although middle managers face a number of challenges in common with supervisory positions, the hallmark of the middle manager's challenge is the balancing of multiple stakeholders' needs (Oshry, 1999). Unlike the line-level supervisor, the middle manager needs to understand the concerns and limitations both of their direct reports and of key employees who report up to those direct reports. In addition to working for a superior, many middle managers will have responsibilities for cross-departmental initiatives such as performance improvement projects, and might also have accountability to internal and external customers. For example, the manager of a marketing department might sit on cross-functional teams with production and financial managers as part of a particular marketing campaign, with external service vendors in designing and delivering the campaign, and with channel representatives in communicating about the launch. All of this adds up to a perpetual balancing act that can prove challenging to a manager's physical and psychological health, particularly if the necessary coping skills are lacking (Peter & Siegrist, 1997).

Pathways to middle management may come from lower levels in the organization or from outside the organization, with the relative numbers of each depending on the nature of the positions as well as the culture of the organization. At the middle-management level and above, the goals of assessment practices more frequently extend beyond hiring and selection decisions. Many organizations involve middle managers in periodic assessments for the purposes of development planning, to identify areas of relative weakness that can be targeted for improvement. Data from these types of assessments can also be used in *succession planning,* identifying emerging organizational needs and the individuals most likely to fill those needs effectively.

## Leadership at Upper Levels

Upper-level leadership refers qualitatively to positions most directly and individually accountable for the success of the organization as a whole. This group can be usefully subdivided into organizational leaders and entrepreneurial leaders.

The titles most commonly associated with upper-level management are president, general manager, and chief officer, although in some organizations persons with vice presidential and even director titles will function as upper-level management. Individuals in these positions typically manage multiple departments or autonomous business units, and will usually have profit and loss responsibility, meaning that they are held directly accountable for the financial performance of the organization. Although middle managers may also have profit and loss responsibility within their departments, the focus at mid-level is more typically on cost controls, and the ultimate financial contribution to the organization might be more difficult to calculate—particularly if the position is in a support department such as marketing or human resources.

At the top levels, hiring decisions are particularly closely tied to the future success of the organization, and can also directly affect the shorter-term perceptions of the organization among its outside stakeholders (Worrell, Davidson, & Glascock, 1993). The boards and upper management in most organizations recognize these realities, and will expend particular effort to ensure that the people holding those positions are the most qualified and capable they can possibly find and afford to employ. Unfortunately, more time and attention often is spent finding a slate of suitable candidates than on constructing the most effective methods for assessing and selecting the top candidate (Sessa & Taylor, 2000; DeVries, 1992). Hiring decisions are often made by current members of the organization or the board, whose methods might be less effective and more prone to conflicts of interest than external professionals with advanced training in personnel selection (Ocasio & Kim, 1999; Westphal & Zajac, 1995; Zajac & Westphal, 1996).

In contrast to the organizational leader, who works within an existing organizational framework, the *entrepreneurial leader* will have ambition to start (or will have started) a new organization, or will be a member of a group of organizational founders. Although many of the business management functions might be similar to those of the organization leader, the entrepreneur will typically need to place greater emphasis on aspects of business growth, culture development, and credibility establishment, and will have a far more intimate involvement with what Schein (1992, p. 53) refers to as the "ultimate survival problem" of the organization.

There are numerous pathways to entrepreneurial leadership. For managers who perceive barriers to advancement that are out of their control (Daily, Certo, & Dalton, 1999), or are facing displacement from their current position (Hisrich, 1990), the path to entrepreneurship might be chosen as a self-imposed promotion to a position of higher responsibility. At the other extreme, some individuals pursue entrepreneurship as a career, starting soon after (or instead of) formal education. For this group, motivations for entrepreneurship can stem from observing the success of entrepreneurial parents (Jacobowitz & Vidler, 1982), or an active desire to avoid company life, particularly for individuals whose interpersonal styles are ill-suited to being a team player or subordinate (Kets deVries, 1985).

Entrepreneurial leaders as a population appear to possess different psychological profiles and skill sets than organization leaders (Rauch & Frese, 2000; Wooten, Timmerman, & Folger, 1999). Whereas an organization leader must be comfortable working within a preexisting framework of rules, policies, and culture, the entrepreneurial leader might choose a career path in part to avoid the imposition of such a structure (Kets deVries, 1985; Feldman & Bolino, 2000). Compared to other managers, entrepreneurs have a relatively greater propensity to assume risk (Stewart & Roth, 2001), and their assessment of the risk potential associated with a given decision tends to be lower than that of managers (Cooper, Woo, & Dunkelberg, 1988). Other characteristics that might distinguish entrepreneurs from other managers, at least at a population level, include achievement motivation (Cooper & Gimeno-Gascon, 1992; Johnson, 1990), innovativeness (Engle, Mah, & Sadri, 1997), and internal locus of control (Rauch & Frese, 2000). Thus far, a specific entrepreneurial personality per se has not been identified (Rauch & Frese, 2000), and attempts to classify entrepreneurs usually articulate several different types, which might relate to the nature of the venture each is attracted to (Miner, 1996, 1997; Smith, 1967).

Goals of assessment are also qualitatively different for entrepreneurial leaders versus organizational leaders. Organizational leaders are typically assessed to support decisions about whether to bring them into the organization, or promote them within the organization, or provide targeted development programs for them. These assessments are usually completed by other members of the organization or by consultants hired by that organization. In contrast, entrepreneurial leaders are assessed to ascertain their ability to successfully launch a proposed venture, usually to support decisions about whether and how to best structure a financial investment (MacMillan, Siegel, & Subba Narasimha, 1985; Sandberg, 1986). As such, the assessment is typically completed by the investing individual or company, or by an assessor hired by the investor.

## ASSESSMENT: METHODS AND RESEARCH

All assessment work typically involves some variation of the following steps: deciding what to look for, deciding how to look for it, conducting the assessments, developing conclusions, and following up. These steps are perhaps best understood through illustration, so a specific case example will be provided.

### Assessment Case: A New CEO for Academy Hospital

Academy Hospital (AH) is a health services organization in Flatfield, a medium-sized city in the U.S. Midwest. The hospital contains a variety of inpatient units and outpatient care providers in six sites scattered across the city and outlying suburbs. The president of Academy, Sharon Crest, will be stepping down in two months, to spend time traveling with her husband. As the original president, she leaves a legacy of developing AH from scratch twenty-four years ago. Though she has enjoyed her tenure, she reports she is ready for a major change, and does not expect to be involved with the hospital in any formal way after she leaves.

In the interest of facilitating as smooth a transition as possible, the board of trustees of Academy has retained a consulting psychologist to assist with the selection process. A slate of candidates, both external and internal, are to be provided with the help of this psychologist and a retained executive search firm.

The board believes that successfully replacing Sharon will be very difficult. She was an extremely popular community leader, someone who constantly pushed for health services for the underserved, and untiringly worked with community leaders to make that happen. Her departure will probably leave community health with a leadership vacuum, at a time when financial pressures at AH and all health care organizations are continuing to increase. Sharon's prominence and reputation also means that her impending departure promises to receive high-profile attention from the press. Already, numerous editorials and several stories have run reflecting her life's work, and speculations—often gloomy—about the future of healthcare in Flatfield.

Hospital and health network CEO positions in today's healthcare climate have been described as among the most challenging executive jobs in the United States. Part of the tremendous challenge comes from the sheer complexity of the work involved. In addition to the intricacy of the U.S. healthcare system itself, there are myriad social and political forces that persistently vie for the CEO's attention. In terms of personnel issues, Academy Hospital has employees spanning multiple unions, as well as a medical department that, though not unionized, nevertheless carries considerable political clout. The city of Flatfield has a well-educated but tight labor market, making competition for entry-level operational talent stiff at best. Add to this a rapidly and wildly changing landscape of medical technology, payor organizations (as well as payment rates and what is covered), corporate compliance policies, standards for data management, and community expectations for addressing real and imagined public health concerns, and a realistic picture of the day-to-day job begins to emerge.

## Deciding What to Look For

The first step in deciding what factors to look for in job candidates is to gain a solid understanding of the requirements of the job. This process should typically begin with gaining an understanding of the organization in which the job is embedded (Frisch, 1998; Sessa & Campbell, 1997). Particularly for higher-level positions, a well-articulated analysis of organizational needs provides essential contextual information to the assessment process (Sessa, Kaiser, Taylor, & Campbell, 1998) This information can be gathered through interviews or meetings with key executives or board members within the organization.

Once the organizational needs are accounted for, the task shifts to *job analysis:* compiling the tasks, responsibilities, activities, and working conditions for the job, and then using that information to describe the knowledge, skills, abilities, and other attributes that are necessary and desirable for effective job performance (Ash, 1988). An analysis of job requirements is typically completed via interviews with key staff including those who hold similar positions, will report up to the person who is hired, or will supervise that person. Occasionally, customers might be included in this data-gathering process, particularly at upper levels in the organization (Sessa et al., 1998).

In terms of the job analysis interview itself, psychologists differ in the amount of structure they impose upon it. The more traditional industrial psychology approach would be to use a highly structured survey, such as the Professional and Managerial Position Questionnaire (Mitchell & McCormick, 1990) or the Common-Metric Questionnaire (Harvey, 1999). Surveys such as these have the advantage of collecting a large amount of information, as well as being relatively reliable methods of collecting job information. However, they have the disadvantage of being tedious and resource-intensive to administer, requiring that considerable time be spent completing highly structured interview or survey tasks. They are also designed to be applicable to all managerial positions, which provides flexibility, but at some expense of capturing unique position-specific facets of a given job.

Due to these disadvantages, a more qualitative approach is often used for job analysis, in which a less-structured interview process is applied. This might involve the psychologist asking key staff a series of questions, the responses to which would then be combined to form a composite description of job demands. This approach is generally indicated for higher-level positions, in which the complexity of the job exceeds the capacity for most preexisting job analysis tools to capture.

For our case study, the psychologist decided to approach the job analysis via semi-structured interviews. Interviews were conducted over the course of four days, and included a half-day session with Sharon, as well as several two-hour sessions with board members, Sharon's direct reports, and community members who worked closely with her. Each interviewee was asked a series of questions to help them identify critical success factors for the position, as well as a number of critical incidents they had witnessed in which Sharon's decisions and actions played an important role in the success or failure of various events. The content of these interviews was then qualitatively analyzed by the psychologist, who then provided the board with a written report describing the organizational needs and challenges, as well as the critical job requirements as he understood them. The job requirements were organized into six major content areas: *strategic vision; charisma; stress resilience; coalition-building; people development;* and *general health administration knowledge*. The specific responsibilities noted by the interviewees were listed under each of these areas.

Once an understanding of the functions and demands of a position has been mapped out, the next step is to construct the assessment plan for measuring these qualities in job candidates. These qualities are often described as a combination of knowledge, skills, abilities, and other behaviors (KSAOs). *Knowledge* refers to the information the individual currently possesses. For our case study, examples would include familiarity with trends in health care financing, an understanding of community organizations and their priorities, and knowledge of the timetable and practical implications of the Health Insurance Portability and Accountability Act (HIPAA). *Skills,* the behavioral component of knowledge, refers to the activities a person can accomplish as a result of their knowledge and experience. For our case, necessary skills could include developing community partnerships (using the knowledge of community organizations and team development), and managing the finances of the organization (using knowledge of corporate finance and accounting). *Abilities* refers to the capacity a person has for acquiring new knowledge and skills, and refers to more global areas such as quantitative or verbal performance. Abilities are often desirable to assess when candidates with particular knowledge or skills are either difficult or impossible to recruit. In such cases, the hiring manager will want to hire someone with the necessary underlying abilities to develop specific knowledge and skills.

Finally, the *other behaviors* domain is used to describe more complex constructs that might not map to a specific job requirement, but are nevertheless helpful or even essential to the job. Common examples of these include interpersonal style, motivation, personality, character, and ethics. *Person-organization fit,* an assessment of the extent to which a particular job candidate appears to have a general profile of style and motivations that meshes well with an organization, is also often placed in this category. For the case study, the interviewees all agreed that a successful candidate would need to have a strong sense of mission and personal dedication to the field of health care. This was felt to be essential in order to help the person weather the inevitably long hours and personal sacrifices that were necessary in the position, and would be expected by the various community leaders with which this person would have frequent contact. This is a good example of a characteristic that cannot be described as a skill or ability per se, but is still deemed essential to the job.

## Deciding How to Look for It

Once there is consensus regarding the specific KSAOs necessary and desirable for a given position, the next step is to develop an *assessment plan*—a structure that will be used with all job candidates to assess their suitability for the position. There are a variety of methods used to assess job candidates, and typically there are a number of choices available for any given domain to be assessed. The most frequently used assessment tools, including what is known about their validity and practicality, are described below.

**Interviews.** Interviews are the most commonly used method for assessment by consulting psychologists (Ryan & Sackett, 1992) as well as other executives (Sessa et al., 1998). In leadership positions, and indeed most positions where a person-organization fit is assessed in addition to ability, hiring managers are often tempted to use an informal, "let's get to know you" approach to the interview. However, a structured interview process, one in which all job candidates receive a common core set of questions, is more desirable for several reasons. Perhaps most importantly, there is ample evidence to suggest that structured interviews will typically outperform informal, unstructured approaches in predicting performance (Conway, Jako, & Goodman, 1995; Hermelin & Robertson, 2001; McDaniel, Whetzel, Schmidt, & Maurer, 1994; Wiesner & Cronshaw, 1988). It should also be noted that informal approaches are far more susceptible to legal challenge than structured approaches, in part because the end result is that two candidates can experience very different interviews for the same position.

Within the structured interview processes there are a variety of approaches, again with some appearing to outperform others. Two frequently cited approaches are the *experience-based* interview, which focuses on past work events (for example, "Tell me about a time when you were faced with a particularly unpopular budgetary constraint in your department . . .") and the *situational* interview, which focuses on solving hypothetical problems (for example, "What would you do if you were faced with the need to cut travel costs in your department?"). Both approaches involve similar construction and scoring procedures: candidates' answers are recorded by the interviewer and then later scored using well-defined scales to rate the quality of the response. This approach allows a quantitative score to be derived from the interview, which is particularly helpful for situations in which there are numerous candidates for a single position. Specifically, whenever more than two candidates are interviewed for a given position, it becomes very difficult to keep track of the relative strengths and weaknesses both within and between candidates without the aid of a more formal accounting process. Scorable measures provide such a process, allowing a more unbiased assessment of the overall profile of candidates against position requirements, as well as each other.

Both situational and experience-based approaches have demonstrated validity across a variety of leadership as well as nonleadership positions (Latham & Sue-Chan, 1999; McDaniel, Whetzel, Schmidt, & Maurer, 1994). Whether one approach is superior to the other is not firmly established; some studies more strongly support situational (McDaniel et al., 1994), others support experience-based (Pulakos & Schmitt, 1995), and still others do not show a significant difference (Campion, Campion, & Hudson, 1994). Both approaches continue to be actively researched, refined, and compared.

Fewer studies have been reported on the use of interviews at the upper levels of management; however, several recent studies suggest their validity with these positions as well. Russell (1990, 2001), using experience-based interviews combined across candidates, peers, and superiors, demonstrated that this approach validly predicts performance at top levels of management, even with a time lag as long as ten years. With regard to entrepreneurs, Smart (1999) found that venture capital firms self-reporting the use of past-oriented interviews had the greatest relative success in terms of their perceived accuracy of the human capital valuation. For the psychologist interested in developing assessment interviewing skills, highly recommended texts include Fear and Chiron (1990), and Smart (1990).

**Biographical Information.** Biographical information, or biodata, refers to efforts to quantify the assessment of past activities and accomplishments, such as school attended, earned GPA, evidence of work during school, and related constructs (Gunter, Furnham, & Drakeley, 1993). The process involves first collecting biographical information about job candidates, or successful and unsuccessful incumbents. These data are then analyzed to determine which indicators (and in what combination) predict job performance. Biodata scores can be obtained through a questionnaire approach, in which the candidate responds to a series of questions about themselves and their work experience, or it can be derived from an experience-based interview, which is transcribed and scored by a trained rater.

An approach conceptually similar to biodata is used by some venture capital firms to estimate the leadership capacity of the entrepreneurial team they are considering investing in. In particular, variables such as quality of educational programs attended, prior track record in a given market, and prior successes in building a comparable business, have been found to validly predict entrepreneurial success; however, the size of the relationship is relatively small. A review by Rauch and Frese (2000) of seven studies found a weighted mean correlation of .09, and also suggested that the magnitude of the relationship is influenced by other aspects of the entrepreneurs' personality, leadership style, and strategy, as well as market-specific considerations.

Concerning other types of leaders, biodata has also demonstrated validity for assessing leadership performance; however, it is relatively infrequently used in practice (Russell, Mattson, Devlin, & Atwater, 1990). A major barrier to more widespread use relates to the fact that biodata assessments have typically been empirically derived. This can lead to questions that are, at best, not perceived as highly job relevant (that is, face valid) to the assessee, and, at worst, might be perceived as needlessly intrusive (Hammer & Kleiman, 1988; Mael, Connerley, & Morath, 1996). However, substantial progress has been made in recent years toward advancing the use of biodata (Stokes & Cooper, 1994), both in terms of psychometrics (see, for example, Mumford, Costanza, Connelly, & Johnson, 1996), and theory development (Kuhnert & Russell, 1990; Dean, Russell, & Muchinsky, 1999), which, in combination with its demonstrated utility, might yield increased use in the future. Additionally, biodata scored from experience-based interviews might be a more palatable assessment tool at higher levels in the organization than other selection tools, such as personality and cognitive ability measures (Russell, 2001).

**Assessment Centers.** Assessment centers involve a standardized series of work-related simulations that people complete and then receive scores based on their performance. The scores are completed by a group of trained observers and assessors, and can be derived from a combination of objective tests and observed behavior (Task Force on Assessment Center Guidelines, 1989). The goal is to gain an evaluation of a person's abilities based on as realistic a sample of their work as possible. (Assessment centers are dealt with in detail elsewhere in this book, and therefore are summarized here only in terms of their relationship to the larger profile of assessment methods used in leadership positions.)

Assessment centers are most frequently used in organizations as a way of gauging supervisory capacity among nonmanagerial employees, as well as for job candidates outside of the hiring organization. However, use of developmental centers is growing at the higher levels, where participants engage in more complex simulations (for example, press conferences) to provide feedback on commensurately more complex skills (Cascio, 1998). Assessment centers are also being used as part of formal succession planning processes in some organizations (Higgs, Papper, & Carr, 2000).

Of the assessment methods described in this chapter, assessment centers are often the most costly, both in terms of candidate time (an assessment might take as long as three days or more), as well as assessor time (multiple assessors are needed to gain consensus, and substantial time is involved in design, setup, and scoring). Despite the high costs, assessment centers are popular tools, due in part to their long track records of criterion-related validity, as well as some compelling evidence for long-term predictive validity. The meta-analysis by Gaugler, Rosenthal, Thornton, and Bentson (1987), covering fifty studies, estimated the assessment center results in their study to have an average corrected $r$ of .37. This same analysis also found that the use of psychologists (versus managers) as assessors significantly improved the predictive validity of the ratings. With regard to long-term prediction, one noteworthy study (Bray & Howard, 1983) found that assessment center results can significantly predict career performance even with time horizons of more than 20 years. In addition to its criterion validity, a well-constructed assessment center will often also enjoy high face validity, in that the relevance of the assessment activities to the job is typically readily apparent to job candidates (Smither, Reilly, Millsap, Pearlman, & Stoffey, 1993).

Despite their demonstrated value, however, assessment centers have also been the subject of controversy. From a psychometric perspective, concerns have been raised about the construct validity of assessment centers, because ratings tend to be influenced more by the specific components of the assessment center (that is, the exercises) than by any underlying dimensions of performance (Fleenor, 1996). From a process perspective, there is no specific assessment center approach recognized as optimal in terms of content and length (Klimoski & Brickner, 1987), and despite the widespread availability of professional guidelines (Task Force on Assessment Center Guidelines, 1989; Joiner, 2000), many organizations apparently do not follow a number of the recommendations these guidelines contain (Spychalski, Quinones, & Gaugler, 1997).

**Cognitive Ability Tests.** Unlike work sample assessments, which attempt to measure skills directly, measures of intellectual or cognitive ability assess an individual's capacity to learn new skills. There are a tremendous number of cognitive ability tests marketed for use in selecting leaders. A survey by Ryan and Sackett (1992) of psychologists from APA Divisions 14, 13, and 12 who conduct individual assessments for personnel decisions, found the Wechsler Adult Intelligence Scale and the Watson-Glaser Critical Thinking Appraisal to be the most frequently used by those in their study. Meta-analytic research suggests that the general mental ability tapped by cognitive assessments is typically the best single predictor of job performance, leading the authors of the study to recommend that general mental ability be considered ". . . the primary personnel measure for hiring decisions" (Schmidt & Hunter, 1998, p. 266). Cognitive ability tests have proven to be remarkably good predictors of job performance across a breadth of leadership positions (Baehr & Orban, 1989; Schmidt & Hunter, 1998), and their predictive validity seems to increase with increasing job complexity (Hunter, 1986).

Other research, however, suggests that cognitive ability does not always predict performance better than other measures, nor does it always predict all aspects of managerial performance as well as other approaches (Baehr & Orban, 1989; Young, Arthur, & Finch, 2000). The potential for cognitive ability tests to cause adverse impact against ethnic minority groups in the selection process has also been cited (Schmitt, Clause, & Pulakos, 1996; Wagner, 1997). These limitations suggest that cognitive ability testing should at most be used as a *component* of a larger assessment battery, rather than a standalone assessment tool, and caution should be exercised in its interpretation when comparing a diverse group of candidates.

**Personality Inventories.** Personality inventories are structured methods used to directly gain an understanding of the assessee's attitudes, motivations, and psychological character. Often similar in procedural structure to clinical personality inventories, these personality inventories can similarly be classified as either objective or projective assessments. Projective assessments involve presenting the assessee with an ambiguous stimulus, such as a picture of two individuals interacting, and then asking the person to describe what he or she believes is going on in the picture. The theory behind projective assessments is that personality structure influences the way individuals perceive, organize, and interpret their environment and experiences (Brown, 1983); stimuli are thus designed to differentiate among assessees according to their methods of interpreting their environment. Objective assessments, in contrast, attempt to assess personality more directly, usually through a series of questions about preferences, attitudes, or values (Cascio, 1998). The two approaches are often compared in terms of their emphasis on quantitative methods, with projective tests typically described as nonquantitative in nature. However, projective techniques with the strongest track records of validly predicting job performance (such as the Thematic Apperception Test) have scoring protocols associated with them, suggesting that quantitative approaches can be usefully applied to projective techniques as well.

According to the Ryan and Sackett survey (1992), the following personality assessments were used by 15 percent or more of the psychologists in their sample: the California Psychological Inventory, the Guilford-Zimmerman Temperament Survey, the Minnesota Multiphasic Personality Inventory, the 16PF, and the Thematic Apperception Test (TAT). Interest in using personality assessments has increased substantially since the time of that survey, partly in reaction to several landmark meta-analytic research studies examining the relationship between the big five personality constructs (Barrick & Mount, 1991), integrity/honesty tests (Ones, Viswesvaran, & Schmidt, 1993), and job performance.

There is also evidence that personality tests can incrementally improve the validity of assessment practices over measures of cognitive ability alone, at least for integrity and for the conscientiousness component of the big five (Schmidt & Hunter, 1998), although these results were not specific to leadership positions per se. Other recent research has shown personality assessments to significantly predict performance in leadership positions, both by themselves and as incremental additions to other assessment practices, such as an assessment center (Goffin, Rothstein, & Johnston, 1996).

Unfortunately, the relationship between personality tests and job performance is often less clear to job applicants, which can make personality assessments more susceptible to arousing applicant suspicion, as well as to perceptions of unfairness (Smither et al., 1993). Organizational leaders also might be less likely to view personality assessments favorably, or even to tolerate them as part of an assessment protocol (Russell, 2001), creating a barrier to their use at higher levels of many organizations.

Many projective tests have not demonstrated high validity in predicting management performance (Reilly & Chao, 1982), particularly when compared to other assessment methods more readily available to nonpsychologist HR professionals. A noteworthy exception can be found in measures of motivation, in particular the Miner Sentence Completion Scale (MSCS) and the Thematic Apperception Test. The MSCS has demonstrated validity in predicting both managerial promotion (Berman & Miner, 1985), and success as an entrepreneur, as part of a larger battery of assessments (Miner, Smith, & Bracker, 1994). The TAT, using the Leadership Motive Pattern scoring methodology of McClelland and Burnham (1976), has also been shown to predict management career success (McClelland & Boyatzis, 1982).

### Selection of an Assessment Approach: Case Example

In preparation for considering candidates for the Academy Hospital CEO position, the psychologist provided the board with a variety of methodological options, including psychological assessments, structured interviewing, and an assessment center. As is common for higher-level positions, concerns were expressed that many of the assessment options would come across as demeaning for a person at the top levels of an organization. Thus, the assessment protocol that was developed focused on a combination of experience-based interviewing and consideration of biographical information.

Interview questions were constructed to assess each of the competency domains, along with scoring guidelines. Exhibit 8.1 provides example questions and a scoring key that was developed for the content area *charisma*. In order to turn this dimension into a measurable construct, an operational definition was developed with the assistance of behavioral descriptions provided by Conger and Kanungo (1988), and Bass (1985). Using these definitions, in conjunction with a set of critical incidents provided through the interviews, a set of questions was generated for assessing this characteristic in candidates interviewed. A scoring key was also developed by examining the critical incidents from the prior CEO's tenure, and coming to consensus regarding what would constitute evidence of various levels of effectiveness.

The board decided to use the psychologist as one of the interviewers in the process. In addition, two of the board members, two community leaders, and one of the departing CEO's direct reports were selected to participate, providing a diversity of interviewers, in terms of gender as well as ethnic and professional background (see recommendations of Deal, Sessa, & Taylor, 1999). Before beginning the interviewing, the psychologist provided each interviewer with an introduction to the materials, some information about the interviewing process, and several sample responses to rate. In collaboration with the psychologist (who attended all components of each interview conducted), the interviewers proceeded to interview, then score, each of the candidates' responses and background information. Once this step was completed, the psychologist met with the interviewers to facilitate a discussion of their ratings, resolve rating discrepancies, and develop consensus on the scores. Once this was finished, the next step was to eliminate any candidates who were not deemed minimally qualified on one or more of the dimensions rated. The remaining candidates were then discussed, and a final candidate was selected based partly on ratings and partly on discussion of nonrated aspects of the candidates' backgrounds and presentation.

The group agreed that the most qualified candidate was Karen, who at the time was serving as the chief financial officer at the hospital. After Karen accepted the employment offer she was provided, the psychologist met with several of the board members, and then with the candidate, to facilitate the construction of a development and transition plan. This plan drew heavily from the results of the selection process itself, as well as the psychologist's familiarity with executive-level training and development options that would be appropriate to the position requirements and a good match for Karen's learning style. The interview process revealed two areas as development needs for Karen: *charisma* and *coalition-building*. To address these needs, Karen agreed to enroll in leadership and negotiations classes provided by the executive development division of the business school of a nearby university, and to work with an executive coach during the three months prior and six months after the transition took place.

**Exhibit 8.1. Sample Interview Questions and Scoring Key for Charisma.**

A. Interview Questions

1. Tell us about an experience you've had working with staff who were discouraged or had even given up hope on resolving a particular problem, but in which you still tried to make some positive strides. Tell us what the situation was, how you decided to address it and why, and the outcome.

2. Tell us about a time when you had to make a decision that you knew would be unpopular with your staff. What was the situation, how did you come to make the decision, how did you communicate the decision to your staff, and what was the outcome?

3. Give us an example of a time when you had to build support to address a concern that your staff did not initially view as particularly important—for example, where their attitude might initially be "if it's not broken, why fix it?" What was the concern, how did you build support, and what was the outcome?

B. Scoring Key

1. (Strength): Candidate provides examples suggesting a clear ability to: (a) perceive and effectively communicate deficiencies in the status quo; (b) effectively turn around severely fragmented or dissatisfied staff by constructing an effective and emotional call to action (for example, putting staff in touch with their sense of mission, personal duty, or calling to the healthcare profession); and (c) build follower trust through leading by example and demonstration of a willingness to put him or herself on the line.

2. (Acceptable): Candidate provides examples of turning around difficult situations and challenging the status quo, but falls short of a "1" due to one of the following: (a) examples were of situations that were not as challenging as those the new CEO is expected to face; or (b) one of the criteria listed under "1" was not met.

3. (Development need): Candidate provides examples of turning around difficult situations, but falls short of a "2" due to either: (a) missing the bar on multiple components outlined under "1"; or (b) resolutions seemed to come as much as a result of tenacity or exercise of position power as on developing influence through trust and interpersonal relationships.

4. (Unacceptable): Candidate provides examples of situations that did not seem particularly challenging, suggested a limited understanding of others' points of view, or were handled in ways that either alienated staff or otherwise placed trust relationships in jeopardy (for example, resolutions came through intimidation—"Do it or else!"—or through sheer tenacity—"We have to do it this way. Period.").

# CONCLUSIONS

Before drawing conclusions, it is worthwhile to note that although assessment is a critical step in effective human resource practices, it is only one step. Many executives who understand the need for careful selection fail to retain their hard-won human capital because they do not pay enough attention to quality of work life, work-life balance, development, and compensation. Furthermore, even the most effective human resource strategy is still embedded within a larger organizational strategy, which might or might not effectively steer the organization toward achieving its mission regardless of the quality of the executives it employs. In other words, effective assessment is a necessary but not sufficient condition for organization effectiveness.

Although the research evidence available on the subject leaves many open questions, a few conclusions can be drawn. First, there is ample evidence that valid selection practices can add substantial bottom-line value to organizations, to a level that well exceeds their typical cost to administer, regardless of the specific type of selection process used (Schmidt & Hunter, 1998). Burke and Frederick (1986), in a study comparing numerous cost accounting approaches to a selection process for district sales managers, found that even the most conservative estimate suggested a gain of several thousand dollars per selected candidate (in 1983 dollars). Russell (2001), in analyzing a protocol for selecting top-level executives, estimated a cost savings of upwards of $3 million per candidate. Organizational research has also demonstrated the positive effects of sound selection practices as part of an effective HR strategy on organizational performance (Terpstra & Rozell, 1993; Huselid, 1995).

Second, the approach to leadership assessment does seem to make a difference in the validity and usefulness of the results. Assessment methods involving structured processes, as well as statistical and mechanical composites, tend to yield better predictive power than less structured methods and ones relying solely on assessor judgment (McDaniel et al., 1994). Assessment methods that either parallel actual work incidents (for example, assessment centers), or that ask candidates to recreate them from memory (for example, biographical and experience-based interviews), tend to outperform the more distal and hypothetical approaches (for example, situational interviewing and general personality testing). If there is a single best predictor of leadership performance, it is probably general cognitive ability, although assessments using multiple approaches including cognitive ability appear to outperform than those using cognitive ability alone (Mount, Barrick, & Strauss, 1999; O'Reilly & Chatman, 1994; Schmidt & Hunter, 1998), and many tools for measuring cognitive ability are hampered by their potential for adverse impact.

Finally, there is still a tremendous need for additional research in this important area of psychological practice (Ryan & Sackett, 1998). As such, practitioners are strongly encouraged to critically evaluate the work of their peers and themselves on a regular basis, to pursue quantitative evaluation of their results, and to communicate those results to the community of professional assessors.

# References

American Educational Research Association, American Psychological Association, & National Council on Measurement in Education. (1999). *Standards for educational and psychological testing.* Washington, DC: American Psychological Association.

American Psychological Association, Committee on Psychological Tests and Assessment. (1996). Statement on disclosure of test data. *American Psychologist, 51,* 644–648.

Ash, R. A. (1988). Job analysis in the world of work. In S. Gael (Ed.), *The job analysis handbook for business, industry, and government* (Vol. I, pp. 3–13). New York: Wiley.

Baehr, M. E., & Orban, J. A. (1989). The role of intellectual abilities and personality characteristics in determining success in higher-level positions. *Journal of Vocational Behavior, 35,* 270–287.

Barrick, M. R., & Mount, M. K. (1991). The big five personality dimensions and job performance: A meta-analysis. *Personnel Psychology, 44,* 1–26.

Bass, B. M. (1985). *Leadership and performance beyond expectations.* New York: Free Press.

Bass, B. M. (1990). *Bass & Stogdill's handbook of leadership: Theory, research, & managerial applications* (3rd ed.). New York: Free Press.

Bennis, W. G. (2000). Foreword. In D. Giber, L. Carter, & M. Goldsmith (Eds.), *Best practices in leadership development handbook: Case studies, instruments, training.* San Francisco: Jossey-Bass.

Berman, F. E., & Miner, J. B. (1985). Motivation to manage at the top executive level: A test of the hierarchic role-motivation theory. *Personnel Psychology, 73,* 507–514.

Bray, D. W., & Howard, A. (1983). *Longitudinal studies of adult psychological development.* New York: Guilford Press.

Brown, F. G. (1983). *Principles of educational and psychological testing* (3rd ed.). Austin, TX: Holt, Rinehart and Winston.

Burke, M. J., & Day, R. R. (1986). A cumulative study of the effectiveness of managerial training. *Journal of Applied Psychology, 71,* 232–245.

Burke, M. J., & Frederick, J. T. (1986). A comparison of economic utility estimates for alternative study estimation procedures. *Journal of Applied Psychology, 71,* 334–339.

Campion, M. A., Campion, J. E., & Hudson, J. P., Jr. (1994). Structured interviewing: A note on incremental validity and alternative question types. *Journal of Applied Psychology, 79,* 998–1002.

Cascio, W. F. (1998). *Applied psychology in human resource management* (5th ed.). Englewood Cliffs, NJ: Prentice Hall.

Conger, J. A., & Kanungo, R. N. (1988). Behavioral dimensions of charismatic leadership. In J. A. Conger & R. N. Kanungo (Eds.), *Charismatic leadership: The elusive factor in organizational effectiveness.* San Francisco: Jossey-Bass.

Conway, J. M., Jako, R. A., & Goodman, D. F. (1995). A meta-analysis of interrater and internal consistency reliability of selection interviews. *Journal of Applied Psychology, 80,* 565–579.

Cooper, A. C., & Gimeno-Gascon, F. J. (1992). Entrepreneurs, process of founding, and new firm performance. In D. L. Sexton & J. D. Kasarda (Eds.), *The state of the art of entrepreneurship* (pp. 301–340). Boston: PWS.

Cooper, A. C., Woo, C., & Dunkelberg, W. (1988). Entrepreneurs' perceived chances for success. *Journal of Business Venturing, 3,* 97–108.

Daily, C. M., Certo, S. T., & Dalton, D. R. (1999). Entrepreneurial ventures as an avenue to the top? Assessing the advancement of female CEOs and directors in the *Inc.* 100. *Journal of Developmental Entrepreneurship, 4,* 19–32.

Deal, J. J., Sessa, V. I., & Taylor, J. J. (1999). *Choosing executives: A research report on the peak selection simulation.* Greensboro, NC: Center for Creative Leadership.

Dean, M. A., Russell, C. J., & Muchinsky, P. M. (1999). Life experiences and performance prediction: Toward a theory of biodata. In G. Ferris (Ed.), *Research in personnel and human resource management* (Vol. 17, pp. 245–281). Greenwich, CT: JAI Press.

DeVries, D. L. (1992). Executive selection: Advances but no progress. *Center for Creative Leadership: Issues and Observations, 12,* 1–5.

Engle, D. E., Mah, J. J., & Sadri, G. (1997). An empirical comparison of entrepreneurs and employees: Implications for innovation. *Creativity Research Journal, 10,* 45–49.

Equal Employment Opportunity Commission. (1978). *Uniform guidelines on employee selection procedures.* Retrieved April 5, 2002, from http://www.dol.gov/dol/esa/public/regs/cfr/41cfr/toc_Chapt60/60_3_toc.htm

Fear, R. A., & Chiron, R. J. (1990). *The evaluation interview.* New York: McGraw-Hill.

Feldman, D. C., & Bolino, M. C. (2000). Career patterns of the self-employed: Career motivations and career outcomes. *Journal of Small Business Management, 38,* 53–67.

Fleenor, J. W. (1996). Constructs and developmental assessment centers: Further troubling empirical findings. *Journal of Business and Psychology, 10,* 319–335.

Fogli, L., & Whitney, K. (1998). Assessing and changing managers for new organizational roles. In R. Jeanneret & R. Silzer (Eds.), *Individual psychological assessment: Predicting behavior in organizational settings* (pp. 285–329). San Francisco: Jossey-Bass.

Freedman, A. M. (1998). Pathways and crossroads to institutional leadership. *Consulting Psychology Journal: Practice and Research, 50,* 131–151.

Frisch, M. H. (1998). Designing the individual assessment process. In R. Jeanneret & R. Silzer (Eds.), *Individual psychological assessment: Predicting behavior in organizational settings* (pp. 135–177). San Francisco: Jossey-Bass.

Garman, A. N., & Corrigan, P. W. (1998). Developing effective team leaders. In P. W. Corrigan & D. G. Giffort (Eds.), *Building teams and programs for effective psychiatric rehabilitation: New directions for mental health services* (pp. 45–54). San Francisco, CA: Jossey-Bass.

Garman, A. N., Zlatoper, K. W., & Whiston, D. L. (1998). Graduate training programs and consulting psychology: A content analysis of doctoral-level programs. *Consulting Psychology Journal: Practice and Research, 50,* 207–217.

Gaugler, B. B., Rosenthal, D. B., Thornton, G. C., & Bentson, C. (1987). Meta-analysis of assessment center validity. *Journal of Applied Psychology, 72,* 493–511.

Goffin, R. D., Rothstein, M. G., & Johnston, N. G. (1996). Personality testing and the assessment center: Incremental validity for managerial selection. *Journal of Applied Psychology, 81,* 746–756.

Gunter, B., Furnham, A., & Drakeley, R. (1993). *Biodata: Biographical indicators of business performance.* New York: Routledge.

Hammer, E. G., & Kleiman, L. A. (1988). Getting to know you. *Personnel Administrator, 34,* 86–92.

Harvey, R. J. (1999). *Development of the common-metric questionnaire.* Retrieved April 5, 2002, from http://www.ipmaac.org/files/harvey.pdf

Hermelin, E., & Robertson, I. T. (2001). A critique and standardization of meta-analytic validity coefficients in personnel selection. *Journal of Occupational & Organizational Psychology, 74,* 253–277.

Higgs, A. C., Papper, E. M., & Carr, L. S. (2000). Integrating selection with other organizational processes and systems. In J. F. Kehoe (Ed.), *Managing selection in changing organizations* (pp. 73–122). San Francisco, CA: Jossey-Bass.

Hisrich, R. D. (1990). Entrepreneurship/intrapreneurship. *American Psychologist, 45,* 209–222.

Hogan, R., Curphy, G. J., & Hogan, J. (1994). What we know about leadership: Effectiveness and personality. *American Psychologist, 49*(6), 493–504.

Hogan, R., Raskin, R., & Fazzini, D. (1990). The dark side of charisma. In K. E. Clark & M. B. Clark (Eds.), *Measures of leadership* (pp. 343–354). West Orange, NJ: Leadership Library of America.

Hunter, J. E. (1986). Cognitive ability, cognitive aptitude, job knowledge, and job performance. *Journal of Vocational Behavior, 29,* 340–362.

Huselid, M. A. (1995). The impact of human resource management practices on turnover, productivity, and corporate financial performance. *Academy of Management Journal, 38,* 635–672.

Jacobowitz, A., & Vidler, D. C. (1982). Characteristics of entrepreneurs: Implications for vocational guidance. *Vocational Guidance Quarterly, 30,* 252–257.

Jeanneret, R. (1998). Ethical, legal, and professional issues for individual assessment. In R. Jeanneret & R. Silzer (Eds.), *Individual psychological assessment: Predicting behavior in organizational settings* (pp. 88–131). San Francisco: Jossey-Bass.

Johnson, B. R. (1990). Toward a multidimensional model of entrepreneurship: The case of achievement motivation and the entrepreneur. *Entrepreneurship Theory and Practice, 14,* 39–54.

Joiner, D. A. (2000). Guidelines and ethical considerations for assessment center operations: International task force on assessment center guidelines. *Public Personnel Management, 29,* 315–331.

Kets deVries, M.F.R. (1985). The dark side of entrepreneurship. *Harvard Business Review, 63,* 160–167.

Klimoski, R., & Brickner, M. (1987). Why do assessment centers work? The puzzle of assessment center validity. *Personnel Psychology, 40,* 243–260.

Kouzes, J. M., & Posner, B. Z. (1993). *Credibility: How leaders can gain and lose it, why people demand it.* San Francisco: Jossey-Bass.

Kuhnert, K. W., & Russell, C. J. (1990). Using constructive developmental theory and biodata to bridge the gap between personnel selection and leadership. *Journal of Management, 16,* 1–13.

Latham, G. P., & Sue-Chan, C. (1999). A meta-analysis of the situational interview: An enumerative review of reasons for its validity. *Canadian Psychology, 40,* 56–67.

Levinson, H. (1980). Criteria for choosing chief executives. *Harvard Business Review, 58,* 113–120.

Lowman, R. L. (Ed.). (1998). *The ethical practice of psychology in organizations.* Washington, DC: American Psychological Association.

MacMillan, I. C., Siegel, R., & Subba Narasimha, P. N. (1985). Criteria used by venture capitalists to evaluate new venture proposals. *Journal of Business Venturing, 1,* 119–128.

Mael, F. A., Connerley, M., & Morath, R. A. (1996). None of your business: Parameters of biodata invasiveness. *Personnel Psychology, 49,* 613–650.

Mahoney, T. A., Jerdee, T. H., & Carroll, S. I. (1965). The job(s) of management. *Industrial Relations, 4,* 97–110.

McClelland, D. C., & Boyatzis, R. E. (1982). Leadership motive pattern and long-term success in management. *Journal of Applied Psychology, 67,* 737–743.

McClelland, D. C., & Burnham, D. (1976). Power is the great motivator. *Harvard Business Review, 54,* 159–166.

McDaniel, M. A., Whetzel, D. L., Schmidt, F. L., & Maurer, S. D. (1994). The validity of employment interviews: A comprehensive review and meta-analysis. *Journal of Applied Psychology, 79,* 599–616.

Miner, J. B. (1996). *The four routes to entrepreneurial success.* San Francisco: Berrett-Koehler.

Miner, J. B. (1997). *A psychological typology of successful entrepreneurs.* Westport, CT: Greenwood Press.

Miner, J. B., Smith, N. R., & Bracker, J. S. (1994). Role of entrepreneurial task motivation in the growth of technologically innovative firms: Interpretations from follow-up data. *Journal of Applied Psychology, 79,* 627–630.

Mitchell, J. L., & McCormick, E. J. (1990). *Professional and managerial position questionnaire.* North Logan, UT: PAQ Services.

Mount, M. K., Barrick, M. R., & Strauss, J. P. (1999). The joint relationship of conscientiousness and ability with performance: Test of the interaction hypothesis. *Journal of Management, 25,* 707–721.

Mumford, M. D., Costanza, D. P., Connelly, M. S., & Johnson, J. F. (1996). Item generation procedures and background data scales: Implications for construct and criterion-related validity. *Personnel Psychology, 49,* 361–398.

Niemiec, R. P., Sikorski, M. F., Clark, G., & Walberg, H. J. (1992). Effects of management education: A quantitative synthesis. *Evaluation and Program Planning, 15,* 297–302.

Ocasio, W., & Kim, H. (1999). The circulation of corporate control: Selection of functional backgrounds of new CEOs in large U.S. manufacturing firms, 1981–1982. *Administrative Science Quarterly, 44,* 532–562.

Ones, D. S., Viswesvaran, C., & Schmidt, F. L. (1993). Comprehensive meta-analysis of integrity test validities: Findings and implications for personnel selection and theories of job performance. *Journal of Applied Psychology, 78,* 679–703.

O'Reilly, C., & Chatman, J. A. (1994). Working smarter and harder: A longitudinal study of managerial success. *Administrative Science Quarterly, 39,* 603–627.

Oshry, B. (1999). *Leading systems: Lessons from the Power Lab.* San Francisco: Berrett-Koehler.

Peter, R., & Siegrist, J. (1997). Chronic work stress, sickness absence and hypertension in middle managers: General or specific sociological explanations? *Social Science & Medicine, 45,* 1111–1120.

Pulakos, E. D., & Schmitt, N. (1995). Experience-based and situational interview questions: Studies of validity. *Personnel Psychology, 48,* 289–308.

Rauch, A., & Frese, M. (2000). Psychological approaches to entrepreneurial success: A general model and an overview of findings. In C. L. Cooper & I. T. Robertson (Eds.), *International review of industrial & organizational psychology* (Vol. 15, pp. 101–141). New York: Wiley.

Reilly, R. R., & Chao, G. R. (1982). Validity and fairness of some alternative employee selection procedures. *Personnel Psychology, 35,* 1–62.

Reither, A. E., & Pappas, T. K. (1998, April). *Managerial training effectiveness: How far have we come?* Poster session presented at the annual meeting of the Society for Industrial and Organizational Psychology, Dallas, TX.

Russell, C. J. (1990). Selecting top corporate leaders: An example of biographical information. *Journal of Management, 16,* 73–86.

Russell, C. J. (2001). A longitudinal study of top-level executive performance. *Journal of Applied Psychology, 86,* 560–573.

Russell, C. J., Mattson, J., Devlin, S. E., & Atwater, D. (1990). Predictive validity of biodata items generated from retrospective life experience essays. *Journal of Applied Psychology, 75,* 569–580.

Ryan, A. M. (1992). Psychologists' evaluations of individual assessments: A comparison on the basis of graduate training and professional affiliation. *Journal of Business and Psychology, 6,* 371–386.

Ryan, A. M., & Sackett, P. R. (1992). Relationships between graduate training, professional affiliation, and individual psychological assessment practices for personnel decisions. *Personnel Psychology, 45,* 363–385.

Ryan, A. M., & Sackett, P. R. (1998). Individual assessment: The research base. In R. Jeanneret & R. Silzer (Eds.), *Individual psychological assessment: Predicting behavior in organizational settings* (pp. 54–87). San Francisco: Jossey-Bass.

Sandberg, W. R. (1986). *New venture performance: The role of strategy and industry structure.* San Francisco: New Lexington Press.

Schein, E. H. (1992). *Organizational culture and leadership: A dynamic view* (2nd ed.). San Francisco: Jossey-Bass.

Schmidt, F. L., & Hunter, J. E. (1998). The validity and utility of selection methods in personnel psychology: Practical and theoretical implications of 85 years of research findings. *Psychological Bulletin, 124,* 262–274.

Schmitt, N., Clause, C. S., & Pulakos, E. D. (1996). Subgroup differences associated with different measures of some common job-relevant constructs. In C. R. Cooper & I. T. Robertson (Eds.), *International review of industrial and organizational psychology* (Vol. 11, pp. 115–140). New York: Wiley.

Sessa, V. I., & Campbell, R. J. (1997). *Selection at the top: An annotated bibliography.* Greensboro, NC: Center for Creative Leadership.

Sessa, V. I., Kaiser, R., Taylor, J. K., & Campbell, R. J. (1998). *Executive selection: A research report on what works and what doesn't.* Greensboro, NJ: Center for Creative Leadership.

Sessa, V. I., & Taylor, J. J. (2000). *Executive selection: Strategies for success.* San Francisco: Jossey-Bass.

Sharf, J. C., & Jones, D. P. (2000). Employment risk management. In J. F. Kehoe (Ed.), *Managing selection in changing organizations* (pp. 271–318). San Francisco: Jossey-Bass.

Smart, B. D. (1990). *The smart interviewer.* New York: Wiley.

Smart, G. H. (1999). Management assessment methods in venture capital: An empirical analysis of human capital valuation. *Journal of Private Equity, 2*(3), 29–45.

Smith, N. R. (1967). *The entrepreneur and his firm: The relationship between type of man and type of company.* East Lansing: Michigan State University Press.

Smither, J. W., Reilly, R. R., Millsap, R. E., Pearlman, K., & Stoffey, R. W. (1993). Applicant reactions to selection procedures. *Personnel Psychology, 46,* 49–76.

Society for Industrial and Organizational Psychology. (1987). *Principles for the validation and use of personnel selection procedures* (3rd ed.). College Park, MD: Author.

Spychalski, A. C., Quinones, M. A., & Gaugler, B. B. (1997). A survey of assessment center practices in organizations in the United States. *Personnel Psychology, 50,* 71–90.

Stewart, W. H., & Roth, P. L. (2001). Risk propensity differences between entrepreneurs and managers: A meta-analytic review. *Journal of Applied Psychology, 86,* 145–153.

Stokes, G. S., & Cooper, L. A. (1994). Selection using biodata: Old notions revisited. In G. S. Stokes, M. D. Mumford, & W. A. Owens (Eds.), *Biodata handbook* (pp. 311–349). Palo Alto, CA: Consulting Psychologists Press.

Task Force on Assessment Center Guidelines. (1989). Guidelines and ethical considerations for assessment center operations. *Public Personnel Management, 18,* 457–470.

Terpstra, D. E., & Rozell, E. J. (1993). The relationship of staffing practices to organizational level measures of performance. *Personnel Psychology, 46,* 27–48.

Wagner, R. K. (1997). Intelligence, training, and employment. *American Psychologist, 52,* 1059–1069.

Westphal, J. D., & Zajac, E. J. (1995). Who shall govern? A CEO/board power, demographic similarity, and new director selection. *Administrative Science Quarterly, 40,* 60–83.

Wiesner, W. H., & Cronshaw, S. F. (1988). A meta-analytic investigation of the impact of interview format and degree of structure on the validity of the employment interview. *Journal of Occupational Psychology, 61,* 275–290.

Wooten, K. C., Timmerman, T. A., & Folger, R. (1999). The use of personality and the five-factor model to predict new business ventures: From outplacement to start-up. *Journal of Vocational Behavior, 54,* 82–101.

Worrell, D. L., Davidson, W. N., & Glascock, J. L. (1993). Stockholder reactions to departures and appointments of key executives attributable to firings. *Academy of Management Journal, 36,* 387–401.

Young, B. S., Arthur., W., Jr., & Finch, J. (2000). Predictors of managerial performance: More than cognitive ability. *Journal of Business and Psychology, 15,* 53–72.

Zajac, E. J., & Westphal, J. D. (1996). Who shall succeed? How CEO/board preferences and power affect the choice of new CEOs. *Academy of Management Journal, 39,* 64–90.

# CHAPTER NINE

# Enhancing Peak Potential
# in Managers and Leaders:

## *Integrating Knowledge and Findings from Sport Psychology*

Sandra Foster
*Success at Work*

Among a consulting psychologist's activities in the service of organizational effectiveness are the appraisal and development of leadership capacities. The consultant might coach for the development of executive presence as well as for the facilitation of the client's mastery of specific functions such as strategic thinking and influencing others. The consultant is informed in this work by behavioral principles (Sperry, 1996), a knowledge of the client's industry and its challenges, perhaps the tenets of cognitive theory translated into specific techniques for increasing reality testing and improving problem-solving capabilities (Shatte, Reivich, & Seligman, 2000), or even the new *broaden-and-build* model advocating the use of positive emotions in the workplace (Frederickson, 2000). This chapter proposes that the consultant could likewise find a valuable resource in the methodologies used to enhance the performance of high-level athletes. It examines the possible beneficial outcomes resulting from the integration of sport psychology performance-enhancement principles, also known as mental training (terminology more commonly used in Canada and Europe than in the U.S.), into organizational consultation, particularly for individuals. Recommendations for training teams and entire organizations are also noted.

## SPORT PSYCHOLOGY: FOCUS OF RESEARCH AND APPLICATIONS

Sport psychology is an interdisciplinary field that brings together those in sport science—coaches, kinesiologists, physical educators—and psychologists. Areas of interest are the study of training and physiological characteristics contributing to success in competition (Davlin, Sands, & Shultz, 2001; Mujika, Busso, Lacoste, & Barale, 1996), sport as an intervention for psychological disorders such as depression (Babyak et al., 2000; Hays, 1999; Singh, Clements, & Fiatarone, 1997), and benefits of sport for youth (Colchico, Zybert, & Basch, 2000; Orlick & McCaffrey, 1991). However, the enhancement of athletic performance through mental training is a primary focus. A relatively new specialty emerging in the 1960s and 1970s (Wiggins, 1984), sport and exercise psychology became Division 47 of the American Psychological Association in 1987 (Williams & Straub, 1993).

The merits of sport psychology and mental training methodology for recreational, elite, and professional athletes are supported by more than two decades of controlled research (Cox, Qui, & Liu, 1993; Rejeski & Thompson, 1993). There is growing evidence for the efficacy of performance enhancement techniques applied with elite (Olympic or professional) athletes, based on numerous survey studies and reports from those associated with national and international sport-related organizations (Anshel & Porter, 1996; Buceta, 2001; Fink, 2001; Gould, Guinan, Greenleaf, Medbury, & Peterson, 1999; Mahoney, Gabriel, & Perkins, 1987; Orlick, 1998a; Samela, 1989). However, the transfer of the methodology of performance enhancement to settings other than sport is more recent (Hays, 2000). The focus here is the contribution of sport psychology principles and techniques to consulting best practices when engagements are focused on the development of competence in individual managers and leaders, and work teams. The literature on this skill transfer from sport to business settings is reviewed, along with the relevant empirical findings from the emerging area of positive psychology.

The quest for the quantification of factors in organizational leadership effectiveness has occupied the attention of business school faculty, consultants, and researchers in Industrial-Organizational (I-O) psychology since World War II (Levinson, 1981, 1991; Moxley & Wilson, 1998; Schein, 1996; Wilhelm, 1996). From the 1970s to the present day, the processes involved in developing expertise and the means for deploying skillful action while competing have been two major questions investigated by sport psychology. The same two areas of inquiry by sport psychologists have been pursued by those striving to bring the best consultation practices to businesses.

## SKILL TRANSFER FROM SPORT TO BUSINESS: REVIEW OF THE LITERATURE

There are no studies that directly compare a sport psychology intervention with an I-O psychology consultation in investigations of managerial acumen or executive success. Only a few studies have been conducted in business settings that empirically test the efficacy of the techniques that sport psychologists routinely use in their performance-enhancement interventions. Nevertheless, a review of the sport psychology literature yields numerous practical applications of mental training skills to business settings that have potential relevance to organizational consulting psychology. From these studies, the reader will discover several factors important to athletes' peak performance that are pertinent to the achievement of corporate leaders. I find (Foster, 2001) that these techniques possess considerable face validity for business clients and are well received by them.

Sport psychologists have identified five major skills of mental training (Gordin and Heil, 1996). These are: (1) the incorporation of mental imagery into the planning for the season, injury recovery, and competition preparation; (2) the use of performance routines in training and competition; (3) the use of positive self-talk to mentally guide performance; (4) activation control strategies; and (5) techniques for sharpening focus and sustaining attention to a task (concentration). The empirical basis for each of these skills is presented in the next several pages. One other area of research in performance enhancement is noted because of its relevance: deliberate practice.

## THE FIRST SKILL: USING MENTAL IMAGERY TO IMPROVE PERFORMANCE

*Man can create anything he imagines.*
—Hill

The utility of imagery in mental practice to enhance athletic performance has long been a research focus of sport psychologists, notably Suinn (1972, 1985, 1993). Likewise, imagery in mental processing has a substantial history in the cognitive science literature. Rieber (1995) provides an historical review of imagery used for initiating and improving creativity and problem-solving. Results of a meta-analysis of the mental practice literature indicate that mental practice, including the use of imagery, has a positive and significant effect on performance (Driskell, Copper, & Moran, 1994).

Suinn (1997) reviews the empirical basis for imagery training and notes several elements that allow an athlete to make the best use of such mental imagery practice. He recommends that simple relaxation procedures precede each session of self-guided mental practice, and that the user, rather than practitioner, specify precisely the content of the imagery. His research also indicates that alternating mental practice with the actual behavioral practice of skills leads to more favorable results. Outcomes from other studies also suggest the value of imagery-based mental training for improving athletic performance in terms of more rapid skill acquisition, the development of effective coping strategies when facing a setback, reduced state somatic and cognitive competitive anxiety, increasing the accuracy of a discrete skill, and effectively establishing a competitive attitude before a race or contest (Gould & Damarjian, 1996; Savoy & Beitel, 1996; Savoy, 1997; Vealey & Walter, 1993; Weinberg & Williams, 1993). This mental training skill might well have merit in business settings. Suinn's prescriptions appear to be transferable to consultation processes for employees developing their sense of themselves as managers (Foster, 2001).

One empirical study investigated the effects of imagery-based mental practice on transfer of training in a Canadian pulp and paper mill (Morin & Latham, 2000). Mental practice consisted of imaginary rehearsal of the specific communication skills taught to the subjects, who were forty-one supervisors and process engineers. A second independent variable was the explicit setting of goals (goal commitment condition), or implicit goal setting (no definite goals set). Those subjects in the mental-practice and the mental-practice-plus-goal-setting conditions evinced higher self-efficacy ratings and improvements in peer ratings of workplace communication skills than employees in the goal-setting-only or control conditions.

This study was noteworthy for its random assignment of subjects to groups and its being conducted in a naturalistic setting. A possible confounder in this investigation was the reliance on subjects' self-report that they, in fact, had not set specific goals for themselves (in the implicit goal-setting condition), apart from the researchers' time with them during the instructions for the imaginary skill rehearsal. Despite this limitation, these results suggest that mental practice using imagery, a commonly used sport psychology technique, could be a helpful procedure in the consultant's tool kit. The benefits of this mental practice would be augmented by clients setting definite goals, as this study's results suggested.

## THE SECOND MAJOR MENTAL TRAINING SKILL: THE CONTRIBUTION OF PERFORMANCE ROUTINES TO PRODUCTIVITY IN BUSINESS

*We are what we repeatedly do. Excellence, then, is not an act but a habit.*
—Aristotle

Olympic and elite athletes around the world rely on performance routines to maximize their adherence to their training regimen and to compete successfully. Orlick (1998b), writing in a trade publication based upon his research in athletic performance enhancement (Kreiner-Phillips & Orlick, 1993; McCaffrey & Orlick, 1989; Orlick & Partington, 1988; Zhang, Ma, Orlick, & Zitzelsberger, 1992), offers several guidelines for success that could translate well into a consultant's work with individuals or teams, including prescribing performance routines. In sport, these are consistent habits of sleep and nutrition, mental and physical preparatory rituals performed before competing or engaging in challenging portions of training, and the proficient allocation of time to practice (Jackson & Baker, 2001; Orlick, 1998b).

Performance routines also incorporate strategies for recovery from intense periods of exertion to avoid overload (Orlick, 1998b), usually called overtraining in sport. Overcommitment—manifesting as overwork (Lowman, 1993)—might be the focus of a consultant's coaching with a rising star or a team. Cogent arguments for the deleterious effects of overwork can be found in examples of athletic overtraining (Lehmann, Foster, & Keul, 1994; McKenzie, 1999). The use of performance routines for both performance enhancement and to help prevent overwork is described by Foster (2002). Sport psychologist Jim Loehr reports on the use of performance routines and the importance of recovery in consultations with corporate clients (Loehr & Schwartz, 2001).

Although there are no empirical studies examining the efficacy of performance routines on the enhancement of work performance, the impact of effective use of time has been the focus of two investigations. Fifty-six supervisors at an Australian manufacturing plant were randomly assigned to a three-day, off-site time-management training session or a no-treatment control group (Orpen, 1995). Time-management techniques included "setting goals, learning time planning, setting priorities for tasks and jobs, dealing with interruptions, using filing systems . . . time diaries . . . and techniques for handling incoming information" (p. 394). Three managers reviewed the diary entries kept by all subjects, and rated those in the trained group as engaging in significantly better use of time than those who were untrained. Self-reports of trained subjects indicated their evaluations of their time management were superior to the reports from untrained employees. While random assignment of subjects was a strong point of this study, providing training on-site and tying training results to actual productivity rather than relying upon raters' evaluations or self-reports could be improvements in a future replication.

In a second study (Barling, Cheung, & Kelloway, 1996), researchers assessed subjects' use of specific time-management behaviors, reflecting either short- or long-term planning, and achievement striving using one dimension of a Type-A measure (Spence, Helmreich, & Pred, 1987) that gauged effective characteristics such as taking work seriously and working hard (Bluen, Barling, & Burns, 1990). When data were analyzed from 102 high and average performers at sixty Canadian car dealerships, short-term planning behaviors—such as setting daily goals—interacting with achievement striving were found to correlate with total number of sales. Regression analyses revealed that the number of years of experience was also a predictor of sales production.

These two investigations, when examined more closely for the factors associated with effective performance, identify not only the effective use of time but also prioritizing, goal-setting, and what sport psychology research has termed goal commitment. These elements are addressed in the section on Focus and Concentration.

Returning to another guideline of Orlick's (1998b), he recommends that athletes evaluate their routines and results, and concludes, *do what works.* This exhortation is a principle found in appreciative inquiry (Cooperrider, 1995; Cooperrider, Barrett, & Srivastva, 1995; Cooperrider, Sorensen, Whitney, & Yaeger, 1999; Sorensen & Yeager, 2002), a model that urges that businesses move away from a problem-based focus of inquiry to the identification of what works. Recent publications illustrate the radical difference in perspective and improved productivity for corporations and nonprofits that apply appreciative inquiry (AI) principles (Hammond, 1996; Watkins & Mohr, 2001).

Sport psychologists and coaches have recognized the powerful effect of identifying the factors of *successful* performance so that they can be replicated in future training and competitions (Thompson, 1998). The similarity of sport psychologists' emphasis on asking *what works* with the focus of appreciative inquiry in strategic planning is noteworthy. Consultants might consider incorporating appreciative inquiry questions (for example, What practices contribute to increased profit? What do our customers like about our service?) into their assessment of the strengths of the executives, teams, and the organization as a unit, based on the positive outcomes of AI principles applied in consultations with British Airways North America, NASA, McDonalds, and DTE Energy Systems (as cited in Watkins & Mohr, 2001).

Another area of research relevant to performance routines and the concept of mastery is that of *deliberate practice* (Ericsson, Krampe, & Tesch-Roemer, 1993; Lehmann & Ericsson, 1999). In the initial investigation (Ericsson et. al., 1993), researchers found that, contrary to the assumption that innate talent accounted for most of the variance related to mastery in music, it was intense practice over a ten-year period that emerged as one of the main characteristics contributing to expert performance. This finding has implications for the design of effective training regimens and performance routines in performing arts, and has been evaluated, along with commitment to sport, in a retrospective study of individual and team practice time spent by national and provincial level athletes (Helsen, Starkes, & Hodges, 1998).

The outcomes from the Lehmann and Ericsson study (1999) suggest that the learning process of proceeding from novice to expert could be refined by incorporating several tactics derived from this line of research: recognizing the importance of practice time and scheduling it; individualizing the training plan for an individual or a team; and improving feedback from master instructor to learner. Similarly, the latter point of seeking feedback has been recommended by consulting psychologists Peterson and Hicks (1995).

While most new managers would balk at the idea of a decade spent in deliberate practice before achieving mastery, they might be persuaded by consultants who make the case by citing the successes of elite athletes who are more likely to train with greater intensity after performance failures (Anshel & Porter, 1996), as well as the reports, noted earlier, of the benefits to Olympic competitors of strategies like performance routines. The consultant could design development plans with an individual client or team, specifying leadership skills to be practiced, regular opportunities when practice could be optimally conducted, and the means for securing regular and specific feedback on skill acquisition progress from someone who has mastered the skills. The consultant could then assist these clients in setting priorities, scheduling effectively using accurate appraisals of time needed for task execution, and adopting techniques for recovery from periods of intense output to help ward off overwork. This approach would parallel a sport psychologist's prescriptions of performance routines for a high-level competitor or team.

## RESEARCH IN THE USE OF SELF-TALK AS A THIRD MENTAL TRAINING SKILL

*Whether you believe you can do a thing or not, you are right.*
—Ford

Self-talk that is positive, self-affirming, and that internally guides successful behavior is a third major mental training skill. Sport psychology quickly adopted strategies from Beck's approach to cognitive therapy (Mahoney et al., 1987; Whelan, Mahoney, & Meyers, 1991) and rational-emotive therapy (RET). Theorists such as Albert Ellis have influenced sport psychologists' approach to self-talk (1982), as well as that of practitioners in the field of consulting psychology (2001). Several empirical studies support the hypothesis that specific self-talk techniques increase athletes' positive mood and self-confidence, and also appear to enhance performance during competition (Clingman & Hilliard, 1990; Gould, Eklund, & Jackson, 1992a, 1992b; Masters & Lambert, 1989; Spink, 1988; Van Raalte, Brewer, Rivera, & Petitpas, 1994; Whelan et al., 1991).

The use of constructive self-talk was tested empirically in a business setting by Neck and Manz (1996), who examined the efficacy of a skills-training package termed *thought self-leadership* (Godwin, Neck, & Houghton, 1999; Neck, Neck, Manz, & Godwin, 1999). The researchers compared the outcomes of trained employees with those waiting to be trained; all were volunteers and were randomly assigned to a treatment condition. The forty-eight subjects worked for the accounting department of America West, a company operating under bankruptcy status at the time. The thought self-leadership (TSL) training consisted of six weekly two-hour sessions of instruction. Subjects learned how to replace cognitive distortions with more functional self-referents (Burns, 1980), how to use positive self-talk in the manner of Butler (1981), and how to imagine the completion of assignments at work and elsewhere using Orlick's approach (1986).

The second author's conceptualization of transforming unhealthy thought patterns into constructive ones (Manz, 1992) was another element of the program, along with a relapse-prevention component. Those trained reported that the TSL instruction helped them in their work, and self-report measures showed higher job-satisfaction scores, less nervousness, and greater enthusiasm at work, when compared to the reports of those not yet trained. Those in the TSL group also perceived the organization's position in the bankruptcy proceedings in a more opportunistic manner than those in the wait-list control group. In their discussion, the authors noted that the findings provided support for the assertion of Judge and Locke (1993) that dysfunctional thinking is a factor in negative affect at work and experiencing less satisfaction with one's job. The investigators also commented on three limitations of the study: that all subjects worked in the same department and that some information might have migrated from those trained to those waiting to be trained; that, since all subjects worked for the accounting department, the generalizability of the findings to employees in other departments was limited; and finally, that no other credible treatment was compared to TSL.

Lange and Grieger (1993) developed a corporate training model that integrated the RET principles of self-motivation and realistic thinking into management consultation. The authors presented a case study to illustrate the promise of such a program. The authors recommended to users both a careful appraisal of employees' ongoing use of the skills taught in the program and follow-up interventions to address possible "resistance" (p. 55) to a fundamental RET principle, that of taking personal responsibility for one's emotional responses and behavior.

Incorporating self-talk as one intervention step—yet extending far beyond simple internal dialogue—is the concept of *explanatory style*. Martin Seligman and his colleagues developed this innovative construct (Abramson, Seligman, & Teasdale, 1978) and posited that explanatory style was the personal explication or understanding of what caused an event, whether good or bad. According to Seligman, explanatory style was not to be confused with motivation, but rather described a person's state of mind, whether optimistic or pessimistic. More than 500 investigations of optimistic explanatory style have been conducted, demonstrating the wide-ranging applicability of training in optimism to sport and business performance enhancement, as well as to improving health status (Peterson & Seligman, 1987; Kamen-Siegel, Rodin, Seligman, & Dwyer, 1991), and fending off depression (Jaycox, Reivich, Gillham, & Seligman, 1994). An instrument for assessing optimistic explanatory style has been created and validated: the Seligman Attributional Style Questionnaire or SASQ (Peterson et al., 1982; Shulman, Castellon, & Seligman, 1989).

In an oft-cited study of nationally ranked swimmers from the University of California at Berkeley, Seligman and his colleagues (Seligman, Nolen-Hoeksema, Thorton, & Thorton, 1990) found that those athletes who scored as pessimistic felt defeated by false feedback from their coaches, who told them they had posted slower times than they actually did. Their performance deteriorated on a second swim. However, performance decrements were not shown by the swimmers who scored as optimists on the SASQ. Explanatory style did not correlate with the coaches' judgments of who would come back after hearing falsely negative times.

There is evidence that optimism is a crucial factor in business success. Seligman and Shulman (1986) tested the hypothesis that explanatory style would predict the performance of Metropolitan Life insurance agents who, like other sales people, frequently experienced negative events during their workdays (rejection by potential customers, contracts not being signed after hours of negotiation, and the stress of cold calling). Even when sales aptitude was taken into account, the most optimistic sales people sold 37 percent more insurance in their initial two years in the business when compared with their more pessimistic counterparts.

In a second prospective study of new hires, retention rates and sales productivity were much higher for those agents testing as optimists on the SASQ. In contrast, pessimistic agents sold fewer policies and were more likely to quit. These findings have been supported by Goleman (1995, 1998), who included optimism as a key factor of emotional intelligence (EI). Although consultants might debate the merits of assessing the full range of EI on either the Goleman instrument or another instrument that is widely used, the Bar-On EQ-i (Bar-On & Parker, 2000; Robins, 2002), they might be convinced of the merits of testing optimism using the SASQ.

Although more empirical research is needed, case reports suggest the benefit to individual corporate clients of teaching optimism skills in a customized fashion after reviewing an employee's score in the six areas of the SASQ (Foster, 2001). Similar findings for individuals and teams are also reported by Stoltz (1997). Extrapolating from various reports and my own experience consulting, I would recommend that optimism skills training for teams involve the following: confidential SASQ results highlighting areas of need; training examples that reflect corporate culture and problems facing the team; and booster sessions to reinforce the use of optimistic explanatory style to guide workday encounters.

## THE FOURTH MAJOR MENTAL TRAINING SKILL: ACTIVATION CONTROL

*Both are foes to tranquility—the inability to change and the inability to endure.*
—Seneca the Younger

The ability to be self-composed under pressure is a valued skill in competitive sport and for business performance. Sport psychologists routinely teach skills that allow athletes to regulate their level of arousal at will, whether the need is to relax, to pump up in order to manifest a burst of energy for a specific task, or to maintain one's pace during an endurance event. Likewise, consultants might include relaxation exercises for management of workplace stressors in their interventions, but might not be familiar with activation techniques. These can be physical, such as moving about to increase heart rate and blood pressure, cognitive, such as imagining speedy movement or feeling inspired by reflecting upon one's dream goal, or environmental, such as lowering ambient room temperature or shifting location. No empirical studies could be found that examined, in a business setting, the specific bipolar approach to teaching activation control that is common to sport psychology, that is, imparting effective skills for both relaxing *and* activating. Further research would shed light on the relevance of this particular training paradigm for managers and aspiring leaders.

Constructs used in this area of sport psychology research can potentially be transferred to leadership training conducted by consultants in organizational settings. As one example, the *zone of optimal functioning* (ZOF), conceived by Hanin (1980), refers to the level of intensity that an individual athlete can specify and learn in order to recreate best performances (Hanin, 1989). In the application of this theory to sport performance, the consultant facilitates the athlete's identification of this optimal state, anchored in the recollection of the circumstances in which it occurred. Mental practice is suggested, whereby the athlete imagines the event in which she experienced this optimal state, and specifies the cues for reaccessing the associated physical sensations and emotion. The athlete is then taught, in the bipolar fashion noted previously, strategies for adjusting arousal (intensity) to match his or her ZOF.

Two studies of distance runners (Morgan, O'Connor, Sparling, & Pate, 1987; Morgan, O'Connor, Ellickson, & Bradley, 1988), and one investigation with soccer players (Krane, 1993), showed support for Hanin's construct in working with athletic performance. Reviewers critical of the studies noted the need for ZOF to have been determined by individual, not group, assessment, and that real-time measures rather than retrospective ones should have been used.

In an attempt to address the limitations of the unidimensional nature of the ZOF concept, catastrophe theory (Thom, 1975) has been cited as a way to understand the activation-performance relationship. Hardy and Fazey (1987) proposed that two factors contributed to level of activation, physiological arousal, and cognitive anxiety. They suggested that cognitive anxiety was the mediator for physiological arousal, meaning that an athlete's cognitive appraisal of his anxiety would be one important factor influencing his performance. The few studies that have been conducted (Hardy, 1990; Hardy & Parfitt, 1992) have generally found support for the predictions elaborated in catastrophe theory.

A consultant could assist an executive client in finding his or her ZOF by employing the retrospective assessment used in Hanin's research (Hanin, 1986). The person wishing to perform optimally is asked to remember a time when he experienced being in charge, effective, on target, and achieving the desired goal. The consultant then directs the client's attention to his body sensations and level of energy or adrenaline associated with this recollection. A key word is selected by the client to cue this memory and the physical sensations associated with this optimal state. While training in the mental skill of activation control is widely practiced in sport psychology, more research would help answer the question of whether such training provides lasting benefit—to those in sport or to those in business.

There are several implications for individuals and teams learning activation control that could have a positive impact on the entire organization. The ability to quickly replicate optimal performance states could mean decreased lag time between the intention to act and the initiation of behavior. To be able to relax at will could enable leaders and their subordinates to manage stressful events occurring during the workday and potentially reduce overall state anxiety. Employees being able to deploy activation skills when they experience diminished energy could permit them, as necessary, to persist in their efforts, say, to meet an important deadline. These three possible outcomes suggest the value of exploring the use of mental training skill in the workplace.

# THE FIFTH MENTAL TRAINING SKILL: FOCUS AND CONCENTRATION

*In every area of effectiveness within an organization, one feeds the*
*opportunities and starves the problems.*
—Drucker

The reports of sport psychologists who have experience working with elite athletes (Gould, Eklund, & Jackson, 1992a; Ogilvie, 1995) indicate that the clarity of long-range goals as well as focus on tactical plans are factors in their success. These reports, compiled from interviews with successful and unsuccessful elite athletes, are suggestive. Bruce Ogilvie, a pioneer in sport psychology, has consulted with professional and Olympic athletes since the 1960s. He has consistently found this relationship between an athlete's clear sense of purpose and goals, and his or her success in qualifying for the Summer or Winter Games (B. Ogilvie, personal communication, August 17, 2001). He describes how these athletes engage in daily reminders, or even reverie, about this purpose during the long months of training, and return to it when feeling discouraged or troubled by self-doubt. He concludes that this clearly defined purpose enhances the athlete's capacity to focus on the task at hand, both in training and during competition, and can serve as the cornerstone for initiating and sustaining effort even under conditions of considerable stress. Echoing these findings about Olympic competitors, survey research on peak performance in business points to success for those who are truly mission-driven (Garfield, 1989).

Discovering, defining, and clearly articulating the *appropriate* mission and organizational values are among the factors contributing to an organization's success when chief executive officers characterize what's working (for example, Gillette's Al Zeien, Pfizer's Bill Steere, Cisco's John Chambers, and Caterpiller's John Fites, quoted in Neff & Citrin, 2001), and when researchers in organizational management delineate their findings (Collins, 2001; Collins and Porras, 1994; Heskett & Schlesinger, 1996). Although a review of the business goal-setting literature and its implications is beyond the scope of this chapter, it can be said that in both business and in sport, mission, purpose, and goal-setting are critically important constructs and practices (Gould, Tammen, Murphy, & May, 1989; Orlick & Partington, 1988; Weinberg, Stitcher, & Richardson, 1994).

Reflecting upon purpose and reviewing goals might direct the athlete's attention to the task, and this might also prove to be the case for individuals and teams at work. What a consultant may also find useful is Nideffer's theoretical model of concentration, and specific strategies of broad versus narrow focus (1992). He defines concentration as the ability to focus on the right target in a given situation, and the capacity to shift from one type of focusing to another in order to maintain an optimal level of performance. Using business examples, an executive is focusing broadly when she appraises her organization's competitive position in a global manner, taking in information from a variety of sources. Narrow focus would be exemplified by her response to certain of the day's events as they unfold within the organization in real time. The consultant could make clients aware of the need for both broad and narrow focus, and coach them in the recognition of cues and tactics for shifting focus.

In practice with business clients, I find the focusing heuristic of Ogilvie (1999) applicable as well. Here, capacity for focus is enhanced not only by clear purpose and goals, but also by the client's savvy management of distractions defined as either internal, within oneself, or external, in the environment and relating to others. In my own consulting practice, I help clients identify internal distractions such as negative emotions, unpleasant physical states, negative thoughts, and neutral but unrelated thoughts (Foster, 2002). Tactics for managing each of these distractions are offered, including the other four mental training skills, along with a model for mindfulness and present-moment awareness that notes the utility of occasional compartmentalization. Skills for managing external distractions include training in the management of time and information flow, effective delegation, and the efficient procurement of outside resources for child and elder care.

# AN EXAMPLE OF THE MAJOR PERFORMANCE-ENHANCEMENT STRATEGIES IN ACTION

My work has been primarily with individual clients, but the skills described in the following example could be employed with functional groups or project teams. A consultant could also promote these skills for optimal performance as an element of organization-wide culture. This example from my practice retains the anonymity of a senior scientist, who, in his 40s at the time of the consultation, was struggling to lead a seven-person team for a large pharmaceutical firm. He had not sought this promotion, but felt supported by his immediate superior, who had sent the client to two management courses taught by an external training firm and encouraged him to seek coaching.

My assessment revealed that the client was an engaging and well-liked man with an average to moderately optimistic explanatory style on the SASQ, a strong technical background, and obvious promise as a leader. He already could delegate effectively to his group of hard-working scientists. Although he was a bright, even brilliant conceptualizer, he had never learned how to organize himself, his time, or his projects. He admitted to last-minute flurries of output while in graduate school, even though his grades were high and faculty reports were glowing. His pattern of erratic focus and working in fits and starts without a plan had persisted into this phase of his career. Therefore, our coaching addressed these deficits and set goals for him to attain and sustain high levels of effective performance as a leader.

The client was encouraged to secure mentoring from his boss, a director, in strategic thinking and goal-setting, and more efficient use of the substantial IT systems in place for tracking and reporting on projects. His boss agreed, and regular meetings were scheduled during which the client could demonstrate his developing skills as planner and implementor, and receive feedback. Our conversations helped him clarify his own sense of purpose at work, even though he was well aware of the corporate mission. An adept visualizer, he was encouraged to use imagery to see himself becoming the leader that his boss had envisioned and the client found himself wishing he could be. With coaching, he developed performance routines for organizing his own work space, setting daily goals for himself at the end of each business day for the next, and establishing regular sleep, eating, and exercise habits that had been missing.

He began to arrive at work at 8 A.M. instead of when it suited him, quickly focused himself using his daily goals and a brief visualization, and employed self-statements to refocus when competing neutral thoughts disrupted his concentration. In the assessment, it was noted that he possessed no strategies for managing information or interactions with his reports. He instituted regular team and one-to-one meetings. He began to allocate specific daily times for returning non-urgent telephone calls and replying to electronic mail. He eventually advised his team about streamlining electronic correspondence by clearly specifying the topic and reply deadline in the subject line.

The results of this intervention would ideally have been measured by a 360-degree instrument, but their use had been discontinued by the organization after complaints about the mishandling of information. Informal evaluations of this client's progress were sought from his direct reports, and his yearly performance review provided another marker. His boss was pleased with the progress he observed, and committed himself to continuing the mentoring. His team's comments suggested they liked the regular contact with him and appreciated his more focused direction of their work.

# SUMMARY

This chapter has described the best practices from sport psychology and mental training, areas of endeavor that are dedicated to the research and application of methods for enhancing performance generally, and which specifically deploy techniques for attaining goals under conditions of intense competition. Empirical studies testing these methods in the workplace are few, and more research is needed to judge their efficacy and explore how best to integrate these skills into the ongoing functions of individual leaders and teams. The chapter suggests that those in consulting psychology can be informed by the outcomes of this domain in which high performance is an expectation and peak experiences are sought and welcomed. I suggest that organizational consultants have much to gain from becoming familiar with the five major mental training skills described in the preceding pages and considering their use during their engagements.

## References

Abramson, L. Y., Seligman, M.E.P., & Teasdale, J. D. (1978). Learned helplessness in humans: Critique and reformulation. *Journal of Abnormal Psychology, 87,* 49–74.

Anshel, M. H., & Porter, A. (1996). Self-regulatory characteristics of competitive swimmers as a function of skill level and gender. *Journal of Sport Behavior, 19,* 91–110.

Babyak, M., Blumenthal, J. A., Herman, S., Khatri, P., Doraiswamy, M., Moore, K., et al. (2000). Exercise treatment for major depression: Maintenance of therapeutic benefit at 10 months. *Psychosomatic Medicine, 62,* 633–638.

Barling, J., Cheung, D., & Kelloway, E. K. (1996). Time management and achievement striving interact to predict car sales performance. *Journal of Applied Psychology, 81,* 821–826.

Bar-On, R., & Parker, J. D. A. (Eds.). (2000). *The handbook of emotional intelligence.* San Francisco: Jossey-Bass.

Bluen, S. D., Barling, J., & Burns, W. (1990). Predicting sales performance, job satisfaction, and depression using the achievement strivings and impatience-irritability dimension of Type A behavior. *Journal of Applied Psychology, 75,* 212–216.

Buceta, J. (2001, October). *Psychological preparation in the immediate period prior to top competitions.* Symposium conducted at the sixteenth annual conference of the Association for the Advancement of Applied Sport Psychology, Orlando, FL.

Burns, D. D. (1980). *Feeling good: The new mood therapy.* New York: Morrow.

Butler, P. E. (1981). *Talking to yourself: Learning the language of self-support.* San Francisco: Harper San Francisco.

Clingman, J. M., & Hilliard, D. V. (1990). Race walkers quicken their pace by tuning in, not stepping out. *The Sport Psychologist, 4,* 25–32.

Colchico, K., Zybert, P., & Basch, C. E. (2000). Effects of after-school physical activity on fitness, fatness, and cognitive self-perceptions. *American Journal of Public Health, 90,* 977–978.

Collins, J. C. (2001). *From good to great.* New York: HarperCollins.

Collins, J. C., & Porras, J. I. (1994). *Built to last: Successful habits of visionary companies.* New York: HarperCollins.

Cooperrider, D. L. (1995). Introduction to appreciative inquiry. *Organizational Development* (5th ed.). Englewood Cliffs, NJ: Prentice Hall.

Cooperrider, D. L., Barrett, F. J., & Srivastva, S. (1995). Social construction and appreciative inquiry: A journey in organizational theory. In D. Hosking, P. Dachler, & K. Gergen (Eds.), *Management and organization: Relational alternatives to individualism* (pp. 157–200). Aldershot, England: Avebury Press.

Cooperrider, D. L., Sorensen, P. F., Jr., Whitney, D., & Yaeger, T. (Eds.). (1999). *Appreciative inquiry: Rethinking human organization toward a positive theory of change.* Champaign, IL: Stipes.

Cox, P. H., Qui, Y., & Liu, Z. (1993). Overview of sport psychology. In R. N. Singer, M. Murphy, & L. K. Tennant (Eds.), *Handbook of research on sport psychology* (pp. 3–31). Old Tappan, NJ: Macmillan.

Davlin, C. D., Sands, W. A., & Shultz, B. B. (2001). The role of vision in control of orientation in a back tuck somersault. *Motor Control, 5,* 337–346.

Driskell, J. E., Copper, C., & Moran, A. (1994). Does mental practice enhance performance? *Journal of Applied Psychology, 79,* 481–492.

Ellis, A. (1982). Self-direction in sport and life. *Rational Living, 17,* 27–33.

Ellis, A. (2001, August). *How I survived 60 years of consulting psychology practice.* Invited address presented at the 109th annual meeting of the American Psychological Association, San Francisco.

Ericsson, K. A., Krampe, R. T., & Tesch-Roemer, C. (1993). The role of deliberate practice in the acquisition of expert performance. *Psychological Review, 100,* 363–406.

Fink, C. (2001, October). *Psychological preparation of the Mexican modern pentathaletes for the Sydney Olympic Games.* Symposium conducted at the sixteenth annual conference of the Association for the Advancement of Applied Sport Psychology, Orlando, FL.

Foster, S. (2001, August). *Adapting performance psychology principles to the enhancement of executives' functioning.* Paper presented at the 109th annual meeting of the American Psychological Association, San Francisco.

Foster, S. (2002). *Stand out and move up: Becoming a peak performer at work.* Manuscript submitted for publication.

Frederickson, B. L. (2000). Why positive emotions matter in organizations: Lessons from the broaden-and-build model. *The Psychologist-Manager Journal, 4*(2), 131–142.

Garfield, C. (1989). *Peak performers.* New York: Avon.

Godwin, J. L., Neck, C. P., & Houghton, J. D. (1999). The impact of thought self-leadership on individual goal performance. *Journal of Management Development, 18,* 153–170.

Goleman, D. (1995). *Emotional intelligence: Why it can matter more than IQ.* New York: Bantam Books.

Goleman, D. (1998). *Working with emotional intelligence.* New York: Bantam Books.

Gordin, R., & Heil, J. (1996). The cardinal skills of mental training. *American Fencing, 49,* 10–11.

Gould, D., & Damarjian, N. (1996). Imagery training for peak performance. In J. L.Van Raalte & B. W. Brewer (Eds.), *Exploring sport and exercise psychology* (pp. 25–50). Washington, DC: American Psychological Association.

Gould, D., Eklund, R. C, & Jackson, S. A. (1992a). 1988 U.S. Olympic wrestling excellence: I. Mental preparation, precompetition cognition, and affect. *The Sport Psychologist, 6,* 358–382.

Gould, D., Eklund, R.C., & Jackson, S.A. (1992b). 1988 U.S. Olympic wrestling excellence: II. Thoughts and affect occurring during competition. *The Sport Psychologist, 6,* 383–402.

Gould, D., Guinan, D., Greenleaf, C., Medbury, R., & Peterson, K. (1999). Factors affecting Olympic performance: Perceptions of athletes and coaches from more and less successful teams. *The Sport Psychologist, 13,* 371–394.

Gould, D., Tammen, V., Murphy, S., & May, J. (1989). An examination of U.S. Olympic sport psychology consultants and the services they provide. *The Sport Psychologist, 3,* 300–312.

Hammond, S. A. (1996). *The thin book of appreciative inquiry.* Plano, TX: Thin Book.

Hanin, Y. L. (1980). A study of anxiety in sports. In W. F. Straub (Ed.), *Sport psychology: An analysis of athlete behavior* (pp. 236–249). Ithaca, NY: Mouvement.

Hanin, Y. L. (1986). The state-trait anxiety research on sports in the USSR. In C. D. Spielberger & R. Diaz-Guerrero (Eds.), *Cross-cultural anxiety* (Vol. 3, pp. 45–64). Bristol, PA: Hemisphere.

Hanin, Y. L. (1989). Interpersonal and intergroup anxiety: Conceptual and methodological issues. In C.D Spielberger & D. Hackfort (Eds.), *Anxiety in sport: An international perspective* (pp. 19–28). Bristol, PA: Hemisphere.

Hardy, L. (1990). A catastrophe model of performance in sport. In J. G. Jones & L. Hardy (Eds.), *Stress and performance in sport* (pp. 81–106). New York: Wiley.

Hardy, L., & Fazey, J. (1987, June). *The inverted-U hypothesis: A catastrophe for sport psychology.* Paper presented at the annual meeting of the North American Society for the Psychology of Sport and Physical Activity, Vancouver, British Columbia, Canada.

Hardy, L., & Parfitt, G. (1992, October). *Different approaches to the study of the anxiety-performance relationship.* Paper presented at the 7th annual meeting of the Association for Advancement of Applied Sport Psychology, Colorado Springs, CO.

Hays, K. F. (1999). *Working it out: Using exercise in psychotherapy.* Washington, DC: American Psychological Association.

Hays, K. F. (2000). Breaking out: Doing sport psychology with performing artists. In M. B. Andersen (Ed.), *Doing sport psychology: Process and practice* (pp. 261–274). Champaign, IL: Human Kinetics.

Helsen, W. F., Starkes, J. L., & Hodges, N. J. (1998). Team sports and the theory of deliberate practice. *Journal of Sport and Exercise Psychology, 20,* 12–34.

Heskett, J. L., & Schlesinger, L. A. (1996). Leaders who shape and keep performance oriented culture. In F. Hesselbein, M. Goldsmith, & R. Beckhard (Eds.), *The leader of the future* (pp.189–198). San Francisco: Jossey-Bass.

Jackson, R. C., & Baker, J. S. (2001). Routines, rituals, and rugby: Case studies of a world class goal kicker. *Sport Psychologist, 15,* 48–65.

Jaycox, L. H., Reivich, K. J., Gillham, J., & Seligman, M.E.P. (1994). Prevention of depressive symptoms in school children. *Behavior Research and Therapy, 32,* 301–316.

Judge, T. A., & Locke, E. A. (1993). Effect of dysfunctional thought processes on subjective well-being and job satisfaction. *Journal of Applied Psychology, 78,* 475–490.

Kamen-Siegel, L., Rodin, J., Seligman, M.E.P., & Dwyer, J. (1991). Explanatory style and cell-mediated immunity in elderly men and women. *Health Psychology, 10,* 229–235.

Krane, V. (1993). *Anxiety and athletic performance: A test of the multidimensional anxiety and catastrophe theories.* Unpublished doctoral dissertation, University of North Carolina, Greensboro.

Kreiner-Phillips, K., & Orlick, T. (1993). Winning after winning: The psychology of ongoing excellence. *The Sport Psychologist, 7,* 31–48.

Lange, A., & Grieger, R. (1993). Integrating RET into management consulting and training. *Journal of Rational-Emotive and Cognitive Behavior Therapy, 11,* 51–57.

Lehmann, A. C., & Ericsson, K. A. (1999). Research on expert performance and deliberate practice: Implications for the education of amateur musicians and music students. *Psychomusicology, 16,* 40–58.

Lehmann, M., Foster, C., & Keul, J. (1994). Overtraining in endurance athletes: A brief review. *Medicine & Science in Sports & Exercise, 25,* 854–862.

Levinson, H. (1981). *Executive.* Cambridge, MA: Harvard University Press.

Levinson, H. (1991). Consulting with top management. *Consulting Psychology Bulletin, 43*(1), 10–15.

Loehr, J., & Schwartz, T. (2001). The making of a corporate athlete. *Harvard Business Review, 79*(1), 120–128.

Lowman, R. L. (1993). *Counseling and psychotherapy of work dysfunctions.* Washington, DC: American Psychological Association.

Mahoney, M. J., Gabriel, T. J., & Perkins, T. S. (1987). Psychological skills and exceptional athletic performance. *Sport Psychologist, 1,* 181–199.

Manz, C. C. (1992). *Mastering self-leadership: Empowering yourself for personal excellence.* Englewood Cliffs, NJ: Prentice Hall.

Masters, K. S., & Lambert, M. J. (1989). The relations between cognitive coping strategies, reasons for running, injury, and performance on marathon runners. *Journal of Exercise and Sport Psychology, 11,* 161–170.

McCaffrey, N., & Orlick, T. (1989). Mental factors related to excellence among top professional golfers. *International Journal of Sport Psychology, 20,* 256–278.

McKenzie, D. C. (1999). Markers of excessive exercise. *Canadian Journal of Applied Physiology, 24,* 66–73.

Morgan, W. P., O'Connor, P. J., Ellickson, K. A., & Bradley, P. W. (1988). Personality structure, mood states, and performance in elite male distance runners. *International Journal of Sport Psychology, 19,* 247–263.

Morgan, W. P., O'Connor, P. J., Sparling, P. B., & Pate, R. R. (1987). Psychological characteristics of elite female distance runners. *International Journal of Sport Medicine, 8,* 124–131.

Morin, L., & Latham, G. P. (2000). The effect of mental practice and goal setting as a transfer of training intervention on supervisors' self-efficacy and communication skills: An exploratory study. *Applied Psychology: An International Review, 49,* 566–578.

Moxley, R. S., & Wilson, P. O. (1998). A systems approach to leadership development. In C. D. McCauley, R. S. Moxley, & E. Van Velsor (Eds.), *The Center for Creative Leadership handbook of leadership development* (pp. 217–241). San Francisco: Jossey-Bass.

Mujika, I., Busso, T., Lacoste, L., & Barale, F. (1996). Modeled responses to training and taper in competitive swimmers. *Medicine & Science in Sports and Exercise, 28,* 251–258.

Neck, C. P., & Manz, C. C. (1996). Thought self-leadership: The impact of mental strategies training on employee cognition. *Journal of Organizational Behavior, 17,* 445–467.

Neck, C. P., Neck, H. M., Manz, C. C., & Godwin, J. (1999). "I think I can; I think I can": A self-leadership perspective toward enhancing entrepreneur thought patterns, self-efficacy, and performance. *Journal of Managerial Psychology, 14,* 477–501.

Neff, T. J., & Citrin, J. M. (2001). *Lessons from the top.* New York: Doubleday.

Nideffer, R. M. (1992). *Psyched to win.* Champaign, IL: Leisure Press.

Ogilvie, B. (1995). Consultation concerns when working with "best" athletes. In K. P. Henschen & W. F. Straub (Eds.), *Sport psychology: An analysis of athlete behavior* (3rd ed., pp. 287–301). Ithaca, NY: Mouvement.

Ogilvie, B. (1999). *User's guide to the competitive styles profile.* Los Gatos, CA: Promind Institute.

Orlick, T. (1986). *Psyching for sport: Mental training for athletes.* Champaign, IL: Leisure Press.

Orlick, T. (1998a). Reflections on sportpsych consulting with individual and team sport athletes at summer and winter Olympic Games. *Sport Psychologist, 3,* 358–365.

Orlick, T. (1998b). *Embracing your potential.* Champaign, IL: Leisure Press.

Orlick, T., & McCaffrey, N. (1991). Mental training with children for sport and life. *The Sport Psychologist, 5,* 322–334.

Orlick, T., & Partington, J. (1988). Mental links to excellence. *The Sport Psychologist, 2,* 105–130.

Orpen, C. (1995). The effect of time-management training on employee attitudes and behavior: A field experiment. *Journal of Psychology, 128,* 393–396.

Peterson, C., & Seligman, M.E.P. (1987). Explanatory style and illness. *Journal of Personality, 55,* 237–265.

Peterson, C., Semmel, A., von Baeyer, C., Abramson, L. Y., Metalsky, G. I., & Seligman, M.E.P. (1982). The attributional style questionnaire. *Cognitive Research and Therapy, 6,* 287–300.

Peterson, D. B., & Hicks, M. D. (1995). *Development first: Strategies for self-development.* Minneapolis, MN: Personnel Decisions International.

Rejeski, W. J., & Thompson, A. (1993). Historical and conceptual roots of exercise psychology. In P. Seraganian (Ed.), *Exercise psychology: The influence of physical exercise on psychological. processes* (pp. 3–35). New York: Wiley.

Rieber, L. P. (1995). A historical review of visualization in human cognition. *Educational Technology Research & Development, 43,* 45–56.

Robins, S. (2002). A consultant's guide to understanding and promoting emotional intelligence in the workplace. In R. L. Lowman (Ed.), *Handbook of organizational consulting psychology* (pp. 159–184). San Francisco: Jossey-Bass.

Samela, J. H. (1989). Long-term intervention with the Canadian men's Olympic gymnastic team. *The Sport Psychologist, 3,* 340–349.

Savoy, C. (1997). Two individualized mental training programs for a team sport. *International Journal of Sport Psychology, 28,* 259–270.

Savoy, C., & Beitel, P. (1996). Mental imagery in basketball. *International Journal of Sport Psychology, 27,* 454–462.

Schein, E. H. (1996). Leadership and organizational culture. In F. Hesselbein, M. Goldsmith, & R. Beckhard (Eds.), *The leader of the future* (pp. 59–69). San Francisco: Jossey-Bass.

Seligman, M.E.P., Nolen-Hoeksema, S., Thorton, N., & Thorton, K. M. (1990). Explanatory style as a mechanism of disappointing athletic performance. *Psychological Science, 1,* 143–146.

Seligman, M.E.P., & Shulman, P. (1986). Explanatory style as a predictor of productivity and quitting among life insurance sales agents. *Journal of Personality and Social Psychology, 50,* 832–838.

Shatte, A. J., Reivich, K., & Seligman, M.E.P. (2000). Promoting human strengths and corporate competencies: A cognitive training model. *The Psychologist-Manager Journal, 4,* 183–196.

Shulman, P., Castellon, C., & Seligman, M. E. P. (1989). Assessing explanatory style: The context analysis of verbatim explanations and the Attributional Style Questionnaire. *Behaviour Research and Therapy, 27,* 505–512.

Singh, N. A., Clements, K. M., Fiatarone, M. A. (1997). A randomized controlled trial of resistance training in depressed elders. *Journal of Gerontology, 52,* M27–M35.

Sorensen, P. F., Jr., & Yaeger, T. F. (2002). Appreciative inquiry as an approach for organizational consulting. In R. L. Lowman (Ed.), *Handbook of organizational consulting psychology* (pp. 605–616). San Francisco: Jossey-Bass.

Spence, J. T., Helmreich, R. L., & Pred, R. S. (1987). Impatience versus achievement striving in the Type A behavior pattern: Differential effects on students' health and academic achievement. *Journal of Applied Psychology, 72,* 522–528.

Sperry, L. (1996). *Corporate therapy and consultation.* New York: Brunner/Mazel.

Spink, K. S. (1988). Facilitating endurance performance: The effect of cognitive strategies and analgesic suggestions. *The Sport Psychologist, 2,* 97–104.

Stoltz, P. G. (1997). *Adversity quotient: Turning obstacles into opportunities.* New York: Wiley.

Suinn, R. M. (1972). Removing emotional obstacles to learning and performance by visuomotor behavioral rehearsal. *Behavior Therapy, 3,* 308–310.

Suinn, R. M. (1985). Imagery applications to performance enhancement. *Behavior Therapist, 8,* 155–159.

Suinn, R. M. (1993). Imagery. In R. N. Singer, M. Murphy, & L. K. Tennant (Eds.), *Handbook of research on sport psychology* (pp. 3–31). Old Tappan, NJ: Macmillan.

Suinn, R. M. (1997). Mental practice in sport psychology: Where we have been, where do we go? *Clinical Psychology: Science and Practice, 4,* 189–207.

Thom, R. ( 1975). *Structural stability and morphogenesis* (D. H. Fowler, Trans.). Menlo Park, CA: Benjamin-Cummings.

Thompson, M. A. (1998). A philosophy of applied sport psychology. In M. A. Thompson, R. A. Vernachhia, & W. E. Moore (Eds.), *Case studies in applied sport psychology.* Dubuque, IA: Kendall/Hunt.

Van Raalte, J. L., Brewer, B. W., Rivera, P. M., & Petitpas, A. J. (1994). The relationship between observable self-talk and competitive junior tennis players' match performance. *Journal of Sport and Exercise Psychology, 16,* 400–415.

Vealey, R., & Walter, S. (1993). Imagery training for performance enhancement. In J. M. Williams (Ed.), *Applied sport psychology: Personal growth to peak performance* (2nd ed., pp. 200–224). Mountain View, CA: Mayfield.

Watkins, J. M., & Mohr, B. J. (2001). *Appreciative inquiry: Change at the speed of imagination.* San Francisco: Jossey-Bass.

Weinberg, R. S., Stitcher, T., & Richardson, P. (1994). Effects of a seasonal goal setting program on lacrosse performance. *The Sport Psychologist, 8,* 166–175.

Weinberg, R. S., & Williams, J. M. (1993). Integrating and implementing a psychological skills program. In J. M. Williams (Ed.), *Applied sport psychology: Personal growth to peak performance* (2nd ed., pp. 274–298). Mountain View, CA: Mayfield.

Whelan, J. P., Mahoney, M. J., & Meyers, A. W. (1991). Performance enhancement in sport: A cognitive behavioral domain. *Behavior Therapy, 22,* 307–327.

Wiggins, D. K. (1984). The history of sport psychology in North America. In J. Silva & R. Weinberg (Eds.), *Psychological foundations of sport* (pp. 9–22). Champaign, IL: Human Kinetics.

Wilhelm, W. (1996). Learning from past leaders. In F. Hesselbein, M. Goldsmith, & R. Beckhard (Eds.), *The leader of the future* (pp. 221–226). San Francisco: Jossey-Bass.

Williams, J. M., & Straub, W. F. (1993). Sport psychology: Past, present, and future. In J. M. Williams (Ed.), *Applied sport psychology: Personal growth to peak performance* (2nd ed., pp. 1–10). Mountain View, CA: Mayfield.

Zhang, L., Ma, Q., Orlick, T., & Zitzelsberger, L. (1992). The effect of mental-imagery training on performance enhancement with 7–10-year-old children. *The Sport Psychologist, 6,* 230–241.

PART THREE

# GROUP LEVEL APPLICATIONS

# CHAPTER TEN

# Successfully Implementing
# Teams in Organizations

Douglas A. Johnson, Michael M. Beyerlein, Joseph W. Huff,
Terry R. Halfhill, and Rodger D. Ballentine
*Center for the Study of Work Teams and*
*Department of Psychology*
*University of North Texas*

There is a disturbingly high failure rate of organizational change efforts involving the implementation of work teams. It is the purpose of this chapter to identify factors related to the success (and failure) of such efforts. The emphasis will be on providing consultants with research-based information about the types of structures and processes that need to be established to ensure the long-term survival of their team interventions. It is assumed that the reader is familiar with effective techniques for team building, so we will not be addressing that topic. We will concentrate instead on identifying the crucial contextual issues related to sustaining a team-based organization after the consultants leave. [For those who are interested in team building, Jossey-Bass/Pfeiffer offers extensive relevant publications to assist consultants.]

The chapter is organized into four major sections. The first section will focus on failures of team-based interventions. It is based on over ten years of research and case studies at the Center for the Study of Work Teams at the University of North Texas. The second section is also based on the Center's research, and will identify the elements of team support systems and the critical role that they play in sustaining teams. The third section is a review of climate measurement issues. The post-implementation assessment of climate is necessary for

*Note:* Part of the research cited in this chapter was funded by a grant (SBR 9422368) from the National Science Foundation.

determining whether or not the organizational environment is conducive to sustaining teams. In the final section, we summarize our findings and state them in the form of implications for consultants as they work with their clients to implement teams.

# WHY DO TEAMS FAIL?

Too many big change initiatives fail. The success rate of work team implementations is similarly quite modest. Because failures often lead to more learning than successes, the Center for the Study of Work Teams has systematically collected reasons for team failures. Even with our passion for teams, we almost titled this section "Teams: Can They Be Sustained?" because in our research at the Center for the Study of Work Teams, nearly half of the implementation attempts we have studied have "failed." There are quote marks around the word "failed" because there is no single outcome that can be labeled that way. One main reason for implementing work teams is to increase the potential of the natural work group to do effective work. Work teams are organized in ways that increase the capabilities of the group as a whole, and promise a number of improvements in hard and soft outcomes. So, we will define "failure" for a team implementation effort as one in which the full potential of that team or group of teams was not reached.

## Types of Team Implementations and Failures

The failures come in many forms and for many reasons. They will be organized here from the big picture down to the local picture, from whole system problems down to problems within the team itself. The point of such an organization is that the macro and the micro aspects of the organization must both be attended to and must be in alignment with each other for sustained success of the team.

Team implementations come in a number of forms, so the failures also appear in a number of ways. A popular and often recommended approach to implementation is socio-technical change (Emery & Trist, 1978; Pasmore, 1988). The socio-technical change approach emphasizes that effective organizational change cannot occur unless both technical and social systems are changed. It is top-down and systematic (Mohrman & Cummings, 1989); it uses an executive steering committee, which does lots of homework to learn about teams and how to proceed with the transformation of the organization. After months of preparatory work, the steering committee sets up design teams and (sometimes) pilot teams. If the operation is large enough, the design teams select the pilot teams after careful assessment of which sites are best prepared to work in teams. We do not have any statistics on the success rate for this approach, but our impression is that it can be fairly successful, *if* all of the steps are thoroughly carried out. Of course, it is complex enough and lasts long enough for all kinds of difficulties to occur to disrupt the implementation effort. We will address several of these difficulties below.

Another form of team implementation is informal, such as grassroots bottom-up efforts. In one company, an engineer led her work group on such a change, and the team was successful enough to convince the plant manager and HR personnel to attempt a plant-wide implementation effort. However, isolated, spontaneous efforts typically have minimal organizational support, and run into lots of problems interfacing with the traditional parts of the organization around them. A former student of ours, Sandra Ellison, identified these problems as stemming from the responses of the *corporate immune system* to radical changes. Just as the white blood cells destroy the strange invader, the corporate immune system attacks anything (such as the informal team) that looks like it does not fit into the familiar dominant system (Ellison, n.d.).

For organizations that are comfortable with change programs, some of the fast-paced change approaches might be appropriate, such as search conferences (Emery & Purser, 1996) and future conferences (Weisbord, 1992). However, Lytle and Rankin (1996) warn against the use of such accelerated methods in traditional settings. The political climate must be mild and fairly agreeable for accelerated methods to succeed. This requirement precludes the use of fast-paced change approaches in many organizations. The choice of implementation approach can be a source of failure unless there is a match between the approach and the type of organization.

Regardless of which implementation method is used, the change from a traditionally organized business to one that is team-based represents a *radical* transformation of the work place. Those who contemplate a transition to teams often do not understand how radical a change it is. The requisite changes needed to make such transformations work might be on a par with such fundamental personal changes as adolescence and marriage. They represent a paradigm shift in how work is organized and managed. Kuhn (1970), the originator of the term *paradigm shift*, suggested that in the sciences, a paradigm shift can only occur when the old guard dies off and the new scientists replace them with a new perspective. For an individual to make a shift in perspective so radical that his or her paradigm or dominant perspective turns 180 degrees is extremely difficult and rare. Consequently, an inadequate understanding of the nature of the transformation will likely lead to an inadequate implementation, and hence to a failure of the change effort.

## Lessons About Team Implementation

Researchers and practitioners have learned many lessons about team implementation since 1990. We consider 1990 to be a watershed year, because in that year, the first systematic attempts to understand teams began to emerge. The

Center for the Study of Work Teams that year held the first of twenty-five conferences on teams, and the book *Self-Directed Work Teams* (Orsburn, Moran, Musselwhite, & Zenger, 1990) was published. What are some of the lessons that we in the Center have learned?

First, we learned that there are many types of teams. These include project teams, quality improvement teams, cross-functional teams, virtual teams, and permanent self-managing work teams. Although self-managing work teams have been the focus of much of the recent interest in teams, they might be appropriate only in certain situations. There are many options, and we found that smart organizations did not *adopt* teams, they *adapted* them, by adjusting the design to fit the setting and goals of the organization.

Second, we learned that it is not wise to introduce teams just for the sake of having teams, or because other organizations are using them. The only point of having teams, as one manager told us, was to "get the work done." The design and maintenance of the teams had to be organized so that improvements in work productivity occurred. Many organizations did not recognize this, and upper management became disenchanted with teams as a consequence of the lack of evidence for a connection between teams and work performance.

Third, thanks mostly to the work of Susan Mohrman and her colleagues (see Mohrman, Cohen, & Mohrman, 1995), we learned that implementing teams in isolation and without support was a major error. Significant attention had to be paid to lateral integration and support systems. Lateral integration meant the goal was to create teams of teams, not just individual teams. Without adequate support from the systems in the teams' environment, they could not be sustained. For example, in some companies, the human resources department represented one of the major barriers to successful implementation of teams, and in others it represented the major champion for the change. In other organizations, the information and communications system was a problem, and in many organizations the management system was a major problem. We discovered that if upper-level managers have little understanding about what the team transformation means, minimize commitment to it, or make little effort to communicate the overarching vision and mission of the initiative to team members, the initiative is likely to be abandoned. A famous example of abandonment is the Digital Equipment Corporation Enfield plant, which was a highly successful pioneer team implementation in the 1980s that was shut down in the 1990s. This may have been an example of the corporate immune system at work. A similar experience occurred at Volvo, as plants at Kalmar and Uddevalla, once famous for teams assembling whole automobiles, were also closed, although the Uddevalla plant reopened a few years later (Nilsson, 2000).

Fourth, we learned about the role of empowerment. By empowerment, we mean vesting employees with the responsibility for taking action. The issue here relates to the difference between redesigning the work to use teams and the empowerment of individuals. We believe this difference is critical, that well-functioning teams represent a significant structural change over and above empowerment. Failure to make that distinction might create some confusion. Of course, there are many potential sources of confusion during a transformation. The meanings of team, change, responsibility, and others, must be clarified to make effective communications possible. Empowerment has some rich definitions, including that of Sandy (1990), which emphasizes provision of support to employees so they can capitalize on the opportunities that empowerment provides. Perhaps even more important is Oshry's point that *every* member of the system has responsibility for systemic transformation (1996). Unfortunately, transformation is often dictated from above, with inadequate participation by the people in lower parts of the hierarchy. When that happens, the transformation is experienced by employees as something that was done *to* them, not *with* them. As a consequence, they develop little commitment to change. One of the more obvious examples of the need for partnering on the change effort is the need to involve union representation in the planning stages. A subtler example is the need to involve employees who do the work in the change. These employees are closest to the work, so their ideas are typically better about the changes needed at that level. In sum, simply ordering employees to be empowered is a recipe for failure.

The reasons for failure noted above are on the macro level, the big picture issues that threaten a whole initiative. This is not an exhaustive list. A good source for a more extensive discussion of the bases of team failure is Hitchcock and Willard (1995). The more experience we gain with team failures, the more important we believe the macro-level issues to be. Organizational context and support systems contradict or undermine teams with more predictable and devastating results than do the internal or micro-level causes of failure. Yet most literature and most practice focus on the micro level.

## Internal Team Health

The internal health of a team depends on a lot of factors. Researchers have studied those factors for over fifty years, though most often in laboratory settings. They have identified a number of threats within the team that will undermine the level of success it achieves, or lead to failure. In a laboratory, a researcher has a lot more control over the situation, so if he or she wants to focus on a particular source of influence on the group, it is fairly clear what the impact of that source is. Hundreds and perhaps thousands of such studies have helped us understand a lot about group dynamics. Other understanding grew out of encounter groups, T-groups, and sensitivity groups, where employees from the same or different work units came together to work on problems of communication, emotion, conflict, and so on. That work continues in both academic and consulting settings. The big problem is that we do not know how to put the whole organization in a lab or T-group, so context is only present from participants' memories. We would learn as much or more by doing interviews or surveys, or better yet, focus groups or observations, to gain an understanding of the group or team within its context.

Attention to context has been emerging in the past few years, but the effort is in its infancy. We have a long way to go to develop our understanding of macro influences (context), and even to develop better tools for studying it. What can we use to guide us in looking at the micro level until the macro approach matures?

## NSF-Supported Study of Teams in Nine Organizations

In our National Science Foundation (NSF)-supported study of teams in nine organizations, we began to see a number of failing teams and failing team-implementation efforts. In most cases, failing teams were doing poorly because of changes at the macro level or lack of appropriate macro-level support. Solving problems at that level tends to be the responsibility of management. However, some of our findings allowed us to identify micro-level problems and influences that a team or facilitator might be able to work on. For example, one lesson from our research was a realization that making a manager a member of the same team he or she supervised, or transforming him or her into a facilitator or coach of that team, were both errors. In one team, the manager was demoted and became a member of the team she had supervised. She resisted the change in role mightily. Other managers in the organization continued to relate to her as though she was still in her old role. The team tried to use peer pressure to enlist her participation in their activities, but she isolated herself. Finally, the team gave up trying to convert her and decided to just wait it out until her retirement in two years. Meanwhile, of course, the team functioned at a mediocre level, which we define as a failure, since they could not achieve high performance levels and their stretch goals.

## Worse Before Better

Another problem is referred to as the *worse before better* dynamic (Keating & Oliva, 2000). Transformation from a work group to a work team, and then to a mature team, takes a lot of learning by team members, as well as team leaders, supervisors, and managers. Formal training typically occurs away from the job, such as in classrooms, on site visits, and at conferences. It takes time. Some of the companies best known for teams put team members through 150 to 200 hours of formal training each year. This practice entails time away from work, so work output typically is reduced in the short run. If production pressures are high enough, managers, and even workers, become increasingly reluctant to take the time for learning, so a reaction sets in from impatience and training time drops off. Consequently, the team becomes less likely to achieve the maturity that is prerequisite for achieving the highest levels of performance, and the value of teaming seems more questionable. On the other hand, if the team is allowed to continue its development, performance will eventually improve beyond its original level (Macy & Izumi, 1993).

## Changes in the Nature of Work

In some cases, as the team matures, the nature of the work changes. Keating and Oliva (2000) described the APEX team at AT&T in detail. They concluded that the product design work that the team was responsible for started with the easy, obvious problems that showed quicker results, then as the team matured, it tackled more challenging problems and the output seemed to slow down. But the nature of the work had changed, and comparison of outputs from the first few years to the later years of the team was as if comparing apples and oranges. On the surface, output looked poorer, and as a consequence, rewards diminished and motivation fell off. Finally, the methodology the team used became inadequate as the problems became more difficult, so challenges could not be met and involvement on the team dropped off.

Typically, transition to a team structure changes the responsibilities of the work group members; when team members become cross-trained and empowered, they have new work responsibilities. At some point, they begin to feel that they ought to be rewarded and compensated for the extra skills, effort, and responsibility now required. When an adjustment in reward is not forthcoming, disaffection can result and effort can diminish. While this is a macro-level issue, it can interact with internal issues that can occur within cross-functional teams and integrated product teams (IPTs). In these types of teams, there are often different job titles for different members. For example, on an IPT, there might be an engineer and an accountant paid at a rate 50 percent higher than the production workers on the team. Such differences might be justified by differences in expertise, but such justification might not eliminate a sense of inequity among the production team members.

Transition to teams takes a long time; so does the related progress on a ladder of empowerment. If the length of that journey is not made clear, team members might have unrealistic expectations about how quickly changes will occur. When the pace of change is slower than expected, they will become disappointed and reduce their effort and their enthusiasm for future steps in the journey.

## Affective Reactions to Change

In our NSF study of teams, which involved over 600 interviews in nine companies, we found a number of team members reporting fear, stress, and pain. Fear emerged in response to downsizing, and loss of projects and customers in other parts of their company. Pain emerged as their expectations about the transition to empowered, high-performance teams were not met. Stress emerged as their workloads increased because of downsizing, increased responsibilities, and time away from work for meetings and training. The fear, stress, and pain were taking a toll on the individuals and on the implementation program. In some cases, management did not seem to be aware of the problem, and in others, although aware, did not know how to respond. Stress management training should be an integral part of a team development program.

Some teams are highly successful. We studied two self-directed teams (they had formal leaders) that were similar to each other and quite successful in two different companies. To contrast them with other teams in our sample, we called them the *happy teams*. They both provided computer-support services to their external customers. They did an excellent job of documenting team learning by capturing knowledge that they acquired in a database. Unfortunately, during the course of the study, one of these teams lost their customers through no fault of their own, and was dissolved as a team. Sometimes it doesn't matter how well the team does; larger events can prevent it from succeeding. However, keeping the team informed about the current business situation and its possible implications for them can reduce the negative impact that such events have on team members.

The change from being a member of a traditional work group to being a fully involved member of a work team requires learning a lot of new behaviors, skills, and concepts, even a new perspective. The training might not take. What might emerge is an ability to talk about the changed role, but a failure to actually engage in it. This is evidence of a subconscious defensive routine (Agrell & Gustafson, 1996), which is described by Argyris and Schön (1974, 1978) as a contrast of "theories in use" to "espoused theories." Although espousing theories while failing to use them is a criticism more commonly aimed at management, team members can be subject to the same shortcoming (Agrell & Gustafson, 1996).

Why teams fail will be a topic of investigation for the foreseeable future. In 1995, Darcy Hitchcock and Marsha Willard published a book on that topic, and at the annual International Conference on Work Teams, the panel presentation of that name is the most heavily attended session nearly every year. We are continuing to endeavor to learn where the potholes are in the road to teams; after all, one definition of wisdom is learning from others' mistakes.

One type of mistake that we observed in the earlier stages of our NSF study was the failure of organizations to properly support their teams after they were implemented. We decided to learn from these mistakes by concentrating on team support systems during the latter part of the study. The results of this research are summarized below.

# THE CRUCIAL ROLE OF TEAM SUPPORT SYSTEMS

Any organization can implement teams, but keeping them working effectively requires continuing organizational support. A support system is a sustained set of interdependent organizational processes that enhances the ability of teams to work collaboratively and effectively. The purpose of this section is to describe research conducted at the Center for the Study of Work Teams (Hall & Beyerlein, 2000; Hall, Beyerlein, & Johnson, 2000) to determine the relationship of support systems and team performance, and to provide guidance to consultants about educating their clients concerning the importance of these systems.

## Categories of Support Systems

A review of the literature was conducted to identify categories of support systems. Models of team effectiveness by Cohen (1994), Gladstein (1984), Hackman (1987), Hackman and Morris (1975), May and Schwoerer (1994), Pearce and Ravlin (1987), Shea and Guzzo (1987), and Sundstrom, De Meuse, and Futrell (1990), were covered in this review. Additionally, the work of Mohrman, Cohen, and Mohrman (1995), which thoroughly outlines the effective design of team-based organizations, was most helpful in this effort. A summary of the findings of this review can be found in Hall and Beyerlein (2000). The review resulted in a taxonomy containing nine types of support systems. Each is briefly described below:

1. *Group Design System.* This system is concerned with clarifying roles, tasks, and boundary functions, and with personnel selection.

2. *Defining Performance System.* This system is concerned with the setting and alignment of performance-related goals.

3. *Information System.* This system is concerned with the mechanisms for providing the necessary information that teams need to make decisions, correct errors, integrate work, and maximize performance.

4. *Performance Appraisal System.* This system is concerned with the accurate identification and measurement of performance-related abilities, as well as the feedback of performance assessments to team members.

5. *Integration System.* This system is concerned with insuring the linkage of interdependent performing units, both vertically and horizontally.

6. *Direct Supervisor Support System.* This system is concerned with the development and utilization of appropriate leadership, communication, and facilitation skills in those who directly supervise teams.

7. *Executive and Manager Support System.* This system is concerned with insuring that leaders develop the organizational context that makes effective teamwork possible.

8. *Training System.* This system is concerned with creating the mechanisms for developing the performance-related knowledge, skills, and abilities of teams.

9. *Reward System.* This system is concerned with reinforcing desirable priorities, goals, and behaviors.

These categories are consistent with the recently published taxonomy of support systems developed by Sundstrom (1999). A comparison of the two support system taxonomies shows that they are remarkably similar, despite the fact that they were developed independently of one another. The Sundstrom version contains two system concepts that are not addressed by our version, Communication Technology, and Facility (physical work environment). Similarly, our version has two unique system concepts, Defining Performance, and Integration. While it can be logically assumed that these systems are all necessary and important ongoing processes for sustaining the long-term success of teams, it is always advisable to conduct empirical research to be sure. The following section contains findings of a recent study (Hall et al., 2000) designed to determine the relationship between support systems and team effectiveness.

## Relationship of Team Support Systems and Team Performance

To determine the relationship between team support systems and team effectiveness, measures of support systems and team performance had to be created. For the support systems measure, items reflecting support activities within each category were written and reviewed by the staff from the Center for the Study of Work Teams. Subsequently, eight external subject matter experts, drawn from academia, industry, and consulting, reviewed the items for content, suggesting revisions and deletions. After preliminary analysis, fourteen items for each of the nine support systems categories were chosen for the final version of the instrument, the Support Systems Survey (SSS). Two responses per item were collected on five-point scales: 1) the extent to which the support activity was present; and 2) its importance.

The performance measure, the Perception of Team Performance (PTP) had been developed previously by Beyerlein (1996) for the NSF project. The PTP asked for team members to rate their team's effectiveness on twenty items. Item ratings were factor analyzed ($N = 255$) using oblimin rotation and principal components extraction. Four stable factors emerged, accounting for 66 percent of the variance. These were: Customer Satisfaction, Psychological Effectiveness (trust, commitment, and satisfaction items), Resource Utilization and Development, and Team Effectiveness. A fifth, overall score, Composite Effectiveness, was created by summing all PTP items. Responses to PTP items could range from zero to 100.

The SSS and the PTP were administered to nearly 400 members of technical and professional teams from six organizations that were participating in the NSF-sponsored team study. Some of the participating organizations were recruited from the ranks of the Center's corporate sponsors. Others were recruited through advertisements on the Center's web site, and through personal contact by Center members. Sample sizes on the various analyses varied from 323 to 379.

Psychometric analyses indicated that both the SSS and the PTP scales had acceptable levels of internal consistency reliability (alphas ranged from .80 to .95). The average correlation between the individual Presence scales was .65, between the individual Importance scales, .70, and between the individual PTP scales, .59. The average correlation between same-scale Importance and Presence scores was only .40. This latter correlation provides evidence of internal validity for the SSS, because it indicates that the subjects were able to conceptually separate their responses to the SSS Importance and the SSS Presence scales.

The SSS Importance ratings correlated only weakly with the PTP scores, with an average $r = .17$. The Importance scores for Group Design, Defining Performance, and Training had the highest individual correlations with PTP Composite Effectiveness (.23, .21, and .21, respectively).

Much stronger findings emerged with the SSS Presence scale scores. Their correlations with PTP Composite Effectiveness were moderately high, ranging from .37 to .63, with an average $r = .51$. The Group Design and Defining Performance Presence scores had the highest correlations with Composite Effectiveness ($r = .63$ and .61, respectively), followed by Information System ($r = .57$), Performance Appraisal ($r = .53$), Integration System ($r = .52$), Direct Supervisor Support ($r = .48$), Executive and Manager Support ($r = .46$), Training System ($r = .43$), and Reward System ($r = .37$). The findings clearly indicate that the presence of team support systems is strongly linked to team performance ratings.

We consider the SSS Presence scales to be more useful for studying support systems than the SSS Importance scales. The Presence scales reflect the extent of actual development of the support systems in each organization, not just opinions about the hypothetical importance of each system. It therefore makes sense that the actual levels of team support are more closely related to team effectiveness than are ratings of support importance. Additionally, each SSS Presence scale score represents a concrete phenomenon—the extent of the actual existence of a given support system. The PTP measure of effectiveness also reflects a relatively concrete phenomenon that is directly observable by the subjects. In contrast, the SSS Importance scores are much more hypothetical and attitudinal in nature, and lack an underlying shared variance of concreteness with the Performance scores. Under these conditions, the greater strength of the Presence-Performance correlations seems to be a reasonable and logical outcome.

**Reward Systems and Performance.** Perhaps the most surprising finding of our research was the relatively low correlation between Reward Systems and performance. This suggests that other support processes might deserve greater priority when implementing teams, but it might also reflect the relative immaturity of many of the teams in the sample. Heneman, Dixon, and Gresham (2000), and Hitchcock and Willard (1995), have suggested that team rewards are not particularly effective until a team is fully mature. About half the teams in our sample were less than three years old. Finally, we need to mention one cautionary note. The SSS and the PTP were administered at the same time, and though they were physically separate instruments with different response formats, the possibility of the existence of some method variance must still be considered.

Our findings suggest that organizations that focus their efforts on developing effective support system processes will increase the likelihood of success for their teams. These results provide empirical support for the theoretical positions taken by Mohrman et al. (1995) and Sundstrom (1999) about the importance of team support systems. They are also consistent with conclusions from the review by Guzzo and Dickson (1996) about the importance of having the proper organizational context for insuring the success of teams.

This research has permitted us to begin the development of a theoretical model of team effectiveness. In our model, support systems are seen primarily as inputs in an input-process-output (I-P-O) model of teams (see Figure 10.1). Unfortunately, these types of graphic displays tend to suffer by having to portray a dynamic, nonlinear, reiterative process in a static, linear way. Our knowledge of team processes suggests that though support systems might be inputs, the processes and outputs they generate reoccur throughout the performance cycle. The value of an I-P-O framework is that it reflects that reiterative process, and reminds us that inputs, processes, and outputs are not just static categories in boxes, but are sustained, reoccurring events that continuously impact one another.

Once the support systems have been effectively implemented, the likelihood is that both the performance and the climate of the organization will improve. An additional step is to establish a monitoring process to regularly assess the state of the organization, so that renewal efforts can be undertaken before any serious deterioration can occur. A critical element to assess is the organization's climate. In the next section, we review the concept of climate and issues concerning its measurement.

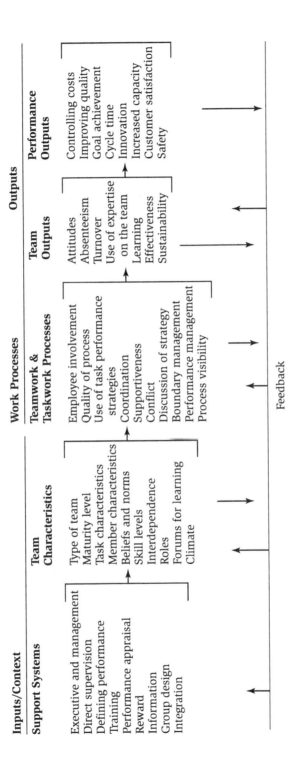

**Figure 10.1 Theoretical Model of Team Effectiveness.**

# ASSESSING PSYCHOLOGICAL AND ORGANIZATIONAL CLIMATE

When practitioners conduct organizational development and change interventions, focus groups, interviews, or surveys are customarily used to capture employee perceptions of their organizational environment. These employee perceptions are commonly labeled as the culture or climate of the organization. Although culture and climate are often used in an interchangeable manner, distinctive differences in construct conceptualization and data gathering methodologies are apparent in the literature (Rousseau, 1988). Climate has been characterized as employee perceptions of the organizational work environment (Rousseau, 1988), whereas culture seems to be a deeper phenomenon, assessing the core values, beliefs, and assumptions held by the organization (Schein, 1992). Although culture has become the prevalent focus of the contemporary literature (Schneider, 2000), a large part of the research that is commonly being conducted by practitioners is more related to the study of climate than the study of culture (Schein, 1992). This section will focus on how climate issues, which have been more frequently studied by practitioners than culture, pertain to the understanding of the organizational context.

## Two Levels of Organizational Climate

Although all climate researchers focus on employee perceptions of their organizational environment, two distinct levels of climate have been established—psychological and organizational. Psychological climate has been conceptualized as an "individual's cognitive representations of relatively proximal situational events, expressed in terms that reflect the psychological meaning and significance of the situation to the individual" (James & Sells, 1981, p. 275). To examine how groups of employees collectively perceive their organization, we need to address the organizational climate(s) of the organization. Traditionally, the term organizational climate was used to describe climate at a different unit of analysis; that is, individual psychological climate perceptions that have been aggregated to the level of the organization (Glick, 1985). More commonly found in practice and literature are alternative definitions of organizational climate that represent units smaller than the whole organization (for example, work team or division). For instance, an *aggregate climate* refers to the aggregation of climate perceptions at some formal subunit of the organization, whereas a *collective climate* is said to exist when a shared perception of climate results from agreement among the employees across climate dimension(s) (Joyce & Slocum, 1984).

The aggregation of psychological climate perceptions flows from the viewpoint that organizational characteristics, such as the size and formal structure of the organization, drive shared meaning in organizations. A variety of aggregation criteria, including employee demographic variables (Schneider, 1975), formal position in the organizational hierarchy (Schneider & Snyder, 1975), organizational structure (Hellriegel & Slocum, 1974; Payne & Pugh, 1976), as well as employee membership in formal units of the organization (Drexler, 1977; Gavin & Howe, 1975; Jones & James, 1979), have been used to create aggregate climates. Most of these studies have demonstrated that mean levels of individual employee climate perceptions differ according to organizational structure. However, little evidence is available to demonstrate differential relationships with outcome variables or internal consistency criteria for aggregate climates (Joyce & Slocum, 1984; Patterson, Payne, & West, 1996).

In response to these less than consistent results, Joyce and Slocum (1984) defined a process to aggregate individual climate perceptions based on the level of statistical agreement among individual climate perceptions. In this case, collective climate refers to those individual employees who agree on their organizational perceptions, but do not necessarily work together in the same formal organizational groups, units, or divisions. Generally, if interrater agreement, such as the within-group agreement statistic ($r_{wg}$; James, Demaree, & Wolf, 1984) or intraclass correlation coefficient (ICC; James, 1982; Shrout & Fleiss, 1979) is sufficient (for example, $r_{wg} > .70$), we can state that a collective climate does exist. Indeed, these collective climates have demonstrated significant relations to job satisfaction, organizational commitment, intent to quit, and job performance (Jackofsky & Slocum, 1988; Joyce & Slocum, 1984; Young & Parker, 1999). In addition, due to their creation by statistical criteria, collective climates also demonstrate internal consistency and mean differences between other collective climates (Joyce & Slocum, 1984).

However, these collective climates are created based purely on a level of statistical agreement, and not upon a priori group membership. It is with this latter point that Payne and colleagues (Patterson et al., 1996; Payne, 1990) have opposed the use of collective climates. They argue that these statistically created groups might only be artifacts of the statistical clustering procedures that were used to create them. Payne (1990) states that such collective climates are essentially meaningless unless they are "rooted in some formal or informally constructed collectivity" (p. 78). As argued by Payne (1990), these collective climates are artificially created and do not seem to represent a meaningful socio-psychological collective. This issue regarding the meaningfulness of collective climates is related to yet another unclear issue surrounding organizational climate; that is, how do individual employees come to share perceptions of their organizational environments?

## From Individual to Organizational Perceptions of Climate

As a possible answer to how individuals might form collective climates, Schneider and Reichers (1983) presented two general alternatives. First, collective climates can arise from sets of individuals who share similar interpretive schemata (for example, values, beliefs, attitudes, needs, goals, or personality attributes; James & James, 1989; James & Sells, 1981). In this case, the similarities in the values, beliefs, and cognitive representations held by the employees help define the collective climate. Second, collective climates should develop from the formal or informal social interaction groups present in the organization. In describing how climates arise out of employee socialization and interactions between group members, Schneider and Reichers (1983) state that "mutual determination and reciprocal causality are the processes through which climates emerge, develop, and change over time" (p. 35).

A limited number of research studies are pertinent to formally testing the two alternatives of collective climate formation identified by Schneider and Reichers (1983). The importance of individual difference variables on climate perceptions has been the focus of a number of discussions by James and colleagues, yet surprisingly little research exists. Indirect support has been indicated by those studies demonstrating that employee demographic variables such as employee age, gender, and tenure influence climate perceptions (Joyce & Slocum, 1984). Direct evidence also exists, but consists of only a few research studies. Johnston (1974) found significant relationships between employee personality characteristics and their perceptions of the relationships between the individuals and organization at large. Jones and James (1979) reported significant correlations between their levels of job involvement and achievement motivation and job perceptions. Finally, James and Sells (1981) reported that employee levels of anxiety, job involvement, and achievement motivation were significant predictors of psychological influence.

The search for the effect of employee interaction patterns has also been an elusive subject of the collective climate literature, with only mixed support available. In a longitudinal study, Jackofsky and Slocum (1988) report finding that collective climates based upon departmental membership were present the first time data were collected for a study, but not the second time. The researchers believe that these results were supportive of the idea of collective climates (Jackofsky and Slocum, 1988, 1990). González-Romá, Peiró, Llorret, and Zoronoza (1999) reported finding two collective climates in their study of 195 office employees. These were upper-level managers, and low-level managers and non-managerial employees. Finally, Patterson et al. (1996) reported finding no evidence for collective climates based upon group interactions in their sample of construction employees.

Only one comprehensive, methodologically rigorous examination of Schneider and Reichers' two plausible explanations for the formation of collective climates (1983) has been conducted. Young and Parker (1999) examined the influence of two individual difference factors that have been discussed by James and colleagues (need strength and work values), and two possible indicators of interaction patterns identified by Schneider and Reichers (work group membership and interaction group membership) on the formation of collective climates. Their study of employees in a small manufacturing environment indicated that employee interaction patterns were the most predictive factor of collective climate perceptions. Specifically, those employee interactions related to employee sensemaking and information-seeking activities, rather than work flow or informal friendship interactions, were most strongly related to the formation of collective climates. Limited evidence also supported the role of employee need strength as being a basis for collective climate formation.

## The Referent Point of Climate Items

A final issue that might help to better understand organizational climate has not received as much attention in the literature as the aggregate and collective climate issues. The reference point included in the climate survey items, whether it pertains directly to the individual, the organization, or an organizational subunit, might represent another conceptualization of organizational climate. As recently described by Chan (1998), a referent-shift model can be applied to the study of climate, where the focus or wording of the items can represent a different level of climate. The following are sample items from the same dimension of Litwin and Stringer's widely used work environment survey (1968, p. 207): (1) "I feel that I am a member of a well functioning team"; and (2) "People are proud of belonging to this organization." The focus of the first statement centers on how the work environment dimension directly impacts the individual employee, and the second item aims at assessing an individual's perception of how the work environment affects others in the organization.

Two studies have examined the role of the climate item referent. Klein, Conn, Smith, and Sorra (2001) report that items worded at the group level had significantly higher within-group agreement than items worded at the individual level. With the use of individual and organizational division-level referents, Altmann et al. (1998) effectively replicated those findings presented by Klein et al. (2001). Altmann et al. (1998) also found evidence that individual referent items were more predictive of individual outcomes (for example, employee satisfaction, motivation, involvement, and performance) than were division-worded items. Preliminary data indicated that division-worded items were more predictive of organizational-level data than were individual-worded items. Such subtle distinctions as wording referent in the climate survey seem to influence within-group agreement, and perhaps collective climate formation. This distinction might prove particularly important when predicting individual versus organizational-level outcome variables.

## Assessing Climates in Teams

A number of practically important issues specifically related to the assessment of climate in team-based interventions exist. The five main issues include:

1. Although the relationship between organizational climate and team-based interventions is not necessarily direct, there are organizational qualities and intervention strategies that can increase or decrease the likelihood of team-based intervention success. For example, the implementation of team support systems can enhance team functioning and viability across multiple organizations.

2. Psychological climate perceptions can be, and commonly are, aggregated to a specific level of the organization (for example, team, division, site, and others). When doing so, we should at least ensure that agreement across employees exists. However, we still might not be forming a true collective climate.

3. Collective climates can be created from the statistical agreement of employee psychological climate perceptions, but we must decline the temptation to rely solely upon statistical agreement. We must understand how employees interact together, because interaction patterns seem to be an important factor related to shared perceptions. In addition, we should note that employee interaction patterns might not conform directly to existing teams, divisions, or other formal organizational units.

4. Recent climate research has examined a number of specific foci of climate, such as innovation, customer service, and safety (Anderson & West, 1998; Schneider, Bowen, Ehrhart, & Holcombe, 2000; Zohar, 2000). These foci relate to the specific duties and functions of teams, rather than teamwork in general. Unlike these specific climate foci, no specific climate for teaming or teamwork has been identified.

5. The climate item referent (the individual, team, or unit) might represent unique employee perceptual processes, and also might differentially predict outcome variables. For example, the individual referent might be most predictive of individual outcomes, and a team or organizational referent might be most predictive of team- and organizational-level outcomes, respectively.

Although the assessment of psychological and organizational climate is a relatively straightforward process, practitioners must be careful when designing climate survey items, as well as the methods of aggregating climate data, to ensure that meaningful collective climates are created. We must be more sensitive to understanding the importance of employee personal variables and interaction patterns, and must not simply aggregate a group of individuals due to their connection in an organizational chart or reliance on a within-group agreement statistic. If we are aware of the five issues listed above, then we will be able to better understand how the organizational context influences employee and team perceptions, attitudes, and behavior.

# IMPLICATIONS FOR ORGANIZATIONAL CONSULTANTS

Consultants can increase the probability of long-term success of their team interventions by applying the lessons we have learned through our research at the Center for the Study of Work Teams. Though following our suggestions below might not absolutely guarantee success, *not* following them will increase the probability of failure.

Teams should never be implemented just for the sake of having teams, or because everyone else is doing it. There always must be a sound business reason for having teams that can be ultimately related to some important organizational outcome. This might sound self-evident, but we have encountered some organizations that have implemented teams without truly understanding why they were doing it. The consultant must conduct a thorough diagnosis to determine if the problems faced by the organization are ones that can be ameliorated by the use of teams.

If teams are an appropriate solution, the consultant must work with the organization to ensure that the design of the teams is tailored to fit the needs of the organization. The appropriate types of teams should be determined during organizational diagnosis. It is very risky to uncritically adopt a team structure that some other organization has employed, even if the other organization has been very successful. The organization must adapt, not adopt.

## Piecemeal versus Integrated Implementations

Teams must not be implemented piecemeal or in isolation. When this happens, the corporate immune system is likely to kill them. An overall system view must be taken by the organization. All levels of the organization must be involved in the implementation, and the appropriate support systems must be put into place. Many organizations do not understand this, because they are used to implementing other types of changes in a piecemeal fashion. Consultants must convince their clients to take the whole-system approach. This might require that consultants use their best sales and influence skills to overcome organizational resistance to such a large-scale change.

Teams inevitably involve empowering employees with increased responsibility for making decisions and then acting on them. Though management has the responsibility of overseeing the implementation, it must learn to practice what it preaches. If management orders employees to be empowered (a contradiction in terms), they will see that no real change is occurring and will have little commitment to teams. The consultant must act as a process observer and facilitator in this situation to ensure that management's deeds match its words.

## Managing the Stress of Team Implementation

The implementation of teams is stressful for team members. The organization must be prepared to assist team members with stress-related problems. Stress management training should be specifically included as part of the team development program.

There are clear implications for organizational consultants from our research on support systems. Teams cannot function effectively without dedicated support. To achieve and maintain effective teams, consultants must be able to assist organizations with planning and implementing team-related changes in the support systems listed earlier in this chapter. They must convince their clients that the transition to a team-based organization is a systemic change that affects everything the organization does, and therefore all of its systems must change. Clients who are unwilling or unable to understand this are setting up themselves (and their consultants) for failure. As soon as the diagnosis indicates that teams are appropriate for the organization's needs, the client must be educated about the system-wide ramifications of a transition to a team-based organization. All too often, clients see team implementations as quick fixes and projects. The reality is that they represent a massive, permanent change in the way the organization operates. Early in the consultation, clients should be educated about the magnitude of change that will be necessary. Clients who are unwilling to commit to such a change can then terminate change efforts before any improper steps are taken, because poorly implemented teams can be very destructive to employee morale. We believe that it is better to leave an existing dysfunctional system in place than it is to implement teams improperly.

## Assess the Organization's Climate

A system to assess the organization's climate should also be a part of the implementation. The assessment of an organization's climate supplies an observation of the structure, practices, and procedures of an organization filtered by employee perceptual processes. Climate perceptions provide organizational decision-makers with a snapshot of how their employees perceive the overall environment, or specific foci (for example, innovation, safety) of the environment. Climate perceptions can also help indicate whether team-based organizational interventions might be needed, or whether such interventions have a good likelihood of success. In addition, employee climate perceptions can be used as a base criterion to detect how well the employees believe an intervention is accomplishing its goals. Although the employee climate assessment process is generally simple and straightforward, the practitioner must make sure not to use a cookie-cutter approach for team intervention issues. That is, there are no general issues that apply to all teams or all organizations that utilize teams. In each case, the necessity of teams and teamwork might exist, but the type and amount of teamwork can vary greatly between organizations. In any case, obtaining employee perceptions of their environmental context is a necessity before conducting a team implementation, or any other organizational development and change initiative.

## Asking the Hard Questions

Finally, as part of the process of educating clients about the significant changes a team implementation will bring, consultants need to ask hard questions of their clients regarding their willingness to commit to the long-term support of their teams. Some examples follow:

Will management be willing to work collaboratively with their employees to determine what they do, how they do it, and with whom they interact?

Will employees be selected and trained for team skills as well as technical skills?

Will team members be allowed to set their own goals and align them with the organization?

Will employees be provided with the on-time information they need to make effective decisions?

Will the performance appraisal system be changed to reflect team performance and to provide useful team feedback?

Will steps be taken to insure that interdependent teams will be able to communicate effectively both vertically and horizontally to prevent the formation of silos?

Will all of the executives truly support the team implementation, and will they see it through despite the inevitable bumps in the road that will occur?

Will the managers be educated and trained regarding their new roles and responsibilities?

Will everyone understand that the nature of leadership will change dramatically, and that they will all need to play different leadership roles at different times?

Will employees be given assistance in dealing with the increased stress that will occur?

Will the organization be willing to completely change its reward system to a team-based version?

Will input from employees be used to understand the areas that need change?

Will employees be surveyed about their perceptions concerning the strengths and growth opportunities for the organizational environment?

Will regular follow-up assessments be made to determine if employee perceptions have changed after the intervention?

Obviously, the above questions do not represent an exhaustive list. Yet if the client cannot answer yes to these few questions, there should be serious concern as to whether a team implementation should take place. Consultants who are willing to confront their clients with these realities will serve them well.

# References

Agrell, A., & Gustafson, R. (1996). Innovation and creativity in work groups. In M. A. West (Ed.), *Handbook of work group psychology* (pp. 317–344). New York: Wiley.

Altmann, R., Huff, J., Baltes, B., LaCost, H., Young, S., & Parker, C. (1998, April). *Psychological and organizational climate perceptions: A field experiment of a contemporary distinction.* Paper presented at the thirteenth annual meeting of the Society for Industrial and Organizational Psychology, Dallas, TX.

Anderson, N. R., & West, M. A. (1998). Measuring climate for work group innovation: Development and validation of the team climate inventory. *Journal of Organizational Behavior, 19,* 235–258.

Argyris, C., & Schön, D. A. (1974). *Theory and practice: Increasing professional effectiveness.* San Francisco: Jossey-Bass.

Argyris, C., & Schön, D. A. (1978). *Organizational learning: A theory of action perspective.* Reading, MA: Addison-Wesley.

Beyerlein, M. M. (1996). *Perceptions of team performance scale.* Unpublished manuscript. Center for the Study of Work Teams, University of North, Texas, Denton, TX.

Chan, D. (1998). Functional differences among constructs in the same content domain at different levels of analysis: A typology of composition models. *Journal of Applied Psychology, 83,* 234–246.

Cohen, S. G. (1994). Designing effective self-managing work teams. In M. M. Beyerlein & D. A. Johnson (Eds.), *Advances in interdisciplinary studies of work teams: Vol. 1. Theories of self-managing work teams* (pp. 67–102). Greenwich, CT: JAI Press.

Drexler, J. A., Jr. (1977). Organizational climate: Its homogeneity within organizations. *Journal of Applied Psychology, 65,* 96–102.

Ellison, S. (n.d.). *Classic blunders in team implementation.* (Available from the Center for the Study of Work Teams, University of North Texas, P.O. Box 311280, Denton, TX 76203-1280).

Emery, F. E., & Trist, E. L. (1978). Analytical model for sociotechnical systems. In W. A. Pasmore & J. J. Sherwood (Eds.), *Sociotechnical systems: A sourcebook* (pp. 120–131). San Diego, CA: Pfeiffer.

Emery, M., & Purser, R. E. (1996). *The search conference: Theory and practice.* San Francisco: Jossey-Bass.

Gavin, J. F., & Howe, J. G. (1975). Psychological climate: Some theoretical and empirical considerations. *Behavioral Science, 20,* 228–340.

Gladstein, D. L. (1984). Groups in context: A model of task group effectiveness. *Administrative Science Quarterly, 29,* 499–517.

Glick, W. H. (1985). Conceptualizing and measuring organizational and psychological climate: Pitfalls in multilevel research. *Academy of Management Review, 10,* 601–616.

González-Romá, V., Peiró, J. M., Llorret, S., & Zoronoza, A. (1999). The validity of collective climates. *Journal of Occupational and Organizational Psychology, 72,* 25–40.

Guzzo, R. A., & Dickson, M. W. (1996). Teams in organizations: Recent research on performance and effectiveness. *Annual Review of Psychology, 47,* 307–338.

Hackman, J. R. (1987). The design of work teams. In J. W. Lorsch (Ed.), *Handbook of organizational behavior* (pp. 315–342). Englewood Cliffs, NJ: Prentice Hall.

Hackman, J. R., & Morris, C. G. (1975). Group tasks, group interaction processes, and group performance effectiveness: A review and integration. In L. Berkowitz (Ed.), *Advances in experimental social psychology* (Vol. 8, pp. 45–99). Orlando, FL: Academic Press.

Hall, C. A., & Beyerlein, M. M. (2000). Support systems for teams: A taxonomy. In M. M. Beyerlein, D. A. Johnson, & S. T. Beyerlein (Eds.), *Advances in interdisciplinary studies of work teams: Vol. 5. Product development teams* (pp. 89–132). Stamford, CT: JAI Press.

Hall, C. A., Beyerlein, M. M., & Johnson, D. A. (2000, April). Relationship of team support systems to team performance. In M. A. Marks (Chair), *What's really in the "P-box" of I-P-O effectiveness models?* Symposium conducted at the meeting of the Society for Industrial and Organizational Psychology, New Orleans, LA.

Hellriegel, D., & Slocum, J. W., Jr. (1974). Organizational climate: Measures, research, and contingencies. *Academy of Management Review, 17,* 255–280.

Heneman, R. L., Dixon, K., & Gresham, M. T. (2000). Team pay for novice, intermediate, and advanced teams. In M. M. Beyerlein, D. A. Johnson, & S. T. Beyerlein (Eds.), *Advances in interdisciplinary studies of work teams: Vol. 7. Team development* (pp. 141–160). New York: Elsevier

Hitchcock, D. E., & Willard, M. L. (1995). *Why teams can fail and what to do about it.* Burr Ridge, IL: Irwin.

Jackofsky, E. F., & Slocum, J. W., Jr. (1988). A longitudinal study of climates. *Journal of Organizational Behavior, 9,* 319–334.

Jackofsky, E. F., & Slocum, J. W., Jr. (1990). Rejoinder to Payne's comment on "A longitudinal study of climates." *Journal of Organizational Behavior, 11,* 81–83.

James, L. A., & James, L. R. (1989). Integrating work environment perceptions: Explorations into the measurement of meaning. *Journal of Applied Psychology, 74,* 739–751.

James, L. R. (1982). Aggregation bias in estimates of perceptual agreement. *Journal of Applied Psychology, 67,* 219–229.

James, L. R., Demaree, R. G., & Wolf, G. (1984). Estimating within-group interrater reliability with and without response bias. *Journal of Applied Psychology, 69,* 85–98.

James, L. R., & Sells, S. B. (1981). Psychological climate: Theoretical perspectives and empirical research. In D. Magnusson (Ed.), *Toward a psychology of situations: An interactional perspective* (pp. 275–295). Hillsdale, NJ: Erlbaum.

Johnston, H. R., Jr. (1974). Some personality correlates of the relationships between individuals and organizations. *Journal of Applied Psychology, 59,* 623–632.

Jones, A. P., & James, L. R. (1979). Psychological climate: Dimensions and relationships of individual and aggregated work environment perceptions. *Organizational Behavior and Human Performance, 23,* 201–250.

Joyce, V. F., & Slocum, J. W., Jr. (1984). Collective climate: Agreement as a basis for defining aggregate climate in organizations. *Academy of Management Journal, 27,* 721–742.

Keating, E. K., & Oliva, E. (2000). A dynamic theory for sustaining process improvement teams in product development. In M. M. Beyerlein, D. A. Johnson, & S. T. Beyerlein (Eds.), *Advances in interdisciplinary studies of work teams: Vol 5. Product development teams* (pp. 245–281). Stamford, CT: JAI Press.

Klein, K. J., Conn, A. B., Smith, D. B., & Sorra, J. S. (2001). Is everyone in agreement? An exploration of within-group agreement in employee perceptions of the work environment. *Journal of Applied Psychology, 86,* 3–16.

Kuhn, T. S. (1970). *The structure of scientific revolutions* (2nd ed.). Chicago: University of Chicago Press.

Litwin, G. H., & Stringer, R. A. (1968). *Motivation and organizational climate.* Cambridge, MA: Harvard University Press.

Lytle, W., & Rankin, W. (1996, March). Fast-paced change. Workshop presented at the 1996 Strategies and Skills Conference for Effective Teaming, Dallas, TX.

Macy, B. A., & Izumi, H. (1993). Organizational change, design, and work innovation: A meta-analysis of 131 North American field studies—1961–1991. *Research in Organizational Change and Development, 7,* 235–313.

May, D. R., & Schwoerer, C. E. (1994). Developing effective work teams: Guidelines for fostering work team efficacy. *Organizational Development Journal, 12,* 29–39.

Mohrman, S. A., Cohen, S. G., & Mohrman, A. M., Jr. (1995). *Designing team-based organizations: New forms for knowledge work.* San Francisco: Jossey-Bass.

Mohrman, S. A., & Cummings, T. G. (1989). *The self-designing organization.* Reading, MA: Addison-Wesley.

Nilsson, T. (2000). A history of teams: The case of Sweden and Volvo. In M. M. Beyerlein (Ed.), *Social indicators research series: Vol. 6. Work teams: Past, present and future* (pp. 275–288). Norwell, MA: Kluwer.

Orsburn, J. D., Moran, M., Musselwhite, E., & Zenger, J. H. (1990). *Self-directed work teams: The new American challenge.* Homewood, IL: Business One Irwin.

Oshry, B. (1996). *Seeing systems: Unlocking the mysteries of organizational life.* San Francisco: Berrett-Koehler.

Pasmore, W. A. (1988). *Designing effective organizations: The socio-technical systems perspective.* New York: Wiley.

Patterson, M., Payne, R., & West, M. (1996). Collective climates: A test of their sociopsychological significance. *Academy of Management Journal, 39,* 1675–1691.

Payne, R. (1990). Madness in our method. A comment on Jackofsky and Slocum's paper, "A longitudinal study of climates." *Journal of Organizational Behavior, 11,* 77–80.

Payne, R., & Pugh, D. S. (1976). Organizational structure and climate. In M. D. Dunnette (Ed.), *Handbook of industrial and organizational psychology* (pp. 1125–1173). Skokie, IL: Rand McNally.

Pearce, J. A., II, & Ravlin, E. C. (1987). The design and activation of self-regulating work groups. *Human Relations, 40,* 751–782.

Rousseau, D. M. (1988). The construction of climate in organizational research. In C. Cooper & I. Robertson (Eds.), *International review of industrial and organizational psychology 1988* (pp. 139–158). New York: Wiley.

Sandy, W. (1990, October). Do more of what matters to your customers. *Modern Office Technology, 35,* 12–14.

Schein, E. H. (1992). *Organizational culture and leadership: A dynamic view* (2nd ed.). San Francisco: Jossey-Bass.

Schneider, B. (1975). Organizational climate: Individual preferences and organizational realities revisited. *Journal of Applied Psychology, 60*, 459–465.

Schneider, B. (2000). The psychological life of organizations. In N. Ashkanasy, C. Wilderom, & M. F. Peterson (Eds.), *Handbook of organizational culture and climate*, (pp. xvii–xxii). San Anselmo, CA: Sage Press.

Schneider, B., Bowen, D. E., Ehrhart, M. G., & Holcombe, K. M. (2000). The climate for service: Evolution of a construct. In N. Ashkanasy, C. Wilderom, & M. F. Peterson (Eds.), *Handbook of organizational culture and climate* (pp. 21–36). San Anselmo, CA: Sage Press.

Schneider, B., & Reichers, A. E. (1983). On the etiology of climates. *Personnel Psychology, 36*, 19–39.

Schneider, B., & Snyder, R. A. (1975). Some relationships between job satisfaction and organizational climate. *Journal of Applied Psychology, 60*, 318–328.

Shea, G. P., & Guzzo, R. A. (1987, Spring). Group effectiveness: What really matters? *Sloan Management Review, 28*, 25–31.

Shrout, P. E., & Fleiss, J. L. (1979). Intraclass correlations: Uses in assessing rater reliability. *Psychological Bulletin, 86*, 420–428.

Sundstrom, E. D. (1999). *Supporting work team effectiveness: Best management practices for fostering high performance.* San Francisco: Jossey-Bass.

Sundstrom, E. D., De Meuse, K. P., & Futrell, D. (1990). Work teams: Applications and effectiveness. *American Psychologist, 45*, 120–133.

Weisbord, M. R. (1992). *Discovering common ground.* San Francisco: Berrett-Koehler.

Young, S. A., & Parker, C. P. (1999). Predicting collective climates: Assessing the role of shared work values, needs, employee interaction, and work group membership. *Journal of Organizational Behavior, 20*, 1199–1218.

Zohar, D. (2000). A group-level model of safety climate: Testing the effect of group climate on microaccidents in manufacturing jobs. *Journal of Applied Psychology, 85*, 587–596.

# CHAPTER ELEVEN

# The Psychoanalytic Approach to Team Development

Pieter Koortzen and Frans Cilliers

*Department of Industrial and Organizational Psychology,
University of South Africa*

This chapter departs from traditional approaches to consulting and organizational psychology, because traditional approaches often look at it solely from a rational and economical view towards work in order to understand concepts such as cognition, perception, motivation, leadership, group norms and stages, organizational structures, culture, and development (see, for example, Robbins, 1997). We will argue that organizational behavior and consultants should not only address the conscious and the, too often, mechanistic approaches to the workplace. This chapter will also address aspects of work that will go beyond simple diagnostic prescriptions to include consulting skills related to processes and dynamics as they unfold in interpersonal, group, and organizational relations.

In our experience, after some intense exposure to the work environment, students and consultants realize that they do not understand the underlying processes and dynamics of behavior in organizations. They are aware that something is happening, but they cannot always say exactly what it is. The results of research may help to explain some of the observed behaviors in organizations, but they do not always explain the "here and now" processes and the unconscious dynamics that we believe are operating in individuals, groups, and organizations. Students and consultants who are not trained in psychodynamic approaches to groups and organizations often feel ineffective, uninformed, and helpless in many dynamic organizational situations such as meetings, team developments, and organizational processes. These feelings result in less effective consultations, emphasizing diagnostic functions and too often conscious interventions, instead of the process and development interventions. Consulting psychologists emphasize behavioral change, which we believe also includes studying relationships in groups and teams, and providing opportunities for exploration and development of relationship processes and dynamics. These consulting tasks might require consultants to acquire new knowledge, skills, and competencies if they wish to facilitate development and growth, and understand and work with behavior processes and dynamics at different levels. This need was expressed by the Society of Consulting Psychology of the American Psychological Association ([APA], 2000) when they issued principles for training at doctoral and postdoctoral levels. These guidelines emphasize the need for training and development of consulting psychologists at individual, group, and organizational levels, as well as the role of both content and process in consultation.

This chapter focuses on a psychoanalytic team development intervention as part of the consulting services offered by consultants at a *group* level. We will describe the roles and competencies of consulting psychologists in team development, provide an overview of the uniqueness of psychoanalytic group consultation, and then describe the approach in more depth. This discussion includes the Tavistock model, the basic assumptions of the model, the relevant concepts evaluated and studied in the approach, the consulting stance, and the methodology and techniques used. We will conclude by reviewing the diagnostic and evaluation process of team development interventions.

# ROLES AND COMPETENCIES OF CONSULTING PSYCHOLOGISTS IN GROUP AND TEAM DEVELOPMENT

The literature on this subject stresses the relevance of the process approach to group and team development, and the training of consulting psychologists. Schein (1987, 1988), for example, distinguishes between three fundamentally different roles in his description of the consulting process, namely the provider of expert information, the diagnostician and prescriber of remedies, and the process consultant, whose focus is on helping the client to help himself or herself. The process consultant uses a systemic approach to broaden the concept of client as the relationship between client and consultant evolves, to include individuals, groups, and organizational units at different times.

The Society for Consulting Psychology uses the three-level model in its training guidelines (APA, 2000) to describe the competencies needed by consulting psychologists. According to them, the core competencies required by psychologists at the group level are group assessment, assessment of functional and dysfunctional group behavior, assessment and development of teams, creating group-level teams in organizations (for example, self-directed work groups), intergroup assessment and intervention, group boundary assessment, and intervention and identity group (racial, gender, ethnic) management in the organizational context. They explain this further by stating that consulting psychology competencies take the group as one of the primary units of analysis. This group-level frame of reference is not only relevant to the internal (that is, interpersonal) relations of task groups, but also addresses phenomena such as role analysis, leader-follower behavior, interpersonal conflict, workflow intergroup relations, diversity, authority dynamics, labor-management relations, and interorganizational relations (APA, 2000).

The guidelines (APA, 2000) have also developed a number of crucial propositions about groups or teams in organizations that should be considered during consultations. First, they state that organizational roles are shaped by group-level forces; second, individuals function as group representatives in organizations whether they intend to or not; third, the internal dynamics of groups cannot be adequately understood independent of the external relations of those same groups; fourth, unconscious processes within individuals, within groups, and between groups affect individual roles, intragroup dynamics, intergroup relations, and interorganizational relations. This suggests that consulting psychologists need to acquire a variety of competencies including diagnostic and assessment competencies, developing and planning of intervention competencies, and implementation and managing intervention competencies. All these competencies should be employed at the intragroup, intergroup, and interorganizational levels of organizational consultation.

Apart from these generic competencies, it is important for consulting psychologists to have knowledge of the different psychological approaches, including the cognitive-behavioral, humanistic and psychoanalytic approaches, to group and team development. Depending on the types of problems experienced by a group or team, a specific approach with its unique theory, models, assumptions, methodology, and techniques might be more appropriate in achieving the required outcomes. In the cognitive-behavioral approach, Goldsmith and Morgan (2000), for example, describe a fourteen-point team intervention model that focuses on analyzing and sharing the perceptions that team members have of the team's performance, the exploration of feelings and self-defeating behaviors of team members, and the identification and implementation of behavioral changes required for effective performance. Myers (1999), from the same approach, believes that consultants should help the leader to promote member participation by coaching and gradually increasing the amount of freedom, candor, and flexibility that will help the team to move to a point of self-management.

Team development interventions from the humanistic approach are often described as group process facilitation. Facilitation is conceptualized by the person-centered approach (Hirschenbaum & Henderson, 1993; Rogers, 1973, 1975a, 1975b, 1982, 1985; Rogers & Stevens, 1967) as a process of providing an open and trusting climate, and an opportunity for learning to take place. The facilitator functions at high levels of specific core behavioral dimensions (also called conditions or interpersonal skills), namely respect (also called unconditional positive acceptance), realness (also called congruence), and empathy. It is believed that these conditions facilitate the exploration of thoughts, feelings, and behaviors in the team, and result in personal growth and learning about ways to change behavior (such as owning of feelings and interpersonal sensitivity), so as to become a more fully functioning or self-actualized person. Research with this model has shown significant enhancements of psychological optimal functioning and relationship-building skills (Bruce-Sanford, 1998; Cilliers, 1984, 1995a, 1995b; Romano, 1998; Romano & Sullivan, 2000).

We believe, however, that knowledge of psychoanalytic theory, models, assumptions, methodologies, and techniques can be more useful to explore conscious and unconscious processes and dynamics in team development. In the next section, we will look at the differences between the three models and the motivation for choosing a specific approach for team development.

# PSYCHOANALYTIC GROUP CONSULTATION

Although we will discuss the psychoanalytic approach to team development in great detail in the next section, it is appropriate to distinguish the approach from the cognitive-behavioral and humanistic approaches, and to motivate the choice of this specific approach in team development. The nature of the team's problems and the goals to be achieved with the team development intervention generally determine the choice of a psychological approach. From the previous discussion, it seems that a cognitive-behavioral approach might be more indicative in situations in which the group's dysfunctional behavior stems from perceptions of themselves, self-defeating behaviors, and an inability to make appropriate behavioral changes themselves.

A facilitative approach is often chosen when there is, for example, a lack of interpersonal sensitivity, acceptance, realness, and empathy in the group. The goal in such a case would be to facilitate the development of these interpersonal conditions and skills, and to teach the skills of relationship building and interpersonal support between individuals in the team.

As consultants, we generally choose to work from a psychoanalytic approach if the team presents conscious and unconscious conflicts (which might be the result of the team's history and unconscious motives), unhealthy splits between team members or exclusion of team members, problematic relationships with leaders or authority figures, integrating diverse individuals into the team, and difficulty in understanding self- and collective anxiety, defenses, and irrational behavioral processes in the team. The goal of the consultation is to assist the team in exploring its conscious and unconscious processes as team members relating with each other and leadership, and to work on interteam and organizational relationships with other parts of the system.

The initial diagnosis and decision to use the approach is based on an assessment of six dimensions, represented by the CIBART mnemonic: unresolved *conflicts* between team members, and between team members and management; unclear *identity* (for example, "Who are we?" and "How do we relate to the rest of the system?"); unclear task, space, and time *boundaries;* problems with authority and *authorization* (for example, taking on roles and exercising authority); *relationships* and *relatedness* problems (for example, mistrust and discrimination); and uncertainty and confusion about the primary *task* of the team.

Although we refer to the approach as the psychoanalytic approach in this chapter, it is obvious that the approach also incorporates systems theory (Colman & Geller, 1985; Fuqua & Newman, 2002) and an object-relations theory. Systems theory looks at the relationships and relatedness of the team with other teams, and object-relations theory (Kets de Vries, 1991) studies relationships between individuals based on what they represent (for example, relationships between white males and African-American females, or workers and management). With this as an introduction to the approach, let us present the approach in more detail.

# THE PSYCHOANALYTIC APPROACH TO TEAM DEVELOPMENT

In the following section, we will discuss the psychoanalytic approach to team development in terms of the assumptions about team development from this approach, the rationale and hypotheses of the psychodynamics of teams and organizations, the Tavistock model and other relevant concepts, the consultancy stance, team development methodology and techniques, and evaluating team development interventions.

## Assumptions about Team Development

A number of assumptions about team development are derived from this approach and are central to the intervention. These assumptions can be summarized as follows:

- Experiential learning is one of the best ways to facilitate adult learning (Neumann, Kellner, & Dawson-Shepherd, 1997). The interventions in this approach therefore take the form of experiential group relations workshops. Adult learning about interpersonal relationships occurs by making use of available opportunities in this dynamic environment.

Team members take responsibility for their own learning by using these opportunities. Consideration of the here-and-now behavior enhances learning. It also provides the consultant with valuable information on the processes and dynamics in the team.

- We also believe that the individual's and team's behavior (such as needs and anxieties) are both conscious and unconscious, and that consultants should work on both levels.

- Human and personality development start with individual intrapersonal awareness, and the consultant also provides opportunities to individuals to study their own dynamics within the team.

- Intrapersonal awareness forms the basis for interpersonal awareness and relationship building.

- A group of workers—or work team—has a unique life of its own with the individuals (the microsystem) forming the basic component.

- Group behavior follows predictable processes as well as specific, collectively developed conventions, thus creating the team's dynamics.

- Group dynamics refers to the study of how individuals and teams relate to each other, and the implied assumptions and myths. Consciously determined policies are sometimes supported and often subverted by less-conscious factors.

- The group process and dynamic consultant interprets this behavior in order to help move the group along its path to maturity and interdependence.

With these assumptions as a background to the psychoanalytic team development approach, the rationale and model according to which the development is being done can be discussed in more detail.

## THE RATIONALE AND HYPOTHESES OF THE PSYCHOANALYTIC APPROACH OF TEAMS AND ORGANIZATIONS

The psychoanalytic view rejects as overly definitive the rational and economic views on work, and believes that statistical analysis gives very little useful information about organizational behavior, teams, or the people working in the system. It also rejects the notion of a grand theory of organizations (Lawrence, 1999; Miller, 1976).

Kets deVries (1991) views work as both a painful burden (for example, in the task that needs to be performed) and a pleasurable activity (for example, in the outcome). The basic questions in understanding work, in this model, are why it is experienced as painful and why people try to avoid it while also experiencing it as pleasurable. The psychoanalytic answer (Kets deVries, 1991) lies in the renunciation of the instincts, giving up the pleasures and freedom of childhood play, and entering life ruled by the reality principle rather than the pleasure principle. If this does not happen, working will be too painful to perform and will be avoided altogether (Kets deVries, 2001). Consequently, employees and teams will never have an opportunity to gain the pleasure associated with accomplishment if they cannot delay gratification or endure the necessary suffering (Lawrence, 1999; Miller, 1976). To study this behavior, this approach focuses on flowing back and forth between theory and case analysis (Kets deVries, 1991; Lawrence, 1999; Miller, 1976, 1983, 1993; Obholzer & Roberts, 1994).

The rationale for studying organizational and team behavior from the psychodynamic approach can be stated as follows: the organization as a system has its own life, which is both conscious and unconscious, with subsystems relating to and mirroring one another. Unresolved conflicts in groups and teams are at times denied and repressed, but continue to influence the relations in the team. Similarly, unresolved conflicts between two team leaders, for example, can be mirrored in conflicts between their teams (Coleman & Bexton, 1975; Czander, 1993; Hirschhorn, 1993; Miller, 1993; Obholzer & Roberts, 1994). This rationale forms the basis for the belief that the study of unconscious behavior and dynamics leads to an understanding of organizational and team behavior. With this knowledge, the consultant can facilitate real organizational change by using the Tavistock model. This model provides a framework for studying the relationships (including the conscious and unconscious dynamics) in teams and organizations.

## THE TAVISTOCK MODEL

The authors have formulated a few basic hypotheses about individuals in team and organizational contexts. These can be described as follows.

The worker (as microsystem) approaches the work situation with unfulfilled conscious and unconscious family-oriented needs that he or she wants to fulfill in the work situation. As an example, some employees might be playing out unfulfilled needs for parental recognition or affection towards the manager, who might be representing male or female authority.

The worker brings unconscious, unresolved conflict, for example with authority, into the organization. Since the role of manager excludes relating to the employee on the level a father or mother would, the individual experiences conflict (a basic experience in this model).

The worker unconsciously plays out a need for power over siblings and the parental figure. Since colleagues are not siblings or parents, the need does not fit the reality of the work situation. This can lead to confusion, anxiety, anger, and aggression, which is another example of basic experiences in this model (Miller, 1976; Obholzer & Roberts, 1994).

Based on these assumptions, Bennis and Shepard (1956), Wheelan (1994), and Colman and Geller (1985) developed two basic psychoanalytic hypotheses about team behavior in the work context. These hypotheses look at teams' attempts to study and overcome anxiety, and to study and explore the projections from the rest of the system. The hypotheses can be described as follows.

First, Bennis and Shepard (1956), and Wheelan (1994), believe that criteria can be established by which phenomena of development, learning, or movement toward maturity of groups or teams can be identified and studied. From this point of view, maturity for the group means something similar to maturity for the person. A mature group or team can be identified by its ability to resolve its internal conflicts, mobilize its resources, and take intelligent action only if it has a way to consensually validate its experience. Individuals can resolve their internal conflicts, mobilize their resources, and take intelligent action only if anxiety does not interfere with their ability to profit from their experience to analyze, discriminate, and foresee.

Anxiety in groups and teams prevents individuals' internal communication systems from functioning appropriately. Under these circumstances, individuals can learn from their experiences only if they are able to overcome their anxiety (Bennis & Shepard, 1956). Similarly, groups or teams need to develop the ability to analyze and study their own anxiety without defensiveness, and to overcome obstacles to valid communication between team members. Using Sullivan's definition of personal maturity (1953), Bennis and Shepard (1956), and Wheelan (1994), contend that a group has reached a state of valid communication or maturity when its members have developed tools for analyzing interpersonal experience, the capacity to differentiate between past and present experiences, and the foresight of relatively near future events.

Second, Colman and Geller (1985) point out the importance of projective processes in groups and teams, which affect individuals and others related to them. Mutual projective processes not only impoverish and distort experience of the self and the perceived world, they also affect the behavior of the world towards the self. Groups, teams, and organizations inevitably create projection systems, in which threatening experiences or feelings are projected on different parts of the system. In a business, for example, incompetence might be projected on the production manager as if the rest of the system has no responsibility for it. This can create personal and interpersonal impoverishment and ineffectiveness. Team development interventions from a psychoanalytic approach offer teams, small groups, and internally divided individuals the chance to resolve some of the anxieties and fantasies observable in those settings. Consultants will therefore try to facilitate the development of maturity and the capacity to understand and explore projections from other parts of the system. A number of basic assumptions about groups or teams have also been identified in this approach. These assumptions represent specific problematic dynamics, which consultants should work with in team development.

# THE BASIC ASSUMPTIONS OF GROUPS AND TEAMS IN THE ORGANIZATION

Bion (1961) identified three basic assumptions to be studied in the individual (which he called the microsystem), the group or team, department or division (the mesosystem), and the organization (the macrosystem). These assumptions have been accepted by consultants working from this approach as the cornerstones of the study of organizational dynamics (Lawrence, 1999).

**Dependency.** The assumption is that the worker, just as a child, unconsciously experiences dependency on an imaginative parental figure or system. Since these needs for parenting, acceptance, and love are not always met, the worker experiences frustration, helplessness, powerlessness, and disempowerment. Typical remarks in this regard are, "Why is the boss not giving us more attention?" and "What do you want me to do?" These expressions, according to Cilliers and Koortzen (2000), are projections of the worker's own anxiety and insecurity, and indicate work and emotional immaturity. Organizationally, it manifests in the need for structure in remarks such as, "We need a committee to investigate," or "We need to structure this department more." This defense against anxiety can also be seen as a manipulation of authority out of its role, for example from supervisor to parental figure, according to the fantasy that then "we will be safe and cared for." Consultants should make teams and leaders aware of this dependency, and provide opportunities to study and possibly move from dependent behavior to more mature behavior.

**Fight or Flight.** The assumption is that the here-and-now of organizational life is filled with anxiety; in trying to get away from this anxiety, the worker unconsciously uses fight or flight as his or her defense mechanism. Fight reactions become manifest in aggression against the self, team members (with envy, jealousy, competition, elimination, boycotting, sibling rivalry, and fighting for a position in the group and privileged relationships with authority figures), or authority itself. Flight reactions become manifest physically in avoidance of others, illness, or resignation. Psychological flight reactions include defense mechanisms such as avoiding threatening situations or emotions in the here-and-now, rationalizing, and intellectualizing. In a meeting, for example, this would mean talking about "them" and "out there" issues, and avoiding looking at what this behavior says about me or the team. During team development interventions, the consultant constantly makes the group aware of its fight or flight reactions. This provides an opportunity for individuals to study and analyze the motivation behind this behavior, and to gain valuable insights into their own behavior.

**Pairing.** The assumption is that in order to cope with anxiety, alienation, and loneliness, the individual or team tries to pair up with perceived powerful individuals or subgroups. The unconscious need, according to Bion (1961) and Lawrence (1999), is to feel secure and to create; the unconscious fantasy is that creation will take place in pairs. Pairing also implies splitting up of the group. This happens when anxiety is experienced because of differences. The individual or team tries to split up the whole and build a smaller system in which he or she can belong and feel secure. This pairing also manifests in ganging up against the perceived aggressor or authority figure. Intrateam conflict and interteam conflict can result from pairings. This behavior can also split the team emotionally, and it is the consultant's task to make the team aware of this behavior and to assist them in studying the underlying anxiety that creates this need for safety and pairing.

**One-ness.** Two additional assumptions were later added to Bion's original assumptions (1961). According to Turquet (1974) the assumption is that team members seek to join a powerful union with an omnipotent force, surrendering the self for passive participation, thus experiencing existence, well-being, and wholeness. It is as if the individual team member gets lost within oceanic feelings of unity. This wish for salvationist inclusion can be seen in a team striving towards cohesion and synergy in which it is believed that problems will be solved by this strong united force. In the South African context, this was observed in teams' attempts to reconcile after the 1994 election. This might, however, lead to a total denial of differences, and consultants need to make teams aware of this dynamic.

**Me-ness.** As the opposite of one-ness, this assumption refers to the risk of living in a contemporary, turbulent society. The individual is pressed more and more into his or her inner reality in order to exclude and deny the perceived disturbing reality of the outer environment. The inner world becomes the comfortable place, and the outer the one to be avoided. The team works on the tacit, unconscious assumption that the group is to be a nongroup. Only people who are present can be related to, because their shared construct in the mind of what the group is about is of an undifferentiated mass. They act, therefore, as though the team has no existence; if it did exist, it would be the source of persecuting experiences. The idea of the group is contaminating, taboo, and impure. The members act as though the group has no reality and that the only reality is that of the individual. The individual's reality exists in a culture of selfishness in which the individual is only aware of his or her personal boundaries, which have to be protected from others. This leads to instrumental transactions with no room for affect (experienced as dangerous, because one would not know where feelings might lead to). This resistance of individuals to become part of the team can affect the team's performance negatively, and consultants need to facilitate the exploration of related feelings, processes, and dynamics in order to achieve more cohesion. For example, in the predominantly black collectivistic South African culture, white team members seem to feel threatened of losing their individuality, and present this kind of resistance. Apart from these basic psychoanalytic concepts, consultants also work with and explore the concepts discussed in the following section.

## Other Relevant Concepts Studied in Tavistock Team Development Interventions

Other relevant concepts studied in the Tavistock approach include anxiety (Menzies, 1993), resistance to change (Lawrence, 1999), boundaries (Czander, 1993), role (Lawrence, 1999), representation (Obholzer & Roberts, 1994), authority (Czander, 1993), leadership and followership (Kets deVries, 2001), relationship and relatedness (Shapiro & Carr, 1991), and group-as-a-whole (Wells, 1980). The discussion about the concepts that follows indicates how the manifestations of these concepts in team behavior can be used to analyze team dynamics, and to explore and work with the behavior in team interventions.

**Anxiety.** Anxiety in this framework is accepted as the basis of all organizational and team behavior (Menzies, 1993). In order to cope with the inevitable anxieties in the workplace, Menzies argues that employees unconsciously need something or someone to contain the anxiety. Employees use defense mechanisms such as projection to ensure that the workplace is safe and accepting. Projection can be defined as the process of putting parts of oneself onto the other person (projection); the identification is based on attributing some of one's own qualities to the other person (Colman & Geller, 1985). Projection can be used to blame management for what goes wrong. An individual or group might expect the manager or management to contain their anxiety about losing their jobs or securing jobs in a difficult labor market, or to negotiate with the unions on their behalf. The system might also expect the existing structures such as laws, regulations, procedures, organizational structures, job descriptions, and idiosyncratic ways of solving problems, to act as containers for anxiety. It is interesting to see that the moment the level of anxiety rises in the system, the need for structure is expressed almost immediately; for example, "Lets make a rule about . . . " or "Why don't you put this in writing and then let's discuss the future. . . ." Rationalization and intellectualization are used to stay emotionally uninvolved, and to feel safe and in control. Assisting the team to study and explore its anxiety can uncover the conscious and unconscious motivation behind many of their self-defeating and ineffective behaviors. Team members need to learn how to identify when there is anxiety in the team, how to analyze and study it, and how to take the necessary steps to contain or ventilate it.

**Resistance to Change.** This is probably one of the most acknowledged concepts among consultants working in this framework. It refers to the system (individual, team, or organization) resisting the exposure of unconscious material (Lawrence, 1999). A team might experience many changes in its lifetime, such as changes in membership or leadership, changes in its identity, or changes to its task, equipment, or technology. These changes can create new challenges and require new skills. It can also impact the perceived safety and security of the team. Consultants need to provide opportunities to study the resulting rational and irrational fears associated with these changes.

**Boundaries.** The individual, team, and organization, considered as interactive parts of the total system, all have boundaries (Czander, 1993; Lawrence, 1999; Hirschhorn, 1993). In the same way that psychoanalysis refers to ego boundaries, thus distinguishing between the individual and the environment, every part of the organizational system operates inside and across its boundaries. The purpose of setting organizational boundaries is to contain anxiety and to make the workplace controllable and pleasant. Examples of basic boundary management in organizations are time, space, and task. Time boundaries are used to structure the working day (starting, going home, meetings) in an endeavor to order, structure, and contain the workplace. The space boundary refers to the workplace itself, for example, knowing exactly where to sit or stand while working, or having one's own desk, cabinet, locker, office, or building. It can be argued that having to work in an open-plan office creates anxiety because of the lack of clear space boundaries. The task boundary refers to knowing what the work content entails. The anxiety about not knowing what to do, and according to which standard, is contained in structures like the individual's job description and the department's structure. Another example of a boundary issue is the forming of the team's identity. Boundaries that are not managed effectively seem to create a lot of anxiety in employees (Kets deVries, 2001). One of the basic tasks of consultants in this regard is to make teams and leaders aware of the lack of boundary management and how it affects team performance. This is often supported with discussions on more effective time and space management, and task boundary management.

**Taking Up a Role and Managing Oneself in a Role.** To take up an organizational or team role implies uncertainty and risk (Czander, 1993; Hirschhorn, 1993; Lawrence, 1999). Anxiety is not simply rooted in a person's internal voices or private preoccupations, but also reflects real threats to professional identity. If the individual's anxiety is too great or too difficult to bear, the person might escape by stepping out of his or her role. Anxiety is transformed along a chain of interactions through the psychological process of projection and introjection. Psychological violence happens inside the individual as a result of the interplay between anxiety caused by real uncertainty and anxiety created by threatening voices within. These mostly parental voices punish the individual, and paradoxically, the individual can feel badly even before he or she has failed in reality. This anxiety chain leads people to violate boundaries and people. When anxiety mobilizes behavior, the individual, at times, experiences other people not as they are, but as the person needs them to be, so that the other person can play a role in the individual's internal drama (Lawrence, 1999). In this regard, consultants often assist team members, leaders, and managers in taking up and staying in their roles; they also make the team aware of unconscious motives and attempts to manipulate the leader out of his or her role, or to disempower a team member with a specific role. This can be detrimental to the functioning of the team.

**Representation.** This occurs whenever one of the team's boundaries is crossed by the individual or team (Obholzer & Roberts, 1994). The crossing of individual (microsystem) boundaries happens in interpersonal communication between two people, such as in a performance appraisal interview between a manager and a subordinate. The crossing of mesosystem boundaries happens in interpersonal or team communication between two people from different departments, or in a meeting between departments (for example, when the human resources department has a planning meeting about training in the production department). The crossing of macrosystem boundaries happens when an individual or team meets with an individual or team from another organization. The issue of representation refers to the authority given to the person crossing the boundary on behalf of someone else, the department, or the organization. Unclear authority boundaries seem to immobilize and disempower representatives to another part of the system. Consultants need to provide opportunities for team members to study the authorization process in their team, or to review how they authorized or disempowered representatives in the past (for example, by giving an unclear task or limiting authority).

**Authorization.** This approach distinguishes between three levels of authorization, namely representative, delegated, or plenipotentiary authority (Czander, 1993; Obholzer & Roberts, 1994). Representative authority implies being restricted in giving and sharing sensitive information about the system across the boundary. Delegated authority refers to more freedom in sharing, but with a clear boundary around the contents thereof. Plenipotentiary authority gives the person freedom to cross the boundary using his or her sense of responsibility when making decisions, and his or her choice of conduct. When an employee is sent to communicate, negotiate, or sell across the boundary of his or her own system without a clear indication of the level of authority, it creates anxiety that hinders rational decision-making and reporting back to colleagues inside the boundary. We have observed that in teams in which the competition is strong, team members have great difficulty in authorizing team members to take up roles on their behalf.

**Leadership.** This approach refers to leadership as managing what is inside the structural boundary in relation to what is outside the boundary (Obholzer & Roberts, 1994). An individual employee takes individual leadership when negotiating a salary increase for himself or herself, or taking an afternoon off. Leadership of followers applies when an individual—not necessarily the designated leader or manager—acts or negotiates on behalf of others in the organization. Leadership also implies followership, another role with a clear boundary in the system (Kets deVries, 2001). Studying the way team members are allowed or not allowed to take up leadership roles in the team needs special attention. It is also important to note how followers empower or disempower the leader; leaders often fail because their followers do not support them. The trust relation between leaders and followers is of prime importance in this process.

**Relationship and Relatedness.** The Tavistock approach is based on the study and understanding of human relationships (Shapiro & Carr, 1991). This implies any type of face-to-face or telephonic interaction in the organization as it happens in the here-and-now. On another more abstract and unconscious level, the organization is always in the mind of the individual, as well as the group (team or department), and so will influence behavior. This is called the relatedness or *the organization in the mind* (Shapiro & Carr, 1991). This concept originates from the basic childhood experience of the family one belongs to. In an organizational context, it seems that the individual's or team's identification with, and fantasies about, the organization and sections of it, can be seen as a driving force for a lot of behavior in the system. Consultants, therefore, need to provide opportunities for the team to study the relationships between team members and the team's relatedness to other teams or departments in the system. Existing relationships might be the result of perceptions teams have about themselves, other teams, and the organization, which, if ineffective, can influence the cooperation and performance of the team.

**Group-as-a-Whole.** The concept of collectivism from analytical psychology (Albertyn, 1999) is also used in the Tavistock approach. It refers to one part of the system acting or carrying emotional energy on behalf of another (Wells, 1980). An example of carrying emotional energy in a team is when one member is mobilized to act out anger experienced by several members towards the leader. The concept of group-as-a-whole can also be studied on the organizational level.

Some researchers (Alderfer, 1977) have found that dynamics in one part of an organization can be reflected in another part of the organization. This author developed the concept of parallel processes, which refers to any apparent resonance or similarities between two engaged social systems. This implies that dynamics that developed collectively in teams and organizations can become manifest in different parts of the system simultaneously. The issue of collectivism also implies that no event happens in isolation, and that there is no coincidence in the behavior of the system (Kets deVries, 1991). Consultants, therefore, need to be cognizant of the fact that manifested behavior in a team might be the result of what is happening elsewhere in the system. Teams and their behavior should therefore be studied in the context of the broader system.

**Projective Identification.** This phenomenon is described by Kets deVries (1991) as a psychological defense against unwanted feelings or fantasies, a mode of communication as well as a type of human relationship. It is considered to occur when covert dynamics in one system get played out in parallel form by another system with which it interacts. For example, the system might deny or reject a conflict that exists, thus altering an uncomfortable experience by imagining that it belongs to someone or something else. Next, the recipient of the attribution or projection is inducted into the situation by subtle pressure to think, feel, and act congruently to the received projection. According to Kets deVries, this phenomenon is not really understood in the consultancy situation, and it might play a large role in the traditional splits (for example, splits between management and the workers) when external consultants work with organizations, as well as when mistrust and suspicion exist between management and labor unions. Consultants need to assist teams to study and make sense of their own thoughts, feelings, and behavior, and to distinguish them from what was dumped on them by other teams and departments. The basic idea is that if this is done for a long enough time period, the team members might start to believe this about themselves and identify with the projection. If the projection is of a negative nature, which it quite often is, it can seriously affect the team members' perceptions of themselves and their capabilities. If incompetence is projected onto workers by management, and workers start to identify with the projection, their performance can deteriorate drastically. Consultants need to assist the team to distinguish between who they really are and what is projected onto them, and to resist identifying with negative projections.

The team dynamics discussed in this section are present in overt and covert ways during a team development intervention. It is the task of the consultant to make the group aware of both conscious and unconscious processes and dynamics, and a specific stance, based on psychoanalytic methodology, is used in this.

# THE CONSULTANCY STANCE

The role of the consultant who works according to the Tavistock model is very different from the general role of the consultant (Czander, 1993). Traditionally, the consultant observes, instructs, or helps to solve problems, but these roles are believed to create dependence on the team and its members. The Tavistock model requires consultants to be actively involved with the group, its members, its tasks, and its experiences. The presence, person, and authority represented by the consultant are seen as part of the team development event, which implies that the team might respond at different levels to the consultant. In our experience, teams sometimes project some of the hostility they feel towards management onto the consultants; this can provide valuable information on the relationship between the two parties in the initial stages of the consultation. A consultant is also required to manage the boundary conditions and to make the team aware of these boundaries (such as task, territory, and time). More specifically, a consultant's role involves the following:

- Investigate why the team needs development, including the conscious and unconscious reasons. The consultant must contract with the team about the desired outcome, and ensure that he or she has the necessary authority to examine problems at all levels in the organization. The consultant must also spend time with the team in order to explain its role, boundaries, and impact on the expectations and experiences within the team.

- Consulting from this stance implies two kinds of verbal interventions, namely the consultant asking questions, and formulating and sharing working hypotheses about what is happening. These inputs operate primarily on the cognitive level of team functioning, but the inputs obviously also elicit cognitive, affective, and interpersonal behavior among team members (Czander, 1993). The questions asked by the consultant are sometimes referred to as licensed stupidity, because they have the freedom to ask naive and sometimes childlike questions to encourage the team to make sense out of nonsense. The consultant's working hypotheses are an interpretation of what might be happening in the here-and-now of the group's experience. Both interventions are meant to stimulate awareness.

- Question the working relationship between himself or herself and the team from his or her role perspective, especially the underlying power issues. (How is the group reacting to the authority of the consultant? Is the group trying to seduce him or her out of role?)

- Help team members realize their interpretations of the situation and exercise their authority to test realities.

- Lead the team into working within boundaries, with himself or herself as the container (an emotional container) of the team's anxiety, but at the same time allow team members to be in their own terms (Neumann et al., 1997).

- Work in continual conditions of subjectivity, and be comfortable, therefore, in using the self as an instrument. This involves the internal disentangling of what is being projected onto the consultant and what is already there.

- Frame the working hypotheses and interpretations on the basis of his or her experience in the role.

More specifically we contend, based on our experience with this approach, that the consultant will work with the following behavior:

- The way individuals and teams manage their anxiety by making use of various defense mechanisms

- The way individuals and teams exercise their authority in the different systems of the team and the organization

- The nature of the interpersonal relationships within the team and the organization

- The relationships and relatedness with authority, peers, and subordinates

- Leadership practices and the management of boundaries

- Intergroup relationships between subsystems or departments

- Identity, roles, tasks, space, time, and structures as boundaries, and the management thereof in coping with anxiety

We also believe that specific outcomes can be achieved by consulting from this approach. This approach offers team members the opportunity to study their intrapersonal functioning (for example, unresolved conflict with authority) and their interpersonal functioning as it manifests itself in relationships with team members and leadership. It also offers an opportunity to reevaluate the way in which individuals and managers attempt to satisfy their power and affiliation needs when relating to others or taking up a role.

At the team level, this approach provides an opportunity for team members to study the here-and-now dynamics, processes, and relations in the team, which result in a keen awareness of underlying dynamics and anxieties, and an openness and willingness to explore and study behavior in the group. If the skills of observation, exploration, and studying of team dynamics can be transferred to the team, team members can empower themselves to analyze and explore their own behavior and team behavior. If a team can stop the formal agenda of a meeting when it becomes aware of anxiety in the team, and spend some time on the underlying processes, dynamics, and relationships, it can be a very valuable process of understanding and resolving the problem. The transferring of observation and exploration competencies can be of great value to team members, and make them less dependent on consultations.

We firmly believe that consultants who intend to work from this approach need intensive training, under supervised conditions, in psychoanalytical theory and practice, and the group relations model, before effective consultancy can take place. Added to this is a sense of self-awareness—consultants have only their observations and feelings as guidelines. It is important that consultants ask what these feelings and reactions mean in terms of team behavior, and why the team is responding to the consultant in a particular manner. The underlying feelings need to be explored and processed in order to understand, for example, the team's dependence or authority issues. Team development workshops are presented by trained group relations consultants who work at specific tasks and in specific formats during different events. This methodology is described as follows.

## Team Development Methodology and Techniques

Although the consultant(s) might work with a team over a long period of time, the team development interventions are often delivered through workshops and training programs that include specific tasks, methods, and techniques to address each of these interventions. These interventions can be described in terms of the primary task of the workshop, and the format and tasks of the different events.

The primary task of a team development workshop is to give members the opportunity to study the behavior of the team(s) they belong to as it happens in the here-and-now. This task is educational and is based on examining the behavior of the team as it unfolds in the present.

In terms of the format, workshops can consist of plenaries, large group events, small group events, intergroup or team events, lectures, and review and application groups. The task of each of these events is very different.

Plenaries allow consultants and team members to plan the following sessions, to give instructions, to set boundaries for different events, and to share information about the learning. Large group events aim to study the behavior of the team as it happens in the here-and-now of the total system. Small group events, on the other hand, focus on studying the behavior of face-to-face interpersonal relations as they happen in the here-and-now.

During intergroup events, team members divide themselves into smaller groups in order to study the relations between groups as they happen in the here-and-now, and in particular, the problems associated with exercising authority on behalf of others across boundaries. Lecturers are also an important part of the workshops, as they might teach specific content on group or team behavior, analyze team behavior, identify dysfunctional team behavior, build interpersonal and team relations, and develop leadership. Towards the end of the workshop review and application, group members are required to look at the various roles they played within the group, and to review their learning experiences (review group). Team members then need to work towards applying these learning roles to other groups within their everyday working lives (application group).

Great care is taken in these events to manage the boundary conditions of time, space, and task in such a way that team members and consultants can effectively work at the specified task. The selection of events to be included in the workshop is based on the initial diagnosis, which is made at the start of the consulting process. The process of diagnosing team dynamics and the evaluation of team interventions is discussed in the following section.

## Diagnosing Teams and Evaluating Team Development Interventions

Traditionally, diagnoses of group behavior and evaluations of psychoanalytic interventions, whether in the context of individual psychoanalysis or group development, have taken the form of case studies in which a diagnosis was made, the intervention was described, and the impact or effect was analyzed qualitatively and thematically. In practice, this mean that the consultants use themselves as the instrument of diagnosis, and the evaluation of the intervention is done by describing behavioral changes on the initially diagnosed problematic dimensions (Hunt & McCollom, 1994; McWilliams, 2000). Although this methodology is widely used, it has received severe criticism in the past. Diagnostic and intervention procedures used by consultants, and the evaluation and research developments in the psychoanalytic field are discussed in the following section.

Gutmann, Ternier-David, and Verrier (1999), and Levinson (1991), describe diagnostic and intervention procedures that can be summarized as consisting of a diagnostic phase, an intervention phase, and a feedback or evaluation phase. Levinson (1991) describes the importance of data gathering in the first phase of the consultation, starting when the first contact is made.

During and after the first meeting, it is important for the consultant to evaluate their own experience (cognitions, emotions, and reactions) of the meeting. McCormick and White (2000) believe that when consultants use themselves as instruments of diagnosis, they should pay attention to their emotional responses to a team or organization, and use these to create diagnostic hypotheses. One's emotional reactions to the team or organization can be indicative of the emotional state of that team or organization. Consultants should also pay close attention to their initial perceptions of the organization, including the negative impressions and feelings about the team or organization. They also stress that consultants should try to understand their common reactions and prejudices so that they can reduce bias in their diagnosis, and at the same time postpone judgment to avoid premature conclusions (McCormick & White, 2000). Finally, they encourage consultants to pay attention to the fantasies and images that occur while gathering information about the system, and use these to create diagnostic hypotheses.

The first meeting will enable the consultant to develop an initial diagnosis of the team or organization, but should be followed by a structured process of gathering information (Levinson, 1991). An effective relationship should be developed with the client in order to gather factual data about the history, policies and procedures, and external information relating to the other teams in the system, the competitors and customers. He also mentions the importance of studying the organizational or team structure and responsibilities, the setting or context in which they operate, and the their main tasks. Lawrence (1999) points out that the consultant should be aware of what is not being said during information-gathering interviews, as well as the discrepancies between how the team presents itself and the behavior manifested in the work context.

Once the initial diagnosis has been made and working hypotheses developed, the consultant will develop a formal plan to study the institution, and an intervention for team development is developed. Gutmann et al. (1999) describe the framework of a workshop in the group relations model as a learning institution. As described in the previous section, a workshop consists of different learning events during which opportunities are provided to study the processes and dynamics in the whole team, the relationships between subsystems in the team and with other teams, and the interpersonal relationships in the team. Consultants present working hypotheses or interpretations of what is happening in the here-and-now, and provide opportunities for the team to explore their dynamics. The exploration leads to either supporting or rejecting the hypotheses, and new insights into their own behavior is facilitated. Alderfer (1980), as well as Hunt and McCollom (1994), suggest that team members should consider collectively alternative explanations of their experience and what is interpreted by the consultant. This will facilitate a collective acceptance or rejection of possible explanations and solutions. The team also learns this methodology of analyzing, exploring hypotheses, and validating, in an attempt to uncover, explore, and understand their own dynamics. This is carried over into the work context.

Gutmann et al. (1999) point out that important work needs to be done between workshops. During this period, team members might start to experiment with alternative ways of relating to each other; decisions that were made during the first workshop might be implemented, and these changes might create anxiety in the team. Consultants should be available to consult during this process.

According to Long (2000), this is the period in which team members should develop the capacity to be in the presence of others and to see them for what they really are. Examples of this can include denying aspects of team members' identity, including their race, gender, and authority. This author believes that team members tend to see others the way they want to and not the way they are. The more the team can work with the reality of other team members, the more the team as a whole will engage reality and hence be able to work. The author also stresses the importance of developing the ability to internalize other team members. The identification with other team members through the task is an important aspect of this. This is especially important after workshops during which interpersonal conflicts were explored and studied. Finally, Long also mentions the importance of developing the capacity to be able to refer to and negotiate with the internalized team members when forming judgments. Consulting during this phase therefore involves assisting team members in establishing new ways of working together and relating. Further workshops can also be presented if the need exists.

The evaluation consists of a thorough analysis of the diagnosis, the intervention, and the outcomes of the intervention (Levinson, 1991). This is normally presented to the team or organization in report form, and includes recommendations for further development. In order to do this evaluation, consultants working from this approach have realized that more systematic methods for gathering data, recording intervention processes, and analyzing the outcomes of the intervention are needed. It may therefore be appropriate to include some of the more recent attempts in this regard.

It is acknowledged by consultants working from this approach that the validity and reliability of research methods attempting to address such questions can be questioned. Care must be taken to provide reasonable checks for the weaknesses of any single method (Baum, 1990; Gummesson, 1991; Shevrin & Dickman, 1980).

Guerin (1997) developed a methodology plan for her study to counter the challenges normally faced by research on phenomena that participants might not be aware of. The researcher used both quantitative and qualitative traditions of research. Data sources in the form of ethnographic observation, participant interviews, and textual coding of recorded meetings permitted triangulation of data. An empirical-analytical method was used for the content analysis of the meeting texts, using the Group Development Observation System

(Wheelan, Verdi, & McKeage, 1994) protocol. The researcher stressed that the unit of analysis for this kind of study was the team in its meeting, rather than any individual or pair of people. By using this lens on the behavior of a team, the analysis process itself departs from contemporary conventions in the study of teams. Throughout the process of data collection, and periodically during the analysis phase, a research journal was maintained for recording observations and noting personal experiences. Guerin (1997) mentions that the personal material in the research journal, while pertinent to the findings narrative, is never directly quoted in the results. The journal, however, was a distinct aid to her in maintaining and observing the self, providing a mechanism for interpreting personal projections and transference reactions.

Wheelan (1994) also describes more systematic methods of observation and analysis. She refers to a process analysis system that, in contrast to content analysis, is less concerned with what is said and more with *how* things are said, the dynamics underlying communications, and the patterns and sequence associated with these dynamics. She refers to the Interaction Process Analysis system developed by Bales (1950) in this regard. This system is used to classify each unit of behavior into one of twelve categories, six of which relate to the socio-emotional dimensions of the group, and six to the group's task. The problem with the system seems to be that it was not designed to capture the range of behaviors generally associated with the various stages of group development.

Apart from using more systematic methods of observation and analysis, and a combination of methods to increase the validity of team development evaluations, a need also exists for the development of valid and reliable instruments. Wheelan (1994) describes a number of instruments already in existence. The Group Development Stage Analyses were created by Carew and Parisi-Carew (1988) and are based on eight characteristics thought to be associated with high-performance teams. These characteristics are productivity, empathy, empowerment, roles and goals, flexibility, open communication, recognition, and morale. Under each characteristic, four options are listed representing a four-stage model of group development. The stages include orientation, dissatisfaction, resolution, and production. The goal of the instrument is to determine the group's stage of development, but no reliability, validity, or norms are reported.

An instrument that is perhaps more valuable to consultants working from the psychoanalytic approach is the Reactions to Group Situations Test by Stock Whitaker (Wheelan, 1994). This fifty-item test indicates individual member preference for certain behaviors in groups. Preference for work, fight, flight, dependency, and pairing are assessed. The findings concerning reliability and validity were not very good, but the instrument might form the basis for further research.

# SUMMARY

Consultants rendering team development services work from a number of psychological approaches depending on the problems the team presents. While the cognitive-behavioral and humanistic approaches are more commonly used in the work context, we believe that unconscious behavior in teams can be studied and explained more effectively from the psychoanalytic approach. This chapter covers the psychoanalytic approach to team development.

The chapter starts with an outline of the roles and competencies of consulting psychologists, indicating the importance of the psychoanalytic approach as part of their competencies and skills when consulting on the group level. As an introduction to psychoanalytic group consultation, a comparison of the approach with other approaches is given. The specific application of the psychoanalytic approach is then discussed in terms of the assumptions about team development, the basic assumptions of groups and teams in the organization, the Tavistock or Group Relations model, and the psychoanalytic concepts studied in team diagnosis and development interventions.

The last part of the chapter covers the methodology used in the approach, including the consultancy stance, the method and techniques used in workshops, and the diagnostic, evaluation, and research methodologies used in the approach.

# References

Albertyn, L. (1999). Group behaviour. In Z. C. Bergh & A. L. Theron (Eds.), *Psychology in work context* (pp. 333–353). Cape Town, South Africa: Oxford University Press.

Alderfer, C. P. (1977). Group and intergroup relations. In J. R. Hackman & J. L. Suttle (Eds.), *Improving life and work: Behavioral sciences approaches to organizational change* (pp. 234–246). Santa Monica, CA: Goodyear Publishing.

Alderfer, C. P. (1980). Consulting to underbounded systems. In C. P. Alderfer & C. L. Cooper (Eds.), *Advances in experiential social processes* (Vol. 2, pp. 267–295). New York: Wiley.

American Psychological Association (2000). Society of Consulting Psychology. *Principles for education and training at the doctoral and post-doctoral level in consulting psychology: Organizational consulting psychology*. Washington, DC: Author.

Bales, R. F. (1950). *Interaction process analysis: A method for the study of small groups*. Reading, MA: Addison-Wesley.

Baum, H. S. (1990). *Organizational membership: Personal development in the workplace*. Albany, NY: State University of New York Press.

Bennis, W. G., & Shepard, H. A. (1956). A theory of group development. *Human Relations, 9,* 415–437.

Bion, W. R. (1961). *Experiences in groups*. New York: Basic Books.

Bruce-Sanford, G. (1998). A simulation model for training in group process. *International Journal of Group Psychotherapy, 48,* 393–396.

Carew, D. K., & Parisi-Carew, E. (1988). *Group development stage analysis: Matching leader behaviors with team development.* (Available from Blanchard Training and Development, Inc., 125 State Place, Escondido, CA 92025).

Cilliers, F. (1984). *'n Ontwikkelingsprogram in sensitiewe relasievorming as bestuursdimensaie* [A development program in sensitive relationship forming as a managerial dimension]. Unpublished doctoral dissertation, Potchefstroom University, Potchefstroom, South Africa.

Cilliers, F. (1995a). Die effek van 'n groeigroepervaring op predikante [The effect of a growth group experience on ministers of religion]. *NG Teologiese Tydskrif, 36*(4), 630–642.

Cilliers, F. (1995b). Fasiliteerderopleiding [Facilitator training]. *Journal of Industrial Psychology, 213,* 7–11.

Cilliers, F., & Koortzen, P. (2000). The psychodynamic view of organizational behavior. *The Industrial-Organizational Psychologist, 38*(2), 59–67.

Colman, A. D., & Bexton, W. H. (1975). *Group Relations Reader 1.* Jupiter, FL: A. K. Rice Institute.

Colman, A. D., & Geller, M. H. (1985). *Group Relations Reader 2.* Jupiter, FL: A. K. Rice Institute.

Czander, W. M. (1993). *The psychodynamics of work and organizations: Theory and application.* New York: Guilford Press.

Fuqua, D. R., & Newman, J. L. (2002). The role of systems theory in consulting psychology. In R. L. Lowman (Ed.), *Handbook of organizational consulting psychology.* San Francisco: Jossey-Bass.

Goldsmith, M., & Morgan, H. (2000). Team building without time wasting. In M. Goldsmith, L. Lyons, & M. Freas (Eds.), *Coaching for leadership* (pp. 103–109). San Francisco: Jossey-Bass.

Guerin, M. L. (1997). Teamwork at Barton Company: A psychodynamic perspective. Retrieved June 2001, from http://www.sba.oakland.edu/ispo/html/1997Guer.htm

Gummesson, E. (1991). *Qualitative methods and management research.* Thousand Oaks, CA: Sage.

Gutmann, D., Ternier-David, J., & Verrier, C. (1999). From envy to desire: Witnessing the transformation. In R. French & R. Vince (Eds.), *Group relations, management, and organization* (pp. 155–172). New York: Oxford University Press.

Hirschenbaum, H., & Henderson, V. L. (1993). *The Carl Rogers reader.* London: Constable.

Hirschhorn, L. (1993). *The workplace within: Psychodynamics of organizational life.* Cambridge, MA: MIT Press.

Hunt, J., & McCollom, M. (1994). Using psychoanalytic approaches in organizational consulting. *Consulting Psychology Journal, 46*(2), 1–11.

Kets deVries, M.F.R. (1991). *Organizations on the couch: Clinical perspectives on organizational behavior and change.* San Francisco: Jossey-Bass.

Kets deVries, M.F.R. (2001). *The leadership mystique: A user's manual for the human enterprise.* Englewood Cliffs, NJ: Prentice Hall.

Lawrence, W. G. (1999). *Exploring individual and organizational boundaries: A Tavistock open systems approach.* London: Karnac.

Levinson, H. (1991). Diagnosing organizations systematically. In M.F.R. Kets deVries (Ed.), *Organizations on the couch: Clinical perspectives on organizational behavior and change* (pp. 45–68). San Francisco: Jossey-Bass.

Long, S. (2000). The internal team: A discussion of the socio-emotional dynamics of team (work). Retrieved June 2001, from http://www.sba.oakland.edu/ispso/html/2000Synposium/ Long2000.htm

McCormick, D. W., & White, J. (2000). Using one's self as an instrument for organizational diagnosis. *Organizational Development Journal, 18*(3), 49–62.

McWilliams, N. (2000). On teaching psychoanalysis in antianalytical times: A polemic. *American Journal of Psychoanalysis, 60*(4), 371–390.

Menzies, I.E.P. (1993). *The functioning of social systems as a defence against anxiety.* London: Tavistock Institute of Human Relations.

Miller, E. J. (1976). *Task and organization.* New York: Wiley.

Miller, E. J. (1983). *Work and creativity. Occasional Paper No. 6.* London: Tavistock Institute of Human Relations.

Miller, E. J. (1993). *From dependency to autonomy: Studies in organization and change.* London: Free Association Books.

Myers, J. R. (1999). To build a team, you've got to tear down walls. *Purchasing, 127*(2), 140–142.

Neumann, J. E., Kellner, K., & Dawson-Shepherd, A. (1997). *Developing organizational consultancy.* New York: Routledge.

Obholzer, A., & Roberts, V. Z. (1994). *The unconscious at work.* New York: Routledge.

Robbins, S. P. (1997). *Essentials of organizational behavior.* Englewood Cliffs, NJ: Prentice Hall.

Rogers, C. R. (1973). *Client-centered therapy.* London: Constable.

Rogers, C. R. (1975a). *Encounter groups.* Harmondsworth, England: Penguin Books.

Rogers, C. R. (1975b). *On becoming a person: A therapist's view of psychotherapy.* London: Constable.

Rogers, C. R. (1982). *Freedom to learn for the 80's.* Columbus, OH: Charles E. Merrill.

Rogers, C. R. (1985). *Carl Rogers on personal power.* London: Constable.

Rogers, C. R., & Stevens, B. (1967). *Person to person: The problem of being human.* Moab, UT: Real People Press.

Romano, J. L. (1998). Simulated group counseling: An experiential training model for group work. *Journal for Specialists in Group Work, 23*(2), 119–132.

Romano, J. L., & Sullivan, B. A. (2000). Simulated group counselling for group work training: A fourth year research study of group development. *Journal for Specialists in Group Work, 25*(4), 366–375.

Schein, E. H. (1987). *Process consultation: Vol. II. Lessons for managers and consultants.* Reading, MA: Addison-Wesley.

Schein, E. H. (1988). *Process consultation: Vol. I. Its role in organization development* (2nd ed.). Reading, MA: Addison-Wesley.

Shapiro, E. R., & Carr, A. W. (1991). *Lost in familiar places: Creating new connections between the individual and society.* New Haven, CT: Yale University Press.

Shevrin, H., & Dickman, S. (1980). The psychological unconscious: A necessary assumption for all psychological theory? *American Psychologist, 35,* 421–434.

Sullivan, H. S. (1953). *The interpersonal theory of psychiatry.* New York: Norton.

Turquet, P. M. (1974). Leadership: The individual and the group. In G. S. Gibbard, J. Harman, & R. Mann (Eds.), *Analysis of groups* (pp. 349–371). San Francisco: Jossey-Bass.

Wells, L. (1980). The group-as-a-whole: A systemic socio-analytical perspective on interpersonal and group relations. In C. P. Alderfer & C. L. Cooper (Eds.), *Advances in experiential social processes* (Vol. 2, pp. 165–198). New York: Wiley.

Wheelan, S. A. (1994). *Group processes: A developmental perspective.* Boston: Allyn & Bacon.

Wheelan, S. A., Verdi, A., & McKeage, R. (1994). *The group development observation systems: Origins and applications.* Philadelphia: PEP Press.

# CHAPTER TWELVE

# Organizational Consulting to Virtual Teams

Joanie B. Connell
*California School of Organizational Studies*
*Alliant International University*

Over the past decade, technological developments have enabled people to communicate vast quantities of information instantaneously across large distances, transforming the workplace into a multinational cybercommunity. Managers are increasingly working with people who are telecommuting from home or working in geographically dispersed locations, using e-mail, voice-mail, the web, and various forms of conferencing (Coovert, 1995; Ellison, 1999; Prieto & Simon, 1997; Reich, 2001). The advantages and disadvantages of the virtual workplace are multiple. Employers save money and employees are more productive and satisfied (Cascio, 2000), yet in some cases, employers lose control, teams become dysfunctional, and employees can no longer separate work from home (Kurland & Bailey, 1999). The technology has so quickly changed the workplace that organizations are now swimming to catch up with the human factors. Managers hunger for guidance on how to virtually manage people and projects, and organizational consultants are well positioned to provide guidance.

There are a number of organizational consulting issues that arise for virtual teams, including: selecting and hiring the right managers and employees for successful remote teamwork, managing communication and trust in virtual environments, measuring productivity of invisible employees, and determining what types of jobs can be done remotely. This chapter will address these issues from both a theoretical and an applied perspective. The chapter begins with an overview of the state of the research on virtual management, defining terms and describing what organizations are currently doing. It then reviews theories and models of differences between the various modes of communication to be referred to throughout the chapter. Finally, the chapter introduces six important issues that arise in organizations as a result of virtual work. The chapter reviews each issue in detail, giving research-derived advice to organizational consultants on how to help virtual teams succeed.

# DEFINING VIRTUAL WORK ENVIRONMENTS

There are a variety of different forms of virtual and remote work environments. Some employees who are being remotely managed, for example, have always been located remotely, such as sales people or employees who work from remote regional offices. Information technology (IT) has changed aspects of these working relationships, but it has not fundamentally redefined their work practices (O'Mahony & Barley, 2000). Teleworkers, on the other hand, are a different category of virtual worker. They perform work at home, or from some remote office space, which could previously only be performed at the office. Recent advances in technology have enabled these types of arrangements. Finally, some virtual employees still work in traditional offices, but use computers, voicemail, faxes, and so on, to augment their business communications. These people are working virtually in some, but not all, aspects of their jobs. Thus, it is important to define the terminology of virtual work to understand the different environments and explore the common themes.

## Telework

Telework, also called remote work, flexiwork, electronic homework, and distance work (Fisher & Fisher, 2001; O'Mahony & Barley, 2000; Qvortrup, 1998), refers to working from remote locations, including home, satellite offices, and shared work centers, as well as mobile work (Kurland & Bailey, 1999; Prieto & Simon, 1997). Satellite offices contain work space for a single company that is typically closer to people's homes and reduces commuting time. Neighborhood, or shared work centers, house employees from multiple companies. Mobile workers travel frequently and work from hotels, cars, airplanes, and so on.

Providing space for teleworkers can increase or decrease costs for companies (Cascio, 2000). Satellite offices can be expensive and require duplication of facilities and staff. On the other hand, these costs can be balanced by eliminating or reducing office space at headquarters. One way that companies can save on the cost of space for part-time office workers is by offering *hotelling*. This is a shared office space for multiple employees who are not in the office simultaneously.

## Telecommuting

The term telecommuting was originally defined by Nilles, Carlson, Gray, and Hanneman (1976) to refer to replacing transportation with the use of communication and information technologies. Although every author seems to have a unique definition of the term, telecommuting has generally come to mean performing office work at home, and this is typically achieved using various forms of information technology (Ellison, 1999; O'Mahony & Barley, 2000). In Europe, the term telework is often used interchangeably with telecommuting, although they also employ the term telework in the broader context explained above.

## Virtual Work

Virtual work refers to working with others using communication tools, such as telephones, computers, pagers, and so on. Virtual work describes work being accomplished via information technology and can include both remote work and office work. Typically, however, the term *virtual team* is used to refer to teams that are geographically dispersed, or, at a minimum, are not located in proximate offices (Kurland & Bailey, 1999). This chapter focuses on the unique issues that arise when team members are working virtually and remotely.

# SPECIAL CHALLENGES THAT ARISE WITH VIRTUAL TEAMS

Organizational consultants encounter certain challenges with virtual teams. These stem from characteristics of the situation and the environment. Distance is one such challenge. When team members and managers do not interact with each other on a face-to-face basis, new methods must be employed to develop trust, monitor performance, inspire teamwork, and maintain culture. In addition, employees must learn to use technology to share information that would otherwise be communicated in person. Furthermore, the isolation of working alone in a remote location can both positively and negatively affect employee satisfaction and productivity. Technology creates a second set of challenges. Communicating via technology, compared to face-to-face, influences communication behaviors, interpersonal relationships, trust, and so on. In addition, virtual employees become dependent on the quality and availability of the communication technology. When it fails, either they have to be technically savvy enough to fix it or contend with delays. Time creates a third set of challenges for virtual teams. When employees work from home and have flexible schedules, or when geographically dispersed employees work from different time zones, it can be hard to coordinate team members and schedule meetings.

The issues stemming from distance and time are intuitively easy to understand. The issues arising from the technology require more explanation. The next section describes how communication media differ theoretically and what effects these differences have been empirically shown to have on potential aspects of business interactions.

## Theoretical Differences Between Communication Media

There is a growing body of research—both empirical and theoretical—on communication media (for a recent review, see O'Mahony & Barley, 2000). Much of the research compares face-to-face (FTF) interactions to computer-mediated communications (CMCs), such as e-mail and computer chat. The majority of empirical studies have been conducted in laboratories, and focus on small group interactions. Results of these studies show that, compared to face-to-face interactions, people communicating via computer tend to exhibit: less inhibition, conformity, and satisfaction with the interaction (Bordia, 1997; Kiesler & Sproull, 1992; Straus, 1997); more open and emotionally expressive behaviors (Baron, 1998; Walther, 1996); greater equalization, efficiency, and self-awareness (Dubrovsky, Kiesler, & Sethna, 1991; Kiesler & Sproull, 1992; Matheson & Zanna, 1988); and different group processes but similar outcomes in decision-making and problem-solving tasks (Gallupe & McKeen, 1990; Reid, Ball, Morley, & Evans, 1997; Weisband, 1992). These research findings have illuminated certain consequential effects of communication media on business interactions, but they might be limited in how much they generalize to the workplace, because many of the studies have been performed on students in laboratories. Also, they have not taken into account the real-world contexts of organizational culture, ongoing relationships, and high-stakes outcomes of organizational decisions.

Theoretically, communication media differ from each other in many ways, including how much social information they transmit, how fast they transmit the information, and how real they feel to the participants. Researchers of communication media have sought to meaningfully categorize the components of communication media for the purpose of comparing and contrasting media effects on human interactions. Three theories stand out in the literature: media richness theory (Daft & Lengel, 1984, 1986), social presence theory (Short, Williams, & Christie, 1976), and the social identity model of deindividuation effects (Postmes, Spears, & Lea, 1998).

**Media Richness.** According to Daft and Lengel (1986), information richness is defined as ". . . the ability of information to change understanding within a time interval. Communication transactions that can overcome different frames of reference or clarify ambiguous issues to change understanding in a timely manner are considered rich. Communications that require a long time to enable understanding or that cannot overcome different perspectives are lower in richness" (p. 560). In order of decreasing richness, the media classifications are: face-to-face, video, telephone, computer-mediated, addressed written communication, unaddressed written communication, and formal numeric text (see also Rice, 1992). Media richness theory has been widely referenced, yet it has been highly criticized because it is not very theoretical in nature, and because media richness on its own cannot account for the differences in behavioral and perceptual outcomes in the different media. Counter claimants argue that the richness of the medium depends, in part, on how the users give meaning to what they receive in the communication. In particular, users of the media, their experience, and the contexts in which the media are being used, interact with the media to form higher or lower levels of richness (Carlson & Zmud, 1999; Contractor & Eisenberg, 1990; Lee, 1994; Markus, 1992; Rice, 1992). Media selection—which medium a person chooses to employ—also affects a person's use of the medium (Fulk, Schmitz, & Steinfield, 1990). In addition, media can take on different forms. For example, e-mail can be used either to send a business letter or a personal correspondence (Yates & Orlikowski, 1992).

**Social Presence.** Social presence theory (Short et al., 1976) was developed in the context of telecommunications, and describes a communication medium by the degree to which it is perceived as conveying the physical presence of the communicating participants. Social presence includes verbal cues (such as timing, pause, and inflection), and nonverbal cues (such as facial expression, gaze, posture, and physical distance). Social presence is often measured in terms of personalness or warmth of the medium, or by the appropriateness of its use for a particular task (Johansen, 1977; Reid, 1977; Rice, 1992). According to this theory, nonverbal cues play a significant role in presence, and therefore people interacting in CMCs are lower in presence than when they interact via telephone, and people communicating via telephone are lower in presence than when they are interacting FTF. Thus, communication media vary in the extent to which they can transmit both a person's message and personal qualities.

**Social Identity Model of Deindividuation Effects (SIDE).** The social identity model of deindividuation effects (SIDE) developed out of a critique of deindividuation theory (Postmes et al., 1998). Many CMC researchers have theorized that the relative (and sometimes complete) anonymity that CMCs afford induces a state of deindividuation which, in turn, encourages uninhibited behavior. In contrast, Postmes et al. suggest that deindividuation causes a sensitivity to situational norms. For example, a computing subculture might have the norm that *flaming* (using particularly aggressive or abusive language) is seen as good and desirable. Also, counter to media richness theory, the SIDE model suggests that CMC might be perceived as a socially rich environment. Due to the absence of individuating information (such as physical and vocal cues of individuals), social norms and group identity cues gain importance. In other words, the seemingly anonymous nature of CMC groups might create an even stronger influence of social identity norms than in face-to-face interactions. The SIDE model is relatively new and has not received much critique or additional support yet, but it is increasingly gaining prevalence.

**Summary.** Differences in social presence, richness, and the influence of situational norms affect many aspects of interpersonal interactions, including perception, trust, inhibition, self-awareness, sense of responsibility, conformity, and so on. Consequently, it is important for consultants to give careful consideration to how business processes will be affected by the transition of intact to virtual teams.

### Diagnosing Issues that Arise from Managers of Virtual Teams

Table 12.1 contains typical questions that managers raise when supervising virtual teams. The Issue(s) column on the right-hand side of the table is designed to help consultants diagnose the issues driving the questions. There are six categories of issues: (1) policy and culture, (2) tools, (3) communication, (4) trust, (5) selection and performance measurement, and (6) employee satisfaction. The next six sections address these issues in detail.

# POLICY AND CULTURE

It is important to distinguish between corporate and team levels when creating policies and culture for remote work. At the corporate level, the focus might be more on cost and liability, whereas at the team level, the focus might be more on individual styles and idiosyncratic needs for tasks being performed. (Team-level culture and policies are discussed in the section on communication.) In both cases, it is important to strike the right balance between flexibility and structure to fit with the existing climate. This might manifest itself in a distinction between implicit and explicit rules for telework. For example, at a law firm I recently studied, there was no formal policy regarding working at home. However, it was implied that only attorneys had the choice of working at home without explicit permission from a supervisor. When asked, employees at all levels of the law firm indicated that they did not want a formal policy because the implicit one worked to their satisfaction; they felt that a written policy would impose unwanted restrictions.

Not surprisingly, there is a dearth of scientifically backed advice on establishing successful policies and cultures for virtual work. Therefore, consulting psychologists, for now, will have to rely on more general organizational knowledge and practical advice from telework specialists. Clearly, this is a rich area for new research.

## Policy

At least three major issues arise for organizational consultants in guiding companies on policies for remote work. The first is the type of culture the company has. For example, the importance of flexibility might outweigh certain risks of not having an explicit policy. The second issue is corporate liability—primarily

Table 12.1. Diagnosing Issues with Sample Questions from Managers.

| Questions from Managers | Issue(s) |
|---|---|
| Can people successfully work remotely in this organization? | Policy and culture, tools |
| How do I know who will be successful at telecommuting? | Selection and performance |
| How do I create a fair system for letting some people telecommute? | Policy and culture |
| How do I know my remote employees are working and not off shopping at the mall? | Selection and performance, trust, communication |
| How do I keep remote employees visible in the organization? | Communication, policy and culture |
| How do I know there is a problem with a remote employee? | Communication, trust |
| How often do I need to see the employees face-to-face? | Communication, employee satisfaction |
| I want to have regular staff meetings, but it is impossible to coordinate everyone's schedules. How do I balance flextime with availability? | Communication, policy and culture, tools, employee satisfaction |
| Some of my team members don't like working remotely. Some complain that they don't feel as much a part of the team as the on-site employees. What should I do? | Communication, employee satisfaction, policy and culture |
| How do I remain accessible remotely? | Communication, policy and culture |
| How do I keep from being interrupted by remote employees calling in, and overwhelmed by the number of e-mails? | Policy and culture, communication, tools |
| One of my employees never responds to my e-mails. What should I do? | Communication, tools, policy and culture |
| One employee e-mails at the last minute to cancel meetings, and I don't get the messages in time. What should I do? | Communication, tools, policy and culture |
| How can multiple employees access documents all at once? | Policy and culture, tools |
| How do I ensure that remote employees internalize the corporate culture? | Communication, policy and culture |
| How do I know remote employees have a safe work space? | Policy and culture, tools |

in terms of worker's compensation for injuries occurring while working at home, and fair and equal treatment of employees. For example, encouraging some employees to telecommute and not others could adversely impact legally protected populations of employees (Miller & Cardy, 2000). This could occur, for instance, if young, single people were encouraged to work at home, but older people with children were not. Other liability issues might arise as a result of people inadvertently documenting communications via e-mail and other virtual tools. A notable example of such a liability was when a Microsoft executive's e-mail about "establishing ownership of the Internet" was entered into evidence against them in their antitrust trial ("U.S. Lawyer Hammers," 1999 P.E1). The third issue is cost to the company. This arises in two forms: (1) impact on productivity and effectiveness (for example, can employees effectively satisfy customers if they are not able to answer their phones?); and (2) the cost of tools and support for remote workers. Although the fear is generally that costs will be higher for teleworkers, the costs might, in fact, be lower if practices such as office sharing or hotelling are adopted (Kurland & Bailey, 1999; Prieto & Simon, 1997).

Because these issues cross a number of boundaries, it is important to involve the appropriate people when drafting virtual work policies. Table 12.2 outlines several policy issues to consider, and which people or departments should be involved. I recommend working primarily with human resources (HR) and involving other departments, such as legal, IT, facilities, safety, and management, in developing guidelines and policies. Other sources of practical suggestions are found in Hoefling (2001) and Nilles (1998).

## Culture

Two fears about corporate culture often arise when organizations consider allowing remote work. The first is how the dispersion of employees will affect the company's culture, and the second is how remote employees will adopt and remain in touch with the culture. These fears can be very real, as organizational consultants well know. It is therefore important to determine what kind of culture exists before setting a program in place (Bray, 1999; Fisher & Fisher, 2001). Some cultures are less conducive to virtual work, such as a culture that is heavily dependent on personal contact with key individuals within the organization (Gainey, Kelley, & Hill, 1999). Even though virtual effects on culture tend to be a significant concern for organizations, there is very little scientific research about these effects. The following paragraphs share what evidence exists, along with experiences from consultants in this area.

Several actions can be taken to minimize the undesirable cultural impact of the dispersion of employees. For one, managers can limit the amount of time employees can spend away from the office. The law firm described previously exhibited a good example of the first technique. They had one office that was

Table 12.2. Corporate-Level Policy Issues to Consider for Telework.

| Policy Issues to Consider and Who to Get Involved | |
| --- | --- |
| Policy Issue | Who to Involve |
| Safety of home office environment, and the limits of company liability for injuries occurring there | Safety<br>Legal |
| Security, network access, tool provision, and support | IT |
| Requirements for being eligible to work at home | HR<br>Legal |
| Selection criteria and guidelines for remote workers | HR<br>Management |
| Types of jobs that are eligible for remote employees | HR<br>Management<br>Legal |
| Training on tools and communication practices for employees and managers, including performance management | HR<br>IT<br>Management |
| Guidelines on how to be successful at working remotely | HR<br>IT<br>Management |
| Inappropriate behavior, grounds for termination | HR<br>Legal |
| Guidelines for setting boundaries between work and home | HR |

located in a geographical region with a particularly high cost of living. As a consequence, people tended to live quite far away from work, and a large number of senior attorneys began telecommuting. This changed the once gregarious culture into one quite barren of social interaction. In addition, the office became void of mentors to train and acculturate junior attorneys. To solve these problems, management and peer pressure mounted to limit the frequency of telecommuting to no more than two days per week.

Second, organizations can keep remote workers in touch with the company culture using virtual methods. For example, Wiesenfeld, Ragurham, and Garud (1998) found that a higher frequency of e-mail communication among home workers corresponded to a greater sense of organizational identity. This finding did not hold for on-site employees. Organizations might also find ways to keep cultural information flowing to employees, for instance, by having regular company meetings and celebrations—face-to-face or virtual (Fisher & Fisher, 2001). Thus, it is advisable to provide important company communications in multiple formats to reach both on-site and remote employees.

In addition to bringing the culture to the remote employees in a virtual format, another way to keep remote employees in touch with the culture is to bring the remote employees to the company for periodic face-to-face interactions. For employees who only work remotely part of the time, flexibility and attention to scheduling may be the only added challenges. For purely remote employees, the tradeoffs between travel costs and acculturation benefits come into question immediately. Culture alone might not be a strong enough reason to fly employees in for costly get-togethers, but when other factors, such as team building, trust, and performance evaluation, are considered, the benefits might justify the costs.

Finally, it is important to take special care to make sure that new employees acculturate before being left entirely on their own (Prieto & Simon, 1997). Many of the organizations I and others have studied require—implicitly or explicitly—employees to work on-site for a minimum amount of time (typically three to six months) before beginning to work remotely on a regular basis (Fisher & Fisher, 2001). In addition, it is advisable to assign new remote employees to work closely with a mentor during the early phase of their employment.

# TOOLS

Organizations vary a great deal in the types of tools they need and can financially justify to support remote employees. For example, a completely virtual startup company that I recently studied employed minimal tools. They required employees to own home computers and telephones, but the company paid for the Internet connection fees and long distance calls. The company communications were entirely by e-mail, phone, instant messaging, twice-yearly face-to-face retreats, and occasional face-to-face meetings with customers. In contrast, I also studied a large networking company with a core business of developing tools for virtual communications. They had a larger tools budget to support thousands of employees, and they had ample access to the technology that they produced. They provided employees with laptop computers, high-speed Internet access, pagers, cell phones, videoconferencing, and toll-free telephone numbers, along with a host of intranet tools for accessing company resources remotely.

As these examples illustrate, there are many different factors to consider when selecting which tools to use to support remote work. Some factors include: what methods of communication are necessary to get the work done from both task and cultural perspectives, what company resources need to be accessed remotely, how securely the information is being accessed or communicated, and what the costs are to the company and whether some of these costs should be shared by employees. Table 12.3 provides a number of suggestions of types of tools and issues to consider. Other practical suggestions are offered by Kurland and Bailey (1999), and Nilles (1998).

Table 12.3. Tools and Issues to Consider for Remote Work Environments.

| Communication | | |
| --- | --- | --- |
| *Tools* | Face-to-face meeting accommodation | Pager |
| | Telephone | E-mail |
| | Mobile phone | Chat |
| | Voicemail | Video camera |
| | Call forwarding | Video at office |
| | Conferencing phones in meeting rooms | |
| | Toll-free phone numbers | |
| | Long-distance access (for example, calling card) | |
| *Issues* | Privacy for confidential calls | Expense |
| | Privacy for confidential e-mails | Company culture |
| | Quality | Types of tasks to be performed |
| | Remote accessibility | |
| | Speed | |
| **File Sharing** | | |
| *Tools* | Intranet | Website |
| | Connectivity to server (dial-up, high-speed dedicated line) | Bulletin board |
| | Software for home access | Project page |
| | File access control software | Important company information (culture, phone numbers, HR, and so forth) |
| *Issues* | Security | |
| | Speed | |
| | Level of access to confidential documents | |
| | File access control (read/write access) | |
| **Costs/What to Provide** | | |
| *Tools* | Company provides everything | |
| | Company provides nothing but access to phones, voicemail, server | |
| | Company provides essentials | |
| | Flexible spending account (employee chooses tools) | |
| | Company matches or shares spending with employees for home equipment | |
| *IT Support* | Support office equipment only | |
| | Support company-provided hardware and software only | |
| | Support everything users need to work remotely (the author has not observed this situation) | |

# VIRTUAL COMMUNICATION

Organizational consulting psychologists can be particularly helpful to organizations by providing guidance on the psychological and behavioral effects of communication media. This section begins with a brief report on the empirical findings of these effects. Then, I will present several suggestions for managers and teams to improve virtual communications.

## Media Effects on Communication

Communication tools can influence interpersonal interactions. The following research describes these effects in more detail.

**Emotions, Inhibition, and Relationship Building.** Communicating virtually can heighten people's emotions and reduce social barriers for openly expressing them. Researchers have theorized that either perceiving fewer social cues or facing stronger situational norms in CMCs leads people to behave with less inhibition (Lea & Spears, 1991; Postmes et al., 1998). Experimental studies show that people tend to express negative emotions more in CMCs, exhibited by the phenomenon of flaming (Lea, O'Shea, Fung, & Spears, 1992). People also express positive emotions more in CMCs by self-disclosing more and becoming more intimate and personal (Walther & Burgoon, 1992). Higher levels of emotion can either facilitate or hinder relationship building. In the business literature, CMC has been associated with lower levels of rapport in negotiations (Moore, Kurtzberg, Thompson, & Morris, 1999), and decreased cohesiveness in and satisfaction with group decision-making (Kiesler & Sproull, 1992; Straus, 1997). As Walther and Burgoon explain, the highs are higher and the lows lower in CMCs. In other words, when the context facilitates liking and friendship, people tend to become even closer than they would be face to face. When the situation obstructs cues associated with trust, then frustration and aggression mount to higher levels than they would in FTF interactions.

**Understanding and Social Norms.** Losing nonverbal channels can make it harder for people to understand each other (Bordia, 1996; Brennan, 1998; Daft & Lengel, 1986; Straus & McGrath, 1994). People have to verbalize what would normally be nonverbal cues (Bordia, 1996). For example, Reid et al. (1997) found that participants in a computer-mediated group decision-making situation shared proportionately more positional and value statements, and fewer factual and inferential statements, than face-to-face participants. In other words, virtual groups tended to focus more on social norms than on facts. Thus, to overcome misunderstanding in CMCs, people more explicitly express social intimations.

**Group Decision-Making Processes and Outcomes.** Communication media tend to affect group decision-making processes. When compared, CMC groups seem to arrive at similar outcomes as FTF groups, but the decision-making process tends to be comprised of different dynamics (Gallupe & McKeen, 1990; Reid et al., 1997; Weisband, 1992). For example, Reid et al. measured increased conversation about social norms in CMC groups as compared to FTF groups, but less convergence of opinions and no differences in final decisions. Many studies also show decreased satisfaction with computer- and video-mediated group interactions (Hiltz & Johnson, 1990; Whittaker & O'Conaill, 1997). For example, CMC has been associated with lower levels of rapport in negotiations (Moore et al., 1999), and decreased cohesiveness in and satisfaction with group decision-making (Kiesler & Sproull, 1992; Straus, 1997). Thus, although the outcomes of FTF and CMC group decision-making tend to be similar, there are differences in the dynamics of and satisfaction with the communications.

## Managing Successful Virtual Communications

As the research implies, it is important for virtual teams to set standards on how to effectively select and use media for different types of interactions. The following four steps are recommended to encourage successful communications in virtual teams: (1) explore the existing culture and individual communication styles; (2) set expectations for media usage; (3) select the appropriate medium for the situation; and (4) fit the communication style to the medium.

**Explore Culture and Individual Styles.** Organizational consultants might find it useful to do their own investigation of the company's culture prior to working with teams on communication practices (Block, 1981; Fisher & Fisher, 2001). If the company's culture is very formal, policies and training might need to be implemented to ensure e-mail communications are exchanged appropriately. To determine what communication practices are appropriate for a particular team, the consultant might assess current practices and individual preferences among team members. One way for the consultant to help teams explore individual differences is to conduct a personality assessment exercise. Although there is no research to date on what types of personalities are associated with media preference and usage, a basic understanding of the principles suggests some predictions. For example, extroverts enjoy going to meetings and become drained spending too much time alone (Kroeger & Thuesen, 1992), and would therefore tend to prefer face-to-face interactions.

**Set Expectations.** One of the biggest complaints I have heard from managers and employees in virtual environments is that they suffer from information overload. At the same time, they often complain that they are not aware of what others are doing. It is therefore useful to set expectations about communications to solicit the right number and type of incoming messages (Fisher & Fisher, 2001). As much as people might want to resist adding structure, experience shows that successful virtual teams rely on it (Cole, 1996; Hoefling, 2001). For example, team members cannot rely on running into their colleagues in the hallway to pass along important but informally communicated information. Table 12.4 outlines recommended practices for setting expectations about virtual communications.

Table 12.4. Recommended Communication Practices for Virtual Teams.

| Manager-Employee Communications | |
| --- | --- |
| *Setting expectations* | Set clear objectives and expectations to facilitate independent work.<br>Set expectations about employee availability and responsiveness. |
| *Monitoring status, performance, well-being* | Check in with remote employees regularly and frequently. |
| *Being accessible* | Choose a medium on which you can be reached for emergencies, and check that medium often. |
| *Avoiding information overload* | Prioritize your media.<br>Filter messages by sender, topic, and so forth, and respond as necessary. |
| **Team Communications** | |
| *Setting expectations* | Set expectations about team member availability and responsiveness, both in terms of time and medium (phone, chat, e-mail).<br>Schedule meetings and available time collectively.<br>Set ground rules for media usage. |
| *Communicating and monitoring status* | Ensure that communications get to all members.<br>E-mail minutes to meetings.<br>Take responsibility to find out what you missed.<br>Make sure you have access to medium, documents, and so forth, in advance of meetings.<br>Make sure remote people have access to everything they need prior to meetings. |
| *Information sharing* | Set up tools and processes for sharing documents. |
| *Avoiding miscommunications and trust breakdowns* | Over-communicate and be exceptionally responsive.<br>Use people's preferred media. |
| *Avoiding information overload* | Decide at the outset which correspondence is appropriate for the entire team. |

Fisher and Fisher (2001) also provide practical tips on structuring communications. Most important is to get the team members talking to each other about their expectations, even if no formal training or presentation is given.

**Select the Appropriate Medium.** Because some forms of interaction are better than others to communicate urgency, emotions, complex information, trust, and rapport, it is important to select the appropriate medium for the particular situation. To put it simply, there are five basic criteria to consider in choosing the right medium: (1) purpose, (2) presence, (3) preexisting relationship, (4) priority, and (5) permanence (Connell & Mendelsohn, 2000). These can be remembered as the *five P's*. The first consideration is that it depends on the purpose of the interaction, or the type of task. For example, because people conform less in e-mail interactions, e-mail might be better than face-to-face for creative tasks, such as brainstorming, but worse for consensus building. The second factor is how much personal presence matters. For example, it is easier to influence others or be a sympathetic friend when nonverbal cues are present (Baumeister, 1982). Third is the degree of familiarity with the person. Trust, for instance, is better built with a new acquaintance face-to-face than via computer (Rocco, 1998). Fourth is how quickly the job needs to get done. E-mail is often slower in terms of getting a response than a phone call or face-to-face meeting. It also tends to take longer to do equivalent tasks via e-mail than face-to-face (Bordia, 1997; Hightower & Sayeed, 1995; Siegel, Dubrovsky, Kiesler, & McGuire, 1986). However, e-mail is good for multitasking and corresponding with people in different time zones. Last is whether or not the transaction should be documented—permanently, and sometimes publicly. In some cases, it is important to maintain a record, such as documenting agreed-upon expectations of the scope of work to be completed on a project. On the other hand, a casual comment written in an e-mail can later be taken out of context and used to deplore the author.

Experienced high performers can be good role models for how to choose the appropriate medium. There is a substantial body of research showing that successful people already select the appropriate medium of communication for the type of communication being made (see review by Rice, 1992). Daft, Lengel, and Trevino (1987) empirically demonstrated that high-performing managers tend to choose the medium that best reduces the equivocality of the message, whereas low-performing managers do not.

**Fit the Communication Style to the Medium.** A number of steps can be taken to counteract potentially negative behavioral and perceptual impacts of virtual communication. Table 12.4 contains recommended communication practices for virtual interactions. The most important theme is to over-communicate when interacting electronically. That means to communicate explicitly, regularly, and frequently (Prieto & Simon, 1997), and be very responsive to others (Hoefling,

2001). In particular, when colleagues and subordinates are out of sight, it is more difficult to monitor their performance and gauge their emotions. Therefore, it is important to set up frequent and regular communication channels for people to apprise each other of their goals, progress, obstacles, and well being. It is also critically important to be responsive to other people's messages. Letting the sender know that the recipient has both received and understood the message is useful in establishing and maintaining trust and avoiding escalating negative emotions.

Even though no technology can replace face-to-face interaction, people adapt to new technologies over time. Research shows that people acculturate to group norms (Lea & Spears, 1991), and gradually warm up relationships in CMCs (Walther, 1995). Moreover, a recent study on partially distributed work groups found that social presence developed over time for remote, as well as local, team members (Burke, Aytes, Chidambaram, & Johnson, 1999). Thus, communicating virtually is experienced as being more familiar and comfortable over time.

# TRUST

Trust is an essential element in any interpersonal relationship, including individual, group, and organizational associations (Berscheid & Reis, 1998; Jones, Couch, & Scott, 1997), and it influences performance at all of these levels in organizations (Shaw, 1997). Virtual communications challenge people's ability to develop and maintain trust (Jarvenpaa & Leidner, 1998; Rocco, 1998). Therefore, it is important for managers to select the appropriate employees to work in virtual teams, set policies and procedures to ensure mutual understanding among team members, and make a special effort to foster trust among team members.

## Select Trusting and Trustworthy Virtual Employees

To successfully manage virtual employees, it is critical to hire trustworthy and responsible people. There is obviously a certain amount of risk in having employees work in unsupervised locations, such as at home, because they are more difficult to monitor. Because of this, it is also important to select managers who are able to trust employees to work autonomously. Managers with a high need for control can strain relationships with their employees and reduce productivity by administering too much surveillance over remote employees (Ellison, 1999). Successful managers of virtual teams should be trusting enough to be able to manage invisible employees, yet be discriminating enough to distinguish which employees are sufficiently responsible to work in such an environment and take action to remove those who are not.

## Set Policies and Procedures to Ensure Mutual Understanding

Hiring trustworthy employees and trusting managers is only the first step. Leaders also need to restructure project management so that productivity is clearly defined and measured by objectives and results (Ellison, 1999; Prieto & Simon, 1997). Making sure team members understand expectations and protocol can greatly reduce mistrust by alleviating confusion, frustration, and disincentive (Jarvenpaa & Leidner, 1998). Consulting psychologists have the tools to train managers on management-by-objective styles and effective communication skills.

Trust is more volatile in virtual team interactions as well, as team members tend to be less forgiving when communicating virtually. For example, Jarvenpaa and Leidner (1998) found that a simple technical problem that prevented one person from responding to another in a timely fashion created distrust, even though the delay was not the person's fault. Therefore, it is important to set expectations about communication protocol at the outset of virtual teaming to avoid such misunderstandings. This example also shows that it is important for virtual team members to be skilled at using the communication tools.

Finally, virtual teams, by their geographically dispersed nature, tend to be comprised of people with diverse cultural backgrounds. In face-to-face interactions, people can be constantly reminded that cultural differences exist by visual cues and nonverbal mannerisms. In electronic interactions, however, cultural differences might not be as evident. As with other social expectations in CMCs, it might be necessary to explicitly express cultural expectations and norms to smooth cross-cultural interactions. Diversity training might be particularly helpful for global teams.

## Foster Trusting Relationships among Team Members

It has been repeatedly shown that trust and cooperation are more difficult to establish and maintain in virtual communications than face-to-face (Jarvenpaa & Leidner, 1998; Moore et al., 1999; Rocco, 1998). For example, it is more difficult to determine whether someone is lying when visual and audio cues are missing. Even though it contradicts research findings, people tend to believe that they are good lie detectors (DePaulo, 1994) and that they must be face-to-face to determine whether they can trust others. This creates an immediate barrier to establishing trust in virtual environments.

In a study of cooperation in situations involving social dilemmas, Rocco (1998) found that participating in a FTF interaction prior to engaging in a series of computer-mediated social dilemma situations increased cooperation, but participating in computer chats did not. Similarly, Moore et al. (1999) examined trust and rapport in an experimental study of e-mail negotiations. They found that negotiators who became acquainted via e-mail prior to negotiations had fewer impasses than participants who did not, and that positive affect associated with rapport mediated this outcome.

In sum, in both of these studies, adding richer social contact before the CMC negotiations led to better outcomes and more cooperation. Thus, if it is at all possible, team members should meet face-to-face prior to working together. If that is not practical, they should attempt to build relationships virtually by exchanging information about each other and engaging in open and thoughtful exchanges prior to working together (Jarvenpaa & Leidner, 1998; Moore et al., 1999). In addition, because trust is such a critical factor in team building, and it is harder to establish electronically, there is good reason for consultants to suggest trust-building exercises for virtual teams. Other practical suggestions are offered by Fisher and Fisher (2001), and Hoefling (2001).

## SELECTION AND PERFORMANCE MEASUREMENT

With all of the previously described challenges that arise in virtual environments, it is critical to select the appropriate people to work on such a team. It is also important to modify traditional management practices to be able to evaluate employees who are less visible. There is little research in these two areas. The following two sections report what is known and suggest what questions still need to be addressed.

### Selection

Despite the advantages of working from home, there is less telecommuting than one might expect. Estimates of the quantity of telecommuters tend to converge at around 10 percent in the U.S., and less in Europe and Japan (McClelland, 1999; O'Mahony & Barley, 2000; Qvortrup, 1998; Sato & Spinks, 1998). This may be, in part, because employees are reluctant to be away from the office for a variety of reasons. In short, telecommuting is not for everyone. Thus, both managers and employees should be given the option to volunteer before the organization begins to select them for such programs (Bray, 1999; Cole, 1996; Prieto & Simon, 1997; Schilling, 1999). To help employees determine if they are appropriate for telecommuting, consultants might find useful the self-screening questionnaire for potential telecommuters provided by the American Health Information Management Association (Fletcher, 1999).

It is important to select for virtual success at three levels: employee, manager, and job. Table 12.5 shows criteria to be considered in selecting potential virtual employees, managers, and jobs (Bray, 1999; Fulk & DeSanctis, 1995; Prieto & Simon, 1997; Schilling, 1999; Staples, Hulland, & Higgins, 1998). It is important to note that very little empirical research about selecting for telework exists, and the criteria in the table are derived primarily from articles based on consulting experience.

Table 12.5. Employee, Manager, and Job Characteristics to Consider for Remote Work.

| Employee | *Enthusiasm* | Is interested in teleworking? |
| | *Tenure* | Has been at the company long enough to be acculturated? Is experienced enough to work independently? |
| | *Performance* | Has good performance and attendance records? |
| | *Trust* | Is reliable, dependable, conscientious? Has good relationships with manager and coworkers? |
| | *Personality* | Is tolerant of isolation, independent, confident, self-motivated, focused, organized, self-disciplined? |
| | *Communication skills* | Communicates well with others? Is not too introverted? |
| | *Technical savvy* | Is proficient with the tools needed to work remotely? |
| Manager | *Enthusiasm* | Is interested in supporting teleworkers? |
| | *Communication skills* | Communicates well with others? Clearly defines expectations? |
| | *Personality* | Tolerance for independence? Not a micromanager? |
| | *Management style* | Task-centered? Manages by objective? |
| | *Technical savvy* | Is proficient with the remote management tools? |
| Job | *Interaction with people* | Requires face-to-face interactions, high level of visibility? Can be done autonomously? |
| | *Remote access to information* | Organization provides remote access to information and other articles needed to perform job? |
| | *Access to physical materials* | Requires access to physical materials, such as lab equipment, mail, products? |
| | *Function* | Job function can be performed remotely? Part-time? |
| | *Flexibility* | Schedule is flexible? |
| | *Need for focus* | High level of focus leads to success at this job? |

As shown in the table, personality, skills, attitudes, tenure, and performance all impact a teleworker's ability to succeed. This is similar for managers, but management style is also very important (Garber, 1999; Prieto & Simon, 1997). Most of these selection criteria are measurable using standard assessment tools and practices, such as personality inventories, ability tests, assessment centers, and performance data. Most of these criteria, however, have not been scientifically validated for successful telework, and further research is needed. In addition to characteristics of the people, characteristics of the job should also be considered. Whether a job can be performed remotely is most effectively determined by a comprehensive job analysis. If that is not feasible, managers and employees can simply assess whether the job functions could be performed remotely. Nilles (1998) offers practical methods for assessing jobs for telework.

## Performance Measurement

Performance measurement changes in two significant ways for virtual teams. First, the emphasis shifts from time and process (input) to objectives and results (output) (Prieto & Simon, 1997). For example, a manager might measure a virtual employee's productivity by whether she achieves particular milestones by the target dates, rather than by observing her presence in the office. Secondly, performance information is communicated differently. Employees must learn to report status virtually, whereas managers need to observe performance and give feedback virtually. These interactions can take the form of e-mail status reports, weekly telephone meetings, and annual FTF performance reviews. Also, managers and other leaders need to find new ways to mentor virtually. Typically, this occurs in more structured ways, such as during regularly scheduled status meetings or in response to questions via e-mail, because spontaneous hallway conversations are not feasible.

Consultants also have the opportunity to guide managers in developing fair policies and cultivating perceptions of equality among remote and local team members. When modifying performance appraisal techniques for telework, it can be challenging to maintain fairness and equality for on-site and remote employees. For example, if a manager has weekly meetings with remote employees and only monthly meetings with on-site employees, it might appear to the on-site employees that they have less time with the manager, even though they have more unscheduled interactions. In addition, it is common for on-site employees to believe that remote employees, especially telecommuters, are not working as hard as office workers, as two recent studies of partially distributed work groups demonstrated (Burke et al., 1999; Duxbury & Neufeld, 1999). These studies showed that office workers might also be envious of telecommuters, and resentful that they themselves cannot telecommute.

In addition to the challenges, there can be benefits to virtual performance evaluation. There is some evidence that people evaluate others' contributions with less bias in CMCs than FTF. For example, in a study of group decision-making, people's ratings of others' contributions were not influenced by how much they liked them in CMCs, as was the case with FTF groups (Weisband & Atwater, 1999). In another study of group decision-making, leaders of computer-mediated teams were better able to differentiate group members on the quality of their decisions than leaders of FTF teams were (Hedlund, Ilgen, & Hollenbeck, 1998). Thus, managers might evaluate employees more objectively in virtual interactions.

## EMPLOYEE SATISFACTION WITH TELEWORK

Employee reactions to telework are mixed. On the positive side, employees typically appreciate the flexibility that remote and home work provides (especially for employees with families), the reduction in commute time, and the ability to be more focused and productive without office distractions (Bray, 1999; Ellison, 1999). On the negative side, employees often complain of isolation, feeling left out of important social and political interactions, and being concerned that the lack of visibility restricts their careers (Duxbury & Neufeld, 1999). In addition, a common complaint that consistently arises for telecommuters is the challenge of creating boundaries between work and home (Ellison, 1999; Nilles, 1998). Being able to access work or be accessed by coworkers at any time of the day or night can increase the number of hours that employees work (Cooper & Lewis, 1999; Prieto & Simon, 1997), and blurs the times when employees are expected to work. Consulting psychologists, therefore, have a number of opportunities for guiding people on how to set up satisfactory boundaries between home and work for both the employees and the organization. Some practical solutions are offered by Fisher and Fisher (2001), and Nilles (1998).

Social isolation is a notable hindrance to employee satisfaction, regardless of whether employees are working at home or in other remote locations (Duxbury & Neufeld, 1999; Ellison, 1999; Prieto & Simon, 1997). Many people report substituting FTF interactions with e-mail or computer chat, but it is clearly not the same (Kraut, Patterson, Lundmark, Kiesler, Mukophadhyay, & Scherlis, 1998; Taha & Calwell, 1993). It would therefore be interesting to research how employees can effectively replace social interactions virtually. Social presence and media richness theories predict that people cannot be as fulfilled with computer-mediated socializing. However, the SIDE model and Walther's (1996) hyperpersonal hypothesis predict otherwise. Socializing virtually has yet to be systematically studied in the context of the workplace. As organizations become more physically dispersed (Reich, 2001), this will become an increasingly important problem to solve.

# IMPLICATIONS OF CONSULTING TO VIRTUAL TEAMS

This chapter opened by citing evidence that the workplace is changing, and that organizations are increasingly turning to information technology to connect geographically dispersed employees in the form of telework. As telework expands, consulting psychologists will encounter the challenges described in this chapter more frequently. Therefore, the first implication for consulting psychologists is that they will need to be more aware of the challenges of virtual work, and be able to diagnose problems resulting from virtual work when they occur. A second implication is that, because consulting psychologists will be dealing with an increasing number of remote workers, they will undoubtedly have to begin employing virtual consulting practices. These practices might range in complexity from coaching by telephone, to holding video-conferenced team-building sessions, to implementing on-line selection systems for telework candidates. As a result, consulting psychologists will need to add experience with technology and technology-driven interventions to their consulting tool kits. They might also develop partnerships with experts in information technology to assist them in conducting virtual interventions.

More implications arise from the different challenges with virtual teams, compared to FTF teams. At a high level, it might seem that the issues are similar. Indeed, consulting psychologists work on issues of trust, communication, selection, performance, and organizational culture for FTF teams too. However, these issues are magnified for virtual teams, and they can take on different forms. The implication is that consulting psychologists will need to be more sensitive to these issues for virtual teams, and tackle them explicitly. For example, whereas a new FTF team might naturally engage in social interactions to build relationships without a consultant intervening, a virtual team would probably need a more structured, explicit approach for socialization to occur. In addition, the virtual team is more at risk of developing mistrust among its team members without the nonverbal channels of communication to mitigate misunderstandings. Therefore, the consultant should more often incorporate trust-building and communication exercises into a virtual team-building intervention than for a FTF intervention.

Furthermore, since the challenges for virtual teams are magnified compared to FTF teams, virtual teams require high-performing members to be successful. The implication for consulting psychologists is that they might need to be more involved in selection and performance measurement for virtual teams. They will also need to utilize, and perhaps develop, methods specifically for selecting and appraising virtual workers.

# SUMMARY

Virtual teams present many unique challenges to organizations. Distance between team members, differing schedules and time zones, and communication technology affect culture, interpersonal dynamics, performance management, satisfaction, productivity, and so on. Organizational consultants, therefore, have a number of areas on which to give guidance: developing tools and policies to support virtual work, selecting and hiring for successful remote teamwork, managing communication and trust in virtual environments, measuring productivity of remote employees, and determining what types of jobs can be done remotely. Known practices in the field of consulting psychology can be used to deal with these issues to some degree. However, as this chapter demonstrates, virtual teams also face unique challenges for which new consulting methods need to be researched and developed.

Although technological developments have enabled fantastic new forms of virtual work, it is hard for organizational research to keep up with corresponding human resource practices. Organizations and consultants are in need of guidance on how to deal with the human side of virtual work. A great deal of advice has been put forth for effectively managing virtual teams, but very little of it is based on empirical research. This chapter is thus, in part, a call for more empirical research on virtual management.

# References

Baron, N. S. (1998). Letters by phone or speech by other means: The linguistics of email. *Language and Communication, 18,* 133–170.

Baumeister, R. F. (1982). A self-presentational view of social phenomena. *Psychological Bulletin, 91,* 3–26.

Berscheid, E., & Reis, H. T. (1998). Attraction and close relationships. In D. T. Gilbert, S. T. Fiske, & G. Lindzey (Eds.), *The handbook of social psychology* (pp. 193–281). New York: McGraw-Hill.

Block, P. (1981). *Flawless consulting: A guide to getting your expertise used.* San Diego, CA: Pfeiffer.

Bordia, P. (1996). Studying verbal interaction on the Internet: The case of rumor transmission research. *Behavior Research Methods, Instruments and Computers, 28,* 149–151.

Bordia, P. (1997). Face-to-face versus computer-mediated communication: A synthesis of the experimental literature. *Journal of Business Communication, 34,* 99–120.

Bray, L. (1999). Consider the alternatives. *Association Management, 51,* 33–37.

Brennan, S. E. (1998). The grounding problem in conversations with and through computers. In S. R. Fussell & R. J. Kreuz (Eds.), *Social and cognitive approaches to interpersonal communication* (pp. 201–225). Hillsdale, NJ: Erlbaum.

Burke, K., Aytes, K., Chidambaram, L., & Johnson, J. J. (1999). A study of partially distributed work groups: The impact of media, location, and time on perceptions and performance. *Small Group Research, 30,* 453–490.

Carlson, J. R., & Zmud, R. W. (1999). Channel expansion theory and the experiential nature of media richness perceptions. *Academy of Management Journal, 42,* 153–170.

Cascio, W. F. (2000). Managing a virtual workplace. *The Academy of Management Executive, 14,* 81–91.

Cole, J. (1996). The art of long distance management. *Getting Results for the Hands-on Manager, 41,* 1.

Connell, J. B., & Mendelsohn, G. A. (2000, April). *On-line management: How to effectively manage employees using computer-mediated communication.* Paper presented at the annual meeting of the Society of Industrial and Organizational Psychology, New Orleans, LA.

Contractor, N. S., & Eisenberg, E. M. (1990). Communication networks and new media in organizations. In J. Fulk & C. W. Steinfield (Eds.), *Organizations and communication technology* (pp. 117–140). Newbury Park, CA: Sage.

Cooper, C. L., & Lewis, S. (1999). Gender and the changing nature of work. In G. N. Powell (Ed.), *Handbook of gender and work* (pp. 37–46). Thousand Oaks, CA: Sage.

Coovert, M. D. (1995). Technological changes in office jobs. In A. Howard (Ed.), *The changing nature of work* (pp. 175–208). San Francisco: Jossey-Bass.

Daft, R. L., & Lengel, R. H. (1984). Information richness: A new approach to managerial behavior and organizational design. *Research in Organizational Behavior, 6,* 191–233.

Daft, R. L., & Lengel, R. H. (1986). Organizational information requirements, media richness and structural design. *Management Science, 32,* 554–571.

Daft, R. L., Lengel, R. H., & Trevino, L. K. (1987). Message equivocality, media selection and manager performance: Implications for information systems. *MIS Quarterly, 11,* 355–366.

DePaulo, B. M. (1994). Spotting lies: Can humans learn to do better? *Current Directions in Psychological Science, 3,* 83–86.

Dubrovsky, V. J., Kiesler, S., & Sethna, B. N. (1991). The equalization phenomenon: Status effects in computer-mediated and face-to-face decision-making groups. *Human-Computer Interaction, 6,* 119–146.

Duxbury, L., & Neufeld, D. (1999). An empirical evaluation of the impacts of telecommuting on intra-organizational communication. *Journal of Engineering and Technology Management, 16,* 1–28.

Ellison, N. B. (1999). Social impacts: New perspectives on telework. *Social Science Computer Review, 17,* 338–356.

Fisher, K., & Fisher, M. D. (2001). *The distance manager: A hands-on guide to managing off-site employees and virtual teams.* New York: McGraw-Hill.

Fletcher, D. M. (1999). Practice brief: Telecommuting. *Journal of the American Health Information Management Association,* Retrieved October 19, 2000, from http://www.ahima.org/search/journal.html

Fulk, J., & DeSanctis, G. (1995). Electronic communication and changing organizational forms. *Organization Science, 6,* 337–350.

Fulk, J., Schmitz, J., & Steinfield, C. W. (1990). A social influence model of technology use. In J. Fulk & C. W. Steinfield (Eds.), *Organizations and communication technology* (pp. 117–140). Thousand Oaks, CA: Sage.

Gainey, T. W., Kelley, D. E., & Hill, J. A. (1999). Telecommuting's impact on corporate culture and individual workers: Examining the effect of employee isolation. *S.A.M. Advanced Management Journal, 64,* 4–10.

Gallupe, R. B., & McKeen, J. D. (1990). Enhancing computer-mediated communication: An experimental investigation into the use of a Group Decision Support System for face-to-face versus remote meetings. *Information and Management, 18,* 1–13.

Garber, P. R. (1999). *Managing by remote control.* Boca Raton, FL: St. Lucie Press.

Hedlund, J., Ilgen, D. R., & Hollenbeck, J. R. (1998). Decision accuracy in computer-mediated versus face-to-face decision-making teams. *Organizational Behavior and Human Decision Processes, 76,* 30–47.

Hightower, R., & Sayeed, L. (1995). The impact of computer-mediated communication systems on biased group discussion. *Computers in Human Behavior, 11,* 33–44.

Hiltz, S. R., & Johnson, K. (1990). User satisfaction with computer-mediated communication systems. *Management Science, 36,* 739–765.

Hoefling, T. (2001). *Working virtually: Managing people for successful virtual teams and organizations.* Sterling, VA: Stylus.

Jarvenpaa, S. L., & Leidner, D. E. (1998). Communication and trust in global virtual teams. *Journal of Computer Mediated Communication, 3*(4). Retrieved October 19, 2001, from http://jcmc.huji.ac.il/vol3/issue4/jarvenpaa.html

Johansen, R. (1977). Social evaluations of teleconferencing. *Telecommunications Policy, 1,* 395–419.

Jones, W. H., Couch, L., & Scott, S. (1997). Trust and betrayal. In R. Hogan, J. Johnson, & S. Briggs (Eds.), *Handbook of personality psychology* (pp. 465–482). Orlando, FL: Academic Press.

Kiesler, S., & Sproull, L. (1992). Group decision making and communication technology. *Organizational Behavior and Human Decision Processes, 52,* 96–123.

Kraut, R. E., Patterson, M., Lundmark, V., Kiesler, S., Mukophadhyay, T., & Scherlis, W. (1998). Internet paradox: A social technology that reduces social involvement and psychological well-being? *American Psychologist, 53,* 1017–1031.

Kroeger, O., & Thuesen, J. M. (1992). *Type talk at work.* New York: Tilden Press.

Kurland, N. B., & Bailey, D. E. (1999). Telework: The advantages and challenges of working here, there, anywhere, and anytime. *Organizational Dynamics, 28,* 53–68.

Lea, M., O'Shea, T., Fung, P., & Spears, R. (1992). "Flaming" in computer-mediated communication: Observations, explanations, implications. In L. Martin (Ed.), *Contexts of computer-mediated communication* (pp. 89–112). London: Harvester Wheatsheaf.

Lea, M., & Spears, R. (1991). Computer-mediated communication, de-individuation and group decision-making. *International Journal of Man-Machine Studies, 34,* 283–301.

Lee, A. S. (1994). Electronic mail as a medium for rich communication: An empirical investigation using hermeneutic interpretation. *MIS Quarterly, 18,* 143–157.

Markus, J. L. (1992). Electronic mail as the medium of managerial choice. *Organizational Science, 5,* 502–527.

Matheson, K., & Zanna, M. P. (1988). The impact of computer-mediated communication on self-awareness. *Computers in Human Behavior, 4,* 221–233.

McClelland, S. (1999). Telework: New form for a working life. *Telecommunications, 33,* 80–81.

Miller, J. S., & Cardy, R. L. (2000). Technology and managing people: Keeping the "human" in human resources. *Journal of Labor Research, 21,* 447–461.

Moore, D. A., Kurtzberg, T. R., Thompson, L. L., & Morris, M. W. (1999). Long and short routes to success in electronically-mediated negotiations: Group affiliations and good vibrations. *Organizational Behavior and Human Decision Processes, 77,* 22–43.

Nilles, J. M. (1998). *Managing telework: Strategies for managing the virtual workforce.* New York: Wiley.

Nilles, J. M., Carlson, F. R., Gray, P., & Hanneman, G. (1976). *The telecommunications-transportation tradeoff: Options for tomorrow.* New York: Wiley.

O'Mahony, S., & Barley, S. R. (2000). Do digital telecommunications affect work and organization? *Research in Organizational Behavior, 21,* 125–161.

Postmes, T., Spears, R., & Lea, M. (1998). Breaching or building social boundaries? Side-effects of computer-mediated communication. *Communication Research, 25,* 689–715.

Prieto, J. M., & Simon, C. (1997). Network and its implications for assessment. In N. Anderson & P. Herriot (Eds.), *International handbook of selection and assessment* (pp. 97–124). New York: Wiley.

Qvortrup, L. (1998). From teleworking to networking: Definitions and trends. In P. J. Jackson & J.M.V.D. Wielen (Eds.), *Teleworking: International perspectives.* New York: Routledge.

Reich, R. B. (2001). *The future of success.* New York: Knopf.

Reid, A. (1977). Comparing telephone with face-to-face contact. In I. de Sola Pool (Ed.), *The social impact of the telephone* (pp. 386–415). Cambridge, MA: MIT Press.

Reid, F.J.M., Ball, L. J., Morley, A. M., & Evans, J. (1997). Styles of group discussion in computer-mediated decision making. *British Journal of Social Psychology, 36,* 241–262.

Rice, R. E. (1992). Task analyzability, use of new media, and effectiveness: A multi-site exploration of media richness. *Organization Science, 3,* 475–500.

Rocco, E. (1998, April 18–23). *Trust breaks down in electronic contexts but can be repaired by some initial face-to-face contact.* Paper presented at the annual meeting of the Computer Human Interaction Special Interest Group of the Association for Computing Machinery, Los Angeles, CA.

Sato, K., & Spinks, W. A. (1998). Telework and crisis management in Japan. In P. J. Jackson & J. M. Van Der Wielen (Eds.), *Teleworking: International perspectives.* New York: Routledge.

Schilling, S. L. (1999). The basics of successful telework networks. *HR Focus, 76,* 9–10.

Shaw, R. B. (1997). *Trust in the balance: Building successful organizations on results, integrity, and concern.* San Francisco: Jossey-Bass.

Short, J., Williams, E., & Christie, B. (1976). *The social psychology of telecommunications.* New York: Wiley.

Siegel, J., Dubrovsky, V., Kiesler, S., & McGuire, T. W. (1986). Group processes in computer-mediated communication. *Organizational Behavior and Human Decision Processes, 37,* 157–187.

Staples, D. S., Hulland, J. S., & Higgins, C. A. (1998). A self-efficacy theory explanation for the management of remote workers in virtual organizations. *Journal of Computer Mediated Communication, 3*(4). Retrieved October 19, 2001, from http://jcmc.huji.ac.il/vol3/issue4/staples.html

Straus, S. G. (1997). Technology, group process, and group outcomes: Testing the connections in computer-mediated and face-to-face groups. *Human-Computer Interaction, 12,* 227–266.

Straus, S. G., & McGrath, J. E. (1994). Does the medium matter? The interaction of task type and technology on group performance and member reactions. *Journal of Applied Psychology, 79,* 87–97.

Taha, L. H., & Calwell, B. S. (1993). Social isolation and integration in electronic environments. *Behaviour and Information Technology, 12,* 276–283.

U.S. lawyer hammers at credibility of witness: Microsoft executive seems unpersuasive. (1999, February 23). *The Washington Post* p. E1.

Walther, J. B. (1995). Relational aspects of computer-mediated communication: Experimental observations over time. *Organization Science, 6,* 186–203.

Walther, J. B. (1996). Computer-mediated communication: Impersonal, interpersonal, and hyperpersonal interaction. *Communication Research, 23,* 3–43.

Walther, J. B., & Burgoon, J. K. (1992). Relational communication in computer-mediated interaction. *Human Communication Research, 19,* 50–88.

Weisband, S. P. (1992). Group discussion and first advocacy effects in computer-mediated and face-to-face decision making groups. *Organizational Behavior and Human Decision Processes, 53,* 352–380.

Weisband, S. P., & Atwater, L. (1999). Evaluating self and others in electronic and face-to-face groups. *Journal of Applied Psychology, 84,* 632–639.

Whittaker, S., & O'Conaill, B. (1997). The role of vision in face-to-face and mediated communication. In K. E. Finn, A. J. Sellen, & S. B. Wilbur (Eds.), *Video-mediated communication* (pp. 23–49). Hillsdale, NJ: Erlbaum.

Wiesenfeld, B. M., Ragurham, S., & Garud, R. (1998). Communication patterns as determinants of organizational identification in a virtual organization. *Journal of Computer Mediated Communication, 3*(4). Retrieved October 19, 2001, from http://www.ascusc.org/jcmc/vol3/issue4/wiesenfeld.html

Yates, J., & Orlikowski, W. J. (1992). Genres of organizational communication: A structurational approach to studying communication and media. *Academy of Management Review, 17,* 299–326.

PART FOUR

# ORGANIZATIONAL LEVEL ISSUES

CHAPTER THIRTEEN

# Assessing Organizations

Harry Levinson
*Chairman Emeritus, The Levinson Institute and*
*Clinical Professor of Psychology Emeritus*
*Harvard Medical School*

Organizations come in a wide variety of shapes, sizes, functions, activities, resources, and intentions. Each, however new and young, quickly establishes a culture, a set of symbols, traditions, customary practices, values, and even local language (in-words and jargon). Some of these are drawn from the industry, service, or tradition of which they are a part; some from the policies, practices, and values of its founder; some from national character; some from the specialties of people employed in their work. In this chapter, I offer my own method of assessing organizations, developed out of more than fifty years of consulting experience, and nearly forty years of teaching graduate seminars on the topic, much of which involved student teams working with organizations.

## CONTEXT FOR ASSESSING ORGANIZATIONS

There are no organizations without people; therefore, an organization can be considered to be a living organism. As an organization ages, like all living organisms, it evolves through a series of recognizable stages (Adizes, 1988; Greiner, 1998), each, as with the developmental sequence of human beings (Erikson, 1963; Levinson, Darrow, Klein, Levinson, & McKee, 1978), with its own dominant issues and theme. It soon develops a character (Levinson, 1997), that set of values that leads to established attitudes, and, in turn, to customary repetitive behaviors. These differentiate one organization from another in the same

315

industry, business, or service. As its components mature, they, too, begin to differentiate themselves, as do children in a family. The subcultures of marketing differ from those of finance. Sometimes, in large organizations, those components vary so widely that their incumbents have difficulty communicating with those in other units.

A classic example is the Roman Catholic Church, a venerable, worldwide institution. Although the individual churches practice the same liturgy, and a parishioner entering any of them would find the service familiar, the social and emotional atmosphere of the churches, even the languages of ordinary discourse, vary widely.

Those consistencies of behavior, organized around the core organizational character, become what one might call an organizational personality. They make for a certain identifiability, that stable sameness that enables those within the organization to recognize they are part of it, and those outside to recognize what the organization is and what it does. A parishioner can always know what practices to expect in a Roman Catholic Church or an orthodox Jewish synagogue or a Muslim mosque. A customer knows what to expect to buy in a Wal-Mart store or what to expect to eat in a Kentucky Fried Chicken restaurant. The differences that then arise in the dispersed components of a large organization, just as the differences that begin to arise very early on among siblings, make for a certain uniqueness within that identifiability.

Consultants to organizations, and consulting techniques and methods, come in as many varieties as the organizations they serve. Most focus on a specific functional area (for example, marketing), or a specific process (for example, tax accounting), or an organization-wide task (for example, design of organizational structure). Each focus tends to be narrow, problem-centered, and governed by equally narrow diagnostic and intervention techniques. For example, financial consultants who specialize in assessing the market for a potential stock issue are unlikely to consider the personality of the director of manufacturing, however important that person is to the profitability of the company, which, in turn, is crucial to the sale price of the stock.

The recommendations that follow such analyses are necessarily equally narrow, a product of the specialty of the consultant's method. Such recommendations rarely take into account the potential unintended consequences or implications beyond the purview of the consultant. For example, a marketing consultant recommended to a major international company that it use the same colors on its packages and the same slogans in its advertising all over the world. The consultant did not take into account the fact that various colors have different meanings in different cultures, as do slogans, idioms, and advertising phrases (Axtell, 1993). Only when the product failed in several countries did the company discover its costly error.

## Precipitating Events for Consultation

Typically, a board of directors, a chief executive, or some intermediate manager, decides the organization or one of its components has a problem. Depending on the executive's own judgment, he will attribute the problem to a cause he suspects. He will then request consultation either by going directly to a consultant or inviting bids for a consultation project. If the company official goes directly to a consultant, that executive is likely to fall back on previous experiences. For example, a major financial organization from time to time senses rumbles of discontent among its employees. Each time the vice president of human resources hears echoes of that disquiet, he calls on the same consulting firm to distribute a questionnaire among the disaffected work group, followed by some limited corrective effort. Some businesses routinely survey their employees at regular intervals to keep abreast of morale (Kraut, 1996). Some will call on experts they have heard at professional meetings, or whose promotional brochures interest them. Some, preoccupied with a problem, might save published articles, procrastinating about that problem for years, before they call the expert featured. Some seek recommendations from peers. Some do not seek consultation until their organizational problems become crises.

## Types of Consultants

Much of the consultation on psychological issues is done by industrial-organizational (I-O) psychologists, some by social psychologists, some by counseling and clinical psychologists, and much by many who are not psychologists. I-O psychologists are involved significantly in macro-organizational problems such as organizational design, organizational climate, selection by objective tests and assessment centers, compensation, performance appraisal methods, job analyses, and similar topics that lend themselves to categories, systems, and measurement (Kraut & Korman, 1999). The second type of consultant works largely with group processes on such issues as conflict resolution, team building, participative management, stress management, and organizational culture (Waclawski & Church, 2002). The third type focuses more heavily on individuals, emphasizing executive selection, career development, coaching, and leadership (Silzer, 2002).

Depending on their skills and training, there is considerable overlap in consultation activities among these types. At one end of the continuum of psychological consultants, the training and emphasis in the first group is heavily concentrated on the scientific (by which they mean measurement), empirical, atheoretical, and rational. At the other end of the continuum is clinical psychology, with its heavy dependence on theory, particularly its attention to the dynamics of personality development, emotions, conceptualization of motivation of which a person or group is unaware, and its effort to understand the sequence, however irrational, that proceeds from feelings to thoughts to behavior. Those who are highly trained in one area are less likely to be equally skilled in another. However, they are all governed by the same code of ethics (Lowman, 1998), by which they are constrained from undertaking consultation in areas for which they are not trained. But, like professionals in other wide-ranging disciplines, too often they are not well enough aware of what they do not know. Equally often, they might not be able to accept the usefulness of another point of view. Between not knowing and not accepting, many do not adequately define the boundaries of their competence.

Often, those who call upon psychologists for consultation cannot differentiate among the specialists. Those who most frequently are the contact persons, namely the directors or vice presidents of human resources, often are no more knowledgeable in this respect than other executives. Therefore, the prospective consultant must herself delimit the nature of the organizational problem and her competence to help resolve it. Unfortunately, too often, some with a limited range of skills are ready to apply them to every problem. That tendency recalls the old saw that if one gives a child a hammer, everything gets hammered.

There is nothing necessarily wrong with being empirical and dealing directly with problems of which an individual is aware. All of us are likely to take an aspirin for a headache or put fuel in the automobile gas tank when the dial reports the fuel to be low. Similarly, employees in an organization can be angry because they feel underpaid, and become enthusiastic when their pay is raised. But if the headache arises repetitively when a person becomes enraged, aspirin will be of little relief, and if the gas is low because of a leak in the tank, putting more in will be of only temporary help. So it is in organizations: when employees feel infantilized, their pent-up feelings can result in poor morale. When surveyed, they might attribute their malaise to poor communication with their higher managements. Without an understanding of the phenomenon of displacement, that is, unwittingly transferring the feelings stimulated by one situation to another, efforts to improve communications might be equally inadequate to raise morale.

The implication, of course, is that when a problem is more than transient or casual, before trying to fix it, the consultant should understand what caused it and why it persists. Primitive peoples might have tried to avert epidemics by propitiating their gods, but doing that is unlikely to relieve the endemic AIDS problem among them.

## Cause-Finding in Assessment

The issue of cause, or *why*, raises the question of what constitutes adequate diagnosis or cause-finding. This chapter describes my particular method for doing so, but there are many possible answers to that question. Here is a list of some:

Who is doing the finding-out?

What is the consultant's specialty?

What is the consultant's competence or reputation in that specialty? (Remember that half of any graduating class is in the bottom 50 percent of that class.)

How narrow or comprehensive is the consultant's focus?

To what degree does the consultant understand what motivates individuals and groups, that is, the why of behavior?

How does the consultant take that understanding into account?

How long will it take to discover the causes, because all behavior has multiple causes?

How much will it cost?

What is the trade-off between the time and cost on the one hand, and tolerating the pain and discomfort on the other?

Who feels the pain most acutely?

Who doesn't want to be bothered?

How long has this pain been going on?

What was done about it before?

Why now?

Who now can do what about it?

Who will be helped by finding the causes? Who will be hurt?

What are the odds on bringing about useful change?

What might be the unintended consequences?

# TOOLS FOR ASSESSMENT

Most psychological efforts to diagnose or assess organizational problems are focused on *part-problems* or processes (Howard, 1994). By part-problems, I mean subjects or topics that are circumscribed, sometimes by a model of an organization, sometimes by a problem. Using models enables consultants to gather and organize their information about an organization into subjects or categories. Among the more prominent models are those of Burke (1994), Hornstein and Tichy (1973), Nadler and Tushman (1988), and Weisbord (1978). However necessary to organize what otherwise would be an overwhelming plethora of data, diagnosis by categories risks boxing in or limiting what the consultant sees, and therefore what she does about it.

By processes, I mean such issues among others, for example, as training (Odiorne & Rummler, 1988), selection (Bray & Byham, 1991), performance appraisal (Milkovich & Wigdor, 1991), building and managing teams (Lawler, 1992), and managing change. In my view, concentrating on processes too often does not take adequately into account the history, structure, and culture of the organization in which the processes take place.

Different types of consultants use many of the same methods: interviews, questionnaires, compilation of organizational statistics, analysis of organizational culture, evaluation of goals, and, in addition, specialized skills in which they are expert. Few take into account the historical evolution of an organization, the impact of its past on the present, its level of energy, the meaning of the problem to the organization members, its adaptive pattern, or the typical repetitive behavioral characteristics it develops. Failure to do so means that often the consultant has an inadequate grasp of the complexity of the problem and limited logic for undertaking specific processes for change.

My preferred assessment or diagnostic procedure goes beyond and ideally integrates both the part-problems and processes (Levinson, 2002a). It is based on Von Bertalanffy's biological conception of a living organism as an open system (1950), and adapted from Menninger's psychiatric case study method (1962). My psychological orientation is psychoanalytic and my basic professional training is clinical. Four years of training in a psychiatric hospital led to a heavy emphasis on diagnosis and the therapeutic use of the hospital environment as a treatment method. This background, taking into account the family background and psychological development of the individual, leads me to consider the impact of the founder on the organization, the concept of organizational evolution, stages in growth, and interactions both with and on the organization's environment, as well as the influence of the environment on the organization, interaction among its components, and adaptive efforts toward internal integration and mastery of the environment for survival. I assume that all organizations, even nonprofits, necessarily compete for resources and acceptance. One way or another, they seek a return on their investment, whether money or energy. The fundamental thrust of an organization is to perpetuate itself.

## PRELIMINARY STAGES OF CONSULTATION

Organizational consultation often begins with a generic proposal from a consultant who offers her services to address a specific area or problem. The proposal may be *cold*. In a cold proposal, the consultant identifies frequent problems in organizations and offers his services, either in a self-initiated visit to a prospective client or by a brochure, to ameliorate or remedy them. The generic proposal might be a response to interest from or a request by an official in an organization. In either case, acceptance of the generic proposal usually leads to an interview by the consultant with one or more persons representing the organization.

In the initial interview, usually the organization's representatives state the problem or issue that needs professional attention, seek to learn about the consultant's training, experience, and previous consultations, and how this problem is proposed to be addressed, and arrive at an estimate of time and cost of the proposed effort. Rarely, the initial interview is a ruse to get the consultant to provide an answer to a problem without formally engaging him to do so.

The consultant concurrently makes a preliminary private assessment of the nature and complexity of the problem, the authority of those who are interviewing him to retain him for a prospective engagement, or who they represent, the likelihood of success in consulting with this problem in this organization at this time, and the competence and resources of the organization to undertake the necessary change.

The consultant should ask why he or she is being considered and learn what other consultants have worked with the organization, on which problems, and with what success. The consultant should also find out what the organization expects from the consultation, and what, if any, constraints there will be on areas, functions, or people to be interviewed, surveyed, or observed. It is also important to learn what makes the consultation important to be undertaken at this particular time, how the information will be fed back to the organization, and how confidentiality will be maintained. The consultant also will need to learn the key figure in the organization to whom he or she will be accountable, and the person or persons to be worked with directly to accomplish the project.

If the preliminary mutual exploration satisfies both parties, the consultant might then submit a preliminary exploratory proposal to sample the problem described which might be a symptom of a more complex issue. The preliminary exploration usually means interviewing several people at different levels in the organization, but sometimes only those at a given level if the problem is attributed to that level. That exploration might lead the consultant to redefine the problem with the management.

For example, the top management of a financial company attributed the seeming lack of interest of the clerical staff and their unrelieved repetition of errors to the management's unwillingness to accept a union. Preliminary interviews with six clericals disclosed that the clerical staff was demotivated by managements' repeated threat over several years to downsize the function. They did not know whether they would continue to have a job in the immediate, let alone the more distant future.

In another example, the superintendent of a school system sought consultation to relieve the high absentee rate among teachers, which he attributed to inadequate salaries that he could not change. Interviews with eight teachers in four elementary schools disclosed that the superintendent practically never visited the classrooms or talked with individual teachers. His motto seemed to be that if they did not make problems for him, he wouldn't bother them. As a result, they felt abandoned.

After the exploration, the consultant might submit a formal proposal describing what is proposed to be done, over what period of time, and at what cost (see Appendix B of Levinson, 2002b, for proposal examples). When that proposal is accepted, preferably in writing, it becomes a formal contract for the consultation. If the consultation continues in phases, and the organization is required to bind its obligations, as, for example, government organizations usually are, the contract might have to be renegotiated at the beginning of each phase. However, I have been engaged in a number of long-term consultations without renegotiation.

## THE ASSESSMENT PROCESS

Following the preliminary stages, the consultant enters the organization. I have summarized the steps in my method and described them in detail elsewhere (Levinson, 1993, 2002a, respectively). In those works, I organize the process into four steps, the first three for gathering data, and the fourth for the inferences drawn from the data. These are:

1. Genetic data (identification and description of the organization, its history, and the reasons for the consultation)

2. Structural data (the formal organization, plant and equipment, finances, personnel demographics and policies, general policies and practices, and time cycles)

3. Process data (information and communications transmission)

4. Interpretative data (how the organization perceives itself and its environment, its basic knowledge and how it makes use of that knowledge, the emotional atmosphere of the organization and its capacity to act, and attitudes about and relationships with multiple stakeholders, things and ideas, the consultant, power, and itself)

The facts and inferences are then integrated into an analysis (depending heavily on the psychological orientation of the consultant), and then into a summary and conclusions.

# The Consultant as a Diagnostic Instrument

The consultant herself is the most important instrument in her work. Therefore, I recommend that the consultant keep a diary of her contacts, activities, impressions, and feelings about the process throughout her consultation. Such a diary is imperative if the consultant is to understand the ups and downs of her relationships in the organization, the resistances and hostilities she encounters, and the efforts of various organizational members to use her for their own organizational purposes.

For example, a consultant observing a machine shop in a steel fabricating company wrote in her diary, "This is the cleanest machine shop I have ever seen. Although the milling machines necessarily create lots of scrap metal, the machine operators repeatedly sweep the floors around their machines. They invited me to don safety glasses and to take an initial cut at a piece of steel. They explained what they were doing even though to do so required that they take time from their work. When the bell rang for the lunch break, they gathered in small cliques around the radios to listen to Paul Harvey, a conservative commentator. They invited me to take my lunch with them."

After feeding back the consultation report to the head of a private school, the leader of the consulting team wrote in her diary, "He constantly interrupted me as I was reading him the report, repeatedly making minor corrections and raising questions about the methods and findings although I had kept him apprised all along in a general way about what we were learning. His continued querulous attitude irritated me and finally I told him that he was quibbling at the expense of learning about the school's problems."

**Transference.** It is especially important for the consultant to understand *transference,* or the unwitting transfer of attitudes toward the consultant from an interviewee's past relationships to power figures (Racker, 1968). Some might regard the consultant suspiciously, others as omnipotent, still others contemptuously. The consultant also must try to understand her own varied feelings about and attitudes toward those organizational members with whom she comes into contact. These feelings are called *countertransference* (Racker, 1968). The consultant might not be aware of her feelings as they occur, but maintaining a diary enables her to review her own behavior and infer those previously unrecognized feelings and attitudes that might have intruded into her work.

For example, the team head above who complained about the querulous client, in a subsequent discussion with me about why she vented her anger at him, came to understand that she overreacted because she identified him with her father, who had corrected her repetitively about trivial aspects of her behavior.

In other situations, a consultant needs to learn why she becomes irritated with a client manager who she thinks is trying to control her, or why she bristles when a director of human resources proposes to fall back on 360-degree feedback whenever a morale problem arises, and similar irritating or frustrating experiences. Sometimes she needs to understand why she prefers some people in an organization over others, and why, perhaps, she gives greater weight to their opinions.

**Subjectivity in Organizational Assessment.** Another reason for maintaining a diary is because all organizational assessment is necessarily subjective. No matter how many instruments a consultant uses and how much statistical data he amasses and reports, inevitably he has had to choose what aspects of the organization to examine, which to pass over or ignore, and how he interprets what he has found. In his final report, he does not merely quote statistics. He explains or gives meaning to his data. It follows that an assessment conclusion necessarily is hypothesis. This, the consultant ultimately reports, is what was done and found (facts); this is what was learned (inferences); this is how the consultant understands them (interpretations); and this is what is recommended (methods to bring about change).

Most consultants, of whatever theoretical orientation, are likely to agree on the facts. They might differ in what they infer from the facts. They certainly will differ in their interpretation of their inferences depending on their specific theoretical orientations, which is why each needs to have a firm theory to guide the work and to keep inferences separate from interpretations. A consultant's recommendations likely will follow preferred methods and the espoused or implicit theory. When reporting back to the organization, the consultant's findings and interpretations are subject to the critical analysis of the organizational members. They might or might not follow the recommendations, or might offer or seek other solutions to their problems. The consultant also might recommend other consultants to deal with problems not within the consultant's area of expertise.

Organizational assessment involves viewing the information gathered from several different vantage points. This is necessary because, given the subjective nature of the process, the overlap of perspectives that become repetitive confirmations assures the assessor (and the organization) of the validity of the findings. The diary is an additional device for checking on oneself, perhaps reinterpreting what one is learning, and reviewing various options for change as the consultant becomes more familiar with the organization's potential for change. It is also a device for maintaining one's professional humility.

There are two other important reasons for maintaining a diary. When something goes awry, when the information gathering is not going as well as it should, the consultant can review the basic organized facts, recheck the inferences derived from them, and review the interpretations. Since all assessment is hypothesis, and all tentative hypotheses (the hunches or temporary understandings) the consultant makes along the way must be checked out, only by being able to review both the data and logic can the consultant maintain a scientific, self-correcting posture.

When a consulting team was returning by car to its home base from its work in the branch office of a public utility company, one of the team members complained about the behavior of the team leader in the regional office they had just visited. He wrote in his diary, "The team leader pressed the local manager to designate his best and his worst crews. The elderly local manager, close to retirement and preoccupied with a sick wife, seemed unable to do so. The team leader abruptly took over, told the manager which of us would ride the gas crew trucks, which the electrical line crew trucks, and which would interview in the office. The manager had no say in the matter. I thought that was an impatient and discourteous way to manage the situation and said so in the car."

**The Detail of Organizational Assessment.**  As I view it, fully elaborated, organizational assessment is highly detailed. It cannot be comprehensive and be otherwise. Such detailed attention often dismays the prospective consultant and leads him to avoidance, in favor of more simple assessment methods, or none at all (Schein, 1999). But complexity does not become simplicity solely by denying it or choosing to ignore it. As a matter of fact, such an outline is extremely helpful to the consultant, especially the beginner, because it tells the consultant what kinds of information to gather, and, in addition, how to order that information so that it leads to logical inferences and conclusions regardless of one's theoretical orientation. Thus, the detailed outline provides both structure and guidance and enables him to continue organizing and integrating his work as it progresses. If the consultant elects not to use it fully, at least he knows what he has chosen to leave out. Furthermore, with experience, the consultant need not always undertake a comprehensive, detailed assessment, as the range of cases in another chapter in this volume illustrates (Levinson, 2002b). A client once asked me how I arrived at a diagnostic conclusion after only five minutes of conversation with him. My reply was, "Five minutes—and forty years of experience before that."

## The Importance of History in Organizational Assessment

My conception of organizational assessment makes much of history. Apart from my clinical orientation that gives important consideration to a person's history, there is good reason for tracing an organization's history. One important reason is that it establishes both the pace of growth and the basic focus of the organization. It is not without good reason that many businesses and other organizations are shedding components that were acquired when it was assumed that expansion (to become a conglomerate if the organization was a business) was wise. There is much contemporary management effort to get back to basics, and to recognize and reassert the fundamental core of the organization. But in consultation, the importance of history largely has been ignored.

Much has been written about more traditional organizational development (OD) consultation and the problems inherent in ignoring history (Coglan, 1997). But even in the early days of OD consultation, few took seriously Greiner's admonition (1967, p. 2) that ". . . future researchers and change agents need to give greater weight to historical determinants of change with special emphasis being attached to the developing relationship between an organization and its environment. It is within this historical and developmental context . . . that we may be able to explain better why a 'planned' change program may succeed in one organization and not in another." Even before there was an OD movement, Meltzer (1944, p. 166) observed that ". . . segmented studies of such problems as illumination, fatigue and monotony do not get at the heart of the realities in industry. The realization of the significance of human attitudes and the development of techniques for human understanding has more to contribute . . . What are the realities of problems of management in industry? Can they be realistically and comprehensively understood without a fairly thorough study of personality organization as they emerge in life situations in industry?"

Not only was history largely ignored in OD consultation, but it continues to be. In the most recent volume of varied OD methods (Waclawski & Church, 2002), there is no reference to history in the index, and none of the chapters discusses organizational history. With rare exceptions (Argyris, 1958), subsequent writings on OD tended not to address problems the consultant encountered in long-term relationships with an organization, and particularly with its key figures. Nor did those writings identify the kinds of feelings the consultant had when she gathered information for assessment and intervention when that effort was extended and comprehensive.

All organizations fundamentally are interactions of people. This implies that, despite nearly 100 years of effort to make management scientific (Taylor, 1911), that is, reduce as much analysis of management practices to numbers as possible, the basic currency of all organizations is people's feelings. No matter how logical or rational organizational decisions presumably are meant to be, almost all decisions ultimately are judgments, and, like all human behavior, judgments necessarily are based on feelings and thoughts.

De Geus (1997) points out that the average life of companies is 12.5 years. He concludes that, "Companies die because their managers focus on the economic activity of producing goods and services, and they forget that their organizations' true nature is that of a community of humans. The legal establishment, business educators, and the financial community all join them in this mistake" (p. 3). Other institutions that are not driven primarily by economic issues do not have the same mortality rate, he adds.

## The Role of Power in Organizations

All organizations are power hierarchies and necessarily must be so. Every organization is headed by a board of directors or an owner. That individual (or they) establish(es) the direction of the organization and is responsible for decisions about the organization. She or they often delegates subsidiary decision-making to executives, and they, in turn, delegate authority to others who are accountable to them. She or they employ(s) people with various levels of authority and control to carry out the policies and practices of the organization. Employees at each level are accountable to or report to a person at the next higher level for the effectiveness of their work. Sometimes people report to more than one person, each of whom has some degree of control over the reporting person. It is crucially important for the consultant to understand where power lies in an organization and how it is distributed, both manifestly and covertly, and not to be prejudiced against its appropriate exercise. Some people in some organizations at some time should indeed be fired, sometimes for their own benefit. True, power often is abused in organizations (Hornstein, 1996), and all too often over-control inhibits innovation and adaptive effort. But attempts to abolish power or to make business organizations more democratic by having employees choose their own leaders (which is not the same as inviting employee participation in some aspects of decision-making), as was the case in some communist political systems, can only lead to organizational chaos. The most conspicuous examples in nonprofit organizations are the elections of abbots in monasteries. There, the effort to balance the interests of all factions results in the compromise choice of the candidate least offensive to any faction, and therefore most nearly acceptable to all of the monks. If that leader is not a skilled manipulator, and most monks are not, that choice leads to organizational paralysis and often to subsequent splits.

All organizations are attack devices. That's one of the reasons so many writers about leadership and organizations offer military and athletic models or metaphors. On the military side, these range from Attila the Hun (Roberts, 1991) through contemporary generals. The athletic model is exemplified by descriptions of highly successful coaches like the University of North Carolina's championship basketball coach Dean Smith (Chadwick, 1999). Schools attack ignorance, churches inveigh against sins, charitable organizations seek to alleviate poverty or strife, heathcare organizations fight illness and death. All living organisms seek to master their environments for their survival and to perpetuate their species. For the organizational consultant, it is important to learn what the organization attacks, how well that attack fits with its purpose, and how effectively it does so.

# Identification with the Organization

All organizations foster identification of their members with the organization. Some go to great lengths, often paternalistically, to further the feeling of being one big family. That identification is necessary if people are to assume initiative, and to act responsively and authoritatively on behalf of the organization's values, standards, and practices. However, when organizational members become overly identified with their employer, they risk becoming narcissistically preoccupied: for example, "We are not only the best, but also, competitors deserve only our condescension." Such an orientation exacerbates dependency and inhibits innovative adaptation in the organization (Schwartz, 1990; Levinson, 1994).

Ideally, power in an organization is organized and implemented in a five-step process, usually beginning with the *ego ideal* of the founder. An ego ideal is one's wishful fantasy about himself at his ideal best (Freud, 1961). However vague that mental picture of oneself, one is always implicitly and unwittingly striving toward it. When transformed into organizational leadership, that personal ideal aspiration becomes an organizational ideal. To the extent to which members of the organization are organized in its pursuit, the organizational ideal becomes their dominant sense of purpose. It addresses the question, "Why are we doing this?" Purpose is then translated into vision: "What is the nature of the field in which we are pursuing our ideal?" Vision, in turn, is narrowed to mission. For example, a company whose founder failed to be accepted to medical school pursued his ego ideal as one who cured illnesses by forming a business that manufactured drugs, his vision. Since he could not manufacture drugs for all illnesses, he then had to choose from among many illnesses those toward which he would direct his efforts: his mission. The mission then had to be refined into goals, or long-term steps toward purpose, and goals, in turn, into objectives, or short-term steps.

Unfortunately, most organizations are not organized as logically as I have outlined in the preceding paragraph. In fact, few are based on solid psychological logic (Jaques, 1996). Many heads of business organizations, especially if they are not the founders and they come from outside the organization, are not clear about the first two issues, purpose and vision. With the usual limited, mechanistic psychological training offered in schools of management, or none at all, they tend to jump into mission and objectives without giving adequate consideration to the more fundamental psychological issues. As a result, they do not build their organizations to last (Collins and Porras, 1994; Collins, 2001). In addition to failing that knowledge, they are intensely preoccupied with reaching quarterly profit goals or other short-term targets to achieve their bonuses and to please the financial community or their boards (Stevenson & Cruikshank, 1998). Their circumscribed focus leads to high leadership turnover about which the business press repetitively complains. Further, when managerial difficulties then arise, they tend to flee repetitively into managerial fads (Levinson, 1985; Shapiro, 1995).

## Next Steps in the Assessment

After the initial mutual exploration and the acceptance of a formal proposal, the consultant speaks at length with the chief executive, or whichever executive is responsible for the unit about which the consultation is proposed. If the accountable executive or manager is not involved, she is unlikely to support the consultation and might even sabotage it. In effect, to enter an organization without her assent is to intrude into her management prerogatives. The consultant should discuss with that person how he plans to assess the organization and how he proposes to go about doing it. This discussion might even be in the nature of a mutual diagnosis. If not already the case, the responsible executive must get to know the consultant and be assured that he or she will continue to be in charge of what is happening in the organization. The consultant must be careful not to undermine the authority of the responsible executive. That executive might help the consultant avoid some problems and even steer the consultant around potential blocks. For example, in my first study in the Kansas Power and Light Company (Levinson, Price, Munden, Mandl, & Solley, 1962), the chief executive recommended that I, not one of my colleagues, interview the union leader only after my team had been accepted in the field. That proved to be a fruitful recommendation.

The responsible executive also might be the best contact for arranging interviews with board members and community influentials. The responsible executive or the person in charge of the human resources function will have to help lay out the plan of the consultation to the extent that the consultant must take into account geographical distribution of functions and locations, as well as the range of work roles that must be sampled. The responsible executive usually is the person who must interface with the organization's many environments and stakeholders (those who have something at stake in their relationship to the organization). She or he also might describe most comprehensively what issues and problems the organization faces, and what its particular achievements have been. Unless there are strong reasons why the consultation report is to be limited to the responsible executive, permission for it to be presented subsequently to all employees can be given at this time. The consultant will inform them of that agreement in his initial presentation to them. The discussion with the responsible executive also will provide the consultant with a perspective on the organization's history and its dominant competitive edge or core competence, for example, what it tries to do better than competing organizations. It also sets the stage for a regularly scheduled conference between the two when the consultant keeps the responsible executive informed about where he is in the organization, and, without violating confidences, tells her or him in a general way what he is doing, for example, interviewing, observing, or examining financial reports. As the consultation progresses, without identifying individuals or groups, the consultant should report general themes arising in the interviews and informal discussions with employees or groups that are likely to appear in the final report. By doing so, the consultant alerts the client executive to what later might be reported so that there are no significant surprises for her or him in the final report.

In my preferred approach, the consultant then prepares a letter to be signed by the chief executive (or approves one that she has written) that is sent to all employees describing the reasons for the approaching consultation and what the consultant will do. That letter should assure the recipients that their privacy will be respected and confidentiality will be maintained both in interviews and observations of their work. Following the distribution of that letter of introduction (see Appendix B of Levinson, 2002a, for examples of all suggested written communications), the consultant then presents an oral statement to the top management group (however that is defined) of what is proposed to be done, emphasizing confidentiality and the agreement about feedback. The consultant follows with similar presentations to successive lower levels in the organization, following the organization's formal accountability structure, allowing for questions and discussion.

**The Company Tour.** The consultant should then tour the physical location(s) of the organization where feasible, and describe in his diary the circumstances of the various work environments and their impact on those who work in them. Some organizations are in one location, some are scattered throughout the same community, and some are dispersed nationally and even worldwide. The September 11, 2001 collapse of the World Trade Center towers illustrated the distribution of several companies in New York and their subsequent dispersal into temporary quarters both within the city and outside of it. Some organizations (for example, Boeing, General Electric, American Red Cross) might have a headquarters in one community and manufacturing or service facilities in several others. Some American companies (for example, Nike, Lucent) have their products manufactured overseas by contractors. Even some Japanese companies are contracting their manufacturing to Chinese firms. Some companies have distant contractors (in India, China, and Ireland) that tally data, or call centers that respond to inquiries. Some universities have branches in foreign countries, as do many religious organizations. Some major medical centers, such as the Cleveland Clinic, have developed local centers to serve populations distant from their headquarters.

**Interviews.** The consultant then will develop a sample of employees to interview and a schedule for interviewing. I prefer to interview all of top management, a 10 percent sample of middle management, and a 5 percent sample of line employees. (It will be helpful early on to interview a long-time employee who is familiar with the evolution of the organization and who can identify the informal power brokers.) Those classifications might be arbitrary, but the consultant should assure both himself and the client organization that he has interviewed a representative sample. I generally include all single-person specialists (for example, a hospital pathologist). I allow at least two hours for senior level employees. Some people might have to be interviewed several times. The most unusual interview in my experience continued for eleven hours. Usually, line-level employees are less verbal than managers and executives, so an hour often suffices. I prefer to dictate summaries of my interview notes in the ten-minute break after each interview, because tape-recorded interviews require four hours of transcription for each hour of interview. If one waits until the end of a working day to dictate from notes, the notes might be cold by then, and much information as well as observations of interviewee behavior will be lost.

A questionnaire that follows the interview outline (both are illustrated in Appendix A of Levinson, 2002a) is then distributed to all employees. Unless the client organization is small or heavily individualized, such as a modest-sized law firm in which everyone is interviewed, the questionnaire provides information beyond that from the interviewees. As with the individual interviewees, the respondents are assured of confidentiality. If, being unfamiliar with the consultant, some respondents doubt his integrity, the consultant can suggest that they call anyone they know in other organizations with which he has worked.

The consultant must be aware of the different capacities for abstract thinking among interviewees, as well as the different languages they speak. Although the managers of an Argentinian client spoke English, for them it was a second language. Therefore they asked for an interpreter to be present during the interviews so that they could be sure they both understood the questions and responded accurately in English. In a Boston hospital, the questionnaire had to be translated into Spanish for the kitchen staff. Similar adaptations must be made for the varied ethnic personnel both in the United States and abroad.

In the process of understanding the organization's history, the consultant should give particular attention to the stages in the organization's growth and how it has coped with crises. For example, for many years, public utilities were protected from competition. That fostered long-term employment and heavy dependence on the employer. When those companies were deregulated and had to become more competitive, that change became a crisis for many managers and executives who were less able to compete. In turn, the organizations were less able to compete and experienced a high turnover in their managerial ranks. Some companies are still recovering from that drastic change in organizational personality. Some dignified, mainline Protestant churches are being outflanked by more fundamentalist churches that foster emotional expression. Medical practice has become more strictly controlled by HMOs at the cost of more personal relationships that formerly characterized most physicians' practices.

Elementary schools are being pressed to test pupils at certain grade intervals, leading teachers to complain about having to teach to the tests.

It will be important to know how the organization is financed. The consultant unfamiliar with interpreting balance sheets might find it advantageous to ask an accountant to help him understand its implications.

When there have been changes in its products or services, and especially when the organization has confronted technological changes both in its internal processes and among its work with clients, parishioners, students, patients, or customers, the consultant might also want to ask for guidance by someone technologically knowledgeable. Though technological change has been a boon for many organizations (Trist & Murray, 1997), even nonprofits, many employees do not have the conceptual capacity to learn the now-required skills. In some cases, recent employees who are computer-knowledgeable have been asked to teach older, higher-level executives (who do not have ten-year-olds at home) how to use their computers. But in a few years, there will be no computer illiterate executives.

## The Organization's Leadership

No organizational issue is more important than leadership. Several dimensions merit examination. The most significant is the personality of the leader and the fit between the leader's characteristic behavior and that now required by the organization's contemporary environment (Silzer, 2002). For example, it is not a new finding that, characteristically, most entrepreneurs have difficulty becoming managers. The freewheeling entrepreneur often finds it difficult to shift from doing as his impulse moves him to the more rigid, impersonal control of people and processes, from selling a product that he invented to a limited audience to catering to a mass market. The manager of a small operation with close relationships among colleagues might find it difficult to enforce impersonally policies and practices that necessarily must transcend friendships. This is a particularly difficult problem in family businesses (Levinson, 1971; Kets deVries, 1996). People in positions of power over others must meet their dependency needs, because followers necessarily depend on leaders, while simultaneously keeping those relationships free of personal ties and obligation (Zaleznik, 1989).

**Choice of the Leader.** In addition to the fit of the personality of the leader to the behavioral requirements of the leadership role, another fundamental issue is how the leader is chosen (Vancil, 1987). Some boards of directors are wise enough to analyze the behavior to be required of a prospective leader and then choose one who fits their projections. Most are not (Levinson, 1980). Some large organizations like General Electric, Citicorp (Levinson & Rosenthal, 1984), and the Roman Catholic Church, keep careful track of promising executive candidates, and rotate them through assignments to test them. Some wise organizations have their board members meet regularly with a diverse number of promising candidates for upward mobility to get to know them personally. Unfortunately, most chief executives are not so wisely chosen, and some are carefully chosen for the wrong reasons. Furthermore, often chief executives endorse favorite candidates for nepotistic or dynastic reasons without an adequate appreciation of what the successor will have to do differently than they did. In any event, the choice of a new leader always involves significant, sometimes drastic, adaptive problems, not only for the new CEO, but also for the followers (and for the consultants who are working in the organization).

There are certain dangers in the selection of executives. The most common in my experience is the promotion of previously successful executives into roles that are conceptually beyond them; they cannot think at the required level of abstraction (Jaques, 1996). Many chief executives, let alone lower-level executives and managers, are in roles that exceed their conceptual capacity. A second major problem is narcissism. All of us necessarily must like ourselves well enough to have self-confidence. But some people like themselves too much and inflate that self-confidence unnecessarily to compensate for their tacit sense of inadequacy. They are particularly attracted to executive roles in which their grandiosity sometimes can be destructive to the organization (Kets deVries, 1989; Maccoby, 2000). Similarly, a third major problem is paranoia. A certain level of suspicion of others' intentions and motives is necessary to survive in competitive executive ranks (Grove, 1996). Too much suspicion, the worry that there are threats behind everyone else's actions, becomes paranoia. A fourth problem is that of dependency. Often an executive succeeds because he is dependent on a stronger leader. The apparent success might mask a dependency that becomes apparent when the dependent executive is promoted to succeed an erstwhile predecessor and proves to be unable to act independently.

**Leadership Dangers.** There are two tragic dangers among those executives who build highly successful organizations. The first, more frequent, is that sometimes those who succeed too well are seduced into excesses that lead to their demise (Miller, 1990). That allegation was made of Ken Lay when Enron collapsed (McLean, 2001). The second, fortunately comparatively rare, concerns executives who lead their organizations into destruction only after the organization has attained a high level of success so that their failure will be spectacular. Some argue that American business organizations are their own worst enemy and are destructive to the country (Weaver, 1988).

If the progenitors of these styles of leadership behavior remain in position long enough, their personal styles lead to similar, characteristic subordinate behavior, or efforts to escape or evade the leader's influence. This can affect entire organizations (Kets deVries & Miller, 1984). Employees frequently complain about the contradictions and confusion in their organizations. Given so many different people in authority, with differing perceptions of reality, differing points of view about appropriate actions, and differing conceptual levels, that reaction should not be surprising.

Just as some people should not be parents, some (perhaps most) should not be managers and executives. Sometimes managerial pathology can be turned to an advantage. Many manipulators become spectacular sales executives. Some narcissists have channeled their grandiosity into building expansive organizations, even though they cannot sustain mechanisms of perpetuation in them (Maccoby, 2000). To be unduly suspicious can undermine trust in others, but many with a paranoid bent might be good at uncovering and guarding against financial trickery. The more dependent person might be a good mentor. Indeed, given the wide range of behaviors, society survives because people find ways to turn even those behaviors that are pathological to their occupational advantage. Organizations should, and often can, do the same.

**Leadership Succession Plans.** Once, during his inauguration, I asked a newly elected college president who his successor was. One of his board members who overheard the question protested that this was no time to ask that question. The president understood the significance of my question and reassured his board member that it was appropriate. The importance of this story is that all organizations should have succession plans. No one can predict when an emergency will require a successor. Without such a plan, turmoil necessarily ensues. Too many chief executives, uneasy about contemplating their departure or denying their mortality, do not institute a plan. The usual accompaniment of that neglect is the absence of a management development program that insures the organization that all of its leaders are being prepared for upward mobility. Such a program is psychological money in the management bank. The consultant should give careful attention to this element of organizational perpetuation, especially if he has to help the chief executive release his constricting grip on the organization (see the example in Chapter 3 of Levinson, 2002a).

**Structure.** Most organizational structures presumably define accountability, designating who reports to whom, and indicating indirect accountability by dotted lines on the organizational chart. Few have structures based on psychological logic. The best such logic that defines and categorizes management activities and relates them both to the requirements of the organization and the levels of conceptual ability that should differentiate them is that of Elliott Jaques (1996).

**Cognitive Processes of Leaders.** Jaques defines all work as the exercise of discretion, judgment, and decision-making (cognitive processes), within limits, in carrying out tasks, driven by values, and bringing skilled knowledge into play in a given role. He describes cognitive processes as those mental processes used to take in information, play with it, pick it over, analyze it, put it together, reorganize it, judge and reason with it, draw conclusions, make plans, arrive at decisions, and take action.

Jaques (1996) posits eight levels of conceptual ability or cognitive power among humans, each defined by how far ahead an individual can think and plan. Fundamentally, this capacity is a given; people are born with it. Those who have the basic capacity, if given the right kind of stimulation, training, and experience, will mature in their cognitive power along predictable lines according to their age. Just as we do physically, we grow cognitively at different rates in specific discontinuous steps.

Those same eight levels, given their universality, become the basis for organizational structure and compensation. Jaques (1996) contends that no organization, however large, should have more than eight levels. Roles should be defined according to the cognitive level required to fulfill their tasks. People should be placed in roles who have the cognitive power to carry out the requirements of those roles. Jaques measures cognitive power in terms of an individual's time horizon (the maximum time span at which an individual is capable of working at any given point in his life, or the person's working capacity).

Although often the case, Jaques contends that no person should report to anyone who is not at a higher conceptual level than he. When a manager reports to another who is at a lower conceptual level, his superior cannot supervise him adequately or add value to his work. This condition is widespread in organizations, which contributes to their ineffectiveness. Also, if the manager to whom one is accountable is more than one conceptual level above him, the conceptual distance between them is so great that the superior can only be bored by the kinds of problems the subordinate brings to him. This means that ideally organizations are structured according to a management accountability hierarchy (Jaques, 1996).

The conceptual level required of an organizational leader will vary with the size of the organization and the complexity of its work. A large multinational corporation will require a chief executive at Stratum VIII (Jaques, 1996), who must be able to anticipate problems fifty years ahead and plan options for dealing with them. That person must project political trends, economic cycles, cultural changes, and shifting market needs, among other forces. To build a nuclear power generating plant requires the capacity to think ahead fourteen years, because that is how long such a project takes from conception to completion. An organization that undertakes to build such plants in various countries requires a chief executive to deal with multiple issues several times more complex. By way of contrast, a secretary, social worker, or teacher must be able to think ahead one year, even though many decisions require far less time, and would be in Jaques' Stratum II. These levels are grouped into three domains: system leadership, organizational leadership, and direct leadership.

Intelligence capacity (IQ) measures usually include tests of vocabulary, memory, attention, logic, and other capacities that are organized as intelligence. Conceptual capacity, as Jaques uses the term, goes beyond IQ. It is the *ability* to grasp and explain matters at different levels of abstraction. The capacity to deal with abstractions not only varies among people, but also with their age, experience, and training. The time line of that growth can be plotted, which is a significant contribution to selection, career development, and assignment. It can be assessed by tracing how far ahead people planned in their previous roles, and now, in their present roles.

Jaques (1996) has delineated the kinds of thought processes, reflected in how people speak and write, which mark their conceptual capacity. These are declarative, cumulative, serial processing, and parallel. Declarative entails putting forth one reason at a time. Cumulative brings together a number of ideas, none of which is sufficient to make the case. Serial is exemplified by a chain of linked reasons, each leading to the next. Parallel addresses the examination of a number of possible positions, each reached serially.

Most charts of organizational structure simply separate roles into line and staff. That makes for inadequate separation of functions and activities, and does not delineate those that are more directly focused on the thrust of an organization and others that support them. Jaques (1996) separates the major functions that constitute that thrust: developing or improving products or services; producing the goods or services; procuring the materials or components needed for doing so; delivering the goods or services; client/customer relations; marketing, in the sense of analysis of needs of the client population, and promotions to encourage the clients or customers to seek the products or services; and new business development. All other roles and functions, however important, are ancillary. Failure to understand this differentiation led one major automobile company to choose a financial executive as CEO, whose failure to understand the importance of styling led to its near demise.

With respect to staff functions like human resources, legal, safety, and accounting, Jaques differentiates their functions into prescribing, auditing, coordinating, monitoring, serving, advising, and collateralizing, and charts how each relates to the others and to operational managers.

## The Organization's Communication System and Methods

If the human skeleton is the analogue for organizational structure, its communication system is analogous to the human nervous system. That mechanism is responsible for perceiving a wide range of data, both from within the organization and the outside. It must process those data, distribute them to their appropriate receptors, and devise the mechanisms for putting them to use.

Communication has three aspects: input, processing, and output. Input refers to what information an organization seeks from outside itself and where it gets that information. Some organizations are heavily involved in trade and professional organizations. Some send their staff to academic training programs; others have significant internal educational programs. Some conduct customer surveys, focus groups, and other customer follow-up activities. Some carefully review their cash register tapes. Those that are publicly held give careful attention to financial news. In short, all organizations are swamped with a plethora of information. Necessarily, they must be selective about what they review and absorb. Some information stops with the chief executive; some goes to those whose specialties require it. Most of it is unshared; much of it is unused.

Two important kinds of information come from inside the organization: that which the organization creates by research or generates by creative innovation; and the feelings and attitudes of employees, and the statistics of their work. Some organizations routinely sample employee feelings and attitudes, some do so in crises, and most not at all.

*Processing* refers to what happens to the information: who gets it and what is done with it. Most organizations rely heavily on the printed word: annual reports, bulletins, manuals, books of policies and procedures, and organizational newspapers and magazines. Some have turned to television and e-mail. Most communications intended to inform employees do not really inform. For example, if a strike is threatening, one might read about the discontent in a community newspaper, but rarely will one find that unease reflected or addressed in a corporate publication. Therefore, most organizational publications, having been spun to present the organization in the best possible light, are not regarded as adequate sources of information about the organization. For financial information about publicly held companies, investors turn not to annual reports, but to the completed public 10K forms submitted to the Securities and Exchange Commission. These usually are available from the corporations themselves. The consultant also should do so.

In addition to financial information, the consultant must learn how the organization gets information about how its employees feel, and what it does about its findings. Of particular importance is how people within the organization communicate with each other, a critical issue not only for efficiency, but also for cooperation and mutual support.

With respect to output, three important aspects of communication should be reviewed by the consultant. How does this organization want the outside world to view it, what does it do to further that wish, and with what success? What does the organization do about the gap between how it is viewed by the outside world and how it wants that world to view it? All organizations go to great lengths, some more aggressively and expensively than others, to impress those audiences in the external world that are important to them. All seek customers, patients, adherents, clients, students, donors, and public approval. In short, all to varying degrees engage in public relations.

**The Psychological Contract.** All people who work in organizations develop implicit psychological contracts with those organizations, and the organizations with them. The psychological contract is not a social contract, a conscious agreement about wages, hours, and working conditions, even if unwritten. It is an evolving, unconscious set of expectations that the individual and the organization have of each other (Levinson et al., 1962). Employees expect the organization to understand their dependency needs, their need to express affection and aggression appropriately in their work roles, and to help them manage change. For its part, the organization expects people to do their work responsibly, to represent the organization well, and to be loyal to its norms and standards. When these mutual expectations are met we can speak of reciprocation; when they are not, even though they are implicit and might be poorly understood on both sides, there is a contractual violation that then leads to symptoms of discontent.

**Communication Problems.** In my experience, most organizations do a poor job of communicating for several reasons: first, as indicated earlier, because they rely too much on the printed word; second, because they do not adequately train their managers in communication techniques; and third, because top management does not interact sufficiently with employees.

Unfortunately, most people do not read much, even about what concerns them. (I find that even consultants don't read much.) When employees do read, too often, they understand only poorly what they read. Wise chief executives create opportunities to hear what their employees have to say, and learn to listen. Some have cross-level meetings with employee groups. Some make it a point to lunch with their employees in the employees' cafeteria. Some create relaxed social occasions where management and employees mix more freely, thus opening communication doors. Some make it a point to visit various locations, particularly to better understand their employees' work and working conditions. The best example I know is what happened to a miner, working deep in a coal mine, who asked his new, helmeted neighbor who he was. The miner was startled to discover that his new companion was the CEO. The miners in that company subsequently knew they had a friend in executive ranks who knew their work problems first-hand, a conviction reemphasized when another time that CEO took his teenaged son into the mine with him, and also worked to upgrade the safety of the mines and the quality of their communities.

Speaking to employees is not a comfortable task for CEOs. The late Thomas J. Watson, Jr., then head of IBM, and Reginald H. Jones, then head of General Electric, spoke of how painful it was for them to learn to do so (Levinson &

Rosenthal, 1984). When I told another CEO that the contemporary business environment now required that he interact with his subordinates, he said simply, "I can't do that." He hid in his office until he was fired.

Chief executives, and often others, must be a presence, especially when there are tragedies. Former New York mayor Rudolph Giuliani demonstrated the importance of being there in the tragic World Trade Center towers collapse (Alter, 2001). Like it or not, they must meet the dependency needs of their people. Willing or not, they are identification figures for their organizations.

# CONCLUSION OF THE ASSESSMENT

## Feedback of the Results of the Assessment

In my experience, three steps are helpful in the feedback process. The first is to prepare a summary of the assessment that can be read in an hour or less to successive audiences in the order in which the consultant presented his initial announcement, followed by an opportunity for questions and discussion. That summary should describe what the consultant did, what was found, what was inferred from the findings, how the consultant understands those inferences, and what remedial action is recommended. Depending on the size of the organization, the number of levels, and the respective cognitive levels of the listeners, different forms of the report might have to be prepared. In some cases, the report might have to be translated and subsequently read by someone who knows a particular language.

As a second step, before presenting the feedback to successive levels, I recommend that two feedback sessions with the chief executive be arranged. I hold these to be an inviolate requirement. I require one meeting the last two hours of the day, during which I read the report to her and ask her how it sounds to those who will hear it, and what factual errors might have to be corrected. The second must take place the first two hours of the next morning. The reason for making it a requirement is simple: no matter how much the chief executive has wanted the assessment, nor how well the consultant has prepared her for the issues that are to be reported, the report inevitably, at least partly, will be seen as an indictment. When the CEO takes that report home to review it further, anger and paranoid feelings will arise. Unless the consultant meets with the CEO immediately the next morning, those feelings will not be dissipated and the consultant might well lose the client. In one instance, I had to hold five supportive feedback sessions with a CEO to clarify several such psychological bruises, the upshot of which was the recognition that his kindly but over-controlling paternalism was neither appreciated nor desired by his employees. He recognized that he no longer fit the contemporary CEO role and resigned.

The third step is to do the actual feedback by reading the report to the successive groups of employees, answering questions and inviting discussion. They should be told what remedial actions or follow-up steps are likely to be taken, these already having been approved by the CEO. Ordinarily, I do not distribute copies of the report to the assembled employees even if the chief executive wants me to do so. The CEO must be made aware of the possible exploitation of the report by whoever wants to cause harm to the CEO or the organization. There is one exception: when I do feedback with the top management level, I distribute numbered copies of the report to facilitate their critical examination, and collect the copies at the end of the session. The reason for doing so is that this group, as with the CEO, is likely to feel most injured, and requires more time to vent their anger, debate the consultant, and question the findings.

## Termination of the Consulting Relationship

All relationships must end. It is best that they end on a warm note. If further consultation is not to follow the assessment, the consultant should take the time formally to say goodbye to those he has interviewed and observed, and to thank them for taking time from their work and for helping him. The consultant should give them permission to call him at a later date, and to speak to anyone from other organizations who might want to ask them about the assessment experience or for a referral for personal help. Unless the consultation has been undertaken for previously agreed on research purposes, if the consultant wishes to publish something about what was learned, the permission of the organization should be obtained. What is written should be carefully disguised so that neither the organization nor anyone in it is recognizable.

# SUMMARY AND CONCLUSIONS

Most organizations are complex. Most organizational problems are even more so. To understand that complexity, a consultant must recognize that consultation is a process and the consultant is an actor in that process. To carry out the role effectively, in most cases, the consultant must recognize the emotional nature of the relationship with members of the consultee organization. The consultant's impact on the organization, whether real or imagined, inevitably evokes many varied feelings. That relationship also stirs up aspects of his own feelings. While interviewing, using questionnaires, observing, or examining data, the consultant must keep a record of his own feelings about his contacts and experiences in the organization. In the last analysis, organizational assessment is a subjective experience. To sustain his own integrity, the consultant must have a device for keeping himself as honest as he can.

Although much organizational consultation is short term and narrowly focused on specific problems, to understand an organization, one must have a sense of its history, its adaptive methods, its relative degree of success, and particularly how it maintains its internal cohesion while focusing its efforts on its aggressive attack on its competitive problems. A detailed outline of what is to be analyzed in what steps, as described in this chapter, will be especially helpful.

# References

Adizes, I. (1988). *Corporate life cycles*. Englewood Cliffs, NJ: Prentice Hall.

Alter, J. (2001, September 24). Grit, guts and Rudi Giuliani, *Newsweek, 32*.

Argyris, C. (1958). Creating effective research relationships in organizations. *Human Organization, 17*, 34–40.

Axtell, R. E. (Ed.). (1993). *Do's and taboos around the world*. (3rd ed.). Janesville, WI: Parker Pen.

Bray, D. W., & Byham, W. C. (1991). Assessment centers and their derivatives. *Journal of Continuing Higher Education, 39*, 8–11.

Burke, W. W. (1994). *Organizational development: A process of learning and changing*. Reading, MA: Addison-Wesley.

Chadwick, D. E. (1999). *The 12 leadership principles of Dean Smith*. New York: Total.

Coglan, D. (Ed.). (1997). Grandmasters of organizational development. *Organizational Development Journal, 15*, 2–90.

Collins, J. C. (2001). *Good to great*. New York: Harper Business.

Collins, J. C., & Porras, J. I. (1994). *Built to last: Successful habits of visionary companies*. New York: HarperCollins.

De Geus, A. (1997). *The living company*. Boston: Harvard Business School Press.

Erikson, E. H. (1963). *Childhood and society* (2nd ed.). New York: Norton.

Freud, S. (1961). Group psychology and the analysis of the ego. *The standard edition of the complete psychological works of Sigmund Freud* (Vol. 18, p. 131). London: Hogarth Press.

Greiner, L. E. (1967). Antecedents of planned organizational change. *Journal of Applied Behavioral Change, 3*, 51–85.

Greiner, L. E. (1998). Evolution and revolution as organizations grow. *Harvard Business Review, 5*, 55–68.

Grove, A. S. (1996). *Only the paranoid survive: How to exploit the crisis points that challenge every company and career*. New York: Doubleday.

Hornstein, H. A. (1996). *Brutal bosses and their prey*. New York: Riverhead Books.

Hornstein, H. A., & Tichy, N. M. (1973). *Organization diagnosis and improvement strategies*. New York: Behavioral Science Associates.

Howard, A. (Ed.). (1994). *Diagnosis for organizational change*. New York: Guilford Press.

Jaques, E. (1996). *Requisite organization: A total system for effective managerial organization and managerial leadership for the 21st century*. (2nd ed.). Falls Church, VA: Cason Hall.

Kets deVries, M.F.R. (1996). *Family Business: Human dilemmas in the family firm*. London: International Thomson Business Press.

Kets deVries, M.F.R. (1989). *Prisoners of leadership*. New York: Wiley.

Kets deVries, M.F.R., & Miller, D. (1984). *The neurotic organization*. San Francisco: Jossey-Bass.

Kraut, A. I. (Ed.). (1996). *Organizational surveys: Tools for assessment and change*. San Francisco: Jossey-Bass.

Kraut, A. I., & Korman, A. K. (Eds.). (1999). *Evolving practices in human resource management: Responses to a changing world of work*. San Francisco: Jossey-Bass.

Lawler, E. E., III. (1992). *The ultimate advantage: Creating the high involvement organization*. San Francisco: Jossey-Bass.

Levinson, D. J., Darrow, C. M., Klein, E. B., Levinson, M. H., & McKee, B. (1978). *Seasons of a man's life*. New York: Ballantine.

Levinson, H. (1971). Conflicts that plague family businesses. *Harvard Business Review, 45*(2), 90–98.

Levinson, H. (1980). Criteria for choosing chief executives. *Harvard Business Review, 58*, 113–120.

Levinson, H. (1985). Fate, fads, and the fickle fingers thereof. *Consulting Psychology Bulletin, 37*, 3–11.

Levinson, H. (1993). The practitioner as diagnostic instrument. In A. Howard (Ed.), *Diagnosis for organizational change*. New York: Guilford Press.

Levinson, H. (1997). Organizational character. *Consulting Psychology Journal: Practice and Research, 49*(4), 246–255.

Levinson, H. (2002a). *Organizational assessment: A step-by-step guide to effective consulting*. Washington, DC: American Psychological Association.

Levinson, H. (2002b). Psychological consultation to organizations: Linking assessment and intervention. In R. L. Lowman (Ed.), *Handbook of organizational consulting psychology* (xx). San Francisco: Jossey-Bass.

Levinson, H., Price, C. R., Munden, K. J., Mandl, H. J., & Solley, C. M. (1962). *Men, management and mental health*. Cambridge, MA: Harvard University Press.

Levinson, H., & Rosenthal, S. (1984). *CEO: Corporate leadership in action*. New York: Basic Books.

Lowman, R. L. (Ed.). (1998). *The ethical practice of psychology in organizations*. Washington, DC: American Psychological Association.

Maccoby, M. (2000). Narcissistic leaders: The incredible pros; the inevitable cons. *Harvard Business Review, 78*, 68–78.

McLean, B. (2001, December 24). Why Enron went bust. *Fortune*, 58–68.

Meltzer, H. (1944). Approach of the clinical psychologist to management relationships. *Journal of Consulting Psychology, 8*, 165–174.

Menninger, K. A. (1962). *A manual for psychiatric case study*. (2nd ed.). Philadelphia: Grune & Stratton.

Milkovich, G. T., & Wigdor, A. K. (Eds.). (1991). *Pay for performance: Evaluating performance appraisal and merit pay*. Washington, DC: National Academy Press.

Miller, D. (1990). *The Icarus paradox*. New York: HarperCollins.

Nadler, D. A., & Tushman, M. L. (1988). A model for diagnosing organizational behavior. In M. L. Tushman & W. L. Moore (Eds.), (2nd ed.) (pp. 148–163). Cambridge, MA: Ballinger.

Odiorne, G. S., & Rummler, G. A. (1988). *Training and development: A guide for professionals*. Chicago: Commerce Clearing House.

Racker, H. (1968). *Transference and countertransference*. Madison, CT: International Universities Press.

Roberts, W. (1991). *Leadership secrets of Attila the Hun*. New York: Warner Books.

Schein, E. H. (1985). *Corporate cultures and leadership*. San Francisco: Jossey-Bass.

Schein, E. H. (1999). *Process consultation revisited: Building the helping relationship.* Reading, MA: Addison-Wesley.

Schwartz, H. S. (1990). *Narcissistic process in corporate decay: The theory of the organizational ideal.* New York: New York University Press.

Shapiro, E. C. (1995). *Fad surfing in the boardroom.* Reading, MA: Addison-Wesley.

Silzer, R. (2002). Selecting leaders at the top: Exploring the complexities of executive fit. In R. Silzer (Ed.), *The 2lst century executive.* San Francisco: Jossey-Bass.

Stevenson, H. H., & Cruikshank, J. L. (1998). *Do lunch or be lunch.* Boston: Harvard Business School Press.

Taylor, F. W. (1911). *The principles of scientific management.* New York: HarperCollins.

Trice, H. M., & Beyer, J. M. (1984). Studying organizational cultures through rites and ceremonials. *Academy of Management Review, 49,* 653–669.

Trist, E. L., & Murray, H. (Eds.) (1997). *The social engagement of social science: A Tavistock anthology:* Philadelphia: University of Pennsylvania Press.

Vancil, R. F. (1987). *Passing the baton: Managing the process of CEO selection.* Boston: Harvard Business School Press.

Von Bertalanffy, L. (1950). An outline of general systems theory. *British Journal of Philosophical Science, 1,* 134–163.

Waclawski, J., & Church, A. H. (Eds.). (2002). *Organizational development: A data-driven approach to organizational change.* San Francisco: Jossey-Bass.

Weaver, P. H. (1988). *The suicidal corporation: How big business fails America.* New York: Simon & Schuster.

Weisbord, M. R. (1978). *Organizational diagnosis: A workbook of theory and practice.* Reading, MA: Addison-Wesley.

Zaleznik, A. (1989). *The managerial mystique.* New York: HarperCollins.

# CHAPTER FOURTEEN

# Organizational Evaluation: Issues and Methods

E. Jane Davidson
*The Evaluation Center*
*Western Michigan University*

Constantly changing market conditions provide a formidable challenge for almost all business organizations in the new millennium (Cotter, 1995; Deevy, 1995). In order to survive in the past, an organization needed a technological or resource advantage that was sustainable, usually because it was difficult to obtain or to imitate (Barney, 1986; Porter, 1988). At the current pace of change, simply having a better product or method is not enough; organizations need to be able to *constantly produce* new and better ways of doing things more effectively than their competitors (Tropman, 1998). Thus, the long-term edge appears to be in the capability of producing advantages rather than in the current advantage itself.

## BUILDING ORGANIZATIONAL LEARNING CAPACITY

How can consulting psychologists help organizations build this capacity to create new and innovative ways of doing business? There is a growing body of theoretical and empirical literature suggesting that the ability constantly to improve and produce competitive advantages depends largely on the organization's ability to *learn* from its own experience (DiBella & Nevis, 1998; Dodgson, 1993; Easterby-Smith, 1997), as well as the experience of others.

New organizational knowledge can come from two possible sources: from within the organization, and from outside it. In order to gather information from outside, organizations need to build capabilities in environmental scanning

(DiBella & Nevis, 1998), and scenario planning (De Geus, 1997). In order to generate knowledge from within the organization, the primary sources are innovation and experimentation with new ideas and methods (Brown & Eisenhardt, 1998; Csikszentmihalyi, 1996), and systematic evaluation of these ideas and methods in order to distinguish which have the greatest value for further development (Davidson, 2001; Sathe & Davidson, 2000; Scriven, 1991).

### The Consulting Psychologist's Role

The focus of this chapter is on the issues a consulting psychologist might encounter when helping an organization with the task of learning through the systematic evaluation of organizational successes and failures. Issues explored will include the practical and methodological challenges of deciding what criteria should be used in an evaluation, how performance against these criteria should be assessed and then condensed into a concise, comprehensible format, as well as which of the various possible approaches to evaluation consulting should be employed.

To illustrate many of the points listed above, a consulting project will be described in which the organizational learning capacity of a small biotechnology startup company was evaluated. This project was somewhat unusual because it involved a whole-organization evaluation at the organizational culture level of analysis, as opposed to the evaluation of a specific intervention, program, or system. However, the general principles and processes are the same as for any other evaluation, so the reader should readily be able to see how they might be applied to another type of evaluand (that is, the organization's intervention program, policies, strategy, etc. being evaluated). The added advantage of using this as an example is that it also allows some further exploration of what it means to build a *learning culture* within an organization—a topic likely to be of interest to consulting psychologists with interests in organization development.

The aim of this chapter is not only to contribute a number of useful methodologies from the discipline of evaluation to the consulting psychologist's tool kit, but also to raise awareness of some of the key political, psychological, and practical issues that are important in this kind of work. I will begin with explanations of some important concepts and definitions (specifically, of evaluation and organizational learning), before exploring and addressing each of the issues mentioned above.

# DEFINITIONS

The literature abounds with definitions of organizational learning, ranging from "the detection and correction of error" (Argyris & Schön, 1978, p. 2) to "the capacity or processes within an organization to maintain or improve performance based on experience" (DiBella & Nevis, 1998, p. 28). Based on a synthesis of the most useful definitions in the literature, the term *organizational learning* is used in this chapter to refer to the purposeful acquisition, creation, evaluation, and dissemination of important knowledge about organizational effectiveness, and the use of that knowledge to improve it. In this chapter, the terms *learning organization* and *learning-enabled organization* are used to refer to organizations that acquire, create, evaluate, and disseminate knowledge more effectively than most organizations, while *learning-impaired* organizations are those that do this poorly.

The term *evaluation,* though used in a myriad of different ways in conversational English, has very specific connotations when used to refer to the core activities of a professional evaluator. Evaluation is the systematic determination of the quality or value of something (Scriven, 1991). This means that the conclusions drawn about a program, project, strategy, organization, or other evaluand are clearly and explicitly evaluative. This is in contrast with the usual forms of *descriptive* organizational research, where the client organization might be presented with a range of metrics from which each individual reader is then expected to draw his or her own conclusions (see, for example, Lawler, Seashore, & Mirvis, 1983).

The importance of translating descriptive data into explicitly evaluative conclusions turns out to be a major practical issue in organizational evaluation. Two important goals for this chapter are to persuade readers of the necessity of moving beyond descriptive research, and to demonstrate that doing so can be done validly. It is argued that the findings of organizational evaluations will be considerably more useful to stakeholders if three extra steps are taken beyond the simple collection and presentation of descriptive data: (1) being explicit about how meritorious or valuable particular results are; (2) being explicit about the relative importance of results on various dimensions; and (3) condensing detailed performance profiles into concise evaluative conclusions. These steps are referred to in this paper as *merit determination, importance determination,* and *synthesis.* Later in the chapter, reasons for the necessity of each will be outlined, as will some of the methods required.

# METHODOLOGICAL AND PRACTICAL ISSUES IN ORGANIZATIONAL EVALUATION

The evaluation of any organization, program, policy, practice, or system is a complex task involving a great many considerations, not all of which can be examined in a chapter of this length. Instead, a subset of issues has been selected that should be of interest to the consulting psychologist working at the organizational level of analysis. The issues presented are a blend of methodological and practical concerns, many of which are strongly linked to the psychology and politics of evaluation consulting in organizations. Questions facing the consulting psychologist include: (1) Against what criteria should any particular evaluand be evaluated?; (2) Is it sufficient simply to present factual results and let others draw their own conclusions about overall quality, value, or effectiveness?; (3) What should constitute *excellent* performance on these criteria, as opposed to *good, mediocre,* or *unacceptable* performance?; (4) How can one determine whether any of these criteria are more important than the others?; (5) How can all this information be combined to provide a concise, understandable summary of (in this case) the organization's learning capacity?; and (6) To what extent (and in what capacity) should organizational members be actively involved in the evaluation process?

## Selecting Appropriate Criteria

There are a number of potential sources of information for determining the criteria against which organizations and programs should be evaluated. The three most critical sources are: (1) the definition of a good program—or, in this case, a good (that is, well-functioning) learning organization; (2) a needs assessment; and (3) a list of other relevant values (Scriven, 1991). The question of what constitutes an excellent program (or, in this case, a highly learning-enabled organization) represents a general set of criteria that can be applied to any organization; the needs assessment is used to uncover organization-specific considerations. Finally, a checklist of other relevant values (such as ethical and legal standards) is needed to ensure that the criterion list is complete.

**Defining a Good Program.** Consulting psychologists necessarily operate under a range of different budgetary and political constraints, each of which might require a quite different approach to defining criteria. Three options are outlined here, along with considerations for choosing which to use. First, an experienced evaluator who has observed many examples of this type of program or organization might be able to list several features that distinguish a well-functioning one from a poorly-functioning one, without conducting a great deal of additional research. This is the fastest and cheapest way of producing a criterion list, although its completeness and accuracy are highly dependent on the consulting psychologist's knowledge.

The second option is to work with members of the client organization to collectively generate a list of criteria. This might be done with a brainstorming exercise, followed by a facilitated discussion in which criteria are sorted for relevance. This option is clearly preferable in the case where client buy-in to the criteria is a major issue, or when there is a strong interest in building organizational members' capacity to think critically about effectiveness, and to evaluate their own programs and interventions. A major downside of this approach is the considerable time and productivity costs to the organization; not only does this lengthen the time line for the entire evaluation, it also requires a considerable allocation of employee time away from their regular jobs.

The third method for identifying criteria that distinguish good programs from poor ones is to obtain this information from the relevant literature. This is a particularly important source when the evaluand is complex, when the consulting psychologist has not conducted multiple evaluations of this type before, and when the client organization does not have the resources to allocate staff time to involvement in the evaluation effort.

**Applied Example: Defining the Learning-Enabled Organization.** The criteria developed for the evaluation described in this chapter were generated using the third strategy described above (drawing on the relevant theoretical and empirical literature), due to the complexity of the organizational learning concept. I began with a review and summary of the relevant theoretical and empirical literature, and then grouped the main findings into similar themes (for full details, see Davidson, 2001). The intent was to produce five to ten major themes that were reasonably distinct and similar in scope (in terms of breadth, specificity, and conceptual level of analysis). These dimensions would provide the basis for distinguishing a learning-enabled organization from a learning-disabled one, and would therefore make valid criteria against which to evaluate an organization's learning capacity.

Using this process, it was found that the five dimensions of organizational learning identified in Senge's well-known framework (1990), namely (1) building personal mastery, (2) challenging mental models, (3) creating a shared vision, (4) team learning, and (5) systems thinking, covered a reasonably large proportion of the concepts unearthed in the organizational learning literature. However, three critical elements of organizational learning were missing that emerged repeatedly in a number of other theoretical and empirical sources. These were (6) external and future scanning (looking beyond the organization to understand both the organization's environment and its possible futures), (7) organizational innovation and experimentation, and (8) the systematic evaluation of successes and failures. The eight major themes, along with their operational subdefinitions (more specific descriptions of the subelements that constituted each major dimension) are outlined in Table 14.1.

**Needs Assessment.** As most organizational consultants know, each client organization has a different set of issues and concerns. Additionally, every group of stakeholders within the organization—from management, marketing, and human resources to front-line workers, union representatives, and customers—has a

Table 14.1. Concepts Underlying the Key Criteria for Evaluating Learning Culture.

| Dimension | Definition | Key Learning Culture Concepts |
|---|---|---|
| Personal Mastery | Maintaining the creative tension between personal vision (ambitious, meaningful goals), and the truth about current performance (DiBella & Nevis, 1998; Sathe, 2000; Senge, 1990) | • Pursuit and attainment of high, inspiring goals<br>• Relentless pursuit of the truth about one's own performance<br>• Shared understanding of the true gap between current and desired performance |
| Mental Models | Challenging and testing deeply ingrained assumptions (Senge, 1990), theories in use (Argyris, 1993), and sacred cows (Sathe, 2000) | • Diversity of thought truly valued<br>• No sacred cows (undiscussables)<br>• Strong sense of trust (for example, safe to criticize) |
| Shared Vision | Sense of shared purpose (Senge, 1990), shared identity and organizational persona (De Geus, 1997) | • Shared vision (and genuine commitment to it)<br>• Long-term commitment to organization, sense of community, and shared identity<br>• People exercise good judgment and common sense in work |
| Team Learning | Team dialogue (Argyris, 1992), synergy (spontaneous, coordinated action; Senge, 1990); knowledge creation and sharing (Nonaka & Takeuchi, 1995) | • Team synergy and intelligence<br>• True dialogue used; few defensive routines<br>• Good cross-project communication |
| Systems Thinking | Understanding interdependence among units (DiBella & Nevis, 1998); seeing causal loops (Senge, 1990) | • Understanding interdependence of different parts of the organization<br>• Looking for systemic causes of problems and causal loops |
| External and Future Scanning | Scanning the external environment (DiBella & Nevis, 1998); creating memories of the future (De Geus, 1997); embracing continuous change | • Awareness of the external environment<br>• Awareness of possible changes in the future<br>• Change seen as a natural part of organizational life |

*(Continued)*

Table 14.1. (*Continued*)

| Dimension | Definition | Key Learning Culture Concepts |
|---|---|---|
| Experimentation | Constant generation of and experimentation with new ideas and methods (Csikszentmihalyi, 1996; Brown & Eisenhardt, 1998) | • Support of risk-taking<br>• Diversity of practice (variety of methods in existence)<br>• Marketplace for ideas<br>• Streamlining and constant improvement |
| Systematic Evaluation | State-of-the-art, systematic evaluation of methods, products, personnel, policies, and programs (Sathe & Davidson, 2000; Scriven, 1991) | • True value focus in personnel evaluation<br>• Flexible use of goals<br>• Use of multiple perspectives<br>• Finger on the pulse of customer needs<br>• Benchmarking quality against competitors, best practice |

different set of opinions as to what the real problem is. How is the consulting psychologist supposed to sift through these concerns and uncover the real needs of the organization, as opposed to the whims and wishes of the various stakeholder groups?

One of the key distinctions that evaluators have learned to make is the one between *wants* and *needs*. A need is something without which *dysfunction* occurs (Scriven, 1991). It might be conscious or unconscious, met or unmet. In contrast, a *want* is a conscious desire for something without which *dissatisfaction* (but not dysfunction) occurs. When conducting a needs assessment, then, it is important to focus on actual performance issues (as evidence of unmet needs), and on instances of excellence (as examples of situations in which needs are being met very well), and looking at contrasts between these success stories and problem areas to find the differences. This is in contrast to the *satisfaction survey* approach, in which the loudest grumble with the most votes tends to be erroneously equated with the area of greatest need for the organization—a potentially costly misattribution.

For a large-scale evaluation, a needs assessment should be comprehensive, and should cover the three levels of organizational analysis—individual, group, and organizational. For a project with a smaller budget or a shorter time line, it might be necessary to focus the needs assessment at the one or two levels that will provide answers to the most pressing questions for the client organization. The main point here is that this decision should be a deliberate rather than a haphazard one, made after thoroughly investigating and considering the organization's true informational needs (which might differ considerably from the initial request made by a single stakeholder or group).

**Applied Example: Conducting the Needs Assessment for Biosleep.** For the case being presented in this chapter, the participating organization (a small biotechnology startup company on the U.S. east coast) had two primary needs. Needs are defined here as levels of performance that were required for the organization to function effectively and survive. First, because the firm's primary consideration was the creation of innovative products that would attract investor funding, the most important need was to have a work environment in which organizational members felt enabled to reach their full potential in adding value to the organization. Of secondary significance, given the knowledge-intensive nature of the enterprise, was the retention of talent.

Other potential outcome variables (such as organizational financial performance and projected long-term survival) were considered, but were excluded from the focus of this evaluation after discussions with the client. The nature of the organization (a startup) meant that both of these variables would have been difficult, time-consuming, and therefore expensive to measure. In addition, distal outcomes such as these are affected by a plethora of extraneous, uncontrollable variables (for example, market fluctuations). In such cases, the pragmatic consulting psychologist often needs to focus an evaluation in light of practical considerations as well as the information needs of the client.

**Other Relevant Values.** The third source of criteria in any evaluation is a checklist of other relevant standards. These include whether the program or organization is operating in accordance with relevant legal and ethical principles (for example, equal opportunity employment practices), as well as adherence to any relevant professional or scientific standards. Criteria such as these are generally used as standalone warning flags, rather than considerations that are weighted and balanced alongside the other criteria. Thus, as long as the program or organization is minimally acceptable on each of them, they are typically not included in the synthesis step. For Biosleep, no evidence was uncovered that suggested violations of legal or ethical standards were present.

## Beyond Data Collection and Description

Is it enough for the consulting psychologist to identify a set of relevant criteria, measure performance against them, and then simply present results, allowing various stakeholder groups to draw their own conclusions based on their own values? Some writers argue that this is the only defensible strategy, since the only alternative is to impose the evaluator's (arbitrary) values on the results (see, for example, Mohr, 1999; Stake, 1998). To use an example from the evaluation of organizational change, this is equivalent to saying that it is a mere matter of opinion whether a mass exodus of top performers is a good or bad outcome, or that it is more or less important than a decrease in morale among the remaining employees. It is true that the task of determining the relative value of these results is challenging, and it requires that multiple perspectives be taken into account. However, this is by no means impossible to do with a level of precision appropriate for the context, as will be shown in this chapter.

In the following sections, I will outline the importance of (and some specific methods for) taking three extra steps beyond the collection and presentation of descriptive data: (1) converting descriptive results into explicit determinations of merit; (2) determining the relative importance of the various results; and (3) combining performance results on the various dimensions of merit to yield more concise evaluative conclusions. These steps are referred to in this chapter as *merit determination, importance determination,* and *synthesis.* I will begin with a discussion of the merit determination step, before moving on to the synthesis issue (importance determination will be addressed under synthesis for the sake of clarity).

**Merit Determination.** More often than not, an evaluation report has to be delivered to stakeholders who do not have substantive expertise in the area of organizational learning. For this audience, there is a need for well-founded, objective, and unambiguous conclusions about the relative efficacy or cost-effectiveness of the results in question. What should constitute excellent performance on the organizational learning capacity criteria, as opposed to good, mediocre, or unacceptable performance? The step from factual results to an explicit statement about program or organizational merit requires the application of relevant values, or standards, to those results (Scriven, 1991).

**General Principles for Merit Determination.** Professional evaluators have struggled for decades with the sticky issue of how to ascribe value to descriptive findings. While there are no hard-and-fast guidelines, there are certainly some simple strategies available that can help the practitioner dispel accusations of subjectivity by detailing exactly the basis on which the conclusions were drawn. While this will not eliminate objections to the conclusions, it can at least shift the debate from "who decides the criteria" (a question implicitly laced with accusations of arbitrariness and the use of personal preferences) to "how are the criteria determined" (a much more constructive dialogue, and one that learning organizations should in any case be engaging in as a matter of course).

On what basis should the merit of particular results be determined? One strong (but misguided) temptation is to ascribe merit on the basis of goal achievement. In other words, are we doing better, worse, or about the same as we had hoped to do? The problem with this as a standard is that the value of achieving the original goal (if indeed goals exist) then has to be justified. After all, clearing an easy target is clearly not as meritorious as a near miss on a tough one. What standards should be used instead?

The answer is to go back to the organization's needs. Almost all organizations operate in an environment that is competitive to some extent. While business organizations obviously compete for customers, even nonprofit and governmental organizations compete with other organizations for scarce resources (funding) and talent. Therefore, a valid source of standards for organizational evaluation is how well an organization (or a program within an organization) is doing relative to competitors in any of the above arenas.

Getting from factual results to explicit conclusions about merit involves two challenging steps. First, the appropriate criteria must be identified with a thorough diagnosis of the organization's performance issues and the factors that drive those issues. As mentioned earlier, this will be done either by the consultant alone, or by the consultant in collaboration with members of the client organization, depending on the goals and resources for the evaluation project. Second, standards must be created for converting raw results on these criteria into explicit statements about how good (or poor) those results are. Again, a broad range of options exists with respect to the extent of client involvement in this process; guidelines for deciding on the right approach will be explored later in the chapter. In the next two subsections, some guidelines are given for the merit determination step, focusing first on outcomes, and then on the drivers of those outcomes.

**Methods for Merit Determination: Outcomes.** An example of how the merit determination step might be done with outcome data is shown in Table 14.2. This broad-brush, rubric-based approach categorizes organizational performance on the criterion in question into one of five categories—excellent, very good, good, satisfactory, and poor—where excellent corresponds to a clear example of best practice or exceptionally good performance, and poor signifies a significant performance problem or area of organizational dysfunction. The consultant's task in this case is to assemble the various different pieces of data and determine which merit category they most closely match.

The scale shown in Table 14.2 is deliberately not balanced so that satisfactory is at the midpoint of the scale. The rationale for this is simple: If an organization's performance on a particular criterion is less than satisfactory, then it is a moot point whether this performance is *somewhat* or *very* poor. This clearly identifies a problem area with a need for action, on which failure to act will lead to poor organizational health, possibly even death. The poor rating in a diagnostic evaluation such as this is both a conversation starter and an alarm bell, not an end in itself.

**Methods for Merit Determination: Drivers.** While the determination of merit is a relatively straightforward task for outcomes such as employee retention, it is considerably more complex for the softer variables in an evaluation of

Table 14.2. Rubric for Converting Retention Data into Determinations of Merit.

| Merit Level | Corresponding Evidence* |
| --- | --- |
| Excellent | • *Extremely low* voluntary turnover (compared to industry average) in past one to two years; mostly *functional* turnover (poorer performers leaving)<br>• Vast majority (more than 90 percent) of employees report a strong intent to stay (that is, would leave only if an *exceptional* opportunity arose)<br>• Very high levels of organizational commitment and loyalty (vast majority scored over 4 on the five-point scale) |
| Very good | • *Very low* dysfunctional voluntary turnover (i.e., better performers leaving) in past one to two years (well below industry average)<br>• Most (more than 70 percent) employees report a strong intent to stay (that is, would leave only if an *exceptional* opportunity arose)<br>• High levels of organizational commitment and loyalty (more than 70 percent scored at least 4 on the five-point scale) |
| Good | • *Low* voluntary turnover in past one to two years (below industry average)<br>• More than half of employees report a strong intent to stay (that is, would leave only if an *exceptional* opportunity arose)<br>• No more than 10 percent of employees report a low intent to stay (that is, are currently looking for alternative work)<br>• Quite high levels of organizational commitment and loyalty (more than 70 percent scored at least 3 on the five-point scale) |
| Satisfactory | • *Acceptable* voluntary turnover in past one to two years (in line with industry average); level of *dysfunctional* turnover (that is, high-performing employees leaving of their own accord) not causing serious problems<br>• Most employees report a strong intent to stay, but a significant number are seriously considering leaving<br>• Acceptable levels of organizational commitment and loyalty (more than half scored at least 3 on the five-point scale) |
| Poor | • Voluntary, dysfunctional employee turnover a *significant* problem<br>• Several (more than 20 percent) high-performing employees report that they are currently looking for work elsewhere<br>• Low levels of organizational commitment and loyalty (fewer than half scored at least 3 on the five-point scale) |

*Note:* Not every single item of evidence needs to be present in any one case.

organizational learning capacity (such as the dimensions of the learning culture). For example, what should we say about an organization that scores 3.5 on a five-point scale measuring Personal Mastery? Determining whether a score of 3.5 is good, very good, or just satisfactory might be criticized as a purely arbitrary decision by a stakeholder who takes exception to your findings, unless there is a solid rationale for the conclusion.

The fact that evaluation consultants come under fire so frequently for even the most innocuous conclusions likely underlies the reluctance of many practitioners to bother with this extra step. When anxiety about adverse consequences to the consultant becomes strong, it is tempting simply to let each of the stakeholder groups draw its own conclusions about what a score of 3.5 means *to them*. The problem, of course, is that responsibility for the difficult step from descriptive results to evaluative conclusions now falls into the hands of people with less expertise in both evaluation and organizational psychology, less familiarity with the measures used, and a higher likelihood of having a personal agenda that would be served by viewing results in a favorable or unfavorable light. For the conscientious evaluator operating under these conditions, the only viable solution is to take responsibility for converting descriptive data into explicit determinations of merit. This means not only stating whether the above result is good, very good, or satisfactory, but also being able to clearly demonstrate how that determination was made, and to enter into a constructive dialogue with anyone who raises valid questions or objections.

The role of the consulting psychologist being advocated in this situation is clearly that of an expert advisor rather than a decision-making facilitator or collector of organizational opinions. The conditions under which one might use a facilitated approach will be discussed in depth later in the chapter. The purpose of this section is to describe some methodological tools that can be used by the evaluation team to convert descriptive results on soft variables into explicit determinations of merit.

One methodological strategy we saw in the evaluation of results on outcomes (see Table 14.2) is the use of industry-specific comparison data. This is considerably more difficult to obtain with organizational culture measures (which often need to be tailored to the client organization) for two main reasons. First, most organizations do not measure these variables on an ongoing basis as they might with some more concrete variables, for example, organizational turnover. Second, those that do measure their culture regularly probably use quite different measurement tools. What, then, should be the principles for determining merit on organizational culture variables?

Two strategies come into play here, each of which feeds into the other. First, qualitative data (such as interview, focus group, and questionnaire comments) should be used to build a better understanding of the quantitative data obtained.

This can be done at two phases in the evaluation. At pilot study stage, respondents selected from a cross-section of the organization should be asked by the consulting psychologist to describe the organizational reality they associate with particular numerical ratings on quantitative items. This process not only allows for a better in-depth understanding of what survey items mean to people in the organization, but also helps ensure that items revised after such input tap what the consulting psychologist intended. Triangulation (that is, using different types of data from different sources to check consistency) should also be a feature of regular data collection. Here, the consulting psychologist can provide opportunities for respondents to give reasons for their ratings. Again, this gives a better sense of what participants really *mean* when their scale scores are, say, 4.0 versus 3.0.

The second strategy available to the evaluation consultant is to *anchor* (or label) the top end of the scale with a clear example of existing best practice on that dimension, and the bottom with a real example of poor performance on this dimension. This ensures that it is clearly possible to achieve scores at either end of the scale, and reduces central-tendency error (excessive bunching of scores around the middle of the scale). It also provides a nonarbitrary basis for inferring that a score of 1 or 2 is consistent with a learning-impaired organization, whereas a score of 4 or 5 is consistent with one that is learning-enabled.

As with the guidelines for outcome variables, the merit determination step for the organizational culture criteria should also be based on a synthesis of qualitative and quantitative data. A general rubric the evaluator might use, possibly in collaboration with organizational members (see the discussion later in this chapter about choosing the most appropriate role for the consulting psychologist), is shown in Table 14.3. Data should be matched with the merit category that best matches the description in the rubric. In the case of wildly discrepant information that makes merit determination ambiguous, the consulting psychologist should go back to the appropriate part of the organization for deeper exploration, rather than simply averaging the evidence (or worse, disregarding some of it).

## Synthesis

A diagnostic evaluation of organizational learning capacity needs to include all twenty-six subdimensions of the learning culture (see Table 14.1), and can encompass many more, depending on the scope of the evaluation. As discussed in the previous section, converting raw results into determinations of merit goes some way toward easing the stakeholder's burden in interpreting them. However, it is clear that even if the merit determination step is done, a profile of performance on the twenty-six subdimensions of organizational learning

Table 14.3. General Rubric for Evaluating Learning Culture Subdimensions.

| Merit Level | Corresponding Evidence |
| --- | --- |
| Excellent | • Clear example of exemplary practice on this dimension<br>• Median scale score at least 4.5 on a five-point scale; almost all scores above 4.0 |
| Very Good | • Clear example of very good practice on this dimension, although improvement is possible on some minor aspects<br>• Median scale score generally between 4.0 and 4.5 on a five-point scale; almost all scores above 3.0 |
| Good | • Promising performance in many respects, but some nontrivial areas for improvement<br>• Median scale score generally between 3.25 and 4.0 on a five-point scale; almost all scores above 2.5, very few higher than 4.0 |
| Satisfactory | • Adequate performance; some fairly substantial areas for improvement<br>• Median scale score generally between 2.75 and 3.25 on a five-point scale; almost all scores above 2.0, very few higher than 3.75 |
| Poor | • Clear example of below satisfactory performance; evidence of serious weaknesses that hinder the organization's ability to learn<br>• Median scale score generally below 2.75 on a five-point scale; almost all scores below 3.5 |

capacity is still too much detail to give a time-pressured executive audience (Cox, 1988). Thus, the evaluator's task is not finished until these results are condensed (that is, synthesized) into a more concise form that meets the needs of the audience (Scriven, 1994). This turns out to be one of the most challenging problems in the discipline of evaluation, and is certainly a critical issue in the evaluation of organizational learning capacity.

Some organizational change and evaluation experts have argued that any attempt to weight the results in terms of importance would be simply an attempt arbitrarily to impose the researcher's values on the data (see, for example, Mohr, 1999; Lawler et al., 1983). The problem of dealing with multiple stakeholders' values has long been debated within the discipline of evaluation, with some authors contending that multiple perspectives simply cannot be synthesized (see, for example, Stake, 1998). There are two major problems with this stance. The first is fundamentally a practical concern. Managers and other decision-makers typically do not have the time, the expertise, or the inclination to sift through all the data, weight it according to what is most important, and synthesize the results themselves.

The second problem with allowing the reader to apply his or her own values and interpret the data relates to validity. The values of the various organizational stakeholders are not simply random perspectives, each of which is equally important. Ultimately, the organization's very survival hinges primarily on meeting the needs of its most important stakeholders—the consumers (Scriven, 1991). The needs, wants, and preferences of employees, management, and stockholders are also important, because they provide the means through which this is accomplished. However, an organization that allows the values of these groups to be placed above those of the consumers (for example, by not being sufficiently explicit about which results have greater value) runs the risk of losing sight of its greatest priority.

Synthesis involves two major components. First, the consulting psychologist needs a way to determine the relative *importance* of the results obtained on multiple dimensions—an independently verifiable method that goes beyond merely asking the opinions of a few stakeholders. Why is it necessary to know the relative importance of the dimensions? If an organization does poorly on one of the most critical aspects of organizational learning, this is clearly much more serious than doing poorly on something of minor importance.

The second phase of synthesis is having a methodology that validly but simply allows multiple subevaluations (how well the organization has done on all the various organizational learning subdimensions) to be combined into a more concise form. This allows for an appropriate presentation of results to a busy audience, and (with the importance weightings) indicates the level of urgency required for improvement.

Most consulting psychologists will agree that clients seldom request information about the methodological details used in the creation of a consulting report. While this is generally true in my experience as well, I find it to be less so for evaluation projects in which I draw explicitly evaluative conclusions. When an organization is told that its performance on one of these dimensions is satisfactory, there is often a much stronger interest in how this result was obtained than if descriptive data are presented. For this reason, I have found it useful to construct my reports in three layers of detail (executive summary, short report, and detailed appendices), with extensive cross-referencing so that the interested reader can easily find explanations of how results were obtained.

In the following sections, each of the above components (importance determination and the combination of subevaluations) will be described, along with illustrative examples from the specific case mentioned earlier in the chapter. For each component, the main challenges are explained, and then practical strategies for dealing with these issues are outlined and illustrated.

**Importance Determination.** How might an evaluator determine which of the eight organizational learning subdimensions are the most important for a particular organization? Clearly this has the potential to vary widely across industry, national or cultural context, and organizational size and stage of development, making a one-size-fits-all approach inappropriate (Davidson, 2001). As with the merit determination step, this turns out to be considerably simpler for outcome variables than for the learning culture dimensions that drive those outcomes.

In the example case of the biotechnology startup company (referred to here as Biosleep), two key outcome variables were included in the evaluation: the extent to which individuals felt enabled to add value in their jobs, and individual intent to leave the organization. The relative importance of these two outcomes was determined using a *potential impact* approach to needs assessment. In-depth discussion with key organizational stakeholders was used to ascertain the severity of negative impact that poor performance on each criterion would have for the organization, and the magnitude of positive impact that good performance would have on the organization. The more dramatic the consequences of high or low performance for an organization and its stakeholders, the more important the outcome was deemed to be. Results of this assessment indicated that the importance of individual ability to add value is extremely high, and that of employee retention is high (see Table 14.4); key organizational stakeholders concurred with this assessment.

Determining the importance of the learning culture dimensions is a considerably more complex procedure. This is because high performance on these dimensions is valuable not in its own right, but primarily because of the potential

Table 14.4. Potential Impact Assessment for Outcome Variables.

| Outcome Variable | Potential Impact of Excellent or Poor Performance | Importance |
|---|---|---|
| Individual ability to add value | • Quality and productivity of the creative process (which drives product quality, and is therefore central to organizational survival) is heavily dependent on each individual's ability to add maximum value in his or her position | Extremely high |
| Employee retention (esp. of top performers) | • Continuity important for the development of a particular product, and desirable across multiple projects due to cumulative learning effects<br>• Employees have high levels of very specific expertise, are hard to replace, and carry significant organizational knowledge | High |

impact it likely has on important outcomes such as those described above. Accordingly, the key to determining the relative importance of these dimensions is tied to looking at the *causal links* between culture dimensions and outcomes.

In the case example in this chapter, I used a combination of qualitative and quantitative evidence to ascertain the strengths of the causal links. Causal analysis involves the systematic elimination of competing explanations, for which potential sources of evidence include scatterplots, correlation and regression analyses, and causal tracing techniques similar to those used by detectives (for more in-depth information about practical causal tracing techniques, see Davidson, 2000; Miles & Huberman, 1994; Scriven, 1974). In this case, a *strong link* was defined as one for which multiple sources of information (for example, correlations, interviews, and causal traces or clues) were strongly indicative of a substantial effect. *Weaker links* were those in which either the size of the effect was less, or not all evidence supported it. *Very weak and nonexistent links* were those for which the evidence was either highly contradictory or insubstantial.

The relative importance of the learning culture dimensions was based on the following guidelines: *Extremely important* dimensions were those with the strongest links to important outcome variables; *very important* dimensions had at least moderate links to the most important outcome variable; *moderately important* dimensions had weak links to both outcome variables; and *desirable* learning culture dimensions had very weak links only to the most important outcome (see Figure 14.1).

**Synthesis.** Condensing the results on the twenty-six subdimensions of the learning culture requires that these performances be combined into a more condensed profile of organizational learning capacity on the eight main learning culture dimensions. For example, Table 14.5 shows that Biosleep was rated very good, very good, and satisfactory on the three subdimensions of Shared Vision. What overall rating should it receive on Shared Vision?

A common response to the synthesis problem is to use a quantitative method in which each rating is converted to a numerical score, and the subdimensional scores are averaged to yield an overall rating. However, such a synthesis system could potentially allow an organization or program scoring very low on a

Table 14.5. Learning Culture Profile for Biosleep on "Shared Vision".

| Dimension | Subdimensions | Performance Rating | | | | |
| | | P | S | G | VG | Ex |
|---|---|---|---|---|---|---|
| Shared Vision | *Shared vision and purpose* | | | | | |
| (*very **important***) | *Shared sense of identity* | | | | | |
| | *Using own good judgment* | | | | | |

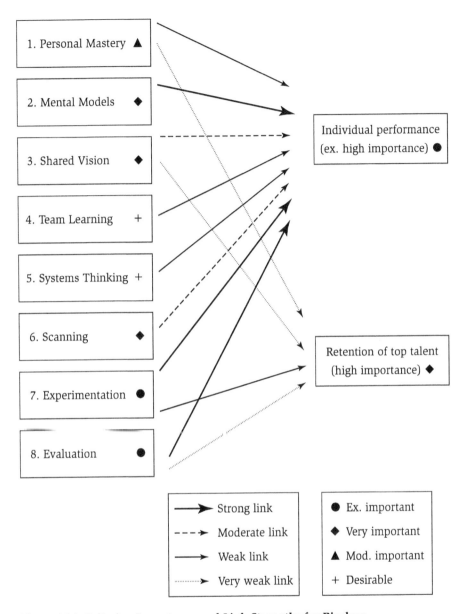

**Figure 14.1 Criterion Importance and Link Strengths for Biosleep.**

relatively important dimension to receive a high overall rating if it does exceptionally well on other dimensions. To use an analogy, this is equivalent to allowing a manager who excels in all the operational and strategic aspects of his or
her job, but consistently fails to provide adequate feedback to subordinates, to
be awarded a bonus for excellent managerial performance. A good synthesis
system must have a valid way of dealing with this problem.

Table 14.6. Guidelines for Synthesizing Subdimensions into Dimensions.

| Dimensional Rating | Median Subdimension Rating[*] | Subdimensions below Good[*] | Subdimensions below Satisfactory[*] |
|---|---|---|---|
| *Excellent* | Excellent | 0 | 0 |
| *Very Good* | Very Good (or better) | 0 | 0 |
| *Good* | Good (or better) | < 35% | 0 |
| *Satisfactory* | Satisfactory (or better) | [no restrictions] | < 35% |
| *Poor* | [no restrictions] | [no restrictions] | [no restrictions] |

[*]Conditions in *all three columns* must be met to receive the corresponding rating.

One solution is to use a *hurdle* principle that requires certain minimal levels of performance for entry into each performance category. Using this principle for the Biosleep case, an algorithm was developed for synthesizing different combinations of subdimension ratings into overall conclusions (see Table 14.6). Full details about how the way in which the algorithm was developed are available in the original study (Davidson, 2001).

For each organizational learning dimension, the median rating on the relevant subdimensions (of which there were between two and five) was the initial criterion used to determine the probable overall rating. The reason for this was twofold: first, it ensured that extreme ratings on one subdimension did not have a disproportionate effect on results; and second, it avoided making the erroneous assumption that the rating categories represented an interval scale (as would have been required had a mean rating been computed).

Using the algorithm in Table 14.2, performances on the twenty-six subdimensions were synthesized to determine merit on the eight main learning culture dimensions. These results are then presented in the form of a prioritized learning culture profile (see Figure 14.2). This allows the client to see at a glance how well the organization is doing on the eight learning culture dimensions, listed in order of importance.

To recap, we have just walked through the first two of three possible synthesis steps—importance determination and partial synthesis. This has allowed us to produce a profile of the organization's learning culture on eight dimensions. Because the dimensions are listed in order of importance, the profile clearly shows where improvements need to be made with the greatest urgency—that is, on those dimensions where importance is greatest and performance is poorest.

As mentioned earlier, one further synthesis step is also possible here, that of combining performance on the eight dimensions above to draw an overall conclusion about the organization's learning capacity. Full details about this step are available elsewhere (Davidson, 2001).

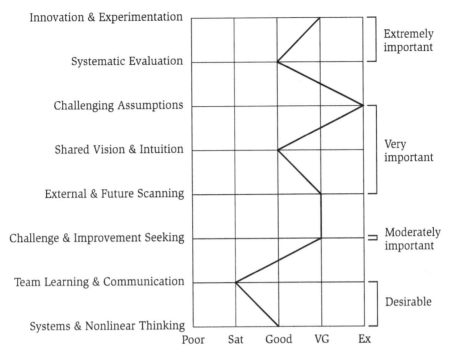

**Figure 14.2 Prioritized Learning Culture Profile for Biosleep.**

## Choosing an Appropriate Evaluation Approach

An important decision for the consulting psychologist in choosing an evaluation approach is the extent to which the evaluation process should involve key stakeholders, and in what capacity. For example, should the consultant be primarily a facilitator of decision-making by stakeholders, an advocate for one or more groups within the organization, or an independent expert delivering an impartial view? In this section, a range of options is briefly outlined, along with guidelines to help the practitioner (or those choosing a practitioner) to make an informed decision.

**Participative and Collaborative Approaches.** There are several versions of highly interactive evaluation currently practiced today, each of which varies in the extent to which decision-making power about the evaluation process is balanced between the evaluation consultant and the participating stakeholders. For example, the consultant's role could be pure facilitation, allowing evaluation participants to make the final decisions on how the evaluation is conducted, and having them alone sign the final report (see, for example, Patton, 1997). This approach maximizes ownership of the evaluation findings, as well as the likelihood that they will be followed up on. Other forms of participatory evaluation typically involve a collaborative effort in which the decision-making power is shared between the consultant and participants (see, for example, Fetterman, Kaftarian, & Wandersman, 1996).

Perhaps the most popular current approach to specifically linking evaluation and organizational learning is evaluative inquiry (Preskill & Torres, 1999). Briefly, evaluative inquiry combines a highly participatory organization development approach (Cummings & Worley, 1999), with Senge's concept of team learning (1990), and some of the more collaborative approaches to evaluation (see, for example, Fetterman et al., 1996; Patton, 1997). An external consultant acts as facilitator and coach, and helps the staff generate questions they have about the organization, and that they feel they need answered in order to advance organizational learning. The group then designs experiments, studies, or evaluations to answer those questions. The eventual aim is that the organization builds its own culture of evaluative inquiry (Owen, 1999), thereby eliminating the need for an external facilitator in the ongoing process.

An important step along the way to becoming a learning organization is certainly the development of an organizational culture in which evaluation is part of everyday organizational life rather than an infrequent event. Highly collaborative approaches focusing on self-evaluation and inquiry, such as Preskill and Torres' (1999), are an important way to build such a culture; however, they do have some important weaknesses. First, such approaches are implicitly based on the assumption that employees are somehow in the best position to decide what ought to be evaluated, and against what standards (if any). Even if the facilitator has substantial subject matter or evaluation expertise, participative inquiry approaches run the risk of gathering only the information the inquiring group *wants*, which may be very different from what the organization as a whole *needs*, especially if that information is seen as potentially threatening or embarrassing to the group carrying out the inquiry, or their superiors (Argyris, 1993). Of course, examination of such issues with the help of a skilled consulting psychologist can be a worthwhile exercise in its own right, especially if it allows organizational members to unlearn dysfunctional beliefs (Imai, Nonaka, & Takeuchi, 1985). However, the consulting psychologist who has committed to an evaluation contract must be mindful of the tradeoffs associated with digressing too far from the agreed-upon task, seeking to renegotiate terms if necessary.

There is a second problem with using a purely collaborative approach to evaluation for organizational learning: it may only allow for incremental improvements in efficiency, rather than in frame-breaking opportunities for innovation. A study of organizational learning in the Organization for Economic Cooperation and Development (OECD; Forss, Cracknell, & Samset, 1994) compared the nature and extent of learning achieved through two approaches to evaluation: involvement and communication. Learning through involvement (that is, a participative approach) was effective for increasing the efficiency, that is, doing things right. However, this approach "neither encourages nor answers questions such as whether the organization does the right things" (p. 588).

**Independent Evaluation.** The opposite end of the continuum from evaluative inquiry is a fully independent evaluation conducted by an outside expert. This approach has several advantages, but also several disadvantages, over the participative and collaborative approaches. For example, research has shown that evaluation reports from external sources give rise to a greater likelihood of new ideas being injected into the organization, leading to greater variation and innovation (Forss et al., 1994). This is consistent with Weiss and Buculavas' finding (1980) that evaluation findings that challenged the status quo were viewed by decision-makers as having higher utility. Both studies serve as useful reminders of the value of external criticism and outside ideas.

There are also strong practical and political reasons why an independent approach might be chosen. First, it is typically far less time-consuming than participatory approaches, which have the added burden of obtaining agreement from multiple stakeholders at multiple decision points throughout the evaluation process. Second, the opportunity costs associated with taking people away from their everyday work are usually substantial.

Independent approaches to evaluation also have the advantage of placing the responsibility for evaluation quality on an individual or team with specific expertise in the area, and experience with other organizations that allows them a broader perspective. In addition, the independent evaluator has a dramatically reduced vested interest in assuring the favorability of results, and is therefore far less likely to be accused of conflict of interest.

The main disadvantages of using an independent evaluator relate to the absence of the benefits of the more collaborative approaches. First, it fails to build the organization's capacity to learn by itself, thereby leaving it largely dependent on external expertise. Second, findings are considerably more likely to be resisted, criticized, and ignored because organizational members might not feel as much a sense of ownership as they would if they had participated in the evaluation. A related issue is the lack of buy-in to changes arising from the evaluation.

**Choosing Among Multiple Evaluative Perspectives.** The above discussion has outlined a number of issues for the consulting psychologist to consider when choosing whether to use a participative and collaborative approach versus a fully independent approach to evaluation. Drawing on these ideas, the following are some simple suggestions for choosing approaches for both a single evaluation project and a longer term commitment.

An independent approach to evaluation is best pursued when (a) there is extreme time pressure to get information quickly, (b) the organization cannot afford to take employees away from their regular work to participate in an evaluation project, (c) accuracy of the evaluation is critical, or (d) the political climate is such that questions are likely to be raised about conflict of interest if the evaluation has heavy internal involvement. Resistance to independent evaluations can be reduced if they make a deliberate point of gathering opinions from all relevant stakeholder groups (as all good evaluations should). The difference between this and a collaborative approach is that organizational members do not have input into decisions about evaluation methodology.

Participative and collaborative approaches (such as evaluative inquiry) are appropriate when (a) there is a need to increase the capacity of individuals and teams to learn about what works in their own organizations, (b) the potential for resistance to findings (or changes arising from those findings) is high, or (c) organizational unlearning is important. In the latter case, organizational stakeholders might be working with faulty assumptions, which they are unlikely to change without directly participating in a joint inquiry and seeing the truth with their own eyes.

## Building Long-Term Learning Capacity: Advice for Organizations

Clearly, each of the approaches described in the previous section has some very important advantages and disadvantages that will make the choice a difficult one in many cases. For the purpose of maximizing the organization's ability to improve its learning capacity, the following long-term strategy is recommended for practitioners wanting to combine the best ideas to improve their own (or their client's) organization's learning capacity.

**Organizational Diagnosis.** Good organizational improvement begins with good diagnosis (Howard, 1994). The organization should obtain an accurate overall assessment of the organization's learning capacity from a consulting psychologist with expertise in evaluation, using the merit determination and synthesis steps outlined in the first half of the chapter. A few key stakeholders should be involved if possible, so that they can learn about the process and explain it to others. This diagnostic evaluation should be used as a starting point for identifying areas where the organization needs to learn and improve.

**Expert-Facilitated Evaluation Interventions.** The second step is to set up one or two expert-facilitated evaluation interventions designed to teach organizational members how to learn about what works (and what they can do better). This is where learning capacity can be built into the organization's competencies. Another worthwhile investment (for larger organizations) is to appoint an internal evaluation consultant to the organizational effectiveness or knowledge management team. There are now many high-quality graduates of organizational and consulting psychology programs who have solid training in evaluation, and would be an excellent resource for ongoing capacity building.

**Integrating the Strategic Plan.** Third, each business unit in the organization should build evaluative learning and improvement into its strategic plan. Performance reviews of the managers running those units should document what their units have learned, and how well their learning capacity is improving. As the old adage says, what gets measured gets done. Many organizations will need assistance from a consulting psychologist with evaluation expertise to develop solid measures of organizational learning.

**Creating a Knowledge Management System.** Organizations that learn generate knowledge. Therefore, one of the most important follow-up tasks a consulting psychologist can assist with is the creation of a knowledge management system for sharing and storing knowledge. Strategies include the creation of user-updateable databases or intranet knowledge hubs (see, for example, Hickins, 1999), the use of internal coaching and job rotation, and the creation of physical spaces where people from different parts of the organization can come together to share knowledge, ideas, and methods (Nonaka & Takeuchi, 1995). This not only reduces the tendency to reinvent the wheel in different parts of the organization, it also helps newcomers get up to speed quickly, and reduces the negative impact caused by the departure of knowledgeable employees.

**Value of the External Evaluation.** Finally, the organization needs to maintain an important underlying belief of the learning organization's culture—the value of the *external eye*. While internal review is an excellent ongoing strategy for organizational learning, the competitive edge cannot be maintained without the occasional injection of an external perspective, preferably from the toughest evaluator it can find.

# CONCLUDING COMMENTS

Consulting psychology is a relatively new profession that is working to establish its own unique identity, and to find roles that have better synergy with training in consulting psychology than with training in related disciplines, such as management or industrial/organizational psychology. This chapter has not only presented a range of issues and methods of interest to consulting psychologists practicing evaluation in organizations, but also has introduced a distinct but related profession, the practitioners of which share a great deal in common with consulting psychologists.

Evaluation, like consulting psychology, is both an art and a science. It requires a broad array of technical and methodological skills on the one hand, and an equally powerful set of interpersonal, political, and critical thinking instincts on the other. It requires the knowledge and tools to analyze complex phenomena from multiple angles at the individual, group, and organizational levels of analysis. At the same time, evaluation consulting demands the ability to deal with an enormous range of emotions provoked by evaluation, including fear, anxiety, resistance, and anger. While the main focus of this chapter has been to present consulting psychologists with a glimpse of what the discipline of evaluation has to offer us, it is equally true that the emerging profession of consulting psychology has a great deal to offer evaluators.

# References

Argyris, C. (1992). Overcoming organizational defenses. *Journal for Quality and Participation, 15*(2), 26–29.

Argyris, C. (1993). *Knowledge for action: A guide to overcoming barriers to organizational change.* San Francisco: Jossey-Bass.

Argyris, C., & Schön, D. A. (1978). *Organizational learning: A theory of action perspective.* Reading, MA: Addison-Wesley.

Barney, J. B. (1986). Organizational culture: Can it be a source of sustained competitive advantage? *Academy of Management Review, 11,* 656–665.

Brown, S. L., & Eisenhardt, K. M. (1998). *Competing on the edge.* Boston: Harvard Business School Press.

Cotter, J. J. (1995). *The 20% solution: Using rapid redesign to create tomorrow's organizations today.* New York: Wiley.

Cox, G. B. (1988). Managerial style: Implications for the utilization of program evaluation information. In F. Dickman, B. R. Challenger, W. G. Emener, & W. S. Hutchison, Jr. (Eds.), *Employee assistance programs: A basic text* (pp. 288–297). Springfield, IL: Thomas.

Csikszentmihalyi, M. (1996). *Creativity.* New York: HarperCollins.

Cummings, T. G., & Worley, C. G. (1999). *Organization development and change* (7th ed.). Cincinnati, OH: South-Western.

Davidson, E. J. (2000). Ascertaining causality in theory-based evaluation. *New Directions for Evaluation, 87,* 17–26.

Davidson, E. J. (2001). The meta-learning organization: A model and methodology for evaluating organizational learning capacity. *Dissertation Abstracts International, 62,* (05A), 1882 (UMI No. 3015945).

De Geus, A. (1997). *The living company.* Boston: Harvard Business School Press.

Deevy, E. (1995). *Creating the resilient organization: A RapidResponse® management program* (pp. 201–214). Englewood Cliffs, NJ: Prentice Hall.

DiBella, A. J., & Nevis, E. C. (1998). *How organizations learn.* San Francisco: Jossey-Bass.

Dodgson, M. (1993). Organizational learning: A review of some literatures. *Organizational Studies, 14,* 375–394.

Easterby-Smith, M. (1997). Disciplines of organizational learning: Contributions and critiques. *Human Relations, 50,* 1085–1113.

Fetterman, D. M., Kaftarian, S. J., & Wandersman, A. (1996). *Empowerment evaluation: Knowledge and tools for self-assessment and accountability*. Thousand Oaks, CA: Sage.

Forss, K., Cracknell, B., & Samset, K. (1994). Can evaluation help an organization to learn? *Evaluation Review, 18*, 574–591.

Hickins, M. (1999). Xerox shares its knowledge. *Management Review, 88*(8), 40–45.

Howard, A. (Ed.). (1994). *Diagnosis for organizational change*. New York: Guilford Press.

Imai, K., Nonaka, I., & Takeuchi, H. (1985). Managing the new product development process: How Japanese companies learn and unlearn. In K. B. Clark, R. H. Hayes, & C. Lorenz (Eds.), *The uneasy alliance: Managing the productivity-technology dilemma* (pp. 337–376). Boston: Harvard Business School Press.

Lawler, E. E., III, Seashore, S. E., & Mirvis, P. H. (1983). Measuring change: Progress, problems, and prospects. In S. E. Seashore, E. E. Lawler, III, P. H. Mirvis, & C. Cammann (Eds.), *Assessing organizational change: A guide to methods, measures, and practices* (pp. 531–546). New York: Wiley.

Miles, M. B., & Huberman, A. M. (1994). *Qualitative data analysis: An expanded sourcebook* (2nd ed.). Thousand Oaks, CA: Sage.

Mohr, L. B. (1999). The impact profile approach to policy merit: The case of research grants and the university. *Evaluation Review, 23*, 212–249.

Nonaka, I., & Takeuchi, H. (1995). *The knowledge-creating company: How Japanese companies create the dynamics of innovation*. New York: Oxford University Press.

Owen, J. M. (1999, November). *Institutionalising an evaluation culture in an organisation*. Paper presented at the annual meeting of the American Evaluation Association, Orlando, FL.

Patton, M. Q. (1997). *Utilization-focused evaluation* (3rd ed.). Thousand Oaks, CA: Sage.

Porter, M. E. (1988). *Competitive advantage: Creating and sustaining superior performance*. New York: Free Press.

Preskill, H., & Torres, R. T. (1999). *Evaluative inquiry for learning in organizations*. Thousand Oaks, CA: Sage.

Sathe, V. (2000). Creating change in mindset and behavior. *Ivey Business Journal, 64*(5), 83–89.

Sathe, V., & Davidson, E. J. (2000). Toward a new conceptualization of culture change. In N. M. Ashkanasy, C. Wilderom, & M. F. Peterson (Eds.), *Handbook of organizational culture and climate* (pp. 279–296). Thousand Oaks, CA: Sage.

Scriven, M. (1974). Maximizing the power of causal investigations: The modus operandi method. In W. J. Popham (Ed.), *Evaluation in education: Current applications* (pp. 68–84). Berkeley, CA: McCutchan.

Scriven, M. (1991). *Evaluation thesaurus* (4th ed.). Thousand Oaks, CA: Sage.

Scriven, M. (1994). The final synthesis. *Evaluation Practice, 15*, 367–382.

Senge, P. M. (1990). *The fifth discipline: The art and practice of the learning organization*. New York: Doubleday.

Stake, R. (1998, November). *Constructivist assault on evaluation constructs*. Paper presented at the annual meeting of the American Evaluation Association, Chicago.

Tropman, J. E. (1998). *The management of ideas in the creating organization*. Westport, CT: Quorum/Greenwood.

Weiss, C. H., & Bucuvalas, M. J. (1980). Truth tests and utility tests: Decision-makers' frames of reference for social science research. *American Sociological Review, 45*, 302–313.

# CHAPTER FIFTEEN

# Leadership Development in Organizational Consulting

Steven W. Graham

*President's Institute for Academic Leadership—University of Missouri System &
Department of Educational Leadership and Policy Analysis
University of Missouri-Columbia*

Debra A. G. Robinson

*Division of Student and International Affairs
University of Missouri-Rolla*

This chapter provides an introduction to leadership development. It focuses on challenges inherent in leadership development, integrating the development activities with the organizational climate, and the role of the consultant. Conceptual frameworks describing organizational and leadership theories are offered to provide a basis for consulting psychologists to understand the various leadership development perspectives. The chapter offers specific suggestions on how consultants can work with various organizations to design an ongoing leadership development process that can be sustained over time.

## LEADERSHIP DEVELOPMENT PRACTICES

Developing leadership potential is one of the essential ingredients of modern organizations. Though leadership development can be expensive and time-consuming, most organizations find it pays off in the long run (Conger, 1993; Conger & Xin, 2000; McNamara & Pennisi, 2000; Van Velsor, McCauley, & Moxley, 1998). Leadership development activities can lead to increased self-awareness, enhanced personal management skills, improved interpersonal skills, increased capacity to employ problem-solving capabilities, and balanced skills in managing change (Van Velsor et al., 1998). Leadership development programs can also play a key role in succession planning by identifying and nurturing talent within organizations. In other instances, new organization-wide leadership development programs are initiated when top management changes or crises occur in the organizations.

Consultants often receive requests for skill training in an attempt to fix something quickly; but short-term skill training done in isolation normally has minimal impact. Identifying the current climate, the long-term needs of the organization, the status of current and future leaders, and the desired outcomes, are necessary steps in designing effective intervention strategies. Furthermore, these steps help the consultant set realistic expectations for the types of programs that are being developed, and offer the opportunity to discuss the follow-up efforts, the challenge assignments, and the continuous support needed for leadership to evolve.

A variety of practices are used to develop leaders, and the extent to which these practices are employed depends on the model of leadership development espoused by the organization. Consultants should understand the organization's history of training efforts and the prevailing culture to determine which leadership practices can be supported and design ongoing programs that increase the potential impact on both the individual and the organization (Hawkins & Petty, 2000; Van Velsor, et al., 1998). In most instances, a combination of multirater assessments, self-assessments, feedback, coaching, mentoring, challenge assignments, and skill training in areas related to emotional intelligence are utilized (Garman, 2002). The combined approaches are generally more effective than a single-strategy approach (Guthrie & Kelly-Radford, 1998).

## What Is Leadership?

For years, both scholars and practitioners have attempted to define the characteristics or talents that comprise good leadership. As a result, there are probably as many definitions of leadership as there are leadership theories. In the early literature, strong leaders were viewed as heroes, and the attention focused on the key personality traits that made them great. Later researchers began to see that leaders often responded differently in different situations, deemphasizing the notion that certain personality attributes were involved. Since that time, those studying leadership have looked at it from an organization-wide perspective, and have attempted to account for the ambiguity, complexity, and interconnected nature of leadership. Though there is no single definition of leadership, John Gardner, who served as the U.S. Secretary of Health, Education, and Welfare, worked for six different presidents, and was the founder of Common Cause, offers a clear and concise one: "Leadership is the process of persuasion or example by which an individual (or leadership team) induces a group to pursue objectives held by the leader or shared by the leader and his or her followers" (Gardner, 1990, p. 1). While Gardner sees leadership characteristics in successful managers, he also cited several distinguishing characteristics between leaders and run-of-the-mill managers. Leaders think longer term, influence constituents beyond their formal jurisdictions, emphasize intangibles such as vision, values, and motivation, have political skills, and think in terms of organizational renewal.

With this general definition of leadership, the following sections provide a basic overview of some of the most commonly debated and researched theories on leadership. They are not intended to cover the entire range of leadership, but instead provide a basis for leadership development activities for consulting psychologists.

## Leadership Practices of Effective Leaders

In an attempt to define effective leaders, Bennis and Nanus (1985) studied a large number of leaders in both business and public service settings. They identified several common themes inherent in these strong leaders, including: the ability to articulate a clear vision; instill a sense of communication; promote trust—demonstrating reliability, consistency, and organizational integrity; and foster a strong and positive self-regard. These leaders were able to empower followers and create a work climate that promoted success. These findings provided a framework to discuss broad behaviors and strategies that could guide the behavior of other leaders. Other researchers have looked for common themes among effective leaders, and many have identified similar categories of traits (Bass, 1985; Bolman & Deal, 1997; Burns, 1978; Conger, 1999; Covey, 1989; Kouzes & Posner, 1993).

Not unlike Bennis and Nanus' common leadership themes (1985), Gardner (1990) articulated the common tasks of successful leadership that include envisioning goals, affirming values, motivating, managing, achieving unity, explaining, serving as a symbol, renewing, and representing the group. These themes were similar to those identified by Bolman and Deal (1997) when they reviewed over two decades of research and literature on leadership. Likewise, a group of noted authorities on leadership (Conger, Kotter, Porter, Bolman, Deal) articulated a similar set of leadership talents and contended that leadership is inherently symbolic and political, and requires intangible human qualities such as ethical commitment, risk-taking, self-knowledge, moral character, and courage (Bolman & Deal, 1994).

Kouzes and Posner (1995) asked hundreds of employees over two decades what they wanted in a leader, and a number of traits consistently received high ratings. At the top of the list were honesty, competence, forward-looking, inspiration, and credibility. Kouzes and Posner's research (1987, 1993, 1995) led them to articulate five key themes that defined effective leadership. In *The Leadership Challenge* they identified key strategies to guide effective leaders, including (1) challenging the process, (2) inspiring a shared vision, (3) enabling others, (4) modeling behaviors, and (5) encouraging the heart. In their book, *Credibility: How Leaders Can Gain and Lose It, Why People Demand It*, they discussed these themes and elaborated on the ones that foster credibility, in their minds, the essential component of leadership.

Kouzes and Posner designed the *Leadership Practices Inventory* (LPI), a multirater instrument to assess leadership behaviors that can be used in leadership development programs. It has been used in a number of large studies of leader behavior, and found to be a reliable and valid measure of leadership behaviors (Fields & Herold, 1997; Kouzes & Posner, 1993; Posner & Kouzes, 1993; Posner & Kouzes, 1994). Furthermore, the LPI has also been used as a measure of transformational and transactional leadership (Fields & Herold, 1997).

**Contingency Theories.** Contingency leadership theories comprise one of the most researched leadership areas. This general area includes some of the most familiar theories, such as Fiedler's contingency theory (1967, 2002), Yukl's multiple linkage model (1971), the Vroom-Yetton model (Vroom, 1973), and House's path-goal theory (1971). These models identified leader behaviors that were effective under specific conditions related to the nature of the followers, the nature of the organizational climate, or the maturity of the organization. Theoretically, leaders in formal positions of authority could master a wide range of leadership practices, and apply them in the appropriate contexts to improve their effectiveness. Another theme among these models was the role of subordinate participation in decision-making.

Contingency theories have also been linked to transformational and charismatic leadership, as they are primarily concerned with the relationship between leaders and followers (Hooijberg & Choi, 1999). Furthermore, these theories often focus on contingent reward behaviors (Waldman & Bass, 1990), are concerned about organizational conditions, performance goals, and organizational structure (Yukl & Howell, 1999), and recognize how charismatic leadership enhances the effects of contingent rewards (Waldman & Bass, 1990). There has also been research suggesting that certain leader behaviors or tactics are effective across different cultures, though some behaviors are uniquely effective based on the cultural context (Dorfman & Howell, 1997; Fu & Yukl, 2000; Yukl & Howell, 1999).

The contingency theories have come under some criticism as research has suggested that there are moderating variables, or *substitute variables,* that strongly influence the effectiveness of these leadership behaviors. In fact, sometimes these substitute variables account for more variance than the leader behaviors themselves (Howell, 1997; Parker, 1999; Leithwood & Duke, 1999). Other research has indicated that some of the earlier studies might have overestimated the effects of manager performance by using self-ratings of manager efficacy (Parker, 1999).

**Transformational Leadership.** One of the most popular leadership theories over the past twenty-five years focused on the notions of transactional, transformational, and charismatic leadership. First articulated by such authors as Burns (1978) and Bass (1985), they suggested that transformational leaders were those who were charismatic, self-confident, visionary, and morally inspiring, and capable of motivating people to go beyond the traditional organizational expectations. These transformational leaders inspired higher levels of commitment to organizational goals, and created conditions in which followers were more effective and accomplished goals beyond those elicited by contingent leader behaviors alone (Waldman & Bass, 1990). Furthermore, leaders who could inspire commitments and collective aspirations from followers were able to acquire additional power, which in turn increased their effectiveness (Leithwood & Duke, 1999). Transformational leadership ultimately raised the ethical aspirations of both leaders and followers, and had a transforming effect on the organization (Burns, 1978). Bennis and Nanus (1985) highlighted this theme and contended that transformational leaders emphasized the inspirational, vision-building nature of their work, and communicated a clear vision for others to follow.

Bass (1985) initially conceptualized transactional leadership and transformational leadership along seven factors, including charisma, inspirational, intellectual stimulation, individualized consideration, contingent rewards, management by expectation, and laissez-faire leadership. Later, the charismatic and inspirational constructs were collapsed into one category, leaving six factors that Bass refered to as a multifactor model of leadership (Avolio & Bass, 1999). These six factors are: (1) charisma/inspirational—provides followers with a clear sense of purpose that energizes followers, creates a shared vision, and provides a role model for ethical behavior; (2) intellectual stimulation—encourages followers to question traditional ways of solving problems and improve work process methods; (3) individualized consideration—requires understanding, and addresses the individual needs of all workers and helps them to develop their full potential; (4) contingent reward—clarifies expectations for followers, and articulates what they can expect if they meet these levels of performance; (5) active management by exception—focuses on monitoring tasks, and provides corrective actions if need be; (6) passive-avoidant leadership—reacts to problems only after they have become serious or ignores them altogether.

In contrast to transformational leadership, transactional leadership focused on an exchange between the leader and the subordinates in which the workers' performance was based on the leader's ability to hand out punishment and rewards through positional or organizational power. According to Bass (1990, 1995), transactional leadership is a prescription for mediocrity, and is often based on administering rewards and punishments or behaving passively. On the other hand, superior leadership performance—transformational leadership—occurs when leaders motivate employees to broaden their interests and embrace the mission of the larger group.

Burns' early notions of transformational and transactional leadership (1978) were seen as a single construct with the two types of leadership falling at opposite ends of the continuum. Research by Avolio and Bass (1999) suggested that the best leaders exhibit both styles, and that a component of the transactional style of leadership can be the basis for creating developmental expectations and developing trust. Their research suggested that certain elements of transactional leadership correlate highly with transformational leadership and provide the basis for a range of effective leadership behavior (Avolio & Bass, 1999; Waldman & Bass, 1990). Often, Bass and Avolio have used the Multifactor Leadership Questionnaire (MLQ) to study transactional leadership (Avolio & Bass, 1999; Waldman & Bass, 1990).

A considerable body of research has examined how transformational leaders inspire followers. Numerous articles have summarized this research and attempted to clarify the findings and linkages with other theories (Conger, 1998; Waldman & Bass, 1990; Conger, 1999; Bass, 1990; Yukl & Howell, 1999). As examples, studies have found links between transformational leadership and contingency theories (Yukl & Howell, 1999), between transformational leadership and contingent-reward behaviors (Avolio & Bass, 1999; Waldman & Bass, 1990), and between organizational and contextual influences, and transformational and charismatic leadership (Fu & Yukl, 2000). Furthermore, Yammarino and Dubinsky (1994) cited positive relationships between transformational leadership and transactional leadership, a link between transformational leadership and a subordinate's performance, a relationship between contingent rewards and a subordinate's performance, and even a link between outcomes of transactional and transformational leadership and a subordinates' performance.

Though the focus on transformational leadership, and the work by Bass and his colleagues, have gained considerable attention, they have also raised a number of questions. Some of these questions include what exactly can be defined and learned regarding transformational leadership behaviors (Conger, 1999), whether the constructs defined by Bass and Avolio are in fact distinct (Hartog & Van Muijen, 1997; Tracey & Hinkin, 1998), and whether transformational leadership corresponds with actual organizational performance (Ross & Offermann, 1997). Conger (1999) suggested there is much still to learn about transformational leadership, and offered other avenues to promote leader development. Likewise, a number of authors have offered cautions about the wholesale acceptance of charismatic leadership, an element of transformational leadership. They have questioned its effectiveness in all situations, even noting the darker side of charismatic leaders (Conger, 1999; Sandowsky, 1995; Yukl & Howell, 1999).

**Emotional Intelligence: Another Aspect of Transformational Leadership.** Goleman's research (1998a, 1998b; see also Robins, 2002) suggested that the key ingredients that separated exceptional leaders from average performers were emotional intelligence factors. While he found that intelligence and technical skills were certainly important to any leader's success, emotional intelligence turned out to be more important among jobs at all levels. His theory is consistent with many of the definitions of transformational leaders that include references to the self-awareness and motivational abilities of transformational leadership (Avolio & Bass, 1999; Conger, 1999). Goleman defined emotional intelligence in five components: self-awareness, self-regulation, motivation, empathy, and social skill. In his research, Goleman (2000) eventually identified six more distinctive leadership styles that stem from components of emotional intelligence. The six styles included coercive, authoritative, affiliative, democratic, pace-setting, and coaching leadership. Apparently, leaders whose companies have the best financial performance use several of these styles interchangeably. Goleman's notion of emotional intelligence has received attention as a means of fostering successful leader behavior, and has been linked to transformational styles of leadership (Megerian & Megerian, 1999).

In *The Seven Habits of Highly Effective People*, Covey (1989) suggested that effective leaders have skills in seven key areas, including being proactive, focusing on a goal or vision, attending to the most important items, developing winning coalitions, seeking understanding and clear communication, synergy, and ongoing professional development. Covey (1990) went on to describe characteristics of principle-centered leaders, and how effective leaders were often guided by personal values and their commitment to living and leading others with integrity. He viewed these principle-centered leaders as continually learning, service-oriented, radiating positive energy, believing in other people, leading balanced lives, seeing life as an adventure, being synergistic, and focusing on self-renewal.

One theme that has gained increasing interest is the notion of servant leadership (Spears, 1998). Greenleaf (1970) proposed that great leaders are servants of those they lead because of a deep sense of personal integrity; they exemplify the ethics of leadership. His basic premise was that the only authority deserving allegiance is that which is freely given by those who are being led. Followers give this authority only to those who have given freely of their services by truly being willing to serve those they lead (Greenleaf, 1970; Oseem, 2001). Other more contemporary authors like Blanchard (1998), Kouzes (1998), and Block (1998) have refined his work and tied servant leadership to citizenship and defining one's own leadership from within.

## Leadership Development from an Organizational Perspective

To be truly effective, many have suggested that leaders must take a broad view of the inner workings of organizations and focus beyond individual leader behaviors and relationships with individual workers (Bolman & Deal, 1997; Morgan, 1997; Yukl & Howell, 1999). For some, it is the larger organizational climate that gives leadership its complexity and meaning. Key elements often include the political climate, the culture of the organization, the core business processes, the organizational structure, the human resources, the organization's ability to address change, the learning practices present in organizations, and the use of technology.

**Crossing Areas.** Bolman and Deal (1997) contended that the most effective leaders are those who work successfully across several key areas, which include the symbolic or cultural frame, the political frame, the structural frame, and the human resources frame. This approach was appealing as a meaningful way to understand the various arenas that leaders must address to be successful (Buono, 1998; Morgan, 1997; Thompson, 2000). The ability to manage all of these organizational elements rather than one set of skills or attributes makes leaders effective. Morgan (1997) also identified several of these areas as critical in understanding complex organizations and how people operate within them.

**Human Resources Perspectives.** Bolman and Deal (1997), and Morgan (1997), discussed the importance of the human resources perspective and the leader's focus on the human side of the enterprise. They noted the inherent conflicts and tensions that exist between management and workers, and offered ways to establish a more worker-oriented framework that enhances involvement. Strategies for improving human resources management include participative management, quality circles, job enrichment, self-managed work teams, and organizational democracy (Bolman & Deal, 1997; Garvin, 1993; Katzenbach & Smith, 1993). Argyris (1991, 1994) identified the importance of getting employees to critically examine ways to improve their work, and the role of leadership in addressing traditional defensive routines and mental traps that prevent people from improving their effectiveness. This notion is also consistent with Bass' intellectual stimulation factor (Avolio & Bass, 1999).

**Organizational Structure.** The organizational structure is another element in effective leadership (Bolman & Deal, 1997; Morgan, 1997; Yukl & Howell, 1999). No specific structure is associated with organizational success. Instead, leaders must build a structure that creates the work processes and relationships that are most effective for the nature of the business or the external environment (Kanter, Stein, & Jick, 1992; Kotter & Heskett, 1992; Morgan, 1997). Furthermore, Bartlett and Ghoshal (1994), and Bartlett and Sumantra (1995a; 1995b), suggested that people and work processes should actually define the organizational structure, not the other way around.

**Shaping the Organizational Culture.** Schein (1992) viewed shaping the organizational culture as the primary function of leadership. Both the formal and informal aspects of organizational culture shape the nature of the day-to-day relations for people in an organization (Deal & Kennedy, 1982; Kanter et al.,

1992; Kofman & Senge, 1993; Kotter & Heskett, 1992; Schein, 1993). The organizational culture is developed throughout the life of the organization by the background habits, values, and beliefs of the organizational members, and by how the organization responds to its external environment. The organizational culture affects who gets promoted, the quality and pace of work, how people interact, and how technology is used. The organizational values and beliefs are subtle and so ingrained that they are often resistant to change. All of this affects the leader's role and effectiveness. Managing the culture can become one of the most effective tools leaders have to work with (Bolman & Deal, 1997; Kanter et al., 1992; Kotter & Heskett, 1992; Schein, 1993).

**Power and Politics.** Power and politics can be viewed as negative by-products of organizational life, the cause of discontent, the reason for the unfair distribution of resources, and the explanation of why things never go as they should. However, power is one of the most important tools of leaders (Bolman & Deal, 1994; Burns, 1978; Kanter, 1983; Pfeffer, 1992). Pfeffer (1992) and Kanter (1989) summarized previous research on power, and contended that a variety of sources increases the leader's influence. These include providing resources, solving organizational problems, coping with uncertainty, being irreplaceable, affecting the decision process, having access to important information, building consensus, having powerful personal characteristics, and establishing effective mentoring relationships.

**Organizational Decision Making and Learning.** Cyert and March (1963), and March and Olsen (1976), challenged management theorists and practicing leaders to look at organizational decision-making and learning in an entirely new light. Expanding on their work, Senge's book *The Fifth Discipline* (1990) brought organizational learning to the forefront for many business leaders, and much of the leadership literature now focuses on organizational learning and how it is fostered. Promoting organizational learning is one of the primary tasks of leaders, in which employees learn to create local knowledge, capture insights from their experiences, and share it with others throughout the organization. For example, many argue that organizations must foster ways to make implicit knowledge concrete, as well as make explicit knowledge part of the common practice or culture (Nonaka & Takeuchi, 1995; Nonaka, Toyama, & Konno, 2001; van Krough, Ichigo, & Nonaka, 2000).

# CONTEMPORARY APPROACHES TO LEADERSHIP DEVELOPMENT

Theories about leadership and organizational behavior often provide the foundation upon which leadership programs are designed. They help foster a broad understanding of leadership and help explain how organizations function.

Effective leadership development programs also focus on critical organizational leadership competencies. Consequently, an important first step in designing leadership development programs is to identify the leadership competencies that are critical for the organization when the program is being developed. Data can be collected around these core competencies, and the program plan can be designed with them as the major focus.

## Leadership Competencies

Zenger, Ulrich, and Smallwood (2000) suggested examining the organization's readiness for change and current leadership efforts before designing new programs. Selecting a leadership framework that matches the broad range of talents needed in an organization can help consultants and organizational leaders view leadership development as an ongoing and emerging process. For example, Kouzes and Posner (1987) created their Leadership Challenge model based on research of the characteristics of admired leaders of business people in the public and private sectors. Their model of leadership development focuses on developing five behaviors that embody these characteristics and can be linked to more organization-specific skills.

Although there are some desirable qualities for all leaders, different skills, perspectives, and values are needed for leaders at various levels in the organization. Charan, Drotter, and Noel (2001) identify and describe six distinct leadership passages in *The Leadership Pipeline.* At each passage up the ladder, people need to acquire a new way of managing and leading, as well as leave behind some of their old ways. They must let go of some things that made them successful in the past in order to learn new skills to be successful at the new level. The characteristics for success at one level might be counterproductive at the next level, particularly as some leaders jump over intermediate levels and have to make rather dramatic shifts. Consultants can play a role in preventing derailment by understanding the skills and perspectives needed at various levels, and helping leaders adapt to and grow into new roles.

## Feedback-Intensive Approaches

As people progress in organizational leadership positions, it becomes increasingly difficult for them to obtain honest feedback. Saporito (1996) contends that senior executives tend to get isolated from real-time, unvarnished feedback about the impact of their individual leadership. Subordinates often feel uncomfortable providing candid feedback to their superiors, but people need candid and constructive information on how they affect others and how they can improve (Chappelow, 1998; Kirkland & Manoogian, 1998). Consultants can provide a valuable service by helping aspiring leaders obtain and use feedback in an effective manner, and helping their peers and subordinates learn to offer constructive feedback.

Feedback-intensive programs provide an opportunity to give and receive feedback in a safe environment. Most leadership development efforts include one or more types of feedback, and multirater feedback is commonly used in organizations for a variety of purposes. It can be one of the most powerful leadership development tools available, and create a readiness to learn on the part of the future leaders. Self-assessment tools can be used in conjunction with the ratings of others as a means to increase self-awareness, and as a way to compare the self-assessment data against the impressions of others. While self- and peer-assessment components are often viewed as threatening, they are often the most highly valued aspects by the conclusion of the development program (Guthrie & Kelly-Radford, 1998).

## Multirater Feedback Approaches

The use of multirater feedback, sometimes referred to as 360-degree feedback, is rapidly growing in organizations. This method is used to obtain information about how aspiring leaders' behaviors are viewed by those above them, below them, and by their peers and colleagues. Top management needs to identify the most important leadership competencies for the organization; otherwise, 360-degree feedback lacks an important frame of reference. Furthermore, consultants should select instruments that are easy to use and interpret, and consistent with organizational culture, rather than just using the most sophisticated tools available. Assessment tools need to be consistent with organizational and desired leadership competencies (Chappelow, 1998).

Critical to this process are the decisions on how to use the assessment data, with whom it will be shared, who is to be included in the data collection process, and how the results will be shared with the program participant who was evaluated. Most experts recommend that the results from the assessment tools only be shared with the participant (Chappelow, 1998). This approach encourages the raters to be candid in their assessments, and creates an atmosphere of growth and development.

Interpreting the feedback data to the aspiring leader is another important step in the process (Fleenor & Prince, 1997), and this is an area where consultants can add value to leadership development efforts. Giving program participants the results with minimal interpretive data is an ineffective way to use 360-degree data, yet it frequently happens. If the debriefing process is handled poorly, people tend to focus on negative parts of an evaluation, dismiss the results as invalid, attempt to find out who said what about them, or feel angry and become less productive. A development plan can be created after the results are shared and integrated with the work context and the competencies required in the organization.

There are numerous multirater feedback instruments on the market today, and some are linked directly to theoretical models that can also serve as the foundation for a leadership development program. For example, the *Leadership Practices Inventory* (LPI) is based on Kouzes and Posner's Leadership Challenge model, and the *Multifactor Leadership Questionnaire* (MLQ) is based on Bass' model of transformational leadership. Covey has an instrument to complement his theory of principled leadership. Other comprehensive instruments that have a strong research base include *Leadership Effectiveness Analysis* by Management Research Group, *Benchmarks* from the Center for Creative Leadership, *Profiler* by Personnel Decisions International (PDI), and *Acumen*.

## Individual Assessment Approaches

Individual assessment tools can be used as a part of the screening and selection process for leadership positions, for developing high-potential employees, and to promote the development of current leaders (Garman, 2002). Assessment tools can also be used to help leaders who are struggling, or at risk of derailing, by providing insight into personal factors that affect their work. Personality assessments are used to provide insight into one's overall personality dimensions, and other instruments focus on specific personal factors related to leadership development, such as motivation and emotional competence. Aptitude, ability, and skill assessment tools can be used in leadership development to enhance the match between a job and skill and ability sets. Assessment tools can be used to assess general cognitive ability as part of the selection process for management positions. Ability batteries can be used to identify specific abilities and combinations of abilities as they relate to success and satisfaction in work roles. Using assessment as a foundation for individual development planning with follow-up coaching is a significant trend in leadership development programs in organizations (Giber, Carter, & Goldsmith, 2000).

## Peer Feedback Experiences

Some programs incorporate feedback to help leaders learn about their interpersonal styles and how their styles affect others. Leaders might ask colleagues or other program participants to provide feedback on specific behaviors they wish to evaluate or competencies they wish to develop, or they might participate in personal growth groups. Developing skills to provide effective, constructive feedback and receive feedback are important for leadership effectiveness.

## Challenge Assignments

People normally grow when they are forced out of their zones of comfort (Ohlott, 1998), and new jobs, temporary positions, and job rotation can provide stretch experiences. Off-site, intensive leadership development programs, international assignments, professional presentations, and professional education can also provide opportunities to push people to new levels of development. Outward Bound, high-ropes courses, mountain treks, and other physical challenge experiences are used to stretch participants out of their traditional roles and facilitate new learning. Although never sought out, hardship experiences and personal life crises also force people to grow and develop. Even work conditions can be difficult for aspiring leaders and their organizations when they present too much challenge and change at one time. However, consulting psychologists can use these naturally occurring experiences to help leaders seek out an appropriate balance of challenge situations that promote growth and help new leaders determine ways to cope with the demands and changes (Moxley & Wilson, 1998).

## Mentoring

Mentors have long been known for their contributions in leadership development (Bell, 2000; Peddy, 1998). Mentor relationships are usually informal relationships based on proximity, common experience, and chemistry between the mentor and protégé. The mentors are usually older, seasoned professionals who take newer professionals under their wings. Mentors often have worked in positions similar to that of the new leaders, and can provide information, guidance, and encouragement that relates specifically to the job. Effective mentors become learning partners by leveling the learning field, fostering acceptance and safety, and bolstering self-direction and independence (Bell, 2000).

Formal mentoring programs have grown in recent years as organizations see the powerful impact that mentors can have on professional growth and leadership development. Having an experienced leader as a guide along the way can facilitate leadership development. Mentors typically do not have line authority over mentees, which allows for more trust and safety in the relationship, and avoids a potential conflict of interest for supervisors (Peddy, 1998).

## Coaching

Coaching (Kilburg, 2002) can enhance leader development. An experienced coach continuously expands one's capacity to produce the results truly desired (Hargrove, 1995). Coaches can help novice leaders stretch beyond their current situations, set and achieve high goals, examine external and internal barriers blocking their success, and serve as sounding boards. Effective coaches can provide honest feedback about discrepancies or ineffective behavior patterns, challenge limiting perspectives, and provide safe environments to vent frustrations. Coaching, combined with assessment, is commonly used for leadership development in organizations, and as a way to foster development among leaders struggling in their roles (Giber et al., 2000).

Coaching can focus on performance, development, or personal transformation. Performance coaching focuses on changing behavior for immediate results, and is useful when people need to produce results under new conditions, or where stress or changes cause breakdowns in a system. Many organizations focus on performance coaching—training their leaders to be performance coaches rather than traditional managers in order to enhance employee productivity and satisfaction (Deeprose, 1995). Developmental coaching focuses on challenging thinking patterns and shifting mental models so that new skills and capabilities can be learned. Kilburg (1996) identified a range of psychological and social competencies within this framework for coaching. Transformational coaching has the most lasting impact, because it focuses on tapping into special talents, energy, and purpose to enable people to achieve goals otherwise unattainable (Hudson, 1999).

## Professional Development Plans

An individual development plan helps the aspiring leader integrate new information into a usable format and creates an appropriate course for development. Without a plan, leadership development activities can become random events that might or might not promote leadership development. Setting a particular course and checking progress allows the leader to develop over time. Most people can successfully change one or two behaviors at a time, so that should be addressed when creating individual development plans (Waagan, 2001). Coaches, mentors, and organizational leaders can help the leader pursue their development plans by writing plans and sharing them with others in the organization. All of these strategies increase the chances of successful implementation for the aspiring leader.

## Skill Training

Some organizations provide a generalized set of leadership training experiences consistent with their cultures. Individual skill training needs to be consistent with the individual development plan to be effective. Skill training should be viewed as part of a total plan and not as one-shot, isolated experiences. Most leadership training programs focus on emotional intelligence—personal and interpersonal competencies. Typical training topics include teamwork, interpersonal skills, managing change, motivating and empowering people, and systems thinking and problem solving (McDonald-Mann, 1998). Various formats can be used, however a large auditorium lecture is not an effective way to teach skills related to personal and interpersonal development. Practice, feedback, and reflection are more important components of the skill development process.

# CURRENT ISSUES IN LEADERSHIP DEVELOPMENT

Leadership development seems to be a rapidly growing enterprise with a trend toward customization, action learning, real-time projects, and involvement of leaders at many levels in the organization. Giber et al. (2000) cited this explosion of interest in leadership development, as companies realize there is a shortage of talented managers and need to build their internal resources to be globally competitive. Companies that successfully build their high-potential employees seem to favor structured leadership development systems that include a combination of formal training, 360-degree feedback, and developmental relationships.

## Trends in Executive Leadership and Education

With the advances in technology, global competition, and changes in organizational life, executive education has become very focused on strategic issues and change management (Conger & Xin, 2000). The preferred program format is customized, in-house, and learner-centered, rather than standardized and university-based. About 75 percent of all executive education dollars in the United States go to customized programs (Fulmer & Vicere, 1995), so public, open-enrollment programs are likely to play a smaller role in executive leadership and education in the future.

Developmental programs are viewed as adding value to the organization rather than serving solely as a benefit to the individual (Stopper, 1998). Program selection is no longer a reward for successful executives to prepare them for promotion to a more senior level, but rather as part of strategic initiatives to build leaders at all levels for rapid change and succession. In these cases, the emphasis is on cascading learning experiences downward in the organization to facilitate translation of big-picture initiatives into actionable goals that can be implemented (Conger & Benjamin, 1999; Fulmer & Vicere, 1995). Managing organizational change programs is often the top priority, followed by implementing new strategic and organizational imperatives, instilling mission, vision, and values of the corporation, and facilitating career transitions of senior managers to executive roles. Accountability in terms of development of organizational competencies, seeking bottom-line results, and cost effectiveness are all additional concerns in organizational leadership development programs (Zenger et al., 2000).

## Diversity and Leadership

Consideration of the issues and barriers women and people of color experience in addition to the traditional leadership challenges is important when designing leadership development programs (Morrison, White, & Van Velsor, 1997; Morrison, 1992). Morrison identified a variety of barriers that affect progression to leadership positions. Prejudice is a dominant barrier, because people tend to view people who are different from the majority group as deficient and potentially unable to perform. Career planning can also be curtailed because of limited exposure to assignments, experiences, and organizational relationships that prepare leaders for senior positions.

Fletcher (1996) suggests that companies can undercut women's strengths inadvertently by assuming people skills are not business skills. Women sometimes work so hard to get results, that they do not spend enough time building critical business alliances and discussing strategy. Since women often take primary responsibility for home and family, balancing career and family becomes more difficult as they move to senior management positions requiring long work hours and more dedication to the organization (Morrison, 1992; Newman, 1993).

Consultants can help leaders and their organizations understand differences and barriers to facilitate change and develop appropriate compensation strategies. Even in developmental processes such as coaching and mentoring, diversity can have an impact (Thomas, 2000). Issues related to managing multiple identities (Bell, 2000) and fitting in (Morrison et al., 1987) can be facilitated through individual coaching, and consultants must be aware of the potential of issues related to social allegiances, preferential treatment, lack of confidence, lack of trust, fear of intimacy, and faulty presumptions of fairness and equal treatment.

## Globalization Issues and Challenges

Globalization is posing new challenges for organizations and leaders (Ensari, 2002; Mullin & Cooper, 2002). Successful global leaders need to possess personal competencies, social competencies, business literacy, and cultural literacy (Rosen & Digh, 2001). Personal literacy encompasses self-awareness, and understanding and acceptance of other attitudes, beliefs, and behaviors. Social literacy requires listening to other people, inspiring greater performance in constructive ways, and creating collaborative learning networks. Business literacy can take leadership to another level, enabling leaders to guide people through change by aligning people, systems, and processes with the visions and goals of the organization. Cultural literacy requires understanding and valuing one's own culture, while looking beyond it for business opportunities, resources, and alliances. Hoppe (1998) noted that there are cross-cultural issues in leadership development, because preferred values and beliefs are not universal.

Leaders need to be culturally self-aware and sensitive to performance in the cultural context (Solomons, Hu-Chan, Marin, & Roberston, 2000). Global leaders can promote cultural literacy by sharing their vision of becoming a world-class organization in a way that excites people, and creating a global road map of where they want to go that is readable around the world. Through a global enterprise strategy, organizations can create global leadership competencies, localize them, develop ongoing feedback systems, and provide development opportunities for leaders at all levels. Virtual multicultural teams and global learning communities can create global management routines and engage executive teams in worldwide conversations about global markets and opportunities. Inclusion of cultural literacy in leadership development programs can bolster the organization's competitive advantage.

## Stategies to Enhance Leadership Development in Organizations

There are a number of specific strategies that consultants can use to increase the chances that an organization's leadership development program will be truly effective. Often these require approaching the task as an ongoing process, and integrating the development program with other key elements of the organization. Modifying the leadership development programs to fit particular organizations greatly increases their likelihood of acceptance and eventual success. A number of these practical strategies, as well as a set of recommendations, are provided in the following section.

**Preparing the Organizational Culture.** Organizational culture is a critical variable that must be considered when creating leadership development programs. Some companies have well-established leadership development programs throughout their organization, and this type of activity becomes second nature to the senior managers. These companies are likely to identify high-potential employees, and provide leadership development opportunities as part of a formal succession planning process and as a means to retain valuable employees. However, in some cases, companies have no history of leadership development initiatives, and only become interested when they have immediate crises that need to be resolved. It is more difficult to design programs in which the efforts will be sustained for this latter type of organization.

**Assessing Support Systems.** As consultants determine the commitment of the organization, they can also assess the support systems in place to promote and sustain new leadership behaviors. Understanding the power structure within the organization, and involving different levels of the organization in leadership development planning and participant selection, can greatly enhance the chances for success in the organization. Some strategies that are helpful include involving important constituents in the program design itself by securing the blessing and support of the participants' immediate supervisors, by communicating concrete results and outcomes to the rest of the organization, by securing a wide range of input in 360-degree assessment practices, and by encouraging the participants to communicate their experiences to important constituent groups.

Though all of these elements take time, they greatly increase the ability to gain organizational support and sustain leadership development efforts. Without organizational support, aspiring leaders who participate in leadership development activities can come back to an organizational culture in which their new insights and behaviors are discouraged. In some cases, leadership development can backfire, and these aspiring leaders can become frustrated and leave or revert back to the old ways in order to be consistent with the organization.

**Assessing Individual Readiness.** Leadership development focuses on increasing individual capabilities in order to enhance organizational functioning. Leadership development activities are usually supported by the organization, but to truly benefit, the individual must also be engaged in and committed to the process. Leadership development programs are more successful for those who participate voluntarily and are ready to fully engage in the required activities and challenging experiences. Individuals must understand that leadership competencies are part of an evolving set of skills that must be nurtured and practiced back on the job. The informal leadership development network that evolves as part of a formal program can provide the opportunities to obtain advice and problem-solving strategies, assistance with challenge experiences, and emotional support for the tougher aspects of the aspiring leaders' duties. The informal coaching relationships that develop can be one of the most valuable components of the leadership program.

# SPECIFIC STRATEGIES AND RECOMMENDATIONS FOR SECURING ORGANIZATIONAL SUPPORT

Depending on the nature of the organization, consultants will find that using some of the following strategies can strengthen the impact of the training and provide some self-sustaining components that will continue to foster leader development. These strategies are a compilation of successful techniques that were identified in actual leadership development programs. They are drawn from the authors' experiences, as well as from a number of documented sources that are identified for each suggested strategy.

- Allow key organizational players to help design the program—most consultants are not intimately familiar with the culture of the organization, nor do they know all the skills and competencies that will be required for leaders. Designing planning efforts to involve influential organizational members will allow them to help shape the program to fit the environment. These advisors can also serve as rich resources for the program, and provide ideas for case studies and find ways to gain organizational support (Manzi & Abramson, 2000; McNamara & Pennisi, 2000; Moxley & Wilson, 1998).

- Address ambiguous areas like emotional intelligence and self-awareness—leadership is more than just learning new managerial practices. It involves emotional and social awareness that allow leaders to make good judgments and build instincts for working with people. These are important components to include in any program (Goleman, 1998a, 1998b; Van Velsor et al., 1998).

- Make sure leadership development activities appropriately address the needs of a diverse population. Expand upon the practices that were developed for white men to include issues that are of importance to women and diverse races. Leadership programs can become an opportunity to educate and expand the perspectives of the majority so they can develop skills necessary to lead and work collaboratively with a diverse workforce. These skills are critical if the organization expects to be globally competitive (Rosen & Digh, 2001; Ruderman & Hughes-James, 1998).

- Address the growing needs and desires for customized programs. Organizations want to include many levels of management to work on real-life issues related to organizational strategy. Hence, the need for traditional, broad-based university executive education programs might decrease and be replaced with in-house, custom programs (Conger & Xin, 2000; Moxley & Wilson, 1998; Van Velsor et al., 1998).

- Refine the process for selecting individual participants—individual readiness and a personal commitment to the program are two of the most critical components for program success. Designing a process that selects individuals who are interested in the personal challenges, have the respect of their colleagues, and have the support of their immediate supervisors, is crucial (Van Velsor & Guthrie, 1998).

- Design development experiences for different levels of leaders. To be effective, experiences should be consistent with the competencies and mental models required for different leadership levels within the organization. Training must address the issues that are important to the participants, and allow them to work with others and learn from experienced, peer-level leaders (Charan et al., 2001; Conger & Xin, 2000).

- Design a comprehensive evaluation process—create an evaluation process that assesses participant needs, program results, ways to improve the program, and clearly demonstrates outcomes. Use a variety of techniques to gather quantitative and qualitative data, as well as personal stories and specific changes in leader behavior (Foxon, 2000; Kraft, 2000; McNamara & Pennisi, 2000; Van Velsor, 1998).

- Foster informal leadership networking across the organization—learning new behaviors often requires emotional support and modifying ideas that others have used to implement change. Participants in a leadership program need informal opportunities to get together that allow them to build networks and offer support to one another to make the most of their new experiences (Latif & Anderson, 2000; Guthrie & Kelly-Radford, 1998).

- Design challenge experiences—challenge experiences that provide a safe environment for learning new skills can be extremely valuable. Participants need to put their new learning into practice, and will need safe supportive opportunities. Once an informal leadership network is in place, it also can offer support as aspiring leaders try new challenges (Ohlott, 1998; Van Velsor et al., 1998).

- Design ongoing follow-up programs that support new learning—leadership development is an emerging process and requires periodic updates for testing new behaviors, obtaining personal support, and reinforcing new ideas. Standalone programs can lose some of their impact over time as participants return to the workplace (Guthrie & Kelly-Radford, 1998; Van Velsor et al., 1998).

- Identify mentors back in the workplace—aspiring leaders need experienced leaders they can talk with about their experiences and working through new challenges. Identifying mentors in the immediate work environment can provide the valuable expertise needed to put new leadership ideas into practice (Moxley & Wilson, 1998; McNamara & Pennisi, 2000; McCauley & Douglas, 2000).

As consultants work with organizations to design leadership development programs, they might face resistance from some people who want quick, tangible results. Others might suggest that leaders are born and not made. To be effective, consultants will need to design programs that are tailored to the organization, engage influential members of the organization, draw on the existing leadership theories that are consistent with the organization, employ self-assessment tools and long-term development, foster supportive yet challenging work assignments, and are self-sustaining. As John Gardner stated, "Most of what leaders have that enables them to lead is learned. Leadership is not a mysterious activity. Most men and women go through their lives using no more than a fraction—usually a small fraction—of the potentialities within them . . . learning to tap that reservoir more effectively is one of the most exciting tasks ahead for mankind" (Gardner, 1990, p. xix).

# SUMMARY

Effective leadership development programs are those that assess individual strengths and weaknesses, offer constructive feedback to participants, and provide ongoing support. Consultants should recognize that in addition to providing the more direct educational components of the program, they will need to work the organizational environment. They will find that building the foundation, tailoring the program to match organizational goals, and creating a network of organizational support, will greatly enhance the likelihood of sustained change and organizational impact.

# References

Argyris, C. (1991). Teaching smart people how to learn. *Harvard Business Review, 69*(3), 99–109.

Argyris, C. (1994). Good communication that blocks learning. *Harvard Business Review, 72*(4), 77–85.

Avolio, B. I., & Bass, B. M. (1999). Re-examining the components of transformational and transactional leadership using the multifactor leadership questionnaire. *Journal of Occupational and Organizational Psychology, 72,* 441–462.

Bartlett, C., & Ghoshal, S. (1994). Changing the role of top management: Beyond strategy to purpose. *Harvard Business Review, 72*(6), 79–88.

Bartlett, C., & Sumantra, G. (1995a). Changing the role of top management: Beyond structure to process. *Harvard Business Review, 73*(1), 86–96.

Bartlett, C., & Sumantra, G. (1995b). Changing the role of top management: Beyond systems to people. *Harvard Business Review, 73*(3), 133–142.

Bass, B. M. (1985). *Transformational leadership: Performance beyond expectations.* New York: Free Press.

Bass, B. M. (1990). From transactional to transformational leadership: Learning to share vision. *Organizational Dynamics, 19*(1), 19–31.

Bass, B. M. (1995). Comment: Transformational leadership. *Journal of Management Inquiry, 4,* 293–297.

Bell, C. R. (2000). Mentoring as partnership. In M. Goldsmith, L. Lyons, & A. Freas (Eds.), *Coaching for leadership* (pp. 131–141). San Francisco: Jossey-Bass.

Bennis, W. G., & Nanus, B. (1985). *Leaders: The strategies for taking charge.* New York: HarperCollins.

Blanchard, K. (1998). Servant leadership revisited. In L. C. Spears (Ed.), *Insights on leadership* (pp. 21–28). New York: Wiley.

Block, P. (1998). From leadership to citizenship. In L. C. Spears (Ed.), *Insights on leadership* (pp. 87–95). New York: Wiley.

Bolman, L., & Deal, T. (1994). Looking for leadership: Another search party's report. *Educational Administration Quarterly, 30*(1), 77–95.

Bolman, L., & Deal, T. (1997). *Reframing organizations: Artistry, choice, and leadership* (2nd ed.). San Francisco: Jossey-Bass.

Buono, A. (1998). Book review: Reframing organizations. *Personnel Psychology, 51,* 507.

Burns, J. M. (1978). *Leadership.* New York: HarperCollins.

Chappelow, C. T. (1998). 360-degree feedback. In C. D. McCauley, R. S. Moxley, & E. V. Van Velsor (Eds.), *The Center for Creative Leadership Handbook of Leadership Development* (pp. 29–65). San Francisco: Jossey-Bass.

Charan, R., Drotter, S., & Noel, J. (2001). *The leadership pipeline.* San Francisco: Jossey-Bass.

Conger, J. A. (1993). The brave new world of leadership training. *Organizational Dynamics, 22*(1), 46–58.

Conger, J. A. (1998). Qualitative research as the cornerstone methodology for understanding leadership. *Leadership Quarterly, 9*(1), 107–121.

Conger, J. A. (1999). Charismatic and transformational leadership in organizations: An insider's perspective on these developing streams of research. *Leadership Quarterly, 10*(2), 145–169.

Conger, J. A., & Benjamin, B. (1999). *Building leaders: How corporations are developing the next generation.* San Francisco: Jossey-Bass.

Conger, J. A., & Xin, K. (2000). Executive education in the 21st Century. *Journal of Management Education, 24*(1), 73–101.

Covey, S. (1989). *The seven habits of highly effective people.* New York: Fireside.

Covey, S. (1990). *Principle-centered leadership.* New York: Fireside.

Cyert, R., & March, J. (1963). *Behavioral theory of the firm.* New York: HarperCollins.

Deal, T. E., & Kennedy, A. A. (1982). *Corporate cultures: The rites and rituals of corporate life.* Reading, MA: Addison-Wesley.

Deeprose, D. (1995). *The team coach.* New York: American Management Association.

Dorfman, P., & Howell, J. (1997). Leadership in western and Asian countries: Commonalities and differences in effective leadership. *Leadership Quarterly, 8,* 233–274.

Ensari, N. (2002). The role of leaders and consultants in fostering international organizations. In R. L. Lowman (Ed.), *Handbook of organizational consulting psychology* (pp. 493–515). San Francisco: Jossey-Bass.

Fiedler, F. E. (1967). *A theory of leadership effectiveness.* New York: McGraw-Hill.

Fiedler, F. E. (2002). Proactive ways to improve leadership performance. In R. L. Lowman (Ed.), *Handbook of organizational consulting psychology.* San Francisco: Jossey-Bass.

Fields, D., & Herold, D. (1997). Using the leadership practices inventory to measure transformational and transactional leadership. *Educational and Psychological Measurement, 57,* 569–579.

Fleenor, J. W., & Prince, J. M. (1997). *Using 360-degree feedback in organizations.* Greensboro, NC: Center for Creative Leadership.

Fletcher, J. K. (1996). *Relational theory in the workplace* (Tech. Rep. No. 77). Wellesley, MA: Wellesley College, Stone Center.

Foxon, M. (2000). Motorola. In D. Giber, L. Carter, & M. Goldsmith (Eds.), *Linkage Inc.'s best practices in leadership development handbook* (pp. 326–366). San Francisco: Jossey-Bass.

Fu, P., & Yukl, G. (2000). Perceived effectiveness of influence tactics in the United States and China. *Leadership Quarterly, 11,* 251–266.

Fulmer, R. M., & Vicere, A. A. (1995). *Executive education and leadership development: The state of the practice.* University Park, PA: Pennsylvania State Institute for the Study of Organizational Effectiveness.

Gardner, J. (1990). *On leadership.* New York: Free Press.

Garman, A. N. (2002). Assessing candidates for leadership positions. In R. L. Lowman (Ed.), *Handbook of organizational consulting psychology* (pp. 185–211). San Francisco: Jossey-Bass.

Garvin, D. (1993). Building a learning organization. *Harvard Business Review, 71*(4), 78–91.

Giber, D., Carter, L., & Goldsmith, M. (Eds.). (2000). *Linkage Inc.'s best practices in leadership development handbook.* San Francisco: Jossey-Bass.

Goleman, D. (1998a). Leadership that gets results. *Harvard Business Review, 76*(2), 78–90.

Goleman, D. (1998b). *Working with emotional intelligence.* New York: Bantam Books.

Goleman, D. (2000). What makes a leader? *Harvard Business Review, 78*(1), 93–102.

Greenleaf, R. K. (1970). *The servant as leader.* Indianapolis, IN: Robert Greenleaf Center.

Guthrie, V. A., & Kelly-Radford, L. (1998). Feedback-intensive programs. In C. D. McCauley, R. S. Moxley, & E. Van Velsor (Eds.), *The Center for Creative Leadership handbook of leadership development* (pp. 66–105). San Francisco: Jossey-Bass.

Hargrove, R. (1995). *Masterful coaching*. San Diego, CA: Pfeiffer.

Hartog, D., & Van Muijen, J. (1997). Transactional versus transformational leadership: An analysis of the MLQ. *Journal of Occupational and Organizational Psychology, 70*(1), 19–37.

Hawkins, B., & Petty, T. (2000). Coaching for organizational change. In M. Goldsmith, L. Lyons, & A. Freas (Eds.), *Coaching for leadership* (pp. 307–315). San Francisco: Jossey-Bass.

Hooijberg, R., & Choi, J. (1999). From Austria to the United States and from evaluating therapists to developing cognitive resources theory: An interview with Fred Fiedler. *Leadership Quarterly, 10*, 653–665.

Hoppe, M. H. (1998). Cross cultural issues in leadership development. In C. D. McCauley, R. S. Moxley, & E. Van Velsor (Eds.), *The Center for Creative Leadership handbook of leadership development* (pp. 336–378). San Francisco: Jossey-Bass.

House, R. (1971). A path-goal theory of leader effectiveness. *Administrative Science Quarterly, 16*, 321–339.

Howell, J. (1997). Substitutes for leadership: Their meaning and measurement—An historical assessment. *Leadership Quarterly, 8*, 113–116.

Hudson, F. M. (1999). *The handbook of coaching: A comprehensive resource guide for managers, executives, consultants, and human resource professionals*. San Francisco: Jossey-Bass.

Kanter, R. M. (1983). *The change masters: Innovation and entrepreneurship in the American corporation*. New York: Simon & Schuster.

Kanter, R. M. (1989). The new managerial work. *Harvard Business Review, 67*(6), 85–92.

Kanter, R. M., Stein, B., & Jick, T. (1992). *The challenge of organizational change*. New York: Free Press.

Katzenbach, J. R., & Smith, D. K. (1993). The discipline of teams. *Harvard Business Review, 71*(2), 111–120.

Kilburg, R. R. (1996). Toward a conceptual understanding and definition of executive coaching. *Consulting Psychology Journal: Practice and Research, 48*(2), 134–144.

Kilburg, R. R. (2002). Individual interventions in consulting psychology. In R. L. Lowman (Ed.), *Handbook of organizational consulting psychology* (pp. 109–138). San Francisco: Jossey-Bass.

Kirkland, K., & Manoogian, S. (1998). *Ongoing feedback: How to get it, how to use it*. Greensboro, NC: Center for Creative Leadership.

Kofman, F., & Senge, P. (1993). Communities of commitment: The heart of learning organizations. *Organizational Dynamics, 22*(2), 5–23.

Kotter, J., & Heskett, J. (1992). *Corporate culture and performance*. New York: Free Press.

Kouzes, J. M. (1998). Finding your voice. In L. C. Spears (Ed.), *Insights on leadership* (pp. 322–325). New York: Wiley.

Kouzes, J. M., & Posner, B. Z. (1987). *The leadership challenge*. San Francisco: Jossey-Bass.

Kouzes, J. M., & Posner, B. Z. (1993). *Credibility: How leaders can gain and lose it, why people demand it*. San Francisco: Jossey-Bass.

Kouzes, J. M., & Posner, B. Z. (1995). *The leadership challenge: How to keep getting extraordinary things done in organizations*. San Francisco: Jossey-Bass.

Kraft, D. (2000). Abbott Laboratories. In D. Giber, L. Carter, & M. Goldsmith (Eds.), *Linkage Inc.'s best practices in leadership development handbook* (pp. 1–36). San Francisco: Jossey-Bass.

Krogh, G., Ichigo, K., & Nonaka, I. (2000). *Enabling knowledge creation: How to unlock the mystery of tacit knowledge and release the power of innovation*. Oxford, England: Oxford University Press.

Latif, M., & Anderson, B. (2000). Barclay's global investors. In D. Giber, L. Carter, & M. Goldsmith (Eds.), *Linkage Inc.'s best practices in leadership development handbook* (pp. 108–136). San Francisco: Jossey-Bass.

Leithwood, K., & Duke, D. (1999). A century's quest to understand school leadership. In J. Murphy & K. Seashore-Louis (Eds.), *Handbook of research on educational administration* (2nd ed., pp. 45–72). San Francisco: Jossey-Bass.

Manzi, L., & Abramson, J. (2000). SmithKline Beechem. In D. Giber, L. Carter, & M. Goldsmith (Eds.), *Linkage Inc.'s best practices in leadership development handbook* (pp. 408–438). San Francisco: Jossey-Bass.

March, J., & Olsen, J. (1976). *Ambiguity and choice in organizations.* Bergen, Norway: Uiversitetsforlaget.

McCauley, C. D., & Douglas, C. A. (2000). Developmental relationships. In D. Giber, L. Carter, & M. Goldsmith (Eds.), *Linkage Inc.'s best practices in leadership development handbook* (pp. 160–193). San Francisco: Jossey-Bass.

McCauley, R. S., Moxley, R. S., & E. Van Veslor (Eds.). *The Center for Creative Leadership handbook of leadership development* (pp.217–241). San Francisco: Jossey-Bass.

McDonald-Mann, D. G. (1998). Skill based training. In C. D. McCauley, R. S. Moxley & E. Van Velsor (Eds.), *The Center for Creative Leadership handbook of leadership development* (pp. 106–126). San Francisco: Jossey-Bass.

McNamara, D., & Pennisi, A. (2000). Colgate-Palmolive. In M. Goldsmith, L. Lyons, & A. Freas (Eds.), *Coaching for leadership* (pp. 188–225). San Francisco: Jossey-Bass.

Megerian, J., & Megerian, L. (1999). Understanding leader emotional intelligence and performance. *Group and Organization Management, 24,* 367–393.

Morgan, G. (1997). *Images of organization* (2nd ed.). Thousand Oaks, CA: Sage.

Morrison, A. M. (1992). *The new leaders: Guidelines on leadership diversity in America.* San Francisco: Jossey-Bass.

Morrison, A. M., & Von Glirow, M. A. (1997). Women and minorities in management. *American Psychologist, 45,* 200–208.

Morrison, A. M, White, R. P., & Van Velsor, E. (1997). *Breaking the glass ceiling: Can women reach the top of America's largest corporations?* (Rev. ed.). Reading, MA: Addison-Wesley.

Mullin, V. C., & Cooper, S. E. (2002). Cross-cultural issues in international organizational consultation. In R. L. Lowman (Ed.), *Handbook of organizational consulting psychology.* San Francisco: Jossey-Bass.

Newman, M. A. (1993). Career advancement: Does gender make a difference? *American Review of Public Administration, 23,* 361–384.

Nonaka, I., & Takeuchi, H. (1995). *The knowledge-creating company: How Japanese companies create the dynamics of innovation.* New York: Oxford University Press.

Nonaka, K., Toyama, R., & Konno, N. (2001). SECl, Ba and leadership: A unified model of dynamic knowledge creation. In I. Nonaka & D. Teece (Eds.), *Managing industrial knowledge: Creation, transfer, utilization* (pp. 13–43). Thousand Oaks, CA: Sage.

Ohlott, P. J. (1998). Job assignments. In C. D. McCauley, R. S. Moxley & E. Van Velsor (Eds.), *The Center for Creative Leadership handbook of leadership developmentØ* (pp. 127–159). San Francisco: Jossey-Bass.

Oseem, M. (2001). The leadership lessons of Mount Everest? *Harvard Business Review, 79*(9), 51–58.

Parker, C. (1999). The impact of leaders' implicit theories of employee participation on tests of the Vroom-Yetton model. *Journal of Social Behavior and Personality, 14*(1), 45–61.

Peddy, S. (1998). *The art of mentoring.* Houston, TX: Bullion Books.

Pfeffer, J. (1992). *Managing with power.* Boston: Harvard Business School Press.

Posner, B., & Kouzes, J. (1993). Psychometric properties of the Leadership Practices Inventory—updated. *Educational and Psychological Measurement, 53*(1), 191–199.

Posner, B., & Kouzes, J. (1994). An extension of the Leadership Practices Inventory to individual contributors. *Educational and Psychological Measurement, 54*, 959–966.

Robins, S. (2002). A consultant's guide to understanding and promoting emotional intelligence in the workplace. In R. L. Lowman (Ed.), *Handbook of organizational consulting psychology* (pp. 159–184). San Francisco: Jossey-Bass.

Rosen, R., & Digh, P. (2001). Developing globally literate leaders. *Training and Development, 55*(5), 70–81.

Ross, S., & Offermann, L. (1997). Transformational leaders: Measurement of personality attributes and work group performance. *Personality and Social Psychology Bulletin, 23*, 1078–1087.

Ruderman, M. N., & Hughes-James, M. W. (1998). Leadership development across race and gender. In C. D. McCauley, R. S. Moxley, & E. Van Velsor (Eds.), *The Center for Creative Leadership handbook of leadership development* (pp. 291–335). San Francisco: Jossey-Bass.

Sandowsky. (1995). The charismatic leader as narcissist: Understanding the abuse of power. *Organizational Dynamics, 23*(4), 57–71.

Saporito, T. J. (1996). Business-linked executive development: Coaching senior executives. *Consulting Psychology Journal: Practice and Research, 48*, 96–103.

Schein, E. H. (1992). *Organizational culture and leadership: A dynamic view* (2nd ed.). San Francisco: Jossey-Bass.

Schein, E. H. (1993). On dialogue, culture, and organizational learning. *Organizational Dynamics, 22*(2), 40–51.

Senge, P. (1990). *The fifth discipline: The art and practice of the learning organization.* New York: Doubleday.

Solomons, J., Hu-Chan, M., Marin, C. E., & Robertson, A. G. (2000). Becoming an effective global leader: Coaching for organizational change. In M. Goldsmith, L. Lyons, & A. Freas (Eds.), *Coaching for leadership* (pp. 327–336). San Francisco: Jossey-Bass.

Spears, L. (1998). *Insights on leadership.* New York: Wiley.

Stopper, W. G. (1998). Agility in action: Picturing the lessons learned from Kodak and 23 other companies. *Human Resource Planning, 21*(1), 11–13.

Thomas, R. R. (2000). Coaching in the midst of diversity. In M. Goldsmith, L. Lyons, & A. Freas (Eds.), *Coaching for leadership* (pp. 349–358). San Francisco: Jossey-Bass.

Thompson, M. (2000). Gender, leadership orientation, and effectiveness: Testing the theoretical models of Bolman & Deal and Quinn. *Sex Roles, 42*, 969–692.

Tracey, J., & Hinkin, T. (1998). Transformational leadership or effective managerial practices? *Group and Organization Management, 23*(3), 220–236.

Van Velsor, E. (1998). Assessing the impact of developmental experiences. In C. D. McCauley, R. S. Moxley & E. Van Velsor (Eds.), *The Center for Creative Leadership handbook of leadership development* (pp. 262–288). San Francisco: Jossey-Bass.

Van Velsor, E., & Guthrie, V. A. (1998). Feedback-intensive programs. In C. D. McCauley, R. S. Moxley, & E. Van Velsor (Eds.), *The Center for Creative Leadership handbook of leadership development* (pp. 66–105). San Francisco: Jossey-Bass.

Van Velsor, E., McCauley, C. D., & Moxley, R. S. (1998). Our view of leadership development. In. C. D. McCauley, R. S. Moxley, & E. Van Velsor (Eds.), *The Center for Creative Leadership handbook of leadership development* (pp. 1–25). San Francisco: Jossey-Bass.

Vroom, V. (1973). *Leadership and decision-making.* Pittsburgh, PA: University of Pittsburgh Press.

Waagan, A. J. (2001). Individual development plans for leaders. *ASTD Performance in Practice*, 2–3.

Waldman, D., & Bass, B. (1990). Adding to contingent-reward behavior. *Group and Organization Management, 15*, 381–394.

Yammarino, F. I., & Dubinsky, A. (1994). Transformational theory: Using levels of analysis to determine boundary conditions. *Personnel Psychology, 47*(4), 787–811.

Yukl, G. (1971). Toward a behavioral theory of leadership. *Organizational Behavior and Human Performance, 6*, 414–440.

Yukl, G., & Howell, J. (1999). Organizational and contextual influences on the emergence and effectiveness of charismatic leadership. *Leadership Quarterly, 10*, 257–284.

Zenger, J., Ulrich, D., & Smallwood, N. (2000). The new leadership development. *Training & Development, 54*(3), 22–27.

PART FIVE

# BRIDGING LEVELS

# CHAPTER SIXTEEN

# Proactive Ways to Improve Leadership Performance

Fred E. Fiedler
*University of Washington*

It is relatively easy to predict who is more likely to become a leader. While there are many exceptions, people who rise to leadership positions come from among those who tend to be taller, more visible, better looking, and who have more leader-like bearing and charisma, as well as social skills. They tend to have the job-related experience, education, and abilities that a given job requires. They also have a better chance to become leaders if they happen to come from prominent, wealthy families (Bass, 1990).

Selecting *effective* leaders turns out to be considerably more difficult (Bass, 1990). Empirical research to identify leaders who will become effective has focused mainly on selecting the most intelligent and experienced individuals, and training them in the skills and behaviors that will supposedly enable them to organize and direct the work of their subordinates. However, despite much effort, we have had little success in finding personal attributes or leadership traits that consistently identify effective leaders, or in training them to become effective.

---

This chapter is a review and reinterpretation of previous research by the author and his associates. I am especially indebted to Judith Fiedler who read, reread, and reread this chapter, and gave me the benefit of her critical comments and suggestions.

# SITUATIONAL FACTORS IN LEADERSHIP MODELS

This chapter suggests that we might have been looking in the wrong place for the answer to this problem. We have ignored the well-established finding that effective leadership depends not only on the leader's personality, ability and certain personal attributes, but also on the leader's immediate work-environment, the leadership situation. In fact, we have paid little attention in our research to the important role that the leadership situation plays in determining the leader's performance, and the specific conditions under which leaders and their subordinates can make the most effective use of their abilities, experience, and job-related personal attributes (see, for example, Fiedler, 1995, 1996).

## Importance of the Leadership Situation

This chapter contends that most selection procedures and training are based on two highly questionable assumptions. These are that (1) the job candidate will naturally make effective use of his or her job-relevant abilities and attributes, and (2) the leader's behavior, job knowledge, and personal attributes can predict leadership performance regardless of the characteristics of the situation in which leadership is to be exercised.

Why is the leadership situation important? As it has been defined in our research (see, for example, Fiedler, 1967; Fiedler & Chemers, 1974), the leadership situation, and specifically *situational control,* indicates the power, control, and influence the leader has over the group process and the task. If the leader lacks situational control (for example, if the group's members do not listen to the leader), the leader's intellectual abilities and task-relevant knowledge cannot affect the group's performance (Blades & Fiedler, 1976). Clearly, the leader's performance depends both on the leader's attributes and on the leadership situation. Thus, we cannot predict leadership performance by looking only at such leader attributes as intellectual abilities or task knowledge (Blades & Fiedler, 1976; Fiedler, 1967, 1995). This chapter presents a number of examples that show the critical importance of the leadership situation in determining the leader's effectiveness, and its consequence for selection and training.

We know that the leader's abilities and personal attributes do not change much over time. However, we have generally ignored the fact that leadership situations *do* change frequently—very often from year to year, and sometimes as often as from day to day or week to week. For example, the leader might get a new boss, key members of the group might retire, leave, or get promoted, or the group might get a new assignment or be faced with an emergency. The typical selection process does not consider these situational factors (Fiedler & Chemers, 1984).

In the usual course of events, candidates are first screened by evaluating their educational background, work history, technical skills, and required abilities.

The survivors of this process are then interviewed by a member of the hiring organization. This process usually includes a closer examination of their previous work history and track record, as well as a highly subjective evaluation of their bearing, attitudes, and personality. In many large organizations, candidates also might have to take tests of mental abilities, personality attributes, and technical knowledge, which are among the most frequently used leader attributes in selecting leaders and managers (Campbell, Sessa, & Taylor, 1995). These factors were also used in our studies.

## Research Findings

Our own research, and that by other investigators (see, for example, Bass, 1990; Ghiselli, 1963; Stogdill, 1948), show that there is little, if any, relationship between leadership performance and the leader's intellectual abilities, technical training, or expertise. Results from our own research are summarized in Tables 16.1 and 16.2.

Table 16.1. Median Correlations and Range of Correlations Between Leaders' Cognitive Resource Measures and Performance.

|  | Performance and | | |
|---|---|---|---|
|  | Median $r$ | Range | No. of Studies |
| Intelligence | 0.16 | 0.35– −0.23 | 13 |
| Amt. of tech. training | 0.00 | 0.17– −0.17 | 7 |
| Leader experience measures |  |  |  |
| Time in service | 0.10 | 0.27–0.00 | 9 |
| Time in job or organization | 0.11 | 0.18–0.011 | 10 |

Table 16.2. Correlations Between Leader Intelligence Scores and Performance in Groups in which Leaders Were Relatively Directive or Nondirective, and Groups Were either Supportive or Not Supportive of Their Leader[1].

|  | Directive Behavior | | | |
|---|---|---|---|---|
|  | High | | Low | |
|  | Group Support | | Group Support | |
|  | High | Low | High | Low |
| Mess steward IQ | .56[2] (13) | −.09 (13) | .21 (11) | −.05 (11) |
| Job experience | .44 (13) | .26 (13) | −.08 (11) | −.37 (11) |
| Job training | .25 (13) | .08 (13) | .24 (11) | −.65[2] (11) |

[1]Substituting Stress for Group Support gave similar results.

[2]Indicates probability level below .05.

*Source of data:* Blades and Fiedler, 1976.

Apparently, selecting and training effective leaders requires much more than selecting the best and the brightest, the most experienced, intelligent, or technically most competent people (Fiedler, 1996). It also demands that leaders have a work environment in which these qualities can operate. Thus, the information provided by the selection process might well tell us about the candidate's *capacity* for performing a given job, but the leadership *situation* determines whether the work environment will enhance or block the leader's effective use of his or her cognitive resources and other task-relevant attributes.

## Illustrative Studies

I have here selected a small number of studies to illustrate some roles played by the leadership situation. I will confine my discussion primarily to organizational settings in which reliably measurable indices of intellectual abilities, experience, and technical competence are available, and the leader's performance can be adequately measured. These studies suggest how the consultant can enable the organization to make maximum use of the leader's job-relevant abilities and attributes. More extensive examples are described in various references (see, for example, Fiedler & Chemers, 1984; Fiedler & Mahar, 1979; Potter & Fiedler, 1981).

## Directive versus Participative Approaches

Leaders typically (but not always) have more job knowledge than their group members, or they might have been given special training or instruction for the job. It is obvious on brief reflection that leaders must also be encouraged to communicate their knowledge or training to members of their group, and to direct them accordingly in performing the assigned task.

Thus, certain organizations (for example, the military or paramilitary) typically encourage the leader to be directive, to tell group members what to do and how to do their jobs. Other organizations encourage a participative management in which the leader is expected to be democratic, to consult with the members of the group, and to include them in the decision-making process. The latter implies that the leader should listen to subordinates and take a relatively passive, more democratic role in making decisions. This participative, nondirective leadership style has been especially endorsed by a number of writers in the organizational development (OD) field (see, for example, Sashkin, 1984). However, neither of these approaches is always effective.

**Simulated Technical Training Experiments.** Two experiments on simulated training by Murphy, Blyth, and Fiedler, (1981) illustrate the point. One simulated training exercise shows that the leader's technical training increases leadership performance only when the organizational climate encourages the leader to direct and participate actively in the work of his group.

Two related experiments examined the effect of training on the performance of decision-making teams under differing styles of leadership. In the first experiment, fifty-six teams of college students participated in a decision-making task. The task of these groups, developed by Lafferty and Pond (1974), was to imagine that their plane had crash-landed in summer in the middle of a desert, and that only fifteen items could be salvaged from the wreck. Their job was to rank these fifteen items in order of their potential usefulness for helping the group to survive. Their performance was evaluated by comparing the group's ranking with the ranking of these items by a team of experts from the U.S. Desert and Tropic Information Center.

The teams worked under four conditions. Leaders in half of the groups were instructed to be autocratic in directing the group's work, and the other half of the leaders were instructed to be democratic and participative in their leadership style. Furthermore, half of the autocratic and half of the democratic leaders were given a short training session on general principles of survival under desert conditions. They were given no specific help on the task. The other leaders were given a lecture covering an irrelevant topic.

The results of this study (see Figure 16.1) clearly showed that the leader's training contributed only if the leader adapted an autocratic, directive

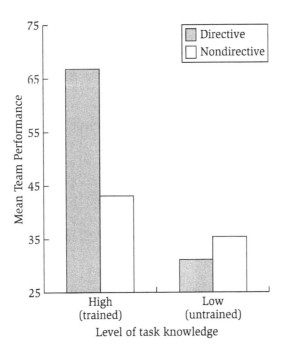

Figure 16.1 Effect of Leaders' Training, Level of Task Knowledge, and Leadership Style on Team's Performance.

leadership style. However, the leader's training contributed substantially to the group's performance only if the leader had received training and had adapted a directive style of management. Neither training by itself nor the style of management alone increased team performance.

The task of a companion study asked teams to decide on methods for surviving a plane crash on an isolated mountain range (Kast & Rosenzweig, 1976). It was designed to determine under what conditions directive or nondirective leadership would be most effective. In this experiment, noncommissioned officers of the New York National Guard ($n = 68$; mean age, 34) were randomly assigned to nineteen three-person groups and one four-person group. As in the first experiment, the task consisted of ranking the value of fifteen salvaged pieces of equipment for helping the group to survive.

In this experiment, all group members, *with the exception of the leader*, were given relevant information about survival in the mountains. Performance was again defined by the similarity of the group's ranking to the ranking by experts in mountain rescue. Half the leaders were instructed to be directive in their leadership style, and the other half were told to be nondirective and participative.

Figure 16.2 shows that training enabled group members to contribute to group performance *only* if the leader was participative and nondirective in his management. Their training had *no* beneficial effect in groups in which the leader was told to adopt a directive, autocratic style. Thus, group members

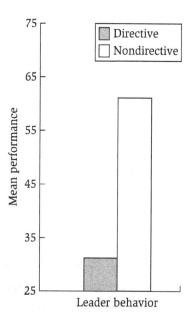

**Figure 16.2. Performance of Groups in which Members Were Given Relevant Task Training and Leaders Were Instructed to Be Directive or Nondirective.**

were able to utilize the knowledge they had gained from training only when the leader encouraged them to participate in the group discussion.

**Army Dining Hall Study.** Leaders who are nondirective and do not communicate their orders and instructions, as well as subordinates who are not supportive of the leader, constitute a barrier between the leader's cognitive resources and task performance. This is seen in a field study of forty-eight army dining halls by Blades (Blades & Fiedler, 1976). In this study, we correlated the dining hall stewards' intelligence scores, job experience, and the scores of a task-ability test, with the rated performance of forty-eight army dining halls under four conditions. The dining hall stewards were rated as relatively directive or nondirective, and their subordinate cooks as supportive or not supportive, as indicated by a group atmosphere score. Leader intelligence contributed to performance only if the dining hall stewards were directive and the group was supportive ($rxy = .56$, $n = 13$, $p < -.05$, one-tailed test). In dining halls in which the stewards were not directive or did not have group support, the correlations between intelligence score and performance were small and nonsignificant (that is, $rxy = -.09$, $-21$, $-.05$). Similarly, the leader's on-the-job experience and task knowledge contributed relatively more when the leader was directive. Thus, low support or nondirective leadership blocked the potential contribution of the leader's intellectual ability and task-knowledge to the task. We found very similar results in other studies (Fiedler & Garcia, 1987).

# THE EFFECT OF STRESS ON PERFORMANCE

Stress is another very important situational factor that determines the degree to which the leader's intellectual ability or experience contributes to the task.

## Job Stress versus Interpersonal Stress

We must differentiate between job stress and interpersonal stress. Our studies show that job stress (which is usually a function of such task characteristics as the complexity of the task, time pressures, physical danger, and so on) tends particularly to affect the use of leader experience.

Interpersonal stress with coworkers, subordinates, and especially with the immediate superior (*boss stress*) appears to arouse a much more emotional reaction in the leader. In contrast to job stress, interpersonal stress tends to evoke a highly emotional reaction that diverts the leader's intellectual focus from the task to the relationship with the immediate superior.

**The Army Division Study.** The effects of boss stress on leader intelligence and experience in the army is particularly well illustrated by a field study by

Borden (1980; see also Fiedler, 1996). Data came from 327 company commanders, platoon leaders, and platoon sergeants of an army infantry division. Borden obtained intelligence test scores, experience (time of army service), and the ratings of stress between the leader and the leader's immediate superior. Two to five of the leader's superiors evaluated the performance of each leader. (Stress with the superior was essentially unrelated to the superior's rating of the leader, presumably because most leaders cannot evaluate how they appear to their subordinates.)

To determine the contribution of leader intelligence and experience to the performance of the leader's unit, Borden separately standardized intelligence, experience, and boss stress ratings for company commanders, platoon leaders, and platoon sergeants. Borden then correlated the leader's standardized intelligence and experience scores with ratings of leadership performance under three levels of stress. Figure 16.3 shows that the more intelligent leaders performed substantially better than less intelligent leaders when stress was low, but they performed substantially less well than less intelligent leaders when stress was

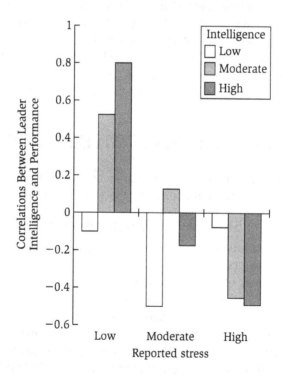

**Figure 16.3. Contribution of Army Troop Leaders' Intelligence under Low, Moderate, and High Stress. The Vertical Axis Shows the Correlation in Standardized Scores Between Leader Intelligence and Performance. (All Interactions Are Highly Significant.)**

high. In other words, high leader intelligence was effectively utilized only when stress was low.

In contrast, Figure 16.4 shows that relatively experienced leaders performed substantially better than inexperienced leaders when stress was high, but less well when stress was low. In other words, stress energized experienced leaders, but was detrimental to inexperienced leaders.

This finding was also supported in a variety of others studies. These included high school basketball teams (Fiedler, McGuire, & Richardson, 1989), officers and petty officers of a large Coast Guard headquarters (Potter & Fiedler, 1981), and teams of college students who performed creative and problem-solving tasks (Fiedler et al., 1989).

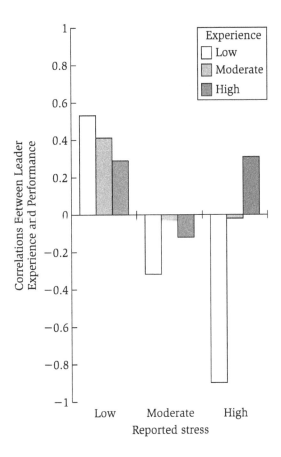

Figure 16.4. Contribution of Army Troop Leaders' Experience to Performance under Conditions of Low, Moderate, and High Stress. The Vertical Axis Shows the Correlation in Standardized Scores Between Leader Experience (Time in Service) and Performance. (All Interactions Are Highly Significant.)

**Fire Captains Study.** The positive effect of stress on experience is especially well illustrated in a study of fire department captains who commanded fire stations in various districts of Seattle (Frost, 1983). In this study, job stress could be measured by the average number of hours per year the company spent at the scene (a measure correlated with a variety of psychosomatic symptoms, as well as job-related injuries and accidents).

For purposes of this study, the fire companies were divided into those located in suburban areas, where the work required relatively few hours at the scene of the fire (low job stress), and companies in downtown and industrial areas, which spent relatively many hours at the scene of the fire (high job stress). The companies were further divided into those in which fire captains reported relatively low stress with their boss, and those in which they reported relatively high stress in their relationship with their boss. We could then compare the performance of the four subgroups of fire captains: those with (1) high experience and low boss stress; (2) high experience and high boss stress; (3) low experience and low boss stress; and (4) low experience and high boss stress.

Fire battalion chiefs, the immediate superiors of fire captains, rated their performance. Figure 16.5 shows that the less experienced fire captains were rated better than experienced captains under low stress, but that experienced captains were rated best when performing under high-stress conditions. The greater the level of stress, the better the performance of experienced fire captains. In this case, differences in intelligence played a very minor role in determining performance.

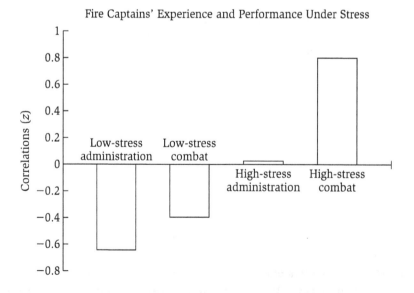

Figure 16.5. **The Effect of Stress on the Fire Captain's Experience and Intelligence in Directing Fire Department Companies.**

One way of intervening in an organization like the fire department would be, of course, to place the more experienced leaders in positions that are normally stressful (for example, districts that see a great deal of fire fighting action), and to place relatively new fire captains into less stressful positions, such as in sub-urban areas in which the need for fire combat is less frequent. In addition, in the case of fire departments, some fire chiefs are notoriously difficult to work with, and others run a more relaxed and stress-free organizations. To the extent possible, the data suggest in this particular case that the organization should place the less-experienced fire captains under the command of fire chiefs who are easy to work with, and the more experienced captains in locations in which job stress tends to be high, and in which, perhaps, the fire chief is more demanding and generates a relatively stressful environment. As in other studies described here, the leadership situation plays a major part in determining leadership performance.

In summary, we know at least some of the situational factors that strongly affect the leader's ability to utilize cognitive resources, and therefore, also the leader's performance. We might not be able to predict leadership performance unless we also know the degree to which the leadership situation is stressful, and how much control and influence the leader will have. However, as the following section shows, we can teach leaders and their superiors to identify work environments in which leaders are likely to perform well, and those in which they are likely to fail. Leaders who learn how to avoid situations in which they are likely to fail are more likely to succeed.

## THE CONTINGENCY MODEL AND SELECTION

The interactions of the leadership situation and leader attributes are by no means limited to such cognitive resources as intellectual abilities, task knowledge, and experience. In fact, the Contingency Model of leadership (Fiedler, 1967, 1993) was one of the earliest, if not the first, of the theories to show that certain leader attributes or traits might correlate with leadership performance on a given task in a positive direction when the leader has high situational control, but in a negative direction when the leader has relatively low situational control, or vice versa.

The main personality measure in the Contingency Model is the Least Preferred Coworker (LPC) score, which measures whether the leader is motivated primarily to develop and maintain a good and supportive relationship with members of the team (high LPC), or is motivated primarily to accomplish the assigned task (low LPC). Task-motivated leaders tend to perform best in situations in which their control and influence is either high or relatively low; relationship-motivated leaders tend to perform best in situations in which their

Table 16.3. Schematic Presentation of the Contingency Model Showing that Different Levels of Situational Control Change Leader Behavior and Performance.

Behavior and Performance of Task-Motivated (Low LPC) and Relationship-Motivated (High LPC) Leaders under Conditions of High, Moderate, and Low Situational Control

| | Situational Control | | |
| --- | --- | --- | --- |
| | High | Moderate | Low |
| Low LPC leader | Considerate | Inconsiderate | Inconsiderate |
| Behavior | Nondirective | Directive | Directive |
| Performance | Good | Poor | Good |
| High LPC leader | Inconsiderate | Considerate | Withdraws |
| Behavior | Directive | Nondirective | Passive |
| Performance | Poor | Good | Poor |

*Note:* Stress and Situational Control have roughly opposite effects. That is, the effect of high Situational Control is similar to the effect of low Stress; the effects of moderate Situational Control and moderate Stress are similar, and the effect of low Situational Control is similar to the effect of high Stress.

control is moderate. This is schematically shown in Table 16.3. Similar relations occur when the leader reports low, moderate, or high stress.

Over 400 studies related to the Contingency Model have been conducted (see, for example, Fiedler, 1967, 1972), and confirmed by three different meta-analyses (Peters, Hartke, & Pohlman, 1985; Schriesheim, Tepper, & Terault, 1994; Strube & Garcia, 1981). These studies show that changes in situational control often markedly increase or decrease leader behavior and performance.

# INTERVENTION STRATEGIES

Although we cannot predict future leadership situations, organizational consultants can teach leaders how to identify or tailor leadership situations for themselves. They can teach leaders to identify situations in which they are likely to succeed and those in which they are likely to fail. They also can teach bosses under which conditions subordinate leaders tend to perform best (see, for example, Fiedler & Mahar, 1979; Fiedler & Chemers, 1984; Fiedler, 1995).

The two important factors in the leadership situation are *stress* and the *control* the leader has over the group process and outcome. Both can be modified. Some suggestions for doing so are listed here. Though not every one of the suggestions will be feasible and practical in every leadership job, and not all of them will work in every situation, some of the changes in the leadership situation do usually work. Indeed, many managers intuitively use these methods for increasing their own performance and that of their subordinates.

## Managing Stress

Managing stress is one way to affect the situation. Some situations are more easily made less stressful than others.

**When Stress Cannot Be Reduced.** Higher-level managers can assign their more experienced supervisors or managers to positions in which stress is likely to be high. This, in fact, is done in many organizations. Since highly experienced leaders appear to perform better in jobs with tight deadlines and complex requirements, they might be seen as troubleshooters in the organization, or startup people when new branches are to be opened. We must remember that a good many leaders not only seek challenging tasks, but also enjoy a certain amount of stress on their job and in their life.

**Stress Reduction.** To reduce stress, organizational consultants and leaders can do the following. Leaders can be trained to reduce stress with their bosses. They can do so by avoiding confrontations and minimizing face-to-face contacts with the superior, rehearsing and role playing potentially threatening interviews, and rewarding and praising superiors for nonthreatening behavior. (How often do bosses get praised by their subordinates?) Consultants can provide stress-reduction training for those who are expected to perform creative and intellectually demanding tasks. Additionally, organizations can give their creative employees job security and a great deal of control over their time and work preferences.

*Lowering stress* will increase the individual's ability to utilize cognitive resources. For example, in a study conducted in a notoriously stressful officer candidate school, stress-reduction sessions included muscle relaxation, breathing, and cognitive restructuring exercises (Smith & Rosenhow, 1988; Link, 1992). The cadets performed in-basket exercises, a management simulation exercise that requires decisions about requests, directives, letters, messages, and so on. The cadets completed these exercises prior to, and again eleven weeks after, completing stress-reduction training. Prior to training in this very stressful environment, the cadets who were relatively more intelligent performed *less well* than those with lower intelligence, a finding consistent with the results of studies already mentioned. However, after receiving stress management training, the more intelligent cadets performed *better* than those with lower intelligence, indicating that the more intelligent cadets had improved in the effective use of their intellectual abilities.

## Controlling the Environment

The situation can also be controlled by changing other aspects of the environment.

**Changing Relations with Subordinates.** A leader can improve interpersonal relations with group members by spending more social time with them, showing concern for their feelings, consulting them, and encouraging them to participate in decisions that concern them. The leader can create more distant relations by being more formal in his or her interactions with group members, using messages and memos to communicate with them, and seeing them by appointment rather than informally.

**Changing the Task Structure.** It is easier to maintain control over group members when the task is laid out by the numbers, the methods and procedures are clearly spelled out, and the objective is clearly specified. It is more difficult to maintain control if the task is vague, and leaves room for argument and different interpretations of the objective (for example, following a blueprint versus developing a policy statement).

A leader can increase the task's structure by gaining expertise about the task, using manuals, obtaining training, and consulting experienced colleagues. He or she can reduce task structure by inviting input from group members and making the job into a group project. A leader can also decrease task structure by asking for jobs that are new and challenging.

**Increasing Position Power.** Leaders can increase their position power by following the book, checking their decisions with the immediate superior, and assuring, as much possible, that all information is channeled through the leader. Sharing information from upper-level managers and sharing decisions tends to lower the leader's authority. (Note, however, that more authority does not necessarily make the leader more successful.)

These and other recommendations, which have been tried successfully in various field studies, are spelled out in greater detail in Fiedler and Chemers (1984) and other sources. Again, the point is that the leader or superior do not have to take a given leadership situation for granted. A well thought-out intervention to change the leadership situation can materially improve performance. Again, it is much easier to change the leadership situation than a leader's personality or cognitive abilities.

# SUMMARY

This chapter has demonstrated that characteristics of the leader alone are insufficient to predict effectiveness on the job. Rather, personal characteristics, which are relatively unchangeable (for example, intelligence and personality characteristics), interact with situational characteristics, which are far more changeable, to determine effectiveness. It follows that organizational consultants should not attempt merely to assess personal characteristics of potential leaders in isolation from the situation in which they are to be placed. The situation as well as the person must be considered. Some aspects of the situation might also be changed. Ways in which situations can be changed were illustrated in the chapter.

# References

Bass, B. M. (1990). *Bass and Stogdill's handbook of leadership: Theory, research, and managerial applications* (3rd ed.). New York: Free Press.

Blades, J. W., & Fiedler, F. E. (1976). *The influence of intelligence, task ability, and motivation on group performance* (Tech. Rep. No. 76-78). Seattle: University of Washington, Organizational Research.

Borden, D. F. (1980). *Leader-boss stress, personality, job satisfaction and performance: Another look at the inter-relationship of some old constructs in the modern large bureaucracy.* Unpublished doctoral dissertation, University of Washington, Seattle.

Campbell, R. J., Sessa, V. I., & Taylor, J. (1995). Choosing top leaders: Learning to do better. *Issues & Observations, 15*(4), 1-5.

Fiedler, F. E. (1967). *A theory of leadership effectiveness.* New York: McGraw-Hill.

Fiedler, F. E. (1972). Predicting the effects of leadership training and experience from the contingency model. *Journal of Applied Psychology, 56*(2), 114-119.

Fiedler, F. E. (1993). The leadership situation and the black box in contingency theories. In M. M. Chemers & R. Ayman (Eds.), *Leadership theory and research: Perspectives and directions* (pp.1-28). Orlando, FL: Academic Press.

Fiedler, F. E. (1995). Cognitive resources and leadership performance. *Applied Psychology: An International Review, 44*(1), 5-28.

Fiedler, F. E. (1996). Research on leadership selection and training. *Administrative Science Quarterly, 41,* 241-250.

Fiedler, F. E., & Chemers, M. M. (1984). *Leadership and effective management.* Glenview, IL: Scott, Foresman.

Fiedler, F. E., & Garcia, J. E. (1987). *New approaches to effective leadership: Cognitive resources and organizational performance.* New York: Wiley.

Fiedler, F. E., & Mahar, L. (1979). A field experiment validating contingency model leadership training. *Journal of Applied Psychology, 64*(3), 247-254.

Fiedler, F. E., McGuire, M. A., & Richardson, M. (1989). The role of intelligence and experience in successful group performance. *Journal of Applied Sport Psychology, 1*(2), 132-149.

Frost, D. E. (1983). Role perceptions and behavior of the immediate supervisor: Moderating effects on the prediction of leadership effectiveness. *Organizational Behavior and Human Performance, 31*, 123-142.

Ghiselli, E. E. (1963). Intelligence and managerial success. *Psychological Reports*, 12, 898.

Kast, F. E., & Rosenzweig, J. R. (1976). *Experiential exercises and cases in management.* New York: McGraw-Hill.

Lafferty, J. C., & Pond, A. W. (1974). *The desert survival problem.* Plymouth, MI: Human Synergistics.

Link, T. G. (1992). *Stress management training: An extension of cognitive resource theory.* Unpublished doctoral dissertation, University of Washington, Seattle.

Murphy, S. E., Blyth, D., & Fiedler, F. E. (1981). Cognitive Resource Theory and the utilization of the leader's and group members technical competence. *Leadership Quarterly, 3*(3), 237-255.

Peters, L. H., Hartke, D. D., & Pohlmann, J. T. (1985). Fiedler's contingency theory of leadership: An application of the meta-analysis procedure of Schmidt and Hunter. *Psychological Bulletin, 97,* 274–285.

Potter, E. H., III, & Fiedler, F. E. (1981). The utilization of staff member intelligence and experience under high and low stress. *Academy of Management Journal, 24*(2), 361–376.

Sashkin, M. (1984). Participative management as an ethical imperative. *Organizational Dynamics, 12,* 4–22.

Schriesheim, C. Tepper, B. J., & Terault, L. A. (1994). Least Preferred Co-Worker score, situational control, and leadership effectiveness: A meta-analysis of contingency model performance predictions. *Journal of Applied Psychology, 79*(4), 561–573.

Smith, R., & Rosenhow, D. (1988). *Trainer's manual for cognitive-affective stress management training.* Unpublished manuscript, University of Washington, Seattle.

Stogdill, R. M. (1948). Personal factors associated with leadership: A survey of the literature. *Journal of Psychology, 25,* 35–71.

Strube, M. J., & Garcia, J. E. (1981). A meta-analytical investigation of Fiedler's contingency model of leadership effectiveness. *Psychological Bulletin, 90,* 307–321.

# CHAPTER SEVENTEEN

# Psychological Consultation to Organizations

## Linking Assessment and Intervention

Harry Levinson

*Chairman Emeritus, The Levinson Institute and
Clinical Professor of Psychology Emeritus
Harvard Medical School*

Psychological consultation to organizations takes many forms and is based on many different assumptions about the causes and precipitants of human behavior.

## VARIETIES OF ORGANIZATIONAL CONSULTATION

Historically, in industrial-organizational (I-O) psychology, organizational change was brought about through the design of work (Jaques, 1996), by evolving selection methods (Kehoe, 2000), attitude survey methods (Kraut, 1996), and various derivatives of organizational development methods (Lawler, 1986). Consultation therefore was focused on practices and procedures. It assumed essentially a reward and punishment motivational model. From the days of the Hawthorne studies (Roethlisberger & Dickson, 1939), it also assumed that manipulations of the work environment would have significant effects on productivity and work satisfaction. Furthermore, it assumed implicitly that top management had the right to manipulate the organization and those who worked in it to attain those ends. Implicit also was a psychology of individual differences and individual comparisons.

To a lesser degree, organizational and industrial consultation involved working with managers and executives in a counseling role. Executive coaching (see, for example, Kilburg, 2000; Hall, Otazo, & Hollenbeck, 1999) recently has reached fad-level proportions. To an even lesser degree, sometimes masked by the executive coaching rubric, clinical relationships have become acceptable to practicing executives (Levinson, 1991; Kets deVries, 1984).

With the development of the group dynamics movement (Bradford, Gibb, & Benne, 1964), much psychological consultation early on took the form of sensitivity training and similar experiences, such as encounter groups, and subsequently, other forms of group process, such as team building. The underlying motivational assumptions were built around self-actualization (Maslow, 1954), group membership, and the honest and accurate expression of feelings. Thus, the implicit theory of motivation was broad and nonspecific (little mention of how one might solve specific problems of people, or apply specific leadership behavior in specific organizational settings). The major techniques advocated were catharsis and group participation in decision-making. Much of the current organizational development movement is derived from this model. Concurrently, there was frequently an assumption of an open system model of organization (Katz & Kahn, 1978), but rarely was this model considered explicitly in detail in published accounts of consultation.

In both modes, the more traditional industrial-organizational and the group dynamics–based, the role of the consultant is essentially temporary and transient. Even when the latter-day organizational development consultant becomes involved in career counseling and the management of human resources, her relationship usually is short-term and technique-oriented. The consultant's observation of group processes and facilitation of group effort tend to be bounded by the discrete meetings in which they occur (Schein, 1987). There is an underlying assumption that motivation is conscious or readily can become so, that one is dealing with learned behavior, and that people effectively can use the feedback of both personal and group psychological data garnered from the group experience to enhance subsequent personal and organizational behavior over extended periods of time (Marrow, 1972).

Many have learned about some aspects of both individual and group behavior from these experiences, and much contemporary consultation on organizational change proliferated from them. However, interest in the experiences themselves (T-groups and some of their more prominent derivatives such as encounter groups) declined. Today, even their once prominent and enthusiastic proponents no longer advocate them. They fell into disuse because the behavioral changes largely were temporary. Also, confidence in the methods decreased as evidence of their ineffectiveness increased (Truax & Carkhuff, 1967). The proponents or trainers, usually without clinical training, failed to take into account the fact that much behavior, particularly that which is troublesome to oneself or others, is characterological (Levinson, 1976a). That is, the behavior is consistent and enduring. Usually, its origins are beyond the awareness of the individual. It is therefore not amenable to enduring, significant change by short-term feedback methods. Another reason why managements backed off and prominent practitioners gave up the methods was the incidence of psychological casualties, denied by the clinically untrained trainers, but familiar to corporate medical departments and the outside clinical consultants who treated them. There are no statistics on the incidence of casualties, but I heard much about them in seminars I was then conducting for physicians employed by organizations.

Few methods for assessing organizational behavior are comprehensive. There is a wide range of such methods, largely focused on part-problems such as organizational development, organizational design, organizational training and staffing, organizational culture, and rewards (Howard, 1994). Some consultants lean heavily on survey techniques, some on role analysis, some on interviews, some on evaluating organizational structure. Few combine their analyses of these part-problems or processes, undertaken with circumscribed methods, into a more comprehensive understanding of an organization that encompasses its history, statistics, characteristic mode of behavior, methods of discovering and solving problems, its crises, adaptive patterns, leadership, ethnographic composition, communications patterns, financial features, competitive posture, relations to its competitors, community, and government, and the variations in its relationships with the consultant, let alone the consultant's involvements with various components of the organization, and his feedback. Even fewer clearly identify their assumptions about motivation, personality, and environment. Therefore, most consultants have difficulty being scientific, for example, establishing fact, making and identifying inferences from fact, and drawing interpretations from those facts and inferences. Their methodological limitations also constrain their interventions. Few consultants discuss a flexible range of intervention methods that they can draw on. Too often, organizational consultation consists of techniques in search of a problem.

## Systems Models

My own consultation model (Levinson, 2002) takes more seriously the concept of the organization as an open system, drawn from biology (Von Bertalanffy, 1950; Fuqua & Newman, 2002). Such a living system seeks to sustain an equilibrium among the multiple forces, inner and outer, acting upon it, and simultaneously pursues a developmental course toward adaptive effectiveness, mastering its environment and maintaining its stability. In this model, adapted and extrapolated from the psychiatric case study method (Menninger, 1962), an organization has a history, characteristic modes of operating, enduring values, recallable crises, and folklore, modes of gathering, processing, and acting on information, leadership, and relative degrees of flexibility. In short, there is an organizational personality. Using this model, and assuming an underlying psychoanalytic theory of motivation, a consultant is responsible for understanding the organization as a whole, in its context, and against its history. This knowledge becomes a base for evaluating the organization's capacity to approach its collective aspirations and its competence for relieving its internal strains, for helping the organization as a whole perceive accurately its self-image against its ideal expectation of itself, and to evolve steps toward more effectively pursuing its adaptation.

To those ends, the consultant must be in a continuing relationship with the organization, as an outside source of knowledge about the organization, about which it is not readily aware (for example, most employees in most organizations know little about their organization's history, let alone its implications for current behavior), and a point of stability for an organization in turbulence (change always implies turbulence). The consultant must have evolved diagnostic and prognostic hypotheses and a mode for working with the organization that simultaneously will respect its integrity and help it move toward a higher adaptive plane. In this chapter, I propose to illustrate some critical intervention issues that usually followed upon that kind of assessment process, or a frame of mind that assumed that process, and the logic that led to the particular consultation activity in each situation. The several illustrative cases exemplify a range of diagnostic and prognostic conclusions from the assessments and subsequent consulting behavior that followed from the psychological logic that was developed. I also note some more important lessons I learned from each.

## The Consultant's Responsibilities

Using this method, the consultant assumes responsibility for gathering, integrating, and assessing information about the organization, sometimes with the help of its internal resources and participants, and defining an intervention based on his assessment and prognosis. Some might feel that this is a physician-patient model in which the know-it-all physician therapeutizes the passive patient. But the reality is that all change agents operate this way, no matter how much they deny it. Each brings his or her own training, prejudices, ignorance, perceptions, methods, and skills. Each does things in, with, and to an organization, based on some (usually tacit) assumptions about himself, about the organization, and about motivation.

With this method, I make my assumptions as explicit as I can, although these illustrative cases are too short to do so in detail here. I make the assessment and prognosis based on clinical psychological training, a classic psychoanalytic theory of motivation (Levinson, 1987), and a biological model of the organization following Von Bertalanffy (1950). That model assumes that the organization is a living organism that evolves a pattern of growth, development, and adaptation, methods for competitive survival, modes of maintaining its equilibrium in the context of social and economic changes, and, to the extent that it coheres, does so around a set of values. Necessarily, it requires processes that have to do with creating or providing products or services, making them known, communicating both internally and with its contextual worlds, and getting, controlling, and expending money. I assume that the organization not only has strengths, but also that there are limits to how and how well it can change. After all, organizations necessarily are heavily influenced by the nature of their leadership, as well as by financial, technical, educational, political, and sociological forces. In consultation practice, this means the consultant undertakes different kinds of interventions under different circumstances, with a specific logic for choosing those interventions that also allow for the consultant's self-correction.

# CASE STUDY: STUCK IN PSYCHOLOGICAL MUD

Here is a classic case, a frequent model for many consultations. Often, consultants are called upon to help with a crisis situation. Too frequently for his professional comfort, he quickly discovers that there is no time for a comprehensive assessment, that he must act to relieve the crisis, and only later follow up with more thorough consideration of broader issues to be dealt with. To complicate matters, when he discovers that the organization for years not only has been in a constricted, rigid managerial pattern, but also controlled from behind the scenes by a dominant board member, he is soon walking on delicate psychological eggs as he tries to help the organization awaken to its realities and adapt to them. He also discovers that if there is frequent organizational change in a long-term consulting relationship, particularly in a large organization, it is wise to train and supervise the internal human resources staff to anticipate, assess, and carry out most of those changes.

The case in point was a large profitable single-industry company that was faced with a predictable, radically changing competitive and governmental environment. Its largely technical employee group and their managers had been over-controlled tightly for years by a succession of authoritarian chief executives. Their resulting dependency was reflected in their reluctance to act unless the action was prescribed by policies or directed by their superiors. They were not noted for bold innovations or imaginative ideas. The company's ethos was one of don't make waves, obedient middle-class conformity, and stable employment. There was strong new leadership in the form of a young executive, promoted from within but shadowed by his predecessor, now chairman, who had appointed him. The new leader not only had the capacity to conceptualize the business environment, but also the ways in which the organization would have to change to master it. Not long before his appointment, and perhaps in anticipation of it, he had been enrolled in a university advanced management program. He was willing to take risks and to encourage others to do so. His vision of where he wanted the organization to go was clear and firm. He could articulate a direction.

The enduring core values of the company, as reflected in the comparisons with other companies in the same industry that the employees made in interviews, had to do with integrity and how change was managed. Both stemmed from the religious orientation of the founder. For example, when changes were made, people rarely were fired. Managing change was left to the CEO, and had largely to do with finding and developing the company's natural resources. It was fundamentally a conservative organization that respected its leadership, but one in which most people did not have information beyond their narrow managerial and technical roles within the half-dozen major tracks (called silos) through which the company pursued its business, and in which, once assigned to one, they remained. Each was headed by a vice president who dominated his track. They had little flexibility to act on their own.

## Results of Consulting Interviews

Getting no innovative movement from his vice presidents after a year of effort, at the insistence of the in-house psychologist, the frustrated CEO asked for consultation. My interviews with the several vice presidents who headed the six tracks and staff functions led me to hypothesize that they were in a depressed rage because of the changes that the new CEO was urging. Historically, and because of their characteristic over-controlled personalities, they were unable to disagree with him, let alone speak up publicly. It was difficult for some to see the competitive handwriting on the environmental wall, and for others to see that the business could be operated differently than it had been for years, and indeed would have to be.

The acute depressive rage that paralyzed the vice presidents was quickly apparent to me in the initial interviews. They were tightly controlled in their curt, deliberate, angry answers to my unwelcomed questions, and had little to say spontaneously about their respective roles. Some became red in the face and responded irritably as I pressed them for information about their work. They said little about the president's proposed innovations. They were not about to express their feelings, especially their anger, and certainly not to a psychologist.

I thought that, to loosen that angry constriction and to begin to open up the organizational system so that consultation could proceed further, rapid action was called for before a comprehensive assessment could be completed. The organization, having been stalled for a year, could not continue to be frozen in its tracks. These circumstances (here necessarily highly condensed) led to the choice of the method of dealing with the depression that allowed the top management group to mourn its past in a way congenial to its characteristic mode of behaving, to face contemporary realities, and to organize around its leadership. The method also had to undo the rigidity of the tracks, open the avenues for the next level of managers to act, and facilitate their identification with their new leader. Whatever other steps had to be taken would follow subsequent in-depth assessment.

## Off-Site Consultation

The top eighty people in the company met off-site for three days under the guidance of another consultant colleague and myself. In the first step, we asked the CEO to start the meeting by tracing the directions from which the organization had come, its current status, and what he anticipated to be its current challenges. We recommended that he deliberately not offer his own recommendations or directions about what changes should be undertaken, as we might ask a CEO to do in other situations. We wanted to encourage contributions from the participants. After his presentation, discussion followed in ten-person small groups, whose participants were drawn from all of the major tracks. Their interaction enabled the participants to anticipate and mourn collectively the losses that might follow any change. It also enabled them to become more closely acquainted with each other, encouraged them to support each other in raising questions about the presentation, and permitted them to discuss their doubts and concerns about what they had heard. They then comprised a plenary session in which feedback and questions from the small groups to the CEO became a new model for interaction with authority.

In my experience, in most such meetings where trust of the leadership has not yet been established, managers usually feel they are being manipulated. In this case, our concern was that they might feel they were being persuaded of the CEO's perception of the industry's future. Therefore, as we recommended, the second step was a presentation by a respected futurist, an economist knowledgeable about the industry but unrelated to the company. His predictions necessarily complemented those of the CEO, because the data about the industry and the economy on which both based their judgments were public, even though most of the participants were not as knowledgeable about them. Discussion in the same small groups, and subsequent questions of the futurist in the plenary session, served to counteract whatever suspicion there might have been about the CEO's picture of the future of the industry and the business.

In the third step, the participants were asked to specify the major problems they thought the company faced, and who should do what about them. They did so in the same small groups and reported back to the CEO in the plenary session. The CEO indicated which problems he could and would do something about, which would require greater thought or policy reformulation, and which would require action by the board.

In the fourth step, the participants were reassigned to small groups composed of executives and managers in the same tracks and departments. They were asked to decide what they were going to do about what they had learned in the meeting on the following Monday morning when they were back on the job. Each group reported subsequently in plenary session. I then summarized what had gone on psychologically, followed by a summary by the CEO of his understanding of the meeting.

We then took the same steps within the respective tracks, including those managers who had been at the top management meeting and the next levels of managers, but not first-line supervisors. It was a mistake not to include them because our assumption that the managers would follow up with their subordinates turned out to be invalid.

The enthusiasm of the managers for the new way of doing business was both remarkable and contagious. Their identification with their new leader and their subsequent interaction with him stimulated their cooperation with each other and undermined the rigidity of the depressed, unyielding vice presidents.

## Supporting the Leader

Using this method also requires that the consultant support the leader. I had to help him understand and accept the turbulence that would take place in the small groups, and the hostile questions or criticisms that would arise when those groups reported in plenary sessions. Although I knew those pointed words would be mild, CEOs in that position inevitably feel them to be harsh. I had to help him experience their long-suppressed anger and formulate his responses in ways that would encourage the participants to redirect their anger into problem-solving efforts. The CEO had to encourage initiative and counteract the heavy dependency of the organization on authority. Later, I would have to help him think through what to do and how to do it with those now-obsolete senior executives who could not change. This phase called for careful management of separating those who had to be separated, so as not to demoralize the organization further and exacerbate the guilt of either those who had to terminate them or their erstwhile subordinates (Tomasko, 1987; Noer, 1993). This method also required supporting the successor executives and managers who took their places, who were new in their roles. They were caught up in their feelings both about usurping these positions and displacing their symbolic fathers (Brockner, Gibb, & Benne, 1985). We had to teach those new executives, some of whom never had been executives or managers before, how to support lower-level people amidst turbulence and change by making their rounds among them, being in touch with them, entertaining their fears and disappointments, and demonstrating care and concern. Simultaneously, we had to teach them to take firm action with some subordinates, often former colleagues and peers, who tested them.

We also had to further the support and development of the internal human resources function so that both training programs and organizational development activities could be undertaken to strengthen the organization's inner capacity for change. I had to abstain carefully from being involved in the selection of people who were moved into new roles, lest I be seen as the power behind the organizational leadership. I had to limit my contribution in that area to helping define criteria for roles and teaching managers to write behavioral job descriptions (Levinson, 1976b). These enabled them to make their own choices with greater assurance. To have become involved in selection in this case would have violated the implied contract that placed me at the side of the whole top management group in its efforts to accomplish its changes. I had not contracted with them to contribute judgments about individuals.

In this organization, there were strong financial resources with which to cope with the inevitable economic ups and downs, and the organizational turbulence during the change process that affects effectiveness and profitability. There was solid technical competence, and people, generally speaking, had relatively high educational levels. The organizational culture (Schein, 1992; Trice & Beyer, 1984; Deal & Kennedy, 1982; Geertz, 1973), while somewhat varied among the respective tracks, was essentially cohesive and internally consistent. There was no history of previous failure or organizational crisis. Over its century-long history, the organization had adapted well. The odds were that it could continue to do so if it pursued change proactively, although one could predict that, like most organizational change in large organizations, it would take a five- to ten-year period during which the major changes would come about.

## Changes in the Company over Time

Actually, the organization went through six major changes over a ten-year period, three of which were precipitated by major changes in the industry. The change processes we introduced were internalized by the human resources personnel who carried out the subsequent changes. The consulting relationship continued for several more years in monthly meetings in support of the top management group, which itself had undergone three significant changes. The initial client CEO, who failed to take seriously my warning about his rivalry with his predecessor, the dominant figure on his board, was summarily fired. The consultation ended when the company spun off most of its major tracks, and contracted its size and function to only one of them.

One important lesson in this consultation was the need to take charge and act in what, in a sense, was an emergency situation, before I could do the usual comprehensive assessment. I had to take my initial clinical impressions seriously and trust myself to be guided by them. I could do that only with the trust of the CEO, who was unable to understand and therefore break out of the bind he was in, and the in-house psychologist, whom he trusted and at whose instance he had invited me to help. Despite his trust, he could not think psychologically enough to grasp my cautions about his relationship with his predecessor until it was too late.

In sum, crisis intervention might have to precede a formal assessment, but assessment can then unfold. Implementation might require developing mechanisms for greater managerial involvement, handling terminations, guilt relief, selection and training of new personnel, and support for the CEO.

# CASE STUDY, U.S. STATE DEPARTMENT: SWAMPED IN A POLITICAL FISH BOWL

A formal consultation process carried on by the consultant, as in the previous case, is preferred. But some consultations are too large to be dealt with by a single consultant or even a large team of consultants. With a necessarily large team, some consultations can be too expensive, which is why many large organizations such as Sears, Roebuck, and IBM use attitude surveys (Kraut, 1996) regularly. Furthermore, without the continuous stability of top management over extended periods of time, issues of who is to implement any consultant's recommendations become bureaucratic fodder. All too often, organizations resist recommendations and reforms by ignoring them. This is especially the case with large governmental organizations. Confronted exactly by that kind of a problem after a relatively cursory assessment did not mean that I, the consultant, declined the opportunity. Instead, I made use of the organization's department heads themselves to pinpoint their issues, and to agree on and make public their recommendations. I learned, incidentally, that using members of an organization's own personnel to make their own assessment was instrumental in getting information, and crucial to the acceptance of those findings by the organization.

## Organizational History

The U.S. Department of State had a long history of chronic attack, often purely political, and low self-confidence as an organization. From time to time there was even political talk of doing away with it altogether. It was ridiculed by successive presidents and a wide range of congressmen and senators. There was little experience in the organization of getting at and solving management problems, nor did people in the organization feel they had any right to do so. The professional staff had been subjected to a variety of consultants, including an aborted sensitivity training program for senior officers. State was, and continues to be, a large, unwieldy, bureaucratic organization in which the major figures were rotated through the system. Some secretaries of state, notably John Foster Dulles and Henry Kissinger, operated as Lone Rangers, ignoring the rest of their organization; some were outmaneuvered by other advisors politically closer to the President; none seemed to hold effective management as a primary goal despite the repetitive criticism. Other agencies were created independent of State that carried out specific international programs, sometimes in conflict with it. The historic tradition of dominance by Ivy League graduates had long since given way to a more democratic ethos that led to recruiting prospective Foreign Service Officers from many other universities. But nothing seemed to affect the rigid barriers between managerial levels, or the manner in which the system undermined its own people. For example, at the time of the consultation, in a consulate, whose staff presumably was immediately the closest to the host country's people, staff observations and recommendations were subject to change by every immediate superior through whom they passed. By the time they reached whatever authority needed that information, there was no knowing how valid it was.

Since the top management leaders were political appointees, there was no extended continuity of leadership and no guarantee that there would be any long-term relationship between any consultant and the organization. Usually, in an organizational consultation, the relationship of the consultant with the top management is crucial. The Department of State operated in a context of multiple international political forces, many in conflict with each other, and often those appointees who were responsible for diplomacy in a given country knew little of that country's culture, traditions, or political currents. State had an extensive internal education program for its professional staff, the Foreign Service Institute, which included such topics and language training, and also sent selected officers to various university programs. However, the policy of rotation, required to broaden officers' experiences, and the fact that no one could know the languages of all of the countries to which he or she might be assigned, limited the immersion of many in different foreign locales, and made many dependent on local translators. There was also the issue of physical danger. Some rarely left their diplomatic compounds, particularly in unstable nations, for fear they might be attacked.

However, the new political leadership at the time of the consultation was strong, felt secure in its role, and, mindful of the criticism, wished to bring about change. The late Elliott Richardson, then undersecretary of state, invited me to consult.

From my previous experience with them, I knew that the officers in the Foreign Service, the elite component of State, were highly educated, had considerable professional competence, and were strongly identified with their role and function. They had a long history and what they regarded to be a noble tradition. They had already organized the Foreign Service Officers Association to make their wishes and feelings felt in the system. Thus, there was some capacity to act in a politically unstable setting that could not provide continuing sanction for consultant-guided action. However, to my mind, given the multiple problems I referred to, prognosis at best was dubious, no matter what the intervention. I could imagine the officers shuddering at the thought of yet another set of recommendations by outsiders that would likely be ignored or shelved as were previous critiques, as they themselves later documented (U.S. Department of State, 1970).

There was an opportunity to act, but by whom and how? True, there was a formal authority structure, but how long would those political appointees remain in place? And if they did, who would be willing to take the necessary action steps? What actions would be most beneficial to the system?

In my judgment, those that would be most effective would cut across bureaucratic barriers to illuminate common concerns, give sanction to initiative, legitimize lower-level initiative to bring about change, and quickly produce visible results as a product of initiative. Ideally, people should discover that they could indeed have an effect, and acquire a degree of competence for doing so. That, in turn, meant that a large number of people had to be involved in cross-level activities that would resolve problems that, though in some cases not major, nevertheless constituted psychological thorns in the organizational body.

That set of factors led to my recommendation that a number of internal task forces gather the data and make the recommendations that followed. I would guide and consult with them. In our first meeting, the officers who were invited to become the heads of the projected task forces questioned the possible usefulness of the project and the sincerity of higher management wishing it on them. When they learned that I, who had respected academic credentials and occasionally had taught in the Foreign Service Institute, was to be involved with them, they accepted the seriousness of the assignment. The deputy undersecretary of state for administration, William B. Macomber, Jr., appointed thirteen task forces, each designed to deal with a topic the project heads had nominated. Two hundred fifty Foreign Service Officers and others participated over a five-month period in what they described as a massive modernization plan. The diverse range of participants, and the range of topics, precluded *group think* (Janis, 1972), or agreement based on pressure to cohere at the expense of individual opinions. The topics they addressed were: career management and assignment policies; performance appraisal and promotion policies; personnel requirements and resources; personnel training; personnel requisites; recruitment and employment; stimulation of creativity; the role of the country director; openness in the foreign affairs community; reorganization of the Foreign Service Institute; the roles and functions of diplomatic missions; a management evaluation system; and management tools.

## The Modernization Effort

"This modernization effort," they later wrote (U.S. Department of State, 1970, p. 1), "is an unusual one. It does not follow the traditional procedures for reforming a large bureaucracy. It is not based on the creation of a new outside study commission, nor does it involve a program developed and imposed in detail by top management. On the contrary, at the request of that management, this reform program has been developed not from the top or from the outside, but from *within*. It is the work of 13 task forces made up of outstanding career professionals from within the Department of State and Foreign Service augmented by distinguished career personnel from other agencies in the American foreign affairs community."

I remained at a distance from the activity, meeting only three times with the project heads: first, to give them official sanction and let them know that there was indeed serious intention from the top managerial level of the department; second, to help them formulate how the task forces should go about gathering information; and third, to insist that they report to the first three levels of the executive hierarchy, to overcome some of the barriers to implementation of their recommendations. There were two reasons for insisting that they themselves report their findings to higher management: they were reluctant for structural and historic reasons to confront their superiors and they wanted me to do so; and there would be no "not invented here" resistances. "Not invented here" refers to organizational members' frequent rejection of external consultants' recommendations because the consultants are assumed to impose solutions that are not derived from experience in the organization.

They subsequently published their findings and more than 500 recommendations in a 600-page volume (U.S. Department of State, 1970). They distributed updates of the action plans, called Management Reform Bulletins, to those who had participated, on how the recommendations were being carried out.

Two earlier meetings with the undersecretary of state and the deputy undersecretary for administration and the three meetings with the task force leaders constituted the entire intervention.

Thus, this consultation was short-term, highly focused, and with limited goals in a turbulent setting. It established precedent and left open an avenue for further consultation when, and if, such might be appropriate and necessary. The task forces had done a commendable job, so I recommended that the heads of the task forces be constituted as an advisory council to pursue continued innovation. However, the deputy undersecretary for administration was reluctant to do so for fear that such an advisory council might become another power center in a setting that already had too many fiefdoms. Two years later, an internal study disclosed that a significant portion of the task force recommendations had been carried out.

Consultation does not always mean that the consultant assess and recommend, or even have a continuing relationship with top management. He or she might well do better, especially in large, complex organizations, to guide the internal managerial personnel to do so. They then acquire a skill for looking at their own organization, and are more likely to implement their own recommendations.

# CASE STUDY: SURVIVING DEMORALIZATION

In the previous case, I maintained a distant relationship to the client system. In this case, I was called on to pick up the pieces. Although a consultant might have neither a relationship with the top management of an organization nor even the usual leverage to help it change, there still might be ways to strengthen it and those who work in it so that both can become more adaptive. This kind of intervention calls for greater imagination and initiative on the part of the consultant, as well as simultaneously helping the client group avoid political problems as they strengthen themselves and the organization. The important lesson for me in this case was that the client's situation was not as hopeless as it seemed at first, and that I had to be more active in helping the client staff arrive at their solutions than was the case in either of the two previous cases.

A large state agency had a narrow functional responsibility. It ran the state's lottery, which meant that it publicly chose the winning numbers each week on television, validated the winning numbers, notified the winners, distributed the winnings, and forwarded books of coupons to retail operations that sold them. It was staffed at the top with political appointees, each of whom was seeking to maximize his political potential, and none of whom had any significant interest in or competence with the activities of the agency. Those activities were managed largely by a civil service cadre who had limited technical competence, and who saw the agency as a device to increase their social and economic status. However, since they could not get direction, guidance, authority, resolution of conflict, or political protection from their superiors, they were demoralized and constantly bickering among themselves. Their management was terrible and they knew it. Apart from the state's mandated administrative processes, their executives initiated few innovations. Performance was appraised by checklist with only limited interaction between the appraiser and appraisee. Almost all employees were rated acceptable. There was no history of organizational success, achievement, or proficiency. There was no tradition, no enduring reputation, or commitment to any kind of professional values, except minimal service to the public. In short, the agency was pasted together by a civil service structure to carry on its nonprestigious, little-valued activity.

A change in top management resulted in greater support for the human resources function, but no significant interest on the part of top management itself to become involved in the managerial functions and activities of the agency. The civil service cadre were like abandoned orphans, left to fend for themselves in a complex political world in which they were vulnerable to possible predatory attacks in the legislature and political maneuvering by their superiors in which they could become potential victims, both as an organization and as individuals.

## Issues in the Organization's Demoralization

The director of human resources asked for the consultation to combat the demoralization, and that agency became the client. The director thought he had sanction to act, but since his superiors were uninterested, he could expect no support from them. Of course, they would not want any activity that would attract public attention or make political waves. There were no consistent efforts to resolve conflicts or to increase the efficiency or effectiveness of the agency. The human resources staff itself was a hopeless, demoralized, disappointed group of people who saw themselves going nowhere.

There was no place to go but up, but to what and how? The civil service people could not move far in the hierarchy; the top-level managers were all political appointees. The only opportunity for upward mobility available to them, I discerned, was to increase their own capacities and skills in their management roles so they could ultimately move out of this agency into other civil service roles or into private management. They could improve the present system and themselves out of enlightened self-interest. Therefore, my task as the consultant, after making this assessment, was to become the ally of the human resources function, which, in turn, became allied with the middle management toward their own self-enhancement.

The function of the human resources department became primarily to build into the system that kind of managerial training and development that would enable people to improve their competences and skills, even to acquire academic or professional credentials, and to prepare themselves as individuals for personal advancement. This meant that they had to learn to solve managerial problems together, to evolve better working modes, to improve their own leadership skills, and to use the agency as a laboratory for increasing their managerial effectiveness. Doing so would enable them to organize around common problems, and to develop cohesion that was mutually profitable to themselves and to the organization. As long as they left top management alone and did not cause those officials any difficulties, that management was not very concerned about what they did and how they did it. It could only profit from the increased effective management below them. The prognosis for such an activity was good.

Here, once again, my consulting role was minimal: assessment and subsequent support of the human resources function. After the assessment and my recommendations, my task was to help that staff define their realities and the avenues for steering among them to do an effective job in the absence of strong leadership. The consultation left the human resources staff in a position to choose the appropriate training and development activities that would be most relevant to the people involved, who could not by themselves see the wider range of managerial functions to which they might aspire. Theirs was now the task of helping their constituents to take advantage of their own wish to improve, by defining the skills they needed in their present roles, as well as those they would have to have to move on or up. In some ways, I served in loco parentis, giving sanction, permission, encouragement, and some direction to the human resources staff that otherwise experienced itself as being alone and rudderless.

There are times, as I learned in this case, where the consultant has to become like a benign father, giving more direct advice and counsel to people who need information, guidance, and direction. He also has to become politically attuned in such poorly governed situations, lest his advice stir up higher-level hostility from superiors who want only not to be disturbed. The issues are the same whether in state government, as in this case, or in a business, church, school, or hospital, where management is fuzzy and leadership only nominal.

## CASE STUDY: THE PASSIVE PRESIDENT

In the preceding case, the consultant had to help the demoralized management group find their way in an ambiguous political situation; in other situations, the consultant becomes an agent of long-term stability for the chief executive officer and the senior management. Assessment in this case disclosed that I was dealing with a highly dependent chief executive who also was subject to the whims of a quarrelsome top management trio that was incompetent to lead. My sense of the situation was that the chief executive had a character problem that called for long-term support and protection. The CEO's problems, I hypothesized, were not going to be dealt with by such techniques as team building alone, nor would the constricted personality characteristics of the technical staff (Roe, 1956) lend themselves to easy give and take. I had to be prepared for the challenges and hostilities, as well as the unrealistic expectations, of an extended relationship.

This manufacturing company of highly technical equipment, a division of a larger corporation, was being torn apart by the seventh president in five years. No sooner were the presidents appointed than they were in the midst of conflicting top management directions and quickly resigned. The new chief, almost immediately after his appointment, had come into conflict with its scientific and technical executives, who were the sources of the organization's innovative ability. They were becoming increasingly demoralized and threatening to resign because of his authoritarian manner. Indeed, some had resigned. The financial vice president of the parent company earlier had been in a seminar with me.

Because there was a telephone strike at the time the consultation was requested, the financial vice president, many miles distant from my office, wired the request for immediate consultation.

## Consulting in the Crisis

In this crisis, my task was to gain immediate information about that group, which I did by interviewing each of the sixteen people in the division's senior management. I then summarized those interviews in a meeting with them and their new chief executive, so that they could check on the validity of my findings and so he had accurate and honest information about how they felt. They were pleased that I accurately had tapped the nature of their feelings and concerns. Because of the urgency of the situation, I did not then interview the corporate top management to whom the division reported. As it soon became evident, the top management trio was itself dysfunctional, which then required me to protect the divisional management from the trio's potentially disruptive intrusion.

The interviews disclosed a cohesive group of scientific and technical people with a previous record of group accomplishment in new technology. They wanted to continue to work with each other. They did not want to be mechanized with traditional management formulae. They were not going to be boxed in or ordered about.

When these data were then reported, the task of the group was to determine what they wanted to do about their feelings and how they wanted to go about doing it. I led a series of half-day meetings, during which they thrashed out some of their concerns about the way they were being managed, the freedom they felt they had to have, and their lack of trust in their chief executive. That executive also took part in these meetings, to respond and be tested by their questions when appropriate.

After each meeting, I met privately with the division chief executive, my client, to review what was going on and what kinds of steps needed to be taken to bolster the effort he was making, and to assure his subordinates of his open interest, concern, and support. He moved from his authoritarian position to a more passive one, which provoked significant concern because he would not interact effectively with his people. It took a great deal of my effort to get him to interact, because he was afraid that he would produce the same kind of reaction that he had stimulated in the first place.

## Results of Diagnosis

My diagnostic hypothesis was that his initial authoritarian over-control was a reaction formation against his underlying passivity. To compensate for his sense of inadequacy and helplessness, he went to the opposite extreme in his behavior. He would demonstrate that he was a strong leader. However, when threatened, he again became passive. He needed my support to take a more active stance. That became my near-term focus. Other consultants with different psychological orientations might formulate other diagnostic hypotheses. Whatever one's orientation, a diagnostic formulation is critical for a systematic intervention plan and process.

Although cohesion between the leader and the followers increased, there was still a significant gap. As they began to accommodate to each other, they also tried to slough over significant differences. It was clear to me that the denial mechanisms were setting in as these generally more passive technical people (Roe, 1956) and their fundamentally passive leader worked out a way not to come to grips with each other. I could see that this accommodation would result in their once again pulling away from each other and barely touching psychologically as they passed each other.

At this point, I chose to risk their anger by pointing out these avoidances and becoming the common enemy. I felt I could do this because I had a strong enough relationship with both the group and the chief executive that they could take that abrasion on my part. I knew also that, given the kinds of people they were, they would be unlikely to become overtly hostile; the leader had the capacity to absorb the hostility of the group if and when it occurred, and to deflect it into problem solving, particularly with my encouragement and support.

There were strong financial, technical, and educational, resources, and a reasonably consistent organizational character. The organization's expensive new products were highly regarded in the marketplace, and the organization had good prospects for becoming profitable. Despite their intrusions, after my resistance, the parent organization trio left it largely autonomous. These factors, together with the strong motivation of the top management group, augured well for the prognosis. Though the organization's history had been a turbulent one, marked by initial success, followed by five years of relatively poor productivity through the series of presidents, it was beginning to experience positive change. They rallied to my provocation, and the interaction became more intense as they worked out some of their problems. The organization began to grow rapidly and ultimately divided itself into two, requiring a new generation of team-building activity to create two separate interactive teams.

However, at this point, the president decided that, in addition to my own work in the company, now three years into the relationship, he also wanted to use a more traditional organizational development consultant who would make lists of issues and paste them on walls or easels, and who also would provide certain kinds of academic social psychological input. He told me that he had been impressed by a young female consultant whose presentation he had seen at an industry meeting. He was quite fearful, however, that if he were to retain her, I would leave him. He was also fearful, hinting that if he did not do so, he would no longer be in charge of himself, but rather be a puppet for me. I inferred that his intention arose from his concern that he might become too dependent on me. I accepted these feelings and the president proceeded with his new program. That activity continued sporadically for about a year and then petered out as its superficiality became apparent to him.

Ultimately, the president became fatally ill and had to retire from his role. Serious conflict at the corporate top management level contributed to the deterioration of the parent organization and therefore of its subsidiaries. The corporate top management yielded to a new, more effective CEO, who promptly closed the unprofitable subsidiary and ended the consultation.

## Problems in the Consultation

There were three additional problems in this consultation. The first was that the married president was carrying on a sexual liaison with his reluctant secretary. I referred her for professional help that enabled her to break off that exploitation. The second problem was the corporate top management trio. Two of the three had been constantly in rivalrous conflict with each other for years. Each had a stake in the corporation, and therefore would not leave, nor could either buy out the other. I recommended to the two that they each get personal psychological help. Instead, they retained a clinically untrained trainer who urged them and their spouses into confrontational behavior that only exacerbated their conflict. When they tried to get the subsidiary president to accept him into the subsidiary, I objected. Fearful that I might abandon the now blossoming subsidiary, they backed off. The third problem was their intrusive attempts to interfere with the management of the subsidiary. I had to rebuff them early on because obviously the president at that time could not.

Among the important things I learned in this case was the need to protect the client. A consultant often might not be able to fend off higher management, and no doubt many consultants do not see that as part of their function. The rationale for doing so stems from clinical experience: one has to act in many different ways for many different clients. In this situation it was possible, partly because of my reputation and partly because they did not want the subsidiary to collapse. In addition to assessment, in the course of managing the consulting relationship, one must bring to bear whatever clinical skill one has.

This case illustrates the varying facets of extended consultation, ranging from crisis response, to supporting a passive CEO, to resolving conflict, to evolving a cohesive team, to protecting both the client organization and its leader from intrusive machinations by higher management, to clinical referrals. It points to the need for having an armamentarium of intervention skills and the competence to manage long-term consulting relationships.

# CASE STUDY: NO WAY

In the preceding cases, I undertook consultation, but sometimes one must not. An issue that arises infrequently in the consultation literature is when not to take on a client. An important aspect of a consultant's decision to do so or not hinges not only on the client's degree of readiness for help but also on his willingness to be helped. A client or client system often has great pain, but is unwilling or unable to do something about it. Sometimes a consultant spends weeks of work assessing a situation only to have the client fail to settle into a course of action. Making the judgment not to enter into consultation is a crucial part of the assessment. This case is illustrative.

A medium-sized service organization had some 300 technical and professional people, with a supporting staff of about twice that number. The chief executive had been exposed to various kinds of organizational development activities and wanted more for his organization. New to his role, he hoped to build a lively and participative organization. All of his key professional staff who would go were sent off to various kinds of group experiences. However, when they came back, nothing much happened in their day-to-day application of what they supposedly had learned.

The organization had a fifty-year history of eminence in its field. Its staff had strong identification with it and its services. Many were preeminent in their disciplines. Many also were professionally and socially close to each other. However, they had long been dominated by a charismatic chief who made certain that no successor would arise from the professional group by reorganizing the structure when it seemed that someone among the group had developed a significant following. He maneuvered his board, most of whom were old friends, into choosing his successor. The staff had no part in choosing their new chief executive, nor did they respect the competence of the person chosen.

The new chief executive engaged a series of consultants, including some from abroad, but he seemed unable to make effective use of any of them. They waited around for him to decide how to use them, and then, bored with waiting, they left. The organization lost many of its key staff, who departed in three successive waves at two-year intervals. Only those remained who had no options to go elsewhere or felt it was too late to do so. Sizing up the situation in the initial meeting, I decided that there was nothing to consult about because there was no client. If the chief executive could not act, and if others in the organization could not do so without being perceived as rebels, then I, the consultant, perforce would be viewed as a fomenter of rebellion. There was little possibility of change. Ultimately, the organization hemorrhaged and desperately sought to be acquired by another, an effort that failed because the chief executive did not want to give up his organization's autonomy. Now diminished in size, reputation, and function, it remains a money-losing shadow of its former self, barely surviving until its financial reserves run out.

Learning to say "Thanks, but no thanks" has to become a fundamental technique for a consultant. Despite the urgent wish to consult, and sometimes the pressure to sustain one's income, it is the better part of wisdom not to allow oneself to be exploited uselessly. In this case, I could have been paid well for not doing very much, but time is too precious to waste in such an exercise in futility. If one has time to spare, better to use it to develop new clients or catch up on professional reading.

# PUBLIC SCHOOL CASE STUDY: NO LONGER A FIT

Most organizational consultations range from helping individuals with career problems to resolving intraorganizational differences, managing change, and helping to formulate new directions. Sometimes, more unusually, the consultant is called upon to assess fundamental elements of a community. For most organizational consultants, this is a long way from their industrial-organizational or clinical paths. Such a task particularly calls for systematic assessment. In this case, it calls specifically for both clinical and sociological understanding.

The superintendent of a public school system in a suburban community sought consultation because he could not understand why his community several times had rejected a bond issue to build a new high school, despite its commitment to a high level of secondary education. He wanted to know how decisions were made in his community. Although he had lived there for some years, that process eluded him.

An assessment disclosed that he had been chosen by one school board to be, in effect, an errand boy for that board, which insisted on making its own decisions. However, another board subsequently was elected, and the new board wanted him to assume more active leadership. Given his established characteristic mode of behavior that had made him the appropriate choice for the previous board, he could not do so. It was quite clear that this rather unaggressive man, who needed to be able to please others, could not engage in that kind of take-charge leadership activity that his situation now demanded.

The subunits of his school system had become empires of their own. He was unwilling and unable to confront and challenge the respective principals and the power structures in the community that supported them. The principals had no reason to allow themselves to be organized into a cohesive system, because each had his or her own domain that he or she viewed as needing to be protected. The financial resources and political structure of the community allowed them to operate independently, because the citizens of each neighborhood were mobilized behind their respective schools. The community had a history of quiet, middle-class, Caucasian personal and social over-control, and of making no waves. When assessment disclosed the aggressive but diplomatic leadership activities that now had to be carried out, the superintendent was so dismayed that he refused to allow the results of the assessment to be presented to his school staff and board, as he had agreed. Instead, he delayed the feedback for six months. By that time, although some of the findings were relatively obsolete, the fundamentals had not changed. He no longer fit the role. He chose to resign.

The situational definition of the kinds of leadership behavior required (Hersey & Blanchard, 1977), based on a comprehensive assessment of that community, clarified the leadership role with such vividness that it was apparent to the client that the redefined role was not his cup of tea. When I emphasized the situational requirements, it allowed the leader to juxtapose himself against those requirements without loss of face. His unrelieved discomfort in that situation made it impossible for him to continue to deny the reality of the assessment that had been offered to him. He chose his own prescription. Prognosis was poor for any intervention while he was in that role.

What was most important here, I learned, was the need for a very careful description of the behavior required in each of what now were two different roles, together with an evaluation of the community context. Once having done that, the next important step was to help him understand that he was not guilty of doing anything wrong, but that his occupational world had changed around him. Confronting a now well-defined reality, without being criticized by the findings, he could choose other options with his head held high.

# CASE STUDY: MANAGEMENT ON THE RUN

In a preceding case, the crucial problem was with the CEO who did not grasp the radical change in his work environment. Here is a situation in which the consultation is frustrated by the personality of the CEO.

There are times when undertaking a consultation is a calculated risk. Without yet having assessed an organization, a consultant might have vague impressions from general knowledge in the community or from having heard of specific incidents about an organization. He or she also might know of an organization's relationship to a larger entity that could influence its practices, or of its heritage that becomes a form of control of the people who operate it. Such organizations often are managed by executives who are not formally trained in management and therefore do not know how they should manage. That is especially true of organizations that are operated by religious denominations. With the best of intentions, one might want to help, but discover too late that he is in a psychological morass, as in this case.

High nursing turnover was the bane of a nun administrator of a rehabilitation hospital. In addition, there was open conflict between the administrator and the medical director. That conflict precipitated the request for consultation by the director of human resources with the grudging consent of the administrator, with the expectation that the consultation would ameliorate the conflict between the two authorities.

## Results of Interviews

My student consulting team interviewed all five of the top management group, nine department heads, a sample of twenty-one ward aides on the three shifts, and a sample of support workers (such as janitors, electricians, and dietary personnel), and reviewed the hospital's various statistics and history. They observed six administrative meetings, and visited the wards where patients were largely aged persons who primarily needed nursing care. Given the debilitated state of most of the chronic patients, they did not interview patients. Diagnostic assessment (Levinson, 2002), primarily the interviews, disclosed inadequately trained people in supervisory roles, inadequate support for those in positions of power, show-and-tell meetings of administrative heads, and the administrator's intolerance of leadership initiative other than her own.

The history of the hospital, according to most of the interviewees, was one of passive acquiescence to that kind of administration that substituted rigid smiles for leadership action, and smoothing, denial behavior in the face of repetitive conflict just below the surface. From early on, it was apparent that the prognosis was guarded because the character of the hospital reflected the character of its administrator, who had been in her role eighteen years and reported to the head of her order many miles away in Nebraska.

The likely conclusions of the assessment were becoming more apparent with each passing day. Efforts by the student team to remain in continuing liaison with the director during the course of the assessment were of little avail. Ordinarily, I prefer to meet at least weekly during a consultation with the chief executive of the client organization, to apprise her in a general way without violating confidences about where the consulting team is in its work, and of the general themes that are arising so that she can be prepared for the conclusions when later they are presented formally. That practice was not to be in this case. She would avoid meetings, make only brief and passing contacts in the halls, and continue to operate in a passive-aggressive way, acting in a clandestine manner behind the scenes. Even the priest-chaplain complained about this style of communication. She would manage to attack people, without their knowing clearly how they had been attacked and with no direct opportunity to respond. With that style of leadership, predictably the consequence was that, in the end, when the report and its recommendations were presented to her, she listened politely and then declined the usual post-feedback discussion with the chief executive that I recommend and the subsequent report to the staff.

Given the kind of organization, it soon was clear that the opportunity for significant organizational and personal change was going to be limited. She would and did flee any kind of involvement with me and members of the consulting team that would have required looking seriously at problems and taking forthright action. She fled from her subordinates in the same way. They had no support. Problems remained unaddressed. However, there needed to be a long enough test of various efforts in order to establish a supportive relationship to make certain that no technical and therapeutic stones were unturned to try to help solve these problems. Systematic assessment frequently serves that purpose.

The most important lesson I learned was not to undertake a consultation without prior discussion with and making a judgment about the authoritative executive. If I will not be comfortable working with that executive and she cannot make use of what I have to offer, there is little point in continuing.

## CASE STUDY: LEARNING TO SAY NO

In contrast to taking a calculated risk, as in the preceding case, there are times when it becomes apparent in the initial interview with the executive who is seeking consultation, that there is no point to undertaking consultation at all. This might be the case when that person does not have the authority to engage a consultant, as is often the case when a pained member of a family business wants to impose consultation on his uninterested authoritarian boss. It also might be the case when some members of a top management group in conflict see no need for consultative help, or, as in the present case, simply want to be rid of the business and each other.

A management consultant who had been trying to rescue a family company of three brothers, one of whom was a seriously ill alcoholic, recommended I consult with the three. He hoped that the highly respected chain of quality shoe stores, founded by their grandfather and long headquartered in the community, was still a good business that might be perpetuated.

My interviews with the three disclosed no way in which they could come together. Each had erected a decades-long wall of anger against the others. None had sufficient leverage to bring the other two into significant discussion. One, more desperate to preserve the business than the others, had assented to organizational assessment; the other two were uninterested. They had engaged the management consultant to help them prepare to sell their business. Their only compromise was to sell the company so they could go their respective ways.

Sometimes, given this kind of history and problem, it is the task of the consultant to indicate that nothing further can be done. None of the parties has the wish or other motivation to save themselves as a group (in this case a family), or the organization as an organization. Sometimes this might be the case because the leader does not know what to do. Even though the words of the assessment are clear and the recommendations are specific, and even with the collaborative help of the consultant, the leadership task is beyond the leader's capacities, competences, and skills. While intellectually he might be capable of understanding whatever might be recommended, psychologically he is inadequate to do so. This often happens with executives who have been number two persons to very powerful leaders, who then have passed their mantle on to long-serving loyal lieutenants (Levinson, 1974). Sometimes those to whom the business has been bequeathed have no interest in running it, especially if they are members of the third or fourth family generation. Sometimes the uniqueness of the founder's insights, technical knowledge, or innovative perception cannot be replicated by those who follow.

Sometimes the chief executive has deteriorated physically or mentally to the point where, although propped up by his staff, he cannot seriously engage in consultation. On one occasion, a chief executive, who had sent several of his executives to my leadership seminars, wanted to follow up with consultation. However, another consultant was already conducting a time-and-motion study in his plant. I demurred, saying that having two different consultants at the same time in the same factory would confuse the employees, and therefore we should wait until the other consultant was finished. An executive accustomed to having his own way, he angrily rejected my position, and my prospective consultation as well.

Whatever the case, the prospective consultant must learn quickly to make the judgment that he cannot undertake the consultation, and, if at all possible, inform the prospective client why. Sometimes he can explain his reasons, but often discretion dictates the statement that the consultant cannot be helpful with this problem.

Saying no might be a problem if one has an established reputation for successful consultation. Prospective clients then have high expectations, particularly if they feel that this consultant is their last resort. Nevertheless, the consultant cannot be motivated by guilt. His major task then might be to help the client manage his disappointment (Zaleznik, 1967).

# CASE STUDY: COMMUNITY MENTAL HEALTH CENTER

The contemporary scene of radically changing demands on organizations raises a different kind of disappointment that requires consultation. Assessment is fundamental to helping the organization create and develop a momentum if it has become somewhat confused about what it is supposed to do. This set of circumstances arises when its economic or philosophical ground is no longer as solid as it once was. What do you do if you have been making buggy whips profitably and you see that people are buying fewer buggies and more autos?

Or what do you do if your organization of highly skilled professionals is now being asked to render new services for which its staff, well-trained for present functions, feels unprepared, perhaps even unwilling, to undertake? What happens to the morale of a proud staff if its prized, hard-earned skills become less valued? In such events, a consultant has a multiple task: not only to help the organization recognize and confront its new reality, but also to help its members mourn the loss of their cherished functions and adapt themselves to new demands. This case is illustrative.

A community mental health center with fifty-seven professionals on its staff and a fifty-year history had a new director who followed a much-beloved charismatic predecessor. The center was in crisis because other community agencies (the police department, the school system, the courts), increasingly sophisticated about psychological aspects of their work, were demanding more varied services. They were not satisfied with the consulting and psychotherapeutic services they were getting. Other public and private community service groups whose work overlapped with that of the center were arising. Budget pressures were mounting and relationships with HMOs were rocky. Some key people had moved on.

In the face of this turbulence, the new director chose to take active control. But that was largely of the budget. There was little quality control of services and little movement toward redefining the center's goals and priorities. There was no overall planning. The center was essentially a fragmented assembly of autonomous subunits. Communication among them was poor despite a large number of meetings. The director had little contact with most of the staff, and never discussed reports from the subunits or attended their meetings. None of their respective heads came to see him informally. There was a lack of overall direction, leadership, and strategy.

The staff had high standards. It wanted to perform well and did so clinically. As individual professionals, they always had. However, they talked around issues and jargonized them rather than solving problems. Their mood was one of harassed but controlled professional concern. Both they and the leader were pained by their situation. They could not seem to attack their internal problems despite the great deal of energy expended on them. The staff had little confidence in their new leader, especially after their sense of loss of his predecessor. They shared the perception that the director required direct control. The frustrated director, not knowing which way to turn first, asked for consultation.

Given the shared pain, and the motivation of both the director and the staff as reflected in the assessment interviews, the prognosis was good, but it would take a long time to implement significant change. My goals as the consultant, after assessment, had to include presentation of reality to the organization, that is, that the community wanted more than the individual and group treatment in which the staff prided itself. The goals also had to include mechanisms for change. There was a need to repair the current functioning of the organization before attempting to modify its basic activities. There also was a need to mobilize the staff behind its leader, and to establish his and their confidence in me.

To present the assessment findings, as is my practice, I met with the director alone, then with the director and department heads, and then with the rest of the staff, followed by a presentation to the board. I made explicit the staff's dedication to its historic professional aspirations, together with its limits in meeting the present community's contemporary demands. My summary pointed to the need to develop upgraded programs that were specifically focused on the community's stated requests, and for expanding the staff's aspirations. I also recommended further differentiating and decentralizing the task groups of the organization, and then integrating them more cohesively for better cooperation. I recommended internal task forces to clarify roles, purposes, and goals of the center, specifically stating what the center could and could not do, and how much it would do in each area. This work was to become the basis for a realistic strategy for the center to respond to the new demands being made on it. I asked the director to concentrate his energies primarily on managing the center, and all of the department heads to do the same in their units. That required that they be trained in management and leadership. Recognizing that clinical supervision alone was no longer enough, and being as conscientious as they were, the opportunity to improve their leadership and management skills attracted their interest.

There was a solid history and tradition here, pain from both inside the organization and complaints from the outside, as well as the wish to meet and sustain higher standards while retaining professional vitality and reputation. These comprised sufficient motivation on the part of highly intelligent people to be able to bring them together. Given an accurate perception of both their internal and external realities from a trusted consultant, they could understand what they had to do. However, had I stopped with assessment and recommendations, they would have felt helpless about how to go about implementing the recommendations. I doubt if there would have been sufficient momentum to move ahead. I learned that confronted by a sense of helplessness, I also had to push. Apparently this consultation worked very well, as reflected in the response of the center's director and staff. Some of the staff, later having moved to other agencies and now in charge of them, asked for similar consultation.

## CASE STUDY: PHARMACEUTICAL RESEARCH AND DEVELOPMENT GROUP

How to use power wisely was the essence of the preceding case. In this one, the question for the consultant is what does he do in the absence of appropriate managerial power. All organizations are power structures. Leadership is the exercise of power that enables a group of people to work together toward a common purpose. Too frequently, power is not exercised well, as was too often evident in the preceding cases. Sometimes it is dissipated in conflict, sometimes in manipulation that leads those in the organization to distrust their leadership, and sometimes in over-control that undermines spontaneity and initiative. Worse still, in some kinds of organizations, those in authoritative roles who presumably are to exercise power eschew even the appropriate exercise of that power. When that happens, turmoil follows and demoralization ensues. What can a consultant do when assessment makes it clear that appropriate authority cannot act to resolve the turmoil? Here is one way.

In a large pharmaceutical company's research and development division of five major research areas, an interdisciplinary team was organized to pursue innovation possibilities in a prospective new field. The members of the team were assigned by their respective area chiefs. Four of them were male Caucasian physicians. The fifth was a small, Asian woman. She had both an M.D. and Ph.D., was highly knowledgeable about research design, and more highly specialized on the topic than her colleagues. She had been nominated by her area chief and appointed by the vice president of research to head the project when its previous director retired. She soon found herself embroiled in unpleasant conflict with the four men, who resented a chief who was a small, Asian woman, and because of three aspects of her person: size, gender, and quiet demeanor; she did not have a particularly authoritative manner. When she called a meeting, one or more failed to attend. They complained that she was not a good manager. They resisted her leadership efforts. When she turned to her area chief, conflict-avoidant as many scientists are, he counseled her to appease them. In desperation, she appealed to the director of human resources for the division.

## Concern About the Leader

The director of human resources interviewed the four men and concluded that they did not want to be led by this small, Asian woman. It was as if to accept her leadership reflected on their masculinity. The director had neither the authority nor the power to resolve the conflict. The project head turned to the corporate vice president of human resources for help. That officer interviewed the five parties and attempted to ameliorate the conflict. When her conciliatory efforts failed, she asked for consultation.

I interviewed all of the participants. Two of the hostile men thought they should have been chosen to head the project. One of them had the support of his empire-building chief, who wanted the project for his own area. That chief was a prominent scientist who was locked into his role by his research reputation, and therefore refractory to higher management control. The other area heads did not want to tangle with him either. Another of the four engaged in oppositional behavior that bordered on the unethical. When the vice president of research had appointed the project head, he had instructed her to recruit scientists to expand the project that likely would have great promise. The project was supported in part by government and foundation funds whose grantors valued and expected high-level science. She set about doing so and invited the four to interview the candidates, all of whom necessarily were better qualified for this research than they. Predictably, they rejected all of the applicants.

As I assessed the organization, I concluded that the vice president of research, himself preoccupied with larger scientific and political issues, had little wish to become involved in interpersonal conflict several levels below him, especially if it involved differences among area heads. The area head to whom the project head reported was weak, as manifested by his lack of support for the project head and his advice to appease the men. Internal efforts to alleviate the problem had not been successful, and one area head indirectly was fostering the conflict for his own purposes. Neither the director of human resources nor the vice president of human resources had power over the team members or their area chiefs. There was no person who could support the project head. She was left to flutter in the political breeze. She did not want to quit, nor did the vice president of human resources want to lose a project head, reputable in her specialty, respected by and well-funded by grantors. She was competent as a manager, a good scientist, and demonstrated enthusiastic imagination for the project. Besides, if she quit, her leaving would contradict the company's oft-stated stance of promoting women and minorities. In addition, the company could be vulnerable to a lawsuit for discrimination.

Although I indicated earlier that it was unwise to undertake consultation if the consultant could not have a continuing relationship with an authoritative executive, there was no such person in this situation. The vice president of human resources was desperate for a solution, as was the project head. I determined that if the power vacuum somehow could be filled and someone could exercise authority, the problem might be resolved. Since those who logically should have exercised their power were not doing so, and there were no other internal mechanisms for dealing with the issue, either I had to withdraw or initiate another mechanism for exercising power. I decided on the latter. I recommended that the division create an advisory committee to the project, comprised of prominent women scientists from outside the company. The director of research, glad not to have to be involved in the problem, agreed. The vice president of human resources, in consultation with the project head, recruited such a panel. The panel members interviewed the five participants, coming to the same conclusions I had reached. When they confronted the four men with their findings, the four, who also were involved in other roles in their respective areas, withdrew further into those roles, contributing only nominally to the project. The advisory committee interviewed and helped select the scientific candidates that the project head had recruited. By supporting the project head, they removed a psychological thorn in the body of the organization. The project head was promoted several times as her project became more successful and autonomous.

## The Consultant's Concerns

Psychological organizational consultants usually are preoccupied with three major concerns. The first is getting people to talk to each other. That might be to resolve conflict, develop cohesion and mutual support, evolve new directions, or mourn losses, and similar issues. Much of that is done with group processes, ranging from activities that precipitate and then resolve conflicts within a group, to those that encourage people to share losses, to challenging outdoor group projects like Outward Bound. Some of that is done by survey methods.

The second concern tends to be with helping organizations counteract authoritarian power, to cope with ineffective leadership, and to help organizations select and develop their personnel. These activities can take the form of collective feedback, as in upward appraisal or 360-degree feedback, or sometimes group encounters. They might also include job analysis, psychological testing, career counseling, and executive coaching, as well as training and development programs.

The third concern is helping organizations cope with or compensate for incompetence or ineffectiveness. This can take the form of organizational assessment, using some of the techniques referred to above. However, to be thorough, such an assessment, as I have reiterated frequently above, should be systematic and comprehensive. It should establish fact, develop inferences from fact, and make use of a theory of motivation to give body to those inferences.

There is one other issue that psychological organizational consultants characteristically avoid: the exercise of power. Characteristically, they fear and decry power as if the existence of power is bad. That doesn't make it disappear. Psychologists view as their major task helping people increase their flexibility to make their own choices and develop their own directions. Much of the time, psychologists should not, cannot, and do not make choices for their clients, although some, however inadvertently and perhaps even unconsciously, urge their clients in one direction or another.

There are times when a client cannot act intelligently on its own behalf, whether this arises because of being too upset, too incapacitated, or frozen into some kind of position from which he cannot break free, as was the situation of the project head in this case. When I presented this case to a group of colleagues, their recommendations almost exclusively were to have the respective participants talk further to each other, or talk more with the higher authorities, although much of that had been done before to no avail. What my colleagues did not see, indeed did not want to see, was the need for the consultant to fill the power vacuum. They, as with most psychologists and most of the scientist-executives in this case, were reluctant to exercise power, and did not see themselves as creators of power. Inevitably, to be successful as organizational consultants, sooner or later, as this case illustrates, they must.

# CASE STUDY: A SIGNIFICANT DIFFERENCE[1]

A significant difference between the mode of consultation illustrated here and that which ordinarily is carried on under the rubric of OD (organizational development) is exemplified by a case developed by David Nadler, Webster Hull, Tom Scanlon, and Bill Englehoff and called the Medteck Corporation. The case begins as follows:

> "We have a basic problem of performance here in the Technical Division." John Torrence (30) Senior Vice President of the Medteck Corporation and director of the company's Technical Division (R&D) was talking with several members of a consulting team that he had brought in to help with the problems in the Division.
>
> "We have a bad case of technical constipation; this Division has not brought out a successful new product in two years. If we don't do something about this problem soon, the whole company is going to be in big trouble."
>
> The Medteck Corporation was founded in 1939 by Paul Torrence, the father of the present chairman and CEO, Arthur Torrence, and the grandfather of the present Senior Vice President for Research and Development, John Torrence. Paul Torrence died in 1968.

The consultation took place in 1972. The issue that it raises continues to be valid. I presented this case to several groups of organizational development consultants and asked them what they would do. Their immediate recommendation was to define the problems, list them on a board or easel, conduct team building, and similar kinds of activities. The problems to be dealt with, they assumed, would arise from the group. Also, they presumed, so would corrective actions. However, from the point of view of comprehensive personality theory (Levinson, 1987), I believe the problem was clearly evident in the first two paragraphs, and corrective action could be much simpler and more direct.

According to my assessment (Levinson, 2002), the client is the thirty-year-old grandson of the entrepreneur. He is likely to be under great pressure to prove himself for two developmental reasons, apart from any other considerations: first, as the grandson in a family business, because of what we have known for a long time about intrafamily conflicts in family businesses (Levinson, 1971); second, because at that point in his chronological time, he is in the intimacy

---

[1]I am indebted to David Nadler for permission to use this case.

stage of psychological development (Erikson, 1963). In that stage, he would likely be concerned with establishing his own track record. His probable sense of urgency for both of these reasons is likely to be exacerbated by the economic realities of the marketplace and the structural interdependencies of the organization; for example, if there are no new products, there is nothing to manufacture or sell.

Furthermore, he himself offers us the metaphor of technical constipation. Unconsciously, he himself senses the problem. The psychoanalytic frame of reference (Levinson, 1976a) enables us to understand that he is talking about a derivative of the anal period of child development. His metaphor refers to stubborn children being toilet trained who won't give. The technicians are holding on; they won't get out new products. We might understand, as a hypothesis, this is their response to the pressure being exerted by the new young boss, operating under the configuration of forces our theory has enabled us to derive. Therefore, rather than get involved in elaborate meetings, problem definitions, team-building efforts, and similar typical OD activities, it would be much simpler and more direct to work with the young executive himself. Helping him to understand his present psychological position is likely to reduce his anxieties and concerns to manageable proportions, and thereby diminish his pressure on the technicians that results, however unconsciously, in their stubborn withholding. More importantly, he would not be subject to his subordinates' likely confrontation and attack that might well exacerbate his guilt and paralyze his initiative.

Without a comprehensive theory of personality that includes an understanding of unconscious motivation, stages of development, and characteristic occupational behavior, a consultant could beat all around the organizational bush with a wide range of techniques, none of which really would get to the core of the problem.

# CONCLUSIONS

These examples illustrate a range of activities that an organizational consultant can undertake, indeed in some instances must undertake, when he or she bases his activities on a comprehensive theory of personality and a comprehensive assessment procedure, both of which lead logically and systematically to the methods of intervention that the consultant chooses. Such interventions are based on his assessment of the historical momentum of the organization, its limits and resources, its adaptive capacity, the quality of its leadership, and its freedom psychologically, sociologically, and economically to act in its own self-interest.

This series of cases highlights some more frequent typical organizational consulting problems, and how they were managed. Some called for greater initiative on the part of the consultant than one ordinarily finds in the consulting literature. When there was an emergency situation, for example, when an organization was frozen into a rigid managerial posture, I undertook more active charge of the steps toward easing the crisis without undermining the organization's stability. In another situation, I kept my distance from the client system, and, as a benign parental figure, guided the client personnel in doing their own assessment, and making and implementing their recommendations. In still another situation, I not only had to coach the dependent client executive to greater flexibility and autonomy, but also had to protect him and his organization from potential threats from top-level executives and predatory consultants. Despite the impulse to help, on occasion I had to be firm in my refusal to undertake a consultation. When, unwittingly, I was so unfortunate as to have become enmeshed, I learned to evaluate my client executive before undertaking a consultation. At times, after assessment and recommendations, I found that I had to give the client organization a big push to get it started in the right direction. Sometimes assessing an organizational problem meant assessing a host community, and when the focal problem involved the unrecognized shift of a role for a significant authoritative person, I had to help that person find his way out of his occupational dilemma. Group processes and other psychological devices won't solve power vacuums; sometimes I, not fearing power, had to initiate an organizational device to exercise power when those in positions of power would not or could not do so. Finally, difficult managerial problems sometimes do not need elaborate group processes. It was enough in one case to help the executive client understand his stage of psychological development and his place in his family constellation.

Not all consultations are likely to be successful (Mirvis & Berg, 1977). Some are calculated risks. In some, the odds are against success, but entering such situations with a carefully considered prognosis enables the consultant to avoid becoming demoralized when the consultation turns out negatively, as, from time to time, inevitably it does. Such a consultation posture makes for maximum flexibility of operation, specificity of assessment hypotheses, and self-correction.

## References

Bradford, L. P., Gibb, J. R., & Benne, K. D. (Eds.). (1964). *T-Group theory and laboratory method: Innovation and re-education.* New York: Wiley.

Brockner, J., Davy, J., & Carter, C. (1985). Layoffs, self-esteem, and survivor guilt: Motivational, affective and attitudinal consequences. *Organizational Behavior and Human Decision Processes, 36,* 229–244.

Deal, T. E., & Kennedy, A. A. (1982). *Corporate cultures: The rites and rituals of corporate life.* Reading, MA: Addison-Wesley.

Erikson, E. H. (1963). *Childhood and society* (2nd ed.). New York: Norton.

Fuqua, D. R. & Newman, J. L. (2002). The role of systems theory in consulting psychology. In R. L. Lowman (Ed.), *Handbook of organizational consulting psychology* (pp. 76–105). San Francisco: Jossey-Bass.

Geertz, C. (1973). *The interpretation of culture*. New York: Basic Books.

Hall, D. T., Otazo, K. L., & Hollenbeck, G. P. (1999). Behind closed doors: What really happens in executive coaching. *Organizational Dynamics, 27*, 39–53.

Hersey, P., & Blanchard, K. H. (1977). *Management of organizational behavior: Utilizing human resources*. Englewood Cliffs, NJ: Prentice Hall.

Howard, A. (Ed.). (1994). *Diagnosis for organizational change*. New York: Guilford Press.

Janis, I. L. (1972). *Victims of groupthink*. Boston: Houghton Mifflin.

Jaques, E. (1996). *Requisite organization: A total system for effective managerial organization and managerial leadership for the 21st century* (2nd ed.). Falls Church, VA: Cason Hall.

Katz, D., & Kahn, R. L. (1978). *The social psychology of organizations*. (2nd ed.). New York: Wiley.

Kehoe, J. F. (Ed.). (2000). *Managing selection in changing organizations*. San Francisco: Jossey-Bass.

Kets deVries, M.F.R. (Ed.). (1984). *The irrational executive: Psychoanalytic explorations in management*. Madison, CT: International Universities Press.

Kilburg, R. R. (2000). *Executive coaching: Developing managerial wisdom in a world of chaos*. Washington, DC: American Psychological Association.

Kraut, A. I. (Ed.). (1996). *Organizational surveys: Tools for assessment and change*. San Francisco: Jossey-Bass.

Lawler, E. E., III. (1986). *High involvement management: Participative strategies for improving organizational performance*. San Francisco: Jossey-Bass.

Levinson, H. (1971, March–April). Conflicts that plague family businesses. *Harvard Business Review, 45*(2), 90–98.

Levinson, H. (1974, November–December). Don't choose your own successor, *Harvard Business Review, 52*(6), 53–62.

Levinson, H. (1976a). *Psychological man*. Boston: Levinson Institute.

Levinson, H. (1976b, July–August). Appraisal of what performance? *Harvard Business Review, 54*(4), 30–46.

Levinson, H. (1987). Psychoanalytic theory in organizational behavior. In J. W. Lorsch (Ed.), *Handbook of organizational behavior*. Englewood Cliffs, NJ: Prentice Hall.

Levinson, H. (1991). Consulting with top management. *Consulting Psychology Bulletin, 43*(1), 10–15.

Levinson, H. (2002). *Organizational assessment: A step-by-step guide to effective consulting*. Washington, DC.: American Psychological Association.

Marrow, A. J. (1972). *The failure of success*. New York: AMACOM.

Maslow, A. H. (1954). *Motivation and personality*. New York: HarperCollins.

Menninger, K. A. (1962). *A manual for psychiatric case study* (2nd ed.). Philadelphia: Grune & Stratton.

Mirvis, P. H., & Berg, D. N. (1977). *Failures in organizational development and change: Cases and essays for learning*. New York: Wiley.

Noer, D. M. (1993). *Healing the wounds: Overcoming the trauma of layoffs and revitalizing downsized organizations*. San Francisco: Jossey-Bass.

Roe, A. (1956). *The psychology of occupations*. New York: Wiley.

Roethlisberger, F. J., & Dickson, W. J. (1939). *Management and the worker*. Cambridge, MA: Harvard University Press.

Schein, E. H. (1987). *Process consultation: Vol. I. Its role in organizational development.* Reading, MA: Addison-Wesley.

Schein, E. H. (1992). *Organizational culture and leadership: A dynamic view* (2nd ed.). San Francisco: Jossey-Bass.

Tomasko, R. L. (1987). *Downsizing: Reshaping the organization for the future.* New York: AMACOM.

Trice, H. M., & Beyer, J. M. (1984). Studying organizational cultures through rites and ceremonials. *Academy of Management Review, 49*(4), 653–669.

Truax, C. B., & Carkhuff, R. R. (1967). *Toward effective counseling and psychotherapy.* Hawthorne, NY: Aldine de Gruyter.

U.S. Department of State. (1970). *Diplomacy in the 70's.* (Department of State Publication 8551, Department and Foreign Service Series 143). Washington, DC: U.S. Government Printing Office.

Von Bertalanffy, L. (1950). An outline of general systems theory. *British Journal of Philosophical Science, 1,* 134–163.

Zaleznik, A. (1967, November–December). Management of disappointment. *Harvard Business Review, 45,* 59–70.

# CHAPTER EIGHTEEN

# Integrating Individual Assessment, Position Requirements, Team-Based Competencies, and Organizational Vision

## *Roles for Consulting Psychologists*

John T. Kulas, Brad A. Haynes, Suzanne M. Kalten,
Pamela J. Hopp, and Rebekah L. Duffala
*Corporate Psychology Resources*

Τhis chapter outlines an integrative approach for human resources-based consultation. *Human resources* (HR) are defined here as being an organization's *person-based capital.* HR systems, then, are organizing frameworks for managing human capital. Using this model, the role of the organizational consulting psychologist is discussed within this context focusing on services, products, and tools that can be used to aid in the management of effective HR systems. Although the model stresses multiple levels (Dansereau, Yammarino, & Kohles, 1999), this chapter uses illustrative examples of model-based consultant strategies that can directly impact the individual employee.

The specific HR system functions that are discussed in this chapter concern the HR responsibilities of employee selection, development, promotion, and succession. Although traditional HR departments also involve such responsibilities as compensation and benefit analyses, Equal Employment Opportunity Commission (EEOC) compliance assurance, and collective bargaining, these responsibilities are not directly addressed here.

The specific model presented here uses an integrated, HR problem-focused approach. It presents a framework for common-source (integrated) tools and services that can help identify an appropriate progression of employees throughout the course of the employee-employer relationship. These approaches are achieved through a consideration of four different perspectives: the individual, position, team or department, and organization.

The role of the consulting psychologist (who can be either internal or external to the organization) is presented as that of being a knowledgeable facilitator of the dynamic progression of employees in, through, and out of organizations. Efficacious HR systems (and consulting psychologists who work within these systems) strive to advise an appropriate course of employee progression and maintain mutual benefit for both the employer and the employees in the HR system and process.

# MODEL OVERVIEW

The consulting psychologist within our model considers the needs of the individual, position, team, and organization, while also coordinating action across these four levels of analysis. The specific model strives for correspondence between individual, position, team, and organizational needs, and conceptualizes the employee-employer relationship ideally as being symbiotic. Rather than being prescriptive, the model is intended to provide a broad framework through which consulting psychologists can approach HR-based consulting.

A comprehensive organizational consulting assessment should consider the needs of the individual, position, team, and organization, and the appropriate course to address particular consulting issues should be based on these assessments. For example, if the individual's career goals are consistent with the vision of the organization, identified developmental needs can result in targeted training of value to both the individual and the organization. In contrast, the chronic developmental needs of individuals whose career goals are inconsistent with the vision of the organization would warrant a different course of action (perhaps outplacement).

# MODEL COMPONENTS

The term *integrated* in our model refers to coordinating individual, position, team, and organizational needs, and taking into account the ways in which the needs of each of these can be mutually beneficial. The consulting psychologist's role in our model is therefore focused both toward identifying needs and to the issue of assessing the correspondence of needs.

## Integrators

Integrated entities are connected to each other by at least one identifiable communality, here termed *integrators*. For example, a car's exhaust, suspension, and steering systems are mechanically integrated in the sense that they share the common purpose of serving the locomotive ability of the vehicle; or, two cultures that are socially integrated might share both a physical proximity and a common fate. Similarly, integrated HR approaches are bound by certain communalities, also referred to here as integrators. The communalities that bind integrated HR approaches from the perspective of the employing organization are: (1) position competency models, (2) team-based competency models, and (3) organizational visions or goals. A fourth integrator to be considered throughout this chapter consists of the career goals of the individual employee.

## Position Competency Model

A primary function of HR management involves an identification of what tasks need to be done (that is, what are the specific job elements in positions), and what skills, knowledge, and abilities are necessary for the successful completion of the identified job elements. This identification is traditionally accomplished through job analytic procedures. The application of job analysis, in fact, dates to the early 1900s, when Hugo Munsterberg began examining tasks and necessary skills of ship captains in an attempt to ensure safer transportation. Using this approach, Munsterberg was able to help select captains who were most capable of, in this case, making critical decisions quickly (Van De Water, 1997).

Competency modeling derives from job analysis procedures, although competency models are typically more tightly aligned with the vision of the organization than are job analyses. Job analysis tends to be strictly descriptive; competency models more commonly consider both current requirements and future needs of a particular position. The scope of competency models can be narrow or broad. They can specify characteristics necessary for successful completion of a particular function, or they can encompass all knowledge, skill, and abilities required to be a successful contributor at any number of tasks or jobs within the organization (Lawler, 1994).

The most important features of competency models are that they help identify the characteristics (also defined as knowledge, skills, abilities, or traits) that are necessary to excel within a particular organizational function, and they align those characteristics with the goals of the organization. In the framework presented in this chapter, competency models can be interpreted as being future- (or vision-) focused job analyses. Some competencies that commonly occur within, for example, managerial-level competency models across organizations include communication, motivation, leadership, business acumen, team-orientation, and interpersonal awareness (McClelland, 1973; Shippmann et al., 2000). Position competency models can be used as integrators of products and services aimed at identifying important skill and knowledge domains of current and future position incumbents.

## Team Competency Model

Team-focused competencies extend position-based competencies by identifying the features of a team that are necessary for it to succeed. These competencies are concerned with the factors important for the success of the team as a whole, not just of the individual team members. The unit of analysis is the team and the characteristics necessary for team success (see, for example, Johnson, Beyerlein, Huff, Halfhill, & Ballentine, 2002).

Some organizations incorporate a team orientation competency into their position competency models. Indeed, team orientation is also often an important competency in position competency models. Team orientation alone, however, does not identify the distinct competencies that are exhibited by the successful team or work group. These team-based competencies might include such factors as shared or common vision, results orientation, accountability, and synergistic interdependence. Note that these concepts relate important features of the team, as a whole, in developing effective performance. Team-based competency models can integrate products and services aimed at identifying current and future team needs. (For additional information regarding team-based competency modeling, see Cannon-Bowers & Salas, 1997, and Militello, Kyne, Klein, Getchell, & Thordsen, 1999.)

## Organizational Vision

An organization's vision differs from the concept of organizational *mission*. The mission of an organization describes its core purpose, whereas the vision is a statement of intended direction, or where the organization would like to be. Stated differently, "Effective visions should describe a future world where the mission is advanced and where goals and strategy are being successfully achieved in lockstep with the organization's guiding philosophy and values" (Levin, 2000, p. 95). Collins and Porras (1994), and Quigley (1994), have further defined vision as being a combination of an organization's mission, philosophy, goals, and strategy. The communication of these vision elements allows members of the organization to share a sense of purpose, direction, and meaning. Due in part to this important communicative feature, vision is frequently associated with the act of organizational leadership.

Organizations occasionally struggle with the idea of a vision statement. Often times vision statements are derived by painstakingly analyzing partial or misguiding information that is more consistent with current trends than with organizational needs. As Levin notes, vision statements often include so many catchy phrases, buzzwords, and "managementese" that they lose power or meaning (Levin, 2000). The important feature of an organizational vision statement is that it encompasses the organization's values, outputs, and goals, and communicates the intentions of the organization. Organizational vision statements can be used as integrators of products and services (such as succession planning systems) aimed at preparing the organization for future needs. For more detailed information regarding the practice of developing an organizational vision, see Larwood, Falbe, Kriger, and Miesing (1995), and Levin (2000). For a presentation of the specific relationship between leadership and vision, see Yukl (1994).

## Career Goals

The fourth integrator considered here differs from the three previously presented integrators. This fourth and final integrator, career goals, is a function solely of the individual applicant, candidate, or employee, and is ideally determined in isolation from the employment context. Although the determination of individual career goals and employment needs is an important feature of the current discussion, the determination of these needs and goals is a difficult procedural objective within the job context. Specifically, organizational incumbents are typically not in a position to be speaking freely of their needs and desires, particularly if they are obviously inconsistent with the vision of the organization. The career goals assessment of the individual might consist of face-to-face interviews with the consulting psychologist, or might include the administration of psychological instruments such as occupational interest inventories (see, for example, Campbell & Holland, 1972).

## Mutual Correspondence of Integrators

The development of the three employer-based integrators ideally occurs with mutual consideration of each. The position and team-based competency models, for example, should complement both each other and the organizational vision. Having accurate, complementary, and organizationally relevant competency models and organizational visions facilitates the consultative requirements of HR systems. Furthermore, fully integrated employer-based integrators enable a more straightforward interpretation of the relative value that organizations and individuals contribute to each other.

Not only can these integrators provide a common ground as a framework within which the consulting psychologist can develop and implement consulting tools, but the integrators also serve as a starting point for identifying potential sources of issues that lead companies to seek consultation. A company, for example, might have created new integrators that are not complementary with each other or might be using outdated integrators. This might be attributable to the organization having rewritten the organizational vision without considering competency models, or having implemented published competency models that were not consistent with the organizational vision. The individual who occupies such a position might experience job stress in working toward the attainment of contradictory (or at least noncomplementary) goals.

The three employer-based integrators, if utilized properly, can effectively drive selection, development, promotion, and succession planning activities. Proper utilization of these integrators includes an initial assessment of mutual correspondence. A lack of correspondence should be addressed through revision of some or all of the integrators. If the integrators correspond with each other, the consulting psychologist can focus attention on the development or revision of integrator-driven tools that assess integrator proficiency. The employee-based career goal integrator generally serves as a basis from which individual measures of fit can be assessed. Fit is defined through an idealized conceptualization of the employer-employee relationship, a concept presented in terms of the employee life cycle.

## Employee Life Cycle

Our model utilizes an interpretive framework referred to as the *employee life cycle*. By this we mean a conceptual representation of the employee-employer relationship in which the stages of an employee's tenure at a particular organization are mapped out. This framework for interpreting the relationship between employers and employees is consistent with the seminal work of Benjamin Schneider (1987). This life cycle is intended to represent a dynamic process whereby the individual is identified, selected, trained, promoted, placed, and outplaced within an organization.

The ideal nature of this employee-employer relationship is presented as being analogous to the biological concept of symbiosis. The following discussion further explores this concept of work-oriented symbiosis of employee-employer relationships (by which is meant an employer-employee relationship that is not merely based on the financial aspects of employment).

**Organizational Symbiosis.** From the biological perspective, a symbiotic relationship consists of at least two distinct organisms that cannot survive without each other. In order to consider mutual benefit of the employee-employer relationship across individual, position, team, and organizational perspectives, the organization must be viewed as a component not only of its raw transformative state (that is, inputs to outputs), but also as an entity that is supported and defined by employees, and that enables the organization to function properly. From the perspective of the consulting psychologist, the nature of the employee-employer relationship is most ideally represented as being symbiotic, as opposed to a parasitic or exploitative relationship. (Note that different biological models might suit different organizations and different individuals better than this symbiotic model. The current discussion, therefore, does not intend to imply that all organizations should strive for symbiosis, but rather that the *consulting psychologist* should strive for symbiosis. Symbiosis here represents the nature of relationship that most considerately suits all client entities—that is, individual, position, team, and organization.) The consulting psychologist can use this concept to recommend a course of action that is in support of the needs of each client entity. The consulting psychologist strives for approaches that can be viewed as being mutually beneficial to the employee's career, as well as the position's effectiveness, the team's sustainability, and the organization's growth.

Note that symbiosis represents an ideal state, one that is not actually realized in practice. Although the *state* of symbiosis might be a frustrating procedural objective, conceptualizing symbiosis as being a guiding principle of HR consultation facilitates and clarifies the role of the consulting psychologist. This concept of mutual benefit can thus serve the consulting psychologist's role of facilitating the relationship between the employee and the employer, and can also guide how the consultant's services can be applied to serve that relationship.

Individual employees benefit and identity from the employee-employer relationship, and the position, team, and organization receive production and identity from the employee. The employee-employer relationship is defined by transactions (in this case consisting of benefits, production, and identity). The concept of symbiosis can be used to guide the consulting psychologist's interpretation of these transactions. At times, the most mutually beneficial course of action for all parties will be outplacement of an individual. In other cases, the most mutually beneficial course of action will be promotion. Any action taken should be implemented to facilitate the individual's progression through the organization, from the perspective not only of the individual, but also of the position and team requirements, as well as that of the organization as a goal-oriented entity.

**Summary.** In summary, symbiosis is defined as an idealized, mutually beneficial relationship through which the employer gains productivity, sustainability, cultural enrichment, and a variety of other criteria of interest, and that support the organization's vision. In turn, the employee gains financial security, skills and knowledge enrichment, and fulfillment of career needs. Likewise, the needs of the position and team are incorporated at this stage of consideration.

# SYMBIOTIC CRITERIA

The nature of symbiosis is not universal across individuals, positions, teams, or organizations. The important features of employment for some individuals might be financial independence, for others camaraderie, and for others skill set or knowledge base expansion. Similarly, although most traditionally defined employment organizations are profit-driven, the goals of other types of organizations differ. For nonprofit organizations, for example, the goals are not monetary, but rather such achievements as impacting the environment or the political climate. Therefore, the consulting psychologist should perform a needs assessment of the individuals, positions, teams, and organizations in the client organization in order to select appropriate criteria against which success of HR programs can be measured. Accurate and organizationally relevant position and team-based competency models and organizational visions define the needs assessment components for the position, team, and organization; career goals speak to the needs of employees as individuals.

There are many nontraditional criteria that might be of interest across all levels. These include job satisfaction (Smith, Kendall, & Hulin, 1969), life satisfaction (Diener, Emmons, Larsen, & Griffin, 1985), contextual performance (Borman & Motowidlo, 1993; Kulas, Roberts, & Finkelstein, 2000), job stress and strain (Bhagat, McQuaid, Lindholm, & Segovis, 1985), values (such as honesty, helping, and fairness; Ravlin & Meglino, 1987), work and family balance (Frone, Russell, & Cooper, 1992), and perceptions of climate and culture (Rousseau, 1988; Schein, 1989; Schneider, 1987).

More traditional forms of criteria that have not traditionally explicitly addressed these multiple levels include, from the individual's perspective, financial compensation and job satisfaction, and, from the position's or organization's perspective, measures of task-based performance, perceived work-group sustainability, and team performance. Note that each of these criteria can have important implications for all the levels (individual, position, group, and organization).

## Aggregation of Information

The criterion of interest in a traditional job analysis is inherent in this model. In his job analytic-based intervention for the job of ship captain, Munsterberg identified what characteristics were most important to ensure safe ship travel (such as making critical decisions accurately and quickly), and then implemented a selection protocol to address the identified needs. Likewise, identifying criteria for assessing the appropriate progression through the employee life cycle is an important step for the consulting psychologist. Although the types of criteria deemed important may be consistent across individual, position, team, and organizational perspectives, this consistency does the consulting psychologist little good unless a method for interpreting data at each of these four different levels is established. Similarly, the interpretation of predictor variables of interest (for example, for selection or promotion of team members) differs across levels of consideration.

The interpretation of information at the individual and position levels is straightforward. Raw scores or relative (normed) scores might be reported, but information derived from the individual, reflecting both individual and position-based needs, can be interpreted without further analysis. The collection and interpretation of information at the team and organizational levels, however, frequently requires further data collection and analyses. Specifically, at the team level, criteria such as team viability and performance can be collected by methods such as utility and viability analyses and team-based 360-degree evaluations, but the aggregation of individual team members' information to the team level is not as straightforward. For example, when aggregating information such as team member personality traits, the consultant must consider not only the desired group, but also the types of tasks the team will encounter. An excellent presentation of the relationship between team members' characteristics, team tasks, and team outcomes can be found in Barrick, Stewart, Neubert, and Mount (1998).

Finally, interpreting information at the team and organizational levels can be facilitated through the development of local norms. In this process, information collected from job incumbents and applicants can be created to provide a snapshot of the organization, team, or department, including the relative strengths and weaknesses across departments, and the progression of performance rating scores from year to year.

## MULTILEVEL PROBLEM-FOCUSED CONSULTATIVE MODELS

The idea of multiple perspectives in problem-focused approaches is consistent with multisource (or 360-degree) feedback application procedures, by which process a comprehensive assessment of the rated individual or team (or organization) can be formed. Likewise, utilizing a multiple perspective approach to consulting strategies allows for comprehensive assessment of an individual's appropriate progression through the employee life cycle. Although we have emphasized the employee life cycle issues, concurrent frameworks can also be applied to the position life cycle, the team life cycle, and the organizational life cycle, as shown in Table 18.1.

The integrated models presented here focus on four different perspectives to be considered when facilitating progression through the individual employee life cycle, or matrix elements A1, A2, A3, and A4 (presented in boldface) in Table 18.1. The asterisked diagonal of the matrix represents common areas of focus for the consulting psychologist. The consultant specializing in individual assessment traditionally has focused on the impact of interventions at the individual level (matrix element A1), the job analyst might concentrate on

Table 18.1 Matrix of Life Cycle (Rows) by Perspective (Columns). The Sixteen Cells Represent Consultant Levels of Consideration.

| Life Cycle (Consultant Focus): | Level of Analysis | | | |
| --- | --- | --- | --- | --- |
| | 1. Individual | 2. Position | 3. Team | 4. Organization |
| A. Individual | **A1*** | **A2** | **A3** | **A4** |
| B. Position | B1 | B2* | B3 | B4 |
| C. Team | C1 | C2 | C3* | C4 |
| D. Organization | D1 | D2 | D3 | D4* |

element B2, the team facilitator or specialist in group dynamics (see, for example, Tuckman & Jensen, 1977) has traditionally focused on element C3, and the OD practitioner has typically focused on element D4. Although focusing on any of these levels in isolation can be appropriate, focusing on only one element across a particular row can result in a kind of consultative myopia. The advantage of an integrated approaches lies in the coordination of consultation tools both *within* a level of analysis (that is, selection, development, promotion, and succession systems that all support the position competency model) and *across* levels of analysis (that is, individual, position, team, and organizational needs that are all addressed in the development or implementation of selection, development, promotion, or succession systems).

# APPLYING THE MODEL IN INTEGRATED HR APPROACHES

Having established the importance and impact of accurate, complementary, and organizationally relevant position competencies, team competencies, and organizational visions, as well as having discussed the importance of individual needs assessment and the ideal nature of the employee-employer relationship, we can now formally consider the role of the four integrators within the context of the employee-employer relationship, and the specific role of the consulting psychologist as a facilitator of this relationship.

The four integrators presented earlier parallel the four levels of analysis mentioned throughout this chapter. These four integrators serve as the theoretical glue for the currently presented framework of consultation. This framework specifically posits that HR products and services should be integrator-driven and focused toward achieving symbiosis of the employer-employee relationship (symbiosis here being operationally defined as a state in which there is congruence between the individual-based integrator (career goals) and the three position, team, and organizational integrators).

The role of the consulting psychologist again starts with a comprehensive understanding and assessment of the integrators. It is the responsibility of the consulting psychologist to ensure that the three employer-based integrator variables are coordinated with each other, as well as being measurable against the needs of the individual employee. Having complementary integrators at all three employer-based levels of analysis facilitates the development and coordination of the consulting psychologist's tool kit.

## Individual Perspectives

The consulting psychologist first considers the needs of the individual within the employee life cycle context, progressing initially from attraction to, and selection into, the organization, and progressing to promotion or outplacement. The individual-level integrator is the communality that binds the stages of employee life, and various consultant tools can be viewed as supporting these different stages. Prior to entry into the organization, for example, an occupational interests can be assessed (Carson & Lowman, 2002). This evaluation can provide an initial screen as to whether or not the applicant or candidate should progress into the organization.

Such an evaluation occurs in the context of the individual's career goals (the individual-level integrator). If the individual's career goals reflect financial motives as being paramount, then other measures might be needed, such as market-based salary surveys, work and family balance evaluation issues, and measures of social adjustment or adaptation. These tools assist employees in determining whether or not personal career needs are being met in the current organization, and whether advancement, continuation, or outplacement is warranted.

## Position Perspectives

HR functions can support the progression of employees through the employee life cycle at each progressive stage. HR-relevant consulting tools that can be useful include psychological tests, screening interviews, and other selection devices. These can provide assessment of the candidate's degree of fit within the framework of the identified position competency model. Similarly, subsequent to candidate selection, the incumbent is assessed via 360-degree appraisals on that dimension, annual performance reviews, and perhaps promotional assessments (such as assessment centers) that are competency-driven. Obtaining an evaluation of the individual's relative competency-related strengths and weaknesses allows for the development, promotion, or outplacement of the incumbent from the perspective of position requirements. Symbiosis is addressed through the creation of individual employee developmental plans that fulfill both individual and position-based needs (for example, attending university classes might contribute to an employee's technical knowledge set, enabling more efficient contributions to be made at work, and also moving the person toward the attainment of a professional degree, which might be consistent with the personal needs of the employee).

## Team Perspectives

The team perspective should concurrently be considered when facilitating the appropriate progression through the employee life cycle. This consideration is advised by the team-based competency model. The sustainability of the work team, for example, is dependent on its competencies. Assessing individuals using the team-based competency model allows for a more comprehensive evaluation of the individual's appropriate progression through the employee life cycle, taking into account the perspectives of the team. This enables consideration not only of how the individuals might perform within their own functional areas of responsibility, but also how the individual's team will be impacted by this individual.

## Organizational Perspectives

Finally, the perspective of the organization as a whole is assessed. This entails, for example, considering whether the candidate espouses values that are consistent with the vision of the organization. Selection criteria here might be more value-driven than the criteria developed in consideration of the position and team-oriented competency models. Normative information regarding relative strengths and deficiencies are considered, and organizational benches are developed (that is, succession planning systems can be implemented). Targeted individuals can thereby be identified and positioned to take over leadership within different organizational functions or departments.

## Building the Consultative Tool Kit

The fundamental integrators also provide a solid foundation for the construction or interpretation of an organization's HR processes. These integrators can act as catalysts for the development of a healthy employer-employee relationship. These approaches might include the implementation of traditional predictor and criterion measures, coaching models, and benchmarking programs. It is important not only to develop and aid in the implementation of HR products and services at multiple levels, but also to utilize directive feedback at each of these levels.

For example, providing individual candidates with feedback regarding performance on a promotional assessment enables candidates to identify strengths and target developmental needs. The feedback process should not be discontinued at this point, however, since information is also available regarding the status of the work group and the norms of the organization.

Specific tools that the organizational consulting psychologist can use in this process include multirater (also known as 360-degree) performance feedback. In such approaches, ratings on specific work behavior are gathered from oneself, subordinate, peer, supervisor, and any other constituent groups of interest. These data, when compared with the individual's self-perceptions, can be used to enhance self-awareness and subsequent behavioral change. Additionally, these instruments can be administered at the team level (involving ratings made on functional work groups instead of individuals), and compared against organizational or industry norms.

The consulting psychologist can obtain considerable information through application and interpretation of information provided from multilevel, integrated HR approaches (for example, 360-degree appraisals, psychological assessments, benchmarking programs). The information can consist of strengths and developmental needs of individual employees, positions, work groups, and the organization itself (including organizational norms). The role of the consultant then consists of evaluating employees' current status in the employee life cycle, taking into account where each perspective suggests that the employee should be. This entails consideration of which specific locations in the cycle would best achieve career goals, position and team requirements, and the organizational vision. In order to further elaborate on the type of information that can be gathered through this multiperspective framework, and how this information can be used, consider the following case study.

### Case Study

Barbara works for the ABC corporation, where she was recently promoted into a managerial position. Barbara's formal training was in electrical engineering, and her recent promotion put her in charge of six computer systems developers. In addition to her responsibilities as a technical manager, Barbara is a member of an eight-member, cross-functional team consisting of marketing, engineering, sales, and distributing personnel. The purpose of the team is to forecast product development, initiate sales programs, and keep internal production costs to a minimum.

Barbara enjoys her responsibilities at ABC, although she is finding the new position to be very stressful. When asked to list what she hopes to receive out of her career, Barbara lists work and family balance as being her top priority. The consulting psychologist who is focused on the individual's relationship with the employing organization (row A in Table 18.1) will note that the proper consultative approach should incorporate Barbara's priorities with the needs of the managerial position, the team, and the organization.

The types of information available to the consulting psychologist consist of Barbara's personal goals and needs, her competency-based selection assessment scores, her performance reviews, performance reviews of her team, and an assessment of her contribution to the culture of the organization, both positive and negative.

The consulting psychologist who is provided with even as little information as is provided in the case of Barbara is faced with the challenging task of integrating these different perspectives. The consultant facilitates not only the attainment of symbiotic relationships across individual, position, group, and organizational requirement levels, but also incorporates each of these perspectives into an organized, digestible proposed plan of action. It is at this point that the consulting psychologist, who is already armed with an integrated, multilevel analytical perspective of HR systems, is required to draw upon knowledge of organizational structure to create a working organizational model.

## Additional Considerations

Throughout this presentation, the notion of mutual benefit has been emphasized. The employee life cycle model incorporates fulfillment of needs of the individual, position, team, and organization through proper placement within the employee life cycle. Additionally, however, it is important to consider the perceived fairness of the HR system and process. Perceptions of procedural and distributive fairness include consideration of the perceived fairness of the HR selection, promotion, and outplacement process, and of the organization's allocation of rewards. Through communicating an established standard against which individuals will be measured (including the position and team competencies, and the organizational vision), all employees are afforded equal opportunity for progression toward these criteria, and, subsequently, through the organizational hierarchy.

Note also that a competent data management function is necessary for integrating and warehousing information at the individual, position, group, and organizational levels. This system provides an important tracking and storage component to keep and retrieve multilevel information. Succession planning interfaces are widely available that allow for the interpretation of data from the perspective of the individual, position, team, and organizational requirements. Once in place, practitioners can, for example, request information about top candidates for a particular position, the prospective team members who should be considered for a project, and what the succession plan is for senior incumbents. This information is typically stored through the use of a software device with multilevel database capabilities.

# SUMMARY AND CONCLUSION

The major contributions of this chapter have been identifying the importance of common metrics to create, define, or implement measuring tools, and the utilization of a specific model of the employer-employee relationship. Across all elements of this framework, the consulting psychologist should consider the impact of actions at multiple organizationally-relevant levels (individual, position, group, and organizational or systemic).

Although the information presented here serves the purpose of organizing, condensing, and integrating an approach for HR-based consulting within organizations, it is not a prescriptive instructional guide for the consulting psychologist. The level of consultation presented in the current chapter has emphasized complexity. This includes the need to combine data from multiple levels, including individual assessment (facilitation of the employee life cycle). The matrix presented in Table 18.1 can be used as a basis for consideration of other organizational consulting needs. The model presented here relates to a broad range of organizational consulting opportunities.

## References

Barrick, M. R., Stewart, G. L., Neubert, M. J., & Mount, M. K. (1998). Relating member ability and personality to work-team processes and team effectiveness. *Journal of Applied Psychology, 83*, 377–391.

Bhagat, R. S., McQuaid, S. J., Lindholm, H., & Segovis, J. (1985). Total life stress: A multimethod validation of the construct and its effect on organizationally valued outcomes and withdrawal behaviors. *Journal of Applied Psychology, 70,* 202–214.

Borman, W. C., & Motowidlo, S. J. (1993). Expanding the criterion domain to include elements of contextual performance. In N. Schmitt & W. C. Borman (Eds.), *Personnel selection in organizations.* (pp. 71–98). San Francisco: Jossey-Bass.

Campbell, D. P., & Holland, J. (1972). A merger in vocational interest research: Applying Holland's theory to Strong's data. *Journal of Vocational Behavior, 2,* 353–376.

Cannon-Bowers, J. A., & Salas, E. (1997). Teamwork competencies: The interaction of team member knowledge, skills, and attitudes. In H. F. O'Neil, Jr. (Ed.), *Workforce readiness: Competencies and assessment.* (pp. 151–174). Hillsdale, NJ: Erlbaum.

Carson, A. D., & Lowman, R. L. (2002). Individual-level variables in organizational consulting. In R. L. Lowman (Ed.), *Handbook of Organizational Consulting Psychology* (pp. 5–26). San Francisco: Jossey-Bass.

Collins, J. C., & Porras, J. I. (1994). *Build to last: Successful habits of visionary companies.* New York: HarperCollins.

Dansereau, F., Yammarino, F. J., & Kohles, J. C. (1999). Multiple levels of analysis from a longitudinal perspective: Some implications for theory building. *Academy of Management Review, 24,* 346–357.

Diener, E., Emmons, R. A., Larsen, R. J., & Griffin, S. (1985). The satisfaction with life scale. *Journal of Personality Assessment, 49,* 71–75.

Frone, M. R., Russell, M., & Cooper, M. L. (1992). Antecedents and outcomes of work-family conflict: Testing a model of work-family interface. *Journal of Applied Psychology, 77,* 65–78.

Johnson, D. A., Beyerlein, M. M., Huff, J. W., Halfhill, T. R., & Ballentine, R. (2002). Successfully implementing teams in organizations. In R. L. Lowman (Ed.), *Handbook of Organizational Consulting Psychology* (pp. 235–259). San Francisco: Jossey-Bass.

Kulas, J. T., Roberts, J. E., & Finkelstein, L. M. (2000). *Development and validation of a five-factor contextual performance scale.* Paper presented at the annual meeting of the American Psychological Society, Miami Beach, FL.

Larwood, L., Falbe, C. M., Kriger, M. P., & Miesing, P. (1995). Structure and meaning of organizational vision. *Academy of Management Journal, 38,* 740–769.

Lawler, E. E., III. (1994). From job-based to competency-based organizations. *Journal of Organizational Behavior, 15,* 3–15.

Levin, I. M. (2000). Vision revisited: Telling the story of the future. *Journal of Applied Behavioral Science, 36,* 91–107.

McClelland, D. C. (1973). Testing for competence rather than for "intelligence." *American Psychologist, 28,* 1–14.

Militello, L. G., Kyne, M. M., Klein, G., Getchell, K., & Thordsen, M. (1999). A synthesized model of team performance. *International Journal of Cognitive Ergonomics, 3,* 131–158.

Quigley, J. V. (1994). *Vision: How leaders develop it, share it and sustain it.* New York: McGraw-Hill.

Ravlin, E. C., & Meglino, B. M. (1987). Effects of values on perception and decision making: A study of alternative work value measures. *Journal of Applied Psychology, 72,* 667–673.

Rousseau, D. M. (1988). The construction of climate in organizational research. In C. L. Cooper & I. Robertson (Eds.), *International review of industrial and organizational psychology 1988* (pp. 139–158). New York: Wiley.

Schein, E. H. (1989). Organizational culture. *American Psychologist, 45,* 109–119.

Schneider, B. (1987). The people make the place. *Personnel Psychology, 40,* 437–453.

Shippmann, J. S., Ash, R. A., Battista, M., Carr, L., Eyde, L. D., Hesketh, B., et al. (2000). The practice of competency modeling. *Personnel Psychology, 53,* 703–740.

Smith, P. C., Kendall, L. M., & Hulin, C. L. (1969). *The measurement of satisfaction in work and retirement: A strategy for the study of attitudes.* Skokie, IL: Rand McNally.

Tuckman, B. W., & Jensen, M.A.C. (1977). Stages of small group development revisited. *Group and Organizational Studies, 2,* 419–427.

Van De Water, T. J. (1997). Psychology's entrepreneurs and the marketing of industrial psychology. *Journal of Applied Psychology, 82,* 486–499.

Yukl, G. (1994). *Leadership in organizations.* Englewood Cliffs, NJ: Prentice Hall.

# PART SIX

# ISSUES IN CONSULTING TO SPECIFIC TYPES OF ORGANIZATIONS AND FOR SPECIFIC TYPES OF CONSULTING

# CHAPTER NINETEEN

# Consulting to For-Profit Organizations

Cecelia L. Brock
*C. L. Brock Consulting Services*

Effective consultants need to have a broad spectrum of capabilities, because the specific abilities needed vary depending on the type of organizational consultation. The primary goal of this chapter is to identify the specific knowledge and abilities important in consulting to for-profit organizations. The chapter briefly reviews the U.S. economic sectors in which consultants are likely to work, key differences in the missions of profit and nonprofit organizations, and how consultants can work with those differences in practical applications. Next, I describe how the missions of for-profit organizations can be analyzed through a business model that I identify as the *Strategic Triangle*. This model has other names, such as the 3 C's, referring to the company, competitors, and customers (Biswas & Twitchell, 1999), and is especially useful with for-profit organizations in helping to analyze companies' relative competitive advantage. Using the Strategic Triangle and a consulting methodology (Lippett & Lippett, 1986) as diagnostic tools, I then review a typical consulting project. In this illustrative example, I specify the knowledge, skills, and consulting roles used to assess, diagnose, and implement certain organizational changes. The capabilities and processes described are not in themselves necessarily unique to consulting with for-profit businesses. What is unique is the distinction of knowledge required. In addition to this extended example, throughout the chapter, I use multiple examples based on actual consulting assignments, and detail a step-by-step process of a consulting project from a business.

# DISTINCTIONS OF THE FOR-PROFIT ORGANIZATION

There are three sectors from which consulting clients can be sought: for-profit businesses, nonprofit organizations, and the public sector (government). Based on diverse missions, each of these sectors has strategies, goals, cultures, power systems, and a language specific to their purpose. Strategy is built on a deliberately chosen direction for an organization to accomplish its purpose or mission. Goals and objectives are established priorities governed by the mission and strategy of an organization, and culture flows from the collective beliefs and ideologies unique to each organizational sector. In for-profit organizations, strategy, goals, culture, and power are shaped in response to the profit-making objectives of the organization.

## Diverse Definitions of Stakeholders in the Various Sectors

In the various sectors, respective stakeholders (investors, customers, and employees) hold different roles and responsibilities. For example, in for-profit organizations, investors generally provide the initial main source of capital, with ongoing investment traditionally including both customers and investors. Sources of capital in the public sector (such as government agencies or institutions) are tax- or revenue-funded. The nonprofit sector is often funded by charitable donations and by other funding agencies. Definitions of other stakeholders, such as recipients of the organization's services and products, also differ between sectors. Government agencies, such as the military, law enforcement, or the Internal Revenue Service, provide services to citizens, but those citizens are not typically viewed as being customers.

Although there are clearly differences deriving from the type of organization, there are also similarities across sectors. Biswas and Twitchell (1999), for example, reported that 80 percent of the organizational issues occurring in nonprofit organizations are the same as those in for-profit companies. Lukas (1998) concurred with this conclusion, noting that management of a nonprofit requires the same attention to quality, production, sales, marketing, finance, human resources (HR), facilities, and customers that for-profit management requires. However, the essential difference between these two sectors centers on their basic reason for being. "Nonprofits must strive for missions that serve either the non-monetary purposes of a group of people or the higher good of humankind" (Biswas & Twitchell, 1999, p. 112).

This nonprofit mission translates to another key cultural and legal distinction, the nondistribution constraint. In nonprofit organizations this means profit is not distributed to stakeholders. Although nonprofit organizations can certainly strive for financial effectiveness, this is only a part of their primary mission. However, the for-profit sector aims to bring value to stakeholders through effective bottom-line results.

Despite the fact that many of the organizational issues that emerge in for-profit and nonprofit organizations are similar, the knowledge and approach required of consultants who specialize in each sector vary. For-profit consultants need to understand the belief systems, values, and power dynamics that typically operate in for-profit organizations. They must understand that the primary objective of for-profit organizations is to bring value through profitability. Goals directed toward the accomplishment and measurement of that objective, as well as other business and marketing ideas, become part of the priority and actions of the collective organization. Often, employees who are perceived to be most directly responsible for generating revenue and profit in such organizations have influential power.

## Profitability—A Key Goal in For-Profit Organizations

Generally, a for-profit organization's primary objective for achieving its mission includes creating value for customers, investors, employees, and other stakeholders. Businesses that emphasize creating value for their stakeholders (especially when competitors are unable to do so) are operating strategically and consistently with their basic mission. When their needs and interests are being met, the various stakeholders are more likely to be supportive of the organization. Sustaining this support creates a mutually beneficial relationship.

Profitability allows a business to achieve its primary goal of producing and distributing value to stakeholders. Profits can be reinvested into the organization to produce more innovative products and services for customers. Company employees are more likely to have a range of benefits, compensation, and other resources available to them when their respective company is making more money. Vendors and suppliers are more likely to receive business if, through its profitability, a company has the resources to expand. Management is likely to receive higher salaries, larger bonuses, and more opportunities for development as they help their respective companies become more profitable. Therefore, when a for-profit organization has enhanced profitability, it adds value to virtually all of the organization's stakeholders. Of course, businesses do not always distribute their proceeds to the satisfaction of all their stakeholders. However, they are more likely to do so as their profit increases, and when the strategic link between mutually beneficial relationships with their stakeholders is understood. Increasing profits without bringing value to internal and external stakeholders is a short-lived strategy for most businesses.

## Power Distribution in Response to the Priorities and Goals of the For-Profit Organization

Power dynamics and relationships are common to all organizations, and an important part of collective organizational knowledge. In for-profit companies, power is directly related and distributed according to the organization's priorities. In that way, power follows the emphasis of an organization's goals and strategy. For example, if a high-technology company designs and sells highly valued and complex technical solutions, they will probably place increased resources, goals, measurement, and visibility on the engineering and sales functions. Likewise, if a sales team is successful in generating substantial added revenue, it will receive visibility and resources for helping the organization achieve one of its key objectives. The value placed on these functions will tend to give individuals who work in these departments increased power. Similarly, if a company's strategy involves high-volume production of a product with a less-complex design function, more emphasis and resources will be placed on the production and operations departments. Since profitability is always a priority in the for-profit organization, measurement and visibility of it will place the finance department in most for-profit organizations in a position of power. If a departmental function or individual is perceived to be directly responsible for critical accomplishments, they will be more likely to have power in the form of resources, rewards, and visibility.

Understanding the power dynamics in for-profit organizations is important for the organizational consultant in virtually all phases of consultation. As a consultant helps an organization defines its issues, contracts with organizational members for specific objectives, collects and analyzes data, and recommends and implements solutions, it is essential for the consultant to gain involvement from those people who hold influence and an interest in the outcomes of the consulting assignment.

## Market-Focused Management—An Essential Strategy in For-Profit Organizations

The mission statement of a business should drive the organization's strategy, internal structure, goals, capabilities, reward systems, culture, and systems of operation. Since satisfying customers is of primary importance to most businesses in fulfilling their missions, the internal organization of a for-profit business must adapt itself to that purpose. This will require understanding the preferences and constraints of customers in order to win market share. Capabilities, roles, and organizational structure within the business must be arranged to serve markets, not just to manage departmental functions. In order to offer an advantage for their customers to purchase their products or services, for-profit organizations must do this better than their competitors. Market-driven management requires a complete understanding of customer applications, requirements, and needs, and is a strategy that promotes accelerated and profitable top-line growth (Ames & Hlavacek, 1997).

## How Language and Culture Flow from the Organization's Mission Statement

Each organization is unique in its own way. This uniqueness is based on many factors, including participation in different market segments, technologies, strategies, and different leadership within respective organizations. Despite company-specific differences, for-profit organizations also have a commonly understood language that flows from their missions and the collective socialization of employees into the world of business. This collective and company-specific knowledge can be gained from several sources, including physical immersion into the culture or academic study.

When I worked as a vice president (VP) of HR for a high-technology, *Fortune* 500 company, for example, I also served as the key senior internal consultant for the organization. This dual role offered both advantages and disadvantages. The largest disadvantage was the difficulty of remaining and being perceived as neutral when I worked on consulting assignments. There was a significant advantage, however, in that my role as VP of HR placed me in many business meetings where I gained important knowledge about for-profit organizations. This knowledge was gained by either observing others as they worked on business issues, or personally engaging in dialogue with business leaders as they attempted to accomplish strategic or operational work. Although the content of business meetings was generally based on the issues of the day, discussions almost always fell into a small group of categories. These categories represented the corporation's shared language, agreements about priorities, and how things were to be accomplished in the business.

These same categories probably form the basis of business discussions in the vast majority of for-profit organizations. From these discussions, a collective understanding tends to create the basis of a language used by most employees. These categories included discussions about strategy, profit and finances, products and technology, marketing and sales, methods of producing the products, the customers, competitors, and the company itself. The specific company issues will vary, but can include discussions about operational processes, employees, or the interdependencies of people or departments. Whether during periods of fast growth, downsizing, reengineering organizational culture, or mergers and acquisitions, the categories of basic topics of discussion do not change.

Similar issues arise in most consultations. In order to effectively consult to for-profit companies, the consultant must have knowledge about the company's specific business, and must understand and use the generic language of its business.

# MODELS FOR ASSESSEMENT AND ANALYSIS

A good model or framework helps internal and external consultants assess information about the specific business entity that is the focus of the consultation, organize the information, and discover what is and is not known about the business. There are numerous business and organizational models that can help a consultant accomplish the assessment of a business or organizational issue. A good summary of organizational or business models that can be applied (generally to business issues) can be found in Biswas and Twitchell (1999). Even if a specific model is not used, some other systematic method of gathering data should be used for assessment and analysis. Some of these same models can be used to help implement strategy. They also can be used as a way to achieve agreement, clarity, and alignment within an organization.

## The Strategic Triangle—The 3 C's:
## Company, Competitors, and Customers

The particular model I will use in this chapter is called the Strategic Triangle, and represents a way to analyze the interactions between the company, its competitors, and its customers. This model is used regularly and for diverse reasons in for-profit organizations, often in the context of business strategy. Executives use this model to create and define strategy for their respective companies. Employees in marketing, sales, engineering, and management use the model to assess their competitive advantage against their competitors. Internal and external consultants can keep this model in mind as they work to develop the organizational capabilities of their client companies. Consulting assignments such as hiring, developing skills of employees, creating reward and benefit systems, changing organizational cultures, developing communication programs, and many other HR and management projects, can be understood as employing a strategy to build organizational capabilities. Business consultants might also find this model useful when creating, and implementing strategy. For instance, it can be used to evaluate how a business compares with its competitors in such areas as technology, products, services, pricing, marketing knowledge, selling capacity, systems capability, operational capability, or overall capability of the organization.

**Company.** The internal resources of a company are made of many constituents. Some of these are: organizational capabilities, structure, assets, processes and culture. A company's competitive advantage is in part determined by the specific advantages its internal resources have over its competition. Different types of consultants will focus on different aspects of the company's internal resources. For example, HR or management consultants will tend to emphasize the core competencies of employees in the organization as a source for enhancing the company's advantage. This approach might be accomplished by focusing on employee development, employment outcomes, cultural factors or compensation programs.

Training and development for instance, can be linked to developing strengths that customers require and competitors do not have. Corporate preferences for cultures that promote collaboration, participative management techniques, and the creation of creative and innovative atmospheres are only effective organizational strategies if they help to accomplish the basic mission: adding value to customers, investors and other constituents. Even employee motivational training can be understood as a competitive strategy when employees bring an attitude to their work that results in marketplace advantage through increased customer satisfaction.

As an internal consultant, I was often faced with the challenge of hiring or developing employee abilities to work with new technologies, new processes or new market segments. I tended to view this challenge through the lens of the Strategic Triangle, attempting to understand how the new capability would affect marketplace objectives. Often the goal was to develop or recruit employees who had the technical capabilities needed to produce an innovative product, or had knowledge of customer preferences or a particular marketplace. Employees were sought who had the technical capability and knowledge base that the company required and competitors did not have.

Developing reward and compensations systems also can be viewed through the Strategic Triangle lens. The reward system is placed in a context of identifying and paying for the accomplishment of both short- and long-term goals that are aligned with market priorities. For example, engineering bonuses might be paid out for innovation, delivery, or customer satisfaction depending on the organization's priorities and objectives. Instead of just designing a well-structured compensation system in recognition of employees' good work, use of the Strategic Triangle context links and defines good work to company objectives such as understanding and meeting the actual needs of the company's customers, having knowledge about competitors and other business goals.

Additionally, a consultant working in for-profit organizations must be cognizant of how compensation schemes can affect not only market priorities, but also the company's finances. While it is essential to financially attract capable employees to an organization, it is important to know that employees' salaries are generally taken out of profits, or the costs are passed along to customers. Therefore, it is also critical to insure that the compensation scheme of the business does not drive the price of services and products to a level which customers cannot afford them, so they become motivated to buy from the competition.

Whether analyzing the internal capability of an organization with the plan of enhancement, or analyzing organizational structure or processes, the goal should always revolve around adapting the internal organization to meet customer and marketplace needs. Internal or external consultants can therefore benefit from using the competitive advantage framework for virtually all of their work.

**Competitors.** Competitive advantage is developed from a company's ability to create value for its customers that exceeds the company's cost of creating it (Porter, 1998). Porter contends that there are two ways to create competitive advantage: cost leadership in a particular industry, and differentiation. Both of these strategies require that a business compare its own operating capabilities and costs against those of competitors. The Strategic Triangle provides a way to analyze those interactions. For example, a business might have internal capabilities such as superior production technologies or distribution networks, referential sourcing relationships, or a superior market positioning that give it advantages over its competitors (Biswas & Twitchell, 1999). It is true that a consultant with an assignment to improve the teamwork among the management team does not necessarily need to understand everything about the competitor's production technologies. Still, it might be important for the consultant to understand the marketing capabilities, selling strategies, and product innovation capabilities of key competitors when deciding what skills and competencies might be missing from that company's own management and executive staff. Even consultation that is apparently tangential to the major competitive needs of the organization can help align the consultant's and client's goals, and result in the consultant using the language of business.

**Customers.** Groups of customers form market segments, and market-driven management is considered a strategic and practical methodology to attain one of the primary goals of for-profit businesses: profitable growth. Consultants can use this knowledge to help develop and coordinate each department's contribution toward that goal. When market-driven management techniques are followed, the day-to-day management activities of the organization are coordinated to meet the specific needs of targeted market segments. Providing highly valued services to customers becomes the job of the entire organization. Engineering and development projects are directed to developing solutions to customer problems; manufacturing is committed to meeting cost targets, quality standards, and delivery cycles; and the sales and marketing personnel are focused on identifying and interpreting customer problems (Ames & Hlavacek, 1997).

Organizational consultants can assist any or all functions of a for-profit organization to gain the capability of becoming more aligned with marketplace requirements. The creation of a sales commission plan, for example, is a typical organizational consulting assignment. Viewed strategically, it not only involves technical compensation expertise, but also provides the opportunity to help employees in the sales and marketing departments be rewarded for knowledge of customer needs and market requirements. In implementing such a project, organizational consultants are advantaged who understand the unique buying processes of their clients' customer base and the special selling and marketing skills required to sell products or services into that marketplace. The consultant benefits from knowing how the company segments its customer base, its sales quota system, and the organization's strategy and goals for growth. Obtaining this type of knowledge is often gained through reading business plans and discussions with the company's employees. The internal consultant has the advantage of working daily with employees to gain this information.

As an internal consultant working in a for-profit organization, my previous role included responsibilities such as creating and implementing performance evaluation systems, sales training, sales and marketing compensation, commission plans, product bonus plans for engineering personnel, leadership development, customer service training, and facilitating strategic planning. All of these assignments necessitated that I actively sought a working knowledge of the company's business issues in order to link my consulting work to the needs of the company's customer base and the internal capabilities of employees. I therefore attended almost all business, marketing, and product reviews, and visited customers with other executives to gain additional business information. Together, the group and I assessed the ease or difficulty of selling products to customers, and analyzed customer's buying processes, and their potential readiness for future products and business conditions.

# TYPES OF FOR-PROFIT ORGANIZATIONAL CONSULTING ASSIGNMENTS

Consulting assignments can be as diverse as the challenges faced by organizational clients. They can be segmented into functional categories such as business strategy, HR, technology, operations management, systems, or reengineering the organization. Consulting engagements can be classified on dimensions other than the functional areas defined above. Kinard (1995) identified these dimensions as: nature of the problem, phases of the analytic process, type of industry, technical processes or models, and geographic area.

The nature of the consulting assignment can also be classified by whether the organizational problem is corrective, progressive, or opportunistic. For example, a *corrective assignment* might require a consultant to assess and recommend solutions about why a company has been losing key employees, market share, or profit. A *progressive assignment* might include team development, aligning belief systems, assessing compensation plans, or other operational processes, even though no particular problem has been identified. This is work that sustains the fundamental status quo in the organization, perhaps implementing minor improvements, but is not attempting to create major changes. *Opportunistic assignments* include finding ways to help an organization leap forward to gain market share, improve an organization's effectiveness, or increase profits.

Assignments can also be based on a particular phase or combination of phases of the consulting process. For instance, a client might request an assessment and not ask for recommended solutions; or an assessment and recommended solutions can be requested without implementation. Assignments also can be generated from the consultant's involvement with a particular industry, such as agriculture, communication, transportation, or oil and gas. Or, engagements might be specialized and rely on technical processes or models. Finally, an assignment might be restricted to one geographic location or take place in multiple sites, including international. Each of these dimensions will affect the actual consulting project and the way the consultant performs the work.

## Technical, Business, and Organizational Development Consulting

A functional segmentation of (business strategy, marketing, finance, operations management, engineering, information technology [IT], HR, and general management) provides an overview of the typical kinds of consulting engagements. These engagements each make use of a consulting methodology and understanding of the particular context in which the problems are embedded. In each such category, the Strategic Triangle provides a useful business context.

**Consultant Engagements in Business Strategy.** Constructing and implementing effective business strategy is an important management function of top executives. In for-profit companies, opportunities to participate in constructing or implementing a strategy are numerous for organizational consultants. A consultant might be engaged to facilitate part or all of a company's strategic planning process. They might be hired to create the process, to obtain information, or to help implement the plan. Helping an organization clarify its values and beliefs, creating an organizational mission statement, identifying the driving forces and critical success factors of an organization, and helping a business identify its strengths, weaknesses, and core capabilities, are all examples of work that consultants perform in the area of strategic planning. An organizational consultant advising on strategy helps the organization answer questions such as: what business are we, or should we be, engaged in, should we diversify or focus on core activities, and how best can we compete with other organizations (Cooper, 2000)? Performing gap and performance audits, turning the planning process into effective operational goals, gaining agreement of those involved, and communicating the strategic plan can also be part of such consulting. The strategic planning process involves virtually every part of an organization, and is an excellent way to identify other opportunities for consulting. Consultants who specialize in one or more functional areas of a business, in contrast, are known as technical business specialists.

**Technical Business Consultants.** When an organization enters a marketplace in which it has very little internal core capability, it might hire a technical business consultant to provide market knowledge about customer specifications and competitive information and to identify potential strategic alliances external to the business. Likewise, if a company is developing a new technology and has not hired the technical capability required to produce the technology, it might contract with a technology consultant.

IT has become one of the fastest growing categories of organizational consulting. It is now viewed as a critical way to create and change businesses, and not just as a support function. IT is used for efficiency and as a way to capture knowledge by most employees, and in every function of the entire organization. IT consulting accounts for one-half of the consulting industry revenues (Cooper, 2000). Much of this work, however, comprises installations of large software systems. Even so, for the management or organizational consultant, it is difficult to think of a business problem that does not include either technology or some type of system required to measure performance against outcomes of an implemented project (Cooper, 2000).

**Organizational Consulting to HR and General Management.** General management and HR consultation, the focus of many organizational consultants, addresses the internal capability of an organization that allows it to execute its strategic business plan. In the Strategic Triangle, the company dimension represents the internal resources of an organization. Similar to the IT consultant, human resources or general management consultants have the ability to positively influence and shape the organization's internal resources and capabilities in order to execute an organization's mission statements. Consulting opportunities for the human resources or general management consultant are extremely varied and can fall into many categories. They can include projects such as implementing general or technical developmental processes for employees. Consultants might assess, refine, or construct organizational systems or processes. Selecting and retaining employees, designing effective reward systems, and dealing with a problem employee, are also typical HR-related consulting assignments. Developing skills and belief systems in traditional management processes, such as planning, problem solving, decision-making, and implementing goals, are important organizational development projects. Work in team building, conflict resolution, collaboration, communications, and clarifying or reengineering a culture can be stimulating and complex consulting assignments (Block, 2001; Carter, Giber, & Goldsmith, 2001; Schein, 1987).

The categories of consulting just discussed are not mutually exclusive (Kennedy, 2000). For instance, a technical consultant with knowledge of a particular market segment might help design a strategic plan. Or, a business consultant who helps create a strategy involving acquisition of other companies might also be an organizational consultant with expertise in managing mergers and acquisitions.

An organizational consultant might choose to specialize in one of these major areas, or remain more of a generalist. Each of the types of consulting engagements just discussed requires both content- and process-oriented knowledge and skills. Some of these areas require more advanced knowledge and specialization than others. Accelerated technology shifts and changes, for example, make it difficult to maintain state-of-the-art specialist skills and knowledge. Even a generalist approach, however, requires solid training in the principles of business management, gained through an academic program or equivalent experience in business (Kinard, 1995; Waldroop & Butler, 2000).

## Translating Consulting Concepts into Financial Ones

There is general consensus that for-profit businesses must manage their costs, cash flow, balance sheets, productivity, and profitability in order to sustain, grow, and create profit for their organizations. Depending on many factors, including the financial awareness of executives and the culture of the company, the importance of financially managing the business is either implicitly or explicitly understood by all departmental functions. Whether financial management is highly visible or not, consulting work can benefit from being framed in the context of solid financial concepts, because that is the language used in business. Many of the assignments already described can be framed in terms of improving productivity, managing costs, or improving profitability. For instance, a consultant might promote a sales training program by projecting the possible increase in actual sales that a new sales training program or a new commission plan might produce.

A simple model for determining the relative value of any organizational consulting project or assignment is the cost-benefit analysis (Biswas & Twitchell,

1999). This model simply identifies and quantifies, in measurable dollars, the benefits of implementing a project compared to the costs of the project. Although this model is used to analyze financial costs compared to financial benefits of a project or venture, it can also be used (and perhaps even more meaningfully) to analyze the qualitative pros and cons of any project. Combining the financial advantages with the less measurable, but important, strategic benefits of a project, and comparing them with the financial costs and negatives of a particular idea, is a good way to assess the benefit of any project.

## Summary of Method, Knowledge, and Skills
## Used in For-Profit Consulting

It is important for a consultant to understand the strategy, mission statement, goals, and culture of a business in order to effectively work with the complexities in business. I have also recommended the use of two models, the Strategic Triangle (which focuses on the relationships between a company, its competitors, and its customers), and a cost-benefit analysis (which emphasizes the financial benefits of a project), to frame their work. Each of these models aligns the consultant's work not only with the language used by their clients, but also with the client's strategic and operational goals.

Although the roles and the consulting steps enacted by consultants are not necessarily unique to for-profit consulting, I briefly outline them here in order to facilitate description of a case study that follows. Lippit and Lippit (1986) provided a continuum of consulting roles that ranged from consultant-centered to client-centered. Consultant-centered work is based on the consultant's expertise and experience, and client-centered projects are based on the client's experience and knowledge. The roles a consultant manifests in his or her work can be based on many factors. Lukas (1998) categorizes these factors as follows: the consultant's skills, the consultant's preferences, the client's preferences, and the specific nature of the assignment and the needs of the client group or organization. These factors determine the role a consultant can adopt, and they also require different skills and capabilities.

Lippitt and Lippitt (1986) describe consulting roles as including those of advocate, expert, educator/trainer, catalyst, and reflector. The advocacy role involves the use of facts, logic, the challenging of assumptions, and thinking. The expert shares expertise, evaluates, and is more likely to make prescriptions. The educator/trainer teaches, making use of research and theory, and helps to identify options. The catalyst helps clients collect and interpret data, raises awareness, and facilitates and guides the process in which the client is engaged. The reflective approach involves listening, empathizing, clarifying, and reflecting. A range of skills are required in order to operate in these various roles. For instance, the skills used to educate and train people emphasize presentation skills and articulation of ideas, whereas the reflector emphasizes listening, understanding, clarifying, and reflecting capabilities. Each step of the consulting process tends to use various skills, or combinations of attributes and skills.

Consultation can also be described as a process approach, encompassing specific, sequential steps. Typical steps in such models include contracting, gathering and analyzing data, planning the work or diagnosis, implementing and monitoring the project, sustaining change and evaluating impact, and terminating the consulting project (see, for example, Cherrington, 1995; Lippitt, Watson, & Westley, 1958, Lippitt & Lippitt, 1986; Lukas, 1998).

In the next section, I recount an actual consulting project to demonstrate consulting in for-profit organizations.

# A CONSULTING ASSIGNMENT—
# USING A MODEL AND A METHOD

In the case example to follow, I demonstrate how the previously described consulting methodology and models are applied. The case concerns an assignment I undertook while working in the dual role of a senior executive and an internal consultant for a *Fortune* 500 high-technology business.

As an internal consultant and vice president of HR and administration, I often received feedback from employees in the organization when they perceived things were not going well. In this particular situation, other members of the executive staff were also receiving similar information. These problems seemed to cover numerous and complex aspects of the business. Some of the identified issues were: employees perceived a lack of clarity about the company direction and whether the organization would be successful in accomplishing its goals; some considered there to be a lack of leadership; there was conflict among various departments, and a lack of respect in interacting with one another; the organization was seen as being unresponsive to its customers; there was a perception of problems with some aspects of the quality of products and services; and finally, employees described a lack of accountability for meeting schedules, and a host of other related problems. Generally, these perceptions were stated in emphatic terms such as: "Management doesn't care about quality," or "This organization has no direction."

## The Methodology, Diagnostic Model, and Consulting Roles

It is easy for consultants to feel lost about where and how to begin working on issues when they are as plentiful and diverse as these were. I considered it essential to follow a consulting methodology and use a diagnostic model. The methodology I followed included the following steps: contracting with the client; data collection, planning, and diagnosis; and implementing solutions and evaluating the impact. As a diagnostic model during the data collection phase, I sorted the diagnostic data into these categories: concerns related to the company's mission, and perceptions that fit into the categories associated with the Strategic Triangle. The mission category was used because it was clear from the data that employees, including some management and other leaders in the company, did not have a clear understanding of the company's direction, did not agree with the stated direction, or thought that the company lacked a clear vision. The Strategic Triangle was used as a model because many of the expressed comments were about the internal processes and interactions of the company, the customers, the vendors, and how the company interacted with its competition. Therefore, initially as the data about problems were collected, they were classified on the basis of relevance to the following categories: the direction or mission of the business, and the three categories (the company, competition, and customers) of the Strategic Triangle. Relevant subcategories of the Strategic Triangle were defined in which to categorize problems. For instance, data about the company were put into subcategories that included, for example, employee perceptions of poor teamwork among departments, and lack of quality in products. Comments about customer responsiveness were placed in the customer category.

Organizational consulting is rarely linear. I used a variety of roles during each phase of the consultation. For example, at one point I worked as a consultant-centered advocate, persuading and recommending. Then, based on circumstances in the group process, I might have quickly shifted to client-focused behavior, listening, clarifying, and reflecting.

**Contracting with the Client.** Typically, the first step in a consulting project is to contract with the client. Although the initial information will necessarily be incomplete, it should be sufficient to develop a written proposal to describe the intended work, including any methodology that might impact current operations, and the projected outcomes, or deliverables, of the consulting project. As an internal consultant, this can be handled by documenting and distributing to clients an agreed-upon plan of action, including the objectives and anticipated outcomes of the project. In this case, the multitude of issues that were being articulated made it difficult to clarify the overriding problems, let alone the specific objectives of the project. Also, it was somewhat unclear at the beginning stages who the client should be defined as.

Defining the stakeholders of a consulting project is an important and often political action in the consulting process. A change process might be initiated by some person or group in the organization without the support of other organizational members whose help will be needed to implement the desired changes. Therefore, it is essential to insure that people who have a vital interest in the outcomes of a project, and also have organizational power to support or undermine the process, be included in agreements early in the consulting process. In a for-profit organization, determining the stakeholders for a project is particularly important. In such settings, people with organizational power include not only the organizational hierarchy, but also employees whose talents are difficult to find, those skilled at accomplishing organizational priorities, and those who are hard to retain. Obtaining this kind of buy-in is especially important in high-technology organizations.

In the case example, because I was a member of the company's executive staff, and because I knew that a change process works most effectively if senior management accepts the problems and supports the recommended changes, I decided to contract with the entire executive team of seven people. I convened an initial meeting with the executive staff to determine if the whole group perceived a need to work through and resolve some of the issues that were emerging in the organization. I also wanted to include other important stakeholders of the possible outcomes of this project. Therefore, I recommended that each senior staff member go to their next departmental meeting and engage their own staff to help clarify some of the issues. My purpose was to gain better information than I then had about the problematic issues, and also to increase the ownership and interest level of a larger group of influential people. In this phase of the project, I worked as a catalyst to help raise awareness of the staff, as I guided the process. Each senior staff member was to return to the next meeting with a list of those issues that their employees thought should be on the division's agenda, and issues that were affecting the particular department's ability to fully execute their objectives. Since I have found that responses to inquiries are often influenced by the way a consulting question is framed, I asked the executive team to frame the issues raised with their staffs in terms that emphasized what the organization might build or develop, as opposed to identifying only what was wrong.

In spite of the attempted neutral framing, each member of the executive staff returned the next week with a long list of divisional and departmental problems very similar to those that had already been articulated. Many hours of debate on how the group should proceed demonstrated a high level of interest and involvement from each of the executive staff. I saw an opportunity based on their ownership of these issues. I suggested that the group embark as a team to assess, create, document, and communicate an improved vision for the organization. The aim was to include the entire organization in this process to help answer questions about where the company was headed and how the group wanted to interact with customers, teammates, and employees.

During this phase, I became an advocate, trying to gain acceptance of my recommendations. I presented facts, challenged assumptions and the thinking about how things had been done in the past, and proposed a plan of how to proceed. It was at this stage that I began documenting objectives, agreements of actions, time frames, individual actions, and projected outcomes of the work. This *contracting* segment of the project was accomplished in a collaborative, action-oriented process. I believe part of the reason the executive staff initially supported this action plan is that they had helped create it, and understood how the group's work could influence the internal organization to become more effective with each other, customers, and vendors. Several of the staff believed strongly in the need to focus on internal processes of the company, including employee attitudes and motivation, in order to adapt processes and beliefs to marketplace needs and requirements. These executives pushed for overall realignment and transformation of the company's values and internal processes.

It was agreed that the understanding, acceptance, and participation of key influential leaders who were involved in the day-to-day problems of the organization, were essential to the success of the project. It was also agreed that it was important for all employees in the organization to see the outcome of this process as a template for how the executive staff expected to manage the company. This project would require the understanding and participation of all employees. More succinctly, the collaborative objectives were to:

- Create a clear vision and direction for the company
- Emphasize the primary importance of effectively working with internal and external customers
- Create continuous improvement as a way of organizational life
- Improve the motivation and involvement of all employees toward excellence
- Offer a process and model that would serve as a template for how the company wanted to function as an organization
- Improve teamwork among the executive staff and among various departments
- Clarify and gain acceptance of a belief system that management believed was essential to sustained success
- Develop a process that would highlight and resolve issues or problems deemed to be inconsistent with the new mission statement and guiding principles

**Data Collection and Diagnosis.** Data collection was an important part of this process because it not only provided important informational content, it also demonstrated to employees that the executive staff wanted their input and participation to help reenergize the organization. Therefore, it was important to set up a process to include those employees. I designed a data collection method involving each member of the executive staff gathering information about the issues from two subordinate management levels. They were to ask some simple questions of their staffs; for example, "What issues do you think should be on the division's agenda?"; "What do you think is needed to be done by the department or organization to become excellent?"; and "What barriers are inhibiting individual and organizational excellence?"

To add to the available data, I also interviewed the executive staff's management team, asking very similar questions. My inquiries were accomplished in either individual meetings or small groups of two or three managers. The purpose of this intervention was to insure that all information about the organization could flow up freely, without fear of retribution. The data collection process in which the executive staff engaged took place at weekly staff meetings. It lasted approximately four weeks, with each executive gaining information from their management staffs and reporting their data at the executive staff meeting. My role was one of a facilitator, listening to and clarifying information. I had introduced the diagnostic model, demonstrating how the information could be sorted into the categories of mission statement, customer, competitor, and company. Patterns and themes in each of these categories were identified. Until the executive staff decided how to proceed on the basis of these findings, it was not possible to move forward. My role in this diagnostic stage moved back and forth between being a catalyst who listened, clarified, and worked toward common group understanding, and being an advocate and expert. I had worked with many organizational interventions, and proposed helping the organization create a revised mission statement, identifying guiding principles for the organization, and a core set of values. I believed the collaborative creation and visible communication of this material could have a large impact on reenergizing and positively transforming this organization. Ideas were included about success criteria as a business, and how the group wanted to work with the company's primary stakeholders: the customers, employees, and suppliers.

**Diagnosis and Implementation.** Sorting the data into the diagnostic model, with a plan to create a new mission statement, business values, and organizational principles, resulted in multiple categories:

- *Mission Statement*: Company direction, leadership, alignment among organizations and the executive staff
- *Company-Related Data*: Employee motivation, development and participation in the company, teamwork, respect, communications, product quality, the importance of profit, integrity in the internal systems and profit
- *Customer-Related Data*: Information about how the company met the customer's needs, responsiveness to customers and the manner in which customers felt they were treated

## Firmly Held Beliefs

From the above categories, the group collaboratively established the *firmly held beliefs* summarized below. The group then attempted to expand these beliefs with full descriptions in order to gain clarity and alignment within the organization.

- Development of a clear mission statement for the organization was central to leadership and direction.

- The company's values included business success criteria and the following assumptions: people were the company's most treasured asset; the firm's products and services determined its success in the marketplace; and sustained profitability is the ultimate measure of success.

- Concerning employees, leadership must operate at all levels of the organization.

- Concerning the company dimensions, the company must continuously improve its products and services.

- Company teamwork was essential for the organization to succeed.

- Concerning the customer, it was necessary to create market leadership, and to focus on creating value for customers in everything that was done.

- The ultimate expression of quality was manifest in having a high level of customer satisfaction and success. That satisfaction results in customers continuing to do business with the company.

Each staff member selected one of these firmly held beliefs based on their interest level and specific departmental function. They were then asked to gather input from their peers and their staffs and write a description of how the company wanted to operate on this dimension. The results of this work were to be presented two weeks after the initial assignment, with the understanding that the group would work as a team to create the final document. By using this process, I hoped to gain ownership from a large group of employees in the creation and communication of an important company document.

This stage of the process was useful in helping to build understanding and teamwork at the executive staff level. It became apparent that there were wide differences in the understanding and emphasis of the topics. The president of the company played an important role in inserting his market-focused business beliefs into the final versions in a very collaborative and convincing manner. However, even though the executive staff began this process with differences in the emphasis that they believed should be placed on specific topics, all were knowledgeable about market-driven management philosophies. This knowledge helped us collectively work together to accomplish the goals.

The group was addressing real problems, always asking ourselves if the material being created would answer the concerns of those voicing them. It specifically focused on difficult issues that had not been resolved, but that were creating conflict in the organization. It was acknowledged, for example, that when executive staff members were in discord, whether there would be a ripple effect downward within their respective organizations. Also reviewed were expectations of each other regarding the importance of communicating openly, with respect, and while attempting to understand the other person's perspective when in conflict. A new problem resolution process among the executive staff was also competent to help resolve conflict. These discussions helped to set constructive attitudes while working with other departmental processes that were perceived to be not working effectively. In this stage I operated as a facilitator and educator, bringing in principles and theories of teamwork and communication.

We talked about believing in what was being created, rather than just going through the motions of creating rhetoric in which no one really believed. The group discussed the importance of the executive staff's setting an example by making sure its actions and words were consistent. All of these discussions, plus the collaborative creation of a growth-oriented mission statement and motivating business values, helped to build teamwork, confidence, and conviction to operate productively at the executive team level.

**Evaluating Impact of the Intervention.** I led a discussion with the executive staff reviewing progress against the original goals for this project. The group realized that it had accomplished several of the intended objectives, including the collaborative creation of a clear vision, direction, and values for the company. Collectively, the executive team also believed it had resolved many differences and improved teamwork. However, the work had not yet taken the form of implementing organizational process changes, or changes in interactions with customers and employees. In order to accomplish these desired changes, it was still necessary to communicate the outcomes of this work to the rest of the organization and gain their support. Management and other employees had participated in the original definition of the issues, and the creation of the vision statements, but had not yet seen the final versions. It was then necessary to begin the process of communicating the final versions of the organization's work at staff meetings, in company documents such as updated employee handbooks, and in company newsletters.

In order to gain more understanding and acceptance of the company vision, I therefore designed a one-day management development session with key leaders in the company. The president of the company took a highly visible role in this meeting. He and each member of the executive staff presented a portion of the newly created vision documents, along with an updated business status on company goals. The leadership group then was divided into teams. They were asked to discuss the material, and then to make a presentation on how clear the information was and how well they thought these concepts were operating within the organization. They also were asked what they could do to help make the mission statement, values, and guiding principles become a template for action and working values in the company. The result of these meetings was enormous support by the leadership for the company's new mission and values statements. The leadership provided valuable feedback in the form of actions they would undertake, and recommended additional actions the executive staff still needed to emphasize.

The organization continued to work with this material on an iterative basis. The original assignment offered opportunities to clarify and refine a company mission statement. It also offered the ability to refine, document, and communicate the values and culture of an organization, to improve team awareness and effectiveness, to provide managerial and leadership development, and to provide a working document about how to operate the business. Training in conflict resolution, problem solving, leadership, and other development programs were implemented in the context of our revised values. I also designed a performance appraisal system for all employees, incorporating the key ideas from the company's new set of core values. The entire organization was measured against these values and guiding principles, and rewarded as they incorporated them into their behavior.

Four months after the initial project results had been communicated to all employees, I designed and implemented a survey, using Likert response format scales to measure a variety of employee perceptions of how well the company's mission statement, values, and guiding principles were operating in the organization. Technical consulting skills such as survey design, quantitative analysis, quantitative and qualitative interpretation, facilitation skills, communication skills, and presentation techniques were required in this part of the assignment. In addition to the Likert scale, I asked for employee comments throughout the survey. The interpretation and presentation of these comments required a working knowledge of the business philosophies and operational processes of this for-profit organization. After the survey was administered, analyzed, and interpreted, I presented the information to the executive staff, the management staff, and all employees in the company in a series of communication and discussion sessions.

It is difficult to evaluate the full impact of this large-scale intervention. As a result of the work, many new processes were implemented to help the organization work in alignment with their revised values. A cross-functional management team was set up to access and respond to customer problems. An employee-relations process was implemented to insure fair treatment and respect for all employees. In an effort to respond more effectively to customer delivery dates, a new project management information system was implemented in the engineering department. Development programs were undertaken for marketing, sales, and customer service personnel, to help them understand and respond to customer requirements. To fully evaluate the impact of the many organizational changes that were implemented, pre- and post-data collection would have been necessary, addressing such issues as quality problems, employee-relations issues and their causes, and customer problems. These types of data were collected and monitored with visibility and organizational interest by responsible departments. However, it was understood that any progress was a result of goals set in that direction after the implementation of the new vision for the organization. Prior to understanding the abundant concerns of employees in the organization, or developing a plan to resolve those issues, the executive staff would probably not have responded positively to data that emphasized additional problems with employees, customers, and quality. However, as an internal consultant, I was able to evaluate the change in perceptions of employees by conducting the same employee survey annually for three years. This data was sorted in two ways: by department, and by perception of organizational consistency with the specific stated company value. The first year, 61 percent of employees agreed or strongly agreed that the organization and employees behaved consistently with the company's stated values. The second year, this increased to 74 percent, and by the third year, it had risen to 83 percent. The executive staff at that point would not have desired or supported more measurement of this project. The culture of this organization was informal, and as a result, I met with individuals and groups periodically to assess their experience of the organization's effectiveness.

The new document was viewed as a template for the type of values that create excellence in organizations. Employees were encouraged to voice their concerns and follow designated processes when they did not think these operational values and guiding principles were operating effectively. I did track employee-relations problems and their causes, however I did not attempt to link this measurement to the work that had been accomplished in this assignment. Instead, I placed my emphasis on creating structures and processes that would further the visibility and adherence to the company values.

# SUMMARY

Consulting to all organizational sectors in a for-profit consultation requires an array of skills and knowledge. This knowledge is based on an understanding of the purpose of for-profit organizations. It is also based on experience or education in business, cultures, and language associated with business, and the power relationships that are inherent in for-profit companies. The Strategic Triangle is a model that helps consultants use the language of business, and frame their work in a context of market-driven management concepts. These concepts and techniques facilitate the goal of accelerating growth and profitability in for-profit organizations.

Not all for-profit organizations are most concerned about the strategic relationship between the internal resources and capabilities of the company, its customers, and competitors. This circumstance might occur, for example, in regulated industries. In addition to all of the required skills and knowledge already identified, an astute assessment of capability is essential for consultants. The ability to assess an organization's needs on a particular organizational issue, and to develop acceptable recommendations to create progressive change, can help a business become more successful. This is true even if the company does not operate using market-driven management concepts or does not have a sophisticated strategy. However, the consultant to for-profit organizations will know that helping an organization implement solutions that will align it with solid strategic and financial management concepts will move it closer to creating and maintaining organizational success.

# References

Ames, C. B., & Hlavacek, J. D. (1997). *Market driven management.* Burr Ridge, IL: Irwin.

Biswas, S., & Twitchell, D. (1999). *Management consulting, a complete guide to the industry.* New York: Wiley.

Block, P. (2001). *Flawless consulting fieldbook & companion: A guide to understanding your expertise.* San Francisco: Jossey-Bass.

Carter, L., Giber, D., & Goldsmith, M. (Eds.). (2001). *Best practices in organization development and change handbook: Culture, leadership, retention, performance, consulting.* San Francisco: Jossey-Bass.

Cherrington, J. O. (1995). Professional attributes of consultants. In S. W. Barcus III & J. W. Wilkinson. (Eds.). *Handbook of management consulting services* (2nd ed., pp. 4-1–4-25). New York: McGraw-Hill.

Cooper, M. (Ed). (2000). *Career guide to the top consulting firms.* Fitzwilliam, NH: Kennedy Information.

Kennedy, A. (2000). The management consulting industry: A top management consultant's perspective. In L. Wong (Ed.), *Careers in management consulting* (pp. 9–10). Boston: Harvard Business School Press.

Kinard, J. C. (1995). The management consulting profession and consulting services. In S. W. Barcus III & J. W. Wilkinson (Eds.), *Handbook of management consulting services consulting* (pp. 2-1–2-10). New York: McGraw-Hill.

Lippitt, G. L., & Lippitt, R. (1986). *The consulting process in action: Skill development* (2nd ed.). San Diego, CA: Pfeiffer.

Lippitt, R., Watson, J., & Westley, B. (1958). *The dynamics of planned change.* Orlando, FL: Harcourt Brace.

Lukas, C. A. (1998). *Consulting with nonprofits*. St. Paul, MN: Amherst H. Wilder Foundation.

Porter, M. E. (1998). *Competitive advantage: Creating and sustaining superior performance*. New York: Simon & Schuster.

Schein, E. H. (1987) *Process consultation: Vol. II. Lessons for managers and consultants*. Reading, MA: Addison-Wesley.

Waldroop, J., & Butler, T. (2000). Is management consulting the right career for you? In L. Wong (Ed.), *Careers in management consulting* (pp. 1–4). Boston: Harvard Business School Press.

# CHAPTER TWENTY

# The Role of Leaders and Consultants in Fostering International Organizations

Nurcan Ensari

*California School of Organizational Studies*
*Alliant International University*

As the world shifts toward a global economy, more and more organizations are becoming international in focus. Increasing trends toward globalization, and concerns about the ability of United States organizations to compete in the global marketplace, are major concerns of managing internationally. Consultants can assist with a variety of internationally oriented assignments. These include working with companies that are in the process of opening new markets in other countries (Fine, 1995), assisting companies develop programs that prepare executives to work abroad, and training employees to work effectively in international assignments. In all of these roles, fostering a better understanding of characteristics of other cultures and their influences in business has become an important consultation concern. Organizational consultants need to be able to help companies manage employees based in other countries, to assist organizations in the process of internationalizing, and to develop diversity initiatives that are integrated into the company's overall business strategy. Both leaders' and consultants' positions and responsibilities are crucial in successful internationalization efforts.

## MANAGING INTERNATIONAL ORGANIZATIONS

The task of managing an international organization raises concerns about cultural values, norms, traditions, political, economic, and legal systems, and language. Marketing a product in Japan, for example, requires a different approach than marketing the same product in the United States. Similarly, a business strategy successfully pursued in Germany might not work in Mexico. Past research has indicated that managerial techniques and styles appropriate for homogeneous work groups do not necessarily work well for diverse organizations composed of people from different cultures with different values, perspectives, and expectations concerning how leaders should behave (James, Chen, & Cropanzano, 1996). Managing a diverse team is a different experience from managing a homogeneous team (Mayo, Meindl, & Pastor, 1996). Thus, leaders in international organizations must not only be sensitive to cultural differences, but must also adopt the appropriate policies and strategies for coping with them.

This chapter examines the sources of these differences by focusing specifically on issues related to intercultural communication, cultural sensitivity, ethnocentrism, and acculturation. I first review information processing and perceptions of leaders as a conceptual approach to understanding leadership in international organizations, and then discuss the role of leaders in these issues. Next, I discuss ways that leaders and consultants can potentially increase their effectiveness in international organizations. Finally, I identify directions for future research. The specific objectives of this chapter are: (1) to discuss the complex nature of organizational internationalization; (2) to make clear what is known, and what still needs to be discovered, about research that can be used in international organizational settings to improve the leader-employee relationship and leadership effectiveness; (3) to provide a framework for understanding diversity issues in international organizations; and (4) to present some strategies for building successful international organizations.

## INFORMATION PROCESSING AND LEADERSHIP PERCEPTIONS

How leaders are perceived, what researchers call leadership perceptions (Pfeffer, 1977), affects how they are accepted by their followers. These perceptions in turn affect the extent to which employees will be committed to the organization (Foti, Fraser, & Lord, 1982). The perception of leaders also affects how leadership behavior can effectively be assessed or measured (Maurer & Lord, 1991; Hogg, 2001). Understanding how people perceive leaders and how they process information also expands our views of how leaders gain and maintain power, adds to our knowledge of how leaders can be more effective, and can help psychologists and consultants in the application of behavioral measurements (Ensari & Murphy, 2001).

Two models have been proposed to explain leadership perceptions.

## The Recognition-Based Model of Explaining Leadership Perceptions

Lord, De Vader, and Alliger (1986) suggested that leadership perceptions are based on the match between a leader's characteristics and the prototype of a leader that people hold (Den Hartog, House, Hanges, Ruiz-Quintanilla, & Dorfman, 1999). When there is a good fit between the leader's observed characteristics and people's abstract ideas of what good leaders should be, that leader is perceived as being more powerful and charismatic, and in turn is given more credit for positive work outcomes (Lord, Foti, & De Vader, 1984). For example, someone who has characteristics that are interpreted to match the prototype of a charismatic leader is likely to be recognized as a charismatic leader (Cronshaw & Lord, 1987; Fraser & Lord, 1988; Lord et al., 1984; Maurer & Lord, 1991).

## The Inference-Based Model of Information Processing

The inference-based model of information processing (Calder, 1977; Meindl & Ehrlich, 1987; Meindl, Ehrlich, & Dukerich, 1985) interprets leadership perceptions differently. It maintains that people perceive leaders based on the outcome of events. For instance, a leader is perceived as being charismatic when the company is successful, whereas business failures are usually, in contrast, attributed to a lack of leadership of the executives. In such circumstances, the perceived executive leadership qualities will be lessened (Lord & Maher, 1993; Shamir, 1992).

## Culture and Leadership Characteristics

Culture also plays an important role in how leadership perceptions are formed and information about them is processed. One's experience with the environment and culture shapes perceptions of the ideal leader by creating perceptual expectations (Shiraev & Levy, 2001). Leaders are constrained by some aspects of culture, but cultures are themselves affected by some behavior or other aspects. Understanding the information processing aspects of culture can improve understanding of the impact of leadership on culture, and how culture, in turn, influences leadership (Emrich, Brower, Feldman, & Garland, 2000).

Despite its importance, information processing of leadership has been considered in only a few studies. Ensari and Murphy (2001) compared leadership perception models across cultures, and examined what constitutes an ideal leader in terms of leader prototypes. This study specifically considered the differences between individualistic and collectivistic societies on the social cognitive processing of perceptions of leader behavior. Leaders in individualistic cultures were perceived as being independent, self-constrained, autonomous entities, whereas in the collectivistic non-Western cultures, the prototype emphasized interdependence between the leader and organization members (Matsumoto, 2000). We argued that in collectivistic cultures, experiencing interdependence promotes perceptions of organizational, collective actions as having been the primary cause of outcomes. Accordingly, we predicted that information processing that is based on *recognition* will dominate in individualistic cultures (Ensari & Murphy, 2001). This is because people in these cultures are more likely to perceive the individuals as the causes of outcomes, and thus make dispositional attributions as compared to situational attributions (Markus & Kitayama, 1991). On the other hand, we predicted that *inference-based processing* would be more likely to be the basis of leadership attributions in collectivistic cultures. This was because collective activities or groups, rather than individual leaders behaviors, are more likely to be seen as the source of outcomes in such cultures.

These predictions were tested in a laboratory experiment in which groups of participants from either a collectivistic culture (Turkey) or an individualistic culture (United States) read a vignette about a prototypical or antiprototypical leader (manipulation of recognition-based processing) whose company had experienced either a slight or high increase in sales (manipulation of inference-based processing). The results supported the predictions. American participants in the study perceived the leader as being more charismatic when he was a prototypical rather than a nonprototypical leader. However, for Turkish participants, the prototypicality of the leader did not play a role in leadership perceptions. In addition, when the company made a high profit, Turkish students perceived the leaders more charismatically than when the company failed, whereas the Americans made equal attributions of charisma to the leader in positive and negative outcome situations. We concluded that the leader's prototypical characteristics were more effective in forming a leadership impression in individualistic cultures, such as in the U.S., whereas people in collectivistic cultures, such as in Turkey, were more likely to make attributions based on the company's performance outcomes.

I believe these results have important implications for understanding leadership in international contexts. As discussed, how leaders are perceived helps to clarify how executives will be able to gain followers' commitments and acceptance for their decisions, and how their characteristics will interact with organizational outcomes. The leader's effectiveness will primarily be based on the leader's characteristics in some cultures, whereas in other cultures, the perception of success will be based on whether support and participation from followers and subordinates was obtained.

As Ensari & Murphy's study (2001) showed, U.S. models of leadership behavior tend to focus on the individual as leader, whereas models used in collectivistic cultures conceptualize leadership as being a function of the group or organization as a whole. Although a leadership style that allows subordinates' participation can be very effective in some cultures (specifically, those in which individuals are educated and responsible for their actions), it can backfire in other cultures (those in which employees are not ready to act independently). For example, in the Russian culture, people seem generally unwilling to participate actively in politics even when democratic freedoms are available to them. This seems to derive from the fact that Russians generally expect a strong, charismatic leader to take care of their problems, rather than needing personally to assume responsibility and act independently (Glad & Shiraev, 1999).

Although leaders who have abilities to accomplish group goals, intellectual skills, strong motivation, and abilities to sustain pressure are more likely to be effective in every culture (Hui & Luk, 1997; Schmidt & Yeh, 1992), certain characteristics or situational contexts dominate in specific types of cultures. Thus, understanding cross-cultural contexts in social cognitive processing has important implications for the study of cross-cultural leadership, as well as for understanding issues of leadership in international organizations.

## THE ROLE OF LEADERS IN INTERNATIONAL ORGANIZATIONS

The role of leaders is altered as organizations change the way they operate internationally. Better understanding of the structure of international organizations, cross-cultural education, training, and development is essential for leaders to operate effectively in a complex, global marketplace.

In increasingly more pluralistic and multicultural work environments, intercultural awareness and skills are vital for leaders who must function in the international scene (Harris & Moran, 1979). This need is more evident in multinational corporations that send representatives to be change agents in multicultural settings. The leaders' challenge in such contexts is to learn to motivate others and to understand the characteristics of others in the new culture, in order to facilitate communication with them, increase effective collaboration, and gain the necessary skills for dealing with cultural differences.

## ROLES AND RESPONSIBILITIES OF CONSULTANTS AND LEADERS IN INTERNATIONAL SETTINGS

This section reviews leaders' and consultants' roles and responsibilities specifically within the context of intercultural communication, cultural sensitivity and ethnocentrism, and acculturation.

## Intercultural Communication

Intercultural communication refers to the exchange of knowledge, ideas, thoughts, concepts, and emotions among people of different cultural backgrounds (Matsumoto, 2000). Communication is perhaps the most important tool in organizational operations and international relations. For leaders in international organizations, although being aware of personal needs, values, standards, and expectations of people from other cultures is an important step toward more effective communication, they should also be willing to revise and expand their images of others as part of the process of change and growth (Harris & Moran, 1979). In this process, leaders might need to change their verbal and nonverbal communication skills, such as their facial expressions, tone of voice, posture, dress, distance, and the like.

Learning appropriate foreign languages is necessary for several reasons. First, many words have different nuances and connotations, and thus translation of an English word into its literal equivalent in another language might change the intended meaning. Even common words for breaking, cutting, eating, and drinking can have entirely different connotations and nuances, and might be used in different contexts, in other cultures (Suzuki, 1978). Similarly, people of different cultures can have different associations with the same word. Thus, it is questionable whether the relationship between words in our own language and their translated equivalents in another are exact equivalents.

Secondly, languages in the world have different systems of reference. In American English, people generally use one of two words, and their derivatives, to describe themselves when talking to others: *I* and *we* (Matsumoto, 2000). Many languages in the world, on the other hand, have much more elaborate systems of reference that depend on the nature of the relationship between people, and the context under which the communication is occurring. For example, in Japanese, reference to self and others is dependent on the status differential between the two people, and group orientation (Matsumoto, 2000). Furthermore, cultural differences have also been documented in a number of other communication areas, such as apologies (Barnlund & Yoshioka, 1990), children's personal narratives (Minami & McCabe, 1995), self-disclosure (Chen, 1995), compliments (Barnlund & Araki, 1985), and interpersonal criticism (Nomura & Barnlund, 1983). For example, past studies indicated that Americans had a higher level of self-disclosure than did the Taiwanese Chinese, and Japanese prefer more direct, extreme forms of apology than Americans, who tend to favor explanation as a form of apology.

People of different cultures structure the world around them differently in the language they use to describe the world. The feelings, associations, connotations, and nuances of language are influenced by the culture. Learning and using the appropriate foreign language transforms leaders into agents of the culture, giving them the opportunity to embody the essence of the culture, and with that, the need to avoid possible conflicts during communication.

Even when people speak the same language, however, cultural differences can still arise because of the differences in nonverbal communication (for example, facial expressions, gestures of the hands, arms, and legs, posture, tone of voice, interpersonal space, touching behaviors, gaze and visual attention). Nonverbal behaviors convey messages during communication just as verbal language do. In Thailand, for example, the head is considered sacred, and the feet the lowest part of the body. Crossing one's legs or unintentionally pointing one's foot at someone can be interpreted as being very negative gestures.

It is therefore important for consultants to learn the foreign system of unspoken, nonverbal behaviors, as well as to learn the verbal language, because nonverbal behaviors are an integral part of the entire communication package. This can help avoid problems of miscommunication. For example, Japanese head nodding does not necessarily mean yes (Matsumoto, 2000). American representatives in many business negotiations have faltered on the interpretation of this behavior, believing that the Japanese have agreed to something and that the deal is closed (Matsumoto, 2000). However, the Japanese head nodding might only be a signal to inform the speaker that the listener is listening.

Personal space is another cultural difference in nonverbal behavior. For instance, Americans prefer to interact with people at a certain physical distance, and interactions with people from Arab or Middle Eastern organizations who try to adjust the distance and get closer might cause an uncomfortable, unsettling situation. Eye contact is another important nonverbal component of interpersonal interaction that varies widely among different cultures. African Americans, for example, generally have greater eye contact when they are speaking, whereas European Americans tend to maintain eye contact when they are listening (Hecht, Ribeau, & Alberts, 1989). As a consequence, the different eye contact patterns can create situations in the workplace in which African American workers are perceived as less attentive when someone else is speaking. In turn, misinterpretation of African American workers' nonverbal behavior can have powerful negative consequences for them, potentially leading to personal conflicts with the speaker and making their working relationship more difficult (Fine, 1995).

**Summary.** Cultural differences in verbal and nonverbal communication have important practical, real-world ramifications in international organizations. With increasing interaction among international organizations around the world, these differences are bound to arise with growing frequency at work situations. The leaders' role in the process of truly appreciating cultural differences in communication and gaining fundamental understanding of culture itself is to study intercultural communication not solely in terms of verbal language, but also in terms of nonverbal behaviors as a microbehavioral system of symbols and signals. Learning verbal and nonverbal language of the appropriate foreign culture precludes possible conflicts, negative emotions associated with misunderstanding, uncertainty, and frustration.

## Cultural Sensitivity and Ethnocentrism

The term *cultural sensitivity* refers to the integration of characteristics of a culture, acquiring knowledge about cultural influences on behavior, and translating such cultural awareness into effective relationships with those from other cultures (Harris & Moran, 1979). Cultural sensitivity enables people to recognize cultural differences; it can help a consultant or manager be at the margins of those differences, and can reduce ethnocentric bias.

People who are physically or psychologically isolated from other cultural groups can erect social barriers to create distance and separation from such differences (Bennett, 1993). Although internationalization brings people from different cultures together, and thereby enables them to acknowledge that cultural differences exist, they might still defend themselves against these differences that can be perceived as being threatening to the self. People can defend themselves against cultural differences by degrading others, holding derogatory, ethnocentric attitudes toward others (out-group bias), and evaluating one's own cultural group as superior (in-group bias). As people increase their intercultural sensitivity, the cultural differences are not only recognized, but also respected. They further acquire new skills (for example, empathy) for relating to and communicating with people of different cultures.

Consequences of ethnocentrism and lack of intercultural sensitivity can be costly for international organizations. Ethnocentric people are unable to go beyond their own cultural filters in interpreting the behaviors of other. Thus, ethnocentrism will increase ignorance of the processes that are necessary to gain a different cultural viewpoint, and thus prevent effective intercultural communication. It often forms the basis of limited and detrimental patterns of thinking about, and dealing with, others in the world. Ethnocentrism can also evoke prejudicial thinking that can induce feelings of anger, contempt, resentment, disdain, or even compassion and closeness. As negative emotions about out-groups reinforce stereotypic attitudes, they serve as the primary motivators for behavior and action, thus forming the basis for discrimination in the workplace.

Leaders are sometimes aware of ethnocentrism, and relate to the world around them through the cultural filters of their own particular culture. Problems arise when they believe that their way of perceiving and interpreting the world is the only way of perceiving and interpreting it, and that other interpretations do not exist. It is important for leaders to consider ways to develop flexibility when interacting with others, and for them to promote flexibility and intercultural sensitivity within the organization. They first need to recognize and appreciate the fact that people of different cultural backgrounds are different. They should then learn to deal with the emotions, judgments of morality, and judgments of personality that are associated with their ethnocentrism (Brislin, 1993). This process might involve learning to put leaders' emotional reactions and moral judgments on hold, and gaining new skills and knowledge to see the world from another person's point of view.

Leaders in international organizations should be flexible and sensitive in their assumptions about people from other cultures, and should promote a better understanding of the other culture throughout the organization in order to minimize the costs of ethnocentrism and prejudice. This need implies many consultative roles.

## Acculturation

Leaders in international organizations sometimes move into an unfamiliar environment, and undergo a social and cultural change. As a result, when arriving in a new culture, people often experience culture shock and problems associated with initial reactions of adjustment to a new culture and new life. Acculturative stress is a distressful, unpleasant, and disruptive psychological reaction to any unfamiliar cultural environment (Shiarev & Levy, 2001). Leaders face challenges when they try to develop new skills or adopt to new rules and roles required in the new cultural setting. They also experience a loss of control when they interact with members of the new culture (Triandis, 1994).

Organizational consultants can be helpful in the important roles of preparing managers, employees, and their families to live and work in another country. Kanter (1995) described global leaders as individuals with the ability to learn from, and leverage, the chaos of the worldwide market. The ability to use cross-cultural interaction not just on a foreign assignment, but also on a daily basis, to enrich knowledge and create a culturally dynamic organization, are important skills for leaders in international organizations (Adler & Bartholomew, 1992). Dalton (1998) listed several skills that are crucial for global leaders to meet the demands of international roles, including: "high levels of cognitive complexity, excellent interpersonal skills, being able to learn from experience and advanced moral reasoning" (p. 386). The challenge is to develop and use these skills while also realizing that the cross-cultural nature of the work requires culture-specific approaches to learning. Some of the assignments that can provide leaders with the opportunity to develop different skills include involvement in long-distance multicultural projects, taking business trips to other countries (learning by doing), working as a member of a cross-cultural team, and managing a major multicountry project (Dalton, 1998). In summary, it is important for the dynamic nature of global work that leaders who face problems associated with acculturation develop a set of skills, competency, and an ability and willingness to learn.

# THE ROLE OF CONSULTANTS IN INTERNATIONAL ORGANIZATIONS

Understanding the complex nature of international organizations is valuable for organizational consultants who need to gain insight into an organization's culture, or in consulting to international organizations. I propose here several strategies and tactics for consultants in international organizations. I primarily discuss how consultants can help leaders to improve the effectiveness of communication in an international setting, increase intercultural sensitivity and reduce ethnocentrism, and deal with problems associated with acculturation. Finally, I will discuss strategies that can help consultants manage change in international organizations.

## Principles of Effective Intercultural Communication

Misunderstandings in intercultural communication can occur for several reasons. These include: the inappropriate assumption of similarities (for example, that all people are the same), language differences, nonverbal misinterpretations, preconceptions and stereotypes, the tendency to evaluate, and high anxiety and tension (Barna, 1997). To overcome these limitations, Spitzberg (1997), as part of a model of intercultural communication competence, has identified several characteristics of individuals considered important in facilitating intercultural communication. Among these are:

- Ability to adjust to different cultures
- Ability to work effectively with different societal systems
- Ability to handle psychological stress
- Skills in interpersonal relationships
- Ability to understand others
- Adaptiveness
- Awareness of self and culture
- Charisma
- Cooperation
- Communication competence
- Interpersonal flexibility and interest
- Managerial ability
- No ethnocentrism
- Self-confidence
- Social adjustment
- Verbal and nonverbal behaviors

Other characteristics associated with effective intercultural communication include: knowledge of alternative interpretations, similarities, and differences, self-disclosure, self-monitoring, social relaxation, adaptation ability, perceived social distance, and attitudes toward the other culture. Past research suggests that although knowledge and skills are necessary components of effective intercultural communication, openness and flexibility in one's thinking and interpretations, and being motivated to communicate effectively and build a successful relationship are essential characteristics (Matsumoto, 2000).

Differences in language can also cause some problems in the implementation of consulting assessments, instruments, and questionnaires in international settings for several reasons (Hoppe, 1998). First, the acceptance level or appeal of certain assessments or instruments can differ in different cultures due to lack of trust among people from different countries, or to ambiguity as to use of the material or in understanding it. Second, dimensions of concepts assessed by the instrument might be culturally biased. Assessment instruments developed by U.S. researchers generally reflect U.S. models of human behavior, therefore it is questionable whether they can be generalized or applied to other cultures. Third, assumptions about the assessment process might not transfer to other cultures. Finally, consultants might experience problems in interpreting the results. For example, if a measure of perceived effective leadership that is developed in the United States is administered in Saudi Arabia, it is almost impossible to make cross-cultural comparisons on that measure, because Saudi Arabians' concept of effective leadership, with its emphasis on respect for authority and position, indirectness in communication with others, tradition, and religion, is totally different than Americans' concept (Feghali, 1997). Therefore, researchers fail to generalize the findings across other cultures.

The emergence of the global marketplace has clearly created international organizations with similar organizational and managerial functions across cultures that face the same challenges no matter where they are located, and that require the same leadership competencies. Consultants therefore need to find ways to address the challenges of generalizability. One piece of practical advice is to use instruments developed in, or competently adopted for, the culture in which the assessment or measurement is to take place (Hoppe, 1998). However, this approach might be difficult to implement, because there is much less propensity in some societies such as China, Japan, or Saudi Arabia, for psychological measurement of people in employment contexts, and the research infrastructure for developing measurements is significantly less extensive in these countries (Hoppe, 1998).

Ideally, instrument translation from one culture to another should be made by translators who are proficient in the terminology of the instruments, and are familiar with their implicit cultural meanings. Finding such people is time-consuming and a difficult process. Obtaining opinions of knowledgeable practitioners and researchers from within the culture, including whether the items on the questionnaire adequately capture the behaviors that are viewed in that culture as effective, can also be helpful (Hoppe, 1998).

Another piece of advice is to look for instruments that have been cross-culturally validated: questionnaires that have been shown to measure what is considered important across many societies, and whose meaning is reasonably equivalent across cultures (Hoppe, 1998). Even when using cross-culturally validated measures, consultants should always discuss operationalization and meaning of items with the recipient.

Consultants who want to use instruments developed in the United States in other countries should be cautious about the international reliability and validity of these instruments. They should identify cross-culturally validated scales if possible, or adjust and add according to local needs, values, and expectations.

## Methods to Increase Intercultural Sensitivity and Reduce Ethnocentrism

One possible consequence of internationalization is ethnocentric attitudes toward people from different cultures. As a result, an individual perceives others from different cultures (out-groups) as distinctively different from those who share the same nationality, ethnicity, or culture with them (in-groups). The formation of in-groups and out-groups can cause individuals to favor the in-group and to discriminate against the out-group. When ethnocentrism and prejudice arise in an international organization, the decrease in effectiveness and productivity of the organization is inevitable.

## Reducing Prejudice

In examining the group formation in international organizations from a social-psychological perspective, the *contact hypothesis* (Allport, 1979) offers ways in which prejudice can be reduced. It simply suggests that interaction between individuals belonging to different groups will reduce ethnic prejudice and intergroup tension. Research supporting the contact hypothesis has yielded an impressive array of data derived from a wide range of social situations, such as the armed services (see, for example, Landis, Hope, & Day, 1984; Roberts, 1953), educational settings (see, for example, Johnson, Johnson, & Maruyama, 1984), the workplace (see, for example, Harding & Hogrefe, 1952; Minard, 1952), and places of residence (see, for example, Wilner, Walkley, & Cook, 1952). Past research suggested that the outcome of contact is favorable when group members are of equal status, pursuing common, superordinate goals, and backed by social and institutional support, and when the interaction is cooperatively interdependent with one another.

When applied in an organizational setting, to achieve a successful intergroup contact and reduce the conflict between the groups, there needs to be positive and functional interdependence between groups. Consultants can attain this interdependence by creating a superordinate goal that neither group can attain on its own and which supersedes other goals each group might have. A single superordinate goal, however, might not be sufficient to reduce intergroup conflict; a series of cumulative superordinate goals are required (Sherif, 1966).

Superordinate goals often generate strong motivations for cooperation, which in many applied settings has been used to reduce intergroup conflict (see, for example, Cook, 1978). *Cooperation* can also increase intergroup attraction and communication, reduce tension, and lead to greater trust and increased satisfaction with group products (Worchel, 1979). The other important factor influencing intergroup contact is the status of group members, which is seen as a basis for generating expectations about oneself and others in social interaction (Cohen, 1982). If there is a status difference between the group members, the high-status group tends to dominate intergroup interaction, which is undesirable for the low-status group. This results in less effort being exerted, and via a self-fulfilling prophecy, lower actual achievement. Thus, in creating a contact situation in an organizational setting, consultants' focus should be in achieving a superordinate goal, cooperation, and equal status, and in reassuring the group members that this contact situation is supported by the leaders of the organization.

**Personalization.** Several models have been proposed to achieve intergroup acceptance. The personalization model (Brewer & Miller, 1984; Ensari & Miller, 2001; Ensari & Miller, in press) suggests that when intergroup relations are more interpersonally oriented, and when individual out-group members are seen as distinct from one another (as opposed to the perception of the out-group as a homogeneous unit), the intergroup conflict can be reduced. In a number of experiments (see, for example, Bettencourt, Brewer, Croak, & Miller, 1992; Ensari & Miller, 2001; Ensari & Miller, in press; Harrington, 1988; Miller, Brewer, & Edwards, 1985), it has been shown that personalized interaction allows in-group members to recognize the personal attributes of out-group members, and to develop more personalized, less homogenized perceptions of them (Fiske & Neuberg, 1989; Islam & Hewstone, 1993).

The author's research is illustrative. Ensari and Miller (in press), for example, conducted laboratory experiments in which they varied levels of personalization. In these studies, a typical or atypical out-group member either disclosed personal and unique information, or gave impersonal and general information to the participant. The social groups used in these experiment were Muslims and secularist groups in Istanbul, Turkey (Study 1), and liberals and conservatives in the United States (Study 2). The results showed that, in a cooperative contact situation, when a typical out-group member disclosed personal information, the participants' ethnocentric attitudes were eliminated. A more interesting finding was that participants not only changed their attitudes toward the out-group person in the contact situations, but also generalized their positive attitudes toward the social category as a whole. The disclosure of personal information had greater beneficial impact on perceptions of the group as a whole—across situations and across persons—when the out-group member in the contact situation was perceived as typical of his or her group. Although personalization or typicality alone provide some benefit, more maximal benefit can be achieved when personalization and typicality are induced simultaneously.

These results suggest that it is beneficial for international organizations to implement the personalization findings in their organizations in an attempt to improve intergroup relations. Consultants might be able to reduce the conflicts created by the intense relations between the workers from different cultural or ethnic groups by endorsing the importance of voluntary interpersonal contact, and creating situations in which the workers have the opportunity to share their individual attributes and interact at an interpersonal level. The personalization model suggests that such contact situations will increase liking and acceptance not only at the personal level, but also at the group level.

**Recategorization.** Another model, espoused by Gaertner and Dovidio (1986), contends that one possible way of reducing ethnocentric bias is to create a new social identity for group members. When this form of *recategorization* is successful, in-group loyalties and concern for the collective welfare can be transferred from the original in-group to the group as a whole. Gaertner and Dovidio claimed that replacing the salience of the intergroup boundaries with the perception of common membership within a superordinate entity can reduce intergroup conflict, because it increases the likelihood that members of these groups will perceive themselves as belonging to one group rather than two. In a number of experiments, Gaertner and his colleagues tested the hypothesis that strategies that increase the salience of a common or superordinate group reduce the salience of prior group boundaries, and thereby contribute to the development of a general sense of unity and identity. Consistently, conditions that enhanced the salience of the common group identity and reduced the salience of the prior in-group identity were found to diminish and eliminate ethnocentric bias in evaluations of fellow group members. To the extent that participants perceived that combined group as a single entity, rather than an aggregate of two separate groups, evaluations of former out-group members became more positive.

**Applications of Recategorization to International Settings.** Such a merger of group identities can also be represented in international work settings, in which workers representing different cultures or ethnic groups are successfully merged into a new functional unit. Consultants can achieve recategorization and implement superordinate goals in several ways. First, within the organizations, they can create work groups composed of group members with different cultural or ethnic backgrounds, and introduce to them a single, common group identity. For instance, group members can be encouraged to work on a common project that requires interdependent cooperation. Second, groups can be reminded of their common interest in the success of the organization as a whole. After all, successful collaboration will improve organizational effectiveness, and, in turn, benefit the group members working for that organization. Alternatively, heterogeneous work teams can be created with accountability to the larger organization. Consultants should emphasize the fact that recategorization does not require elimination of former group identities. Having a common, superordinate group identity does not eliminate the distinctions between the ethnic groups in international organizations. Instead, the common group identity enhances the relative salience of common group membership over differentiated categories. As a result, loyalties to the superordinate group enhance individuals' sense of responsibility and efficacy in ways to promote collective interests.

## Strategies for Improving Acculturation

Leaders' reactions to acculturation vary at both the societal and individual level (Triandis, 1994). They might minimize the cultural differences by shifting toward the new culture, repressing their own (assimilation strategy), emphasize the ways in which their own culture is different (separation strategy), neither maintain their own culture nor contact with the other culture (marginalization strategy), or integrate to the new culture by valuing aspects of both culture (integration strategy) (Triandis, Kashima, Shimada, & Villareal, 1986).

Perhaps the best strategy that consultants can put into place is the integration of a strategy of acculturation in which leaders in an international setting participate in the new culture while also maintaining their own. In this case, these leaders retain their own culture and also learn the new culture. Berry, Kim, Minde, and Mok (1992) presented cross-cultural evidence that this approach is the most desirable one for the mental health of participants.

When leaders interact with members of the new culture, they must develop skills, such as learning the language, customs, traditions, organizational rules, and regulations of the other culture. Americans who do business in Japan, for example, can benefit if they take the time to study in depth Japanese business operations, norms, and values. For instance, one fundamental distinction between Asian and American cultures is the definition of self. The United States is an individualistic culture that stresses the importance of individual goals over group goals, whereas Asian cultures are we-oriented, and personal goals are subordinated to the goals of the group (Triandis, 1994).

Another implementation example relates to the distinction between the two cultures in familial responsibilities. In Asian cultures, it is usual to see family members all work in the family business, even if the children would prefer a different career (Fine, 1995). Asian parents are obligated to care for their children, feed them, educate them, provide financial support, and so on. Recognition of these distinctions between the two cultures helps leaders who work in Asia to understand why Asians cannot conceptualize their individual self-identity separate from their group identity, why conformity to authority and obedience are high in Asian cultures, how cooperation, as opposed to competition, is a more effective tool to increase work team performances, and why organizations are responsible for not only paying wages, but also for ensuring that workers have housing, schools, and so on. In other words, the interdependence of the individual to the group and family is a critical concept in understanding motivation and decision-making in Asian cultures.

## Enhancing Acculturation

The acculturation experience can offer many constructive inputs to the leader from the host culture and people, if expatriate leaders take the time to learn and to listen. The consultant's responsibility is to provide leaders with information about the new culture by gathering external information from several sources such as national government, regional organizations, chambers of commerce, trade associations, universities, magazines, and newspapers. When external sources are unreliable, consultants can conduct surveys to provide leaders with dependably accurate, available, and inexpensive information. Typical questions a consultant might raise in gathering external information concern the economy (for example, is it growing rapidly, or slowly?), money and finance, planning (for example, what will be the effect of company activities?), taxes, resources, and facilities (for example, how available are land, water, transport, and so on?), labor (for example, are wages high or low?), and foreign assistance (for example, how available is assistance from foreign countries?) (Walsh, 1973).

Another strategy to enhance cultural awareness is to implement a variety of educational interventions related to cultural differences. Consultants to international organizations can organize celebrations that honor different cultures, develop awareness-training workshops that are efficient and interesting to the audience, or offer a course on understanding and learning other cultures, that is available not only to leaders, but also to workers throughout the organization. In addition, they can maintain a resource library that includes films, articles, and books that can be used to increase knowledge about other cultures.

**Warnings.** In addition, consultants should warn leaders against overshooting, moving toward the new culture to an extreme degree (for example, by changing names), and against extreme maintenance and protection of their own culture. Overshooting can cause loss of in-group identity, which has negative consequences for the individual's self-esteem and self-respect. When leaders protect their own culture to an extreme degree, on the other hand, it might cause social rejection, or even discrimination against them. As a result, leaders might become even more extreme in manifesting their own culture than those who have not attempted to relate to the other culture (ethnic affirmation). For example, some African Americans who work in Europe dress and behave in ways that are more African than the Africans (Triandis et al., 1986). Hence, neither total rejection nor extreme protection of one's own culture is a desirable process for leaders in international settings to adopt.

## Change Strategies

Internationalization often entails new interventions, new insights, new attitudes, and new people. In turn, it leads to an organizational change that challenges leaders. The leader's role in change management is to be a source of innovation and creativity in achieving goals, to analyze the new techniques for forecasting major organizational decisions, and to develop more effective policies and strategies for change. Management in international work environments requires appropriate adaptation of corporate objectives and procedures, and attention to personal and personnel aims in multicultural settings (Harris & Moran, 1979).

To manage and foster change in international organizations, Harris and Moran (1979) provided some tips that are helpful in intercultural situations. The first step they recommend that consultants follow is to *describe and identify the desired changes*. Consultants should determine what exactly is to be changed: is it a change in structure (for example, the system of authority, communication, and so on), technology (for example, tools, computers), tasks (for example, activities, research), processes (for example, techniques, methods, and so on), environment, people, or a combination of these? Next, they need to identify the *antecedents of the change* (Why did the change occur? What are the factors that led to these alterations?), and also examine the *impact of change on the organization* (Why will the organization benefit from this innovation? What are the positive and negative consequences of the change for the organization?). Furthermore, the responsibilities of consultants include *determining available material and resources to foster the change*, and *identifying people who promote or resist the change*. Consultants should determine the ways in which the driving forces can be enforced, and the resisting forces weakened. To develop strategies to increase the driving forces and decrease the restraining forces, consultants should investigate the rationale for the change, and anticipate arguments against the change, and develop counterarguments. However, creative ideas for modification or alteration of the change plan should always be allowed. To create a *readiness for change,* consultants should involve leaders who have to implement the change in the planning process, and provide the complete case to them.

Despite all these attempts to implement the change, the change plans can be rejected or abandoned. In that case, consultants should create *alternative plans or strategies* to undertake, and promote related changes to strengthen the current one. Once the change is accepted and functioning, consultants should identify what needs to be done, what steps should be followed, when and where it is to be done, and set realistic time frames for bringing about the change. Finally, the effectiveness of the change should be *objectively evaluated*, and further modifications or alterations should be made accordingly. Collection of data on the situation might be helpful to support the change, and eventually to evaluate it.

# SUGGESTIONS FOR FUTURE RESEARCH

Cross-cultural implementation of assessments and instruments that are developed in the United States is troublesome due to cultural differences in understanding the items, using the method of implementation, and interpreting the results. One strategy to deal with the generalizability issue is to find instruments that are cross-culturally validated. Unfortunately, there are very few cross-culturally reliable and valid instruments that are available for consultants and researchers, and the equivalence of most of the questionnaires that are being used outside of the United States has not been checked (Hoppe, 1998). Thus, future research should address this generalizability issue carefully, and check the international reliability and validity of the instruments developed and used in the United States.

## Ethnocentric Bias

The results of social psychological experiments exploring ways in which ethnocentric bias can be reduced have potentially useful implications for how groups formed within an international organization can work together and manage to reap the benefits of internalization without the costs of intergroup conflict. There are a number of reasons, however, that the translation of findings from basic research to applications in real-world settings still requires additional research and theory.

First, neither the personalization model nor the common in-group identity model have been studied in organizational settings. Their applicability in the international work environment is therefore unknown. The practicality of implementing interpersonal-oriented relationships between workers in an international organization also raises an important concern.

Second, social psychologists have studied the consequences of cooperative, interdependent contact as a tool for improving intergroup relations without much consideration of the outcomes on group performance. Therefore, the moderating effects of group structure, group effectiveness, or group composition on organizational performance still need to be studied. Similarly, it is unclear whether interventions that lower ethnocentric bias also promote greater organizational effectiveness.

Third, even though the application of these approaches creates desirable outcomes for the organization in the short run, future studies should address the impact of these models on process and performance over time. They should also identify situations in which the positive outcomes are obtained in the long run.

Finally, social psychological experiments studied groups in which status relationship differences among the groups was a constant feature of the experimental design. However, there is often an objectively recognized status hierarchy in organizations. There is now considerable evidence that the status hierarchy moderates the effects of team structure and function (see, for example, Marcus-Newhall, Miller, Holtz, & Brewer, 1993). Thus, the role of status hierarchy in the organizational context should be examined in future research.

## Acculturation

Although integration strategy appears to be a far better approach than the others from the point of view of mental health (Berry et al., 1987), future research should examine situations in which this is not the case. For example, when there is a social hierarchy in the work setting (such as when there are both members of lower- and higher-status social categories), workers might prefer the assimilation strategy in which they adopt the new culture and reject their own.

Another factor that plays an important role in acculturation of leaders is the length of time spent in the new culture. Those who spent only a short period of time in the new culture might hold different values and assumptions than those who had the opportunity to contact with people of the new culture, and make progress toward integration.

# SUMMARY AND CONCLUSION

This chapter has considered a variety of ways in which organizational consultants can become more effective in international organizational contexts. By knowing and making use of social psychological findings on group research, they can design approaches that are likely to be more effective in bringing about organizational change. Because most large organizations are increasingly global rather than national in scope, knowledge of relevant literature has moved for organizational consultants from nice-to-know to obligatory. The result is likely over time to be improved consulting and improved organizations.

# References

Adler, N. J., & Bartholomew, S. (1992). Managing globally competent people. *Academy of Management Executive, 6,* 52–65.

Allport, G. W. (1979). *The nature of prejudice.* Reading, MA: Addison-Wesley. (Original work published 1954)

Barna, M. (1997). Stumbling blocks in intercultural communication. In L. Samovar & R. Porter (Eds.), *Intercultural communication: A reader* (pp. 370–379). Belmont, CA: Wadsworth.

Barnlund, D. C., & Araki, S. (1985). Intercultural encounters: The management of compliments by Japanese and Americans. *Journal of Cross-Cultural Psychology, 16,* 9–26.

Barnlund, D. C., & Yoshioka, M. (1990). Apologies: Japanese and American styles. *International Journal of Intercultural Relations, 14,* 193–206.

Bennett, M. J. (1993). Towards ethnorelativism: A developmental model of intercultural sensitivity. In P. Michael Paige (Ed.), *Education for the intercultural experience* (pp. 179–196). Yarmouth, ME: Intercultural Press.

Berry, J. W., Kim, U., Minde, T., & Mok, D. (1987). Comparative studies of acculturative stress. *International Migration Review, 21,* 185–206.

Bettencourt, B. A., Brewer, M. B., Croak, M., & Miller, N. (1992). Cooperation and the reduction of intergroup bias: The role of reward structure and social orientation. *Journal of Experimental Social Psychology, 28,* 301–319.

Brewer, M. B., & Miller, N. (1984). Beyond the contact hypothesis: Theoretical perspectives on desegregation. In N. Miller & M. B. Brewer (Eds.), *Groups in contact: The psychology of desegregation* (pp. 281–302). Orlando, FL: Academic Press.

Brislin, R. (1993). *Understanding culture's influence on behavior.* Orlando, FL: Harcourt Brace.

Calder, B. J. (1977). Endogenous-exogenous versus internal-external attributions: Implications for the development of attribution theory. *Personality and Social Psychology Bulletin, 3,* 400–406.

Chen, G. M. (1995). Differences in self-disclosure patterns among Americans versus Chinese: A comparative study. *Journal of Cross-Cultural Psychology, 26,* 84–91.

Cohen, E. G. (1982). Expectation states and interracial interaction in school settings. *Annual Review of Sociology, 8,* 209–235.

Cook, S. W. (1978). Interpersonal and attitudinal outcomes in cooperating interracial groups. *Journal of Research and Development in Education, 12,* 97–113.

Cronshaw, S. F., & Lord, R. G. (1987). Effects of categorization, attribution, and encoding processes on leadership perceptions. *Journal of Applied Psychology, 72,* 97–106.

Dalton, M. A. (1998). Developing leaders for global roles. In C. D. McCauley, R. S. Moxley, & E. Van Velsor (Eds.), *The Center for Creative Leadership handbook of leadership development* (pp. 336–378). San Francisco: Jossey-Bass.

Den Hartog, D. N, House, R. J., Hanges, P. J., Ruiz-Quintanilla, S. A., & Dorfman, P. W. (1999). Culture specific and cross-culturally generalizable implicit leadership theories: Are attributes of charismatic/transformational leadership universally endorsed? *Leadership Quarterly, 10,* 219–256.

Emrich, C. G., Brower, H. H., Feldman, J. M., & Garland, H. (2000). *Images in words: Presidential rhetoric, charisma, and greatness.* Paper presented at the meeting of the Academy of Management, Toronto, Ontario, Canada.

Ensari, N., & Miller, N. (2001). Decategorization and the reduction of bias in the crossed categorization paradigm. *European Journal of Social Psychology, 31,* 193–216.

Ensari, N., & Miller, N. (in press). Out-group must not be so bad: The effects of disclosure, typicality and salience on out-group bias. *Journal of Personality and Social Psychology.*

Ensari, N., & Murphy, S. (2001). *Cross-cultural variations in leadership perceptions and attribution of charisma to the leader*. Manuscript submitted for publication.

Feghali, E. (1997). Arab cultural communication patterns. *International Journal of Intercultural Relations, 21*, 345–378.

Fine, M. G. (1995). *Building successful multicultural organizations*. Westport, CT: Quorum/ Greenwood.

Fiske, S. T., & Neuberg, S. L. (1989). Category-based and individuating processes as a function of information and motivation: Evidence from our laboratory. In D. Bar-Tal, C. F. Graumann, A. W. Kruglanski, & W. Stroebe (Eds.), *Stereotyping and prejudice: Changing conceptions* (pp. 83–104). New York: Springer-Verlag.

Foti, R. J., Fraser, S. L., & Lord, R. G. (1982). Effects of leadership labels and prototypes on perceptions of political leaders. *Journal of Applied Psychology, 67*, 326–333.

Fraser, S. L., & Lord, R. G. (1988). Stimulus prototypicality and general leadership impressions: Their role in leadership and behavioral ratings. *Journal of Psychology, 122*, 291–303.

Gaertner, S., & Dovidio, J. (1986). *Prejudice and racism*. Orlando, FL: Academic Press.

Glad, B., & Shiraev, E. (Eds.). (1999). *The Russian transformation*. New York: St. Martin's Press.

Harding, J., & Hogrefe, R. (1952). Attitudes of white department store employees towards negro co-workers. *Journal of Social Issues, 8*, 18–28.

Harrington, H. J. (1988). *The effects of personal contact on intergroup relations*. Unpublished doctoral dissertation, University of Southern California, Los Angeles.

Harris, P. R., & Moran, R. T. (1979). *Managing cultural differences*. Houston, TX: Gulf.

Hecht, M. L., Ribeau, S., & Alberts, J. K. (1989). An Afro-American perspective on interethnic communication. *Communication Monographs, 56*, 385–410.

Hogg, M. A. (2001). A social identity theory of leadership. *Personality and Social Psychology Review, 5*, 184–200.

Hoppe, M. H. (1998). Cross-cultural issues in leadership development. In C. D. McCauley, R. S. Moxley, & E. Van Velsor (Eds.), *The Center for Creative Leadership handbook of leadership development* (pp. 336–378). San Francisco: Jossey-Bass.

Hui, C. H., & Luk, C. L. (1997). Industrial/organizational psychology. In J. W. Berry, M. H. Segall, & C. Kagitcibasi (Eds.), *Handbook of cross-cultural psychology: Social behavior and applications* (Vol. 3, pp. 371–411). Needham Heights, MA: Allyn & Bacon.

Islam, M. R., & Hewstone, M. (1993). Dimensions of contact as predictors of intergroup anxiety, perceived out-group variability, and out-group attitude: An integrative model. *Personality and Social Psychology Bulletin, 19*, 700–710.

James, K., Chen, D.-L., & Cropanzano, R. (1996). Culture and leadership among Taiwanese and U.S. workers: Do values influence leadership ideals? In M. N. Ruderman, M. W. Hughes-James, & S. E. Jackson (Eds.), *Selected research on work-team diversity* (pp. 33–52). Greensboro, NC: Center for Creative Leadership.

Johnson, D. W., Johnson, R. T., & Maruyama, G. (1984). Goal interdependence and interpersonal attraction in heterogeneous classrooms: A meta-analysis. In N. Miller & M. Brewer (Eds.), *Groups in contact: The psychology of desegregation* (pp. 187–212). Orlando, FL: Academic Press.

Kanter, R. M. (1995). *World class: Thriving locally in the global economy*. New York: Simon & Schuster.

Landis, D., Hope, R. O., & Day, H. R. (1984). Training for desegregation in the military. In N. Miller & M. Brewer (Eds.), *Groups in contact: The psychology of desegregation* (pp. 213–242). Orlando, FL: Academic Press.

Lord, R. G., De Vader, C., & Alliger, G. (1986). A meta-analysis of the relation between personality traits and leadership perceptions: An application of validity generalization procedures. *Journal of Applied Psychology, 71*, 402–410.

Lord, R. G., Foti, R. G., & De Vader, C. (1984). A test of leadership categorization theory: Internal structure, information processing, and leadership perceptions. *Organizational Behavior and Human Performance, 34*, 343–378.

Lord, R. G., & Maher, J. P. (1993). *Leadership and information processing.* New York: Routledge.

Marcus-Newhall, A., Miller, N., Holtz, R., & Brewer, M. B. (1993). Cross-cutting category membership with role assignment: A means of reducing intergroup bias. *British Journal of Social Psychology, 32*, 125–146.

Markus, H. R., & Kitayama, S. (1991). Culture and the self: Implications for cognition, emotion, and motivation. *Psychological Review, 98*, 224–253.

Matsumoto, D. (2000). *Culture and psychology.* Belmont, CA: Wadsworth.

Maurer, T. J., & Lord, R. G. (1991). An exploration of cognitive demands in group interaction as a moderator of information processing variables in perceptions of leadership. *Journal of Applied Social Psychology, 21*, 821–839.

Mayo, M. C., Meindl, J. R., & Pastor, J. C. (1996). The cost of leading diversity: Effects of group diversity on leader's perceptions. In M. N. Ruderman, M. W. Hughes-James, & S. E. Jackson (Eds.), *Selected research on work-team diversity* (pp. 9–31). Greensboro, NC: Center for Creative Leadership.

Meindl, J. R., & Ehrlich, S. B. (1987). The romance of leadership and the evaluation of organizational performance. *Academy of Management Journal, 30*, 91–109.

Meindl, J. R., Ehrlich, S. B., & Dukerich, J. M. (1985). The romance of leadership. *Administrative Science Quarterly, 30*, 78–102.

Miller, N., Brewer, M. B., & Edwards, K. (1985). Cooperative interaction in desegregated settings: A laboratory analogue. *Journal of Social Issues, 41*, 63–79.

Minami, M., & McCabe, A. (1995). Rice balls and bear hunts: Japanese and North American family narrative patterns. *Journal of Child Language, 22*, 423–445.

Minard, R. D. (1952). Race relationships in the Pocahontas coal fields. *Journal of Social Issues, 25*, 29–44.

Nomura, N., & Barnlund, D. C. (1983). Patterns of interpersonal criticism in Japan and United States. *International Journal of Intercultural Relations, 7*, 1–18.

Pfeffer, J. (1977). The ambiguity of leadership. *Academy of Management Review, 2*, 104–112.

Roberts, H. W. (1953). The impact of military service upon the racial attitudes of Negro servicemen in World War II. *Social Problems, 1*, 65–69.

Schmidt, S., & Yeh, R. S. (1992). The structure of leader influence. *Journal of Cross-Cultural Psychology, 23*, 251–264.

Shamir, B. (1992). Attribution of influence and charisma to the leader: The romance of leadership revisited. *Journal of Applied Social Psychology, 22*, 386–407.

Sherif, M. (1966). *Group conflict and cooperation.* New York: Routledge.

Shiraev, E., & Levy, D. (2001). *Introduction to cross-cultural psychology: Critical thinking and contemporary applications.* Needham Heights, MA: Allyn & Bacon.

Spitzberg, B. (1997). A model of intercultural communication competence. In L. Samovar & R. Porter (Eds.), *Intercultural communication: A reader* (pp. 379–391). Belmont, CA: Wadsworth.

Suzuki, T. (1978). *Japanese and the Japanese: Words in culture.* Tokyo: Kodansha International.

Triandis, H. C. (1994). *Culture and social behavior.* New York: McGraw-Hill.

Triandis, H. C., Kashima, Y., Shimada, E., & Villareal, M. (1986). Acculturation indices as a means of confirming cultural differences. *International Journal of Psychology, 21*, 43–70.

Walsh, J. E., Jr. (1973). *Guidelines for management consultants in Asia.* Tokyo: Asian Productivity Organization.

Wilner, D. M., Walkley, R. P., & Cook, S. W. (1952). Residential proximity and intergroup relations in public housing projects. *Journal of Social Issues, 8*, 45–69.

Worchel, S. (1979). Cooperation and the reduction of intergroup conflict: Some determining factors. In W. G. Austin & S. Worchel (Eds.), *The social psychology of intergroup relations* (pp. 262–273). Pacific Grove, CA: Brooks/Cole.

# CHAPTER TWENTY-ONE

# Assessment and Intervention Issues in International Organizational Consulting

Ann M. O'Roark
*Private Practice*

Cultural competence in international organizational consulting involves more than practicing social etiquette that encourages participation in assessment and intervention activities (Sue, 1978; Sue & Zane, 1987; Sue, Arredondo, & McDavis, 1992; Holcomb-McCoy & Myers, 1999). While genuine, appropriate behavior is considered germane to effectiveness in every consulting venture (American Psychological Association, Society of Consulting Psychology [APA/SCP], 2000), working with international clients and multicultural work-groups brings the U.S. consultant's credibility and relevance under intensified scrutiny (Pasa, Kabasakal, & Bodur, 2001; Hofstede, Neuijen, Ohavy, & Sanders, 1990). The challenge for the organizational consulting psychologist is to temper interventions with consideration of the client's *zeitgeist* (spirit of the time), *ortgeist* (spirit of the place), *weltanschauung* (outlook on the world), and *erliebnistypus* (experience balance). Knowledge from culture orientation profiling, organizational culture analysis, and individual employee assessments sets the stage for effective, noninvasive consulting.

The compelling, vital need for concentrated attention to cultural competence is illustrated in the September 11, 2001, suicide attacks on U.S. landmarks that killed thousands of civilians and hundreds of military personnel. This example of extreme consequences when people fail to comprehend cultures that vary from their own assumptions of good and bad behavior, right and wrong lifestyles, is a sharp reminder for all U.S. psychologists—scientists, academicians, and practitioners of every specialization—of the importance of their

516

international work and our professional commitment to "strive to help the public in developing informed judgments and choices concerning human behavior" (APA, 2001, p. 6). Consulting psychologists are in the business of "increasing knowledge of behavior and people's understanding of themselves and others and to the use of such knowledge to improve the condition of individuals, organizations, and society" (p. 6).

Psychologists are asked to "prevent or minimize harm to others through acts of commission or omission in their professional behavior . . . [and instructed that] [w]hen conflicts occur among psychologists' obligations or concerns, they [are to] attempt to resolve these conflicts and to perform their roles in a responsible fashion that avoids or minimizes harm" (APA, 2002, p. 6). In light of these professional obligations, cultural competency for international organizational consultants becomes more than polite, good manners, and assumes dimensions of diplomacy with a backbone of specialized knowledge in psychology, psychometrics, and organizational consulting theory and methods.

# BASIC CULTURAL ISSUES

Valid cross-cultural exchange in international organizational consulting hinges on minimizing overt and unconscious bias. Intervention modes, as well as many standardized tests typically used by U.S. consulting psychologists in formal assessment work, potentially contaminate diagnostic processes and consulting outcomes (Dana, 2001a). In Western or Euro-American cultures, the organizational psychologist interprets information about behavior, performance, and competence of individuals, work groups, or organizations, by working with normative tables that provide comparison exemplars in order to benchmark performance against known excellent, average, or poor performances, and to establish standards and parameters for acceptable behavior (Barclay, 1991). Absence of culturally appropriate exemplars, role models, or culture-specific normative statistics can negate the validity of assessment reports and intervention strategies.

Whether an international consultant is called upon for expert, assessment, or intervention work, cultural sensitivity and *consideration* prove critical in the management of the consultation project, as strongly as consideration and relationship behaviors did in the 1950s Ohio State leadership studies (Bass, 1981). This stream of organizational leadership research, adapted for indigenous organizational consulting by Japan's respected Professor Mitsumi (1985), points out the necessity for managers and leaders to attend to both task and consideration aspects of organizational productivity (Blanchard & Hersey, 1977; Bass, 1990, in press). Consideration issues affecting cultural competence are important in two major organizational consulting functions addressed here: *assessment* and *intervention*.

Assessment problems discovered in the transfer of Euro-American methods to other cultures are described as deeply embedded in U.S. psychological science and thinking. Technical and procedural issues are compounded and masked by the dominance of American management theory in international associations during the final decades of the twentieth century (Pasa et al., 2001). The promulgation of U.S. concepts resulted in an impression that a good manager in the United States would also be a good manager in other countries. Chen (1996, p. 165) cautioned that "there are no one-size-fits-all international managers who can be effective across several cultures, especially among cultures with many cultural differences." More subtle, but equally pervasive, biases in Anglo (American) academic and scientific methods are cultural assumptions underlying quantitative techniques, as is illustrated by the proposed reformulation of the null hypothesis to assert as truth that there are cultural differences, as opposed to the standard no-difference stipulation (Cuéllar, 2000; Dana, 2001b; Malgady, 2000; Van de Vijver & Hambleton, 1996).

# CURRENT NEED FOR ORGANIZATIONAL CONSULTING PSYCHOLOGISTS

With or without quick resolution of issues surrounding statistical methods, unbiased research hypotheses, and interpretation of ethical proscriptions, greater numbers of consulting psychologists who were raised and trained in the United States are being called upon to provide organizational consultation to businesses, agencies, and industries in other countries, companies operating in the United States that are owned by groups from non-U.S. countries, and organizations with multicultural work group constituencies (Hodgson & White, 2001). Small and mid-sized businesses of every sort across the country increasingly rely on international suppliers and consumers. Countless U.S. service firms employ greater numbers of immigrants for jobs such as housekeeping, lawn and yard maintenance, taxi driving, restaurants, and repairs on durable goods and appliances. The American Management Association reports that since the 1960s, the percentage of U.S. companies exposed to international competition increased from 7 to 80 percent (Greenberg, 1998).

## Cultural Competence Training

Dana (2001b) states that U.S. psychologists in all areas of professional practice rely on workshops, continuing education courses, and in-service training to gain cultural competence. He adds that much of this training is didactic, superficial, or out of context, and calls for integration and integumentation of cultural training into doctoral programs, and for post-degree continuing education courses that clarify how practitioners can apply new research findings. Dana commends curricula that are multicultural rather than Eurocentric, and the assessment courses that compare protocols from diverse cultural populations, examining conclusions drawn from both high-inference procedures where little standardized interpretation is available, and from low-inference instruments where little interpretation is required.

## Cultural Competency Criteria

At least five different self-report instruments are being used to assess cultural competence of psychological service providers (Dana, 2001a). In general, cultural competence is considered to comprise two functional clusters: attitudes and beliefs, and knowledge and skills (Arredondo et al., 1996). Initially, questions associated with a comprehensive model of thirty-one multicultural competencies (Sue et al., 1992) were used to describe three characteristics: awareness of one's own cultural values and biases, awareness of the client's world view, and knowledge of credible, acceptable interventions.

A national survey completed with the Multicultural Counseling Competence and Training Survey (MCCTS) reported responses of predominantly white American (90 percent) professional psychologists and counselors. Self-perceived competence in working with African Americans, Hispanic Americans, Asian Americans, and American Indians or Alaska natives was reported to be 38 percent, 26 percent, 16 percent, and 8 percent, respectively (Dana, 2000). "Cultural competence begins with a service delivery style or social etiquette that is acceptable to clients. . . . More specifically, each cultural/racial group has a distinct preference for certain behaviors and an emotional climate conveying a sense of being understood that includes how affect is expressed as well as the pace, kind and extent of assessment services" (Dana, 2001b, pp. 461–462).

Standards for competence (Dana, 2001b; Dana, Behn, & Gonwa, 1992) that were developed by the Western Interstate Commission for Higher Education (WICHE) for the California Cultural Competence Task Force (Dana, 2001b), and included in the subsequent California plan are: access—that is, language accessibility, linguistically appropriate written information, and responsiveness of the specialty service provider; quality of care—competent evaluation, diagnosis, and intervention; and quality management—utilization, evaluation of outcomes, and continuous improvement plans. Although not directed to organizational consulting per se, I contend that these same factors are equally applicable to competent practice of international consulting psychology.

## Consultant Bias

Dana (2001b) urges assessment practitioners and consultants to examine and understand their own cultural identities, to engage in explicit training to develop cultural knowledge and skills, and to make opportunities for in vivo experiences in other cultural communities. A further recommendation is to work toward obtaining fluency in a relevant language, something that psychologists trained outside the U.S. typically acquire in early education and schooling. Jaris Draguns (2001), recipient of the American Psychological Association award for distinguished contributions to the advancement of international psychology, writes that "the development of a truly international psychology is obstructed at this point by the massive disregard of contributions that are published in languages other than English" (p. 1019), and proposes eleven suggestions to overcome linguistic isolation of psychologists who disseminate their ideas and findings in languages other than English.

The significance of the consultant's *self* is an established variable in studies of client-perceived efficacy and utilization of psychological services (Combs & Gonzalez, 1997; Purkey, 1970). Acknowledging the potential for the self inadvertently to cause harm through acts of omission or commission, whether from ignorance or arrogant assumption, the international organizational consultant takes time to hone the *self-as-instrument* (Combs, Miser, & Whitaker, 1999; Covey, 1992; Combs & Snygg, 1959).

# INTERNATIONAL CONSULTING LITERATURE

Growing numbers of consultants, perhaps eager to be identified with an age of maturing internationalism in corporate business, invoke the word international as often as possible in résumés listing clients and work experiences. Providing psychological services in the United States to a firm with a corporate headquarters in Munich, or with branch operations in places such as Zurich, Beijing, or Sydney, however, does not bestow cultural competence in the design and delivery of organizational interventions anywhere or everywhere in the global economic village outside U.S. boundaries. Consulting psychologists who take seriously the professional injunction to do no harm (APA, 1992, 2001) are proactive, not only in compliance with guidelines being established for the practice of consulting psychology (CP) (APA/SCP, 2000a), but also with cultural competencies.

Those who choose to work transnationally benefit from becoming informed about psychology and psychological services across a spectrum of cultures. The goal is not an exhaustive knowledge of all practices in all cultures and subcultures, but rather familiarity with primary social variables and diversities. It is beyond the scope of this chapter to provide a thorough review of information currently available on ethnic and national characteristics. Representative of accumulating data applicable to international organizational consulting is a comparison of managers from twelve areas of the world (Bass, Burger, Doktor, & Barrett, 1979). The twelve geographic areas included in this pioneering research that was, and remains, of practical use for consultants are: the United States, Britain, the Netherlands, Belgium, Germany and Austria, Scandinavia, France, Italy, Iberia, Latin America, India, and Japan. A recent, widely acclaimed extension of international data, known as Project GLOBE, is presented by House et al. (1999).

# International Knowledge Base

Information about the efficacy of international consulting projects is accumulating, as recent reports in the *Consulting Psychology Journal: Practice and Research* are indicative of (Chen, 1996; Davis, 1997; Plummer, 1998; Mullin & Cooper, 1998; Kaminstein, Smith, & Miller, 2000; Fisher & Alford, 2000).

The *International Psychology Reporter* provides brief cross-cultural perspectives. In Vol. 5, No. 3/4, eleven countries are profiled in terms of cultural background and current psychological activity: China, Israeli, Switzerland, France, South Africa, Azerbaijan, Chile, Cyprus, Oman, South Korea, and Norway. Perloff (American Psychological Association, Division of International Consulting Psychology [APA/ICP], 2001) writes: "It is difficult to understand the Korean management system clearly without understanding the importance of its family system . . . One of the unique aspects of Korean management is management by family" (p. 34). Likely, consultants with experience in consulting to family businesses would be better prepared for assignments in South Korea. Other brief reports also contain information useful for consultants who work in the region; for example, Oman has changed from rural and traditional to modern without accompanying intellectual or technology advances (APA/ICP, 2001); in Cyprus, seminars are needed to help the public appreciate psychology better, and organizational psychology is not included in the list of topics taught in colleges (APA/ICP, 2001); Azerbaijan lists applied psychology—personnel selection and military psychology—among their valued studies (APA/ICP, 2001).

Other sources for articles about international consulting include: the *International Psychologist (IP)*, newsletter of the International Council of Psychologists; *Journal of Cross-Cultural Psychology; Advances in Global Leadership;* the *Academy of Management Review (AMR);* the *Journal of Social Issues (JSI);* and *Applied Psychology: An International Review (AP:IR). AP:IR* attempts to reduce bias in theoretical models by publishing lead articles with complementary pieces from a range of countries (see, for example, Fiedler, 1995, with seven commentaries from the United States [2], Germany [2], France [1], Japan [1], and India [1]).

# Assessment in International Contexts

The next section in this chapter reviews advances in adapting psychological measures as assessment instruments for international applications, progress on formulation of etic (universal) assessment dimensions, and the use of calibration consultation as an approach with potential to reduce cultural bias in organizational assessments. Calibration is defined as refining the accuracy of an instrument by comparison with a known standard, which is often the elusive, critical variable in cross-cultural work.

The final section of the chapter presents a consulting process that includes cultural components, and proposes the utility of adapting U.S. models and procedures associated with organizational culture, conflict, and decision-making for use in projects conducted with non-U.S. cultures. Modifying a U.S. emic conceptualization so that it becomes appropriate for use in multicultural situations, or in a different culture, is psychologically complex and sensitive work. Ancient efforts to achieve this level of cross-cultural sensitivity are most obvious in Egyptian syncretism. Traditional human-form gods were given the animal heads of the gods from merged cults: Ra, the sun god, the executive-king-administrator role model, was merged with falcon-headed Horus, god of the lower Nile.

According to the inner logic of Eastern Confucian philosophy, growth (development) of the human conceptualizing process includes both a deepening process and a broadening process (Tu, 1984; Gielen, 1989). In this sense, exporting of Anglo organizational conceptual models and standard U.S. intervention techniques needs to be closely examined and prepared for use in the other culture. In the Confucian philosophy, the broadening process leads from the self to an expanding universe of relationships: the family, the community, the country, the world, and ultimately, the universe. In international organizational consulting, the broadening process expands from emic, or a culturally specific universe of assumptions, hypotheses, and prescriptive recommendations, along a continuum that includes multicultural adaptations, and progresses into more etic, or culturally general conceptualizations (Dana, 2001a).

The Eastern deepening process focuses on conceptual transformation that is based, in part, upon the integration of body, mind, heart, and spirit, as demonstrated by attaining virtues such as *jen* (human-heartedness), *li* (propriety), *i* (righteousness), *chung* (loyalty), *hsin* (trustworthiness), and *chung jang* (the doctrine of the golden mean) (Gielen, 1989). For organizational consultants, the deepening process begins by being conscious of value systems active in the client workplace, and of where clients fit along a continuum of culture orientation: Anglo or Euro-American, assimilated, bicultural, marginal, transitional, or traditional (culture orientation that is not Euro-American) (Dana, 2000). In the intervention section of this chapter, the culture calibration/action research model (see Figure 21.1) introduces both breadth and depth to international consulting.

## International Assessment Issues

This section reviews progress in adaptations of U.S. emic assessment instruments for international application, developments in the validation and recognition of etic universal assessment dimensions, and the use of calibration consultation as an approach with potential to reduce cultural bias. In psychological consulting, calibration refers to assessment procedures associated with action research methods (French & Bell, 1973), and preparation of heuristic criteria, can be practical targets for performance improvements, can be used with interventions intended to facilitate adjustment within a desired range, and can verify outcome efficacy (O'Roark, 1995). In international organizational consulting, calibration assessment promotes cultural competency by an assuming up front that organizational intervention strategy and tactics need to build around a central focal image of desired range and efficacy that is determined by an assessment of extant social and organizational culture.

## Psychological Testing and Assessment

A strong argument is made that "optimal knowledge is obtained from a sophisticated integration of information derived from a multimethod assessment battery" (Meyer et al., 2001, p. 155). The authors draw a distinction between psychological testing and psychological assessment. Psychological testing is described as a "relatively straightforward" process of administering a particular scale to obtain a specific score. Psychological assessment is defined as administering a variety of tests, using data obtained from multiple assessment methods, and interpreting the data in the framework of history, presages, observations, and the client's reasons for requesting consultation, as well as social, economic, and cultural conditions. Meyer et al. (2001) conclude that "the ultimate factor, given that tests do not think for themselves, is found to lie in the judgment of the psychologist-assessor" (p. 153).

This meta-analysis is encouraging for international consultants, because it documents strong positive evidence for the validity of psychological tests and formal assessment procedures. It is worth the effort and time required to adapt and apply the assessment tools of our trade for international and multicultural work. Moreover, Kim (2001) serves as a concrete example of the benefits from outsider-insider collaborations in his MIT dissertation research into the succession rules for CEO in large Japanese institutions and agency. Kim reports the advantages of being a cultural outsider who can take a comparative perspective, by using a U.S. succession model to contrast with the results of qualitative and quantitative insider data (Japanese emic) about succession rules.

## Environmental Pressures

Cultural competency relies on assessment competency. The international organizational consultant builds cultural competency by engaging in an honest assessment of self-biases (Dana, 2001b), and conducting a systematic, methodical assessment of environmental pressures (Barclay, 1991; Murray, 1943). Barclay describes environmental pressure as the total of environmental and cultural factors that shape and mold behavior in a given setting. Murray (1938) developed the Thematic Apperception Test (TAT) as a projective measure of *environmental pressure* on individual thinking and behaving. Tell-Me-a-Story (TEMAS) (Constantino, Malgady, & Rogler, 1988) is a non-Anglo emic (assessment tool) that has grown out of the TAT. TEMAS, primarily used with Spanish-speaking children, is also adapted for use with adult populations.

## Projective Tests

Projective assessments use ambiguous images, many of which include no cultural content, such as the Rorschach inkblots (Rorschach, 1921), the Hand Test (Wagner, 1962), and the Holtzman Inkblot Technique (Holtzman, 1972). Since few U.S. organizational consultants work with projective techniques, little is published about advantages and disadvantages of using ambiguous images to overcome language and cultural barriers. A major objection to assessment with projective instruments is that most are high-inference (relying heavily on interpretation or judgment by the assessor), as opposed to low-inference assessment tools such as objective self-report questionnaires and surveys (Dana, 2001b).

Projective assessment techniques were used pivotally in an organizational consultation with a telephone cables production plant (Dubey, Agrawal, & Palia, 2001). B. L. Dubey of Punjab University and Anil Agrawal, CEO of the cables production company, reported success with an organizational development program in Chandigarth, India, that began with an employee assessment battery to determine training interventions. The Somatic Inkblot Series (SIS) (Cassell, 1980, 1994), a projective measure, was administered along with other tests, for example, the Myers-Briggs Type Indicator (MBTI) (Myers & McCaulley, 1989). A pre- and post-project climate survey showed improvement in employee satisfaction ratings in eleven categories. Notable changes included: training and development, 1999 = 25 percent, 2000 = 83 percent; aware of organizational goals and objectives, 1999 = 23 percent, 2000 = 66 percent; growth prospect, 1999 = 31 percent, 2000 = 74 percent; remuneration, 1999 = 12 percent, 2000 = 40 percent.

## Objective Measures

The traditional process of adapting educational and psychological tests for use in a second language involved back-translation, a translating of items previously translated into a target language back into the source language. The process emphasized the literal translation of each word, giving little attention to the constructs being measured, and "is often less adequate than constructing a new item based on an equivalent cross-cultural conceptual definition of the . . . dimension being measured" (Spielberger, Moscoso, & Brunner, in press, p. 7).

Several cycles of translation and back-translation are found to be necessary before an adequate adaptation can be developed for items with words that cannot be translated from the source language without changing the grammatical construction (Spielberger & Sharma, 1973). Idiomatic expressions pose the problem of translating both concept and feeling connotations, rather than a literal exchange of words. At times, there are no words in a target language with the equivalent meaning of key words in the source language. Cross-cultural equivalence of theoretical concepts that are being assessed is now considered essential for accurate data collection (Spielberger, Moscoso, & Brunner, 2001).

## Essential Cross-Cultural Equivalence

Construct equivalence is one of three essential considerations when developing a cross-cultural adaptation of any type of test, survey, or questionnaire, and consultants need to choose situations, vocabulary, and expressions that can be adapted easily across language groups and cultures (Hambleton, 1994; 2002). The other two considerations in adapting an instrument are the state-trait distinction (Anastasi, 1988; Spielberger, 1966; Lonner, 1990), and item intensity-specificity (Anastasi, 1988; Spielberger, Gorsuch, & Lushene, 1970). The importance of the state-trait distinction (a transitory condition, as contrasted with a relatively stable characteristic) is reinforced by discovery during test translations that in Spanish there are two forms of the verb *to be, ser* and *estar* (Spielberger & Diaz-Guerrero, 1982). *Ser* denotes a permanent characteristic of a person or situation, and *estar* means a temporary condition. The Hindi language also has two verbs, *rahahun* and *rahtahun,* that refer to, respectively, a current and variable state, and a more lasting and permanent trait condition.

The need to convey an appropriate feeling-level connotation of words becomes quickly apparent in translation of questionnaires and surveys from one language to another. Certain words carry intense or minimal emotional charges, as noted in measures of angry feelings that can range from mild irritation to rage or fury (Spielberger, Moscoso, & Brunner, 2002). The better test will use idioms and words proven to be cultural equivalents, and be one where the scoring process takes into consideration technical and methodological problems and other factors that influence the interpretation of test results (Hambleton, in press).

## Widely Used U.S. Tests

Few psychological tests used in organizational consultation have widespread use comparable to that of the Minnesota Multiphasic Personality Inventory-2 (MMPI-2), a clinical measure of psychopathology. Butcher, Coelho, and Tsai (in press) have discussed the successful adaptation of the MMPI-2 for twenty-two languages. Even so, major problems and issues related to internationally accepted clinical diagnostic classifications remain unresolved. Dana (2001a) cautions clinical assessors that "test bias occurs whenever a standard test used for . . . diagnosis has not been demonstrated to have conceptual, linguistic, and metric equivalence for cultural or racial populations not represented adequately in the [U.S.] normative data" (p. 109).

Fewer conceptual and interpretive issues surround measures of three basic emotions: anxiety, anger, and curiosity (Spielberger, Ritterband, Sydeman, Reheiser, & Unger, 1995). These are personality factor variables that activate the autonomic nervous system and have relevance for organizational productivity and workplace cultures, especially in times of intensified social anxiety or workplace stress (O'Roark, 2000). The characteristics appear to be etic, that is, universally experienced (Spielberger, Moscoso, & Brunner, 2000), and are relatively uncluttered with cultural complexities. Spielberger's State-Trait Anxiety Inventory (STAI) (1983) reports perhaps the greatest number of validated adaptations. The test is available in fifty languages and dialects for cross-cultural research (Spielberger, Sydeman, Owen, & Marsh, 1999).

## U.S. Leadership Programs and Assessment of Non-Nationals

A comparison of assessment scores from U.S. managers and internationals working in the United States ($n = 652$ and 65, respectively), from a standard assessment battery used in leadership training (O'Roark & Capobianco, 1992), showed common patterns and significant differences in pairwise analysis. The internationals' (Europe $n = 13$: Austria, Belgium, France, England; Canada $n = 30$; South America $n = 9$: Argentina, Brazil, Chile, Bolivia, Peru; Caribbean $n = 13$: Barbados, Bermuda, Jamaica, Puerto Rico) responses on the *California Personality Inventory* (CPI; English language) (Gough, 1995) followed a pattern similar to that of the U.S. nationals, with averages somewhat below those obtained by U.S. managers.

Significant differences ($p \leq .01$) on eleven of twenty CPI scales were found: Dominance, Capacity for Status, Responsibility, Well-Being, Tolerance, Achievement by Conformance, Achievement by Independence, Intellectual Efficiency, and Psychological Mindedness. These internationals also reported Myers-Briggs Type Indicator (Myers & McCaulley, 1989), Thinking preferences with 20 percent greater frequency, and reported higher average scores on FIRO-B (Schutz, 1977) scales Expressed Inclusion and Expressed Control.

International participants and U.S. participants also shared common highs and lows on the CPI: high—Dominance, Achievement by Conformance, and Achievement by Independence; and low—Feminine-Masculine (reflecting stronger masculine scores), Flexibility, and Intellectual Effeciency. The greatest variability in scores was found on the Social Presence scale. Capobianco (2001) reports results from additional data (1996–2001) from fifty-six international participants (forty-five men and eleven women) that produced a pattern of CPI scores comparable to the earlier international group. One difference noticed in the CPI profile of the recent group of internationals is that Independence moved up to become the second highest scale. The policy of this leadership training program is to review assessment results with internationals who demonstrate comfort with the English language, and to stress a caveat that their scores on U.S. English language instruments might not provide a valid picture of their personality structure. A valid assessment picture of characteristics for the international would come from their responses to questionnaires adapted to their first language.

## Universal Characteristics: Etics

A logical approach for the international consultant seeking to determine best-fit assessment procedures and organizational interventions might begin with determination of broad cultural characteristics, such as the tight versus loose cultures described by Triandis (1987). This very general information can alert a consultant to how to modify project expectations and delivery style. For example, when working in a nation with a *tight* culture, social norms are strongly implemented. *Loose*-culture countries are more relaxed about norms, and often include groups with diverse interaction expectations. Triandis (1987) describes tight cultures as being those in which self-identity is absorbed by group identity.

The tight-loose distinction incorporates *collectivism* versus *individualism,* a variable frequently mentioned when discussing contrasts between Eastern and Western cultures (Chen, 1996). Chen noted that the word individualism has a negative connotation in Chinese (illustrative of emotional qualities that are bonded to words). He concluded that what gets in the way of American expatriates being effective in assessment and selection of management personnel in a host country is their failure to consider five major cultural parameters proposed by Hofstede (1980, 1993).

Hofstede (1980) initially proposed four dimensions of variability that discriminated between national origins of employees: Individualism versus Collectivisim; Power Distance; Uncertainty Avoidance; and Masculinity-Femininity. Among Hofstede's early findings were three cultural distinctions: U.S. nationals, Western Europeans, Canadians, Australians, and New Zealanders were the lowest scorers on Power Distance, indicating a preference not to have great status differences between levels in the organizational hierarchy; Japanese employees and U.S. workers were highest on the Masculinity scale, indicating ambitiousness and desire for success; and U.S. employees were highest on Individualism, indicating value for independence and autonomy.

His later study (Hofstede, 1993) used five scales: Power Distance; Individualism; Masculinity; Uncertainty Avoidance; and Long-Term Orientation, also called Confucian Work Dynamism (Pasa et al., 2001; Bond, 1988; Schwartz, 1994). China, Hong Kong, and Russia were high on Power Distance, with Russia being very high; the U.S. was low on this dimension. The U.S. again was very high on Individualism, China and Hong Kong were very low, and samples from Japan and Russian scored average on the scale. Findings from the Masculinity scale showed the U.S., Hong Kong, and Japan to be high, with Japan very high; China and Russia were average.

Uncertainty Avoidance obtained very high scores from Japan and Russia, average scores from China, low scores from the U.S., and very low scores from Hong Kong. Long-Term Orientation received very high scores from China and Hong Kong, high scores from Japan, and very low scores from the U.S. and Russia (Hofstede, 1993). Three additional etics appear in studies conducted with cultures in Asia, the Middle East, and Africa: Paternalism (Schwartz, 1994); abstractive versus associative thinking (Chen, 1996), and developing country versus developed country (Adler & Boyacigiller, 1995; Kanungo & Mendonca, 1996).

## Discovering the Meanings Behind Concepts

Hui and Triandis (1985) concluded that semantic differential scales have particular utility in international consulting. The process can be used to discover the meanings attached to concepts, words, or persons. Factor analysis shows that an *evaluation* scale accounts for 50 to 75 percent of variances in meaning (Osgood, Suci, & Tannenbaum, 1957). Polarized rating items used to assess the evaluation scale include, for example, good versus bad, wise versus foolish, clean versus dirty, and true versus false. Usually, three differential scales are assessed: evaluation, potency, and activity. At least three polarized rating items are included for each scale, allowing a five- or seven-point range between opposite ends of paired words.

Consider the following example:

Leadership (concept of interest)

| | | | | | | | |
|---|---|---|---|---|---|---|---|
| Bad | 1 | 2 | 3 | 4 | 5 | 6 | 7x | Good |
| Dirty | 1 | 2 | 3 | 4 | 5x | 6 | 7 | Clean |
| Harmonious | 1 | 2x | 3 | 4 | 5 | 6 | 7 | Dissonant |

The Harmonious/Dissonant scale is reverse scored. Total points derived from the x marks on the polarized word sets (all part of the *evaluation* scale) are calculated as follows: $7 + 5 + 6 = 18$ points (scale range = 3 to 27). The mean score here, 6, indicates a positive view of leadership. Word pairs for the *potency* scale might be: hard versus soft; light versus heavy; and strong versus weak. Paired dichotomies for assessing the *activity* scale might be: active versus passive; fast versus slow; and moving versus still. Six other factor scales are seldom assessed: *stability, tautness, novelty, receptivity, aggressiveness,* and *unassigned.* Selection of word pairs in the target language will prove critical in conducting a semantic differential assessment for determining cross-cultural equivalence of the meanings of concepts.

## Assessment-Intervention Questions

A third technique appropriate for inclusion in a culture calibration process is an *assessment-intervention* set of questions developed by Dana (1997, p. 123):

Question 1. Is there an etic (universal) instrument that measures the variable(s) of interest?

If NO: Question 2. What is the culture orientation of the client(s)?

| *Anglo* | *assimilated* | *bicultural* | *marginal* | *transitional* | *traditional* |
|---|---|---|---|---|---|
| 1 | 2 | 3 | 4 | 5 | 6 |

*Euro-American culture orientation*           *not Euro-American*

If traditional:

Question 3. Is an [organizational culture] diagnosis necessary?

If YES: Question 4. Is an emic, indigenous questionnaire available?

If NO: Question 5. What norms will be used? [How can norms be validated locally?]

Question 6. Is cross-culture integration stress present in the organization?

If YES: Question 7. Is diagnosis necessary?

An additional question for the U.S. international organizational consultant would be: Is an emic stress assessment instrument available? Is a U.S. questionnaire adapted, or adaptable? For example, among many stress assessment tools described in the U.S. literature, the Job Stress Survey (JSS) (Spielberger & Vagg, 1999; O'Roark, in press) is one that has been translated into several languages. It is easily modified to accommodate organizational, industry, or national cultures, and can facilitate both individual and organizational diagnosis. Two factors imbedded within the thirty survey items sort stressors into those associated with work pressures (structure, flow, deadlines) and lack of support (supervision, coworkers, policies).

The JSS also provides information on stressors in terms of their frequency of occurrence in the workplace and their severity of impact on the worker. Internal norms can be generated around ratings provided by those responding to the survey, and in comparison with norms established in several cultures, such as Japan, Spain, Mexico, and the Netherlands. Stress assessment results can assist the consultant in making particularized, that is, informed, recommendations for intervention.

## Calibration Consultation

Widely cautioned against using U.S. emics as a baseline of comparisons, international consultants calibrate cultural dimensions generally accepted as etic. The international consultant can frame broad characteristics from firsthand observations, library research, and information available from the U.S. Diplomatic Service. Locally relevant emic assessment materials are collected, along with other pertinent organizational background information. When possible, the consultant collects semantic differential information about the meanings associated with concepts relevant to the project. Calibration consultation as a full-cycle action research process is shown in Figure 21.1: the International Organizational Consultation Process (IOCP).

# INTERNATIONAL INTERVENTION ISSUES

Warfare and disaster relief are extreme examples of U.S. international intervention. The exporting of U.S. management and production techniques falls somewhere in the middle range of these extremes. James Michener chronicles

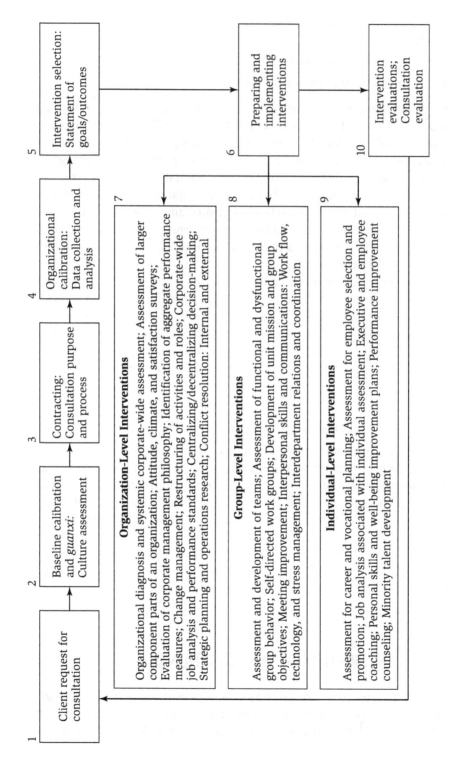

**Figure 21.1.** **International Organizational Consulting Process: A Ten-Step Strategy for International Organizational Consulting Incorporating Calibration Consultation, Action Research, Levels of Intervention Services, and Evaluations.**

1 Client request for consultation

2 Baseline calibration and *guanxi*: Culture assessment

3 Contracting: Consultation purpose and process

4 Organizational calibration: Data collection and analysis

5 Intervention selection: Statement of goals/outcomes

6 Preparing and implementing interventions

10 Intervention evaluations; Consultation evaluation

**Organization-Level Interventions**

7 Organizational diagnosis and systemic corporate-wide assessment; Assessment of larger component parts of an organization; Attitude, climate, and satisfaction surveys; Evaluation of corporate management philosophy; Identification of aggregate performance measures; Change management; Restructuring of activities and roles; Corporate-wide job analysis and performance standards; Centralizing/decentralizing decision-making; Strategic planning and operations research; Conflict resolution: Internal and external

**Group-Level Interventions**

8 Assessment and development of teams; Assessment of functional and dysfunctional group behavior; Self-directed work groups; Development of unit mission and group objectives; Meeting improvement; Interpersonal skills and communications: Work flow, technology, and stress management; Interdepartment relations and coordination

**Individual-Level Interventions**

9 Assessment for career and vocational planning; Assessment for employee selection and promotion; Job analysis associated with individual assessment; Executive and employee coaching; Personal skills and well-being improvement plans; Performance improvement counseling; Minority talent development

religious missionary interventions in several of his epic novels, especially *Hawaii*, reissued in 1994, and *Alaska*. Margaret Mead (1969) reported cultural disintegration and tragic human consequences after well-intentioned missionaries and World War II naval personnel intervened in Pacific islanders' traditional belief systems.

## Culture Assessment as First-Order Calibration Business

Burdick and Lederer portrayed a positive side of American contributions abroad in *The Ugly American* (Lederer & Burdick, 1999). In this 1954 novel, a U.S. diplomat on duty in the Far East offered what consultants would call a management engineering intervention, but only after months of observing the stooped backs of women who swept their doorways daily with short-handled brooms. Only after he'd built mutual regard and gained an understanding relationship with his host country did he presume to intervene. He ordered U.S. brooms with long handles that were then made available to the local women. The women quickly discovered that they had fewer backaches when sweeping with the longer-handled brooms.

## *Guanxi:* Establishing and Using Relationships

The difference between missionary conversions from traditional belief systems, post-World War II aftermaths, and the interventions recorded in *The Ugly American,* can be summed up by a Chinese word, *guanxi,* short for *guanxixue.* It's about the "instrumental quality of one's relationships and the ability of one to use them" (Davis, 1997, p. 110), and getting to know and understand clients before trying to do business or make changes in their behaviors, organizations, or value systems. Davis describes *guanxi* in terms of a Chinese folk saying: "If you know someone in the kitchen, it's easier to eat; if you know someone in the court, it's easier to become an official" (p. 110). Davis reports that cultivating and nurturing good *guanxi* motivates many business practices in China and other Eastern and Middle Eastern countries.

*Guanxi*-relationship building is shown in Figure 21.1, IOCP step 2, but more likely begins even before step 1. Some form of contact precedes the request for service from a client. This request is as important to consulting outcomes as it is in the success of clinical and counseling helping services (Combs, Miser, & Whitaker, 1999). With each presenting problem or initial service request, baseline calibration (culture assessment and *guanxi*-relationship building) is already in process. Steps 1 and 2 in the IOCP overlap and are ideally complete before a project contract is finalized. Using intelligence, that is, information, from culture assessment and relationship building, step 3, the international consultant, adapts conceptual models, prepares structured interviews, and tailors data collection materials. Data collection, step 4, initiates the primary organizational consultation, and is the first phase of the U.S. action research process.

## Using a Systematic, Scientific Method: The IOCP

The IOCP enlarges upon a U.S. consulting method known as action research (French & Bell, 1973; Lippitt & Lippitt, 1978). The action research intervention model can be traced to two independent sources: Kurt Lewin and John Collier, both working to improve interracial and cross-cultural relations. Kurt Lewin (1951), a pioneer social psychologist, applied action research to his work in intergroup relations and to eradicate prejudice. John Collier, a commissioner of U.S. Indian Affairs from 1933 to 1945, was assigned to diagnose problems and recommend programs to improve race relations. He found ethnic relations to be a difficult challenge that required a joint effort by scientists (social psychologists), administrators, and the groups being served. Collier called the form of research he developed to investigate practical problems *action research,* and applied his strategy systematically to gather data for determining proposals for solutions that were relevant and feasible (French & Bell, 1973). In IOCP, as in action research, selection of interventions and objectives, step 5, becomes a joint effort between consultant(s) and client(s), as are conclusions about project progress or redirection. Joint determination of a client organization's needs, critical problems, and solution-interventions serves as a safeguard against imposing U.S. concepts and practices in inappropriate situations. Preparation for international interventions (step 6) requires special attention to consultant aids, such as adaptation of handout materials to the first language of the clients, and of culture-correct slides, overheads, and activities.

Three levels of interventions (see Figure 21.1 boxes 7, 8, and 9) that consultants offer to organizational clients are individual services, group services, and corporate services (APA/SCP, 2000b). The services listed under each heading are representative only, and the activities will not be appropriate in every culture. Every consulting contract does not include interventions at each organizational level. Interventions are evaluated at the end of the intervention or at the conclusion of all contracted services (step 10).

When the overall consultation is evaluated, results from the earlier organizational data collections are compared with post-project data in order to calibrate progress. Based on pre-post-data analysis and qualitative evaluations (self-reported comments, interviews, third-party observations), recommendations for the future are prepared for the client.

## Analyzing Organizational Culture

International consultants will also confront issues rooted in a specific organization's culture that are unique beyond environment and social influences. Organizational culture, in contrast with the broader identity groups such as family, community, and regional and national cultures, is reflective of the values and assumptions shared by employees of a particular organization about what is right, what is good, and what is important (Pasa et al., 2001). Defined as a select set of variables experienced by persons associated with an organization, workplace cultures provide compelling individual and group member orientations (Pasa et al., 2001; Hofstede et al., 1990; House et al., 1999; Schein, 1992).

Contrasts between corporate structures (that is, centralization versus decentralization, decision-making and decision-implementation processes, specialization, and formalization) and underlying values and attitudes in organizations result in differences in companies and groups in the same part of the world, confirming the existence of significant differences in organizational cultures (Tayeb, 1994; Schein, 1992). Schein concludes that distinctive organizational cultures arise wherever values, beliefs, and behaviors are perpetuated by the organization's structure and shared by its members. He emphasizes that taken-for-granted assumptions are typically held by persons in organizations with stable membership and a history of shared learning. Schein describes culture as a pattern of assumptions invented or discovered by a group as it learns how to cope with the problems of external adaptation and internal integration. These strategies worked well enough that they are considered the correct way to perceive, think, and feel in relation to those problems.

## Organizational Culture: Influence by Tasks and Founders

In studies conducted outside of the United States, businesses have been found to develop similar organizational cultures if they have similar task environments (Tayeb, 1988), and there is a comparable level of industrialization (Kanungo & Jaeger, 1990). Also similar to U.S. research findings (Levinson, 1994), organizational culture in non-U.S. cultures was found to vary according to the values of founders or strong leaders (Hofstede et al., 1990).

U.S. psychologists entering international organizational consulting have an advantage due to their long-standing history of assessing organizational cultures in the United States (Hughes & Flowers, 1976; Kilmann & Saxton, 1983; Kilmann, 1987; Quinn, Faeman, Thompson, & McGrath, 1990; Quinn, 1992; Schneider, 1995; Dennison, 1995). Theoretical approaches to surveying organizational cultures range from developmental, to behavioral, to typographic. While these are respectable starting points, all need adapting and validation if they are to become useful and relevant for international consulting.

## Developmental Model: Organizational Culture and Values

Hughes and Flowers (1976) built a developmental model of organizational culture based on an assumption that humans are open-system types of organisms. The model hypothesizes an emerging process marked by the progressive subordination of earlier value systems to higher-order value systems (Graves, 1970). Seven sets of collective value systems that comprise the Hugh and

Flowers model are called tribalistic, egocentric, conformist, manipulative, materialistic, sociocentric, and existential.

*Tribalistic* values cultures are collaborations that came into being without awareness, thought, or purpose, and continue through shared beliefs, myths, traditions, or superstitions. *Egocentric* values organizational cultures are associated with an awareness of life and death, accompanied by active survival efforts. Power ethics and competitive behaviors prevail. In *conformist* values cultures, self-discipline, self-sacrifice, and authority figures dominate. *Manipulative* values cultures emphasize education and science, and independence from predetermined fate. The *materialism* culture is characterized by efficiency, calculated risks, and a drive to get more of the wealth. In a *sociocentric* culture, the first concern is with relationships, and getting along becomes more important than getting ahead. The *existential values* organization focuses on restoring the world so that life can continue. Values are associated with the work process, potentials for growth, creativity, and quality of life.

## Organizational Culture Typology Models

Quinn (1992) defines four types of organizational cultures based on an organization's information processing methods: market, clan, adhocracy, and hierarchy. Market cultures emphasize efficiency, productivity, aggressiveness, and initiative. Clan cultures stress relationships, broadmindedness, cooperation, fairness, forgiveness, and social equality. Adhocracy companies are open to transformation and growth, and promote adaptability, autonomy, creativity, and experimentation. The hierarchy culture is noted for an emphasis on stability and execution of regulations. This culture values cautiousness, economy, formality, logic, and orderliness. Schneider (1995) proposes a typology derived from his research into the literature on organizational culture, organizational effectiveness, and individual psychodynamics. He defines culture as "the way we do things around here in order to succeed" (p. 6), and concludes it is important because it limits an organization's strategy, provides consistency (order and structure), determines conditions for internal effectiveness, and sets patterns for internal relationships. The four types of core cultures contrasted in Schneider's Organizational Culture Survey (OCS) are called collaboration, control, cultivation, and competence.

## Organizational Culture and Change Analysis

A questionnaire designed to identify where organizational change is needed in functional and behavioral dimensions is the *Dennison Organizational Culture Survey* (DOCS) (Dennison, 1995; Dennison & Neale, 1996). Dennison argues that the first step in a process designed to create cultural change and organizational transformation is diagnosing the current culture. In order to translate a culture profile into change-action, a set of suggestions, called levers for change, are prepared for characteristics associated with corporate effectiveness: *mission, consistency, involvement,* and *adaptability.* DOCS gathers multirater information about corporate management functions that influence business performance: Mission includes strategic direction and intent, goals and objectives, and vision. Consistency includes core values, agreement, and coordination and integration. Involvement includes empowerment, team orientation, and capability development. Adaptability includes organizational learning, customer focus, and creating change.

## Priority Needs: Conflict Models

Encounters with conflict are inevitable whenever differences exist, and typically begin with a degree of surprise (O'Roark, 2000; Horney, 1945). Engaging in international consulting escalates exposure to surprising differences, and to strong conflicts of values, assumptions, opinions, norms, goals, priorities, and even information. With the specific injunction in the psychological code of conduct (APA, 2001, p. 6) that "when conflicts occur among psychologists obligations or concerns, they are to attempt to resolve these conflicts and to perform their roles in a responsible fashion that avoids or minimizes harm," consulting psychologists need to rely heavily on conceptual theories and intervention procedures associated with scientifically supported definitions of the nature of conflict, conflict management, and conflict resolution. The international consultant is endowed with a vast consulting literature on complexities surrounding intrapersonal, interpersonal, and organizational conflict, as well as emic techniques for intervening in first-party (my conflict), second-party (another's conflict), and third-party conflict (outsider mediation of other's conflicts) situations.

The first conflict issues are interpersonal and are resolved in the context of the consultant's beliefs, values, and philosophy about being a psychologist. U.S. psychologist and international specialist Brewster (1994) calls for psychologists to "reexamine . . . [conflict] theories and assumptions if psycholog[ists are] to contribute to understanding . . . [aimed at] reducing lethal conflict and promoting peace. Current and recent events remind us that potentialities for escalating hatred and destructive conflict between 'us' and 'them' may be more deeply rooted and require more compensatory attention than the liberal ideologies shared by many psychologists and social scientists have assumed" (p. 326). That is, we should pay more attention to oversimplifications in *caring organization* concepts, and forgiveness versus justice and repatriation.

Further dramatizing the conflict issues and value choices facing a consultant who engages in international work, Kelman (1994, p. 326) of Yale expresses an opinion that "an independent state is not entitled to international legitimacy unless it guarantees for the protection of minority rights." Does the U.S. consulting psychologist accept work in countries that do not guarantee protection for human rights? Does the U.S. consulting psychologist travel to countries that refuse visa admissions to certain other countries, such as Indonesia's refusal to admit Portuguese citizens? The answer relies on the informed judgment of each professional.

When the consultant resolves personal conflicts and issues associated with international assignments, there will be conflict situations in process within the organizations for which the consultant provides services. Adding to a not new, but rapidly growing, body of literature on international conflict issues, Worchel and Coutant (1994) provide data from organizational studies suggesting that conflict between groups is necessary for groups to establish their identity and independence, but is avoided when the focus is on performance and individual freedom. They state that intragroup conflict is not tolerated in early stages of identity formation, but is acceptable, and at times encouraged, at later stages of organizational life, when productivity is emphasized.

Heuristic assessment tools that lend themselves to adaptation by international consultants describe trait, behavioral, and developmental phases of the conflict phenomenon, and human behavior under conflict conditions (Lewin, 1951; Blake & Mouton, 1964; Satir, 1967; Deutsch, 1969; Hall, 1973; Thomas & Kilman, 1989; Capobianco, Davis, & Kraus,1999). Conflict management styles were simply addressed earlier by descriptions of the tough battler, the objective thinker, the friendly helper, a model attributed to National Training Laboratories instructor Richard Wallen in the late 1960s. Since then, conflict styles have been assessed and described in more formal and detailed models, frequently based on managerial grid profiles developed by Blake and Mouton (1964).

A multidimensional approach to analyzing conflict management behavior is found in the Conflict Management Survey (Hall, 1973), which assesses four levels of organizational conflict management. Personal, interpersonal, group, and intergroup conflicts are associated with Blake and Mouton's managerial grid types (9/1 win-lose; 1/9 yield-lose; 1/1 lose-leave; 5/5 compromise; 9/9 synergistic). Glaser and Glaser (1996) credit Blanchard and Hersey, as well as Blake and Mouton, when describing five negotiating styles assessed in their survey: defeat (win at any cost); collaborate (creatively problem solve); accommodate (build friendly relationships); withdraw (take whatever you can get); and compromise (split the difference).

Illustrative of a behavioral-developmental approach to conflict management is the *Conflict Dynamics Profile* (Capobianco, Davis, & Kraus, 1999). The survey provides information about how an individual's self-perceptions differ from the observations of others across three stages of a conflict experience. Items obtain reports about behaviors when a conflict is just beginning, when it is fully underway, and after it is over. Behaviors are classified as active-constructive, passive-constructive, active-destructive, and passive-destructive. This conflict model is similar to a continuum of anger styles described by Day (1980) and attributed to Catherine Bond. Anger is also found to be integrally associated with conflict in recent studies of so-called psychological vital signs, emotional states, and personality traits (Spielberger, Ritterband, Sydeman, Reheiser, & Unger, 1995; O'Roark, 2000).

## Decision-Making, Leadership, Disaster Management

Issues that continue to be frequently addressed during international applied psychology conventions, thus suggesting psychological services being requested, are decision-making, leadership, disaster management, organizational culture change, technology, and gender. Heller, Pusie, Strauss, & Wilpert, 1998) has been involved in cross-cultural studies called Decisions in Organizations for more than twenty years. Underachievement by mid-level managers has been shown to be associated with too little involvement in decision-making, and decision-making processes are found intertwined with leadership approaches. Bass (1981, 1985, 1990, in press) reports that transformational leadership is an etic phenomena. The studies indicate that providing employees with inspirational motivation, intellectual stimulation, and personal attention, coupled with being a strong role model with a strong vision of the future, is universally successful.

Safety and disaster management are continuing topics of interest. Decision-making has been studied in conjunction with major disasters such as the explosion and subsequent fire onboard the North Sea oil production platform Piper Alpha, which caused 168 deaths in 1988 (Flin, 2001). Naturalistic decision-making (NDM), based on research from aviation, medicine, and the energy sector, suggests that at times of disaster, best decisions depend on situation awareness, intuitive decision-making (relying on automatic, learned response patterns), and current team mental models.

Organizational culture change, technology impacts, and gender topics continue as issues of emphasis and discussion, reflecting the more active areas in the field of applied organizational psychology (European Congress of Psychology, 2001).

# CONCLUSION AND IMPLICATIONS FOR ORGANIZATIONAL CONSULTANTS

Figure 21.2 represents considerations of the international organizational consultant that influence selection of both assessment and intervention activities. The preliminary culture calibration and analysis of the organizational culture will provide guidelines for the conduct of the consulting work. The business or purpose of the organization, distinguished in terms of primary outputs—industry, service, government, not-for-profit, and international—is plotted in terms of the activity zones of the consultant's work: expert resource, organizational-level interventions, work group interventions, individual

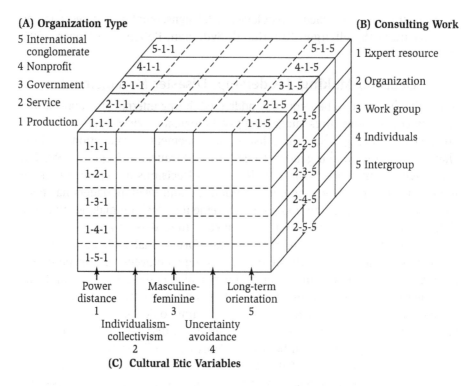

Figure 21.2. Calibration Contexts. Variables Influencing Intervention Tactics:
(A) Type of Organization: Production, Service, Government, Non-Profit,
International Conglomerate (Euro-American or Traditional); (B) Type of Consulting
Work: Expert Resource, Organization, Group, Individual Intervention, Intergroup
Relations; (C) Etic: Culture Variables: Power Distance; Individualism-Collectivism;
Masculine-Feminine; Uncertainty Avoidance; Long-Term Orientation.

interventions, and intergroup interventions. These situation-awareness variables are further refined in terms of etic variables: power distance, individualism-collectivism, masculine-feminine, uncertainty avoidance, and long-term orientation (Confucian Dynamism).

Cultural competence of international organizational consultants involves consideration of prerequisite issues: the consultant's own cultural identity and biases; the discovery of the client culture's preferences for certain behaviors and emotional climates; and the relevance of U.S. ethical codes, literature, research, and consulting standards to a particular consulting venture. Assessment issues discussed include: the importance of multimethod approaches and the interpretative function of the consultant; considerations when selecting and adapting U.S. tests and questionnaires; the need for cross-cultural equivalence of concepts, and a way to determine the meaning of a concepts in another culture; and the benefits of including a preliminary culture-calibration phase in an International Organizational Consulting Process.

Suggestions for the collection of preliminary calibrations of baseline information include: assessing macroculture characteristics in terms of etics such as Hofstede's five universal variables (1993); the meaning of key concepts via semantic differentials (Hui & Triandis, 1985); and culture orientation(s) and cross-cultural integration stress via Dana's seven questions (1997).

Intervention issues surrounding international organizational consulting, discussed here in the context of the IOCP model, highlight the importance of building, maintaining, and using relationships (*guanxi*), and of applying an action research strategy that aids in the cultivation of cultural competence and consultation effectiveness. Two types of interventions that are likely to be critical zones in international organizational development are presented: organizational culture diagnosis and conflict management/resolution models. Adaptations of tactical approaches should be culturally appropriate for interventions at any of the three levels described in guidelines for consulting psychologists.

A practical tactical methodology is the contextual modular approach (Macnab, 1991) developed in Australia. Macnab's "contextual modular . . . [approach] aims to ensure that the person is seen and heard in context, and that [intervention] takes constant account of past, present and possible contexts" (p. 13). After becoming acquainted with issues in international organizational consulting, and as a consultant steps out to practice international organizational assessment or intervention, three questions are uppermost in the consultant's mind: What is the full nature of the client's request or problem? What help or intervention will be appropriate? What specific protocols and procedures are necessary to prepare for that intervention?

# References

Adler, N. K., & Boyacigiller, N. (1995). Going beyond traditional HRM scholarship. In R. N. Kanungo (Ed.), *New approaches to employee management: Volume 3. Employee management in developing countries* (pp. 1–13). Greenwich, CT: JAI Press.

American Psychological Association. (1992). Ethical principles of psychologists and code of conduct. *American Psychologist, 47*, 1597–1611.

American Psychological Association. (2002). *Draft ethics code,* anastasi.apa.org.draftethicscode/draftcode.clin

American Psychological Association, Division of International Psychology (Division 52). (2001). Cross cultural perspective. *International Psychology Reporter, 5*(3/4), 18–36.

American Psychological Association, Society of Consulting Psychology, Education and Training Committee. (2000). *Principles for education and training at the doctoral and post-doctoral level in consulting psychology/organizational.* Washington, DC: Author.

Anastasi, A. (1988). *Psychological testing* (6th ed.). Old Tappan, NJ: Macmillan.

Arredondo, P., Toporek, R., Brown, S. P., Jones, J., Locke, D. C., Sanchez, J., & Stadler, H. (1996). Operationalization of the multicultural counseling competencies. *Journal of Multicultural Counseling and Development, 24*, 42–78.

Barclay, J. R. (1991). *Psychological assessment: A theory and systems approach.* Malabar, FL: Krieger.

Bass, B. M. (1981). *Stogdill's handbook of leadership: A survey of theory and research.* New York: The Free Press.

Bass, B. M. (1985). *Transformational leadership: Performance beyond expectation.* New York: Free Press.

Bass, B. M. (1990). *Bass and Stogdill's handbook of leadership: Theory, research, and managerial applications* (3rd ed.). New York: Free Press.

Bass, B. M. (in press). *Stogdill's handbook of ledership: A survey of theory and research, revised and expanded* (4th ed.). New York: Free Press.

Bass, B. M., Burger, P. C., Doktor, R., & Barrett, G. V. (1979). *Assessment of managers: An international comparison.* New York: Free Press.

Blake, R. R., & Mouton, J. S. (1964). *The managerial grid.* Houston, TX: Gulf.

Blake, R. R., & Mouton, J. S. (1976). *Consultation.* Menlo Park, CA: Addison-Wesley.

Blanchard, K., & Hersey, P. (1977). *Management of organizational behavior.* Englewood Cliffs, NJ: Prentice Hall.

Bond, M. H. (1988) Finding universal dimensions of individual variation in multi-cultural studies of values. The Rokeach and Chinese values surveys. *Journal of Personality and Social Psychology, 55,* 1009–1015.

Brewster, M. (1994, July). Ethnic identity, nationalism, and the need for distinctive inclusion [Abstract]. *23rd International Congress of Applied Psychology, Madrid, Spain, 326.*

Butcher, J. N., Coelho, J. R., & Tsai, M. (in press). International adaptations of MMPI-2. In R. K. Hambleton, C. D. Spielberger, & P. F. Merenda (Eds.), *Adapting educational and psychological tests for cross-cultural assessment.* Hillsdale, NJ: Erlbaum.

Capobianco, S. (2001). *Foreign LDP participants—1996–2001: Computer-analysis sheet.* St. Petersburg, FL: Eckerd College Management Development Institute.

Capobianco, S., Davis, M., & Kraus, L. (1999). *Conflict dynamics profile.* St. Petersburg, FL: Eckerd College, Management Development Institute.

Cassell, W. A. (1980). *Body symbolism and the Somatic Inkblot Series.* Anchorage, AK: Aurora.

Cassell, W. A. (1994). The Somatic Inkblot Series: Continuing Rorschach's conceptualization. *Journal of Projective Psychology and Mental Health, 1–2,* 3–14.

Chen, Z. (1996). An American guide to working with Chinese managers: Enhancing effectiveness through cultural understanding. *Consulting Psychology Journal: Practice and Research, 48,* 162–170.

Combs, A. W., & Gonzalez, D. M. (1997). *Helping relationships: Basic concepts for the helping professions* (4th ed.). Needham Heights, MA: Allyn & Bacon.

Combs, A. W., Miser, A. B, & Whitaker, K. S. (1999). *On becoming a school leader.* Arlington, VA: Association for Supervision and Curriculum Development.

Combs, A. W., & Snygg, D. (1959). *Individual behavior: A perceptual approach to behavior.* New York: HarperCollins.

Constantino, G., Malgady, R. G., & Rugler, L. H. (1988). *TEMAS (Tell-Me-A-Story) manual.* Los Angeles: Western Psychological Services.

Covey, S. R. (1992). *Principle-centered leadership.* New York: Simon & Schuster/First Fireside Edition.

Cuéllar, I. (2000). Acculturation as a moderator of personality and psychological assessment. In R. H. Dana (Ed.), *Handbook of cross-cultural and multicultural personality assessment* (pp. 113–129). Hillsdale, NJ: Erlbaum & Associates.

Dana, R. H. (1997). Multicultural assessment and cultural identity: An assessment-intervention model. *World Psychology, 3*(1–2), 121–142.

Dana, R. H. (2000). An assessment-intervention model for research and practice with multicultural populations. In R. H. Dana (Ed.), *Handbook of cross-cultural and multicultural personality assessment* (pp. 5–16). Hillsdale, NJ: Erlbaum.

Dana, R. H. (2001a). Clinical diagnosis of multicultural populations in the United States. In L. A. Suzuki, J. G. Ponterotto, & P. J. Meller (Eds.), *Handbook of multicultural assessment: Clinical, psychological, and educational applications* (2nd ed., pp. 101–131). San Francisco: Jossey-Bass.

Dana, R. H. (2001b). Multicultural issues in assessment. In B. Bolton (Ed.), *Handbook of measurement and evaluation in rehabilitation* (3rd ed., pp. 449–469). Gaithersburg, MD: Aspen.

Dana, R. H., Behn, J. D., & Gonwa, T. (1992). A checklist for examination of cultural competence in social service agencies. *Research in Social Work Practice, 2,* 220–233.

Davis, D. D. (1997). Change management and consulting in Chinese organizations. *Consulting Psychology Journal: Practice and Research, 49,* 108–121.

Day, J. (1980). *A working approach to human relations in organizations.* Pacific Grove, CA: Brooks/Cole.

Dennison, D. R. (1995). *Toward a Theory of Organizational Culture and Effectiveness.* Greensboro, NC: Discovery Learning.

Dennison, D. R., & Neale, W. S. (1996). *Dennison Organizational Culture Survey: Guide.* Greensboro, NC: Discovery Learning.

Deutsch, M. (1969). Conflicts: Productive and destructive. *Journal of Social Issues, 25,* 7–42.

Draguns, J. G. (2001). Toward a truly international psychology: Beyond English only. *American Psychologist, 56*(11), 119–130.

Dubey, B. L., Agrawal, A., & Palia, R. S. (2001). Personality profile and HRD intervention in a telephone cables company. *SIS Journal of Projective Psychology and Mental Health, 8,* 127–134.

European Congress of Psychology. (2001). *Abstracts: VII European congress of psychology.* London: British Psychological Society.

Fiedler, F. E. (1995). Cognitive resources and leadership performance. *Applied Psychology: An International Review, 44,* 5–28.

Fisher, C. J., & Alford, R. J. (2000). Consulting on culture: A new bottom line. *Consulting Psychology Journal: Practice and Research, 52,* 206–217.

Flin, R. (2001). Naturalistic decision making: Implications for safety [Abstract]. *Abstracts: VII European Congress of Psychology,* 82.

French, W. L., & Bell, C. H. (1973). *Organization development: Behavioral science interventions for organization improvement.* Englewood Cliffs, NJ: Prentice Hall.

Gielen, U. P. (1989). Studies of moral reasoning in Chinese societies: An introduction. *International Psychologist, 29,* 61–64.

Glasser, R., & Glaser, C. (1996). *Negotiating style profile.* San Francisco: Organization Design and Development.

Gough, H. G. (1995). *CPI: Introduction to form 434.* Palo Alto, CA: Consulting Psychologists Press.

Graves, C. W. (1970). Levels of existence: An open system of values. *Journal of Humanistic Psychology,* 131–155.

Greenberg, E. R. (1998, December). AMA global survey on key business issues. *Management Review,* 27–38.

Hall, J. (1973). *Conflict management survey.* The Woodlands, TX: Teleometrics International.

Hambleton, R. K. (1994). Guidelines for adapting educational and psychological tests: A progress report. *European Journal of Psychological Assessment, 10,* 229–244.

Hambleton, R. K. (in press). Issues, designs, and technical guidelines for adapting tests in multiple languages and cultures. In R. K. Hambleton, P. F. Merenda, & C. D. Spielberger (Eds.), *Adapting educational and psychological tests for cross-cultural assessment.* Hillsdale, NJ: Erlbaum.

Heller, F., Pasic, E., Strauss, G., & Wilpert, B. (1988). *Organizational Participation: Myth & Reality.* Oxford, England: Oxford University Press.

Hodgson, P., & White, R. P. (2001). *Relax: It's only uncertainty. Lead the way when the way is changing.* Englewood Cliffs, NJ: Prentice Hall.

Hofstede, G. (1980). *Culture's consequences: International differences in work-related values.* Thousand Oaks, CA: Sage.

Hofstede, G. (1993). Cultural constraints in management theories. *Academy of Management Executive, 7,* 81–94.

Hofstede, G., Neuijen, B., Ohavy, D. D., & Sanders, G. (1990). Measuring organizational cultures: A quantitative and qualitative study across twenty cases. *Administrative Science Quarterly, 35,* 286–316.

Holcomb-McCoy, C. C., & Myers, J. E. (1999). Multicultural competence and counselor training: A national survey. *Journal of Counseling and Development, 77,* 294–302.

Holtzman, W. H. (1972). *Holtzman Inkblot Technique* (HIT). San Antonio, TX: Psychological Corporation.

Horney, K. (1945). *Our inner conflicts.* New York: Norton.

House, R., Hanges, P. J., Ruiz-Quintanilla, S. A., Dorfman, P. W., Javidan, M. Dickson, M., et al. (1999). Cultural influences on leadership and organizations: Project GLOBE. *Advances in Global Leadership, 1,* 171–233.

Hughes, C. L., & Flowers, V. S. (1976). *Value systems analysis.* Dallas, TX: Center for Values Research.

Hui, C. H., & Triandis, H. C. (1985). Measurement in cross-cultural psychology. *Journal of Cross-Cultural Psychology, 16,* 131–152.

Kaminstein, D., Smith, K. K., & Miller, R. (2000). Quiet chaos: An organizational consultation in Mandela's South Africa. *Consulting Psychology Journal: Practice and Research, 52*(1), 49–62.

Kanungo, R. N., & Jaeger, A. M. (1990). Introduction: The need for indigenous management in developing countries. In A. M. Jaeger & R. N. Kanungo (Eds.), *Management in developing countries.* London: Routledge.

Kanungo, R. N., & Mendonca, M. (1996). Cultural contingencies and leadership in developing countries. *Sociology of Organizations, 14,* 263–295.

Kelman, H. (1994, July). National self-determination and ethnic cleansing: Some lethal consequences of ethnic nationalism [Abstract]. *23rd International Congress of Applied Psychology,* Madrid, Spain, 326.

Kilmann, R. H. (1987). *Beyond the quick fix: Managing five tracks to organizational success.* San Francisco: Jossey-Bass.

Kilmann, R. H., & Saxton, M. J. (1983). *The Kilmann-Saxton culture-gap survey.* Pittsburgh, PA: Organizational Design Consultants.

Kim, H. (2001). *Succession rules for CEO in large Japanese institutions and agency.* Unpublished doctoral dissertation. Massachusetts Institute of Technology, Boston.

Lederer, W. J., & Burdick, E. (1999). *The ugly American.* New York: Norton.

Levinson, H. (1994). Why the behemoths fell: Psychological roots of corporate failure. *The American Psychologist, 49*(5), 428–436.

Lewin, K. (1951). *Field theory in social science: Selected theoretical papers* (D. Cartwright, Ed.). New York: HarperCollins.

Lippitt, R., & Lippitt, G. L. (1978). *The consulting process in action: Skill development.* Chicago: Chakiris & Pirsein Associates.

Lonner, W. J. (1990). An overview of cross-cultural testing and assessment. In R. W. Bislin (Ed.), *Applied cross-cultural psychology, Cross-cultural research and methodology series, Vol. 14* (pp. 56–76). Thousand Oaks, CA: Sage.

Macnab, F. (1991). *Psychotherapy: New directions for clinical practice.* Melbourne, Australia: Spectrum.

Malgady, R. G. (2000). Myths about the null hypothesis and the path to reform. In R. H. Dana (Ed.), *Handbook of cross-cultural and multicultural personality assessment* (pp. 49–62). Hillsdale, NJ: Erlebaum.

Mead, M. (1969). Research with human beings: A model derived from anthropological field practice. *Daedalus, 98,* 361–386.

Meyer, G. J., Finn, S. E., Eyde, L. D., Kay, G. G., Moreland, K. L., Dies, R. R., et al. (2001). Psychological testing and psychological assessment: A review of evidence and issues. *The American Psychologist, 56,* 128–165.

Mitsumi, J. (1985). *The behavioral science of leadership: An interdisciplinary Japanese research program.* Ann Arbor: University of Michigan Press.

Mullin, V. C., & Cooper, S. E. (1998). Cross-cultural consultation in a South African cancer setting. *Consulting Psychology Journal: Practice and Research, 50*(1), 47–58.

Murray, H. A. (1938). *Explorations in personality.* New York: Oxford University. Press.

Murray, H. A. (1943). *Thematic apperception test manual.* Cambridge, MA: Harvard University Press.

Myers, I. B., & McCaulley, M. H. (1989). *Manual: A guide to the development and use of the Myers-Briggs Type Indicator.* Palo Alto, CA: Consulting Psychologists Press.

O'Roark, A. M. (1995). Occupational stress and informed interventions. In C. D. Spielberger, I. G. Sarason, J.M.T. Brebner, E. Greenglass, P. Laungani, & A. M. O'Roark (Eds.), *Stress and emotion: Anxiety, anger, and curiosity.* Washington, DC: Taylor & Francis.

O'Roark, A. M. (2000). *The quest for executive effectiveness: Turning vision inside-out. Charismatic-participatory leadership.* Nevada City, CA: Symposium Press.

O'Roark, A. M. (in press). *Creating the optimal challenge: Using the Job Stress Survey to calibrate workplace productivity.* Tampa, FL: Center for Research in Behavioral Medicine and Health Psychology.

O'Roark, A. M., & Capobianco, S. (1992, July). Leaders-in-training: Cross-cultural comparison of personality characteristics. Paper presented at the *23rd Congress of the International Union of Psychological Science, Brussels,* Belgium.

Osgood, C. E., Suci, G. J., & Tannenbaum, P. H. (1957). *The measurement of meaning.* Urbana: University of Illinois Press.

Pasa, S. F., Kabasakal, H., & Bodur, M. (2001). Society, organisations, and leadership in Turkey. *Applied Psychology: An International Review, 50,* 559–589.

Plummer, D. L. (1998). Approaching diversity: Training in the year 2000. *Consulting Psychology Journal: Practice and Research, 50,* 181–189.

Purkey, W. W. (1970). *Self-concept and student achievement.* Englewood Cliffs, NJ: Prentice Hall.

Quinn, R. E. (1992). *Beyond rational management: Mastering the paradoxes and competing demands of high performance.* San Francisco: Jossey-Bass.

Quinn, R. E., Faeman, S. R., Thompson, M. P., & McGrath, M. R. (1990). *On becoming a master manager: A competency framework.* New York: Wiley.

Rorschach, H. (1921). *Rorschach Psychodiagnostic Test.* Zurich, Switzerland: Hans Huber.

Satir, V. (1967). *Conjoint family therapy: A guide to theory and technique.* Palo Alto, CA: Science and Behavior Books.

Schein, E. H. (1992). *Organizational culture and leadership: A dynamic view* (2nd ed.). San Francisco: Jossey-Bass.

Schneider, W. E. (1995). Productivity improvement through cultural focus. *Consulting Psychology Journal: Practice and Research, 47,* 3–27.

Schutz, W. (1977). *FIRO-B.* Palo Alto, CA: Consulting Psychologists Press.

Schwartz, S. H. (1994). Cultural dimensions of values: Towards an understanding of national differences. In U. Kim, H. C. Triandis, C. Kagitcibasi, S. C. Choi, & G. Yoon (Eds.), *Individualism-collectivisim: Theoretical and methodological issues* (pp. 85–119). Thousand Oaks, CA: Sage.

Spielberger, C. D. (1966). Theory and research on anxiety. In C. D. Spielberger (Ed.), *Anxiety and behavior* (pp. 3–22). Orlando, FL: Academic Press.

Spielberger, C. D. (1983). *Manual for the State-Trait Anxiety Inventory: STAI (Form Y)*. Palo Alto, CA: Consulting Psychologists Press.

Spielberger, C. D., & Diaz-Guerrero, R. (1982). Cross-cultural anxiety: An overview. In C. D. Spielberger and R. Diaz-Guerrero (Eds.), *Cross-cultural anxiety* (Vol. 2). New York: McGraw-Hill.

Spielberger, C. D., Gorsuch, R. L., & Lushene, R. E. (1970). *STAI manual for the State-Trait Anxiety Inventory*. Palo Alto, CA: Consulting Psychologists Press.

Spielberger, C. D., Moscoso, M. S., & Brunner, T. M. (2002). Cross-cultural assessment of emotional states and personality traits. In R. K. Hambleton, C. D. Spielberger, & P. F. Merenda (Eds.), *Adapting educational and psychological tests for cross-cultural assessment*. Hillsdale, NJ: Erlbaum.

Spielberger, C. D., Ritterband, L. M., Sydeman, S. J., Reheiser, E. C., & Unger, K. K. (1995). Assessment of emotional state and personality traits: Measuring psychological vital signs. In J. N. Butcher (Ed.), *Clinical personality assessment: Practical approaches* (pp. 42–58). New York: Oxford University Press.

Spielberger, C. D., & Sharma, S. (1973). Development of the Hindi edition of the State-Trait Anxiety Inventory. *Indian Journal of Psychology, 48,* 11–20.

Spielberger, C. D., Sydeman, S. J., Owen, A. E., & Marsh, B. J. (1999). Measuring anxiety and anger with the State-Trait Anxiety Inventory (STAI) and the State-Trait Anger Expression Inventory (STAXI). In M. E. Maruish (Ed.), *The use of psychological testing for treatment planning and outcomes assessment*. Hillsdale, NJ: Erlbaum.

Spielberger, C. D., & Vagg, P. (1999). *Professional manual for the Job Stress Survey (JSS)*. Odessa, FL: Psychological Assessment Resources.

Sue, D. W. (1978). Eliminating cultural oppression in counseling. *Journal of Counseling Psychology, 25,* 419–428.

Sue, D. W., Arredondo, P., & McDavis, R. J. (1992). Multicultural counseling competencies/standards: A pressing need. *Journal of Counseling and Development, 70,* 477–486.

Sue, S., & Zane, N. (1987). The role of culture and cultural techniques in psychotherapy: A critique and reformulation. *The American Psychologist, 42,* 37–45.

Tayeb, M. (1994). Organizations and national culture: Methodology considered. *Organizational Studies, 15,* 429–446.

Thomas, K. W., & Kilmann, R. H. (1989). Thomas-Kilmann conflict mode instrument. Tuxedo, NY: Xicom.

Triandis, H. C. (1987). Individualism and social psychological theory. In. C. Kagitçibasi (Ed.), *Growth and progress in cross-cultural psychology* (pp. 78–84). Berwin, PA: Swets North America.

Tu, W. M. (1984). *Confucian ethics today: The Singapore challenge*. Singapore: Curriculum Development Institute of Singapore.

Van de Vijver, F., & Hambleton, R. K. (1996). Translating tests: Some practical guidelines. *European Psychologist, 1,* 89–99.

Wagner, E. (1962). *The Hand Test: Manual for administration, scoring and interpretation*. Los Angeles, CA: Western Psychological Services.

Worchel, S., & Coutant, D. (1994, July). The importance of conflict for group identity [Abstract]. *23rd International Congress of Applied Psychology, Madrid, Spain,* 331.

# CHAPTER TWENTY-TWO

# Cross-Cultural Issues in International Organizational Consultation

Virginia Mullin
*Mullin & Associates*

Stewart Cooper
*Valparaiso University*

W hat is needed to be known in order to become an international organizational consulting psychologist? How culturally sophisticated do you need to be? What types of attitudes are most useful? What kind of professional skills are needed? This chapter seeks to address these questions. It begins by discussing the changing international and intranational contexts that underlie the need for internationally competent consultants. Next, some of the contributions of organized psychology and multiculturalism are addressed. Later sections describe the results of a survey of organizational consultants who have engaged in international cross-cultural consultation. This is then followed by a presentation of a model for conducting cross-cultural consultation, and a case example of its application. The conclusion integrates the central themes of the chapter.

## CONSULTING SKILLS FOR INTERNATIONAL CONSULTATION

To be effective in consulting internationally, the consultant will utilize the majority of the skills valued by consultants generally. However, these skills will be utilized in different ways within the context of the particular cultural milieu in which the consultation occurs. Helpful backgrounds for international consultation include training in clinical or counseling psychology, or in industrial-organizational (I-O) or social psychology, as well as a working familiarity with international business. Indeed, when accompanied by post-degree training and supervision, these are the most common pathways to successfully transition to consulting psychology.

## Training Needs in Organizational Consulting

In most international consultation projects, cross-cultural factors are important, but are not the primary foci of intervention. However, very few organizational consultants have received training in multicultural work. Daugherty (2000) noted that organizational consultants are ill-equipped to be effective in multicultural and cross-cultural settings. He articulates three main issues about this. Specifically, he views the current United States social, economic, and political systems as unprepared and inadequate to address social, ethnic, and other forms of diversity. Further, he contends that most consultation models and techniques are derived from a Euro-American framework that does not always fit cultures that differ from this on any significant dimensions. Finally, Daugherty comments that the pressures for relevance, inclusiveness, and equal access to opportunities will continue to increase in the upcoming years. Anthony Marsella (2001) takes a similar perspective: "A very basic truth [is that] western psychology is rooted in an ideology of individualism, rationality, and empiricism that has little resonance in many of the more than 5000 cultures found in today's world. More than 85 percent of the world's six billion people are from non-western ethnic and cultural traditions" (p. 7).

The implications of the above clearly are manifested in the field of international consultation. Organizational consultants engaged in such work are challenged to develop necessary knowledge and skills that were not included in their training, and that might not be present in their existing personal psychology. Marsella (2001) also argues that internationalizing the psychology curriculum is an important first step toward resolving the global challenges. He argues for a new psychology curriculum that incorporates greater attention to indigenous psychologies of such great cultural traditions as China, Islam, India, and Native Americans. In addition, he encourages teaching of post-modernism, feminist theory, and social constructivism, because they point out the biases and abuses of the entrenched power of the dominant culture.

The authors have consulted on the nature and level of training in multicultural psychology in graduate psychology programs in South Africa and Australia. We found the amount of curricular and applied resources allocated to this area to be very small.

A particular area in which the above plays out is the globalization of business; the greater international networking of commerce and the growing diversity of the world's work force have resulted in an increase in the need for, and use of, international consultation (Black & Gregersen, 1999). These authors comment that while many U.S. companies send managers overseas, far too many times this does not work out. Moreover, they point out that this attrition rate, both overseas and upon return home, is very costly to the corporation. One cause for this apparent deficit is that selection, training, and support services are often the domain of the company's human resources (HR) department, yet, according to one study, few HR managers (11 percent) have ever traveled abroad themselves or have personal experience with a global assignment (Black & Gregersen, 1999).

Consultants with knowledge of multicultural psychology have much to offer these HRDs and global corporations. Cultural sensitivity and skills learned from training to practice effectively in the United States can be expanded to meet the needs of companies struggling to be successful in global situations. Rather than viewing other countries homogeneously or stereotypically, consultants can help corporations and their executives be aware that the majority of the countries of the world have ethnically diverse populations.

This diverse ethnicity is not always addressed internally by countries. For example, though Canada and Australia have an official policy of multicultural-ism, all signs and teaching materials exist only in the mainstream languages. Thus, the existing deficits and increased need for multiculturalism within soci-eties worldwide exist even in the more progressive nations. International busi-ness is growing more dependent on cross-cultural knowledge and understanding (Sue, Bingham, Porche-Burke, & Vasquez, 1999).

Some authors (see, for example, Jackson & Holvino, 1988; O'Roark, 2000; Trompenaars & Hampden-Turner, 1998) recognize the importance of the incor-poration of multicultural factors into global consultation. Leaders in business, service, and government organizations face expanding interconnectedness with the world as international competition increases. According to O'Roark, one in five jobs is already tied, directly or indirectly, to international trade. So, execu-tives who limit their field of vision to previous markets are doomed to under-achievement or even failure (O'Roark, 2000).

Globalization is an incremental process that develops over time. Ayman, Kriecker, and Masztal (1994) visualized a pattern of corporate progression from nationalism to globalism that is reflected in leadership style and management practices. With the first step into internationalism, organizational leaders typi-cally demonstrate an ethnocentric attitude. Their style of thinking remains authoritarian, and corporate control continues to be centralized. Often, when offices or operations are located in at least two countries and positions are filled locally by the host country, the company moves from ethnocentric to polycen-tric internationalism. Corporate headquarters begin to keep a hands-off attitude. Regiocentric internationalism allows for collaborative planning for business in multiple neighboring countries. Globalization is one step further. Employment of different nationals at all locations and management levels is common for truly global organizations (O'Roark, 2000). At each stage of this progression, an organizational consultant with expertise in cross-cultural and multicultural issues can help ensure success.

Skills beyond social etiquette and polite conversation are required for the success of consultants working internationally, whether in high-level corporate settings in world-class cities or with remote healthcare or non-profit organizations in Third World countries. Instruction in such skills is being addressed in programs ranging from graduate schools to corporate in-house commercial ventures in global training and relocation, designed for managers who are relocating overseas or frequently travel abroad. As one example, Berlitz International Inc. is a commercial program that has combined its well-known intensive language instruction with cross-cultural briefings (see www.berlitz.com; Berlitz, 1999). The Berlitz programs were designed in response to the large amount of money lost annually due to failed foreign assignments, as a result of the inability to adapt to a foreign culture rather than management weaknesses. The Berlitz program includes training in verbal and nonverbal communications, role playing, and topics such as Communicating Across Cultures and Raising Global Awareness (Berlitz, 1999).

Black and Gregersen (1999) have suggested that companies that manage their overseas executives successfully follow certain guidelines (utilizing either internal or external programs) by focusing on knowledge creation and global leadership development in international assignments. Success is further enhanced by assigning overseas posts to those whose technical skills are matched or exceeded by their cross-cultural abilities, and ending with a repatriation process to help managers readjust to American life.

# ORGANIZED PSYCHOLOGY AND MULTICULTURALISM

The need to prepare organizational psychologists for multicultural work is beginning to be addressed by organized psychology and by the largest association of psychologists in the world, the American Psychological Association (APA). Historically, psychology, particularly professional psychology, has been criticized for being overly intrapsychic and overly based on male and Western European cultures, and simultaneously ignoring the significant impacts of environment and culture (Lewis, Lewis, Daniels, & D'Andrea, 1998; Marsella, 2001).

Other theorists have contributed to the current multicultural zeitgeist. Some have articulated models of racial identity (see, for example, Cross, 1991; Helms, 1990; Sue & Sue, 1990). Others (see, for example, Hackney & Cormier, 1996) call for greater attention to cross-cultural process variables such as time, distance, touch, and communication style. Still others articulate the tremendous input of sex (Miller, 1986).

One of the most significant developments in this field was the identification of key attitudes, knowledge, and skills thought to underlie effective cross-cultural work (Sue, Arredondo, & McDavis, 1992). This approach provides a central organizer for the field. A related model focusing on possible professional roles, primarily in counseling and psychotherapy, was offered by Atkinson, Thompson, and Grant (1993). These authors contended that psychologists should use one of eight professional roles depending on whether the client's (consultee's) situation requires prevention or intervention, whether the solution was externally or internally focused, and the degree of the consultee's acculturation to the dominant, Western culture.

The American Psychological Association, through its directorates, task forces, and divisions, has taken three major steps in response to the changing multicultural context of professional psychology and society. The first step was the development of the Guidelines for Providers of Psychological Services to Ethnic, Linguistic, and Culturally Diverse Populations (American Psychological Association, 1993). These guidelines were the product of a task force on the delivery of services to ethnic minority populations established by the APA's Board of Ethnic Minority Affairs in 1988. The guidelines include nine principles that have relevance to those consulting in international contexts, which by their very nature are inherently cross-cultural. The principles cover domains such as education, research, and practice, and incorporate attention to family, spiritual beliefs, language, customs, and socio-political considerations.

Additionally, three of APA's divisions, Counseling Psychology (Division 17), the Society for the Psychology of Women (Division 35), and the Society for the Psychological Study of Ethnic Minority Issues (Division 45), sponsored two national multicultural summits in January 1999 and February 2001.

A third major action from APA is currently in process and is being advanced by these same divisions. Appointed members of each of the three divisions are meeting to develop a comprehensive set of standards for multiculturally sensitive practice, teaching, and research. The intent is to create standards that will apply across a diversity of applications of psychology, including those relevant to organizational consultation.

# FOUNDATIONAL CONCEPTS AND THEORIES

Having tools to assess organizational culture is an important starting place for organizational consultants doing international work. Schein (1990) defined culture as "a pattern of basic assumptions invented, discovered, or developed by a given group as it learns to cope with its problems of external adaptation and internal integration that has worked well enough to be considered valid and, therefore is to be taught to new members as the correct way to perceive, think, and feel in relation to those problems" (p. 11). Schein's model (1985, 1990) identified a number of underlying dimensions of organizational culture. These included the organization's relationship to the environment, the nature of human activity, the nature of reality and truth, the nature of time, the nature of human nature, the nature of human relationships, and homogeneity versus diversity. The consultant immersed in cross-cultural settings can utilize these concepts to better understand the consultee and the client system.

Organizational consultants need to consider other cultural aspects in their consultations. *Artifacts,* the day-to-day representations of culture found in commonly used objects, are also relevant. In organizations, these can include seemingly superficial factors such as dress codes, annual reports, role and mission statements, and the interpersonal rituals people engage in, such as socially sanctioned greetings and ways of expressing agreement. Manifestations of the organization's culture include climate, group norms, roles, systems, politics, and values. Whether or not a consultation is successful might highly depend on the consultant's understanding of, and acting with respect for, the organizational client's culture (Daugherty, 2000). Moreover, organizational culture has very real bottom-line impacts. For example, Fisher and Alford (2000) present empirical evidence on the role of organizational culture on corporate success. Specifically, healthy organizational cultures in their study generated better profitability, market share, and sales growth. Similarly, Swartz-Kulstad and Martin (1999) elaborated five cultural and contextual domains—ethnocultural orientation, family environment, community environment, communication style, and language—that impact organizational effectiveness. They demonstrated that the more successful psychologically based consulting interventions likely take all five of these domains into account. Additionally, it is important for consultants to realize that individuals are influenced by various levels of proximal to distal culture. Neville and Mobley (2001) describe the different effects of micro-, meso-, and macrosystems, ideas initially developed by Bronfenbrenner (1988).

The concept of individual or group *acculturation* is closely related to the idea of organizational culture. Specifically, acculturation is the process of change that occurs when two cultures come into contact with each other (Sciarri, 1999). Williams and Berry (1991) described acculturation as the extent to which a member of a nondominant group adopts the beliefs, values, customs, and institutions of the dominant culture. Theories of racial identity formation can also be helpful to the organizational consultant engaged in international consultation. The Minority Identity Development Model (Atkinson, Morten, & Sue, 1993) explains how those from nonwhite groups develop a personal identity when in an environment that devalues their cultural, ethnic, and racial background.

The cultural background of the consultation is equally critical to the success or failure of cross-cultural consultation in international contexts. Denzin and

Lincoln (1994) contend that consultants must be aware of their own personal histories and how these backgrounds can interact with the worldview embodied by the client organization. Levinson (1994) stated that "organizational dynamics recapitulate the family structure and actions of the culture in which they are embedded" (p. 429). As with a family, the organization consists of interrelated subsystems. These subsystems might be determined by organizational purpose, power dynamics among groups, commonly held values, and other factors (Levinson).

Several other theoretical models are specifically helpful to multicultural and international consultants. Geert Hofstede (1991) developed his Five-Dimensional Model in carrying out a fifty-country empirical investigation for IBM that involved 116,000 respondents. Four of his five dimensions (Power Index [PDI], Individualism [IDV], More Aggressive for Success [Masculinity, MAS], and Uncertainty Avoidance [UAI]) were assessed in most settings (see also Hackney & Cormier, 1996; Mullin & Cooper, 1998).

In Hofstede's model (1991), the PDI assesses the extent to which the less-powerful members of society accept that power is distributed unequally. Individualism (IDV), the second factor, indicates whether a culture is more individualistic or collectivistic in its orientation. In the latter type of society, people emphasize the life of the extended family or clan, and prioritize relationships over tasks and fulfilling obligations to the group. The third factor, MAS, contrasts values of achievement and success with caring for others and quality of life. UAI measures the extent to which people show much anxiety and stress and an inner urge to work hard, versus a higher level of relaxation, with lower stress and less value placed on hard work.

Trompenaars and Hampden-Turner (1998) presented an alternative but overlapping model of culture including a set of dichotomies, some of which overlap with Hofstede's theories. For example, the Individual versus Communitarianism differential might be important to help the consultant understand why, in some countries (in Africa, for example), people show up in a group to a meeting, while in other countries, only one representative is sent. Also, in some Asian countries, the group is represented by sending a different participant each time a meeting convenes. Attitude toward the Environment was a second cultural dichotomy in this model that is useful. For example, in the U.S., the environment is considered to be of service to the corporation, whereas in many Asian cultures, the corporation serves the environment.

## Nonverbal Behavior

Theories of nonverbal aspects of behavior, another important dimension of organizational culture, abound in multicultural and international settings. Ivey, Ivey, and Simek-Morgan, 1997, for example, identified six nonverbal communication areas: time, eye contact, body language, voice tone, speech rate, and physical space. In the case of time, Western cultures, such as Switzerland and Germany, prize punctuality, whereas others (for example, Mexico and some Third World countries) value time flexibility. Furthermore, Oosterwal (1994) noted that in many cultures, one must wait for an appropriate time to approach certain subjects. For example, dinnertime is considered off limits for business discussions in France and other locations. Trompenaars and Hampden-Turner (1998) emphasize that a country's worldview of time, that is, past-oriented or future-oriented, will dictate how progressive a proposal or consultation should be.

The importance of eye contact ranges from being only an element of cultural politeness to a display of demonstrated power distance. As an illustration, one of the authors mistakenly assumed that a Zulu interviewee was depressed because of his downward glance and avoidance of direct eye contact with the consultants. However, they were informed that this is how persons from rural cultures demonstrate respect to those with the Doctor title. Such modifications to communication are very common in high-context cultures. Additionally, it is not uncommon for persons from high-context cultures to value normative politeness, in which an open demonstration of assertiveness, uncertainty, or annoyance would be taboo, especially with someone in a position of respect and status (Mullin, Cooper, & Eremenco, 1998).

Body language misuse can be a problem in any culture, but hand gestures in particular can convey many unintended messages. There are fewer universals of interpretation with body language than there are with eye contact and facial expressions. Therefore, consultants are advised to exercise caution in three ways. First, they should avoid gestures as much as possible, unless they are thoroughly familiar with their local meaning. Second, they should learn to use gestures appropriate to the host country. When in doubt, they should ask for their meaning (Oosterwal, 1994).

Vocal tone and speech rate also varies among cultures, and might be misinterpreted as to meaning and intent. In line with the social politeness described above, Asians, for example, might consider United States consultants as brash, loud, and noisy. On the other hand, consultants from the United States might find people in client organizations from high-context cultures to be too indirect and nonassertive in their communications (Oosterwal, 1994). Knowledge of appropriate interpersonal physical space when interacting multiculturally or internationally is also important. For example, Leong (1993) noted that a consultant can often learn the status of employees in a Japanese organization by observing where they physically stand in relation to the CEO.

Motivation also differs from one culture to another. Maslow's *hierarchy of needs* (1970) might not be as useful in many parts of the world as in Western-based cultures. For example, some people work for monetary rewards and others for positive regard and support of their colleagues. In Japan, the top rung would be occupied by the concept of harmonious relationships. Their term for individual translates to "person among others," not unlike the African concept of *Ubuntu* ("I am a person because of others.").

Specialized multicultural models are relevant in particular consulting applications. In healthcare, for example, Herselman (1996) compares the differences between Western and traditional systems of medicine. He contrasts medical practices in Western cultures, in which the mind-body connection is compartmentalized, with the unification seen in traditional cultures. As opposed to the separate role relegated in Western cultures, in traditional medicine, the role of religion is integrated into the medical system. This is common in Africa, where the healer, or Sangoma, is also a religious figure, and combines spirituality with knowledge of folk medicine.

Additionally, due to the collectivism of traditional societies, the family is much more involved in health-related decision-making in non-Western cultures. Choices about an individual's treatment might be deferred to the family or community, even if opposed to the wishes of the patient. Moreover, in the pluralistic medical approach of traditional societies, etiological beliefs have a spiritual basis, whereas in the biological approach of the West, the beliefs are physiologically based. Finally, patients in traditional societies have a high expectation of the relationship with the medical profession, whereas in the West, the expectation is low to moderate. Herselman's model is very useful for international health consultation.

## THE CROSS-CULTURAL CONSULTING MODEL

Organizational consultation models presented in the literature have often lacked attention and sensitivity to multicultural and cross-cultural issues. Jackson and Hayes (1993) identified several cultural factors important in consultation. These include the importance of integrating multicultural concerns into consultation, given the increase in ethnically diverse organizations and their belief that cultural differences inevitably create struggles within individuals, organizations, and communities. They also noted that the consultants' overall effectiveness might well be dictated by their own personal cultural competencies. Their work suggests that cultural dynamics can generate resistance and tension during the consultation process, and that cultural differences can and do impact formal and informal communication patterns, structures, and power dynamics within organizations (see also Daugherty, 2000; Lewis et al., 1998; Sue, Ivey, & Pedersen, 1996).

Chasnoff and Muniz (1989) presented an interesting and important model for multicultural training, based on their Cultural Awareness Hierarchy approach. We have adopted this six-factor model to international consultation, and have added a more fluid, systemic perspective to it.

The first factor in this model refers to focusing on the personal and interpersonal aspects of oneself that influence the consultant's self-awareness in a cultural context. The emphasis in Level I of the model is on people apart from their cultures. The systems expansion of this level is the focus on the person-in-relation. People always live in relational and environmental contexts, and to effectively understand and intervene within these contexts, these must be understood and taken into consideration.

The second level of skills relates to the technical or professional skills or competencies important for success in the consultant's own culture. Two important parameters of this dimension are competence and politics. The organizational consultant operating in international contexts needs to have the requisite competencies for success, and be involved in a project in which the sociopolitical factors surrounding it are conducive to success. Similarly, the involved consultees must have adequate and appropriate technical or professional skills. Chasnoff and Muniz (1989) state that if not careful, the consultant or consultees might misattribute problems that exist or evolve to cultural factors, rather than viewing them as difficulties due to technical or other skill deficits. The systems expansion of this level is the understanding and application of the notion that desired skills emerge and decline in a context. For example, a facility with computers is essential for many jobs today, but this was not the case five years ago.

Issues in Level III, termed Factors Beyond Culture, include poverty, racism, international relations, organizational health, and sexism, most of which are more prevalent in cross-cultural consultation than in monocultural consultation. The need for the consultant to avoid making negative judgments based on cultural indoctrination is high, and the likelihood of their perceptions being impacted by their own personal cultural biases is large. Beyond being careful from an individual stance, the consultant conducting international work must avoid collisions with consultees who share their cultural background or priorities. The systems expansion of this level is the utilization of a more complex framework of microsystems, exosystems, and macrosystems, with the awareness that the culture plays out differently with each of these.

Levels IV through VI of Chasnoff and Muniz's model (1989) address factors related more to the personhood of the consultant. Level IV identifies the need to understand one's own culture and its impact on one's personal and professional beliefs and values. The importance of this self-knowledge cannot be overemphasized, as it is only when a person understands his or her own influences that they can transcend the culture of another. The systems expansion of this level is the paradigmatic shift from viewing one's own culture as fixed to recognizing it as an ongoing constructive narrative that is being influenced by exposure to persons, ideas, and customs from different cultures. Level V relates to the extent to which one's own culture is multi- or monocultural, addressing the myth of cultural homogeneity (see also Naisbitt, 1984). Some cultures have great uniformity, others are melting-pot-type societies, and still others value diversity. The systems expansion of this level emerges from the destruction of the myth of homogeneity of any given country's culture. While there are exceptions, the majority of societies have some level of multiculturalism. So, awareness and use of etic (personal) and emic (group) factors must be utilized. Finally, Level VI is the development of the skills to focus nonjudgmentally and helpfully on the other culture. This entails advancing from awareness to acceptance to valuation of cultural differences. The systems expansion of this level is similar to the previous one. Consultants must avoid the trap of overgeneralization, and should both assess and respond to real differences among subgroups and other important characteristics.

Not all consultants will be capable of international cross-cultural consultation. High self-awareness, high sensitivity to other cultures, sufficient professional and interpersonal skills, and attitudinal and behavioral flexibility are key factors for success. Not everyone can develop these, but many can.

There are several implications of our interpretation of this model to consultation practice. We do believe that it is important to apply all steps of the expanded Hierarchy model in consulting to organizations. Second, we believe it is important for the consultant to maintain some level of neutrality with regard to the diverse cultures encountered within the organization. The more different the culture is from one's own, the greater the challenge can be. A third suggestion is to confirm assumptions made about other cultures with people from that culture. The consultant's own cultural background determines what can and cannot be seen and experienced. It is very easy to project distortions of culture onto those different from ourselves. Another suggestion is to always remember that individuality exists even with monocultures. No matter how closely a given person might fit with a particular group, there are always unique aspects and differences at the individual level. Finally, we believe it is important to honor and cherish the positive contributions of one's personal culture. All groups to which we belong have positives to offer to others, to organizations, to communities, society, and the world.

A recent expansion of multicultural counseling therapy to organizational development (OD) supports the above recommendations. Sue, Ivey, and Pedersen (1996) suggest that enhancing the corporate climate and the relations among different organizational levels is appropriate for Euro-American companies. However, for companies in other cultures, techniques specifically applicable to that culture should be considered. For example, use of a smoke ceremony to promote health in Australian Aboriginal communities is common. Employment of such a technique when consulting with a subsidiary located in an Aboriginal community might be highly prized and effective.

Lewis et al. (1998) also note the importance of considering whether an OD intervention will occur in a low- or high-context culture. Most consultants from the U.S., they contend, are affected by our dominant low-context culture, which values time limits and an orientation toward task accomplishment. Such approaches create conflict with many world cultures, which are high-context with fluid time and a greater relational emphasis. Communication in low- versus high-context cultures also differs. In low-context cultures, messages are direct and explicit, with words conveying most of the information. In contrast, in high-context cultures, indirect and differential communication might be preferred, as are nonverbal cues.

One additional factor in international consultation concerns the nature of expected and necessary interactions between the consultant and the client system. At times, the organizational consultant working in international contexts engages in behaviors that are contrary to a stringent avoidance of multiple relationships. For example, engaging in a more personal relationship is often important for the success of consultation in a high-context culture. As an illustration, gift giving is very important in Hindu culture, whereas not meeting in a social context might be viewed as an insult in other cultures such as Latin America.

## CASE ILLUSTRATION OF THE MODELS

An illustrative application of the models discussed in this chapter involved us, as consultants from the United States, working with Western-trained European ancestry physicians and well-educated, urban Black nurses to provide medical and psychosocial treatment to rural, low, Black patients with cancer. The setting for the intervention was an Apartheid hospital (named after the architect of Apartheid), which had exclusively served White patients until the election of Nelson Mandela as president of South Africa. The project was based on assessing quality of life as associated with the treatment being provided. Cella's quality-of-life survey served as the basis for this work (Cella, 1988). Thus, this was an internal, cross-cultural healthcare consultation, which involved significant multicultural issues as well. Details of the project are available through several previously published articles (Mullin & Cooper, 1998; Mullin, Cooper, & Eremenco, 1999; Mullin, Cella, et al, 2000; Cooper & Mullin, 2001). What follows are our perceptions of how the models we have presented in this chapter guided our work on this project.

Certain materials served as general background context for our work. These included the APA's *Guidelines for Providers of Psychological Services to Ethnic, Linguistic, and Culturally Diverse Populations* (APA, 1993), Bronfenbrenners's concept of person-in-context (1988), and the primacy of the need to know and demonstrate culturally relevant knowledge, attitudes, and skills (Sue, Arredondo, & McDavis, 1992).

Other writings served to guide the process of our consultation. These process guides included the importance and impacts of acculturation (Williams & Berry, 1991), and of racial identity (Sue & Sue, 1990). Of even more importance, Schein's dimensions of organizational culture (Schein, 1985) were especially helpful, because significant differences on most of these dimensions differentiated us from the consultees, as well as their clients from both them and us.

Still other models were directly employed as part of the consultation. Specifically, we had the consultees rate themselves and their patients on Hofstede's factors of individualism/collectivism, power distance, communication style, and uncertainty avoidance, and the related dimensions of goals from interaction with a professional, and focus of verbal and nonverbal behaviors discussed by Hackney and Cormier (1996). The work by Ivey, Ivey, and Simek-Morgan (1997) was also very helpful on the nonverbal behavior dimensions. In addition to these, the specialized cross-cultural health model offered by Herselman (1996) was of significant assistance in the project. Feedback from the consultees indicated that our using the above conceptual frameworks was quite helpful in their adjustment to the huge change in their client constituency and the environmental context of their work.

Finally, adaptations of several specific models and suggestions promoted our professional development in international consultation. Specifically, our expansion of the six-level hierarchical model of Chasnoff and Muniz (1989) was very productive. Additionally, while no recent practitioners writing about the topic of multicultural consultation (see, for example, Jackson & Hayes, 1993; Lewis, Lewis, Daniels, & D'Andrea, 1998; Sutton, 2000) have offered comprehensive models for such work, several have offered sound recommendations, and we used many of them. Suggestions from Daugherty (2000) on integrating cross-cultural considerations within the entry, diagnosis, and intervention phases of consultation were particularly affirming to read, as our actions in these stages were entirely consistent with his recommendations. Olweny's work (1994) on conducting research in international cross- and multicultural settings makes many similar suggestions.

# ORGANIZATIONAL CONSULTANTS FOSTERING MULTICULTURALISM IN THE WORKPLACE

Given the trends towards globalization and diversification of the work force (O'Roark, 2000), there are times when consultants working in international contexts are asked to help deal directly with multicultural issues. Three models, Jackson and Holvino's multicultural OD models (1988), Sue's Cultural Diversity Training Model (1991), and Sue's Multiple Dimensions of Cultural Competence

Model (2001), are recommended for use by organizational consultants. Enhancing organizations to become more multicultural requires the consultant to engage in a variety of roles in addition to consultation. Such additional roles as change agent, instructor, advocate, and facilitator of the formation and action of disempowered groups are necessary (Atkinson, Thompson, & Grant, 1993).

We believe it is important for the organizational consultant working in international contexts to recognize the inherent institutional discrimination imposed by the dominant (and often male-oriented) culture (see, for example, Axelson, 1985). The knowledge and skills of a sensitive and aware consultant can be invaluable in fostering a positive OD change process by a culturally competent consultant (Cross, Bazron, Dennis, & Isaacs, 1999).

To assist in such positive change, Oosterwal (1994) provides a number of specific suggestions that warrant presentation. He recommends that consultants can suggest the following actions to leaders of organizations wanting to embrace multiculturalism in the workplace: leaders can attend holiday festivities of the different ethnic and cultural groups, show a warm interest in others' religion and spirituality, organize projects through which different groupings of people can meet, actively combat prejudice in the workplace, evaluate the organization's commitment to diversity, and develop an organization-wide vision statement on diversity.

# CONCLUSION

Organizational consultants engaged in international work are inherently operating in cross-cultural, and often, multicultural situations. It is also clear that a synergy is emerging from the growing interdependency of the global community, enhanced international communications systems, and the rising interest in the globalization of psychology. With conscientiousness and adequate training, we believe such professionals might possess some of the best skills and are best positioned to assist many organizations and their associated work forces. We agree with Marsella's emphasis on the internationalization of psychology, and the impact of events and contributions of other cultures on everyone's lives in a world community (Marsella, 2001).

In the global economy of today, it is a competitive necessity to have a work force that is fluent in the ways of the world. Consultants working cross-culturally or with multicultural societies can be the catalyst for executives to have the confidence to try out new languages, experiment with different customs, interact with many levels of a different society with a respect of diverse viewpoints, and develop a collaborative negotiation style.

# References

American Psychological Association. (1993). Guidelines for providers of psychological services to ethnic, linguistic, and culturally diverse populations. *American Psychologists, 48,* 45–48.

Atkinson, D. R., Morten, G., & Sue, D. W. (1993). *Counseling American minorities: A cross-cultural perspective* (4th ed.). Dubuque, IA: Brown & Benchmark.

Atkinson, D. R., Thompson, C. E., & Grant, S. K. (1993). A three dimensional model for counseling racial/ethnic minorities. *The Counseling Psychologist, 21,* 257–277.

Axelson, J. A. (1985). *Counseling and development in a multicultural society.* Pacific Grove, CA: Brooks/Cole.

Ayman, R., Kreicker, N. A., & Masztal, J. (1994). Defining global leadership in business environments. *Consulting Psychology Journal: Practice and Research, 46,* 64–67.

Berlitz. (1999). *Global training and relocation.* Princeton, NJ: Berlitz.

Black, J. S., & Gregersen, H. B. (1999). The right way to manage expats. *Harvard Business Review, 77,* 52–62.

Bronfenbrenner, V. (1988). Interacting systems in human development. In N. Bolgan, A. Caspi, G. Doeney, & M. Moorehand (Eds.), *Persons in context: Developmental process.* Cambridge, England: Cambridge University Press.

Cella, D. F. (1988). Quality of life during and after cancer treatment. *Comprehensive Therapy, 14,* 69–75.

Chasnoff, R., & Muniz, P. (1989). The cultural awareness hierarchy: A model of OD intervention in cross-cultural settings. In W. Sikes, A. Drexler, & J. Gant (Eds.), *The evolving practice of organizational development.* Alexandria, VA: NTL Institute of Applied Behavior Science.

Cooper, S. E., & Mullin, V. C. (2001). Cancer patient quality of life in underserved populations in South Africa. *Journal of Psychosocial Oncology, 19,* 39–56.

Cross, T. L., Bazron, B. V., Dennis, K. W., & Isaacs, M. R. (1999). *Towards a culturally competent system of care* (Vol. I). Washington, DC: Georgetown University, Child Development Center, National Technical Assistance Center for Children's Mental Health.

Cross, W. (1991). *Shades of black.* Philadelphia: Temple University Press.

Daugherty, A. M. (2000). *Psychological consultation and collaboration in school and community settings* (3rd ed.). Pacific Grove, CA: Brooks/Cole.

Denzin, N. K., & Lincoln, Y. S. (1994). Introduction: Entering the field of qualitative research. In N. K. Denzin & Y. S. Lincoln (Eds.), *Handbook of qualitative research.* Thousand Oaks, CA: Sage.

Fisher, C. J., & Alford, R. J. (2000). Consulting on culture: A new bottom line. *Consulting Psychology Journal: Practice and Research, 52,* 206–217.

Hackney, H. L., & Cormier, L. S. (1996). *The professional counselor: A process guide to helping* (2nd ed.). Needham Heights, MA: Allyn & Bacon.

Helms, J. (1990). *Black and white racial identity.* Westport, CT: Greenwood Press.

Herselman, S. (1996). Some problems in health communication in a multicultural clinical setting: A South African experience. *Health Communications, 8,* 153–170.

Hofstede, G. (1991). *Cultures and organizations: Software of the mind.* New York: McGraw-Hill.

Ivey, A. E., Ivey, M. B., & Simek-Morgan, L. (1997). *Counseling and psychotherapy.* Needham Heights, MA: Allyn & Bacon.

Jackson, D. N., & Hayes, D. H. (1993). Multicultural issues in consultation. *Journal of Counseling and Development, 72,* 144–147.

Jackson, D. N., & Holvino, E. (1988). Developing multicultural organizations. *Journal of Religion and Applied Behavioral Sciences, 9,* 14–19.

Leong, F.T.L. (1993). The career counseling process with racial-ethnic minorities: The case of Asian Americans. *The Career Development Quarterly, 42,* 26–40.

Levinson, H. (1994). Why the behemonths fell: Psychological roots of corporate failure. *The American Psychologists, 49,* 428–436.

Lewis, J. A., Lewis, M. D., Daniels, J. A., & D'Andrea, M. J. (1998). *Community counseling: Empowerment strategies for a diverse society* (2nd ed.). Pacific Grove, CA: Brooks/Cole.

Marsella, A. J. (2001). Essay: Internationalizing the psychology curriculum. *Psychology International, 12,* 7–8.

Maslow, A. H. (1970). *Motivation and personality* (2nd ed.). New York: HarperCollins.

Miller, J. B. (1986). *Toward a new psychology of women* (2nd ed.). Boston: Beacon Press.

Mullin, V. C., Cella, D., Chang, C.-H., Eremenco, S., Mertz, M., Lent, L., et al. (2000). Development of three African language translations of the FACT-G. *Quality of Life Research, 9,* 139–149.

Mullin, V. C., & Cooper, S. E. (1998). Cross-cultural consultation in a South African cancer setting. *Consulting Psychology Journal: Practice and Research, 50,* 47–58.

Mullin, V. C., Cooper, S. E., & Eremenco, S. (1999). Communication in a South African cancer setting: Cross-cultural implications. *International Journal of Rehabilitation and Health, 4,* 69–82.

Naisbitt, J. (1984). *Megatrends* (2nd ed.). New York: Warner Books.

Neville, H. A., & Mobley, M. (2001). Social idealities in contexts: An ecological model of multicultural counseling psychology processes. *The Counseling Psychologist, 29,* 471–486.

Olweny, C. (1994). The ethics and conduct of cross-cultural research in developing countries. *Psych-Oncology, 3,* 11–20.

Oosterwal, G. (1994). *Community in diversity: A workbook.* Benton Harbor, MI: Patterson.

O'Roark, A. M. (2000). *The quest for executive effectiveness: Turning vision inside-out. Charismatic-participatory leadership.* Nevada City, CA: Symposium.

Schein, E. H. (1985). *Organizational culture and leadership: A dynamic view.* San Francisco: Jossey-Bass.

Schein, E. H. (1990). Organizational culture. *American Psychologist, 45*(2), 109–119.

Sciarri, D. T. (1999). *Multiculturalism in counseling.* Itasca, IL: Peacock.

Sue, D. W. (1991). A model for cultural diversity training. *Journal of Counseling and Development, 70,* 99–105.

Sue, D. W. (2001). Multidimensional cultural competence. *The Counseling Psychologist, 29,* 790–821.

Sue, D. W., Arredondo, P., & McDavis, R. J. (1992). Multicultural competencies/standards: A pressing need. *Journal of Counseling and Development, 70,* 477–486.

Sue, D. W., Bingham, R. P., Porche-Burke, L., & Vasquez, M. (1999). The diversification of psychology: A multicultural revolution. *The American Psychologist, 54,* 1061–1069.

Sue, D. W., Ivey, A. E., & Pedersen, P. B. (1996). *A theory of multicultural counseling and therapy.* Pacific Grove, CA: Brooks/Cole.

Sue, D. W., & Sue, D. (1990). *Counseling the culturally different: Theory and practice* (2nd ed.). New York: Wiley.

Sutton, M. (2000, October). Cultural competence: It's not just political correctness. It's good medicine. Retrieved October 2000, from http://www.aofb.org/pm/2000/000/58cult.html

Swartz-Kulstad, V. L., & Martin, W. E., Jr. (1999). Impact of culture and context on psychosocial adaptation: The cultural and contextual guide process. *Journal of Counseling & Development, 77*, 281–293.

Trompenaars, F., & Hampden-Turner, C. (1998). *Riding the waves of culture: Understanding diversity in global business*. New York: McGraw-Hill.

Williams, C. L., & Berry, J. W. (1991). Primary prevention of acculturative stress among refugees. *The American Psychologist, 46*, 632–641.

# CHAPTER TWENTY-THREE

# Consulting with Healthcare Organizations

Ira M. Levin
*California School of Organizational Studies*
*Alliant International University*
*&*
*Cap Gemini Ernst & Young LLC*

Over the past decades, healthcare has been one of the fastest growing industries in the U.S. economy (Goldman & Dubow, 1996). It therefore presents an important market niche for organizational consulting psychologists. This chapter focuses on some of the special organizational issues that organizational consultants need to keep in mind when working with healthcare organizations. I write from the perspective of an organizational consulting psychologist who has specialized in work with this industry.

## OVERVIEW OF THE CHAPTER

I will first review some of the major trends influencing the healthcare industry, and the healthcare industry's responses to them. Next, I will describe some of the common cultural attributes of healthcare organizations, as well as their implications for working with the organizations identified. Finally, some of the opportunities for organizational consulting psychologists to work with healthcare organizations to help them address key challenges they face will be examined, and examples of successful practices will be offered.

The chapter will focus primarily on consulting with healthcare organizations within the United States. The majority of international healthcare systems are national systems in which nearly all care is funded and administered through the country's federal government. In Canada, for example, physicians are paid on a fee-for-service basis in which the mandated fee schedule is negotiated between the provincial government and the medical association (Fooks, 1999). This is similar to the managed care model that has been developing within the United States, except that the American system continues to combine private with public funding, administration, and delivery of care.

# OVERVIEW OF THE HEALTHCARE INDUSTRY SECTORS

The healthcare industry in the United States is very heterogeneous, comprised of a wide array of different enterprises and entities. These include hospital organizations, physician groups, and insurance companies, as well as a variety of other specialty care providers, including long-term care facilities and ambulatory care clinics. Historically, they have operated independently of one another and in a rather fragmented way (Starr, 1982). However, while operating, at least in principle, autonomously, the three industry sectors are clearly interconnected. Hospitals, for example, need physicians to admit patients and provide inpatient care, and physicians require hospitals to provide acute-level care to their patients. Both require third-party payers such as health insurance companies to reimburse them for care provided.

## Sectors in the Healthcare Industry

The largest sector of the industry consists of *provider* organizations. These include hospital organizations, as well as physician and other clinical care groups. Within the hospital group, there are both *for-profit* publicly traded companies and *not-for-profit* hospitals. The not-for-profit hospitals can be further divided into *faith-based organizations,* spanning the religious denominations, academic medical centers, and community hospitals. In addition, the provider segment includes clinical care groups, of which physician organizations are the largest (Kongstevdt & Plocher, 1996). There are also a variety of different organization and business models for physician practice organizations (PPOs). These can be established as for-profit partnerships, limited liability companies, business corporations, or not-for-profit corporations or foundations. The other major sector within healthcare, payers, includes the traditional indemnity health insurers as well as the various types of managed care organizations. Federal and state governments are other large payers that provide health insurance coverage to the elderly through the U.S. Medicare program, and to the poor through the Medicaid program. Hospitals also contract with physician practices to provide medical care services to their patients. Sometimes, primary care physician groups contract with physician specialty groups for better clinical care coordination and increased power in their contracting with health insurers and hospitals. This creates a web of different entities that are tied together operationally, in terms of the delivery of care, but which often maintain separate governance and management structures, and have different cultures and goals (Williams & Van Der Reiss, 1997). This complexity causes the healthcare industry to be more complex than organizations in other industries.

# CONTEMPORARY TRENDS AND ISSUES INFLUENCING THE HEALTHCARE INDUSTRY

The trillion-dollar healthcare system in the United States has been described as highly fragmented and unstable (Coddington, Moore, & Fischer, 1996). Kongstevdt, Lutz, Shaman, and Stanford (1999) likened it to a chaotic system because it operates in a highly turbulent market environment, and acts similar to a nonlinear system in that the various entities that comprise it, though highly interdependent, are loosely coupled (Cohen & March, 1974). Often, these various entities have competing goals. It is a highly complex industry that has been in the throes of a rapid and dramatic transformation over the past decade, with little indication that the pace and magnitude of change will slow any time soon (Robinson, 1999). The traditional U.S. healthcare system that was dominated by the professional medical guild and financed by an indemnity insurance industry has been shattered beyond recognition. A variety of market forces are driving this change. These include the rise of managed care, increasing consumerism and changing population demographics, new emerging information and biomedical technology, and a shifting regulatory and political environment.

## Managed Care

Managed care is rapidly dominating the healthcare financing and delivery system in the United States (Fox, 1996). In 1976, only about six million people received their care through health maintenance organizations (HMOs); by 1995, this number had increased to fifty-six million (American Association of Health Plans, 1995). This trend toward increased use of HMOs is expected to continue for the next couple of decades.

**Defining Managed Care.** The term managed care has been variously defined, but here we use it to refer to a type of organization or a set of procedures by which responsibility for financial risk for the healthcare of prepaid members is assumed. In this approach, member healthcare premiums are used to pay for the costs of providing healthcare. As a result, managed care includes the active management of both the *delivery system* through which care is provided *and* of the medical care itself that is delivered to patients (Abbey, 1996). Since health insurance premiums collected in this manner are prepaid, rather than having fees paid for services actually rendered, as in the traditional indemnity health insurance model, HMOs in theory can be expected to promote wellness, the early identification of disease, and the management of healthcare service utilization (Fox, 1996). Managed care techniques are used by the federal government-funded Medicare and Medicaid programs by establishing fixed schedules of reimbursement for healthcare services provided. Managed care organizations contract with hospitals and medical care professionals to provide healthcare services to their members according to set reimbursement structures and payment levels. As a result, managed care companies have had enormous influence on what types of care and treatments are provided. This contrasts sharply to the past practices in which health insurers paid physicians and hospitals for whatever nonexcluded services they delivered.

Managed care has also shifted the balance of power within the medical profession away from physician specialists to primary care physicians, who have become the gatekeepers of patient care (Kongstvedt, 1996). Managed care has pushed for increased consistency in medical care practice patterns, in order to eliminate unexplained and costly variations in the delivery of medical care. This threatens to reduce further physician and other medical care provider autonomy and control over patient care. Due to managed care's success in reducing some of the costs of medical care, its influence on the U.S. healthcare system can be expected to continue for years to come. However, this influence is beginning to be tempered by groups of consumers not shy about expressing, including through the legislative process, their displeasures with the restrictions placed on medical care by managed care companies. Such groups are demanding increased government intervention into and regulation of the healthcare system to combat what has been referred to as the corporatization of healthcare (Botelho, 1998). They have put increasing political pressure on their federal and state legislators to move more health-related decisions back to their doctors and away from some anonymous business manager or faceless bureaucrat.

**Consumerism in Medical Care.** The rise in healthcare consumerism is another environmental factor driving change in the U.S. healthcare system. More informed, empowered, and assertive consumers are taking greater control over their healthcare needs. The baby boomer generation is leading the way in taking control over its own healthcare and the spending of its healthcare dollars (Institute for the Future, 2000). As employers shift the cost burden of healthcare delivery more to them, employees are spending more time and money making their own healthcare decisions. The overall experience, not only the quality or price of care and service, is becoming one of the main factors considered in healthcare consuming decisions (Pine & Gilmore, 2001). This is pushing healthcare organizations to focus more on improvements in their service patterns and processes.

Some hospitals and clinics have been experimenting with *mass customization,* in which standardized modules of healthcare can be combined in different ways for different buyers (Pine & Gilmore, 2001). Patients and their families are not only being referred to as guests by some healthcare facilities, but also are being treated as such. In some cases, hospital rooms have been designed to look and feel more like home, and surgical care center waiting rooms offer an array of different entertainment options, from the traditional reading materials to video cassettes and stereophonic equipment. Patients in such settings are being exposed to fewer moves within the care setting itself.

**Use of the Internet.** The Internet has also provided an efficient means for consumers to educate themselves on medical research and treatments, and is a potent factor in the modern healthcare environment. More and more, consumers come to their healthcare providers armed with considerable medical information on assessment and treatment. Recognizing this appetite for information, the pharmaceutical industry has sponsored increasing amounts of direct-to-consumer advertising. There has also been a growing consumer interest in holistic and alternative medical therapies, including acupuncture, chiropractic services, biofeedback, and herbal remedies (Eisenberg, 1993). In some cases, health insurers have been pushed to providing coverage for these new treatment modalities and healthcare delivery systems. In England and Germany, it has been reported (Goldman & Dubow, 1996) that 25 percent of all healthcare practitioners are alternative therapists. This new consumerism in the healthcare market has been forcing healthcare organizations to become much more responsive to their customers' wants and needs, not only to reengineer patient care and service processes, but also to look for opportunities to reinvent them. More and more of my own healthcare consulting clients have been focusing attention on ways to improve their organization's customer relationships and customer service.

**Information Technology.** Advances in information technology and biomedical technology are also exerting enormous influence on the healthcare industry. The Internet, or more broadly, the array of emerging connective technologies, are altering the traditional doctor-patient relationship, which has historically been the cornerstone of healthcare. The growth of medical and health information websites offer mind-boggling amounts of information to consumers, turning medical research and treatment protocols into a near public commodity. An estimated one-third of the current ninety-two million-plus Internet users seek health-related information (Conte, 1999). Patients with similar medical conditions are now able to convene in chat rooms and other forms of on-line discussion forums, to discuss treatments they are receiving and provide medical care information to each other. In addition, this trend toward a connected health economy offers other innovations that will alter the financing and delivery of care. Electronic medical records, on-line patient scheduling and appointments, on-line receipt of test results, and tracking of health plan claims are already in the early stages of use. In the very near future, physicians will be able to peruse the latest medical journals, reference clinical protocols, and receive consults from other physicians across the country, or for that matter across the world, all at the touch of their computer, or a button on their wireless device. As more healthcare organization performance data becomes available on-line, consumers will be able to make more informed quality-of-care and cost decisions through comparison shopping of hospital and other provider cost, cure, and survival rates. This will increase dramatically the competitiveness of the healthcare marketplace.

**Impact of Innovation.** Biomedical innovations, from mechanical hearts to drugs that operate at the genetic level, are changing the face of medical treatment. Many medical procedures that once required hospitalization are now routinely performed on an outpatient basis, increasing the importance of ambulatory care in the mix of services offered.

Due to managed care's restrictions on the length of hospital stays, and the movement of many medical treatments to ambulatory care centers, the average U.S. hospital today loses money, and faces enormous challenges to discover new operating efficiencies without lessening the quality of care (Mango & Shapiro, 2001). From robots assisting in the operating room and filling prescriptions in the pharmacy, to the miniaturization of devices for diagnosing, treating, and monitoring medical conditions, technology is altering the very nature of medical care. Technological innovations like these will likely impact the healthcare provider labor force in coming years.

Fewer healthcare professionals will be needed to deliver a higher quality of care, and the skill sets required of these providers will change significantly (Goldman & Dubow, 1996). New technologies are emerging at such a rapid pace that many healthcare executives are overwhelmed by the array of choices, the capital investment required, and how quickly an accepted technology becomes outdated. They also face the challenge of integrating new technologies with their existing information systems. In addition, implementing new information and biomedical technologies requires broad-based business and clinical process redesigns to realize the anticipated benefits and value. The healthcare industry has not, compared to other industries, invested highly in information technology. This is predicted to change over the next decades as technology is increasingly integrated into healthcare delivery, especially concerning clinical information systems and business technologies (Coddington et al., 1996).

Technological advances in medical care have also increased life expectancy and the longevity of chronically ill patients. According to the 2000 U.S. census report (U.S. Bureau of the Census, 2000), the U.S. population is both aging and living longer. Elderly Americans are expected to increase from a little over 20 percent of the general population in 1990 to nearly 40 percent in 2050. By that year, the average life expectancy in the U.S. is expected to climb to eighty-two. Seniors and the chronically ill have the highest healthcare needs, and are the most costly to treat, adding financial pressures to the U.S. healthcare system (Saphir, 1999). As the first million baby boomers reach age sixty-five in the year 2011, a huge increase in the demand for healthcare-related services is expected. Seniors, especially baby boomers, not only want quality of care, but also comfort, convenience, and comprehensive one-stop shopping (Goldman & Dubow, 1996). This will push healthcare delivery organizations to search for new and innovative ways to organize their operations to meet this anticipated future increased demand and high levels of expectations for services.

## Legislative and Regulatory Factors

The healthcare industry also has had to respond to shifts in public policy, expressed through the enactment of new laws and regulations. Because healthcare represents a significant portion of the U.S. gross domestic product, and access to affordable, quality care is considered by many in the United States to be an inherent right, it is not surprising that healthcare issues shape the political agenda and generate enormous public policy debate (Abbey, 1996). During the last decade, for example, the number of Washington, D.C.-based healthcare-related lobbying groups, associations, and coalitions nearly tripled from the previous decade (National Health Council, 1993). Such groups, representing a diverse spectrum of political agendas and interests, are all trying to influence national healthcare policy. Legislation and regulatory actions tend to have cumulative and interfering effects on the industry. For example, the Balanced Budget Act of 1997, which reduced federal reimbursement for Medicare and Medicaid recipients, placed enormous financial pressures on hospital and health insurance organizations (Ferman, 2000). As a result, many acute care facilities were forced to find more effective ways to manage patient care processes, because the loss of revenue put them at greater financial risk. Some health insurance companies decided to exit the elder care products market entirely, rather than absorb this increased financial exposure.

Healthcare organizations are also regulated by a combination of different entities. For example, the Joint Commission on Accreditation of Healthcare Organizations (JCAHO) establishes and monitors performance standards of provider organizations, and its actions create enormous impact on these organizations. When the JCAHO expanded its accreditation criteria to include a continuous quality improvement (CQI) approach in the late 1980s and early 1990s, provider organizations were forced to grapple with quickly applying industrial quality management methods and tools to their operations (Berwick, Godfrey, & Roessner, 1990; Hertz, Reimann, & Bostwick, 1994). Most healthcare organizations have established internal compliance officers, and have dedicated staff to educate their managers about new regulatory requirements, interpret their operational implications, and oversee the implementation of new procedures and practices to comply with them. Shifting government legislation and the actions of regulatory agencies led one of my healthcare senior executive clients to liken healthcare management to the croquet game in *Alice in Wonderland,* in which the rules of the game keep shifting as the game is being played.

# THE HEALTHCARE INDUSTRY'S RESPONSE TO ITS NEW CONDITIONS

The various forces driving change within healthcare have produced an expanding movement toward integration and consolidation in the form of mergers, acquisitions, and other forms of strategic alliances and partnerships. Pressures to deliver high-quality, cost-effective healthcare have pushed hospitals, physician groups, and insurance companies to try to gain more direct control over both the pricing and delivery of healthcare through integration (Judge & Reyman, 2001). Integrated healthcare systems combine physicians, hospitals, and other medical services with health plans to provide the complete spectrum of medical care for customers (Coddington et al., 1996). According to Coddington et al. (1996), hospitals and medical practices are merging in record numbers. Hospitals are either purchasing or aligning themselves with primary care physician practices. Health plans are purchasing or forming exclusive contractual arrangements with physician practice groups, and in some instances purchasing hospitals. Some hospitals are establishing their own healthcare plans, or looking to acquire existing health plans. At the same time, hospitals and health plans are forming new risk-sharing and other types of joint-venture relationships (Kongstvedt & Plocher, 1996).

The reasons for all this integration and consolidation activity include: (1) an attempt to obtain a stronger, less-vulnerable market position; (2) increased access to capital; (3) risk sharing; and (4) improved operating efficiencies and improved quality of care through better coordination and sharing of successful practices (Coddington et al., 1996; Labb, 1999; Judge & Reyman, 2001). In addition, the prospect of impending reform of the American healthcare system, whether through increased government regulation or marketplace-driven reform, has added to this drive for increased alignment among the various entities comprising the industry (Kongstvedt & Plocher, 1996). The result is a blurring, and in some cases, a disintegration of the traditional boundaries among the different types of healthcare organizational entities, and the creation of new organizational forms.

## Forms of Integrated Health Systems

Typically, integrated health systems fall into one of three broad categories (Kongstvedt & Plocher, 1996): IPAs, partnerships, and managed care organizations. Each will briefly be discussed in this section.

**IPAs.** Independent practice association's (IPAs) are legal entities comprised only of independently practicing physicians who unite for the sole purpose of collectively contracting with one or more health plans to deliver medical services. The IPA and its member physicians are often at risk for some portion of medical costs, so the group is paid a fixed per patient payment (often referred to as a *capitation rate*), regardless of the actual costs of providing the defined services. A variation of this is the group practice without walls (GPWW), which is composed of private practice physicians who agree to aggregate their practices into a single legal entity, but with the physicians continuing to practice in their own independent locations. Physician practice management organizations (PPMs) are organizations that provide a variety of management for care delivery support functions (for example, billing and collections, contract negotiation and administration, information technology services, and so on), but remain relatively uninvolved with the clinical aspects of the physician practice. In many cases, physicians and small physician groups might remain virtually independent practitioners.

**Partnerships.** A second form of integration consists of partnerships between physicians and hospitals, or plans that otherwise integrate these two groups. The physician-hospital organization (PHO) is an entity by which a hospital and its admitting physician groups can negotiate, together with third-party payers. PHOs actively manage the relationship between medical staff, hospitals, and managed care companies, who supply their members as patients. PHOs are often considered the first step on the evolutionary ladder toward vertical integration with regard to hospitals and physicians, because, though they increase integration, they tend still to preserve the independence and autonomy of physicians.

Another integration form is the foundation model in which a hospital creates a not-for-profit foundation, and actually purchases physician practices and places those practices into the foundation. The foundation is governed by its own board, which is independent from the hospital's board or any physician group's board. While the foundation owns and manages the medical practices, the physicians as a group have an exclusive contract for services with the foundation. This makes the foundation the only source of revenue for the physicians.

**Managed Care Organizations.** A third form of integration relates to the different forms of managed care companies. One is the health maintenance organization (HMO) (Boland, 1993; Wagner, 1996). This type of organization is, in effect, a healthcare system responsible both for the financing and provision of a broad range of health services to an enrolled population of members. It is both a health insurer and a healthcare delivery system.

HMOs can either contract with a select group of medical care providers who receive reimbursement for services they provide to enrolled members, or might employ physicians who serve the health plan's members. The former is often referred to as a preferred provider organization (PPO), and the latter a staff model (Kongstvedt & Plocher, 1996). A variation is the group model, in which an HMO contracts with a multispecialty physician group to provide all physician services to the HMO's members. Managed care issues in the mental health area present special challenges (see, for example, Lowman & Resnick, 1994).

**Multihospital Systems.** In addition to these different forms of integration, large multihospital systems are continuing to merge and acquire each other, although the pace of such combinations has slowed somewhat over the last couple of years (Lando, 2000). Large multihospital systems, which for many years operated in a highly decentralized federation-type model in which local management control over operations was allowed, are now consolidating and integrating their services to realize greater economies of scale. Typically, these new hospital systems will concentrate acute care services in one location, establish centers of excellence at a small number of locations, and offer a range of services at many locations, if the local market demands them (Coddington et al., 1996).

In addition, many of these hospital systems are experimenting with new types of operating models. For example, certain operational support services, such as human resources, supply chain management, information technology services, and patient financial services, might be consolidated under a single management structure, sometimes referred to as shared services (Schulman, Dunleavy, Harmer, & Lusk, 1999), funded through budgetary allocations from each of the hospitals. This organizational unit provides these shared services to all hospitals, and other services, such as marketing, physician recruitment, and facilities management, remain under the control of local hospital management. Many of these newly formed integrated healthcare systems are also considering outsourcing some of their nonclinical functions, such as information technology, finance, housekeeping, and even laboratory services, in order to concentrate more on their core clinical services and the delivery of healthcare (Chyna, 2000a).

All of this integration and consolidation activity by healthcare organizations offers considerable opportunities for organizational consulting psychologists. Such services can include helping determine the most appropriate and effective organizational design and management structure for these new organizational forms, as well as helping to facilitate the organizational change process associated with the new design's implementation. Key interventions might include role analysis and negotiation (Harrison, 1972), responsibility charting (Dayal & Thomas, 1968), and team development (Dyer, 1977) for the new cross-entity leadership teams. Before examining in more detail opportunities for organizational consulting psychologists in the healthcare industry, it is important to gain an understanding of the unique attributes of typical healthcare organizations.

# HEALTHCARE ORGANIZATIONAL CULTURES

Organizational culture theorists acknowledge that the business environment or industry within which an organization exists can exert significant influence on the development of its culture (Deal & Kennedy, 1982; Collins & Porras, 1994; Schein, 1992). Although numerous definitions of organizational culture abound, it is commonly understood to be the underlying assumptions, shared beliefs, values, and general worldview that influence a group's behavior and actions (Ott, 1989; Schein, 1992). Organizational culture is the deep structure of organizations rooted in the values, beliefs, and assumptions held by their members (Dennison, 1996). Since the healthcare industry is so heterogeneous, the cultures of the various organizational entities comprising it are also quite diverse. For example, the cultures of for-profit organizations (Brock, 2002) are typically different from those of not-for-profit organizations, in that for-profits tend to have a more results orientation and bottom-line mentality than the not-for-profits, who tend to be more mission focused, more political in their decision-making, and tend to operate with a lesser sense of urgency. However, there are also differences within the non-profit environment. Even the cultures of two Catholic not-for-profit hospital systems can be remarkably different depending on the origins and heritage of their religious sponsoring community and the organization's history of adapting to emergent environmental challenges (Levin, Felice, Proctor, & Thibault, 2000). The culture of academic health centers is based on a system that places the physician as its main focus. The hospital is the physicians' workshop, the medical school is the physicians' classroom, and the various specialty departments often operate in the manner of separate fiefdoms (Solit & Nash, 1996).

There are also cultural differences between physicians, insurers, and hospital management (Labb, 1999). These different professional groups comprise what can be considered organizational subcultures (Martin & Siehl, 1983). Physicians tend to be scientists first and foremost (see, for example, Lowman, 1991). They highly value their autonomy, and hold themselves accountable primarily to their professional community and their patients. The value of autonomy is at the heart of physicians' overall sense of professionalism (Hall, 1968), and is a key component driving overall job satisfaction in their work (Hadley & Mitchell, 1997). Hoff and Mandel (2001) found that only 36 percent of physician executives in managed care organizations expressed a dual commitment to their profession and the organization within which they worked; the majority expressed commitment only to their profession. Health insurers' orientation is to the business of healthcare, and their expertise is in financial analysis and planning, actuarial forecasting, claims processes, and marketing. Their focus, particularly when they are a publicly traded enterprise, is achieving financial goals. Hospital management's expertise centers on management and operations, and many hospitals contain a strong community service orientation. For them, business performance includes managing an array of financial, clinical, community, and employee goals and issues. Hospital executives are continually challenged to bridge the business and clinical worlds.

Despite these internal differences among significant groups in medical institutions, the cultures of healthcare organizations have much in common. Healthcare organizational cultures tend first and foremost to be humanistic, high-touch, and highly affiliation-oriented. The core business of healthcare organizations is helping people, and this mission is often what attracts people to the healthcare professions. A client of mine, for example, once referred to his decision to work in healthcare as having been a calling. Also found in many healthcare organizations is reverence for specialized expertise. Advanced degrees, licenses, and certifications commonly adorn business cards and offices. Generally, there is a high regard in healthcare organizations for developing and maintaining collegial relationships; direct conflict and confrontation are often avoided. This is especially true in relationships between hospital and health plan executives and their medical staff. Generally, healthcare business executives are very careful not to alienate their medical staff for fear they will choose to practice elsewhere.

Nonphysician executives and managers in this type of organization often have little formal authority over physicians, even in organizations in which physicians are employees. In one large HMO, for example, there was an explicit rule that physicians were never allowed to report to nonphysicians. This produced some very unusual organizational structures and often confusing lines of authority. Even the hospital's chief medical officer, one of the most senior executive roles in this organization, had minimal formal authority over that hospital's physicians. As a result, informal influence and selling of ideas, rather than formal authority, is often the predominant method of getting others to act in accordance with organizational goals and imperatives. Consensus building and the surety of touching all the bases are important prerequisites for decision-making.

## Case Example

An example from a large multifacility hospital is illustrative. The corporate office executive management team in this hospital was under enormous pressure from its board to reduce operating costs in light of declining Medicare reimbursement. Medical supplies became a focal point for reducing costs. An assessment had uncovered that the different hospitals in the system were maintaining a large number of different supplier contracts for the same types of supplies. A task force comprised of supply managers and physicians from each of the different hospitals in the system was formed to examine the issue and make recommendations. After six months of research and analysis, the task force recommended negotiating new bulk purchasing contracts with a small number of different vendors. This approach was estimated to result in savings of nearly two million dollars. Management approved the task force's recommendations, and their implementation began. However, after six months, only a fraction of the cost savings had been realized. It was discovered that large numbers of hospitals were still buying from their old vendors at the request of their medical staffs. Clearly, physician behavior had not been changed as a result of the executive management's edict.

I was engaged as a consultant by executive management to help them address this problem. After reconvening the task force, we developed an extensive educational campaign directed at the medical staff. Small teams of physician task force members first held meetings with formal physician leaders at each of the hospitals, and then conducted town-hall-type meetings with the medical staff. During these meetings, the task force's work was reviewed and the rationale for their recommendations was explained in great detail, including how the quality of supplies, and not simply cost, was used as the selection criteria. While 100 percent physician compliance was never achieved, the hospital system was able to realize close to a 60 percent reduction in costs associated with this one medical supply item within one year. This illustrates how healthcare organizations function more by persuasion and influence, rather than by command and control. A former client executive characterized this way of getting things done as *guided autonomy*, in which parameters are established for what needs to get done, but groups are left considerable leeway for how to get it done.

Healthcare organizational cultures are also very reactive and tend to flourish on crises. It is quite common for hospital organizations to mobilize quite late to prepare themselves for a JCHAO accreditation survey visit, and to proudly recount how they prepared themselves in such a short time. Problems and issues in such approaches are addressed in the here-and-now with little long-term perspective. The daily work life of most healthcare executives is filled with a seemingly endless stream of emergent management demands. This cultural characteristic may be an artifact traced to the medical profession's subculture, in which physicians and nurses are trained and socialized to attend to detail, to diagnose quickly, and to respond rapidly and effectively to healthcare emergencies. As a result of these cultural factors, long-range planning in many healthcare organizations is not a highly valued organizational competency, and therefore, business plans tend to be very tactical and operational in nature.

Meetings are commonly packed tight with agenda items and highly task-oriented. Little, if any, time is available for substantive examination or debate of issues, or for reflection and learning. Again, action and doing are the primary focus. As a healthcare consultant, for example, I often have had to settle for as little as fifteen minutes per topic with executive management groups to introduce and discuss a complex problem. Considerable attention is needed in such contexts to plan crisply effective ways to approach agenda items, including sending out materials in advance for review. Often, these pre-meeting materials need to include questions that focus the review on a few critically important issues or questions that will be discussed in the meeting. Consultants in such contexts need to accept that smaller segments of work and more bounded decisions are the likely reality in their work with such client groups. More strategic issues, such as managing a change process or facilitating an executive team's development, need to be addressed at off-site sessions planned specifically for that purpose.

A key consequence of the strong humanistic and relationship orientation of healthcare organizational cultures, in combination with the need to use influence rather than control to get things done, is that most decision-making processes in healthcare organizations tend to be consensus driven, and the preferred healthcare managerial styles, highly participative. Physicians' high regard and respect for autonomy, independence, and control over their medical practice make most physician organizations more akin to Grecian democracies than a traditional for-profit organization. It is not uncommon for only a single physician to stall or block the implementation of a new policy or procedure, even if it is administrative in nature. Implementing any type of change in such settings therefore first takes time to build consensus among what may be different goals, competing interests, and agendas of the various constituencies. In my experience, top-down approaches to change in such contexts rarely work.

Healthcare organizations tend to be rather risk averse and conservative. This cultural trait also appears linked to the professional, subcultural roots of medical training and socialization processes. Physicians and other clinical care providers are socialized to apply the scientific method to problem solving, and to explore as many options as possible before acting. This approach is analogous to the methods used by physicians in medical practice, in which data collection and analysis (for example, diagnostic tests) usually precede action (for example, treatment).

This cultural tendency tends to exhibit itself in healthcare organizational cultures in what has colloquially been termed *analysis paralysis,* and by the persistent desire to pilot innovations before deciding on a broader-based implementation. On its surface, this cautiousness seems paradoxical to the cultural qualities of reactiveness and crisis orientation discussed earlier, but organizational cultures are rich and complex, and often consist of seemingly contradictory qualities (Levin, Felice et al., 2000; Martin, 1992).

# CONSULTING OPPORTUNITIES AND CHALLENGES

The movement toward increased mergers, consolidation, integration, and partnerships within the healthcare industry clearly offers a wide variety of consulting opportunities for organizational consulting psychologists. Shortell (1988) reported that the primary reason many of the integration efforts and strategic alliances failed was that they did not achieve a sense of *systemness,* or commonality across the combined institution. In such settings, the former entities were unable to create a singular vision or cohesiveness to operate as a more efficient entity. In addition to organizational design issues, the newly integrated or affiliated entities need to develop a shared vision, values, and goals (Collins & Porras, 1994; Marks & Mirvis, 1998). Coddington et al. (1996) found that hospital administrators, health plan executives, and physician leaders all recognized the importance of building a new culture that fosters cohesiveness and shared commitment. Following the formation of a new integrated health system, an important way of beginning this shared culture building is to develop a shared mission, vision, and preferred culture for the new health system. Establishing shared strategic goals, designing new operating models, and reaching agreement on how the success of the new organization will be measured (see, for example, Levin, Proctor, & Thibault, 2001) all can contribute to a united vision of the newly combined enterprise.

## Large Group Interventions

One approach that has proved successful in medical settings is the use of a series of large group interventions (Bunker & Alban, 1997). This approach can be effective in facilitating the discovery of common ground among diverse constituencies, and in leveraging the strong humanistic and relationship orientation of healthcare organizational cultures. It is also consistent with a highly consensus-driven and participative style of managing. Such interventions typically include multiday working sessions conducted off-site with cross-sectional representation of key stakeholder groups from across the full organizational system. These representatives are brought together to plan change and prioritize actions.

Although there are a variety of different approaches and models of large group interventions (Jacobs, 1994; Weisbord & Janoff, 1995; Emery & Purser, 1996), they share some basic premises. One is that people will support what they help create. Providing members from the different constituencies within healthcare organizations meaningful opportunities to influence and shape what will impact them helps to build their commitment to it.

Related to this premise is the notion that implementation of change will be more effective if there is no split between the designers of change and the implementers of change. Second, it is assumed that the synthesis of diverse perspectives on issues will produce higher-quality and more innovative solutions to issues impacting the organization.

In my own work with healthcare organizations, I have used several variations of this type of intervention, often involving more than 200 stakeholders, including board members, executives, managers, clinicians, and community members. The range of purposes have included creating alignment around a future vision and goals, developing new business strategies, constructing an agenda for change, redesigning the organization, and recreating a variety of different business, administrative, and patient care processes. Of course, in large organizations, this large group is still only a representative one. Such sessions still need to plan a process for taking the work produced to the different organizational constituencies for further review, input, and refinement (Levin, 2000).

## Key Success Factors in Large Group Work Sessions

There are a variety of key success factors for conducting large group work sessions in healthcare organizations.

**Commitment to Honor Outcomes.** First, it is important to gain the commitment of the executive leadership in order to honor the outcomes produced. They need to understand that through this type of process they will have as much influence on outcomes achieved as other participants, but no more. If senior leadership does not value this type of participation or is uncomfortable with it, then this type of intervention is inappropriate. If some decisions already have been made and are not open to discussion or revision, these facts need to be conveyed to participants at the beginning of the experience so that their expectations can be managed effectively. I therefore sometimes begin these large group sessions by reviewing the *givens,* those things that are already decided and beyond the scope of the work together.

**Having the Relevant Decision-Makers Present.** A second success factor is ensuring that key decision-makers are in the room. Key leadership needs to participate actively in the session; otherwise, the experience actually can become a disempowering one for those who do participate. A few years ago, for example, when conducting a redesign session with a large hospital organization, several top executives left during the afternoon of the first day to address a crisis back home. A majority of them did not return until just before the session concluded. Their absence was viewed by participants as a sign of their lack of commitment to the process, and seriously undermined the credibility of the redesign efforts.

**Clearly Defined Purpose and Expected Outcomes.** Third, the large group session needs to have clearly defined purposes and specific outcomes that are expected to be achieved. Process-related outcomes such as building trust and cooperation, although important, are not tangible enough outcomes for these types of action-oriented cultures to warrant the investment in resources, time, and energy of busy and expensive healthcare professionals. Concrete outcomes can include creating a shared vision for the future, establishing goals that will serve as milestones in realizing that vision, or redesigning the patient care process and developing an implementation plan. It is also advisable to create for the session a single theme that summarizes the session's focus. Examples of such themes include: reinventing our organization together, or building a foundation for future success.

**Selecting the Right People.** Fourth, it is critical to select the right people to participate in such interventions. I generally use four major criteria for choosing participants. These center on selecting participants who: (1) can contribute substantively to achieving the defined purpose; (2) are expected to implement the outputs of the session; (3) will be directly impacted by the changes created; and (4) have informal influence within their respective constituencies, and can be employed as change agents.

**Structuring Productive Conversations.** A fifth success factor is to assure that the session is designed in such a way as to structure and promote productive conversations among the participants. In such contexts, diverse perspectives will be voiced, genuinely considered, and constructively challenged, critiqued, and reconciled. Creative combinations of small and large group structured activities are used to facilitate such conversations. In addition, the design has to promote creativity and the perception of new possibilities.

I and others (see, for example, Bunker & Alban, 1997) have found that it is important to build into the design semistructured time for reflection and pondering the information and ideas generated at such meetings. Although there is always pressure in healthcare organizations to move quickly, it is important to allow sufficient soak time for people to think about issues discussed and ideas being considered. This can be as simple as assigning overnight thought homework, or separating working days by a period of time that allows participants to digest what has taken place thus far. There is research that supports the idea that breakthrough ideas often come when people work very hard for a while and then take a break to allow their minds creatively to synthesize the components (Bunker & Alban, 1997).

One design approach I have effectively used in organizational consulting is to have a small client work group develop prior to the conduct of the session a *straw model* of whatever needs to get done in the session. This model might be a draft vision, statement of values, preferred culture profile, or draft operating model redesign. Then, when the larger group is convened, it can react to, critique, refine, and build upon this straw model. This approach has been well received by healthcare executives, because it tends to accelerate the process and help assure that a concrete product will be produced. The approach is also very congruent with the healthcare organizational cultural characteristics of being reactive action-oriented and preferring analytical approaches to problem solving, as discussed earlier.

**Focus on the Future.** A sixth success factor is to focus these collective intense working efforts on the future, rather than rehashing past or current problems and issues. Seligman and Csikszentmihalyi (2000) suggested that this more positive psychological approach to facilitating change tends to generate energy and momentum because it is based on potential, hope, and desire. Cooperrider and Srivastva (1987), as well as Lippitt (1998), have also proposed that an unencumbered exploration of possibilities leads to imaginative and innovative solutions, and increased energy to see those solutions through. Finally, it is critically important to manage the logistical details associated with conducting one of these large group events. Such logistics include being sure that pre-work materials get out to all participants, that the space to be used is compatible with the requirements of the session design, that meals and refreshments arrive on time, that instructions and materials for activities are accessible when needed, and that the room's audio system is effective enough to ensure all participants can hear each other.

**Contingency Planning.** Comprehensive contingency planning is also necessary. This can include simple matters, as, for example, making certain that there are back-up bulbs for presentation projectors and handouts in case of electrical power outages. Of course, not all contingencies can be planned for. A session I held several years ago abruptly and prematurely ended when a major thunderstorm outside caused the ceiling to leak excessively. When logistical matters are planned and managed properly, no one notices, but when they have not been, they can create serious distractions from the work.

These types of large group sessions hold considerable promise for helping newly integrated healthcare organizations build shared identity, goals, and commitment to the new enterprise. Formal research is important to evaluate the effectiveness of such programs. This should go beyond simple post-session evaluations that are typically used to assess whether identified objectives were achieved. Feedback on participants' perceived usefulness of the session and the extent to which goals were actually achieved should be obtained. Such research can also usefully focus on the sustainability of changes initiated during the session and the achievement of longer-range objectives. In addition, such research might help the consultant understand the specific design features that did and did not contribute significantly to a successful outcome.

# OTHER CONSULTING OPPORTUNITIES

Another opportunity area for organizational consulting psychologists involves the redesign of organizational incentive programs in healthcare contexts. Incentives need to be aligned toward achieving goals that are in the best interests of the new system or entity, so that risk is shared, as well as rewards (Kongstvedt, 1996; Nebeker & Tatum, 2002). These incentives need to be designed in ways that balance cost and quality of care. For example, the traditional fee-for-service models of care rewarded overutilization of services, and fostered an adversarial relationship between payers and providers (Coddington et al., 1996). There simply was not much economic incentive to see more patients. On the other hand, capitation or previously-agreed-upon per member per month (PMPM) rates encourage limitation of care, and do nothing to encourage management of care (Cook & Edsall, 1994). Integrated systems that employ salaried physicians often report that physician productivity declines when income is no longer tied to how hard they work (Collins & Buntz, 1995).

Coddington et al. (1996), for example, described a reimbursement arrangement that a newly affiliated health plan and hospital kept in place after their coming together. In this arrangement, physicians were incentivized to discharge patients from the hospital as quickly as possible. When this led to earlier discharges, the health plan realized all the savings because their medical costs were being reduced. Although the physicians on this plan had an incentive to minimize admissions and length of stay, they had no incentive to limit the use of resources once the patient was admitted, and were found to be driving up expenses through the use of expensive medical tests and supplies. The solution involved moving to a gainsharing arrangement based on a target cost per discharge, and adjusted for the severity of the cases. If the average cost per discharge exceeded the target, the health plan and hospital jointly absorbed the shortfall. If the cost per discharge was below the target, both entities shared in the gain.

A large HMO's efforts provide another example of aligning incentives with desired outcomes. The HMO implemented a performance development program for its physicians that was tied to the achievement of specific, concretely defined goals. The overall compensation structure included a large bonus component tied to both the organization's overall performance and the provider's individual performance. Organizational performance measures that were used included both financial targets, for example, operating margins, and population-relevant quality-of-care outcomes, for example, vaccination rates, neonatal care outcomes, and rates of preventive care procedures. Individual physician performance goals in this example included utilization management, the degree of compliance with utilization of an agreed-upon generic drug formulary, peer satisfaction, and patient satisfaction measures.

HMO patient satisfaction was measured with a brief survey tool that was administered to patients immediately after each HMO visit. It focused primarily on satisfaction with the overall experience of care, including waiting time, and how well the physician listened to the patient's concerns and explained the medical actions taken. The patient satisfaction feedback process also encouraged physicians to work with the nurses, medical assistants, and receptionists to ensure that the overall patient experience was positive. They had an incentive to do so since their bonuses now depended on its success.

Designing this system required several months to educate physicians regarding the drivers of organizational performance and participation in performance goal-setting activities. A weakness of this program, identified after implementation, was the program's primary focus on the physician. Other members of the provider team also significantly affected patient satisfaction. Eventually, this problem was addressed by designing a patient care team-based component to the bonus plan that included the nursing staff and medical assistants. This seemingly minor adjustment in the program proved to be rather complex to implement because the nonphysician providers' pay structures were governed by existing collective bargaining agreements. Including them in the incentive plan took months of negotiations with the labor unions.

## The Client Contract Process in Healthcare Organizations

In all organizational consulting, the client contracting process is considered integral to the success of the consulting relationship (Block, 1981; Nielsen, 1984). Contracting is commonly understood to be the process of reaching formal agreement between the consultant and client about the scope and nature of work to be performed, the desired outcomes to be produced, the approach and methods to be used, the timing of the work, fee arrangements, and respective roles and expectations. Weisbord (1973) defined contracting as consisting of a shared understanding of mutual expectations, written and verbal, which describes what each presumes from the working relationship, how much time each will invest when and at what cost, and the ground rules under which both parties will operate.

**Client Definition Issues.** Contracting with organizational clients is often a continual and repetitive process. The consulting literature (see, for example, Engdahl, 1995; French & Bell, 1978) identifies a key issue during this phase of the consulting process to be determining who is the client. The client usually includes one or more individuals in the prospective client system who have the power to authorize the consulting engagement, make decisions that facilitate the implementation of changes emanating from the engagement, and make resources available to support the consulting work.

In organizational consulting, determining who is the client is not always a straightforward or simple task (Robinson-Kurpius, Newman, & Fuqua, 2002). In healthcare organizations, particularly those that have moved toward increased integration or are engaged in strategic partnerships, considerable diffusion of authority has often occurred. Competing goals and interests among the diverse constituencies comprising an organization often follow from that. It is not always obvious in such contexts who can truly authorize a potential consulting project. Due to the high levels of interdependence among the different entities and business areas within healthcare organizations, very few consulting engagements will have impact only within the scope of authority of a single entity or specific business area. Even if the work appears to be confined within a specific business domain under the leadership of an identified executive, it is likely that the impact of changes produced will require some level of commitment and support from other organizational areas.

Jamieson (1995) identified four types of organizational members with whom a consultant might need to contract. These included: (1) *direct clients,* with whom the consultant works most closely; (2) *sponsors* of the consulting work, whose visible leadership and active support is required, but who typically are not involved in the actual work of the engagement; (3) *key players* in the organization's power system, whose commitment and support is needed for effective change to occur (these are often formal and informal leaders who can either help make things happen or prevent them from happening); and (4) other organizational members who might be involved with the later stages of the work, or are required to operate under the changed conditions. Due to the interrelated, multiple constituencies and the diffuse lines of authority across them, it is extremely important for the consultant working with healthcare organizations to determine the key organizational members whose input and agreement is needed before any contracting is complete and the engagement actually gets underway.

**Case Example.** Some years ago I was contacted by an executive vice president and chief operating officer (COO) of a large hospital system, and asked to assist him in redesigning his organization's patient care processes. He wanted to strengthen the integration of operations across the institution's entire continuum of care. I naively assumed that, due to his senior level in the organization, he would be my client, and that my contracting primarily would be with him. Less than a month into the effort, however, I learned that many of the improvements he wanted to see implemented required changed behavior among a diverse group of clinical staff. Although most inpatient services (for example, hospital nursing and other ancillary patient care services, such as housekeeping, social work, and patient discharge planning and home health) reported to him, others (for example, medical staff, outpatient nursing, health education, skilled nursing facilities, and laboratory services) did not.

In fact, my client had no formal authority over any of the areas outside of the immediate hospital organization. These other areas reported to the medical staff leadership, and in the case of the skilled nursing facilities, to an alliance partner that was a completely separate organization with their own independent management structure. Hospital nursing, though formally accountable to the COO, was influenced informally by their relationships with the physicians. After a few instances in which physicians and managers from the alliance partner organization did not show up for scheduled work sessions, and my requests for organizational performance information were not responded to, I realized the error. I then needed to initiate a whole new entry and contracting process with the leadership of the medical staff and the alliance partner organization, with the sponsorship of the COO.

Working effectively with healthcare organizations will often require multiple contracting meetings with leaders representing the various organizational constituencies. The consultant's goals during this collective contracting process is to build an understanding of the scope and nature of the work to be performed by integrating and synthesizing perspectives, and to obtain a broad-based commitment for the proposed work. After first meeting one-on-one with the key team players, I have often brought them together to ensure that there is shared understanding, agreement, and commitment. An added benefit of multiple contracting is being able to engage each client as an active sponsor within their respective constituencies for building broader stakeholder commitment.

## SUMMARY AND CONCLUSION

Virtually all healthcare organizations, in both the public and private sectors, are grappling with massive and radical change. They are experimenting with new organizational arrangements and operating models to help them adapt to and manage this onslaught of change. Leading and facilitating change effectively will be essential to healthcare organizations' ability to survive and prosper in the future. However, doing so in a situation in which professional autonomy is valued, consensus is required, and roles and accountabilities are often ambiguous, makes it a daunting challenge. Healthcare organizations of the future need to develop and nurture a stronger enterprise-wide perspective, reflective of their newly formed integration, alliances, and partnerships. They will need to establish a broad-based commitment to enterprise-wide goals and interests, which take precedence over prior allegiance to the interests of the former entities and different constituencies that comprise the enterprise. Meaningful opportunities for equal participation in the rewards and risks of working toward common goals need to be established. As Judge and Reyman (2001) noted, carefully constructed legal contracts are not sufficient to guarantee success in healthcare organizational alliances or other forms of integration. What is also required is disciplined attention to leadership, governance, and organizational issues, and the application of appropriately designed behaviorally based solutions to enable integration or alliance success.

I argue that organizational consulting psychologists are uniquely qualified to provide assistance in these areas. However, it is imperative that consultants choosing to work in this industry stay current on the various trends and issues occupying executives' attention, and stay attuned to the cultural idiosyncracies of the organizations that comprise the industry. This work also demands flexibility and a genuine openness for discovering how to work most effectively with a particular organization. It is wise for the consultant not to be too attached to personally preferred solutions or those that have worked in the past. Above all, it is important to remember that many of those who work in healthcare view their work as being as much a social mission as a business.

Consulting with healthcare organizations can be very rewarding for those who learn to navigate the complexities inherent within and among organizations in this industry. After all, there are few other industries that provide so essential a set of products and services, and the work of which has such a profound impact on the well-being of our society.

# References

Abbey, F. (1996). Managed care and health care reform: Evolution or revolution? In P. Kongstvedt (Ed.), *The managed health care handbook* (pp. 16–29). Gaithersburg, MD: Aspen.

American Association of Health Plans. (1995). *Patterns in HMO enrollment.* Washington, DC: Author.

Berwick, D., Godfrey, A. B., & Roessner, J. (1990). *Curing health care: New strategies for quality improvement.* San Francisco: Jossey-Bass

Block, P. (1981). *Flawless consulting: A guide to getting your expertise used.* San Diego, CA: Pfeiffer.

Boland, P. (1993). *Making managed care health care work: A practical guide to strategies and solutions.* Gaithersburg, MD: Aspen.

Botelho, R. J. (1998). Negotiating partnerships in healthcare: Contexts and methods. In A. L. Suchman, R. J. Botelho, & P. Hinton-Walker (Eds.), *Partnerships in healthcare: Transforming relational process* (pp. 19–49). Rochester, NY: University of Rochester Press.

Brock, C. L. (2002). Consulting to for-profit organizations. In R. L. Lowman (Ed.), *Handbook of organizational consulting psychology* (pp. 469–492). San Francisco: Jossey-Bass.

Bunker, B. B., & Alban, B. T. (1997). *Large group interventions: Engaging the whole system for rapid change.* San Francisco: Jossey-Bass.

Chyna, J. T. (2000a). From alliances to outsourcing: Making good connections. *Healthcare Executive, 15*(3), 12–17.

Chyna, J. T. (2000b). Physician-health system partnerships: Strategies for finding common ground. *Healthcare Executive, 15*(2), 12–17.

Coddington, D. C., Moore, R. D., & Fischer, E. A. (1996). *Making integrated health care work.* Englewood, CO: Center for Research and Ambulatory Healthcare Administration.

Cohen, M. D., & March, J. G. (1974). *Leadership and ambiguity.* New York: McGraw-Hill.

Collins, H., & Buntz, D. (1995). Effective income distribution for employed physicians. *Healthcare Financial Management, 6,* 27–28.

Collins, J. C., & Porras, J. I. (1994). *Built to last: Successful habits of visionary companies.* New York: HarperCollins.

Conte, C. (1999). *Networking for better care: Health care in the information age.* Washington, DC: Benton Foundation.

Cook, J. V., & Edsall, R. L. (1994). Family physicians should be paid for managing. *Family Practice Management, 2*(1), 4–38.

Cooperrider, D. L., & Srivastva, S. (1987). Appreciative inquiry in organizational life. In W. Pasmore & R. Woodman (Eds.), *Research in organization change and development* (Vol. 1, pp. 129–169). Greenwich, CT: JAI Press.

Dayal, I., & Thomas, J. (1968). Operation KPE: Developing a new organization. *Journal of Applied Behavioral Science, 4,* 473–506.

Deal, T. E., & Kennedy, A. A. (1982). *Corporate cultures: The rites and rituals of corporate life.* Reading, MA: Addison-Wesley.

Dennison, D. R. (1996). What is the difference between organizational culture and organizational climate? A native's point of view on a decade of paradigm wars. *Academy of Management Review, 21*(3), 619–654.

Dyer, W. G. (1977). *Team building: Issues and alternatives.* Reading, MA: Addison-Wesley.

Eisenberg, P. (1993). Unconventional medicine in the U.S: Prevalence, cost, and patterns of use. *New England Journal of Medicine, 328*(4), 246.

Emery M., & Purser, R. E. (1996). *The search conference: Theory and practice.* San Francisco: Jossey-Bass.

Engdahl, R. A. (1995). Entry. In W. J. Rothwell, R. Sullivan, & G. N. McLean (Eds.), *Practicing organization development: A guide for consultants* (pp. 75–103). San Diego, CA: Pfeiffer.

Ferman, J. (2000). Healthcare agenda for the 106th Congress. *Healthcare Executive, 15*(3), 62.

Fooks, C. (1999). Will power, cost control, and health reform in Canada. In F. Powell & A. Wesson (Eds.), *Health care systems in transition: An international perspective* (pp. 151–172). Thousand Oaks, CA: Sage.

Fox, P. D. (1996). An overview of managed care. In P. Kongstvedt (Ed.), *The managed health care handbook* (pp. 3–15). Gaithersburg, MD: Aspen.

French, W. L., & Bell, C. H. (1978). *Organization development* (2nd ed.). Englewood Cliffs, NJ: Prentice Hall.

Goldman, E., & Dubow, M. (1996). *Future health: New dimensions in strategic thought: 20/20 foresight: 21st century health care delivery systems.* Washington, DC: Ernst & Young.

Hadley, J., & Mitchell, R. (1997). Effects of HMO market penetration on physicians' work effort and satisfaction. *Health Affairs, 16*(6), 99–111.

Hall, R. H. (1968). Professionalization and bureaucratization. *American Sociological Review, 33,* 92–104.

Harrison, R. (1972). Role negotiation: A tough minded approach to team development. In W. W. Burke & H. A. Hornstein (Eds.), *The social technology of organization development* (pp. 84–96). Fairfax, VA: NTL Learning Resources Group.

Hertz, H. S., Reimann, C. W., & Bostwick, M. C. (1994). The Malcolm Baldridge national quality award concept: Could it help stimulate or accelerate health care quality improvement? *Quality Management in Health Care, 2*(4), 63–72.

Hoff, T. J., & Mandell, J. (2001). Exploring dual commitment among physician executives in managed care/practitioner application. *Journal of Healthcare Management, 46*(2), 4–21.

Institute for the Future. (2000). *Health and healthcare 2010: The forecast, the challenge.* San Francisco: Jossey-Bass.

Jacobs, R. (1994). *Real time strategic change.* San Francisco: Berrett-Koehler.

Jamieson, D. (1995). Start-up. In W. J. Rothwell, R. Sullivan, & G. N. McLean (Eds.), *Practicing organization development: A guide for consultants* (pp. 105–137). San Diego, CA: Pfeiffer.

Judge, W. Q., & Reyman, J. A. (2001). The shared leadership challenge in strategic alliances: Lessons from the U.S. healthcare industry. *The Academy of Management Executive, 15*(2), 71–79.

Kongstvedt, P. (1996). Primary care in open panels. In P. Kongstvedt (Ed.), *The managed health care handbook* (pp. 104–118). Gaithersburg, MD: Aspen.

Kongstvedt, P., Lutz, J., Shaman, H., & Stanford, J. (1999). *Equilibrium at the edge: Planning in chaotic managed care markets.* Washington, DC: Ernst & Young.

Kongstvedt, P., & Plocher, D. (1996). Integrated health care delivery systems. In P. Kongstvedt (Ed.), *The managed health care handbook* (pp. 46–64). Gaithersburg, MD: Aspen.

Labb, D. A. (1999). Integrated healthcare delivery: How are we shaping up? *Healthcare Executive, 14,* 8–12.

Lando, M. (2000). The framework for a successful merger. *Healthcare Executive, 15*(3), 6–11.

Levin, I. M. (2000). Vision revisited: Telling the story of the future. *Journal of Applied Behavioral Science, 36,* 91–107.

Levin, I. M., Felice, L., Proctor, D., & Thibault, T. (2000). *Merging organization cultures: An assessment and integration approach.* Panel at session presented the Society for Industrial/Organizational Psychology Annual Meeting, New Orleans, LA.

Levin, I. M., Proctor, D., & Thibault, T. (2001). The making of Ascension Health. *Health Progress, 82*(3), 48–52.

Lippitt, L. L. (1998). *Preferred futuring: Envision the future you want and unleash the energy to get there.* San Francisco: Berrett-Koehler.

Lowman, R. L. (1991). *The clinical practice of career assessment: Interests, abilities, and personality.* Washington, DC: American Psychological Association.

Lowman, R. L., & Resnick, R. J. (Eds.). (1994). *The mental health professional's guide to managed mental health care.* Washington, DC: American Psychological Association.

Mango, P. D., & Shapiro, L. A. (2001). Hospitals get serious about operations. *The McKinsey Quarterly, 2,* 74–85.

Marks, M. L., & Mirvis, P. H. (1998). *Joining forces: Making one plus one equal three in mergers, acquisitions, and alliances.* San Francisco: Jossey-Bass.

Martin, J. (1992). *Cultures in organizations: Three perspectives.* New York: Oxford University Press.

Martin, J., & Siehl, C. (1983, Autumn). Organization culture and counterculture: An uneasy symbiosis. *Organizational Dynamics,* 52–64.

National Health Council. (1993). *Health groups in Washington: A directory* (12th ed.). Washington, DC: Author.

Nebeker, D. M., & Tatum, B. C. (2002). Understanding organizational processes and performance: A continuous improvement model for consulting psychologists. In R. L. Lowman (Ed.), *Handbook of organizational consulting psychology* (pp. 668–691). San Francisco: Jossey-Bass.

Nielsen, E. H. (1984). *Becoming an OD practitioner.* Englewood Cliffs, NJ: Prentice Hall.

Ott, J. S. (1989). *The organizational culture perspective.* Florence, KY: Dorsey Press.

Pine, B. J., & Gilmore, J. H. (2001). Welcome to the experience economy. *Health Forum Journal, 44*(5), 10–16.

Robinson, J. C. (1999). *The corporate practice of medicine: Competition and innovation in health care.* Berkeley, CA: University of California Press.

Robinson-Kurpius, S. E., Newman, J. L., & Fuqua, D. R. (2002). *Issues in the ethical practice of consulting psychology.* San Francisco: Jossey-Bass.

Saphir, A. (1999). Forever young: Long term care industry must reinvent itself to keep boomers, minorities happy. *Modern Healthcare, 29*(31), 28–30.

Schein, E. H. (1992). *Organization culture and leadership: A dynamic view (2nd ed.).* San Francisco: Jossey-Bass.

Schulman, D. S., Dunleavy, J. R., Harmer, M. J., & Lusk, J. S. (1999). *Shared services: Adding value to business units.* New York: Wiley.

Seligman, M.E.P., & Csikszentmihalyi, M. (2000). Positive psychology: An introduction. *American Psychologist, 55,* 5–14.

Shortell, S. (1988). The evolution of hospital systems: Unfulfilled promises and self-fulfilling prophesies. *Medical Care Research & Review, 22*(11), 177–214.

Solit, R. L., & Nash, D. B. (1996). Academic health centers and managed care. In P. Kongstvedt (Ed.), *The managed health care handbook* (pp. 215–233). Gaithersburg, MD: Aspen.

Starr, P. (1982). *The social transformation of American medicine.* New York: Basic Books.

U.S. Bureau of the Census. (2000). *Population projections of the U.S. by age, sex, race, and ethnic origin 2000–2050.* Washington DC: Author.

Wagner, E. R. (1996). Types of managed care organizations. In P. Kongstvedt (Ed.), *The managed health care handbook* (pp. 33–45). Gaithersburg, MD: Aspen.

Weisbord, M. R. (1973). The organization development contract. *OD Practitioner, 5*(2), 1–4.

Weisbord, M. R., & Janoff, S. (1995). *Future search.* San Francisco: Berrett-Koehler.

Williams, E. D., & Van Der Reis, L. (1997). *Health care at the abyss: Managed care vs. the goals of medicine.* Buffalo, NY: William S. Hein.

# CHAPTER TWENTY-FOUR

# Organizational Consulting on Healthy Lifestyles

Paul Lloyd and Louis Veneziano
*Southeast Missouri State University*

The six leading causes of death in the United States—coronary heart disease (CHD), stroke, lung cancer, colon cancer, diabetes, and chronic obstructive pulmonary disease (COPD)—were responsible for 43 percent of all deaths in 1998 (Doyle, 2001). These diseases are also referred to as *lifestyle diseases,* a term deriving from the fact that lifestyle characteristics, such as stress, poor diet, obesity, lack of exercise, and cigarette smoking, have been found to significantly heighten the risk of an individual developing them. In fact, changes in lifestyle account for much of the change in mortality rates among these six diseases during the past twenty years (Blair et al., 1989).

The specialty area of psychological consulting on healthy lifestyles can have a direct impact on the bottom line for organizations and alleviation of these lifestyle diseases. Employer examples include the DuPont Corporation (Bertera, 1990), the City of Mesa, Arizona (Aldana, Jacobson, Harris, Kelley, & Stone, 1994), The Travelers Corporation (Golaszewski, Snow, Lynch, Yen, & Solomita, 1990), and Steelcase (Yen, Edington, & Witting, 1994). That there are ample opportunities for corporate cost reductions is illustrated by a finding that in the United States, the direct costs for employers as a result of workers suffering from work-related stress or depression is over $12 billion (Greenberg, Finkelstein, & Berndt, 1995).

Organizational consulting psychologists, by virtue of their education and training, are well equipped to provide a wide variety of services to help organizations realize improved cost-benefit ratios on health-related expenditures, and to help senior organizational leaders provide a healthy culture for both employees and executive staff. Since consultation includes the professional practice of providing expert advice and services in a particular field, there are ample opportunities for consulting psychologists to help organizations develop and implement successful health promotion programs.

On the organizational level, consultants can assist employers in developing corporate cultures that promote long-term healthy lifestyles (Wilson & Wagner, 1997). Organizational consultants can use their skills in gaining entry at the top management level, conducting needs assessments, working with groups to design and implement specific intervention programs, and assisting companies to develop motivational strategies and perform ongoing assessments of changes in culture and healthy lifestyles.

There is little doubt that lifestyle diseases have an adverse effect on organizations. Health problems are likely to result in decreased productivity among the employees of any organization. Employees with health problems, especially chronic health problems, are more likely to be absent from work. Such absences not only result in lost productivity, but also contribute to lower levels of productivity among workers who aren't absent, by increasing their work load, increasing stress, and decreasing morale (Lloyd, Hoover, Wheeler, & Blair, 1998). Employees with health problems can also experience higher turnover rates. Finally, employer medical costs can be reduced if fewer employees experience chronic illnesses (Gebhardt & Crump, 1990).

This chapter is organized around lifestyle diseases and work-related health promotion topics integrated with individual, group, and organizational levels of consultation involving interventions at the primary, secondary, and tertiary levels of prevention (see Table 24.1). Such consultative efforts can help companies develop a preventive management philosophy and healthy corporate culture, and can assist in the systematical implementation of such a program (Lloyd & Atella, 2000).

# PRINCIPLES OF CONSULTATIVE INTERVENTIONS

The discussion of consultation interventions will be guided by five principles (Quick, Quick, Nelson, & Hurrell, 1997). First, we contend that there is a direct correlation between the health of the individual and the health of the organization in which they are involved. We also believe that individuals are responsible for their own health, and managers within organizations are responsible for the health of the people they supervise. Our third premise is that individuals deal with stress in unique ways. Fourth, individuals and organizations are dynamic. Finally, we offer the premise that distress among individuals and organizations is inevitable and cannot be avoided.

Table 24.1. Organizational Health Prevention Models.

|  | Primary | Secondary | Tertiary |
|---|---|---|---|
| *Individual* | • Physical fitness assessment<br>• Personal wellness profile | • Smoking cessation<br>• Stress management<br>• Nutrition<br>• Communication skills | • Job redesign<br>• Participative management<br>• Learned optimism training |
| *Group* | • Facility assessment<br>• Back safety<br>• Ergonomic review<br>• Nutrition | • Specific group interventions<br>• Weight reduction program | • Smoking cessation programs<br>• Conflict resolution |
| *Organization* | • Smoke-free environment<br>• Lung cancer screenings | • Cholesterol reduction<br>• Hypertension monitoring<br>• Diversity training | • Employee assistance programs<br>• Preventive stress management |

## Levels of Consultation

Different health prevention consultation efforts can be used depending on which of the three organizational consultation levels—individual, group, or organizational—is being addressed.

**Individual Level.** At the individual level, psychological consultants can assist organizations in reducing the adverse effects of the lifestyle diseases by attempting to reduce significant risk of developing one of the six primary lifestyle diseases. To the extent that stress reduction at the individual level also lowers the likelihood of developing such diseases, they can design programs and interventions to lower individual levels of stress. Consultants can help employees alter those aspects of their lifestyle, for example, cigarette smoking and sedentary behavior, that are known to place them at risk for the development of one of the six lifestyle diseases.

**Group Level.** The importance of workplace groups on productivity has been central to theories of effective management since the pioneering studies of the Hawthorne Western Electric Works in the 1920s (Roethlisberger & Dickson, 1939). Although it is generally conceded that conflicts arising from workplace groups can never be totally eliminated, such conflicts, and the resultant stress that they engender, can be significantly reduced. Group-level interventions can include, for example, in-service training programs on such topics as disease prevention, conflict resolution, and communication skills. Social support groups can also be important in disease prevention and stress reduction efforts.

**Organizational Level.** The internal structure and demands of the organization can either add to or modulate the level of stress experienced in the workplace. Programs are likely to contribute to disease prevention that streamline work demands, decrease job frustrations, and promote development of healthy coping techniques. In attempting to adjust the demands placed on employees, organizational consultants examine the structure and process of work, and attempt to eliminate wasted time, unnecessary tasks, and workplace clutter. In job redesign, the streamlining technique is combined with skills evaluation to better match workers and tasks. Attempting to ensure that employees have the skills and interests needed to perform a task well can modulate work stress. As morale increases from organizational-level interventions, workers' job satisfaction level and desire to perform well can also be affected (see, for example, Matheson & Ivancevich, 1987).

# HEALTH PREVENTION MODELS

Health prevention and promotion models used by organizational consulting psychologists derive from preventative concepts originated in the field of public health (Caplan, 1963). The three levels of prevention differ in the following three respects: (1) the size and nature of the target population; (2) the effectiveness; and (3) costs of the interventions.

## Primary Prevention

Primary prevention efforts are directed to preventing a problem from ever occurring (Shinn & Toohey, 2001). Mass inoculation against an infectious disease, for example, is intended to keep most people in the target population from ever developing a disease. Physical exercise is another example of a primary preventive approach that has been demonstrated to benefit employees' overall health, relieve stress, and promote social relationships between employees. Heightened mental energy, improved self-esteem, improved memory, and greater self-awareness are other work-related benefits of exercise. Some research has suggested that if 25 percent of employees reduce health risk factors by staying physically fit, companies can save as much as 15 percent on medical expenses annually (Storer, 2001; Lloyd & Wheeler, 1994).

Primary prevention programs in the workplace involve helping employees develop healthier lifestyles. For example, providing all employees with basic nutritional information can potentially lessen the adverse effects of faulty eating habits on the development of such diseases as coronary heart disease and diabetes. Providing all workplace groups with communication skills training can reduce the amount of group-related stress that exacerbates the six lifestyle diseases. Assisting an organization to develop a smoke-free environment or an incentive-based employee physical fitness program can reduce the risk of all employees to the adverse effects of cigarette smoking and physical activity.

## Secondary Prevention

Secondary prevention efforts are targeted to interventions with high-risk individuals (Pearson & Koretz, 2001). Secondary prevention efforts are addressed only to those individuals who are known to be at heightened risk for developing the problem in question. The successes of such programs are based on being able to correctly identify high-risk individuals, and then providing them with interventions that prevent them from developing the problem. Examples of such programs include smoking cessation programs and weight reduction programs (Shiffman, Henning & Mason, 1998; Brownson, Erikson, Davis, & Warner, 1997; Visscher & Seidell, 2001).

In developing such programs, reliable means must be developed to identify at-risk individuals. Self-identification or routine assessment on a regular basis can be used to identify them. In general, secondary prevention programs are not as effective as primary prevention programs, and they are more expensive (Smith, Schwebel, Dunn, & McIver, 1993). However, secondary prevention programs are more effective than tertiary prevention programs, and they are less expensive (Smith et al.).

## Tertiary Prevention

Tertiary prevention efforts are designed to treat individuals who have already developed a problem, and to attempt to keep the problem from becoming more pronounced in one of two ways: (1) lessen the adverse effects of the condition; and (2) prevent the problem from recurring (Munoz, 2001). An example of the first subtype of tertiary prevention is to assist an individual with hypertension in losing weight, and to increase their physical activity level. An example of the second subtype of tertiary prevention is helping an individual who has suffered a heart attack stop smoking in an attempt to prevent another heart attack. Although the research indicates that tertiary prevention programs are most expensive and least effective (Smith et al., 1993), organizations can assist their employees affected by conditions needing tertiary care or prevention.

## Relative Effectiveness of Prevention Efforts

A significant body of research has indicated that in terms of effectiveness, primary prevention efforts are more effective than secondary prevention efforts, which in turn are more effective than tertiary prevention efforts. In terms of cost effectiveness, tertiary prevention efforts are most expensive, secondary prevention efforts are less expensive, and primary prevention efforts are least expensive (Smith et al., 1993).

Even though research consistently demonstrates that in terms of the tertiary model of prevention, primary prevention efforts are most effective and least expensive, there are at least two reasons why interventions should not be restricted solely to primary prevention efforts. First, it might be years before the true effects of primary prevention efforts are realized. Second, immediate problems, either in the form of at-risk individuals (secondary prevention) or individuals with a problem (tertiary prevention), need to be attended to.

# SPECIFIC CHRONIC DISEASES

In this section, several exemplary diseases will be discussed. The goal is to illustrate ways in which the organizational consultant can assist.

## Coronary Heart Disease

Coronary heart disease (CHD) is the term describing a group of conditions directly related to the flow of oxygen to the heart muscle. It ranges from mild angina (chest pain or pressure) with physical exertion, to irreversible damages to the quality of the heart muscle (myocardial injury), to eventual cardiac arrest, in which the heart stops functioning completely and death results (Guyton & Hall, 2000). Statistically in America, someone experiences a heart attack once every twenty seconds, and death from a heart attack occurs about once every minute (Nutrition Screening Initiative, 2001).

Some causes of CHD include smoking and lung disorders. Many other lifestyle choices affect the quality of the heart muscle and the blood vessels surrounding it (Guyton & Hall, 2000). The four most significant are the following: cholesterol levels in the blood, short- and long-term stress levels, diet in relation to body weight, and physical activity (Young, 1994).

**Coronary Heart Disease and Healthy Lifestyle.** Staying fit, eating a balanced diet, and maintaining tolerable stress levels are lifestyle changes that are difficult for most people to enact. Such changes require a certain amount of hard work and willpower to prevent a disease that one might never even develop. However, even slow, small changes can be better than doing nothing at all (Lloyd et al., 1998).

The main components of the healthy heart lifestyle correlate directly with the four main causative factors of CHD. The healthy heart lifestyle focuses on managing diet (weight as well as cholesterol), increasing physical activity, and coping effectively with stress (Dusseldorp, van Elderen, Maes, Meulman, & Kraaij, 1999). A heart-healthy diet can be accomplished by following the food guide pyramid; that is, being careful to avoid fatty foods, oils, and foods with high salt content (Steptoe, Kerry, Rink, & Hilton, 2001). A heart-healthy activity level can be accomplished by thirty minutes of strenuous daily activity (Burn, Naylor, & Page, 1999; Lee, 2001). And of course, a healthy heart lifestyle does not include smoking (He, 1999).

There are no ideal universal recommendations for the level of stress that needs to be maintained to prevent CHD. With planning and training, however, it is thought that the effects of stress can be managed, especially when attempting to deal with long-term or chronic stressors (Orth-Gomer, 2000). Of all the lifestyle changes recommended for preventing coronary heart disease, managing stress is the one factor that can make the difference between life and death in an individual who already has symptoms of CHD (Ornish, 1998). CHD will occur in some individuals despite any precautions, but the Stockholm Female Coronary Risk indicated that individuals who experience chronic stress are almost ten times more likely to die from the disease state (Orth-Gomer, 2000).

Researchers at Duke Medical Center have found that stress management helped significantly reduce the risk of surgery or heart attacks. According to these researchers, those who participated in a stress management program were less likely to have additional heart problems than those who received only medical treatment (Blumenthal et al., 1997).

**Organizational Consultation and Coronary Heart Disease.** Consulting psychologists can assist organizations in a variety of ways to lessen the likelihood that workers will succumb to CHD. Consulting psychologists can assist organizations in developing a multimodal treatment protocol to help workers who have CHD, by encouraging organizational clients to develop programs in individualized nutritional counseling, individualized physical activity, weight reduction, smoking cessation, and individualized instruction in stress management techniques.

In order to prevent stress associated with workgroup problems from reaching levels that could contribute to CHD among susceptible individuals, consulting psychologists can provide communication skills training and stress management training for all workgroups in an organization (Margolis, McLeroy, Runyan, & Kaplan, 1983). If the results of an organization-wide diagnosis indicate low levels of employee morale and high levels of employee alienation, consulting psychologists could also assist an organization in developing a participative management program (Dracoup et al., 1994). Such a program can raise levels of employee morale and decrease levels of employee alienation. By reducing levels of stress, such a program can conceivably lessen the adverse effects of stress on individuals susceptible to the development of coronary heart disease.

# Stroke

Strokes are the leading cause of death and disability in the United States. They occur when part of the brain is deprived of oxygen and is damaged. A blood clot, a wandering clot, or an aneurysm can cause strokes. Each year, stroke affects 600,000 to 750,000 people in the United States (see, for example, Everson, Lynch, Kaplan, Lakka, Sivenius, & Salonen, 2001).

There are many factors that increase an individual's chance of having a stroke. Hypertension, atrial fibrillation, history of cardiac disease and stroke, smoking, high cholesterol, high blood pressure, and stress can increase the likelihood of stroke (McKeown & Jacques, 2001).

There are some risk factors that an individual cannot prevent or control for stroke, including heredity, age, gender, and race. Family history, older age, being male, and being African American all increase the risk of stroke (Goldstein et al., 2001).

**Stroke and Healthy Lifestyle.** Stress, or the inability to manage stress, is one of the most significant risk factors for stroke. However, studies have found that the general public does not even associate stress as a risk factor for stroke. Biochemicals degrade the immune system, digestive tract, and lungs, and weaken the heart. Stress management techniques not only help the individual, but also benefit the organization that he or she works for (Ornish et al., 1998). Biofeedback (Stein, 2001) might also be helpful in preventing adverse physical reactions associated with stress potentially influencing strokes.

## Organizational Consultation and Stroke Prevention

Aerobic fitness programs and exercise fitness rooms in workplaces can significantly reduce the risk for stress and the chance of stroke for employees. When organizations encourage employees to participate in recreational sports and activities, this provides another opportunity for employees to release stress in a positive way. Stretching and flexibility lower an individual's state of arousal. Muscle strength training can be effective in relaxing tense muscles, releasing frustration, and helping to improve self-image. Physically relaxing just before a meeting can promote relaxation and decrease stress (see, for example, Blumenthal et al., 2000; Billings, 2000).

Consulting psychologists can determine which workplace groups have high stress levels by administering stress measures (see, for example, Vagg & Spielberger, 1999). Those workplace groups with the highest measured stress levels can then be targeted for intensive instruction in stress reduction techniques, such as conflict resolution and communication skills training (Palmer & Dryden, 1995).

Organizations can hold stress management workshops to teach a variety of techniques to cope with stress, and reduce the risk for stroke and other diseases.

Education is one approach that has proven to be extremely effective in helping people modify their lifestyle to reduce the chance of recurrent strokes (Blumenthal et al., 1999; Marmot & Bosma, 1997; Lloyd & Blair, 1992).

## Lung Cancer

Lung cancer is the second most commonly occurring cancer among both men and women. Lung cancer is fatal for 86 percent of its victims within five years of a diagnosis (Thun, Apicella, & Henley, 2000). Women now have a higher risk than ever before of developing this disease. It is now the leading cause of cancer death among women. While lifestyle characteristics contribute to the development of nearly every type of cancer, lifestyle characteristics have a particularly pernicious effect with respect to the development of lung cancer. It has been estimated that nearly 80 percent of cases of lung cancer could be prevented. It is generally agreed that the vast majority of cases of lung cancer can be attributed to smoking and exposure to second-hand smoke (Ichiro & Colditz, 1999).

Lifestyle factors clearly cause people to be at a heightened risk of developing cancer. These factors include diet, sedentary lifestyle, alcohol consumption, cigarette smoking, and general stress (Donatelle, 2002). Smoking remains the single biggest risk factor for lung cancer. Lung cancer occurs most often in people over fifty years of age who have long histories of cigarette smoking (Viswesvaran & Schmidt, 1992).

**Lung Cancer Prevention.** Eliminating smoking is part of the prevention process when dealing with lung cancer. It is known that high-demanding jobs produce a lot of stress in the lives of workers. Smoking is a common way to relieve stress. This addiction can have many negative side effects for business. The smell of smoke can affect employees and cause their production to go down, and the person who smokes is more likely to catch colds and other respiratory illnesses, and ultimately lung cancer (Rose, Chassin, Presson, & Sherman, 1996).

Since cigarette smoking is the most significant risk factor for the development of lung cancer, developing smoking cessation programs can help prevent the disease. (Zelman, Brandon, Jorenby, & Baker, 1992; Orleans et al., 1991; Lloyd, Blair, & Hoover, 1994). Viswesvaran and Schmidt (1992) provided a review of the effectiveness of such programs. Once a person has quit smoking, it is important to avoid situations in which smoking occurs as much as possible. This prevents further lung damage, decreases irritation to the lungs, and helps control susceptibility to COPD (Hays, 2000).

To the extent that smoking is a response to stress, providing conflict resolution and communication skills training to those work groups in an organization that exhibit high levels of conflict and stress (Mermelstein, Cohen, Lichtenstein, Baer, & Kamarck, 1986) in theory might help decrease smoking. Creating totally smoke-free work environments can decrease the frequency with which smokers will actually smoke, thereby lowering their risk, and also eliminating exposure of nonsmokers to the hazardous effects of second-hand smoke (Breslau & Peterson, 1996). Work groups can also be provided with information on where a person can get medical and emotional help. This might include pamphlets on counseling, group therapy, or medical services. These suggestions are not expensive, and can improve the quality of life and work for each employee.

## Diabetes

Each year, companies spend millions of dollars in healthcare for diabetic patients. Over 16 million Americans each year are diagnosed with diabetes. Diabetes is the most rapidly growing chronic disease in America, and is the leading cause of blindness, amputations, kidney disease, obesity, heart disease, and stroke (Whittemore, 2000).

Diabetes is a metabolic disorder in which the body either does not produce enough insulin, or does not properly use the insulin that is produced. Insulin is a hormone needed to convert sugar, starches, and other foods into energy necessary for daily life. There are two major types of diabetes: Type I, known as insulin-dependent, or juvenile, diabetes; and Type II, known as non-insulin dependent diabetes. Individuals with Type I diabetes do not produce enough insulin. Consequently, their blood-sugar level becomes elevated, which if left untreated, can create a host of physical problems. It is reported that 90 percent of patients with diabetes have Type II diabetes, which occurs when the body makes too much sugar, and either does not produce enough or cannot properly use insulin (Surwit et al., 2002). This type most often begins with people over the age of twenty, and typically occurs later in life. Symptoms can include frequent infections, blurred vision, cuts and bruises that heal slowly, tingling or numbness in the hands or feet, and recurring skin, gum, or bladder infections. Type II diabetes can usually be treated with diet, medication, or insulin (Wing, Goldstein, & Acton, 2001).

There are several risk factors for the development of diabetes. The most prominent risk factors include being over the age of forty-five, being overweight, not exercising regularly, and having a family history of the disorder. In addition, African Americans, Hispanic Americans, Native Americans, Asians, and Pacific Islanders all have heightened risks of developing diabetes. It is recommended that an individual be tested for diabetes if they fall under one of these categories, or if there is a family history of high cholesterol, high blood pressure, or heart disease (Pascale, Wing, Butler, Mullen, & Bononi, 1995).

Although a cure has not yet been found for diabetes, there are many ways in which diabetes can be controlled. By eating healthy meals and exercising regularly, diabetics can keep their blood-sugar levels low. By taking medications as instructed, and by eliminating smoking, a patient can take an active role in treatment. Diabetics need to check their blood-sugar level every day, visit their doctor regularly, wash and check their feet for sores daily, and minimize alcohol intake (Defay, Delcourt, Ranvier, Lacroux, & Papoz, 2001).

**Organizational Consultation and Diabetes.** Consultants can help prevent diabetes in the workplace by arranging training seminars on diagnosis and prevention. In addition to providing nutritional information, such seminars can address dietary habits (Hu et al., 2001). Since physical inactivity is a risk factor for diabetes, consulting psychologists can help organizations develop incentive-based physical fitness programs for all employees.

## Chronic Obstructive Pulmonary Disease

Of the six lifestyle-related diseases, chronic obstructive pulmonary disease (COPD) is ranked as the fourth leading cause of death among Americans. COPD is the permanent obstruction of airflow from the lungs, causing a loss of lung function. In 1998, 113,000 Americans died of COPD (Mayo Clinic, 2002). Among the several risk factors associated with COPD, the most significant is smoking cigarettes (Doyle, 2001).

Most of the people who suffer from COPD have either chronic bronchitis or emphysema (Barnes, 2000). Chronic bronchitis occurs when there is an inflammation and thickening of the bronchial tubes in the lungs. Emphysema is the result of damage to the alveoli, tiny sacs of air located on the walls of the lungs, which become inflamed as they lose elasticity, and might even rupture (Barnes, 2000). When this happens it becomes difficult to completely exhale, thus trapping air inside the lungs (Duren-Winfield, Berry, Jones, Clark, & Sevick, 2000).

**COPD and Healthy Lifestyle.** Lifestyle interventions assist those who suffer from COPD. Sufferers of COPD can greatly benefit from exercising for at least five to fifteen minutes, three or four times a day, either walking or riding a stationary bicycle. Also recommended are breathing exercises, using a humidifier, drinking plenty of fluids, and changing work environments (Donatelle, 2002). Another treatment is oxygen therapy, which involves the use of an oxygen concentrator to increase oxygen-rich air in the living environment, resulting in easier breathing. All of these techniques are only used to treat and control COPD, and will not permanently cure a person of COPD (Beauchesne, 2001).

While COPD cannot be cured, it can be prevented. The most important preventive measure is to avoid smoking and smoke-filled atmospheres (Barnes, 2000). It is also important to avoid air pollution and extreme variations in temperature and humidity. Finally, lifestyle changes such as changing jobs to work in a healthier environment or moving to a less polluted, lower altitude area should be considered (Narsavage, 1997). Smoking is by far the greatest risk factor for COPD. Smoking causes 80–90 percent of the COPD cases that affect nearly 16 million people (Boyle & Waters, 2000).

A well-rounded health promotion and disease prevention plan can be quite effective in preventing and coping with COPD. Sedentary behavior contributes to 23 percent of the deaths from nine key chronic illnesses, of which COPD is one. Exercise is a fundamental part of rehabilitation for chronic lung disease. Many people believe the myth that people with COPD do not exercise because they are short of breath. Actually, regular exercise can help COPD sufferers feel less short of breath. It increases muscle strength and endurance, cardiopulmonary endurance, and the ability to fight infection, and also decreases shortness of breath, side effects of medicine, depression, and blood-sugar levels. Presentations by specialists in COPD rehabilitation can help show employees with COPD beneficial exercises (Cooper, 2001).

The benefits of an exercise program definitely outweigh the costs involved. When a fitness plan is started, employee absenteeism decreases, turnover is reduced, and employees show a more positive attitude towards work and have better relationships at work. In addition, disability claims decrease, productivity increases, and health insurance costs are lowered (Gebhardt & Crump, 1990; Lloyd, Blair, Wheeler, & Munz, 1998).

**Organizational Consultation and Chronic Obstructive Pulmonary Disease.** Consulting psychologists can assist organizations in numerous ways to decrease the likelihood that workers will develop COPD. The following combinations of level of consultation and type of preventive intervention can be discussed: secondary preventive interventions at the individual consultative level; tertiary preventive interventions at the group consultative level; and primary preventive interventions at the organizational consultative level.

Since cigarette smoking is the most significant risk factor associated with the development of COPD, consulting psychologists can assist organizations in developing individualized smoking cessation programs for workers who smoke. Incorporating a relapse prevention component into a standard smoking cessation program can enhance its effectiveness (Petty, 2000). Because many people smoke cigarettes because of the calming effects nicotine has on the peripheral nervous system, being part of a work group in which there is a significant amount of conflict can be very stressful, and might result in a former smoker returning to the habit. Consequently, consulting psychologists might provide a variety of assessment and intervention programs to decrease stress (see, for example, Gift, Moore, & Soeken, 1992).

# CONCLUSIONS

Consulting psychologists potentially have much to offer organizations in terms of helping their workers attain healthier lifestyles in three types of preventative efforts (primary, secondary, and tertiary), and at three levels (individual, group, and organizational). Having employees with healthier lifestyles will have a positive effect on an organization in a number of respects, including: increased productivity, decreased absenteeism, decreased turnover, decreased costs associated with recruitment and training, and decreased expenditures for medical services.

This chapter has demonstrated ways that consultants can potentially lessen the negative effects of lifestyle characteristics associated with diseases that are among the leading causes of death in the United States today (coronary heart disease, stroke, lung cancer, diabetes, and chronic obstructive pulmonary disease). Especially important are lifestyle characteristics, such as smoking, physical inactivity, and poor dietary habits.

Stress is also a contributing factor to these lifestyle diseases. Consulting psychologists have much to offer organizations in helping workers alter their lifestyles and manage stress. This chapter has provided a conceptual framework that integrates two principles that can serve as a guide for the types of consultative services that psychologists could provide to organizations.

# References

Aldana, S. G., Jacobson, B. H., Harris, C. J., Kelley, P. L., & Stone, W. J. (1994). City of Mesa: Influence of a mobile worksite health promotions program on health care costs. *American Journal of Preventive Medicine, 9,* 378–382.

Barnes P. J. (2000). Medical progress: Chronic obstructive pulmonary disease. *New England Journal of Medicine, 343,* 269–280.

Beauchesne, C. F. (2001). Management of chronic obstructive pulmonary disease: A review. *Journal of Pharmacy Practice, 16,* 126–139.

Bertera, R. L. (1990). The effects of workplace health promotion on absenteeism and employment costs in a large industrial population. *American Journal of Public Health, 80,* 1101–1105.

Billings, J. H. (2000). Maintenance of behavior change in cardiorespiratory risk reduction: A clinical perspective from the Ornish program for reversing coronary heart disease. *Health Psychology, 19,* 70–75.

Blair, S. N., Kohl, H. W., Paffenberger, R. S., Clark, D. G., Cooper, K. H., & Gibbons, L. W. (1989). Physical fitness and all-cause mortality. *Journal of the American Medical Association, 262,* 2395–2401.

Blumenthal, J. A., Jiang, W., Babyak, M. A., Krantz, D. S., Frid, D. J., Coleman, R. E., et al. (1997). Stress management and exercise training in cardiac patients with myocardial ischemia: Effects on prognosis and evaluation of mechanisms. *Archives of Internal Medicine, 19,* 2213–2223.

Blumenthal, J. A., Sherwood, A., Babyak, M., Thurston, R., Tweedy, D., Georgiades, A., et al. (1999). Mental stress and coronary heart disease. *North Carolina Medical Journal, 60*(2), 95–99.

Blumenthal, J. A., Sherwood, A., Gullete, E., Babyak, M., Waugh, R., Georgiades, A., et al. (2000). Exercise and weight loss reduce blood pressure in men and women with mild hypertension. *Archives of Internal Medicine, 160,* 1947–1957.

Boyle, A. H., & Waters, H. F. (2000). COPD: Focus on prevention: Recommendations of the national lung health education program. *Heart and Lung, 29,* 446–449.

Breslau, N., & Peterson, E. (1996). Smoking cessation in young adults: Age at initiation of cigarette smoking and other suspected influences. *American Journal of Public Health, 86,* 214–220.

Brownson, R. C., Erikson, M. P., Davis, R. M., & Warner, K. E. (1997). Environmental tobacco smoke: Health effects and policies to reduce exposure. *Annual Review of Public Health, 18,* 163–185.

Burn, G. E., Naylor, P., & Page, A. (1999). Assessment of stages of changes for exercise within a worksite lifestyle screening program. *American Journal of Health Promotion, 13*(3), 143–145.

Caplan, G. (1963). Types of mental health consultation. *American Journal of Orthopsychiatry, 33,* 470–481.

Cooper, C. B. (2001). Exercise in chronic pulmonary disease: Aerobic exercise prescription. *Medicine & Science in Sports & Exercise, 33,* 671–679.

Defay, R., Delcourt, C., Ranvier, M., Lacroux, A., & Papoz, L. (2001). Relationship between physical activity, obesity and diabetes mellitus in a French elderly population. *International Journal of Obesity, 25,* 512–518.

Donatelle, R. (2002). *Access to health.* Menlo Park, CA: Benjamin-Cummings.

Doyle, R. (2001). Lifestyle blues. *Scientific American, 284*(4), 30.

Dracoup, K., Baker, D., Dunbar, S., Dacey, R., Brooks, N., Johnson, J., et al. (1994). Management of heart failure: Counseling, education, and lifestyle modification. *Journal of the American Medical Association, 272,* 1442–1446.

Duren-Winfield, V., Berry, M. J., Jones, S. A., Clark, D. H., & Sevick, M. A. (2000). Cost effective-ness analysis for the REACT study. *Western Journal of Nursing Research, 22,* 460–475.

Dusseldorp, E., van Elderen, T., Maes, S., Meulman, J., & Kraaij, V. (1999). A meta-analysis of psychoeducational programs for coronary heart disease patients. *Health Psychology, 18,* 506–519.

Everson, S. A., Lynch, J. W., Kaplan, G. A., Lakka, T. A., Sivenius, J., & Salonen, J. T. (2001). Stress-induced blood pressure reactivity and incident stroke in middle-aged men. *Stroke, 32,* 1263–1270.

Gebhardt, D., & Crump, C. (1990). Employee fitness and wellness programs in the workplace. *American Psychologist, 45,* 262–272.

Gift, A., Moore, T., & Soeken, K. (1992). Relaxation to reduce dyspnea and anxiety in COPD patients. *Nursing Research, 41,* 242–246.

Golaszewski, T., Snow, D., Lynch, W., Yen, L., & Solomita, D. (1990). The Travelers: A benefit-to-cost analysis of a worksite health promotion program. *Journal of Occupational Medicine, 32,* 9–12.

Goldstein, L. B., Adams, R., Becker, K., Furberg, C. D., Gorelick, P. B., Hademenos, G., et al. (2001). Primary prevention of ischemic stroke: A statement for healthcare professionals from the stroke council of the American Heart Association. *Circulation, 103,* 163–182.

Greenberg, P. E., Finkelstein, S. N., & Berndt, E. R. (1995). Economic consequences of illness in the workplace. *Sloan Management Review, 34,* 1–17.

Guyton, A. C., & Hall, J. E. (2000). *Textbook of medical physiology* (10th ed.). Philadelphia: Saunders.

Hays, J. T. (2000). Tobacco dependence treatment in patients with heart and lung disease: Impli-cations for intervention and review of pharmacological therapy. *Journal of Cardiopulmonary Rehabilitation, 20,* 215–223.

He, J. (1999). Passive smoking and the risk of coronary heart disease—A meta-analysis of epidemiologic studies. *The New England Journal of Medicine, 340,* 920–927.

Hu, F., Manson, J. E., Stamfer, M., Colditz, G., Simin, L., Solomon, C., et al. (2001). Diet, lifestyle, and the risk of type 2 diabetes mellitus in women. *The New England Journal of Medicine, 345,* 790–797.

Ichiro, K., & Colditz, G. (1999). Workplace exposure to passive smoking and risk of cardiovascular disease: Summary of epidemiologic studies. *Environmental Health Perspectives, 107,* 847–852.

Lee, I. M. (2001). Preventing coronary heart disease: The role of physical activity. *The Physician and Sports Medicine, 29*(2), 37–52.

Lloyd, P. J., & Atella, M. (2000). Positive leadership that inspires: Theoretical and empirical perspectives from positive psychology, existential theory, and hardiness research. *The Psychologist-Manager Journal, 4,* 155–165.

Lloyd, P. J., & Blair, S. N. (1992, July). *Depression, fitness & successful aging.* Paper presented at the 25th International Congress of Psychology, Brussels, Belgium.

Lloyd, P. J., Blair, S. N., & Hoover, M. W. (1994, June). *Stress buffers, physical fitness and depression.* Paper presented at the American College of Sports Medicine Annual Meeting, Indianapolis, IN.

Lloyd, P. J., Blair, S. N., Wheeler, R. J., & Munz, D. M. (1992, May). *Factor structure of psychosocial measures.* Paper presented at the American College of Sports Medicine Annual Meeting, Dallas, TX.

Lloyd, P. J., Hoover, M. W., Wheeler, R. J., Blair, S. N. (1998). Managing the bottom line via managing employee stress. *The Psychologist-Manager Journal, 2,* 83–92.

Lloyd, P. J., & Wheeler, R. J. (1994, August). *Psychosocial and physical stress buffers for depressive symptoms.* Paper presented at the American Psychological Association Annual Convention, Los Angeles.

Margolis, L. H., McLeroy, K. R., Runyan, C. W., & Kaplan, B. H. (1983). Type A behavior: An ecological approach. *Journal of Behavioral Medicine, 6,* 245–258.

Marmot, M. G., & Bosma, H. (1997). Contribution of job control and other risk factors to social variations in coronary heart disease incidence. *Lancet, 350,* 235–240.

Matheson, M. T., & Ivancevich, J. M. (1987). *Controlling work stress.* San Francisco: Jossey-Bass.

Mayo Clinic. (2002). *Chronic obstructive pulmonary disease: A matter of life and breath.* Retrieved December 27, 2001, from http://www.mayoclinic.com

McKeown, N. M., & Jacques, P. (2001). Whole grain intake and risk of ischemic stroke in women. *Nutrition Reviews, 59*(5), 149.

Mermelstein, R. M., Cohen, S., Lichtenstein, E., Baer, J. S., & Kamarck, T. (1986). Social support and smoking cessation and maintenance. *Journal of Consulting and Clinical Psychology, 54,* 447–453.

Munoz, R. E. (2001). How shall we ensure that the prevention of onset of mental disorders becomes a national priority? *Prevention and Treatment, 4,* Article 26. Retrieved December 27, 2001, from http://journals.apa.org /prevention/volume4/pre0040026c.html

Narsavage, G. L. (1997). Promoting function in clients with chronic lung disease by increasing their perception of control. *Holistic Nursing Practice, 12*(1), 17–26.

Nutrition Screening Initiative. (2001). Nutritional strategies efficacious in the prevention or treatment of coronary heart disease. *Geriatric Nursing, 22,* 47–58.

Orleans, T., Schoenbach, V., Wagner, E., Quade, D., Salmon, M., Pearson, D., et al. (1991). Self-help quit smoking interventions: Effects of self-help materials, social support instructions, and telephone counseling. *Journal of Consulting and Clinical Psychology, 59,* 439–438.

Ornish, D. (1998). *Love & survival: The healing power of intimacy and love.* New York: HarperCollins.

Ornish, D., Scherwitz, L. W., Billings, J. H., Gould, L., Merritt, T., Sparler, S., et al. (1998). Intensive lifestyle changes for reversal of coronary heart disease. *Journal of the American Medical Association, 280,* 2001–2007.

Orth-Gomer, K. (2000). Marital stress worsens prognosis in coronary heart disease: The Stockholm female coronary risk study. *Journal of the American Medical Association, 284,* 3008–3015.

Palmer, S., & Dryden, W. (1995). Stress management interventions in the workplace: A counseling psychologist's experience and concerns. *Counseling Psychology Review, 10,* 17–21.

Pascale, R., Wing, R., Butler, B., Mullen, M., & Bononi, P. (1995). Effects of a behavioral weight loss program stressing calorie restriction versus calories plus fat restriction in obese individuals with NIDDM or a family history of diabetes. *Diabetes Care, 18,* 1241–1247.

Pearson, J. L., & Koretz, D. S. (2001). Opportunities in prevention research at NIMH: Integrating prevention with treatment research. *Prevention and Treatment, 4,* Article 18. Retrieved December 11, 2001, from http://journals.apa.org/prevention/volume4 /pre0040018c.html

Petty, T. L. (2000). COPD interventions for smoking cessation and improved ventilatory function. *Geriatrics, 55,* 30–39.

Quick, J. C., Quick, J. D., Nelson, D. L., & Hurrell, J. J. (1997). *Preventive stress management in organizations.* Washington, DC: American Psychological Association.

Roethlisberger, F. J., & Dickson, W. J. (1939). *Management and the worker.* Cambridge, MA: Harvard University Press.

Rose, J., Chassin, L., Presson, C., & Sherman, S. (1996). Prospective predictors of quit attempts and smoking cessation in young adults. *Health Psychology, 15,* 261–268.

Shiffman, S., Mason, K. M., & Henning, J. E. (1998). Tobacco dependence treatments: Review and prospectus. *Annual Review of Public Health, 19,* 335–358.

Shinn, M., & Toohey, S. M. (2001). Refocusing on primary prevention. *Prevention and Treatment, 4.* Retrieved November 4, 2001, from: http://journals.apa.org /prevention/volume4/ pre0040021c.html

Smith, G. B., Schwebel, A. I., Dunn, R. L., & McIver, S. D. (1993). The role of psychologists in the treatment, management, and prevention of chronic mental illness. *American Psychologist, 48,* 966–971.

Stein, F. (2001). Occupational stress, relaxation therapies, exercise and biofeedback. In F. Stein, & S. Cutler, *Psychosocial occupational therapy* (2nd ed., pp. 235–245). Albany, NY: Delmar.

Steptoe, A., Kerry, S., Rink, E., & Hilton, S. (2001). The impact of behavioral counseling on stage of change in fat intake, physical activity, and cigarette smoking in adults at increases risk of coronary heart disease. *American Journal of Public Health, 91,* 265–269.

Storer, T. W. (2001). Exercise in chronic pulmonary disease: Resistance exercise prescription. *Medicine & Science in Sports & Exercise, 33,* 680–686.

Surwit, R. S., van Tilburg, M. A., Zucker, N., McCaskill, C., C., Parekh, P., Feinglos, M. N., et. al. (2002). Stress management improves long-term glycemic control in Type 2 diabetes. *Diabetes Care, 25,* 30–34.

Thun, M. J., Apicella, L. F., & Henley, J. (2000). Smoking vs. other risk factors as the cause of smoking attributable deaths. *Journal of the American Medical Association, 284,* 706–712.

Vagg, P. R., & Spielberger, C. D. (1999). The Job Stress Survey: Assessing perceived severity and frequency of occurrence of generic sources of stress in the workplace. *Journal of Occupational Health Psychology, 4*(3), 288–292.

Visscher, T. L., & Seidell, J. C. (2001). The public health impact of obesity. *Annual Review of Public Health, 22,* 355–375.

Visweswaran, C., & Schmidt, F. (1992). A meta-analytic comparison of the effectiveness of smoking cessation methods. *Journal of Applied Psychology, 77,* 554–561.

Whittemore, R. (2000). Strategies to facilitate lifestyle change associated with diabetes mellitus. *Journal of Nursing Scholarship, 32*(3), 225–232.

Wilson, B., & Wagner, D. (1997). Developing organizational health at the worksite. *American Journal of Health Studies, 13*(2), 105–108.

Wing, R., Goldstein, M., & Acton, K. (2001). Behavioral science research in diabetes: Lifestyle changes related to obesity, eating behavior, and physical activity. *Diabetes Care, 24*(1), 117–123.

Yen, L., Edington, D. W., & Witting, P. (1994). Steelcase: Corporate medical claim cost distributions and factors associated with high-cost status. *Journal of Occupational Medicine, 36,* 505–515.

Young, D. R. (1994). Can cardiorespiratory fitness moderate the negative effects of stress on coronary artery disease risk factors? *Journal of Psychosomatic Research, 38,* 451–459.

Zelman, D., Brandon, T. H., Jorenby, D., & Baker, T. B. (1992). Measures of affect and nicotine dependence predict differential response to smoking cessation treatments. *Journal of Consulting and Clinical Psychology, 60,* 943–952.

# CHAPTER TWENTY-FIVE

# Appreciative Inquiry as an Approach for Organizational Consulting

Peter F. Sorensen, Jr. and Therese F. Yaeger
*Benedictine University*

This chapter presents an introduction to, and brief overview of, the current state of knowledge pertaining to an approach to organizational change and consulting called appreciative inquiry (AI). It defines AI, presents a brief history of its development, its theoretical foundations, the process of applying AI, and areas of application, including global and international OD. It also reviews criticisms of AI and includes a current bibliography.

## WHAT IS APPRECIATIVE INQUIRY?

AI encompasses many aspects. It reflects a paradigm shift in organizational consulting. It is an organizational development (OD) approach that falls clearly within the Lewinian tradition of value-based change (Cooperrider & Srivastva, 1987). It is also an approach based on a specific and developing theory of change, as well as a developing methodology for its application. It is a process in OD that implies a specific set of consulting skills. It is an approach that has grown from a method of organizational consulting practiced and developed by a small core of people in the 1980s to a widespread phenomenon by the beginning of the 21st century. For example, the First International Conference on AI was held in Baltimore, Maryland, in October 2001, with more than 500 attendees.

AI is an important approach for organizational consultants for several reasons:

- It is a major departure from more traditional consulting, and, at the same time, represents an approach that returns to the core values of the field.
- Its popularity is increasing.
- It is an approach that is being used internationally.
- It can be combined with a variety of interventions.

# HISTORY OF AI

A brief chronology of important events in the development of AI follows:

*History of Appreciative Inquiry*

| | |
|---|---|
| 1980 | Cleveland Clinic Project |
| 1987 | "Appreciative Inquiry in Organizational Life" |
| 1987 | Roundtable project |
| 1987 | SIGMA Center for Global Change |
| 1992 | Imagine Chicago |
| 1996 | The Avon Project |
| | *OD Practitioner* |
| | United Religions Initiative |
| | *The Thin Book of Appreciative Inquiry* published |
| 1998 | GTE/ASTD award |
| 1999 | *Appreciative Inquiry: Rethinking Human Organization Toward a Positive Theory of Change*—Cooperrider's work with the Dalai Lama |
| 2000 | New millennium issue of *OD Practitioner* |
| | European AI Network |
| 2001 | *Appreciative Inquiry*—First book in Jossey-Bass new organizational development series |

AI began in 1980 with a team of action researchers from Case Western Reserve University in a study of the Cleveland Clinic, a healthcare organization. The researchers were struck by the nature of the constructive, positive environment of the organization, which was noted for exceptional levels of performance. The curiosity concerning the characteristics of this high-performance work environment served as the catalyst for the development of a new approach to organizational change and consulting based on a positive rather than problem-oriented change model.

In 1987, the first formal statement of AI appeared in the series on *Research in Organizational Change and Development*. The article by David Cooperrider and Suresh Srivastva (1987), "Appreciative Inquiry in Organizational Life," stands as one of the most important initial statements about AI. This article set forth some of the basic AI constructs, including the idea of the positive image, a central concept in AI. It also presented several basic premises pertaining to the emerging theory of affirmation that provides the foundation for AI. These statements included the ideas that a proper understanding of organizational life necessitates understanding the positive aspects of the organization, that organizations can be altered and changed, a positive future can be envisioned, positive imagery can be created and worked toward, and that organizations need reaffirming, not just fixing.

The year 1987 also saw the creation of the SIGMA Center, the Social Innovations in Global Management Center, a group dedicated to the application of AI to global social problems, and the consulting application of AI in the Round Table Project (Rainey, 1996; Mann, 1997). The 1990s followed with a series of important projects and publications, including: the first application of AI to a community project, which was to serve as a model for numerous later metropolitan applications (Bowling, Ludema, & Wyss, 1997); the beginning of the United Religions Initiative (Chaffee, 1997; Gibbs & Ackerly, 1997; Odell, 2000); the first journal issue devoted solely to AI, a double issue of *OD Practitioner*; the first primer on AI, called *The Thin Book of Appreciative Inquiry* (Hammond, 1996); and the first reader in AI (Cooperrider, Sorensen, Whitney, & Yaeger, 2000). The beginning of the new millennium saw a second special issue of the *OD Practitioner* devoted to AI, as well as a special issue of *The Organizational Development Journal* that included a number of articles on international applications of AI. The new millennium also saw the initiation of the European AI Network, the beginning of the new Jossey-Bass series in OD, which began with an AI book (Watkins & Mohr, 2001), and the first international conference on AI.

## THEORETICAL FOUNDATIONS

The role of positive imagery was introduced by the Cooperrider and Srivastva article (1987). Cooperrider (1990) extended the development of the rationale for the role of positive imagery. In addition to the concept of positive imagery, five principles were identified as central to AI's theory of change: the Construction-ist Principle (the idea that reality is socially constructed), the Principle of Simul-taneity (suggesting that inquiry and change occur simultaneously, and that the process of inquiry changes the nature of what is being studied), the Poetic Principle (contending that human organizations can be viewed as an open book), the Anticipatory Principle (suggesting that an organization's collective image of the future guides its behavior), and the Positive Principle (which advo-cates that the more positive the question, the longer-lasting and more success-ful the change effort will be) (Cooperrider & Whitney, 2001).

## The AI Process

The AI process has been described as consisting of four stages: 1) *discovery*, the identification of what an organization is, individually and collectively, and help-ing to find the positive change core (what is the organization best at?); 2) *dream*, the envisioning of the organization's greatest potential for positive influence and impact on the world (what is possible or might be?); 3) *design*, the creation of an organization in which the positive change core is reflected in the strategies, processes, systems, decisions, and collaborations of the orga-nization (what should be the ideal?); and 4) *destiny*, the creation of action (Cooperrider & Whitney, 2001).

In comparison to other approaches to organizational consulting, the AI dis-covery phase essentially serves as a diagnosis phase, except that in AI, the diag-nosis focuses solely on the strengths of the organization. This concentration on strengths rather than problem identification is a major and primary difference from other models of consulting.

There are a number of variations on this process (Watkins & Mohr, 2001; Rainey, 1996; Williams, 1996), but the 4-D Cycle described above is the model most frequently cited in the AI literature. Although the process of implement-ing AI varies, a major theme in most case studies is the recollection of peak experiences. Peak experience is described by Bushe (2001): "I have found that an AI, where people listen to each other's stories about micro moments in orga-nizational life where the best in us is touched, can create a unique climate for collective dreaming where the focus of ridicule and repression are momentar-ily suspended. There is something about telling one's story of 'peak' organiza-tional experiences, and listening to others . . ." (p. 119).

The positive question is also a central part of the AI discovery phase (Ludema, 2000). A typical format calls for one-on-one interviews built on the following typical AI questions:

- What attracted you to the organization?
- Without being humble, what do you value most about yourself, the organization, and your work?

- Looking at your entire experience, can you recall a time when you felt most alive, most involved, or most excited about working at this organization?

Interviews are then summarized into themes and reported back to the entire group, which sets the stage for the remaining phases.

One of the first large-scale applications of AI provides an illustration of a possible application of the process (Rainey, 1996). The AI intervention was undertaken at LeadShare, a partnership of nearly 400 accountants and management consultants that was ranked among the top accounting firms in Canada. The process was undertaken in anticipation of changes in key executive positions. The objectives were to ensure minimum disruption and to help prepare for future leadership. The project was entitled the Roundtable Initiative to indicate leadership without hierarchy, shared resources, and cross-functional networks. The objective of the intervention was to deal effectively with major transitions in key executives through a process designed to assist the organization in envisioning a collectively desired future and collaboratively translating the vision into reality.

The AI initiative at LeadShare included the development of the AI interview protocol, data collection, thematic analysis of the data, data feedback, and identification of future direction. More specifically, the process involved:

1. Development of the AI interview, focusing on innovation, partnership equality, speed to market, and valuing diversity

2. Nearly 400 AI interviews conducted with junior members of the firm

3. Analysis of the interviews for major themes

4. Presentation of the interview results to all members at the next annual meeting; the results served as the basis for creating the vision and direction for the future.

An additional illustration of the application of AI involves the completion of organizational culture profiles, identifying when the organization was successful and at its best, that is, so-called peak experiences. An example of the AI peak experience approach includes a project involving work with a public healthcare organization experiencing significant problems. In this case, the identification of peak experience profiles led to the realization that the organization at one time had been one of the leading centers in the country. This realization then became the focus for the change strategy (Akinyele, Sorensen, & Yaeger, 2001).

If AI involves an unconditional positive approach to change, how does it deal with organizational problems? As addressed by Watkins and Mohr (2001), AI attempts to solve problems by identifying and building on what is going right in the organization. In a gender issue case, for example, rather than employing traditional educational means for dealing with the issue at one organization, AI interviews were conducted with all 3,000 employees of the organization, asking for stories about when men and women were working constructively together. The AI process resulted in public recognition for the organization as being one of the best in dealing with gender issues (Watkins & Mohr).

# CURRENT APPLICATIONS

Based on AI's theoretical foundation, it represents a fundamental shift in thinking about organizations, and consequently is a major shift in the organizational change or consulting process. (Cooperrider & Whitney, 2001). However, the conditions under which AI is the consulting model of choice are not yet clearly defined or empirically validated. Golembiewski's review (1998) identifies AI as situationally, not universally, relevant, but no studies were found addressing this issue. Meanwhile, the list of applications continues to grow (see, for example, Cooperrider, Sorensen, Whitney, & Yaeger, 2000; Sorensen, Yaeger, & Nicoll, 2000; Cooperrider, Sorensen, Yaeger, & Whitney, 2001).

AI has been employed as an independent intervention, with other OD approaches, and as a modification of other approaches in applications, including:

- Survey feedback (Sharkey, Sorensen, & Yaeger, 1998; Sharkey, 1999; Cooke & Hartmann, 1989; Williams, 1996)
- Gender issues (Bunker, 1990; Watkins & Mohr, 2001)
- Quality and customer relations (Cooperrider & Whitney, 2001)
- Union-management relations (Whitney & Cooperrider, 2000)
- Community involvement (Cooperrider, 1996a, 1996b; Sena & Booy, 1997)
- Leadership transformation (Rainey, 2001; Srivastva & Cooperrider, 1990, 1998)

Recently the four-stage process has been integrated with large group and large-scale change approaches. This approach to AI is referred to as the AI Summit, and has been used with such organizations as Nutrimental, Hunter Douglas, GTE, Red Cross, British Airways, and the United Religions Initiative (Whitney & Cooperrider, 2000).

Team building is one area that has received continued, ongoing attention, with the work of Gervase Bushe (Bushe, 1998, 1995; Bushe & Coetzer, 1995). Bushe developed a theory of small group and team development using an AI format, which used the development of a shared, generative image of teamwork applied to work with both new teams and ongoing teams. Research based on experimental designs reported by Bushe (1995) indicates that AI is superior to traditional team building interventions. The effectiveness of AI in team building has been supported by field experiments comparing AI to traditional team-building methods (R. L. Head, 2000).

A number of studies have also reported positive results using AI in organizational culture change or renewal. One of the most frequently cited applications is the AI application at GTE Corporation. After fourteen months of using such a program, significant and measurable changes in stock prices and morale were attributed to the intervention (Cooperrider & Whitney, 2001). Significant improvements in performance data have been reported for Nutrimental and Hunter Douglas, among other corporations (Cooperrider & Whitney, 2001).

What accounts for the apparent success of AI interventions? In a review of fifty AI articles, Yaeger and Sorensen (2001) identified ten major themes that emerged as contributing to the power of AI, including: the power of the positive question; the positive emphasis of the AI interview; the focus on the future; positive outcomes; and the replacement of a focus on the negative with identification and appreciation of the positive.

One of the classic problems confronting the organizational consultant is the commonly encountered problem referred to as resistance to change. It is here that AI creates one of the most important contributions for effective consulting. T. C. Head (2000) set forth an AI explanation of why the approach can be effective in addressing four of the primary reasons for employee resistance.

## GLOBAL AND INTERNATIONAL ORGANIZATIONAL CONSULTING

Head, Sorensen, Preston, and Yaeger (2001) have suggested the value of AI in international consulting contexts. One of the ongoing arguments in the field of international consulting is the extent to which OD interventions might be inappropriate, or might need to be modified, to be consistent with the national cultural values of the host country (Yaeger, 2001). In a review of the use and effectiveness of OD interventions in twelve countries, Head et al. (2001) reported a relationship between the compatibility of national cultural values and the core values of OD, with the level of use and effectiveness of OD. The authors also contended that AI might very well transcend differences in national values, and has universal application. The position appears to have received support, based on responses to the Organizational Culture Inventory, a measure of organizational culture. Current research (Sharkey, Yaeger, & Sorensen, 2001) involving Chinese and Japanese executives has suggested that executives from a range of diverse cultures responded similarly to U.S. samples in describing organizational peak experiences deriving from AI models. A second frequently cited project in the international context is one conducted by Avon Mexico directed toward creating high-quality cross-gender relationships (Cooperrider & Whitney, 2001).

Other AI organizational change case studies have been reported. To date there have been few field experiments of AI. The few so far reported in the literature have reported positive outcomes. Jones (1998) reported a field experiment involving ninety fast food restaurants, comparing AI to traditional change methods. He found the AI-based interventions to be significantly more effective than other change methods (Jones). A second field experiment by White-Zappa (2001) reported similarly positive results using AI in two healthcare systems.

An additional application, which links AI to traditional survey feedback (Sorensen, Sharkey, Head, & Spartz, 2001), was reported for five organizations: three private hospitals, a large financial institution, and a government agency. Each of the studies reported findings relating AI's performance patterns with patterns consistent with high performance.

# CRITICISMS OF AI

To date, little systematic criticism has been directed at AI. Golembiewski (2000) identified four concerns about the AI literature. First, he suggested that AI overstates real but qualified differences. Golembiewski contended that traditional OD consulting has always incorporated those things that work in an organization: the positive aspects of the organization. The distinction between AI and other OD consulting strategies is not in the exclusion of the positive elements of the organization, but in a balance of the positive elements and a focus on the things that need to change. Second, Golembiewski contended that AI is insufficiently integrated with other relevant theories and practices, particularly work that deals with conflict. He also noted that there was insufficient research objectively to assess AI. Finally, Golembiewski noted that the work to date has suffered from an absence of the kind of constructive criticism that is needed to evaluate and develop its tenets.

Several of these points, especially the first and last, are well taken. The dominant use of AI thus far appears to be used most frequently as a front-end intervention, rather than as part of a process that places the consultant in a continuing role in the implementation of change. Of course this concern is not unique to AI, as a number of large group change strategies similarly have focused primarily on the startup of the initiation of the change process.

With regard to Golembiewski's comments regarding lack of linkages to other theories and practices, this is a valid criticism in terms of tightly defined OD interventions. On the other hand, we believe the development of AI theory has been exceptional in building on, and linking to, a much broader area of ideas, literature, and research. AI also represents an important restoration of action research that is a major and critical link to the core of OD theory and practice. AI also links clearly with the values and tradition of the foundation of the field—the works of Maslow, McGregor, and, with particular significance, Kurt Lewin.

Lack of relevant empirical research is an area of concern. The AI research that does exist, including field experiments both in total systems change and team development, has been highly supportive of the effectiveness of AI. Nevertheless, the literature continues to be dominated by anecdotal stories of success. The lack of serious, sustained research efforts appears to be critical if AI is to be better understood and developed, and if it continues to be a major approach to organization consulting. Along with the lack of research literature, AI would benefit from a constructive critique, one that would provide alternative views on the further development and refinement of AI.

Whether or not AI is situation-specific in its applications is not at all clear. AI has been used in a broad range of situations, and the boundaries of its application are not defined. There is emerging evidence that AI might work well under very different conditions, suggested by its recent applications to international and cross-cultural situations (Head, Sorensen, Preston, & Yaeger, 2001).

## SUMMARY AND CONCLUSIONS

In this review article we have provided an overview of a relatively new approach to organizational change and consulting called AI by providing the history, theoretical foundations, process, and applications. We have also noted international AI applications and critiques of the theory.

We believe the evidence to date suggests that AI can provide an effective front end application in organizational change projects, and has incorporated large group methods with the AI Summit. AI can also be used with other classic OD interventions such as team building, culture change, and survey feedback.

The reporting of AI's effectiveness is to a large extent case-oriented and anecdotal at this time. It still needs more rigorous, systematic evaluation. However, the field experiments that have been reported for AI to date consistently suggest favorable outcomes.

Questions clearly remain, however. More rigorous reporting of evaluation research is still needed, along with research on the sustainability of change initiatives using AI. More clarity is needed on the role and responsibility of the organizational consultant using AI. Is the consultant role only responsible for front-end activities, with no responsibility for ongoing work, or is the consultant responsible for the traditional OD roles working with the organization through the entire change process? Finally, there is a need for research and a better understanding, particularly regarding the global application of AI across national and cultural boundaries.

For the organizational consultant, AI appears to be an exceptionally promising approach to organizational change. In the brief period of fifteen years from its first formal statement by Cooperrider and Srivastva (1987), AI has become a global phenomenon in organizational change.

# References

Akinyele, A., Sorensen, P. F., Jr., & Yaeger, T. F. (2001, October). *Recreating high performance cultures with AI.* Paper presented at the First International Conference on Appreciative Inquiry, Baltimore, MD.

Bowling, C., Ludema, J., & Wyss, E. (1997). *Vision twin cities appreciative inquiry report.* Cleveland, OH: Case Western Reserve University, Department of Organizational Behavior.

Bunker, B. B. (1990). Appreciating diversity and modifying organizational cultures: Men and women at work. In S. Srivastva & D.L. Cooperrider (Eds.), *Appreciative management and leadership: The power of positive thought and action in organization* (Rev. ed., pp. 126–149). Euclid, OH: Williams Custom Publishing.

Bushe, G. R. (1995). Advances in appreciative inquiry as an organization development intervention. *Organization Development Journal, 13,* 14–22.

Bushe, G. R. (1998). Appreciative inquiry with teams. *Organization Development Journal, 16,* 41–50.

Bushe, G. R. (2001). Five theories of change embedded in appreciative inquiry. In D. L. Cooperrider, P. F. Sorensen, T. Yaeger, & D. Whitney (Eds.), *Appreciative inquiry: An emerging approach for organization development* (pp. 117–127). Champaign, IL: Stipes.

Bushe, G. R., & Coetzer, G. (1995). Appreciative inquiry as a team development intervention: A controlled experiment. *Journal of Applied Behavioral Science, 31,* 13–30.

Chaffee, P. (1997). Ring of breath around the world: A report of the united religions initiative global conference. *United Religions, A Journal of the United Religions Initiative, 4,* 1–8.

Cooke, R., & Hartmann, J. (1989). *Interpreting the culture styles measured by the organizational culture inventory: Organizational Culture Inventory leader's guide,* Plymouth, MI: Human Synergistics.

Cooperrider, D. L. (1990). Positive image, positive action: The affirmative basis of organizing. In S. Srivastva, & D. L. Cooperrider (Eds.), *Appreciative management and leadership: The power of positive thought and action in organization* (Rev. ed., pp. 91–125). Euclid, OH: Williams Custom Publishing.

Cooperrider, D. L. (1996a). The child as agent of inquiry. *Organization Development Practitioner, 28*(1–2), 5–11.

Cooperrider, D. L. (1996b). Resources for getting appreciative inquiry started: An example of an OD proposal. *Organization Development Practitioner, 28*(1–2), 23–33.

Cooperrider, D. L., Sorensen, P. F., Jr., Whitney, D., & Yaeger, T. F. (2000). *Appreciative inquiry: Rethinking human organization toward a positive theory of change.* Champaign, IL: Stipes.

Cooperrider, D. L., Sorensen, P. F., Jr., Yaeger, T. F., & Whitney, D. (Eds.) (2001). *Appreciative inquiry: An emerging direction for OD.* Champaign, IL: Stipes.

Cooperrider, D. L., & Srivastva, S. (1987). Appreciative inquiry in organizational life. In W. Pasmore & R. Woodman (Eds.), *Research in organizational change and development* (Vol. 1, pp. 129–169). Greenwich, CT: JAI Press.

Cooperrider, D. L., & Whitney, D. (2001) A positive revolution in change: Appreciative inquiry. In D. L. Cooperrider, P. F. Sorensen, Jr., T. F. Yaeger, & D. Whitney (Eds.), *Appreciative inquiry: An emerging direction for OD* (pp. 9–29). Champaign, IL: Stipes.

Gibbs, C., & Ackerly, S. (1997, June). *United religions initiative global summit summary report.* Paper presented at the United Religions Initiative Global Summit Summary Report, San Francisco.

Golembiewski, B. (2000). Three perspectives on appreciative inquiry. *OD Practitioner: Journal of the Organization Development Network, 32*(1), 53–58.

Golembiewski, R. T. (1998). Appreciating appreciative inquiry: Diagnosis and perspectives on how to do better. In W. Pasmore & R. Woodman (Eds.), *Research in organizational change and development* (Vol. 11, pp. 1–45). Greenwich, CT: JAI Press.

Hammond, S. A. (1996). *The thin book of appreciative inquiry.* Plano, TX: Thin Book.

Head, R. L. (2000). Appreciative inquiry as a team-development intervention for newly formed heterogeneous groups. *OD Practitioner: Journal of the Organization Development Network, 32*(1), 59–66.

Head, T. C. (2000). Appreciative inquiry: Debunking the mythology behind resistance to change. *OD Practitioner: Journal of the Organization Development Network, 32*(1), 27–35.

Head, T. C., Sorensen, P. F., Jr., Preston, J., & Yaeger, T. F. (2001). Is appreciative inquiry the philosopher's stone? In D. L. Cooperrider, P. F. Sorensen, Jr., T. F. Yaeger & D. Whitney (Eds.), *Appreciative inquiry: An emerging approach for organization development* (pp. 363–378). Stipes.

Jones, D. A. (1998). A field experiment in appreciative inquiry. *Organization Development Journal, 16,* 69–78.

Ludema, J. D. (2000). Power of the unconditional positive question. In P. Reason & H. Bradbury (Eds.), *Handbook of action research* (pp.189–199). Thousand Oaks: Sage.

Mann, A. J. (1997). An appreciative inquiry model for building partnerships. *Global Social Innovations, Journal of the GEM Initiative, 1,* 41–44.

Odell, M. (2000). An appreciative inquiry conversation guide: Creating a small forum in which leaders of the world religions can gather in mutual respect and dialogue. *Global Social Innovations, Journal of the GEM Initiative, 1,* 23–26.

Rainey, M. A. (1996). An appreciative inquiry into the factors of culture continuity during leadership transition. *Organization Development Practitioner, 28,* 34–41.

Rainey, M. A. (2001). An appreciative inquiry into the factors of culture continuity during leadership transition: A case of LeadShare, Canada. In D. L. Cooperrider, P. F. Sorensen, T. Yaeger, & D. Whitney (Eds.), *Appreciative inquiry: An emerging approach for organization development* (pp. 205–215). Champaign, IL: Stipes.

Sena, S. O., & Booy, D. (1997). Appreciative inquiry approach to community development: The world vision Tanzania experience. *Global Social Innovations, Journal of the GEM Initiative, 1,* 7–12.

Sharkey, L. (1999). Changing organizational culture through leadership development: A case in leadership transformation. *OD Journal,* 29–37.

Sharkey, L., Sorensen, P. F., Jr., Yaeger, T., (1998, June). *Integrating traditional and contemporary approaches to change: Culture, survey feedback and appreciative inquiry.* Paper presented at the Creating Healthy Organization Cultures Conference, Chicago, IL.

Sharkey, L., Yaeger, T. F., and Sorensen, P. F., Jr. (2001). Appreciative inquiry in a *Fortune* 50 global organization: Extending the concept of AI to Japan. In D. L. Cooperrider, P. F. Sorensen, Jr., T. F. Yaeger, & D. Whitney, D. (Eds.), *Appreciative inquiry: An emerging direction for OD* (pp. 441–447). Champaign, IL: Stipes.

Sorensen, P. F., Jr., Sharkey, L., Head, R., Spartz, D. (2001). Appreciative inquiry meets the logical positivist. In D. L. Cooperrider, P. F. Sorensen, Jr., T. F. Yaeger, & D. Whitney (Eds.), *Appreciative inquiry: An emerging direction for OD* (pp. 341–347). Champaign, IL: Stipes.

Sorensen, P. F., Jr., Yaeger, T. F., & Nicoll, D. (2000). Appreciative inquiry 2000: Fad or important new focus for OD? *OD Practitioner: Journal of the Organization Development Network, 32*(1), 3–5.

Srivastva, S., & Cooperrider, D. L. (Eds.). (1990). *Appreciative management and leadership: The power of positive thought and action in organizations.* San Francisco: Jossey-Bass.

Srivastva, S., & Cooperrider, D. L. (Eds.). (1998). *Organizational wisdom and executive courage.* San Francisco: New Lexington Press.

Watkins, J. M., & Mohr, B. J. (2001). *Appreciative inquiry: Change at the speed of imagination.* San Francisco: Jossey-Bass.

White-Zappa, B. (2001). *Hopeful corporate citizenship: A quantitative and qualitative relationship between organizational hope, appreciative inquiry and organizational citizenship behavior.* Unpublished doctoral dissertation, Benedictine University Lisle, IL.

Whitney, D., & Cooperrider, D. L. (2000). The appreciative inquiry summit: An emerging methodology for whole system positive change. *OD Practitioner: Journal of the Organization Development Network, 32*(2), 13–26.

Williams, R. F. (1996). Survey guided appreciative inquiry: A case study. *Organization Development Practitioner, 28*(1–2), 43–51.

Yaeger, T. F. (2001). Globalizing organization development: Convergence or divergence? In P. F. Sorensen, Jr., T. C. Head, T. F. Yaeger, & D. L. Cooperrider (Eds.), *Global and international organization development* (3rd ed., pp. 81–92). Champaign, IL: Stipes.

Yaeger, T. F., & Sorensen, P. F., Jr. (2001). What matters most in appreciative inquiry: Review and thematic assessment. In D. L. Cooperrider, P. F. Sorensen, Jr., T. F. Yaeger, & D. Whitney (Eds.), *Appreciative inquiry: An emerging direction for organization development* (pp. 129–142). Champaign, IL: Stipes.

# PART SEVEN

# MEASUREMENT, EVALUATION, AND EFFECTIVENESS ISSUES

# CHAPTER TWENTY-SIX

# Interventions That Work
# (and Some That Don't)

## *An Executive Summary of the Organizational Change Literature*

Terry R. Halfhill, Joseph W. Huff, Douglas A. Johnson,
Rodger D. Ballentine, and Michael M. Beyerlein
*Center for the Study of Work Teams and Department of Psychology*
*University of North Texas*

Consulting psychologists are often called on to create lasting organizational change by modifying the structure, process, or technology of an organization. However, a wide variety of organizational change approaches exist, and a variety of outcomes can be targeted. This choice of interventions and outcomes can leave practitioners unsure of the specific interventions that should be employed in the attempt to reach specified intervention goals. For example, if turnover is high in the organization, what type of organizational intervention would be most effective in retaining employees? Likewise, if performance needs to be improved, what interventions increase lagging performance metrics? Can the same interventions target both of these outcomes? Additional factors might also need to be considered by the practitioner, such as whether the intervention fits within the existing framework of the organizational structure. Having a broad knowledge of the organizational change and development literature is essential for effective intervention strategy selection and implementation.

The purpose of this chapter is to provide a summary of the empirical literature regarding organizational change and its impact on various organizational outcomes. Unlike traditional reviews that synthesize individual studies (see, for example, Armenakis & Bedeian, 1999), this review analyzes findings from several qualitative and quantitative reviews. Although substantial agreement exists on how best to classify outcome measures, there is little agreement on the best way to categorize specific interventions. Therefore, we organize this chapter by major outcome variables, specifically productivity, withdrawal behaviors (that is, absenteeism, turnover), and individual attitudes. Together, our review includes the results of nearly 600 studies from the last forty years, reporting more than 1,300 relationships between organizational interventions and outcomes.

# WHAT IS ORGANIZATIONAL CHANGE AND DEVELOPMENT (OCD)?

Many broad and varying definitions of organizational change exist, and nearly as many terms are used to describe change efforts. The terms organizational development, organizational transformation, and organizational innovation are used interchangeably to refer to change procedures at the organizational level. Thus, any initiative associated with these three broad terms can fall into the scope of organizational change. Some definitions of organizational change distinguish between planned and unplanned change (Porras & Robertson, 1992; Robertson, Roberts, & Porras, 1993), and others make more finite distinctions between concepts such as *collaboration of organizational members* (Beer, 1980), *top-management supported* (French & Bell, 1984), and *involving a change agent* (Bennis, 1966).

Another dimension of organizational change is the degree of pervasiveness of the initiative. Organizational change can be as simple as installing new technology or changing employee schedules to make them more flexible. Or it can be more extensive, such as initiatives involved in flattening the organizational chart, or aligning the organization to work in a collaborative work system that requires marked changes to the basic structure of the organization itself. In addition, many change initiatives are not implemented alone; often they entail multiple initiatives that are implemented simultaneously.

To help conceptualize the categories of change initiatives, researchers have created classification systems to help reduce the overall number of categories of OCD interventions. Of the six articles reviewed in the current chapter, the simplest intervention classification scheme was created by Neuman, Edwards, and Raju (1989). They used only two main categories: human processes and technostructural interventions. Perhaps the most comprehensive attempt to categorize the various change initiatives were the four general categories used by Macy and Izumi (1993): organizational structure changes, human resources directed change, technological changes, and total quality management (TQM)-related change initiatives. Porras and Robertson (1992), and Robertson et al. (1993), used the earlier categorization scheme identified by Porras (1987) to define four categories of interventions: organizing arrangements, social factors, technology, and social setting. Guzzo, Jette, and Katzell (1985) divided the

OCD interventions into a more finely grained set of eleven categories originally identified by Katzell, Bienstock, and Faerstein (1977). The categories used by each of the six reviewed studies are presented in more detail in Table 26.1.

Instead of attempting to develop a wide-ranging classification system, we took a more pragmatic approach. We defined the categories of organizational change based on those intervention categories that are contained within the core set of review studies that are included in the current study. Using this approach, we began with Guzzo et al.'s eleven categories (1985) and determined whether the remaining studies provided data that would fit within these categories. We identified two additional intervention categories: interventions that included self-directed work teams (SDWTs), and those that included more than one intervention. This resulted in thirteen total categories. This categorization helps answer the question, "What intervention can be used for a specific outcome?" We believe that this approach is more informative for practitioners.

## OCD Theory

The topic of OCD is in a very early stage, perhaps no older than thirty years (the point at which researchers departed from the case study approach to OCD, and began treating the organization as the unit of analysis). As a result, the OCD literature lacks an abundance of theory, and existing theory is not firmly buttressed. Nevertheless, many studies can be integrated.

## Individual versus Organizational Change

One of the more salient features of OCD theory for practitioners is the notion of individual versus organizational change. This issue addresses the question of whether individual attitudes and behavior must change in order to achieve any lasting organizational change. We do not attempt to definitively answer the question in this chapter, because there is not enough empirical evidence available for either side of the argument. However, available data do provide thought-provoking insight into the question, which might be of use to those attempting to create change in organizational contexts.

Porras and Robertson (1992) published a qualitative review of the organizational change literature, and Robertson et al. (1993) published a quantitative review of very similar studies. The model presented by Porras and Robertson states that the environment impacts the work setting, which is defined using the four categories listed in Table 26.1. All of the variables included in the four work design categories have an impact on individual cognitions, which affects on-the-job behavior, and in turn affects organizational performance. Thus, at the heart of the Porras and Robertson model is the underlying assumption that change in the individual is at the core of organizational change. Additionally, any lasting successful change results when members alter their on-the-job behavior in appropriate ways.

Table 26.1. OCD Intervention Classification Taxonomies Used by the Six Reviewed Studies.

| Review and Category | Definition and Examples |
|---|---|
| *Neuman et al. (1989)* | *From Friedlander and Brown (1974)* |
| • Human processes | Interventions to help improve human functioning and process: training, participation in decision-making, RJPs, team building, grid OD, feedback |
| • Technostructural | Interventions that improve work content and method, and the relationship between workers: job (re)design and enlargement, job enrichment, and work schedule changes |
| • Multifaceted | More than one human process or technostructural intervention |
| *Macy and Izumi (1993)* | *Defined by Macy and Izumi (1993)* |
| • Structural | Significant change occurred in the organization's hierarchical structure (for example, self-directed work teams, changes in goal setting, feedback, compensation systems) |
| • Human resources | Changes employed within the organization's existing hierarchical structure (for example, employee and manager training, job enrichment, team building, selection methods) |
| • Technological | Changes in the mechanical, informational, and process technologies (for example, office computer hardware and software, improved manufacturing systems, computerized process and control systems) |
| • Total quality management | Changes to improve the quality of organizational products and services (for example, increased customer focus, customer and supplier partnerships, employee inspection of materials, processes, and outputs) |
| *Porras and Robertson (1992); Robertson et al. (1993)* | *Defined by Porras (1987)* |
| • Organizing arrangements | Formal elements of organizations designed to provide coordination and control (for example, reward systems, formal organizational structures) |

*(Continued)*

Table 26.1. *(Continued)*

| Review and Category | Definition and Examples |
|---|---|
| • Social factors | Characteristics of individuals and groups (for example, interaction patterns, attitudes) |
| • Technology | Any process related to the transformation of inputs into outputs (for example, work flow, job design or redesign) |
| • Social setting | Characteristics of the physical space and layout |
| *Pasmore et al. (1982)* | |
| • Autonomous work groups | Teams control their own activities—rewards, training, promotion, and so forth. |
| • Technical skill development | Acquisition of new skills |
| • Action groups | Purpose is to eliminate all status differentials between management and labor |
| • Changes to reward system | To align with organizational objectives |
| • Employee quality inspection | Formation of quality circles |
| • Technological changes | Joint optimization with social systems |
| • Team formation | Includes training and structural changes |
| • Facilitative leadership | Leader training and delegation of authority |
| • Operator maintenance | Includes training and autonomy for end users of equipment |
| *Guzzo et al. (1985)* | *From Katzell, et al. (1977)* |
| • Recruitment and selection | Realistic job previews only (all other interventions were correlational studies) |
| • Training and instruction | Behavioral modeling, HR programs, management seminars |
| • Appraisal and feedback | Formal and informal systems of appraisal and feedback |
| • Management by objectives | Variety of interventions specifying objectives and tying rewards to objective attainment |
| • Goal setting | Setting difficult, yet attainable, goals; worker goal formation not necessary |
| • Financial compensation | Monetary rewards tied to individual, group, or organizational performance |
| • Work redesign | Job enrichment |
| • Decision-making techniques | Any improvement to decision making (primarily manager focused) |
| • Supervisory methods | Retraining and role redefinition of supervisors |
| • Work rescheduling | Use of flextime or compressed work weeks |
| • Socio-technical interventions | Integrated HR changes; joint consideration of social and technological demands |

A model presented by Macy and Izumi (1993) holds that it might be more effective to begin with the desired organizational outcome and work backward toward an appropriate intervention. This would imply that individual behavioral change might not be necessary to achieve organizational change.

Several of the tables in the Porras and Robertson article (1992) demonstrated that in almost half of the relevant studies, a work setting change took place in the absence of any behavioral change, individual behavioral change was not necessary for change in all outcomes, and individual behavioral change was not necessary for a change in organizational outcomes. According to these findings, organizational change occurred in the absence of individual behavioral change.

Furthermore, Robertson et al. (1993) reported a .53 correlation between individual behavior and organizational outcome effect sizes (effect sizes are statistics used to indicate the magnitude of an outcome). They interpreted these results as supporting the proposition that individual behavioral change is positively associated with organizational outcome change. Upon closer inspection however, it becomes clear that this hypothesis was tested by correlating two effect sizes. This correlation simply implies that both *effect sizes* were probably positive in direction and small to moderate in magnitude, which would have resulted in a moderately high correlation.

Again, we do not believe that, on the basis of presently available empirical evidence, it is possible to provide a definitive answer to the question of individual versus organizational change. However, we believe practical advice can still be offered. In many cases, organizational change can occur in the absence of individual behavioral change.

## METHODS USED IN THE CURRENT REVIEW

The current chapter synthesizes six influential qualitative and quantitative reviews of the consulting psychology literature related to OCD. Although a comprehensive review of all material on organizational change is beyond the scope of this chapter, one comprehensive meta-analytic review of all organizational development and change studies would be useful to our field, and we call upon potential authors to integrate all of the research in this general area.

Six separate reviews are included, because no single review had a large enough scope to represent multiple date ranges, theoretical approaches, and a broad range of interventions and organizational outcomes. For example, one meta-analysis assessed the impact of a variety of organizational change interventions from ninety-eight research studies, yet focused solely on productivity as the outcome measure (Guzzo et al., 1985). Another meta-analytic review also included a large number of research studies ($n = 126$), but focused only on attitudinal outcomes (Neuman et al., 1989). Other studies were more constrained by the number of studies available, or the change initiatives reviewed. Porras and Robertson (1992), and Robertson et al.(1993), examined seventy-two and forty-seven studies, respectively, covering a variety of change initiatives and outcome variables. Pasmore, Frances, Haldeman, and Shani's review (1982) included 134 studies, yet focused only on socio-technical system-based interventions. Finally, Macy and Izumi (1993) assessed the impact of multiple change initiatives on financial measures, individual attitudes, and employee withdrawal behaviors for 131 research studies. Although Macy and Izumi provided the most comprehensive review of the area conducted to date, their review still does not include all of the pertinent research studies from the literature. Table 26.2 lists the studies and their features included in the present review.

We now focus on methodological issues related to reviewing the organizational change and development literature. First, we make a distinction between the review of individual studies and reviews of review studies, in an attempt to bolster the methodological and statistical rigor of the current review. Therefore, the current methods are akin to a qualitative analysis of a number of qualitative and quantitative reviews. Thus, our unit of analysis is the review level, rather than the individual study level. In addition, four of the six review articles that we include in formulating our results used meta-analysis. In the case of the two qualitative reviews, we attempt to interpret the results with the same metric, an effect size, as is commonly reported in meta-analytic research. Due to the influence of meta-analysis and our adherence to the interpretation of organizational change initiatives as effect sizes, we briefly describe meta-analytic methods.

Meta-analysis refers to the statistical analysis of "a large collection of analysis results from individual studies for the purpose of integrating the findings. It connotes a rigorous alternative to the casual, narrative discussions of research studies which typify our attempts to make sense of the rapidly expanding research literature" (Glass, 1976, p. 3). Meta-analysis utilizes a set of decision processes and statistical procedures to accumulate the results of multiple, independent, correlational, and experimental research studies that are related to the same set of research questions. Unlike more traditional qualitative reviews that use some sort of counting procedure to summarize whether interventions do or do not work, meta-analysis utilizes the summary statistics from individual studies as data points. One general assumption of meta-analysis is that each study reviewed provides a differing estimate of the underlying relationship within the general population of research studies, referred to as *rho* ($\rho$). By sampling multiple studies from the same general population, one can better estimate the relationship between variables of interest for the population.

Although the outcomes presented are more statistically robust, meta-analysis raises its own concerns and issues. First, the decisions made by researchers to

Table 26.2. Studies Included in the Current Review.

| Brief Reference | Dates Inclusive | Study Type | Outcome Categories | Number of Studies | Number of Effect Sizes |
|---|---|---|---|---|---|
| Guzzo et al. (1985) | 1971–1981 | Quantitative | Performance<br>• Combined<br>• Output<br>• Withdrawal<br>• Disruptions | 98 | 330;<br>$n = 37,371$ |
| Macy and Izumi (1993) | 1961–1991 | Quantitative | Performance<br>• Overall financial performance<br>Quantity<br>Quality<br>Cost<br>• Behavioral performance (mostly withdrawal)<br>• Attitudes<br>Work environment<br>Group characteristics<br>Individual characteristics | 131 | 506; N/A |
| Neuman et al. (1989) | 1950–1986 | Quantitative | Attitudes<br>• Overall satisfaction<br>General satisfaction<br>Facet satisfaction<br>• Other attitudes<br>Attitudes toward self<br>Attitudes toward others<br>Attitudes toward job<br>Attitudes toward organization | 126 | 238;<br>$n = 40,633$ |
| Pasmore et al. (1982) | 1970s | Qualitative | Performance<br>Withdrawal<br>Attitudes | 134 | N/A; N/A |
| Porras and Robertson (1992) | | Qualitative | | 63 | N/A; N/A |
| Robertson et al. (1993) | 1959–1988 | Quantitative | Work setting<br>Individual behavior<br>Organizational outcomes | 47 | 302;<br>$n = 29,611$ |

include or not include specific studies (the issue of *inclusion criteria* ) can influence the results of meta-analyses. Although such criteria can also influence qualitative reviews, inclusion criteria are commonly more complicated in meta-analytic reviews. In the case of the four meta-analyses reviewed here, the inclusion criteria varied from Neuman et al.'s least restrictive (1989) to Macy and Izumi's most restrictive (1993). A list of each study and their inclusion criteria are included in Table 26.3.

Second, without necessary statistical data, a study cannot be included in a meta-analytic investigation. Therefore, studies reporting anecdotally on the effectiveness of an intervention are excluded. This can severely reduce the

Table 26.3. Inclusion Criteria across Studies Included in Current Review.

| Study | Inclusion Criteria |
|---|---|
| Guzzo et al. (1985) | 1. Experimental methodology<br>2. Objective measures of productivity<br>3. Organization; not laboratory study<br>4. U.S. company<br>5. Between 1971 and 1981<br>6. Necessary data |
| Macy and Izumi (1993) | 1. North American organization<br>2. Longitudinal design<br>3. Naturalistic field setting<br>4. At least fifteen employees per organization affected<br>5. Pre-post or experimental control design<br>6. Published research study between 1961 and 1991<br>7. Necessary data |
| Neuman et al. (1989) | 1. Ongoing organization<br>2. Intervention primary independent variable (IV)<br>3. Satisfaction or job attitudes dependent variable (DV)<br>4. Necessary data |
| Pasmore et al. (1982) | 1. STS intervention<br>2. North American emphasis<br>3. Primarily studies from 1970s |
| Porras and Robertson (1992) | 1. Published research study between 1975 and 1988<br>2. Field study<br>3. Participants, design, and methodology reported<br>4. Statistical data presented |
| Robertson et al. (1993) | 1. Published research study<br>2. Ongoing organization<br>3. Necessary data |

number of usable studies from any more general population of interest. For example, both Pasmore et al. (1982), and Porras and Robertson (1992), are qualitative reviews, which place much less emphasis on the quality of the data reviewed. In such qualitative studies, data such as reports acknowledging that an intervention was effective could be used. However, in the four meta-analytic studies included here, only those studies with statistical data that could be converted into a metric of effect size (for example, $r$, $g$, or $d$) were included. Therefore, the number of usable studies from any more general population of interest is also reduced. For example, Macy and Izumi (1993) identified approximately 1,800 published studies conducted between 1961 and 1991 on the subject of organizational change. Of these 1,800 studies, only 500 remained after applying their inclusion criteria. In the end, it was determined that 131 of these 500 studies met the criteria for inclusion in the meta-analysis.

Third, meta-analytic techniques vary in their use of parameter estimation formulae, assumptions, and the rules used for integrating individual studies (Hedges & Olkin, 1985; Rosenthal, 1986). As advocated by Hunter, Schmidt, and Jackson (1982), all of the included studies calculated individual effect size statistics for each outcome variable, rather than collapsing across outcomes. Three of the four meta-analyses (Guzzo et al., 1985; Macy & Izumi, 1993; Robertson et al., 1993) utilized only experimental research in their reviews. Neuman et al. (1989) used a validity generalization approach (Raju & Burke, 1983) that included correlational studies in their sample. In addition, the three meta-analyses corrected only for sampling error, but Neuman et al. (1989) corrected for multiple sources of artifactual variance (for example, sampling error, range restriction, predictor and criterion reliability). Finally, Macy and Izumi (1993) varied the formulae used to calculate effect sizes, depending on whether the study used between-subjects or within-subjects experimental designs. Thus, the number and variety of studies included in meta-analytic studies varies. For example, Porras and Robertson (1992) included sixty-three studies in their qualitative review. In contrast, only forty-seven studies were included in Robertson et al.'s quantitative review (1993).

Fourth, the manner in which the various predictors and criterion are defined or aggregated can alter the manner in which results are interpreted and how easily they can be compared across meta-analyses and qualitative reviews alike. Since intervention schemas are not yet standardized, no common taxonomies exist with which to categorize the various predictor variables. The manner in which dependent variables are defined or categorized can influence a single review's results and the interpretations made from that review. For example, Pasmore et al. (1982) placed absenteeism and turnover into two separate outcome categories. Macy and Izumi (1993), in contrast, created an aggregated variable they termed behavioral performance, which included absenteeism, turnover, and other forms of counterproductive employee behavior. In either case, the use of nonequivalent predictor and criterion categories restricts the ability to generalize across the various reviews. Consumers of the literature must attempt to integrate categorical schemes to find the commonalities between studies.

All this implies, as in the case of qualitative literature reviews, that meta-analytic results from two or more studies examining the same literature base can yield different results. The decisions made by the researcher(s) can influence the number and type of studies reviewed, the types of predictors and criteria use, and the basis for computing the results. Although the results of meta-analyses are more statistically rigorous than qualitative reviews, the quality and generalizability of the results are no better than the quality of the studies that were included in the meta-analysis. Therefore, it is imperative for researchers who use meta-analytic techniques to fully document all of their procedures and the specific choices made during all stages of the analysis.

Finally, a brief discussion of the most common metric used to describe meta-analytic study findings is necessary. Meta-analyses commonly summarize their findings with a statistic that is called the *d*-effect (Hedges & Olkin, 1985; Rosenthal, 1986). Although two variants of the *d*-effect exist, either can be generally interpreted as consisting of the standard deviation change between two means. In experimental studies, this difference is interpretable as being the difference between the experimental and control groups, and can be either positive or negative, representing either positive or negative changes. For example, suppose that a manufacturing company decides to implement teams in the organization, and that they currently have two production lines. Levels of productivity are similar between the two production lines. After the intervention (team training, goal setting, and so forth), productivity increases 30 percent for the line that received the intervention. Let us further assume that productivity did not change for the production line that did not receive the intervention. The distance between the two mean scores (post-intervention line 1 and line 2) is the *d*-effect. In addition, *d*-effects vary in magnitude. Cohen (1969) defined five ranges of effect sizes based on different magnitude ranges. These criteria of the magnitude of effect sizes will be used in this chapter, and are shown in Table 26.4.

Table 26.4. Common *d*-Effect Intervals.

| Degree of Improvement | *d*-Effect Size |
| --- | --- |
| Very small improvement | .01–.24 |
| Small improvement | .25–.49 |
| Marginal improvement | .50–.74 |
| Large improvement | .75–.99 |
| Very large improvement | 1.00 or larger |

# RESULTS

## Common Intervention Steps

For beginning practitioners and those tasked with their first change effort, it might be helpful to illustrate intervention steps that are common to many change efforts. In a review of sixteen different change theories presented from 1958 to 1983, Porras and Robertson (1992) document the implementation steps common across procedural theories of change. Additionally, Edgar Schein authored a practical handbook *Process Consultation: Vol. I. Its Role in Organization Development (1988),* in which he documented the steps he used when helping organizations. Considerable overlap exists between these sources and the five steps described below.

1. *Role Definition*—This step includes client selection, entry into the organization, and the contracting of roles. Often, management does not know exactly what is wrong; they simply know that *something* is wrong. In this type of situation, it is important that the change agent help clarify issues and subsequently define the consultant's role. There are also instances in which management knows exactly what is wrong, and this is precisely why a consultant was asked to help. Sometimes the organization is not aware of, or does not know, what services are available to them. In such cases, the change agent is responsible for linking the appropriate intervention or strategy with the desired organizational outcome.

2. *Diagnosis/Assessment*—This step includes formulating a comprehensive assessment model and strategy for diagnosis. Schein (1988) considered assessment itself a form of intervention, and warned the consultant not to lose sight of the importance of the type and form of questions asked of organizational employees.

3. *Planning*—This step often includes two stages. In the first stage, the change agent identifies appropriate interventions based on the gap between current and ideal levels of organizational effectiveness, or a lack of alignment between organizational systems. Stage two involves selecting the intervention, and can be influenced by variables such as an organization's readiness to change, the power and influence of the change agent, and the available leverage points for change.

4. *Intervention*—This stage consists of implementing the intervention.

5. *Monitoring*—This stage includes monitoring and feedback, stabilization, and integration over time. The focus of monitoring is to ensure that post-intervention levels of performance are maintained, and to reimplement interventions as necessary.

## Productivity and Financial Outcomes

Guzzo et al. (1985) quantitatively reviewed the effects of nearly 100 OD studies on productivity; Macy and Izumi (1993) quantitatively reviewed the effects of 131 field studies on three categories of financial outcomes. This section addresses the findings of these studies in detail, and provides a summary.

In the Guzzo et al. research (1985), an intervention program was defined as being an experimental treatment or change in one or more independent variables. Productivity was defined as having three components: (1) *output*—quantity, quality, and cost effectiveness; (2) *withdrawal*—turnover and absenteeism; and (3) *disruption*—accidents, strikes, and other costly disturbances. Organizational context variables included the size of the organization, the type of organization (private, government, and other), and the type of worker (managerial or professional, blue-collar labor, sales, and clerical). Organizational design variables included the number of weeks between the initiation of an intervention project and the collection of the dependent measure(s), and whether control groups (true, nonequivalent, other, and self- or repeated measures) were used.

The overall effect of all interventions in the Guzzo et al. study on productivity (1985) was statistically significant ($d = .44$). This indicates that OD interventions in the studies they aggregated were associated with an increase of nearly one-half standard deviation in productivity over workers not exposed to the interventions. More specifically, training, goal setting, socio-technical system (STS), work design, and appraisal and feedback interventions had the highest impact on productivity, while providing financial incentives did not affect productivity.

The interventions differentially affected types of productivity. The effect size for measures of withdrawal behaviors (absenteeism, turnover) was significantly lower than the average of all types of productivity. Additionally, withdrawal behaviors were only affected by interventions that addressed supervisory methods and work rescheduling. Disruptions were significantly affected by goal-setting interventions only. Most interventions significantly affected output, but failed to affect withdrawal.

In general, change efforts had greater impact in small rather than large organizations ($d = .63$, compared to .42), and in government rather than other types of organizations ($d = .54$, compared to .38). Interventions were more effective with sales ($d = .62$) and managerial ($d = .68$) employees than with labor ($d = .27$) and clerical ($d = .22$) employees. Effect sizes were smaller if the design included a randomized control group ($d = .23$), and larger if the organization was implementing two or more contrasting interventions ($d = .72$). Time since the intervention revealed a small, statistically significant negative relationship ($r = -.10$, $p < .05$), indicating that the effects of the intervention get weaker as time increases.

Macy and Izumi (1993) also reviewed the literature on organizational change and its relationship to financial outcomes. Similarly to Guzzo et al. (1985), they defined financial outcomes as *quantity* (output, sales, actual dollars, and productivity), *quality* (rejects, repairs, defects, customer returns, rework, yield, and scrap), and *costs* (repairs, errors, downtime, labor costs, overtime, recruitment and training costs, and office and manufacturing supplies). This meta-analysis only included those studies with longitudinal research designs that were conducted in work settings. The included studies had to have reported appropriate statistics for analysis, and have collected data at two points in time, or have used a post-intervention only with a control group. Although the restrictive inclusion criteria limited the number of studies, it allowed for more informed inferences about linking interventions with outcomes. Additionally, the individual, group, and organizational levels of analysis were each represented by approximately one-third of the studies. TQM studies were not included due to a lack of methodological rigor in published accounts (for a review, see Hackman & Wageman, 1995).

The mean $d$-effect size for all financial indicators in the Macy and Izumi study (1993) was 1.27, nearly three times the Guzzo et al. estimate (1985). This might be in part due to the authors' having included only those studies with longitudinal designs, perhaps extracting a more pure effect size. On the other hand, most of the outcome data (75 percent) were collected less than two years after the intervention was introduced, a relatively short time period, given the nature of change and its tendency to decrease over time. Additionally, absenteeism and turnover, two variables seemingly unaffected by many interventions, were considered behavioral outcomes, not financial measures. Although the cost category had the largest effect size ($d = 3.64$), it also had a very large standard deviation (SD = 13.68). After the authors removed one outlier from the analysis, the effect size reduced considerably ($d = 1.08$). If the authors were to recalculate the overall mean effect size after accounting for the outlier in the cost category, it would be substantially less than 1.27. Quantity and quality also exhibited effect sizes above one standard deviation (1.13 and 1.08, respectively, with no outliers removed).

Organizations implementing multiple interventions across design categories (structural, human resources, and technological) showed larger outcomes than organizations implementing fewer interventions simultaneously. Effect sizes were larger for manufacturing organizations, which also had the greatest number of average interventions. The most effective change strategy was the simultaneous implementation of a combination of interventions from all three categories (structural, human resources, and technological). The next most effective strategy was to implement a structural intervention, followed by a combination of human resources and structural interventions.

Overall, the effect of OD interventions on productivity is reported to be small according to Guzzo et al. (1985), and very large according to Macy and Izumi

(1993). The actual effect is likely somewhere between .44 and 1.27, but as Guzzo et al. (1985) note, "Cohen (1969) characterizes this as an effect large enough to be visible to the naked eye" (p. 289). The effects vary with the type of productivity that is being measured. Quantity and quality are more likely to change than absenteeism or turnover. Training, goal setting, and STS interventions had the most powerful effects, and realistic job previews had negligible effects. Reward systems changes were not significant overall, but in some isolated cases, reward system changes did have a significant impact on outcomes. This finding is undoubtedly due to enormous variations in the results of the studies. As the authors note, although incentive plans are often more complicated than they look, if done correctly, they can have tremendous effects on output (for a review, see DeMatteo, Eby, & Sundstrom, 1998).

Interventions are more strongly associated with productivity when the organization is smaller, governmental in nature, and aimed at managerial or professional employees, or sales employees. There is also support for the simultaneous integration of multiple change initiatives.

## Employee Withdrawal Behaviors (Tardiness, Absenteeism, and Turnover)

Although employee withdrawal behaviors are commonly categorized as a performance or productivity dimension, we believe that there are both theoretical and practical advantages to separating employee withdrawal behaviors from more direct indicators of performance. First, the withdrawal literature is quite voluminous, and specific models have defined the antecedents and stages included in employee withdrawal. Although withdrawal behaviors are commonly aggregated, specific models exist for lateness (Blau, 1994), absenteeism (Steers & Rhodes, 1978, 1984), and turnover (Hom & Griffeth, 1995; Mobely, Griffeth, Hand, & Meglino, 1979). The common theme uniting the study of withdrawal behavior was the underlying assumption that the primary cause of employee withdrawal is employee dissatisfaction (and other negative employee attitudes). In all three areas, researchers assumed that employees attempt to avoid dissatisfying or uninvolving work (Hom & Griffeth, 1995). Second, we argue that it is practically important to separate withdrawal behavior from employee performance and productivity. In many cases, practitioners may appropriately wish to target a specific outcome, or perhaps even a specific category of withdrawal (for example, turnover) or performance (for example, quality), because that is the problem of interest to the organization. Unless the same interventions affect each outcome in exactly the same manner, separating the two categories, and perhaps further demarcating the subcategories, should be attempted. Thus, the current results separate withdrawal from performance; however, further divisions of withdrawal behavior seem unlikely, because no information is provided for lateness or tardiness. In addition, only one of the reviews (Pasmore et al., 1982) divided withdrawal into absence and turnover. Macy and Izumi (1993) combined all withdrawal behaviors, including measures of counterproductivity, into a single outcome that they termed *behavioral performance*.

Three of the six review studies included data relevant to the examination of employee withdrawal (Guzzo et al., 1985; Macy & Izumi, 1993; Pasmore et al., 1982). Across the eleven intervention categories defined by Guzzo et al., only ten had sufficient data ($n \geq 5$) in which to examine effectiveness; decision-making had insufficient data. Two of the remaining ten intervention types, supervisory methods and work schedules, demonstrated significant effects on reducing employee withdrawal. In both cases, the average effect sizes could be considered very small improvements ($d = .11$ for supervisory methods, and $d = .10$ for work rescheduling). Three interventions (employee training, financial compensation, and work redesign) demonstrated small to moderate effect sizes (with respective $d$ estimates of .68, .34, and .28), but it must be noted that the confidence intervals included the value of zero, suggesting the possibility of no effect at all, or that possible moderator variables exist for these relationships. Thus, the results of Guzzo et al. would suggest that the various categories of OCD interventions either do not readily influence employee withdrawal, or that the relationship is more complex than a direct effects model can affect or capture. These results strongly contrast with the much more positive effects of the OCD interventions for other performance criteria, thus supporting our decision to separate withdrawal from the larger category of performance.

Overall, the results of the Macy and Izumi (1993) meta-analysis suggest a more positive picture of the effectiveness of OCD interventions in reducing employee withdrawal. For the fifty-five studies that targeted withdrawal behavior, the mean reported effect size was large and positive ($d = .89$). The meta-analysis also had a large standard deviation (SD = 2.07). These results suggest that some interventions were effective, although other interventions were either ineffective or counterproductive. Macy and Izumi broke down the effect sizes to the level of two of their four intervention categories, structural changes and human resource changes, and a combination of both changes. They reported that the largest effect size for withdrawal behavior was for structural design interventions ($d = 1.43$, SD = 2.90); human resource-based changes resulted in much smaller effect sizes, but the standard deviation was much smaller ($d = .45$, SD = .20). Finally, those eleven studies that used a combination of both structural and HR changes demonstrated a moderately high average effect size ($d = .66$), although it was highly variable (SD = 1.78). This suggests that one or more moderators are likely present for those studies utilizing structural changes and a combination of structural- and HR-based change initiatives. In a follow-up set of analyses, goal setting seemed to be the one change initiative than demonstrated a consistent positive impact on withdrawal behavior across studies.

To explore the moderating effects of organizational type, Macy and Izumi (1993) divided their total sample of 131 studies into three categories: manufacturing employers ($n = 46$), nonmanufacturing, for-profit employers ($n = 51$), and nonmanufacturing, nonprofit employers (n = 34). In the case of withdrawal behavior, the average $d$-effect sizes varied only slightly between the types of employers. The average $d$-effect sizes were .89 across employers, .93 for the manufacturing sample, .95 for the nonmanufacturing, for-profit companies, and .72 for the nonmanufacturing, nonprofit employers. Standard deviations ranged from 1.5 to 3 times as large as the average effect sizes. This further suggested that unidentified moderator variables existed for withdrawal behavior.

Finally, Pasmore et al. (1982) divided employee withdrawal into absenteeism and turnover in their qualitative review of socio-technical system (STS)-based change. When examining the results of the nine most popular STS interventions, the results for absenteeism and turnover were similar. In the case of absenteeism, Pasmore et al. (1982) reported that 100 percent of those studies using employee training and compensation system changes were successful in decreasing absenteeism, and that the development of self-directed work teams (SDWTs) was effective in 86 percent of the cases. Similar effects were indicated for employee turnover. Employee training and the implementation of technology were reported to effectively reduce turnover in all of the organizations employing the two interventions. Modifying the reward system and introducing SDWTs are reported to be the next two most effective interventions, effective in 91 percent and 81 percent of organizations employing these interventions, respectively. Overall, employee training, modification of reward systems, and the introduction of SDWTs were reported to be the most effective interventions to reduce withdrawal (in that order).

A general conclusion is suggested about the effectiveness of OCD interventions on employee withdrawal. It seems clear from the results that the effects are generally positive in nature, yet have a large degree of variability. Even though many of the effect sizes ranged from small to medium (Guzzo et al., 1985), to large (Macy & Izumi, 1993), the degree of variability was quite large (two to three times the size of the mean effect sizes). Nonetheless, it appears that at least three interventions, goal setting, supervisory methods, and work rescheduling resulted in positive effects for employee withdrawal. However, the practitioner must be careful when attempting to decrease withdrawal behaviors. The large standard deviations found for many of the intervention categories suggest that interventions might not work or might be counterproductive. Clearly, a number of moderating variables exist in the case of employee withdrawal.

## Job Satisfaction and Other Attitudes

Neuman et al. (1989) conducted a meta-analysis on 126 studies that employed OCD interventions aimed at assessing satisfaction and other employee attitudes.

They defined OCD as Beckhard (1967) did: "An effort which is planned, organization wide and managed from the top to increase organization effectiveness and health through planned interventions in the organization's processes, using behavioral science knowledge" (p. 20). Neuman et al., distinguished between three different types of interventions: (1) *human processes interventions* (lab training, involvement in decision-making, goal setting, management by objectives [MBO], realistic job previews [RJPs], team building, and survey feedback); (2) *technostructural interventions* (job design or enlargement, job enrichment, and flextime or flexible working hours); and (3) *multifaceted interventions* (combinations of one or more human processes or technostructural approaches). Satisfaction was defined as either *general satisfaction* or *facet satisfaction* (for example, satisfaction with pay, coworkers, and advancement opportunities). Nonsatisfaction attitudes were divided into four categories: (1) *attitudes about self* (self-identity and decision-making); (2) *attitudes about others* (interpersonal trust of coworkers, social support, and peer support); (3) *attitudes about the job* (commitment, job involvement); and (4) *attitudes about the organization* (organizational commitment, attitude toward the company, and organizational trust).

Overall, the mean corrected correlation coefficient for all the OCD interventions on all attitudes (both job satisfaction and other attitudes) was .33, but the confidence interval included .00, indicating that the interventions were situationally specific, and in general did not affect attitudes. OCD interventions had a larger impact on nonsatisfaction attitudes, especially attitudes toward others, the job, and the organization. The corrected mean correlation for all human processes interventions was .37. More specifically, goal setting or MBO significantly affected all three outcome variables (all attitudes, overall satisfaction, and overall other attitudes), whereas survey feedback did not affect any of the three. Relationships among technostructural interventions and attitudes were lower than for human processes interventions, and only attitude toward the job was significantly related to this type of intervention. Of the three technostructural categories, only flexible working hours or compressed work week was significantly related to an outcome measure—overall other attitudes.

Interestingly, multifaceted interventions (those that included at least one human processes and one technostructural intervention) were significantly related to all attitudes in which data were available. These categories included all attitudes, overall and facet satisfaction, overall other attitudes, and attitude toward the job. In other words, multifaceted interventions were related to satisfaction and attitudes.

As with the Guzzo et al. study (1985), Neuman et al. (1989) found that interventions aimed at supervisory employees were more effective than those directed at other types of employees. Satisfaction and attitudes (outcomes) were higher for manufacturing than nonmanufacturing organizations. Also similar to the Guzzo et al. study, outcomes from studies of technostructural interventions with less methodological rigor had relatively larger effects than outcomes from more rigorous studies. Conversely, for team building or grid OD interventions, methodological rigor was significantly related to outcomes.

Macy and Izumi (1993) also assessed the impact of organizational change on individual attitudes, and their findings were more austere than those of Neuman et al. (1989). None of the interventions correlated significantly with any of the attitudinal outcomes. Not only were attitudinal outcomes weak in comparison to other outcomes, but standard deviations were typically twice the effect size, indicating the contextual nature of attitude change. One exception occurred when both human resources and structural design interventions overlapped. The effect size in this instance was substantial ($d = .76$), but so was the standard deviation (SD = 1.13).

A summary of the data from the studies cited above is presented in Table 26.5.

Table. 26.5. Relationship Between Common Interventions and Outcomes.

| Common Interventions | Overall Range[1] | Withdrawal | | Productivity | | Individual Attitudes | |
|---|---|---|---|---|---|---|---|
| | | Absen-teeism | Turnover | Quality | Quantity | Job Satisfaction | Other Attitudes |
| Appraisal and feedback[2] | .0–.35 | xs | xs | s | s | xs | xs |
| Flextime | .0–.42 | xs | xs | s | s | xs | s |
| Goal setting | .40–.75 | xs–s | xs–s | m | m | s | m |
| Job enrichment | .0–.12 | xs | xs | m | m | xs | xs |
| MBO | .12–.43 | xs | xs | xs | xs | s | m |
| Multiple interventions | .38–1.80 | xs–xl | xs–xl | s–xl | s–xl | xs–s | xs–s |
| Reward systems | .0–.57 | xs | xs | xs | xs | xs | xs |
| RJP | .0–.20 | N | N | N | N | xs | xs |
| SDWTs | .0–.78 | xs | xs | l | l | xs | xs |
| STS | .0–.62 | xs | xs | m | m | N | N |
| Team building | .12–.58 | xs | xs | m | m | xs–m | xs |
| Training | .56–.85 | xs | xs | m–l | m–l | xs | s |
| WorkDesign/ redesign | .11–.42 | xs | xs | m | m | xs | xs |

[1]Range of overall effect size for intervention (several $d$-effects are estimated from reported correlations).

[2]Average effect sizes, xs = .01–.24 (or the lower bound of the confidence interval included .00, indicating a nonsignificant effect), s = .25–.49, m = .50–.74, l = .75–.99, xl = 1.00 and higher. N = not observed.

# DISCUSSION

In this review, several issues have been identified that are of considerable importance to practicing organizational consulting psychologists. Perhaps most important is the finding that a widely accepted taxonomy of interventions does not currently exist. However, based on our review, such a taxonomy might not be necessary at this point. Too few studies exist of appropriate quality to piece together such a taxonomy. What scientists and practitioners might need most are quality intervention studies that report results of specific interventions, and groups of interventions, for targeted outcomes. This will build the repertoire of empirical studies, eventually enabling the building of a more statistically robust taxonomy.

Even if we had an appropriate number of quality intervention studies, little standardization exists on operational definitions of interventions. Suppose, for example, that two practitioners operationally define participation differently. One defines it as employee involvement; another, as consisting of the implementation and training of quality circles. Additionally, two researchers might use different terms to refer to similar interventions (that is, SDWTs and autonomous work teams). Of the six studies examined, five different taxonomies were used to classify the change initiatives. We would likely have viewed six classification categories, if two studies had not been conducted by the same set of colleagues (Porras & Robertson, 1992; Robertson et al., 1993). Thus, no standardized set of interventions, definitions, or larger categorization scheme exists in the literature. This implies that a large amount of conceptual and definitional work still needs to be conducted in the area.

A contributing factor to this lack of consensus in OCD intervention typologies is the fact that no systemic theory of change has been developed for the OCD literature. Since the interventions used by OCD researchers and practitioners are so varied and represent a number of theoretical approaches, developing a common theme is difficult. We believe that the identification of a common set of steps or stages for the various OCD interventions is a useful first step. However, more research needs to be conducted that helps to identify the commonalities between OCD interventions, as well as identifying parallel interventions that have similar effects upon organizational outcomes. At the present time, both researchers and practitioners alike examine OCD interventions at the basic intervention level, and only later develop categories that are based upon similarities in the outcomes produced by the interventions.

## Impact of Categories on OCD Practitioners

When standardized categories summarizing the OCD interventions are widely accepted, we wonder whether they will be too broad for practitioners to make decisions about linking interventions and outcomes. For example, interventions that target changes in employee work schedules, including flexible work schedules (flextime), compressed work weeks, and telecommuting, can all be categorized into the general class of work schedule interventions. These work schedule interventions can further be classified into categories such as technostructural interventions (Neuman et al., 1989), and structural interventions (Macy & Izumi, 1993). However, the results might vary even at the basic intervention level. For example, within the narrow category of work schedule interventions, Baltes, Briggs, Huff, Wright, and Neuman (1999) found that flexible work schedules were most strongly related to changes in employee absenteeism, productivity, and satisfaction with work schedules. However, compressed work week interventions most strongly affected employee job satisfaction, supervisor-rated performance, and satisfaction with work schedules. In addition, Baltes et al. reported evidence for differences in moderator variables between the two work schedule interventions.

Such results are problematic for the current attempt to summarize the OCD literature in a relatively succinct manner. Even though our results have attempted to categorize at the most basic type of intervention level, certain details and intricacies have likely been overlooked. Thus, we suggest that all OCD practitioners need to become familiar with the specific relevant category of literature, such as work schedule interventions, when they plan to conduct such an intervention. It also increases the need for a broad meta-analysis to be conducted that reviews all of the common intervention types on specific organizational outcomes (for example, attitudes, performance, withdrawal).

## OCD Practice Implications

Turning now to specific findings of this review, we believe much has been learned that will help practitioners link appropriate interventions with targeted outcomes. For example, goal setting, MBO, team building, training, and work design or redesign, had favorable effects overall. Additionally, when organizations implemented multiple interventions simultaneously, the potential for positive change was unparalleled by any single intervention category. However, this favorable depiction of positive change might be somewhat misleading. When the targeted outcome addressed productivity issues such as quality and quantity, results were indeed favorable. When the targeted outcome addressed individual attitudes such as satisfaction, few results were favorable. Finally, when the targeted outcome addressed withdrawal behaviors such as absenteeism and turnover, a few substantive $d$-effects were accompanied by very large standard deviations.

**Attitudes versus Organizational Outcomes.** Collectively, our findings suggest that individual attitudes and behaviors are generally difficult to change, and that organizational outcomes (for example, productivity) are more readily influenced by OCD interventions. This pattern of results supports the theoretical contention that individual change might not be necessary to achieve desired organizational change. Clearly, this question deserves further empirical consideration.

**Methodological Rigor.** It might be assumed that the degree of methodological rigor would be related to the success of the intervention, but the data do not consistently support this contention. Previous research has proposed that rigor might positively enhance OCD outcomes, because more stringent methodologies are more likely to generate the expected change (see, for example, Bullock & Syvantek, 1983). Others have suggested that lower methodological rigor employed during the evaluation process might inflate the effect sizes found in the OCD literature (see, for example, Terpstra, 1981). Of the six studies included in the current review, Guzzo et al. (1985) and Neuman et al. (1989) assessed methodological rigor. Guzzo et al. examined the influence of research design, a common definition of study rigor, on the size of the average $d$-effect sizes collapsed across intervention and outcome categories. They reported that mean $d$-effects were smallest when studies were rigorous, and largest when the studies were less rigorous. Neuman et al. reported a positive relationship between methodological rigor and average effect size. However, Neuman et al. used a more comprehensive assessment of methodological rigor than did Guzzo et al., thus the results might not be directly comparable. An alternative investigation of rigor will be discussed next to help infer a common theme in the OCD literature.

We could compare the results presented by the four meta-analyses to attempt to infer whether the rigor levels of the studies included have any influence on the effect sizes of the various OCD interventions. Of the four meta-analyses, only Neuman et al. (1989) included nonexperiemntal studies in their analyses. All other meta-analyses required that all studies be experimental. Macy and Izumi (1993) required the most restrictive inclusion criteria, in which studies did not only need to be experimental in nature, but also needed to be longitudinal in assessing OCD outcomes. Thus, we will use Neuman et al. to represent an analysis of primary studies with relatively low levels of methodological rigor and studies included by Macy and Izumi as a higher level of rigor. In order to compare the results of the two studies, only the attitudinal outcomes are reviewed here.

Simply stated, we found a very small difference between the Macy and Izumi (1993) outcomes and the outcomes reported by Neuman et al. (1989). For the category of overall employee attitudes, the one category most comparable between the two studies, Macy and Izumi reported an average $d$-effect size of .42, with a standard deviation of .85, suggesting that the effect of OCD interventions on employee attitudes varied considerably among the studies. Neuman et al. reported a more substantial, corrected effect size of approximately .68;

however, the confidence interval also included zero, suggesting situational influences on the effectiveness of OCD interventions on employee attitude change. Taken together, these results do not help much in clarifying the role of methodological rigor on the effect size of OCD interventions. More and less rigorous findings on criteria resulted in rather modest effects, and the variance of the mean effects was quite high. In addition, we have only examined the influence of OCD interventions on aggregated employee attitudes, and have not been able to examine more specific attitudes, such as measures of employee performance or withdrawal. Thus, no clear picture of the effects of methodological rigor has been discovered.

**Comprehensiveness of Intervention.** The use of the five common intervention steps could serve as another measure of the rigor of study implementation. Although relevant data were not available from the six current reviews, there is some evidence to suggest that the comprehensiveness of the implementation strategy might influence the strength of the outcome effects. In a review of the organizational training literature, Bennett (1996) identified that the quality of the implementation process was a key moderator of the effectiveness of training programs. This was especially pronounced in the case of including a needs assessment process. Although the vast majority of training initiatives included the needs assessment step, those that did not were markedly less effective than those that did. It might also be the case that any other four of the commonly identified intervention steps might also have some impact on the effectiveness of OCD interventions. Future researchers might benefit from specifying the steps taken, or excluded, during intervention processes. Measures of the implementation steps or strategies can be included as a moderator variable in order to assess whether the methodological rigor of the intervention process has had a significant impact on the effectiveness of the OCD intervention.

**Effects of Multiple Change Efforts.** Finally, most of the reviews in this chapter found that multiple change efforts were more effective than single interventions. Many readers would agree that this trend is related to the concept of organizations as open systems (Katz & Kahn, 1978). Systems (for example, structural, technostructural, HR, and human processes) are embedded in the organization, and a change in one system will likely affect, to some degree, its surrounding systems. This conceptualization is somewhat nonspecific, however, and a more practical model would suggest key linkages among interventions embedded in different systems. Some preliminary work has already been done in this area. Macy and Izumi (1993) examined the multiple implementations in their review, and discovered from statistical clustering techniques that certain interventions seemed to be implemented together. This does not necessarily mean that these clusters of interventions are from juxtaposed systems, but in many cases, the selection of multiple interventions comes from experts in the field who have grouped them according to logical categories. We also note that the selection of multiple interventions can also be driven by organizational members (and some practitioners) with no apparent logic.

Macy and Izumi (1993) report that five main clusters of interventions resulted from their analyses. Structural changes that involved hierarchical factors, physical layout, job classification systems, and multiskill training comprised the first cluster of interventions. The second intervention cluster addressed the implementation of teams within the current organizational structure. The third cluster was comprised of interventions that utilized autonomous or semi-autonomous teams, and job enrichment or enlargement. The fourth cluster resulted from those interventions attempting to modify the goal-setting process. The fifth cluster was related to implementing recognition and formal financial reward systems.

## SUMMARY AND CONCLUSION

Our review of six influential organizational change and development reviews has led us to several conclusions. A widely accepted taxonomy of intervention categories currently does not exist. Individual attitudes and behaviors are difficult to change via interventions, while measures of productivity appear more amenable to change efforts. We found little support for the theoretical contention that individual attitudes and behavior must change in order to achieve lasting organizational change. In fact, based on the data we reviewed, we maintain that organizational change can be achieved without individual change. Our findings relating methodological rigor and success of OCD initiatives were inconclusive. There appear to be five intervention steps that are common across many change initiatives. These intervention steps should be considered in both practice and research.

### References

Armenakis, A. A, & Bedeian, A. G. (1999). Organizational change: A review of theory and research in the 1990s. *Journal of Management, 25*(3), 293–315.

Baltes, B. B., Briggs, T. E., Huff, J. W., Wright, J. A., & Neuman, G. A. (1999). Flexible and compressed workweek schedules: A meta-analysis of their effects on work-related criteria. *Journal of Applied Psychology, 84,* 496–513.

Beckhard, R. (1967). The confrontation meeting. *Harvard Business Review, 45,* 149–153.

Beer, M. (1980). *Organizational change and development: A systems view.* Santa Monica, CA: Goodyear Publishing.

Bennett, W. R., Jr. (1996). *A meta-analytic review of factors that influence the effectiveness of training in organizations.* Unpublished doctoral dissertation, Texas A&M University, College Station, TX.

Bennis, W. G. (1966). *Changing organizations*. New York: McGraw-Hill.

Blau, G. J. (1994). Developing and testing a taxonomy of lateness behavior. *Journal of Applied Psychology, 79,* 959–970.

Bullock, R. J., & Syvantek, R. T. (1983). Positive-findings bias in positive findings research. *Academy of Management Proceedings, 43,* 221–224.

Cohen, J. (1969). *Statistical power analysis for the behavioral sciences*. Orlando, FL: Academic Press.

DeMatteo, J. S., Eby, L. T., & Sundstrom, E. (1998). Team-based rewards: Current empirical evidence and directions for future research. *Research in Organizational Behavior, 20,* 141–183.

French, W. L., & Bell, C. H. (1984). *Organization development: Behavioral science interventions for organization improvement* (3rd ed.). Englewood Cliffs, NJ: Prentice Hall.

Friedlander & Brown. (1974). Organizational development. *Annual Review of Psychology, 25,* 313–341.

Glass, G. V. (1976). Primary, secondary, and meta-analysis of research. *Educational Researcher, 5,* 3–8.

Guzzo, R. A., Jette, R. D., & Katzell, R. A. (1985). The effects of psychologically based intervention programs on worker productivity: A meta-analysis. *Personnel Psychology, 38,* 275–291.

Hackman, J. R., & Wageman, R. (1995). Total quality management: Empirical, conceptual, and practical issues. *Administrative Science Quarterly, 40,* 309–342.

Hedges, L. V., & Olkin, I. (1985). *Statistical methods for meta-analysis*. Orlando, FL: Academic Press.

Hom, P. W., & Griffeth, R. W. (1995). *Employee turnover*. Cincinnati, OH: South-Western.

Hunter, J. E., Schmidt, F. L., & Jackson, G. B. (1982). *Meta-analysis: Cumulating research findings across studies*. Thousand Oaks, CA: Sage.

Katz, D., & Kahn, R. L. (1978). *The social psychology of organizations* (2nd ed.). New York: Wiley.

Katzell, R. A., Bienstock, P., & Faerstein, P. H. (1977). *A guide to worker productivity experiments in the United States 1971–75*. New York: New York University Press.

Macy, B. A., & Izumi, H. (1993). Organizational change, design, and work innovation: A meta-analysis of 131 North American field studies—1961–1991. *Research in Organizational Change and Development, 7,* 235–313.

Mobely, W. H., Griffeth, R. W., Hand, H. H., & Meglino, B. M. (1979). Review and conceptual analysis of the employee turnover process. *Psychological Bulletin, 86,* 493–522.

Neuman, G. A., Edwards, J. E., & Raju, N. S. (1989). Organizational development interventions: A meta-analysis of their effects on satisfaction and other attitudes. *Personnel Psychology, 42,* 461–483.

Pasmore, W. A., Frances, C., Haldeman, J., & Shani, A. (1982). Sociotechnical system: A North American reflection on empirical studies of the seventies. *Human Relations, 35,* 1179–1204.

Porras, J. L. (1987). *Stream analysis: A powerful way to diagnose and manage organizational change*. Reading, MA: Addison-Wesley.

Porras, J. L., & Robertson, P. J. (1992). Organizational development: Theory, practice, and research. In M. D. Dunnette & L. M. Hough (Eds.), *Handbook of industrial/organizational psychology* (2nd ed., Vol 3, pp. 719–822). Palo Alto, CA: Consulting Psychologists Press.

Raju, N. S., & Burke, M. J. (1983). Two new procedures for studying validity generalization. *Journal of Applied Psychology, 68,* 382–395.

Robertson, P. J., Roberts, D. R., & Porras, J. I. (1993). Dynamics of planned organizational change: Assessing empirical support for a theoretical model. *Academy of Management Journal, 36,* 619–634.

Rosenthal, R. (1986). *Meta-analytic procedures for social research.* Thousand Oaks, CA: Sage.

Schein, E. H. (1988). *Process consultation: Vol. I. Its role in organization development* (2nd ed.). Reading, MA: Addison-Wesley.

Steers, R. M., & Rhodes, S. (1978). Major influences on employee attendance: A process model. *Journal of Applied Psychology, 63,* 391–407.

Steers, R. M., & Rhodes, S. (1984). Knowledge and speculation about absenteeism. In P. S. Goodman & R. S. Atkin (Eds.), *Absenteeism: New approaches to understanding, measuring, and managing employee absence* (pp. 229–275). San Francisco: Jossey-Bass.

Terpstra, D. E. (1981). Relationship between methodological rigor and reported outcomes in organizational development evaluation research. *Journal of Applied Psychology, 66,* 541–543.

# CHAPTER TWENTY-SEVEN

# Assessing the Impact of Organizational Consulting

Paul C. Winum, Tjai M. Nielsen, and Robert E. Bradford
*RHR International*

M ost psychologists who provide consulting services within organizational settings are motivated by the same desire as our colleagues who work in the other arenas where the art and science of psychology is applied: the desire to make a constructive difference. Just as our clinical counterparts labor to assist their clients in successfully meeting the personal challenges of living with others and with themselves, organizational consulting psychologists seek to enhance the effectiveness of organizations and the people who work in them. But how do we know if and when we are making a difference that matters? What are methods to assess consulting impact that have been used historically, and what approaches and tools are needed for today and the future? The authors' attempt to address these questions is the subject of this chapter. Specifically, we will summarize why it is especially important to evaluate the results of consulting efforts, and what some of the challenges to doing so are. Next, we will present some of the types of outcomes often sought by organizational leaders who utilize the services of consulting psychologists, and review literature on some past approaches to evaluating consulting interventions. Finally, we will offer some case illustrations and recommendations for the further development of outcome evaluation for psychologists who provide consultation to organizations.

# WHY EVALUATING CONSULTING IMPACT IS IMPORTANT

Aside from personal motivations to make a difference, why is the evaluation of consulting impact so important? There are three main reasons: (1) our clients demand it; (2) our economic and professional viability depend on it; and (3) the ethics of our profession require it.

These three reasons are closely interconnected. Most organizations face imposing challenges with limited resources. Whether a not-for-profit human service organization, government agency, educational institution, or *Fortune* 500 multinational corporation, organizations today function in a demanding and highly competitive landscape in which the pressures to deliver superior performance are greater than ever. Consulting psychologists are one among many groups of service professionals who compete for the mind share, time, and budget resources of organizations. Executives and managers within those organizations must make prudent decisions about investing those resources in ways that will yield the greatest return on investment.

Psychologists who understand and can help deliver the outcomes and results that organizational leaders are working to achieve offer significant value. The need for accountability in organizational consulting has never been higher, just as it is critical in the clinical arena (Cone, 2000). Consultants who aren't able to make compelling connections between their services and desired organizational outcomes will be marginalized. Unlike some professional service providers, such as accountants and lawyers, consulting psychologists do not provide services that organizations are required to have by law. There is no captive market in organizational consulting. Furthermore, budgetary constraints are present in almost every type of organization. Psychologists who want to remain in business must show how their services contribute tangible, cost-effective value to the organization's ability to execute its mission. Thus, the ability to assess the impact and demonstrate the value of consultation is an increasing imperative if we are to serve our clients well and remain economically viable.

The third reason why we must develop our focus on evaluating the impact of our consultation is that our professional code of ethics requires it. The most recent version of the American Psychological Association (APA)'s *Ethical Principles of Psychologists and Code of Conduct* (1992) contains several general principles and standards that we believe require consulting psychologists to pay careful attention to the impact of their interventions and their presence in organizations. In our view, the principles of competence, professional and scientific responsibility, and concern for others' welfare all contain language that urges examination of the effect of our conduct and methods on our organizational clients. The general standards on evaluation, assessment, or intervention address the duty to provide evidence of the usefulness and proper application of techniques. Although these ethical principles and standards are at this writing under revision (with input from the Division of Consulting Psychology), there have also been other efforts to explore the particularly complex ethical challenges inherent in organizational consultation (Lowman, 1998; Newman, 1993; Newman, Gray, & Fuqua, 1996). These authors have delved into many of the moral and ethical dilemmas that confront psychologists consulting in organizations, but each in their own way address the responsibility to engage in collaborative dialogue with our clients about their organizations' purposes, and how our services will be utilized to achieve desired ends.

## The Challenges of Outcome Evaluation in Organizational Consulting

Warner Burke, in his book *Organization Development: A Normative View* (1987), aptly compared the evaluation process of OD practice with an annual physical examination, in that most people agree that it is important, but few people want to go to the expense and trouble of making it happen. The cost of doing a thorough evaluation of organizational consultation is clearly one major impediment. Most organizations don't have much of a budget for engaging consulting psychologists, much less for evaluating the results of their efforts. Furthermore, except for those with access to the resources of a university, most practicing consulting psychologists have severe limitations on their capacity to support outcome research in their work. Also, many psychologists who have gravitated toward organizational consulting are more drawn to practice than to research, and often have deficits in both motivation and skills for doing it. With time, money, and even motivation in short supply, it is easy to see how evaluation studies of impact often get left out of the service mix.

Even in situations in which both the consultant and the organization are committed to assessing the impact of consultation and have the resources to do it, there are challenges associated with the difficulty of measuring so-called soft or multidetermined outcomes such as leadership, morale, or process improvement. Also, as Burke (1987) notes, there are many constituents in organizations—sponsoring executives, managers, employees, shareholders, customers, and others—with different vested interests and varied perspectives about the benefits and appropriate focus of consultation and its evaluation. Some stakeholders believe they know what will constitute a good outcome and that it will be self-evident. Others favor a rigorous, scientifically valid measurement methodology. However, organizations present a plethora of challenges to sound experimental design. The impossibility of controlling the variables that contribute to changes in organizations makes sound experimental design difficult at best. Cook, Campbell, and Peracchio (1990) provided a thorough treatment of the issues of manipulability, validity, and causality in field research, and examined a host of threats to the application of results from one setting to the next. No wonder

Blanton (2000) challenged the practicality of using standard psychological research methods in organizational consultation. This territory is extremely complex, with many subtle elements in the terrain. Good maps and aerial photographs are tough to come by.

Despite these challenges and forces of resistance, the imperative remains to develop commitments from our clients to assess the impact of organizational consulting efforts and assemble the resources to design and fund these efforts appropriately. Investments in this regard will yield rich dividends for our clients and contribute to the continued development of our practice and profession. A good beginning is to consider and understand what organizations are trying to accomplish and the outcomes that matter to them.

# THE OUTCOMES THAT MATTER TO ORGANIZATIONS

Before addressing the question of how psychologists might assess the impact of organizational consultation, it is worth considering the types of outcomes that organizations value and consider important. Describing the outcomes that matter to organizations can be difficult because they depend so strongly on the characteristics of the organization itself. In our experience, hard-driving, bottom-line, low-margin businesses will have much different outcome requirements than not-for-profit social organizations. However, all organizations, regardless of the business they are in, have some core interrelated dimensions that can be used as a basic taxonomy for organizing our discussion of outcome evaluation. These basic dimensions can be characterized as *mission, people, structure* and *systems,* and every organization has desired outcomes that can be related to one or more of these dimensions.

The mission dimension pertains to the mission or purpose of the organization, and the strategy or strategies to achieve that mission. The people dimension addresses the human resources who devise and implement the mission and strategy. The structure dimension is concerned with how the work of the organization is divided, and how the various components work in concert. The systems dimension relates to the various mechanisms that integrate the mission, people, and structure dimensions (for example, communication, technology, and compensation). For each of these dimensions, there are outcomes that are needed for effective and efficient organizational functioning. The following list contains examples of outcomes or desired states related to these organizational dimensions:

*Mission Dimension*

- All members of the organization are clear and aligned about the mission and strategy of the organization.
- The strategy of the organization co-evolves with conditions in the external environment.

- The desired values and culture of the organization are behaviorally evidenced throughout the organization.

### People Dimension

- The selection of people into the organization results in a highly competent work force.

- Talented individuals are retained by the organization.

- New employees of the organization are well oriented, trained, and integrated into the organization such that they rapidly reach high levels of productivity.

### Structure Dimension

- There is efficiency and minimal redundancy in the use of resources.

- Departments operate with the resources and authority they need to execute their tasks well.

- Assignments and responsibilities change to keep up with changes in the size of the organization.

### Systems Dimension

- Employees are informed in a timely manner about what they need to know to do their jobs effectively.

- The compensation system enables the organization to offer salary and benefits that effectively reinforce desired job performance.

- The accounts payable process results in just-in-time payments.

The outcomes listed above are of a very general nature. Depending on the organization, more specific outcomes related to each dimension are commonly articulated. For example, many *Fortune* 500 companies with whom we have worked have dozens of very specific quantitative outcome objectives in each of the organizational dimensions listed, and have identified specific metrics to gauge whether or not those objectives are achieved.

## The Role of the Consultant

The role of the consultant also has a bearing on the decision about what outcomes will be sought and measured. Some consulting firms do analysis and recommendations only. They will provide a careful examination of the issues and make suggestions for improvement, but they will not implement the solutions. In these circumstances, we have found the perception that good advice and well-constructed recommendations have been provided is probably a good outcome measure. Other consultants are more focused on *how* to implement the changes the organization desires. In these cases, the outcome might very well center on the successful implementation of the desired change. There might or might not be an expectation that the change will produce a desired result, but the consultant is held accountable for the implementation itself (for example, IT consulting).

Finally, there are organizational consultants who promise to do whatever is necessary to achieve a desired end result. They are often careful to negotiate the definition of the outcome fully with the organization itself, with the measure of success being the achievement of the result. Not many consultants are willing to take this stance, and it does pose the question of management roles, but organizations are increasingly asking for hard results from consultants, so it seems likely that demands for actual measurable outcomes will become increasingly important.

These three scenarios make it obvious that what is desired as an outcome is often less a concrete fact than a negotiated agreement. Organizations will sometimes ask for outcomes that are impossible, or so improbable that it would be unwise to even attempt them without further refinement (for example, "Make a good manager out of him."). At other times, they ask for outcomes that bear little likely relationship to the work being done (for example, "Raise the stock price by 5 percent as a result of your intervention."). There are also times when organizations know more about what they do not want than what they do want (for example, "This team is not working together well and needs to be fixed."). It is important for organizational consultants to clarify carefully, and thoroughly understand the outcomes desired and the resources necessary to achieve them.

Having come to an understanding that organizations will vary in their outcome expectations and will sometimes make unreasonable demands, it is also possible to classify outcomes according to the types of outcomes on which consulting psychologists are typically engaged to work: process outcomes, specific outcomes, long-range outcomes, and unreasonable outcomes.

## Process Outcomes

Process outcomes are those results that derive from the consulting relationship itself. Process outcomes are the benefits derived from the consultation process. The facts that the consultant is an outsider, has unique experience or knowledge, and often has a different perspective, can be valuable to organizations. Although these types of outcomes are often difficult to measure, client executives usually have no difficulty knowing when they have benefited from the consulting process and when they have not.

The first process outcome that organizations appreciate and often seek from consultants is clear thinking about the nature of the problem and its resolution. Schein, in his seminal book *Process Consultation* (1969), refers to the fact that managers often need help in diagnosing their own needs. In many cases, executives have lived with, or have been part of the problem so long, that they have difficulty removing themselves from it or maintaining objectivity about it.

They appreciate the consultant who can get to the heart of the issue and bring clarity to what has been frustrating and sometimes emotionally charged. In addition, the consultant often defines the issue differently than the organization might have assumed. In most cases, problems are less the result of a single individual than the operation of old patterns that are no longer effective. Often, changing the way problems have been defined will present new ideas about their probable resolution. Organizations appreciate such reframing. This process can restore hope.

A second process outcome is the addition of expertise and perspective about human resource issues. Most businesses are adept in dealing with machinery, distribution systems, financial systems, and other relatively predictable and manageable interactions. They know that if they manipulate X, there is a better than average chance that the result they desire (Y) will occur. In dealing with people, however, the same principle does not apply, and expectations for change can be unreasonable and even idealistic. Consulting psychologists can provide a valuable service by providing perspectives regarding human motivation, managing change, and serving as a sounding board regarding decisions that will significantly affect people.

A third process outcome is the consultants describing or helping to modify the processes that create, and continue to support, the issues of concern. In many cases, organizational problems result from systems that once worked well, but have outlived their usefulness. Such difficulties manifest gradually over time, and organizations often have difficulty determining the signs or solutions. Organizational consultants provide such perspective and can suggest ways to move beyond the difficulty. In many cases, business people are excellent problem solvers, but they might not have as good diagnostic skills, so they might be trying to resolve the wrong issue. The consultant's ability to define the problem in terms of ongoing systems, and to describe the heart of the issue clearly, often allows the organization to solve the problem itself.

For example, in one company, the presenting problem was a lack of depth and talent in mid-management. The CEO had actually demanded more and better talent at that level for some time, but could not seem to get it. After looking at the organization, the consultants determined that the COO (who was a very close and personal friend of the CEO) was not competent in the job. For some years, the COO had hired individuals of lesser talent, seemingly to cover his own lack of ability. The presenting problem was clear, but the system issues behind the problem were not clear and presented considerable complexity in constructing a resolution. Organizations might find the consultant's information difficult to absorb, but they generally appreciate the clarification of the issue from a systems perspective. Process outcomes include consultation around modifying the processes involved in selecting, integrating, rewarding, and planning for the succession of people.

## Specific Outcomes

It is our experience that consulting psychologists are frequently engaged by organizations to assist in the attainment of specific outcomes in any of the core dimensions of organization classified earlier. Specific outcomes are results that are identifiable, measurable, and commonly understood by all concerned. There is often a specific issue that needs resolution through the behavior of the organization's employees. The issue is typically obvious to all, and commonly understood to need resolution. The problem is that the organization has not been able to resolve it. While there might be many reasons why the issue persists, the desired result is typically not in doubt. Three major types of specific outcomes are discussed below.

The first type of specific outcome is that targeted toward a narrow, but specified result. For example, in one company the credit department had set credit limits so high that sales were lost with little obvious benefit in return. The credit department rather stubbornly held to the standards in spite of heated demands by senior executives that they loosen the limits. In this case, the solution was straightforward (credit limits had to be eased), but the reasons for its resistance were certainly less than clear (why is the credit department so reluctant to change?). It is probable that after some negotiation, the desired result would center on relaxed credit standards with support and follow-through from the credit department. The consultant then would be free to identify the problem, identify and propose solutions, or actually manage the solution depending on the preference of the consultant.

Other examples of targeted outcomes include improving the performance of managers and faltering executives, executive integration into new situations, increasing cross-departmental cooperation, reducing territorial conflicts, and decreasing management distrust or even incompetence. We have found that most large organizations have many such issues. Organizational consultants will likely find themselves in high demand if they can develop a reputation for resolving these types of issues successfully.

Another type of specific outcome occurs when an organization wants an identified business result to occur. Examples include requests to increase sales, lower costs, raise the stock price, have 10 percent less turnover, have a higher percentage of internal promotions, and increase the percentage of successful offers to desirable candidates. These outcomes are ambiguous, because what leads to their attainment is multifaceted. In addition, the outcome is a desired state rather than the resolution of an identified problem. It is easy in this category for organizations to request unreasonable outcomes, and for consultants to tackle issues that should be more clearly defined. While the desired outcome is clear, the underlying dynamics of the issue typically are not, and the attainment of the outcome can be complex indeed. There is no question, however, that these outcomes are highly desired by most organizations.

The last type of specific outcome is related to comparisons either to an ideal or across a range of participants. For example, it is not unusual for companies (especially those merging) to ask for an assessment to identify their most capable managers. If there are too many managers and some must go, the organization wants to be sure to retain the best ones. They typically ask for a ranking based on specified criteria for retention. It is also common for companies to ask for assessments against various benchmarks. Organizations sometimes set goals for employee surveys, for example, with targets established for particular categories. For example, organizations often want employee satisfaction at a high level, and might set specific quantitative targets. Department and regional managers in such circumstances are often held accountable for employee survey results, and might hire organizational consultants to help them. It is also common for organizations to set targets based on performance data from comparable organizations in their industry. They often know what the target looks like, but might not know how to get there. Consultants who can provide such a road map are well appreciated.

## Long-Range Outcomes

Organizations will often request outcomes that involve changes within the organization over considerable time. While there might be specific outcomes within the long-range goal, the outcomes desired are grander and much more complex. Two types of long-range goals are described below.

We will call the first type *betterment outcome*. These outcomes describe a desire to make something better than it is currently. Examples include better morale, more teamwork, closer integration, better communication, and so on. These outcomes describe a situation in which there might not be a particular problem, but management believes that it could be done better than it is currently. They are typically long-range in nature because there is seldom a defined outcome, and the intervention can go on for some time. In fact, interventions can go on indefinitely if management is unusually perfectionistic or idealistic. The now faded concept of reengineering (Hammer and Champy, 1993) would fall in this category.

The second type we will call *change outcome*. Change outcomes are requests to directly change something about the organization. Examples include requests to change the culture from collegial to performance, change individual executive skills (for example, the ability to listen, work better with others), change leadership (for example, assisting with the integration of a new CEO, work on leadership style), or company reorganization with changes in lines of reporting authority or responsibility. The measure of success here involves the successful transition from one organizational state to another. These types of outcomes are usually straightforward in principle and highly desirable, but might be difficult to implement. They almost always occur over extended periods of time.

## Unreasonable Outcomes

It is important to understand that organizations can and will make unreasonable demands of their organizational consultants. They often assume, wrongly, that with enough effort and know-how, anything can be done. They assume that people can be influenced, directed, or otherwise convinced, to do things that might not be perceived to be in their best interests. It is not unusual for organizations to ask the consultant to address these unreasonable expectations.

Examples of unreasonable outcomes might include goals such as making people happy with management decisions, developing employee loyalty to the organization, creating a cohesive atmosphere, developing more cooperation, raising the stock price, and so on. These are frequently products of unclear thinking, resulting in a desire to shoot at something even if the target is not in sight. In addition, these outcomes are probably impossible even in the long term. The development of such things as loyalty, cohesion, or cooperation will always be problematic, depending on the circumstances at the time. Although organizations will ask for these unreasonable outcomes and find them desirable if achieved, the wise consultant will think more than twice about entering into them.

The process of clearly defining the desired outcomes for any psychological consultation engagement is a critical component that will greatly influence the design of interventions and the ultimate success of the endeavor. In our view, best consulting practice dictates that this process be undertaken in collaboration with the key constituents in the organization who will be significantly affected by the consultation, and only after thoughtful, careful assessment and diagnosis.

# MEASURING THE IMPACT OF CONSULTING

Assessing the impact of consulting services is something many organizations would like to do. They want to know what kind of return they are receiving on their investment. In our experience, impact is assessed very informally. Assessing impact typically involves verbal reports from recipients and the organizational sponsor, or satisfaction and performance surveys. These data provide anecdotal evidence regarding perceived impact, but can fall short in demonstrating specific outcomes of the consulting services provided.

There are many reasons for a lack of rigor in this area, two of which include a lack of time and tools. First, when a project has ended or is nearing completion, a lot of employee and organizational time has already been devoted. Thus, the idea of taking more time and effort to assess impact receives little adherence. Second, there is a paucity of tools that can be used to effectively assess impact for the vast variety of interventions conducted. While these are salient reasons for the lack of impact assessment, most consultants and organizations would agree that assessing more accurate and business-oriented outcomes is important.

At present, there is a relative scarcity of specific tools and methods for assessing consulting in the field of consulting psychology. However, there has been some research in areas such as organizational development and I-O psychology that might provide valuable information about assessing consulting impact. In the following section, we discuss specific methods for evaluating the outcomes that matter within the basic dimensions of mission, people, structure, and systems. We review and summarize a broad range of relevant studies falling within this taxonomy. Our attempt is to uncover useful tools and methodologies that can be used by consultants and organizations alike to more accurately assess the impact of consulting services. It is not within the scope of this chapter to conduct a comprehensive review of these areas. We simply discuss potential tools and past work that consulting psychologists can incorporate in their tool kits.

# EVALUATING THE OUTCOMES THAT MATTER

The next sections describe outcomes for each organizational dimension in the taxonomy of desired outcomes.

## Mission

Consulting psychologists implement a variety of interventions designed to contribute to the various desired outcomes within the mission dimension. Outcomes in this dimension include: a clear understanding of the organizational mission and strategy; alignment of strategy with the external environment; and organizational values represented by behavior. Many interventions exist for attempting to achieve these results, as do methods to assess their impact.

One outcome that falls under this dimension includes people in an organization exhibiting behaviors that represent the values and culture of the organization. One type of intervention that could possibly be used to facilitate the realization of this outcome would include the implementation of a 360-degree feedback (Huet-Cox, Nielsen, & Sundstrom, 1999a) or survey program designed to assess specific behaviors that represent organizational values. For example, a key organizational value might include open communication. In this case, the 360-degree survey would include items describing specific behaviors promoting or demonstrating open communication such as "Consistently shares vital company or departmental information"; or "Provides constructive performance feedback." The assessment of these behaviors would likely be followed by feedback given to employees based on the survey results. In most 360-degree feedback programs, this is followed by the creation of development plans, which serve as road maps to improving specific key competencies (Huet-Cox, Nielsen, & Sundstrom, 1999b).

A very practical method for assessing the outcomes of such interventions involves readministering surveys and comparing results from the initial administration. Once the second set of survey results are tallied, analyses can be used to determine the existence of significant differences (for example, ANOVA, MANOVA) or relationships (for example, correlation). This type of outcome assessment would provide very specific indicators of intervention impact.

Another intervention example under the *mission* dimension includes the development of an effective organizational strategy that is aligned with the competitive environment. In this case, strategy is defined as ". . . a patterned stream of decisions which focus on resource allocations in an attempt to reach a market position consistent with a firm's environment" (Mintzberg, 1973, p. 45). A consulting psychologist might intervene with a training program focused on strategy alignment, or work individually with those responsible for strategic decisions. One way to assess the impact of such an intervention would be to get verbal or written feedback from each participant in the program. This feedback would center on participants' perceptions of greater knowledge and ability to align internal strategy with the environment. The percentage of participants who felt that they knew a lot more about strategy alignment after the training would indicate the degree of impact. Another method for measuring impact would be to test each participant's knowledge regarding strategy alignment. A final method for assessing impact would be to use and compare surveys assessing strategy, environment, and performance. Lukas, Tan, and Hult (2001) used surveys to determine the relationship between the environment, strategic orientation, and the performance of 330 electronics firms in China. The authors used correlational analyses to determine the strength of these relationships. Results indicated that most firms demonstrated high environment-strategy coalignment, but that this coalignment only had mixed implications on organizational performance. Another study related to strategy that used surveys to measure impact examined the relationship between board appointments and board involvement in strategic decision-making (Carpenter & Westphal, 2001). This study hypothesized that directors who were assigned to other boards from similar companies would be more involved in strategic decisions for the focal company. After analyzing data from 263 CEOs and 564 corporate directors, results supported the authors' hypotheses. Though assessing impact using surveys is valuable, some executives might want other outcome measures involving financial performance.

Henderson (1999) examined firm strategy, age dependence, and financial performance of U.S.-based computer firms. This study analyzed financial data to assess the impact of specific strategies. While Henderson used fairly complex statistical techniques and models in his analyses, this study demonstrated one method for using financial data as an outcome assessment. While there are relatively few examples in the literature describing outcome assessments within the mission dimension, there are many more within the people dimension.

## People

In our experience, consulting psychologists are consistently called upon to help achieve outcomes within the people dimension. Some outcomes that matter within this dimension include whether, as the result of consulting, a highly competent work force was selected, whether talented employees were retained, and as a result of training, the extent to which employees reached and maintained high levels of productivity.

Most companies want to select the very best people. Consulting psychologists are frequently used to implement selection systems or augment a current selection system. There are several ways to assess the impact of such consulting interventions.

The degree of employee retention can be a key indicator of impact. In addition, the success of people selected within the organization by consulting efforts can offer another key measure of impact. Most organizations maintain relevant records consistently, so outcome assessment becomes a matter of accessing archival records. An alternative method of evaluating selection impact involves the measurement of person-organization fit. One key goal of employee selection is selecting people whose values are aligned with those of the organization. Chatman (1991) assessed the impact of a selection system by measuring person-organization fit using the Organizational Culture Profile (Chatman & Caldwell, 1991). Although this assessment of impact, as with others, was survey-based, it differed from others in that it did not directly assess the job performance of those selected. There are also several other techniques, such as utility analysis, that can be used to assess the monetary impact of selection systems (Cascio, 1991).

Many organizations invest significant amounts of money on selection, and the executives who lead these companies justifiably expect a return on their investment. However, few personnel selection programs are evaluated using such criteria, even though methods for doing so have long been available (see, for example, Brogden, 1949; Cronbach & Gleser, 1965). The numerous techniques used to assess the *utility* of a selection program provide valuable information that can potentially be used by consulting psychologists as outcome measures for selection programs they provide for client organizations. Utility can be defined as, "the degree to which its [i.e., the selection system] use improves the quality of the individuals selected beyond what would have occurred had that device not been used" (Cascio, 1991, p. 298). Quality, then, can be defined as, ". . . the proportion of individuals in the selected group who are considered successful . . . the average standard score on the criterion for the selected group, or the dollar payoff to the organization resulting from the use of a particular selection procedure" (Cascio, 1991, p. 298).

**Evaluating Selection Outcomes.** Consulting psychologists are often tasked with facilitating this process. For example, a selection test might be developed by a consulting psychologist to aid in the selection of computer programmers for a large software firm. There are several different methods for assessing the impact of this test. One method might involve interviewing each hiring manager after an employee has been selected to gather feedback on how things are going. Another method involves calculating the retention percentage of all those selected using a particular test. But, what if a senior executive wants to know the financial impact of this specific selection technique? One method for providing this type of impact assessment involves conducting a utility analysis (see, for example, Russell, 2001; Schmidt & Hunter, 1998; Thornton, Murphy, Everest, & Hoffman, 2000). Schmidt, Hunter, McKenzie, and Muldrow (1979) used this technique in a very similar situation. They estimated the impact of using a valid selection test for computer programmers. Results indicated that given certain parameters, a more valid selection procedure demonstrated an average gain in productivity of $64,725 per employee selected over nine years.

Consulting psychologists also frequently develop and utilize assessment centers for management selection (Goldsmith, 1990; Hough & Oswald, 2000; Thomas, Dickson, & Bliese, 2001). Assessment centers are typically expensive, and many organizations want to know what impact they are having. One method for measuring the impact of an assessment center is to calculate the net financial gain for the organization. Cascio and Ramos (1986) did just that by examining the impact of assessment centers in selecting first-level management. The authors examined a selection group comprised of 1,116 managers with an average tenure of 4.4 years. Employing utility analysis, the authors identified a net financial gain for the organization of $13 million by using the assessment center.

Russell (2001) examined, longitudinally, the impact of selecting top-level executives using competency ratings. Russell looked at the performance of ninety-eight executives over time. Using the Brogden-Cronbach-Gleser (BCG) Model (Brogden, 1949; Cronbach & Gleser, 1965), the author concluded that each executive selected using the competency procedure would account for an additional $3 million in additional profit per year.

In another, more dramatic, example, Hunter and Hunter (1984) examined entry-level jobs for the federal government. They concluded that substituting a less valid selection procedure for one that's highly valid would result in productivity losses costing approximately $3.12 billion. Utility can be calculated using several different methods.

There are several techniques for assessing utility, and each has its own advantages and disadvantages. The Taylor-Russell Utility Model (Taylor &

Russell, 1939) makes use of a validity coefficient that is based on current employees who were assessed prior to hire. The model classifies hired employees into successful and unsuccessful categories, and assumes they make equal contributions. This utility model is most appropriate for assessing the impact of selecting people for positions where differences in performance and ability beyond the minimum needed do not add any benefit to the organization.

**Other Outcome Evaluation Models.** The Naylor-Shine Model (Naylor & Shine, 1965) makes an assumption of linearity between validity and utility. This approach implies that "... the higher the validity, the greater the increase in average criterion score for the selected group over that observed for the total group" (Cascio, 1991, p. 299). This model is generally more useful than the Taylor-Russell Utility Model in assessing the utility of selection systems.

The BCG Model (Brogden, 1949; Cronbach & Gleser, 1965) assumes that the relationship between test scores and job performance is linear. This seems to be a logical assumption that can be made in the vast majority of selection situations. A key component of this model is the use of $SD_y$, the standard deviation of dollar-valued job performance in the selection group, in the estimation equation. One initial drawback to this model was the lack of appropriate methods for estimating $SD_y$. However, several alternative estimation methods have since been developed that make the use of this model more manageable.

Finally, the Schmidt-Hunter Global Estimation Procedure (Schmidt, Hunter, Pearlman, & Shane, 1979) reasons that job performance represented in dollar amounts is normally distributed. This model, then, permits a more reasonable method for estimating $SD_y$.

The results presented in some of these studies demonstrated that there are approaches to assessing the financial impact of selection services provided by consulting psychologists. However, utility analysis can also be used to assess the financial impact of other interventions such as training (Morrow, Jarrett, & Rupinski, 1997), changes in pay-level policies (Klaas & McClendon, 1996), and quality circles (Barrick & Alexander, 1992). There are many other ways to assess the impact of consulting services, but different utility analyses clearly provide methods for assessing their financial impact.

Organizations also want productive new hires to stay with the company as long as possible. One intervention that an organizational consulting psychologist might use to increase the likelihood of this desired outcome involves the use of realistic job previews (RJPs) (Phillips, 1998). A consultant might design a program that effectively previews different positions for possible candidates. Methods for assessing the impact of an RJP intervention include calculating the rate of attrition from the recruitment process, analyzing performance reviews for each candidate hired, using a survey to assess job satisfaction, and calculating turnover of selected candidates. All of these techniques for impact assessment were used in studies reviewed by Phillips. This author conducted a meta-analysis on studies reporting the impact of RJPs, and found that the RJP method was related to lower attrition from the selection process, lower turnover, higher job satisfaction, and higher levels of performance.

Having a multicultural work force is another desired organizational outcome falling within the people dimension. One intervention for achieving a multicultural work force involves the implementation of diversity programs. Consulting psychologists frequently implement diversity programs (see, for example, Wright, Ferris, Hiller, & Kroll, 1995). Wright et al. assessed the impact of diversity programs using a unique technique called the *event study methodology,* which is commonly used in financial economics research (see, for example, Dodd & Warner, 1983). This technique involves the analysis of a firm's stock price immediately surrounding the announcement of an event of interest. In this case, the authors analyzed stock price fluctuation connected to recognition announcements by the Department of Labor for exemplary affirmative action programs. Many other methods exist for assessing the impact of interventions within the people dimension, but we now turn our focus to the structure dimension.

## Structure

The structure dimension includes desired organizational outcomes such as efficiency and minimal redundancy in the use of resources, adequate information technology, effective technical systems, an organizational hierarchy that facilitates decision-making and performance, and role responsibilities that keep up with changes in the organization. Many organizations don't have the internal capacity to realize these desired outcomes (Dewett & Jones, 2001; Pickering & King, 1995; Prahalad & Hamel, 1990), so they rely on consulting psychologists for help.

The CEO of an organization might believe, for example, that her company is not operating as efficiently and effectively as she might hope. In an effort to find out what might be happening, she calls on a trusted advisor to conduct an organizational study and make specific recommendations for improvement. After an extensive and detailed analysis of the organization, the advisor recommends the implementation of a different information technology infrastructure. The CEO heeds this advice, and a new information technology (IT) system is in place within months. Assessing the impact of a new IT system on the organization is also done by consulting psychologists. Several methods for assessing the impact of IT systems are described by Dewett and Jones (2001) in a review. Impact was assessed in this study by measuring the codification of employees' knowledge base (Anand, Manz, & Glick, 1998; Rockart & Short, 1989), efficiency improvement (Pickering & King, 1995; DeSanctis & Gallupe, 1987), innovation promotion (Davidow & Malone, 1992; Prahalad & Hamel, 1990), specialization (Barabba &

Zaltman, 1990), formalization (Huber, 1990), decentralization (Fulk & Dutton, 1984), and learning (Cohen & Levinthal, 1990).

## Systems

Similar in some ways to the structure dimension is the systems dimension. Desired outcomes within the systems dimension include keeping employees informed in a timely manner, maintaining compensation systems that support effective job performance, and sustaining administrative mechanisms to fully support the organization.

A common intervention employed by consulting psychologists to achieve desired systems outcomes involves reward structures (Lawler, 1990, 2000). For example, work team performance has been linked to the way team members are rewarded (DeMatteo, Eby, & Sundstrom, 1998; Sundstrom, De Meuse, & Futrell, 1990). In some organizations, work team members are rewarded for individual performance, which works in opposition to many of the dynamics promoting work team performance. An intervention to create better team performance might involve implementing a team-based reward structure. Once an intervention such as this takes place, its impact must be assessed. One option for the consultant would be the use of surveys for measuring team member perceptions of fairness. Dulebohn and Martocchio (1998) assessed the impact of an incentive-based pay plan by measuring team member perceptions of procedural and distributive justice after the intervention. Another method for assessing impact would be to assess team and individual performance before implementing a new reward system and after.

Another intervention within the system dimension involves the implementation of skill-based pay. Murray and Gerhart (1998) examined the impact of implementing skill-based pay systems in a manufacturing organization. They assessed impact by measuring production, quality, and labor cost. Each of these was measured using the organization's archival records. Labor cost was measured as actual wage expense divided by the quantity of good parts produced. Quality was measured by the percentage of defective units in the total units allowed through the production process. Productivity was measured as labor hours per part.

## Interventions and Outcomes in OD

The field of consulting psychology has often not focused on establishing methods for assessing the impact of organizational consulting. However, several other fields have evaluated outcomes and offer useful methods for consulting psychologists. One such field is organizational development (OD) and change. Several significant reviews (see, for example, Guzzo, Jette, & Katzell, 1985; Macy & Izumi, 1993; Neuman, Edwards, & Raju, 1989; Pasmore, Frances, Halderman, & Shani, 1982; Porras & Robertson, 1992) have been conducted that summarize common organizational interventions and methods for assessing their impact. We attempt to review these studies to offer further methods for assessing the impact of organizational consulting.

**Types of Interventions.** The plethora of initiatives, interventions, and techniques are almost too numerous to count. However, past reviews of over 400 organizational development and change studies (Guzzo et al., 1985; Macy & Izumi, 1993; Neuman et al., 1989; Pasmore et al., 1982; Porras & Robertson, 1992) have provided specific and distinct categories of interventions. For example, Neuman et al. separated interventions into three categories: (1) human processes—interventions to help improve human functioning and process, such as training, participation in decision-making, team building, grid organizational development, and feedback; (2) technostructural—interventions that improve work content and method, the relationship between workers, job redesign, enlargement, and enrichment and work schedule changes; and (3) multifaceted—interventions involving multiple approaches.

Macy and Izumi (1993) created four categories of types of interventions: (1) structural—significant changes in an organization's hierarchical structure, such as self-directed work teams, changes in goal setting, feedback, and compensation systems; (2) human resources—changes employed with the organization's existing hierarchical structure, such as employee and manager training, job enrichment, team building, and selection; (3) technological—changes in the mechanical, informational, or process technologies, such as office computers, software, improved manufacturing systems, and computerized process and control systems; and (4) total quality management (TQM)—changes to improve the quality of organizational products and services, such as increased customer focus, customer and supplier partnerships, employee inspection of materials, process, and outputs. Although studies in these reviews ($n > 400$) included specific interventions, they also included specific outcome measures. We now review these outcome measures to help identify methods or key metrics for assessing the impact of consulting services. Guzzo et al. (1985) reviewed almost 100 intervention studies in an attempt to identify which interventions had the greatest impact. This review labeled the key criterion as productivity, and divided it into three specific outcomes: (1) output, including quantity, quality, and cost effectiveness; (2) withdrawal, referring to turnover and absenteeism; and (3) disruption, including accidents, strikes, and other costly disturbances. Results indicated a positive relationship between specific interventions and most of the outcome measures ($d = .44$).

**Other Reviews.** In another review of the organizational change literature, Macy and Izumi (1993) examined 131 studies, looking at the connection between organizational change initiatives and financial outcomes. Similar to the Guzzo et al. Study (1985), Macy and Izumi defined outcomes as: (1) quantity (output, sales, actual dollars, and productivity); (2) quality (rejects, repairs, defects, customer service returns, rework, yield, and amount of scrap); and (3) costs (repairs, errors, downtime, labor costs, overtime, recruitment and training costs, and office and manufacturing supplies). The majority of this outcome data was collected within two years of the interventions. Results indicated a strong relationship between the initiatives undertaken and the outcome variables ($d = 1.27$).

Pasmore et al. (1982) conducted a qualitative analysis of studies examining socio-technical system-based change. The key outcomes assessed in this review were categorized as turnover and absenteeism. Findings indicated that 100 percent of the studies that used both training and compensation system changes as interventions were able to decrease absenteeism and employee turnover. However, the magnitude of the effects were highly variable. While this review considered studies with relatively objective criteria, other reviews have analyzed studies utilizing job satisfaction and more attitudinal data as criteria.

Neuman et al. (1989) considered 126 studies that used organizational change initiatives to improve employee satisfaction and other attitudes. Employee satisfaction included satisfaction with pay, coworkers, and advancement opportunities. Attitudes included those about self (self-identity and decision-making), others (interpersonal trust of coworkers, social support, and peer support), the job (commitment and job involvement), and the organization (organizational commitment, attitude toward the company, and organizational trust). Results indicated that the organizational interventions employed were more positively related to attitudes than satisfaction.

The wide variety of outcome measures speaks to the widely varied contexts in which organizational interventions were used. For example, studies varied by organizational size, type (that is, public, private, and governmental), worker type (that is, managerial, blue collar, sales, and clerical), and length of time between intervention and outcome assessment. Each of these factors, along with many others, would be involved in determining which outcome measures would be most appropriate for specific consulting situations.

# IMPLICATIONS AND RECOMMENDATIONS FOR CONSULTING PSYCHOLOGISTS

In this chapter, the case for assessing the impact of consulting endeavors delivered by psychologists in organizational settings has been presented, along with a variety of methods and examples for doing so. The outcome evaluation process should be an essential aspect of high-quality consulting, not just an add-on or afterthought following consulting intervention. Well-developed organizational consulting practice dictates that consultants engage in thoughtful dialogue, examination, and articulation of the outcomes and results their clients are seeking, prior to proceeding with any intervention or programmatic design. The clarification and articulation of desired outcomes should inform the design of services and interventions.

In reviewing the literature on outcome evaluation in consulting, it is clear that there is a need for much more in the way of both research and practical methods that consulting psychologists can use in applied organizational settings. The field of consulting psychology can certainly borrow from I-O psychologists, who have historically evidenced a more empirical approach to their work, and, consequently, have constructed a more substantial case literature.

As we proceed in developing our focus and capability on assessing the impact of psychologically informed consultation to organizations, it is important to note an important caveat. Not all consultation provided by psychologists to organizations readily lends itself to quantitative or utility analysis. There are many instances in which consulting psychologists contribute advice and counsel that enriches or reframes the perspectives of an executive or manager that cannot adequately be measured by simple outcome or financial metrics. For example, psychologists are consulted by CEOs or board committees to consider the merits of a proposed merger or acquisition. In our experience, the value contributed by consulting psychologists is critical judgments about the formidable difficulties that would be posed by attempting to integrate the cultures and management teams of the respective organizations. As a result of the psychologists' analysis and recommendations, the merger discussions are halted and the CEO or board committee terminates the deal. In such cases, it is impossible to determine the effects had the deal gone through. In other examples; consulting psychologists can be asked to provide input regarding the termination of a key manager, employees' reaction to the closing of a plant, or the likely effects of a major organizational restructuring. Executives who retain the services of consulting psychologists in such cases call upon them to render opinions or help think through key decisions that involve matters of judgment and conscience. These matters do not lend themselves to any methods of simple outcome evaluation.

In summary, we are not advocating a human factors approach to outcome evaluation in all circumstances where consulting psychologists provide services to organizations. Even the best-trained and experienced psychologists cannot engineer precisely desired outcomes in the complex landscape of organizational practice. We believe, however, that consulting psychologists have a duty to commit ourselves, much more rigorously than ever before, to the examination and refinement of the explicit and implicit outcomes organizations seek, and to the assessment of the impact we have when we apply the science and art of psychology in organizational settings. We also believe this commitment will improve the quality and impact of the consultation and organizational effectiveness.

# References

American Psychological Association. (1992). Ethical principles of psychologists and code of conduct. *American Psychologist, 47,* 1597–1611.

Anand, V., Manz, C. C., & Glick, W. H. (1998). An organizational memory approach to information management. *Academy of Management Review, 23,* 796–809.

Barabba, V. P., & Zaltman, G. (1990). *Hearing the voice of the market.* Boston: Harvard Business School Press.

Barrick, M. R., & Alexander, R. A. (1992). Estimating the benefits of a quality circle intervention. *Journal of Organizational Behavior, 13,* 73–80.

Blanton, J. S. (2000). Why consultants don't apply psychological research. *Consulting Psychology Journal: Practice and Research, 52,* 235–247.

Brogden, H. E. (1949). When testing pays off. *Personnel Psychology, 2,* 171–183.

Burke, W. W. (1987). *Organization development: A normative view.* Reading, MA: Addison Wesley.

Carpenter, M. A., & Westphal, J. D. (2001). The strategic context of external network ties: Examining the impact of director appointments on board involvement in strategic decision making. *Academy of Management Journal, 44,* 639–660.

Cascio, W. F. (1991). *Applied psychology in personnel management* (4th ed.). Englewood Cliffs, NJ: Prentice Hall.

Cascio, W. F., & Ramos, R. A. (1986). Development and application of a new method for assessing job performance in behavioral economic terms. *Journal of Applied Psychology, 71,* 20–28.

Chatman, J. A. (1991). Matching people and organization: Selection and socialization in public accounting firms. *Administrative Science Quarterly, 36,* 459–484.

Chatman, J. A., & Caldwell, D. M. (1991). People and organizational culture: A Q-sort approach to assessing person-organization fit. *Academy of Management Journal, 34,* 487–516.

Cohen, W. M., & Levinthal, D. A. (1990). Absorptive capacity: A new perspective on learning and innovation. *Administrative Science Quarterly, 35,* 128–152.

Cone, J. D. (2000). *Evaluating outcomes: Empirical tools for effective practice.* Washington, DC: American Psychological Association.

Cook, D. T., Campbell, D. T., & Peracchio, L. (1990). Quasi experimentation. In M. D. Dunnette & L. M. Hough (Eds.), *Handbook of industrial and organizational psychology* (2nd ed., Vol. 1, pp. 491–576). Palo Alto, CA: Consulting Psychologists Press.

Cronbach, L. J., & Gleser, G. C. (1965). *Psychological tests and personnel decisions* (2nd ed.). Urbana: University of Illinois Press.

Davidow, W. H., & Malone, M. S. (1992). *The virtual corporation.* New York: HarperCollins.

DeMatteo, J. S., Eby, L. T., & Sundstrom, E. (1998). Team-based rewards: Current empirical evidence and directions for future research. *Research in Organizational Behavior, 20,* 141–183.

DeSanctis, G., & Gallupe, B. (1987). A foundation for the study of group decision support systems. *Management Science, 33,* 116–132.

Dewett, T., & Jones, G. R. (2001). The role of information technology in the organization: A review, model, and assessment. *Journal of Management, 27,* 313–346.

Dodd, P., & Warner, J. (1983). On corporate governance. *Journal of Financial Economics, 11,* 401–438.

Dulebohn, J. H., & Martocchio, J. J. (1998). Employee perceptions of the fairness of work group incentive pay plans. *Journal of Management, 24,* 469–488.

Fulk, J., & Dutton, W. (1984). Videoconferencing as an organizational information system: Assessing the role of electronic meetings. *Systems, Objectives, and Solutions, 4,* 105–118.

Goldsmith, R. F. (1990). Utility analysis and its application to the study of the cost-effectiveness of the assessment center method. In K. R. Murphy & F. E. Saal (Eds.), *Psychology in organizations: Integrating science and practice* (pp. 95–110). Hillsdale, NJ: Erlbaum.

Guzzo, R. A., Jette, R. D., & Katzell, R. A. (1985). The effects of psychologically based intervention programs on worker productivity: A meta-analysis. *Personnel Psychology, 38,* 275–291.

Hammer, M., & Champy, J. (1993). *Reengineering the corporation.* New York: HarperCollins.

Henderson, A. D. (1999). Firm strategy and age dependence: A contingent view of the liabilities of newness, adolescence, and obsolescence. *Administrative Science Quarterly, 44,* 281–314.

Hough, L. M., & Oswald, F. L. (2000). Personnel selection: Looking toward the future— Remembering the past. *Annual Review of Psychology, 51,* 631–664.

Huber, G. P. (1990). A theory of the effects of advanced information technologies on organizational design, intelligence, and decision making. *Academy of Management Review, 15,* 47–71.

Huet-Cox, G. D, Nielsen, T. M., & Sundstrom, E. (1999a). Get the most from 360-degree feedback: Put it on the Internet. *HR Magazine, 44*(5), 92–103.

Huet-Cox, G. D., Nielsen, T. M., & Sundstrom, E. (1999b). Getting results from Internet-based 360-degree feedback through coaching. *Human Resource Professional, 12*(6), 23–28.

Hunter, J. E., & Hunter, R. F. (1984). Validity and utility of alternative predictors of job performance. *Psychological Bulletin, 96,* 72–98.

Klaas, B. S., & McClendon, J. A. (1996). To lead, lag or match: Estimating the financial impact of pay level policies. *Personnel Psychology, 49,* 121–141.

Lawler, E. E., III. (1990). *Strategic pay: Aligning organizational strategies and pay systems.* San Francisco: Jossey-Bass.

Lawler, E. E., III. (2000). *Rewarding excellence: Pay strategies for the new economy.* San Francisco: Jossey-Bass.

Lowman, R. L. (Ed.). (1998). *The ethical practice of psychology in organizations.* Washington, DC: American Psychological Association.

Lukas, B., Tan, J., & Hult, G.T.M. (2001). Strategic fit in transitional economies: The case of China's electronics industry. *Journal of Management, 27*(4), 409–429.

Macy, B. A., & Izumi, H. (1993). Organizational change, design, and work innovation: A meta-analysis of 131 North American field studies—1961–1991. *Research in Organizational Change and Development, 7,* 235–313.

Mintzberg, H. (1973). Strategy-making in three models. *California Management Review, 16,* 44–53.

Morrow, C. C., Jarrett, M. Q., & Rupinski, M. T. (1997). An investigation of the effect and economic utility of corporate-wide training. *Personnel Psychology, 50,* 91–119.

Murray, B., & Gerhart, B. (1998). An empirical analysis of a skill-based pay program and plant performance outcomes. *Academy of Management Journal, 41,* 68–78.

Naylor, J. C., & Shine, L. C. (1965). A table for determining the increase in mean criterion score obtained by using a selection device. *Journal of Industrial Psychology, 3,* 33–42.

Neuman, G. A., Edwards, J. E., & Raju, N. S. (1989). Organizational development interventions: A meta-analysis of their effects on satisfaction and other attitudes. *Personnel Psychology, 42,* 461–483.

Newman, J. L. (1993). Ethical issues in consultation. *Journal of Counseling and Development, 72,* 148–156.

Newman, J. L., Gray, E. A., & Fuqua (1996). Beyond ethical decision making. *Consulting Psychology Journal: Practice and Research, 48,* 230–236.

Pasmore, W. A., Frances, C., Haldeman, J., & Shani, A. (1982). Sociotechnical system: A North American reflection on empirical studies of the seventies. *Human Relations, 35,* 1179-1204.

Phillips, J. M. (1998). Effects of realistic job previews on multiple organizational outcomes: A meta-analysis. *Academy of Management Journal, 41,* 673-690.

Pickering, J. M., & King, J. L. (1995). Hardwiring weak ties: Interorganizational computer-mediated communication, occupational communities, and organizational change. *Organization Science, 6,* 479-486.

Porras, J. L., & Robertson, P. J. (1992). Organizational development: Theory, practice, and research. In M. D. Dunnette & L. M. Hough (Eds.), *Handbook of industrial/organizational psychology* (2nd ed., Vol. 3, pp. 719-822). Palo Alto, CA: Consulting Psychologists Press.

Prahalad, C. K., & Hamel, G. (1990). The core competencies of the corporation. *Harvard Business Review, 68,* 43-59.

Rockart, J. F., & Short, J. E. (1989). IT in the 1990s: Managing organizational interdependencies. *Sloan Management Review, 30,* 17-33.

Russell, C. J. (2001). A longitudinal study of top-level executive performance. *Journal of Applied Psychology, 86,* 560-573.

Schein, E. H. (1969). *Process consultation: Its role in organization development.* Reading, MA: Addison-Wesley.

Schmidt, F. L., & Hunter, J. E. (1998). The validity and utility of selection methods in personnel psychology: Practical and theoretical implications of 85 years of research findings. *Psychological Bulletin, 124,* 262-274.

Schmidt, F. L., Hunter J. E., McKenzie, R. C., & Muldrow, T. W. (1979). Impact of valid selection procedures on work-force productivity. *Journal of Applied Psychology, 66,* 609-626.

Schmidt, F. L., Hunter, J. E., Pearlman, K., & Shane, G. S. (1979). Further tests of the Schmidt-Hunter Bayesian validity generalization procedure. *Personnel Psychology, 32,* 257-281.

Sundstrom, E., De Meuse, K. P., & Futrell, D. (1990). Work teams: Applications and effectiveness. *American Psychologist, 45,* 120-133.

Taylor, H. C., & Russell, J. T. (1939). The relationship of validity coefficients to the practical effectiveness of tests in selection. *Journal of Applied Psychology, 23,* 565-578.

Thomas, J. L., Dickson, M. W., & Bliese, P. D. (2001). Values predicting leader performance in the U.S. Army Reserve Officer Training Corps Assessment Center: Evidence for a personality-mediated model. *Leadership Quarterly, 12,* 181-196.

Thornton, G. C., Murphy, K. R., Everest, T. M., & Hoffman, C. C. (2000). Higher cost, lower validity and higher utility: Comparing the utilities of two tests that differ in validity, costs and selectivity. *International Journal of Selection and Assessment, 8,* 61-75.

Wright, P., Ferris, S. P., Hiller, J. S., & Kroll, M. (1995). Competitiveness through management of diversity: Effects on stock price valuation. *Academy of Management Journal, 38,* 272-287.

# CHAPTER TWENTY-EIGHT

# Understanding Organizational Processes and Performance

## *A Continuous Improvement Model for Consulting Psychologists*

Delbert M. Nebeker
*California School of Organizational Studies*
*Alliant International University*

B. Charles Tatum
*Department of Psychology*
*National University*

The purpose of this chapter is to describe a new model for understanding organizational functioning that can be used by consulting psychologists in helping business owners, managers, and corporate leaders improve their organizations' effectiveness. Consulting psychologists are often called upon to assess the needs of organizations and suggest strategies for change and improvement (American Psychological Association, 2000). To do this, they need competencies in a variety of areas, because their consulting activities might be at one or more of three different levels within organizations. The first level is the individual level within organizations (for example, personal and career development, assessment of job skills, or performance appraisal). The second is at the group level. Here, organizational consultants might also work with groups or teams (for example, team development, assessment of group dynamics, or identity group management). The third level organizational consultants might deal with is the organization as a whole (for example, organizational diagnosis, assessment surveys of culture and climate, or change management). Regardless of the level or the nature of the consulting task, we believe that the best results usually occur when the psychologist works within the framework of an established theory or model. One purpose of this chapter is to present a model of organizational processes that organizational consultants can use to better understand and improve organizational functioning. We call this model the Continuous Improvement Model (CIM). The model is shown in Figure 28.1. We developed the CIM to serve as an analytic tool for consultants, practitioners, and

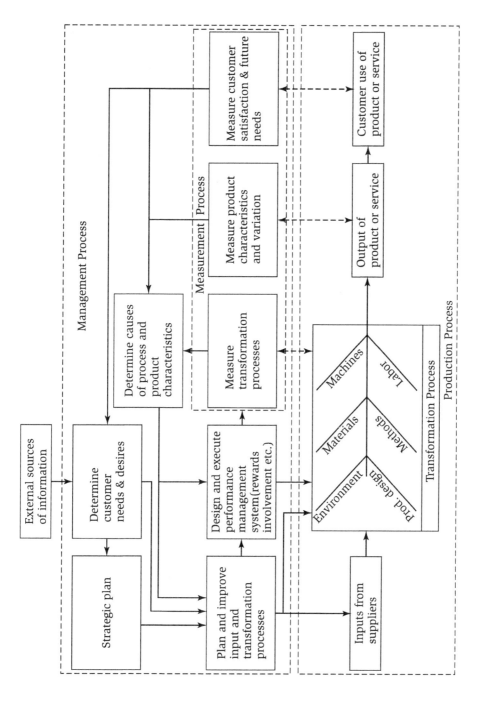

**Figure 28.1 The Continuous Improvement Model, Showing Both the Production and Management Processes and the Relationship Between the Two.**

researchers. It serves as a map of the essential functions that all organizations and consulting psychologists should be striving to improve. The CIM grew out of our own consulting and research experiences, as well as the research and theory of others. It is designed to focus attention on key organizational processes, and how they are interconnected as a system, in determining organizational efficiency and effectiveness.

The CIM focuses on two vital functions of the organization—production and management—and is intended as a road map or guide for consulting psychologists. The model is based on sound organizational theory and recent scientific evidence, and embraces the goals of the scientist-practitioner approach to consulting. By analyzing organizations using the CIM, and following the steps described in this chapter, consultants can better understand and assess the needs of their client organizations, and suggest scientifically valid improvements to quality, productivity, and competitiveness. This chapter begins with a discussion of organizations as systems. We then describe the CIM in more detail, along with some ideas about how it can be used to guide the thinking of consulting psychologists.

## ORGANIZATIONS AS SYSTEMS

Organizations have been a dominant feature of civilization for thousands of years. Power and authority have been exercised in formal, organized institutions from the earliest history of humanity. Organizations are perhaps even more important in our modern, technological society than in past, pre-industrial societies. Business organizations, in particular, have become more complex, and are a fundamental driver of the increased standard of living in the modern world (Strank, 1983). Because organizations are such a central part of everyday life, the proper functioning of organizations is a major interest of psychology and business today. The effective performance of these institutions is vital to our well-being, but, unfortunately, there is much room for improvement in how modern organizations and institutions function.

Organizations function as *systems* (Fuqua & Newman, 2002). A system is defined as a set of elements, relationships, interdependencies, and interacting functions, which comprise a purposeful means for achieving an objective. An organization is considered an *open system* (Katz & Kahn, 1978). It has boundaries that differentiate it from other systems, but it must constantly receive a multitude of inputs from its external environment (for example, people, energy, raw materials, tools, equipment, information, and so on) in order for the system to achieve its objectives. An organization takes its inputs and transforms them into outputs with value added; these outputs are then returned to the environment. To survive and prosper, an organization must produce outputs valued by the environment. In other words, it must create or generate something of value to its customers or clients (Williams, DuBrin, & Sisk, 1985). To accomplish this objective, an organization must integrate and coordinate functions at several levels (individuals, groups, large aggregations) successively and simultaneously.

## Individuals

Managing the individuals within an organization is a complex process that involves many activities (for example, career development, personnel selection, coaching, mentoring, job training). Perhaps one of the most difficult tasks at the individual level is performance appraisal. Organizations struggle with devising systems that measure individual work performance accurately and fairly, while meeting the needs of both employees and management. There is no perfect system, obviously, but many of the inherent problems can be avoided by adopting new approaches developed within the past two decades that emphasize multisource rating and a focus on the customer (Lepsinger & Lucia, 1997). These techniques, such as 360-degree feedback, are not only used to evaluate individuals, but have also been adapted to organizational development, cultural change efforts, and team development (Lepsinger & Lucia).

## Groups

Managing groups and teams within the organization has become more of an imperative in the last ten to twenty years (Guzzo, Salas et al., 1995; Lepsinger & Lucia, 1997), and there has been considerable research interest in teams in recent years (Brannick, Salas, & Prince, 1997). Many organizations today structure their work tasks around groups in an attempt to maximize the synergy and creativity that often flows from people working together. Of course, to get superior performance from a group or team, the individuals must be able to, among other things, communicate, cooperate, coordinate, adapt, and make decisions, not only with each member of the group, but also with other groups (Brannick & Prince, 1997). There are serious challenges for the consultant when helping to develop effective groups (for example, selecting compatible individuals, managing group conflict, dealing with issues of equity). One of the more difficult tasks is measuring the group results. Recent advances have been made in constructing teamwork measures using survey techniques (Hallam & Campbell, 1997), critical incidents methodologies with behaviorally anchored scales (Dickinson & McIntyre, 1997), and analyzing knowledge, skills, and abilities (Cannon-Bowers & Salas, 1997).

## Organizations

Often, changes made at the individual or group level, though improving the effectiveness of the individual or the group, have no overall impact on organizational outcomes (Harris, 1994). For example, a training program might improve the job knowledge of the trainees, but unless this knowledge is put to use back at the job site, there will be no noticeable change at the organizational level (for example, no increase in productivity, no improvement in customer satisfaction, no more sales). Part of the job of the consulting psychologist is to help the client find useful ways to measure organizational outcomes and link those outcomes to improvements at the other levels (Pritchard, 1994).

Given the complex nature of organizations, and the difficulties in coordinating change efforts at multiple levels, the consulting psychologist has a very challenging role when working with managers and leaders of businesses and institutions. Exercising that role requires a clear understanding of the nature and function of organizations. We believe that the CIM in Figure 28.1 provides a useful theoretical framework and systems view for understanding the complex character of most organizations. As such, it can help guide the consultant through the many issues and problems commonly encountered. The model is composed of two major processes: management and production. These two processes overlap with two of the five subsystems described by Katz and Kahn (1978), and are vital to the integrating and coordinating mechanisms that "bring the system together for unified functioning" (p. 29). The internal process flow between and within management and production is a sequence of supplier-customer relationships that serves to generate a product or service. We will explain the model by covering each of the major elements of the model sequentially. Our model suggests that most organizations are repeating cycles of processes that flow in a grand loop. Therefore, organizational improvement is based on entering this loop, analyzing the organization's functioning, and then adjusting organizational elements to bring about the desired improvement. We can enter the iterative processes of the model at any convenient point. However, because production is the primary purpose for most organizations, and most consultants will enter an existing organization that has some form of a production process, we begin our more detailed explanation of the model with a discussion of the production process.

# THE PRODUCTION PROCESS

The core of any organization is its production process. Often, people think of production in terms of manufacturing a product. Here we use the term more generically to describe any process that generates an output (for example, goods, services, policies, ideas, and social benefits). We believe that designing and improving production systems requires developing efficient ways to predict the performance of the production systems, and identify the effects of important design parameters on system performance. The increasing complexity of modern, automated production systems, with their high capital cost, is forcing system designers to develop formal models to assess system performance, and to evaluate the main parameters of the design (Buzacott & Shanthikumar, 1991).

Figure 28.1 depicts a production process as a system in which inputs are received from suppliers and then transformed into outputs. These outputs are usually, but not only, products or services. These outputs then are typically delivered to customers. Depending on the nature and objectives of an organization, its essential inputs can take many forms. Information, energy, raw materials, human resources, land, capital, parts and subassemblies (in factories), and people (for example, students in schools, and patients in treatment centers) are just a few examples of possible inputs.

The transformation processes an organization performs are the necessary conversions of its inputs into usable products or services (for example, assemble parts into subassemblies or completed products, provide financial services to bank customers, educate students, or diagnose and treat patients). Outputs are the goods and services produced for use outside of the focal organization. They are intended for delivery to the marketplace or the served sector of the society, geography, or economy. Directly or indirectly, they are also intended to help the receiving organization achieve its purpose (Mundel, 1982). The expected output of the above examples can be expressed in terms of products such as bicycles or battleships, completed financial transactions, educated students, diagnosed, treated, or healed patients, creative ideas, or scientific discoveries.

## Inputs

The raw materials, parts, or information used in the production process begin with the supplier(s) of these inputs. The quality of the output can be no better than the quality of the materials or parts used in the production of the output. The purchaser (organization) cannot guarantee quality to its customers if the raw materials or parts purchased from the supplier(s) are substandard or defective. Quality assurance of parts and materials purchased from the supplier(s) is the key to the manufacturer's own quality assurance. It is also important to the smooth planning of manufacturing operations, raising productivity, and planning cost cutting (Ishikawa, 1985).

Occasionally, suppliers ship materials as soon as they are produced, without regard to quality. The purchaser, also without performing inspection, sends everything to the manufacturing division. If the manufacturing division is concerned with the quality, it has no alternative except to engage in 100 percent inspection and select only those materials and parts acceptable for manufacturing. In an even worse situation, the manufacturing division might not engage in 100 percent inspection and might use defective parts in manufacturing. Even if the organization was to engage in inspection at the point of receiving, and send only good parts to the manufacturing division, this would impose a serious burden on the purchaser. Therefore, excessive costs are added to the production process. The supplier could engage in 100 percent inspection, but if its methods are not statistically stable and capable, its inspection probably cannot be trusted either. The ideal state is one in which the supplier only produces good parts. To achieve this, statistical quality control is employed by the supplier to ensure stable and capable production of materials before entering into the production process of our target organization. In such instances, shipping inspection by the supplier is usually no longer required, and the purchaser can be confident that the inputs are of high quality. However, inspection might still be required if the quality of the materials used might affect the safety of the users (for example, blood supplies).

## Transformation Processes

The sequence of steps and activities that converts inputs into an output is known as the transformation process. Before a transformation process can be improved, it must be stable, predictable, or under control. If it is not predictable or under control, it is not understood. If a process is not understood, then attempts to improve it are, at best, only random guesses. Process analysis is a procedure used to help establish process control. It helps clarify the relationship between causal factors in the process (for example, environmental factors, materials, machines, product design, methods, and labor) and effects (for example, quality, cost, and productivity). Process control attempts to discover causal factors that hinder the smooth and efficient functioning of the manufacturing process, and introduce unwanted variation into the product or service (Breyfogle, 1999). It thus endeavors to find technology that can engage in preventative control (Ishikawa, 1985). By preventative control, we mean a process that is predictable and in which all output meets the purchaser's specifications.

Quite often a large number of factors will be involved in the instability of a process. When this happens, a disciplined approach is necessary in order to establish and maintain statistical control. One of the simplest tools used in process analysis is the cause-and-effect (fishbone) diagram (see the box in Figure 28.1 labeled Transformation Process). The rudiments of a cause-and-effect diagram depicted in this box suggest that transformational processes produce not only products or services, but also quantifiable *outcomes* associated with the products or services. All the factors included in the diagram are potential *causes* of those outcomes. For example, suppose a client has identified an important quality characteristic (for example, roundness of a metal shaft, or typographical errors in written publications). Also suppose we want to help our client improve or control this characteristic in the product or service. To do this, we would want to identify the major causes for the quality characteristic (for example, materials, machines, methods of work, and so on). Next, we would identify detailed subcauses for each of the major causes. We continue doing this until we have defined and linked the relationships of the possible causal factors that lead to the source of the quality characteristic (roundness or errors). It is important to check that all possible causes are included in the analysis.

In addition to detailing the causal structure of the outcome, other values of the cause-and-effect diagram are as an educational tool, a guide for focusing attention in discussions concerning the pursuit of quality improvement, a working document that is updated as additional information is accumulated, and an indication of the level of the understanding of the process. If a detailed diagram cannot be constructed, it indicates that the level of knowledge of the process is currently too shallow (Brumbaugh & Heikes, 1991).

There are many possible measures of process quality. These include waste, yield, labor hours, energy consumption, and so on. Additional process improvement tools are available in addition to cause-and-effect diagrams. Discussion of them is beyond the scope of this chapter. Many of them are part of statistical quality control (SQC), and can be used to ensure quality within an acceptable quality level (see, for example, Montgomery, 2000).

## Outputs

The outputs from a process are the products or services that are created by the transformation process. Once a product or service is created, it is transferred to an internal or external customer. We have argued that the quality of the output (product or service) is dependent on the inputs received from the suppliers and the effectiveness of the transformation process.

In our example above, the metal shaft might be the finished product. Suppose one of our client's goals is to produce round shafts with minimal variance in roundness and within their customer's specifications. How well they accomplished this goal determines the degree of quality of the process. Our goal as consulting psychologists is to help them produce a quality product. In addition, we probably want to consider the cost of the production (for example, labor, material, energy, and so on). In other words, the amount of variation in the product and the cost of production will determine quality.

## Customer Use of Products

In order to produce an output that meets the requirements of the customer, it is necessary to define, monitor, and control the inputs and transformation process. To do this, the organization needs to know how the customer will use the product or service. Learning how the customer uses the product, as well as assessing customer satisfaction and future needs, is part of management's responsibility. This information forms the foundation for all attempts to analyze and improve the production process. This information is collected as part of the management process.

# THE MANAGEMENT PROCESS

An organization's management is continually in the process of planning, organizing, leading, and controlling organizational resources to achieve specific objectives (Williams et al., 1985). Planning involves determining customer needs and desires, and developing strategic and transformational plans to meet these needs and desires (for example, developing new technology to improve the production process). Organizing and leading involve the design and execution of the performance management system within the organization (for example, organizational structures, rewards, and involvement opportunities). Controlling involves, first, the measurement of the transformation process, product characteristics, product variation, customer satisfaction, and future needs of the customer, and second, the adjustment of the transformational system to meet organizational objectives. Management is responsible for the entire system and its various processes. Traditionally, in larger organizations, management is divided into three levels: top, middle, and first line. Each of these levels is part of the management process that oversees the production process. How efficient and effective the management process is will determine how well the production process will function.

Managers have a challenging task. In an organization focused on quality, they must take responsibility for the processes used, and constantly seek to improve them. This necessitates a fundamental change in how organizations are viewed by people who manage them and those who work in them. Managers must realize that the systems they create and perpetuate control the great majority of process variability (Gitlow, Gitlow, Oppenheim, & Oppenheim, 1989). Workers also have responsibility in the process, in addition to performing their jobs. Their responsibility is to communicate to management the information they have about the system.

The CIM presented here is based on a cybernetic view of organizations (Sigler, 1999; Strank, 1983) within an open system (that is, systems of control and communication, linking feedback and action across organizational boundaries). Management in this approach is viewed in terms of both control and goal achievement. Jankowicz (1973) identified two types of control activities. The first is *classic feedback*, in which the deviation of output against the goal is measured, and corrective action is taken. The second occurs when control actions are initiated on the basis of information reaching the managers via established input mechanisms from outside the organization (for example, customer satisfaction or need surveys). Disturbances arise both within and outside of the organization. Therefore, feedback and corrective actions are initiated from both internal and external regulation processes.

An organization can enter the cybernetic loop at any point in the model. For example, a new organization might want to begin with the assessment of customer needs. An established organization might want to start with the assessment of customer satisfaction, because, presumably, it already has a good idea of its customers' needs. Starting with customer satisfaction and then moving backward to view other areas is analogous to looking through a microscope at an ever-increasing magnification. Customer satisfaction is a macro-view of product or service quality. For more microscopic views of the product or service, one must probe deeper into the organization.

## Determining Customer Needs

The most important customers to any organization are its external ones, those that purchase or use its products or services. External customer needs and desires must be understood. This can be determined by measuring customer satisfaction and future needs, and by obtaining information from external sources (for example, consumer reports, government studies, marketing analyses). Because the quality chain can break down at any unit in the flow of work, the internal customers must also be well-served in order to satisfy the external customers. Neverending or continuous improvement is probably the most powerful concept to guide management. An organization must recognize, throughout its ranks, that the purpose of all work and all efforts to improve is to better serve customers. This means that an organization must know how well its outputs are performing in the eyes of the customer, through measurement and feedback.

## Strategic Plan

The information that has been gathered and analyzed regarding customer needs and desires is used to guide the strategic plan. Strategic planning involves making strategic decisions about major plans for the organization. Strategic planning is one of the most often written-about subjects in organization and management. There are thousands of books that could be cited as models for the strategic process. The majority of these share much in common with the process we describe (see, for example, Anthony, 1985; Miller & Dess, 1997; Thompson & Strickland, 1999). The most popular approaches generally include five key elements: (1) conducting an industry and competitive analysis; (2) developing a long-term strategic vision (often three to five years, but sometimes as many as ten to twenty years); (3) setting objectives for the organization; (4) crafting a strategic course of action to reach the objectives; and (5) implementing the strategy (Thompson & Strickland, 1999).

A strategic plan is intended to provide the framework for all that the organization does. It establishes the criteria for major investment decisions (for example, opening a new plant, new product or service development, budgetary allocation). It also serves as the basis to evaluate the performance of the organization and its managers. Anthony (1985) recommends the following steps in creating a strategic plan:

1. Perform an environmental analysis, from which a forecast is made regarding changes, trends, and so on.

2. Perform a customer and market analysis to see how the market is changing, and develop a customer profile of tomorrow. Key assumptions made about the future are established, based on the forecast, and serve as the basis for developing the strategic plan.

3. Perform an internal assessment that attempts to determine the strengths and weaknesses of the organization as it now exists.

4. Outline the role and mission of the organization in view of the environment it faces and the resources it has or can reasonably expect to obtain. The mission provides the ultimate rationale for the organization's existence. It gives the organization identity.

5. Identify three or four major areas in which the organization plans to focus its efforts in the next three to five years. This reflects the mission and the forecast.

6. Develop a way to implement the strategic plan from the development of operational objectives, and take corrective action.

## Determining Causes of Process and Product Characteristics

If an organization is to improve its processes, it must first determine the causes of process variation. This can be accomplished through the use of process analysis and control activities (Gitlow et al., 1989). For example, suppose an organization has hired a consultant to help solve problems the organization is experiencing in shipping the wrong products to customers. The consultant might identify several possible causes: the method for identifying different products, errors by personnel, and equipment errors (both software and hardware). If employee errors are the most likely general cause, the consultant would examine personnel more closely, in order to identify subcauses. These might include the amount of training provided to employees, the level of ability of employees, and employees' attention to detail. Furthermore, the consultant might determine that the amount of personnel training is the most important subcause, and select it for even more detailed analysis. Getting at this root cause allows us to peel back the layers of a problem, as one would peel off the layers of an onion, to get to the heart of the problem.

Another method of determining causes of process capability and product characteristics is to use what is known as a *Pareto chart*. Sometimes several events (for example, steps in a process) create a problem, and it is unclear which event or step is the major cause. A Pareto chart is used to identify and prioritize which events produced the problem. The concept behind this tool is often referred to as Pareto's Law. It states that 80 percent of errors come from 20 percent of the possible causes. These 20 percent are the vital few versus the trivial many. The process of arranging data, classifying it, and tabulating it in a Pareto chart helps to determine the most important problem to be worked on (Gitlow et al., 1989). Examples of other tools that can be used to improve processes are histograms, control charts, run charts, affinity diagrams, and scatter diagrams (Ishikawa, 1990).

## Measurement Processes

**Levels of Measurement: Individual, Group, and Organization.** Developing good measures of organizational processes is vital to organizational success. From a management perspective, all levels of an organization must be integrated so the system as a whole can function optimally. Properly designed measurement systems help to accomplish this. Pritchard (1994) presents a useful structure for linking the different levels. In Pritchard's terminology, outputs from more molecular levels become inputs to the more molar levels. Other inputs are added as we move up the hierarchy. So, for example, the behavior of individuals (for example, engineering knowledge) is combined with existing technology (computer-assisted design programs) to produce group-level outputs (for example, better engineering designs from the engineering team). Likewise, group-level outputs (better designs) are combined with the manufacturing capabilities to produce company-wide outputs (for example, high-performance motorcycles). Measurement of input and output must occur at all levels; management's role is to optimize the system as a whole.

The data needed for these measures are collected from the measurement process. As seen in Figure 28.1, the measurement process includes measure of: (a) customer satisfaction and future needs, (b) product characteristics and variation, and (c) the transformation process. For example, the data collected on customer satisfaction can be used to help improve both transformation processes and product characteristics. When a consultant's objective is to improve a production process, it is often valuable to begin data analysis with customer satisfaction. The results from this analysis can be use to trace problems back to causal or contributing areas of the organization's processes.

**Measure Customer Satisfaction and Future Needs.** Customer satisfaction must become the focus of corporate thinking. Providing customers with goods and services that meet their expectations and needs at a price they are willing to pay is paramount. This can only be done by continually improving quality in a never-ending cycle.

Through increased consumer education and media attention customers are becoming more sophisticated. They are making more explicit demands and know what they want and what they expect to pay for it. Consumers are motivated to get the most value for their dollars. To satisfy customers organizations must market quality products at a fair price (Deming, 1986). When customers are satisfied work and revenue will increase in the long run; but satisfying customers must be the primary goal, *not* just increasing revenue or balancing the budget.

There are various methods that can be used for the purpose of measuring customer satisfaction and determining their future needs (see Tatum & Nebeker, 2002, for specific examples). These methods can be used for both internal and external measurement. Some of these methods include customer surveys, quality panel techniques (that is, focus groups), in-depth interviews or follow-up phone calls, and surveying trade associations. No matter what method is used, whether the customer is external or internal, or how extensive the data collection, it is important to keep very close to the customer.

If a problem is identified with customer satisfaction and future needs regarding an organization's product, the next step would be to increase measurement refinements for the identified product characteristics to determine where improvements in the process can be made.

**Measure Product Characteristics and Variation.** Performance measurements can help improve product characteristics and variation if they incorporate statistical quality control techniques (Montgomery, 2000). SQC is often thought of as a collection of some useful statistical tools to measure and monitor the quality of production processes. However, SQC is more than that; it is a way of thinking about production systems as a deterministic, scientific endeavor that emphasizes the necessity for careful thinking, observation, and experimentation to improve production processes. Without adopting the proper conceptual framework, the tools and techniques cannot be used to full effectiveness. The aim of SQC is producing actions that improve underlying (causal) processes, and this requires both an understanding of the processes and an understanding of the way to use the tools and techniques of SQC for continual improvement of the system (Ishikawa, 1985).

SQC can be used to control variation. Variation can be thought of as deviation from the target objective. Although every process displays variation, some processes display controlled variation, and others display uncontrolled variation. Controlled variation (often referred to as common-cause variation) is inherent in the process itself, and is characterized by a stable and consistent pattern of variation over time (Shewhart, 1931; Montgomery, 2000). An example of common-cause variation can be seen in a manufacturing process making a discrete part. Each part produced has measurable dimensions or characteristics.

Some of these parts are periodically selected and measured. The specific measurements vary from part to part because the materials, machines, operators, and methods all interact to produce variation. Such common variation is relatively consistent over time, because it is composed of a myriad of small randomly occurring variations that are always present in a process and affect all elements of the process.

Conversely, the causes of uncontrolled variation (that is, special-cause variation) lie outside of the system, and are characterized by a pattern of variation that changes over time (Shewhart, 1931; Montgomery, 2000). Examples of special-cause variation include: procedures not suited to requirements, poor product design, machines out of order, and machines not suited to requirements. SQC allows the consultant to determine if a process is in statistical control by using one or more tools (for example, control charts, histograms, graphs, and so on). Although, it has not been empirically verified, some authors estimate that common-cause variation causes about 85 percent of the problems in a process; the remaining 15 percent is caused by special-cause variation (Gitlow et al., 1989).

Deming (1975, p. 5) has written, "It is good management to reduce the variation in any quality characteristic, whether this characteristic be in a state of control or not, and even when few or no defectives are being produced." If variation is reduced, parts will be more reliable. Customer satisfaction will increase, because customers will get what they want and know what to expect. Process output and capability will be known with greater certainty, and the results of any changes to the process will be more predictable.

Therefore, management must constantly attempt to reduce process variation around desired characteristic specifications (target objectives), in order to achieve the degree of uniformity required to get products to function during their life cycle, as promised to the customer. For example, if a company had an average deviation of 5 percent from its target value, it might try to reduce this to a 3 percent average, then to 2 percent, and, ultimately, to reduce the variation to as close to zero as possible.

After all special causes of variation have been eliminated from a process, *process capability* is the extent to which the natural behavior of the process can meet established or customer specifications for the product (Brassard & Ritter, 1994; Montgomery, 2000; Gitlow et. al., 1989). A process is capable if virtually all of the expected output falls within the upper and lower specification limits (that is, the maximum and minimum tolerances allowed by design). If any expected outputs from a process fall outside of the specification limits, the process is not considered capable. A process' capability is defined as the ratio of the difference between the upper specification limit of a product (USL) and the lower specification limit (LSL) to the expected range of products produced by the process. When the upper and lower specification limits for a product characteristic are equal to plus or minus three standard deviations from the process' mean, or within an interval of six sigma or standard deviations ($6\sigma$), the process is said to be capable. $C_p$ is the simple index ratio that is used to summarize a process' ability to meet two-sided specification limits. The formula for computing $C_p$ is shown in Equation 1 (Brassard & Ritter, 1994).

$$C_p = (USL - LSL)/6\sigma \qquad (1)$$

A process capability index of 1.0 indicates that a process will generate approximately three units out of specification for every 1,000 (Gitlow et. al., 1989). A $C_p$ of 1.33 or higher is considered good.

The *capability* of a process depends upon both the *conformity* of the product and the *stability* of the process (Wheeler & Chambers, 1986). A stable process is one that displays a reasonable degree of statistical control—that is, we can predict, within limits, how the process will perform in the future. A process must be stable before it can be capable.

A variety of tools can be used to assess the stability and capability of a process. One measurement method that aids in measuring and stabilizing a process is the control chart. The control chart seeks to determine if a sequence of data can be used for predictions of what will occur in the future. It is a statistical tool that is constructed by drawing samples of data from a process (for example, manufacturing parts, processing documents, maintaining equipment). Figure 28.2 is an example of a control chart that shows the variation over time of a product characteristic (for example, a metal shaft with an intended diameter

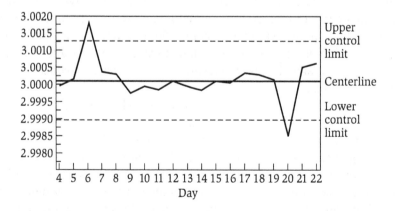

**Figure 28.2 Example of a Control Chart with Upper and Lower Control Limits Calculated from Production Data. Day 6 and Day 20 Are Both Shown as Out of Control, and Suggest That Special Causes Were Likely to Have Occurred on Those Days. Elimination of These Special Causes in the Future Is Likely to Improve Quality.**

of 3.00 cm). The data plotted are daily averages of samples taken randomly from all shafts produced each day. It has a centerline that represents the process grand mean (3.0025), and upper and lower control limits (3.0013 and 2.9989, respectively) that provide information on the process variation (mean $+3\sigma$ and $-3\sigma$, respectively). The control chart is useful in detecting special-cause variation, because it can detect a deviation in a product or service characteristic that is not caused by the typical process, but rather by some unusual event or condition. These changes are signaled by any abnormal points on the graph (for example, a point above the upper control limit or below the lower control limit) from which the data have been collected (Ishikawa, 1990). In making a control chart, the sample data are averaged, and each value then becomes a point on the control chart that represents the characteristics of that given sample. When a given sample or set of samples is outside the control limits, as seen on days 6 and 20, it signals that something has changed. The process for those data was significantly different than would have been expected, based on repeated samples of data. Once a signal has been detected, then causes can be investigated using a flow chart or cause-and-effect diagram. A process that has special causes influencing variation is not stable, and therefore is not generally considered capable. The special-cause variation must be identified and corrected for the process to be capable of meeting customer requirements.

There are a number of sophisticated methods that one can use (for example, $C_p$ index) to assess the capability of a stable process. However, the simplest and easiest method is to plot a histogram of values directly from the control chart. The horizontal axis of the histogram can show the purchaser's specification limits, and the relationship between the histogram and these limits will portray the capability of the stable process (Wheeler & Chambers, 1986). If all the values of the histogram are within the specification limits, the process is capable. Process capability is greater when the histogram occupies a smaller proportion of the specification range.

**Measuring the Transformation Processes.** The responsibility for quality in any transformation process must lie with the operators of that process (that is, the producers). To fulfill this responsibility, however, people must be provided with the tools necessary to know whether the process is capable, and whether the process is meeting the requirements at any point in time, and to make correct adjustments to the process or inputs when they are not meeting the requirements. Statistical quality control can also be used to help improve the transformation process.

The first step in measuring the transformation process is to establish an operational definition. Operational definitions establish a language for process improvement, and put communicable meaning into a process, product, service, job, or specification (Margenau, 1950; Gitlow et al., 1989). Specifications such as defective, safe, round, and so on, have no communicable meaning until they are operationally defined. An operational definition consists of a criterion to be applied to an object or group, a test of the object or group, and a decision as to whether or not the object or group met the criterion.

Next, the process and its inputs and outputs must be identified. Many processes are easily understood and related to known procedures (for example, drilling a hole, compressing tablets, servicing a customer, delivering a lecture, and so on). In many situations, however, it can be extremely difficult to define the process (for example, diagnosing a patient's illness). Process definition is important because the nature of the inputs and outputs change with the scope of the process.

Once the process is specified, the Shewhart cycle (Deming, 1986) can be used to aid management in the pursuit of continuous and neverending process improvement. The Shewhart cycle, a derivative of the scientific method aimed at improving processes, was later renamed the *Deming cycle* by the Japanese. The Shewhart (or Deming) cycle is also known as the PDCA cycle, because it is composed of four basic stages: a plan stage (P), a do stage (D), a check stage (C), and an act stage (A). A group develops a plan (P), which is then implemented on a small-scale or trial basis (D); they then monitor the effects of the trial plan (C), and then take appropriate actions (A). These actions can lead to a new or revised plan (process modifications), so the PDCA cycle continues forever in a cycle of neverending improvement.

The PDCA cycle operates by recognizing that problems (opportunities for improvement) in a process are determined by the difference between customer (internal or external) needs and process performance. If the difference is large, customer dissatisfaction might be high, and there is great opportunity for improvement. If the difference is small, the consequent opportunity for improvement is diminished. It is usually desirable to continually attempt to decrease the difference between customer needs and process performance, assuming, of course, that the cost of such attempts is not greater than the benefits.

Statistical tools that can be used to measure the transformational processes are the cause-and-effect diagram or Ishikawa fishbone diagram (see Figure 28.1 for a simplified example), histograms, Pareto diagrams, control charts, run charts, and scatter diagrams (Brassard & Ritter, 1994; also see Konoske & Tatum, 1992, for examples of using these tools in a nonmanufacturing environment). These tools can be used to measure the efficiency of a process, such as the amount of waste and scrap generated, labor hours used and lost, and the cost of capital and energy needed for the process (the amount or variation in each of these measures can indicate the efficiency of the process).

The tools used are chosen because of the type of study being performed (enumerative versus analytic), and what information is desired. An enumerative study is a statistical investigation on a static population; that is, a group of units that exist in a given time period and location (Montgomery, 2000; Gitlow et al.,

1989). This study uses random sampling procedures and describes the characteristics of the static population being studied. For example, the goal might be to estimate the average number of sick days per employee in the XYZ company in 2002. There is no reference to the past or to the future. Tools that might be used for such purposes are histograms and descriptive statistics, such as means and standard deviations.

An analytic study is a statistical investigation that leads to an action on a dynamic process; that is, a process that has a past, present, and future. Process improvement actions based on a process' past behavior are rational only if the process' past behavior was stable, hence predictable to the future (Gitlow et al., 1989). Samples in analytic studies are almost always judgment samples (expert opinions). Examples of tools that might be used in an analytic study are control charts, and a variation of a control chart called a run chart (Brassard & Ritter, 1994).

Prevention of failure in a transformation process is not possible if the process definition, inputs, and outputs are not properly documented and agreed upon. The documentation of procedures will allow reliable data about the process itself to be collected and analyzed, and action taken to improve the process and avoid failure or nonconformance with the requirements. The target in the operation of any process is the total avoidance of failure. If the idea of no failures or error-free work is not adopted, at least as a target, then it will never be achieved (Oakland, 1990).

# PLAN AND IMPROVE INPUTS AND TRANSFORMATION PROCESSES

As illustrated in Figure 28.1, three different sources of information influence the plan to improve the input and transformation processes. These are (1) determining causes of process and product characteristics, (2) determining customer needs and desires, and (3) the strategic plan. These are used to make decisions regarding the planning and improvement of inputs (for example, "Are our materials of high enough quality to meet customer requirements?" and "Should we change suppliers?") and transformation processes (for example, "How efficient are our methods?" and "Do we need to replace our equipment?").

# DESIGN AND EXECUTE PERFORMANCE MANAGEMENT SYSTEMS

Performance management systems direct the performance of employees by motivating desired job performance (behavior). Performance management systems are designed to motivate employees to perform all expected behavior (meeting minimal expected standards), but also to exhibit what is called *extra-role behavior*. This refers to a desire by employees to go above and beyond what is nominally expected of them (Steers & Porter, 1987).

Selection and training are also important in a performance management system. Management's performance hinges on their subordinate's performance (employees who do not have the appropriate abilities will not be able to perform effectively). Therefore, organizations must select employees carefully to ensure they possess adequate abilities and are willing to exhibit "extra-role behavior." If it is not feasible to select employees who already have these abilities, then an efficient and effective training program is especially important.

Ultimately, performance management systems are governed by the strategic plan. In our CIM model, the strategic plan influences how the input and transformation processes are improved. This in turn will influence the decision regarding which tools will be used to motivate the desired behavior. As stated previously, part of the strategic plan provides the criteria for investment decisions, and also serves as the basis for compensating and rewarding employees. For example, an organization would like its employees to accept only inputs that meet the organization's criteria of quality for the manufacturing of a product. The organization could encourage this behavior by rewards that are given for doing so (for example, measuring the use of quality inputs, and then rewarding employees based on how well they use quality inputs).

In addition, the causes of process and product characteristics will have an impact on the performance management system. For example, suppose an organization's product (output) is of poor quality. Along with other possibilities, the consultant can examine the causal factors determining employee skills. If broader skills could improve quality, then a performance management system might be instituted that incorporates a skill-based pay system. Under this system, employees are rewarded for the acquisition of new skills.

In summary, the organization needs to do three things before it can specify the content of its performance management system. It must decide on its approach to gaining competitive advantage, develop a plan to improve the input and transformation processes, and determine the behavioral causes of process and product characteristics. In other words, the design of a performance management system begins with a focus on the individual and organizational behaviors that are needed in order for the organization to be successful (Lawler, 1990).

## Reward Systems

If an organization is to be quality driven, then its reward system must reflect a management philosophy of reward (Lawler, 1990). Employees must be rewarded for quality as well as efficiency. This approach to management calls for some new approaches to compensation as well, simply because it calls for a different relationship between people and their work organization (Lawler, 2000).

Belcher (1991) observed that of all the management processes, reward systems are the slowest to change. This is not surprising, because changes in reward systems directly affect the financial well-being of employees, and therefore can be traumatic. This slowness to change is unfortunate because reward practices probably have a greater impact on employees' behaviors than almost anything else that management does (Belcher, 1991).

Reward systems affect organizational performance and individual behavior largely through the impact that they have on people's beliefs and expectations about how they are and will be rewarded. For a reward system to be effective, it must do at least three things. First, employees must value the rewards that the organization offers. Second, employees must expect that their performance and behavior will lead to the rewards they value. Third, employees must expect they can perform the behaviors required to achieve the desired rewards. Expectations are particularly important in influencing motivation, but they also have an important influence on organizational culture, the ability of an organization to attract and retain the right members, and on organizational structure. In order to be effective, a pay system must impact perceptions and beliefs in ways that produce desired organizational behaviors (Lawler, 1990, 2000).

## Employee Involvement

Many authors contend that today's organizations need new approaches to management (Lawler, 2000). Because workers are much more mobile and willing to change employment, they argue that these approaches must foster employee commitment and employee involvement rather than emphasize top-down control. In terms of organizational functioning, this means decidedly less hierarchy, the making of decisions at the lowest level possible, and a greater emphasis on employee development (Lawler, 1990, 2000).

Organizations of all kinds are pursuing a culture that is characterized by high involvement and teamwork at all levels. This work is showing that employee involvement in a variety of forms is effective at improving organizational productivity, financial performance, and employee satisfaction (see, for example, Lawler, 2000, 1991; Levine, 1995; Mohrman, Lawler, & Ledford, 1996). A study conducted by the U.S. General Accounting Office (GAO) in 1987 found that over 80 percent of the responding firms had some form of employee involvement activity underway. However, many of these efforts have not lived up to expectations or stood the test of time. An analysis of the GAO data by the Center for Effective Organizations at the University of Southern California in 1989 led to a conclusion that only 25 percent of the companies have made significant changes in the way most of their employees are managed (Lawler, Ledford, & Mohrman, 1989).

This finding is not surprising, because many companies tend to mechanically add or plug in employee involvement programs without considering the need to change other systems (for example, selection, promotion, information sharing, job design) that might be contradictory to the new programs. In this situation, powerful forces, in the form of the traditional systems, can undermine the involvement effort. Fortunately, companies are beginning to recognize that real cultural change (for example, a change from a culture in which employees at the working level make few decisions, to a culture in which employees at the working level are empowered to make decisions) can only occur when they rethink the basic management assumptions that underlie the systems and practices of the organization (Belcher, 1991).

There are a variety of ways to integrate employee involvement in the workplace. Process action teams (PATs) are teams of process specialists that address critical business needs (for example, reducing the number of billing errors to no more than one per thousand bills) by creating an efficient and effective process for that need.

Self-managed work teams (SMT) (Cohen, Ledford, & Speitzer, 1996) are small groups of employees that effectively manage their own work area. They carry out virtually all of the functions formerly reserved for management (for example, goal setting, scheduling, customer relations, problem solving, capital planning, discipline, hiring, and even firing).

Quality circles (Miller, 1989) are small groups of workers who perform quality control activities on a volunteer basis within their work area. They work as part of a company-wide effort for quality control, using quality control techniques for self- and mutual development purposes. The basic ideas behind quality circle activities are carried out as part of a company-wide quality control program. They are designed to contribute to the improvement and development of the enterprise, respect humanity and build a worthwhile-to-live-in, pleasant work area, and exercise human capabilities fully, and eventually draw out boundless possibilities for improvement (Ishikawa, 1985).

Suggestion systems are another successful way to encourage employee involvement (Savageau, 1996). These systems not only elicit ideas from employees, but also have a structure for review and implementation. Having suggestions reviewed and implemented by a team of employees and management allows employees to have input into which ideas will be implemented and how this will be accomplished.

# CONCLUSIONS

As shown in Figure 28.1, the CIM is composed of two major processes: the management process and the production process. When practicing continuous improvement, the focus of the process is on the customer, first determining the customers' needs and desires. These are then used as direct input for developing a strategic plan and improving input and transformation processes.

Once a plan has been developed for improving input and transformation processes, this information can be used to design and execute the performance management system. The performance management system will directly affect the measurement process in the management process, and the transformation process in the production process.

The measurement process (measures of transformation processes, product characteristics, product variation, customer satisfaction, and future needs of customers) directly affects the production process (transformation process, outputs, and customer use) and the management process (determining causes of process and product characteristics, and determining customer needs and desires).

The CIM can be viewed as mapping a loop of continual process improvement. As an organization continuously improves, substantial benefits can be earned. These include increases in productivity, improvements in quality, decreases in the cost of production, reductions in the prices paid by the customer, and increases in workers' morale (Gitlow & Gitlow, 1987). What organization wouldn't find these benefits attractive?

# References

American Psychological Association, Society of Consulting Psychology, Education and Training Committee (2000). *Principles for education and training at the doctoral and post-doctoral level in consulting psychology/Organizational.* Retrieved November 6, 2001, from http://www.apa.org/divisions/div13/

Anthony, W. P. (1985). *Practical strategic planning.* Westport, CI: Quorum Greenwood.

Belcher, J. G., Jr. (1991). *Gain sharing: The new path to profits and productivity.* Houston, TX: Gulf.

Brannick, M. T., & Prince, C. (1997). An overview of team performance measurement. In M. T. Brannick, C. Salas, & C. Prince (Eds.), *Team performance assessment and measurement: Theory, methods, and applications* (pp. 3–18). Hillsdale, NJ: Erlbaum.

Brannick, M. T., Salas, E., & Prince, C. (1997). *Team performance assessment and measurement: Theory, methods, and applications.* Hillsdale, NJ: Erlbaum.

Brassard, M., & Ritter, D. (1994). *The memory jogger II: A pocket guide for continuous improvement.* Methuen, MA: Goal.

Breyfogle, F. W. (1999). *Implementing six sigma: Smarter solutions using statistical methods.* New York: Wiley.

Brumbaugh, P. S., & Heikes, R. G. (1991). Statistical quality control. In G. Salvendy (Ed.), *Handbook of industrial engineering* (2nd ed., pp. 2252–2281). New York: Wiley.

Buzacott, J. A., & Shanthikumar, J. G. (1991). Models of production systems. In G. Salvendy (Ed.), *Handbook of industrial engineering* (2nd ed., pp. 1989–2024). New York: Wiley.

Cannon-Bowers, J. A., & Salas, E. (1997). A framework for developing team performance measures in training. In M. T. Brannick, C. Salas, & C. Prince (Eds.) *Team performance assessment and measurement: Theory, methods, and applications* (pp. 45–62). Hillsdale, NJ: Erlbaum.

Cohen, S. G., Ledford, G. E., & Speitzer, G. M. (1996). A predictive model of self-managing work team effectiveness. *Human Relations, 49,* 643–676.

Deming, W. E. (1975). On some statistical aids to economic production. *Interfaces, 5,* 1–15.

Deming, W. E. (1986). *Out of the crisis.* Cambridge, MA: MIT.

Dickinson, T. L., & McIntyre, R. M. (1997). A conceptual framework for teamwork measurement. In M. T. Brannick, C. Salas, & C. Prince (Eds.) *Team performance assessment and measurement: Theory, methods, and applications* (pp. 19–44). Hillsdale, NJ: Erlbaum.

Fuqua, D. R., & Newman, J. L. (2002). The role of systems theory in consulting psychology. In R. L. Lowman (Ed.), *Handbook of organizational consulting psychology* (pp. 76–105). San Francisco: Jossey-Bass.

Gitlow, H. S., & Gitlow, S. J. (1987). *The Deming guide to quality and competitive position.* Englewood Cliffs, NJ: Prentice Hall.

Gitlow, H. S., Gitlow, S. J., Oppenheim, A., & Oppenheim, R. (1989). *Tools and methods for the improvement of quality.* Burr Ridge, IL: Irwin.

Guzzo, R. A., & Salas, E., & Associates. (1995). Team effectiveness and decision making in organizations. San Francisco: Jossey-Bass.

Hallam, G., & Campbell, D. (1997). The measurement of team performance with a standardized survey. In M. T. Brannick, C. Salas, & C. Prince (Eds.) *Team performance assessment and measurement: Theory, methods, and applications* (pp. 217–241). Hillsdale, NJ: Erlbaum.

Harris, D. H. (Ed.). (1994). *Linkages: Understanding the productivity paradox.* Washington, DC: National Academy Press.

Ishikawa, K. (1985). *What is total quality control? The Japanese way* (D. J. Lu, Trans.). Englewood Cliffs, NJ: Prentice Hall.

Ishikawa, K. (1990). *Guide to quality control.* White Plains, NY: Quality Resources.

Jankowicz, A. (1973). Strategic management control. *International Journal of Systems Science, 1,* 24–39.

Katz, D., & Kahn, R. L. (1978). *The social psychology of organizations* (2nd ed.). New York: Wiley.

Konoske, P. J., & Tatum, B. C. (1992). *Structured problem solving and the basic graphic methods within a total quality leadership setting: Case study.* (NPRDC Report No. TR 92-8). San Diego, CA: Navy Personnel Research and Development Center.

Lawler, E. E., III. (1990). *Strategic pay: Aligning organizational strategies and pay systems.* San Francisco: Jossey-Bass.

Lawler, E. E., III. (1991). *High-involvement management: Participative strategies for improving organizational performance.* San Francisco: Jossey-Bass.

Lawler, E. E., III. (2000). *Rewarding excellence: Pay strategies for the new economy.* San Francisco: Jossey-Bass.

Lawler, E. E., III., Ledford, G. E., Jr., & Mohrman, S. A. (1989). *Employee involvement in America: A study of contemporary practice.* Houston, TX: American Productivity and Quality Center.

Lepsinger, R., & Lucia, A. D. (1997). *The art and science of 360° feedback.* San Diego, CA: Pfeiffer.

Levine, D. I. (1995). *Reinventing the workplace: How business and employees can both win.* Washington, DC: Brookings Institution.

Margenau, H. (1950). *The nature of physical reality.* New York: McGraw-Hill.

Miller, A., & Dess, G. (1997). *Strategic management* (2nd ed.). New York: McGraw-Hill.

Miller, T. R. (1989). The quality circle phenomenon: A review and appraisal. *SAM Advanced Management Journal, 54,* 4–8.

Mohrman, S. A., Lawler, E. E., III, & Ledford, G. E. (1996). Do employee involvement and TQM programs work? *Journal for Quality and Participation, 19*(1), 6–10.

Montgomery, D. C. (2000). *Introduction to statistical quality control* (4th ed.). New York: Wiley.

Mundel, M. E. (1982). Productivity measurement and improvement. In G. Salvendy (Ed.), *Handbook of industrial engineering* (pp. 1.5.1–1.5.28). New York: Wiley.

Oakland, J. S. (1990). *Total quality management.* Oxford, England: Butterworth-Heinemann.

Pritchard, R. D. (1994). Decomposing the productivity paradox linkages. In D. H. Harris (Ed.), *Understanding the productivity paradox* (pp. 161–192). Washington, DC: National Academy Press.

Savageau, J. (1996). World class suggestion systems still work. *Journal for Quality and Participation, 19*(2), 86–89.

Shewhart, W. A. (1931). *Economic control of quality of manufactured product.* New York: Van Nostrand Reinhold.

Sigler, J. (1999). Systems thinking: Organizational and social systems. *Futurics, 23*(1–2), 39–67.

Steers, R. M., & Porter, L. W. (1987). *Motivation and work behavior* (4th ed.). New York: McGraw-Hill.

Strank, R.H.D. (1983). *Management principles and practice: A cybernetic approach.* Newark, NJ: Gordon & Breach.

Tatum, B. C., & Nebeker, D. M. (2002). A strategic approach to measuring organizational performance. In R. L. Lowman (Ed.), *Handbook of organizational psychology* (pp. 692–730). San Francisco: Jossey-Bass.

Thompson, A. A., & Strickland, A. J. (1999). *Strategic management* (11th ed.). New York: McGraw-Hill.

Wheeler, D. J., & Chambers, D. S. (1986). *Understanding statistical process control.* Knoxville, TN: SPC Press.

Williams, J. C., DuBrin, A. J., & Sisk, H. L. (1985). *Management and organization* (5th ed.). Cincinnati, OH: South-Western.

# CHAPTER TWENTY-NINE

# A Strategic Approach to Measuring Organizational Performance

## Tools for the Consulting Psychologist

**B. Charles Tatum**
*Department of Psychology*
*National University*

**Delbert M. Nebeker**
*California School of Organizational Studies*
*Alliant International University*

The importance of measuring an organization's performance has come of age. New approaches and techniques promise to revolutionize the way organizations monitor their past and mold their future (see, for example, Becker, Huselid, & Ulrich, 2001; Fitz-Enz, 2000; Felix & Riggs, 1983; Kaplan & Norton, 1996; Nebeker, Tatum, & Wolosin, 1996). In another chapter of this volume (Nebeker & Tatum, 2002), we introduce a model of organizations as processes guided by a strategic plan designed to transform inputs into customer satisfaction. A central part of this model is the requirement to have measures of processes and outcomes focused on leveraging all an organization's assets to accomplishing its strategic objectives. This chapter concerns that process.

## MULTIPLE MEASURES AND APPROACHES

In their book *Translating Strategy into Action: The Balanced Scorecard,* Kaplan and Norton (1996) described a mythical encounter with the pilot of a modern jet aircraft. The pilot of the craft only had one instrument in the cockpit. The instrument measured air speed very accurately, but there were no other instruments to measure altitude, fuel consumption, or anything else that might be important for navigating the plane. When the pilot was asked why there was only one instrument, he said that he could only concentrate on one thing at a time, and air speed must get his attention at the moment. Later, when he had perfected his skills at controlling air speed, he would add other instruments and develop his skills in those areas.

Fortunately, this encounter was mythical. Nobody would try to fly a jet with only one instrument, and certainly nobody would voluntarily ride in a jet with such a cockpit. But, sadly, many managers of organizations that are at least as complex as a jet plane attempt to navigate their business using a very limited measurement instrument—the quarterly financial report. Even if the financial report is considered to be composed of many instruments, such reports only focus on the financial performance of the organization. Furthermore, such reports are retrospective, showing what has already happened. They lag organizational decisions by several months or even years. What is equally important is to identify the leading indicators of organizational health and vitality. Value chains identify organizational processes that are not directly economic, but tell whether they are creating value for the organization. Kaplan and Norton (1996), and others (Eccles, 1991; Kraft, Jauch, & Boatwright, 1996; Martin, 1997; Quinn, 1978), point out that financial accounting models need to be expanded to incorporate many intangible and intellectual assets of a company (for example, high quality products, motivated and skilled employees, and satisfied customers). These intangible assets must be considered because they are often more critical to success than the physical and tangible elements considered in traditional financial accounting.

Consulting psychologists are often called upon to assist organizations in assessing their performance at the individual, group, and organizational level (American Psychology Association, 2000). Corporate leaders, business owners, and operational managers want to assess their past performance, evaluate their potential for future success, and appraise their competitive position. In short, they want instruments to help them navigate their organizations through the complexities of this modern, fast-paced information age. The role of consulting psychologists is to help these leaders and managers define effectiveness for their organization, and to select the right set of measures for assessing their progress towards improved performance. Consulting psychologists need the many measurement tools available so they can help organizations build an instrument panel that provides information on all aspects of the organization (financial and nonfinancial, tangible and intangible, physical and intellectual). Designing a broad array of measures will ensure that the organization, unlike the mythical pilot described by Kaplan and Norton (1996), will not be restricted in their ability to reach their destination.

## Consulting Psychologists' Roles

An important role of consulting psychologists, then, is to help organizations measure their performance and achieve their strategic goals. Often performance is interpreted to mean organizational effectiveness. There is no single definition of organizational effectiveness, however. Because organizations differ in strategy and purpose, their definitions of effectiveness will also differ. In this chapter, organizational effectiveness is used to refer to an organization's overall performance.

Cameron (1980) described four major approaches to evaluating organizational performance. First, effective organizations can be defined as those in which internal functioning is smooth and free of major problems. Such characteristics as trust and benevolence toward individual workers, smooth information flow, and freedom from conflict between work units would typify such an organization. Second, effective organizations can be seen as those that are able to keep their *strategic constituencies* satisfied. Strategic constituencies are groups of people who have a stake in the organization, such as customers, workers, and stockholders. Third, an organization can be described as effective if it is successful in accomplishing its goals, usually with respect to outputs or production (although, as we will demonstrate, the other three approaches might be sources for goals as well). Fourth, an organization can be considered effective if it is successful in acquiring the resources it needs from the environment. In particular, this approach emphasizes successful competition for scarce resources. In turn, these resources are then transformed in a way that is profitable to the organization.

From this vantage point, the approach we suggest for improving organizational effectiveness can be used to improve the organization from a variety of perspectives. What we emphasize is an integrated, holistic approach based on the strategic objectives of the firm. If an organization is to perform well, be competitive, and survive, it needs to identify and then collect a well-chosen set of measures linked to a strategic plan. If the plan is well conceived, it will naturally suggest a set of primary objectives. These objectives can be converted to measures. Additional objectives can be linked to the strategic plan based on their linkage to the primary objectives. For example, if improving service quality and customer satisfaction are part of the strategic plan for the organization, then they are naturally prime candidates for measuring the performance of the organization. Likewise, those things that can be shown to lead to or predict service quality and customer satisfaction become additional measures and leading indicators of service quality and customer satisfaction. Collecting measures of both types not only helps the organization assess where they are, but also helps to predict where they are headed. In our view, organizational effectiveness can only be captured by measuring the organization's attainment of its explicit and implicit objects—its total performance (Steers, 1975).

This chapter will introduce a typology of organizational effectiveness that portrays the breadth and depth of organizational performance. We then suggest some sample measures for capturing these aspects of performance and integrating them into a unified whole. Finally, we present a technique (called performance indexing) for organizing this information in a way that allows for easy decision-making and policy changes.

# BASIC MEASUREMENT ISSUES

Before we present the proposed typology and indexing technique, it is worthwhile to review some basic measurement concepts and recommendations for good measurement practices.

## Purpose of Measures

In order to measure organizational performance, we need to understand that there are two aspects of performance that need to be included in any system that attempts to assess organizational performance. Until now we have used one of these terms, *effectiveness*, without a more precise meaning. Another term we want to introduce is *efficiency*. When an organization's performance is assessed, two questions must be answered: is the organization doing the right things, and is it doing things right (Sink, Tuttle, & DeVries, 1984). If the organization is doing the right things, it is achieving its primary outcome goals. Its goals are its chief markers for success. The degree to which the organization successfully accomplishes these goals makes it *effective*. If the organization is doing things right, it is doing whatever it is doing *efficiently*. It is using its resources economically to accomplish its primary goals. The answers to neither of these questions can be considered sufficient to measure organizational performance. We maintain that both are necessary. Clearly it is possible to do things efficiently but to be doing the wrong things. It is also possible to be accomplishing the right things but to be doing so inefficiently. We will describe both effectiveness and efficiency measures in the approach we take here.

## Criteria for Good Measures

For any organizational performance measure to have value, it must have certain measurement properties that make it useful. Three such properties are (1) standardization, (2) reliability, and (3) validity. These properties are extensively discussed in the psychological literature, so we will not expound on them here. There are several good sources that discuss the merits of these properties (see, for example, Allen & Yen, 1979; Nunnally & Bernstein, 1994). We will note that standardization (the uniformity of the measurement conditions) ensures that the procedures used to measure performance are consistently applied. Standardization is necessary for reliability. Reliability is the characteristic of the resulting measure that shows how dependable and consistent the measure is when the underlying construct is stable; in other words, when the measure has a minimum of measurement error. Without reliability, there can be no validity. Validity refers to how well a measure captures what it is intended to capture (Allen & Yen, 1979). Validity is the most important property of a measure, and is built from standardization and reliability. However, though standardization and reliability are necessary for validity, they are not sufficient to establish it. Generally, the validity of a measure is established by: (1) construct validity (showing strong correlations with other known measures of the same characteristic); (2) criterion validity (able to predict future performance from the measure); or (3) content validity (showing a logical or conceptual connection between the content of the measure and the desired characteristic).

## Sources of Measurement

Performance measures and information about how an organization performs can be obtained from several sources. These are discussed in this section.

**Objective Sources.** Most organizations have systems that generate quantifiable performance data. For example, if an organization makes machine parts, or repairs engines, or tracks grant funding requests, the organization probably has systems in place that monitor the outputs (for example, automated tracking, manual record keeping). The measurements that are routinely taken from these systems can be used as measures of organizational performance.

**Subjective Sources.** Some types of information cannot be measured objectively. For example, a customer's level of satisfaction with a product, or the quality of work performed by a research team, inherently entail subjective judgments. Many important elements of an effective organization can only be assessed by pooling expert judgment or public opinion. These subjective measures are not necessarily less desirable measures than the objective measures discussed above. If measures are valid, reliable, and standardized, it really does not matter whether they derive from objective or subjective sources. An employee survey, for example, if properly conducted, can tell an organization a great deal about its climate or culture, despite the fact that the source of the data is subjective opinions.

**Archival Data.** Both of the above sources of data can be found in most organizations. When they are collected and maintained in archival records of the organization, they can be readily available. Records of revenue, expenses, production, customer satisfaction, sick leave use, absenteeism, turnover, or accident rates are often maintained by organizations. These archival data can be used to build indices of organizational performance. For example, if an organization identifies low absenteeism as an important factor in reaching its strategic objective, then archival records can allow the organization to monitor it on a regular basis. It is important to recognize that just because a measure is readily available does not make it appropriate to use. Measures might not have the desired properties mentioned above, or they might not match the strategic objectives of the organization to make them useable. In such cases, alternative measures will need to be developed.

## Types of Performance Measures

Performance measures are usually divided into five classes (Behn, 1995; Straight, 2000): input, process, output, outcome, and impact. Performance measures are indicators of an organization's effectiveness, and document the relationships between resources (inputs), internal operations (processes), and results (outputs, outcomes, and impacts).

**Input Measures.** These are measures of the resources that go into an organization or program that are used to produce goods or deliver services. Examples are the number of hours worked by nurses in a hospital, the amount of electricity consumed in a factory, or the number of reams of paper used at a print shop.

**Process Measures.** These are measures of how well the production process for goods or services works. Process measures are indicators of the degree of control that organizations have over their internal operations. Process measures are often efficiency measures, and are usually composed of the ratio of output to input measures. For example, tons of steel produced per labor hour, or its reciprocal (labor hours required to produce a ton of steel), are measures of the efficiency of a steel production system. Process (efficiency) measures can be used to diagnose problems and streamline work procedures. For example, there are usually several steps (processes) involved in processing a delivery order in a government contract office (for example, write statement of work, develop cost estimate, obtain technical review, make request for quote, negotiate with contractor). Each of these processes, in turn, can be broken down into subprocesses, and each subprocess can be broken down into sub-subprocesses. Any or all of these processes and subprocesses can be measured, and these measures can be used to improve efficiency. For instance, if the contracting office measures the time required to complete each step, these times can be used to diagnose the bottlenecks in the system (for example, writing a statement of work takes longer than the other process). If changes are made to streamline parts of the process, the process measures can help verify whether these changes had a positive effect (that is, training on how to write a statement of work reduced the time by 50 percent).

The variability in process measures can also be indicative of improvements, by showing, for example, reduced variation in defects or task time. For instance, providing training to a government contract monitor to write a statement of work might reduce the variation in writing times from contract to contract, which is a reflection of a more stable, consistent process. Process measures help us improve our products and services by making the production or delivery process more efficient. It is important to realize, however, that process measures do not reflect the attributes of the products and services directly. Nevertheless, process measures are critical if an organization wants to continually improve its performance.

**Output Measures.** These are measures that reflect important characteristics of the end-product or service (for example, defects per thousand, reliability of electronic components, on-time delivery).

**Outcome Measures.** These measures reflect progress toward strategic goals or mission objectives. For example, if the organization has a strategic plan that specifies certain strategic goals (for example, increased sales, improved health status of employees, enhanced operational readiness), outcome measures can be used to determine whether these goals are being met. As another example, if the organization's mission was to conduct consumer research, outcome measures would indicate how well it was performing its mission. Often, in both the private and public sector, the strategic goals are couched in terms of customer satisfaction with the end-product or service. In this case, the outcome is some measure that shows that the customer was happy (or unhappy) with the product or service received (for example, repeat business, letters of praise, reduced complaints, high ratings on satisfaction surveys).

**Impact Measures.** These measures typically relate more to government-sponsored programs than individual organizations. These are measures of the changes in a target population, or benefits to society, as a result of a program (for example, reduced pregnancy rates among teenaged girls, improved health benefits for retired persons, better reading skills for primary school children).

## A TYPOLOGY OF MEASURES WITH EXAMPLES

Most organizations collect and process an enormous amount of data every day. Identifying things to measure is usually not the problem. The problem, more typically, is to convert the data into useful information that can be used to make decisions, plan, and act. The typology shown in Figure 29.1 is a way of classifying performance measures into categories that make sense to those who own and operate organizations. These categories represent all the important areas that require attention from an organization if it is to improve and achieve future growth and success. Figure 29.1 reveals that there are four major areas of

**Organizational Performance**

| Resource Development | Stakeholder Relations | Productivity | Financial Performance |
|---|---|---|---|
| The extent to which the organization develops its human and physical resources. This includes its ability to:<br><br>• Attract, select, train, motivate, and retain quality people<br>• Acquire the physical and technological resources needed to produce quality products and services | The extent to which the organization establishes and maintains excellent relationships with its stakeholders. These stakeholders include:<br><br>• Employees<br>• Customers<br>• The public at large<br>• Government regulators<br>• Suppliers<br>• Stockholders and investors | The extent to which the organization improves the quality of its processes (efficiency) and products. This includes:<br><br>• Increasing output per input<br>• Improving processes<br>• Increasing product conformance to standards<br>• Improving product attributes<br>• Improving timeliness | The extent to which the organization produces financial value for its owners and investors. This includes such things as:<br><br>• Profitability<br>• Return on investment<br>• Improvement in the ratio of market value to book value<br>• Meeting financial targets and budgets |

**Figure 29.1. Typology of Concepts and Terminology Related to Organizational Effectiveness.**

*Note:* Figure 29.1 is a typology rather than a taxonomy. Taxonomies are empirically derived, hierarchical systems, whereas typologies are classifications based on theoretical and intuitive categories (see Rich, 1993, for more details on the distinction between taxonomies and typologies).

organizational effectiveness (resource development, stakeholder relations, productivity, and ultimately, financial performance), which are then organized into subareas. This classification is based on practical considerations, and is intended as a heuristic for organizing effectiveness measures. Other researchers have suggested classifications that are somewhat different, but compatible with the typology proposed here (see, for example, Kaplan & Norton, 1996; Pritchard, 1994; Quinn, 1978; Steers, 1975; Thor, 1994). If an organization selects measures based on a strategic plan, using this classification, they can be confident that they have a comprehensive measurement system that reflects total organizational performance.

## Resource Development

The first area in Figure 29.1 is resource development. Measures of resource development are important to an organization's effectiveness because, before an organization can be efficient, it must develop the quality of its resources. In addition to increasing efficiency, developing quality resources creates more opportunities to improve the quality of products and services. Resource development can be subdivided into two general areas: employee development and technology development. Each of these areas can be broken down into smaller areas, as shown in Figure 29.1 and Table 29.1.

**Employee Development.** It is common to hear that employees are an organization's most valuable resource. Certainly, any organization that wants to deliver quality goods and services needs a highly skilled and dedicated work force. How can an organization tell if it is adequately developing its human talent? It must measure and improve in five major areas: recruitment, selection, training, motivation, and retention.

Employee development requires that an organization hire sufficient high-quality personnel to fill all its necessary positions. The success of recruitment is measured in terms of the selection ratio (the number of people hired over the numbered of qualified applicants). Generally, a high selection ratio will increase the quality of the employees hired.

Selection, as compared to recruitment, refers to hiring the right person for the job. Better selection will improve an organization's performance for three reasons: (1) employees who have appropriate abilities for a job will perform more effectively at it; (2) good selection procedures will lower costs (for example, if people are retained longer, the cost of recruitment and new-employee training goes down); and (3) good selection avoids many legal problems resulting from unfair hiring procedures (Dessler, 1988).

Improving the selection process is complicated and requires information on the cost of the selection methods, validity and reliability of the methods, costs of recruiting and training, estimates of the dollar value of high-performing

Table 29.1. Definitions and Examples of Organizational Effectiveness Measures—Resource Development.

**Resource Development:** Measures of how well the organization is improving the future quality of its employees and technology

*Employee development:* How well the organization is developing its human capital by improving its recruitment, selection, training, motivation, and retention activities

| Category | Examples |
|---|---|
| *Recruitment:* The degree to which the organization improves its recruitment efforts | *Recruitment:* Number of qualified applicants per open position, average recruitment costs per position |
| *Selection:* The degree to which the organization improves its selection ratio, and improves validity and cost-effectiveness of selection | *Selection:* Selection ratio (the number of people hired divided by the number of qualified applicants), average costs of selection methods, average validity of selection procedures, percentage hired with valid selection tests, average validity of training courses, utility of selection processes |
| *Training:* The degree to which training programs are cost effective (ratio of training effectiveness to training cost) | *Training:* Number of hours of training per employee, number of hours of training in first year of employment |
| *Motivation:* The degree to which employees put forth their best efforts to reach organizational goals | *Motivation:* Percentage of employees eligible for incentive pay, percentage of employees who receive performance feedback from multiple sources, percentage of employees whose merit increase or incentive pay is tied to performance |
| *Retention:* The degree to which employees performing at satisfactory levels choose to remain with an organization | *Retention:* Voluntary turnover rates, intention to leave, exit interview attitudes |

*(Continued)*

Table 29.1. Definitions and Examples of Organizational Effectiveness Measures
—Resource Development (*Continued*).

**Resource Development:** Measures of how well the organization is improving the future quality of its employees and technology

*Technology development*: How well an organization develops its technology base, enhances its work methods, and improves its physical resources

| Category | Examples |
|---|---|
| *Work methods:* The extent to which the work methods and processes are upgraded and refined | *Work methods:* Time since last upgrade, frequency of process analyses, comparisons with processes used by other organizations (benchmarking), percentage of work tasks employing new technology |
| *Physical resources and capital investments:* The extent to which the facilities, tools, and equipment function properly, are regularly maintained, and are upgraded | *Physical resources and capital investments:* Age of physical resources, percentage of equipment off-line for repair, percentage of preventative maintenance jobs missed, average age of equipment, capital investments per employee |

employees' contributions to the organization, and the selection ratio mentioned above. With this information, utility analysis (see, for example, Cascio & Ramos, 1986; Schmidt, Hunter, McKenzie, & Muldrow, 1979) can be conducted to estimate the value of alternative selection methods. A utility analysis of an organization's selection procedures will show, in dollars, the effectiveness of the current procedures. A utility analysis can also be used as a metric to measure the degree of improvement resulting from changes in the selection procedures. For example, if the organization adopts a new, more expensive selection test with a higher validity, a utility analysis can show whether the new test is cost effective.

To improve its effectiveness, an organization needs to know if its training program is effective. In order to have coordinated, methodical, cohesive, and accountable training programs that share symmetry with the organization's objectives, there are two critical steps required: (1) conduct a needs assessment, and (2) demonstrate training effectiveness. In general, firms that give more training to new employees are more effective (Becker et al., 2001). Therefore, measuring the number of hours of training per employee per year can be a predictor of organizational effectiveness. It is also important to know whether the training is meeting critical needs. Measures can be developed to assess the effectiveness of training programs by measuring the learning and behavioral outcomes of the training courses. If an organization is using its resources wisely, then it should be able to show improved cost-effectiveness of training over time.

Worker motivation mostly derives from a combination of effective leadership and rewarding employee accomplishments in ways that are valued by the employees. Successful firms have higher percentages of employees who are given regular performance appraisals, have merit or incentive pay tied to performance, are evaluated by multiple sources, and are eligible for and earn substantial incentive pay (Becker et al., 2001). If the organization does not have direct measures for worker motivation, these measures can be good indicators of the motivation of the work force.

Finally, retention is a critical employee development concern. Unnecessary turnover can be costly. The cost of not retaining good employees is large, not only in terms of dollars (Bertrand, 1989; Sager, 1990), but also in terms of work attitudes and job involvement (Brockner, Grover, & Blonder, 1988; Krackhardt & Porter, 1985). Measuring turnover rate and the symptoms of employee withdrawal (for example, intention to quit, job satisfaction, attitudes toward life) can lead to retaining those employees who make a significant contribution to success and survival.

**Technology Development.** Technology development refers to using resources for developing technology in the workplace. It consists of the physical and informational resources by which people bring about some desired result (for example, manufacturing a product or delivering a service). Technology development concerns enhancing work methods and improving the use of physical resources.

If an organization wants to improve effectiveness, it should have a thorough understanding of the methods and processes that are used to create its products or deliver its services. The first step is to identify the types of work methods that must be performed. Second, the organization needs to select the specific work methods best suited to its operation. Finally, the organization should assess the effectiveness of its work methods. Ineffective work methods can be either improved or replaced. Table 29.1 suggests some measures for making decisions about upgrading and refining work methods.

The physical resources of an organization are its facilities, tools, and equipment. As with the work methods, an organization needs to know if its physical resources are sufficient and operational. Organizations need a plan for continuously improving these resources or investing in new ones. Table 29.1 gives sample measures for monitoring physical resources.

## Stakeholder Relations

The second major area shown in Figure 29.1 concerns stakeholder relations. A *stakeholder* refers to anyone who has a vital interest in the organization.

Stakeholder relations refers to the effectiveness of an organization in satisfying its stakeholders. This area is important because it is a reflection of the organization's long-term survival. The payoff for improving stakeholder relations is not immediate; rather, improving stakeholder relations helps to secure a future for the organization. As shown in Figure 29.1 and Table 29.2, which both list the major stakeholders, stakeholder relations can be subdivided into six general areas: employee quality of work life, customer relations, public relations, government relations, supplier relations, and stockholders and investors.

**Employee Quality of Work Life.** Quality of work life (QWL) addresses how the relationship between individuals and features of their physical, social, and economic work environment affects on- and off-the-job attitudes and behaviors (Wood, Rasmussen, & Lawler, 1975). Employee QWL can be measured in many different ways for many different attributes, as shown in Table 29.2. Macy and Mirvis (1978) demonstrated that certain behaviors associated with QWL (for example, absenteeism, accidents, and grievances) are costly to the organization in terms of lost productivity, costs of replacement, hiring, and training. They showed that substantial cost savings could occur if these behaviors were more effectively managed. Natural measures of employee QWL include employee behavior and satisfaction.

**Customer Relations.** Customer relations refers to the relationships an organization has to its external customers (internal customers are addressed either under employee QWL or process improvement efforts discussed below). External customers are people who buy or use the organization's products or services. Effective organizations listen to what their customers want, are customer oriented, and satisfy the requirements of the customer without ignoring price, profit, quality, and cost control (Ishikawa, 1985). Customer satisfaction surveys help an organization evaluate how it is meeting the needs and preferences of its customers.

**Public Relations.** Organizations must be concerned with their image and reputation in the eyes of all their stakeholders (for example, citizens, taxpayers, public interest groups, and political activists). Private organizations are especially concerned with how they are perceived by their shareholders and owners. Public organizations are more concerned with the perceptions of legislators, sponsors, citizens, and taxpayers (who are, in a sense, like voting shareholders in a corporation). Without a good image and a sound reputation, the organization's long-term survival is put in jeopardy. A positive image aids survival by attracting and maintaining funding, keeping current customers content, and building a base of support from the taxpayers. Surveys of these publics can assess the reputation and goodwill that the organization possesses.

**Table 29.2 Definitions and Examples of Organizational Effectiveness Measures—Stakeholder Relations.**

**Stakeholder Relations:** Measures of the extent to which the organization establishes and maintains excellent relationships with it stakeholders

| Category | Examples |
|---|---|
| *Employee quality of work life:* The extent to which employees are satisfied with their physical, social, and economic work environment | *Employees quality of work life:* Employee cultural and climate surveys, records of sick leave, absenteeism rates, job satisfaction surveys |
| *Customer relations:* The extent to which the organization satisfies the needs and preferences of external customers | *Customer relations:* Customer satisfaction surveys (addressing general perceptions of the organization, rather than specific perceptions of products or services), focus groups, unsolicited letters |
| *Public relations:* The degree to which the outside public (shareholders, legislators, citizens, sponsors, taxpayers) has a positive image of the organization | *Public relations:* Public opinion surveys, citizen complaints, media publicity, letters to the editor, unsolicited letters |
| *Government relations:* The degree to which the organization complies with government regulations and policies | *Government relations:* Inspection team reports, grievance files, complaints registered, fines levied, penalties assessed, documented compliance, court decisions |
| *Supplier relations:* The degree that suppliers understand, support, and cooperate with the organization in working to meet organizational goals | *Supplier relations:* Average number of years that suppliers have worked with the company, percentage of suppliers who supply quality data on their own production process, average supplier conformance to quality standards |
| *Stockholder and investor relations:* The degree of support and good will with stockholders and investors who are not in operational control of the organization | *Stockholder and investor relations:* Stockholder approval ratings of management, investor and banker willingness to provide funding to the organization |

**Government Relations.** All organizations must comply with government regulations. There are specific agencies that ensure organizations are complying with regulations governing their type of business. For instance, the Departments of Commerce and Justice (fair trade), Securities Exchange Commission (stock transactions), Internal Revenue Service (taxes), Environmental Protection Agency (pollution), and Equal Employment Opportunity Commission (employee discrimination) are only a few of the regulatory bodies with which relations are critical to an organization's success. If organizations fail to comply with these regulations, the government has the legal authority to administer penalties, fines, and even closure. Measures on this dimension can be related to the extent of investigative and legal activity taken by these agencies.

**Supplier Relations.** Suppliers have a stake in the organization's survival and long-term growth. Many U.S. companies, and most government agencies, have a policy of purchasing supplies and awarding service contracts to the lowest bidder. As Deming (1986) has pointed out, focusing on purchase price without regard to quality is a bad practice, because it lowers the quality of the finished product and can drive good suppliers out of business. Deming also notes the drawbacks of maintaining several suppliers and renegotiating contracts frequently. A more sensible and cost-effective approach is to establish a long-term supplier relationship with a single source. This recommendation strikes many as a risky proposition (what happens when your single supplier misses a critical deadline or goes out of business?). Deming acknowledges that the strategy is not without risk, but contends that the advantages far outweigh the disadvantages. The key to good customer-supplier relationships, according to Deming, is an arms-around rather than an arm's-length philosophy. The supplier should be viewed as a partner rather than an adversary.

**Shareholder and Investor Relations.** Maintaining good relationships with the nonmanaging owners and investors in an organization is critical to the organization's long-term success. Shareholders vote to support or replace key officers. They make decisions to buy or sell their stock. Most large companies have a department to provide information to current and potential shareholders in order to maintain good relations with the shareholders. Similar activities are undertaken with other important investors, whether they are venture capitalists or bankers loaning money.

## Productivity

The next major area shown in Figure 29.1 is productivity. Of the measures we have considered so far, productivity is the first of the more tangible areas. Productivity improvement is critical to organizational success, and without improvement in productivity at the national level, there is no real hope for improving our standard of living. Productivity measurement in the United States, especially in the private sector, is therefore well developed. Productivity is generally defined as the ratio of production outputs (goods and services) to organizational inputs (for example, labor, capital, energy, and material). However, the terms used in discussing productivity can be confusing, and are not always used consistently. Terms such as efficiency, performance, effectiveness, and quality are sometimes used interchangeably with productivity (for example, Gormley & Weimer, 1999; Straight, 2000; Tatum, Shaw, & Main, 1996; Thor, 1994). For our purposes, productivity within an organization is expressed as a ratio of quality outputs to inputs, and measures of productivity fall into two general areas: process quality (that is, efficiency) and output quality.

**Process Quality (Efficiency).** As noted above, efficiency is doing things right; that is, using resources in an economically and rationally sound fashion. Process quality refers to the efficiency of a process. In the traditional organization, process quality is often less than optimal. This inefficiency is often the result of the *stovepipe* structure, in which each department or business unit functions on its own with its own management hierarchy (Rumor & Brace, 1991). A more useful approach is a horizontal, or *systems,* view, which cuts across functional boundaries and is organized around processes that include inputs to the system, the transformation of these inputs into an output (product or service), and the delivery of the output to a customer (see Nebeker & Tatum, 2002). To achieve the greatest efficiency in transforming the inputs into the outputs, the organization must be able to measure quantities of inputs and outputs, and must be able to measure improvement efforts in the process of transforming the inputs into outputs. Efficiency is usually expressed as an output to input ratio. Table 29.3 provides definitions and examples of measures of output quantity, input quantity, and process improvements (also see Nebeker, Neuberger, & Hulton, 1983; Thor, 1994).

It is important to note that the measures of input and output quantity are expressed in nonfinancial terms (at the organizational level, the financial equivalents are shown in the section on financial performance). These measures, in principle, could be expressed in dollar values, but only if the organization can be sure that these are constant dollars. If the dollar values do not remain stable (for example, the cost of materials fluctuates substantially), then it is not a good idea to express these inputs as dollar values, and we recommend the use of nonfinancial quantities.

It is also important to note that effectively measuring output units has typically been a challenge for white-collar organizations. It is often difficult to identify and quantify what the specific output units are. The best advice that can be given to any organization is to let the customer define your outputs. After a company's customer has indicated the specific products or services required, then it is time

Table 29.3. Definitions and Examples of Organizational Effectiveness Measures—Productivity.

**Productivity: Measure the extent to which the organization is improving the quality of its processes (efficiency) and the quality of its products**

| Category | Examples |
| --- | --- |
| *Process quality (efficiency):* Measures showing the improvement in the productivity of production processes by reducing input consumption and increasing output generation | |
| *Number of units of output per units of input* | *Output per input:* Labor productivity (units produced per labor hour compared to the baseline), total factor productivity (total unit cost compared to the baseline, adjusted for PPI), material productivity (material costs per unit compared to the baseline) |
| *Process improvements:* Data generated by tools and techniques for improving the internal operations (processes) of the organization | *Process improvements:* Time per unit of output spent in rework, scrap and waste rates compared to the baseline |
| *Output quality:* Measures showing the degree to which each unit of output possesses desirable characteristics | |
| *Conformance to standards:* Inspection of output (end product) to detect flaws, spot defects, or observe variations from standards | *Conformance to standards:* Number of production processes in control, amount of time spent on inspection, percentage of units passing inspection, flaws or defects per thousand, number of reliability tests passed, uniformity of product (revealed by control chart data) |
| *Product and service attributes:* Properties of the output that the end-user (customer) determines to be of value | *Product and service attributes:* Average product customer satisfaction ratings, number of customer complaints, number and content of unsolicited customer letters, product return rate, reorder rate or second purchase rate, warranty return rate, percentage of market share |
| *Timeliness:* Extent to which products or services arrive on time, are used during critical periods, or meet customer deadlines | *Timeliness:* Percentage of time product or service delivered on time (just-in-time), number of items spoiled due to expired shelf life, number of units delivered by deadline or ahead of schedule, average cycle time |

to investigate ways to measure the quantity of this output. Guidelines provided by the Bureau of Labor Statistics (BLS) can be helpful in quantifying outputs. The BLS publishes an annual report from its Federal Productivity Measurement System (FPMS) that summarizes labor productivity trends for twenty-eight broad governmental functions (U.S. Department of Labor, 1993b, 1993c, 1993d). Several sources provide guidelines for developing output measures (U.S. Department of Labor, 1993a; Forte, 1993; Thor, 1994). Some of these guidelines are:

- Output measures should reflect the final products and services of an organization. Final products and services are outputs that are consumed by customers or agencies outside the boundaries of the organization. For example, a library purchases books and periodicals, catalogs these materials, and then lends them to individuals and other institutions. The outputs are the books and periodicals lent. The purchasing and cataloging activities are intermediate tasks, and would not be classified as outputs.

- If sets of output measures are not homogeneous (that is, they are not of equivalent complexity or they do not have the same labor requirements), then a weighting factor can be applied to the measures. For example, if a printing shop measures pages of documentation, it can distinguish between long-run pages and short-run pages by assigning different values to the measures.

- Output measures should reflect regularly reoccurring processes (for example, periodic audits, frequent requests, regularly scheduled maintenance), rather than processes that occur infrequently or on a one-time basis. Repetitive processes can be checked for consistency and stability, whereas nonrepetitive processes are subject to unexpected variation and instability.

- Measures should reflect outputs that are related to the workloads of the organization, and not work performed by third parties or outsourcing agencies. If an organization contracts out its janitorial services, for example, it can measure the processing of the contract (work that the organization performs), but should not measure the custodial work performed by the contractor. The cost of the contracted work would not be considered as part of the organization's labor productivity.

- For organizations that work on a fiscal year basis, performance measures should be scaled by fiscal year. For example, if it takes five years to build a ship, it would be improper to count one ship built in the fifth year and zero in each of the first four years. Instead, it would be better to measure the portion completed in each year, or to break the shipbuilding process into major steps and measure the completion of steps in each year.

- Process improvement measures should not be overlooked as a vital part of measuring productivity. The imperative of every organization should be to continuously improve the quality and efficiency of each process within that organization (see Nebeker & Tatum, 2002, for a detailed model of organizational improvement). Process improvement begins with knowing the customer's requirements, then working backward from that point and making improvements to each process and sub-process that contributes to meeting these customer requirements. There are many tools and techniques available for process improvement. Some of the more useful tools are presented in Table 29.3.

**Output Quality.** In addition to measuring efficiency (the quality of the process), the organization also needs to measure the quality of the end products and services. These measures form an important dimension of productivity. Quality is the degree to which each unit of output possesses desirable characteristics (Nebeker, Neuberger, & Hulton, 1983). The more desirable characteristics a product has, the higher the quality. A higher-quality product that costs the same as a lower-quality product (or consumes the same inputs as a lower-quality product) is worth more to the consumer and has improved productivity. Quality ultimately is based on the customers' reaction to the product or service. If the customer is satisfied, then the product or service has desirable characteristics. Table 29.3 provides definitions and examples of three important areas of output quality: end-product inspection, product and service attributes, and timeliness.

Although end-product inspection, the first category, cannot create quality products and services, it can uncover and correct defects, and prevent them from reaching the customer. The problem with end-product inspection as a quality control method is that, when defects are found, the only corrective actions available are reworking the product or consigning it to scrap. In either case, productivity suffers and costs rise. The yield is lower due to the extra labor involved in the rework and the cost of the material that has to be scrapped. In addition, products that have been adjusted or reworked are more likely to break down, which is exactly the opposite of quality assurance (Ishikawa, 1985).

Self-inspection by each worker in the process is preferred to end-product inspection. Self-inspection moves the quality assurance further upstream, and allows corrective and preventative actions to take place at an earlier, less costly, stage of the process. Self-inspection makes people more aware of problems and leads to earlier identification and corrective action.

Product and service attributes, the second category, refers to those properties of the output that the consumer or end-user determines to be of value. Some of these properties are meeting customer desires (for example, an end-user might desire certain extra features, such as an MS Windows interface for a software application), uniformity (for example, a sponsor might want research reports written in a standardized form), fitness for use (for example, a customer requires that their financial audit be presented in a standard format), and reliability (for example, a consumer might demand consistent data processing of its mailing list). The measures shown in Table 29.3 are not mutually exclusive measures, and an organization should use those that are feasible and that fit into their strategic plan.

Finally, timeliness involves the time criticality of delivery (for example, supplies are delivered when needed), the shelf life of inventory (for example, pharmaceuticals are used before their effective date expires), and meeting milestones and deadlines (for example, delivering a product on an agreed-upon schedule).

## Financial Performance

The final area shown in Figure 29.1 is financial performance. Many experts suggest that the ultimate goal of management is to maximize value for the owners of, and investors in, a company. Financial performance refers to the principal financial ratios that show how well the organization is providing financial value to its owners (profitability in the private sector and budgetability in the public sector). As with productivity, these financial results can be expressed as ratios of output to input (that is, ratios between the revenues generated and the costs to produce the product or service). (See Table 29.4 for definitions and examples of financial performance.)

**Solvency and Profitability.** Livingstone (1990) notes that the most common measures of performance for a company (the so-called bottom line) can be grouped into four categories, all measured as ratios: (1) short-term solvency, (2) long-term solvency, (3) profit-to-sales ratios, and (4) return on investment (ROI). These measures are generally, but not exclusively, associated with for-profit organizations. The first two are concerned with solvency or liquidity, the last two are principally concerned with measuring the profitability of the organization. Each of these measures tells a different story about the organization: where it has been, or where it might be headed. It is beyond the scope of this chapter to discuss the relative merits and demerits of these measures (see Livingstone, 1990, and Thor, 1994, for a more thorough discussion of these profitability measures). Suffice it to say that they can all be of value. The question that a consulting psychologist must answer is what do they say about the organization's strategic performance.

**Budgetability.** While private sector organizations are usually associated with profit measures, public sector organizations and not-for-profit organizations can benefit from similar quasi-profit measures. Publicly owned utilities, transportation systems, and hospitals, for example, function much like private corporations, with some restrictions. Many true public-sector organizations can sometimes

Table 29.4. Definitions and Examples of Organizational Effectiveness Measures—Financial Performance.

**Financial Performance:** Measures of the extent to which the organization produces financial value for its owners and investors

| Category | Examples |
|---|---|
| *Solvency:* Measure of liquidity and payment of long-term debt | |
| *Short-term solvency*: Measures of the liquidity of the organization and its cash flow | *Current ratio:* Current assets/current liabilities. *Accounts receivable turnover:* Credit sales/accounts receivable *Accounts payable turnover:* Cost of goods sold/accounts payable |
| *Long-term solvency*: Measures of the firms ability to meet its obligations to pay interest on long-term debt | *Debt-to-equity ratio:* Long-term debt/owner debt. *Debt ratio:* Long-term debt/owner equity |
| *Profitability:* Measures used in private-sector organizations that show the total earnings (income), or some profitability ratio (earnings to investment, earning to sales, earnings per share, and so on) | *Gross profit:* Gross profit/sales *Operating expenses:* Operating expense/sales *Net income:* Net income/sales *Price/earnings ratio (P/E):* The share price divided by the dollars earned *Earnings per share (EPS):* Net earnings (with appropriate adjustments)/shares outstanding *Return on equity (ROE):* Net income–preferred dividends)/ common equity *Return on sales (ROS):* Net earnings/sales *Market to book ratio:* Market price per common share/book value per common share |
| *Budgetability:* Measures used in public-sector organizations that show conformance to the financial budget | *Budget variance or savings:* Ratio of budget allocations to expenditures while maintaining appropriate quantity and quality of products and services *Budget growth:* Ratio of budget allocation to the baseline |

generate revenue through sales of goods or services to help supplement their budgets (for example, the National Park Service collects user fees). However, government and not-for-profit businesses have no private individual owners or stockholders who invested their money in the business in exchange for a share of the profits. Therefore, there are no owners to accrue equity, no earnings to be distributed, no earnings per share, and no profitability calculations. Whatever might be considered as revenue in excess of expenses is reinvested or returned to customers (in the form of lower prices) instead of to owners.

Most organizations in the public sector are concerned with staying within a budget. Ideally, when an organization chooses among alternative business strategies, it should be able to accurately forecast future revenues and costs, and thereby achieve some degree of control over both. In the public sector, however, improving budgetability normally means trying to control and reduce costs relative to a mostly fixed source of revenue. Success is measured in terms of staying within budget, increasing the services provided within the budget (without adversely affecting the product or service), or enhancing revenues without increasing costs. Table 29.4 outlines these facets of budgeting.

Once the earnings, revenues, and costs are measured, the financial success can be assessed by examining the ratio of income dollars to expenses. As the ratio increases, the financial performance of the organization improves. It is important to note, however, that financial performance is not necessarily the same as productivity. Improved profitability does not necessarily mean that the organization is more productive. Profitability can be influenced by factors that are independent of the output to input productivity ratio (for example, price increases because of higher demand or lower supply can increase the revenue more than they increase costs). Likewise, low profitability does not necessarily imply that the organization is less productive, for much the same reason (for example, if the customer negotiated a lower price for a product, or competition drove the price down, this would lower revenue without necessarily reflecting a productivity decline).

# PERFORMANCE INDEXING: INTEGRATING MEASURES INTO AN OVERALL PERFORMANCE MEASURE

The chapter thus far has laid out a broad array of measures and placed them into a practical typology. At this point, the discussion turns toward how to select appropriate measures for a particular organization, and how to organize this set of measures into a framework that will allow the user to plan, make decisions, and take action. This can be accomplished by what we call *performance indexing*. Performance indexing refers to a set of steps that can guide the user through a process for obtaining and using measures that mirror the performance of the whole organization. The end product is the performance index table, which summarizes a wide variety of measures and gives a numerical snapshot of the effectiveness of the organization. First, some background information will be provided.

## Multiple Measures (a Family of Measures)

The typology in Figure 29.1, and the accompanying measurement options in Tables 29.1–29.4, present a smorgasbord of potential performance measures. In general, it is good to have multiple measures of the same object or characteristic. Multiple measures allow the observer to triangulate (a term borrowed from mapping that refers to finding a position or location by using two or more fixed points). Rarely is there a single measure that captures the concept perfectly, and it is only through the convergence of multiple measures that we begin to get a clear picture of the true nature of the thing we wish to illuminate. This notion of triangulation is most clearly expressed in the idea of 360-degree feedback (Lepsinger & Lucia, 1997). Gathering information from many different raters or sources provides a more complete portrait of a person's job behavior. As Lepsinger and Lucia put it, "It is like having a full-length portrait, a profile, a close-up shot of the face, and a view from the back all at once" (pp. 9–10).

Thor (1994) contends that measures should be expressed in *families,* and managers should bundle related sets of measures (he recommends that each family should consist of collections of four to six related measures). This notion of bundling measures into families has been advanced by others as well, and is a well-accepted principle of organizational measurement (Bhargava & Dubelaar, 1994). For example, the *balanced scorecard* of Kaplan and Norton (1996) advocates bundling measures into four groups (financial, customer, internal, and innovation). Gormley and Weimer (1999) suggest a similar idea with their concept of the *organizational report card,* and Epstein and Henderson (1989) propose an empirical technique for bundling measures called Data Envelopment Analysis (DEA). Regardless of the approach, the key point is that measures should be combined in meaningful ways to capture important dimensions of organizational effectiveness. Of course, the measures selected should meet the standards of validity and reliability discussed above (see Bhargava & Dubelaar, 1994, for a discussion of psychometric properties of organizational measures).

## Multiple Levels

Organizations can be measured at several levels at once. At the top of an organization, measures tend to be broad in their scope and stretch over a long time horizon (quarters, years, decades). At the lowest levels of the organization (for example, work groups on the factory floor, sales clerks in a retail outlet), the measures are more specific and the time frame is shorter (minutes, hours, days). In addition, data can be aggregated at different levels. For example, data can be obtain at the individual level (individual responses to a survey, number of sick days, number of units produced), group level (average survey response from a division, number of parts assembled by a team), or organizational level (average level of job satisfaction for the company, annual profit, quarterly sales figures).

It is very important to understand the linkages between these levels, because changes at one level might not necessarily translate into changes at another level. This problem is sometimes referred to as the *productivity paradox* (Harris, 1994). For example, Hackman and Oldham (1980) showed that introducing job enrichment at the individual level had little effect at the organizational level unless managers and supervisors supported the intervention. The measures suggested in this chapter cut across these different levels: some individual, some team, some organizational.

Which measures to use at which levels is determined by the strategic purpose for which the measures are intended. But even if the strategy focuses on changing financial performance, it would be a mistake to ignore other measures that are leading indicators (that is, indicators that precede and predict important outcomes) of future financial performance. Measures should be selected in meaningful bundles (families) so that an accurate evaluation of both current and future performance can be estimated. With many possible measures being monitored, it is difficult to know how to provide an overall evaluation of whether the organization is improving without a way of combining the different measures into a summated evaluation. Total organizational effectiveness can only be expressed by combinations of measures reflecting many different factors and levels of organizational performance. However, if one set of measures is improving, but another set is declining, how can an organization determine its overall performance? In addition, how can an organization compare measures that are expressed in different units and at different levels of aggregation? The performance indexing technique presented below offers one solution to this problem. The intention of performance indexing is to provide a means to weight and combine a number of different organizational measures into an aggregate index that can be used to give an overall summary of organizational performance. It also provides the basis for determining the value of performance improvement that can be used to reward organizational members.

## Performance Indexing: A Practical Example

This section describes a general methodology for developing a measurement system. Many methods that underlie this methodology are similar to several other measurement approaches (see, for example, Baumol, 1977; Chang & De Young, 1995; Gormley & Weimer, 1999; Kaplan & Norton, 1996; Jones, Powell, & Roberts, 1990/1991; Nebeker & Tatum, 1996; Pritchard, Jones, Roth, Stuebing, & Ekeberg, 1989; Pritchard & Roth, 1991), but the specific method presented was influenced most by the objectives matrix approach described by

Felix and Riggs (1983). There are important differences, however, between the present approach and that of Felix and Riggs. These differences will be elaborated upon later in this section.

Performance indexing combines several diverse measures into one overall score of organizational performance by converting the different measures into a common metric, and then weighting each score to obtain an overall performance index. This index can be tracked over time to see changes in overall organization performance measured against strategic objectives.

Figure 29.2 shows an example of a performance index table (with the procedural steps and sample data) for a hypothetical software development organization. Although Figure 29.2 might appear intimidating at first glance, it is quite simple in concept and design. The steps required to build a performance index table are shown on the right-hand margin of the figure. Each step is described using examples taken from our hypothetical software organization.

One of the difficulties of previous methods to combine performance measures is the problem of double-counting of either inputs or outputs. This presents the greatest difficulty with inputs or expenses, because so many of the performance ratios use expenses or inputs as a divisor. This problem can reduce the accuracy of the combined score. To avoid double-counting in our example, the inputs are not included until the very last step, at which point they are included as a total expense.

**Step 1: Preplanning.** Following the advice of Tuttle and Sink (1984), the first step requires gathering background data on the organization, so that a systems diagram of the organization can be constructed. This should be based on the strategic plan for the organization, and should include input from key stakeholders (for example, top management, major customers). The diagram will help guide the selection of *key result areas* (step 2), and should contain the following information: (1) environmental demands on the organization, (2) strategic opportunities for the organization, (3) inputs into the organization, (4) outputs from the organization, (5) the impacts the outputs have outside the organization (for example, on customers, the community, sponsors), and (6) significant internal processes.

**Step 2: Identifying Key Result Areas.** Many organizations have a mission and values statement, and a strategic plan for accomplishing their goals. From these documents and the diagram developed in step 1, top management can discern the key performance areas that are absolutely essential for meeting the organization's mission and strategic goals. These broad performance areas are the key result areas (Tuttle & Sink, 1984; Tuttle & Weaver, 1986), and must be established by the top management of the organization as the first step in creating a performance index table (see Tuttle, Wilkinson, & Mathews, 1985, for excellent

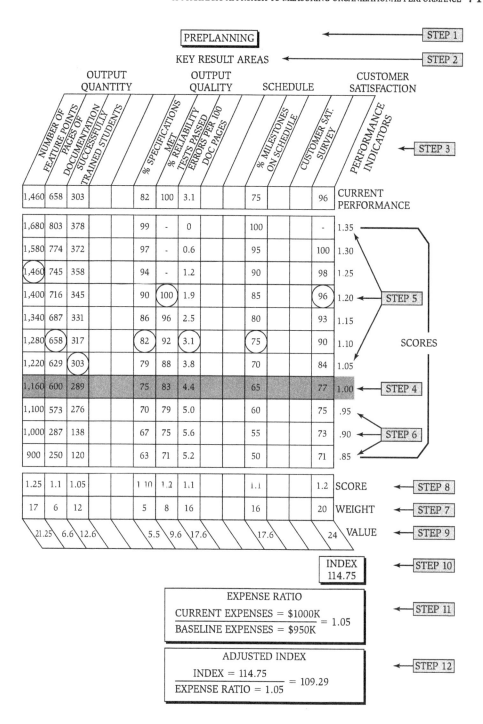

**Figure 29.2  Performance Index Table for a Hypothetical Software Development Organization (Adapted from Felix & Riggs, 1983).**

examples of the process used to generate key result areas). Key result areas are the families described by Thor (1994). In our hypothetical software organization, the key result areas are listed across the top of the table, and are labeled output quantity, output quality, schedule, and customer satisfaction. In other words, for this organization, given the resources available, its mission and goals are accomplished by maximizing the output of its operation, continuously improving the quality of its products and services, meeting its delivery schedules, and satisfying its customers. All of these key result areas reflect some aspect of the outputs or outcomes of the organization. In other words, in this example, the family of measures are results-oriented rather than process-oriented.

**Step 3: Developing Performance Indicators.** The key result areas are the broadly conceived areas that significantly affect the mission and strategic goals of the organization. These key result areas are not useful unless there are specific indicators (measures) that tell the organization how it is performing in these key areas. Performance indicators are the specific ways in which the key result areas are assessed; they are the specific measures that are bundled together into a family and provide quantitative indices of each key result area. Each key result area must have at least one performance indicator, but ideally there should be several (Thor, 1994, recommends four to six). Tables 29.1–29.4 give many alternative measures that can be used as potential performance indicators, or an organization can develop its own. As a rule, the more performance indicators there are for a key result area, the more confidence an organization can have that it has meaningfully evaluated that area. However, if too many performance indicators are used, it becomes difficult to understand how they all work together as a reflection of the key result area.

Confidence in the indicators is also increased if the performance indicators are stable (reliable), measure what they are supposed to measure (valid), and are collected in a systematic and orderly fashion (standardized). Standardization, reliability, and validity are easier to establish if an organization has been collecting data on performance indicators for several years. Organizations in the initial stages of developing performance indicators should try to choose indicators that have shown good measurement properties in other settings. With a set of completely untested indicators, assessment of reliability, validity, and standardization must be established after some history with the measures.

Figure 29.2 shows the performance indicators under each key result area for the hypothetical software organization. For example, under the key result area of output quantity, there are three indicators: (1) number of feature points (a concept used by software developers to count the useful features of a software product); (2) number of pages of documentation; and (3) number of successfully trained students. These three performance indicators capture the essence of what is meant by output quantity in this organization.

To illustrate the process, the first indicator will be considered in more detail. Feature points are used in the software development industry to measure productivity (Jones, 1988), and are similar to function points developed at IBM (Albrecht, 1979). Each feature point represents a significant feature (for example, output of data, creation of a master file, and so on) of the software product delivered to the customer. Obviously, the more feature points delivered, the more work completed, and the greater the output quantity. Thus, for the software organization in this example, delivering software features to the customer is an important part of its mission. Similarly, documenting the software, and training people to use the software, are significant parts of the organization's mission.

Just as with the key result area of output quantity, the other areas have performance indicators. For example, specification adherence, reliability of the software, and software defects, are indicators of quality. Likewise, meeting milestones is an indicator of the key result area for schedule, and a survey of customer satisfaction measures the key result area for customer satisfaction. With respect to schedules and customer satisfaction, it would be better if there was more than a single indicator for each of these, but sometimes it is difficult for an organization to come up with even a single indicator (because the technology is new, the area has not been measured before, and so on). In such cases, it is better to start out with a single indicator, and then develop additional indicators over time as the company gains more experience in measuring key result areas.

**Step 4: Establishing Baseline Performance Levels.** Once all of the performance indicators are identified, it is necessary to establish a baseline level of performance for each indicator (that is, the level of performance to which future performance is compared). Past performance (that is, the level of performance up until now), or some target level of performance (for example, performance mandated by, or negotiated with, some stakeholder) becomes the baseline. The absolute values of the baseline performance for each indicator is entered into the matrix in the shaded row toward the bottom marked with the number 1.00 on the right-hand margin. As seen in Figure 29.2, in our hypothetical software organization, the baseline level of customer satisfaction is 77, and this number appears in the column labeled Customer Satisfaction Survey and the row labeled Step 4. Similarly, the baseline level for % Milestones on Schedule is 65 percent, and this number also appears on the same row.

The baseline level of performance for each performance indicator needs to be carefully selected. Ideally, the baseline level is a stable and accurate reflection of the organization's current state. Usually, the baseline level is computed from data collected over a lengthy period. Often, the baseline levels are established by data collected every quarter for a period spanning three to five years. Obviously, the longer the period of data collection, the more confidence the organization has that these measurements are a stable and accurate reflection of their current capability. If an organization plans to use historical data, but does not have existing measures, it should undergo a period of data collection to establish a stable baseline of performance. This will, of course, delay the development of the performance indexing, but this method is only as good as the data that are entered.

**Step 5: Establishing Performance Goals.** After determining a baseline level of performance on all of the indicators, the next step is to set appropriate improvement goals for performance levels above the baseline level. As shown in Figure 29.2, there are seven rows above the 1.00 row that are marked with scores ranging from 1.05 to 1.35 on the right-hand margin. Each successive row represents an increasing level of performance above the baseline performance. In the best case, these goal levels are determined empirically by known relationships between performance and the value of each successive level. However, establishing these successive goal levels can be based on expert judgment, or be estimated by a committee or group of stakeholders knowledgeable about the relationships between performance and value. In any case, the best approach is to enter a high goal in the top row (score of 1.35), which represents approximately a 35 percent increase in the value of the indicator. Then the values for each descending row (scores 1.30 to 1.05) should be selected so they represent progressively less-difficult goals proceeding downward to the baseline (score 1.00).

The top row should be a goal that is very difficult to meet, a goal that, if met, would mean that the organization had increased its outputs or outcomes substantially. For example, suppose that the last column of the table, Customer Satisfaction, is obtained by a survey in which customers rate the organization's software products and services on a 1 to 100 scale. Obviously, obtaining a score of 100 is the best score this organization can achieve. Therefore, 100 is the highest goal, and is the value placed in the top row in the Customer Satisfaction column. It is not always this easy to determine what the highest goal should be, but the idea is to pick values that express substantial improvement in outputs or outcomes. In some cases, substantial improvement might even occur before performance reaches the 1.35 level (for example, see the reliability tests column in Figure 29.2).

Selecting the values for the intermediate rows is not necessarily a simple process. The easiest way to do it is simply to take the difference between the value in the baseline and the value in the top row (maximum performance), and divide this number into equal intervals. This approach assumes, however, that the value of improving from one goal level to the next is equal. This is not always the case, because the value of achieving progressively higher levels of performance is often a nonlinear function of the goal level. For example, it might not be of much value to reduce the defects in a product from ninety-nine per thousand to ninety-eight per thousand, but it might be exceptionally valuable to go from two per thousand to one per thousand. Considerable thought must be given to how the range of values for the rows between the baseline and the top row ought to be distributed. When it is much more valuable to achieve the higher-level goals, the increments at the higher levels can be made smaller than the increments at the lower levels. In this way, the higher goals are given more importance, and thereby encourage more effort to make improvements at the high end of the scale.

Figure 29.2 shows this nonlinear scaling for the customer satisfaction indicator. Note how customer satisfaction increments become progressively smaller as we go from a score of 1.00 to 1.35. The assumption is that as customer satisfaction gets closer to the maximum goal of 100 percent, the value of a one-point improvement is greater to the organization. In Figure 29.2, we can see that a two-unit increase in customer satisfaction at the high end of the scale (for example, from 96 to 98) is as valuable as a six-unit increase at the low end of the scale (for example, from 77 to 84). Alternatively, for percentage milestones on schedule, for each increment in the scores from 1.00 to 1.35, there is an equal increment in the level of the performance indicator. This shows that there is equal value to each 5 percent improvement all along the milestone scale.

**Step 6: Setting Lower Performance Levels.** Although performance decrements are unpleasant, performance does sometimes deteriorate from past levels. The three rows below the baseline row, as shown in Figure 29.2, are included in the performance index table to cover those occasions in which performance drops below the baseline level. These lower levels send a message to the organization that something is amiss and corrective action must be taken. The values that are selected for these levels will be determined by the mission and strategic goals of the organization, and by what message is to be conveyed when performance drops to these levels. If the mission is to satisfy the customer above all else, then falling below the baseline level of customer satisfaction is a very serious problem. In this case, the levels below the baseline row should be scaled in very small increments, so that the message is clear that even small decreases in performance are unacceptable. On the other hand, if it is common for the delivery schedule to slip, and this is not a serious problem for the organization or its customers, then the values selected for the bottom three rows might be less constrained than for some of the other indicators. In all cases, the organization wants to stress that falling below baseline performance is not good, and that each successive drop in performance below the baseline row creates a greater problem for the organization.

**Step 7: Assigning Weights to Performance Indicators.** Not all performance indicators are equally important to the mission, vision, and strategic goals of the organization. In our hypothetical software organization, documentation and meeting specifications might not be as important as customer satisfaction and increasing feature point output. Assigning weights to the performance indicators is a way of denoting the relative importance of the indicators. The recommended procedure for a performance index table is to start with 100 points, and to distribute those points to the various indicators in proportion to the relative importance of the indicators. In Figure 29.2, we have assigned 20 of the available 100 points to customer satisfaction, and only 5 points to meeting specifications. The other indicators are likewise assigned points so that the total adds up to 100. If there are many more indicators than shown here, it would be possible to use 1,000 points (instead of 100) to distribute across the indicators as weights.

How does an organization decide what weight to give a particular indicator? There are both analytic and nonanalytic methods for assigning weights. Analytic methods involve devising a rational scheme for judging how much weight to give each indicator. For example, it might be possible to determine what proportion of the budget is allocated to efforts supporting each of the performance indicators. If this information is available, the weights can be tied to the budget numbers. If 20 percent of the budget goes toward customer support, it might make sense to assign a weight of 20 to customer satisfaction. If only 5 percent of the budget goes towards ensuring that the programs meet the specifications, perhaps a weight of 5 is reasonable. It should be noted, however, that in order for this method to work optimally, the budget allocation process itself must be rational, and must indeed reflect the strategic importance of each indicator.

Nonanalytic methods for assigning weights rely on group consensus and expert opinion. The typical approach here is to bring together a group of people (for example, top management, or an executive committee) who are intimately involved in the management and operations of the organization, and brainstorm on what is important and what weights should be assigned. There are systematic procedures for bringing about consensus (for example, the Nominal Group Technique; Mosley & Green, 1974). These nonanalytic methods can be very time consuming, but experience has shown that these methods can also be quite accurate, and the results well accepted.

**Step 8: Assigning Scores to Performance Indicators.** At the completion of steps 1 through 7, the performance index table is ready to use. At this point, the organization knows the current and desired level of performance on each indicator for the baseline performance period. Baseline performance levels are entered in the shaded row (step 4). Because performance for each indicator is measured on a different metric or numbering scheme (for example, feature points are measured as raw units, schedules are measured as percentages, customer satisfaction as survey ratings), the numbers for the indicators must be converted to a common metric. This is done by assigning a common score to all indicators falling along the same row. With regard to baseline performance, all the indicators in that row are assigned the score 1.00. At that point, it no longer matters that baseline performance for feature points is 1,160, for schedule it is 65, and for customer satisfaction it is 77. All the numbers in the baseline row are reassigned a score of 1.00. In a similar vein, all the numbers in the three rows above the baseline are scored as 1.15, and all the numbers three rows below the baseline are scored as .85.[1]

The advantage of performance indexing is not only that the organization can view its overall performance at present, but it can also compare future performance to this present performance. Because the baseline performance numbers are forced to take on the score of 1.00, the organization can determine whether future performance rises above or falls below this score. To make this comparison, it is necessary to wait a period of time (for example, one quarter or one year) and then recalculate the performance levels on each of the indicators.

When these new numbers are available, the numbers for each indicator that are just below the calculated number can be circled. For example, suppose that after one year, the feature points indicator is recalculated and it is discovered that the software company is producing 1,500 units, whereas a year earlier only 1,160 units were produced. This is obviously an improvement, but how much of an improvement? As shown in Figure 29.2, the number just below 1,500 is 1,460, and so that number is circled. The reason the lower number is selected is because it is a conservative estimate of the improvement, and because the table values are goals; 1,500 exceeds the goal of 1,460, but does not reach the next highest goal of 1,580. After the appropriate number in the table has been circled, the row is then followed from left to right to determine the score for that number. (To preserve the precise differences in performance on the new scale, it would be a simple matter of interpolation to make the score reflect the continuous levels of the indicator.) In the example, 1,460 feature points gets a score of 1.25. It is then known that the feature point indicator has improved from 1.00 to 1.25 over a one-year period.

If there was only one indicator, there would be no advantage to assigning the scores 1.00 and 1.25 to these feature point numbers. However, with multiple indicators, the scores become a common metric that can be compared across

---

[1]This range of scores from .85 to 1.35 is different from the scores shown in the Objectives Matrix. Felix and Riggs (1983) use a 1–10 point scale. The matrix (table) shown in Figure 29.2 uses a range of scores that is indexed to the proportion of change for each from the baseline. This is done so the results are scaled as proportional improvement. The Felix and Riggs method does not allow this, and distorts change calculations.

diverse sets of measures. Imagine that during that same one-year period, meeting schedule went from 65 percent of the time to 75 percent of the time, as shown in Figure 29.2. This is an improvement, but is it as much of an improvement as was observed for feature points? This cannot be determined by simply looking at the absolute numbers for each indicator, but it can be determined at a glance by comparing the scores. Because the goal of 75 (but not 80) was met, the score for the schedule indicator is 1.10. Because a score of 1.10 on schedule is not as high as a score of 1.25 on feature points, it must be concluded that, based on the beginning assumptions, the company improved more on feature points than it did on meeting the schedule.

The rest of the indicators are converted to scores in a similar manner, and it is possible to tell how much relative improvement (or slippage) there was for each indicator. Those scores for each indicator are then entered in the row at the bottom of the table labeled Score. In addition, the actual number for each indicator is entered in the row at the top of the table labeled Current Performance.

**Step 9: Compute Weighted Values for Performance Indicators.** As useful as the previous step was in helping to compare relative improvement in performance indicators, this next step is even more valuable. This step allows the company to see improvements in performance indicators relative to their importance to the organization. Although it is useful to know that the company improved its performance in feature points, it is more important to the organization to see improvements in customer satisfaction. Calculating the weighted values for each indicator supplies its relative importance. To obtain the weighted value, the score for each performance indicator is multiplied by its given weight, and the result is entered in the bottom row labeled Value, as shown in Figure 29.2. This number adjusts the score of each indicator by the weighted importance of the indicator, and tells the company how important the improvement is relative to the overall mission, vision, and goals of the organization. In the present illustration, it can be seen that despite the fact that customer satisfaction received a lower score than feature points (1.20 versus 1.25), the weighted value is higher (24 versus 21.25). The difference in weighted value reflects the fact that customer satisfaction was determined to be more important to the organization than output of feature points, and thus the lower score is adjusted upward by the weighting.

**Step 10: Calculate an Index.** The next step in constructing a performance index table is to add all of the values along the bottom row of the table and place that number in the box labeled Index. The index is a number that reflects total performance of the organization for the period being evaluated. In the current example, the index number is 114.75, which is the index number for the one-year period following the baseline. The index is a reflection of the overall improvement over the baseline period. The number 100 is the baseline index, because this is the number that would result if all of the values for the baseline performance were added. Any index that exceeds 100 reflects an improvement in performance, and any score that falls below 100 reflects a decline. Thus, the index number indicates clearly and quantitatively whether the organization has improved (index > 100) or declined ( index < 100) during any given period following the baseline.

**Step 11: Calculating a Current-to-Baseline Expense Ratio.** The next step requires that the total expenses during the current and baseline periods be entered in the expense ratio box. These figures need to be expressed in constant, preferably current, dollars. The ratio of the current expenses (in this example $1,000,000) to baseline expenses ($950,000) expresses how much change has occurred in expenses (an increase of 1.05 in constant dollars).

**Step 12: Adjusting the Performance Index.** The performance index is then divided by the expense ratio to adjust the performance index for changes in expenses. In the example, current expenses are 1.05 times those in the baseline period. As a result, the final performance index is 114.75 divided by 1.05. This equals 109.29. Despite the increase in expenses during the current period, the organization's overall performance has improved in meeting its strategic objectives. Obviously, this is only one example. It is possible, and perhaps desirable, that expenses might decline between the baseline and current performance. In this second case, the total performance of the organization would be even higher than the performance shown in the first example.

**Summing Up.** Once the basic principles of performance indexing are understood, an organization can make many adjustments and create many variations. For example, the base costs can be adjusted by the Producer Price Index (PPI) to convert the costs into today's dollars. As another example, if an organization is made up of several relatively independent departments, each department can create its own performance index table, and these different tables can be combined (rolled up) into one larger table for the organization as a whole. As a final example, performance indexing allows an organization to make different adjustments to the inputs so that certain cost categories can be included or excluded. The flexibility and utility of performance indexing makes it an ideal tool for measuring productivity in most environments, particularly in a white-collar environment in which performance is hard to measure and improvements difficult to judge. Although there are other measurement methodologies (see, for example, Felix & Riggs, 1983; Jones et al., 1990; Kaplan & Norton, 1996; Nebeker & Tatum, 1996; Pritchard et al., 1989; Pritchard & Roth, 1991), performance indexing as described here provides an excellent entrée into the confusing and complicated world of organizational performance and effectiveness.

# CONCLUSIONS

This chapter is an introduction to the complex field of measuring organizational performance. We have shown that performance can be divided into four distinct areas (resource development, stakeholder relations, productivity, and financial performance), and we have given many examples of how each of these areas can be measured. Although it is impossible to provide examples that apply to all organizations, most of the measures discussed are general enough to apply to a wide range of organizations. The important point is that measures of organizational performance should be selected from these four areas in harmony with the organization's strategic plan so that total organizational performance can be monitored and improved. Effective organizations realize that there must be a balance between these areas. If one aspect of the organization is performing optimally (for example, spending is within budget parameters), but another area is performing poorly (for example, human resources are not being effectively used), then, ultimately, the overall ability of the organization to perform will be compromised.

Reviewing the measures set forth in this chapter provides the organization with some tools for assessing where its strengths and weaknesses lie. Reviewing these measures should cause an organization to think about areas not previously attended to that are important to achieving the organization's goals. We do not wish to convey the idea that every organization should adopt all of these proposed measures, nor do we believe that this document contains an exhaustive list of performance measures. Each organization should decide which measures are most relevant for its goals and needs, and customize and develop its own measures if these do not suit its purposes. If an organization does develop its own performance measures, we hope that the examples presented here serve as a useful guide. At the very least, an organization should select or develop measures from each of the four major areas (resource development, stakeholder relations, productivity, and financial performance). Adopting the performance indexing methodology proposed here will aid the organization in selecting the right measures, and in using those measures to become more productive, profitable, and competitive. Unlike the mythical pilot who flies with only one gauge, organizations today need many measurement instruments, organized in an orderly fashion, if they are to navigate successfully through the treacherous air space of today's complex information society.

# References

Albrecht, A. J. (1979, October). Measuring application development productivity. *Proceedings of the Joint SHARE/GUIDE/IBM Application Development Symposium* (pp. 83–92). Monterey, CA.

Allen, M. J., & Yen, W. M. (1979). *Introduction to measurement theory.* Pacific Grove, CA: Brooks/Cole.

American Psychological Association, Society of Consulting Psychology (2000). *Guidelines for education and training at doctoral and post-doctoral level in consulting psychology.* Retrieved October 28, 2001, from http://www.apa.org/divisions/div13/Guidelines.html

Baumol, W. J. (1977). *Economic theory and operations analysis.* Englewood Cliffs, NJ: Prentice Hall.

Becker, B. E., Huselid, M. A., & Ulrich, D. (2001). *The HR scorecard: Linking people, strategy, and performance.* Boston: Harvard Business School Press.

Behn, R. D. (1995). The big question of public management. *Public Administration Review, 55,* 313–324.

Bertrand, K. (1989, November). Is sales turnover inevitable? *Business Marketing, 26.*

Bhargava, M., & Dubelaar, C. (1994). Reconciling diverse measures of performance: A conceptual framework and test of a methodology. *Journal of Business Research, 31,* 235–246.

Brockner, J. Grover, S. L., & Blonder, M. D. (1988). Predictors of survivors job involvement following layoffs: A field study. *Journal of Applied Psychology, 73,* 436–442.

Cameron, K. S. (1980). Critical questions in assessing organizational effectiveness. *Organizational Dynamics, 9,* 66–80.

Cascio, W. F., & Ramos, R. A. (1986). Development and application of a new method for assessing job performance in behavioral economic terms. *Journal of Applied Psychology, 71,* 20–28.

Chang, R. Y., & De Young, P. (1995). *Measuring organizational improvement impact.* San Francisco: Jossey-Bass.

Deming, W. E. (1986). *Out of the crisis.* Cambridge, MA: MIT.

Dessler, G. (1988). *Personnel management* (4th ed.). Englewood Cliffs, NJ: Prentice Hall.

Eccles, R. G. (1991, January). The performance measurement manifesto. *Harvard Business Review,* 131–137.

Epstein, M. K., & Henderson, J. C. (1989). Data envelope analysis for managerial control and diagnosis. *Decision Sciences, 20,* 90–119.

Felix, G. H., & Riggs, J. L. (1983). Productivity measurement by objectives. *National Productivity Review, 2*(4), 386–393.

Fitz-Enz, J. (2000). *The ROI of human capital: Measuring the ecomonic value of employee performance.* New York: American Management Association.

Forte, D. (1993). Measuring federal government productivity. In W. F. Christopher & C. G. Thor (Eds.), *Handbook for productivity measurement and improvement* (7-3.1–7-3.16). Washington, DC: Productivity Press.

Gormley, W. T., & Weimer, D. L. (1999). *Organizational report cards.* Cambridge, MA: Harvard University Press.

Hackman, J. R., & Oldham, G. R. (1980). *Work redesign.* Reading, MA: Addison-Wesley.

Harris, D. H. (Ed.). (1994). *Linkages: Understanding the productivity paradox.* Washington, DC: National Academy Press.

Ishikawa, K. (1985). *What is total quality control? The Japanese way* (D. J. Lu, Trans.). Englewood Cliffs, NJ: Prentice Hall.

Jones, C. (1988). *A short history of function points and feature points.* Cambridge, MA: Software Productivity Research.

Jones, S. D., Powell, R., & Roberts, S. (1990/1991, Winter). Comprehensive measurement to improve assembly-line work group effectiveness. *National Productivity Review,* 45–55.

Kaplan, R. S., & Norton, D. P. (1996). *Translating strategy into action: The balanced scorecard.* Boston: Harvard Business School Press.

Krackhardt, D., & Porter, L. W. (1985). When friends leave: A structural analysis of the relationship between turnover and stayers' attitude. *Administrative Science Quarterly, 30,* 242–261.

Kraft, K. L., Jauch, L. R., & Boatwright, E. W. (1996). Assessing organizational effectiveness in the service sector. *Journal of Professional Services Marketing, 14,* 101–111.

Lepsinger, R., & Lucia, A. D. (1997). *The art and science of 360° feedback.* San Diego, CA: Pfeiffer.

Livingstone, J. L. (1990). Accounting and management decision making. In E.G.C. Collins & M. A. Devanna (Eds.), *The portable MBA* (pp. 109–137). New York: Wiley.

Macy, B. A., & Mirvis, P. H. (1978). A methodology for assessment of quality of work life and organizational effectiveness in behavioral-economic terms. *Administrative Science Quarterly, 21,* 212–226

Martin, R. (1997). Do we practice quality principles in the performance measurement of critical success factors? *Total Quality Management, 8,* 429–444.

Mosley, D. C., & Green, T. B. (1974, March). Nominal grouping as an organizational development intervention technique. *Training and Development Journal,* 30–37.

Nebeker, D. M., Neuberger, B. M., & Hulton, V. N. (1983). *Productivity improvement in a purchasing division: Evaluation of a performance contingent reward system (PCRS)* (NPRDC Report No. TR 83-34). San Diego, CA: Navy Personnel Research and Development Center.

Nebeker, D. M., & Tatum, B. C. (1996). *Approaches to measuring quality and productivity for gain sharing: Measuring total organizational value* (NPRDC Report No. TR 96-33). San Diego, CA: Navy Personnel Research and Development Center.

Nebeker, D. M., & Tatum, B. C. (2002). Understanding organizational processes and performance: A continuous improvement model for consulting psychologists. In R. L. Lowman (Ed.), *Handbook of organizational consulting psychology* (668–691). San Francisco: Jossey-Bass.

Nebeker, D. M., Tatum, B. C., & Wolosin, D. G. (1996). *Examples of white collar measurement using a typology of organizational effectiveness.* (NPRDC Report No. TR 96-30). San Diego, CA: Navy Personnel Research and Development Center.

Nunnally, J. C., & Bernstein, I. H. (1994). *Psychometric theory* (3rd ed.). New York: McGraw-Hill.

Pritchard, R. D. (1994). Decomposing the productivity paradox linkages. In D. H. Harris (Ed.), *Understanding the productivity paradox* (pp. 161–192). Washington, DC: National Academy Press.

Pritchard, R. D., Jones, S. D., Roth, P. L., Stuebing, K. K., & Ekeberg, S. E. (1989). The evaluation of an integrated approach to measuring organizational productivity. *Personnel Psychology, 42,* 69–115.

Pritchard, R. D., & Roth, P. G. (1991). Accounting for nonlinear utility functions in composite measures of productivity and performance. *Organizational Behavior and Human Decision Processes, 50,* 341–359.

Quinn, R. E. (1978). Towards a theory of changing: A means-end model of the organizational improvement process. *Human Relations, 31,* 395–416.

Rich, P. (1993). The organizational taxonomy: Definition and design. *Academy of Management Review, 17,* 758–781.

Rumor, G. A., & Brace, A. P. (1991, January). Managing the white space. *Training,* 55–70.

Sager, J. K. (1990). How to retain salespeople. *Industrial Marketing Management, 19,* 155–166.

Schmidt, F. L., Hunter, J. E., McKenzie, R. C., & Muldrow, T. W. (1979). Impact of valid selection procedures on work-force productivity. *Journal of Applied Psychology, 64,* 609–626.

Sink, D. S., Tuttle, T. C., & DeVries, F. J. (1984). Productivity measurement and evaluation: What is available? *National Productivity Review, 3*(3), 265–287.

Steers, R. M. (1975). Problems in the measurement of organizational effectiveness. *Administrative Science Quarterly, 20,* 546–558.

Straight, R. L. (2000). Performance metrics: Avoiding the pitfalls. *Public Administration Quarterly, 4,* 495–516.

Tatum, B. C., Shaw, K. N., & Main, R. E. (1996). *Integrating measurement approaches in gain sharing and total quality* (NPRDC Report No. TR 96-31). San Diego, CA: Navy Personnel Research and Development Center.

Thor, C. G. (1994). *The measure of success: Generating a high performing organization.* Essex Junction, VT: Oliver Wight.

Tuttle, T. C., & Sink, D. S. (1984). Taking the threat out of productivity measurement. *National Productivity Review, 3*(1), 24–32.

Tuttle, T. C., & Weaver, C. N. (1986). *Methodology for generating efficiency and effectiveness measures (MGEEM): A guide for Air Force measurement facilitators* (Report No. AFHRL-TP-86-36). Brooks Air Force Base, TX: Air Force Human Resources Laboratory, Manpower and Personnel Division.

Tuttle, T. C., Wilkinson, & Mathews, R. E. (1985). *Field test of the methodology for generating efficiency and effectiveness measures* (Report No. AFHRL-TP-84-54). Brooks Air Force Base, TX: Air Force Human Resources Laboratory, Manpower and Personnel Division.

U.S. Department of Labor, Bureau of Labor Statistics, Office of Productivity and Technology (1993a). *Description of output indicators by function for the federal government, fiscal year 1991.* Washington, DC: Author.

U.S. Department of Labor, Bureau of Labor Statistics, Office of Productivity and Technology (1993b). *Developing output indicators for federal productivity measurement.* Washington, DC: Author.

U.S. Department of Labor, Bureau of Labor Statistics, Office of Productivity and Technology (1993c). Labor productivity trends for federal government functions and the measured total. In *Productivity measures for selected industries and government service.* Washington, DC: Author.

U.S. Department of Labor, Bureau of Labor Statistics, Office of Productivity and Technology (1993d). *Productivity statistics for federal government functions.* Washington, DC: Author.

Wood, M., Rasmussen, J. E., & Lawler, E. E., III. (1975). *Federally sponsored research on the quality of working life: Planning, support, and products.* Seattle, WA: Battelle Memorial Institute, Human Affairs Research Centers.

PART EIGHT

# PROFESSIONAL
# PRACTICE ISSUES

# CHAPTER THIRTY

# Issues in the Ethical Practice of Consulting Psychology

Jody L. Newman
*Department of Educational Psychology*
*University of Oklahoma*

Sharon E. Robinson-Kurpius
*Division of Psychology in Education*
*Arizona State University*

Dale R. Fuqua
*College of Education*
*Oklahoma State University*

The purpose of this chapter is to identify and examine what we believe to be the most central ethical issues in the practice of consulting psychology in organizational contexts. Although some of these issues have already been thoroughly discussed elsewhere in terms of their application to more traditional applied contexts, for example, psychotherapy, our discussion of these issues here explores the more unique features of their application in organizational consultation. Other issues included in this chapter derive uniquely from organizational consultation, and we examine their implications for consulting psychology practice.

## WHO IS THE CLIENT?

A distinguishing feature of consulting relationships is their triadic nature (Brown, Pryzwansky, & Schulte, 1991). Typically, consulting relationships are conceptualized as involving three parties, the consultant, the consultee system, and the client group(s) served by the consultee. Depending on the size and nature of the consultee organization, the number of individuals comprising the organization itself and the client system it serves can be considerable. Furthermore, an organization's client system, though highly likely to be affected by consultation intervention (either directly or indirectly), frequently has no voice in the consultation process (Robinson & Gross, 1985; Snow &

Gersick, 1986). This condition creates an unusual circumstance for consultants, in that they bear responsibility for the impact of change on a group with whom they might never have had personal contact (Brown et al., 1991; Fannibanda, 1976; Gallesich, 1982; Newman & Robinson, 1991; Snow & Gersick, 1986; Tokunaga, 1984). In some situations, this matter can be effectively addressed by including representatives of the client system served by an organization in the consulting process, if such an option is possible. At other times, the only option might be to attempt to anticipate the impact of intervention(s) on members of the client system and make all provisions possible to protect their interests.

## Competing Interests

A practical difficulty of this situation identified by Newman (1993) relates to the potential threats to the "objectivity, quality, accuracy and relevance" (p. 148) of data regarding an organization's clients obtained indirectly through the consultee system. This is particularly true in those cases where consultee and client interests are competitive. For example, it might be in the best economic interests of an airline to overbook reservations in order to compensate for people who cancel reservations at the last minute or fail to show up for flights. For customers, however, the practice of overbooking can mean extensive difficulties related to delays or disruptions of travel plans. This example illustrates the need for the consultant to anticipate the potential meaning of an intervention for the client system early enough to contract for access to the client system. Failure to do so represents a passive denial of responsibility.

Competing interests might similarly emerge among different subsystems within the organization that make delineation of the client in consultation, along with corresponding lines of consultant responsibility, difficult. For example, during times of economic distress and downsizing, the competition for limited or shrinking resources often fosters competitive relationships within organizations. Unless some shared vision of the greater good can be cultivated, thereby encouraging collaboration among subsystems within the organization, the relative cost and benefit of change efforts are more likely to be evaluated by individuals and units in terms of their own compartmentalized and immediate interests. Defining *moral competition* in such cases might prove to be the most significant intervention of all. Here, we are asking not just that the consultant behave in an ethical way, nor only that the consultant develop a moral character. We are defining the consultation intervention as the resolution of an internal moral conflict within the organization. Internal competition can indeed become dysfunctional. One manifestation of this dysfunction can be conflict with the purposive structure (that is, goals, values, philosophies) of the organization. The resolution of this internal structural conflict might best be addressed by initiating a moral dialogue.

## Focus of the Consultation

Identifying the client in organizational consultation is also often complicated by the fact that the individual who makes the initial contact with the consultant might not be the focus of consultation, or even an active participant in the process (Snow & Gersick, 1986). This situation is illustrated by a chief executive officer (CEO) arranging for consultation on behalf of a specific unit within the organization. Is the client the individual who hires the consultant and bears financial responsibility for the services provided, or the individuals or units who are to be the focus of the intervention? Whose definition of the problem should guide the consultation process? How should differences in perspectives regarding the nature of problems and their solutions be addressed and resolved? These are very difficult issues that have important implications for the ultimate process and outcome of consultation. We recommend that consultants, through open discussions with participants, ensure that issues like these are addressed thoroughly with all relevant parties. Furthermore, consultants should ensure that they clarify the nature of their relationships with all parties involved in the consultation process, as well as their respective responsibilities to each party.

## Intervention Level

Another factor that can potentially complicate definition of the client relates to the level at which intervention is focused (Koocher & Keith-Spiegel, 1998). The predominant conceptual frameworks used in organizational consultation are largely influenced by systems theory, which argues for defining problems in terms of systems constructs, with the emphasis on altering the structure of organizations as the primary means of achieving lasting change. A competing perspective is to focus on attempting to change the behavior of individuals or groups within the organization. There are clearly times when intervention at this level is appropriate (Fuqua & Newman, 1985), such as when the problem is related specifically to a skill deficit in an identifiable person. Each of these perspectives would have very different implications for defining who the client is. Relatedly, there might be disagreement within the organization regarding the locus of the problem and the appropriate focus of intervention. Again, clarification of these issues early in the consulting relationship is recommended in order to avoid confusion and misunderstanding by potential participants.

# INFORMED CONSENT

Freeman (2000) defined informed consent in terms of four essential elements that include: (1) the competence of participants to make rational decisions regarding whether or not to participate; (2) the voluntary nature of participation; (3) access to full information regarding the purposes, potential risks and benefits, and likely outcomes of participation; and (4) the ability to comprehend relevant information; that is, the information is presented in an easily understandable form. Like most ethical issues, informed consent, as applied in organizational consulting psychology, is often complicated by the complexity of the organizational context. For example, the hierarchical nature of organizations introduces potentially serious threats to the requirement that participation in the consultation process be truly voluntary. Typically, there is a notable power differential among individuals and groups within an organization. Since consultation is often arranged for one or more sectors of the organization by another sector, for example, the CEO, it must be questioned whether members for whom the consultation has been arranged are truly free to decline to participate. Even if they are, do they accurately *perceive* that such freedom exists? In reality, organizations routinely pressure members to participate, either directly or indirectly. By their very nature, "organizations necessarily are, in part, systems of compliance, coercion, and public accountability" (Mirvis & Seashore, 1979, p. 767). In our experience, blatant attempts to coerce members into participating in the consultation process are fairly rare. In many ways, because they represent such flagrant violations of the principle of informed consent, consultants might find these offenses easier to address than more subtle forms of pressure or coercion that might appear ambiguous or open to interpretation. In a similar vein, members of the organization might attribute a level of power to the consultant that might make them reluctant to decline to participate. In any of these cases, consultants must seriously consider the threat of such dynamics to the rights of members within the organization to freely choose not to participate, and to do so without fear of retribution. The absence of fear of retribution is a high standard, because power inequalities, both real and imagined, must be overcome to achieve the standard.

## Issues in Compliance Elicitation

It is worth noting that efforts by organizations to elicit compliance by members with regard to participation in the consultation process do not necessarily stem from bad or malicious motives. On the contrary, such efforts can be the result of a genuine desire to foster broad representation of organizational units in the change process, and to promote inclusion of individuals and groups within the organization. In many cases, the concept of informed consent might be unfamiliar to organizational leaders and members. For this reason, ensuring that individuals' rights to informed consent are protected requires that consultants assume a proactive role in discussing the meaning and practical implications of this very important concept with all involved. This discussion can and should be empowering to participants.

An important question that arises in this context is whether or not an individual retains his or her right to informed consent in an organizational setting. Mirvis and Seashore (1979), addressing organizational research specifically, questioned the meaning of informed consent when individuals' contracts for employment stipulate participation in such activities. In organizational consultation, does organizational-level informed consent exist? Can a representative of the organization provide consent on behalf of organizational members that supersedes their individual rights? These are important and difficult questions. Although organizations can legally mandate participation in a consultation process as a condition of employment, we urge that consulting psychologists be extremely cautious in endorsing or participating in any practice that undermines individuals' moral and ethical rights to self-determination. As an ethical matter, individuals do not inherently forfeit their rights to informed consent merely as a function of their employment by the organization. Given the central role of informed consent in other domains of psychological practice, its thoughtful application in organizational contexts is imperative.

As a general ethical principle, informed consent has received considerable attention in the ethical literature. Likewise, the Ethical Principles of Psychologists and Code of Conduct (American Psychological Association [APA], 1992) ascribe a fairly prominent role to informed consent, although generally address only one-on-one situations. One of the results of this kind of attention has been that psychologists, as well as institutions in which they work, have taken great care to develop policies and written contracts thoroughly delineating the conditions relevant to informed consent that anticipate and satisfy relevant legal and mandatory ethical requirements. As noted by Jordan and Meara (1999), the focus has been largely on the specific information to which a client is rightly entitled. However, these authors pointed out that "there is yet a more subtle but equally important ethical issue that concerns *how* the client will be told" (p. 143); that is, from a moral perspective, *how* the truth is spoken is as relevant as *what* truth is spoken. By focusing exclusively on the content of informed consent, important relational and process dimensions might be overlooked. The relationship between the consultant and participants might be reduced to a legal agreement based on the consultant's responsibilities and participants' rights. The risk exists that participants might be perceived, or perceive themselves, as passive recipients of the services being provided, as opposed to active, responsible, and mutually involved parties to the relationship (Jordan & Meara, 1999). Part of organizational consultation is empowering participants to assume active roles in, and accept responsibility for, what happens to them in their work lives. A major mechanism for achieving this kind of empowerment is the nature of the working relationships that are negotiated between the consultant and members of the consultee system.

# CONFIDENTIALITY

The fundamental role of confidentiality among the ethical principles in psychology is well captured by the following statement:

> Except for the ultimate precept—above all, do no harm—there is probably no ethical value in psychology that is more inculcated than confidentiality. Whether psychologists are engaging in research; assessing children, families, employees, criminal defendants, or others; or providing any of the several forms of psychological intervention—regardless of whether they are employed in private or public settings—they know that they bear responsibility for protecting information disclosed to them in the context of a professional relationship. Yet, there is probably no ethical duty more misunderstood or honored by its breach rather than by its fulfillment [Bersoff, 1999, p. 149].

Despite the central role that confidentiality has played in our general discourse regarding professional ethics, relatively little has been written regarding its specific application in organizational contexts. Not surprisingly, protecting the confidentiality of information obtained from participants involved in the consultation process presents a variety of special challenges (Newman & Robinson, 1991). For example, the fact that numerous individuals might be involved in the consultation process and have legitimate access to the data collected creates real limitations on the extent to which confidentiality can be ensured.

Consequently, consultants must openly acknowledge the very real constraints that exist with respect to their ability to ensure confidentiality. Individuals' rights to informed consent are contingent on their understanding of these constraints. At the same time, it is important that consultants do all they can to maximize the likelihood that confidentiality will become a norm in circumstances where sensitive data exist or where disclosure might result in harm to organizational members. Engaging participants in open dialogue regarding issues of confidentiality early in the process is an important step in cultivating a norm of confidentiality. Ongoing discussion of confidentiality issues as they emerge is also essential. Defining confidentiality as a shared responsibility between the consultant and members of the consultee system promotes a collaborative approach to handling such matters.

## Power Differentials

Special sensitivity to the potential impact of the power differential among various organizational members is necessary. Consultants should anticipate that some less-powerful members of the organization might feel uncomfortable at the prospect of sharing information that might be perceived as personally risky, such as discontent with organizational policies, concerns about the competence of a supervisor, and so forth. Threats of sanctions for sharing such information might or might not be real. Nevertheless, the consultant has an obligation to do everything possible to protect participants from negative consequences that might result from their participation in the consultation process. As noted earlier, part of ensuring informed consent is delineating the potential costs, benefits, and risks of participating with organizational members. Occasionally, a given participant might request to share information privately with the consultant. This situation creates an interesting dilemma for the consultant. On the one hand, by declining to hear the information privately, the consultant risks losing access to information that might be essential to understanding the issues that are the focus of consultation. Temporary or permanent damage to the consultant's relationship with the individual wishing to share the information can also occur. On the other hand, by agreeing to listen to the privately shared information, the consultant might discover that he or she is in possession of critical information regarding organizational difficulties that cannot be used due to the promise of confidentiality to the sharer of the information. Agreeing to enter into a private relationship with that individual might also undermine trust in the consultant's relationships with other organizational participants. Generally, a desirable outcome in this case would be to convince the individual of the value in openly sharing the information so that it can be available for inclusion and use in the consultation process. Obviously, there might be times when the individual decides that the potential risks of sharing the information openly are too great, in which case the consultant has another decision to make. Such situations reflect the complex nature of confidentiality in organizational contexts. Addressing this complexity, Lowman (1998) noted that there are times when psychologists are forced to balance competing ethical interests and obligations. In some circumstances, it might be possible to determine a course of action that meets the needs and interests of all parties. When such is not the case, Lowman suggested that the psychologist might need to consider satisfying (that is, good enough) rather than optimizing (that is, optimal) solutions. Of course, this is an important moral (as well as professional) judgment.

# DUAL RELATIONSHIPS

Dual or multiple role relationships have been defined as "those situations in which the psychologist functions in more than one professional relationship, as well as those in which the psychologist functions in a professional role and another definitive and intended role (as opposed to a limited and inconsequential role growing out of and limited to a chance encounter)" (Sonne, 1994, p. 336). Specific risks associated with such relationships delineated in the current ethics code include loss of objectivity, and exploitation of the client by the psychologist. Koocher and Keith-Spiegel (1998) identified additional risks as "confusion, feelings of rejection and abandonment, and misrepresentation of communications that result in a distortion of the relationship" (p. 174). For the most part, risks associated with dual relationships have been discussed in the context of psychotherapeutic relationships. Although the nature and extent of their impact might be somewhat different when applied to consultation, consultants must be cognizant of the potential harm that can result from their failure to effectively manage relationships within the organization. Furthermore, consultants must recognize that harm might result not only to individuals directly involved in the dual relationship, but to other members of the organizational system as well.

It could be argued that dual relationships constitute a special issue in consulting psychology because, in many respects, they might be more the norm than the exception. For example, it is quite common for a consulting contact to emerge through a pre-existing relationship between the consultant and a member of the consultee system, such as a former colleague or student. Furthermore, the nature of consulting relationships often requires extended or repetitive periods during which the consultant is working closely with members of the consultee system. By its very nature, this kind of extensive interaction between individuals inevitably might lead, in some cases, to the development of relationships that might be more personal and more reciprocal in nature than might generally be true of what is permitted in the context of traditional psychotherapeutic relationships. In addition, consulting relationships, by definition, focus on work-related problems. The consultant and members of the consultee system are professionals in their respective domains. The doctor-patient dimension is absent from the consulting relationship in that there is no presumption of psychological or behavioral impairment of participants. The consultant and organizational participants bring to the relationship different areas of expertise, all of which are needed to effectively complete the goals and objectives of consultation. This is not to say the consultant will not encounter members within an organization who are in need of psychological assistance. On the contrary, such encounters should be expected. However, the consultant's relationships with such individuals will not typically be therapeutic in nature. In cases where psychotherapy is indicated, appropriate referrals should be made. Because consulting relationships are distinct in fundamental ways from psychotherapeutic relationships, concerns regarding the potential impact of dual relationships on participants in consultation might be somewhat different in either or both degree and kind.

## Professional Judgment

The major implication of the forgoing discussion is that issues related to dual relationships in organizational consultation are likely to require more from the consulting psychologist in the way of professional judgment. For example, consider the case in which a consultant is hired on the basis of his or her relationship with a member of the consultee system. The consultant in this case needs to be aware of several potential pitfalls. First, how might the consultant's perspective be influenced by information received from the individual with whom a previous relationship existed? Second, what, if any, expectations might this individual have in terms of access to or influence on the consultant? Third, how might others in the organization perceive the consultant's relationship with this individual, and how might their perceptions affect their relationships with the consultant?

More broadly, consultants must be aware that the emergence of dual or multiple relationships poses a continuous threat when consulting with organizations. Consider the example discussed earlier regarding the individual requesting to share information privately with the consultant. Suppose the information pertains to concerns that a particular manager has a drinking problem that is affecting his or her performance on the job. If the consultant agrees to receive the information confidentially, what are the potential effects of such a decision? It could be said that a dual relationship with the sharer of the secret has been created. The consultant now has one relationship with the individual that is open and known by others, and another relationship with the same individual that is private, based upon information unavailable to other participants. The dual nature of this relationship might govern not only the way the consultant relates to the sharer of the secret, but to others as well. The consultant's perceptions of (and relationship to) the manager are probably forever changed. Furthermore, the possession of both public and private information is likely to influence how the consultant interacts with other members of the consultee system. It should also be noted that consultants' involvements in dual relationships might not always be volitional. It is easily foreseeable that information such as that in the above example might be shared spontaneously, without prior authorization, by the consultant. The implications for the consultant's relationships with members of the consultee system would be largely the same.

## Bartering

An evolving issue pertaining to dual relationships relates to the form of compensation received in exchange for consulting services. In the past few years, a small number of consultants have reported accepting stock options or other ownership interests in exchange for their services. This kind of arrangement is akin to bartering, and might introduce a variety of potential ethical problems (APA, 1992, sect. 1.18). It is possible that ownership interests in a company could affect the consultant's judgment as it relates to pursued goals and objectives. For example, consider the situation in which a consultant holds an increasing share of stock in a company while consulting with that company regarding downsizing options for staff that will be terminated. Providing placement services for employees targeted for layoffs might be presented as a helpful but expensive program. The consultant clearly has two roles in the decision-making process. The first is an ownership role in which cash dividends might be lost as a result of providing the placement program. The second role is as a process helper obligated to act in the best interests of all of those who will be affected by the decision. Admittedly, it might be possible for a consulting psychologist to objectively weigh the competing interests associated with these two roles. However, this practice of compensation by ownership interests does seem to create a potential conflict of roles and interests that we believe can and should be avoided.

Given the complex pattern of relationships that exists in organizational consultation, the potential for harm resulting from dual relationships is substantial. Consultants must be keenly sensitive to the fact that the threat of dual relationships must be an ongoing concern. In light of the potentially grave consequences of dual relationships for individuals and organizations alike, we concur with the strong position advocated by Lowman (1998): "While some dual relationships (such as sexually exploitive ones) are obviously and egregiously wrong, others, more subtle and difficult to detect, may create conditions no less problematic. Dual relationships, while not per se unethical, create considerable opportunity for conflict and exploitation and are best avoided. At the least, they need to be identified and ethically managed. Such relationships need not actually be destructive to the parties involved to be a problem or to create a perception of difficulties" (p. 129).

# CONSULTANT COMPETENCE

The issue of competence has been the focus of ongoing attention and concern in psychology for some time. Given the diverse nature of psychological practice, a single set of competency standards is recognized as impractical. A more realistic approach has been to focus efforts on delineating dimensions of competency within specialty areas of psychology. Such efforts have been complicated, however, by confusion regarding what constitutes a specialty or subspecialty, a proficiency, or an area of expertise within the discipline of psychology (Koocher & Keith-Spiegel, 1998). Defining competency in organizational consulting psychology, in particular, has been an interesting challenge. Unlike other, more established specialty areas, consulting psychology has not had the benefit of established training programs and well-defined academic curricula that typically reflect, directly or indirectly, essential competency areas. Until recently, there have been no formal training programs specifically designed to prepare consulting psychologists. In the absence of such programs, there have not really been effective, systematic efforts to define and articulate specific competencies for consulting psychologists. Psychologists who engage in consulting psychology have, historically, been psychologists whose primary training has been in other specialties, such as counseling, clinical, or I-O psychology (Robinson-Kurpius, Fuqua, Gibson, Kurpius, & Froehle, 1995). Thus, the competencies of psychologists engaged in the practice of organizational consulting psychology have themselves been diverse in nature and scope. There has not been a single profile or professional training path for consulting psychologists.

## Personal Responsibility

A major theme of this chapter is the emphasis on the personal responsibility of the organizational consultant in ensuring ethical practice. There is perhaps no area in which this requirement is more crucial than in the area of competence. The inherent complexity of the organizational context, and the multiplex of needs and demands that exist within an organization, create the opportunity to provide a broad range of consulting services. Frankly, there are some real pressures placed upon consulting psychologists from the market place to do it all. Consultants must be cautious in judgments regarding which of those needed services they can rightly provide as a function of their training and experience, or without further supervision. It is incumbent on consultants to know their specific competencies, and to limit their work to areas appropriately matched to those competencies. Consultants must be willing to decline to provide services for which they are not qualified. A basic reality is that no one is qualified to provide every kind of service needed by even a medium-sized organization. Consulting psychologists whose primary training is in other specialties are reliant on competencies defined by those specialties, and must, therefore, extrapolate competencies from those specialties and apply them to the consulting context. This process places a heavy burden on the individual consulting psychologist for making judgments regarding his or her specific competencies in the consulting arena. It should also be noted that clients served by consulting psychologists are often relatively naïve regarding what services they can appropriately request from a consulting psychologist. In that sense, these clients are *dependent consumers;* that is, they are reliant upon the consultant to assist them in identifying those services that can realistically and appropriately be part of the consulting contract.

Fortunately, a significant step toward defining competencies in the area of consulting psychology has recently been made in the form of *Principles for Education and Training at the Doctoral and Post-Doctoral Level in Consulting Psychology (APA, 1999),* developed specifically to delineate competencies relevant to the practice of organizational consulting psychology. An important feature of the *principles* is their acknowledgement that required competencies can largely be acquired through channels other than completion of a formal training program specifically designated as consulting psychology. The *principles* concede that considerable training relevant for consulting psychology can be acquired through programs in other specialty areas within psychology. Another important feature of the proposed *principles* is that they emphasize intended competencies or *end states,* as opposed to delineating required coursework or curricula. This approach acknowledges that there are multiple avenues to acquiring required competencies. A third quality of the *principles* is their endorsement of the scientist-practitioner philosophy of training, embracing the notion that the practice of consulting psychology must be guided by the science of psychology.

Recommended competencies in the proposed *principles* have been organized around three broad areas of expertise: individual, group, and organizational. An underlying assumption of this framework is that at least minimal knowledge and skill within each area is required to effectively respond to the complex demands of the organizational context. Furthermore, it is assumed that consultants to organizations will routinely be called upon to utilize competencies from all three areas simultaneously, and in an integrative manner.

Consulting psychologists should familiarize themselves with these *principles,* and apply them in evaluating their own areas of competence. Accurate self-assessment might be the single most potent safeguard against violation of the competence principle. For those consulting psychologists who determine that they lack requisite knowledge and skill in a given area, there are many potential avenues for remediating such deficits, such as formal coursework, supervised practice, apprenticeships, and so forth. The importance of self-monitoring in the area of competence cannot be overemphasized. Reliance on external governing bodies to ensure competent practice is unrealistic and impractical.

## MANAGEMENT VERSUS HELPING PERSPECTIVES

Although it has not been well addressed in the literature, there has been some historical tension between management and psychology. Management has historically emphasized production systems approaches to organizations, while psychology has emphasized human factors and human process issues. While there has been progress in integrating these perspectives, some tendency toward separation still exists. Consulting psychologists who work in business settings often acquire considerable knowledge about management systems and theories. Managers who wish to be effective will likewise acquire some human process skills. Nevertheless, psychologists typically place substantial emphasis on the quality of human life, whereas most managers are at least somewhat more narrowly focused on concerns about production.

When consultants do emphasize quality-of-life indicators, they run the risk of being referred to as soft, or by some other term intended to reflect a basic naïveté about the hard facts of business life. Frankly, we believe that a little softness in this sense in organizational life can be a good thing. Most psychologists trying to earn consulting contracts in business organizations, however, do not want to be thought of as soft by their colleagues or potential clients. There is some tension, therefore, in integrating the two positions; that is, wanting to improve the quality of life for people in the organization and for the client system, and also wanting to earn contracts awarded primarily by managers who are very concerned about profitability.

## Psychologists versus Managers

At a recent conference attended primarily by consulting psychologists, someone made a statement to the effect that "Maybe every consultant should have an MBA." This statement reflects the awareness by those who consult in organizational settings that business models for management are different from psychological models for helping and change. This statement mirrors the common perception that organizational consultation is influenced heavily by management practices and perspectives. Although there are very strong arguments against this perspective, the historical differences in psychological and management positions are the main concern here.

One difference in the perspectives of management and psychology is the outcome orientation. Overgeneralizing for the purpose of illustration, managers generally have a strong tendency to focus on production, believing they must convince others that by improving production, the organization will be able to increase the quality of life for members. Psychologists, on the other hand, tend to focus more on process and human factors. Consulting psychologists have, historically, spent much time trying to help managers focused on production to shift their perspectives to include the role and function of human factors and processes as they relate to production. In a sense, the perceived challenge has often been to convince managers that the improvements in the quality of life for members of the organization will lead to enhanced productivity. Thus, OD and other kinds of developmental models have often been marketed to managers as a means of enhancing production. Fortunately, improved theories of organizational behavior have helped both psychology and management to develop more mature understandings of the relationship between the quality of life in an organization and the production potential of that organization. There is now acknowledgment of a reciprocal relationship between quality of life and productivity.

Exclusively emphasizing either profit motives or social interests is naïve. These dimensions are intricately related. Consulting psychology practiced in the marketplace can lead to increasingly humanized work settings that will be optimally profitable. In this context, the fact that most consulting contracts are awarded by those in management positions might lead to conflicts of interest within the organization. The consultant can find him- or herself in the position of helping to develop management strategies that might increase profitability at the cost of employee welfare. Is this an activity in which psychologists should participate? Should behavioral science be used to help manipulate employees into positions not in their best interests?

Proactively, consulting psychologists use empirically based behavioral theory to help organizations maximize their potential. They educate managers about sound organizational principles from a behavioral perspective. They take responsibility for the impact of their interventions on all those affected by the change. They encourage the valuing of inclusion in planning change, because it leads to better outcomes, in addition to protecting the dignity of those with less power in the system. They refrain from profiting from the avoidable misery of others.

The ethical and moral implications of working in a free market economy can be serious. Managers will sometimes make short-term, profit-oriented decisions that can be harmful to employees or clients. Sometimes, profit motives can drive decision-making at the top levels of an organization. There are often motives for excluding people from the planning process. Restrictions of access to information are sometimes necessary. Competitive norms might lead individuals to socially destructive behaviors. Economic self-interests might compete with motives to build strong, healthy communities. Consultants have to be aware of these realities prior to entering the system.

There is a very natural partnership between business interests and consulting psychology. People spend substantial portions of their time living and working in organizations. The knowledge base of consulting psychology is extremely relevant to building and maintaining healthy social systems. Principles of planned human change can be easily transported across settings, and the clinical skills possessed by psychologists can be invaluable in managing organizations. However, there is a constant potential for values conflicts between psychology and free enterprise. The ethical practice of consulting psychology in such settings requires an intimate knowledge of the moral and ethical foundations of our practice.

# LEVEL OF INTERVENTION

One of the key factors that determines the nature of relationships in organizational consultation is the level of the change effort (Newman, 1993; Newman & Robinson, 1991; Snow & Gersick, 1986). Consultants might intervene with individuals, small groups, organizational units, whole organizations, or any combination of these. This potential variability in intervention levels has dramatic implications for the ethical practice of consulting psychology.

Because of the complexity of organizations and the interrelatedness of organizational subsystems, interventions focused at the individual level can have profound implications for others in the organization. As a simple example, suppose a CEO invites a consultant into an industrial setting to help with some management problems. In an initial meeting, the consultant learns that a newly promoted vice president for operations has experienced problems with subordinates and been the target of numerous complaints. The CEO asks for executive coaching as an intervention for helping the vice president cope with the social demands of the job. Now, this might be a reasonable request for services, but who is the client here? Does the VP have the right to refuse participation? If the intervention is unsuccessful, who will be harmed? What, if any, responsibility does the consultant have to the subordinates who are directly involved? Generally, what questions must be answered before the service contract is confirmed?

In the preceding example, if the consultant agrees to the request for service *as presented*, she or he enters into a contract in which the CEO and the vice president are cast as clients. Of course, the accessibility of each participant to data generated in the intervention must be carefully defined. A major problem, however, relates to the subordinates with whom the original complaints resided. What impact is the intervention likely to have on them? In fact, the vice president already has an inordinate access to power relative to the subordinates. What, if any, rights do the subordinates have in this situation? How could any social intervention with the vice president be delivered without seriously affecting subordinates in the process? It seems imperative to again point out that the consultant retains a broad moral responsibility for his or her impact on the system. This can conflict, though, with the relationship configuration of the contract. The consultant might agree with the premise that some discomfort might be experienced by the subordinates, but that eventually they stand to benefit from the increased skill development of the vice president. This seems reasonable, but who has the right to commit the subordinates to the risk and discomfort of an incompetent superior in the learning stages? What are the moral implications of such a commitment? In very specific terms, how should the consultant share in this inherent moral responsibility?

According to Kralj (2001), "Coaching at the executive level of organizations most often includes a blend of individual, team, and organizational interventions" (p. 108). Furthermore, the interdependent, systemic nature of organizations means that wherever the consultant enters or contracts with an organization, the effects of intervening and the intervention itself will likely have broader organizational effects. How does the consultant share responsibility for these widespread organizational effects? Is it possible, from a moral perspective, to extricate oneself from residual effects of an organizational intervention? We believe the answer is no. Few consulting psychologists would deny our unequivocal response to this question. The next question is much more difficult. Given the premise that consultants are responsible for the broadest implications of their interventions and their inevitable impact on the quality of life for others, how do consulting psychologists exercise their moral responsibility to the client system?

Consultants often find themselves in the paradoxical situation of having moral responsibility for intervention effects they cannot foresee or control. This is an impossible situation, but it gets worse. By the nature of the contract, the consultant might be limited to a single person or group of people in terms of confidentiality parameters. Consequently, it is possible that the consultant might identify some systemic outcome that has strongly negative implications for some other sector(s) of the organization, but is restricted from directly intervening due to parameters of confidentiality. In such a case, the consultant endeavors to influence the consultee individual or group to intervene as an indirect route of influence, but ultimately forfeits the right to intervene directly due to the pre-eminence of confidentiality in almost all cases. This situation seems incredible, but it carries with it the full force of professional ethical codes, and, even more importantly, civil law.

Many dimensions of organizational life are affected by the hierarchical nature of organizations. The uneven distribution of power across levels creates a great potential for abuse of those with less power. In many organizations, substantial inequalities of power are observed horizontally as well as vertically. Communication is not evenly distributed across levels of an organization, so it is easy for those with less information to be at risk for mistreatment of some kind. As noted earlier, informed consent requires full disclosure of information regarding what is being consented to prior to the consent. In contexts in which information about a change process is unevenly distributed, personal consent to participate is questionable. It is a very important observation that mistreatment of the less powerful members of an organization is not only immoral—it is also extremely poor organizational strategy. We contend that any lack of inclusion of the least powerful members of an organization will lead to reduced functioning. Though special consideration of those with restricted access to power is a moral mandate for psychologists, it is also an essential component in building effective organizations.

The importance of having clear and mutually understood contracts for the consulting relationship cannot be overestimated. Experienced consultants anticipate the potential ethical issues imposed by contracts developed within multi-leveled organizations, and try to help the consultee accommodate them at the contractual stage of the relationship. The parameters of confidentiality and the difficult issues associated with this concept in organizational contexts are addressed at length elsewhere in this chapter. Having a clear sense of personal and professional values prior to contracting with clients is essential in avoiding compromising moral situations. Once the situation develops, one's objectivity is already threatened, and the advice of outside professionals might be required to design a reasonable course of action.

# ETHICAL ISSUES IN ORGANIZATIONAL ASSESSMENT

It has been argued for many years that effective organizational interventions are necessarily based on valid and reliable information (Argyris, 1970). The complex and varied structures of organizations can create complicated assessment targets and objectives. Systems-level change efforts can require extensive databases in problem definition, intervention, and operational phases. Many ethical principles (most notably, confidentiality, informed consent, and competency) are necessary to adequately comprehend the range of ethical dilemmas posed by assessment activities in the organizational setting. The fact that system-, group-, and individual-level assessment data are often required in consultation activities can multiply the ethical challenges presented.

Concerning individual-level assessment, legal requirements and issues can have a strong bearing on assessment practices. Carroll, Schneider, and Wesley (1985), addressing I-O psychologists in particular, made a compelling observation regarding the relationship of the law and ethics:

> Even though I-O psychologists have legitimate concerns about the legal aspects of their work, they also should be aware that morality, at times, supersedes legality. Ethically speaking, they should be more concerned with trying to ensure fair treatment of those whom they may affect than with what is merely legal. Morality may require going beyond what is merely legally acceptable. And because of the strong emphasis on legality in the I-O area, it may be even more important that psychologists who work in that field be aware of ethical issues. For when legality is overemphasized, ethics tend to be ignored [p. 155].

Employees, as members of organizations, have certain protections under the law, but the ethical standard for their treatment must include consideration that goes well beyond their legal rights. Employing organizations can legally require participation of employees in planned change efforts against their best interests. We believe psychologists must be extraordinarily careful about participating in, or even tolerating, the use of coercion to force submission to assessment procedures. It is easily seen that the use of coercion for these purposes can violate the most basic principle of doing no harm. Protecting the welfare of others requires even more assertive positions in such circumstances.

## Power and Authority Issues

One of the persistent problems in applying the principle of informed consent to assessment in the organizational context is the unequal distribution of power and authority that is typical of most organizations. Power does not necessarily follow lines of authority, either. Individuals in organizations are very creative in building bridges of influence that give them access to power on an informal basis. Informal access to power is not always easily seen or understood by those external to the organization, which can be devastating to a consultant at times. The problem of power distribution is that once one is perceived as being powerful, this perception is not easily changed. A manager might formally indicate that employees are free to decline participation in an assessment without prejudice, but can employees distinguish the formal permission from the informal wishes of a person perceived and validated as someone who has power over their employment and career? More pointedly, can an external consultant control the private perceptions of power and influence that existed prior to his or her entry into the system, and that will persist after the consultation process is completed? If not, can the element of coercion truly be removed so that informed consent can truly be given prior to submitting to assessment procedures? Incidentally, this dilemma is not limited to assessment procedures.

Confidentiality of assessment data is another difficult issue in organizational consultation. In individual relationships, the psychologist can ensure that confidentiality is maintained. In organizational work, a consultant's ability to ensure confidentiality is quite limited. First, assessment data in organizational contexts must usually be shared to have their optimal effects. Once the data are shared, the psychologist loses the ability to personally ensure confidentiality, and must share the responsibility with others in the setting.

There are other problems related to ensuring confidentiality of assessment data in organizational settings. Suppose that a manager is evaluated using survey data as part of a leadership development program, and two units express dissatisfaction with the manager. The manager might not have access to data identifying individuals, but only to aggregate data at the unit level. After the consultation has been completed and the consultant has exited the system, the manager might still have access to the unit identities of his or her critics. The potential for retaliative harm here is obvious. As part of an intervention, identifying specific units might seem essential, but it creates an exposure to potential harm that might not be realized until well after the consultant has lost all influence in the system.

Furthermore, suppose that a consultant agrees to share some assessment data with a management team for planning purposes, but first asks the team to agree to maintain strict confidentiality of the shared information. After the completion of the consultation intervention, though, the consultant cannot remove access to the information. Multiple uses of the information might be made after the consultant leaves, even though the group maintains the rules of confidentiality. In this case, the consultant cannot ensure informed consent due to the uses of the data unknown to the consultant. Furthermore, expecting others who have vested interests to respect the psychological principle of confidentiality is not very realistic in organizations where conflicts of interest across levels are routine. Even when the initial intentions are good, there is a tendency for deterioration of the commitment over time and contexts.

# ETHICS OF INTERVENTION

The range of services that psychologists might provide in the consulting role vary widely. It is difficult to accurately characterize consulting psychology as a homogeneous set of integrated activities. In reality, consulting psychologists engage in a wide variety of interventions in organizational settings. The interventions that consulting psychologists market to an often naïve public are central to understanding the most essential parameters of ethical practice. Section 1.06 of the APA ethics code states that "Psychologists rely on scientifically and professionally derived knowledge when making scientific or professional judgments or when engaging in scholarly or professional endeavors" (APA, 1992, p. 1600). An essential question relates to the knowledge base underlying the practice of consulting psychology. A more pointed question might ask, is there a research base for consulting psychology? Gibson and Froehle (1991) reviewed the research literature and reported a substantial empirical database for organizational interventions. They reiterated the ethical principle above: "It is imperative for consulting practitioners to remain flexible and to incorporate research findings into the decision rules they use when selecting organizational interventions" (p. 18). Gibson and Froehle admirably pushed the standard even higher by stating that "consultants will increasingly be expected to accurately anticipate negative residual effects as well as direct positive effects that are likely to accompany a particular intervention design when conducted under a particular set of conditions and circumstances" (p. 18). This is not to say that professional judgment is unimportant. Newman (1993) pointed out that although empirical data cannot provide hard and fast recipes for selecting consulting interventions, the empirical literature can be useful in delineating both technical and ethical parameters of interventions.

Blanton (2000) reported that a sample of members of the Society of Consulting Psychology ranked empirical studies relatively low in terms of value to their practice. This survey was based on only an 11 percent response rate, so it must be viewed cautiously, but it does reinforce the idea that existing empirical research is not totally prescriptive in terms of consulting practices. It would also be interesting to actually observe what consultants are doing (in addition to self-reports) to see if their selected interventions can be related to empirical bases in the literature.

Blanton (2000) also identified four factors that she believed contributed to the limited use of empirical research as a basis for practice: (1) the quantity of research available is inadequate; (2) research is not relevant to the practice of most consultants; (3) theory and concepts in consulting psychology are poorly defined; and (4) consultation is a dialectic practice, not an applied technology. To the extent these propositions are accurate, a great deal of responsibility must reside with the practitioner. As reflected in Section 1.06 of the APA ethics code, the consulting psychologist is ethically obligated to access the most current empirical evidence (APA, 1992). Beyond that, though, it is clear that well-supported theory, personal experience, shared experience, and sound reasoning are all meaningful sources of professional judgment in developing, selecting, and applying interventions that optimize outcomes for organizational clients. The value, then, of providing extensive dialogues among more and less experienced consultants seems enormous. We see little value in arguing the relative importance of empirical research, theory, and experience, as we believe that each is necessary in ensuring competent and ethical practice. The key to the ethical practice of consulting psychology seems to be to integrate the best of the existing knowledge base in a particular context. This ability to demonstrate the validity of interventions has important legal and ethical implications for consulting psychologists.

## Empirical Findings and Professional Judgment

Despite the growing empirical database related to organizational intervention, however, considerable professional judgment is still involved in the recommendations consultants must make regarding intervention. What information should be disclosed to the consultee organization or its representative(s)? Is the consultee entitled to an understanding of the distinction between empirical evidence and professional judgment based on experience as the basis for selecting a particular intervention? What are the implications of promoting an untried intervention over some other interventions that have been demonstrated to be at least partially successful in empirical studies? How flexible should the consultant be in helping a consultee with a preferred or chosen intervention when she or he has reason to believe that the consultee-preferred option is less likely to be effective? It is unethical to withhold relevant information about the efficacy of interventions from a consultee when it is available in the literature. This is especially true when access to the information might reasonably be expected to affect consultee decision-making. It also is critical to present that kind of technical information in a form understandable to the consultee.

The nature of the consultee system in the consideration of interventions necessitates considerable ethical deliberation. For example, what if a consultant is working with a management team when it becomes clear that a staff development program for advancing current staff into management positions will be much more expensive than simply hiring experienced staff from outside the company. By its nature, this decision is value laden. If the consultant's contract limits the consultant's responsibility to the team, what responsibility does the consultant have ethically to others in the organization who will experience lost opportunities if outside managers are hired as a cost-reduction strategy? Will these staff people be harmed? What are the consequences financially to the company? Should the consultant be responsible for the broader economic health of the company as this decision gets made? If the managerial team has personal profit investments (for example, profit sharing motives) that differ from those of other organizational members, should the consultant promote a more inclusive decision-making model? What if the organization is unionized and there is a competitive culture? Is the consultant then relieved of moral and ethical responsibility to union members? We contend that he or she is not. These kinds of conflicts of interests within the consultee system are almost routine. Consultants have a moral and ethical responsibility to protect the interests of all those who will be affected by interventions they help design and promote. Consulting psychologists should refuse to engage in interventions that have the potential to harm organizational members in any way. From a process point of view, pointing out the philosophical and values implications of interventions, and including such implications in deliberations, are imperative. Assisting the consultee group in taking responsibility for the moral implications of their choices is central to effective psychological consultation in organizations.

Some have made the distinction between *technical adequacy* and *ethical adequacy* as the concepts apply to interventions (Newman, 1993; Snow & Gersick, 1986). Broadly speaking, the technical adequacy of an intervention is based on the extent to which the objectives for its use are met. The ethical adequacy of an intervention would involve a general consideration of its impact in protecting the welfare, generally defined, of all those affected by the intervention. In practice, these two concepts are highly interdependent and complementary. Organizational outcomes will likely be enhanced by a careful and thorough consideration of both dimensions. This perspective, consistently addressed in the consultation process, has the potential to move beyond adherence to a marginally relevant set of behavioral guidelines for ethical conduct, toward creating a helping process that is fundamentally moral in its character. This is what ethics in the organizational context should be about.

## ASPIRING TO MORAL AND ETHICAL INFLUENCE

It might seem a little peculiar to hear organizational consultation described as a moral enterprise, but this premise is fundamental to the discussion presented in this chapter. Carroll et al. (1985) asserted that "issues that are moral arise when a person's welfare can be affected by another" (p. 2). Clearly, others' welfare is constantly being affected in organizational consultation, and in the case of large, complex organizations that serve substantive client systems, the potential impact of organizational interventions can be phenomenal. An important question to be considered by consulting psychologists, both individually and collectively as a profession, is: What role should moral and ethical considerations play in consulting psychology practice? Likewise, Newman, Gray, and Fuqua (1996) posed several related, yet more specific, questions including the following: Should consultation be used as a vehicle for helping an organization define what it considers to be right and good? What, if any, responsibility does a consultant have for facilitating consideration of such matters by members of an organization? What should the nature of moral discourse be in organizations engaged in the consulting process?

## Moral Decisions and Moral Obligations

There are two assumptions implicit in these questions. The first assumption is that the person of the consultant is inherently and intricately linked to his or her professional judgments, decisions, and conduct. The importance of this notion is, perhaps, best exemplified by the concept of virtue ethics. *Virtue ethics* and *principle ethics* have been conceptualized as distinct but complementary perspectives (Jordan & Meara, 1999). Principle ethics refer to the prioritization and application of universal principles in the analysis and resolution of specific ethical dilemmas. The Ethical Standards section of the Ethical Principles of Psychologists and Code of Conduct (APA, 1992) largely represents an attempt to operationalize principle ethics. The focus in the case of principle ethics is on a specific action designed to respond to the guiding question, What shall I do? By contrast, virtue ethics emphasize the character of the actor (that is, internal traits, habits, personal values) in response to the question, Who shall I be? As with Jordan and Meara, we believe that principle ethics play an essential role in guiding professional practice. However, given the diverse nature of the professional activities of psychologists, and the complex nature of most ethical dilemmas, it is neither feasible nor even desirable that a professional ethics code specifically addresses the full range of possible dilemmas that professional psychologists might encounter in the course of their practice. Consequently, the effectiveness of any ethics code in fostering high standards of ethical practice will inevitably be highly influenced by the character and motives of those applying it. In making this very point, Newman et al. (1996) suggested that "it is the steward of the principles who determines their impact more so than the content of the principles themselves" (p. 231).

The second assumption implicit in these questions is that the consultant bears some degree of personal responsibility to ensure that moral and ethical considerations are part of the dialogue that occurs during consultation. This is perhaps a more controversial issue. Not all consulting psychologists would necessarily agree that actively promoting the exploration and examination of moral and ethical issues *in the course* of organizational consultation is necessary, or even appropriate. While we acknowledge and respect perspectives different from our own, we believe that organizational consultation is an inherently moral enterprise, with potentially life-changing implications for those who are directly or indirectly affected by it. For example, even seemingly minor changes in an organization's leave policy can have a significant impact on the personal and family lives of employees. Similarly, reductions in services to reduce costs by a mental health agency can create serious hardships for clients who might lack access to alternative sources of help. These kinds of organizational decisions have clear and potentially profound moral implications for individuals who might have no involvement in the decision-making process. Equally important, what might the potential implications of such decisions be for those who do participate in the decision-making process? Have they participated in the decision-making process only after a full and informed consideration of the potential moral and ethical implications of the decision(s) being made?

Although there are reasonable grounds for debating a consultant's personal responsibility for moral issues arising during, or deriving from, a consulting relationship, abdicating responsibility for the moral outcomes for others is unethical. Some consulting psychologists might be reluctant to actively promote the consideration of moral and ethical issues by participants in routine consulting contacts, and probably for a variety of different reasons. Furthermore, in most cases, there is nothing in the APA ethics code that specifically requires a consulting psychologist to actively facilitate consideration of the moral and ethical implications of decisions made by an organization. Thus, a consulting psychologist who chooses not to embrace the kind of advocacy role being advanced here would likely be in compliance with mandatory ethics, that is, the "minimum requirements for professional performance via prescriptive guidelines and behavioral rules" (Newman et al., 1996, p. 230).

Striving to achieve a minimum standard of performance in the ethical arena is inadequate. We would suggest that the profession of organizational consulting psychology, as well as those who are served or affected by it, would benefit substantially from pursuit of a much higher standard. *Aspirational ethics* provide a more useful guiding framework in this regard, with their emphasis on pursuing *maximal* moral and ethical outcomes. Aspirational ethics serve as the basis for the Preamble and the General Principles sections of the APA ethics code. They differ from mandatory ethics, which tend to consist of enforceable rules, in that they are intended to reflect higher, more general ideals to which psychologists are encouraged to aspire. Aspirational ethics should challenge psychologists, both individually and collectively, to seek the highest possible moral and ethical outcomes in every situation.

Some consulting psychologists might be concerned that organizational members might resist efforts to introduce a moral discourse into the consulting process. Granted, some degree of reluctance by organizational participants might, at times, be inevitable. However, it is possible that initial reluctance might be more related to unfamiliarity with the process than resistance to the process itself. It has often been our observation that, once participants understand the purpose of the dialogue, they actively and meaningfully engage in the discussion. More often than not, people care about the moral implications of what they are doing, and value the opportunity to explore them in a thoughtful way. However, what about those less common cases in which there is real resistance to addressing moral and ethical issues? This situation can create difficult decisional demands for the consulting psychologist. Should the consulting psychologist honor the resistance and proceed with the consultation contract as requested? Should attempts be made to overcome the resistance? Should the contract be declined or discontinued? These are difficult questions. In coming to one's own personal answers, the consulting psychologist must carefully consider the implications of various decisional alternatives for all of those involved, including him or herself. We believe that just as one's practice is shaped by one's character, one's character is likewise shaped and reshaped by one's practice. It is very difficult, if not impossible, to compartmentalize decisions or actions; that is, it is difficult to maintain high ethical standards in some contexts and simultaneously compromise standards in others. Decisions and actions become part of identity and character.

Generally, the structure of an organization is greatly shaped by its own moral standards and values (Levinson, 1997). Organizational members' behavior and welfare are substantially affected by the structure of the organization. Operating within a healthy culture of clearly expressed and common values is essential to optimizing human outcomes. Thus, resistance to addressing moral issues should be seen as diagnostic, in that moral and functional considerations are typically similar.

We believe that the ambition to have a single set of prescriptive ethical guidelines for the profession of psychology has been irreversibly frustrated by the escalating breadth of psychological practice. Focusing specifically on organizational contexts, consider the range of potential settings in which a consulting psychologist might work, and the potential range of moral and ethical challenges he or she might encounter: for example, pharmaceutical companies, prisons, law firms, police departments, human service agencies, schools, hospitals, and so forth. While the APA has taken the responsibility for developing and maintaining a code of ethics very seriously, the increasingly complex and varied nature of psychological practice complicates such efforts. As we write this chapter, a special task force is actively engaged in the process of revising the current APA ethics code. Representatives of the Society of Consulting Psychology have submitted a written response to an initial draft of the new code, and have attended a meeting of the task force, in efforts to ensure that the interests of consulting psychologists are reflected in the upcoming code. Specific issues that have been presented for consideration by the task force include: (1) conflicts between ethics and organizational demands; (2) boundaries of competence; (3) informed consent; (4) describing the nature and results of psychological services; (5) third-party requests for services; (6) multiple relationships; (7) group and individual interventions; (8) conflicts of interest; (9) interruption of services; and (10) termination of professional relationships. Despite such efforts, however, framers of the revised code must ultimately produce a document with broad applicability across the many and highly varied domains of psychological practice. Consulting psychologists seeking ethical guidance beyond that provided in the APA ethics code should look to ethics codes in related areas, such as those associated with organizational development and the National Training Laboratory (Lowman, 1991).

# CONCLUSION

An attempt has been made here to portray the ethical foundations of consulting psychology as much more than a set of prescriptive or prohibitive behavioral guidelines. Every interaction the consultant has with a consultee has ethical implications. An infinite number of intentional or unintentional omissions by the consultant will have ethical implications for the consulting relationship(s). We have tried to frame consulting psychology as an inherently moral enterprise that has the potential to increase the quality of life for many people. Clearly, this is an emphasis on aspirational ethics in the context of organizational helping. This emphasis transcends the focus of mandatory ethics on compliance with minimum required standards. By focusing on virtue ethics in addition to principle ethics, we have attempted to underscore the importance of personal accountability for the impact of both the consulting process and outcome on those who participate in, or are affected by, consultation. Given the inherent limitations of external regulation in achieving ethical practice, we believe that self-monitoring and self-governance are the most potent and promising mechanisms for pursuing the aspirational goals discussed in this chapter.

## References

American Psychological Association. (1992). Ethical principles of psychologists and code of conduct. *American Psychologist, 47*, 1597–1611.

American Psychological Association, Society of Consulting Psychology, Education and Training Committee. (1999). *Principles for education and training at the doctoral and post-doctoral level in consulting psychology, Organizational consulting psychology.* Retrieved September 30, 2001, from http://www.apa.org/divisions/div13/

Argyris, C. (1970). *Intervention theory and method.* Reading, MA: Addison-Wesley.

Bersoff, D. N. (1999). Confidentiality, privilege, and privacy. In D. N. Bersoff (Ed.), *Ethical conflicts in psychology* (2nd ed., pp. 149–150). Washington, DC: American Psychological Association.

Blanton, J. S. (2000). Why consultants don't apply psychological research. *Consulting Psychology Journal: Practice and Research, 52*, 235–247.

Brown, D., Pryzwansky, W. B., & Schulte, A. C. (1991). *Psychological consultation.* Needham Heights, MA: Allyn & Bacon.

Carroll, M. A., Schneider, H. G., & Wesley, G. R. (1985). *Ethics in the practice of psychology.* Englewood Cliffs, NJ: Prentice Hall.

Fannibanda, D. K. (1976). Ethical issues of mental health consultation. *Professional Psychology: Research and Practice, 7,* 547–552.

Freeman, S. J. (2000). *Ethics: An introduction to philosophy and practice.* Belmont, CA: Wadsworth.

Fuqua, D. R., & Newman, J. L. (1985). Individual consultation. *The Counseling Psychologist, 13,* 390–395.

Gallesich, J. (1982). *The profession and practice of consultation.* San Francisco: Jossey-Bass.

Gibson, G., & Froehle, T. C. (1991). Empirical influences on organizational consultation. *Consulting Psychology Bulletin, 43,* 13–22.

Jordan, A. E., & Meara, N. M. (1999). Ethics and the professional practice of psychologists: The role of virtues and principles. In D. N. Bersoff (Ed.), *Ethical conflicts in psychology* (2nd ed., pp. 141–145). Washington, DC: American Psychological Association.

Koocher, G. P., & Keith-Spiegel, P. (1998). *Ethics in psychology: Professional standards and cases* (2nd ed.). New York: Oxford University Press.

Kralj, M. M. (2001). Coaching at the top: Assisting a chief executive and his team. *Consulting Psychology Journal: Practice and Research, 53,* 108–116.

Levinson, H. (1997). Organizational character. *Consulting Psychology Journal: Practice and Research, 49*(4), 246–255.

Lowman, R. L. (1991). Ethical human resource practice in organizational settings. In D. Bray (Ed.), *Working with organizations and their people* (pp. 194–218). New York: Guilford Press.

Lowman, R. L. (Ed). (1998). *The ethical practice of psychology in organizations.* Washington, DC: American Psychological Association.

Mirvis, P. H., & Seashore, S. E. (1979). Being ethical in organizational research. *American Psychologist, 34,* 766–780.

Newman, J. L. (1993). Ethical issues in consultation. *Journal of Counseling and Development, 72,* 148–156.

Newman, J. L., Gray, E. A., & Fuqua, D. R. (1996). Beyond ethical decision making. *Consulting Psychology Journal: Practice and Research, 48,* 230–236.

Newman, J. L., & Robinson, S. E. (1991). In the best interests of the consultee: Ethical issues in consultation. *Consulting Psychology Bulletin, 43,* 23–29.

Robinson, S. E., & Gross, D. R. (1985). Ethics of consultation: The Canterville ghost. *The Counseling Psychologist, 13,* 444–465.

Robinson-Kurpius, S. E., Fuqua, D. R., Gibson, R. G., Kurpius, D. J., & Froehle, T. C. (1995). An occupational analysis of consulting psychology: Results of a national survey. *Consulting Psychology Journal, 47,* 75–88.

Snow, D. L., & Gersick, K. E. (1986). Ethical and professional issues in mental health consultation. In F. V. Mannino, E. J. Trickett, M. F. Shore, M. G. Kidder, & G. Levin (Eds.), *Handbook of mental health consultation* (pp. 393–431). Rockville, MD: National Institute of Mental Health.

Sonne, J. L. (1994). Multiple relationships: Does the new ethics code answer the right questions? *Professional Psychology: Research and Practice, 25,* 336–343.

Tokunaga, H. T. (1984). Ethical issues in consultation: An evaluative review. *Professional Psychology: Research and Practice, 15,* 811–821.

# CHAPTER THIRTY-ONE

# Recommendations for Managing Consultants

## The View from Inside the Corporation

Karen M. Grabow
*Land O'Lakes, Inc.*

I t has become axiomatic that a requirement of success in business is to obtain the customers' perspective. One of the most influential proponents of seeing the company's products and services through the customers' eyes has been General Electric, one of the most successful businesses in the United States (see, for example, Casner, 1988; Duncan, 1989; Welch, 2001). Led by this example and others, corporations have implemented programs and processes to determine their customers' criteria for a successful engagement, and then to monitor performance against those criteria.

Consultants are more likely to satisfy their clients—to have more successful engagements and long-term consulting relationships—if they understand how the client views them (see, for example, Ulvila, 2000). What do clients view as the critical success factors of the consultant-client relationship?

I conducted interviews on this question with executives in multibillion dollar businesses that engage a wide variety of consultants. The senior leaders interviewed were all officers responsible for selecting and directing consultants in projects of strategic significance to their businesses. These leaders appreciated the value consultants could add to their businesses, but also understood the need to be cautious about which consultants they engaged to perform which services, and how they should manage those consultants. One senior officer expressed it this way: "Consultants are an incredible resource available to us at an incredible price."

Some of the consulting engagements discussed in these interviews were major in scope, some were small. Some were seen by the corporate clients as wildly successful, some as having been disappointing. The consultants involved in these engagements represented a wide variety of disciplines: psychology, communications, accounting, compensation and benefits, information systems, and business strategy. Regardless of the type of consultant or problem, though, common themes ran through the interviews describing the critical success factors.

The interview format followed a *critical incident* approach (Flanagan, 1954), in which the executives were asked to describe specific consulting engagements that were either very successful or notably unsuccessful. The interviews began this way: "Tell me about your most successful consulting engagement . . . [an] engagement in which the partnership clicked, deeper understanding resulted, solutions emerged, and your business benefited significantly. What was the project? What was the outcome? What factors made it go so well?" All of the interviewees also were asked about projects that disappointed: "Now tell me about the consulting engagement that worked least well," and so forth.

Adhering strictly to the interview protocol was often difficult, especially when interviewing the most senior executives, who often lapsed quickly into giving advice, rather than, as requested, being descriptive. But the advice given was often of high quality, borne of decades of experience as a discerning client.

On the basis of these interviews, I created a set of recommendations for managing consultants. These guidelines might prove useful for corporate project managers in improving the success rate of their consulting projects.

Some of these recommendations might seem self-evident. Recognize, however, that intelligent people in highly successful major corporations and well-regarded, successful consulting groups have sometimes failed to do these things, or have failed to do them right.

# RECOMMENDATION 1: CONSIDER CAREFULLY WHETHER OR NOT TO CALL IN A CONSULTANT

Before engaging an organizational consultant, clients need to think about when and whether one is needed. The first recommendation relates to what I call *the paradox of consulting scope*. This refers to a complicated fact of consultation: the tougher the decision to be made, the more a company benefits from outside objectivity, analysis, and methodology. However, the tougher the decision to be made, the more critical it also is to secure the buy-in of those who will have to implement the final recommendations.

The following were viewed by those interviewed as being appropriate reasons to use consultants:

- To provide a specific technical expertise.

- To provide arms and legs. Corporate executives see consultants as bringing unlimited energy, thus being able to drive a process that would likely take internal resources significantly longer because of their other commitments. Consultants can develop a more rapid timeline regardless of what else is going on inside the organization.

- To gather intelligence. Consultants can typically get access to information about how world-class organizations do things that internal corporate resources cannot (especially when the organization is interested in the practices of key competitors).

- To determine how to make changes in direction when internal people are heavily invested in the status quo.

In contrast, the following were viewed by the respondents as *not* being good reasons to use consultants:

- To implement a strategy devised by the consultants. Consultants who implement a strategy that they devised sometimes gloss over problems, or are reluctant to tweak the strategy they recommended.

- To bolster one side of a political dispute. The consultant will invariably get caught in the crossfire.

Implications of the first recommendation for the organizational consultant are several. First, it is probably important for organizational consultants to understand the purpose(s) for which they were engaged. The consultation approach might differ, for example, if the consultants were engaged to be arms and legs, or for their technical expertise. Second, they need to recognize the implications for the consultative approach of the client's purposes. If, for example, the consultant is engaged to be the arms and legs of the organization, the client is buying speed. Momentum is important in such engagements, and consultants in such circumstances need to make sure the client will provide sufficient horsepower to provide information needed by the consultants at the time it is needed. The consultant will also need sufficient access to the appropriate internal resources to take the handoff when the work is complete. If the project is to have an impact after the consultant leaves the site, the consultant will need to work with the appropriate internal managers who are in a position to implement the communication, training, and policy adjustments necessary to implement the recommendations. Similarly, consultants called upon to implement a strategy they have recommended, or invited into a political dispute, should recognize that project could be fraught with peril.

# RECOMMENDATION 2: SELECT THE RIGHT GROUP FOR THE TASK

It is tempting and easy for clients to stick with the people and personalities they trust—and equally tempting for consultants to say yes to every project that comes their way. Many consultants work hard to provide full service.

Even full-service consultants, however, have functional roots; every consultant has been trained in a particular discipline, and most consulting groups initially work from the discipline that produced its founders. Savvy clients want to know the group's disciplinary foundation.

A consulting firm's roots generally represent the area of its greatest strength—the source of its competitive edge over competing firms—despite the fact that many firms have hired people from a wide range of different disciplines in order to market themselves as broadly capable. Executives, however, generally seek to use consultants where they will make the most difference.

It is important to understand the core strength of a consulting firm. For example, was the firm an accounting firm that conducted financial audits, which then grew into helping their clients solve the problems they uncovered? Or, was it a firm of psychologists who began with psychological assessment and branched out into organization development (OD), and now take a participative approach to strategy development? Was it a firm with technology roots that grew into organizational design and change management?

The following case example is illustrative of several issues in this domain. A consulting firm had established its brand identity among managers as being a good place to go for coaching services. This firm has a coaching program that appears to be much like those offered by other vendors. The consultants meet with individuals needing coaching, to define the goals of the coaching and determine who in their work environment can provide the most useful feedback. Then the consultants conduct interviews to gather specific and detailed feedback about how the individual is seen by others in the organization. The person being coached then receives feedback from the interviews, and the goals of the coaching are redefined. Then, over a period of several months, the consultant-coaches provide skill-building training, using videotaped role plays as a central feature of their coaching, as well as being useful as part of a before-and-after evaluation. Clients using this program report liking that it is very well-defined. The process follows clearly articulated steps. The firm's well-packaged, clearly defined process constitutes a selling point for many clients. They understand the program, and can sell it to their bosses and others.

This approach is a typical one used by consultants from many disciplines. The roots of this particular coaching organization, however, are in theater. This group was seen as being particularly strong at helping people whose issues are related to self-presentation. For a high-ranking executive with an excessively no-nonsense style, this consulting approach was viewed as being a terrific fit. The consultants helped him loosen up, develop social patter, and smile more often. For another sharp executive whose mind outraced her mouth, this group also worked wonders. Through feedback and practice, they taught her to slow down, collect her thoughts, and present her ideas with much more impact.

Another executive, upon hearing about and witnessing these successful transformations, decided that his number two executive, who I will call Sam, needed coaching, and sent him to the same group. Sam's issue involved interpersonal dynamics. In a world given to teams, partnerships, and alliances, Sam still viewed sharing information and resources as threatening. Meanwhile, his own people were suffering. They felt overworked and underappreciated, and their relationships with other parts of the organization were difficult, to say the least.

The theater-based consultants knew they could help Sam. They would assist him communicate more effectively with his peers. They would help him recognize when he used words that alienated others, put others on the defensive, and interfered with collaboration. They also proposed to help him learn the steps of the collaborative process.

Instead of working with that group, however, Sam was redirected to a different consultant, a psychologist-coach. The psychologist also obtained feedback and used videotaped role plays, though he was weaker than the theater-based consultants in helping Sam to learn to present himself in a way that would not invite conflict. However, the psychologist added another dimension to the coaching. The psychologist-coach helped Sam recognize his super-competitive nature, and to understand the ways that drive was likely to be expressed in his day-to-day work life. He helped Sam learn to think about how his peers were likely to view situations, and how to negotiate more effectively once he had an understanding of their drives and needs.

Here were two different consultants with apparently similar, but really significantly different, approaches borne of their different disciplines. Unless consultants market their unique strengths, clients might not be using the best resource to get the outcome they are after.

A more complex example occurred a few years back, when companies, besieged by spiraling healthcare costs, began transitioning their healthcare benefits to managed care programs. A healthcare benefits consultant, a recognized expert in the esoteric areas of healthcare models and actuarial statistics, was brought into one firm to analyze the company's demographics and claims experience, identify the right managed care program, and help to set the short- and long-term healthcare strategy.

This consultant did a great job in his area of expertise, but he was not the right person to sell the program to the organization. He convened task forces of senior managers representative of the organization's various businesses. He proceeded to try to facilitate the task forces' discussion of the benefits challenges in a way that ensured the task forces endorsed the consultant's solution. The participants in those meetings felt manipulated. They also felt their questions were met with defensiveness. Those managers went back to their organizations all over the country frustrated and distrustful, angry about what they saw as being forced to make changes that were not in the best interest of their teams. (This is an example also of why it is often unwise to use consultants to implement the strategies they themselves devised.)

At that point, the company turned to an expert in OD consulting. When this person established a process in which the senior managers obtained complete information about the proposed recommendations and the underlying business case, and were the ultimate decision-makers, the organization fell into line behind the benefits expert's proposal.

In short, no consultant or consulting group can do everything, and informed clients will not expect them to do so. Most clients would prefer to have the kind of relationship with the consultant in which the appropriate expert is recommended for a project outside of the consultant's core expertise. Of course, it is important for consultants to be straightforward with their clients about any products or firms with whom they have a business relationship.

It potentially increases the value of the consultant-client partnership if clients can count on consultants to help them think beyond their own boundaries to help meet all of the organization's needs. In such circumstances, clients would likely be more willing to call consultants just to think together about projects that are starting to emerge, rather than feeling that they were being viewed as an opportunity to sell more consulting services. Thinking together presents a great opportunity to better understand the company's needs, and to define innovative, exciting projects.

Potential clients need to understand the consultant's strengths and unique expertise. They need to be clear in their own minds about what differentiates one consulting group from another with similar offerings. The consultant's packaging and marketing should showcase those differentiators in a way that no prospective client can miss.

# RECOMMENDATION 3: CLEARLY ARTICULATE THE PURPOSE OF THE WORK

Over and over again, when a consulting engagement was described by the corporate executives interviewed as having been less than successful, it was unclear from the beginning of the project what the client was trying to accomplish—or the purpose of the consulting had changed in the middle of the process.

Being clear about the mission in any particular project might not sound difficult, except that many times when consultants are called in, clients are not yet sure what their direction should be, or there are mixed perceptions of the purpose within the organization. Such organizations are often in some sort of turmoil; for example, something or someone is broken, they are expanding or changing their structure, processes, or managers, or they are starting up a new unit or new business.

In one major corporation, it has happened twice in a five-year period that many months into strategic and sweeping consulting engagements, the project sponsors were replaced mid-project with new leaders. The new leaders had not been a part of the effort up to that point, but were expected to bring the project to a successful conclusion and then implement the recommendations. Less dramatic shifts occur with some frequency, such as when a coaching client sinks further and further into performance trouble, or when a decision-maker decides to tighten the project budget by reducing the project scope, or, perhaps most commonly, when the project expands beyond the original issues without a corresponding expansion in budget.

Consulting engagements, in short, often do not come in nice, neat packages. They might not follow any format learned in graduate school. Consultants need to expect that things might change, and when changes occur, they explicitly need to readdress the purpose and scope of the work. They also need to maintain the discipline to have a detailed discussion with the client about the goals and scope of the project every time changes of direction occur.

## RECOMMENDATION 4: LAY OUT THE STATEMENT OF WORK AND DELIVERABLES UP-FRONT AND EVERY TIME THEY CHANGE

Our interviews with corporate executives revealed that getting very explicit at the outset of a consulting engagement can avoid later disagreement with clients about what they will be provided for the consulting fee. Not infrequently, a client pushes the consultant to make a series of small requests that then balloon into major changes, a situation often experienced by systems analysts, who call it *scope creep*. This might result in the consultant following the project where it leads, and incurring extra expenses beyond those spelled out in the original proposal.

To establish appropriate expectations on both sides, expectations about deliverables need to be made as explicit as possible. Corporate project managers, for example, are advised to ask the consultant such questions as: how many interviews will there be? what will the interview content be? will the interviews be on site? and what will happen to the raw data? One particularly important question for clients to ask is, when will this project end? The problems that come to consultants are often problems that tend to linger, and many of our executive interviewees believe that consultants often do not aspire to go away as soon as possible.

Another topic needing explicit attention concerns identifying the specific items for which the client will be billed. Travel expenses, for example, is a term that needs to be defined. Who will travel, to and from where, and for what purpose?

In one corporation, the project manager gasped when, in support of a $100,000 project, the company was billed another $30,000 in travel. On another project, the out-of-town consultants rented furnished apartments. Such an arrangement might have been less expensive in the long run than hotel rooms, but it sounded extravagant to the surprised project sponsor.

There are three additional topics that can cause considerable client concern in this area: level setting, boilerplate, and administration.

Consultants frequently build into their project plans level-setting time, that is, a period at the beginning of the project when the consultants interview the clients about their views of the issues, and then come back and review with the client what they have heard. This practice can be maligned as "taking our watch and telling us what time it is," but is nonetheless important.

Seasoned organizational clients know the importance of this period. Typically, all clients view themselves as being different, and will, to some extent, resent a consultant's implications that they are just like the last company the consultant worked with in their industry. They want the consultant to take the time to understand the company's uniquenesses. But this phase is often frustrating for the client's employees, who ask, "why are we paying them money to ask us questions and then tell us what we already know?" It therefore helps to discuss explicitly at the beginning of the consultation how long the getting acquainted phase should take, and how much benefit each side should get out of it.

Boilerplate is another topic requiring some consultant finesse. Clients often want to see an example of what they can expect the final product to look like, and they know there is a template and methodology that consultants typically use on projects such as theirs. Indeed, consultants are often hired because they have a standard methodology to apply to problems such as theirs. On the other hand, clients become cynical and unhappy if it appears that the consultant already had the answer to the client's concerns before the consulting work was undertaken. One company called this practice *plug and chug,* when it appeared that the consultant used a search-and-replace word processing command in the final report to insert their company's name in place of the name of the last client with a similar problem. A related client gripe concerns consultants who squeeze forty pages of content into a 120-page deliverable. Time and money are two resources never in sufficient supply. Consultants who are respectful of both are valued partners.

One organization talked about a recent project in which they engaged a consulting group for a relatively undirected project. This dot-com client asked the consultant to evaluate the technology and organizational structure underlying their website. The consultant conducted a project that culminated in a presentation of very general commentary about how other organizations manage and support their retail websites. A second consulting group then came in and conducted a one-day briefing, essentially delivering in a day what the other group had delivered in eight weeks. The follow-up business readily went to the second group.

It is sometimes best to give the client what they need, not what they asked for. When consultants are asked to perform an extensive study for which the answer is already known, it is best gently to push back on the client. Recommending a more direct (and cheaper) approach as a starting point might result in more business in the long run.

Finally, while it might seem trivial or obvious, project administration requires considerable attention. In most corporations, successful executives are operationally excellent. That means that deadlines and budgets are expected to be met every time. Project managers are evaluated very harshly if the deadlines or budgets are surpassed, even when the work quality is acceptable.

In many consulting groups, billings are the primary administrative preoccupation such that consultants frequently try to do too much. In such cases, the client's deadlines and budgets might well fall by the wayside. Because those executives who engage consultants generally prefer not to fall by the wayside themselves, it would be wise for both client and consultant to be clear up-front about which deliverables and deadlines are important. For more satisfying and productive engagements, both clients and consultants should have the same expectations about deliverables before the work is done.

## RECOMMENDATION 5: ASSESS THE CREDENTIALS AND EXPERIENCE OF EVERY CONSULTANT WHO WILL WORK ON A PROJECT

This recommendation suggests that it is not enough for an organization to hire a consulting firm with a good reputation. Consulting firms often sell themselves as having broad, comprehensive expertise. Typically, the consulting group decides on the staffing for a particular project.

I argue that the decision of staffing a project should involve the client. As one internal advice-giver warned, "In any five-person consulting team, you can expect two to three who are players; one or two who are brand new, terribly bright, but inexperienced persons, and one floater, definitely not a star. When we're paying the kind of money we typically pay for consultants, we believe we deserve a uniformly solid team. We cannot reasonably expect to pick from the firm's entire roster of consultants, but we believe we should demand at least minimum levels of relevant and successful experience. The consultants should be people who are not only solid, but who also have some understanding of our industry."

Newly graduated consultants are best positioned carefully. Clients see their obvious intelligence and high energy, but sometimes their inexperience in the business world makes them appear impractical, ineffective presenters, not very good at relating to corporate senior decision-makers. Even if a project looks relatively straightforward, one that a relatively inexperienced person could handle, projects often become complicated once the project begins. New graduates should rarely be sent out alone.

On the other hand, even a firm's strong consultants sometimes reach the point of burnout, at which point their work gets sloppy. Corporate project managers are therefore advised personally to interview members of a consulting team as carefully as they would interview potential members of their own team. They are told not only to meticulously check consultants' references, but also to assess the chemistry with the business partners and leaders, that is, to have the key senior decision-makers meet the consultants up-front. More than one manager has described large projects in which good work was done, but in their presentations, the consultants made enemies among the senior leadership team. That unfortunate chemistry often significantly affects the senior leaders' evaluation of what was done, or the recommendations. Consultant-client chemistry is important even if the consultation is highly technical.

Most managers engaging consultants know to watch out for the consultative equivalent of bait-and-switch. This occurs, for example, when the people who show up to do the work are not the people with whom the client had been dealing up to that point. Clients understandably want consultants to be explicit about exactly who will be on the team, and their past experience.

Those interviewed recommended asking about the consultant's alliances. One leader described a project in which she had hired a consultant to prioritize the company's opportunities for web-based systems. She had asked the consultant to analyze the potential payback of a long list of potential projects, and then to recommend software vendors in the areas of greatest payback. This leader was quite perturbed when she later learned that a recommended vendor was one in which the consultant had a business interest. If she had known about that at the outset of the project, she would have been more comfortable with the recommendation and more trusting of the consultant thereafter.

To sum up, consultants need to make sure that their new, young, smart apprentices are not front-and-center when the client's senior people are present, to be straightforward about any business alliances they have when recommending other vendors (and to do so promptly, before making the recommendation), and to do their own chemistry checks to be sure the staff consultants will play well to the internal decision-makers. In the long run, good chemistry is as important to the consultant as it is to the client.

# RECOMMENDATION 6: HAVE A SINGLE POINT OF CONTACT IN THE BUSINESS, AND FREQUENT, DIRECT CONTACT

Clients sometimes make consultants' lives difficult by presenting them with multiple interfaces. It is not unusual in coaching assignments, for example, for the consultant to deal both with corporate leaders and human resources (HR) staff. It can feel like a waste of time to repeat progress reports for both parties, but a far more problematic situation can occur when the leaders and HR have different views of the goals, the course of the work, or the results.

In one illustrative coaching engagement, the HR representative had thought the consultant was working with a problematic manager, but, because of calendar problems, the work was significantly delayed. The HR person had worked hard to persuade the boss of this individual to try coaching with him, rather than giving up on the person altogether. She discovered the work was not happening when the boss called her, more impatient than ever, and more determined about termination. If the HR person and the consultant had communicated regularly, the prognosis of the coaching work would probably have been far more optimistic.

On a recent successful project consultation, the senior leader spent time late in the day or early in the morning with the top two members of the consulting team every time they were on site. This allowed him to get very frequent updates on the team's progress, as well as to ensure that he knew quickly when his people were not providing what the consultants needed. These regular meetings also provided him the opportunity to give feedback to the consultants about how he and his people felt the consultation was going.

This same leader was managing a very difficult consulting project when it became apparent to him that the consulting project leader was not up to the assignment. Because he was monitoring the work so closely, he was able to quickly inform the consulting practice's senior partners, who made a project leadership change. The project was salvaged. Although it is not pleasant to hear that a consulting project or team are not on track, it is far better to be aware of clients' opinions, especially when negative, early enough to do something about it. Staying close to the business leaders throughout the project can prevent unhappiness at the project's end.

# RECOMMENDATION 7: WORK ALONGSIDE THE CONSULTANT

Consulting projects need to be partnerships, the executives we interviewed said, and should not be one-sided. But too often, clients, especially more junior client managers, seem to view consultants, as people in days gone by used to view physicians, as being wise, all-knowing, revered professionals, whose expertise is not to be questioned.

This mindset is aggravated by the fact that often, before calling in a consultant, the client managers have been struggling with the problem themselves, and have been unable to come up with a satisfactory answer on their own. Consultants can themselves encourage this reverence with what is sometimes called *consultantspeak* (abstruse technical language and acronyms), with overly complex presentations with lots of arrows, or by traveling in packs, sometimes outnumbering their clients. Corporate project teams should learn not to worship the consultant. Consultants are a specialized resource, but it is the person who called them, not the consultant, who is ultimately responsible for the end product. This two-way partnership is critical to the project's success. Consultants bring in their technical expertise, but clients are the experts on the organization, the culture, and how things work there.

On one recent project, for example, a consulting group was asked to help strengthen and restructure a group whose mission was in an area of emerging technology. The consulting group brought in people with expertise in this new field, and performed well. The employees who worked in the group, and who had been working hard for some time to meet the challenges without help, however, stepped back and let the consultants work. They developed a dependence on the consultants, conveying to their management the distinct impression that they needed the outside expertise to keep going. This was financially gratifying for the consultants, but not career-healthy or esteem-building for the internal managers. Furthermore, what the consultants designed was a staff almost twice the size of the structure ultimately implemented. The company's style was lean and the consultant's bias was caution, a common style difference between clients and consultants.

In the most successful organizational consulting engagements of this type, internal staff are full partners to the consultants from the very beginning of the project. To facilitate smooth working relationships among the outside and inside resources on the project team, it helps to clarify roles up-front. Subteams made up of internal and external partners should formally be assigned to each of the various project steps.

It is no doubt flattering when the client stands back and allows the consultant to operate relatively independently. But it is not in the long-term best interest of the client or the project to go it alone or to be worshipped.

# RECOMMENDATION 8: GET THE INFORMATION NEEDED TO IMPLEMENT THE CONSULTANTS' RECOMMENDATIONS

Consultants are usually generalists. They typically specialize in approaches that work across companies. They present the 50,000-foot view, industry overviews, and theory.

Clients need help, however, to get from where they now are to where they need to go. The effective consultant helps position the client to implement their recommendations. To do that, it is wise for the consultant to think about the ultimate implementation of the project while writing the proposal, when talking with the client about the statement of work and deliverables, and along the way as the project progresses.

This includes getting answers to questions such as: how does the client actually do what you recommend? what are the risks? and what are the transition steps? how can these recommendations be tested to see if they will actually work?

The implications for consultants are clear. Even though implementation details might not be the consultant's expertise or interest, effective consultants recognize that their clients need to figure out how to turn recommendations into reality for the organization. Consultants do not need to slog through these details with them, but it is best to ensure clients have what they will need to operationalize the recommendations at the project's end. The most incisive recommendations mean nothing to the organization if work begun by a consultant cannot be sustained when the consultant leaves.

# SUMMARY

Corporate senior executives with significant experience overseeing consulting assignments large and small have learned how to manage consultants to ensure project success. Consultants who integrate these executives' recommendations into their own project management approach will have more smooth-running projects and happier clients.

# References

Casner, L. J. (1988). *Successful training strategies: Twenty-six innovative corporate models.* San Francisco: Jossey-Bass.

Duncan, W. J. (1989). *Great ideas in management: Lessons from the founders and foundations of managerial practice.* San Francisco: Jossey-Bass.

Flanagan, J. C. (1954). The critical incident technique. *Psychological Bulletin, 51,* 327–358.

Ulvila, J. S. (2000). Building relationships between consultants and clients. *American Behavioral Scientist, 43,* 1667–1680.

Welch, J. (2001). *Jack: Straight from the gut.* New York: Warner Books.

# Principles for Education and Training at the Doctoral and Post-Doctoral Level in Consulting Psychology/Organizational

Education and Training Committee,
Division 13, American Psychological Association[1]

## PURPOSE OF THE PRINCIPLES

This document outlines the expected competencies to be obtained by persons receiving training at the doctoral or post-doctoral level in Consulting Psychology (CP). It was prepared to assist faculty and academic administrators in designing doctoral or post-doctoral programs in CP.

### Working Model and Assumption of the Principles

**Areas of Training Affected.** Although there are other applications of CP for which alternative or additional competencies may be relevant (e.g., health-related CP), the specific areas of expertise addressed in this document relate to CP as it is applied to the organizational CP. These *Principles* are not intended to replace, usurp, or conflict with training policies or principles that have been developed and approved for other areas of practice such as those in I/O, clinical, counseling, or school psychology.

**Non-Exclusivity.** These *Principles* also recognize that there are appropriate ways other than doctoral training in CP to become proficient in the competencies here

---

[1]Education & Training Committee, Division 13, APA, Rodney L. Lowman (Chair), Clayton Alderfer, Michael Atella, Andrew Garman, David Hellkamp, Richard Kilburg, Paul Lloyd, and Ann O'Roark. Reprinted by permission.

described. Academic training in areas such as Industrial/Organizational Psychology (e.g., Society for Industrial and Organizational Psychology, 1985) and Clinical or Counseling Psychology can provide considerable training that is relevant for the practice of CP. These *Principles* are intended to assist in the specific development of doctoral and post-doctoral programs in CP.

**Scientist-Practitioner Assumptions.** Consistent with the orientation of Division 13 of APA, these *Principles* assume that the practice of CP is guided by the *science* of psychology in evaluating and assessing the effectiveness of CP interventions and its assessment methodologies. It is therefore assumed that the fully trained consulting psychologist is competent to conduct and/or to evaluate and to utilize scientific-based research in the practice of CP. The effective consulting psychologist has in-depth knowledge of the major theoretical models in psychology and of their particular methodologies and applications as they apply to individual, group, and organizational consulting domains.

The profession of CP embraces a scientist-practitioner model of training, including training in traditional research skills (e.g., statistics, research design and the like). No single model of empirical research, however, is assumed to have a monopoly on truth by the endorsement of the "scientist-practitioner" model of consultation. CP trainees learn, e.g., not just about research methodologies but also about the role of the consultant as an active participant in the consulting process at hand. Action research, e.g., is often important in CP in being able to apply complex constructs in practice.

**Evolving Field.** The practice of CP has evolved over time and involves a body of knowledge and methods of service delivery. These *Principles* have been created to reflect the current state of the field and to provide a conceptual framework for the development of training programs. It is expected that these *Principles* will continue to change over time to keep pace with advances in research and practice.

## Competencies and Competency Domains

These *Principles* are organized around a set of core competencies needed for the practice of CP in work and organizational contexts. The document intentionally identifies intended competencies (or "end states") rather than presenting "model curricula" or specific recommended course work since there are multiple ways to obtain the desired competencies. Indeed, innovation in doctoral and post-doctoral training methodologies in helping students achieve these competencies is encouraged.

The desired CP competencies for the doctoral-level consulting psychologist are organized into three broad domains of psychological expertise that are assumed to be important in becoming competent as a consulting psychologist: *individual, group,* and *organizational.* This organizing system is primarily intended for organizational and conceptual purposes in thinking about curriculum design issues; we assume that to some degree competencies in each domain will interact with one another and that the effective practice of CP draws simultaneously on competencies learned at each of the levels.

To illustrate, for example, assessment is considered to be a pivotal CP competency in all three of these consulting levels. Ryan and Zeran (1972) have usefully defined assessment as: "a disciplined way of analyzing as precisely as possible an existing situation by determining the nature of the elements which combine and relate to make the situation what it is, establishing interrelationships among the elements, and synthesizing a new whole to provide means of optimizing system outcomes." A format for describing assessment competencies for specialization in organizational consulting can be summarized in terms of dual, nested continua: the scientist-practitioner model and a progression of learning from theory to practice under each area of emphasis. Skills to be developed in assessment, regardless of level, include identifying (observing, using logical deduction), integrating (classifying), and inferring (matching evidence to goals and assessment schema), in order to assist individuals in implementing change or improving understanding. The pervasive aspect of the competence, across the three interactive domains—individual, group, and organizational—is recognition of *psychological assessment* as an overarching framework-construct.

Similarly, process consultation (e.g., Schein, 1999) is important in all these domains (individual, group, and organizational). Process skills are needed in a number of specific content areas and speak to specialized expertise that psychologists bring to organizational consulting. Process skills are essential in both effective and organizational assessment and in most forms of intervention. As a final example, across all types of consulting relationships, psychologists are able to build constructive and collaborative relationships with a variety of types of people and organizational representatives. They maintain both objectivity and personal engagement as they work with clients to further their specific consultative goals.

Finally, multi-cultural/international competencies are ones that cut across multiple levels. Fully trained consulting psychologists are expected to develop appropriate understanding of and sensitivity to multi-cultural/international issues in all of their work.

So, although competencies do not always neatly fit within a single level, the grouping by categories serves as a useful organizing metric in thinking through the issues of how best to train people to become consulting psychologists. Within each of the three domains a series of specific competencies will be identified consistent with the three-level model. Illustrative competencies include:

*Primarily Individual-Level Core Competencies:*

- Individual assessment for purposes of career and vocational assessment
- Individual assessment for purposes of employee selection or development
- Job analysis for purposes of individual assessment
- Executive and individual coaching
- Individual-level intervention for job- and career-related problems

*Primarily Group-Level Core Competencies:*

- Assessment of functional and dysfunctional group behavior
- Assessment and development of teams
- Creating group-level teams in organizations (e.g., self-directed work groups)
- Intergroup assessment and intervention
- Group boundary assessment and intervention
- Identity group (racial, gender, ethnic) management in the organizational context

*Primarily Organizational/Systemic-Level Core Competencies:*

- Organizational diagnosis including systemic assessment of the entire organization or large component parts of the organization
- Attitude, climate, and satisfaction surveys
- Evaluation of corporate management philosophy, organizational culture and nature of systemic stressors
- Work-flow and project planning activities
- Identification of aggregate performance measures
- Assessment of organizational values and management practices
- Organizational-level interventions
- Change management of organizational systems

In the following sections of this document the core CP competencies are elaborated and illustrated. The competencies described here necessarily constitute a selective listing of skills important in becoming a consulting psychologist.

**I. Individual Domain Consulting Psychology Competencies.** In the individual domain, consulting psychologists are skilled in performing assessments and interventions centered on persons as separate entities in organizational and work contexts. Consulting psychologists are expected to have the knowledge, skills, and abilities to assess and intervene with individuals in nonclinical work- and career-related contexts and to be able to differentiate situations requiring assessment or intervention with abnormal psychological conditions and those with the more normal range of behavior.

**A. *Individual-Level Assessment.*** Doctoral-level consulting psychologists understand and can competently employ individual-level assessment methods and techniques appropriate for the types of problems and issues confronted by individuals in work, career, and organizational contexts. They are competent in psychometric issues in individual assessment, and procedures for conducting valid individual-level assessments and evaluations for purposes of career assessment, personnel selection, personal development, and in the context of determining appropriateness for, and specific needs of, coaching and counseling of persons in the work and career context. Such assessments are based on relevant evaluations using, as appropriate, psychological tests and other assessment procedures and include understanding of the legal and regulatory context in which individual assessments occur. The fully trained consulting psychologist is able to understand intrapsychic individual-level dynamics affecting observed behavior and can integrate these characteristics into the client's situational context. CP individual-level assessment skills do not normally include assessment of abnormal personality or mental dysfunction except to the extent that the consulting psychologist is expected to be able to differentiate the needs of persons whose characteristics may require a different type of intervention (e.g., referral for a formal mental health evaluation or intervention).

Fully trained doctoral-level consulting psychologists are competent in individual-level assessment methodologies and are skilled in the administration and interpretation of a representative-level sample of relevant instruments and in providing feedback to individuals completing such measures. These *Principles* intentionally do not specify a list of assessment devices, procedures, or psychological tests (e.g., specific measures of occupational interests, abilities, and personality traits) in which fully trained consulting psychologists must become competent, since any such list would quickly become outdated or irrelevant. What is important is that the consulting psychologist have meta-skills in individual-level psychological test administration, interpretation, and feedback and experience administering, interpreting, and providing feedback with a sufficiently large number of scientifically-sound instruments that new tests can quickly be mastered as they become available. Consulting psychologists working at the individual level are able to define relevant assessment questions, to choose appropriate instrumentation, competently to administer the relevant tests, and to provide competent feedback, including behaviorally-based feedback, to all relevant parties. Feedback includes helping the individual(s) assessed (and other relevant parties, such as third parties) understand the results and limitations of the assessment, helping to place the results in the appropriate organizational context, addressing the affective aspects of such feedback, and helping identify the relevant implications of the results of the assessment.

Thus, consulting psychologists are able to identify the strengths and limitations of each of several assessment methods: empirical methods (e.g., behavioral, content analysis), psychometric methods (cognition-learning, affect-behavior, conation-willing, i.e., integrative decision-making), and more intuitive methods (projective and other). The history of the development of each methodology is supplemented with detailed exposure to preferred techniques, emphasizing the strengths and limitations that pertain to diagnostic outcomes specific to CP: classification for description, evaluation, placement; classification for performance competency; and classification for consultant-intervention, therapeutic recommendations, or referral for clinical treatment.

At the individual level, the consulting psychologist understands and is able to integrate the various components of psychological assessment (e.g., test results, behavioral observational data, relevant background and life history information) and to synthesize these data into pragmatically relevant results. The consulting psychologist is skilled in a range of individual-level assessment procedures (e.g., objective, projective, structured observation, ethnographic field methods, interviews, etc.), and applies skilled synthesis-level thinking to produce integrated results that are germane to the referral question(s) for which the assessment was undertaken.

**B. Individual-Level Interventions.** Fully trained consulting psychologists are able to successfully implement a range of interventions that focus on the individual level. These interventions can be classified as follows:

*1. Educational.* Consulting psychologists should know how to provide educational-based interventions for individuals. The *goal* of such activities would be to promote the acquisition and use of new knowledge by clients. The range and depth of such educational interventions will vary greatly and may incorporate various modalities including face-to-face and various telecommunications-based formats.

*2. Training.* Practitioners should know how to provide training interventions for individuals. The goals of such activities are to assist individuals in developing and strengthening skills relevant to the workplace. The range and types of skills applicable to jobs are enormous, and it is not expected that organizational consulting psychologists be able to demonstrate competency in all of them. However, practitioners should be able to assess problems and design skill-building interventions that will help clients manage the challenges that they face.

*3. Coaching.* Practitioners should know how to provide competent, assessment-anchored coaching and other individual-level interventions. The goals of such activities include helping clients to improve their abilities to diagnose problems that they are confronting in the workplace, to change problematic attitudes, values, beliefs, and behaviors that may interfere with their performance, and to improve their skills, self-awareness, and self-efficacy in their work-related roles. Coaching may include education and training interventions as part of a package of activities that are usually negotiated and delivered to a client in the context of a formal agreement.

*4. Counseling.* Consulting psychologists are able to provide counseling interventions for individuals. The *goal* of such activities is to help individuals overcome internal psychological or behavioral barriers to the performance of their roles in the workplace. Although consulting psychologists should be familiar with and able to apply an array of counseling theories and methods, they are not necessarily expected to be prepared to conduct mental health treatment with clients. Rather, consulting psychologists refer such clients to appropriately prepared colleagues when they believe that such care is necessary.

*Foci for Individually Directed Interventions.* CP training programs prepare practitioners to intervene with individuals in the workplace who may be encountering a wide variety of problems and issues. To be sure and inevitably, the academic and practice aspects of the programs will not be able to expose students to the full array of difficulties and challenges that clients may present to them once they leave school. However, there are some foci for individual interventions that are reasonable to expect programs to include in their curriculum. These can include such specific applications as those depicted in the list below.

*Representative Individually Oriented Consulting Competencies*

Career management

Coaching on managerial roles and behaviors

Fostering the development of leadership and followership behavior

Technical roles in organizations

Interpersonal relationships and psychosocial challenges in organizations

Intrapsychic aspects of work such as motivation, resistance to change, and emotional management

Crisis management concerning individual behavior in organizations

Individual performance in relationship to groups and organizations

Role conflict management

Assisting individuals to work effectively in globally oriented, culturally diverse organizations

Course work and practicum experiences in CP training programs integrate theory, research, technical skills and implementation methods, and approaches to evaluating individually based interventions. Graduates are prepared to design, implement, and evaluate these approaches.

***C. Self-Awareness, Self-Management, and Professional and Psychological Maturity.*** Most individual-level assessment and intervention methods reasonably assume certain personal characteristics. Consulting psychologists' graduate training programs, which should include one-on-one supervision relevant for learning individual intervention skills, should assist graduates in developing the capacity for self-directed reflection, the ability to receive critical feedback from clients and colleagues, and the willingness to change behavior as needed to work effectively with individuals in work-related contexts. Graduates of CP programs are expected to have been exposed to models and methods for accomplishing these tasks and to have demonstrated a reasonable ability to implement them before graduating. The capacity for developing self-awareness and self-management can be strengthened and deepened in a wide variety of ways, and the curriculum of each program should demonstrate how the faculty assists students to achieve the level of professional and psychological maturity necessary for effective practice in the field.

**II. Group-Level Consulting Psychology Competencies.** Group-level consulting psychology competencies take the group as the primary unit of analysis. The group-level frame of reference, however, does not pertain only to the internal (i.e., interpersonal) relations among task groups. It also addresses such phenomena as role analysis, leader-follower behavior, interpersonal conflict, workflow intergroup relations, diversity, authority dynamics, labor-management relations and inter-organizational relations. Crucial propositions are: (1) roles in organizations are shaped by group-level forces; (2) individuals in organizations function as group representatives, whether or not they intend to do so; (3) the internal dynamics of groups cannot be adequately understood independently of the external relations of those same groups; and (4) unconscious processes within individuals, within groups and between groups affect individual roles, intragroup dynamics, intergroup relations, and inter-organizational relations.

Effective doctoral and post-doctoral education programs in consulting psychology prepare consulting psychologists to carry out interventions with groups embedded in organizations. This education includes knowledge about: (1) the self in relation to these phenomena, (2) relevant concepts and theories, (3) specific case studies and statistical research results, and (4) appropriate social technologies. Effective intervention depends upon favorable confluence among all four of these elements. If any one is missing, or if all are not brought together in a congruous fashion, then education is incomplete.

*Types of Group-Level Assessment and Interventions.* This section elaborates specific types of group-level assessment and intervention approaches in which the consulting psychologist is expected to be trained.

A. *Role Analysis and Renegotiation.* The goals of these activities are to enable individuals in roles within organizations to understand the forces that shape their roles and to adjust those forces that cause dysfunctional consequences for themselves and the organization.

Consulting psychologists who provide this service should be able to establish their own roles in relation to the work, know several versions of role theory (including those that take account of group-level processes), understand the empirical research on role dynamics in organizations, and be able properly to diagnosis and assist clients in analyzing and renegotiating their roles.

B. *Group Formation and Development.* The goals of these activities are to enable group leaders and members to form the group, establish productive relations between the leader and members, develop constructive relations among peers within the team, and fashion cooperative relations between the focal team and other groups and organizations with whom the team must relate in order to perform effectively.

Consulting psychologists who provide this service should understand their own predispositions toward authority and group dynamics; know one or more sophisticated theories of group and intergroup dynamics; understand the empirical research on groups in organizations; and be able properly to diagnosis problems of the team, design interventions to address those problems, and assist the leader, team members and others who may be appropriate to implement the interventions. They are further able to identify both optimal, positive models of functioning and those that are dysfunctional and pathology-driven.

C. *Work Groups and Intergroup Problem Solving* The goal of these activities is to assist two or more identified groups with improving their relationship in order to carry out interdependent work assignments more effectively. Intervention may apply to peer groups (such as engineering and production or production and sales) that have different functions along a flow of work or to groups at different hierarchical levels (such as between field units and headquarters, between entities attempting to merge, or between labor and management).

Consulting psychologists who provide these services should understand their own predispositions toward authority and intergroup relations (especially those that involve ethnocentric forms of conflict) and be prepared to determine whether they can work alone or should join with one or more additional consultants to provide the service. In situations in which teamwork among consultants is called for, consultants who work together should be prepared to manage their relations with one another and in relation to the client in ways that enhance rather than diminish the quality of service. They should be knowledgeable about intergroup theories, informed about the empirical research concerning the specific intergroup problems presented, and prepared to assess and intervene in a manner that utilizes multiple group perspectives.

*D. Identity Groups and Intergroup Relations.* The goal of these activities is to eliminate group-level forces that result in members of some identity groups within organizations being treated unfairly by members of other identity groups on such matters as work assignments, salaries, and promotional opportunities. Identity group membership is defined in terms of birth and biology, including variables as race, ethnicity, gender, family, generation, and sexual orientation. Interventions to alter unfairness among identity groups include both forms of education to change the knowledge and self-awareness of individuals and procedures to alter the distribution of authority and power among identity groups within organizations.

Consulting psychologists who provide these services should have a thorough understanding of their own identities in those areas in which they provide services and a demonstrated capacity to work cooperatively with members of related identity groups to effect change (e.g., whites with blacks, women with men, etc.). They should be highly knowledgeable about theory and research concerning the identity groups about which they provide services. They should be able to develop group-level interventions appropriate to the conditions found in organizations facing groups in their areas of expertise.

*E. Group-Level Interventions.* Consulting psychologists apply what they have learned about groups to address specific issues and problems within the organizational context. Relevant areas include, e.g., managing group conflict, enhancing group functioning so that it is better aligned with organizational objectives, assisting groups in creating conditions of social support to ameliorate the effects of organizational and occupational stress, and helping organizations design work groups that effectively bridge individual and organizational needs.

### III. Organizational/Systemic-Level Consulting Psychology Competencies.

This domain focuses on interventions in which entire organizations are the targeted intervention level or in which the organization itself is integral in effecting changes to segments of the larger organization. Consulting psychologists often play prominent roles in conducting organization-level interventions, including surveys (organizational culture assessments and other employee opinion surveys); organizational strategic planning; change management programs; organization effectiveness/development programs and other types of research and evaluation functions. Competencies to be learned in conjunction with this domain of intervention include the following:

*A. Organization Theory and Design.* Prior to practicing organization-level assessments and interventions, consulting psychologists need to have a solid theoretical foundation from which to work. Training in organizational theory, behavior, and design are the foundations on which effective intervention are built. Relevant topic areas include: organizational theory: modern and historical (e.g., scientific management, the human relations movement, and open systems theory, organizational diagnostic theory); organizational structure and design (e.g., legal structures; centralization/decentralization, matrix configurations); organizational ecology (e.g., the effects of size, growth, market and life cycle); organizational effectiveness (financial indicators; industry benchmarking); globalization (economic, social, and legal challenges; multilingual and multicultural issues); organizational diagnosis; and organizational culture and ethics.

**B. *Organizational Assessment Competencies:* Organizational Diagnosis.** The goal of organizational diagnosis is to develop a widely shared understanding of a system by its members by using the methods of applied behavioral science.

The phases of organizational diagnosis include entry, data collection, analysis, and feedback. Consulting psychologists who provide this service should be prepared to develop a sound contract for the work and then carry out structured and unstructured observation, individual and group interviews, organic and standard questionnaires, and archival searches. Having obtained data from multiple sources and in various forms, they should be able to conduct appropriate qualitative and statistical analyses and to integrate the results. They should then be able to present their findings, first orally in appropriately designed meetings and then in writing. A full-blown organizational diagnosis potentially addresses all of the foregoing areas of group-level inquiry (i.e., roles, teams, work-flow, and identity groups) as well as organizational/systemic constructs. The requirements for proper preparation in each of those areas apply to organizational diagnosis as well. Conversely, the methods of organizational diagnosis also apply to the conceptually focused areas of inquiry.

Developing expertise in organizational surveying and other assessment methodologies requires a combination of theory and applied practice. Skills to be mastered include systematic data collection efforts including survey design implementation and evaluation. In learning to design surveys, attention should be paid to item design and item/survey evaluation. Practice in developing surveys, pilot testing them on representative samples, and evaluating these pilots should be covered through a combination of class projects and practica. Expertise in general survey design topics should also be addressed, including the effects of factors such as survey length, methods of distribution (anonymity, paper-and-pencil vs. IVR), and management (database theory and design, data security).

In teaching implementation of survey projects, skills in client definition and contracting are critical. Consulting psychologists also learn project skills, including managing a project from initial conceptualization to implementation and outcomes evaluation. As part of this process, consulting psychologists consider such issues as: incorporation of key stakeholders, development and execution of communication plans, formative and summative evaluations, and continuous quality and operational improvement of the process itself. Additionally, consideration and costing of alternative organizational assessment procedures should be covered, helping students learn how to effectively evaluate the cost-benefits of alternative strategies.

Relevant expertise in evaluating diagnostic techniques includes the use of statistics to examine reliability (test-retest and internal consistency) and validity (content, construct, criterion) of assessment devices. Classical test methods, and item-based methods such as IRT, should be covered in conjunction with this work. Consulting psychologists also learn a variety of diagnostic assessment methodologies, including those associated with the use of the psychologist him- or herself as an instrument for accurate organizational diagnosis.

**C. Organizational Change.** The organizational change domain focuses on working with organizations undergoing changes that are atypical for that organization in amount, quality, or both. A thorough understanding of client preferences concerning perceived change needs, organization design, theories of organizational change (including drivers of both organizational inertia and organizational resilience), and an understanding of the characteristic psychological processes change evokes, and how to manage those reactions, provides the foundation for effective intervention. Organizational change approaches and theories of change necessarily incorporate knowledge and theories in the individual, group, and organizational domains, developmental theories, incorporation of the organization's history, and change management theories and practice. Positive approaches (e.g., those based on appreciative inquiry) are as important as those oriented to dysfunction.

The foundation of organizational change should also include overviews of legal structures in organizations and organizational change (e.g. incorporation, mergers and acquisitions), as well as the influences of market systems on organizational survival. The history of employment and conventional "psychological contracts" will also be helpful. The value and limitations of person-centered interventions, such as career outplacement and severance, and open communication strategies, are also relevant. In addition, coursework and practical experience in project management skills are relevant.

**D. Organizational Effectiveness/Development.** The organization development domain focuses on strategies for enhancing the effectiveness of existing organizational structures. This domain overlaps with organizational change, but is distinct in its greater focus on incremental, rather than dramatic, transformational, change. Competency in this area will require skills to be developed in assessment, implementation design and execution, and evaluation. Under assessment, methods of assessing organizational effectiveness should be covered, including common financial measurements of effectiveness (e.g. ROI, RONA). Students need to learn how to determine and demonstrate the value to be added by their work. They also need to learn to translate complex psychologically grounded procedures into terms the client can understand and use. Methods for establishing continuous evaluation strategies and heightening general awareness of these strategies, including total quality management approaches, should also be taught.

### IV. Others

*A. Research/Evaluation.* The behavioral sciences are most clearly distinguished from fad and pop psychology by their discipline of research and evaluation. Consulting psychologists need to learn methods of evaluating their organizational interventions to assure that clients are maximizing their return on investment.

Evaluation coursework should include an understanding of both quantitative and qualitative methods. Related to quantitative methods, a grounding in multivariate statistics, regression, and time series designs, as well as a basic understanding of structural equations and hierarchical linear modeling, should be part of the curriculum. Related to qualitative methods, students should learn sound case study methodologies, as well as methods for codifying, synthesizing and summarizing qualitative information. Practical experience in conducting research should be emphasized, including active participation in real-life research projects, either in the classroom, on practica or—ideally—both.

*B. Professional Issues Training.* Across all domains of training, consulting psychologists need to become versed in the professional practice aspects of the discipline. These issues include but are not limited to: ethics, confidentiality, defining the nature of the client, licensure requirements and expectations, issues in interacting with other professionals, including psychologists and non-psychologists, informed consent, and legal issues. In many situations, the existing literature on ethics and professional practice issues relates more to the practice of clinical and counseling psychology rather than to the many complicated issues in consulting psychology. Therefore, consulting psychologists need to be trained in how such matters apply to, and are affected by, the practice of consulting psychology.

## References

Ryan, T. A., & Zeran, F. R. (1972). *Organization and administration of guidance services.* Danville, IL: Interstate Printers & Publishers.

Society for Industrial and Organizational Psychology. (1985). *Principles for education and training at the doctoral level in industrial/organizational psychology.* Bowling Green, OH: Author.

Schein, E. (1999). *Process consultation revisited: Building the helping relationship.* Reading, MA: Addison-Wesley.

# ABOUT THE EDITOR

**Rodney L. Lowman** is systemwide dean of the California School of Organizational Studies and director of the Organizational Consulting Center at Alliant International University. He has served as president of the Society of Consulting Psychology (Division 13 of the American Psychological Association), the Society of Psychologists in Management, and as editor of *The Psychologist-Manager Journal*. Dr. Lowman is the author of numerous journal articles, monographs, and books, including such major works in the field of industrial-organizational and consulting psychology as *The Ethical Practice of Psychology in Organizations, Counseling and Psychotherapy of Work Dysfunctions,* and *The Clinical Practice of Career Assessment: Interests, Abilities, and Personality.*

A Ph.D. graduate of Michigan State University with training in both I/O and clinical psychology (clinical internship, The Texas Research Institute of Mental Sciences), Dr. Lowman served on the faculties of The University of Michigan and University of North Texas and holds (or has held) adjunct or consulting faculty appointments in the Department of Psychology, Rice University, and the Divisions of Medical Psychology and Occupational Medicine at Duke University Medical Center. He is a Fellow of APA (Division 13 and 14) and a Diplomate of the American Board of Assessment Psychology.

# ABOUT THE CONTRIBUTORS

**Rodger D. Ballentine** is codirector for the Center for the Study of Work Teams and an adjunct professor of psychology at the University of North Texas. He received his Ph.D. in industrial-organizational psychology from North Carolina State University. He has more than twenty years of experience developing and implementing personnel and training systems. His areas of expertise include organizational surveys, job analysis and occupational taxonomies, productivity and performance assessment systems, advanced training and education technologies, and collaborative work systems. Since joining the Center in 1994, he has championed the development of education, research, information, and corporate sponsor programs. Furthermore, Rodger manages collaborative work system design and implementation consultative services in conjunction with mentoring graduate students.

**Michael M. Beyerlein** is director of the Center for the Study of Work Teams (www.workteams.unt.edu) and professor of psychology in the Industrial/Organizational psychology program at the University of North Texas. He received his Ph.D. in industrial-organizational psychology from Colorado State University. His research interests include all aspects of collaborative work systems, organization transformation, work stress, creativity and innovation, knowledge management and the learning organization, and complex adaptive systems. He has published in a number of research journals, and has been a member of the editorial boards for *TEAM Magazine* and *Quality Management Journal.* Currently, he is senior editor of the JAI Press annual series of books *Advances in Interdisciplinary Studies of Work Teams.* He is also organizing the launch of a new series of books for Jossey-Bass on collaborative work systems. In addition, he has been coeditor with Steve Jones on two ASTD case books about teams, and edited a book on the global history of teams, *Work Teams: Past, Present and Future.* He has been involved in change projects at the Center for the Study of Work Teams with such companies as Boeing, Shell, NCH, AMD, Westinghouse, and Xerox, and with government agencies such as Veterans Affairs, DCMAO, EPA, and the City of Denton.

**Robert E. Bradford** is a consulting psychologist based in Palo Alto, California. He has also worked as an area vice president at RHR International and has worked in corporate assessment and development for more than twenty-five years. Dr. Bradford was the chief executive officer of a nonprofit human service organization, and received his Ed.D. in counseling psychology from Texas A&M University in Commerce, Texas.

**Cecelia L. Brock** is currently a consultant to for-profit businesses and a managing member of an international venture capital company. In these roles, she specializes in all phases of organizational work, including startup, fast growth, strategic planning, downsizing, restructuring, mergers, acquisitions. She has over fifteen years at the vice president level in *Fortune* 500, high-technology companies creating and implementing effective business strategies. Dr. Brock has a Ph.D. in human and organizational systems, and a master's degree in human development, from the Fielding Graduate Institute, and an undergraduate degree in business. She also has a two-year certificate in counseling from UCSD. She has received training in conflict resolution through the San Diego Mediation Center, and has specialized in individual and organizational conflict resolution. She is also certified in strategic planning and organizational consulting.

**Andrew D. Carson** is senior project director at Riverside Publishing in Itasca, Illinois, where he manages development of the fifth edition of the Stanford-Binet Intelligence Scales. He also maintains a part-time consulting practice in vocational psychology and publishes VocationalPsychology.com. In addition to areas of expertise in career development and vocational psychology, he has published extensively on the nature of abilities and their relations to the interest and personality domains. He earned a Ph.D. in counseling psychology from the University of Texas at Austin in 1990.

**Frans Cilliers** holds a D.Phil. in industrial/organizational psychology from Potchefstroom University in South Africa. He is a registered psychologist (category: industry) with the South African Board for Psychology, and is a professor in the department of industrial psychology at the University of South Africa in Pretoria. His teaching focuses on psychological wellness and group behavior, with a special interest in the psychodynamic stance. He has attended a number of international group relations training events and uses this model in his research activities. He also works as a consultant for various South African and international organizations; these consultancies include team building, and coping with change and transformation. He supervises master's and doctoral research in wellness, organizational dynamics, and psychometrics from a quantitative and qualitative stance. He has published a number of research articles in all the above fields.

**Joanie B. Connell** received her Ph.D. from the University of California, Berkeley in social psychology, with an emphasis in industrial/organizational psychology. She received her bachelors degree in electrical engineering from Harvard University, and has had several years' experience working as an electrical and human factors engineer for a variety of high-tech companies, including Tandem Computers, Cypress Semiconductor, and Cisco Systems. She also worked as a human resource consultant for Personnel Decisions International, where she consulted with a number of *Fortune* 100 companies in the information technology and financial industries. Dr. Connell currently teaches consulting psychology and remote management at Alliant International University, and consults with the University's Organizational Consulting Center. Her primary research interests focus on the effects of technology on interpersonal interactions in organizations, improving telework and telemanagement practices, and interpersonal perception. Dr. Connell has teleworked in several different capacities.

**Stewart Cooper** has served as director of counseling services for the past thirteen years, and is professor of psychology and director of graduate psychology programs at Valparaiso University. He earned his B.A. in psychology, as well as an M.S. in counseling and a Ph.D. in counseling and research methodology at Indiana University. Before joining the staff at Valparaiso University, he was a staff psychologist at the University of Missouri at Rolla. Dr. Cooper holds a diplomate in counseling psychology from the American Board of Professional Psychology, and is a Fellow of Division 13 (Consulting) of the American Psychological Association.

**E. Jane Davidson** is associate director of the Evaluation Center and assistant professor of sociology at Western Michigan University, where she is primarily working on the development of a new university-wide interdisciplinary Ph.D. program in evaluation. She is also co-chair of the Business and Industry Topical Interest Group in the American Evaluation Association. Jane has worked in a variety of internal and external consulting roles in government and private sector organizations. Her primary research and consulting interests lie in the use of evaluation as a tool to improve organizational learning capacity, and the development of evaluation-specific methodologies to help build organizational effectiveness.

**Rebekah L. Duffala** is a research associate with Corporate Psychology Resources. She is responsible for the synthesis and implementation of 360-degree feedback reports, item development, and technical report writing. Currently, she is also involved in writing public relations material for a firm in Atlanta, Georgia. Rebekah received her B.S. in psychology from Berry College.

**Nurcan Ensari** is an assistant professor in the California School of Organizational Studies, Alliant International University. She received her Ph.D. from the University of Southern California, and completed post-doctoral work at the Kravis Leadership Institute, Claremont McKenna College. Her primary research interests are in leadership perceptions, charismatic leadership, cross-cultural differences, nonverbal behaviors, and leadership emergence. She has also published a number of journal articles, and has given conference presentations within the area of group processes and intergroup relations, specifically on the role of personalization and typicality in reducing intergroup bias, and multiple categorization.

**Fred E. Fiedler** is Professor Emeritus of Psychology and of Management and Organization at the University of Washington in Seattle, where he taught and directed the Organizational Research Group from 1969 until his retirement in 1993. From 1951 to 1969 he taught and directed the Group Effectiveness Research Laboratory at the University of Illinois in Urbana. Dr. Fiedler is best known for his development of the Contingency Model of Leadership Effectiveness and his more recent work on cognitive resource theory. He has authored and co-authored eight books and over 350 scientific papers, and received nine national and international awards for his work. He has consulted with government agencies, private business and industry, and military services both in the United States and abroad.

**Sandra Foster** is a performance enhancement psychologist based for years in San Francisco and relocated to Genoa, Italy in June 2002. She began her coaching career in Silicon Valley in the mid-1980s working with new managers in computer firms, entrepreneurs, and the first wave of employees of software startup companies. She later coached emerging leaders in banking, advertising, and Internet startups. Drawing on her training in flute, voice, and ballet, Sandra also provides performance coaching for actors, dancers, and musicians. After completing one year of postdoctoral education in sport psychology and sport medicine, she began assisting athletes with competition preparation and the psychological recovery from sport-related injury. Dr. Foster is certified as a sport psychology consultant by the Association for the Advancement of Applied Sport Psychology (AAASP) and is listed with the U.S. Olympic Committee Sport Psychology Registry. She served as acting assistant professor and consulting associate professor at Stanford University, where she received her doctorate. The coauthor of two books on sport psychology, she has also written numerous articles that have been published in professional and trade journals.

**Arthur M. Freedman** is a consulting psychologist specializing in organizational development. He is the director of the AU/NTL MSOD and the MSHRM programs in the Department of Public Administration, School of Public Affairs, American University (Washington, D.C.). He has consulted throughout North America as well as Sweden, Russia, Western Europe, Zimbabwe, and Israel. He is on the Board of Directors and a fellow of the Society of Consulting Psychology (Division 13, APA) and past-president of the Society of Psychologists in Management. His most recent book, with R. E. Zackrison, is *Finding Your Way in the Consulting Jungle* (Jossey-Bass, 2001). He has been a member of the NTL Institute since 1969. He earned his BS and MBA at Boston University and his Ph.D. in clinical psychology from the University of Chicago.

**Dale R. Fuqua** is a regents research professor in the College of Education at Oklahoma State University. He currently teaches courses in multivariate research methods, multiple regression, measurement, statistics, and research design. He is a past-president of the Society of Consulting Psychology. He has a long history of interests in organizational behavior and consultation as a means of improving the quality of work life.

**Andrew N. Garman** directs the Center for Health Care Entrepreneurship at Rush University, provides consultation to the human resources departments of Rush-Presbyterian-St. Luke's Medical Center and the Rush System for Health, and teaches in the department of Health Systems Management, Rush University, and the department of Industrial/Organizational Psychology, the Chicago School of Professional Psychology. Prior to joining Rush, Dr. Garman held positions with the Illinois Institute of Technology, the University of Chicago, and the Federal Reserve Bank of Chicago. Dr. Garman received a Psy.D. in clinical psychology from the College of William and Mary and an M.S. in personnel and human resource development from the Illinois Institute of Technology.

**Karen M. Grabow** is vice president of human resources for Land O'Lakes, Inc. Prior to Land O'Lakes, Dr. Grabow served as vice president of human resources at Target Stores and vice president of organizational effectiveness at Personnel Decisions, International. Dr. Grabow earned her Ph.D. in industrial/organizational and counseling psychology from the University of Minnesota. She and her husband have two daughters and live in Minneapolis, Minnesota.

**Steven W. Graham** is interim associate vice president for academic affairs and director of the President's Academic Leadership Institute at the University of Missouri System, and professor in the department of educational leadership and policy analysis at the University of Missouri-Columbia. He has over fifteen years of administrative experience as director of continuing professional education and associate dean for graduate studies, and has written approximately seventy articles or papers on manager coaching, college outcomes, industry training and evaluation, adult learning and development, and continuing professional education.

Dr. Graham earned a bachelor's degree in psychology from Coe College, and a master's degree in college personnel and a doctoral degree in higher education administration from the University of Iowa.

**Terry R. Halfhill** received a B.S. from the University of Pittsburgh, an M.A. from Towson University, and a Ph.D. in industrial/applied psychology from the University of Tennessee, Knoxville. He is currently an assistant professor of psychology at the University of North Texas. His research interests include group composition and work team issues, and the role of technology in virtual team settings. Dr. Halfhill has served as a consultant in various organizations, including the U.S. Army, U.S. Air Force, State of Tennessee Department of Human Services, and Petroleum Authority of Thailand.

**Brad A. Haynes** is an active management consultant and researcher in Atlanta, Georgia. He obtained his M.A. in industrial/organizational psychology from Austin Peay State University. His areas of work experience include competency modeling, assessment center development, and 360-degree feedback. Currently he is working on Internet technology applications to deliver competency-based, multimedia-based training and feedback.

**Pamela J. Hopp** has a B.S. in psychology from Duke University. She has extensive applied experience as project manager for 360-degree feedback processes, assessment centers, attitude surveys, and competency modeling projects. Currently, she is working towards her Ph.D. in industrial/organizational psychology at Colorado State University.

**Joseph W. Huff** received his B.A. from Bowling Green State University, his M.A. in experimental psychology from New Mexico State University, and Ph.D. in industrial-organizational psychology from Northern Illinois University. He is currently an assistant professor of psychology in the industrial-organizational psychology program at the University of North Texas. Prior to joining the University of North Texas faculty, he was employed by National Computer Systems (NCS) in Rosemont, Illinois, as a program evaluator. A sample of supported clients includes the Food Marketing Institute, Internal Revenue Service, Movie Gallery, and Pep Boys. His main research interests include the assessment of psychological and organizational climate, as well as comprehending the structure and meaning of employee job attitudes.

**Douglas A. Johnson** received his bachelor's degree in psychology from San Diego State University and his Ph.D. in industrial-organizational psychology from the University of California at Berkeley. He is professor of psychology and director of the industrial-organizational psychology program at the University of North Texas. He is cofounder and associate director of the University's Center for the Study of Work Teams. He is a member of the Society for Industrial and Organizational Psychology and the Society of Consulting Psychology of the American Psychological Association. For the past eight years, he has served as the coeditor of the JAI Press book series *Advances in Interdisciplinary Studies of Work Teams.* He participated in the creation of the first branch office of Personnel Decisions International, and has been an active part-time consultant with them since 1990. His clients have included AT Plastics, The Associates, Boeing, Brinker International, Waste Management, Inc., and Zale Corporation.

**Suzanne M. Kalten** received her bachelor's degree at Hofstra University before obtaining her master's in philosophical and religious studies and Psy.D. in clinical and professional psychology from the University of Denver. She has served as an adjunct professor of psychology and philosophy, a clinical intern at Vanderbilt University, and a post-doctoral fellow in behavioral medicine at the Medical University of South Carolina. Her current interests encompass individual assessment, competency modeling, and executive coaching.

**Sheila Kampa** is a consultant with RHR International in New York and associate clinical professor of psychology at the Gordon F. Derner Institute of Advanced Psychological Studies. She earned a Ph.D. in counseling psychology at Western Michigan University with an emphasis in consulting and organizational development. Her special interests are in executive leadership and development as a way of enhancing executive and organizational performance. She has been a coach to senior-level executives in a variety of organizations in international trade, retailing, energy, pharmaceuticals, and healthcare. She has also conducted research on the efficacy of coaching as a consultation tool. She has written articles on executive coaching for scholarly journals, and is in the process of writing a second book chapter. Sheila is a member in Divisions 13 (Society of Consulting Psychology), 14 (Society for Industrial and Organizational Psychology), and 17 (Counseling Psychology) of the American Psychological Association.

**Richard R. Kilburg** received his Ph.D. in clinical psychology from the University of Pittsburgh in 1972, and completed postgraduate work in mental health administration at Harvard University, and a master's degree in professional writing from Towson University in 1992. He has held positions in the department of psychiatry of the University of Pittsburgh, as director of the Champlain Valley Mental Health Council, a community mental health center in Burlington, Vermont, the American Psychological Association, and has been in private practice as a clinician and consultant. Currently, he is the senior director of the Office of Human Services, a multiprogram service component of human resources that meets the developmental needs of the faculty and staff of the Johns Hopkins University, located in Baltimore, Maryland. He has published widely in the fields of management, professional impairment, and executive coaching. His three previous books were *Professionals in Distress: Issues, Syndromes, and Solutions in Psychology, How to Manage Your Career in Psychology,* and *Executive Coaching: Developing Managerial Wisdom in a World of Chaos,* all published by the American Psychological Association. He was the founding president of the Society of Psychologists in Management (SPIM), and is a Fellow of Division 13, the consulting psychology division of APA. He is the recipient of the 2002 Distinguished Contribution to Psychology in Management Award given by the Society of Psychologists in Management.

**Pieter Koortzen** holds a D.Com. in industrial/organizational psychology from the University of South Africa. He is a licensed psychologist (categories: industry and counseling) with the South African Board for Psychology. He is an associate professor in the department of industrial psychology at the University of South Africa in Pretoria where he teaches courses in personality in the work context, interpersonal development, group relations, and diversity. He also supervises master's and doctoral research in industrial mental health, group and team dynamics, and diversity. He has attended a number of national and international group relations training events, and uses the Tavistock model in research and consulting activities. In his private practice, he renders group dynamic facilitation, interpersonal development, and trauma debriefing consulting services to South African organizations.

**John T. Kulas** is coordinator of statistical and research services for Corporate Psychology Resources in Atlanta, Georgia. His team is responsible for the development and psychometric evaluation of customized selection, promotion, and training systems for domestic and international client organizations. His prior work affiliations include NCS/London House and SBC, Inc. He received his M.A. and Ph.D. in industrial/organizational psychology at Northern Illinois University.

**E. Skipton Leonard** is a vice president and executive consultant in Personnel Decisions International's Washington D.C. office. He is a past-president and fellow of the Society of Consulting Psychology and the founding editor of *Consulting Psychology Journal.* Dr. Leonard is currently an adjunct professor in the AU/NTL Master of Science in Organization Development and formerly an adjunct associate professor at George Mason University's graduate psychology department. He is especially interested in helping organizations develop executive leadership and talent, build high-performing teams, and behave more adaptively, creatively, and strategically in rapidly changing market conditions.

**Ira M. Levin** is a professor on the faculty of the San Francisco Bay Campus, California School of Organization Studies, Alliant International University, and is a principal and national practice leader for organization transformation in the Healthcare Consulting Practice of Cap Gemini Ernst & Young LLC. He has over twenty years of experience consulting with healthcare organizations in such areas as strategic repositioning, post-merger integration, culture development, board and executive team effectiveness, leadership development, human resources strategy, and organizational design. He earned a Ph.D. in organizational psychology from the University of Illinois at Chicago, an M.S. in clinical/counseling psychology from the Illinois Institute of Technology and a B.S. in psychology from the University of Illinois.

**Harry Levinson** is clinical professor emeritus, department of psychiatry, Harvard Medical School; chairman emeritus of the Levinson Institute; and former head of the section on organizational mental health at the Massachusetts Mental Health Center. Dr. Levinson created, and for fourteen years directed, the division of industrial mental health at the Menninger Foundation. He has been a visiting professor at the Sloan School of Management, Massachusetts Institute of

Technology, University of Kansas, Florida Atlantic University, and Thomas Henry Carroll-Ford Foundation Distinguished Visiting Professor in the Harvard Business School. He has lectured at other universities, both in the United States and abroad. Dr. Levinson has received numerous awards for his work with business, academic, and government institutions, including the Perry L. Rohrer Consulting Psychology Practice Award for outstanding achievement in psychological consultation, the Massachusetts Psychological Association's Career Award, the Society of Psychologists in Management's first award, and the Organizational Development Professional Award for Excellence. In 1992, he was named co-recipient of the American Psychological Association Award for distinguished professional contribution to knowledge, and in 2000, he received the American Psychological Foundation Gold Medal Award for life achievement in the application of psychology. He is past president of the Kansas Psychological Association and of the American Board of Professional Psychology. Dr. Levinson has authored many articles and chapters in books edited by others. In addition, he has edited or written sixteen books. The latter include *Men, Management and Mental Health* (Harvard University Press), *The Exceptional Executive* (Harvard University Press), *The Great Jackass Fallacy* (Harvard University Press), *Organizational Diagnosis* (Harvard University Press), *Ready, Fire, Aim* (The Levinson Institute), *Psychological Man* (The Levinson Institute), *CEO: Corporate Leadership in Action* (Basic Books), and *Organizational Assessment* (American Psychological Association).

**Paul Lloyd** is president of Lloyd & Associates and professor of psychology at Southeast Missouri State University. Dr. Lloyd has extensive administrative experience at the University, including as director of the Center for Health Professions. During 1991–1992, he was a visiting scholar at the Cooper Institute in Dallas, Texas. His scholarly works include a chapter on evaluation of preventive and rehabilitative exercise programs, published by the American College of Sports Medicine. Consultation clients include medical centers, governmental agencies, mental health centers, businesses, and universities. He is a fellow of the American Psychological Association (APA) and the American Psychological Society (APS). He is a past-president of the Society of Consulting Psychology, and currently serves on the APA Council of Representatives. Paul is also past-president of the Society of Psychologists in Management (SPIM) and Psi Chi, the national honor society in psychology.

**Susan Albers Mohrman** is senior research scientist at the Center for Effective Organizations in the Marshall School of Business at the University of Southern California. Her research, publications, and consulting focus on organizational design, human resource management, and organizational change and capability development. Her latest books include *Designing Team-Based Organizations; Creating a Strategic Human Resources Function; Tomorrow's Organization:*

*Crafting Winning Capabilities in a Dynamic World;* and *Organizing for High Performance.* She has served on the Board of Governors of the Academy of Management and is on the Board of the Human Resource Planning Society.

**Virginia Mullin** is president of Mullin and Associates Consultation. With a doctorate in clinical health psychology, she launched her consultation career with work in a South African hospital. Since then, consultations have included many community and human services groups, including Head Start schools. Assessments continue to be a primary interest, as well as international venues, which include more than thirty-five countries. Dr. Mullin has served the Society of Consulting Psychology (Division 13 of the American Psychological Association) in various capacities for the past few years, and is the liaison coordinator for an international organizational development association.

**Delbert M. Nebeker** is a professor in the California School of Organizational Studies, Alliant International University. He previously served as the director of the Organizational Systems Department at the Navy Personnel Research and Development Center (NPRDC) in San Diego, California, and as an associate professor of management at San Diego State University. For the last twenty-eight years, he has been helping public and private organizations improve their organizational effectiveness. He specializes in organizational diagnosis and the design of organizational reward systems to increase employee involvement and organizational productivity. His work was cited as being exemplary by the U.S. Office of Personnel Management in its 1981 *Exemplary Practices in Federal Productivity.* He has served numerous clients, both in the public and private sectors. Dr. Nebeker is the author of over sixty professional journal publications and government technical reports. He served on the editorial board of *Organizational Behavior and Human Decision Processes* for eleven years, and has received many awards and honors. These include the 1979 Military Psychology Award from the American Psychological Association. He is also a member of the prestigious Society for Organizational Behavior. He received his Ph.D. in psychology from the University of Washington.

**Jody L. Newman** is a professor in the department of Educational Psychology at the University of Oklahoma. She teaches in the counseling psychology program. Her teaching areas include professional ethics, measurement, and evaluation. Her research and scholarship has focused on ethics in consultation, career psychology, and gender issues. She has served as liaison to women and secretary of the Society of Consulting Psychology.

**Tjai M. Nielsen** is a consulting psychologist with RHR International's Atlanta office, and has worked with organizations in various industries including service, chemical, insurance, and manufacturing. His doctorate is in industrial/

organizational psychology from the University of Tennessee in Knoxville. Dr. Nielsen's published research is in the areas of work team effectiveness, 360-degree feedback, and web-based approaches to assessment and development.

**Ann M. O'Roark** is a consulting psychologist with twenty-five years in private practice, who has specialized in assessment, strategic planning, and leadership. Her Ph.D., M.Ed., and postdoctoral work was at the University of Florida; her B.A., at the University of Kentucky (PKB), with additional training at the C. G. Jung Institute, Zurich. Dr. O'Roark has served as Deputy Secretary, Education and Arts Cabinet, and Assistant State Treasurer in Kentucky. She has also served on the boards of the International Council of Psychologists, the Society of Psychologists in Management, as president and treasurer of the Division of Consulting Psychology (APA13), and as administrative officer for the Society for Personality Assessment. She is a Fellow in the American Psychological Association (APA) and a Diplomate of the American Board of Assessment Psychology (ABAP). She has presented papers in Australia, Austria, Belgium, Canada, England, Holland, India, Israel, Italy, Japan, Mexico, Portugal, the Philippines, Scotland, Singapore, Spain, and the United States.

**Shani Robins** is an adjunct faculty member in the California School of Organizational Studies, Alliant International University. He completed his B.A. in psychology and philosophy at UCLA, his M.A. and Ph.D. in cognitive experimental psychology at the University of California, Santa Barbara, a two-year postdoctoral National Institute of Mental Health Fellowship at the University of California, Irvine, was a visiting scholar at the University of California, Berkeley, and has additionally completed a Ph.D. respecialization in clinical psychology at the California School of Professional Psychology, San Diego at Alliant International University. He has consulted and published extensively and has given numerous invited talks and international conference presentations on the topic of cognition-emotion interactions and their applications to the workplace. He is currently investigating the influence of wisdom on emotions and has developed a wide variety of organizational programs, interventions, and workshops for dealing with anger, conflict, and stress. In addition to his academic research, teaching, and consulting, he also maintains a clinical practice at the Cognitive Therapy Institute in San Diego, California.

**Debra A. G. Robinson** is associate vice chancellor for student and international affairs at the University of Missouri-Rolla. She is also a program director and leader for the coach certification program at the Hudson Institute of Santa Barbara, a senior consultant with Harshman & Associates in St. Louis, and a principal in the Global Consulting Partnership. She has written articles and made presentations at national and international meetings on leadership development and related topics.

Dr. Robinson earned a bachelor's degree in psychology from the University of Illinois in Springfield, and master's and doctoral degrees in counseling psychology from the University of Illinois in Champaign-Urbana.

**Sharon E. Robinson-Kurpius** is a professor in the counseling psychology program at Arizona State University. She is a past-president of the Society of Consulting Psychology, and recently received an award for her distinguished service to the Society for the past twenty years. She teaches professional ethics, and has written several papers on the topic of ethics in consultation. She has also published extensively in the area of women's health.

**Peter F. Sorensen, Jr.,** is professor and director of the Ph.D. program in organization development and the management and organizational behavior program at Benedictine University. He is chair of the OD&C division of the Academy of Management. Peter was an invited, distinguished scholar at the first Academy of Management conference on global change, and has received the outstanding OD Consultant of the Year award from the OD Institute. His recent publications include *Global and International Organization Development*, and *Appreciative Inquiry: An Emerging Direction for OD*, and is coauthor of a forthcoming book on global OD published by Jossey-Bass.

**B. Charles Tatum** received his Ph.D. as a research psychologist in 1973 from the University of New Mexico. During his twenty-three years as a teacher and researcher, he has authored over twenty professional publications and thirty conference papers. Dr. Tatum spent twelve years working for the federal government as a personnel research psychologist for the Navy Personnel Research and Development Center in San Diego, California. During his career as a researcher for the U.S. Navy, he has studied performance measurement, work productivity, quality, and reward systems. In addition to his scientific interest in these areas, Dr. Tatum has also applied his knowledge to help organizations become more efficient and effective. He has consulted with many private and government organizations (for example, the Department of Defense, U.S. Navy, Federal Aviation Administration, McDonnell-Douglas, the San Diego Community College District, and Howard County, Maryland) to help them develop programs for improving productivity, quality, and work motivation. He has administered questionnaires, conducted interviews, presented workshops, and delivered training to both public and private organizations on a variety of topics, including performance measurement, productivity improvement, quality enhancement, and work incentives. Dr. Tatum is currently the chair of the department of psychology at National University in La Jolla, California.

**Louis Veneziano** is a professor of criminal justice and psychology at Southeast Missouri State University. He received his doctorate in clinical psychology from Auburn University, and he has worked in a variety of applied settings with diverse clinical populations. His consultative experiences primarily involve program evaluation efforts. He is a well-published scholar, with over thirty journal articles and 100 paper presentations at professional conferences. His research interests lie at the interface between the fields of criminal justice and psychology.

**Randall P. White** is a principal in the Executive Development Group LLC, Greensboro, North Carolina, and an adjunct professor at the Fuqua School of Business, Duke University. He also teaches at the Johnson Graduate School of Management, Cornell University. His interest in where leaders come from, how they develop, and their eventual success is borne out in his writing. His books include *Breaking the Glass Ceiling* (1987), *The Future of Leadership* (1996), and *Relax, It's Only Uncertainty* (2001). Randy has also written in both popular and scientific outlets on leadership and coaching. He is a frequent speaker for a variety of industry groups. For twelve years he developed programs and research on leadership at the Center for Creative Leadership. He is a fellow in Division 13 (Society of Consulting Psychology) of the American Psychological Association.

**Paul C. Winum** is an area vice president and managing director of RHR International Company, a management psychology firm established in 1945. Dr. Winum has worked in both private sector and nonprofit organizations for more than twenty years in executive, management, and consulting roles. His doctorate is in counseling psychology from the University of Notre Dame, and he serves as a board member of the Society for Consulting Psychology of the American Psychological Association.

**Therese F. Yaeger** is the associate director of the Ph.D. program in organization development at Benedictine University, where she also teaches OD, management, and organizational behavior courses. She has authored more than fifty papers and presentations, including coauthoring three books. She is an editorial associate of the *OD Journal* and Chicago's *ASTD Training Today*, and has been a guest editor for the *OD Practitioner* and the *OD Journal*. She frequently presents at conferences, such as the Academy of Management, the OD Institute, and the OD Network, and is a track chair for the Midwest Academy of Management.

# NAME INDEX

# SUBJECT INDEX